Commentary
on the
OLD TESTAMENT

Commentary
on the
OLD TESTAMENT
IN TEN VOLUMES

by

C. F. KEIL and F. DELITZSCH

Translated from the German by James Martin

VOLUME VI

Proverbs, Ecclesiastes, Song of Solomon

by F. DELITZSCH

Three Volumes in One

WILLIAM B. EERDMANS PUBLISHING COMPANY
Grand Rapids, Michigan

COMMENTARY ON THE OLD TESTAMENT
by C. F. Keil and F. Delitzsch
Translated from the German

Volumes translated by James Martin
THE PENTATEUCH
JOSHUA, JUDGES, RUTH
THE BOOKS OF SAMUEL
THE BOOKS OF THE KINGS
THE PROPHECIES OF ISAIAH
THE PROPHECIES OF EZEKIEL
THE TWELVE MINOR PROPHETS

Volumes translated by Andrew Harper
THE BOOKS OF THE CHRONICLES

Volumes translated by Sophia Taylor
THE BOOKS OF EZRA, NEHEMIAH, ESTHER

Volumes translated by Francis Bolton
THE BOOK OF JOB
THE PSALMS

Volumes translated by M. G. Easton
PROVERBS OF SOLOMON
THE SONG OF SONG AND ECCLESIASTES
THE BOOK OF DANIEL

Volumes translated by David Patrick
THE PROPHECIES OF JEREMIAH, VOL. I

Volumes translated by James Kennedy
THE PROPHECIES OF JEREMIAH, VOL. II

ISBN 0-8028-8040-1

Reprinted, February 1980

TRANSLATOR'S PREFACE

HE volume which is here presented to English readers is the first of three which will contain the Solomonic writings. They form the last section of the "Keil and Delitzsch" series of Commentaries on the Books of the Old Testament Scriptures. The remaining volume on the Proverbs, as well as that on Ecclesiastes and the Canticles, which has also been prepared by Delitzsch, and is now in course of publication in Germany, will be issued with as little delay as possible.

In this translation I have endeavoured accurately to reproduce the original, so as to bring the student as much as possible into direct contact with the learned commentator himself. Any explanatory notes or words I have thought it right to add are enclosed in square brackets [ ], so as to be easily distinguishable. The Arabic and Syriac words occurring in the original have been, with very few exceptions, printed in English characters. In their vocalization I have followed the system of Forbes in his *Arabic Grammar*, so that the student will be readily able to restore the original. When nothing depends on the inflection of these words, the consonants only are printed.

It might appear superfluous in me to speak in commendation of the great work which is now drawing to a close; but a translator, since he has necessarily been in close fellowship with the author, may be expected to be in a position to offer an opinion on the character of the work on which he has been engaged; and I am sure that all my *collaborateurs* will concur with me in speaking of the volumes which form this commentary as monuments of deep

and careful research into the meaning of the sacred Scriptures.
Whether or not we can in all cases accept the conclusions reached
by the respected authors, no one can fail to see how elaborate and
minute the investigation has been.   These volumes are the ripest
fruits of life-long study of the Old Testament.   Their authors are
exegetes who have won for themselves an honoured place in the
foremost rank for their profound acquaintance with the Hebrew
and its cognate languages.   With a scholarship of rare compass
and accuracy, they combine a reverent sympathy with the sacred
Scriptures, and a believing appreciation of its saving truths.

  The satisfaction I have had in the study of this work, and in
spending so many of my leisure hours in rendering it into English,
is greatly heightened by the reflection, that I have been enabled in
this way to contribute to the number of exegetical works within
reach of the English student.   The exegetical study of God's word,
which appears to be increasingly drawing the attention of theologians, and which has been so greatly stimulated by the Translations issued by the publishers of this work, cannot fail to have the
most beneficial results.   The minister of the gospel will find such
study his best and truest preparation for his weighty duties as an
expounder of Scripture, if prosecuted in the spirit of a devout
recognition of the truth, that " bene orasse est bene studuisse."
Thus is he led step by step into a thorough and full understanding
of the words and varying forms of expression used by those " holy
men of old, who spake as they were moved by the Holy Ghost."

AUTHOR'S PREFACE

———◆———

THE preparation of this Commentary on the *Mishle*, which was begun in 1869 (not without previous preparation), and twice interrupted by providential events, extended into the winter of 1872. There is now wanting to the completion of the Commentary on the Old Testament, undertaken by Dr. Keil and myself, only the Commentary on the Canticles and Ecclesiastes, which will form the concluding volume.

In the preparation of this Commentary on the Proverbs, I am indebted in varied ways to my friends Fleischer and Wetzstein. In the year 1836, Fleischer entered on his duties as Professor at Leipzig by delivering a course of lectures on the Book of the Proverbs of Solomon. I was one of his hearers, and am now so fortunate as to be able from his own MS. (begun 13th May, completed 9th September 1836) to introduce this beloved teacher into the number of interpreters of the Book of Proverbs. The assistance contributed by Wetzstein begins at chapter xxx., and consists in remarks on Mühlau's work on the Proverbs of Agur and Lemuel (1869), which my Dorpat friend placed at my disposal.

The exegetical apparatus has in the course of this work extended far beyond the list given at pp. 50, 51. I obtained the Commentary of the Caraite Ahron b. Joseph (1294), which was printed at Koslow (Eupatoria) in 1835, and had lent to me from the library of Dr. Hermann Lotze the Commentary by the Roman poet Immanuel [born at Rome about 1265], who was intimately associated with Dante, printed at Naples in 1487, and equal in value to a MS. Among the interpreters comprehended in the *Biblia Rabbinica*, I made use also of the Commentary of the Spanish

9

Menachem b. Salomo Meîri (1447), which first appeared in the
Amsterdam *Bibelwerk*, and came under my notice in a more handy
edition (Fürth, 1844) from the library of my dear friend and
companion in study, Baer. To him I owe, among many other
things, the comparison of several MSS., particularly of one brought
from Arabia by Jacob Sappir, which has come into his possession.

In making use of the *Græcus Venetus*, I was not confined
to Villoison's edition (1784). The only existing MS. (found in
Venice) of this translation one of my young friends, von Gebhardt,
has compared with the greatest care with Villoison's printed edition,
in which he has found many false readings and many omissions.
We have to expect from him a critical, complete edition of this
singular translation, which, both as regards the knowledge its
author displays of the Hebrew language and his skill in the Greek
language, remains as yet an unsolved mystery.

The Index [1] (to the words etymologically explained in this Commentary) has been prepared by Dr. Hermann Strack, who, by his
recently-published *Prolegomena ad Vetus Testamentum Hebraicum*,
has shown himself to be a Hebraist of rare attainments.

Bacon, in his work *De Augmentis Scientiarum* (viii. 2), rightly
speaks[2] of Solomon's proverbs as an unparalleled collection. May
it be granted me, by the help of God, to promote in some degree
the understanding of this incomparable Book, as to its history, its
language, and its practical lessons!

LEIPZIG, 30*th October* 1872.

---

[1] Will be given with vol. ii.

[2] [In hoc genere autem nihil invenitur, quod ullo modo comparandum sit
cum aphorismis illis, quos edidit rex Salomon ; de quo testatur Scriptura *cor
illi fuisse instar arenæ maris :* sicut enim arenæ maris universas orbis oras circumdant, ita et sapientia ejus omnia humana, non minus quam divina, complexa
est. In aphorismis vero illis, præter alia majis theologica, reperies liquido
haud pauca præcepta et monita civilia præstantissima, ex profundis quidem
sapientiæ penetralibus scaturientia, atque in amplissimum varietatis campum
excurrentia.]

TABLE OF CONTENTS

INTRODUCTION.

THE OLDER BOOK OF PROVERBS, I.—XXIV.

THE BOOK OF PROVERBS

INTRODUCTION.

THE Book of Proverbs bears the external title סֵפֶר מִשְׁלֵי, which it derives from the words with which it commences. It is one of the three books which are distinguished from the other twenty-one by a peculiar system of accentuation, the best exposition of which that has yet been given is that by S. Baer,[1] as set forth in my larger *Psalmencommentar.*[2] The memorial word for these three books, viz. Job, Mishle (Proverbs), and Tehillim (Psalms), is אמ״ת, formed from the first letter of the first word of each book, or, following the Talmudic and Masoretic arrangement of the books, תא״ם.

Having in view the superscription מִשְׁלֵי שְׁלֹמֹה, with which the book commences, the ancients regarded it as wholly the composition of Solomon. The circumstance that it contains only 800 verses, while according to 1 Kings v. 12 (iv. 32) Solomon spake 3000 proverbs, R. Samuel bar-Nachmani explains by remarking that each separate verse may be divided into two or three allegories or apothegms (*e.g.* xxv. 12), not to mention other more arbitrary modes of reconciling the discrepancy.[3] The opinion also of R. Jonathan, that Solomon first composed the Canticles, then the Proverbs, and last of all Ecclesiastes, inasmuch as the first corresponds[4] with the spring-time of youth, the second with the wis-

---

[1] Cf. *Outlines of Hebrew Accentuation, Prose and Poetical,* by Rev. A. B. Davidson, D.D., Professor of Hebrew, Free Church College, Edinburgh, 1861, based on Baer's *Torath Emeth,* Rödelheim 1872.

[2] Vol. ii., ed. of 1860, pp. 477–511.

[3] *Pesikta,* ed. Buber (1868), 34*b*, 35*a*. Instead of 800, the Masora reckons 915 verses in the Book of Proverbs.

[4] *Schir-ha-Schirim Rabba,* c. i. f. 4*a*.

dom of manhood, and the third with the disappointment of old
age, is founded on the supposition of the unity of the book and
of its Solomonic authorship.

At the present day also there are some, such as Stier, who
regard the Book of Proverbs from first to last as the work of
Solomon, just as Klauss (1832) and Randegger (1841) have ventured to affirm that all the Psalms without exception were composed by David. But since historical criticism has been applied
to Biblical subjects, that blind submission to mistaken tradition
appears as scarcely worthy of being mentioned. The Book of
Proverbs presents itself as composed of various parts, different
from each other in character and in the period to which they
belong. Under the hands of the critical analysis it resolves itself
into a mixed market of the most manifold intellectual productions
of proverbial poetry, belonging to at least three different epochs.

1. *The external plan of the Book of Proverbs, and its own testimony as to its origin.*—The internal superscription of the book, which
recommends it, after the manner of later Oriental books, on account
of its importance and the general utility of its contents, extends
from ver. 1 to ver. 6. Among the moderns this has been acknowledged by Löwenstein and Maurer; for ver. 7, which Ewald,
Bertheau, and Keil have added to it, forms a new commencement
to the beginning of the book itself. The book is described as
" The Proverbs of Solomon," and then there is annexed the statement of its object. That object, as summarily set forth in ver. 2,
is practical, and that in a twofold way : partly moral, and partly
intellectual. The former is described in vers. 3–5. It presents
moral edification, moral sentiments for acceptance, not merely to
help the unwise to attain to wisdom, but also to assist the wise.
The latter object is set forth in ver. 6. It seeks by its contents
to strengthen and discipline the mind to the understanding of
thoughtful discourses generally. In other words, it seeks to gain
the moral ends which proverbial poetry aims at, and at the same
time to make familiar with it, so that the reader, in these
proverbs of Solomon, or by means of them as of a key, learns to
understand such like apothegms in general. Thus interpreted, the
title of the book does not say that the book contains proverbs of
other wise men besides those of Solomon ; if it did so, it would
contradict itself. It is possible that the book contains proverbs

other than those of Solomon, possible that the author of the title
of the book added such to it himself, but the title presents to
view only the Proverbs of Solomon. If i. 7 begins the book, then
after reading the title we cannot think otherwise than that here
begin the Solomonic proverbs. If we read farther, the contents
and the form of the discourses which follow do not contradict this
opinion; for both are worthy of Solomon. So much the more
astonished are we, therefore, when at x. 1 we meet with a new
superscription, מִשְׁלֵי שְׁלֹמֹה, from which point on to xxii. 16 there is
a long succession of proverbs of quite a different tone and form—
short maxims, Mashals proper—while in the preceding section of
the book we find fewer proverbs than monitory discourses. What
now must be our opinion when we look back from this second
superscription to the part i. 7–ix., which immediately follows the
title of the book? Are i. 7–ix., in the sense of the book, not the
" Proverbs of Solomon "? From the title of the book, which
declares them to be so, we must judge that they are. Or are they
" Proverbs of Solomon"? In this case the new superscription (x. 1),
" The Proverbs of Solomon," appears altogether incomprehensible.
And yet only one of these two things is possible: on the one side,
therefore, there must be a false appearance of contradiction, which
on a closer investigation disappears. But on which side is it? If
it is supposed that the tenor of the title, i. 1-6, does not accord
with that of the section x. 1–xxii. 6, but that it accords well with
that of i. 7–ix. (with the breadth of expression in i. 7–ix., it has also
several favourite words not elsewhere occurring in the Book of
Proverbs; among these, עָרְמָה, subtilty, and מְזִמָּה, discretion, i. 4),
then Ewald's view is probable, that i.–ix. is an original whole written
at once, and that the author had no other intention than to give it
as an introduction to the larger Solomonic Book of Proverbs beginning at x. 1. But it is also possible that the author of the title
has adopted the style of the section i. 7–ix. Bertheau, who has
propounded this view, and at the same time has rejected, in opposition to Ewald, the idea of the unity of the section, adopts this
conclusion, that in i. 8–ix. there lies before us a collection of the
admonitions of different authors of proverbial poetry, partly original
introductions to larger collections of proverbs, which the author
of the title gathers together in order that he may give a comprehensive introduction to the larger collection contained in x. 1–xxii.
16. But such an origin of the section as Bertheau thus imagines

is by no means natural; it is more probable that the author, whose object is, according to the title of the book, to give the proverbs of Solomon, introduces these by a long introduction of his own, than that, instead of beginning with Solomon's proverbs, he first presents long extracts of a different kind from collections of proverbs. If the author, as Bertheau thinks, expresses indeed, in the words of the title, the intention of presenting, along with the " Proverbs of Solomon," also the " words of the wise," then he could not have set about his work more incorrectly and self-contradictorily than if he had begun the whole, which bears the superscription " Proverbs of Solomon " (which must be regarded as presenting the proverbs of Solomon as a key to the words of the wise generally), with the " words of the wise." But besides the opinion of Ewald, which in itself, apart from internal grounds, is more natural and probable than that of Bertheau, there is yet the possibility of another. Keil, following H. A. Hahn, is of opinion, that in the sense of the author of the title, the section i.–ix. is Solomonic as well as x.–xxii., but that he has repeated the superscription " Proverbs of Solomon" before the latter section, because from that point onward proverbs follow which bear in a special measure the characters of the Mashal (Hävernick's *Einl.* iii. 428). The same phenomenon appears in the book of Isaiah, where, after the general title, there follows an introductory address, and then in ii. 1 the general title is repeated in a shorter form. That this analogy, however, is here inapplicable, the further discussion of the subject will show.

The introductory section i. 7–ix., and the larger section x.–xxii. 16, which contains uniform brief Solomonic apothegms, are followed by a third section, xxii. 17–xxiv. 22. Hitzig, indeed, reckons x.–xxiv. 22 as the second section, but with xxii. 17 there commences an altogether different style, and a much freer manner in the form of the proverb; and the introduction to this new collection of proverbs, which reminds us of the general title, places it beyond a doubt that the collector does not at all intend to set forth these proverbs as Solomonic. It may indeed be possible that, as Keil (iii. 410) maintains, the collector, inasmuch as he begins with the words, " Incline thine ear and hear words of the wise," names his own proverbs generally as " words of the wise," especially since he adds, " and apply thine heart to my knowledge ;" but this supposition is contradicted by the superscription of a fourth section, xxiv. 23 ff., which follows. This short section, an appendix to the

third, bears the superscription, " These things also are לַחֲכָמִים."
If Keil thinks here also to set aside the idea that the following
proverbs, in the sense of this superscription, have as their authors
" the wise," he does unnecessary. violence to himself. The ל is
here that of authorship ; and if the following proverbs are composed by the חֲכָמִים, " the wise," then they are not the production
of the one חָכָם, " wise man," Solomon, but they are " the words
of the wise " in contradistinction to " the Proverbs of Solomon."

The Proverbs of Solomon begin again at xxv. 1 ; and this
second large section (corresponding to the first, x. 1–xxii. 16)
extends to xxix. This fifth portion of the book has a superscription, which, like that of the preceding appendix, commences
thus : " Also (גַּם) these are proverbs of Solomon which the men of
Hezekiah king of Judah collected." The meaning of the word
הֶעְתִּיקוּ is not doubtful. It signifies, like the Arameo-Arabic נסח,
to remove from their place, and denotes that the men of Hezekiah
removed from the place where they found them the following
proverbs, and placed them together in a separate collection. The
words have thus been understood by the Greek translator. From
the supplementary words αἱ ἀδιάκριτοι (such as exclude all διάκρισις)
it is seen that the translator had a feeling of the important literary
historical significance of that superscription, which reminds us of the
labours of the poetical grammarians appointed by Pisistratus to edit
older works, such as those of Hesiod. The Jewish interpreters, simply
following the Talmud, suppose that the " also" (גַּם) belongs to the
whole superscription, inclusive of the relative sentence, and that it
thus bears witness to the editing of the foregoing proverbs also by
Hezekiah and his companions ;[1] which is altogether improbable, for
then, if such were the meaning of the words, " which the men of
Hezekiah," etc., they ought to have stood after i. 1. The superscription xxv. 1 thus much rather distinguishes the following collection from that going before, as having been made under Hezekiah.
As two appendices followed the " Proverbs of Solomon," x. 1–xxii.
16, so also two appendices the Hezekiah-gleanings of Solomonic
proverbs. The former two appendices, however, originate in general from the " wise," the latter more definitely name the authors :
the first, xxx., is by " Agur the son of Jakeh ;" the second, xxxi.

[1] *Vid. B. Bathra*, 15a. From the fact that Isaiah outlived Hezekiah it is there
concluded that the Hezekiah-*collegium* also continued after Hezekiah's death.
Cf. Fürst on the *Canon of the O. T.* 1868, p. 78 f.

1–9, by a " King Lemuel." In so far the superscriptions are clear.
The names of the authors, elsewhere unknown, point to a foreign
country; and to this corresponds the peculiar complexion of these
two series of proverbs. As a third appendix to the Hezekiah-collection, xxxi. 10 ff. follows, a complete alphabetical proverbial poem
which describes the praiseworthy qualities of a virtuous woman.

We are thus led to the conclusion that the Book of Proverbs
divides itself into the following parts :—(1) The title of the book,
i. 1–6, by which the question is raised, how far the book extends
to which it originally belongs; (2) the hortatory discourses, i. 7–ix.,
in which it is a question whether the Solomonic proverbs must be
regarded as beginning with these, or whether they are only the
introduction thereto, composed by a different author, perhaps the
author of the title of the book; (3) the first great collection of
Solomonic proverbs, x.–xxii. 16; (4) the first appendix to this
first collection, " The words of the wise," xxii. 17–xxiv. 22 ; (5)
the second appendix, supplement of the words of some wise men,
xxiv. 23 ff. ; (6) the second great collection of Solomonic proverbs,
which the " men of Hezekiah" collected, xxv.–xxix. ; (7) the first
appendix to this second collection, the words of Agur the son
of Jakeh, xxx. ; (8) the second appendix, the words of King
Lemuel, xxxi. 1–9 ; (9) third appendix, the acrostic ode, xxxi.
10 ff. These nine parts are comprehended under three groups :
the introductory hortatory discourses with the general title at their
head, and the two great collections of Solomonic proverbs with
their two appendices. In prosecuting our further investigations,
we shall consider the several parts of the book first from the point
of view of the manifold forms of their proverbs, then of their
style, and thirdly of their type of doctrine. From each of these
three subjects of investigation we may expect elucidations regarding
the origin of these proverbs and of their collections.

2. *The several parts of the Book of Proverbs with respect to the
manifold forms of the proverbs.*—If the Book of Proverbs were a
collection of popular sayings, we should find in it a multitude of
proverbs of one line each, as *e.g.*, " Wickedness proceedeth from
the wicked" (1 Sam. xxiv. 13) ; but we seek for such in vain. At
the first glance, xxiv. 23*b* appears to be a proverb of one line; but
the line " To have respect of persons in judgment is not good,"
is only the introductory line of a proverb which consists of several

lines, ver. 24 f. Ewald is right in regarding as inadmissible a comparison of the collections of Arabic proverbs by Abu-Obeida, Meidani, and others, who gathered together and expounded the current popular proverbs, with the Book of Proverbs. Ali's Hundred Proverbs are, however, more worthy of being compared with it. Like these, Solomon's proverbs are, as a whole, the production of his own spirit, and only mediately of the popular spirit. To make the largeness of the number of these proverbs a matter of doubt were inconsiderate. Eichhorn maintained that even a godlike genius scarcely attains to so great a number of pointed proverbs and ingenious thoughts. But if we distribute Solomon's proverbs over his forty years' reign, then we have scarcely twenty for each year; and one must agree with the conclusion, that the composition of so many proverbs even of the highest ingenuity is no impossible problem for a "godlike genius." When, accordingly, it is related that Solomon wrote 3000 proverbs, Ewald, in his *History of Israel*, does not find the number too great, and Bertheau does not regard it as impossible that the collection of the " Proverbs of Solomon" has the one man Solomon as their author. The number of the proverbs thus cannot determine us to regard them as having for the most part originated among the people, and the form in which they appear leads to an opposite conclusion. It is, indeed, probable that popular proverbs are partly wrought into these proverbs,[1] and many of their forms of expression are moulded after the popular proverbs; but as they thus lie before us, they are, as a whole, the production of the technical *Mashal* poetry.

The simplest form is, according to the fundamental peculiarity of the Hebrew verse, the *distich*. The relation of the two lines to each other is very manifold. The second line may repeat the thought of the first, only in a somewhat altered form, in order to express this thought as clearly and exhaustively as possible. We call such proverbs *synonymous* distichs; as *e.g.* xi. 25 :

A soul of blessing is made fat,
And he that watereth others is himself watered.

Or the second line contains the other side of the contrast to the statement of the first; the truth spoken in the first is explained in the second by means of the presentation of its contrary. We call such proverbs *antithetic* distichs; as *e.g.* x. 1 :

[1] Isaac Euchel († 1804), in his *Commentary on the Proverbs*, regards xiv. 4a and xvii. 19b as such popular proverbs.

> A wise son maketh his father glad,
> And a foolish son is his mother's grief.

Similar forms, x. 16, xii. 5. Elsewhere, as xviii. 14, xx. 24, the antithesis clothes itself in the form of a question. Sometimes it is two different truths that are expressed in the two lines; and the authorization of their union lies only in a certain relationship, and the ground of this union in the circumstance that two lines are the minimum of the technical proverb—*synthetic* distichs; *e.g.* x. 18:

> A cloak of hatred are lying lips,
> And he that spreadeth slander is a fool.

Not at all infrequently one line does not suffice to bring out the thought intended, the begun expression of which is only completed in the second. These we call *integral* (*eingedankige*) distichs; as *e.g.* xi. 31 (cf. 1 Pet. iv. 18):

> The righteous shall be recompensed on the earth—
> How much more the ungodly and the sinner!

To these distichs also belong all those in which the thought stated in the first receives in the second, by a sentence presenting a reason, or proof, or purpose, or consequence, a definition completing or perfecting it; *e.g.* xiii. 14, xvi. 10, xix. 20, xxii. 28.[1] But there is also a fifth form, which corresponds most to the original character of the Mashal: the proverb explaining its ethical object by a resemblance from the region of the natural and every-day life, the παραβολή proper. The form of this *parabolic* proverb is very manifold, according as the poet himself expressly compares the two subjects, or only places them near each other in order that the hearer or reader may complete the comparison. The proverb is

---

[1] Such integral distichs are also xv. 3, xvi. 7, 10, xvii. 13, 15, xviii. 9, 13, xix. 26, 27, xx. 7, 8, 10, 11, 20, 21, xxi. 4, 13, 16, 21, 23, 24, 30, xxii. 4, 11, xxiv. 8, 26, xxvi. 16, xxvii. 14, xxviii. 8, 9, 17, 24, xxix. 1, 5, 12, 14. In xiv. 27, xv. 24, xvii. 23, xix. 27, the second line consists of one sentence with לְ and the infin.; in xvi. 12, 26, xxi. 25, xxii. 9, xxvii. 1, xxix. 19, of one sentence with כִּי; with כִּי אִם, xviii. 2, xxiii. 17. The two lines, as xi. 31, xv. 11, xvii. 7, xix. 7*ab*, 10, xx. 27, form a conclusion *a minori ad majus*, or the reverse. The former or the latter clauses stand in grammatical relation in xxiii. 1, 2, 15 f., xxvii. 22, xxix. 21 (cf. xxii. 29, xxiv. 10, xxvi. 12, xxix. 20, with hypoth. perf., and xxvi. 26 with hypoth. fut.); in the logical relation of reason and consequence, xvii. 14, xx. 2, 4; in comparative relation, xii. 9, etc. These examples show that the two lines, not merely in the more recent, but also in the old Solomonic Mashal, do not always consist of two parallel members.

least poetic when the likeness between the two subjects is expressed by a verb; as xxvii. 15 (to which, however, ver. 16 belongs) :

> A continual dropping in a rainy day
> And a contentious woman are alike.

The usual form of expression, neither unpoetic nor properly poetic, is the introduction of the comparison by כְּ [as], and of the similitude in the second clause by כֵּן [so]; as x. 26 :

> As vinegar to the teeth, and as smoke to the eyes,
> So is the sluggard to them who give him a commission.

This complete verbal statement of the relation of likeness may also be abbreviated by the omission of the כֵּן; as xxv. 13, xxvi. 11 :

> As a dog returning to his vomit—
> A fool returning to his folly.

We call the parabolic proverbs of these three forms *comparisons.* The last, the abbreviated form of the comparative proverb, forms the transition to another kind of parabolic proverb, which we will call, in contradistinction to the comparative, the *emblematic,* in which the contrast and its emblem are loosely placed together without any nearer expression of the similitude ; as *e.g.* xxvi. 20, xxvii. 17, 18, 20. This takes place either by means of the copulative *Vav,* וְ, as xxv. 25—

> Cold water to a thirsty soul,
> And good news from a far country.[1]

Or without the *Vav ;* in which case the second line is as the subscription under the figure or double figure painted in the first; *e.g.* xxv. 11 f., xi. 22 :

> A gold ring in a swine's snout—
> A fair woman and without understanding.

These ground-forms of two lines can, however, expand into forms of several lines. Since the distich is the peculiar and most appropriate form of the technical proverb, so, when two lines are not sufficient for expressing the thought intended, the multiplication to

---

[1] This so-called *Vav adæquationis,* which appears here for the first time in the Proverbs as the connection between the figure and the thing itself without a verbal predicate (cf., on the other hand, Job v. 7, xii. 11, xiv. 11 f.), is, like the *Vav,* וְ, of comparison, only a species of that *Vav* of association which is called in Arab. *Waw alajam'a,* or *Waw alam'ayat,* or *Waw al'asatsaḥab* (*vid.* at Isa. xlii. 5); and since usage attributes to it the verbal power of *secum habere,* it is construed with the accus. *Vid.* examples in Freytag's *Arabum Proverbia,* among the recent proverbs beginning with the letter ك (*k*).

four, six, or eight lines is most natural. In the *tetrastich* the
relation of the last two to the first two is as manifold as is the
relation of the second line to the first in the distich. There is,
however, no suitable example of four-lined stanzas in antithetic
relation. But we meet with *synonymous* tetrastichs, *e.g.* xxiii. 15 f.,
xxiv. 3 f., 28 f.; *synthetic,* xxx. 5 f.; *integral,* xxx. 17 f., especially
of the form in which the last two lines constitute a proof passage
beginning with כִּי, xxii. 22 f., or פֶּן, xxii. 24 f., or without exponents,
xxii. 26 f.; *comparative* without expressing the comparison, xxv.
16 f. (cf., on the other hand, xxvi. 18 f., where the number of lines
is questionable), and also the *emblematical,* xxv. 4 f. :

> Take away the dross from the silver,
> And there shall come forth a vessel for the goldsmith ;
> Take away the wicked from before the king,
> And his throne shall be established in righteousness.

Proportionally the most frequently occurring are tetrastichs, the
second half of which forms a proof clause commencing with כִּי
or פֶּן. Among the less frequent are the *six-lined,* presenting (xxiii.
1–3, xxiv. 11 f.) one and the same thought in manifold aspects,
with proofs interspersed. Among all the rest which are found in
the collection, xxiii. 12–14, 19–21, 26–28, xxx. 15 f., xxx. 29–31,
the first two lines form a prologue introductory to the substance
of the proverb ; as *e.g.* xxiii. 12–14 :

> O let instruction enter into thine heart,
> And apply thine ears to the words of knowledge.
> Withhold not correction from the child ;
> For if thou beatest him with the rod—he dies not.
> Thou shalt beat him with the rod,
> And deliver his soul from hell.

Similarly formed, yet more expanded, is the *eight-lined* stanza,
xxiii. 22–28 :

> Hearken unto thy father that begat thee,
> And despise not thy mother when she is old.
> Buy the truth and sell it not :
> Wisdom, and virtue, and understanding.
> The father of a righteous man greatly rejoices,
> And he that begetteth a wise child hath joy of him.
> Thy father and thy mother shall be glad,
> And she that bare thee shall rejoice.

The Mashal proverb here inclines to the Mashal ode ; for this
octastich may be regarded as a short Mashal song,—like the alpha-

betical Mashal psalm xxxvii., which consists of almost pure tetrastichs.

We have now seen how the distich form multiplies itself into
forms consisting of four, six, and eight lines; but it also unfolds
itself, as if in cne-sided multiplication, into forms of three, five,
and seven lines. *Tristichs* arise when the thought of the first line
is repeated (xxvii. 22) in the second according to the synonymous
scheme, or when the thought of the second line is expressed by
contrast in the third (xxii. 29, xxviii. 10) according to the antithetic scheme, or when to the thought expressed in one or two
lines (xxv. 8, xxvii. 10) there is added its proof. The parabolic
scheme is here represented when the object described is unfolded
in two lines, as in the comparison xxv. 13, or when its nature is
portrayed by two figures in two lines, as in the emblematic proverb xxv. 20 :

> To take off clothing in cold weather,
> Vinegar upon nitre,
> And he that singeth songs to a heavy heart.

In the few instances of *pentastichs* which are found, the last
three lines usually unfold the reason of the thought of the first
two: xxiii. 4 f., xxv. 6 f., xxx. 32 f.; to this xxiv. 13 forms an
exception, where the כִּי before the last three lines introduces the
expansion of the figure in the first two. As an instance we quote
xxv. 6 f. :

> Seek not to display thyself in the presence of the king,
> And stand not in the place of the great.
> For better that it be said unto thee, " Come up hither,"
> Than that they humble thee in the presence of the prince,
> While thine eyes have raised themselves.

Of *heptastichs* I know of only one example in the collection,
viz. xxiii. 6-8 :

> Eat not the bread of the jealous,
> And lust not after his dainties ;
> For he is like one who calculates with himself :—
> " Eat and drink," saith he to thee,
> And his heart is not with thee.
> Thy morsel which thou hast eaten must thou vomit up,
> And thou hast wasted thy pleasant words.

From this heptastich, which one will scarcely take for a brief
Mashal ode according to the compound strophe-scheme, we see
that the proverb of two lines can expand itself to the dimensions

of seven and eight lines. Beyond these limits the whole proverb ceases to be מָשָׁל in the proper sense ; and after the manner of Ps. xxv., xxxiv., and especially xxxvii., it becomes a Mashal ode. Of this class of Mashal odes are, besides the prologue, xxii. 17–21, that of the drunkard, xxiii. 29–35 ; that of the slothful man, xxiv. 30–34 ; the exhortation to industry, xxvii. 23–27 ; the prayer for a moderate portion between poverty and riches, xxx. 7–9 ; the mirror for princes, xxxi. 2–9 ; and the praise of the excellent wife, xxxi. 10 ff. It is singular that this ode furnishes the only example of the alphabetical acrostic in the whole collection. Even a single trace of original alphabetical sequence afterwards broken up cannot be found. There cannot also be discovered, in the Mashal songs referred to, anything like a completed strophe-scheme ; even in xxxi. 10 ff. the distichs are broken by tristichs intermingled with them.

In the whole of the first part, i. 7–ix., the prevailing form is that of the extended flow of the Mashal song ; but one in vain seeks for strophes. There is not here so firm a grouping of the lines ; on the supposition of its belonging to the Solomonic era, this is indeed to be expected. The rhetorical form here outweighs the purely poetical. This first part of the Proverbs consists of the following fifteen Mashal strains : (1) i. 7–19, (2) 20 ff., (3) ii., (4) iii. 1–18, (5) 19–26, (6) 27 ff., (7) iv. 1–v. 6, (8) 7 ff., (9) vi. 1–5, (10) 6–11, (11) 12–19, (12) 20 ff., (13) vii., (14) viii., (15) ix. In iii. and ix. there are found a few Mashal odes of two lines and of four lines which may be regarded as independent Mashals, and may adapt themselves to the schemes employed ; other brief complete parts are only waves in the flow of the larger discourses, or are altogether formless, or more than octastichs. The octastich vi. 16–19 makes the proportionally greatest impression of an independent inwoven Mashal. It is the only proverb in which symbolical numbers are used which occurs in the collection from i. to xxix. :

> There are six things which Jahve hateth,
> And seven are an abhorrence to His soul :
> Haughty eyes, a lying tongue,
> And hands that shed innocent blood ;
> An heart that deviseth the thoughts of evil,
> Feet that hastily run to wickedness,
> One that uttereth lies as a false witness,
> And he who soweth strife between brethren.

Such *numerical* proverbs to which the name מִדָּה has been given by later Jewish writers (see my *Gesch. der jüd. Poesie,* pp. 199, 202) are found in xxx. With the exception of xxx. 7–9, 24–28 (cf. Sir. xxv. 1, 2), the numerical proverb has this peculiarity, found also in most of the numerical proverbs of Sirach (Sir. xxiii. 16, xxv. 7, xxvi. 5, 28), that the number named in the first parallel line is in the second (cf. Job v. 9) increased by one. On the other hand, the form of the *Priamel*[1] is used neither in the Book of Proverbs nor in that of Sirach. Proverbs such as xx. 10 ("Diverse weights, diverse measures—an abomination to Jahve are they both") and xx. 12 ("The hearing ear, the seeing eye—Jahve hath created them both"), to be distinguished from xvii. 3, xxvii. 21, and the like, where the necessary unity, and from xxvii. 3, where the necessary resemblance, of the predicate is wanting, are only a weak approach to the Priamel,—a stronger, xxv. 3, where the three subjects form the preamble ("The heaven for height, and the earth for depth, and the heart of kings—are unsearchable"). Perhaps xxx. 11–14 is a greater mutilated Priamel. Here four subjects form the preamble, but there is wanting the conclusion containing the common predicate. This, we believe, exhausts the forms of the Mashal in the collection. It now only remains to make mention of the *Mashal chain, i.e.* the ranging together in a series of proverbs of a similar character, such as the chain of proverbs regarding the fool, xxvi. 1–12, the sluggard, xxvi. 13–16, the talebearer, xxvi. 20–22, the malicious, xxvi. 23–28—but this form belongs more to the technics of the Mashal *collection* than to that of the Mashal *poetry.*

We now turn to the separate parts of the book, to examine more closely the forms of their proverbs, and gather materials for a critical judgment regarding the origin of the proverbs which they contain. Not to anticipate, we take up in order the separate parts of the arrangement of the collection. Since, then, it cannot be denied that in the introductory pædagogic part, i. 7–ix., notwithstanding its rich and deep contents, there is exceedingly little of the technical form of the Mashal, as well as generally of technical form at all. This part, as already shown, consists not of proper Mashals, but of fifteen Mashal odes, or rather, perhaps, Mashal discourses, didactic poems of the Mashal kind. In the flow of these discourses separate Mashals intermingle, which may either be regarded as independent, or, as

---

[1] [From *præambulum,* designating a peculiar kind of epigram found in the German poetry of the fifteenth and sixteenth centuries.]

i. 32, iv. 18 f., can easily be so understood. In the Mashal chains of chap. iv. and ix. we meet with proverbs that are synonymous (ix. 7, 10), antithetic (iii. 35, ix. 8), integral, or of one thought (iii. 29, 30), and synthetic (i. 7, iii. 5, 7), of two lines and of four lines variously disposed (iii. 9 f., 11 f., 31 f., 33 f.) ; but the parabolic scheme is not at all met with, separate proverbs such as iii. 27 f. are altogether without form, and keeping out of view the octastich numerical proverb, vi. 16–19, the thoughts which form the unity of separate groups are so widely expanded that the measure of the Mashal proper is far exceeded. The character of this whole part is not concentrating, but unfolding. Even the intermingling proverbs of two lines possess the same character. They are for the most part more like dissolved drops than gold coins with sharp outline and firm impress ; as *e.g.* ix. 7 :

> He that correcteth the mocker getteth to himself shame ;
> And he that rebuketh the sinner his dishonour.

The few that consist of four lines are closer, more compact, more finished, because they allow greater space for the expression ; *e.g.* iii. 9 f. :

> Honour Jahve with thy wealth,
> And with the first-fruits of all thine income :
> And thy barns shall be filled with plenty,
> And thy vats shall overflow with must.

But beyond the four lines the author knows no limits of artistic harmony ; the discourse flows on till it has wholly or provisionally exhausted the subject ; it pauses not till it reaches the end of its course, and then, taking breath, it starts anew. We cannot, moreover, deny that there is beauty in this new springing forth of the stream of the discourse with its fresh transparent waves ; but it is a peculiar beauty of the rhetorically decomposed, dissolved Mashal, going forth, as it were, from its confinement, and breathing its fragrance far and wide.

The fifteen discourses, in which the Teacher appears twelve times and Wisdom three times, are neither of a symmetrically chiselled form nor of internally fashioned coherence, but yet are a garland of songs having internal unity, with a well-arranged manifoldness of contents. It is true that Bertheau recognises here neither unity of the contents nor unity of the formal character ; but there is no Old Testament portion of like extent, and at the same time of more systematic internal unity, and which bears throughout a like formal impress, than this. Bertheau thinks that he has discovered in certain passages a greater art in the form; and certainly there are several sections which consist of just ten verses. But this is a mere accident; for the first Mashal ode consists of groups of 1, 2, and 10 verses, the second of 8 and 6 verses, the third of 10 and 12, the fourth of 10 and 8, the fifth of 2 and 6, etc.—each group forming a complete sense. The 10 verses are met with six times, and if iv. 1–9 from the Peshito, and iv. 20–27 from the LXX., are included, eight times, without our regarding these decades as strophes, and without our being able to draw any conclusion regarding a particular author of these decade portions. In i. 20–33, Bertheau finds indeed, along with the regular structure of verses, an exact artistic formation of strophes (3 times 4 verses with an echo of 2). But he counts instead of the stichs the Masoretic verses, and these are not the true formal parts of the strophe.

We now come to the second part of the collection, whose superscription מִשְׁלֵי שְׁלֹמֹה can in no respect be strange to us, since the collection of proverbs here commencing, compared with i. 7–ix., may with special right bear the name *Mishle*. The 375 proverbs which are classed together in this part, x.–xxii. 16, without any comprehensive plan, but only according to their more or fewer conspicuous common characteristics (Bertheau, p. xii), consist all and every one of distichs; for each Masoretic verse falls naturally into two stichs, and nowhere (not even xix. 19) does such a distich proverb stand in necessary connection with one that precedes or that follows; each is in itself a small perfected and finished whole. The tristich xix. 7 is only an apparent exception. In reality it is a distich with the disfigured remains of a distich that has been lost. The LXX. has here two distichs which are wanting in our text. The second is that which is found in our text, but only in a mutilated form:

ὁ πολλὰ κακοποιῶν τελεσιουργεῖ κακίαν,
[He that does much harm perfects mischief,]
ὃς δὲ ἐρεθίζει λόγους οὐ σωθήσεται.
[And he that uses provoking words shall not escape.]

Perhaps the false rendering of

מרע רבים ישלם־רע
מרדף אמרים לא ימלט:

The friend of every one is rewarded with evil,
He who pursues after rumours does not escape.

But not only are all these proverbs distichs, they have also, not indeed without exception, but in by far the greatest number, a common character in that they are *antithetic*. Distichs of predominating antithetic character stand here together. Along with these all other schemes are, it is true, represented : the synonymous, xi. 7, 25, 30, xii. 14, 28, xiv. 19, etc. ; the integral, or of one thought, xiv. 7, xv. 3, etc., particularly in proverbs with the comparative מִן, xii. 9, xv. 16, 17, xvi. 8, 19, xvii. 10, xxi. 19, xxii. 1, and with the ascending אַף כִּי [much more], xi. 31, xv. 11, xvii. 7, xix. 7, 10, xxi. 27 ; the synthetic, x. 18, xi. 29, xiv. 17, xix. 13 ; the parabolic, the most feebly represented, for the only specimens of it are x. 26, xi. 22 ; besides which I know not what other Bertheau could quote. We shall further see that in another portion of the book the parabolic proverbs are just as closely placed together as are the antithetic. Here almost universally the two members of the proverbs stand together in technical parallelism as thesis and antithesis ; also in the synonymous proverbs the two members are the parallel rays of one thought ; in the synthetic two monostichs occur in loose external connection to suffice for the parallelism as a fundamental law of the technical proverb. But also in these proverbs in which a proper parallelism is not found, both members being needed to form a complete sentence, verse and members are so built up, according to Bertheau's self-confirmatory opinion, that in regard to extent and the number of words they are like verses with parallel members.

To this long course of distichs which profess to be the *Mishle* of Solomon, there follows a course, xxii. 17–xxiv. 22, of " words of the wise," prefaced by the introduction xxii. 17–21, which undeniably is of the same nature as the greater introduction, i. 7–ix., and of which we are reminded by the form of address preserved throughout in these " words of the wise." These " words of the wise " comprehend all the forms of the Mashal, from those of two lines in xxii. 28, xxiii. 9, xxiv. 7, 8, 9, 10, to the Mashal song xxiii. 29-35. Between these limits are the tetrastichs, which are the most popular form, xxii. 22 f., 24 f., 26 f., xxiii. 10 f., 15 f., 17 f., xxiv. 1 f., 3 f., 5 f., 15 f., 17 f., 19 f., 21 f.,—pentastichs, xxiii. 4 f., xxiv. 13 f., and hexastichs, xxiii. 1-3, 12–14, 19–21, 26–28, xxiv. 11 f. ;—of tristichs, heptastichs, and octastichs are at least found one specimen of each, xxii. 29, xxiii. 6–8, xxiii. 22–25. Bertheau maintains that there is a difference between the structure of these

proverbs and that of the preceding, for he counts the number of
the words which constitute a verse in the case of the latter and of
the former; but such a proceeding is unwarrantable, for the remarkably long Masoretic verse xxiv. 12 contains eighteen words;
and the poet is not to be made accountable for such an arrangement,
for in his mind xxiv. 11 f. forms a hexastich, and indeed a very
elegant one. Not the *words* of the Masoretic verse, but the *stichs*
are to be counted. Reckoning according to the *stichs*, I can discover no difference between these proverbs and the preceding. In
the preceding ones also the number of the words in the stichs
extends from two to five, the number two being here, however,
proportionally more frequently found (*e.g.* xxiv. 4*b*, xxiv. 8*a*, 10*b*);
a circumstance which has its reason in this, that the symmetry of
the members is often very much disturbed, there being frequently
no trace whatever of parallelism. To the first appendix to the
" Proverbs of Solomon " there follows a second, xxiv. 23 ff., with
the superscription, " These things also to the wise," which contains
a hexastich, xxiv. 23*b*–25, a distich, ver. 26, a tristich, ver. 27, a
tetrastich, ver. 28 f., and a Mashal ode, ver. 30 ff., on the sluggard
—the last in the form of an experience of the poet like Ps. xxxvii.
35 f. The moral which he has drawn from this recorded observation is expressed in two verses such as we have already found at
vi. 10 f. These two appendices are, as is evident from their commencement as well as from their conclusion, in closest relation to
the introduction, i. 7–ix.

There now follows in xxv.–xxix. the second great collection of
" Proverbs of Solomon," " copied out," as the superscription mentions, by the direction of King Hezekiah. It falls, apparently, into
two parts; for as xxiv. 30 ff., a Mashal hymn, stands at the end
of the two appendices, so the Mashal hymn xxvii. 23 ff. must be
regarded as forming the division between the two halves of this
collection. It is very sharply distinguished from the collection
beginning with chap. x. The extent of the stichs and the greater
or less observance of the parallelism furnish no distinguishing
mark, but there are others worthy of notice. In the first collection
the proverbs are exclusively in the form of distichs; here we have
also some tristichs, xxv. 8, 13, 20, xxvii. 10, 22, xxviii. 10, tetrastichs, xxv. 4 f., 9 f., 21 f., xxvi. 18 f., 24 f., xxvii. 15 f., and
pentastichs, xxv. 6 f., besides the Mashal hymn already referred to.
The kind of arrangement is not essentially different from that in

the first collection; it is equally devoid of plan, yet there are here some chains or strings of related proverbs, xxvi. 1-12, 13-16, 20-22. A second essential distinction between the two collections is this, that while in the first the *antithetic* proverb forms the prevailing element, here it is the *parabolic*, and especially the *emblematic ;* in xxv.–xxvii. are sentences almost wholly of this character. We say *almost*, for to place together proverbs of this kind exclusively is not the plan of the collector. There are also proverbs of the other schemes, fewer synonymous, etc., than antithetic, and the collection begins in very varied quodlibet : xxv. 2, an antithetic proverb; xxv. 3, a priamel with three subjects; xxv. 4 f., an emblematic tetrastich ; xxv. 6 f., a pentastich ; xxv. 8, a tristich ; xxv. 9 f., a tetrastich, with the negative פֶּן ; xxv. 11, an emblematic distich (" Golden apples in silver caskets—a word spoken in a fitting way "). The antithetic proverbs are found especially in xxviii. and xxix.: the first and the last proverb of the whole collection, xxv. 2, xxix. 27, are antithetic; but between these two the comparative and the figurative proverbs are so prevalent, that this collection appears like a variegated picture-book with explanatory notes written underneath. In extent it is much smaller than the foregoing. I reckon 126 proverbs in 137 Masoretic verses.

The second collection of Solomon's proverbs has also several appendices, the first of which, xxx., according to the inscription, is by an otherwise unknown author, Agur the son of Jakeh. The first poem of this appendix presents in a thoughtful way the unsearchableness of God. This is followed by certain peculiar pieces, such as a tetrastich regarding the purity of God's word, xxx. 5 f.; a prayer for a moderate position between riches and poverty, vers. 7-9 ; a distich against slander, ver. 10 ; a priamel without the conclusion, vers. 11-14 ; the insatiable four (a *Midda*), ver. 15 f. ; a tetrastich regarding the disobedient son, ver. 17 ; the incomprehensible four, vers. 18-20 ; the intolerable four, vers. 21-23 ; the diminutive but prudent four, vers. 24-28 ; the excellent four, vers. 29-31 ; a pentastich recommending prudent silence, ver. 32 f. Two other supplements form the conclusion of the whole book : the counsel of Lemuel's mother to her royal son, xxxi. 2-9, and the praise of the virtuous woman in the form of an alphabetical acrostic, xxxi. 10 ff.

After we have acquainted ourselves with the manifold forms of the technical proverbs and their distribution in the several parts of the collection, the question arises, What conclusions regarding the origin of these several parts may be drawn from these forms found in them? We connect with this the conception of Ewald, who sees represented in the several parts of the collection the chief points of the history of proverbial poetry. The "Proverbs of Solomon," x. 1–xxii. 16, appear to him to be the oldest collection, which represents the simplest and the most ancient kind of proverbial poetry. Their distinguishing characteristics are the symmetrical two-membered verse, complete in itself, containing in itself a fully intelligible meaning, and the quick contrast of thesis and antithesis. The oldest form of the technical proverb, according to Ewald, is, according to our terminology, the antithetic distich, such as predominates in x. 1–xxii. 16. Along with these antithetic distichs we find here also others of a different kind. Ewald so considers the contrast of the two members to be the original fundamental law of the technical proverb, that to him these other kinds of distichs represent the diminution of the inner force of the two-membered verse, the already begun decay of the art in its oldest limits and laws, and the transition to a new method. In the "Proverbs of Solomon," xxv.–xxix., of the later collection, that rigorous formation of the verse appears already in full relaxation and dissolution: the contrast of the sense of the members appears here only exceptionally; the art turns from the crowded fulness and strength of the representation more to the adorning of the thought by means of strong and striking figures and forms of expression, to elegant painting of certain moral conditions and forms of life; and the more the technical proverb is deprived of the breath of a vigorous poetic spirit, so much the nearer does it approach to the vulgar proverb; the full and complete symmetry of the two members disappears, less by the abridgment of one of them, than by the too great extension and amplification of the two-membered proverb into longer admonitions to a moral life, and descriptions relating thereto. So the proverbial poetry passes essentially into a different form and manner. "While it loses in regard to internal vigorous brevity and strength, it seeks to gain again by means of connected instructive exposition, by copious description and detailed representation; breaking up its boldly delineated, strong, and yet simply beautiful form, it rises to oratorical display, to attractive eloquence, in which, indeed, though the properly poetical and the artistic gradually disappears, yet the warmth and easy comprehension are increased." In chap. i.–ix., the introduction of the older collection, and xxii. 17–xxiv., of the first half of the supplement to the older collection (xxv.–xxix. is the second half), supplied by a later writer, the great change is completed, the growth of which the later collection of the " Proverbs of Solomon," particularly in xxv.–xxix., reveals. The symmetry of the two members of the verse is here completely destroyed ; the separate proverb appears almost only as an exception ; the proverbial poetry has passed into admonition and discourse, and has become in many respects lighter, and more flexible, and flowing, and comprehensible. " It is true that on the side of this later form of proverbial poetry there is not mere loss. While it always loses the excellent pointed brevity, the inner fulness and strength of the old proverbs, it gains in warmth, impressiveness, intelligibility ; the wisdom which at first strives only to make its existence and its contents in endless manifoldness known, reaches this point at last, that having become clear and certain, it now also turns itself earnestly and urgently to men." In the later additions, chap. xxx. xxxi., appended altogether externally, the proverbial poetry has already disappeared, and given place to elegant descriptions of separate moral truths. While the creative passes into the background, the whole aim is now toward surprising expansion and new artistic representation.

This view of the progressive development of the course of proverbial poetry is one of the chief grounds for the determination of Ewald's judgment regarding the parts that are Solomonic and those that are not Solomonic in the collection. In x. 1–xxii. 16 he does not regard the whole as Solomon's, as immediately and in their present form composed by Solomon ; but the breath of the Solomonic spirit enlivens and pervades all that has been added by other and later poets. But most of the proverbs of the later collection (xxv.–xxix.) are not much older than the time of Hezekiah ; yet there are in it some that are Solomonic, and of the period next to Solomon. The collection stretches backward with its arms, in part indeed, as the superscription, the " Proverbs of Solomon," shows, to the time of Solomon. On the other hand, in the introduction, i.–ix., and in the first half of the appendix (xxii. 17–xxiv.), there is not found a single proverb of the time of Solomon ; both portions belong to two poets of the seventh century B.C., a new era, in which the didactic poets added to the older Solomonic collection longer pieces of their own composition. The four small pieces, xxx. 1–14, 15–33, xxxi. 1–9, 10 ff., are of a still later date ;

they cannot belong to an earlier period than the end of the seventh or the beginning of the sixth century B.C. We recognise the penetration, the sensibility, the depth of thought indicated by this opinion of Ewald's regarding the origin of the book ; yet for the most part it is not supported by satisfactory proof. If we grant that he has on the whole rightly construed the history of proverbial poetry, nevertheless the conclusion that proverbs which bear in themselves the marks of the oldest proverbial poetry belong to the Solomonic era, and that the others belong to a period more nearly or more remotely subsequent to it, is very fallacious. In this case much that is found in Sirach's Book of Proverbs must be Solomonic ; and the משלי אסף of Isaac Satanow,[1] the contemporary of Moses Mendelssohn, as well as many other proverbs in the collection מלין דרבנן, and in the poetical works of other Jewish poets belonging to the middle ages or to later times, might be dated back perhaps a thousand years. Along with the general course of development the individuality of the poet is also to be taken into account ; an ancient poet can, along with the formally completed, produce the imperfect, which appears to belong to a period of art that has degenerated, and a modern poet can emulate antiquity with the greatest accuracy. But Ewald's construction of the progress of the development of proverbial poetry is also in part arbitrary. That the two-membered verse is the oldest form of the technical proverb we shall not dispute, but that it is the two-membered antithetic verse is a supposition that cannot be proved ; and that Solomon wrote only antithetic distichs is an absurd assertion, to which Keil justly replies, that the adhering to only one form and structure is a sign of poverty, of mental narrowness and one-sidedness. There are also other kinds of parallelism, which are not less beautiful and vigorous than the antithetic, and also other forms of proverbs besides the distich in which the thought, which can in no way be restrained within two lines, must necessarily divide itself into the branches of a greater number of lines. Thus I must agree with Keil in the opinion, that Ewald's assertion that in the Hezekiah-collection the strong form of the technical proverb is in full dissolution, contains an exaggeration. If the

---

[1] [Isaac Ha-Levi was born at Satanow (whence his name), in Russian Poland, 1732, died at Berlin 1802. Besides other works, he was the author of several collections of gnomes and apothegms in imitation of the Proverbs. *Vid.* Delitzsch *Zur Gesch. der Jüd. Poesie*, p. 115.]

first collection, x. 1–xxii. 16, contains only two (x. 26, xi. 22) figurative proverbs, while it would be altogether foolish to deny that these two, because they were figurative proverbs, were Solomonic, or to affirm that he was the author of only these two, so it is self-evident that the Hezekiah-collection, which is principally a collection of figurative proverbs, must contain many proverbs in which a different kind of parallelism prevails, which has the appearance of a looser connection. Is it not probable that Solomon, who had an open penetrating eye for the greatest and the smallest objects of nature, composed many such proverbs? And is e.g. the proverb xxvi. 23,

> Dross of silver spread over a potsherd—
> Burning lips and a wicked heart,

less beautiful, and vigorous, and worthy of Solomon than any antithetic distich? If Ewald imagines that the 3000 proverbs which Solomon wrote were all constructed according to this one model, we are much rather convinced that Solomon's proverbial poetry, which found the distich and the tetrastich as forms of proverbs already in use, would not only unfold within the limits of the distich the most varied manifoldness of thought and form, but would also within the limits of the Mashal generally, run through the whole scale from the distich up to octastichs and more extensive forms. But while we cannot accept Ewald's criteria which he applies to the two collections, x. 1–xxii. 16 and xxv.–xxix., yet his delineation of the form and kind of proverbial poetry occurring in i.–ix., xxii. 17 ff., is excellent, as is also his conclusion, that these portions belong to a new and more recent period of proverbial poetry. Since in xxii. 17–21 manifestly a new course of " Words of the Wise " by a poet later than Solomon is introduced, it is possible, yea, not improbable, that he, or, as Ewald thinks, another somewhat older poet, introduces in i. 7–ix. the " Proverbs of Solomon" following, from x. 1 onward.

But if Solomon composed not only distichs, but also tristichs, etc., it is strange that in the first collection, x.–xxii. 16, there are exclusively distichs ; and if he constructed not only contrasted proverbs, but equally figurative proverbs, it is as strange that in the first collection the figurative proverbs are almost entirely wanting, while in the second collection, xxv.–xxix., on the contrary, they prevail. This remarkable phenomenon may be partly explained if we could suppose that not merely the second collection, but both of them, were arranged by the " men of Hezekiah," and that the whole collection of the Solomonic proverbs was divided by them into two collections according to their form. But leaving out of view other objections, one would in that case have expected in the first collection the proportionally great number of the antithetic distichs which stand in the second. If we regard both collections as originally one whole, then there can be no rational ground for its being divided in this particular way either by the original collector or by a later enlarger of the collection. We have therefore to regard the two portions as the work of two different authors. The second is by the " men of Hezekiah ;" the first cannot be by Solomon himself, since the number of proverbs composed, and probably also written out by Solomon, amounted to 3000; besides, if Solomon was the author of the collection, there would be visible on it the stamp of his wisdom in its plan and order : it is thus the work of another author, who is certainly different from the author of the introductory Mashal poems, i. 7–ix. For if the author of the title of the book were not at the same time the author of the introduction, he must have taken it from some other place ; thus it is inconceivable how he could give the title " Proverbs of Solomon," etc., i. 1–6, to poems which were not composed by Solomon. If i. 7–ix. is not by Solomon, then these Mashal poems are explicable only as the work of the author of the title of the book, and as an introduction to the " Proverbs of Solomon," beginning x. 1. It must be one and the same author who edited the " Proverbs of Solomon " x. 1–xxii. 16, prefixed i. 7–ix. as an introduction to them, and appended to them the " Words of the Wise," xxii. 17–xxiv. 22 ; the second collector then appended to this book a supplement of the " Words of the Wise," xxiv. 23 ff., and then the Hezekiah-collection of Solomonic proverbs, xxv.–xxix.; perhaps also, in order that the book might be brought to a close in the same form in which it was commenced, he added[1] the non-Solomonic proverbial poem xxx. f. We do not, however, maintain that the book has this origin, but only this, that on the supposition of the non-Solomonic origin of i. 7–ix. it cannot well have any other origin. But the question arises again, and more emphatically, How was it possible that the first collector left as gleanings to

[1] Zöckler takes xxiv. 23 ff. as a second appendix to the first principal collection. This is justifiable, but the second superscription rather suggests two collectors.

the second so great a number of distichs, almost all parabolical, and besides, all more than two-lined proverbs of Solomon? One can scarcely find the reason of this singular phenomenon in anything else than in the judgment of the author of the first collection as the determining motive of his selection. For when we think also on the sources and origin of the two collections, the second always presupposes the first, and that which is singular in the author's thus restricting himself can only have its ground in the freedom which he allowed to his subjectivity.

Before we more closely examine the style and the teaching of the book, and the conclusions thence arising, another phenomenon claims our attention, which perhaps throws light on the way in which the several collections originated; but, at all events, it may not now any longer remain out of view, when we are in the act of forming a judgment on this point.

3. *The repetitions in the Book of Proverbs.*—We find not only in the different parts of the collection, but also within the limits of one and the same part, proverbs which wholly or in part are repeated in the same or in similar words. Before we can come to a judgment, we must take cognizance as closely as possible of this fact. We begin with " The Proverbs of Solomon," x.-xxii. 16; for this collection is in relation to xxv.-xxix. certainly the earlier, and it is especially with respect to the Solomonic proverbs that this fact demands an explanation. In this earlier collection we find, (1) whole proverbs repeated in exactly the same words: xiv. 12 = xvi. 25;—(2) proverbs slightly changed in their form of expression: x. 1 = xv. 20, xiv. 20 = xix. 4, xvi. 2 = xxi. 2, xix. 5 = xix. 9, xx. 10 = xx. 23, xxi. 9 = xxi. 19;—(3) proverbs almost identical in form, but somewhat different in sense: x. 2 = xi. 4, xiii. 14 = xiv. 27;—(4) proverbs the first lines of which are the same: x. 15 = xviii. 11;—(5) proverbs with their second lines the same: x. 6 = x. 11, x. 8 = x. 10, xv. 33 = xviii. 12;—(6) proverbs with one line almost the same: xi. 13=xx. 19, xi. 21=xvi. 5, xii. 14 = xiii. 2, xiv. 31 = xvii. 5, xvi 18 = xviii. 12, xix. 12 = xx. 2; comp. also xvi. 28 with xvii. 9, xix. 25 with xxi. 11. In comparing these proverbs, one will perceive that for the most part the external or internal resemblance of the surrounding has prompted the collector to place the one proverb in this place and the other in that place (not always indeed; for what reason *e.g.* could determine

the position of xvi. 25 and xix. 5, 9, I cannot say); then that the proverb standing earlier is generally, to all appearance, also the earlier formed, for the second of the pair is mostly a synonymous distich, which generally further extends antithetically one line of the first: cf. xviii. 11 with x. 15, xx. 10, 23 with xi. 1, xx. 19 with xi. 13, xvi. 5 with xi. 21, xx. 2 with xix. 12, also xvii. 5 with xiv. 31, where from an antithetic proverb a synthetic one is formed; but here also there are exceptions, as xiii. 2 compared with xii. 14, and xv. 33 with xviii. 12, where the same line is in the first case connected with a synonymous, and in the second with an antithetic proverb; but here also the contrast is so loose, that the earlier-occurring proverb has the appearance of priority.

We now direct our attention to the second collection, xxv.-xxix. When we compare the proverbs found here with one another, we see among them a disproportionately smaller number of repetitions than in the other collection; only a single entire proverb is repeated in almost similar terms, but in an altered sense, xxix. 20 = xxvi. 12; but proverbs such as xxviii.12, 28, xxix.2, notwithstanding the partial resemblance, are equally original. On the other hand, in this second collection we find numerous repetitions of proverbs and portions of proverbs from the first:—(1) Whole proverbs perfectly identical (leaving out of view insignificant variations): xxv. 24 = xxi. 9, xxvi. 22 = xviii. 8, xxvii. 12 = xxii. 3, xxvii. 13 = xx. 16;—(2) proverbs identical in meaning, with somewhat changed expression: xxvi. 13 = xxii. 13, xxvi. 15 = xix. 24, xxviii. 6 = xix. 1, xxviii. 19 = xii. 11, xxix. 13 = xxii. 2;—(3) proverbs with one line the same and one line different: xxvii. 21 = xvii. 3, xxix. 22 = xv. 18; cf. also xxvii. 15 with xix. 13. When we compare these proverbs with one another, we are uncertain as to many of them which has the priority, as e.g. xxvii. 21 = xvii. 3, xxix. 22 = xv. 18; but in the case of others there is no doubt that the Hezekiah-collection contains the original form of the proverb which is found in the other collection, as xxvi. 13, xxviii. 6, 19, xxix. 13, xxvii. 15, in relation to their parallels. In the other portions of this book also we find such repetitions as are met with in these two collections of Solomonic proverbs. In i. 7–ix. we have ii. 16, a little changed, repeated in vii. 5, and iii. 15 in viii. 11; ix. 10a = i. 7a is a case not worthy of being mentioned, and it were inappropriate here to refer to ix. 4, 16. In the first appendix of " the Words of the Wise," xxii. 17–xxiv. 22, single lines often repeat themselves in another connection; cf. xxiii. 3 and 6, xxiii. 10 and xxii. 28, xxiii. 17 f. and xxiv. 13 f., xxii. 23 and xxiii. 11, xxiii. 17 and xxiv. 1. That in such cases the one proverb is often the pattern of the other, is placed beyond a doubt by the relation of xxiv. 19 to Ps. xxxvii. 1 ; cf. also xxiv. 20 with Ps. xxxvii. 38. If here there are proverbs like those of Solomon in their expression, the presumption is that the priority belongs to the latter, as xxiii. 27 cf. xxii. 14, xxiv. 5 f. cf xi. 14, xxiv. 19 f. cf. xiii. 9, in which latter case the justice of the presumption is palpable. Within the second appendix of " the Words of the Wise," xxiv. 23 ff., no repetitions are to be expected on account of its shortness ; yet is xxiv. 23 repeated from the Solomonic Mashal xxviii. 21, and as xxiv. 33 f. are literally the same as vi. 10 f., the priority is presumably on the side of the author of i. 7–ix., at least of the Mashal in the form in which he communicates it. The supplements xxx. and xxxi. afford nothing that is worth mention as bearing on our present inquiry,[1] and we may therefore now turn to the question, What insight into the origin of these proverbs and their collection do the observations made afford ?

From the numerous repetitions of proverbs and portions of proverbs of the first collection of the " Proverbs of Solomon" in the Hezekiah-collection, as well as from another reason stated at the end of the foregoing section of our inquiry, we conclude that the two collections were by different authors ; in other words, that they had not both " the men of Hezekiah" for their authors. It is true that the repetitions in themselves do not prove anything against the oneness of their authorship ; for there are within the several collections, and even within i.–ix. (cf. vi. 20 with i. 8, viii.

---

[1] Quite the same phenomenon, Fleischer remarks, presents itself in the different collections of proverbs ascribed to the Caliph Ali, where frequently one and the same thought in one collection is repeated in manifold forms in a second, here in a shorter, there in a longer form. As a general principle this is to be borne in mind, that the East transmits unchanged, with scrupulous exactness, only religious writings regarded as holy and divine, and therefore these Proverbs have been transmitted unchanged only since they became a distinct part of the canon ; before that time it happened to them, as to all in the East that is exposed to the arbitrariness of the changing spirit and the intercourse of life, that one and the same original text has been modified by one speaker and writer after another. Thus of the famous poetical works of the East, such e.g. as Firdusi's *Schah-Nameh* [*Book of the Kings*] and Sadi's *Garden of Roses*, not one MS. copy agrees with another.

10 f. with iii. 14 f.), repetitions, notwithstanding the oneness of their authorship. But if two collections of proverbs are in so many various ways different in their character, as x. 1–xxii. 16 and xxv.–xxix., then the previous probability rises almost to a certainty by such repetitions. From the form, for the most part anomalous, in which the Hezekiah-collection presents the proverbs and portions of proverbs which are found also in the first collection, and from their being otherwise independent, we further conclude that "the men of Hezekiah" did not borrow from the first collection, but formed it from other sources. But since one does not understand why "the men of Hezekiah" should have omitted so great a number of genuine Solomonic proverbs which remain, after deducting the proportionally few that have been repeated (for this omission is not to be explained by saying that they selected those that were appropriate and wholesome for their time), we are further justified in the conclusion that the other collection was known to them as one current in their time. Their object was, indeed, not to supplement this older collection; they rather regarded their undertaking as a similar people's book, which they wished to place side by side with that collection without making it superfluous. The difference of the selection in the two collections has its whole directing occasion in the difference of the intention. The first collection begins (x. 1) with the proverb—

> A wise son maketh glad his father,
> And a foolish son is the grief of his mother;

the second (xxv. 2) with the proverb—

> It is the glory of God to conceal a thing,
> And the glory of kings to search out a matter.

The one collection is a book for youth, to whom it is dedicated in the extended introduction, i. 7–ix.; the second is a people's book suited to the time of Hezekiah ("Solomon's Wisdom in Hezekiah's days," as Stier has named it), and therefore it takes its start not, like the first, from the duties of the child, but from those of the king. If in the two collections everything does not stand in conscious relation to these different objects, yet the collectors at least have, from the commencement to the close (cf. xxii. 15 with xxix. 26), these objects before their eyes.

As to the *time* at which the first collection was made, the above considerations also afford us some materials for forming a judgment. Several pairs of proverbs which it contains present to us essentially the same sayings in older and more recent forms. Keil regards the proverbs also that appear less original as old-Solomonic, and remarks that one and the same poet does not always give expression to the same thoughts with the same pregnant brevity and excellence, and affirms that changes and reproductions of separate proverbs may proceed even from Solomon himself. This is possible; but if we consider that even Davidic psalms have been imitated, and that in the " Words of the Wise" Solomonic proverbs are imitated,—moreover, that proverbs especially are subject to changes, and invite to imitation and transformation,—we shall find it to be improbable. Rather we would suppose, that between the publication of the 3000 proverbs of Solomon and the preparation of the collection x.–xxii. 16 a considerable time elapsed, during which the old-Solomonic Mashal had in the mouths of the people and of poets acquired a multitude of accretions, and that the collector had without hesitation gathered together such indirect Solomonic proverbs with those that were directly Solomonic. But did not then the 3000 Solomonic proverbs afford to him scope enough? We must answer this question in the negative; for if that vast number of Solomonic proverbs was equal in moral-religious worth to those that have been preserved to us, then neither the many repetitions within the first collection nor the proportional poverty of the second can be explained. The " men of Hezekiah" made their collection of Solomonic proverbs nearly 300 years after Solomon's time; but there is no reason to suppose that the old book of the Proverbs of Solomon had disappeared at that time. Much rather we may with probability conclude, from the subjects to which several proverbs of these collections extend (husbandry, war, court life, etc.), and from Solomon's love for the manifold forms of natural and of social life, that his 3000 proverbs would not have afforded much greater treasures than these before us. But if the first collection was made at a time in which the old-Solomonic proverbs had been already considerably multiplied by new combinations, accretions, and imitations, then probably a more suitable time for their origination could not be than that of Jehoshaphat, which was more related to the time of Solomon than to that of David. The personality of Jehoshaphat, inclined toward the promotion of the public worship of God, the edification of the people, the administration of justice; the dominion of the house of David recognised and venerated far and wide among neighbouring peoples ; the tendencies of that time towards intercourse with distant regions ; the deep peace which followed the subjugation of the confederated nations,—all these are features which stamped the time of Jehoshaphat as a copy of that of Solomon. Hence we are to expect in it the fostering care of the *Chokma*. If the author of the introduction and editor of the older book of Proverbs lived after Solomon and before Hezekiah, then the circumstances of the case most suitably determine his time as at the beginning of the reign of Jehoshaphat, some seventy years after Solomon's death. If in i.–ix. it is frequently said that wisdom was seen openly in the streets and ways, this agrees with 2 Chron. xvii. 7–9, where it is said that princes, priests, and Levites, sent out by Jehoshaphat (compare the Carolingian *missi*), went forth into the towns of Judah with the book of the law in their hands as teachers of the people, and with 2 Chron. xix. 4, where it is stated that Jehoshaphat himself " went out through the people from Beer-sheba to Mount Ephraim, and brought them back unto the Lord God of their fathers." We have an evidence of the fondness for allegorical forms of address at that time in 2 Kings xiv. 8–11 (2 Chron. xxv. 17–21), which is so far favourable to the idea that the allegorizing author of i.–ix. belonged to that epoch of history.

This also agrees with the time of Jehoshaphat, that in the first collection the kingdom appears in its bright side, adorned with righteousness (xiv. 35, xvi. 10, 12, 13, xx. 8), wisdom (xx. 26), grace and truth (xx. 28), love to the good (xxii. 11), divine guidance (xxi. 1), and in the height of power (xvi. 14, 15, xix. 12) ; while in the second collection, which immediately begins with a series of the king's sayings, the kingdom is seen almost only (with exception of xxix. 14) on its dark side, and is represented under the destructive dominion of tyranny (xxviii. 15, 16, xxix. 2), of oppressive taxation (xxix. 4), of the Camarilla (xxv. 5, xxix. 12), and of multiplied authorities (xxviii. 2). Elster is right when he remarks, that in x.–xxii. 16 the kingdom in its actual state corresponds to its ideal, and the warning against the abuse of royal power lies remote. If these proverbs more distinguishably than those in xxv.–xxix. bear the physiognomy of the time of David and Solomon, so, on the other hand, the time of Jehoshaphat, the son and successor of Asa, is favourable to their collection ; while in the time of Hezekiah, the son and successor of Ahaz, and father and predecessor of Manasseh, in which, through the sin of Ahaz, negotiations with the world-kingdom began, that cloudy aspect of the kingdom which is borne by the second supplement, xxiv. 23–25, was brought near.

Thus between Solomon and Hezekiah, and probably under Jehoshaphat, the older Book of Proverbs contained in i.–xxiv. 22 first appeared. The "Proverbs of Solomon," x. 1–xxii. 16, which formed the principal part, the very kernel of it, were enclosed on the one side, at their commencement, by the lengthened introduction i. 7–ix., in which the collector announces himself as a highly gifted teacher and as the instrument of the Spirit of revelation, and on the other side are shut in at their close by "the Words of the Wise," xxii. 17–xxiv. 34. The author, indeed, does not announce i. 6 such a supplement of "the Words of the Wise;" but after these words in the title of the book, he leads us to expect it. The introduction to the supplement xxii. 17–21 sounds like an echo of the larger introduction, and corresponds to the smaller compass of the supplement. The work bears on the whole the stamp of a unity; for even in the last proverb with which it closes (xxiv. 21 f., "My son, fear thou Jahve and the king," etc.), there still sounds the same key-note which the author had struck at the commencement. A later collector, belonging to the time subsequent to Hezekiah, enlarged the work by the addition of the Hezekiah-portion, and by a short supplement of "the Words of the Wise," which he introduces, according to the law of analogy, after xxii. 17–xxiv. 22. The harmony of the superscriptions xxiv. 23, xxv. 1, favours at least the supposition that these supplements are the work of one hand. The circumstance that "the Words of the Wise," xxii. 17–xxiv. 22, in two of their maxims refer to the older collection of Solomonic proverbs, but, on the contrary, that "the Words of the Wise," xxiv. 23 ff., refer in xxiv. 23 to the Hezekiah-collection, and in xxiv. 33 f. to the introduction i. 7–ix., strengthens the supposition that with xxiv. 23 a second half of the book, added by another hand, begins. There is no reason for not attributing the appendix xxx.–xxxi. to this second collector; perhaps he seeks, as already remarked above, to render by means of it the conclusion of the extended Book of Proverbs uniform with that of the older book. Like the older collection of "Proverbs of Solomon," so also now the Hezekiah-collection has "Proverbs of the Wise" on the right and on the left, and the king of proverbial poetry stands in the midst of a worthy retinue. The second collector distinguishes himself from the first by this, that he never professes himself to be a proverbial poet. It is possible that the proverbial poem of the " virtuous woman," xxxi. 10 ff., may be his work, but there is nothing to substantiate this opinion.

After this digression, into which we have been led by the repetitions found in the book, we now return, conformably to our plan, to examine it from the point of view of the forms of its language and of its doctrinal contents, and to inquire whether the results hitherto attained are confirmed, and perhaps more fully determined, by this further investigation.

4. *The Book of the Proverbs on the side of its manifoldness of style and form of instruction.*—We commence our inquiry with the relation in which x.–xxii. 16 and xxv.–xxix. stand to each other with reference to their forms of language. If the primary stock of both of these sections belongs indeed to the old time of Solomon, then they must bear essentially the same verbal stamp upon them. Here we of course keep out of view the proverbs that are wholly or partially identical. If the expression חַדְרֵי־בָטֶן (the chambers of the body) is in the first collection a favourite figure (xviii. 8, xx. 27, 30), coined perhaps by Solomon himself, the fact that this figure is also found in xxvi. 22 is not to be taken into account, since in xxvi. 22 the proverb xviii. 8 is repeated. Now it cannot at all be denied, that in the first collection certain expressions are met with which one might expect to meet again in the Hezekiah-collection, and which, notwithstanding, are not to be found in it. Ewald gives a list of such expressions, in order to show that the old-Solomonic dialect occurs, with few exceptions, only in the first collection. But his catalogue, when closely inspected, is unsatisfactory. That many of these expressions occur also in the introduction i. 1–ix. proves, it is true, nothing against him. But מַרְפֵּא (health), xii. 18, xiii. 17, xiv. 30, xv. 4, xvi. 24, occurs also in xxix. 1 ; רָדַף (he pursueth), xi. 19, xii. 11, xv. 9, xix. 7, also in xxviii. 19 ; נִרְגָּן (a tattler), xvi. 28, xviii. 8, also in xxvi. 20, 22 ; לֹא יִנָּקֶה (not go unpunished), xi. 21, xvi. 5, xvii. 5, also in xxviii. 20. These expressions thus supply an argument for, not against, the linguistic oneness of the two collections. The list of expressions common to the two collections might be considerably increased, e.g. : נִפְרָע (are unruly), xxix. 18, *Kal* xiii. 18, xv. 32 ; אָץ (he that hastens), xix. 2, xxi. 5, xxviii. 20, xxix. 19 ; מִדְוָנִים (of contentions), xxi. 9 (xxv. 24), xxi. 19, xxiii. 29, xxvi. 21, xxvii.

25. If it may be regarded as a striking fact that the figures
of speech מְקוֹר חַיִּים (a fountain of life), x. 11, xiii. 14, xiv. 27,
xvi. 22, and עֵץ חַיִּים (a tree of life), xi. 30, xiii. 12, xv. 4, as
also the expressions מְחִתָּה (destruction), x. 14, 15, xiii. 3, xiv. 28,
xviii. 7, x. 29, xxi. 15, יָפִיחַ (he uttereth), xii. 17, xiv. 5, 25, xix.
5, 9 ; סִלֵּף (perverteth), xiii. 6, xix. 3, xxi. 12, xxii. 12, and סֶלֶף
(perverseness), xi. 3, xv. 4, are only to be found in the first collection, and not in that by the " men of Hezekiah," it is not a
decisive evidence against the oneness of the origin of the proverbs
in both collections. The fact also, properly brought forward by
Ewald, that proverbs which begin with יֵשׁ (there is),—e.g. xi. 24,
" There is that scattereth, and yet increaseth still,"—are exclusively
found in the first collection, need not perplex us ; it is one peculiar
kind of proverbs which the author of this collection has by preference gathered together, as he has also omitted all parabolic
proverbs except these two, x. 26, xi. 22. If proverbs beginning
with יֵשׁ are found only in the first, so on the other hand the parabolic Vav and the proverbial perfect, reporting as it were an experience (cf. in the second collection, besides xxvi. 13, xxvii. 12,
xxix. 13, also xxviii. 1, xxix. 9), for which Döderlein[1] has invented
the expression aoristus gnomicus,[2] are common to both sentences.
Another remark of Ewald's (Jahrb. xi. 28), that extended proverbs
with אִישׁ are exclusively found in the Hezekiah-collection (xxix.
9, 3, xxv. 18, 28), is not fully established ; in xvi. 27–29 three
proverbs with אִישׁ are found together, and in xx. 6 as well as in
xxix. 9 אִישׁ occurs twice in one proverb. Rather it strikes us that
the article, not merely the punctatorially syncopated, but that expressed by ה, occurs only twice in the first collection, in xx. 1, xxi.
31 ; oftener in the second, xxvi. 14, 18, xxvii. 19, 20, 22. Since,
however, the first does not wholly omit the article, this also cannot
determine us to reject the linguistic unity of the second collection with the first, at least according to their primary stock.

But also what of the linguistic unity of i. 1–ix. with both of these,
maintained by Keil ? It is true, and merits all consideration, that
a unity of language and of conception between i. 1–ix. and x.-
xxii. 16 which far exceeds the degree of unity between x.-xxii. 16
and xxv.-xxix. may be proved. The introduction is bound with the

---

[1] Reden u. Aufsätze, ii. 316.

[2] A similar thing is found among German proverbs, e g. : Wer nicht mitsass,
auch nicht mitass (Whoso sat not, ate not).

first collection in the closest manner by the same use of such ex-pressions as אָגַר (gathereth), vi. 8, x. 5 ; אִישׁוֹן (the middle, *i.e.* of the night, deep darkness), vii. 9, xx. 20 ; אַחֲרִית (the end), v. 4, xxiii. 18, xxiv. 14 ; אַכְזָרִי (fierce), v. 9, xvii. 11 ; בִּינָה (under-standing), i. 2, xvi. 16 ; תְּבוּנָה (understanding), ii. 6, iii. 19, xxi. 30 ; זָרָה (an adulteress), v. 3, xxii. 14, xxiii. 33 ; חֲסַר לֵב (lacking understanding), vi. 32, vii. 7, xii. 11 ; יוֹסֵף לֶקַח (will increase learning), i. 5, ix. 9, xvi. 21, 23 ; יָפִיחַ (uttereth), vi. 19, xiv. 5, xix. 5, 9 ; נָלוֹז (perverted), iii. 32, xiv. 2 ; מְדָנִים (contention), vi. 14, 19, x. 12 ; מַרְפֵּא (health), iv. 22, xii. 18, xiii. 17, xvi. 24 (deliverance, xxix. 1) ; נִסַּח (are plucked up), ii. 22, xv. 25 ; לֹא יִנָּקֶה (shall not be unpunished), vi. 29, xi. 21, xvi. 5 ; הֵעֵז (strengthened, *i.e.* the face), vii. 13, xxi. 29 ; עֵץ חַיִּים (tree of life), iii. 18, xi. 30, xiii. 12, xv. 4 ; עָרַב (becometh surety) and תָּקַע (striketh hands) occurring together, vi. 1, xvii. 18, xxii. 26 ; פְּתִים and פְּתָאִים (simplicity, folly), i. 22, 32, viii. 5, ix. 6, xxiii. 3 ; קָרַץ (to wink with the eyes), vi. 13, x. 10 ; קָרֶת (a city), viii. 3, ix. 3, 14, xi. 11 ; רֵאשִׁית (the beginning), i. 7, xvii. 14 ; שֵׂכֶל טוֹב (good understanding), iii. 4, xiii. 15 ; יִשְׁכְּנוּ־אָרֶץ (shall dwell in the land), ii. 21, x. 30 ; שַׁלַּח מָדוֹן (sendeth forth strife), vi. 14, xvi. 28 ; תַּהְפֻּכוֹת (evil words), ii. 12, vi. 14, x. 31, xvi. 28 ; תּוֹרָה (instruction), i. 8, iii. 1, iv. 2, vii. 2, xiii. 14 ; תּוּשִׁיָּה (counsel), iii. 21, viii. 14, xviii. 1 ; תַּחְבֻּלוֹת (prudent measures), i. 5, xx. 18, xxiv. 6 ;—and these are not the only points of contact between the two portions which an attentive reader will meet with. This relation of i. 1–ix. 18 to x.–xxii. 16 is a strong proof of the internal unity of that portion, which Bertheau has called in question. But are we therefore to conclude, with Keil, that the introduction is not less of the old time of Solomon than x.–xxii. 16 ? Such a conclusion lies near, but we do not yet reach it. For with these points of contact there are not a few expressions exclusively peculiar to the introduction ;—the expressions מְזִמָּה sing. (counsel), i. 4, iii. 21 ; עָרְמָה (prudence), i. 4, viii. 5, 12 ; מְלִיצָה (an enigma, obscure maxim), i. 6 ; מַעְגַּל (a path of life), ii. 9, iv. 11, 26 ; מַעְגְּלָה, ii. 15, 18, v. 6, 21 ; אִישׁוֹן (the apple of the eye), vii. 2, 9 ; גַּרְגְּרוֹת (the throat), i. 9, iii. 3, 22 ; the verbs אָתָה (cometh), i. 27, פִּלֵּס (make level or plain), iv. 26, v. 6, 21, and שָׂטָה (deviate), iv. 15, vii. 25. Peculiar to this section is the heaping together of synonyms in close connection, as " con-gregation" and " assembly," v. 14, " lovely hind" and " pleasant roe," v. 19; cf. v. 11, vi. 7, vii. 9, viii. 13, 31. This usage is, however, only a feature in the characteristic style of this section altogether different from that of x. 1–xxii. 16, as well as from that of xxv.–xxix., of its disjointed diffuse form, delighting in repetitions, abounding in synonymous parallelism, even to a repetition of the same words (cf. *e.g.* vi. 2), which, since the linguistic and the poetic forms are here inseparable, we have already spoken of in the second part of our introductory dissertation. This fundamental diversity in the whole condition of the section, notwithstanding those numerous points of resemblance, demands for i. 1–ix. an altogether different author from Solomon, and one who is more recent. If we hold by this view, then these points of resemblance between the sections find the most satisfactory explanation. The gifted author of the introduction (i. 1–ix.) has formed his style, without being an altogether slavish imitator, on the Solomonic proverbs. And why, then, are his parallels confined almost exclusively to the section x. 1–xxii. 16, and do not extend to xxv.–xxix.? Because he edited the former and not the latter, and took pleasure particularly in the proverbs which he placed together, x. 1–xxii. 16. Not only are expressions of this section, formed by himself, echoed in his poetry, but the latter are for the most part formed out of germs supplied by the former. One may regard xix. 27, cf. xxvii. 11, as the germ of the admonitory addresses to the son. and xiv. 1 as the occasion of the allegory of the wise and the foolish woman, ix. Generally, the poetry of this writer has its hidden roots in the older writings. Who does not hear, to mention only one thing, in i. 7–ix. an echo of the old שְׁמַע (hear), Deut. vi. 4–9, cf. xi. 18–21? The whole poetry of this writer savours of the Book of Deuteronomy. The admonitory addresses i. 7–ix. are to the Book of Proverbs what Deuteronomy is to the Pentateuch. As Deuteronomy seeks to bring home and seal upon the heart of the people the תּוֹרָה of the Mosaic law, so do they the תּוֹרָה of the Solomonic proverbs.

We now further inquire whether, in the style of the two supplements, xxii. 17–xxiv. 22 and xxiv. 23 ff., it is proved that the former concludes the Book of Proverbs edited by the author of the general introduction, and that the latter was added by a different author at the same time with the Hezekiah-collection. Bertheau places both supplements together, and attributes the introduction to them, xxii. 17–21, to the author of the general introduction, i. 7–ix. From the fact that in ver. 19 of this lesser introduction ("I have taught thee, אַף־אָתָּה, even thee ") the pronoun is as emphatically repeated as in xxiii. 15 (לִבִּי נַם־אָנִי, cf. xxiii. 14, 19), and that נָעִים (sweet), xxii. 18, also occurs in the following proverbs, xxiii. 8, xxiv. 4, I see no ground for denying it to the author of the larger general intro-duction, since, according to Bertheau's own just observation, the linguistic form of the whole collection of proverbs has an influence on the introduction of the collector; with more justice from שְׁלִישִׁים, xxii. 20 [only in *Keri*], as the title of honour given to the col-lection of proverbs, compared with נְגִידִים, viii. 6, may we argue for the identity of the authorship of both introductions. As little can the contemporaneousness of the two supplements be shown from the use of the pronoun, xxiv. 32, the שִׁית לֵב (*animum ad-vertere*, xxiv. 32), and יִנְעַם (shall be delight) xxiv. 25, for these verbal points of contact, if they proved anything, would prove too much : not only the contemporaneousness of the two sup-plements, but also the identity of their authorship ; but in this case one does not see what the superscription גַּם־אֵלֶּה לַחֲכָמִים (these also of the wise men), separating them, means. Moreover, xxiv. 33 f. are from vi. 10 f., and nearer than the comparison of the first supplement lies the comparison of יִנְעַם with ii. 10, ix. 17, אָדָם חֲסַר לֵב (a man lacking understanding) with xvii. 18, יַעַמְדֻהוּ with xxii. 14,—points of contact which, if an explanatory reason is needed, may be accounted for from the circumstance that to the author or authors of the proverbs xxiv. 23 ff. the Book of Proverbs i. 1–xxiv. 22 may have been perfectly familiar. From imitation also the points of contact of xxii. 17–xxiv. 22 may easily be explained ; for not merely the lesser introduction, the proverbs themselves also in part strikingly agree with the prevailing language of i. 1–ix.: cf. אַשֵּׁר בַּדֶּרֶךְ (go straight forward in the way), xxiii. 19, with iv. 14 ; חָכְמוֹת (wisdom), xxiv. 7, with i. 20, ix. 1; and several others. But if, according to i. 7, we conceive of the older Book of Proverbs as accompanied with, rather than as without דִּבְרֵי חֲכָמִים (words of wise men), then from the similarity of the two superscriptions xxiv. 23, xxv. 1, it is probable that the more recent half of the canonical book begins with xxiv. 23, and we cannot therefore determine to regard xxiv. 23 ff. also as a com-ponent part of the older Book of Proverbs ; particularly since xxiv. 23*b* is like xxviii. 21*a*, and the author of the introduction can scarcely have twice taken into his book the two verses xxiv. 33 f., which moreover seem to stand in their original connection at vi. 10 f.

The supplements to the Hezekiah-collection, xxx. f., are of so peculiar a form, that it will occur to no one (leaving out of view such expressions as דַּעַת קְדֹשִׁים, knowledge of the Holy, xxx. 3, cf. ix. 10) to ascribe them to one of the authors of the preceding proverbs. We content ourselves here with a reference to Mühlau's work, *De Proverbiorum quæ dicuntur Aguri et Lemuelis origine atque indole*, 1869, where the Aramaic-Arabic colouring of this in all probability foreign section is closely investigated.

Having thus abundantly proved that the two groups of proverbs bearing the inscription מִשְׁלֵי שְׁלֹמֹה are, as to their primary stock, truly old-Solomonic, though not without an admixture of imitations; that, on the contrary, the introduction, i. 7–ix., as well as the דִּבְרֵי חֲכָמִים, xxii. 17–xxiv. and xxx. f., are not at all old-Solomonic, but belong to the editor of the older Book of Proverbs, which reaches down to xxiv. 22, so that thus the present book of the poetry of Solomon contains united with it the poems of the older editor, and besides of other poets, partly unknown Israelites, and partly two foreigners particularly named, Agur and Lemuel; we now turn our attention to the DOCTRINAL CONTENTS of the work, and ask whether a manifoldness in the type of instruction is noticeable in it, and whether there is perceptible in this manifoldness a progressive development. It may be possible that the Proverbs of Solomon, the Words of the Wise, and the Proverbial poetry of the editor, as they represent three eras, so also represent three different stages in the development of proverbial poetry. However, the Words of the Wise xxii. 17–xxiv. are so internally related to the Proverbs of Solomon, that even the sharpest eye will discover in them not more than the evening twilight of the vanishing Solomonic Mashal. There thus remain on the one side only the Proverbs of Solomon with their echo in the Words of the Wise, on the other the Proverbial Poems of the editor; and these present themselves as monuments of two sharply defined epochs in the progressive development of the Mashal.

The common fundamental character of the book in all its parts is rightly defined when we call it a Book of Wisdom. Indeed, with the Church Fathers not only the Book of Sirach and the Solomonic Apocrypha, but also this Book of Proverbs bears this title, which seems also to have been in use among the Jews, since Melito of Sardes adds to the title " Proverbs of Solomon," ἡ καὶ Σοφία; since, moreover, Eusebius (*H. E.* iv. 22) affirms, that not only Hegesippus and Irenæus, but the whole of the ancients, called the Proverbs of Solomon Πανάρετος Σοφία.[1] It is also worthy of observation that it is called by Dionysius of Alexandria ἡ σοφὴ βίβλος, and by Gregory of Nazianzum ἡ παιδαγωγικὴ σοφία. These names not only express praise of the book, but they also denote at the same time the circle of human intellectual activity from which it emanated. As the books of prophecy are a product of the נְבוּאָה, so the Book of the Proverbs is a product of the חָכְמָה, σοφία, the human effort to apprehend the objective σοφία, and thus of φιλοσοφία, or the studium sapientiæ. It has emanated from the love of wisdom, to incite to the love of wisdom, and to put into the possession of that which is the object of love—for this end it was written. We need not hesitate, in view of Col. ii. 8, to call the Book of Proverbs a " philosophical" treatise, since the origin of the name φιλοσοφία is altogether noble : it expresses the relativity of human knowledge as over against the absoluteness of the divine knowledge, and the possibility of an endlessly progressive advancement of the human toward the divine. The characteristic ideas of a dialectic development of thought and of the formation of a scientific system did not primarily appertain to it—the occasion for this was not present to the Israelitish people : it required fructification through the Japhetic spirit to produce philosophers such as Philo, Maimonides, and Spinoza. But philosophy is every-where present when the natural, moral, positive, is made the object of a meditation which seeks to apprehend its last ground, its legi-timate coherence, its true essence and aim. In this view C. B. Michaelis, in his *Adnotationes uberiores in Hagiographa*, passes from the exposition of the Psalms to that of the Proverbs with the words, " From David's closet, consecrated to prayer, we now pass into Solomon's school of wisdom, to admire the greatest of philo-sophers in the son of the greatest of theologians." [2]

---

[1] This name [meaning " wisdom, including all virtue "], there are many things to show, was common in Palestine. The Jerusalem Talmud, in a passage quoted by Krochmal, *Kerem Chemed*, v. 79, divides the canon into נבואה, תורה, and חכמה. Rashi, in *Baba bathra*, 14b, calls Mishle (Proverbs) and Koheleth (Ecclesiastes) ספרי חכמה. The Book of Koheleth is called (*b. Megilla*, 7a), according to its contents, חכמתו של שלמה. The Song bears in the Syriac version (the Peshito) the inscription *chekmetho dechekmotho*.

[2] " In hoc genere," says Lord Bacon, *De Augmentis Scientiarum*, viii. 2, "nihil invenitur, quod ullo modo comparandum sit cum aphorismis illis, quos edidit rex Salomon, de quo testatur Scriptura, cor illi fuisse instar arenæ maris.

When we give the name φιλοσοφία to the tendency of mind to which the Book of Proverbs belongs, we do not merely use a current scientific word, but there is an actual internal relation of the Book of Proverbs to that which is the essence of philosophy, which Scripture recognises (Acts xvii. 27, cf. Rom. i. 19 f.) as existing within the domain of heathendom, and which stamps it as a natural product of the human spirit, which never can be wanting where a human being or a people rises to higher self-consciousness, and begins to reflect on the immediate self-consciousness and its operations in their changing relation to the phenomena of the external world. The mysteries of the world without him and of the world within him give man no rest, he must seek to solve them ; and whenever he does that, he philosophizes, *i.e.* he strives after a knowledge of the nature of things, and of the laws which govern them in the world of phenomena and of events ; on which account also Josephus, referring to Solomon's knowledge of nature, says (*Ant.* viii. 2. 5), οὐδεμίαν τούτων φύσιν ἠγνόησεν οὐδὲ παρῆλθεν ἀνεξέταστον ἀλλ᾽ ἐν πάσαις ἐφιλοσόφησεν. Cf. Irenæus, *Cont. Her.* iv. 27. 1 : *eam quæ est in conditione* (κτίσει) *sapientiam Dei exponebat physiologice.*

The historical books show us how much the age of Solomon favoured philosophical inquiries by its prosperity and peace, its active and manifold commercial intercourse with foreign nations, its circle of vision extending to Tarshish and Ophir, and also how Solomon himself attained to an unequalled elevation in the extent of his human and secular knowledge. We also read of some of the wise men in 1 Kings v. 11, cf. Ps. lxxxviii. lxxxix., who adorned the court of the wisest of kings ; and the מָשָׁל, which became, through his influence, a special branch of Jewish literature, is the peculiar poetic form of the חָכְמָה. Therefore in the Book of Proverbs we find the name דִּבְרֵי חֲכָמִים (words of the wise) used for מְשָׁלִים (proverbs) ; and by a careful consideration of all the proverbs in which mention is made of the חֲכָמִים, one will convince

Sicut enim arenæ maris universas orbis oras circumdant, ita et sapientia ejus omnia humana non minus quam divina complexa est. In aphorismis vero illis præter alia magis theologica reperies liquido haud pauca præcepta et monita civilia præstantissima, ex profundis quidem sapientiæ penetralibus scaturientia atque in amplissimum varietatis campum excurrentia." Accordingly, in the same work Bacon calls the Proverbs of Solomon " insignes parabolas s. aphorismos de divina atque morali philosophia."

himself that this name has not merely a common ethical sense, but begins to be the name of those who made wisdom, *i.e.* the knowledge of things in the depths of their essence, their special lifework, and who connected themselves together in oneness of sentiment and fellowship into a particular circle within the community. To this conclusion we are conducted by such proverbs as xiii. 20—

> He that walketh with wise men becomes wise,
> And whoever has intercourse with fools is destroyed;

xv. 12—

> The scorner loveth not that one reprove him :
> To wise men he goeth not ;—

and by the contrast, which prevails in the Book of Proverbs, between לֵץ (mocker) and חָכָם (wise), in which we see that, at the same time with the striving after wisdom, scepticism also, which we call free thought, obtained a great ascendency in Israel. Mockery of religion, rejection of God in principle and practice, a casting away of all fear of Jahve, and in general of all δεισιδαιμονία, were in Israel phenomena which had already marked the times of David. One may see from the Psalms that the community of the Davidic era is to be by no means regarded as furnishing a pattern of religious life : that there were in it גּוֹיִם (Gentile nations) which were in no way externally inferior to them, and that it did not want for rejecters of God. But it is natural to expect that in the Solomonic era, which was more than any other exposed to the dangers of sensuality and worldliness, and of religious indifference and free-thinking latitudinarianism, the number of the לֵצִים increased, and that scepticism and mockery became more intensified. The Solomonic era appears to have first coined the name of לֵץ for those men who despised that which was holy, and in doing so laid claim to wisdom (xiv. 6), who caused contention and bitterness when they spake, and carefully avoided the society of the חכמים, because they thought themselves above their admonitions (xv. 12). For in the psalms of the Davidic time the word נָבָל is commonly used for them (it occurs in the Proverbs only in xvii. 21, with the general meaning of low fellow, Germ. *Bube*), and the name לֵץ is never met with except once, in Ps. i. 1, which belongs to the post-Davidic era. One of the Solomonic proverbs (xxi. 24) furnishes a definite idea of this newly formed word :

> An inflated arrogant man they call a scorner (לֵץ),
> One who acts in the superfluity of haughtiness.

By the self-sufficiency of his ungodly thoughts and actions he
is distinguished from the פֶּתִי (simple), who is only misled, and
may therefore be reclaimed, xix. 25, xxi. 11; by his non-recog-
nition of the Holy in opposition to a better knowledge and better
means and opportunities, he is distinguished from the כְּסִיל (foolish, stupid), xvii. 16, the אֱוִיל (foolish, wicked), i. 7, vii. 22, and
the חֲסַר לֵב (the void of understanding), vi. 32, who despise truth
and instruction from want of understanding, narrowness, and
forgetfulness of God, but not from perverse principle. This
name specially coined, the definition of it given (cf. also the
similarly defining proverb xxiv. 8), and in general the rich and
fine technical proverbs in relation to the manifold kinds of wisdom
(בִּינָה, xvi. 16; מוּסַר, i. 8; תְּבוּנוֹת, xxi. 30; מְזִמּוֹת, v. 2; תַּחְבֻּלוֹת, i. 5,
xii. 5; the תּוּשִׁיָּה first coined by the Chokma, etc.), of instruction
in wisdom (לֶקַח, i. 5; תּוֹרָה, iv. 2, vi. 23; רָעָה, to tend a flock, to
instruct, x. 21; חָנַךְ, xxii. 6; הוֹכֵחַ, xv. 12; לָקַח נְפָשׁוֹת, to win souls,
vi. 25, xi. 30), of the wise men themselves (חָכָם, xii. 15; נָבוֹן, x. 13;
מוֹכִיחַ, a reprover, preacher of repentance, xxv. 12, etc.), and of the
different classes of men (among whom also אָדָם אַחֲרִי, one who steps
backwards [retrograder], xxviii. 23)—all this shows that חָכְמָה was
at that time not merely the designation of an ethical quality, but
also the designation of a science rooted in the fear of God to which
many noble men in Israel then addicted themselves. Jeremiah
places (xviii. 18) the חָכָם along with the כֹּהֵן (priest) and נָבִיא
(prophet); and if Ezek. (vii. 26) uses זָקֵן (old man) instead of
חָכָם, yet by reference to Job xii. 12 this may be understood. In
his " Dissertation on the popular and intellectual freedom of Israel
from the time of the great prophets to the first destruction of
Jerusalem" (*Jahrbücher*, i. 96 f.), Ewald says, " One can scarcely
sufficiently conceive how high the attainment was which was reached
in the pursuit after wisdom (philosophy) in the first centuries after
David, and one too much overlooks the mighty influence it exerted
on the entire development of the national life of Israel. The more
closely those centuries are inquired into, the more are we astonished
at the vast power which wisdom so early exerted on all sides as the
common object of pursuit of many men among the people. It first
openly manifested itself in special circles of the people, while in the
age after Solomon, which was peculiarly favourable to it, eagerly
inquisitive scholars gathered around individual masters, until ever
increasing schools were formed. But its influence gradually pene-

trated all the other pursuits of the people, and operated on the most
diverse departments of authorship." We are in entire sympathy
with this historical view first advanced by Ewald, although we must
frequently oppose the carrying of it out in details. The literature
and the national history of Israel are certainly not understood if one
does not take into consideration, along with the נְבוּאָה (prophecy), the
influential development of the חָכְמָה as a special aim and subject of
intellectual activity in Israel.

And how was this *Chokma* conditioned—to what was it directed ?
To denote its condition and aim in one word, it was universalistic,
or humanistic. Emanating from the fear or the religion of Jahve
(דֶּרֶךְ ה׳, the way of the Lord, x. 29), but seeking to comprehend
the spirit in the letter, the essence in the forms of the national life,
its effort was directed towards the general truth affecting mankind
as such. While prophecy, which is recognised by the *Chokma* as a
spiritual power indispensable to a healthful development of a people
(בְּאֵין חָזוֹן יִפָּרַע עָם, xxix. 18), is of service to the historical process into
which divine truth enters to work out its results in Israel, and from
thence outward among mankind, the *Chokma* seeks to look into the
very essence of this truth through the robe of its historical and
national manifestation, and then to comprehend those general ideas
in which could already be discovered the fitness of the religion of
Jahve for becoming the world-religion. From this aim towards the
ideal in the historical, towards the everlasting same amid changes,
the human (I intentionally use this word) in the Israelitish, the
universal religion in the Jahve-religion (Jahvetum), and the universal morality in the Law, all the peculiarities of the Book of
Proverbs are explained, as well as of the long, broad stream of the
literature of the *Chokma*, beginning with Solomon, which, when the
Palestinian Judaism assumed the rugged, exclusive, proud national
character of Pharisaism, developed itself in Alexandrinism. Bertheau is amazed that in the Proverbs there are no warnings given
against the worship of idols, which from the time of the kings
gained more and more prevalence among the Israelitish people.
" How is it to be explained," he asks (*Spr.* p. xlii.), " if the
proverbs, in part at least, originated during the centuries of conflict
between idolatry and the religion of Jahve, and if they were collected at a time in which this conflict reached its climax and stirred
all ranks of the people—this conflict against the immorality of the
Phœnician-Babylonian religion of nature, which must often have

led into the same region of the moral contemplation of the world
over which this book moves?!" The explanation lies in this, that
the *Chokma* took its stand-point in a height and depth in which it
had the mingling waves of international life and culture under it
and above it, without being internally moved thereby. It naturally
did not approve of heathenism, it rather looked upon the fear of
Jahve as the beginning of wisdom, and the seeking after Jahve as
implying the possession of all knowledge (xxviii. 5, cf. 1 John ii. 20);
but it passed over the struggle of prophecy against heathendom, it
confined itself to its own function, viz. to raise the treasures of general religious-moral truth in the Jahve-religion, and to use them for
the ennobling of the Israelites as men. In vain do we look for the
name יִשְׂרָאֵל in the Proverbs, even the name תּוֹרָה has a much more
flexible idea attached to it than that of the law written at Sinai
(cf. xxviii. 4, xxix. 18 with xxviii. 7, xiii. 14, and similar passages);
prayer and good works are placed above sacrifice, xv. 8, xxi. 3, 27,
—practical obedience to the teaching of wisdom above all, xxviii. 9.
The Proverbs refer with special interest to Gen. i. and ii., the
beginnings of the world and of the human race before nations took
their origin. On this primitive record in the book of Genesis, to
speak only of the מִשְׁלֵי שְׁלֹמֹה, the figure of the tree of life (perhaps
also of the fountain of life), found nowhere else in the Old Testament, leans; on it leans also the contrast, deeply pervading the
Proverbs, between life (immortality, xii. 28) and death, or between
that which is above and that which is beneath (xv. 24); on it also
many other expressions, such, *e.g.*, as what is said in xx. 27 of the
"spirit of man." This also, as Stier (*Der Weise ein König*, 1849,
p. 240) has observed, accounts for the fact that אָדָם occurs by far
most frequently in the Book of Job and in the Solomonic writings.
All these phenomena are explained from the general human
universal aim of the *Chokma*.

When James (iii. 17) says that the " wisdom that is from above
is first pure, then peaceable, gentle, easy to be entreated, full of
mercy and good fruits, without partiality, and without hypocrisy,"
his words most excellently designate the nature and the contents of
the discourse of wisdom in the Solomonic proverbs, and one is
almost inclined to think that the apostolic brother of the Lord,
when he delineates wisdom, has before his eyes the Book of the
Proverbs, which raises to purity by the most impressive admonitions. Next to its admonitions to purity are those especially to

peacefulness, to gentle resignation (xiv. 30), quietness of mind (xiv. 33) and humility (xi. 2, xv. 33, xvi. 5, 18), to mercy (even toward beasts, xii. 10), to firmness and sincerity of conviction, to the furtherance of one's neighbour by means of wise discourse and kind help. What is done in the Book of Deuteronomy with reference to the law is continued here. As in Deuteronomy, so here, love is at the bottom of its admonitions, the love of God to men, and the love of men to one another in their diverse relations (xii. 2, xv. 9); the conception of צְדָקָה gives way to that of charity, of alms-giving (δικαιοσύνη = ἐλεημοσύνη). Forgiving, suffering love (x. 12), love which does good even to enemies (xxv. 21 f.), rejoices not over the misfortune that befalls an enemy (xxiv. 17 f.), retaliates not (xxiv. 28 f.), but commits all to God (xx. 22),—love in its manifold forms, as that of husband and wife, of children, of friends,—is here recommended with New Testament distinctness and with deepest feeling. Living in the fear of God (xxviii. 14), the Omniscient (xv. 3, 11, xvi. 2, xxi. 2, xxiv. 11 f.), to whom as the final Cause all is referred (xx. 12, 24, xiv. 31, xxii. 2), and whose universal plan all must subserve (xvi. 4, xix. 21, xxi. 30), and on the other side active pure love to man—these are the hinges on which all the teachings of wisdom in the Proverbs turn. Frederick Schlegel, in the fourteenth of his *Lectures on the History of Literature*, distinguishes, not without deep truth, between the historico-prophetic books of the Old Testament, or books of the history of redemption, and the Book of Job, the Psalms, and the Solomonic writings, as books of aspiration, corresponding to the triple chord of faith, hope, charity as the three stages of the inner spiritual life. The Book of Job is designed to support faith amid trials; the Psalms breathe forth and exhibit hope amid the conflicts of earth's longings; the Solomonic writings reveal to us the mystery of the divine love, and the Proverbs that wisdom which grows out of and is itself eternal love. When Schlegel in the same lecture says that the books of the Old Covenant, for the most part, stand under the signature of the lion as the element of the power of will and spirited conflict glowing in divine fire, but that in the inmost hidden kernel and heart of the sacred book the Christian figure of the lamb rises up out of the veil of this lion strength, this may specially be said of the Book of Proverbs, for here that same heavenly wisdom preaches, which, when manifested in person, spake in the Sermon on the Mount, New Testament love in the midst of the Old Testament.

It is said that in the times before Christ there was a tendency to apocryphize not only the Song of Solomon and Ecclesiastes, but also the Book of Proverbs, and that for the first time the men of the Great Synagogue established their canonicity on the ground of their spiritual import; they became perplexed about the Proverbs, according to *b. Sabbath*, 30*b*, on account of such self-contradictory proverbs as xxvi. 4, 5, and according to *Aboth de-Rabbi Nathan*, c. 1, on account of such secular portions as that of the wanton woman, vii. But there is no need to allegorize this woman, and that self-contradiction is easily explained. The theopneustic character of the book and its claim to canonicity show themselves from its integral relation to the Old Testament preparation for redemption; but keeping out of view the book as a whole, it is self-evident that the conception of a practical proverb such as xiv. 4 and of a prophecy such as Isa. vii. 14 are very different phenomena of the spiritual life, and that in general the operation of the Divine Spirit in a proverb is different from that in a prophecy.

We have hitherto noted the character of the instruction set forth in the Proverbs according to the marks common to them in all their parts, but in such a way that we have taken our proofs only from the "Proverbs of Solomon" and the "Words of the Wise," with the exclusion of the introductory proverbial poems of the older editor. If we compare the two together, it cannot be denied that in the type of the instruction contained in the latter, the *Chokma*, of which the book is an emanation and which it has as its aim (לָדַעַת חָכְמָה, i. 2), stands before us in proportionally much more distinctly defined comprehension and form; we have the same relation before us whose adumbration is the relation of the instruction of wisdom in the Avesta and in the later Minochired (Spiegel, *Parsi-Grammatik*, p. 182 ff.). The *Chokma* appears also in the "Proverbs of Solomon" as a being existing in and for itself, which is opposed to ambiguous subjective thought (xxviii. 26); but here there is attributed to it an objectivity even to an apparent personality : it goes forth preaching, and places before all men life and death for an eternally decisive choice, it distributes the spirit to those who do not resist (i. 23), it receives and answers prayer (i. 28). The speculation regarding the *Chokma* is here with reference to Job xxviii. (cf. Prov. ii. 4, iii. 14 f., viii. 11, 19), and particularly to xxviii. 27, where a demiurgic function is assigned to wisdom, carried back to its source in eternity : it is the medium by which the world was created, iii. 19 ; it was before the creation of the world with God as from everlasting, His son of royal dignity, viii. 22–26 ; it was with Him in His work of creation, viii. 27–30 ; after the creation it remained as His delight, rejoicing always before Him, and particularly on the earth among the sons of men, viii. 30 f. Staudenmaier (*Lehre von der Idee*, p. 37) is certainly not on the wrong course, when under this rejoicing of wisdom before God he understands the development of the ideas or life-thoughts intimately bound up in it—the world-idea. This development is the delight of God, because it represents to the divine contemplation the contents of wisdom, or of the world-idea founded in the divine understanding, in all its activities and inner harmonies; it is a calm delight, because the divine idea unites with the fresh and ever young impulse of life, the purity, goodness, innocence, and holiness of life, because its spirit is light, clear, simple, childlike, in itself peaceful, harmonious, and happy; and this delight is experienced especially on the earth among the sons of men, among whom wisdom has its delight; for, as the divine idea, it is in all in so far as it is the inmost life-thought, the soul of each being, but it is on the earth of men in whom it comes to its self-conception, and self-conscious comes forth into the light of the clear day. Staudenmaier has done the great service of having worthily estimated the rich and deep fulness of this biblical theologumenon of wisdom, and of having pointed out in it the foundation-stone of a sacred metaphysics and a means of protection against pantheism in all its forms. We see that in the time of the editor of the older Book of Proverbs the wisdom of the schools in its devotion to the chosen object of its pursuit, the divine wisdom living and moving in all nature, and forming the background of all things, rises to a height of speculation on which it has planted a banner showing the right way to latest times. Ewald rightly points to the statements in the introduction to the Proverbs regarding wisdom as a distinct mark of the once great power of wisdom in Israel; for they show us how this power learned to apprehend itself in its own purest height, after it had become as perfect, and at the same time also as self-conscious, as it could at all become in ancient Israel.

Many other appearances also mark the advanced type of instruction contained in the introduction. Hitzig's view (*Sprüche*, p. xvii. f.), that i. 6–ix. 18 are the part of the whole collection

which was earliest written, confutes itself on all sides; on the contrary, the views of Bleek in his *Introduction to the Old Testament*,
thrown out in a sketchy manner and as if by a diviner, surprisingly
agree with our own results, which have been laboriously reached
and are here amply established. The advanced type of instruction in the introduction, i.–ix., appears among other things in this,
that we there find the allegory, which up to this place occurs in
Old Testament literature only in scattered little pictures built up
into independent poetic forms, particularly in ix., where without
any contradiction אֵשֶׁת כְּסִילוּת [a simple woman, v. 13] is an allegorical person. The technical language of the *Chokma* has extended itself on many sides and been refined (we mention these
synonyms : תּוּשִׁיָה, מוּסָר, מְזִמָּה, עָרְמָה, בִּינָה, דַּעַת, חָכְמָה) ; and the seven
pillars in the house of wisdom, even though it be inadmissible to
think of them as the seven liberal arts, yet point to a division into
seven parts of which the poet was conscious to himself. The
common address, בְּנִי [my son], which is not the address of the
father to the son, but of the teacher to the scholar, countenances
the supposition that there were at that time בְּנֵי חֲכָמִים, *i.e.* scholars of
the wise men, just as there were " sons of the prophets " (נְבִיאִים),
and probably also schools of wisdom. "And when it is described
how wisdom spake aloud to the people in all the streets of Jerusalem, in the high places of the city and in every favourable place,
does not one feel that such sublime descriptions could not be
possible unless at that time wisdom were regarded by the people as
one of the first powers, and the wise men truly displayed a great
public activity?" We must answer this question of Ewald's in
the affirmative.

Bruch, in his *Weisheitslehre der Hebraer*, 1851, was the first to
call special attention to the *Chokma* or humanism as a peculiar
intellectual tendency in Israel; but he is mistaken in placing
it in an indifferent and even hostile relation to the national law
and the national cultus, which he compares to the relation of
Christian philosophy to orthodox theology. Oehler, in his *Grundzüge der alttestamentl. Weisheit*, which treats more especially of
the doctrinal teachings of the Book of Job, judges more correctly;
cf. also his comprehensive article, *Pädagogik des A. T.* in Schmid's
Pädagogischer Encyclopädie, pp. 653–695 (partic. 677–683).

5. *The Alexandrian Translation of the Book of Proverbs.*—Of

highest interest for the history of the Book of Proverbs is the relation of the LXX. to the Hebrew text. One half of the proverbs of Agur (xxx. of the Hebrew text) are placed in it after xxiv. 22, and the other half after xxiv. 34; and the proverbs of King Lemuel (xxxi. 1-9 of the Hebrew text) are placed after the proverbs of Agur, while the acrostic proverbial poem of the virtuous woman is in its place at the end of the book. That transposition reminds us of the transpositions in Jeremiah, and rests in the one place as well as in the other on a misunderstanding of the true contents. The translator has set aside the new superscription, x. 1, as unsuitable, and has not marked the new beginning, xxii. 17; he has expunged the new superscription, xxiv. 23, and has done the same to the superscription, " The words of Agur " (xxx. 1), in two awkward explanations (λόγον φυλασσόμενος and τοὺς ἐμοὺς λόγους φοβήθητι), and the superscription, "The words of Lemuel" (xxxi. 1), in one similar (οἱ ἐμοὶ λόγι εἴρηνται ὑπὸ Θεοῦ), so that the proverbs of Agur and of Lemuel are without hesitation joined with those of Solomon, whereby it yet remains a mystery why the proverbs beginning with "The words of Agur" have been divided into two parts. Hitzig explains it from a confounding of the columns in which, two being on each page, the Hebrew MS. which lay before the translator was written, and in which the proverbs of Agur and of Lemuel (names which tradition understood symbolically of Solomon) were already ranked in order before ch. xxv. But besides these, there are also many other singular things connected with this Greek translation interesting in themselves and of great critical worth. That it omits i. 16 may arise from this, that this verse was not found in the original MS., and was introduced from Isa. lix. 7; but there are wanting also proverbs such as xxi. 5, for which no reason can be assigned. But the additions are disproportionately more numerous. Frequently we find a line added to the distich, such as in i. 18, or an entire distich added, as iii. 15; or of two lines of the Hebrew verse, each is formed into a separate distich, as i. 7, xi. 16; or we meet with longer interpolations, extending far beyond this measure, as that added to iv. 27. Many of these proverbs are easily re-translated into the Hebrew, as that added to iv. 27, consisting of four lines:

כי דרכי מימינים ידע יהוה
ועקשים דרכי משמאילים

הוא יפלם מעגלותיך
ארחותיך בשלום יצליח:

But many of them also sound as if they had been originally
Greek; *e.g.* the lines appended to ix. 10, xiii. 15; the distich, vi.
11; the imperfect tristich, xxii. 14; and the formless trian, xxv.
10. The value of these enlargements is very diverse; not a few
of these proverbs are truly thoughtful, such as the addition to
xii. 13—

> He who is of mild countenance findeth mercy;
> He who is litigious crushes souls—

and singularly bold in imagery, as the addition to ix. 12—

> He who supports himself by lies hunts after (רעה) the wind,
> He catches at fluttering birds;
> For he forsakes the ways of his own vineyard,
> And wanders away from the paths of his own field,
> And roams through arid steppes and a thirsty land,
> And gathers with his hand withered heath.

The Hebrew text lying before the Alexandrian translators had
certainly not all these additions, yet in many passages, such as
xi. 16, it is indeed a question whether it is not to be improved from
the LXX.; and in other passages, where, if one reads the Greek,
the Hebrew words naturally take their place, whether these are not
at least old Hebrew marginal notes and interpolations which the
translation preserves. But this version itself has had its gradual
historical development. The text, the κοινή (*communis*), proceeds
from the Hexaplar text edited by Origen, which received from him
many and diverse revisions; and in the times before Christ, perhaps
(as Hitz. supposes), down to the second century after Christ, the
translation itself, not being regarded as complete, was in the progress of growth, for not unfrequently two different translations of
one and the same proverb stand together, as xiv. 22, xxix. 25
(where also the Peshito follows the LXX. after which it translates),
or also interpenetrate one another, as xxii. 8, 9. These doubled
translations are of historical importance both in relation to the
text and to the interpretation of it. Along with the Books of
Samuel and Jeremiah, there is no book in regard to which the
LXX. can be of higher significance than the Book of Proverbs;
we shall seek in the course of our exposition duly to estimate the
text[1] as adopted by Bertheau (1847) and Hitzig (1858) in their

---

[1] Cf. also J. Gottlob Jäger's *Observationes in Proverbiorum Salomonis Ver-
sionem Alexandrinam*, 1788; de Lagarde's *Anmerkungen zur griech. Uebersetzung*

commentaries, and by Ewald in his *Jahrb.* xi. (1861) and his commentary (2d ed. 1867). The historical importance of the Egyptian text-recension is heightened by this circumstance, that the old Syrian translator of the Solomonic writings had before him not only the original text, but also the LXX.; for the current opinion, that the Peshito, as distinguished from the Syro-Hexaplar version, sprang solely from the original text with the assistance of the Targum, is more and more shown to be erroneous. In the Book of Proverbs the relation of the Peshito and Targum is even the reverse; the Targum of the Proverbs, making use of the Peshito, restores the Masoretic text,—the points of contact with the LXX. showing themselves here and there, are brought about [1] by the Peshito. But that Jerome, in his translation of the Vulgate according to the *Hebræa veritas*, sometimes follows the LXX. in opposition to the original text, is to be explained with Hitzig from the fact that he based his work on an existing Latin translation made from the LXX. Hence it comes that the two distichs added in the LXX. to iv. 27 remain in his work, and that instead of the one distich, xv. 6, we have two :—*In abundanti* (after the phrase בְּרֹב instead of בֵּית of the Masoretic text) *justitia virtus maxima est, cogitationes autem impiorum eradicabuntur. Domus* (בֵּית) *justi plurima fortitudo, et in fructibus impii conturbatio;* for Jerome has adopted the two translations of the LXX., correcting the second according to the original text.[2]

der Proverbien, 1863 ; M. Heidenheim's *Zur Textkritik der Proverbien*, in his *Quarterly Journal for German and English Theological Criticism and Investigation*, No. VIII. (1865), and IX., XI. (1866). The text of the LXX. (cf. Angelo Mai's *Classici Auctores*, t. ix.) used by Procopius in his Ἑρμηνεία εἰς τὰς παροιμίας is peculiar, and here and there comes near to the Hebrew original. The *scholion* of Evagrius in the Σχόλια εἰς τὰς παροιμίας of Origen, edited by Tischendorf in his *Notitia*, 1860, from a MS. of Patmos, shows how soon even the Hexaplar text became ambiguous.

[1] Cf. Dathe, *De ratione consensus Versionis Syriacæ el Chaldaicæ Proverbiorum Salomonis* (1764), edited by Rosenmüller in his *Opuscula*. Maybaum, in the Treatise on the Language of the Targum to the Proverbs and its relation to the Syriac, in Merx's *Archiv*, ii. 66-93, labours in vain to give the priority to that of the Targum: the Targum is written from the Peshito, and here and there approaches the Hebrew text; the language is, with few differences, the Syriac of the original.

[2] The Ethiópic translation, also, is in particular points, as well as on the whole, dependent on the LXX., for it divides the Book of Proverbs into proverbs (παροιμίας), i. - xxiv., and instructions (παιδεῖαι) of Solomon, xxv.- xxxi. *Vid.* Dillmann in Ewald's *Jahrb.* v. 147, 150.

The fragments of the translations of Aquila, Symmachus, Theodotion, etc., contained in Greek and Syrian sources, have been
recently collected, more perfectly than could have been done by
Montfaucon, by Fried. Field, in his work *Origenis Hexaplorum quæ
supersunt*, etc. (Oxonii, 1867, 4). Of special interest is the more
recent translation of the original text, existing only in a MS. laid up
in the Library of St. Mark [at Venice], executed in bold language,
rich in rare and newly invented words, by an unknown author, and
belonging to an age which has not yet been determined (*Græcus
Venetus*) : cf. d'Ansse de Villoison's *nova versio Græca Proverbiorum, Ecclesiastis, Cantici Canticorum*, etc., *Argentorati*, 1784 ; and
also the *Animadversiones* thereto of Jo. Ge. Dahler, 1786.

The literature of the interpretation of the Book of Proverbs is
found in Keil's *Einleitung in das A. T.* (1859), p. 346 f. [*Manual
oj Historico-Critical Introduction to the Old Testament*, translated
by Professor Douglas, D.D., Free Church College, Glasgow.
Edinburgh : T. & T. Clark. Vol. i. p. 468 f.]. The most important
of the older linguistic works on this book is the commentary of
Albert Schultens (*Lugduni Batavorum*, 1748, 4), whose service to
the cause of Semitic philology and O. T. exegesis Mühlau has
brought to remembrance in the Lutheran *Zeitschrift*, 1870, 1 ;
Vogel's abstract (*Halæ*, 1769), prefaced by Semler, does not alto-
gether compensate for the original work. From the school of
Schultens, and also from that of Schröder, originate the *Anmer-
kungen* by Alb. Jac. Arnoldi, maternal grandson of Schultens, a
Latin edition of which was published (*Lugduni Bat.* 1783) by
Henr. Alb. Schultens, the grandson of Schultens by his son.
Among the commentaries of English interpreters, that in Latin
by Thomas Cartwright (*Amstelredami*, 1663, 4), along with the
Exposition of the Book of Proverbs by Charles Bridges (4th ed.,
London, 1859), hold an honourable place. The *Critical Remarks
on the Books of Job, Proverbs*, etc., by D. Durell (Oxford, 1772, 4),
also merit attention. Of more recent commentaries, since Keil gave
his list of the literature of the subject, have been published those of
Elster (1858) and of Zöckler (1867), forming a part of the theo-
logico-homiletical *Bibelwerk* edited by J. P. Lange. Chaps. xxv.-
xxix. Rud. Stier has specially interpreted in two works entitled *Der*

Weise ein König ["The Wise Man a King"], and *Salomonis Weisheit in Hiskiastagen* [" Solomon's Wisdom in the Days of Hezekiah "], 1849 ; and chapters xxx. xxxi. in a work entitled *Die Politik der Weisheit* [" The Politics of Wisdom "], 1850. Part III. (1865) of the new exegetico-critical *Aehrenlese* [" Gleanings"] of Fried. Böttcher, edited by Mühlau, furnishes 39 pages of remarks on the Proverbs. Leop. Dukes, author of the Rabbinical *Blumenlese* ["Anthology "], 1844, and the *Schrift zur rabbinischen Spruchkunde*, 1851, has published (1841) a commentary to the Proverbs in Cahen's French *Bibelwerk*. There also is furnished a list of Jewish interpreters down to the appearance of L. H. Loewenstein's Commentary (1838), which contains valuable contributions to the critical confirmation of the Masoretic text, in which Heidenheim's MS. remains, and also the Codex of 1294 mentioned in my preface to Baer's edition of the Psalter, and in the *Specimen Lectionum* of Baer's edition of Genesis, are made use of. Among Malbim's best works are, after his Commentary on Isaiah, that on the Mishle (Warsaw, 1867). [*Vide* Preface.]

I.

THE OLDER BOOK OF PROVERBS

I.-XXIV.

SUPERSCRIPTION AND MOTTO, I. 1-7.

THE external title, *i.e.* the Synagogue name, of the whole collection of Proverbs is מִשְׁלֵי (*Mishle*), the word with which it commences. Origen (Euseb. *H. E.* vi. 25) uses the name Μισλώθ, *i.e.* מִשְׁלוֹת, which occurs in the Talmud and Midrash as the designation of the book, from its contents. In a similar way, the names given to the Psalter, תְּהִלִּים and תְּהִלּוֹת, are interchanged.

This external title is followed by one which the Book of Proverbs, viewed as to its gradual formation, and first the older portion, gives to itself. It reaches from i. 1 to ver. 6, and names not only the contents and the author of the book, but also commends it in regard to the service which it is capable of rendering. It contains " Proverbs of Solomon, the son of David, king of Israel." The books of the נבואה and חכמה, including the Canticles, thus give their own titles; among the historical books, that of the memoirs of Nehemiah is the only one that does so. מִשְׁלֵי has the accent *Dechî*, to separate[1] it from the following complex genitive which it governs, and מֶלֶךְ יִשְׂרָאֵל is made the second hemistich, because it belongs to שְׁלֹמֹה, not to דָּוִד.[2] As to the fundamental idea of the word מָשָׁל, we refer to the derivation given in the *Gesch. der jud. Poesie*, p. 196, from מָשַׁל, Aram. מְתַל, root תל, Sanskr. *tul* (whence *tulâ*, balance, similarity), Lat. *tollere;* the comparison of the Arab. *mathal* leads to the same

---

[1] Norzi has erroneously accented משלי with the accent *Munach*. The מ is besides the Masoretic *majusculum*, like the ב, שׁ, and א at the commencement of the Law, the Canticles, and Chronicles.

[2] If it had belonged to דוד, then the sentence would have been accented thus : מִשְׁלֵי שְׁלֹמֹה בֶּן־דָּוִד מֶלֶךְ יִשְׂרָאֵל׃

conclusion.   " מָשַׁל signifies, not, as Schultens and others after him affirm, *effigies ad similitudinem alius rei expressa*, from מָשַׁל in the primary signification *premere, premente manu tractare ;* for the corresponding Arab. verb *mathal* does not at all bear that meaning, but signifies to stand, to present oneself, hence to be like, properly to put oneself forth as something, to represent it; and in the Hebr. also to rule, properly with עַל to stand on or over something, with בְּ to hold it erect, like Arab. *kam* with *b*, *rem administravit* [*vid. Jesaia*, p. 691]. Thus *e.g.*, Gen. xxiv. 2, it is said of Eliezer : הַמּשֵׁל בְּכָל־אֲשֶׁר־לֹו, who ruled over all that he (Abraham) had (Luther: was a prince over all his goods). Thus מָשָׁל, figurative discourse which represents that which is real, similitude ; hence then parable or shorter apothegm, proverb, in so far as they express primarily something special, but which as a general symbol is then applied to everything else of a like kind, and in so far stands figuratively. An example is found in 1 Sam. x. 11 f. It is incorrect to conclude from this meaning of the word that such memorial sayings or proverbs usually contained comparisons, or were clothed in figurative language ; for that is the case in by far the fewest number of instances : the oldest have by far the simplest and most special interpretations " (Fleischer). Hence *Mashal*, according to its fundamental idea, is that which stands with something = makes something stand forth = representing. This something that represents may be a thing or a person ; as *e.g.* one may say Job is a *Mashal*, *i.e.* a representant, similitude, type of Israel (*vide* the work entitled עֵץ החיים, by Ahron b. Elia, c. 90, p. 143) ; and, like Arab. *mathal* (more commonly *mithl* = מֶשֶׁל, cf. מִשֶׁל, Job xli. 25), is used quite as generally as is its etymological cogn. *instar* (*instare*). But in Hebr. Mashal always denotes representing discourse with the additional marks of the figurative and concise, *e.g.* the section which presents (Hab. ii. 6) him to whom it refers as a warning example, but particularly, as there defined, the gnome, the apothegm or maxim, in so far as this represents general truths in sharply outlined little pictures.

Ver. 2. Now follows the statement of the object which these proverbs subserve ; and first, in general,

> To become acquainted with wisdom and instruction,
> To understand intelligent discourses.

They seek on the one side to initiate the reader in wisdom and instruction, and on the other to guide him to the understanding of intelligent discourses, for they themselves contain such discourses in which there is a deep penetrating judgment, and they sharpen the understanding of him who engages his attention with them.[1] As Schultens has already rightly determined the fundamental meaning of יָדַע, frequently compared with the Sanskr. *vid*, to know (whence by gunating,[2] *vêda*, knowledge), after the Arab. *wad'a*, as *deponere, penes se condere*, so he also rightly explains חָכְמָה by *soliditas* ; it means properly (from חָכַם, Arab. *hakm*, R. *hk*, *vide* under Ps. x. 8, to be firm, closed) compactness, and then, like πυκνότης, ability, worldly wisdom, prudence, and in the higher general sense, the knowledge of things in the essence of their being and in the reality of their existence. Along with wisdom stands the moral מוּסָר, properly discipline, *i.e.* moral instruction, and in conformity with this, self-government, self-guidance, from יָסַר = וָסַר, cogn. אָסַר, properly *adstrictio* or *constrictio ;* for the מ of the noun signifies both *id quod* or *aliquid quod* (ὅ,τι) and *quod* in the conjunctional sense (ὅτι), and thus forms both a concrete (like מֹאסָר = מוֹסֵר, fetter, chain) and an abstract idea. The first general object of the Proverbs is דַּעַת, the reception into oneself of wisdom and moral edification by means of education and training; the second is to comprehend utterances of intelligence, *i.e.* such as proceed from intelligence and give expression to it (cf. אִמְרֵי אֱמֶת, xxii. 21). בִּין, *Kal*, to be distinguished (whence בֵּין, between, *constr.* of בֵּין, space between, interval), signifies in *Hiph.* to distinguish, to understand ; בִּינָה is, according to the sense, the *n. actionis* of this *Hiph.*, and signifies the understanding as the capability effective in the possession of the right criteria of distinguishing between the true and the false, the good and the bad (1 Kings iii. 9), the wholesome and the pernicious.

Vers. 3–5. In the following, 2*a* is expanded in vers. 3–5, then 2*b* in ver. 6. First the immediate object :

> 3 To attain intelligent instruction,
>   Righteousness, and justice, and integrity ;
> 4 To impart to the inexperienced prudence,
>   To the young man knowledge and discretion
> 5 Let the wise man hear and gain learning,
>   And the man of understanding take to himself rules of conduct.

---

[1] לָרַעַת is rightly pointed by Löwenstein with *Dechî* after Cod. 1294; *vide* the rule by which the verse is divided, *Torath Emeth*, p. 51, § 12.

[2] [Guna = a rule in Sanskrit grammar regulating the modification of vowels.]

With דַּעַת, denoting the reception into oneself, acquiring, is interchanged (cf. ii. 1) קַחַת, its synonym, used of intellectual reception
and appropriation, which, contemplated from the point of view of
the relation between the teacher and the learner, is the correlative of תֵּת, παραδιδόναι, *tradere* (ix. 9). But מוּסַר הַשְׂכֵּל is that
which proceeds from *chokma* and *musar* when they are blended
together : discipline of wisdom, discipline training to wisdom ; *i.e.*
such morality and good conduct as rest not on external inheritance,
training, imitation, and custom, but is bound up with the intelligent knowledge of the Why and the Wherefore. הַשְׂכֵּל, as xxi. 16,
is *inf. absol.* used substantively (cf. הַשְׁקֵט, keeping quiet, Isa. xxxii.
17) of שָׂכַל (whence שֵׂכֶל, *intellectus*), to entwine, involve ; for the
thinking through a subject is represented as an interweaving,
complicating, configuring of the thoughts (the syllogism is in like
manner represented as אֶשְׁכֹּל, Aram. סְגוֹל, a bunch of grapes), (with
which also סָכָל, a fool, and הִסְכִּיל, to act foolishly, are connected, from
the confusion of the thoughts, the entangling of the conceptions ;
cf. Arab. *'akl*, to understand, and מִעְקָּל). The series of synonyms
(cf. xxiii. 23) following in 3*b*, which are not well fitted to be the
immediate object to לָקַחַת, present themselves as the unfolding of
the contents of the מוּסַר הַשְׂכֵּל, as meaning that namely which is
dutiful and right and honest. With the frequently occurring
two conceptions, צֶדֶק וּמִשְׁפָּט (ii. 9), (or with the order reversed as
in Ps. cxix. 121) is interchanged מִשְׁפָּט וּצְדָקָה (or with the order
also reversed, xxi. 3). The remark of Heidenheim, that in צֶדֶק the
conception of the *justum*, and in צְדָקָה that of the *aequum* prevails,
is suggested by the circumstance that not צֶדֶק but צְדָקָה signifies
δικαιοσύνη (cf. x. 2) in the sense of liberality, and then of alms-
giving (ἐλεημοσύνη) ; but צֶדֶק also frequently signifies a way of
thought and action which is regulated not by the letter of the law
and by *talio*, but by love (cf. Isa. xli. 2, xlii. 6). *Tsedek* and *ts'dakah*
have almost the relation to one another of integrity and justice
which practically brings the former into exercise. מִשְׁפָּט (from
שָׁפַט, to make straight, to adjust, cf. שבט, Arab. *sabita*, to be smooth)
is the right and the righteousness in which it realizes itself, here
subjectively considered, the right mind.[1] מֵישָׁרִים (defect. for מישׁרים,
from יָשַׁר, to be straight, even) is plur. *tantum* ; for its sing. מֵישָׁר

---

[1] According to Malbim, מישׁפט is the fixed objective right, צדק the righteousness which does not at once decide according to the letter of the law, but always
according to the matter and the person.

(after the form מֵיטַב) the form מִישׁוֹר (in the same ethical sense, *e.g.*
Mal. ii. 6) is used : it means thus a way of thought and of conduct that is straight, *i.e.* according to what is right, true, *i.e.*
without concealment, honest, *i.e.* true to duty and faithful to one's
word.

Ver. 4. This verse presents another aspect of the object to be
served by this book : it seeks to impart prudence to the simple.
The form פְּתָאִים[1] (in which, as in גּוֹיִם, the י plur. remains unwritten)
is, in this mongrel form in which it is written (cf. vii. 7, viii. 5,
ix. 6, xiv. 18, xxvii. 12), made up of פְּתָיִם (i. 22, 32, once written
plene, פְּתָיִים, xxii. 3) and פְּתָאִים (vii. 7). These two forms with י
and the transition of י into א are interchanged in the plur. of
such nouns as פְּתִי, segolate form, " from פָּתָה (cogn. פָּתַח), to be
open, properly the open-hearted, *i.e.* one whose heart stands open
to every influence from another, the harmless, good-natured,—a
vox media among the Hebrews commonly (though not always, cf.
e.g. Ps. cxvi. 6) *in malam partem :* the foolish, silly, one who
allows himself to be easily persuaded or led astray, like similar
words in other languages — Lat. *simplex*, Gr. εὐήθης, Fr. *naïv ;*
Arab. *fatyn*, always, however, in a good sense : a high and noble-
minded man, not made as yet mistrustful and depressed by sad
experiences, therefore *juvenis ingenuus, vir animi generosi*" (Fl.).
The פְּתָאִים, not of firm and constant mind, have need of עָרְמָה ;
therefore the saying xiv. 15, cf. viii. 5, xix. 25. The noun עָרְמָה
(a fem. segolate form like חָכְמָה) means here *calliditas* in a good
sense, while the corresponding Arab. 'aram (to be distinguished
from the verb *'aram*, עָרַם, to peel, to make bare, *nudare*) is used only
in a bad sense, of malevolent, deceptive conduct. In the parallel
member the word נַעַר is used, generally (collectively) understood,
of the immaturity which must first obtain intellectual and moral
clearness and firmness ; such an one is in need of *peritia et sollertia*,
as Fleischer well renders it ; for דַּעַת is experimental knowledge,
and מְזִמָּה (from זָמַם, according to its primary signification, to press
together, *comprimere ;* then, referred to mental concentration : to
think) signifies in the sing., *sensu bono*, the capability of comprehending the right purposes, of seizing the right measures, of projecting the right plans.

Ver. 5. In this verse the infinitives of the object pass into inde-

[1] Like עֳפָאִים, Ps. civ. 12, וְכִצְבָאִים, 1 Chron. xii. 8, cf. *Michlol*, 196a. In
vers. 22, 32, the mute א is wanting.

pendent sentences for the sake of variety. That יִשְׁמַע cannot mean *audiet*, but *audiat*, is shown by ix. 9; but וְיֹסֶף is jussive (with the tone thrown back before לֶקַח; cf. x. 9, and xvi. 21, 23 where the tone is not thrown back, as also 2 Sam. xxiv. 3) with the consecutive *Vav* (וְ) (= Arab. ـ, *f*): let him hear, thus will he . . . or, in order that he. Whoever is wise is invited to hear these proverbs in order to add learning (*doctrinam*) to that which he already possesses, according to the principle derived from experience, ix. 9, Matt. xiii. 12. The segolate לֶקַח, which *in pausa* retains its ◌ֶ (as also בֶּטַח, יֵשַׁע, צֶמַח, מֶלֶךְ, צֶדֶק, קֶדֶם, and others), means reception, and concretely what one takes into himself with his ear and mind; therefore learning (διδαχή with the object of the ἀποδοχή), as Deut. xxxii. 2 (parallel אִמְרָה, as iv. 2 תּוֹרָה), and then learning that has passed into the possession of the receiver, knowledge, science (Isa. xxix. 24, parall. בִּינָה). Schultens com pares the Arab. *lakah*, used of the fructification of the female palm by the flower-dust of the male. The part. נָבוֹן (the *fin.* of which is found only once, Isa. x. 13) is the passive or the re-flexive of the *Hiph.* הֵבִין, to explain, to make to understand : one who is caused to understand or who lets himself be informed, and thus an intelligent person—that is one who may gain תַּחְבֻּלוֹת by means of these proverbs. This word, found only in the plur. (probably connected with חֹבֵל, shipmaster, properly one who has to do with the חַבָּלִים, ship's ropes, particularly handles the sails, LXX. κυβέρνησιν), signifies guidance, management, skill to direct anything (Job xxxii. 7, of God's skill which directs the clouds), and in the plur. conception, the taking measures, designs, in a good sense, or also (as in xii. 5) in a bad sense; here it means guiding thoughts, regulating principles, judicious rules and maxims, as xi. 14, prudent rules of government, xx. 18, xxiv. 6 of stratagems. Fl. compares the Arab. *tedbîr* (guidance, from דָּבַר, to lead cattle), with its plur. *tedâbîr*, and the Syr. *dubôro*, direction, management, etc.

Ver. 6. The mediate object of these proverbs, as stated in ver. 2*b*, is now expanded, for again it is introduced in the infinitive con-struction :—The reader shall learn in these proverbs, or by means of them as of a key, to understand such like apothegms generally (as xxii. 17 ff.) :

> To understand proverb and symbol,
> The words of wise men and their enigmas.

In the *Gesch. der jüd. Poesie*, p. 200 f., the derivation of the noun מְלִיצָה is traced from לִיץ, primarily to shine, Sanskr. *las*, frequently with the meanings *ludere* and *lucere;* but the Arab. brings near another primary meaning. " מליצה, from Arab. root *las, flexit, torsit,* thus properly *oratio detorta, obliqua, non aperta;* hence לֵץ, mocker, properly *qui verbis obliquis utitur:* as *Hiph.* הֵלִיץ, to scoff, but also *verba detorta retorquere, i.e.* to interpret, to explain" (Fl.). Of the root ideas found in חִידָה, to be sharp, pointed (חַד, perhaps related to the Sanskr. *katu,* sharp of taste, but not to *acutus*), and to be twisted (cf. אָחַד, אָגַד, עָקַד, harmonizing with the at present mysterious *catena*), the preference is given to the latter already, Ps. lxxviii. 2. " The Arab. *hâd*, to revolve, to turn (whence *hid,* bend, turn aside.!), thence חִידָה, στροφή, cunning, intrigue, as also enigma, dark saying, *perplexe dictum*" (Fl.) The comparison made by Schultens with the Arab. *hidt* as the name of the knot on the horn of the wild-goat shows the sensible fundamental conception. In post-biblical literature חידה is the enigma proper, and מְלִיצָה poetry (with הַלָּצָה of poetical prose). The *Græc. Venet.* translates it ῥητορείαν.

Ver. 7. The title of the book is followed by its motto, symbol, device :

> The fear of Jahve is the beginning of knowledge ;
> Wisdom and discipline is despised by fools.

The first hemistich expresses the highest principle of the Israelitish *Chokma,* as it is found also in ix. 10 (cf. xv. 33), Job xxviii. 28, and in Ps. cxi. 10 (whence the LXX. has interpolated here two lines). רֵאשִׁית combines in itself, as ἀρχή, the ideas of *initium* (accordingly J. H. Michaelis : *initium cognitionis, a quo quisquis recte philoso-phari cupit auspicium facere debet*) and *principium, i.e.* the basis, thus the root (cf. Mic. i. 13 with Job xix. 28).[1] Wisdom comes from God, and whoever fears Him receives it (cf. Jas. i. 5 f.). יִרְאַת יְהוָה is reverential subordination to the All-directing, and since designedly יהוה is used, and not אֱלֹהִים(הָ), to the One God, the Creator and Governor of the world, who gave His law unto Israel, and also beyond Israel left not His holy will unattested ; the reverse side of the fear of Jahve as the Most Holy One is שִׂנְאַת רָע, viii. 13 (post-biblical יִרְאַת חֵטְא). The inverted placing

---

[1] In Sirach i. 14, 16, the Syr. has both times רִישׁ חכמתא ; but in the second instance, where the Greek translation has πλησμονὴ σοφίας, שֹׂבַע חָכְמָה (after Ps. xvi. 11) may have existed in the original text.

of the words 7b imports that the wisdom and discipline which
one obtains in the way of the fear of God is only despised by the
אֱוִילִים, i.e. the hard, thick, stupid; see regarding the root-word
אול, coalescere, cohærere, incrassari, der Prophet Jesaia, p. 424, and
at Ps. lxxiii. 4. Schultens rightly compares παχεῖς, crassi pro
stupidis.[1] בָּזוּ has the tone on the penult., and thus comes from
בּוּ; the 3d pr. of בָּזָה would be בָּזוּ or בָּזְיוּ. The perf. (cf. ver. 29)
is to be interpreted after the Lat. oderunt (Ges. § 126).

FIRST INTRODUCTORY MASHAL DISCOURSE, I. 8–19.

WARNING AGAINST FELLOWSHIP WITH THOSE WHO SIN AGAINST
THEIR NEIGHBOUR'S LIFE AND PROPERTY.

Vers. 8, 9. After the author has indicated the object which his
Book of Proverbs is designed to subserve, and the fundamental
principle on which it is based, he shows for whom he has intended
it; he has particularly the rising generation in his eye:

> 8 Hear, my son, thy father's instruction,
> And refuse not the teaching of thy mother;
> 9 For these are a fair crown to thy head,
> And jewels to thy neck.

"My son," says the teacher of wisdom to the scholar whom he has,
or imagines that he has, before him, addressing him as a fatherly
friend. The N. T. representation of birth into a new spiritual life,
1 Cor. iv. 15, Philem. 10, Gal. iv. 19, lies outside the circle of
the O. T. representation; the teacher feels himself as a father
by virtue of his benevolent, guardian, tender love. Father and
mother are the beloved parents of those who are addressed. When
the Talmud understands אָבִיךָ of God, אִמֶּךָ of the people (אֻמָּה),
that is not the grammatico-historic meaning, but the practical
interpretation and exposition, after the manner of the Midrash.
The same admonition (with נְצֹר, keep, instead of שְׁמַע, hear, and
מִצְוַת, command, instead of מוּסַר, instruction) is repeated in vi.
20, and what is said of the parents in one passage is in x. 1
divided into two synonymous parallel passages. The stricter

[1] Malbim's explanation is singular: the sceptics, from אֱוִילִי, perhaps! This
also is Heidenheim's view.

musar, which expresses the idea of sensible means of instruction
(discipline), (xiii. 24, xxii. 15, xxiii. 13 f.), is suitably attributed to
the father, and the *torah* to the mother, only administered by the
word ; Wisdom also always says תּוֹרָתִי (my *torah*), and only once,
viii. 10, מוּסָרִי (my *musar*).

Ver. 9. הֵם, which is also used in the neut. *illa, e.g.* Job xxii.
24, refers here to the paternal discipline and the maternal teaching.
These, obediently received and followed, are the fairest ornament
of the child. לִוְיָה, from לָוָה, to wind, to roll, Arab. *lawy* (from לֹ,
whence also לוּל = לָלוּ, as הוּד, to boil up, = דְּוִדוּ), means winding,
twisted ornament, and especially wreath ; a crown of gracefulness
is equivalent to a graceful crown, a *corolla gratiosa*, as Schultens
translates it ; cf. iv. 9, according to which, Wisdom bestows such a
crown.[1] עֲנָקִים (or עֲנָקוֹת, Judg. viii. 26) are necklaces, jewels for
the neck ; denom. of the Arab. *'unek*, and Aram. עוּנַק, the neck
(perhaps from עָנַק = עוּק, to oppress, of heavy burdens ; cf. αὐχήν,
the neck).   גַּרְגְּרוֹת is, like *fauces*, the throat by which one swallows
(Arab. *g'arg'ara, tag'ary'ara*), a plur. extensive (Böttcher, § 695),
and is better fitted than גָּרוֹן to indicate the external throat ;
Ezekiel, however, uses (xvi. 11) *garon*, as our poet (iii. 3, 22,
vi. 21) uses *garg'roth*, to represent the front neck.[2]

Ver. 10. The general counsel of ver. 9 is here followed by a
more special warning :

> My son, if sinners entice thee
> Consent thou not.

The בְּנִי[3] (my son) is emphatically repeated. The intensive form
חַטָּאִים signifies men to whom sin has become a habit, thus vicious,
wicked.   פִּתָּה (*Pi.* of פָּתָה, to open) is not denom., to make or wish
to make a פְּתִי ; the meaning, to entice (harmonizing with πείθειν),
פִּתָּה obtains from the root-meaning of the *Kal*, for it is related
to it as *pandere (januam)* to *patere :* to open, to make accessible,
susceptible, namely to persuasion. The warning 10b is as brief
as possible a call of alarm back from the abyss. In the form תֹּבֵא
(from אָבָה, to agree to, to be willing, see Wetstein on Job, p. 349)

[1] In לִוְיַת חֵן the חֵן has the conjunctive accent *shalsheleth*, on account of
which the *Pesiq* accent (׀) is omitted. This small *shalsheleth* occurs only eight
times. See *Torath Emeth*, p. 36.

[2] The writing varies greatly. Here and at vi. 21 we have לְגַרְגְּרֹתֶךָ; at iii. 3,
עַל־גַּרְגְּרוֹתֶיךָ ; iii. 22, לְגַרְגְּרֹתֶיךָ. Thus according to the Masora and correct texts.

[3] The accent *Pazer* over the בְּנִי has the force of *Athnach*.

the preformative א is wanting, as in תֹּמְרוּ, 2 Sam. xix. 14, cf. Ps. cxxxix. 20, Ges. § 68, 2, and instead of תִּבֶה (= תֹּאבֶה, 1 Kings xx. 8) is vocalized not תֹּבֶא (cf. xi. 25), but after the Aram. תֹּבֵא (cf. יֵעֲלִי); see Gen. xxvi. 29, and *Comment. on Isaiah*, p. 648; Gesen. § 75, 17.

Vers. 11–14. Of the number of wicked men who gain associates to their palliation and strengthening, they are adduced as an example whom covetousness leads to murder.

> 11 If they say, " Go with us, we will lurk for blood,
>   Lie in wait for the innocent without cause;
> 12 Like the pit we will swallow them alive
>   And in perfect soundness like them that go down to the grave.
> 13 We find all manner of precious treasure,
>   Fill our houses with spoil.
> 14 Thou shalt cast thy lot amongst us,
>   We all have only one purse."

Ver. 11. The verb אָרַב signifies *nectere*, to bind fast (from רַב, close, compact), (see under Isa. xxv. 11), and particularly (but so that it bears in itself its object without ellipse) *insidias nectere = insidiari*. Regarding לְדָם Fleischer remarks : " Either elliptically for לִשְׁפָּךְ־דָם (Jewish interp.), or, as the parallelism and the usage of the language of this book rather recommend, *per synecd.* for : for a man, with particular reference to his blood to be poured out (cf. our saying ' *ein junges Blut*,' a young blood = a youth, with the underlying conception of the blood giving colour to the body as shining through it, or giving to it life and strength), as Ps. xciv. 21." As in post-biblical Heb. בָּשָׂר וָדָם (or inverted, αἷμα καὶ σάρξ, Heb. ii. 14), used of men as such, is not so used in the O. T., yet דָם, like נֶפֶשׁ, is sometimes used synecdochically for the person, but never with reference to the blood as an essentially constituent part of corporealness, but always with reference to violent putting to death, which separates the blood from the body (cf. my *System der bib. Psychologie*, p. 242). Here לְדָם is explained by לְדָמִים, with which it is interchanged, Mic. vii. 2 : let us lurk for blood (to be poured out). The verb צָפַן is never, like טָמַן (to conceal), connected with חֲבָלִים, מוֹקְשִׁים, פַּח, רֶשֶׁת—thus none of these words is here to be supplied; the idea of gaining over one expressed in the organic root צף (whence צָפָה, *diducendo obducere*) has passed over into that of restraining oneself, watching, lurking, hence צפן (cog. Aram. כְּמַן) in the sense of *speculari, insidiari*, interchanges with צפה (to spy), (cf. Ps. x. 8, lvi. 7 with xxxvii. 32). The adv. חִנָּם (an old accus. from

חֵן) properly means in a gracious manner, as a free gift (δωρεάν, gratis = gratiis), and accordingly, without reward, also without cause, which frequently = without guilt; but it never signifies *sine effectu qui noceat, i.e.* with impunity (Löwenst.). We have thus either to connect together נָקִי חִנָּם, "innocent in vain" (as אֹיְבַי חִנָּם, my enemies without a cause, Lam. iii. 52) : his innocence helps him nothing whom God protects not against us notwithstanding his innocence (Schultens, Bertheau, Elster, and others) ; or connect חנם with the verb (lie in wait for), for which Hitzig, after the LXX., Syr., Rashi,[1] Ralbag, Immanuel, rightly decides in view of 1 Sam. xix. 5, xxv. 31 ; cf. also Job ix. 17, where the succession of the accents is the same (*Tarcha* transmuted from *Mugrash*). Frequently there are combined together in this חנם (cf. Isa. xxviii. 14 f.), that which the author thinks, and that which those whom he introduces as speaking think.

Ver. 12. The first clause of this verse Hitzig translates : " as the pit (swallows) that which lives." This is untenable, because כְ with the force of a substantive (as *instar*, likeness) is regarded as a preposition, but not a conjunction (see at Ps. xxxviii. 14 f.). חַיִּים (the living) is connected with נִבְלָעֵם, and is the accus. of the state (حَال, according to the terminology of the Arab. gram- marians) in which they will, with impunity, swallow them up like the pit (the insatiable, xxvii. 20, xxx. 16), namely, while these their sacrifices are in the state of life's freshness,[2] " the living," —without doubt, like Ps. lv. 16, lxiii. 10, cxxiv. 3, in fact and in expression an allusion to the fate of the company of Korah, Num. xvi. 30, 33. If this is the meaning of חיים, then תְּמִימִים as the parallel word means *integros* not in an ethical sense, in which it would be a synonym of נקי of ver. 11*b* (cf. xxix. 10 with Ps. xix. 14), but in a physical sense (*Græc. Venet.* καὶ τελείους; Parchon as Rashi, בריאים ושלמים, *vid.* Böttcher, *De Inferis,* § 293). This physical sense is claimed for תֹּם, Job xxi. 23, for תָּם probably, Ps. lxxiii. 4, and why should not תמים, used in the law regarding sacrifices (*e.g.* Ex. xii. 5, " without blemish ") of the faultlessness of the victim,

---

[1] [Rashi, *i.e.* Rabbi Salomo Isaaki, of Troyes, died A.D. 1105. Ralbag, *i.e.* Rabbi Levi ben Gershon, usually referred to by Christian writers as Master Leo de Bannolis, or Gersonides, a native of Banolas near Gerona, died about 1342.]

[2] Only in this sense is the existing accentuation of this verse (cf. the Targ.) to be justified.

also signify such an one אֲשֶׁר אֵין־בּוֹ מְתֹם (Isa. i. 6)? In the midst
of complete external health they will devour them like those that
go down to the grave (cf. Ps. xxviii. 1, lxxxviii. 5, with Isa.
xiv. 19), *i.e.* like those under whose feet the earth is suddenly
opened, so that, without leaving any trace behind, they sink into
the grave and into Hades. The connection of the finite with the
accus. of place, Ps. lv. 16, lies at the foundation of the genitive
connection יוֹרְדֵי בוֹר (with the tone thrown back): those that go
down to the grave.

Vers. 13, 14.[1] To their invitation, bearing in itself its own condemnation, they add as a lure the splendid self-enriching treasures
which in equal and just fellowship with them they may have the
prospect of sharing. הוֹן (from הִין, *levem*, then *facilem esse, être
aisé, à son aise*) means *aisance*, convenience, opulence, and concretely that by which life is made agreeable, thus money and
possessions (Fleischer in Levy's *Chald. Wörterbuch*, i. 423 f.). With
this הוֹן with remarkable frequency in the *Mishle* יָקָר (from יָקַר,
Arab. *wakar, grave esse*) is connected in direct contrast, according
to its primary signification; cf. xii. 27, xxiv. 4: heavy treasures
which make life light. Yet it must not be maintained that, as
Schultens has remarked, this oxymoron is intended, nor also that
it is only consciously present in the language. מָצָא has here its
primitive appropriate signification of attaining, as Isa. x. 14 of
reaching. שָׁלָל (from שָׁלַל, to draw from, draw out, from שַׁל,
cf. שָׁלָה, שָׁלַף, Arab. *salab, Comm. on Isa.* p. 447) is that which is
drawn away from the enemy, *exuviæ*, and then the booty and
spoil taken in war generally. נְמַלֵּא, to fill with anything, make
full, governs a double accusative, as the *Kal* (to become full of
anything) governs only one. In ver. 14, the invitation shows
how the prospect is to be realized. Interpreters have difficulty
in conceiving what is here meant. Do not a share by lot and a
common purse exclude one another? Will they truly, in the distribution of the booty by lot, have equal portions at length, equally
much in their money-bags? Or is it meant that, apart from the
portion of the booty which falls to every one by lot, they have a
common purse which, when their business is ebbing, must supply
the wants of the company, and on which the new companion can
maintain himself beforehand? Or does it mean only that they will

[1] Here, in ver. 14, גּוֹרָלְךָ is to be written with *Munach* (not *Metheg*) in the
second syllable; *vid. Torath Emeth*, p. 20. *Accentuationssystem*, vii. § 2.

be as mutually helpful to one another, according to the principle τὰ τῶν φίλων κοινά (*amicorum omnia communia*), as if they had only one purse? The meaning is perfectly simple. The oneness of the purse consists in this, that the booty which each of them gets, belongs not wholly or chiefly to him, but to the whole together, and is disposed of by lot; so that, as far as possible, he who participated not at all in the affair in obtaining it, may yet draw the greatest prize. This view harmonizes the relation between 14*b* and 14*a*. The common Semitic כִּיס is even used at the present day in Syria and elsewhere as the name of the Exchange ("*Börse*") (plur. *akjâs*); here it is the purse ("*Kasse*") (χρημάτων δοχεῖον, Procop.), which is made up of the profits of the business. This profit consists not merely in gold, but is here thought of in regard to its worth in gold. The apparent contradiction between distributing by lot and having a common purse disappears when the distribution by lot of the common property is so made, that the retaining of a stock-capital, or reserve fund, is not excluded.

Ver. 15. After the men are described against whose enticements a warning is given forth, the warning is emphatically repeated, and is confirmed by a threefold reason :

> My son! go not in the way with them.
> Keep back thy foot from their path.

If בְּדֶרֶךְ (in the way), taken alone, cannot be equivalent to בדרך אֶחָד (in one way), so is אִתָּם (with them) to be regarded as its determination.[1] Foot (not feet), as eye, hand, etc., is used where the members come less under consideration than what they unitedly bring about (iv. 26 f.). נְתִיבָה, from נָתַב, signifies properly that which is raised, especially the (raised) footstep.

Ver. 16. The *first* argument to enforce the warning :

> For their feet run to the evil,
> And hasten to shed blood.

That this is their object they make no secret (ver. 11 ff.); but why is it that such an object as this should furnish no ground of warning against them, especially as on this beginning the stamp of that which is morally blamable is here impressed with לָרַע ?

---

[1] The Arab. grammarians regard this as half determination, and call it *takhsys;* that אִתָּם has with them the force of a virtually co-ordinated attributive ; while, according to the Arab. gram., it is also possible that בְּדֶרֶךְ, "in one way," is equivalent to on the common way, for in the indetermination sometimes there lies the conception not merely of *âhad,* but of *weahad.*

Besides, this circular movement of the thoughts is quite after the manner of this poet ; and that ver. 16 is in his style, vi. 18 shows. The want of this distich (16*b* = Rom. iii. 15) in LXX. B. א. weighs heavier certainly than the presence of it in LXX. A. (Procop., Syro-Hexap.), since the translation is not independent, but is transferred from Isa. lix. 7 ; but if for the first time, at a later period, it is supplied in the LXX., yet it has the appearance of an addition made to the Hebr. text from Isa. lix. 7 (Hitzig, Lagarde) ; cf. *Comm. on Isaiah*, xl.–lxvi. לִשְׁפָּךְ is always pointed thus ; for, as a regular rule, after לְ as well as מ the aspiration disappears ; but in Ezek. xvii. 17 בִּשְׁפֹּךְ is also found, and in this case (cf. at Ps. xl. 15) the punctuation is thus inconsequent.

Ver. 17. The *second* argument in support of the warning.

> For in vain is the net spread out
> In the eyes of all (the winged) birds.

The interpretation *conspersum est rete*, namely, with corn as a bait, which was put into circulation by Rashi, is inadmissible ; for as little as הִזָּה (*Hiph.* of נָזָה) can mean to strew, can זָרָה mean to spread. The object is always that which is scattered (*gestreut*), not that which is spread (*bestreut*). Thus, *expansum est rete*, but not from מָזַר, *extendere*, from which מְזֹורָה[1] in this form cannot be derived (it would in that case be מְזוּרָה), but from זָרָה, pass. of זֶרָה, to scatter, spread out. The alluring net, when it is shaken out and spread, is, as it were, scattered, *ventilatur*. But if this is done incautiously before the eyes of the birds to be caught, they forthwith fly away. The principal stress lies on the בְּעֵינֵי (before the eyes) as the reason of the חִנָּם (in vain), according to the saying of Ovid, *Quæ nimis apparent retia, vitat avis*. The *applicatio similitudinis* lying near, according to J. H. Michaelis, is missed even by himself and by most others. If the poet wished to say that they carried on their work of blood with such open boldness, that he must be more than a simpleton who would allow himself to be caught by them, that would be an unsuitable ground of warning ; for would there not be equally great need for warning against fellowship with them, if they had begun their enticement with more cunning, and reckoned on greater success ? Hitzig, Ewald, Zöckler, and others, therefore interpret חנם, not in the sense of

---

[1] The MS. Masora remarks לית וחסר, and hence מְזֹרה is written defectively in the *Erfurt*, 1, 2, 3, *Frankf.* 1294, in the edition of Norzi and elsewhere.

in vain, inasmuch as they do not let themselves be caught; but: in
vain, for they see not the net, but only the scattered corn. But
according to the preceding, הָרָשֶׁת (the net) leads us to think only
either of the net of the malicious designs, or the net of the alluring
deceptions. Thus, as Ziegler has noticed, the warned ought to
make application of the similitude to himself : Go not with them,
for their intention is bad; go not with them, for if the bird flees
away from the net which is spread out before it, thou wilt not
surely be so blind as suffer thyself to be ensnared by their gross
enticements. בַּעַל כָּנָף : the furnished with the wing (wings in
Eccles. x. 20); בַּעַל forms the idea of property (lord).

Ver. 18. The causal conj. כִּי (for) in vers. 16 and 17 are
co-ordinated ; and there now follows, introduced by the conj. ו
(" and "), a *third* reason for the warning :

> And they lie in wait for their own blood,
> They lay snares for their own lives.

The warning of ver. 16 is founded on the immorality of the conduct of the enticer ; that of 17 on the audaciousness of the seduction as such, and now on the self-destruction which the robber and
murderer bring upon themselves : they wish to murder others, but,
as the result shows, they only murder themselves. The expression
is shaped after ver. 11, as if it were : They lay snares, as they
themselves say, for the blood of others ; but it is in reality for
their *own* blood : they certainly lie in wait, as they say ; but not, as
they add, for the innocent, but for their own lives (Fl.). Instead
of לְדָמָם, there might be used לְדְמֵיהֶם, after Mic. vii. 2 ; but לְנַפְשָׁם
would signify *ipsis* (post-biblical, לְעַצְמָם), while לְנַפְשְׁתָם leaves un-
obliterated the idea of the life : *animis ipsorum ;* for if the O. T.
language seeks to express *ipse* in any other way than by the personal pronoun spoken emphatically, this is done by the addition of
נֶפֶשׁ (Isa. liii. 11). וְהֵם was on this account necessary, because ver.
17 has another subject (cf. Ps. lxiii. 10).

Ver. 19. An *epiphonema* :

> Such is the lot of all who indulge in covetousness ;
> It takes away the life of its owner.

This language is formed after Job viii. 13. Here, as there, in
the word אָרְחוֹת, the ideas of action and issue, manner of life and
its result, are all combined. בֶּצַע signifies properly that which is
cut off, a piece, fragment broken off, then that which one breaks
off and takes to himself — booty, gain, particularly unjust gain

(xxviii. 16). בֹּצֵעַ בֶּצַע is he who is greedy or covetous. The subject to יִקָּח is בֶּצַע, covetousness, πλεονεξία (see Isa. lvii. 17). As Hosea, iv. 11, says of three other things that they take away לֵב, the understanding (νοῦς), so here we are taught regarding unjust gain or covetousness, that it takes away נֶפֶשׁ, the life (ψυχή) (לְקַח נֶפֶשׁ, to take away the life, 1 Kings xix. 10, Ps. xxxi. 14). בְּעָלָיו denotes not the possessor of unjust gain, but as an inward conception, like בַּעַל אַף, xxii. 24, cf. xxiii. 2, xxiv. 8, Eccles. x. 11, him of whom covetousness is the property. The sing. נֶפֶשׁ does not show that בְּעָלָיו is thought of as sing.; cf. xxii. 23, Ps. xxxiv. 23; but according to iii. 27, xvi. 22, Eccles. viii. 8, this is nevertheless probable, although the usage without the suffix is always בֹּצֵעַ בֶּצַע, and not בַּעֲלֵי (of plur. intens. בְּעָלִים).

SECOND INTRODUCTORY MASHAL DISCOURSE, I. 20-33.

DISCOURSE OF WISDOM TO HER DESPISERS.

After the teacher of wisdom has warned his disciples against the allurements of self-destroying sin, whose beastly demoniacal nature culminates in murder and robbery, he introduces Wisdom herself saying how by enticing promises and deterring threatenings she calls the simple and the perverse to repentance. Wisdom is here personified, *i.e.* represented as a person. But this personification presupposes, that to the poet wisdom is more than a property and quality of human subjectivity: she is to him as a divine power, existing independently, to submit to which is the happiness of men, and to reject which is their destruction. And also to the public appearance of wisdom, as it is here represented, there must be present objective reality, without which the power of conviction departs from the figure. The author must think on historical and biographical facts, on human organs (as 2 Chron. xvii. 7-9, cf. Wisd. vii. 27), through which, without words and in words, Wisdom delivers such addresses. But the figure cannot be so historical that it sustains only the relation to a definite time, and not to all time; it is a call to repentance, going forth to all time and to all places, which, divested of all the accidents of its externality, he here refers to its invisible divine background, when he begins in these words:

20 Wisdom cries, sounding loudly in the streets,
   She causes her voice to be heard in the chief streets.
21 Over the places of greatest tumult she calleth ;
   In the porches of the gates, in the city, she speaketh forth her words.

Ver. 20. Looking to its form and vocalization, חָכְמוֹת may be an Aramaizing abstract formation (Gesen. ; Ew. 165, c; Olsh. 219, b) ; for although the forms אָחוֹת and גְּלוֹת are of a different origin, yet in רַבּוֹת and הוֹלֵלוֹת such abstract formations lie before us. The termination *úth* is here, by the passing over of the u into the less obscure but more intensive o (cf. יְהוֹ in the beginning and middle of the word, and יְהוּ יְהוֹ at the end of the word), raised to *óth*, and thereby is brought near to the fem. plur. (cf. חַכְמוֹת, xiv. 1, *sapientia*, as our plur. of the neut. *sapiens*, חָכְמָה), approaching to the abstract. On the other hand, that חָכְמוֹת is sing. of abstract signification, is not decisively denoted by its being joined to the plur. of the predicate (for תָּרֹנָּה here, as at viii. 3, is scarcely plur. ; and if רָאמוֹת, xxiv. 7, is plur., חָכְמוֹת as the numerical plur. may refer to the different sciences or departments of knowledge) ; but perhaps by this, that it interchanges with תְּבוּנוֹת, Ps. xlix. 4, cf. Prov. xi. 12, xxviii. 16, and that an abstract formation from חָכְמָה (fem. of חָכָם, חֲכַם), which besides is not concrete, was unnecessary. Still less is חָכְמוֹת = חָכְמַת a singular, which has it in view to change חָכְמָה into a proper name, for proof of which Hitzig refers to תְּהֹמוֹת, Ps. lxxviii. 15; the singular ending *óth* without an abstract signification does not exist. After that Dietrich, in his *Abhandl.* 1846, has shown that the origin of the plur. proceeds not from separate calculation, but from comprehension,[1] and that particularly also names denoting intellectual strength are frequently plur., which multiply the conception not externally but internally, there is no longer any justifiable doubt that חָכְמוֹת signifies the all-comprehending, absolute, or, as Böttcher, § 689, expresses it, the full personal wisdom. Since such intensive plurals are sometimes united with the plur. of the predicate, as *e.g.* the monotheistically interpreted *Elohim*, Gen. xxxv. 7 (see *l. c.*), so תָּרֹנָּה may be plur. On the other hand, the idea that it is a *forma mixta* of תָּרֹן (from רָנַן) and תִּרְנֶה (Job xxxix. 23) or תָּרְנֶה, the final sound in *ah* opposes. It may, however, be the emphatic form of the 3d fem. sing. of רָנַן ; for, that the

---

[1] In the Indo-Germanic languages the s of the plur. also probably proceeds from the prep. sa (sam) = συν. See Schleicher, *Compend. der vergl. Gram.* § 247.

Hebr. has such an emphatic form, corresponding to the Arab. *taktu-banna*, is shown by these three examples (keeping out of view the suspicion of a corruption of the text, Olsh. p. 452), Judg. v. 26, Job xvii. 16, Isa. xxviii. 3 ; cf. תִּשְׁלַחְנָה, Obad. 13 (see Caspari, *l.c.*), an example of the 2d masc. sing. of this formation. רָנַן (with רָנָה) is a word imitative of sound (*Schallwort*), used to denote " a clear-sounding, shrill voice (thence the Arab. *rannan*, of a speaker who has a clear, piercing voice) ; then the clear shrill sound of a string or chord of a bow, or the clear tinkle of the arrow in the quiver, and of the metal that has been struck" (Fl.). The meaning of רְחֹבוֹת is covered by *plateæ* (Luke xiv. 21), wide places ; and חוּץ, which elsewhere may mean that which is without, before the gates of the city and courts, here means the " open air," in contra-distinction to the inside of the houses.

Ver. 21. הֹמִיּוֹת (plur. of הוֹמִי, the ground-form of הוֹמֶה, from הָמֵי =הָמָה), " they who are making noise ;" for the epithet is poetically used (Isa. xxii. 2) as a substantive, crowded noisy streets or places. רֹאשׁ is the place from which on several sides streets go forth : cf. *ras el-ain*, the place where the well breaks forth ; *ras en-nahr*, the place from which the stream divides itself ; the sing. is meant dis-tributively as little as at viii. 2. פֶּתַח, if distinguished from שַׁעַר (which also signifies cleft, breach), is the opening of the gate, the entrance by the gate. Four times the poet says that Wisdom goes forth preaching, and four times that she preaches publicly ; the בָּעִיר used in five places implies that Wisdom preaches not in the field, before the few who there are met with, but in the city, which is full of people.

Ver. 22. The poet has now reached that part of his introduction where he makes use of the very words uttered by Wisdom :

> How long, ye simple, will ye love simplicity,
> And scorners delight in scorning,
> And fools hate knowledge ?

Three classes of men are here addressed : the פְּתָיִם, the simple, who, being accessible to seduction, are only too susceptible of evil ; the לֵצִים, mockers, *i.e.* free-thinkers (from לִיץ, Arab. *lus, flectere, torquere*, pro-perly *qui verbis obliquis utitur*) ; and the כְּסִילִים, fools, *i.e.* the men-tally imbecile and stupid (from כָּסַל, Arab. *kasal*, to be thick, coarse, indolent). The address to these passes immediately over into a de-claration regarding them ; cf. the same enallage, i. 27 f. עַד־מָתַי has the accent *Mahpach*, on account of the *Pasek* following ; *vid. Torath*

Emeth, p. 26. Intentionally, Wisdom addresses only the פְּתִים, to whom she expects to find soonest access. Between the futt., which express the continuing love and hatred, stands the perf. חָמְדוּ, which expresses that in which the mockers found pleasure, that which was the object of their love. לָהֶם is the so-called *dat. ethicus*, which reflexively refers to that which is said to be the will and pleasure of the subject; as we say, " I am fond of this and that." The form תְּאֵהֲבוּ, Abulwalîd, Parchon, and Kimchi regard as *Piel;* but תְּאֵהֲבוּ instead of תְּאֵהֲבוּ would be a recompensation of the virtual doubling, defacing the character of the *Piel.* Schultens regards it as a defectively written *Paiël* (in Syr.), but it is not proved that this conjugation exists in Hebr.; much rather תְּאֵהֲבוּ is the only possible *Kal* form with תֶּאֱהֲבוּן without the pause, regularly formed from תֶּאֱהֲבוּ (*vid.* Ewald, § 193, *a*). The division by the accent *Mercha-Mahpach* of the two words תאהבו פתי is equal in value to the connecting of them by *Makkeph; vid.* Baer's *Psalterium.* p. x. In codd., and also in correct texts, תאהבו is written with the accent *Galgal* on the first syllable, as the servant of the *Mercha-Mahpach.* The *Gaja* is incorrectly here and there placed under the תְּ.

Ver. 23. To the call to thoughtfulness which lies in the complaint " How long?" there follows the entreaty :

> Turn ye at my reproof !
> Behold ! I would pour out my Spirit upon you,
> I would make you to know my words.

23*a* is not a clause expressive of a wish, which with the particle expressive of a wish, which is wanting, would be תָּשׁוּבוּ־נָא, or according to xxiii. 1 and xxvii. 23 would be שׁוֹב תָּשׁוּבוּ. The הִנֵּה, introducing the principal clause, stamps 23*a* as the conditional clause ; the relation of the expressions is as Isa. xxvi. 10, Job xx. 24. תָּשׁוּבוּ[1] is not equivalent to *si convertamini,* which would require תִּפְנוּ, but to *si revertamini;* but לְתוֹכַחְתִּי[2] does not therefore mean at my reproof, *i.e.* in consequence of it (Hitzig, after Num. xvi. 34), but it is a *constructio prægnans :* turning and placing yourselves under my reproof. With תוכחת there is supposed an ἔλεγχος (LXX., Symm.) : bringing proof, conviction, punishment. If

---

[1] In the *Hagiographa* everywhere written *plene,* with exception of Job xvii. 10.

[2] The *Metheg* belongs to the ת, under which it should be placed (and not to the ל), as the commencing sound of the second syllable before the tone-syllable ; cf. ver. 25.

they, leaving their hitherto accustomed way, permit themselves to be warned against their wickedness, then would Wisdom cause her words to flow forth to them, *i.e.* would without reserve disclose and communicate to them her spirit, cause them to know (namely by experience) her words. הַבִּיעַ (from נָבַע, R. נב; *vid. Genesis*, p. 635) is a common figurative word, expressive of the free pouring forth of thoughts and words, for the mouth is conceived of as a fountain (cf. xviii. 4 with Matt. xii. 34), and the ῥῆσις (*vid.* LXX.) as ῥεῦσις; only here it has the Spirit as object, but parallel with דְּבָרַי, thus the Spirit as the active power of the words, which, if the Spirit expresses Himself in them, are πνεῦμα καὶ ζωή, John vi. 63. The addresses of Wisdom in the Book of Proverbs touch closely upon the discourses of the Lord in the Logos-Gospel. Wisdom appears here as the fountain of the words of salvation for men; and these words of salvation are related to her, just as the λόγοι to the divine λόγος expressing Himself therein.

Vers. 24–27. The address of Wisdom now takes another course. Between vers. 23 and 24 there is a pause, as between Isa. i. 20 and 21. In vain Wisdom expects that her complaints and enticements will be heard. Therefore she turns her call to repentance into a discourse announcing judgment.

24 Because I have called, and ye refused;
   Stretched out my hand, and no man regarded;
25 And ye have rejected all my counsel,
   And to my reproof have not yielded:
26 Therefore will I also laugh at your calamity,
   Will mock when your terror cometh;
27 When like a storm your terror cometh,
   And your destruction sweeps on like a whirlwind;
   When distress and anguish cometh upon you.

Commencing with יַעַן (which, like מַעַן, from עָנָה, to oppose, denotes the intention, but more the fundamental reason or the cause than, as לְמַעַן, the motive or object), the clause, connected with גַּם־אֲנִי, *ego vicissim*, turns to the conclusion. As here יַעַן קָרָאתִי (as the word of Jahve) are connected by גַּם־אֲנִי to the expression of the *talio* in Isa. lxvi. 4, so also מֵאֵן, with its contrast אָבָה, Isa. i. 19 f. The construction *quoniam vocavi et renuistis* for *quoniam quum vocarem renuistis* (cf. Isa. xii. 1) is the common diffuse (*zerstreute*) Semitic, the paratactic instead of the periodizing style. The stretching out of the hand is, like the "spreading out" in Isa. lxv. 2, significant of striving to beckon to the wandering, and to bring them near. Regarding

הַקְשֵׁיב, viz. אָזְנוֹ, to make the ear stiff (R. קש), *arrigere*, incorrectly explained by Schultens, after the Arab. *kashab, polire*, by *aurem purgare, vid. Isaiah*, p. 257, note.

Ver. 25. פָּרַע is synonymous with נָטַשׁ, i. 8; cf. iv. 15 פְּרָעֵהוּ, turn from it. Gesenius has inaccurately interpreted the phrase פרע ראש of the shaving off of the hair, instead of the letting it fly loose. פרע means to loosen (= to lift up, syn. הֵחֵל), to release, to set free; it combines the meanings of loosening and making empty, or at liberty, which is conveyed in Arab. by فرع and فرغ. The latter means, intrans., to be set free, therefore to be or to become free from occupation or business; with من of an object, to be free from it, *i.e.* to have accomplished it, to have done with it (Fl.). Thus: since ye have dismissed (*missum fecistis*) all my counsel (עֵצָה as לֵדָה, from יָעַץ, وعظ), *i.e.* what I always would advise to set you right. אָבָה combines in itself the meanings of consent, i. 10, and compliance, i. 30 (with לְ), and, as here, of acceptance. The principal clause begins like an echo of Ps. ii. 4 (cf. Jer. xx. 7).

Vers. 26, 27. שָׂחַק, as xxxi. 25 shows, is not to be understood with בְּ; בְּ is that of the state or time, not of the object. Regarding אֵיד, *calamitas opprimens, obruens* (from אוד = آد, to burden, to oppress), see at Ps. xxxi. 12. בֹּא is related to יֶאֱתֶה as arriving to approaching; פַּחְדְּכֶם is not that for which they are in terror,—for those who are addressed are in the condition of carnal security,—but that which, in the midst of this, will frighten and alarm them. The *Chethib* שאוה is pointed thus, שָׁאֲוָה (from שָׁאָה = שָׁוָה, as רָאָה, רָאֲוָה, זָעָה after the form דְּאָבָה, אַהֲבָה); the *Keri* substitutes for this infinitive name the usual particip. שֹׁאָה (where then the *Vav* is יתיר, " superfluous"), crashing (fem. of שֹׁאֶה), then a crash and an overthrow with a crash; regarding its root-meaning (to be waste, and then to sound hollow), see under Ps. xxxv. 8. סוּפָה (from סוּף = סָפָה), sweeping forth as a (see x. 25) whirlwind. The infinitive construction of 27a is continued in 27b in the finite. "This syntactical and logical attraction, by virtue of which a *modus* or *tempus* passes by ו or by the mere parallel arrangement (as ii. 2) from one to another, attracted into the signification and nature of the latter, is peculiar to the Hebr. If there follows a new clause or section of a clause where the discourse takes, as it were, a new departure, that attraction ceases, and the original form of expression is resumed; cf. i. 22, where after the accent *Athnach* the future is returned to, as here

in 27c the infinitive construction is restored" (Fl.). The allite-
rating words צָרָה וְצוּקָה, cf. Isa. xxx. 6, Zeph. i. 15, are, related to
each other as narrowness and distress (Hitzig); the Mashal is fond
of the stave-rhyme.[1]
Vers. 28–31. Then—this sublime preacher in the streets continues—distress shall teach them to pray:

> 28 Then shall they call on me, and I will not answer;
> They shall early seek after me, and not find me;
> 29 Because that they hated knowledge,
> And did not choose the fear of Jahve.
> 30 They have not yielded to my counsel,
> Despised all my reproof:
> 31 Therefore shall they eat of the fruit of their way,
> And satiate themselves with their own counsels.

In the full emphatic forms, יִקְרָאֻנְנִי, they shall call on me, יְשַׁחֲרֻנְנִי,
they shall seek me, and יִמְצָאֻנְנִי, they shall find me, the suffix נִי may
be joined to the old plur. ending ûn (Gesenius, Olshausen, Böttcher);
but open forms like יְבָרְכֶנְהוּ, He will bless him, יְכַבְּדֶנִי, He will
honour me (from יְכַבְּדֵנִי), and the like, rather favour the conclusion
that נ is epenthetic (Ew. § 250, b).[2] The address here takes the
form of declaration: Stultos nunc indignos censet ulteriori alloquio
(Mich.). It is that laughter and scorn, ver. 26, which here sounds
forth from the address of the Judge regarding the incorrigible. שִׁחֵר
is denom. of שַׁחַר, to go out and to seek with the morning twilight,
as also בִּקֵּר, Ps. xxvii. 5, perhaps to appear early, and usually (Arab.)
bakar (I. II. IV.), to rise early, to be zealous (Lane: "He hastened
to do or accomplish, or attain the thing needed"). Zöckler, with
Hitzig, erroneously regards vers. 29, 30 as the antecedent to ver. 31.
With וְיֹאכְלוּ, "and they shall eat," the futt. announcing judgment
are continued from ver. 28; cf. Deut. xxviii. 46–48. The conclusion
after תַּחַת כִּי, "therefore because," or as usually expressed (except

---

[1] Jul. Ley, in his work on the Metrical Forms of Hebrew Poetry, 1866, has
taken too little notice of these frequently occurring alliteration staves; Lagarde
communicated to me (8th Sept. 1846) his view of the stave-rhyme in the Book
of Proverbs, with the remark, "Only the Hebr. technical poetry is preserved to
us in the O. T. records; but in such traces as are found of the stave-rhyme, there
are seen the echoes of the poetry of the people, or notes passing over from it."

[2] In the Codd. יִקְרָאֻנְנִי is written; in this case the Metheg indicates the tone
syllable: vid. Torath Emeth, p. 7 note, p. 21 note; and Accentssystem, ii. § 1, note.
In יְשַׁחֲרֻנְנִי the Rebia is to be placed over the ר. In the Silluk-word יִמְצָאֻנְנִי it
appears undoubtedly that the form is to be spoken as Milel, i.e. with tone on
the penult.

here and Deut. iv. 37, cf. Gen. iv. 25), תַּחַת אֲשֶׁר (ἀνθ᾽ ὧν), is otherwise characterized, Deut. xxii. 29, 2 Chron. xxi. 12; and besides,
תחת אשר stands after (e.g. 1 Sam. xxvi. 21; 2 Kings xxii. 17; Jer.
xxix. 19) oftener than before the principal clause. בָּחַר combines
in itself the meanings of *eligere* and *diligere* (Fl.). The construction of אָבָה לְ (to be inclining towards) follows that of the analogous
שָׁמַע לְ (to hear). Each one eats of the fruit of his way—good fruit
of good ways (Isa. iii. 10), and evil fruit of evil ways. "The מִן,
31*b*, introduces the object from which, as a whole, that which one
eats, and with which he is satisfied, is taken as a part, or the object
from which, as from a fountain, satisfaction flows forth" (Fl.). In
correct texts, וְיֹאכְלוּ has the accent *Dechi*, and at the same time
Munach as its servant. Regarding the laws of punctuation, according to which וּמִמֹּעֲצֹתֵיהֶם (with *Munach* on the tone-syllable, *Tarcha*
on the antepenult, and *Metheg* before the *Chateph-Pathach*) is to be
written, see Baer's *Torath Emeth*, p. 11, *Accentssystem*, iv. § 4.
Norzi accents the word incorrectly with *Rebia Mugrash*. With
the exception of Prov. xxii. 22, the pluralet [1] מֹעֵצוֹת has always the
meaning of ungodly counsels.

Vers. 32, 33. The discourse is now summarily brought to a
close:

> 32 For the perverseness of the simple slays them,
> And the security of fools destroys them.
> 33 But whoever hearkeneth to me dwells secure,
> And is at rest from fear of evil.

Of the two interpretations of שׁוּב, a turning towards (with אֶל and
the like, conversion) or a turning away (with מֵאַחֲרֵי or מֵעַל, desertion), in מְשׁוּבָה the latter (as in the *post-Bib.* תְּשׁוּבָה, repentance, the
former) is expressed; apostasy from wisdom and from God are con-
joined. שַׁלְוָה is here *carnalis securitas;* but the word may also denote
the external and the internal peace of the righteous, as שַׁאֲנָן, whence
שַׁלְאֲנָן, Job xxi. 23, as a superlative is formed by the insertion of the לְ
of שַׁלֵו, is taken *in bonam et malam partem.* שַׁאֲנָן is, according to
the Masora (also in Jer. xxx. 10, xlvi. 27, xlviii. 11), 3d perf. *Pilel*
(Ewald, § 120, *a*), from the unused שָׁאַן, to be quiet: he has attained
to full quietness, and enjoys such. The construction with מִן follows
the analogy of הֵנִיחַ מִן (to give rest from), שָׁקַט מִן (to rest from), and
the like. The negative interpretation of מִן, *sine ullo pavore mali*

---

[1] [A plur. denoting unity in the circumstances, and a similarity in the relations of time and space.]

(Schultens, Ewald), is unnecessary; also Job xxi. 9 may be explained by "peace from terror," especially since שָׁלוֹם is derived from the root שׁל, *extrahere*. פַּחַד רָעָה, "fear of evil," one may perhaps distinguish from פחד רע as the genitive of combination.

THIRD INTRODUCTORY MASHAL DISCOURSE, II.

EARNEST STRIVING AFTER WISDOM AS THE WAY TO THE FEAR OF GOD AND TO VIRTUE.

The admonition so far has almost wholly consisted of warning and threatening. The teacher, directing back to the discipline of the paternal home, warns against fellowship in the bloody deeds of the covetous, which issue in self-murder; and Wisdom holds up before her despisers the mirror of the punishment which awaits them. Now the admonition becomes positive. The teacher describes separately the blessings of the endeavour after wisdom; the endeavour after wisdom, which God rewards with the gift of wisdom, leads to religious and moral knowledge, and this guards men on the way of life from all evil. The teacher accordingly interweaves conditions and promises:

1 My son, if thou receivest my words,
   And keepest my commandments by thee;
2 So that thou inclinest thine ear unto wisdom,
   Turnest thine heart to understanding;—
3 Yea, if thou callest after knowledge,
   To understanding directest thy voice;
4 If thou seekest her as silver,
   And searchest for her as for treasures:
5 Then shalt thou understand the fear of Jahve,
   And find the knowledge of God.
6 For Jahve giveth wisdom:
   From His mouth cometh knowledge and understanding.
7 He preserves for the upright promotion;
   A shield for such as walk in innocence.
8 For He protects the paths of justice,
   And guards the way of His saints.

The first אִם, with that which it introduces, vers. 1, 2, is to be interpreted as an exclamation, "O that!" (*O si*), and then as an optative, as Ps. lxxxi. 9, cxxxix. 19. אִם . . . כִּי, vers. 3–5, with the inserted connecting clauses, would then be confirmatory, "for then." But since this poet loves to unfold one and the same thought in ever new forms, one has perhaps to begin the conditional premisses with ver. 1, and to regard כִּי אִם as a new commencement. Hitzig takes this כִּי אִם in the sense of *imo :* "much more if thou goest to meet her, *e.g.* by curious inquiry, not merely permittest her quietly to come to thee." אִם would then preserve its conditional meaning; and כִּי, as in Job xxxi. 18, Ps. cxxx. 4, since it implies an intentional negative, would receive the meaning of *imo.* But the sentences ranged together with אִם are too closely related in meaning to admit such a negative between them. כִּי will thus be confirmatory, not mediately, but immediately; it is the "for = yes" of confirmation of the preceding conditions, and takes them up again (Ewald, § 356 *b*, cf. 330 *b*) after the form of the conditional clause was given up. The צָפֵן, which in i. 11, 18 is the synonym of צָפָה, *speculari*, presents itself here, 1*b*, 7*a*, as the synonym of טָמַן, whence מַטְמֹנִים, synon. of צְפוּנִים, *recondita;* the group of sounds, צף, צם, טם (cf. also דף, in Arab. *dafan*, whence *dafynat*, treasure), express shades of the root representation of pressing together. The inf. of the conclusion לְהַקְשִׁיב, to incline (Gr. Venet. ὡς ἀκροῷτο), is followed by the accus. of the object אָזְנֶךָ, thine ear, for הקשיב properly means to stiffen (not to purge, as Schultens, nor to sharpen, as Gesenius thinks); cf. under Ps. x. 17. With חָכְמָה are interchanged בִּינָה, which properly means that which is distinguished or separated, and תְּבוּנָה, which means the distinguishing, separating, appellations of the capacity of distinguishing in definite cases and in general; but it does not represent this as a faculty of the soul, but as a divine power which communicates itself as the gift of God (*charisma*).

Vers. 3–8. Instead of כִּי אִם there is an old אַל תִּקְרִי [1] (read not so, but thus), כִּי אֵם (if thou callest understanding mother), which supposes the phrase כִּי אִם (LXX.) as traditional. If אִם were intended (according to which the Targ. in the *Bibl. rabbinica*, but not in Norzi's text, translates), then 3*b* would correspond; *vid.* vii. 4, cf. Job xvii. 14. Thus: Yea, if thou callest for understanding, *i.e.* callest her to thee (xviii. 6), invitest her to thee (ix. 15). The ק of בְּקֵשׁ is, with the exception of the imper. (*e.g.* בַּקְשׁוּ), always without the *Dagesh.* Ver. 4*b* belongs to the ideas in the Book of Job found in these introductory discourses, cf. Job iii. 21, as at ver.

[1] Regarding this formula, see Strack's *Prolegomena*, pp. 66–70.

14, Job iii. 22 (Ewald, *Sprüche*, p. 49). הָפַשׂ (חִפֵּשׂ), *scrutari*, proceeds, as חָפַשׂ shows, from the primary meaning of a ditch, and is thus in its root-idea related to חָפַר (to dig, search out). In the principal clause of ver. 5 the 'יִרְאַת ה, as Ps. xix. 10, is the fear of Jahve as it ought to be, thus the reverence which is due to Him, the worshipping of Him as revealed. 'ה and אֱלֹהִים are interchanged as קְדשִׁים and 'ה at ix. 10. דַּעַת is knowledge proceeding from practice and experience, and thus not merely cognition (*Kenntnis*), but knowledge (*Erkenntnis*). The thoughts revolve in a circle only apparently. He who strives after wisdom earnestly and really, reaches in this way fellowship with God; for just as He gives wisdom, it is nowhere else than with Him, and it never comes from any other source than from Him. It comes (ver. 6) מִפִּיו (LXX. erroneously מִפָּנָיו), *i.e.* it is communicated through the medium of His word, Job xxii. 22, or also (for λόγος and πνεῦμα lie here undistinguished from one another) it is His breath (Book of Wisdom vii. 25 : ἀτμὶς τῆς τοῦ Θεοῦ δυνάμεως καὶ ἀπόρροια τῆς τοῦ παντοκράτορος δόξης εἰλικρινής); the inspiration (נשמת) of the Almighty (according to Job xxxii. 8) gives men understanding. In ver. 7*a*, whether וְצָפַן (*Chethîb*) or יִצְפֹּן (*Kerî*) is read, the meaning is the same. The former is the expression of the completed fact, as ἡτοίμασεν, 1 Cor. ii. 9, and is rightly preferred by LXX. and Syr., for one reluctantly misses the copula (since the thought is new in comparison with ver. 6). לַיְשָׁר ם should be written with the accent *Dechî*. The Chokma-word (besides in Proverbs and Job, found only in Mic. vi. 9 and Isa. xxviii. 29) תּוּשִׁיָּה is a *Hiphil* formation (with the passing over of *ô* into *û*, as in תּוּגָה) from הוֹשָׁה (whence the pr. names יוֹשָׁה and יוֹשַׁוְיָה) = (Arab.) *wasy* and *âsy*, to re-establish, to advance, *Hiph.* of יָשָׁה = וְשָׁה, to stand, and thus means furtherance, *i.e.* the power or the gift to further, and concretely that which furthers and profits, particularly true wisdom and true fortune.[1] The derivation from יֵשׁ (viii. 21) is to be rejected, because " the formation would be wholly without analogy, so much the more because the י of this word does not represent the place of the ו, as

---

[1] I was formerly in error in regarding the word as a *Hophal* formation, and in assigning to it the primary signification of being in a state of realized existence, of reality, in contradistinction to appearance only. The objection of J. D. Michaelis, *Supplem.* p. 1167, *Non placent in linguis ejusmodi etyma metaphysica*, etc., does not apply here, since the word is a new one coined by the *Chokma*, but all the shades of meaning are naturally derived from the funda-

is seen from the Arab. ليس and the Syr. ܐܝܟ " (Fl.);[1] and
the derivation of שָׁוָה = וָשָׁה, to be smooth (Hitzig), passes over
without any difficulty into another system of roots.[2] In the
passage under consideration (ver. 7), תּוּשִׁיָּה signifies advancement
in the sense of true prosperity. The parallel passage 7a clothes
itself in the form of an apposition : (He) a shield (מָגֵן, n. instr. of
גָּנַן, to cover) for הֹלְכֵי תֹם, pilgrims of innocence (Fl.), i.e. such as
walk in the way (the object-accus., as vi. 12, for which in x. 9 בְּ)
of innocence. תֹּם is whole, full submission, moral faultlessness,
which chooses God with the whole heart, seeks good without exception: a similar thought is found in Ps. lxxxiv. 12. לִנְצֹר, 8a, is
such an inf. of consequence as לְהַקְשִׁיב (ver. 2), and here, as there,
is continued in the finite. The " paths of justice" are understood
with reference to those who enter them and keep in them ; parallel,
" the way of His saints" (חָסִיד, he who cherishes חֶסֶד, earnest
inward love to God), for that is just אֹרַח־צְדָקָה (xii. 28) : they are
הֹלְכֵי צְדָקוֹת (Isa. xxxiii. 15). Instead of the Mugrash, the conjunctive Tarcha is to be given to וְדַרְכּוֹ.

Vers. 9–11. With the אָז repeated, the promises encouraging
to the endeavour after wisdom take a new departure :

9 Then shalt thou understand righteousness, and justice,
   And uprightness ; every way of good.
10 For wisdom will enter into thine heart,
   And knowledge will do good to thy soul ;
11 Discretion will keep watch over thee,
   Understanding will keep thee.

---

mental signification " furtherance " (cf. Seneca, Deus stator stabilitorque est).
" תּוּשִׁיה, from Arab. âsy and wasy, to further by word and deed, to assist by
counsel and act, to render help, whence the meanings auxilium, salus, and
prudens consilium, sapientia, easily follow ; cf. Ali's Arab. proverb, واساك من
تغافل—' He furthers thee, who does not trouble himself about thee.' "

[1] The Arab. أيس (almost only in the negative ليس = יֵשׁ לֹא), of the
same signification as יֵשׁ, with which the Aram. אִית (אִיתַי) is associated, presupposes an أس (= أسّ), to be founded, to found, and is rightly regarded
by the Arabs as an old segolate noun in which the verbal force was comprehended.

[2] The Arab. وسي and سوى are confounded in common usage (Wetstein,
Deutsch. Morgenl. Zeitschr. xxii. 19), but the roots יש and שו are different ;
וש and אש, on the contrary, are modifications of one root.

Regarding the ethical triad מֵישָׁרִים [righteousness, rightness], מִשְׁפָּט [judgment], and צֶדֶק [rectitude], vid. i. 3. Seb. Schmid is wrong in his rendering, *et omnis via qua bonum aditur erit tibi plana*, which in comparison with Isa. xxvi. 7 would be feebly expressed. J. H. Michaelis rightly interprets all these four conceptions as object-accusatives; the fourth is the summarizing asyndeton (cf. Ps. viii. 7) breaking off the enumeration : *omnem denique orbitam boni ;* Jerome, *bonam :* in this case, however, טוֹב would be genitive (vid. xvii. 2). מַעְגָּל is the way in which the chariot rolls along; in עֵגֶל there are united the root-conceptions of that which is round (גל) and rolling (גל). Whether כִּי, ver. 10, is the argumentative "because" (according to the versions and most interpreters) or "for" ("denn," J. H. Michaelis, Ewald, and others), is a question. That with כִּי = "for" the subject would precede the verb, as at vers. 6, 21, and i. 32 (Hitzig), determines nothing, as ver. 18 shows. On the one hand, the opinion that כִּי = "because" is opposed by the analogy of the כִּי, ver. 6, following אָז, ver. 5; the inequality between vers. 5-8 and ver. 9 ff. if the new commencement, ver. 9, at once gives place to another, ver. 10; the relationship of the subject ideas in vers. 10, 11, which makes ver. 11 unsuitable to be a conclusion from ver. 10. On the contrary, the promise not only of intellectual, but at the same time also of practical, insight into the right and the good, according to their whole compass and in their manifoldness, can be established or explained quite well as we thus read vers. 10, 11 : For wisdom will enter (namely, to make it a dwelling-place, xiv. 33 ; cf. John xiv. 23) into thine heart, and knowledge will do good to thy soul (namely, by the enjoyment which arises from the possession of knowledge, and the rest which its certainty yields). דַּעַת, γνῶσις, is elsewhere fem. (Ps. cxxxix. 6), but here, as at viii. 10, xiv. 6, in the sense of τὸ γνῶναι, is masc. In ver. 11 the contents of the אז תבין (ver. 9) are further explained. שָׁמַר עַל, of watching (for Job xvi. 16 is to be interpreted differently), is used only by our poet (here and at vi. 22). Discretion, *i.e.* the capacity of well-considered action, will hold watch over thee, take thee under protection ; understanding, *i.e.* the capacity in the case of opposing rules to make the right choice, and in the matter of extremes to choose the right medium, will be bestowed upon thee. In תִּנְצְרֶכָה, as in Ps. lxi. 8, cxl. 2, 5, Deut. xxxiii. 9, etc., the first stem letter is not assimilated, in order that the word may have a fuller sound; the writing ־בָּה for ־ך is meant to affect the eye.[1]

Vers. 12–15. As in vers. 10, 11, the אָז תָּבִין ("then shalt thou understand," ver. 5) is expanded, so now the watching, preserving, is separately placed in view:

> 12 To deliver thee from an evil way,
>   From the man who speaks falsehood;
> 13 (From those) who forsake the ways of honesty
>   To walk in ways of darkness,
> 14 Who rejoice to accomplish evil,
>   Delight in malignant falsehood—
> 15 They are crooked in their paths,
>   And perverse in their ways.

That דֶּרֶךְ רָע is not genitival, *via mali*, but adjectival, *via mala*, is evident from דרך לֹא־טוֹב, xvi. 29. From the evil way, *i.e.* conduct, stands opposed to the false words represented in the person of the deceiver; from both kinds of *contagium* wisdom delivers. תַּהְפֻּכוֹת (like the similarly formed תַּהְבֻּלוֹת, occurring only as plur.) means misrepresentations, viz. of the good and the true, and that for the purpose of deceiving (xvii. 20), *fallaciæ*, *i.e.* intrigues in conduct, and lies and deceit in words. Fl. compares Arab. *ifk*, a lie, and *affak*, a liar. לְהַצִּילְךָ has *Munach*, the constant servant of *Dechî*, instead of *Metheg*, according to rule (*Accentssystem*, vii. § 2). הָעֹזְבִים (ver. 13) is connected with the collective אִישׁ (cf. Judg. ix. 55); we have in the translation separated it into a relative clause with the abstract present. The vocalization of the article fluctuates, yet the expression הָעֹזְבִים, like ver. 17 הָעֻזְבַת, is the better established (*Michlol* 53*b*); הָעֹזְבִים is one of the three words which retain their *Metheg*, and yet add to it a *Munach* in the tone-syllable (*vid.* the two others, Job xxii. 4, xxxix. 26). To the "ways of honesty" (*Geradheit*) (cf. the adj. expression, Jer. xxxi. 9), which does not shun to come to the light, stand opposed the "ways of darkness," the ἔργα τοῦ σκότους, Rom. xiii. 12, which designedly conceal themselves from God (Isa. xxix. 15) and men (Job xxiv. 15, xxxviii. 13, 15).

Ver. 14. In this verse the regimen of the מִן, 12*b*, is to be regarded as lost; the description now goes on independently. Whoever does not shrink back from evil, but gives himself up to deceit, who finally is at home in it as in his own proper life-element,

---

[1] For the right succession of the accents here, see *Torath Emeth*, p. 49, § 5; *Accentuationssystem*, xviii. § 3.

and rejoices, yea, delights in that which he ought to shun as something destructive and to be rejected. The neut. רָע is frequently an attributive genit., vi. 24, xv. 26, xxviii. 5 ; cf. טוֹב, xxiv. 25, which here, since תַּהְפֻּכוֹת are those who in themselves are bad, does not separate, but heightens : *perversitates non simplices aut vulgares, sed pessimæ et ex omni parte vitiosæ* (J. H. Michaelis). With אֲשֶׁר (οἵτινες), ver. 15, this part is brought to a conclusion. Fleischer, Bertheau, and others interpret אָרְחֹתֵיהֶם, as the accus. of the nearer definition, as σκολιὸς τὸν νοῦν, τὰς πράξεις ; but should it be an accus., then would we expect, in this position of the words, עִקֵּשׁוּ (Isa. lix. 8 ; Prov. x. 9, cf. ix. 15). עִקְּשִׁים is the pred. ; for אֹרַח, like דֶּרֶךְ, admits of both genders. וּנְלוֹזִים carries in it its subject הֵם ; לוּז, like the Arab. *l'd, l'dh*, is a weaker form of לִיץ, *flectere, inclinare*, intrans. *recedere :* they are turned aside, inclined out of the way to the right and left in their walk (בְּ as xvii. 20).

Vers. 16–19. With the resumption of לְהַצִּילְךָ, the watchful protection which wisdom affords to its possessors is further specified in these verses :

16 To save thee from the strange woman,
   From the stranger who useth smooth words ;
17 Who forsakes the companion of her youth,
   And forgets the covenant of her God ;
18 For she sinks down to death together with her house,
   And to the shadow of Hades her paths—
19 All they who go to her return not again,
   And reach not the paths of life

The subject here continued is the fourfold wisdom named in vers. 10, 11. זָר signifies *alienus*, which may also be equivalent to *alius populi*, but of a much wider compass—him who does not belong to a certain class (*e.g.* the non-priestly or the laity), the person or thing not belonging to me, or also some other than I designate ; on the other hand, נָכְרִי, *peregrinus*, scarcely anywhere divests itself of the essential mark of a strange foreign origin. While thus אִשָּׁה זָרָה is the non-married wife, נָכְרִיָּה designates her as non-Israelitish. Prostitution was partly sanctioned in the cultus of the Midianites, Syrians, and other nations neighbouring to Israel, and thus was regarded as nothing less than customary. In Israel, on the contrary, the law (Deut. xxiii. 18 f.) forbade it under a penalty, and therefore it was chiefly practised by foreign women (xxiii. 27, and cf. the

exception, Ruth ii. 10),[1]—an inveterate vice, which spread itself
particularly from the latter days of Solomon, along with general
ungodliness, and excusing itself under the polygamy sanctioned
by the law, brought ruin on the state. The *Chokma* contends
against this, and throughout presents monogamy as alone corresponding to the institution and the idea of the relation. Designating marriage as the " covenant of God," it condemns not only
adulterous but generally promiscuous intercourse of the sexes,
because unhallowed and thus unjustifiable, and likewise arbitrary
divorce. Regarding the ancient ceremonies connected with the
celebration of marriage we are not specially informed; but from
ver. 17, Mal. ii. 14 (Ewald, Bertheau, Hitzig, but not Köhler), it
appears that the celebration of marriage was a religious act, and
that they who were joined together in marriage called God to
witness and ratify the vows they took upon themselves. The perf.
in the attributive clause אֲמָרֶיהָ הֶחֱלִיקָה proceeds on the routine
acquired in cajoling and dissembling: who has smoothed her
words, *i.e.* learned to entice by flattering words (Fl.).

Vers. 17–19. אַלּוּף, as here used, has nothing to do with the
phylarch-name, similar in sound, which is a denom. of אֶלֶף; but it
comes immediately from אָלַף, to accustom oneself to a person or
cause, to be familiar therewith (while the Aram. אֲלַף, יְלַף, to learn,
Pa. to teach), and thus means, as the synon. of רֵעַ, the companion
or familiar associate (*vid.* Schultens). Parallels such as Jer. iii. 4
suggested to the old interpreters the allegorical explanation of the
adulteress as the personification of the apostasy or of heresy.
Ver. 18*a* the LXX. translate: ἔθετο γὰρ παρὰ τῷ θανάτῳ τὸν
οἶκον αὐτῆς : she (the dissolute wife) has placed her house beside
death (the abyss of death). This שָׁתָה [ἔθετο] is perhaps the
original, for the text as it lies before us is doubtful, though, rightly
understood, admissible. The accentuation marks בֵּיתָהּ as the subject, but בַּיִת is elsewhere always masc., and does not, like the rarer
אֹרַח, ver. 15, admit in usage a double gender; also, if the fem.
usage were here introduced (Bertheau, Hitzig), then the predicate,
even though ביתה were regarded as fem., might be, in conformity
with rule, שָׁח, as *e.g.* Isa. ii. 17. שָׁחָה is, as in Ps. xliv. 26, 3d pr.
of שׁוּחַ, Arab. *sâkh*, to go down, to sink; the emendation שָׁחָה

---

[1] In Talmudic Heb. אֲרְמִית (Aramean) has this meaning for the Biblical
נָכְרִיָּה.

(Joseph Kimchi) does not recommend itself on this account, that
שָׁחָה and שָׁחַח mean, according to usage, to stoop or to bend down ;
and to interpret (Ralbag, הִשְׁפִּילָה) שָׁחָה transitively is inadmissible.
For that reason Aben Ezra interprets ביתה as in apposition : to
death, to its house; but then the poet in that case should say אֶל־שְׁאוֹל,
for death is not a house.   On the other hand, we cannot perceive
in ביתה an accus. of the nearer definition (J. H. Michaelis, Fl.) ;
the expression would here, as 15a, be refined without purpose.
Böttcher has recognised ביתה as permutative, the personal subject :
for she sinks down to death, her house, *i.e.* she herself, together
with all that belongs to her; cf. the permutative of the subject,
Job xxix. 3, Isa. xxix. 23 (*vid.* comm. *l.c.*), and the more particular
statement of the object, Ex. ii. 6, etc.   Regarding רְפָאִים, shadows
of the under-world (from רָפָה, synon. חָלָה, weakened, or to become
powerless), a word common to the Solomonic writings, *vid. Comment. on Isaiah*, p. 206.   What ver. 18b says of the person of the
adulteress, ver. 19 says of those who live with her ביתה, her house-
companions.   בָּאֶיהָ, " those entering in to her," is equivalent to
בָּאִים אֵלֶיהָ ; the participle of verbs *eundi et veniendi* takes the
accusative object of the finite as gen. in *st. constr.*, as *e.g.* i. 12,
ii. 7, Gen. xxiii. 18, ix. 10 (cf. Jer. x. 20).   The יְשׁוּבוּן, with the
tone on the ult., is a protestation : there is no return for those who
practise fornication,[1] and they do not reach the paths of life from
which they have so widely strayed.[2]

Vers. 20–22.   With לְמַעַן there commences a new section, co-ordinating itself with the לְהַצִּילְךָ (" to deliver thee") of vers. 12, 16,
unfolding that which wisdom accomplishes as a preserver and guide :

> 20 So that thou walkest in the good way,
>   And keepest the right paths.
> 21 For the upright shall inhabit the land,
>   And the innocent shall remain in it.
> 22 But the godless are cut off out of the land,
>   And the faithless are rooted out of it.

---

[1] One is here reminded of the expression in the *Æneid*, vi. 127–129 :

> *Revocare gradum superasque evadere ad auras,*
> *Hoc opes, hoc labor est.*

See also an impure but dreadful Talmudic story about a dissolute Rabbi,
b. Aboda zara, 17a.

[2] In correct texts וְלֹא־יַשִּׂיגוּ has the *Makkeph*.   *Vid. Torath Emeth*, p. 41 ;
Accentuationssystem, xx. § 2.

Wisdom—thus the connection—will keep thee, so that thou shalt not fall under the seductions of man or of woman ; keep, in order that thou . . . לְמַעַן (from מַעַן מַעֲנֶה =, tendency, purpose) refers to the intention and object of the protecting wisdom. To the two negative designations of design there follows, as the third and last, a positive one. טוֹבִים (contrast to רָעִים, xiv. 19) is here used in a general ethical sense : the good (*Guten*, not *Gütigen*, the kind). שָׁמַר, with the object of the way, may in another connection also mean to keep oneself from, *cavere ab* (Ps. xvii. 4) ; here it means : carefully to keep in it. The promise of ver. 21 is the same as in the Mashal Ps. xxxvii. 9, 11, 22 ; cf. Prov. x. 30. אֶרֶץ is Canaan, or the land which God promised to the patriarchs, and in which He planted Israel, whom He had brought out of Egypt; not the earth, as Matt. v. 5, according to the extended, unlimited N. T. circle of vision. יִתָּרוּ (*Milel*) is erroneously explained by Schultens : *funiculis bene firmis irroborabunt in terra.* The verb יָתַר, Arab. *watar*, signifies to yoke (whence יֶתֶר, a cord, rope), then intrans. to be stretched out in length, to be hanging over (*vid.* Fleischer on Job xxx. 11) ; whence יֶתֶר, residue, Zeph. ii. 9, and after which the LXX. here renders ὑπολειφθήσονται, and Jerome *permanebunt.* In 22b the old translators render יִסְּחוּ as the fut. of the pass. נָסַח, Deut. xxviii. 63 ; but in this case it would be יִנָּסְחוּ. The form יִסְּחוּ, pointed יִסָּחוּ, might be the *Niph.* of סָחַח, but סָחַח can neither be taken as one with נָסַח, of the same meaning, nor with Hitzig is it to be vocalized יֻסְּחוּ (*Hoph.* of נסח) ; nor, with Böttcher (§ 1100, p. 453), is יִסְּחוּ to be regarded as a veritable *fut. Niph.* יִסְּחוּ is, as at xv. 25, Ps. lii. 7, active : *evellant;* and this, with the subj. remaining indefinite (for which J. H. Michaelis refers to Hos. xii. 9), is equivalent to *evellentur.* This indefinite " they " or " one " ("*man*"), Fleischer remarks, can even be used of God, as here and Job vii. 3,—a thing which is common in Persian, where *e.g.* the expression rendered *hominem ex pulvere fecerunt* is used instead of the fuller form, which would be rendered *homo a Deo ex pulvere factus est.* בּוֹגְדִים bears (as בֶּגֶד proves) the primary meaning of concealed, *i.e.* malicious (treacherous and rapacious, Isa. xxxiii. 1), and then faithless men.[1]

---

[1] Similar is the relation in Arab. of *labbasa* to *libâs* (לְבוּשׁ) ; it means to make a thing unknown by covering it ; whence *telbîs*, deceit, *mulebbis*, a falsifier.

FOURTH INTRODUCTORY MASHAL DISCOURSE, III. 1–18.

EXHORTATION TO LOVE AND FAITHFULNESS, AND SELF-SACRI-
FICING DEVOTION TO GOD, AS THE TRUE WISDOM.

The foregoing Mashal discourse seeks to guard youth against
ruinous companionship ; this points out to them more particularly
the relation toward God and man, which alone can make them
truly happy, vers. 1–4.

> 1 My son, forget not my doctrine,
>   And let thine heart keep my commandments ;
> 2 For length of days, and years of life,
>   And peace, will they add to thee.
> 3 Let not kindness and truth forsake thee :
>   Bind them about thy neck,
>   Write them on the tablet of thy heart,
> 4 And obtain favour and true prudence
>   In the eyes of God and of men.

The admonition takes a new departure. תּוֹרָתִי and מִצְוֹתַי refer
to the following new discourse and laws of conduct. Here, in the
midst of the discourse, we have יִצֹּר and not יִנְצֹר ; the non-assimi-
lated form is found only in the conclusion, e.g. ii. 11, v. 2. The
plur. יֹסִיפוּ (ver. 2) for תּוֹסֵפְנָה (they will bring, add) refers to the
doctrine and the precepts ; the synallage has its ground in this, that
the fem. construction in Hebrew is not applicable in such a case ;
the vulgar Arab. also has set aside the forms jaktubna, taktubna.
" Extension of days" is continuance of duration, stretching itself
out according to the promise, Ex. xx. 12 ; and " years of life" (ix.
11) are years—namely, many of them—of a life which is life in
the full sense of the word. חַיִּים has here the pregnant signification vita vitalis, βίος βιωτός (Fl.). שָׁלוֹם (R. שׁל) is pure well-being,
free from all that disturbs peace or satisfaction, internal and external contentment.

Ver. 3. With this verse the doctrine begins ; אַל (not לֹא) shows
that 3a does not continue the promise of ver. 2. חֶסֶד (R. חס,
stringere, afficere) is, according to the prevailing usage of the language, well-affectedness, it may be of God toward men, or of men
toward God, or of men toward one another—a loving disposition, of
the same meaning as the N. T. ἀγάπη (vid. e.g. Hos. vi. 6). אֱמֶת
(from אֱמֶנֶת), continuance, a standing to one's promises, and not

falsifying just expectations; thus fidelity, πίστις, in the inter-related sense of *fides* and *fidelitas*. These two states of mind and of conduct are here contemplated as moral powers (Ps. lxi. 8, xliii. 3), which are of excellent service, and bring precious gain; and 4*b* shows that their ramification on the side of God and of men, the religious and the moral, remains radically inseparable. The suffix ◌ָם does not refer to the doctrine and the precepts, but to these two cardinal virtues. If the disciple is admonished to bind them about his neck (*vid.* i. 9, cf. iii. 22), so here reference is made, not to ornament, nor yet to protection against evil influences by means of them, as by an amulet[1] (for which proofs are wanting), but to the signet which was wont to be constantly carried (Gen. xxxviii. 18, cf. Cant. viii. 6) on a string around the neck. The parallel member 3*c* confirms this; 3*b* and 3*c* together put us in mind of the *Tephillim* (phylacteries), Ex. xiii. 16, Deut. vi. 8, xi. 18, in which what is here a figure is presented in external form, but as the real figure of that which is required in the inward parts. לוּחַ (from לָהַח, Arab. *ľah*, to begin to shine, *e.g.* of a shooting star, gleaming sword; *vid.* Wetzstein, *Deutsch. morgenl. Zeitzschr.* xxii. 151 f.) signifies the tablet prepared for writing by means of polish; to write love and fidelity on the tablet of the heart, is to impress deeply on the heart the duty of both virtues, so that one will be impelled to them from within outward (Jer. xxxi. 33).

Ver. 4. To the admonitory imper. there follows here a second, as iv. 4, xx. 13, Amos v. 4, 2 Chron. xx. 20, instead of which also the *perf. consec.* might stand; the counsellor wishes, with the good to which he advises, at the same time to present its good results. שֵׂכֶל is (1 Sam. xxv. 3) the appearance, for the Arab. *shakl* means *forma*, as uniting or binding the lineaments or contours into one figure, σχῆμα, according to which שֵׂכֶל טוֹב may be interpreted of the pleasing and advantageous impression which the well-built external appearance of a man makes, as an image of that which his internal excellence produces; thus, favourable view, friendly judgment, good reputation (Ewald, Hitzig, Zöckler). But everywhere else (xiii. 15; Ps. cxi. 10; 2 Chron. xxx. 22) this phrase means good, *i.e.* fine, well-becoming insight, or prudence; and שֵׂכֶל

---

[1] Fleischer is here reminded of the giraffe in the Jardin des Plantes, the head of which was adorned by its Arabic keeper with strings and jewels, the object of which was to turn aside the *'ain* (the bad, mischievous look) from the precious beast.

has in the language of the *Mishle* no other meaning than *intellectus*, which proceeds from the inwardly forming activity of the mind. He obtains favour in the eyes of God and man, to whom favour on both sides is shown; he obtains refined prudence, to whom it is on both sides adjudicated. It is unnecessary, with Ewald and Hitzig, to assign the two objects to God and men. In the eyes of both at the same time, he who carries love and faithfulness in his heart appears as one to whom חֵן and שֵׂכֶל טוֹב must be adjudicated.

Vers. 5-8. Were "kindness and truth" (ver. 3) understood only in relation to men, then the following admonition would not be interposed, since it proceeds from that going before, if there the quality of kindness and truth, not only towards man, but also towards God, is commended:

> 5 Trust in Jahve with thy whole heart,
> And lean not on thine own understanding.
> 6 In all thy ways acknowledge Him,
> And He will make plain thy paths.
> 7 Be not wise in thine own eyes;
> Fear Jahve, and depart from evil.
> 8 Health will then come to thy navel,
> And refreshing to thy bones.

From God alone comes true prosperity, true help. He knows the right way to the right ends. He knows what benefits us. He is able to free us from that which does us harm: therefore it is our duty and our safety to place our confidence wholly in Him, and to trust not to our own judgment. The verb בָּטַח, Arab. *bath*, has the root-meaning *expandere*, whence perhaps, by a more direct way than that noted under Ps. iv. 6, it acquires the meaning *confidere*, to lean with the whole body on something, in order to rest upon it, strengthened by עַל, if one lean wholly—Fr. *se reposer sur quelqu'un;* Ital. *riposarsi sopra alcuno,*—like הִשָּׁעֵן with אֶל, to lean on anything, so as to be supported by it; with עַל, to support oneself on anything (Fl.). דָּעֵהוּ (the same in form as שָׂאֵהוּ, Num. xi. 12) is not fully represented by "acknowledge Him;" as in 1 Chron. xxviii. 9 it is not a mere theoretic acknowledgment that is meant, but earnest penetrating cognizance, engaging the whole man. The practico-mystical דָּעֵהוּ, in and of itself full of significance, according to O. and N. T. usage, is yet strengthened by *toto corde*. The heart is the central seat of all spiritual soul-strength; to love God with the whole heart is to concentrate the whole inner life on the active

contemplation of God, and the ready observance of His will. God
requites such as show regard to Him, by making plain their path
before them, *i.e.* by leading them directly to the right end, removing all hindrances out of their way. אָרְחֹתֶיךָ has *Cholem* in the first
syllable (*vid.* Kimchi's *Lex.*).[1] " Be not wise in thine own eyes"
is equivalent to *ne tibi sapiens videare ;* for, as J. H.
Michaelis remarks, *confidere Deo est sapere, sibi vero ac suæ sapientiæ, desipere.*
" Fear God and depart from evil" is the twofold representation of
the εὐσέβεια, or practical piety, in the *Chokma* writings : Prov. xvi.
6, the Mashal psalm xxxiv. 10, 15, and Job xxviii. 28 cf. i. 2.
For סָר מֵרָע, the post-biblical expression is יְרֵא חֵטְא.

Ver. 8. The subject to תְּהִי (it shall be) is just this religious-
moral conduct. The conjectural reading לִבְשָׂרֶךָ (Clericus), לִשְׁרֵךָ
= לִשְׁאֵרְךָ (Ewald, Hitzig), to thy flesh or body, is unnecessary ; the
LXX. and Syr. so translating, generalize the expression, which is
not according to their taste. שֹׁר, from שָׁרַר, Arab. *sarr*, to be fast,
to bind fast, properly, the umbilical cord (which the Arabs call *surr*,
whence the denom. *sarra*, to cut off the umbilical cord of the new-
born) ; thus the navel, the origin of which coincides with the
independent individual existence of the new-born, and is as the
firm centre (cf. Arab. *saryr*, foundation, basis, *Job*, p. 487) of the
existence of the body. The system of punctuation does not, as a
rule, permit the doubling of ר, probably on account of the prevailing half guttural, *i.e.* the uvular utterance of this sound by the
men of Tiberias.[2] לְשָׁרֶךָ here, and שָׁרֵּךְ at Ezek. xvi. 4, belong to the
exceptions ; cf. the expanded duplication in שָׁרְרֵךְ, Cant. vii. 3, to
which a chief form שֹׁר is as little to be assumed as is a הָרָר to
הַרְרֵי. The ἅπ. γεγρ. רִפְאוּת, healing, has here, as מַרְפֵּא, iv. 22, xvi.
24, and תְּרוּפָה, Ezek. xlvii. 12, not the meaning of restoration from
sickness, but the raising up of enfeebled strength, or the confirming of that which exists ; the navel comes into view as the middle
point of the *vis vitalis.* שִׁקּוּי is a *Piel* formation, corresponding to
the abstract *Kal* formation רְפָאוּת ; the Arab. سَقَى, used transit.
(to give to drink), also سَقَّى (cf. *Pu.* Job xxi. 24) and أَسْقَى, like

---

[1] In the *st. constr.* ii. 19, and with the grave suff. ii. 15, ŏ instead of ō is in
order ; but Ben-Asher's אָרְחֹתִי, Job xiii. 27, cf. xxxiii. 11, is an inconsistency.

[2] See my work, *Physiologie u. Musik in ihrer Bedeutung für Grammatik beson-
ders die hebräische,* pp. 11–13.

the Hebr. הִשְׁקָה (*Hiph.* of שָׁקָה, to drink); the infin. سَقَى means, to the obliterating of the proper signification, distribution, benefaction, showing friendship, but in the passage before us is to be explained after Job xxi. 24 (the marrow of his bones is well watered; Arnheim—full of sap) and xv. 30. Bertheau and Hitzig erroneously regard ver. 8 as the conclusion to ver. 7, for they interpret רפאות as the subject; but had the poet wished to be so understood, he should have written וּתְהִי. Much rather the subject is devotion withdrawn from the evil one and turned to God, which externally proves itself by the dedication to Him of earthly possessions.

> Ver. 9 Honour Jahve with thy wealth,
> And with the first-fruits of all thine increase:
> 10 Then shall thy barns be filled with plenty,
> And thy vats overflow with must.

It may surprise us that the Chokma, being separated from the ceremonial law, here commends the giving of tithes. But in the first place, the consciousness of the duty of giving tithes is older than the Mosaic law, Gen. xxviii. 22; in this case, the giving of tithes is here a general ethical expression. עָשַׂר and מַעֲשֵׂר do not occur in the Book of Proverbs; in the post-biblical phraseology the tithes are called חֵלֶק הַגָּבֹהַּ, the portion of the Most High. כַּבֵּד, as the Arab. *wakkra*, to make heavy, then to regard and deal with as weighty and solemn (*opp.* קָלַל, to regard and treat as light, from קַל = Arab. *hân*, to be light). הוֹן, properly lightness in the sense of *aisance*, opulency, forms with כַּבֵּד an *oxymoron* (*fac Jovam gravem de levitate tua*), but one aimed at by the author neither at i. 13 nor here. מִן (in מֵהוֹנֶךָ and 'מֵר, ver. 9) is in both cases partitive, as in the law of the Levitical tenths, Lev. xxvii. 30, and of the *Challa* (heave-offering of dough), Num. xv. 21, where also רֵאשִׁית (in Heb. vii. 4, ἀκροθίνια) occurs in a similar sense, cf. Num. xviii. 12 (in the law of the *Theruma* or wave-offering of the priests), as also תְּבוּאָה in the law of the second tenths, Deut. xiv. 22, cf. Num. xviii. 30 (in the law of the tenths of the priests). Ver. 10. With ו *apodosis imperativi* the conclusion begins. שָׂבַע, satisfaction, is equivalent to fulness, making satisfied, and that, too, richly satisfied; תִּירוֹשׁ also is such an accusative, as verbs of filling govern it, for פָּרַץ, to break through, especially to overflow, signifies to be or become overflowingly full (Job i. 10). אָסָם (from אָסַם,

Chald. אָסַן, Syr. *âsan*, to lay up in granaries) is the granary, of the same meaning as the Arab. *âkhzan* (from *khazan* = חָסַן, Isa. xxiii. 18, *recondere*), whence the Spanish *magazen*, the French and German *magazin*. יֶקֶב (from יָקַב, Arab. *wakab*, to be hollow) is the vat or tub into which the must flows from the wine-press (נַת or פּוּרָה), λάκκος or ὑπολήνιον. Cf. the same admonition and promise in the prophetic statement of Mal. iii. 10–12.

Vers. 11, 12. The contrast here follows. As God should not be forgotten in days of prosperity, so one should not suffer himself to be estranged from Him by days of adversity.

> 11 The school of Jahve, my son, despise thou not,
>   Nor loathe thou His correction;
> 12 For Jahve correcteth him whom He loveth,
>   And that as a father his son whom he loveth

Vid. the original passage Job v. 17 f. There is not for the Book of Job a more suitable motto than this tetrastich, which expresses its fundamental thought, that there is a being chastened and tried by suffering which has as its motive the love of God, and which does not exclude sonship.[1] One may say that ver. 11 expresses the problem of the Book of Job, and ver. 12 its solution. מוּסַר, παιδεία, we have translated "school," for יִסַּר, παιδεύειν, means in reality to take one into school. *Ahndung* [punishment] or *Rüge* [reproof] is the German word which most corresponds to the Hebr. תּוֹכַחַת or תּוֹכֵחָה. קוּץ בְּ (whence here the prohibitive תָּקֹץ with אַל) means to experience loathing (disgust) at anything, or aversion (vexation) toward anything. The LXX. (cited Heb. xii. 5 f.), μηδὲ ἐκλύου, nor be faint-hearted, which joins in to the general thought, that we should not be frightened away from God, or let ourselves be estranged from Him by the attitude of anger in which He appears in His determination to inflict suffering. In 12a the accentuation leaves it undefined whether יְהֹוָה as subject belongs to the relative or to the principal clause; the traditional succession of accents, certified also by Ben Bileam, is כִּי אֶת אֲשֶׁר יֶאֱהַב יְהוָה, for this passage belongs to the few in which more than three servants (viz. *Mahpach, Mercha*, and three *Munachs*) go before the *Athnach*.[2] The further peculiarity is here to be observed, that אֶת,

---

[1] Here Procop. rightly distinguishes between παιδεία and τιμωρία.

[2] *Vid. Torath Emeth*, p. 19; *Accentuationssystem*, vi. § 6; the differences between Ben-Asher and Ben-Naphtali in the Appendixes to *Biblia Rabbinica*; Dachselt's *Biblia Accentuata*, and Pinner's *Prospectus*, p. 91 (Odessa, 1845).

although without the *Makkeph*, retains its *Segol*, besides here only in Ps. xlvii. 5, lx. 2. 12*b* is to be interpreted thus (cf. ix. 5*b*): " and (that) as a father the son, whom he loves." The וּ is explanatory, as 1 Sam. xxviii. 3 (Gesenius, § 155, 1*a*), and יִרְצֶה (which one may supplement by אֹתוֹ or בּוֹ) is a defining clause having the force of a clause with אֲשֶׁר. The translation, *et ut pater qui filio bene cupit*, is syntactically (cf. Isa. xl. 11) and accentually (*vid.* 13*b*) not less admissible, but translating " and as a father he holds his son dear," or with Hitzig (after Jer. xxxi. 10, a passage not quite syntactically the same), " and holds him dear, as a father his son " (which Zöckler without syntactical authority prefers on account of the 2d modus, cf. *e.g.* Ps. li. 18), does not seem a right parallel clause, since the giving of correction is the chief point, and the love only the accompanying consideration (xiii. 24). According to our interpretation, יוֹכִיחַ is to be carried forward in the mind from 12*a*. The LXX. find the parallel word in יכאב, for they translate μαστιγοῖ δὲ πάντα υἱὸν, ὃν παραδέχεται, and thus have read יִכְאַב or וַיִּכְאָב.

Vers. 13–15. Such submission to God, the All-wise, the All-directing, who loves us with fatherly affection, is wisdom, and such wisdom is above all treasures.

> 13 Blessed is the man who has found wisdom,
> And the man who has gained understanding;
> 14 For better is her acquisition than the acquisition of silver,
> And her gain than fine gold.
> 15 More precious is she than corals;
> And all thy jewels do not equal her value.

The imperfect יָפִיק, which as the *Hiph.* of פּוּק, *exire*, has the general meaning *educere*, interchanges with the perfect מָצָא. This bringing forth is either a delivering up, *i.e.* giving out or presenting, Isa. lviii. 10, Ps. cxl. 9, cxliv. 13 (cf. נָפַק, Arab. *nafaḳ*, to give out, to pay out), or a fetching out, getting out, receiving, viii. 35, xii. 2, xviii. 22. Thus 13*a* reminds one of the parable of the treasure in the field, and 13*b* of that of the goodly pearl for which the ἔμπορος who sought the pearl parted with all that he had. Here also is declared the promise of him who trades with a merchant for the possession of wisdom; for סַחְרָהּ and סַחַר (both, as Isa. xxiii. 3, 18, xlv. 15, from סָחַר, the latter after the forms זֶרַע, נֶטַע, without our needing to assume a second primary form, סָחַר) go back to the root-word סָחַר, to trade, go about as a trader,

with the fundamental meaning ἐμπορεύεσθαι (LXX.); and also
the mention of the pearls is not wanting here, for at all events the
meaning "pearls" has blended itself with פְּנִינִים, which is a favourite
word in the Mashal poetry, though it be not the original meaning
of the word. In 14b כֶּסֶף is surpassed by חָרוּץ (besides in the
Proverbs, found only in this meaning in Ps. lxviii. 14), which
properly means ore found in a mine, from חָרַץ, to cut in, to dig
up, and hence the poetic name of gold, perhaps of gold dug out
as distinguished from molten gold. Hitzig regards χρυσός as
identical with it; but this word (Sanskr. without the ending *hir*,
Zend. *zar*) is derived from *ghar*, to glitter (*vid.* Curtius). תְּבוּאָתָהּ
we have translated "gain," for it does not mean the profit which
wisdom brings, the tribute which it yields, but the gain, the possession of wisdom herself.

Ver. 15. As regards פְּנִינִים, for which the *Kethîb* has פְּנִיִּים, the
following things are in favour of the fundamental meaning
"corals," viz.: (1.) The name itself, which corresponds with the

Arab. فَنّ; this word, proceeding from the root-idea of shooting
forth, particularly after the manner of plants, means the branch
and all that raises or multiplies itself branch-like or twig-like
(Fleischer). (2.) The redness attributed to the פנינים, Lam. iv. 7,
in contradistinction to the pure whiteness attributed to snow and
milk (*vid.* at Job xxviii. 18). The meaning of the word may, however, have become generalized in practice (LXX. *in loc.* λίθων
πολυτελῶν, *Græc. Venet.* λιθιδίων); the meaning "pearls," given
to it in the Job-Targum by Rashi, and particularly by Bochart,
lay so much the nearer as one may have wrought also corals
and precious stones, such as the carbuncle, sardius, and sapphire,
into the form of pearls. יְקָרָה, in consequence of the retrogression
of the tone, has *Munach* on the *penult.*, and that as an exception, as
has been remarked by the Masora, since in substantives and proper
names terminating in הָ‑ the נסוג אחור, *i.e.* the receding of the tone,
does not elsewhere appear, *e.g.* יָפָה הִיא, Gen. xii. 14, בָּרָה הִיא,
Cant. vi. 9, צָרָה הִיא, Jer. xxx. 7. "חֵפֶץ is first *abstr.*, a being inclined to something, lust, will, pleasure in anything, then also
concr., anything in which one has pleasure, what is beautiful,

precious; cf. شَهِيّ ,نَفِيس, hence جَارَة نَفِيسَة, precious stones "
(Fleischer). שָׁוָה with בְּ means to be an equivalent (purchase-price,

exchange) for anything ; the most natural construction in Arab. as well as in Hebr. is that with לְ, to be the equivalent of a thing (vid. at Job xxxiii. 27) ; the בְּ is the *Beth pretii*, as if one said in Arab. : *biabi anta* thou art in the estimate of my father, I give it for thee. One distinctly perceives in vers. 14, 15, the echo of Job xxviii. This tetrastich occurs again with a slight variation at viii. 10, 11. The Talmud and the Midrash accent it so, that in the former the expression is וכל־חפצים, and in the latter וכל־חפציך, and they explain the latter of precious stones and pearls (אבנים טובות ומרגליות).

Vers. 16–18. That wisdom is of such incomparable value is here confirmed :

> 16 Length of days is in her right hand ;
> In her left, riches and honour.
> 17 Her ways are pleasant ways,
> And all her paths are peace.
> 18 A tree of life is she to those that lay hold upon her,
> And he who always holdeth her fast is blessed.

As in the right hand of Jahve, according to Ps. xvi. 11, are pleasures for evermore, so Wisdom holds in her right hand " length of days," viz. of the days of life, thus life, the blessing of blessings ; in her left, riches and honour (viii. 18), the two good things which, it is true, do not condition life, but, received from Wisdom, and thus wisely, elevate the happiness of life—in the right hand is the chief good, in the left the προσθήκη, Matt. vi. 33. Didymus : *Per sapientiæ dextram divinarum rerum cognitio, ex qua immortalitatis vita oritur, significatur; per sinistram autem rerum humanarum notitia, ex qua gloria opumque abundantia nascitur.* The LXX., as between 15a and 15b, so also here after ver. 16, interpolate two lines : " From her mouth proceedeth righteousness ; justice and mercy she bears upon her tongue,"—perhaps translated from the Hebr., but certainly added by a reader.

Ver. 17. דַּרְכֵי־נֹעַם are ways on which one obtains what is agreeable to the inner and the outer man, and which it does good to enjoy. The parallel שָׁלוֹם is not a genitive to נְתִיבוֹת to be supplied ; the paths of Wisdom are themselves שָׁלוֹם, for she brings well-being on all sides and deep inward satisfaction (peace). In regard to נְתִיבָה, *via eminens, elata,* Schultens is right (vid. under i. 15) ;[1] נְתִיבוֹתֶיהָ has *Munach*, and instead of the *Metheg, Tarcha,* vid. under i. 31b.

[1] The root is not תב, to grope, but נת ; whence Arab. *natt,* to bubble up, *natâ,* to raise oneself, to swell up, etc.

The figure of the tree of life the fruit of which brings immortality, is, as xi. 30, xv. 4 (cf. xiii. 12), Rev. ii. 7, taken from the history of paradise in the Book of Genesis. The old ecclesiastical saying, *Lignum vitæ crux Christi*, accommodates itself in a certain measure, through Matt. xi. 19, Luke xi. 49, with this passage of the Book of Proverbs. הֶחֱזִיק בְּ means to fasten upon anything, more fully expressed in Gen. xxi. 18, to bind the hand firm with anything, to seize it firmly. They who give themselves to Wisdom, come to experience that she is a tree of life whose fruit contains and communicates strength of life, and whoever always keeps fast hold of Wisdom is blessed, *i.e.* to be pronounced happy (Ps. xli. 3, *vid.* under Ps. cxxxvii. 8). The predicate מְאֻשָּׁר, blessed, refers to each one of the תֹּמְכֶיהָ, those who hold her, cf. xxvii. 16, Num. xxiv. 9. It is the so-called distributive singular of the predicate, which is freely used particularly in those cases where the plur. of the subject is a participle (*vid.* under ver. 35).

FIFTH INTRODUCTORY MASHAL DISCOURSE, III. 19-26.

THE WORLD-CREATIVE WISDOM AS MEDIATRIX OF DIVINE PROTECTION.

O son, guard against seducers (i. 8 ff.); listen to the warning voice of Wisdom (i. 20 ff.); seek after Wisdom: she is the way to God, comes from God, and teaches thee to shun the wicked way and to walk in the way that is good (ii.); thou shalt obtain her if, renouncing self-confidence, thou givest thyself unreservedly to God (iii. 1–18)—these are the four steps, so far, of this introductory παραίνεσις. Each discourse contributes its own to present vividly and impressively what Wisdom is and what she procures, her nature and her blessings. From her hand come all good gifts of God to men. She is the tree of life. Her place between God and men is thus that of a mediatrix.

Vers. 19, 20. This place of a mediatrix—the speaker here now continues—she had from the beginning. God's world-creating work was mediated by her:

> 19 Jahve hath by wisdom founded the earth,
> Established the heavens by understanding.

20 By His knowledge the water-floods broke forth,
And the sky dropped down dew.

That wisdom is meant by which God planned the world-idea, and
now also wrought it out; the wisdom in which God conceived the
world ere it was framed, and by which also He gave external
realization to His thoughts; the wisdom which is indeed an attribute of God and a characteristic of His actions, since she is a
property of His nature, and His nature attests itself in her, but
not less, as appears, not from this group of tetrastichs, but from
all that has hitherto been said, and from the personal testimony,
viii. 22 ff., of which it is the *præludium*, she goes forth as a divine
power to which God has given to have life in herself. Considered
apart from the connection of these discourses, this group of verses,
as little as Jer. x. 2, Ps. civ. 24, determines regarding the attributive interpretation; the Jerusalem Targum, I., when it translates,
Gen. i. 1, בראשׁית by בְּחוּכְמָא (בְּחוּכְמְתָא), combines viii. 22 with such
passages as this before us. יִסַד (here with the tone thrown back)
properly signifies, like the Arab. *wasad*, to lay fast, to found, for one
gives to a fact the firm basis of its existence. The parallel *Pil.* of כּוּן
(Arab. *kân*, cogn. כהן, see on *Isaiah*, p. 691) signifies to set up, to
restore; here equivalent to, to give existence.

Ver. 20. It is incorrect to understand 20*a*, with the Targ., of
division, *i.e.* separating the water under the firmament from the
water above the firmament; נִבְקַע is spoken of water, especially of its
breaking forth, Gen. vii. 11, Ex. xiv. 21, cf. Ps. lxxiv. 15, properly
dividing itself out, *i.e.* welling forth from the bowels of the earth;
it means, without distinguishing the primordial waters and the later
water-floods confined within their banks (cf. Job xxxviii. 8 f., Ps.
civ. 6–8), the overflowing of the earth for the purpose of its pro-
cesses of cultivation and the irrigation of the land. תְּהוֹמוֹת (from
הָמָה = הוּם, to groan, to roar) are chiefly the internal water stores
of the earth, Gen. xlix. 25, Ps. xxxiii. 7. But while 20*a* is to be
understood of the waters under the firmament, 20*b* is to be interpreted of those above. שְׁחָקִים (from שָׁחַק, Arab. *shak*, *comminuere*,
attenuare) properly designates the uppermost stratum of air thinly
and finely stretching itself far and wide, and then poetically the
clouds of heaven (*vid.* under Ps. lxxvii. 18). Another name, עֲרִיפִים,
comes from עָרַף, which is transposed from רָעַף (here used in 20*b*),
Arab. *r'af*, to drop, to run. The טַל added on the object accusative
represents synecdochically all the waters coming down from heaven

and fructifying the earth. This watering proceeds from above (וְרַעֲפוּ); on the contrary, the endowing of the surface of the earth with great and small rivers is a fundamental fact in creation (נִבְקָעוּ).

Vers. 21-22. From this eminence, in which the work of creation presents wisdom, exhortations are now deduced, since the writer always expresses himself only with an ethical intention regarding the nature of wisdom :

> 21 My son, may they not depart from thine eyes—
> Preserve thoughtfulness and consideration,
> 22 And they will be life to thy soul
> And grace to thy neck.

If we make the synonyms of wisdom which are in 21b the subject *per prolepsin* to אַל־יָלֻזוּ (Hitzig and Zöckler), then 19-20 and 21-22 clash. The subjects are wisdom, understanding, knowledge, which belong to God, and shall from Him become the possession of those who make them their aim. Regarding לוז, *obliquari, deflectere*, see under ii. 15, cf. iv. 21; regarding תֻּשִׁיָּה (here *defective* after the Masora, as rightly in Vened. 1515, 1521, and Nissel, 1662), see at ii. 7; יָלֻזוּ for תְּלֹזְנָה, see at iii. 2b. The LXX. (cf. Heb. ii. 1) translate without distinctness of reference : υἱὲ μὴ παραρρυῇς (παραρυῇς), let it not flow past, *i.e.* let it not be unobserved, hold it always before thee; the Targ. with the Syr. render לָא נִזֵּל, *ne vilescat*, as if the words were אַל־יָזֻלּוּ. In 22a the *synallage generis* is continued : וְיִהְיוּ for וְתִהְיֶינָה. Regarding גֻּרְגְּרֹת, see at i. 9. By wisdom the soul gains life, divinely true and blessed, and the external appearance of the man grace, which makes him pleasing and gains for him affection.

Vers. 23-26. But more than this, wisdom makes its possessor in all situations of life confident in God :

> 23 Then shalt thou go thy way with confidence,
> And thy foot shall not stumble.
> 24 When thou liest down, thou art not afraid,
> But thou layest thyself down and hast sweet sleep.
> 25 Thou needest not be afraid of sudden alarm,
> Nor for the storm of the wicked when it breaketh forth.
> 26 For Jahve will be thy confidence
> And keep thy foot from the snare.

The לְבֶטַח (cf. our "*bei guter Laune*" = in good cheer), with לְ of the condition, is of the same meaning as the conditional adverbial accusative בֶּטַח, x. 9, i. 33. Ver. 23b the LXX. translate ὁ δὲ πούς σου οὐ μὴ προσκόψῃ, while, on the contrary, at Ps. xci. 12 they make the person the subject (μήποτε προσκόψῃς τὸν κ.τ.λ.) ; here also we retain more surely the subject from 23a, especially since for the intrans. of נָגַף (to smite, to push) a *Hithpa.* הִתְנַגֵּף is used Jer. xiii. 16. In ver. 24 there is the echo of Job xi. 18, and in ver. 25 of Job v. 21. 24b is altogether the same as Job v. 24b: *et decumbes et suavis erit somnus tuus = si decubueris, suavis erit.* The hypothetic perf., according to the sense, is both there and at Job xi. 18 (cf. Jer. xx. 9) oxytoned as *perf. consec.* Similar examples are vi. 22, Gen. xxxiii. 13, 1 Sam. xxv. 31, cf. Ewald, § 357a. עָרְבָה (of sleep as Jer. xxxi. 26) is from עָרֵב, which in Hebr. is used of pleasing impressions, as the Arab. ʿariba of a lively, free disposition. שֵׁנָה, *somnus* (*nom. actionis* from יָשֵׁן, with the ground-form *sina* preserved in the Arab. *lidat*, vid. *Job*, p. 284, note), agrees in inflexion with שָׁנָה, *annus.* אַל, ver. 25a, denies, like Ps. cxxi. 3, with emphasis: be afraid only not = thou hast altogether nothing to fear. Schultens rightly says : *Subest species prohibitionis et tanquam abominationis, ne tale quicquam vel in suspicionem veniat in mentemve cogitando admittatur.* פַּחַד here means terror, as i. 26 f., the terrific object; פִּתְאֹם (with the accus. *om*) is the virtual genitive, as xxvi. 2 חִנָּם (with accus. *am*). Regarding שֹׁאָה, see under i. 27. The genitive רְשָׁעִים may be, after Ps. xxxvii. 17, the *genit. subjecti*, but still it lies nearer to say that he who chooses the wisdom of God as his guiding star has no ground to fear punishment as transgressors have reason to fear it ; the שֹׁאָה is meant which wisdom threatens against transgressors, i. 27. He needs have no fear of it, for wisdom is a gift of God, and binds him who receives it to the giver: Jahve becomes and is henceforth his confidence. Regarding בּ *essentiæ*, which expresses the closest connection of the subject with the predicate which it introduces, see under Ps. xxxv. 2. As here, so also at Ex. xviii. 4, Ps. cxviii. 7, cxlvi. 5, the predicate is a noun with a pronominal suffix. כֶּסֶל is, as at Ps. lxxviii. 7, Job xxxi. 24, cognate to מִבְטָח and מִקְוֶה,[1] the object and ground of confidence. That the word in other connections may mean also foolhardiness, Ps. xlix. 14, and folly, Eccles. vii. 25 (cf. regarding כְּסִיל, which in Arab. as *belîd* denotes the dull, in Hebr. fools, see under i. 22), it follows that it proceeds from the fundamental con-

---

[1] According to Malbim, תִּקְוָה is the expectation of good, and כֶּסֶל, confidence in the presence of evil.

ception of fulness of flesh and of fat, whence arise the conceptions of dulness and slothfulness, as well as of confidence, whether confidence in self or in God (see Schultens *l.c.*, and Wünsche's *Hosea*, p. 207 f.). לֶכֶד is taking, catching, as in a net or trap or pit, from לָכַד, to catch (cf. Arab. *lakida*, to fasten, III. IV. to hold fast); another root-meaning, in which Arab. *lak* connects itself with *nak*, נך, to strike, to assail (whence *al-lakdat*, the assault against the enemy, *Deutsch. Morgenl. Zeitsch.* xxii. 140), is foreign to the Hebr. Regarding the מִן of מלכד, Fleischer remarks : "The מִן after verbs of guarding, preserving, like שׁמר and נצר, properly expresses that one by those means holds or seeks to hold a person or thing back from something, like the Lat. *defendere, tueri aliquem ab hostibus, a periculo.*" [1]

SIXTH INTRODUCTORY MASHAL DISCOURSE, III. 27-35.

EXHORTATION TO BENEVOLENCE AND RECTITUDE.

The promise in which it terminates, designates the close of the fifth discourse. The sixth differs from it in this, that, like none of the preceding, it adds proverb to proverb. The first series recommends love to one's neighbour, and the second warns against fellowship with the uncharitable.

Vers. 27, 28. The first illustration of neighbourly love which is recommended, is readiness to serve :

---

[1] Hitzig rejects iii. 22–26 as a later interpolation. And why ? Because iii., which he regards as a complete discourse, consists of twice ten verses beginning with בְּנִי. In addition to this symmetry other reasons easily reveal themselves to his penetration. But the discourses contained in chap. i.–ix. do not all begin with בני (*vid.* i. 20); and when it stands in the beginning of the discourse, it is not always the first word (*vid.* i. 8); and when it occurs as the first word or in the first line, it does not always commence a new discourse (*vid.* i. 15 in the middle of the first, iii. 11 in the middle of the fourth); and, moreover, the Hebr. poetry and oratory does not reckon according to verses terminated by *Soph Pasuk*, which are always accented distichs, but they in reality frequently consist of three or more lines. The rejected verses are in nothing unlike those that remain, and which are undisputed ; they show the same structure of stichs, consisting for the most part of three, but sometimes also only of two words (cf. iii. 22*b* with i. 9*b*, 10*b*), the same breadth in the course of the thoughts, and the same accord with Job and Deuteronomy.

27 Refuse no manner of good to him to whom it is due
When it is in thy power to do it.

28 Say not to thy neighbour, "Go, and come again,
To-morrow I will give it," whilst yet thou hast it.

Regarding the intensive plur. בְּעָלָיו with a sing. meaning, see under i. 19. The form of expression without the suffix is not בַּעַל but בַּעַל טוֹב; and this denotes here, not him who does good (בעל as Arab. *dhw* or *sahab*), but him to whom the good deed is done (cf. xvii. 8), *i.e.* as here, him who is worthy of it (בעל as Arab. *âhl*), him who is the man for it (Jewish interp.: מִי שֶׁהוּא רָאוּי לוֹ). We must refuse nothing good (nothing either legally or morally good) to him who has a right to it (מִן מְנַע as Job xxii. 7, xxxi. 16),[1] if we are in a condition to do him this good. The phrase יֶשׁ־לְאֵל יָדִי, Gen. xxxi. 29, and frequently, signifies: it is belonging to (practicable) the power of my hand, *i.e.* I have the power and the means of doing it. As זֵד signifies the haughty, insolent, but may be also used in the neuter of insolent conduct (*vid.* Ps. xix. 14), so אֵל signifies the strong, but also (although only in this phrase) strength. The *Keri* rejects the plur. יָדֶיךָ, because elsewhere the hand always follows לְאֵל in the singular. But it rejects the plur. לְרֵעֶיךָ (ver. 28) because the address following is directed to one person. Neither of these emendations was necessary. The usage of the language permits exceptions, notwithstanding the *usus tyrannus*, and the plur. לרעיך may be interpreted distributively: to thy fellows, it may be this one or that one. Hitzig also regards לרעיך as a singular; but the mas. of רֵעִיה, the ground-form of which is certainly *ra'j*, is רֵעֶה, or shorter, רֵעַ. לֵךְ וָשׁוּב does not mean : forth! go home again! but : go, and come again. שׁוּב, to come again, to return to something, to seek it once more.[2] The ו of וְיֵשׁ אִתָּךְ is, as 29*b*, the conditional : *quum sit penes te, sc. quod ei des.* "To-morrow shall I give" is less a promise than a delay and putting off, because it is difficult for him to alienate himself from him who makes the request. This

---

[1] Accentuate אַל־תִּמְנַע טוֹב, not אַל־תִּמְנַע־טוֹב. The doubling of the *Makkeph* is purposeless, and, on the contrary, the separating of טוֹב from מִבְּעָלָיו by the *Dechi* (the separating accent subordinate to *Athnach*) is proper. It is thus in the best MSS.

[2] Thus also (Arab.) *raj'* is used in Thaalebi's *Confidential Companion*, p. 24, line 3, of Flügel's ed. Admission was prevented to one Haschmid, then angry he sought it once more; he was again rejected, then he sought it not again (Arab. *flm yraj'*), but says, etc. Flügel has misunderstood the passage. Fleischer explains *raj'*, with reference to Prov. iii. 28, by *revenir à la charge.*

holding fast by one's own is unamiable selfishness; this putting off
in the fulfilment of one's duty is a sin of omission—οὐ γὰρ οἶδας,
as the LXX. adds, τί τέξεται ἡ ἐπιοῦσα.

Ver. 29. A second illustration of neighbourly love is harmless-
ness :

> Devise not evil against thy neighbour,
> While he dwelleth securely by thee.

The verb חָרַשׁ, χαράσσειν, signifies to cut into, and is used of the
faber ferrarius as well as of the *tignarius* (*Isaiah*, p. 463), who
with a cutting instrument (חֹרֵשׁ, Gen. iv. 22) works with metal or
wood, and from his profession is called חָרָשׁ. But the word means
as commonly to plough, *i.e.* to cut with the plough, and חֹרֵשׁ is
used also of a ploughman, and, without any addition to it, it always
has this meaning. It is then a question whether the metaphorical
phrase חָרַשׁ רָעָה signifies to fabricate evil, cf. *dolorum faber, men-
dacia procudere*, ψευδῶν καὶ ἀπατῶν τέκτων, and the Homeric κακὰ
φρεσὶ βυσσοδομεύειν (Fleischer and most others), or to plough evil
(Rashi, Ewald, etc.). The Targ., Syriac, and Jerome translate
חשׁב, without deciding the point, by *moliri;* but the LXX. and
Græcus Venet. by τεκταίνειν. The correctness of these renderings is not supported by Ezek. xxi. 36, where חָרָשֵׁי מַשְׁחִית are not
such as fabricate destruction, but smiths who cause destruction;
also מַחֲרִישׁ, 1 Sam. xxiii. 9, proves nothing, and probably does not at
all appertain to חרשׁ *incidere* (Keil), but to חרשׁ *silere*, in the sense
of *dolose moliri*. On the one hand, it is to be observed from Job
iv. 8, Hos. x. 13, cf. Ps. cxxix. 3, that the meaning *arare malum*
might connect itself with חָרַשׁ רָעָה; and the proverb of Sirach vii.
12, μὴ ἀροτρία ψεῦδος ἐπ᾽ ἀδελφῷ σου, places this beyond a doubt.
Therefore in this phrase, if one keeps before him a clear perception
of the figure, at one time the idea of fabricating, at another that
of ploughing, is presented before us. The usage of the language
in the case before us is more in favour of the latter than of the
former. Whether יָשַׁב אֵת means to dwell together with, or as
Böttcher, to sit together with, after Ps. i. 1, xxvi. 4 f., need not
be a matter of dispute. It means in general a continued being
together, whether as sitting, Job ii. 13, or as dwelling, Judg. xvii.
11.[1] To take advantage of the regardlessness of him who imparts

---

[1] Accentuate וְהוּא־יוֹשֵׁב לָבֶטַח. It is thus in correct texts. The *Rebia
Mugrash* is transformed, according to the *Accentuationssystem*, xviii. § 2.

to us his confidence is unamiable. Love is doubly owing to him
who resigns himself to it because he believes in it.

Ver. 30. A third illustration of the same principle is peaceable-
ness:

> Contend not with a man without a cause,
> When he has inflicted no evil upon thee.

Instead of תָּרוּב, or as the *Kerî* has amended it תָּרִיב, the abbreviated
form תָּרֹב or תֵּרֶב would be more correct after אַל; רוּב or רִיב (from
רב, to be compact) means to fall upon one another, to come to
hand-blows, to contend. Contending and quarrelling with a
man, whoever he may be, without sufficient reason, ought to be
abandoned; but there exists no such reason if he has done me no
harm which I have to reproach him with. גָּמַל רָעָה with the accus.
or dat. of the person signifies to bring evil upon any one, *malum
inferre*, or also *referre* (Schultens), for גָּמַל (cogn. גָּמַר) signifies to
execute, to complete, accomplish,—both of the initiative and of the
requital, both of the anticipative and of the recompensing action;
here in the former of these senses.

Vers. 31, 32. These exhortations to neighbourly love in the
form of warning against whatever is opposed to it, are followed by
the warning against fellowship with the loveless:

> 31 Be not envious toward the man of violence,
>   And have no pleasure in all his ways.
> 32 For an abhorrence to Jahve is the perverse,
>   But with the upright is His secret.

The conceptions of jealousy and envy lie in קִנֵּא (derived by Schultens from קָנָא, Arab. *kaná, intensius rubere*) inseparable from each
other. The LXX., which for תקנא reads תקנה (κτήσῃ), brings the
envy into 31*b*, as if the words here were וְאַל־תִּתְחַר, as in Ps. xxxvii.
1, 7 (there the LXX. has μὴ παραζήλου, here μηδὲ ζηλώσῃς).
There is no reason for correcting our text in accordance with this
(substituting תִּתְחַר for תִּבְחַר as Hitzig does), because בְּכָל־דְּרָכָיו would
be too vague an expression for the object of the envy, while
אַל־תבחר altogether agrees with it; and the contrary remark, that
בְּחַר בַּכֹּל is fundamentally no בחר, fails, since (1) בחר frequently expresses pleasure in anything without the idea of choice, and (2)
"have not pleasure in all his ways" is in the Hebrew style equivalent to "in any one of his ways;" Ewald, § 323*b*. He who does
"violence to the law" (Zeph. iii. 4) becomes thereby, according to
the common course of the world, a person who is feared, whose autho-

rity, power, and resources are increased, but one must not therefore envy him, nor on any side take pleasure in his conduct, which in all respects is to be reprobated; for the נָלוֹז, *inflexus, tortuosus* (*vid.* ii. 15), who swerves from the right way and goes in a crooked false way, is an object of Jahve's abhorrence, while, on the contrary, the just, who with a right mind walks in the right way, is Jahve's סוֹד—an echo of Ps. xxv. 14. סוֹד (R. סד, to be firm, compressed) means properly the being pressed together, or sitting together (cf. the Arab. *wisâd, wisâdt,* a cushion, divan, corresponding in form to the Hebr. יְסוֹד) for the purpose of private communication and conversation (הִוָּסֵד), and then partly the confidential intercourse, as here (cf. Job xxix. 4), partly the private communication, the secret (Amos iii. 7). LXX., ἐν δὲ δικαίοις [οὐ] συνεδριάζει. Those who are out of the way, who prefer to the simplicity of right-doing all manner of crooked ways, are contrary to God, and He may have nothing to do with them; but the right-minded He makes partakers of His most intimate intercourse, He deals with them as His friends.

Ver. 33. The prosperity of the godless, far from being worthy of envy, has as its reverse side the curse:

> The curse of Jahve is in the house of the godless,
> And the dwelling of the just He blesseth.

מְאֵרָה (a curse), like מְסִלָּה (a highway, from סָלַל), is formed from אָרַר (cf. Arab. *harr, detestari, abhorrere,* a word-imitation of an interjection used in disagreeable experiences). The curse is not merely a deprivation of external goods which render life happy, and the blessing is not merely the fulness of external possessions; the central-point of the curse lies in continuous disquiet of conscience, and that of the blessing in the happy consciousness that God is with us, in soul-rest and peace which is certain of the grace and goodness of God. The poetic נָוֶה (from נוה = Arab. *nwy, tetendit aliquo*) signifies the place of settlement, and may be a word borrowed from a nomad life, since it denotes specially the pasture-ground; cf. xxiv. 15 (Fleischer). While the curse of God rests in the house of the wicked (*vid.* Köhler on Zech. v. 4), He blesses, on the contrary, the dwelling-place of the righteous. The LXX. and Jerome read יְבָרֵךְ, but יְבָרֵךְ is more agreeable, since God continues to be the subject.

Ver. 34. His relation to men is determined by their relation to Him.

As for the scorners, He scorneth them,
But to the lowly He giveth grace.

Most interpreters render the verse thus: "If the scorner He (even He, in return) scorneth, so He (on the other hand) giveth grace to the lowly." For the sequence of the words in the consequence, in which the precedence of the verb is usual, *e.g.* Lev. xii. 5, we are referred to xxiii. 18, cf. xxiv. 14; but why had the poet placed the two facts in the relation of condition and consequence? The one fact is not the consequence but the reverse of the other, and accordingly they are opposed to each other in coordinated passages, Ps. xviii. 26 f. The *Vav* in such antitheses has generally the meaning of "and on the other hand," *e.g.* Job viii. 20, while the LXX., Targ., Syriac, and Jerome altogether pass over the אִם as if it did not exist. Ziegler translates: "Truly! the scorner He scorneth;" but an affirmative אִם does not exist, the asseveration after the manner of an oath is negative. Bertheau's expedient would be more acceptable, by which he makes the whole of ver. 34 the protasis to ver. 35; but if this were intended, another subject would not enter into ver. 35. Thus 34*a* and 34*b* are two independent parallel passages; אִם־לַלֵּצִים is the protasis: if as regards the scorners, *i.e.* if His conduct is directed to the scorners, so He scorneth. The לְ denotes relation, and in this elliptical usage is like the לְ of superscription, *e.g.* Jer. xxiii. 9. הוּא is the emphatic αὐτός: He on the contrary, and in a decisive way (Ewald, § 314*ab*). Instead of יָלִיץ there might have been used יְלִיצֵם (for הֵלִיץ, where it occurs as a governing word, has the accusative, xix. 28, Ps. cxix. 51), but we do not miss the object: if it relates to scorners (thus also Löwenstein translates), so it is He in return who scorneth. The LXX. renders it: κύριος ὑπερηφάνοις ἀντιτάσσεται, ταπεινοῖς δὲ δίδωσι χάριν; cf. Jas. iv. 6, 1 Pet. v. 5. הוּא is used as a name of God (*Deutsch. Morgenl. Zeitschr.* xvi. 400), on which account it is rendered like יהוה by κύριος. A ὑπερήφανος (appearing above others, *i e.* overbearing) is the לֵץ, according to the definition xxi. 24. The expression of the *talio* is generalized in ἀντιτάσσεται (resists them). For עניים the *Kerî* has עֲנָוִים: עָנָו (from עָנָה, the ground-form עָנַו, Arab. 'anaw) is the lowly (ταπεινός), or he who bends himself, *i.e.* the gentle and humble, the patient, and the passive עָנִי, he who is bowed down, the suffering; but the limits of the conception are moveable, since in עָנִי is presupposed the possession of fruit-virtues gained in the school of affliction.

Ver. 35. This group of the proverbs of wisdom now suitably closes with the fundamental contrast between the wise and fools :

The wise shall inherit honour,
But fools carry away shame.

If we take וּכְסִילִים as the object, then we can scarcely interpret the clause : shame sweeps fools away (Umbreit, Zöckler, Bertheau), for הֵרִים [Hiph. of רוּם] signifies (Isa. lvii. 14, Ezek. xxi. 31) "to raise up anything high and far," not "to sweep away." Preferable is the rendering : τοὺς δ᾽ ἄφρονας ὑψοῖ ἀτιμία (Grœc. Venet., and similarly Jerome), i.e. only to it do they owe their celebrity as warning examples (Ewald), to which Oetinger compares "whose glory is in their shame," Phil. iii. 19 ;[1] but קָלוֹן is the contrary of כָּבוֹד (glory, Hab. ii. 16), and therefore is as much an object conception as is the latter, 35a. If it is the object, then if we take מֵרִים from מֵר after the form of לֵץ, Neh. xiii. 21 = מְמִירִים (Hos. iv. 7), it might be rendered : Yet fools exchange shame (Löwenstein). But מוּר, like the Arab. mrr, transire, means properly to pass over or to wander over; it is intransitive, and only in Hiph. signifies actively to exchange. מֵרִים thus will be the participle of הֵרִים ; the plur. taken distributively (fools = whoever is only always a fool) is connected with the singular of the predicate. This change in the number is here, however, more difficult than at iii. 18, and in other places, where the plur. of the part. permits the resolution into a relative clause with quicunque, and more difficult than at xxviii. 1, where the sing. of the predicate is introduced by attraction; wherefore מרים may be an error in transcribing for מרימים or מרימי (Böttcher). J. H. Michaelis (after the Targ. and Syr.) has properly rendered the clause : " stulti tollunt ignominiam tanquam portionem suam," adding " quœ derivato nomine תרומה dicitur." הרים signifies, in the language of the sacrificial worship and of worship generally, to lift off from anything the best portion, the legitimate portion due to God and the priesthood (vid. at iii. 9); for which reason Rashi glosses מרים by מפריש לו, and Ralbag by מגביה לו. See xiv. 29. Honour is that which the wise inherit, it falls to them unsought as a possession, but fools receive shame as the offal (viz. of their foolish conduct). The fut. and part. are significantly interchanged. The life of the wise ends in glory, but

---

[1] Jona Gerundi renders it otherwise : " But shame raises the fools high ;" i.e. only the infamous, he who has no sense of honour, makes much advancement out of fools.

fools inherit shame; the fruit of their conduct is shame and evermore shame.

SEVENTH INTRODUCTORY MASHAL DISCOURSE, IV.-V. 6.

RECOLLECTIONS OF HIS FATHER'S HOUSE.

The means are not yet exhausted by which the teacher of wisdom seeks to procure acceptance for his admonitions and warnings, and to give them emphasis. He has introduced the importance of his person in order that he might gain the heart of the disciple, and has presented as speaker, instead of himself, the revered person of Wisdom herself, who seeks to win, by means of warnings and promises, the souls of men. Chap. iv. 1–4. He now confirms and explains the command to duty which he has placed at the beginning of the whole (i. 8). This he does by his own example, for he relates from the history of his own youth, to the circle of disciples by whom he sees himself surrounded, what good doctrine his parents had taught him regarding the way of life:

1 Hear, ye sons, the instruction of a father,
   And attend that ye may gain understanding;
2 For I give to you good doctrine,
   Forsake not my direction!
3 For I was a son to my father,
   A tender and only (son) in the sight of my mother.
4 And he instructed me, and said to me:
   "Let thine heart hold fast my words:
   Observe my commandments and live!"

That בָּנִים in the address comes here into the place of בְּנִי, hitherto used, externally denotes that בני in the progress of these discourses finds another application: the poet himself is so addressed by his father. Intentionally he does not say אֲבִיכֶם (cf. i. 8): he does not mean the father of each individual among those addressed, but himself, who is a father in his relation to them as his disciples; and as he manifests towards them fatherly love, so also he can lay claim to paternal authority over them. לָדַעַת is rightly vocalized, not לְדַעַת. The words do not give the object of attention, but the design, the aim. The combination of ideas in דַּעַת בִּינָה (cf. i. 2), which appears to us singular, loses its strangeness when we remember that דַעַת means, according to its etymon, deposition or reception into the conscience and life. Regarding לֶקַח, apprehension, reception, lesson = doctrine, vid. i. 5. נְתַתִּי is the perf., which denotes as fixed and finished what is just now being done, Gesenius, § 126, 4. עָזַב is here synonym of נָטַשׁ, i. 8, and the contrary of שָׁמַר, xxviii. 4. The relative *factum* in the perfect, designating the circumstances under which the event happened, regularly precedes the chief *factum* וַיֹּרֵנִי; see under Gen. i. 2 f. Superficially understood, the expression 3a would be a platitude; the author means that the natural legal relation was also confirming itself as a moral one. It was a relation of many-sided love, according to 3a: he was esteemed of his mother—לִפְנֵי, used of the reflex in the judgment, Gen. x. 9, and of loving care, Gen. xvii. 18, means this—as a tender child, and therefore tenderly to be protected (רַךְ as Gen. xxxiii. 13), and as an only child, whether he were so in reality, or was only loved as if he were so. יָחִיד (Aq., Sym., Theod., μονογενής) may with reference to number also mean *unice dilectus* (LXX. ἀγαπώμενος); cf. Gen. xxii. 2, יְחִידְךָ (where the LXX. translate τὸν ἀγαπητόν, without therefore having יְדִידְךָ before them). לפני is maintained by all the versions; לְבְנֵי is not a variant.[1] The instruction of the father begins with the jussive, which is pointed[2] יִתְמָךְ to distinguish it from יִתְמֹךְ on account of the ŏ. The LXX. has incorrectly ἐρειδέτω, as if the word were יסמך; Symmachus has correctly κατεχέτω. The imper. וֶחְיֵה is, as vii. 2, Gen. xx. 7, more than וְתִחְיֶה; the teacher seeks, along with the means, at the same time their object: Observe my commandments, and so become a partaker of life! The Syriac, however, adds וְתוֹרָתִי כְּאִישׁוֹן עֵינֶיךָ [and my instruction as the apple of thine eye], a clause borrowed from vii. 2.

Vers. 5, 6. The exhortation of the father now specializes itself:

5 Get wisdom, get understanding;
Forget not and turn not from the words of my mouth.

---

[1] In some editions לְבְנֵי is noted as *Keri* to לפני, but erroneously and contrary to the express evidence of the Masora, which affirms that there are two passages in which we ought to read not לפני, but לבני, viz. Ps. lxxx. 3 and Prov. iv. 3.

[2] The writing of יִתְמָךְ with the grave *Metheg* (*Gaja*) and *Kamets-Chatuph* (ŏ) is that of Ben Asher; on the other hand, יִתְמֹךְ with *Cholem* (ŏ) and the permanent *Metheg* is that of Ben Naphtali; vid. Michlol 21a (under the verbal form 25), § 30.

6 Forsake her not, so shall she preserve thee;
   Love her, so shall she keep thee.

Wisdom and understanding are (5a) thought of as objects of
merchandise (cf. xxiii. 23, iii. 14), like the one pearl of great
price, Matt. xiii. 46, and the words of fatherly instruction (5b),
accordingly, as offering this precious possession, or helping to the
acquisition of it. One cannot indeed say correctly אַל־תִּשְׁכַּח מַאֲמְרֵי־פִי,
but אַל־תִּשְׁכַּח מִשְׁמֹר אֲמָרֵי־פִי (Ps. cii. 5); and in this sense אַל־תִּשְׁכַּח
goes before, or also the accus. object, which in אַל־תִּשְׁכַּח the author
has in his mind, may, since he continues with אַל־תֵּט, now not
any longer find expression as such. That the אֲמָרֵי־פִי are the
means of acquiring wisdom is shown in ver. 6, where this continues
to be the primary idea. The verse, consisting of only four words,
ought to be divided by *Mugrash*;[1] the *Vav* (ו) in both halves of
the verse introduces the *apodosis imperativi* (cf. *e.g.* iii. 9 f., and
the *apodosis prohibitivi*, iii. 21 f.). The actual representation of
wisdom, ver. 5, becomes in ver. 6 personal.

VERS. 7–9. Referring to ver. 5, the father further explains that
wisdom begins with the striving after it, and that this striving is
itself its fundamental beginning:

7 The beginning of wisdom is " Get wisdom,"
   And with [*um*, at the price of] all thou hast gotten get understanding.
8 Esteem her, so shall she lift thee up;
   She will bring thee honour if thou dost embrace her.
9 She will put on thine head a graceful garland,
   She will bestow upon thee a glorious diadem.

In the motto of the book, i. 7, the author would say that the fear
of Jahve is that from which all wisdom takes its origin. יִרְאַת יְהֹוָה
(i. 7) is the subject, and as such it stands foremost. Here he
means to say what the beginning of wisdom consists in. רֵאשִׁית חָכְמָה
is the subject, and stands forth as such. The predicate may also
be read קְנֹה־חָכְמָה (=קְנוֹת), after xvi. 16. The beginning of wisdom is (consists in) the getting of wisdom; but the imperative
קְנֵה, which also Aq., Sym., Theod. (κτῆσαι), Jerome, Syr., Targ.
express (the LXX. leaves ver. 7 untranslated), is supported by 7b.
Hitzig, after Mercier, De Dieu, and Döderlein, translates the verse

---

[1] According to correct readings in codd. and older editions, וְתִשְׁמְרֶךָ has
also indeed *Rebia Mugrash*, and אֱהָבֶהָ, *Mercha* (with *Zinnorith*); *vid. Torath
Emeth*, p. 47, § 6; *Accentuationssystem*, xviii. § 1, 2; and regarding the *Zinnorith*, see *Liber Psalmorum Hebraicus* by S. Baer, p. xii.

thus : " the highest thing is wisdom ; get wisdom," which Zöckler approves of ; but the reasons which determine him to this rendering are subtleties : if the author had wished himself to be so understood, he ought at least to have written the words רֵאשִׁית הַחָכְמָה. But רֵאשִׁית חָכְמָה is a genitive of relation, as is to be expected from the relativity of the idea רֵאשִׁית, and his intention is to say that the beginning of wisdom consists in the proposition קְנֵה חָכְמָה (cf. the similar formula, Eccles. xii. 13) ; this proposition is truly the *lapis philosophorum*, it contains all that is necessary in order to becoming wise. Therefore the Greek σοφία called itself modestly φιλοσοφία; for ἀρχὴ αὐτῆς the Book of Wisdom has, vi. 18, ἡ ἀληθεστάτη παιδείας ἐπιθυμία. In 7*b* the proposition is expressed which contains the *specificum* helping to wisdom. The בְּ denotes price : give all for wisdom (Matt. xiii. 46, 44) ; no price is too high, no sacrifice too great for it.

Ver. 8. The meaning of the ἀπ. γεγρ. סַלְסֵל is determined by רוֹמֵם in the parallel clause ; סָלַל signifies to raise, exalt, as a way or dam by heaping up ; the *Pilpel*, here tropical : to value or estimate highly. Böttcher interprets well : hold it high in price, raise it (as a purchaser) always higher, make offer for it upon offer. The LXX. (approved by Bertheau), περιχαράκωσον αὐτήν, circumvallate it, *i.e.* surround it with a wall (סֹלְלָה)—a strange and here unsuitable figure. Hold it high, says the author, and so it will reward[1] thee with a high place, and (with chiastic transposition of the performance and the consequence) she will honour[2] thee if (ἐάν) thou lovingly embracest her. חִבֵּק is used of embracing in the pressure of tender love, as in the Canticles ii. 6, viii. 3 ; the *Piel* is related to the *Kal* as *amplexari* to *amplecti*. Wisdom exalts her admirers, honours her lovers, and makes a man's appearance pleasant, causing him to be reverenced when he approaches. Regarding לִוְיַת־חֵן, *vid.* i. 9. מִגֵּן, to deliver up (Gen. xiv. 20), to give up (Hos. xi. 8), is connected in the free poetic manner with two accusatives, instead of with an accus. and dat. LXX. has ὑπερασπίσῃ, but one does not defend himself (as with a shield) by a wreath or crown.

---

[1] Löwenstein has rightly וּתְרוֹמְמֶךָ, *vid.* my preface to Baer's *Genesis*, p. vii.

[2] We read תְּכַבֵּדְךָ, not תְּכַבְּדֶךָ (Hahn) or תְּכַבְּדָה (Löwenstein); the tone lies on the *penult.*, and the tone-syllable has the point *Tsere*, as in וַיְנַדֵּךְ, Deut. xxxii. 7 ; *vid. Michlol* 66*b*.

Vers. 10–12. There is no reason for the supposition that the warning which his father gave to the poet now passes over into warnings given by the poet himself (Hitzig); the admonition of the father thus far refers only in general to the endeavour after wisdom, and we are led to expect that the good doctrines which the father communicates to the son as a *viaticum* will be further expanded, and become more and more specific when they take a new departure.

> 10 Hearken, my son, and receive my sayings,
>   So shall the years of life be increased to thee.
> 11 In the way of wisdom have I taught thee,
>   Guided thee in the paths of rectitude.
> 12 When thou goest, thy step shall not be straitened;
>   And if thou runnest, thou shalt not stumble.

Regarding קַח (of לָקַח) of appropriating reception and taking up *in succum et sanguinem*, vid. i. 3; regarding שְׁנוֹת חַיִּים, years not merely of the duration of life, but of the enjoyment of life, iii. 2; regarding מַעְגָּל (מַעְגְּלָה), path (track), ii. 9; regarding the בְּ of הוֹרָה, of the department and subject of instruction, Ps. xxv. 8. The perfects, ver. 11, are different from נָתַתִּי, 2a; they refer to rules of life given at an earlier period, which are summarily repeated in this address. The way of wisdom is that which leads to wisdom (Job xxviii. 23); the paths of rectitude, such as trace out the way which is in accordance with the rule of the good and the right. If the youth holds to this direction, he will not go on in darkness or uncertainty with anxious footsteps; and if in youthful fervour he flies along his course, he will not stumble on any unforeseen obstacle and fall. יֵצַר is as a metaplastic fut. to צָרַר or צוּר, to be narrow, to straiten, formed as if from יָצַר. The Targ. after Aruch,[1] לֹא תשנק ארחך, thou shalt not need to bind together (*constringere*) or to hedge up thy way.

Vers. 13–17. The exhortations attracting by means of promises, now become warnings fitted to alarm:

> 13 Hold fast to instruction, let her not go;
>   Keep her, for she is thy life.
> 14 Into the path of the wicked enter not,
>   And walk not in the way of the evil.

---

[1] [R. Nathan ben Jechiel, A.D. 1106, who is usually styled by the Jewish writers בַּעַל עָרוּךְ, *Auctor Aruch*, author of a Talmudical Lexicon.]

15 Avoid it, enter not into it;
  Turn from it and pass away.
16 For they cannot sleep unless they do evil,
  And they are deprived of sleep unless they bring others to ruin.
17 For they eat the bread of wickedness,
  And they drink the wine of violence.

Elsewhere מוּסָר means also self-discipline, or moral religious education, i. 3; here discipline, *i.e.* parental educative counsel. תֶּרֶף is the segolated fut. apoc. *Hiph.* (indic. תִּרְפֶּה) from *tarp*, cf. the imper. *Hiph.* הֶרֶף from *harp.* נִצְרָהָ is the imper. *Kal* (not *Piel*, as Aben Ezra thinks) with *Dagesh dirimens;* cf. the verbal substantive נִצְרָה, Ps. cxli. 3, with similar *Dagesh,* after the form יִקְּהָה, Gen. xlix. 10. מוּסָר (elsewhere always masc.) is here used in the fem. as the synonym of the name of wisdom: keep her (instruction), for she is thy life,[1] *i.e.* the life of thy life. In ver. 14 the godless (*vid.* on the root-idea of רָשַׁע under Ps. i. 1) and the habitually wicked, *i.e.* the vicious, stand in parallelism; בּוֹא and אָשַׁר are related as entering and going on, *ingressus* and *progressus.* The verb אָשַׁר signifies, like יָשַׁר, to be straight, even, fortunate, whence אֶשֶׁר = Arab. *yusâr,* happiness, and to step straight out, ix. 6, of which meanings אִשֵּׁר is partly the intensive, as here, partly the causative, xxiii. 19 (elsewhere causative of the meaning, to be happy, Gen. xxx. 13). The meaning *progredi* is not mediated by a supplementary צְעָדָיו; the derivative אָשׁוּר (אַשּׁוּר), a step, shows that it is derived immediately from the root-idea of a movement in a straight line. Still less justifiable is the rendering by Schultens, *ne vestigia imprimas in via malorum;* for the Arab. *áththr* is denom. of *ithr,* אֵתֶר, the primitive verb roots of which, *athr,* אָשַׁר=אתר, are lost.

Ver. 15. On פְּרָעֵהוּ, avoid it (the way), (*opp.* אָחַז, Job xvii. 9; תָּמֹךְ, Ps. xvii. 5), see under i. 25. שָׂטָה, elsewhere (as the Arab. *shatt,* to be without measure, insolent) used *in malam partem,* has here its fundamental meaning, to go aside. מֵעָלָיו (expressed in French by *de dessus,* in Ital. by *di sopra*) denotes: so that thou comest not to stand on it. עָבַר means in both cases *transire,* but the second instance, " to go beyond (farther) " (cf. 2 Sam. xv. 22, and under Hab. i. 11), coincides with " to escape, *evadere.*"

Ver. 16. In the reason here given the perf. may stand in the con-

---

[1] Punctuate כִּי הִיא ; the *Zinnorith* represents the place of the *Makkeph, vid. Torath Emeth,* p. 9.

ditional clauses as well as in Virgil's *Et si non aliqua nocuisses,
mortuus esses ;* but the fut., as in Eccles. v. 11, denotes that they
(the רָעִים and the רְשָׁעִים) cannot sleep, and are deprived of their
sleep, unless they are continually doing evil and bringing others
into misery ; the interruption of this course of conduct, which has
become to them like a second nature, would be as the interruption
of their diet, which makes them ill. For the *Kal* יִכְשׁוֹלוּ, which
here must have the meaning of the person sinning (cf. ver. 19),
and would be feeble if used of the confirmed transgressors, the
Kerî rightly substitutes the *Hiphil* יַכְשִׁילוּ, which occurs also 2 Chron.
xxv. 8, there without an object, in the meaning to cause to fall, as
the contrast of עָזַר (to help).

Ver. 17. The second כִּי introduces the reason of their bodily
welfare being conditioned by evil-doing. If the poet meant : they
live on bread which consists in wickedness, *i.e.* on wickedness as
their bread, then in the parallel sentence he should have used the
word חָמָם ; the genitives are meant of the means of acquisition :
they live on unrighteous gain, on bread and wine which they
procure by wickedness and by all manner of violence or injustice.
On the etymon of חָמָם (Arab. *hamas, durum, asperum, vehementem
esse*), *vid.* Schultens; the plur. חֲמָסִים belongs to a more recent
epoch (*vid.* under 2 Sam. xxii. 49 and Ps. xviii. 49). The change
in the tense represents the idea that they having eaten such bread,
set forth such wine, and therewith wash it down.

Vers. 18, 19. The two ways that lie for his choice before the
youth, are distinguished from one another as light is from darkness :

> 18 And the path of the just is like the brightness of the morning light,
> 　Which shines more and more till the perfect day.
> 19 The way of the wicked is deep darkness,
> 　They know not at what they stumble.

The Hebr. style is wont to conceal in its *Vav* (ו) diverse kinds of
logical relations, but the *Vav* of 18*a* may suitably stand before
19*a*, where the discontinuance of this contrast of the two ways
is unsuitable. The displacing of a *Vav* from its right position is
not indeed without example (see under Ps. xvi. 3); but since
ver. 19 joins itself more easily than ver. 18 to ver. 17 without
missing a particle, thus it is more probable that the two verses are
to be transposed, than that the ו of וְאֹרַח (ver. 17) is to be prefixed to
דֶּרֶךְ (ver. 18). Sinning, says ver. 16, has become to the godless as

a second nature, so that they cannot sleep without it; they must continually be sinning, adds ver. 17, for thus and not otherwise do they gain for themselves their daily bread. With reference to this fearful self-perversion to which wickedness has become a necessity and a condition of life, the poet further says that the way of the godless is בָּאֲפֵלָה,[1] as deep darkness, as the entire absence of light: it cannot be otherwise than that they fall, but they do not at all know whereat they fall, for they do not at all know wickedness as such, and have no apprehension of the punishment which from an inward necessity it brings along with it; on the contrary, the path of the just is in constantly increasing light—the light of knowledge, and the light of true happiness which is given[2] in and with knowledge. On בַּמֶּה vid. under Isa. ii. 22; it is מִכְשׁוֹל, σκάν-δαλον, that is meant, stumbling against which (cf. Lev. xxvi. 37) they stumble to their fall. נֹגַהּ,[3] used elsewhere than in the Bible, means the morning star (Venus), (Sirach l. 4, Syr.); when used in the Bible it means the early dawn, the light of the rising sun, the morning light, 2 Sam. xxiii. 4, Isa. lxii. 1, which announces itself in the morning twilight, Dan. vi. 20. The light of this morning sunshine is הוֹלֵךְ וָאוֹר, going and shining, i.e. becoming ever brighter. In the connection of הוֹלֵךְ וָאוֹר it might be a question

---

[1] In good MSS. and printed copies the כ has the *Pathach*, as Kimchi states the rule in *Michlol* 45a: כל כאבנים פתח, כל באפלה פתח.

[2] Hitzig inverts the order of vers. 18 and 19, and connects the כִּי of 16a immediately with ver. 19 (for the way of the wicked . . .). He moreover regards vers. 16, 17 as an interpolation, and explains ver. 16 as a gloss transforming the text of ver. 19. "That the wicked commit wickedness," says Hitzig, "is indeed certain (1 Sam. xxiv. 14), and the warning of ver. 15 ought not to derive its motive from their energy in sinning." But the warning against the way of the wicked is founded not on their energy in sinning, but on their bondage to sin: their sleep, their food and drink—their life both when they sleep and when they wake—is conditioned by sin and is penetrated by sin. This foundation of the warning furnishes what is needed, and is in nothing open to objection. And that in vers. 16 and 19 לֹא יֵדְעוּ and לֹא יָדְעוּ, נִגְזְלָה and יִכָּשֵׁלוּ and יִכְשׁוֹלוּ, בָּאֲפֵלָה seem to be alike, does not prove that ver. 16 originated as a parallel text from ver. 19—in the one verse as in the other the thoughts are original.

[3] Böttcher, under 2 Sam. xxiii. 4, explains נֹגַהּ of the brightness striking against, conquering (cf. נגף, נגח) the clouds; but *ferire* or *percutere* lies nearer (cf. נגע, Ezek. xvii. 10, נכה, Ps. cxxi. 6, and the Arab. *darb*, used of strong sensible impressions), as Silius, iv. 329, says of the light: *percussit lumine campos.*

whether אוֹר is regarded as gerundive (Gen. viii. 3, 5), or as participle (2 Sam. xvi. 5, Jer. xli. 6), or as a participial adjective (Gen. xxvi. 13, Judg. iv. 24) ; in the connection of וְהָלוֹךְ וָאוֹר, on the contrary, it is unquestionably the gerundive: the partic. denoting the progress joins itself either with the partic., Jon. i. 11, or with the participial adjective, 2 Sam. iii. 1, 2 Chron. xvii. 12, or with another adjective formation, 2 Sam. xv. 12, Esth. ix. 4 (where וְגָדוֹל after וְגָדֵל of other places appears to be intended as an adjective, not after 2 Sam. v. 10 as gerundive). Thus וָאוֹר, as also וָטוֹב, 1 Sam. ii. 26, will be participial after the form בּוֹשׁ, being ashamed (Ges. § 72, 1) ; cf. בּוֹם, Zech. x. 5, קוֹם, 2 Kings xvi. 7. " נְכוֹן הַיּוֹם quite corresponds to the Greek τὸ σταθηρὸν τῆς ἡμέρας, ἡ σταθηρὰ μεσημβρία (as one also says τὸ σταθηρὸν τῆς νυκτός), and to the Arabic قَائِمَة النَّهَار and قَائِمَة الظَّهِيرَة. The figure is probably derived from the balance (cf. Lucan's *Pharsalia*, lib. 9 : *quum cardine summo Stat librata dies*) : before and after midday the tongue on the balance of the day bends to the left and to the right, but at the point of midday it stands directly in the midst" (Fleischer). It is the midday time that is meant, when the clearness of day has reached its fullest intensity,—the point between increasing and decreasing, when, as we are wont to say, the sun stands in the zenith (=Arab. *samt*, the point of support, *i.e.* the vertex). Besides Mark iv. 28, there is no biblical passage which presents like these two a figure of gradual development. The progress of blissful knowledge is compared to that of the clearness of the day till it reaches its midday height, having reached to which it becomes a knowing of all in God, xxviii. 5, 1 John ii. 20.

Vers. 20–22. The paternal admonition now takes a new departure :

> 20 My son, attend unto my words,
>   Incline thine ear to my sayings.
> 21 Let them not depart from thine eyes ;
>   Keep them in the midst of thine heart.
> 22 For they are life to all who get possession of them,
>   And health to their whole body.

Regarding the *Hiph.* הַלּיז (for הַלְיז), ver. 21, formed after the Chaldee manner like הַלִּין, הַנִּיח, הַפִּיג, *vid.* Gesenius, § 72, 9 ;—Ewald, § 114, *c*, gives to it the meaning of " to mock," for he interchanges it with הֵלִיץ, instead of the meaning to take away, *efficere ut recedat* (cf. under ii. 15). This supposed causative meaning it has also here : may they = may one (*vid.* under ii. 22) not remove them from thine eyes; the object is (ver. 20) the words of the paternal admonition. Hitzig, indeed, observes that "the accusative is not supplied;" but with greater right it is to be remarked that יַלִּיזוּ (fut. *Hiph.* of לוז) and יָלֻחוּ (fut. *Kal* of *id.*) are not one and the same, and the less so as הֵלִיץ is not, like הֵלִין, intrinsically transitive. Here and there יָלִיז occurs, but the masoretical and grammatical authorities (*e.g.* Kimchi) demand יָלִיזוּ. The plur. לְמֹצְאֵיהֶם is continued, 22*b*, in the sing., for that which is said refers to each one of the many (iii. 18, 28, 35). מָצָא is fundamentally an active conception, like our "*finden*," to find; it means to attain, to produce, to procure, etc. מַרְפֵּא means, according as the מ is understood of the "that = *ut*" of the action or of the "what" of its performance, either health or the means of health; here, like רְפָאוּת, iii. 8, not with the underlying conception of sickness, but of the fluctuations connected with the bodily life of man, which make needful not only a continual strengthening of it, but also its being again and again restored. Nothing preserves soul and body in a healthier state than when we always keep before our eyes and carry in our hearts the good doctrines; they give to us true guidance on the way of life: "Godliness has the promise of this life, and of that which is to come." 1 Tim. iv. 8.

Vers. 23–27. After this general preface the exhortation now becomes special :

23 Above all other things that are to be guarded, keep thy heart,
   For out from it life has its issues.
24 Put away from thee perverseness of mouth,
   And waywardness of lips put far from thee.
25 Thine eyes should look straight forward,
   And thine eyelids look straight to the end before thee.
26 Make even the path of thy feet,
   And let all thy ways be correct.
27 Turn not aside to the right and to the left ;
   Remove thy foot from evil.

Although מִשְׁמָר in itself and in this connection may mean the object to be watchfully avoided (*cavendi*) (*vid.* under ii. 20*b*) : thus the usage of the language lying before us applies it, yet only as denoting the place of watching or the object *observandi ;* so that it is not to be thus explained, with Raschi and others: before all from which one has to protect himself (*ab omni re cavenda*), guard thine heart; but: before all that one has to guard (*præ omni re custodienda*), guard it as the most precious of possessions committed to thy trust. The heart, which according to its etymon denotes that which is substantial (*Kernhafte*) in man (cf. Arab. *lubb*, the kernel of the nut or almond), comes here into view not as the physical, but as the intellectual, and specially the ethical *centrum*.

Ver. 24. The תּוֹצָאוֹת are the point of a thing, *e.g.* of a boundary, from which it goes forth, and the linear course proceeding from thence. If thus the author says that the תּוֹצְאוֹת חַיִּים go out from the heart,[1] he therewith implies that the life has not only its fountain in the heart, but also that the direction which it takes is determined by the heart. Physically considered, the heart is the receptacle for the blood, in which the soul lives and rules; the pitcher at the blood-fountain which draws it and pours it forth; the chief vessel of the physically self-subsisting blood-life from which it goes forth, and into which it disembogues (*Syst. der bib. Psychol.* p. 232). What is said of the heart in the lower sense of corporeal vitality, is true in the higher sense of the intellectual soul-life. The Scripture names the heart also as the intellectual soul-centre of man, in its concrete, central unity, its dynamic activity, and its ethical determination on all sides. All the radiations of corporeal and of soul life concentrate there, and again unfold themselves from thence; all that is implied in the Hellenic and Hellenistic words νοῦς, λόγος, συνείδησις, θυμός, lies in the word καρδία; and all whereby בָּשָׂר (the body) and נֶפֶשׁ (the spirit, *anima*) are affected comes in לֵב into the light of consciousness (*Id.* p. 251). The heart is the instrument of the thinking, willing, perceiving life of the spirit; it is the seat of the knowledge of self, of the knowledge of God, of the knowledge of our relation to God, and also of the law of God impressed on our moral nature; it is the workshop of our individual spiritual and ethical form of life brought about by self-activity,—the life in its higher and in its lower sense goes out from it, and receives from it the impulse of the direction which it takes; and how earnestly, therefore, must we feel ourselves admonished, how sacredly bound to preserve the heart in purity (Ps. lxxiii. 1), so that from this spring of life may

---

[1] The correct form here is כִּי־מִמֶּנּוּ, with the *Makkeph* to כִּי.

go forth not mere seeming life and a caricature of life, but a true life well-pleasing to God! How we have to carry into execution this careful guarding of the heart, is shown in ver. 24 and the golden rules which follow. Mouth and lips are meant (ver. 24) as instruments of speech, and not of its utterance, but of the speech going forth from them. עִקְּשׁוּת, *distorsio*, refers to the mouth (vi. 12), when what it speaks is disfiguring and deforming, thus falsehood as the contrast of truth and love (ii. 12); and to the lips לְזוּת, when that which they speak turns aside from the true and the right to side-ways and by-ways. Since the *Kametz* of such *abstracta*, as well of verbs ע"ו like רְמוּת, Ezek. xxxii. 5, as of verbs ל"ה like גְּלוּת, Isa. xlv. 13, חָזוּת, Isa. xxviii. 18, is elsewhere treated as unalterable, there lies in this לְזוּת either an inconsistency of punctuation, or it is presupposed that the form לְזוּת was vocalized like שְׁבוּת = שְׁבִית, Num. xxi. 29.

Ver. 25. Another rule commends gathering together (concentration) in opposition to dissipation. It is also even externally regarded worthy of consideration, as Ben-Sira, ix. 5, expresses it: μὴ περιβλέπου ἐν ῥύμαις πόλεως — purposeless, curious staring about operates upon the soul, always decentralizing and easily defiling it. But the rule does not exhaust itself in this meaning with reference to external self-discipline; it counsels also straightforward, unswerving directness toward a fixed goal (and what else can this be in such a connection than that which wisdom places before man?), without the turning aside of the eye toward that which is profitless and forbidden, and in this inward sense it falls in with the demand for a single, not squinting eye, Matt. vi. 22, where Bengel explains ἁπλοῦς by *simplex et bonus, intentus in cœlum, in Deum, unice.* נֹכַח (R. נך) means properly fixing, or holding fast with the look, and נֶגֶד (as the Arab. *najad*, to be clear, to be in sight, shows) the rising up which makes the object stand conspicuous before the eyes; both denote here that which lies straight before us, and presents itself to the eye looking straight out. The naming of the עַפְעַפִּים (from עִפְעֵף, to flutter, to move tremblingly), which belongs not to the seeing apparatus of the eye but to its protection, is introduced by the poetical parallelism; for the eyelids, including in this word the twinkling, in their movement follow the direction of the seeing eye. On the form יַישִׁרוּ (fut. *Hiph.* of יָשַׁר, to be straight), defective according to the Masora, with the *Jod* audible, cf. Hos. vii. 12, 1 Chron. xii. 2, and under

Gen. viii. 17; the softened form הַיְשִׁיר does not occur, we find only הֵישִׁיר or הוֹשִׁיר.

Ver. 26. The understanding of this rule is dependent on the right interpretation of פַּלֵּס, which means neither "weigh off" (Ewald) nor "measure off" (Hitzig, Zöckler). פֶּלֶס has once, Ps. lviii. 3, the meaning to weigh out, as the denom. of פֶּלֶס, a level, a steel-yard;[1] everywhere else it means to make even, to make level, to open a road: vid. under Isa. xxvi. 7, xl. 12. The admonition thus refers not to the careful consideration which measures the way leading to the goal which one wishes to reach, but to the preparation of the way by the removal of that which prevents unhindered progress and makes the way insecure. The same meaning appears if פֶּלֶס, of cognate meaning with תִּכֵּן, denoted first to level, and then to make straight with the level (Fleischer). We must remove all that can become a moral hindrance or a dangerous obstacle in our life-course, in order that we may make right steps with our feet, as the LXX. (Heb. xii. 13) translate. 26b is only another expression for this thought. הָכִין דַּרְכּוֹ (2 Chron. xxvii. 6) means to give a direction to his way; a right way, which keeps in and facilitates the keeping in the straight direction, is accordingly called דֶּרֶךְ נָכוֹן; and "let all thy ways be right" (cf. Ps. cxix. 5, LXX. κατευθυνθείησαν) will thus mean: see to it that all the ways which thou goest lead straight to the end.

Ver. 27. In closest connection with the preceding, 27a cautions against by-ways and indirect courses, and 27b continues it in the briefest moral expression, which is here הָסֵר רַגְלְךָ מֵרָע instead of סוּר מֵרָע, iii. 7, for the figure is derived from the way. The LXX. has other four lines after this verse (27), which we have endeavoured to retranslate into the Hebrew (Introd. p. 47). They are by no means genuine; for while in 27a right and left are equivalent to by-ways, here the right and left side are distinguished as that of truth and its contrary; and while there [in LXX.] the ὀρθὰς τροχιὰς ποιεῖν is required of man, here it is promised as the operation of God, which is no contradiction, but in this similarity of expression betrays poverty of style. Hitzig disputes also the genuineness of the Hebrew ver. 27. But it continues explanatorily ver. 26, and is related to it, yet not as a gloss, and in the general

[1] The Arabic word *teflis*, said to be of the same signification (a balance), and which is given in the most recent editions of Gesenius' Lexicon, has been already shown under Job xxxvii. 16 to be a word devoid of all evidence.

relation of 26 and 27*a* there comes a word, certainly not unwelcome, such as 27*b*, which impresses the moral stamp on these
thoughts.

That with ver. 27 the admonition of his father, which the poet,
placing himself back into the period of his youth, reproduces, is
not yet concluded, the resumption of the address בְּנִי, v. 1, makes
evident ; while on the other hand the address בָּנִים in v. 7 shows
that at that point there is advance made from the recollections of
his father's house to conclusions therefrom, for the circle of young
men by whom the poet conceives himself to be surrounded. That
in v. 7 ff. a subject of the warning with which the seventh address
closes is retained and further prosecuted, does not in the connection
of all these addresses contradict the opinion that with v. 7 a new
address begins. But the opinion that the warning against adultery
does not agree (Zöckler) with the designation זָר, iv. 3, given to
him to whom it is addressed, is refuted by 1 Chron. xxii. 5, 2
Chron. xiii. 7.

Chap. v. 1–6. Here a fourth rule of life follows the three already
given, iv. 24, 25, 26–27 :

> 1 My son, attend unto my wisdom,
>   And incline thine ear to my prudence,
> 2 To observe discretion,
>   And that thy lips preserve knowledge.
> 3 For the lips of the adulteress distil honey,
>   And smoother than oil is her mouth ;
> 4 But her end is bitter like wormwood,
>   Sharper than a two-edged sword.
> 5 Her feet go down to death,
>   Her steps cleave to Hades.
> 6 She is far removed from entering the way of life,
>   Her steps wander without her observing it.

Wisdom and understanding increase with the age of those who
earnestly seek after them. It is the father of the youth who here
requests a willing ear to his wisdom of life, gained in the way of
many years' experience and observation. In ver. 2 the inf. of the
object is continued in the *finitum*, as in ii. 2, 8. מְזִמּוֹת (*vid.* on its
etymon under i. 4) are plans, projects, designs, for the most part
in a bad sense, intrigues and artifices (*vid.* xxiv. 8), but also used
of well-considered resolutions toward what is good, and hence of
the purposes of God, Jer. xxiii. 20. This noble sense of the word
מְזִמָּה, with its plur., is peculiar to the introductory portion (i.–ix.)

of the Book of Proverbs. The plur. means here and at viii. 12 (placing itself with חָכְמוֹת and תְּבוּנוֹת, vid. p. 68) the reflection and deliberation which is the presupposition of well-considered action, and שָׁמֹר is thus not otherwise than at xix. 8, and everywhere so meant, where it has that which is obligatory as its object: the youth is summoned to careful observation and persevering exemplification of the *quidquid agas, prudenter agas et respice finem.* In 2b the *Rebia Mugrash* forbids the genitive connection of the two words וְדַעַת שְׂפָתֶיךָ; we translate: *et ut scientiam labia tua tueantur.* Lips which preserve knowledge are such as permit nothing to escape from them (Ps. xvii. 3b) which proceeds not from the knowledge of God, and in Him of that which is good and right, and aims at the working out of this knowledge; *vid.* Köhler on Mal. ii. 7. שְׂפָתֶיךָ (from שָׂפָה, Arab. *shafat,* edge, lip, properly that against which one rubs, and that which rubs itself) is fem., but the usage of the language presents the word in two genders (cf. 3a with xxvi. 23). Regarding the pausal יִנְצֹרוּ for יִצְּרוּ, *vid.* under iii. 1, ii. 11. The lips which distil the honey of enticement stand opposite to the lips which distil knowledge; the object of the admonition is to furnish a protection against the honey-lips.

Ver. 3. זָרָה denotes the wife who belongs to another, or who does not belong to him to whom she gives herself or who goes after her (*vid.* ii. 16). She appears here as the betrayer of youth. The poet paints the love and amiableness which she feigns with colours from the Canticles, iv. 11, cf. v. 16. נֹפֶת denotes the honey flowing of itself from the combs (צוּפִים), thus the purest and sweetest; its root-word is not נוּף, which means to shake, vibrate, and only mediately (when the object is a fluid) to scatter, sprinkle, but, as Schultens has observed, a verb נָפַת = Arab. *nafat,* to bubble, to spring up, *nafath,* to blow, to spit out, to pour out. Parchon places the word rightly under נָפַת (while Kimchi places it under נוּף after the form בֹּשֶׁת), and explains it by חלות דבש היצאים מי הכוורת קודם ריסוק (the words דבש היוצא should have been used): the honey which flows from the cells before they are broken (the so-called virgin honey). The mouth, חֵךְ = Arab. *hink* (from חָנַךְ, Arab. *hanak, imbuere, e.g.,* after the manner of Beduins, the mouth of the newly-born infant with date-honey), comes into view here, as at viii. 7, etc., as the instrument of speech: smoother than oil (cf. Ps. lv. 22), it shows itself when it gives forth amiable, gentle, impressive words (ii. 16, vi. 24); also our "schmeicheln" (= to flatter, caress) is equivalent to to make smooth and fair; in the language of weavers it means to smooth the warp.

Vers. 4, 5. In verse 4 the reverse of the sweet and smooth external is placed opposite to the attraction of the seducer, by whose influence the inconsiderate permits himself to be carried away: her end, *i.e.* the last that is experienced of her, the final consequence of intercourse with her (cf. xxiii. 32), is bitter as wormwood, sharp as a two-edged sword. The O. T. language regards bitterness and poison as related both in meaning and in reality; the word לַעֲנָה (Aq. ἀψίνθιον = wormwood) means in Arab. the curse. חֶרֶב פִּיּוֹת is translated by Jerome after the LXX., *gladius biceps;* but פִּיפִיּוֹת means double-edged, and חֶרֶב שְׁנֵי פִיּוֹת (Judg. iii. 16) means a double-edged sword. Here the plur. will thus poetically strengthen the meaning, like ξίφος πολύστομον, that which devours, as if it had three or four edges (Fl.). The end in which the disguised seduction terminates is bitter as the bitterest, and cutting as that which cuts the most: self-condemnation and a feeling of divine anger, anguish of heart, and destructive judgment. The feet of the adulteress go downward to death. In Hebr. this *descendentes ad mortem* is expressed by the genitive of connection; מָוֶת is the genitive, as in יֹרְדֵי בוֹר, i. 12; elsewhere the author uses יֹרְדוֹת אֶל, vii. 27, ii. 18. Death, מָוֶת (so named from the stretching of the corpse after the stiffness of death), denotes the condition of departure from this side as a punishment, with which is associated the idea of divine wrath. In שְׁאוֹל (sinking, abyss, from שָׁאַל, R. שׁל, χαλᾶν, *vid.* under Isa. v. 14), lie the ideas of the grave as a place of corruption, and of the under-world as the place of incorporeal shadow-life. Her steps hold fast to Hades is equivalent to, they strive after Hades and go straight to it; similar to this is the Arab. expression, *hdhâ âldrb yâkhdh âly âlbld:* this way leads straight forward to the town (Fl.).

Ver. 6. If we try to connect the clause beginning with פֶּן with 5*b* as its principal sentence: she goes straight to the abyss, so that by no means does she ever tread the way of life (thus *e.g.* Schultens), or better, with 6*b*: never more to walk in the way of life, her paths fluctuate hither and thither (as *Gr. Venet.* and Kamphausen in Bunsen's *Bibelwerk,* after Bertheau and Ewald, translate); then in the former case more than in the latter the difference of the subject opposes itself, and in the latter, in addition, the לֹא תֵדַע, only disturbing in this negative clause. Also by the arrangement of the words, 6a appears as an independent thought. But with Jewish expositors (Rashi, Aben-Ezra, Ralbag, Malbim, etc.) to interpret תְּפַלֵּס, after the Talmud (b. Moëd katan 9a) and Midrash, as an address is impracticable; the warning: do not weigh the path of life, affords no meaning suitable to this connection—for we must, with Cartwright and J. H. Michaelis, regard 6a as the antecedent to 6b: ne forte semitam vitæ ad sequendum eligas, te per varios deceptionum mœandros abripit ut non noveris, ubi locorum sis ; but then the continuation of the address is to be expected in 6b. No, the subject to תפלס is the adulteress, and פֶּן is an intensified לֹא. Thus the LXX., Jerome, Syr., Targ., Luther, Geier, Nolde, and among Jewish interpreters Heidenheim, who first broke with the tradition sanctioned by the Talmud and the Midrash, for he interpreted 6a as a negative clause spoken in the tone of a question. But פֶּן is not suitable for a question, but for a call. Accordingly, Böttcher explains: viam vitæ ne illa complanare studeat! (פִּלֵּס in the meaning complanando operam dare). But the adulteress as such, and the striving to come to the way of life, stand in contradiction: an effort to return must be meant, which, because the power of sin over her is too great, fails; but the words do not denote that, they affirm the direct contrary, viz. that it does not happen to the adulteress ever to walk in the way of life. As in the warning the independent פֶּן may be equivalent to cave ne (Job xxxii. 13), so also in the declaration it may be equivalent to absit ut, for פֶּן (from פָּנָה, after the forms פַּ = Arab. banj, עַיִן = Arab. 'asj) means turning away, removal. Thus: Far from taking the course of the way of life (which has life as its goal and reward)—for פִּלֵּס, to open, to open a road (Ps. lxxviii. 50), has here the meaning of the open road itself—much rather do her steps wilfully stagger (Jer. xiv. 10) hither and thither, they go without order and without aim, at one time hither, at another time thither, without her observing it; i.e. without her being concerned at this, that she thereby runs into the danger of falling headlong into the yawning abyss. The unconsciousness which the clause לֹא תֵדָע expresses, has as its object not the falling (Ps. xxxv. 8), of which there is here nothing directly said, but just this staggering, vacillation, the danger of which she does not watch against. נָעוּ has Mercha under the ע with Zinnorith preceding; it is Milra [an oxytone] (Michlol 111b); the punctuation varies in the accentuation of the form without evident reason:

Olsh. § 233, p. 285. The old Jewish interpreters (and recently also Malbim) here, as also at ii. 16, by the זָרָה [strange woman] understand heresy (מינות), or the philosophy that is hostile to revelation; the ancient Christian interpreters understood by it folly (Origen), or sensuality (Procopius), or heresy (Olympiodorus), or false doctrine (Polychronios). The LXX., which translates, ver. 5, רגליה by τῆς ἀφροσύνης οἱ πόδες, looks toward this allegorical interpretation. But this is unnecessary, and it is proved to be false from v. 15–20, where the זָרָה is contrasted with the married wife.

EIGHTH INTRODUCTORY MASHAL DISCOURSE, V. 7–23.

WARNING AGAINST ADULTERY AND COMMENDATION OF MARRIAGE.

With v. 1–6, which like iv. 20 commences it once more, the seventh discourse is brought to a conclusion. The address בְּנִי is three times repeated in similar connections, iv. 10, 20, v. 1. There is no reason for breaking off the fatherly admonition (introduced with the words, "And he said to me," iv. 4), which was addressed to the author in the period of his youth, earlier than here, where the author again resumes the שִׁמְעוּ בָנִים with which he had begun (iv. 1) this seventh narrative address. That after the father has ceased speaking he does not express himself in a rounded manner, may be taken as a sign that toward the end he had become more and more unmindful of the *rôle* of the reporter, if this וְעַתָּה בָנִים following, with which he realizes for his circle of hearers the admonition which had been in part addressed to himself, does not prove the contrary.

Vers. 7–11. The eighth discourse springs out of the conclusion of the seventh, and connects itself by its reflective מֵעָלֶיהָ so closely with it that it appears as its continuation; but the new beginning and its contents included in it, referring only to social life, secures its relative independence. The poet derives the warning against intercourse with the adulteress from the preceding discourse, and grounds it on the destructive consequences.

> 7 And now, ye sons, hearken unto me,
> And depart not from the words of my mouth.

8 Hold thy path far from her neighbourhood,
  And come not to the door of her house !
9 That thou mayest not give the freshness of thy youth to another,
  Nor thy years to the cruel one ;
10 That strangers may not sate themselves with thy possessions,
  And the fruit of thy toils come into the house of a stranger,
11 And thou groanest at the end,
  When thy flesh and thy body are consumed.

Neither here nor in the further stages of this discourse is there any reference to the criminal punishment inflicted on the adulterer, which, according to Lev. xx. 10, consisted in death, according to Ezek. xvi. 40, cf. John viii. 5, in stoning, and according to a later traditional law, in strangulation (חֶנֶק). Ewald finds in ver. 14 a play on this punishment of adultery prescribed by law, and reads from ver. 9 f. that the adulterer who is caught by the injured husband was reduced to the state of a slave, and was usually deprived of his manhood. But that any one should find pleasure in making the destroyer of his wife his slave is a far-fetched idea, and neither the law nor the history of Israel contains any evidence for this punishment by slavery or the mutilation of the adulterer, for which Ewald refers to Grimm's *Deutsche Rechtsaltertümer.* The figure which is here sketched by the poet is very different. He who goes into the net of the wanton woman loses his health and his goods. She stands not alone, but has her party with her, who wholly plunder the simpleton who goes into her trap. Nowhere is there any reference to the husband of the adulteress. The poet does not at all think on a married woman. And the word chosen directs our attention rather to a foreigner than to an Israelitish woman, although the author may look upon harlotry as such as heathenish rather than Israelitish, and designate it accordingly. The party of those who make prostitutes of themselves consists of their relations and their older favourites, the companions of their gain, who being in league with her exhaust the life-strength and the resources of the befooled youth (Fl.). This discourse begins with וְעַתָּה, for it is connected by this concluding application (cf. vii. 24) with the preceding.

Vers. 8, 9. In verse 8, one must think on such as make a gain of their impurity. מֵעַל, Schultens remarks, with reference to Ezek. xxiii. 18, *crebrum in rescisso omni commercio:* מִן denotes the departure, and עַל the nearness, from which one must remove himself to a distance. Regarding הוֹד (ver. 9), which primarily, like our

Pracht (*bracht* from *brechen* = to break) [pomp, magnificence],
appears to mean fulness of sound, and then fulness of splendour,
see under Job xxxix. 20; here there is a reference to the freshness
or the bloom of youth, as well as the years, against the sacrifice of
which the warning is addressed—in a pregnant sense they are the
fairest years, the years of youthful fulness of strength. Along
with אַחֵרִים the *singulare-tantum* אַכְזָרִי (*vid.* Jer. l. 42) has a collective
sense; regarding the root-meaning, *vid.* under Isa. xiii. 9. It is
the *adj. relat.* of אַכְזָר after the form אַכְזָב, which is formed not
from אַף זָר, but from an unknown verb כָּזַר. The ancients referred
it to death and the devil; but the אכזרי belongs to the covetous
society, which impels ever anew to sin, which is their profit, him
who has once fallen into it, and thus brings bodily ruin upon him:
they are the people who stand far aloof from this their sacrifice,
and among them are barbarous, rude, inexorably cruel monsters
(*Unmenschen*) (*Græcus Venetus*, τῷ ἀπανθρώπῳ), who rest not till
their victim is laid prostrate on the ground and ruined both bodily
and financially.

Ver. 10. This other side of the ruin ver. 10 presents as an image
of terror. For הוֹד refers to the person in his stately appearance,
but כֹּחַ to his possessions in money and goods; for this word, as well
as in the strikingly similar passage Hos. vii. 9, is used as the
synonym of חַיִל (Gen. xxxiv. 29, etc.), in the sense of ability,
estate. This meaning is probably mediated by means of a meto-
nymy, as Gen. iv. 12, Job xxxi. 39, where the idea of the capability
of producing is passed over into that of the produce conformable
to it; so here the idea of work-power passes over into that of the
gain resulting therefrom. וַעֲצָבֶיךָ (and thy toils) is not, like כֹּחֶךָ,
the accusative governed by יִשְׂבְּעוּ; the carrying over of this verb
disturbs the parallelism, and the statement in the passage besides
does not accord therewith, which, interpreted as a virtual predicate, presents 10*b* as an independent prohibitive clause: *neve sint
labores tui in domo peregrini*, not *peregrina;* at least נָכְרִי according
to the usage of the language is always personal, so that בֵּית נָכְרִי
(cf. Lam. v. 2), like מַלְבּוּשׁ נכרי, Zeph. i. 8, is to be explained after
עִיר נָכְרִי, Judg. xix. 12. עֶצֶב (from עָצַב, Arab. 'asab, to bind fast,
to tie together, then to make effort, ποιεῖν, *laborare*) is difficult
work (x. 22), and that which is obtained by it; Fleischer compares
the Ital. *i miei sudori*, and the French *mes sueurs*.

Ver. 11. The fut. יִשְׂבְּעוּ and the יְהִי needed to complete 10*b* are continued in ver. 11 in the *consec. perf.* נָהַם, elsewhere of the hollow roaring of the sea, Isa. v. 30, the growling of the lion, xxviii. 15, here, as also Ezek. xxiv. 23, of the hollow groaning of men; a word which echoes the natural sound, like הוּם, הָמָה. The LXX., with the versions derived from it, has καὶ μεταμεληθήσῃ, *i.e.* וְנִחַמְתָּ (the *Niph.* נִחַם, to experience the sorrow of repentance, also an echo-word which imitates the sound of deep breathing)—a happy *quid pro quo*, as if one interchanged the Arab. *naham, fremere, anhelare,* and *nadam, pœnitere.* That wherein the end consists to which the deluded youth is brought, and the sorrowful sound of despair extorted from him, is stated in 11*b*: his flesh is consumed away, for sensuality and vexation have worked together to undermine his health. The author here connects together two synonyms to strengthen the conception, as if one said: All thy tears and thy weeping help thee nothing (Fl.); he loves this heaping together of synonyms, as we have shown at p. 33. When the blood-relation of any one is called שְׁאֵר בְּשָׂרוֹ, Lev. xviii. 6, xxv. 49, these two synonyms show themselves in subordination, as here in close relation. שְׁאֵר appears to be closely connected with שְׁרִירִים, muscles and sinews, and with שֹׁר, the umbilical cord, and thus to denote the flesh with respect to its muscular nature adhering to the bones (Mic. iii. 2), as בָּשָׂר denotes it with respect to its tangible outside clothed with skin (*vid.* under *Isaiah,* p. 418).

Vers. 12–14. The poet now tells those whom he warns to hear how the voluptuary, looking back on his life-course, passes sentence against himself.

> 12 And thou sayest, "Why have I then hated correction,
> And my heart despised instruction!
> 13 And I have not listened to the voice of my teachers,
> Nor lent mine ear to my instructors?
> 14 I had almost fallen into every vice
> In the midst of the assembly and the congregation!"

The question 12*a* (here more an exclamation than a question) is the combination of two: How has it become possible for me? How could it ever come to it that . . . Thus also one says in Arab.: *Kyf f'alat hadhâ* (Fl.). The regimen of אֵיךְ in 12*b* is becoming faint, and in 13*b* has disappeared. The *Kal* נָאַץ (as i. 30, xv. 5) signifies to despise; the *Piel* intensively, to contemn and reject (R. נץ, *pungere*).

Ver. 13. שָׁמַע בְּ signifies to cleave to anything in hearing, as

רָאָה בְ is to do so in seeing; שָׁמַע לְ yet more closely corresponds with the classic ἐπακούειν, obedire, e.g. Ps. lxxxi. 9; שָׁמַע בְּקוֹל is the usual phrase for "hearken!"

Ver. 14. כִּמְעַט with the perf. following is equivalent to: it wanted but a little that this or that should happen, e.g. Gen. xxvi. 10. It is now for the most part thus explained : it wanted but a little, and led astray by that wicked companionship I would have been drawn away into crime, for which I would then have been subjected to open punishment (Fl.). Ewald understands רָע directly of punishment in its extreme form, stoning; and Hitzig explains כָּל־רָע by "the totality of evil," in so far as the disgraceful death of the criminal comprehends in it all other evils that are less. But בְּכָל־רָע means, either, into every evil, misfortune, or into every wickedness; and since רָע, in contradistinction to לב (Hitzig compares Ezek. xxxvi. 5), is a conception of a species, then the meaning is equivalent to in omni genere mali. The reference to the death-punishment of the adulteress is excluded thereby, though it cannot be denied that it might be thought of at the same time, if he who too late comes to consider his ways were distinctly designated in the preceding statements as an adulterer. But it is on the whole a question whether בכל־רע is meant of the evil which follows sin as its consequence. The usage of the language permits this, cf. 2 Sam. xvi. 8, Ex. v. 19, 1 Chron. vii. 23, Ps. x. 6, but not less the reference to that which is morally bad, cf. Ex. xxxii. 22 (where Keil rightly compares with 1 John v. 19); and הָיִיתִי (for which in the first case one expected נָפַלְתִּי, I fell into, vid. xiii. 17, xvii. 20, xxviii. 14) is even more favourable to the latter reference. Also בְּתוֹךְ קָהָל וְעֵדָה (cf. on the heaping together of synonyms under 11b), this paraphrase of the palam ac publice, with its בְּתוֹךְ (cf. Ps. cxi. 1, 2 Chron. xx. 14), looks rather to a heightening of the moral self-accusation. He found himself in all wickedness, living and moving therein in the midst of the congregation, and thereby giving offence to it, for he took part in the external worship and in the practices of the congregation, branding himself thereby as a hypocrite. That by the one name the congregation is meant in its civil aspect, and by the other in its ecclesiastical aspect, is not to be supposed : in the congregation of the people of the revealed law, the political and the religious sides are not so distinguished. It is called without distinction קָהָל and עֵדָה (from יָעַד). Rather we would say that קהל is the whole ecclesia, and עדה the whole of its representatives; but also the great general council bears sometimes the one name (Ex. xii. 3, cf. 21) and sometimes the other (Deut. xxxi. 30, cf. 28) —the placing of them together serves thus only to strengthen the conception.

Vers. 15–17. The commendation of true conjugal love in the form of an invitation to a participation in it, is now presented along with the warning against non-conjugal intercourse, heightened by a reference to its evil consequences.

> 15 Drink water from thine own cistern,
>   And flowing streams from thine own fountain.
> 16 Shall thy streams flow abroad,
>   The water-brooks in the streets!
> 17 Let them belong to thyself alone,
>   And not to strangers with thee.

One drinks water to quench his thirst; here drinking is a figure of the satisfaction of conjugal love, of which Paul says, 1 Cor. vii. 9, κρεῖσσόν ἐστι γαμῆσαι ἢ πυροῦσθαι, and this comes into view here, in conformity with the prevailing character of the O. T., only as a created inborn natural impulse, without reference to the poisoning of it by sin, which also within the sphere of married life makes government, moderation, and restraint a duty. Warning against this degeneracy of the natural impulse to the πάθος ἐπιθυμίας authorized within divinely prescribed limits, the apostle calls the wife of any one τὸ ἑαυτοῦ σκεῦος (cf. 1 Pet. iii. 7). So here the wife, who is his by covenant (ii. 17), is called "cistern" (בּוֹר)[1] and "fountain" (בְּאֵר) of the husband to whom she is married. The figure corresponds to the sexual nature of the wife, the expression for which is נְקֵבָה; but Isa. li. 1 holds to the natural side of the figure, for according to it the wife is a pit, and the children are brought out of it into the light of day. Aben-Ezra on Lev. xi. 36 rightly distinguishes between בור and באר: the former catches the rain, the latter wells out from within. In the former, as Rashi in *Erubin* ii. 4 remarks, there are מים מכונסים, in the latter מים חיים. The post-biblical Hebrew observes this distinction less closely (*vid.* Kimchi's *Book of Roots*), but the biblical throughout; so far the *Keri*, Jer. vi. 7, rightly changes בור into the form בַּיִר, corresponding to the Arab. *byar*. Therefore בור is the cistern, for the making of which חָצֵב, Jer. ii. 13, and באר the well, for the formation of which

---

[1] The LXX. translate ἀπὸ σῶν ἀγγείων, *i.e.* מְבּוּרֶיךָ (*vid.* Lagarde).

חפר, Gen. xxi. 30, and ברה, xxvi. 25, are the respective words usually employed (*vid.* Malbim, *Sifra* 117*b*). The poet shows that he also is aware of this distinction, for he calls the water which one drinks from the בור by the name מים, but on the other hand that out of the באר by the name נוֹזְלִים, running waters, *fluenta;* by this we are at once reminded of Cant. iv. 15, cf. 12. The בור offers only stagnant water (according to the *Sohar,* the בור has no water of its own, but only that which is received into it), although coming down into it from above; but the באר has living water, which wells up out of its interior (מִתּוֹךְ, 15*b*, intentionally for the mere מן), and is fresh as the streams from Lebanon (נֵל, properly *labi,* to run down, cf. אָזַל, *placide ire,* and generally *ire;* زال, *loco cedere, desinere;* زل, IV., to cause to glide back, *deglutire,* of the gourmand). What a valuable possession a well of water is for nomads the history of the patriarchs makes evident, and a cistern is one of the most valuable possessions belonging to every well-furnished house. The figure of the cistern is here surpassed by that of the fountain, but both refer to the seeking and finding satisfaction (cf. the opposite passage, xxiii. 27) with the wife, and that, as the expressive possessive suffixes denote, with his legitimate wife.

Ver. 16. Here we meet with two other synonyms standing in a similar relation of progression. As עַיִן denotes the fountain as to its point of outflow, so מַעְיָן (*n. loci*) means water flowing above on the surface, which in its course increases and divides itself into several courses; such a brook is called, with reference to the water dividing itself from the point of outflow, or to the way in which it divides, פֶּלֶג (from פָּלַג, Job xxxviii. 25), Arab. *falǵ* (as also the Ethiop.) or *falj,* which is explained by *nahar saghayr* (Fl.).[1] We cannot in this double figure think of any reference to the generative power in the *sperma;* similar figures are the waters of Judah, Isa. xlviii. 1, and the waters of Israel flowing forth as if from a bucket, Num. xxiv. 7, where זרע is the parallel word to מים, cf. also the proper name מוֹאָב (from מוֹ = מוֹי from מָוָה, *diffluere*), *aqua h.e. semen patris,* and שָׁגֵל, Deut. xxviii. 30, = Arab. *sajal* (whence *sajl* = דְּלִי, *situla*), which is set aside by the *Kerî.* Many interpreters

---

[1] The latter idea (*vid.* under Ps. i. 3) lies nearer, after Job xxxviii. 25: the brook as dividing channels for itself, or as divided into such; *falǵ* (*falaj*) signifies, according to the representation Isa. lviii. 8, also like *fajr,* the morning-light (as breaking forth from a cleft).

have by חוּצָה and בָּרְחֹבוֹת been here led into the error of pressing into the text the exhortation not to waste the creative power in sinful lust. The LXX. translates יָפֻצוּ by ὑπερεκχείσθω; but Origen, and also Clemens Alexandrinus, used the phrase μὴ ὑπερεκχείσθω, which is found in the Complut., Ald., and several codd., and is regarded by Lagarde, as also Cappellus, as original: the three Göttingen theologians (Ewald, Bertheau, and Elster) accordingly make the emendation אַל־יָפֻצוּ. But that μή of the LXX. was not added till a later period; the original expression, which the Syro-Hexapl. authorizes, was ὑπερεκχείσθω without μή, as also in the version of Aquila, διασκορπιζέσθωσαν without μή (vid. Field). The Hebrew text also does not need אל. Clericus, and recently Hitzig, Zöckler, Kamphausen, avoid this remedy, for they understand this verse interrogatively—an expedient which is for the most part and also here unavailing; for why should not the author have written אִם יפצו? Schultens rightly remarks: nec negationi nec interrogationi ullus hic locus, for (with Fleischer and von Hofmann, Schriftbeweis, ii. 2, 402) he regards ver. 16 as a conclusion: tunc exundabunt; so that he strengthens the summons of ver. 15 by the promise of numerous descendants from unviolated marriage. But to be so understood, the author ought to have written וִיפֻצוּ. So, according to the text, יפצו as jussive continues the imper. שְׁתֵה (15a), and the full meaning according to the connection is this: that within the marriage relation the generative power shall act freely and unrestrained. חוּץ and רְחֹבוֹת denote (i. 20) the space free from houses, and the ways and places which lead towards and stretch between them; חוץ (from חוץ, Arab. khass, to split, seorsim ponere) is a very relative conception, according as one thinks of that which is without as the contrast of the house, the city, or the country. Here חוץ is the contrast of the person, and thus that which is anywhere without it, whereto the exercise of its manly power shall extend. The two figurative expressions are the description of the libero flumine, and the contrast, that restriction of self which the marriage relation, according to 1 Cor. vii. 3–5, condemns.

Ver. 17. That such matters as these are thought of, is manifest from this verse. As זרע comprehends with the cause (sperma) the effect (posterity), so, in ver. 16, with the effusio roboris virilis is connected the idea of the beginnings of life. For the subjects of ver. 17 are the effusiones seminis named in ver. 16. These in their

effects (ver. 17) may belong to thee alone, viz. to thee alone
(לְבַדֶּךָ, properly in thy separateness) within thy married relation,
not, as thou hast fellowship with other women, to different family
circles, Aben-Ezra rightly regards as the subject, for he glosses
thus : הַפְּלָגִים שֶׁהֵם הַבָּנִים הַכְּשֵׁרִים, and Immanuel well explains יִהְיוּ־לְךָ
by יִתְיַחֲסוּ לְךָ. The child born out of wedlock belongs not to the
father alone, he knows not to whom it belongs; its father must for
the sake of his honour deny it before the world. Thus, as Grotius
remarks : *ibi sere ubi prolem metas.* In וְאֵין the יהיו is continued.
It is not thus used adverbially for לֹא, as in the old classic Arabic
lyas for *l'* (Fl.), but it carries in it the force of a verb, so that יהיו,
according to rule, in the sense of וְלֹא יִהְיוּ = וְלֹא הָיוּ, continues it.

Vers. 18-20. With ver 18 is introduced anew the praise of
conjugal love. These three verses, 18-21, have the same course
of thought as 15-17.

> 18 Let thy fountain be blessed,
>   And rejoice in the wife of thy youth.
> 19 The lovely hind and the graceful gazelle—
>   May her bosom always charm thee;
>   In her love mayest thou delight thyself evermore.
> 20 But why wilt thou be fascinated with a stranger,
>   And embrace the bosom of a foreign woman?

Like בּוֹר and בְּאֵר, מָקוֹר is also a figure of the wife; the root-word is
קוּר, from כר, קר, the meanings of which, to dig and make round,
come together in the primary conception of the round digging out
or boring out, not קוּר = קָרַר, the *Hiph.* of which means (Jer. vi. 7)
to well out cold (water). It is the fountain of the birth that is
meant (cf. מָקוֹר of the female עֶרְוָה, *e.g.,* Lev. xx. 18), not the pro-
creation (LXX., ἡ σὴ φλέψ, viz. φλὲψ γονίμη); the blessing
wished for by him is the blessing of children, which בָּרוּךְ so much
the more distinctly denotes if בָּרַךְ, Arab. *barak,* means to spread
out, and בֵּרֵךְ thus to cause a spreading out. The מִן, 18*b*, explains
itself from the idea of drawing (water), given with the figure of a
fountain; the word בְּאִשָּׁה found in certain codices is, on the contrary,
prosaic (Fl.). Whilst שָׂמַח מִן is found elsewhere (Eccles. ii. 20,
2 Chron. xx. 27) as meaning almost the same as שָׂמַח בְּ; the former
means rejoicing from some place, the latter in something. In the
genitive connection, " wife of thy youth " (cf. ii. 17), both of these
significations lie : thy youthful wife, and she who was chosen by
thee in thy youth, according as we refer the suffix to the whole
idea or only to the second member of the chain of words.

Ver. 19. The subject, 19a, set forth as a theme courts love for her who is to be loved, for she presents herself as lovely. אַיֶּלֶת is the female of the stag, which may derive its name אַיָּל from the weapon-power of its horns, and יַעֲלָה (from יָעַל, Arab. *w'al*, to climb), that of the wild-goat (יָעֵל); and thus properly, not the gazelle, which is called צְבִי on account of its elegance, but the chamois. These animals are commonly used in Semitic poetry as figures of female beauty on account of the delicate beauty of their limbs and their sprightly black eyes. אֲהָבִים signifies always sensual love, and is interchanged in this erotic meaning (vii. 18) with דּוֹדִים. In 19b the predicate follows the subject. The *Græc. Venet.* translates as if the word were דּוֹדֶיהָ, and the *Syr.* as if it were דרכיה, but Aquila rightly translates τίτθοι αὐτῆς. As τίτθος is derived (*vid.* Curtius, *Griech. Etymologie*, Nr. 307) from *dhâ*, to suck (causative, with *anu*, to put to sucking), so דַּד, שַׁד, תַּד, Arab. *thady* (commonly in dual *thadjein*), from שָׁדָה, Arab. *thdy*, *rigare*, after which also the verb יְרַוֻּךָ is chosen: she may plentifully give thee to drink; figuratively equivalent to, refresh or (what the Aram. רַוִּי precisely means) fascinate[1] thee, satisfy thee with love. דַּדִּים also is an erotic word, which besides in this place is found only in Ezekiel (xxiii. 3, 8, 21). The LXX. obliterates the strong sensual colouring of this line. In 19c it changes תִּשְׁגֶּה into חשגה, πολλοστὸς ἔσῃ, perhaps also because the former appeared to be too sensual. Moses ha-Darshan (in Rashi) proposes to explain it after the Arab. ساكى, to cover, to cast over, to come over anything (III. = עסק, to employ oneself with something): engage thyself with her love, *i.e.* be always devoted to her in love. And Immanuel himself, the author of a Hebrew Divan expatiating with unparalleled freedom in erotic representations, remarks, while he rightly understands חשגה of the fascination of love: קורא התמדת חשקו אפילו באשתו שגגה, he calls the husband's continual caressing of the wife an error. But this moral side-glance lies here at a distance from the poet. He speaks here of a morally permissible love-ecstasy, or rather, since תמיר excludes that which is extraordinary, of an intensity of love connected with the feeling of superabundant happiness. שָׁגָה properly signifies to err from the way, therefore figuratively, with בְ of a matter, like

---

[1] Many editions have here בְּבַל־; but this *Dagesh*, which is contrary to rule, is to be effaced.

delirare ea, to be wholly captivated by her, so that one is no longer in his own power, can no longer restrain himself—the usual word for the intoxication of love and of wine, xx. 1 (Fl.).

Ver. 20. The answer to the Why? in this verse is: no reasonable cause,—only beastly sensuality, only flagitious blindness can mislead thee. The ב of בְּזָרָה is, as 19*b* and Isa. xxviii. 7, that of the object through which one is betrayed into intoxication. חֵק (thus, according to the Masora, four times in the O. T. for חֵיק) properly means an incision or deepening, as חֵק (from חֵק, *cohibere*), the front of the body, the part between the arms or the female breasts, thus the bosom, Isa. xl. 11 (with the swelling part of the clothing, *sinus vestis*, which the Arabs call *jayb*), and the lap; חִבֵּק (as iv. 8), to embrace, corresponds here more closely with the former of these meanings; also elsewhere the wife of any one is called אשת חיקו or השכבת בחיקו, as she who rests on his breast. The ancients, also J. H. Michaelis, interpret vers. 15–20 allegorically, but without thereby removing sensual traces from the elevated N. T. consciousness of pollution, striving against all that is fleshly; for the *castum cum Sapientia conjugium* would still be always represented under the figure of husband and wife dwelling together. Besides, though זרה might be, as the contrast of חבמה, the personified lust of the world and of the flesh, yet 19*a* is certainly not the חבמה, but a woman composed of flesh and blood. Thus the poet means the married life, not in a figurative sense, but in its reality—he designedly describes it thus attractively and purely, because it bears in itself the preservative against promiscuous fleshly lust.

Vers. 21–23. That the intercourse of the sexes out of the married relationship is the commencement of the ruin of a fool is now proved.

> 21 For the ways of every one are before the eyes of Jahve,
> And all his paths He marketh out.
> 22 His own sins lay hold of him, the evil-doer,
> And in the bands of his sins is he held fast.
> 23 He dies for the want of correction,
> And in the fulness of his folly he staggers to ruin.

It is unnecessary to interpret נכח as an adverbial accusative: straight before Jahve's eyes; it may be the nominative of the predicate: the ways of man (for אִישׁ is here an individual, whether man or woman) are an object (properly, fixing) of the eyes of Jahve. With this the thought would suitably connect itself: *et omnes orbitas ejus ad amussim examinat;* but פֶּלֶס, as the denom. of פֶּלֶס, Ps. lviii. 3, is not connected with all the places where the verb is united with the obj. of the way, and Ps. lxxviii. 50 shows that it has there the meaning to break through, to open a way (from פל, to split, cf. Talmudic מְפֻלָּשׁ, opened, accessible, from פלשׁ, ܦܠܰܫ, *perfodere, fodiendo viam, aditum sibi aperire*). The opening of the way is here not, as at Isa. xxvi. 7, conceived of as the setting aside of the hindrances in the way of him who walks, but generally as making walking in the way possible: man can take no step in any direction without God; and that not only does not exempt him from moral responsibility, but the consciousness of this is rather for the first time rightly quickened by the consciousness of being encompassed on every side by the knowledge and the power of God. The dissuasion of ver. 20 is thus in ver. 21 grounded in the fact, that man at every stage and step of his journey is observed and encompassed by God: it is impossible for him to escape from the knowledge of God or from dependence on Him. Thus opening all the paths of man, He has also appointed to the way of sin the punishment with which it corrects itself: "his sins lay hold of him, the evil-doer." The suffix יו‎— does not refer to אִישׁ of ver. 21, where every one without exception and without distinction is meant, but it relates to the obj. following, the evil-doer, namely, as the explanatory permutative annexed to the "him" according to the scheme, Ex. ii. 6; the permutative is distinguished from the apposition by this, that the latter is a forethought explanation which heightens the understanding of the subject, while the former is an explanation afterwards brought in which guards against a misunderstanding. The same construction, xiv. 13b, belonging to the *syntaxis ornata* in the old Hebrew, has become common in the Aramaic and in the modern Hebrew. Instead of יִלְכְּדֻהוּ (ver. 22), the poet uses poetically יִלְכְּדֻנוֹ; the interposed ‍נ may belong to the emphatic ground-form יִלְכְּדוּן, but is epenthetic if one compares forms such as קָבְנוֹ (R. קב), Num. xxiii. 13 (cf. p. 73). The חַטֹּאתוֹ governed by חַבְלֵי, *laquei* (חֶבְלֵי, *tormina*), is either *gen. exeg.:* bands which consist in his sin, or *gen. subj.:* bands which his sin unites, or better, *gen. possess.:* bands which his sin brings with it. By these bands he will be held fast, and so will die: he (הוּא referring to the person described) will die in insubordination (Symm. δι'

ἀπαιδευσίαν), or better, since אֱיִן and רֹב are placed in contrast: in
want of correction. With the יִשְׁגֶּה (ver. 23b), repeated purposely
from ver. 20, there is connected the idea of the overthrow which
is certain to overtake the infatuated man. In ver. 20 the sense
of moral error began already to connect itself with this verb.
אִוֶּלֶת is the right name of unrestrained lust of the flesh. אולת is
connected with אֻגּל, the belly; אוּל, Arab. *âl*, to draw together, to
condense, to thicken (*Isaiah*, p. 424). *Dummheit* (stupidity) and
the Old-Norse *dumba*, darkness, are in their roots related to each
other. Also in the Semitic the words for blackness and darkness
are derived from roots meaning condensation. אֱויל is the mind
made thick, darkened, and become like crude matter.

NINTH INTRODUCTORY MASHAL DISCOURSE, VI. 1–5.

WARNING AGAINST INCONSIDERATE SURETYSHIP.

The author does not return to the subject of chastity till the
twelfth discourse, vi. 20 ff. Between the eighth and the twelfth
three other groups of moral proverbs are introduced, which are
neither connected with one another nor with the eight discourses
which precede them. Must we therefore, with Hitzig and Kamphausen, hold vi. 1–5, 6–11, 12–19, to be an interpolation here
introduced from some other place? We find here the fondness
for synonyms and words similar in sound peculiar to the author of
the introduction, vi. 2, 3, 5, and meet with the same interchange of
words, vi. 4, cf. iv. 25, and figurative expressions, vi. 18, cf. iii. 29
(חרש), word-formations, vi. 10 (חִבֻּק), cf. iii. 8 (שִׁקּוּי), ideas, vi. 12,
cf. iv. 28 (עקשות פה), vi. 14, cf. ii. 12, 14 (תהפכות), and constructions,
vi. 12 (הולך עקשות פה), cf. ii. 7 (הלכי תם); like delineations of character, vi. 18b, cf. i. 16, and threatenings, vi. 15, cf. i. 26 f., iii. 25—as
many marks of identity of the authorship as could be expected.
And what had moved the interpolators to introduce the three
groups of proverbs, vi. 1–5, 6–11, 12–19, just here? In vain
does Hitzig seek to extract from chap. v. certain words and ideas
common to it with chap. vi. which shall make it clear that the
groups of proverbs in question are here an interpolation; the points
of contrast are not prominent. If now the poet has already in iii.

1-18, but still more in iii. 27 ff., connected together all manner of rules of life without any close or visible connection, it is not strange if at vi. 1, where besides the בני denotes the new section, he breaks off to a new subject out of the fulness of his matter; and the connection wanting between vi. 1 and v. 23, as well as between iii. 27 and iii. 26, does not therefore warrant critical suspicion.

Vers. 1-5. The author warns against suretyship; or rather, he advises that if one has made himself surety, he should as quickly as possible withdraw from the snare.

> 1 My son, if thou hast become surety for thy neighbour,
>   Hast given thy hand for another :
> 2 Thou art entangled in the words of thy mouth,
>   Ensnared in the words of thy mouth.
> 3 Do this then, my son, and free thyself—
>   For thou hast come under the power of thy neighbour—
>   Go, instantly entreat and importune thy neighbour.
> 4 Give no sleep to thine eyes,
>   And no slumber to thine eyelids ;
> 5 Tear thyself free like a gazelle from his hand,
>   And as a bird from the hand of the fowler.

The chief question here is, whether ל after עָרַב introduces him for whom or with whom one becomes surety. Elsewhere עַרב (R. רב, whence also אָרַב, *nectere*, to twist close and compact) with the accusative of the person means to become surety for any one, to represent him as a surety, xi. 15, xx. 16 (xxvii. 13), Gen. xliii. 9, xliv. 33 (as with the accusative of the matter, to pledge anything, to deposit it as a pledge, Jer. xxx. 21, Neh. v. 3, = שִׂים, Arab. *wad'a*, Job xvii. 3); and to become surety with any one is expressed, xvii. 18, by עָרב לִפְנֵי. The phrase עַרב ל is not elsewhere met with, and is thus questionable. If we look to ver. 3, the רֵעַ (רֵעֶה) mentioned there cannot possibly be the creditor with whom one has become surety, for so impetuous and urgent an application to him would be both purposeless and unbecoming. But if he is meant for whom one has become surety, then certainly לְרֵעֶךָ is also to be understood of the same person, and ל is thus *dat. commodi;* similar to this is the Targumic עֲרַבוּתָא עַל, suretyship for any one, xvii. 18, xxii. 26. But is the זָר, 1*b*, distinguished from רֵע, the stranger with whom one has become surety? The parallels xi. 15, xx. 16, where זר denotes the person whom one represents, show that in both lines one and the same person is meant; זר is in the Proverbs equivalent to אַחֵר, each different from the person in the discourse, v. 17, xxvii. 2,—thus, like רֵעַ, denotes not the friend, but generally him to whom one stands in any kind of relation, even a very external one, in a word, the fellow-creatures or neighbours, xxiv. 28 (cf. the Arab. *sahbk* and *karynk*, which are used as vaguely and superficially). It is further a question, whether we have to explain 1*b* : if thou hast given thine hand to another, or for another. Here also we are without evidence from the usage of the language; for the phrase תָּקַע כַּף, or merely תָּקַע, appears to be used of striking the hand in suretyship where it elsewhere occurs without any further addition, xvii. 18, xxii. 26, xi. 15; however, Job xvii. 3, נִתְקַע לְיָד appears the same : to strike into the hand of any one, *i.e.* to give to him the hand-stroke. From this passage Hitzig concludes that the surety gave the hand-stroke, without doubt in the presence of witnesses, first of all of the creditor, to the debtor, as a sign that he stood for him. But this idea is unnatural, and the "without doubt" melts into air. He on whose hand the stroke falls is always the person to whom one gives suretyship, and confirms it by the hand-stroke. Job also, *l.c.*, means to say : who else but Thou, O Lord, could give to me a pledge, viz. of my innocence? If now the זֵר, ver. 1*b*, is, as we have shown, not the creditor,[1] but the debtor, then is the לְ the *dat. commodi*, as 1*a*, and the two lines perfectly correspond. תָּקַע properly means to drive, to strike with a resounding noise, cogn. with the Arab. *wak'a*, which may be regarded as its *intrans.* (Fl.); then particularly to strike the hand or with the hand. He to whom this hand-pledge is given for another remains here undesignated. A new question arises, whether in ver. 6, where נוֹקַשׁ (*illaqueari*) and נִלְכַּד (*comprehendi*) follow each other as Isa. viii. 15, cf. Jer. l. 24, the hypothetical antecedent is continued or not. We agree with Schultens, Ziegler, and Fleischer against the continuance of the אִם. The repetition of the בְּאִמְרֵי פִיךָ (cf. ii. 14) serves rightly to strengthen the representation of the thought: thou, thou thyself and no other, hast then ensnared thyself in the net; but this strengthening of the expression would greatly lose in force

---

[1] A translation by R. Joseph Joel of Fulda, 1787, whose autograph MS. Baer possesses, renders the passage not badly thus :—" My son, if thou hast become surety for thy friend, and hast given the hand to another, then thou art bound by thy word, held by thy promise. Yet do what I say to thee, my son: Be at pains as soon as thou canst to get free, otherwise thou art in the power of thy friend; shun no trouble, be urgent with thy friend."

by placing ver. 2 in the antecedent, while if ver. 2 is regarded as the conclusion, and thus as the principal proposition, it appears in its full strength.

Ver. 3. The new commencement needs no particle denoting a conclusion; the אֵפוֹא, making the summons emphatic (cf. 2 Kings x. 10, frequently in interrogative clauses), connects it closely enough. זֹאת, *neut.*, refers to what follows. The וְ before הִנָּצֵל is explanatory, as we say in familiar language: Be so good as tell me, or do me the favour to come with me; while no Frenchman would say, *Faites-moi le (ce) plaisir et venez avec moi* (Fl.).[1] The clause כִּי בָאתָ [2] is not to be translated: in case thou art fallen into the hand of thy neighbour; for this is represented (vers. 1, 2) as having already in fact happened. On two sides the surety is no longer *sui juris:* the creditor has him in his hand; for if the debtor does not pay, he holds the surety, and in this way many an honourable man has lost house and goods, Sirach xxix. 18, cf. viii. 13;—and the debtor has him, the surety, in his hand; for the performance which is due, for which the suretyship avails, depends on his conscientiousness. The latter is here meant: thou hast made thy freedom and thy possessions dependent on the will of thy neighbour for whom thou art the surety. The clause introduced with כִּי gives the reason for the call to set himself free (הִנָּצֵל from נצל, R. צל, של, to draw out or off); it is a parenthetical sentence. The meaning of הִתְרַפֵּס is certain. The verb רָפַס (רָפַשׂ, רָפַס) signifies to stamp on, *calcare, conculcare;* the *Kamûs*[3] explains *rafas* by *rakad balarjal.* The *Hithpa.* might, it is true, mean to conduct oneself in a trampling manner, to tread roughly, as הִתְנַבֵּא, and the medial *Niph.* נִבָּא, to conduct oneself speaking (in an impassioned manner); but Ps. lxviii. 31 and the analogy of הִתְבּוֹסֵס favour the meaning to throw oneself in a stamping manner, *i.e.* violently, to the ground, to trample upon oneself,—*i.e.* let oneself be trampled upon, to place oneself in the attitude of most earnest humble prayer. Thus the *Græc. Venet.*

[1] For the right succession of the accents here (three serviles before the *Pazer*), *vid. Torath Emeth*, p. 30; *Accentuationssystem*, xii. § 4. According to Ben-Naphtali, *Mercha* is to be given to the זֹאת.

[2] The *Zinnorith* before the *Mahpach* in these words represents at the same time the *Makkeph*. But Ben-Naphtali differs here from Ben-Asher, for he adopts the *Makkeph* and rejects the *Zinnorith; vid. Torath Emeth*, p. 16, and my *Psalmencomm.* Bd. ii. (1860), p. 460, note 2.

[3] [El-Feyroozábádee's *Kâmus*, a native Arabic Lexicon; *vid.* Lane's *Arab. Lex.* Bk. i. pt. 1, p. xvii.]

πατήθητι, Rashi (" humble thyself like to the threshold which is trampled and trode upon"), Aben-Ezra, Immanuel ("humble thyself under the soles of his feet"); so Cocceius, J. H. Michaelis, and others: *conculcandum te præbe.* וּרְהַב is more controverted. The Talmudic-Midrash explanation (*b. Joma,* 87*a*; *Bathra,* 173*b*, and elsewhere): take with thee in great numbers thy friends (רְהַב = הַרְבֵּה), is discredited by this, that it has along with it the explanation of התרפס by (יד) חַתֵּר פַּס, *solve palmam* (*manus*), *i.e.* pay what thou canst. Also with the meaning to rule (Parchon, Immanuel), which רהב besides has not, nothing is to be done. The right meaning of רְהַב בְּ is to rush upon one boisterously, Isa. iii. 5. רָהַב means in general to be violently excited (Arab. *rahiba*, to be afraid), and thus to meet one, here with the accusative: assail impetuously thy neighbour (viz. that he fulfil his engagement). Accordingly, with a choice of words more or less suitable, the LXX. translates by παρόξυνε, Symm., Theodotion by παρόρμησον, the *Græc. Venet.* by ἐνίσχυσον, the Syr. (which the Targumist copies) by גרג (*solicita*), and Kimchi glosses by: lay an arrest upon him with pacifying words. The Talmud explains רֵעֶיךָ as plur.;[1] but the plur., which was permissible in iii. 28, is here wholly inadmissible: it is thus the *plena scriptio* for רֵעֶךָ with the retaining of the third radical of the ground-form of the root-word (רָעָה = רָעַ'), or with י as *mater lectionis*, to distinguish the pausal-form from that which is without the pause; cf. xxiv. 34. LXX., Syr., Jerome, etc., rightly translate it in the sing. The immediateness lying in לְ (cf. ὕπαγε, Matt. v. 24) is now expressed as a duty, ver. 4 f. One must not sleep and slumber (an expression quite like Ps. cxxxii. 4), not give himself quietness and rest, till the other has released him from his bail by the performance of that for which he is surety. One must set himself free as a gazelle or as a bird, being caught, seeks to disentangle itself by calling forth all its strength and art.

Ver. 5. The naked מִיָּד is not to be translated " immediately ;" for in this sense the word is rabbinical, not biblical. The versions (with exception of Jerome and the *Græc. Venet.*) translate as if the word were מִפַּח [out of the snare]. Bertheau prefers this reading, and Böttcher holds צָיָד [a hunter] to have fallen out after מִיָד. It is not a parallelism with reservation; for a bird-catcher is not at

---

[1] There is here no distinction between the *Kethîb* and the *Kerî.* The Masora remarks, " This is the only passage in the Book of Proverbs where the word is written with *Yod* (י) ;" it thus recognises only the undisputed רֵעֶיךָ.

the same time a gazelle-hunter. The author, if he has so written, has conceived of מִיד, as at 1 Kings xx. 42, as absolute, and connected it with הִנָּצֵל : tear thyself free like the gazelle from the hand into which thou hast fallen (Hitzig); according to which, the section should be accentuated thus : הנצל כצבי מיד. צְבִי, Aram. טַבְי, Arab. *zaby*, is the gazelle (Arab. *ghazâl*), so called from its elegance ; צִפּוֹר, the bird, from its whistling (צפר, Arab. *safar*, R. צף, cf. Arab. *saffârat*, the whistling of a bird), Arab. *safar*, whistler (with prosthesis, *'aṣafwar*, warbler, *Psalm.* p. 794). The bird-catcher is called יָקוֹשׁ (from יָקַשׁ, after the form יְבֻל, cog. קוֹשׁ, Isa. xxix. 21, נָקַשׁ, R. קשׁ), after the form בָּנוֹד (fem. בְּנוֹדָה), or יָקוֹשׁ ; one would think that the *Kametz*, after the form *kâtwl* (*vid.* under Isa. i. 17), must here be fixed, but in Jer. v. 26 the word is vocalized יְקוֹשִׁים.

TENTH INTRODUCTORY MASHAL DISCOURSE, VI. 6–11.

CALL TO THE SLUGGARD TO AWAKE.

Altera parænesis (remarks J. H. Michaelis) *ad debitorem potius directa, sicut prima ad fidejussorem.* But this connection is a subtle invention. These brief proverbial discourses, each of which forms a completed whole, have scarcely been *a priori* destined for this introduction to the Salomonic Book of Proverbs edited by the author ; but he places them in it; and that he so arranges them that this section regarding sluggards follows that regarding sureties, may have been occasioned by accidental points of contact of the one with the other (cf לְךָ,6a, with 3b; שֵׁנוֹת . . . תְּנוּמוֹת, ver. 10, with ver. 4), which may also further determine the course in which the proverbs follow each other.

Vers. 6–8. As Elihu (Job xxxv. 11) says that God has set the beasts as our teachers, so he sends the sluggard to the school of the ant (*Ameise*), so named (in Germ.) from its industry (*Emsigkeit*) :

> 6 Go to the ant, sluggard ;
>   Consider her ways, and be wise !
> 7 She that hath no judge,
>   Director, and ruler :
> 8 She prepareth in summer her food,
>   Has gathered in harvest her store.

The *Dechî* written mostly under the לְ separates the inseparable. The thought, Go to the ant, sluggard! permits no other distinction than in the vocative; but the *Dechî* of לֵךְ אֶל־נְמלה is changed into *Munach* [1] on account of the nature of the *Athnach*-word, which consists of only two syllables without the counter-tone. The ant has for its Hebrew-Arabic name נְמָלָה, from the R. נם (*Isaiah*, p. 687), which is first used of the sound, which expresses the idea of the low, dull, secret,—thus of its active and yet unperceived motion; its Aramaic name in the Peshîto, ܫܘܫܡܢܐ, and in the Targ. שׁוּמְשְׁמָנָא (also Arab. *sumsum, simsim*, of little red ants), designates it after its quick activity, its busy running hither and thither (*vid.* Fleischer in Levy's *Chald. Wörterb.* ii. 578). She is a model of unwearied and well-planned labour. From the plur. דְּרָכֶיהָ it is to be concluded that the author observed their art in gathering in and laying up in store, carrying burdens, building their houses, and the like (*vid.* the passages in the Talmud and Midrash in the Hamburg *Real-Encyclopädie für Bibel und Talmud*, 1868, p. 83 f.). To the ant the sluggard (עָצֵל, Aram. and Arab. עטל, with the fundamental idea of weight and dulness) is sent, to learn from her to be ashamed, and to be taught wisdom.

Ver. 7. This relative clause describes the subject of ver. 8 more fully: it is like a clause with גַּם כִּי, *quamquam*.[2] The community of ants exhibits a peculiar class of workers; but it is not, like that of bees, composed of grades terminating in the queen-bee as the head. The three offices here named represent the highest judiciary, police, and executive powers; for קָצִין (from קָצָה, to distinguish), with the ending *in*, *vid. Jesurun*, p. 215 s.) is the judge; שֹׁטֵר (from שׂטר, Arab. *satr*, to draw lines, to write) is the overseer (in war the director, controller), or, as Saalschütz indicates the province of the *schotrim* both in cities and in the camp, the office of police; מֹשֵׁל (*vid. Isaiah*, p. 691), the governors of the whole state organism subordinated to the *schoftim* and the *schotrim*. The Syr., and the Targ. slavishly following it, translate קצין by חַצְדָּא (harvest), for they interchange this word with קציר.

Ver. 8. In this verse the change of the time cannot be occasioned by this, that קַיִץ and קָצִיר are distinguished as the earlier and the

---

[1] Cod. 1294 accentuates לֵךְ אל־נמלה; and that, according to Ben-Asher's rule, is correct.

[2] Ver. 7 is commonly halved by *Rebia;* but for the correct accentuation, *vid. Torath Emeth*, p. 48, § 3.

later period of the year; for קַיִץ (= Arab. ḳayt, from ḳât, to be glowing hot, cf. Arab. ḳghyyṭ of the glow of the mid-day heat) is the late summer, when the heat rises to the highest degree; but the son of the Shunammite succumbed to the sun-stroke in the time of harvest (2 Kings iv. 18 f.). Löwenstein judiciously remarks that תָּכִין refers to immediate want, אָגְרָה to that which is future; or, better, the former shows them engaged in persevering industry during the summer glow, the latter as at the end of the harvest, and engaged in the bringing home of the winter stores. The words of the procuring of food in summer are again used by Agur, Prov. xxx. 25; and the Aramaic fable of the *ant and the grasshopper*,[1] which is also found among those of Æsop and of Syntipas, serves as an illustration of this whole verse. The LXX. has, after the " Go to the ant," a proverb of five lines, ἢ πορεύθητι πρὸς τὴν μέλισσαν. Hitzig regards it as of Greek origin; and certainly, as Lagarde has shown, it contains idiomatic Greek expressions which would not occur to a translator from the Hebrew. In any case, however, it is an interpolation which disfigures the Hebrew text by overlading it.

Vers. 9–11. After the poet has admonished the sluggard to take the ant as an example, he seeks also to rouse him out of his sleepiness and indolence:

> 9 How long, O sluggard, wilt thou lie?
>   When wilt thou rise up from thy sleep?
> 10 " A little sleep, a little slumber,
>   A little folding of the hands to rest!"
> 11 So comes like a strong robber thy poverty,
>   And thy want as an armed man.

Vers. 9, 10. The awakening cry, ver. 9, is not of the kind that Paul could have it in his mind, Eph. v. 14. עָצֵל has, as the vocative, *Pasek* after it, and is, on account of the *Pasek*, in correct editions accentuated not with *Munach*, but *Mercha*. The words, ver. 10, are not an ironical call (sleep only yet a little while, but in truth a long while), but *per mimesin* the reply of the sluggard with which he turns away the unwelcome disturber. The plurals with מְעַט sound like self-delusion: yet a little, but a sufficient! To fold the hands, *i.e.* to cross them over the breast, or put them into the bosom, denotes also, Eccles. iv. 5, the idler. חִבּוּק, *complicatio*

[1] *Vid.* Goldberg's *Chofes Matmonim*, Berlin 1845; and Landsberger's Berlin Graduation Thesis, *Fabulæ aliquot Aramææ*, 1846, p. 28.

(cf. in Livy, *compressis quod aiunt manibus sidere;* and Lucan, ii. 292, *compressas tenuisse manus*), is formed like שִׁפּוּ, iii. 8, and the *inf.* שְׁכַב like חָסַר, x. 21, and שְׁפַל, xvi. 19. The *perf. consec.* connects itself with the words heard from the mouth of the sluggard, which are as a hypothetical antecedent thereto : if thou so sayest, and always again sayest, then this is the consequence, that suddenly and inevitably poverty and want come upon thee.   That מְהַלֵּךְ denotes the *grassator, i.e.* vagabond (Arab. *dawwar,* one who wanders much about), or the robber or foe (like the Arab. *'aduww,* properly *transgressor finium*), is not justified by the usage of the language ; הֵלֵךְ signifies, 2 Sam. xii. 4, the traveller, and מְהַלֵּךְ is one who rides quickly forward, not directly a κακὸς ὁδοιπόρος (LXX.).

Ver. 11. The point of comparison, 11*a*, is the unforeseen, as in quick march or assault (Böttcher), and 11*b* the hostile and irretrievable surprise ; for a man in armour, as Hitzig remarks, brings no good in his armour : he assails the opponent, and he who is without defence yields to him without the possibility of withstanding him.   The LXX. translate כאיש מגן by ὥσπερ ἀγαθὸς δρομεύς (cf. δρομεύς = מני־ארג, Job vii. 6, LXX., Aq.), for what reason we know not. After ver. 11 they interpose two other lines : " but if thou art assiduous, thy harvest will come to thee as a fountain, but want will go away ὥσπερ κακὸς δρομεύς."   Also this " bad runner " we must let go ; for Lagarde's retranslation, ומחסרך כחש באיש נמג, no one can understand.   The four lines, vers. 10, 11, are repeated in the appendix of Words of the Wise, xxiv. 33 f. ; and if this appendix originated in the time of Hezekiah, they may have been taken therefrom by the poet, the editor of the older Book of Proverbs.   Instead of כמהלך, מתהלך is there used (so comes forward thy poverty, *i.e.* again and again, but certainly moving forward); and instead of מחסרך, מחסריך is written, as also here, ver. 6, for משנתך is found the variant משנתיך with Jod as *mater lectionis* of the pausal *Segol.*

ELEVENTH INTRODUCTORY MASHAL DISCOURSE, VI. 12–19.

WARNING AGAINST DECEIT AND MALICE.

There follows now a *third* brief series of instructions, which run

to a conclusion with a deterring prospect similar to the foregoing.

12 A worthless man, a wicked man,
   Is he who practiseth falsehood with his mouth ;
13 Who winketh with his eyes, scrapeth with his foot,
   Pointeth with his fingers.
14 Malice is in his heart,
   He deviseth evil at all times,
   He spreadeth strife.
15 Therefore suddenly his destruction shall come,
   Suddenly shall he be destroyed, and there is no remedy.

It is a question, what is the subject and what the predicate in
ver. 12. Thus much is clear, that upon him who is here described
according to his deceitful conduct the sentence of condemnation
shall fall. He who is so described is thus subject, and אָדָם בְּלִיַּעַל
is without doubt predicate. But does the complex subject begin
with אִישׁ אָוֶן ? Thus e.g. Hitzig : " A worthless man is the wicked
man who . . . ." But the interchange of אדם and אִישׁ is a sign of
parallel relation ; and if 12b belonged attributively to אִישׁ אָוֶן, then
since אִישׁ הָאָוֶן is not used, it ought at least to have been continued
by הַהֹלֵךְ. The general moral categories, 12a, are thus predicates,
as was indeed besides probable ; the copious division of the subject
demands also in point of style a more developed predicate. xvi.
27 is simpler in plan, and also logically different. There the
expression is, as is usual, אִישׁ בליעל. Since אדם און is not possible,
the author uses instead בליעל. This word, composed of בְּלִי and יַעַל
(from יַעַל, וְעַל, to be useful, to be good for), so fully serves as one
word, that it even takes the article, 1 Sam. xxv. 25. It denotes
worthlessness, generally in a chain of words in the genitive, but
also the worthless, Job xxxiv. 18 ; and it is to be so taken here,
for אָדָם does not form a constructivus, and never governs a genitive. בליעל is thus a virtual adjective (as nequam in homo nequam);
the connection is like that of אדם רָשָׁע, xi. 7, and elsewhere, although
more appositional than this pure attributive. Synonymous with
בליעל is אָוֶן (from an, to breathe), wickedness, i.e. want of all moral
character. Thus worthless and wicked is he who practiseth deceit
with his mouth (cf. iv. 24), i.e. who makes language the means of
untruthfulness and uncharitableness. עִקְשׁוּת פֶּה is meant in a moral
sense, but without excluding that distortion of the mouth which
belongs to the mimicry of the malicious. It is the accus. of the
object ; for הָלַךְ is also bound in a moral sense with the accusative

144   THE BOOK OF PROVERBS.

of that which one practises, *i.e.* dealing with, exercises himself in,
ii. 7, xxviii. 18, Isa. xxxiii. 15.

Ver. 13. קֹרֵץ בְּעֵינָיו is translated according to the sense : who
winks (*nictat*) with his eyes; but that is not the proper meaning of
the word, for קרץ is used not only of the eyes, x. 10 (cf. xvi. 30,
qui oculos morsicat or *connivet*), Ps. xxxv. 19, but also of the lips,
xvi. 30. Thus Löwenstein's explanation : who opens up the eyes,
is incorrect. The verb קרץ unites in it the meanings of قرص, to
pinch off with a sharp implement, and قرض, with a blunt instrument (Arab. *mikrad*, pincers). It means to pince, to nip, as Arab.
kars, pincer,—e.g. kars balskyn alarsasat, he cuts off with the knife
the leaden seal,—hence frequently, to nip together the eyes, provincially: to wink ("*zwickern*," frequent. of " *zwicken*," to nip) with
the eyes—the action of the deceiver, who thereby gives the sign to
others that they help or at least do not hinder him from bantering and mocking, belying and deceiving a third person (Fl.) ; cf.
Ali's proverb, " O God, pardon to us the culpable winking with the
eye (*ramzat*)," and Fleischer's notes thereon, the *Proverbs of Ali*,
p. 100 f.

That the words which follow, מֹלֵל בְּרַגְלָיו, are meant of discourse,
i.e. the giving of signs, with the feet, and, so to say, significant *oratio
pedestris* (LXX., Aben-Ezra, Bertheau, Hitzig, and others), is very
improbable, since the usage of language has set apart the *Piel* מֹלֵל
for the meaning *loqui*, and מולל admits another suitable signification,
for מולל means in Talmudic *fricare, confricare,—e.g.* המולל מלילות, he
who grinds the parched ears of corn (*b. Beza* 12*b* ; *Ma'seroth*, iv. 5),
—after which Syr., Targ., תָּכַס (stamping), Aq. τρίβων, Symm.
προστρίβων, Jerome, (*qui*) *terit pede*, and Rashi משפשף (grinding,
scratching) ; it means one who scrapes with his feet, draws them
backwards and forwards on the ground in order thereby to give a
sign to others; also the Arab. مَلّ, *levem et agilem esse*, which as the
synonym of أسرع is connected with فى of the way, signifies properly to move the feet quickly hither and thither (Fl.).[1] מרה

[1] The root-idea of the Arab. *mall* is unquietness of motion ; the Arab. noun
mallt signifies the glow with its flickering light and burning: glowing ashes,
inner agitation, external haste; Arab. *malil* (מָלִל) is the feverish patient, but
also one quickly hastening away, and generally an impatient or hasty person
(*vid.* Wetstein in Baudissin in his *Job. Tischendorfianus*, vii. 6). The grinding

appears here, in accordance with its primary signification (*projicere*, sc. *brachium* or *digitum* = *monstrare*), connected with בְּאֶצְבְּעֹתָיו; another expression for this scornful, malicious δακτυλοδεικνεῖν is שֹׁלֵחַ אֶצְבַּע, Isa. lviii. 9.

Ver. 14. In this verse is continued the description of the subject, only once returning to the *particip.* The clauses are arranged independently, but logically according to the complex conception of the subject. תַּהְפֻּכוֹת are just the knaveries, *i.e.* the malicious wickedness which comes to light in word and deportment as עִקְּשׁוּת פֶּה. Regarding the double figure of the smithy and of agriculture underlying חרשׁ, *machinari*, vid. at iii. 29, and regarding the omission of the הוּא to חֹרֵשׁ, at Ps. vii. 10   The phrase שְׁלַח מְדָנִים (as ver. 19, xvi. 28), to let loose disputes, so that they break forth, reminds us rather of the unfettering of the winds by Æolus than of the casting in of the apple of discord.   Instead of מדנים the *Kerî* has מִדְיָנִים; on the other hand, מְדָנִים remains uncorrected vi. 19, x. 12.   The form מִדְיָנִים occurs once, xviii. 18, and its *constr.* מִדְיְנֵי once, xix. 13.   Everywhere else the text has מדונים, for which the *Kerî* has מִדְיָנִים, xviii. 19, xxi. 9, 19, xxiii. 29, xxv. 24, xxvi. 21, xxvii. 15.   The forms מִדְיָן and מָדוֹן are also recognised: the former stands alone without any analogous example; the latter is compared at least with מָצָד, Arab. *masâd* (*Psalmen*, p. 163, 3). Probably these two forms are warranted by Gen. xxv. 2, cf. xxxvii. 28, 36, where מְדָן and מִדְיָן occur as the names of two sons of Abraham by Keturah.   But the national name מִדְיָנִים is no reason for the seven times laying aside of the regular form מְדוֹנִים, *i.e.* מְדֹנִים, which is the plur. of מָדוֹן after the forms מְאוֹרִים, מְעוֹרִים, although מְדֻנִּים, after the forms מְצֻקִּים, מְבֻשִּׁים, is also found.

Ver. 15. With the 14th verse the description terminates.   A worthless and a wicked person is he who does such things.   The point lies in the characteristic out of which the conclusion is drawn: therefore his ruin will suddenly come upon him, etc.   Regarding אֵיד, the root-meaning of which is illustrated by Amos ii. 13, *vid.* at i. 26.   פִּתְאֹם is an old accus. of an absol. פֶּתַא, of the same meaning as פֶּתַע, used as an adverbial accus., both originating in the root-idea of splitting, opening, breaking out and breaking forth.   " Shall be

is made by means of a quick movement hither and thither; and so also is speaking, for the instrument of speech, particularly the tongue, is set in motion. Only the meaning *præcidere, circumcidere*, does not connect itself with that root-idea: מָל in this signification appears to be a *nüance* of מַר, *stringere*.

broken to pieces" (as a brittle potter's vessel, Ps. ii. 9, Isa. xxx. 14,
Jer. xxix. 11) is a frequent figure for the destruction (שֶׁבֶר) of an
army (cf. Arab. *ânksar âljysh*), of a city or a state, a man. וְאֵין
continues the יְשֻׁבֵּר as xxix. 1 : there shall be as it were no means
of recovery for his shattered members (Fl.). Without the *Vav* this
אֵין מַרְפֵּא would be a clause conceived of accusatively, and thus
adverbially : without any healing.

Vers. 16–19. What now follows is not a separate section (Hitzig),
but the corroborative continuation of that which precedes. The
last word (מדנים, strife) before the threatening of punishment, 14*b*,
is also here the last. The thought that no vice is a greater
abomination to God than the (in fact satanical) striving to set men
at variance who love one another, clothes itself in the form of the
numerical proverb which we have already considered, pp. 12, 13.
From that place we transfer the translation of this example of a
Midda :—

> 16 There are six things which Jahve hateth,
>   And seven are an abhorrence to His soul:
> 17 Haughty eyes, a lying tongue,
>   And hands that shed innocent blood ;
> 18 An heart that deviseth the thoughts of evil,
>   Feet that hastily run to wickedness,
> 19 One that uttereth lies as a false witness,
>   And he who soweth strife between brethren.

The sense is not, that the six things are hateful to God, and the
seventh an abomination to Him besides (Löwenstein) ; the *Midda*-
form in Amos i. 3–ii. 6, and in the proverb in Job v. 19, shows
that the seven are to be numbered separately, and the seventh is
the *non plus ultra* of all that is hated by God. We are not to
translate : *sex hæcce odit*, for הֵמָּה, הֵנָּה (הֵן, הֵם) points backwards and
hitherwards, but not, as אֵלֶּה, forwards to that immediately following;
in that case the words would be שֵׁשׁ אלה, or more correctly שֵׁשׁ האלה.
But also Hitzig's explanation, " These six things (viz. vers. 12–15)
Jahve hateth," is impossible ; for (which is also against that *hæcce*)
the substantive pronoun הָהֵנָּה (הָהֵנָּה, הָהֵמָּה) הנה, המה is never, like the
Chald. הִמּוֹן (הִמּוֹ), employed as an accus. in the sense of אֶתְהֶן, אֶתְהֶן, אֶתְהֶן,
it is always (except where it is the virtual gen. connected with a
preposition) only the nom., whether of the subject or of the predicate ; and where it is the nom. of the predicate, as Deut. xx. 15,
Isa. li. 19, substantival clauses precede in which הנה (המה) repre-

sents the substantive verb, or, more correctly, in which the logical copula resulting from the connection of the clause itself remains unexpressed. Accordingly, שְׂנֵא ה׳ is a relative clause, and is therefore so accentuated here, as at xxx. 15 and elsewhere : *sex (sunt) ea quæ Deus odit, et septem (sunt) abominatio animæ ejus.* Regarding the statement that the soul of God hates anything, *vid.* at Isa. i. 14. תועבות, an error in the writing occasioned by the numeral (*vid.* xxvi. 25), is properly corrected by the *Keri*; the poet had certainly the singular in view, as iii. 32, xi. 1, when he wrote תועבת. The first three characteristics are related to each other as mental, verbal, actual, denoted by the members of the body by means of which these characteristics come to light. The virtues are taken all together as a body (organism), and meekness is its head. Therefore there stands above all, as the sin of sins, the *mentis elatæ tumor*, which expresses itself in *elatum (grande) super-cilium :* עֵינַיִם רָמוֹת, the feature of the רָם, haughty (cf. Ps. xviii. 28 with 2 Sam. xxii. 28), is the opposite of the feature of the עֵינים שַׁח, Job xxii. 29 ; עַיִן is in the O. T. almost always (*vid.* Cant. iv. 9) fem., and adjectives of course form no dual. The second of these characteristics is the lying tongue, and the third the murderous hands. דָּם־נָקִי is innocent blood as distinguished from דָּם הַנָּקִי, the blood of the innocent, Deut. xix. 13.[1]

Ver. 18. The fourth characteristic is a deceitful heart. On חֹרֵשׁ, *vid.* ver. 14, iii. 29, and on אָוֶן, ver. 12. The fifth : feet running with haste to evil; לָרָעָה as לָרַע in Isa. lix. 7, echoing the distisch i. 16, as here, 17b and 18b. The connection מְהַר לָרוּץ, *propere cucurrit* (contrast אַחַר ?), is equivalent to רָץ מַהֵר.

Ver. 19. The sixth : " A speaker of lies, a tongue of falsehood," is hateful to God. It is one subject which is thus doubly characterized. כְּזָבִים are fictions, and שֶׁקֶר is the disfiguring (*deformatio*) of the actual facts. They are purposely placed together in this connection. The derivations of these synonyms are obscure ; Fürst gives to the former the root-idea of spinning (properly knot-ting together), and to the latter that of painting. כזבים is introduced

---

[1] The writing דָּם follows the Masoretic rule, *vid.* Kimchi, *Michlol* 205b, and Heidenheim under Deut. xix. 10, where in printed editions of the text (also in Norzi's) the irregular form דָּם נקי is found. Besides, the *Metheg* is to be given to דָּם־, so that one may not read it *dom*, as *e.g.* שֵׁשׁ־מֵאוֹת, Gen. vii. 11, that one may not read it שֵׁשׁ־.

to support שֶׁקֶר.[1] It would also be verbally permissible to interpret
עֵד שָׁקֶר in the sense of עֵדוּת שֶׁקֶר, like xxv. 18, as in apposition to
כֹּזְבִים; but in the nearest parallel, xiv. 15, the idea is personal, for it
is said of the עֵד שֶׁקֶר that he breathes out lies. In that place there
can be no doubt that the clause is a verbal one, and יָפִיחַ *finitum*, viz.
Hiph. of פּוּחַ. This *Hiph.* signifies elsewhere also *sufflare*, xx. 8,
afflare, Ps. x. 5, Ezek. xxi. 36, *perflare*, Cant. iv. 16, *anhelare*
(*desiderare*), Ps. xii. 6, Hab. ii. 3, but with כֹּזְבִים, *efflare*, a synonym
to דִּבֶּר, as הִבִּיעַ and הֵפִיחַ, which has (cf. xii. 17) no secondary meaning in use, but is mostly connected with כֹּזְבִים, not without reference
to the fact that that which is false is without reality and is nothing
more than הֶבֶל וְרוּחַ. But what kind of a form is יָפִיחַ, where it
is not, as xiv. 5, the predicate of a verbal clause, but in connection
with כֹּזְבִים, as here and at xiv. 25, xix. 5, 9 (once with אֱמוּנָה, xii. 17),
is the subject of a substantival clause? That which lies nearest is
to regard it as a noun formed from the *fut. Hiph.* Such formations
we indeed meet only among proper names, such as יָקִים, יָכִין, יָאִיר;
however, at least the one *n. appell.* יָרִיב (an adversary) is found,
which may be formed from the *Hiph.* as well as from the *Kal.*
But should not the *constr.* of יָפִיחַ after the form יָרִיב be יְפִיחַ? One
does not escape from this consideration by deriving יָפִיחַ, after the
forms יָשִׁישׁ, יָדִיד, יָחִיל, יָנִיעַ, and the like, from a secondary verb יָפַח, the
existence of which is confirmed by Jer. iv. 31, and from which also
יֶפַח, Ps. xxvii. 12, appears to be derived, although it may be reduced
also, after the form יָרֵב (with יָרִיב), to הֵפִיחַ. But in this case also one
expects as a connecting form יְפִיחַ like יְדִיד, as in reality יְפַח from יֶפַח
(cf. שְׂמֵחַ, אֲבֵל, from אָבֵל, שָׂמֵחַ). Shall it now be assumed that the
Kametz is treated as fixed? This were contrary to rule, since it is
not naturally long. Thus the connection is not that of the genitive.
But if יָפִיחַ were a substantive formed with the preformative of the
second *modus* like יַלְקוּט [1 Sam. xvii. 40], or were it a participial
intensive form of active signification such as נָבִיא, then the verbal
force remaining in it is opposed to the usage of the language.
There remains nothing further, therefore, than to regard יָפִיחַ as an
attributive put in the place of a noun: one who breathes out; and
there is a homogeneous example of this, for in any other way we
cannot explain יוֹסִיף, Eccles. i. 18. In 19*b* the numeral proverb
reaches its point. The chief of all that God hates is he who takes

---

[1] Isaak Albo thus distinguishes these synonyms in his dogmatic, bearing the
title סֵפֶר עִקָּרִים, ii. 27.

a fiendish delight in setting at variance men who stand nearly related. Thus this brief proverbial discourse rounds itself off, coming back again to 14*b* as a refrain.

TWELFTH INTRODUCTORY MASHAL DISCOURSE, VI. 20 ff.

WARNING AGAINST ADULTERY, BY REFERENCE TO ITS FEARFUL
CONSEQUENCES.

After these three smaller sections, the teacher of wisdom returns here to the theme of the eighth: Warning against sins of the flesh, whose power and prevalence among men is so immeasurably great, that their terrible consequences cannot sufficiently be held up before them, particularly before youth.

> 20 Keep, my son, the commandment of thy father,
> And reject not the instruction of thy mother.
> 21 Bind them to thy heart evermore,
> Fasten them about thy neck.

The suff. -*ēm* refers to the good doctrine (cf. vii. 3) pointed out by מִצְוָה and תּוֹרָה; the masc. stands, as is usual (*e.g.* i. 16, v. 2), instead of the fem. Regarding the figure, reminding us of the Tefillin and of Amuletes for perpetual representation, *vid.* under iii. 3. Similarly of persons, Cant. viii. 6. The verb עָנַד (only here and Job xxxi. 36) signifies to bend, particularly to bend aside (Arab. *'ind*, bending off, going aside; accus. as adv., aside, *apud*), and to bend up, to wind about, *circumplicare*.

Ver. 22. The representation of the good doctrine is now personified, and becomes identified with it.

> When thou walkest, it will guide thee;
> When thou liest down, it will keep watch over thee;
> And when thou wakest, it will talk with thee.

The subject is the doctrine of wisdom, with which the representation of wisdom herself is identified. The futures are not expressive of a wish or of an admonition, but of a promise; the form of the third clause shows this. Thus, and in the same succession as in the *schema* Deut. vi. 7, cf. xi. 19, are the three circumstances of the outward life distinguished: going, lying down, and rising up. The punctuation בְּהִתְהַלֶּכְךָ, found here and there, is Ben-Naphtali's variant; Ben-Asher and also the *Textus rec.* reject the *Metheg* in this case, *vid.* Baer's *Metheg-Setzung*, § 28. The verb נָחָה, with its *Hiph.* in a strengthened *Kal*-signification, is more frequently found in the Psalms than in the Proverbs; the Arab. نجا shows that it properly signifies to direct (*dirigere*), to give direction, to move in a definite direction. שָׁמַר with עַל, to take into protection, we had already ii. 11; this author has favourite forms of expression, in the repetition of which he takes delight. With lying down, sleeping is associated. וַהֲקִיצוֹתָ is, as Ps. cxxxix. 18, the *hypoth. perf.*, according to Ewald, § 357*a*: *et ut expergefactus es, illa te compellabit.* Bertheau incorrectly: she will make thee thoughtful. But apart from the fact that there is no evidence of the existence of this *Hiph.* in the language of the Bible, the personification demands a clearer figure. שִׂיחַ (שׂוּחַ) signifies mental speech and audible speech (Gen. xxiv. 63, poet., in the Talmudic[1] a common word); with בְּ, speaking concerning something (*fabulari de*), Ps. lxix. 13; with the accus., that which is said of a thing, Ps. cxlv. 5, or the address, briefly for לְ שִׂיחַ, Job xii. 8 (as מִן with accus. iv. 9 = לְ מֵן): when thou art awake, wisdom will forthwith enter into conversation with thee, and fill thy thoughts with right matter, and give to thy hands the right direction and consecration.

Ver. 23. Since in הִיא the idea of wisdom and of wholesome doctrine lie in one another, the author can proceed with proof:

> For a lamp is the commandment, and instruction a light (Jerome, *et lex lux*);
> And a way of life, disciplinary reproofs.

That תורה has here not the positive, specifically Israelitish sense, but the generalized sense of instruction in conformity with truth regarding the will of God and the duty of man, *vid.* p. 42. This instruction mediated by man, but of divine origin, is אוֹר, light, which enlightens the man who submits to it; and the commandment, מִצְוָה, which directs men in every case to do what is right, and forbids that which is wrong (including the prohibition Lev. iv. 2), is נֵר, a lamp which, kindled at that light, enlightens all the darkness of ignorance with reference to human conduct and its consequences.

---

[1] The conjecture thrown out by Wetstein, that (Arab.) *shykh* is equivalent to מָשִׁיחַ (מסיח), speaker, is untenable, since the verb *shakh*, to be old, a so-called *munsarif*, *i.e.* conjugated throughout, is used in all forms, and thus is certainly the root of *shykh*.

אוֹר and נר are related to each other as general and particular, primary and derivative. Löwenstein accentuates incorrectly וְתוֹרָה אוֹר instead of וְתוֹרָה אוֹר (as the Cod. 1294 and the 3 Erfurt Codd.); *vid.* on the retrogression of the tone, not existing here, under iii. 15. The gen. מוּסָר denotes the object or character of the admonition : not disciplinary in the external sense of the word, but rather moral, having in view discipline in the sense of education, *i.e.* moral edification and elevation. Such corrections are דֶּרֶךְ חַיִּים, the way to true life, direction how to obtain it.

Ver. 24. The section thus closes :

> To keep thee from the vile woman,
> From the flattery of the strange tongue.

Regarding the genitive connection אֵשֶׁת רָע, a woman of a wicked character, *vid.* under ii. 14 ; and regarding the adjectival connection לְשׁוֹן נכריה, under ver. 17 ; the strange tongue is the tongue (לָשׁוֹן) of the strange (foreign) woman (*vid.* p. 81), alluring with smooth words (ii. 16). Ewald, Bertheau : from her of a smooth tongue, the stranger, as Symm., Theod., ἀπὸ λειογλώσσου ξένης ; but חֶלְקַת is a substantive (Gen. xxvii. 16), and as a fem. adject. form is without an example. Rather חלקת לָשׁוֹן is to be regarded as the first member and נכריה as the second of the *st. constr.*, for the former constitutes one idea, and לשׁון on this account remains unabbreviated ; cf. Ps. lxviii. 22, Isa. xxviii. 1 ; but (1) this syntactical phenomenon is yet problematical, *vid.* Friedr. Philippi, *Wesen und Ursprung des St. Constr.* p. 17 ; and (2) the supposition of such an anomaly is here unnecessary.

The *procemium* of these twelve proverbial discourses is now at an end. Wisdom herself begins striking the note of the Decalogue :

> 25 Long not for her beauty in thy heart,
> And let her not catch thee with her eyelids ;
> 26 Because for a harlot one cometh down to a piece of bread,
> And a man's wife lieth in wait for a precious soul.

The warning 25*a* is in the spirit of the " thou shalt not covet," Ex. xx. 17, and the ἐν τῇ καρδίᾳ αὐτοῦ, Matt. v. 28, of the Preacher on the Mount. The Talmudic proverb הרהורי עבירה קשׁו מעבירה (*Joma* 29*a*) means only that the imagination of the sinful act exhausts the body even more than the act itself. The warning, " let her not catch thee with her eyelids," refers to her (the adulteress's) coquettish ogling and amorous winking. In the reason

added, beginning with כִּי בְעַד־ (thus it is to be punctuated), there is
the appositional connection אִשָּׁה זוֹנָה, Gesen. § 113; the idea of זוֹנה
goes over into 26b. "בְּכַּר לֶחֶם [= כִּרְכָּר, R. כר, to round, vid. at
Gen. xlix. 5], properly a circle of bread, is a small round piece of
bread, such as is still baked in Italy (pagnotta) and in the East
(Arab. kurs), here an expression for the smallest piece" (Fl.).
בְּעַד (constr. of בַּעַד), as Job ii. 4, Isa. xxxii. 14, is used in the
sense of ὑπέρ, pro, and with עַד there is connected the idea of the
coming down to this low point. Ewald, Bertheau explain after
the LXX., τιμὴ γὰρ πόρνης ὅση καὶ ἑνὸς ἄρτου, γυνὴ δὲ ἀνδρῶν
τιμίας ψυχὰς ἀγρεύει. But nothing is said here of price (reward); the parallelism is synonymous, not antithetic: he is doubly
threatened with loss who enters upon such a course. The adulterer squanders his means (xxix. 3) to impoverishment (vid. the
mention of a loaf of bread in the description of poverty 1 Sam.
ii. 36), and a man's wife (but at the same time seeking converse
with another) makes a prey of a precious soul; for whoever consents to adulterous converse with her, loses not perhaps his means,
but certainly freedom, purity, dignity of soul, yea, his own person.
צוּד comprehends—as צִירוֹן, fisher's town [Zidon], Arab. syâd, hunter
and fisher, show—all kinds of hunting, but in Hebr. is used only
of the hunting of wild beasts. The root-meaning (cf. צְדִיָּה) is to
spy, to seize.

Vers. 27–29. The moral necessity of ruinous consequences
which the sin of adultery draws after it, is illustrated by examples
of natural cause and effect necessarily connected:

> 27 Can one take fire in his bosom
>   And his clothes not be burned?
> 28 Or can any one walk over burning coals
>   And his feet not be burned?
> 29 So he that goeth to his neighbour's wife,
>   No one remains unpunished that toucheth her.

We would say: Can any one, without being, etc.; the former is the
Semitic "extended (paratactic)[1] construction." The first אִישׁ has
the conjunctive Shalsheleth. חָתָה signifies to seize and draw forth
a brand or coal with the fire-tongs or shovel (מַחְתָּה, the instrument
for this); cf. Arab. khât, according to Lane, "he seized or snatched

---

[1] [The παρατακτικὸς χρόνος denotes the imperfect tense, because it is still
extended to the future.]

away a thing;" the form יַחְתֶּה is *Kal*, as יֶחֱנֶה (*vid.* Köhler, *De Tetragrammate*, 1867, p. 10). חֵיק (properly indentation) is here not the lap, but, as Isa. xl. 11, the bosom.

Ver. 28. A second example of destructive consequences naturally following a certain course is introduced with אִם of the double question. גֶּחָלִים (from גֶּחָל, after the form פֶּחָם, but for which נַחֶלֶת is used) is the regular modification of *gahhalîm* (Gesen. § 27, 2). The fem. וְרַגְלָיו is followed here (cf. on the other hand i. 16) by the rhythmically full-sounding form תִּכָּוֶינָה (retaining the distinction of gender), from כָּוָה, Arab. *kwy*, to burn so that a brand-mark (כִּי, Isa. iii. 24, *cauterium*) remains.

Ver. 29. The instruction contained in these examples here follows : τὸ εἰς πῦρ καὶ εἰς γυναῖκα ἐμπεσεῖν ἴσον ὑπάρχει (Pythagoras in Maximi *Eclog.* c. 39). בּוֹא אֶל is here, as the second in Ps. li. 1, a euphemism, and נָגַע בְּ, to come in contact with, means, as נגע אֶל, to touch, Gen. xx. 6. He who goes in to his neighbour's wife shall not do so with impunity (יִנָּקֶה). Since both expressions denote fleshly nearness and contact, so it is evident he is not guiltless.

Vers. 30, 31. The thief and the adulterer are now placed in comparison with one another, in such a way that adultery is supposed to be a yet greater crime.

> 30 One does not treat the thief scornfully if he steals
>   To satisfy his craving when he is hungry ;
> 31 Being seized, he may restore sevenfold,
>   Give up the whole wealth of his house.

For the most part 30*a* is explained : even when this is the case, one does not pass it over in the thief as a bagatelle. Ewald remarks : בּוּז לְ stands here in its nearest signification of overlooking, whence first follows that of contemning. But this " nearest " signification is devised wholly in favour of this passage ;—the interpretation, " they do not thus let the thief pass," is set aside by Cant. viii. 1, 7 ; for by 31*b*, cf. Cant. viii. 7*b*, and 34*a*, cf. Cant. viii. 6*a*, it is proved that from ver. 30 on, reminiscences from the Canticles, which belong to the literature of the Chokma, find their way into the Mashal language of the author. Hitzig's correct supposition, that בּוּז לְ always signifies positive contemning, does not necessitate the interrogative interpretation : " Does not one despise the thief if . . . ? " Thus to be understood, the author ought to have written אַף כִּי or גַם כִּי. Michaelis rightly : *furtum licet merito pro infami* *in republica habetur, tamen si cum adulterio comparatur, minus pro-brosum est.* Regarding נֶפֶשׁ in the sense of appetite, and even throat and stomach, *vid. Psychologie*, p. 204. A second is, that the thief, if he is seized (but we regard וְנִמְצָא not as the *hypoth. perf.*, but as the *part. deprehensus*), may make compensation for his crime. The fut. יְשַׁלֵּם thus to be understood as the potential lies near from this, that a sevenfold compensation of the thing stolen is unheard of in the Israelitish law ; it knows only of a twofold, fourfold, fivefold restoration, Ex. xxi. 37, xxii. 1–3, 8 (cf. Saal-schütz, *Mos. Recht*, p. 554 ff.). This excess over that which the law rendered necessary leads into the region of free-will : he (the thief, by which we are now only to think of him whom bitter necessity has made such) may make compensation sevenfold, *i.e.* superabundantly ; he may give up the whole possessions (*vid.* on הוֹן at i. 13) of his house, so as not merely to satisfy the law, but to appease him against whom he has done wrong, and again to gain for himself an honoured name. What is said in vers. 30 and 31 is per-fectly just. One does not contemn a man who is a thief through poverty, he is pitied ; while the adulterer goes to ruin under all circum-stances of contempt and scorn. And : theft may be made good, and that abundantly ; but adultery and its consequences are irreparable.

Vers. 32, 33. Here there is a contrast stated to ver. 30 :

32 He who commits adultery (*adulterans mulierem*) is beside himself,
   A self-destroyer—who does this.
33 He gains stripes and disgrace,
   And his reproach is never quenched.

נָאַף, which primarily seems to mean *excedere*, to indulge in excess, is, as also in the Decalogue, cf. Lev. xx. 10, transitive : ὁ μοιχεύων γυναῖκα. Regarding being mad (*herzlos = heartless*) = *amens* (*excors, vecors*), *vid. Psychologie*, p. 254. מַשְׁחִית נַפְשׁוֹ is he who goes to ruin with wilful perversity. A self-murderer—*i.e.* he intends to ruin his position and his prosperity in life—who does it, viz. this, that he touches the wife of another. It is the worst and most inextinguishable dishonouring of oneself. Singularly Behaji : who annihilates it (his soul), with reference to Deut. xxi. 12, Eccles. iv. 17, where עשׂה would be equivalent to בִּטֵּל, καταργεῖν, which is untrue and impossible.[1] נֶגַע refers to the corporal punishment in-

[1] Behaji ought rather to have referred to Zeph. iii. 19, Ezek. vii. 27, xxii. 14 ; but there עשׂה את means *agere cum aliquo*, as we say : *mit jemandem abrechnen* (to settle accounts with any one).

flicted on the adulterer by the husband (Deut. xvii. 8, ⊤xi. 5); Hitzig, who rejects ver. 32, refers it to the stripes which were given to the thief according to the law, but these would be called מַכּוֹת (מַכָּה). The punctuation נֶגַע־וְקָלוֹן is to be exchanged for נֶגַע וְקָלוֹן (Löwenstein and other good editors). מָצָא has a more active signification than our *" finden "* (to find) : *consequitur, τυγχάνει.*

Vers. 34, 35. One who has been stolen from is to be appeased, but not the injured husband.

> 34 For jealousy is the fury of a husband,
> And he spareth not in the day of vengeance.
> 35 He regardeth not any ransom,
> And is not contented though thou offerest to him gifts ever so great.

The connection marks קִנְאָה as the subject ; for it respects carnal intercourse with another's wife. Jealousy is not usually חֵמָה, the glow of anger (from יָחַם, as שֵׁנָה from יָשֵׁן), but חֲמַת־גֶּבֶר (*constr.* as שְׁנַת), the glow of a man's anger, who with the putting forth of all his manly strength will seek satisfaction to his wounded honour. גֶּבֶר, here significant for אִישׁ, with the fundamental idea of strength, firmness; cf. Arab. *jabr,* to make fast, to put right again something broken in pieces, particularly a broken vessel, hence *Algebra,* properly the operation by which an incomplete magnitude is completed (Fl.). The following וְלֹא־יַחְפֹּל (with the orthophonic *Dagesh,* as ver. 25 יַחְפֹּד, and with *Makkeph*) is connected with נבר, with definite reference to the man whom the faithless guest has made a cuckold. When the day comes in which the adultery brought to light demands and admits of vengeance, then, wounded in his right and in his honour, he knows no mercy ; he pays no regard to any atonement or recompense by which the adulterer seeks to appease him and induce him not to inflict the punishment that is due : he does not consent, even though thou makest ever so great the gift whereby thou thinkest to gain him. The phrase נָשָׂא פָנִים, πρόσωπον λαμβάνειν, signifies elsewhere to receive the countenance, *i.e.* the appearance and the impression of a man, *i.e.* to let it impress one favourably ; here it is used of the כֹּפֶר, *i.e.* the means by which covering, *i.e.* non-punishment, pardon of the crime, impunity of the guilty, is obtained. Regarding אָבָה, to consent to, *vid.* at i. 10. שֹׁחַד, Aram. שׁוּחַד, is a gift, particularly bribery. That the language may again finally assume the form of an address, it beautifully rounds itself off.

THIRTEENTH INTRODUCTORY MASHAL DISCOURE, VII.

WARNING AGAINST ADULTERY BY THE REPRESENTATION OF ITS ABHORRENT AND DETESTABLE NATURE AS SEEN IN AN EXAMPLE.

The fearful desolation which adultery, and in general the sin of uncleanness, occasions in the life of the individual who is guilty of it, as well as in society, does not suffer the author of this discourse, directed to youth, to abandon his theme, which he has already treated of under different aspects. He takes up his warning once more, strengthens it by an example he himself had witnessed of one who fell a sacrifice to this sin, and gives it a very impressive conclusion, ver. 24 ff.

The introduction first counsels in general to a true appreciation of these well-considered life-rules of wisdom.

> 1 My son, keep my words,
>   And treasure up my commandments with thee.
> 2 Keep my commandments, and thou shalt live ;
>   And my instruction as the apple of thine eye.
> 3 Wind them about thy fingers,
>   Write them on the tablet of thy heart.

The LXX. has after ver. 1 another distich ; but it here disturbs the connection. Regarding צָפַן, *vid.* at ii. 1 ; אִתָּךְ refers, as there, to the sphere of one's own character, and that subjectively. Regarding the *imper.* וֶחְיֵה, which must here be translated according to its sense as a conclusion, because it comes in between the objects governed by שְׁמֹר, *vid.* at iv. 4. There וֶחְיֵה is punctuated with *Silluk;* here, according to Kimchi (*Michlol* 125a), with *Segol-Athnach,* וֶחְיֶה, as in the *Cod. Erfurt.* 2 and 3, and in the editions of Athias and Clodius, so that the word belongs to the class פתחין באתנח (with short instead of long vowel by the pausal accent): no reason for this is to be perceived, especially as (iv. 4) the *Tsere* (ê from *aj*) which is characteristic of the *imper.* remains unchanged. Regarding אִישׁוֹן הָעַיִן, Arab. *insân el-'ain,* the little man of the eye, *i.e.* the apple of the eye, named from the miniature portrait of him who looks into it being reflected from it, *vid.* at Ps. xvii. 8 ; the ending *ôn* is here diminutive, like Syr. *achuno,* little brother, *b'runo,* little son, and the like. On ver. 3, *vid.* at vi. 21, iii. 3. The תפילין של יד

---

¹ [תפילין, *prayer-fillets, phylacteries.*]

were wound seven times round the left arm and seven times round
the middle finger. The writing on the table of the heart may be
regarded as referring to Deut. vi. 9 (the *Mezuzoth*).[1]

Vers. 4, 5. The subject-matter of this earnest warning are the
admonitions of the teacher of wisdom, and through him of Wisdom
herself, who in contrast to the world and its lust is the worthiest
object of love, and deserves to be loved with the purest, sincerest
love:

> 4 Say to wisdom: " Thou art my sister!"
>   And call understanding " Friend;"
> 5 That they may keep thee from the strange woman,
>   From the stranger who useth smooth words.

The childlike, sisterly, and friendly relationship serves also to picture forth and designate the intimate confidential relationship to
natures and things which are not flesh and blood. If in Arabic
the poor is called the brother of poverty, the trustworthy the
brother of trustworthiness, and *abu, um* (אָם), *achu, ucht*, are used
in manifold ways as the expression for the interchangeable relation
between two ideas; so (as also, notwithstanding Ewald, § 273*b*, in
many Hebr. proper names) that has there become national, which
here, as at Job xvii. 14, xxx. 29, mediated by the connection of the
thoughts, only first appears as a poetic venture. The figurative
words of ver. 4 not merely lead us to think of wisdom as a personal
existence of a higher order, but by this representation it is itself
brought so near, that אָם easily substitutes itself, ii. 3, in the place
of אָם. אֲחֹתִי of Solomon's address to the bride brought home is
in its connection compared with Book of Wisdom viii. 2. While
the *óth* of אָחוֹת by no means arises from abstr. *úth*, but *achóth* is
derived from *achajath*, מוֹדָע (as Ruth ii. 1, cf. מוֹדַעַת, iii. 2), here by
Mugrash מוֹדָע, properly means acquaintance, and then the person
known, but not in the superficial sense in which this word and the
Arab. *ma'arjat* are used (*e.g.* in the Arabic phrase quoted by
Fleischer, *kanna ashaab sarna m'aaraf—nous étions amis, nous
en sommes plus que de simples connaissances*), but in the sense of
familiar, confidential alliance. The *infin.* לְשָׁמְרֶךָ does not need for
its explanation some intermediate thought to be introduced: *quod
eo conducet tibi ut* (Mich.), but connects itself immediately as the
purpose: bind wisdom to thyself and thyself to wisdom thus

---

[1] [=the *door-posts*, afterwards used by the Jews to denote the passages of
Scripture written on the door-posts.]

closely that thou mayest therewith guard thyself. As for the rest,
vid. ii. 16; this verse repeats itself here with the variation of one
word.

How necessary it is for the youth to guard himself by the help
of wisdom against the enticements of the wanton woman, the
author now shows by a reference to his own observation.

> 6 For through the window of my house,
>   From behind the lattice I looked out;
> 7 Then saw I among the simple ones,
>   Discerned among the young people, a youth devoid of
>   understanding.

כִּי refers indeed to the immediately following clause, yet it actually
opens up the whole following exemplification. The connection
with ver. 5 would be closer if instead of the extended Semitic
construction it were said : *nam quum . . . prospicerem vidi, etc.*
חַלּוֹן (from חָלַל, to bore through) is properly a place where the
wall is bored through. אֶשְׁנָב (from שָׁנַב = Arab. *shaniba*, to be
agreeable, cool, fresh) is the window-lattice or lattice-window, *i.e.*
lattice for drawing down and raising up, which keeps off the rays
of the sun. נִשְׁקַף signifies primarily to make oneself long in order
to see, to stretch up or out the neck and the head, καραδοκεῖν,
Arab. *atall, atal'a,* and *tatall'a* of things, *imminere,* to overtop, to
project, to jut in; cf. Arab. *askaf* of the ostrich, long and bent, with
respect to the neck stretching it up, *sakaf,* abstr. crooked length.
And בְּעַד is thus used, as in Arab. *duna,* but not *b'ad,* is used : so
placed, that one in relation to the other obstructs the avenue to
another person or thing : "I looked forth from behind the lattice-
window, *i.e.* with respect to the persons or things in the room,
standing before the lattice-window, and thus looking out into the
open air" (Fleischer). That it was far in the night, as we
learn at ver. 9, does not contradict this looking out; for apart
from the moon, and especially the lighting of the streets, there
were star-lit nights, and to see what the narrator saw there was
no night of Egyptian darkness. But because it was night 6*a* is
not to be translated : I looked about among those devoid of experience (thus *e.g.* Löwenstein); but he saw among these, observed
among the youths, who thus late amused themselves without, a
young man whose want of understanding was manifest from
what further happened. Bertheau: that I might see, is syntactically impossible. The meaning of וָאֵרֶא is not determined by the

אָבִינָה following, but conversely אָבִינָה stands under the operation of וְ (=וְאָבִינה, Neh. xiii. 7), characterizing the historic *aorist*. Regarding פְּתִי, *vid.* at i. 4. בָּנִים is the masc. of בָּנוֹת, Arab. *benât* in the meaning maiden. בַּבָּנִים has in correct texts, according to the rules of the accents, the ב *raphatum*.[1]

Now follows, whither he saw the young fop [*Laffen*] then go in the darkness.

> 8 Going up and down the street near her corner,
>   And he walked along the way to her house,
> 9 In the twilight, when the day declined,
>   In the midst of the night and deep darkness.

We may interpret עֹבֵר as appos.: *juvenem amentem, ambulantem,* or as the predicate accus.: *vidi juvenem . . . ambulantem;* for that one may so express himself in Hebrew (cf. *e.g.* Isa. vi. 1, Dan. viii. 7), Hitzig unwarrantably denies. The passing over of the *part.* into the *finite,* 8b, is like ii. 14, 17, and that of the *inf.* i. 27, ii. 8. שׁוּק, Arab. *suk* (dimin. *suweika,* to separate, from *sikkat,* street, alley), still means, as in former times, a broad street, a principal street, as well as an open place, a market-place where business is transacted, or according to its etymon: where cattle are driven for sale. On the street he went backwards and forwards, yet so that he kept near to her corner (*i.e.* of the woman whom he waited for), *i.e.* he never withdrew himself far from the corner of her house, and always again returned to it. The corner is named, because from that place he could always cast a look over the front of the house to see whether she whom he waited for showed herself. Regarding פִּנָּה for פִּנְתָה, *vid.* at Ps. xxvii. 5: a primary form פֵּן has never been in use; פִּנִּים, Zech. xiv. 10, is plur. of פִּנָּה. אֵצֶל (from אָצַל, Arab. *wasl,* to bind) is, as a substantive, the side (as the place where one thing connects itself with another), and thus as a preposition it means (like *juxta* from *jungere*) beside, Ital. *allato.* וְדֶרֶךְ is the object. accus., for thus are construed verbs *eundi* (*e.g.* Hab. iii. 12, Num. xxx. 17, cf. xxi. 22).

Ver. 9. The designations of time give the impression of progress to a climax; for Hitzig unwarrantably denies that נֶשֶׁף means the twilight; the Talmud, *Berachoth* 3b, correctly distinguishes תרי נשפי two twilights, the evening and the morning twilight. But the idea is not limited to this narrow sense, and does not need this,

[1] Regarding the Targ. of vii. 6, 7, *vid.* Perles, *Etymologische Studien,* 1871, **p.** 9.

since the root-word נָשַׁף (*vid.* at Isa. xl. 24) permits the extension of the idea to the whole of the cool half (evening and night) of the entire day; cf. the parallel of the adulterer who veils himself by the darkness of the night and by a mask on his countenance, Job xxiv. 15 with Jer. xiii. 16. However, the first group of synonyms, בְּנֶשֶׁף בְּעֶרֶב יוֹם (with the *Cod. Frankf.* 1294, to be thus punctuated), as against the second, appears to denote an earlier period of the second half of the day; for if one reads, with Hitzig, בְּעֶרֶב יוֹם (after Judg. xix. 9), the meaning remains the same as with בְּעֶרֶב יוֹם, viz. *advesperascente die* (Jerome), for עֶרֶב = Arab. *gharab*, means to go away, and particularly to go under, of the sun, and thus to become evening. He saw the youth in the twilight, as the day had declined (κέκλικεν, Luke xxiv. 29), going back-wards and forwards; and when the darkness of night had reached its middle, or its highest point, he was still in his lurking-place. אִישׁוֹן לָיְלָה, apple of the eye of the night, is, like the Pers. *dili scheb*, heart of the night, the poetic designation of the middle of the night. Gusset incorrectly: *crepusculum in quo sicut in oculi pupilla est nigredo sublustris et quasi mistura lucis ac tenebrarum.* אִישׁוֹן is, as elsewhere לֵב, particularly the middle; the application to the night was specially suitable, since the apple of the eye is the black part in the white of the eye (Hitzig). It is to be translated according to the accus., *in pupilla noctis et caligine* (not *caliginis*); and this was probably the meaning of the poet, for a ב is obviously to be supplied to וַאֲפֵלָה.

Finally, the young man devoid of understanding sees his waiting rewarded: like meets like.

> 10 And, lo, a woman coming to meet him,
>   In the attire of an harlot and of subtle heart.
> 11 Boisterous is she, and ungovernable;
>   Her feet have no rest in her own house.
> 12 At one time before her door, at another in the street,
>   And again at every corner she places herself on the watch.

" Ver. 12 (Hitzig) expresses what is wont to be, instead of a single event, ver. 11, viz. the custom of a street harlot. But she who is spoken of is not such an one; lurking is not applicable to her (cf. Job xxxi. 9), and, ver. 11, it is not meant that she is thus inclined." But Hitzig's rendering of ver. 11, " she was boisterous . . . in her house her feet had no rest," is inaccurate, since neither וְהִיא nor שָׁכְנוּ is used. Thus in vers. 11 and 12 the poet gives a characteristic of the woman, introduced by וְהִנֵּה into the frame of his picture, which goes beyond that which then presented itself to his eyes. We must with ver. 12 reject also ver. 11; and even that would not be a radical improvement, since that characteristic lying behind the evident, that which was then evident begins with וּנְצֻרַת לֵב (and subtle in heart). We must thus suppose that the woman was not unknown to the observer here describing her. He describes her first as she then appeared. שִׁית Hitzig regards as equivalent to שָׁוִית, similitude (from שָׁוָה), and why? Because שִׁית does not mean " to lay against," but " to place." But Ex. xxxiii. 4 shows the contrary, and justifies the meaning attire, which the word also has in Ps. lxxiii. 6. Meîri less suitably compares 2 Kings ix. 30, but rightly explains תקון (dressing, ornament), and remarks that שִׁית elliptical is equivalent to בְּשִׁית. It is not the nominative (Bertheau), but the accusative, as תבנית, Ps. cxliv. 12, Ewald, § 279d. How Hitzig reaches the translation of ונצרת לב by " and an arrow in her heart " (et saucia corde[1]), one can only understand by reading his commentary. The usage of the language, iv. 23, he remarks, among other things, would stamp her as a virtuous person. As if a phrase like נָצַר לֵב could be used both sensu bono and sensu malo! One can guard his heart when he protects it carefully against moral danger, or also when he purposely conceals that which is in it. The part. נָצוּר signifies, Isa. i. 8, besieged (blockaded), Ezek. xvi. 12, protected, guarded, and Isa. xlviii. 6, lxv. 4, concealed, hidden. Ewald, § 187b, refers these three significations in the two passages in Isaiah and in the passage before us to צָרַר, Niph. נָצַר (as נָגַל); but (1) one would then more surely take צוּר (cf. נָמוֹל, נְבְכִים) as the verbal stem; (2) one reaches the idea of the concealed (the hidden) easier from that of the preserved than from that of the confined. As one says in Lat. homo occultus, tectus, abstrusus, in the sense of κρυψίνους, so it is said of that woman נְצֻרַת לֵב, not so much in the sense of retenta cor, h.e. quæ quod in corde haberet non pandebat, Fr. retenue (Cocc.), as in the sense of custodita cor, quæ intentionem cordis mentemque suam callide novit premere (Mich.): she is of a hidden mind, of a concealed nature; for she feigns fidelity to her husband and flatters her paramours as her only beloved, while in truth she loves none, and each of them is to her only a means to an end, viz. to the indul- gence of her worldly sensual desire. For, as the author further

[1] Virgil's Æneid, iv. 1.

describes her, she is הֹמִיָּה (fem. of הֹמֶה = הֹמִי, as i. 21, Isa. xxii. 2), *tumultuosa*, externally as internally impetuous, because full of intermingling lust and deceit (*opp.* ἡσύχιος, 1 Pet. iii. 4, 1 Tim. ii. 11), and סֹרָרֶת, self-willed, not minding the law of duty, of discretion, or of modesty (from סָרַר, Arab. *sharr, pervicacem, malum esse*). She is the very opposite of the noiseless activity and the gentle modesty of a true house-wife, rude, stubborn, and also vagrant like a beast in its season (Hos. iv. 14): *in domo ipsius residere nequeunt pedes ejus;* thus not οἰκουρός or οἰκουργός (Tit. ii. 5), far removed from the genuine woman-like εἴσω ἥσυχον μένειν δόμων[1]—a *radt*, as they call such a one in Arab. (Wünsche on Hos. xii. 1), or as she is called in Aram. נִפְקַת בָּרָא.

Ver. 12. This verse shows how she conducts herself when she wanders abroad. It is no common street-walker who is designated (no "*Husterin*," Arab. *kahbt*, after which also the female demon-name (Arab.) *se'alâ* is explained), but that licentious married wife, who, no better than such a strumpet when she wanders abroad, hunts after lovers. The alternating פַּעַם (properly a stroke) Fleischer compares with the Arab. synonyms, *marrt*, a going over, *karrt*, a going back, *una volta, una fiata, une fois* (Orelli, *Synon. der Zeit und Ewigkeit*, p. 51). Regarding חוּץ, *vid.* at v. 16: it is the free space without, before the house-door, or also before the gate of the city; the parallelism speaks here and at i. 20 more in favour of the former signification.

Ver. 13. After this digression the poet returns to the subject, and further describes the event as observed by himself.

> And she laid hold on him and kissed him;
> Put on a bold brow and said to him.

The verb נָשַׁק is here, after its primary signification, connected with the dat.: *osculum fixit ei.* Thus also Gen. xxvii. 26 is construed, and the *Dagesh* in לֹ is, as there, *Dag. forte conj.*, after the law for which the national grammarians have coined the technical name אָתֵי מֵרַחִיק (*veniens e longinquo*, "coming out of the distance," *i.e.* the attraction of a word following by one accented on the penult.). The penult.-accenting of נִשְׁקָה is the consequence of the retrogression of the accent (נסוג אחור), which here, where the word from the first had the penult. only with Metheg, and thus with half a tone, brings with it the dageshing of the לֹ following, as the original

[1] Eurip. *Herac.*

penultima-accenting of וְהֶחֱזִיקָה does of the בּו which follows it, for the reading בוֹ by Löwenstein is contrary to the laws of punctuation of the *Textus receptus* under consideration here.[1] As בּו and לּ have received the doubling *Dagesh*, so on the other hand, according to Ewald, § 193*b*, it has disappeared from הֵעֵזָה (written with *Raphe* according to Kimchi, *Michlol* 145*a*). And as נשקה has the tone thrown back, so the proper pausal וַתֹּאמַר is accented on the ult., but without attracting the לּ following by dageshing, which is the case only when the first of the two words terminates in the sound of *ā* (*āh*). הֵעֵז פָּנָיו is said of one who shows firmness or hardness of countenance (Arab. *slabt alwajh*), *i.e.* one who shows shamelessness, or, as we say, an iron forehead (Fl.).

She laid hold on him and kissed him, both of which actions were shameless, and then, assuming the passivity and modesty befitting the woman, and disregarding morality and the law, she said to the youth :

14 " To bring peace-offerings was binding upon me,
    To-day have I redeemed my vows.
15 Therefore am I come out to meet thee,
    To seek thy face, and have found thee."

We have translated זִבְחֵי שְׁלָמִים " peace-offerings," proceeding on the principle that שֶׁלֶם (sing. only Amos v. 22, and on the Phœnician altar at Marseilles) denotes contracting friendship with one (from שָׁלֵם, to hold friendly relationship), and then the gifts having this in view; for the idea of this kind of offering is the attestation and confirmation of communion with God. But in view of the derivatives שֶׁלְמֹנִים and שִׁלּוּם, it is perhaps more appropriate to combine שֶׁלֶם with שִׁלֵּם, to discharge perfectly, and to translate it thank-payment-offering, or with v. Hofmann, a due-offering, where not directly thank-offering; for the proper eucharistic offering, which is the expression of thanks on a particular occasion, is removed from the species of the *Shelamim* by the addition of the words עַל־תּוֹדָה (Lev. vii. 12–25). The characteristic of the *Shelamim* is the division of the flesh of the sacrifice between Jahve and His priests on the one side, and the person (or persons) bringing it on the other side : only one part of the flesh of the sacrifice was Jahve's, consumed by fire (Lev. iii. 16) ; the priests received one part ; those who brought the offering received back another part

[1] *Vid.* Baer's *Torath Emeth*, p. 29 sq., and *Psalmen-Commentar* under Ps. lii. 5.

as it were from the altar of God, that they might eat it with holy joy along with their household. So here the adulteress says that there was binding upon her, in consequence of a vow she had taken, the duty of presenting peace-offerings, or offerings that were due; to-day (she reckons the day in the sense of the *dies civilis* from night to night) she has performed her duties, and the שַׁלְמֵי נֶדֶר have yielded much to her that she might therewith regale him, her true lover; for with עַל־כֵּן she means to say that even the prospect of the gay festival which she can prepare for him moved her thus to meet him. This address of the woman affords us a glimpse into the history of the customs of those times. The *Shelamim* meals degenerated in the same manner as our *Kirmsen*.[1] Secularization lies doubly near to merrymaking when the law sanctions this, and it can conceal itself behind the mask of piety. Regarding שִׁחַר, a more exact word for בִּקֵּשׁ, *vid.* at i. 28. To seek the countenance of one is equivalent to to seek his person, himself, but yet not without reference to the wished-for look [*aspectus*] of the person.

Thus she found him, and described to him the enjoyment which awaited him in eating and drinking, then in the pleasures of love.

16 " My bed have I spread with cushions,
       Variegated coverlets, Egyptian linen;
17 I have sprinkled my couch
       With myrrh, aloes, and cinnamon.
18 Come then, we will intoxicate ourselves with love till the morning,
       And will satisfy ourselves in love."

The noun עֶרֶשׂ, from עָרַשׂ, = Arab. 'arash, *œdificare, fabricari*, signifies generally the wooden frame; thus not so much the bed within as the erected bed-place (cf. Arab. 'arsh, throne, and 'arysh, arbour). This bedstead she had richly and beautifully cushioned, that it might be soft and agreeable. רָבַד, from רב, signifies to lay on or apply closely, thus either *vincire* (whence the name of the necklace, Gen. xli. 42) or *sternere* (different from רָפַד, Job xvii. 13, which acquires the meaning *sternere* from the root-meaning to raise up from under, *sublevare*), whence מַרְבַדִּים, cushions, pillows, *stragulæ*. Böttcher punctuates מַרְבַּדִּים incorrectly; the ב remains aspirated, and the connection of the syllables is looser than in מִרְבֶּה; Ewald, § 88d. The חֲטֻבוֹת beginning the second half-verse is in no case an adjective to מרבדים, in every case only *appos.*, pro-

[1] [*Kirmse* = anniversary of the dedication of a church, village *fête*.]

bably an independent conception; not derived from חָטַב (cogn.
חָצַב), to hew wood (whence Arab. *ḥatab*, fire-wood), according to
which Kimchi, and with him the *Græc. Venet.* (περιξύστοις), understands it of the carefully polished bed-poles or bed-boards, but
from חָטַב = Arab. *khaṭeba*, to be streaked, of diverse colours (*vid.*
under Ps. cxliv. 12), whence the Syriac *machtabto*, a figured
(striped, checkered) garment. Hitzig finds the idea of coloured
or variegated here unsuitable, but without justice; for the pleasantness of a bed is augmented not only by its softness, but also by the
impression which its costliness makes on the eye. The following
אֵטוּן מִצְרָיִם stands in an appositional relation to חֲטֻבוֹת, as when one
says in Arabic *taub-un dîbâg'-un*, a garment brocade = of brocade.
אֵטוּן (after the Syr. for אֵטוּ, as אֵמוּן) signifies in the Targum the
cord (*e.g.* Jer. xxxviii. 6), like the Arab. *tunub*, Syr. (*e.g.* Isa. liv. 2)
tûnob; the root is טן, not in the sense of to bind, to wind (Dietr.),
but in the sense of to stretch; the thread or cord is named from
the extension in regard to length, and אטן is thus thread-work,
whether in weaving or spinning.[1] The fame of Egyptian manufactures is still expressed in the Spanish *aclabtea*, fine linen cloth,
which is equivalent to the modern Arabic *el-ḳobtije* (*ḳibtije*); they
had there particularly also an intimate acquaintance with the dye
stuffs found in the plants and fossils of the country (Klemm's
Culturgeschichte, v. 308-310).

Vers. 17, 18. These verses remind us of expressions in the
Canticles. There, at iv. 14, are found the three names for spicery
as here, and one sees that מר אהלים are not to be connected geni-
tively: there are three things, accented as in the title-verse i. 3.
The myrrh, מֹר (*Balsamodendron myrrha*), belongs, like the frankincense, to the species of the *Amyris*, which is an exotic in
Palestine not less than with us; the aromatic quality in them does
not arise from the flowers or leaves, so that Cant. i. 13 leads us
to think of a bunch of myrrh, but from the resin oozing through
the bark (*Gummi myrrhæ* or merely *myrrha*), consisting of bright
glossy red or golden-yellow grains more or less transparent.
אֲהָלִים (used by Balaam, Num. xxiv. 6) is the Semitic Old-Indian
name of the aloë, *agaru* or *aguru;* the aromatic quality is in the
wood of the *Aquilaria agallocha*, especially its root (*agallochum* or

---

[1] Hence perhaps the Greek ὀθόνη, which Fick in his *Vergl. Wörterbuch* connects with the Arab. verb-root *vadh*, to bind, wind, clothe, but not without
making thereto interrogation marks.

lignum aloes) dried in the earth,—in more modern use and commerce the inspissated juice of its leaves. קִנָּמוֹן is κιννάμωμον (like
מֹר, a Semitic word[1] that had come to the Greeks through the
Phœnicians), the cinnamon, *i.e.* the inner rind of the *Laurus cinnamomum.* The myrrh is native to Arabia; the aloë, as its name
denotes, is Indian; the cinnamon in like manner came through
Indian travellers from the east coast of Africa and Ceylon (Tapro-
bane). All these three spices are drugs, *i.e.* are dry apothecaries'
wares; but we are not on that account to conclude that she perfumed (Hitzig) her bed with spices, viz. burnt in a censer, an
operation which, according to Cant. iii. 6, would rather be designated קִטַּרְתִּי. The verb נוּף (only here as *Kal*) signifies to lift
oneself up (*vid.* under Ps. xlviii. 13), and transitively to raise and
swing hither and thither (=הֵנִיף); here with a double accusative,
to besprinkle anything out of a vessel moved hither and thither.
According to this sense, we must think of the three aromas as
essences in the state of solution; cf. Ex. xxx. 22–33, Esth. ii. 12.
Hitzig's question, "Who would sprinkle bed-sheets with perfumed
and thus impure water?" betrays little knowledge of the means by
which even at the present day clean linen is made fragrant. The
expression רְוֶה דוֹדִים sounds like שְׁכַר דודים, Cant. v. 1, although
there דודים is probably the voc., and not, as here, the accus.; רְוֶה is
the *Kal* of רָוָה, v. 19, and signifies to drink something copiously in
full draughts. The verbal form עָלַם for עָלַץ is found besides only
in Job xx. 18, xxxix. 13; the *Hithpa.* signifies to enjoy oneself
greatly, perhaps (since the *Hithpa.* is sometimes used reciprocally, *vid.* under Gen. ii. 25) with the idea of reciprocity (Targ.
חַד לְחַד). We read *bo°habim* with *Chateph-Kametz* after Ben-
Asher (*vid.* Kimchi's *Lex.*); the punctuation בְּאָהָבִים is that of
Ben-Naphtali.

The adulteress now deprives the youth of all fear; the circumstances under which her invitation is given are as favourable as
possible.

19 " For the man is not at home,
            He has gone on a long journey.

---

[1] Myrrh has its name מֹר from the bitterness of its taste, and קְנָם appears to
be a secondary formation from קָנֶה, whence קָנֶה, reed; cf. the names of the
cinnamon, *cannella*, Fr. *cannelle.* *Cinnamum* (κίνναμον) is only a shorter form
for *cinnamomum.* Pliny, *Hist. Nat.* xii. 19 (42), uses both forms indiscrimi-
nately.

20 He has taken the purse with him ;
He will not return home till the day of the full moon."

It is true that the article stands in הָאִישׁ, Arab. *alm'ar-fat*, *i.e.* serves
to define the word : the man, to whom here κατ' 'ἐξοχήν and alone
reference can be made, viz. the husband of the adulteress (Fl.) ;
but on the other side it is characteristic that she does not say אִישִׁי
(as *e.g.* Gen. xxix. 32), but ignores the relation of love and duty
in which she is placed to him, and speaks of him as one standing
at a distance from her (Aben-Ezra). Erroneously Vogel reads בְּבֵיתָהּ
after the Targ. instead of בְּבֵיתוֹ. We say in Hebr. אֵינוּ בביתו, *il n'est
pas chez soi*, as we say לָקַח בְּיָדוֹ, *il a pris avec soi* (cf. Jer. xxxviii.
10). מֵרָחוֹק Hitzig seeks to connect with the verb, which, after
Isa. xvii. 13, xxii. 3, is possible; for the Hebr. מרחוק (מִמֶּרְחָק), far
off, has frequently the meaning from afar, for the measure of
length is determined not from the point of departure outward, but
from the end, as *e.g.* Homer, *Il.* ii. 456 : ἕκαθεν δέ τε φαίνεται
αὐγή, from afar the gleam is seen, *i.e.* shines hither from the distance. Similarly we say in French, *il vient du coté du nord*, he
comes from the north, as well as *il va du coté du nord*, he goes
northwards. But as we do not say : he has gone on a journey far
off, but : on a distant journey, so here מרחוק is virtually an adj.
(*vid.* under Isa. v. 26) equivalent to רְחֹקָה (Num. ix. 10) : a
journey which is distant = such as from it he has a long way back.
Michaelis has well remarked here : *ut timorem ei penitus adimat,
veluti per gradus incedit.* He has undertaken a journey to a
remote point, but yet more : he has taken money with him, has
thus business to detain him ; and still further : he has even determined the distant time of his return. צְרוֹר־הַכֶּסֶף (thus to be written
after Ben-Asher, *vid.* Baer's *Torath Emeth*, p. 41) is the purse
(from צָרַר, to bind together), not one of many, but that which is his
own. The terminus precedes 20*b* to emphasize the lateness; *vid.*
on כֵּסֶא under Ps. lxxxi. 4. *Græc. Venet.* τῇ ἡμέρᾳ τοῦ καιροῦ, after
Kimchi and others, who derive כסא (כסה) from the root כם, to
reckon, and regard it as denoting only a definite time. But the two
passages require a special idea; and the Syr. *kêso*, which in 1 Kings
xii. 32, 2 Chron. vii. 10, designates the time from the 15th day
of the month, shows that the word denotes not, according to the
Talmud, the new moon (or the new year's day), when the moon's
disk begins to cover itself, *i.e.* to fill (יתכסה), but the full moon,
when it is covered, *i.e.* filled ; so that thus the time of the night-

scene here described is not that of the last quarter of the moon
(Ewald), in which it rises at midnight, but that of the new
moon (Hitzig), when the night is without moonlight. Since
the derivation of the word from כסא (כסה), to cover, gives the
satisfactory idea of the covering or filling of the moon's disk, we
do not seek after any other; Dietrich fixes on the root-idea of
roundness, and Hitzig of vision (כסא = סכה, שׂכה; *vid.*, on the contrary, under Ps. cxliii. 9). The לְ is that of time at which, in
which, about which, anything is done; it is more indefinite than בְּ
would be. He will not return for some fourteen days.
The result:—

> 21 She beguiled him by the fulness of her talking,
> By the smoothness of her lips she drew him away.

Here is a climax. First she brought him to yield, overcoming
the resistance of his mind to the last point (cf. 1 Kings xi. 3);
then drove him, or, as we say, hurried him wholly away, viz. from
the right path or conduct (cf. Deut. xiii. 6, 11). With הִטַּתּוּ
(= הִטַּתְהוּ) as the chief *factum*, the past imperf. is interchanged,
21*b*. Regarding לֶקַח, see above, p. 56. Here is the rhetoric of
sin (Zöckler); and perhaps the לֶקַח of 20*a* has suggested this anti-
phrastic לֶקַח to the author (Hitzig), as חֵלֶק (the inverted לֶקַח, formed
like שֵׁפֶל, which is the *abstr.* of שָׁפָל as that is of חָלָק) and תַּדִּיחֶנּוּ are
reciprocally conditioned, for the idea of the slippery (Ps. lxxiii. 18)
connects itself with חלק.
What followed:—

> 22 So he goes after her at once
> As an ox which goeth to the slaughter-house,
> And as one bereft of reason to the restraint of fetters,
> 23 As a bird hastens to the net,
> Without knowing that his life is at stake—
> Till the arrow pierces his liver.

The *part.* הֹלֵךְ (thus to be accentuated according to the rule in
Baer's *Torath Emeth*, p. 25, with *Mercha* to the tone-syllable and
Mahpach to the preceding open syllable) preserves the idea of the
fool's going after her. פִּתְאֹם (suddenly) fixes the point, when he
all at once resolves to betake himself to the rendezvous in the
house of the adulteress, now a κεπφωθείς, as the LXX. translates,
i.e., as we say, a simpleton who has gone on the lime-twig. He
follows her as an ox goes to the slaughter-house, unconscious that

he is going thither to be slaughtered ; the LXX. ungrammatically destroying the attributive clause : ὥσπερ δὲ βοῦς ἐπὶ σφαγὴν ἄγεται. The difficulties in וּכְעֶכֶס (thus punctuated, after Kimchi, with a double *Segol*, and not וּכְעֶכֶס, as is frequently the case) multiply, and it is not to be reconciled with the traditional text. The ox appears to require another beast as a side-piece ; and accordingly the LXX., Syr., and Targ. find in עֶכֶס a dog (to which from אֱוִיל they also pick out אַיָּל, a stag), Jerome a lamb (*et quasi agnus* כֶּבֶשׂ), Rashi a venomous serpent (perhaps after ἔχις?), Löwenstein and Malbim a rattlesnake (נחש מְצַלְצֵל after עֶכֶס); but all this is mere conjecture. Symmachus' σκιρτῶν (ἐπὶ δεσμῶν ἄφρων) is without support, and, like the favourite rendering of Schelling, *et sicut saliens in vinculum cervus* (אַיָּל), is unsuitable on account of the unsemitic position of the words. The noun עֶכֶס, plur. עֲכָסִים, signifies, Isa. iii. 18, an anklet as a female ornament (whence ver. 16 the denom. עָכַס, to make a tinkling of the anklets). In itself the word only means the fetter, *compes*, from עָכַס, Arab. 'akas, 'akash, *contrahere, constringere* (*vid.* Fleischer under Isa. lix. 5) ; and that it can also be used of any kind of means of checking free movement, the Arab. 'ikâs, as the name of a cord with which the camel is made fast by the head and forefeet, shows. With this signification the interpretation is : *et velut pedicâ* (= וּכְבֶעֶכֶס) *implicatus ad castigationem stulti*, he follows her as if (bound) with a fetter to the punishment of the fool, *i.e.* of himself (Michaelis, Fleischer, and others). Otherwise Luther, who first translated " in a fetter," but afterwards (supplying לְ, not כְּ) : " and as if to fetters, where one corrects fools." But the ellipsis is harsh, and the parallelism leads us to expect a living being in the place of עֶכֶס. Now since, according to Gesenius, עֶכֶס, fetter, can be equivalent to a fettered one neither at Isa. xvii. 5, xxi. 17, nor Prov. xxiii. 28 (according to which עֶכֶס must at least have an active personal signification), we transpose the nouns of the clause and write וּכְאֱוִיל אֶל־מוּסָר עֶכֶס, he follows her as a fool (*Psychol.* p. 292) to correction (restraint) with fetters ; or if אֱוִיל is to be understood not so much physically as morally, and refers to self-destroying conduct (Ps. cvii. 7) : as a madman, *i.e.* a criminal, to chains. The one figure denotes the fate into which he rushes, like a beast devoid of reason, as the loss of life ; and the other denotes the fate to which he permits himself to be led by that woman, like a criminal by the officer, as the loss of freedom and of honour.

Ver. 23. The confusion into which the text has fallen is continued in this verse. For the figure of the deadly arrow connects itself neither with that of the ox which goes to the slaughter-house, nor with that of the madman who is put in chains : the former is not killed by being shot; and with the latter, the object is to render him harmless, not to put him to death. The LXX. therefore converts אֱוִיל into אַיָּל, a stag, and connects the shooting with an arrow with this : ἢ ὡς ἔλαφος τοξεύματι πεπληγὼς εἰς τὸ ἧπαρ. But we need no encroachment on the text itself, only a correct placing of its members. The three thoughts, ver. 23, reach a right conclusion and issue, if with כְּמַהֵר צִפּוֹר אֶל־פָּח (here *Mercha-mahpach*) a new departure is begun with a comparison : he follows her with eager desires, like as a bird hastens to the snare (*vid.* regarding פַּח, a snare, and מוֹקֵשׁ, a noose, under Isa. viii. 15). What then follows is a continuation of 22*a*. The subject is again the youth, whose way is compared to that of an ox going to the slaughter, of a culprit in chains, and of a fool; and he knows not (*non novit*, as iv. 19, ix. 18, and according to the sense, *non curat*, iii. 6, v. 6) that it is done at the risk of his life (בְנַפְשׁוֹ as 1 Kings ii. 23, Num. xvii. 3), that his life is the price with which this kind of love is bought (הוּא, *neut.*, as not merely Eccles. ii. 1 and the like, but also *e.g.* Lev. x. 3, Esth. ix 1)—that does not concern him till (עַד = אֲשֶׁר עַד or עַד כִּי) the arrow breaks or pierces through (פִּלַּח as Job. xvi. 13) his liver, *i.e.* till he receives the death-wound, from which, if not immediately, yet at length he certainly dies. Elsewhere the part of the body struck with a deadly wound is called the reins or loins (Job, etc.), or the gall-bladder (Job xx. 25); here the liver, which is called כָּבֵד, Arab. *kebid*, perhaps as the organ in which sorrowful and painful affections make themselves felt (cf. Æschylus, *Agam.* 801: δῆγμα λύπης ἐφ᾽ ἧπαρ προσικνεῖται), especially the latter, because the passion of sensual love, according to the idea of the ancients, reflected itself in the liver. He who is love-sick has *jecur ulcerosum* (Horace, *Od.* i. 25. 15); he is diseased in his liver (*Psychol.* p. 268). But the arrow is not here the arrow of love which makes love-sick, but the arrow of death, which slays him who is ensnared in sinful love. The befooled youth continues the disreputable relation into which he has entered till it terminates in adultery and in lingering disease upon his body, remorse in his soul, and dishonour to his name, speedily ending in inevitable ruin both spiritually and temporally.

Vers. 24, 25. With וְעַתָּה, as at v. 7, the author now brings his narrative to a close, adding the exhortation deduced from it:

24 And now, ye children, give ear unto me,
   And observe the words of my mouth!
25 Let not thine heart incline to her ways,
   And stray not in her paths.

The verb שָׂטָה (whence *jêst*, like *jêt*, iv. 15, with long *ê* from *i*) the author uses also of departure from a wicked way (iv. 15); but here, where the portraiture of a faithless wife (a סוֹטָה) is presented, the word used in the law of jealousy, Num. v., for the trespass of an אֵשֶׁת אִישׁ is specially appropriate. שׂטה is interchanged with תָּעָה (cf. Gen. xxi. 14): wander not on her paths, which would be the consequence of straying on them. Theodotion: καὶ μὴ πλανηθῇς ἐν ἀτραποῖς αὐτῆς, with καί, as also Syr., Targ., and Jerome. The Masora reckons this verse to the 25 which have אל at the beginning and ואל at the middle of each clause (*vid.* Baer in the *Luth. Zeitschrift*, 1865, p. 587); the text of Norzi has therefore correctly וְאַל, which is found also in good MSS. (*e.g.* the Erfurt, 2 and 3).

Vers. 26, 27. The admonition, having its motive in that which goes before, is now founded on the emphatic *finale*:

26 For many are the slain whom she hath caused to fall,
   And many are her slain.
27 A multiplicity of ways to hell is her house,
   Going down to the chambers of death.

The translation "for many slain has she laid low" (Syr., Targ., Jerome, Luther) is also syntactically possible; for רַבִּים can be placed before its substantive after the manner of the demonstratives and numerals (*e.g.* Neh. ix. 28, cf. אחד, Cant. iv. 9), and the accentuation which requires two servants (the usual two *Munachs*) to the *Athnach* appears indeed thus to construe it. It is otherwise if רבים here meant *magni* (thus *e.g.* Ralbag, and recently Bertheau), and not *multi*; but רבים and עֲצֻמִים stand elsewhere in connection with each other in the signification many and numerous, Ps. xxxv. 18, Joel ii. 2, Mic. iv. 3. "Her slain" are those slain by her; the part. pass. is connected with the genitive of the actor, *e.g.* ix. 18; cf. (Arab.) *katyl âlmhabbt*, of one whom love kills (Fl.). With ver. 27 cf. ii. 18, ix. 18. In 27a, בֵּיתָהּ is not equivalent to בביתה after viii. 2, also not elliptical and equivalent to דרכי ביתה; the former is unnecessary, the latter is in no case established by Ps.

xlv. 7, Ezra x. 13, nor by Deut. viii. 15, 2 Kings xxiii. 17 (see, on the other hand, Philippi's *Status Constructus*, pp. 87–93). Rightly Hitzig has: her house forms a multiplicity of ways to hell, in so far as adultery leads by a diversity of ways to hell. Similarly the subject and the predicate vary in number, xvi. 25, Ps. cx. 3, Job xxvi. 13, Dan. ix. 23, and frequently. If one is once in her house, he may go in this or in that way, but surely his path is to destruction : it consists of many steps to hell, such as lead down (דרך, fem. Isa. xxxvii. 34, masc. Isa. xxx. 21) to the extreme depths of death (cf. Job ix. 9, "chambers of the south " = its remotest regions veiling themselves in the invisible) ; for חֶדֶר (Arab. *khiddr*) is the part of the tent or the house removed farthest back, and the most private (Fl.). These חַדְרֵי־מָוֶת, cf. עִמְקֵי שְׁאוֹל, ix. 18, approach to the conception of גֵּיהִנֹּם, which is afterwards distinguished from שְׁאוֹל.

FOURTEENTH INTRODUCTORY MASHAL DISCOURSE VIII.

A DISCOURSE OF WISDOM CONCERNING HER EXCELLENCE AND HER GIFTS.

The author has now almost exhausted the ethical material; for in this introduction to the Solomonic Book of Proverbs he works it into a memorial for youth, so that it is time to think of concluding the circle by bending back the end to the beginning. For as in the beginning, i. 20 ff., so also here in the end, he introduces Wisdom herself as speaking. There, her own testimony is delivered in contrast to the alluring voice of the deceiver ; here, the daughter of Heaven in the highways inviting to come to her, is the contrast to the adulteress lurking in the streets, who is indeed not a personification, but a woman of flesh and blood, but yet at the same time as the incarnate ἀπάτη of worldly lust. He places opposite to her Wisdom, whose person is indeed not so sensibly perceptible, but who is nevertheless as real, coming near to men in a human way, and seeking to win them by her gifts.

1 Doth not Wisdom discourse,
   And Understanding cause her voice to be heard?
2 On the top of the high places in the way,
   In the midst of the way, she has placed herself.

> 3 By the side of the gates, at the exit of the city,
> At the entrance to the doors, she calleth aloud.

As הִנֵּה points to that which is matter of fact, so הֲלֹא calls to a consideration of it (cf. xiv. 22); the question before the reader is doubly justified with reference to i. 20 ff. With חכמה, תבונה is interchanged, as *e.g.* ii. 1–6; such names of wisdom are related to its principal name almost as אלהים, עליון, and the like, to יהוה. In describing the scene, the author, as usual, heaps up synonyms which touch one another without coming together.

Ver. 2. By מְרֹמִים Hitzig understands the summit of a mountain, and therefore regards this verse as an interpolation; but the "high places" are to be understood of the high-lying parts of the city. There, on the way which leads up and down, she takes her stand.

עֲלֵי = علىٰ, old and poetic for עַל, signifies here "hard by, close to," properly, so that something stands forward over the edge of a thing, or, as it were, passes over its borders (Fl.). The בֵּית, Hitzig, as Bertheau, with LXX., Targ., Jerome, interpret prepositionally as a strengthening of בְּין (in the midst); but where it once, Ezek. i. 27, occurs in this sense, it is fully written בֵּית לְ. Here it is the *accus. loci* of the substantive; "house of the ascent" (Syr. *bêth urchotho*) is the place where several ways meet, the uniting point, as אֵם הדרך (Ezek. xxi. 26), the point of departure, exit; the former the crossway, as the latter the separating way. Thus Immanuel: the place of the frequented streets; Meïri: the place of the ramification (more correctly, the concentration) of the ways. נִצָּבָה signifies more than קָמָה (she raises herself) and עָמְדָה (she goes thither); it means that she plants herself there.

Ver. 3. In this verse Bertheau finds, not inappropriately, the designations of place: on this side, on that side, and within the gate. לְיַד, at the hand, is equivalent to at the side, as Ps. cxl. 6. לְפִי, of the town, is the same as לְפֶתַח, ix. 14, of the house: at the mouth, *i.e.* at the entrance of the city, thus where they go out and in. There are several of these ways for leaving and entering a city, and on this account מְבוֹא פְתָחִים are connected: generally where one goes out and in through one of the gates (doors). מְבוֹא, fully represented by the French *avenue*, the space or way which leads to anything (Fl.). There she raises her voice, which sounds out far and wide; *vid.* concerning תָּרֹנָּה (*Græc. Venet.* incorrectly, after Rashi, ἀλαλάξουσι), at i. 20.

Now begins the discourse. The exordium summons general attention to it with the emphasis of its absolute truth:

> 4 " To you, ye men, is my discourse addressed,
>   And my call is to the children of men !
> 5 Apprehend, O ye simple ones, what wisdom is;
>   And, ye fools, what understanding is.
> 6 Hear, for I will speak princely things,
>   And the opening of my lips is upright.
> 7 For my mouth uttereth truth,
>   And a wicked thing is an abomination to my lips.
> 8 The utterances of my mouth are in rectitude,
>   There is nothing crooked or perverse in them.
> 9 To the men of understanding they are all to the point,
>   And plain to those who have attained knowledge."

Hitzig rejects this section, 4–12, as he does several others in viii. and ix., as spurious. But if this preamble, which reminds us of Elihu, is not according to every one's taste, yet in respect of the circle of conception and thought, as well as of the varying develop- ment of certain fundamental thoughts, it is altogether after the manner of the poet. The terminology is one that is strange to us ; the translation of it is therefore difficult ; that which is given above strives at least not to be so bad as to bring discredit on the poet. The tautology and flatness of ver. 4 disappears when one under- stands אִישִׁים and בְּנֵי אָדָם like the Attic ἄνδρες and ἄνθρωποι ; vid. under Isa. ii. 9, liii. 3 (where אִישִׁים, as here and Ps. cxli. 4, is equivalent to בְּנֵי אִישׁ, Ps. xlix. 3, iv. 3). Wisdom turns herself with her discourses to high and low, to persons of standing and to the *proletariat*. The verbal clause 4*a* interchanges with a noun clause 4*b*, as frequently a preposition with its noun (*e.g.* ver. 8*a*) completes the whole predicate of a semistich (Fl.).

Ver. 5. Regarding אָרְמָה, *calliditas*, in a good sense, *vid.* at i. 4 ; regarding פְּתָאִים, those who are easily susceptible of good or bad, according to the influence that is brought to bear upon them, *vid.* also i. 4 ; and regarding כְּסִילִים, the intellectually heavy, dull persons in whom the flesh burdens the mind, *vid.* at i. 22. לֵב is parallel with ערמה, for the heart (according to its Semitic etymon, that which remains fast, like a kernel, the central-point) is used for the under- standing of which it is the seat (*Psychol.* p. 249), or heartedness =intelligence (cf. חסר־לב, vi. 32=ἄνους or ἄλογος). We take ערמה and לב as objective, as we have translated : that which is in both, and in which they consist. Thus הֵבִין, which is a favourite word with this author, has both times the simple transitive meaning of the gain of understanding into the nature and worth of both; and we neither need to interpret the second הָבִינוּ in the double transitive meaning, " to bring to understanding," nor, with Hitzig, to change it into הָכִינוּ[1] [direct, *i.e. applicate*].

Ver. 6. That to which Wisdom invites, her discourse makes practicable, for she speaks of נְגִידִים. Hitzig interprets this word by *conspicua*, manifest truths, which the *Grœc. Venet.* understands to be ἐναντία, after Kimchi's interpretation: truths which one makes an aim and object (נֶגֶד) on account of their worth. Fürst, however, says that נגיד, from נָגַד, Arab. *najad*, means to be elevated, exalted, and thereby visible (whence also הִגִּיד, to bring to light, to bring forward); and that by נגידים, as the plur. of this נגיד, is to be understood *princeps* in the sense of *principalia*, or *prœstantia* (LXX. σεμνά; Theodot. ἡγεμονικά; Jerome, *de rebus magnis*) (cf. νόμος βασιλικός of the law of love, which surpasses the other laws, as kings do their subjects), which is supported by the similar expression, xxii. 20. But that we do not need to interpret נגידים as *abstr.*, like מֵישָׁרִים, and as the *acc. adverb.*: in noble ways, because in that case it ought to be נגידות (Berth.), is shown by xxii. 20, and also xvi. 13; cf. on this neuter use of the masc., Ewald, § 172a. " The opening of my lips (*i.e.* this, that they open themselves, not: that which they disclose, lay open) is upright " is to be regarded as *metonymia antecedentis pro conseq.*: that which I announce is . . .; or also as a poetic attribution, which attributes to a subject that which is produced by it (cf. iii. 17b): my discourse bearing itself right, brings to light (Fl.). xxiii. 16, cf. 31, is parallel both in the words and the subject; מֵישָׁרִים, that which is in accordance with fact and with rectitude, uprightness (*vid.* at i. 3), is a word common to the introduction (i.–ix.), and to the first appendix to the first series of Solomonic Proverbs (xxii. 17–xxiv. 22), with the Canticles. In Cant. v. 16 also, as here (cf. v. 3, Job vi. 30), the word palate [*Gaumen*] is used as the organ of speech.

Ver. 7. כִּי continues the reason (begun in ver. 6) for the Hearken! (cf. i. 15–17, iv. 16 f.); so that this second reason is co-ordinated with the first (Fl.). Regarding אֱמֶת, *vid.* at iii. 3; הָגָה, here of the palate (cf. Ps. xxxvii. 30), as in xv. 28 of the heart, has not hitherto occurred. It signifies quiet inward meditation, as well as also (but only poetically) discourses going forth from

---

[1] *Vid.* the *Hebr. Zeitschrift*, החלוץ, 1856, p. 112.

it (*vid.* at Ps. i. 2). The contrary of truth, *i.e.* moral truth, is רֶֽשַׁע,
wickedness in words and principles,—a segolate, which retains its
Segol also *in pausa*, with the single exception of Eccles. iii. 16.
Vers. 8, 9. The בְּ of בְּצֶדֶק is that of the close connection of a
quality with an action or matter, which forms with a substantive
adverbia as well as virtual *adjectiva*, as here : *cum rectitudine (con-
juncta i. e. vera) sunt omnia dicta oris mei* (Fl.) ; it is the בְּ of the
distinctive attribute (Hitzig), certainly related to the בְּ *essentiæ*
(iii. 26, according to which Schultens and Bertheau explain),
which is connected with the abstract conception (*e.g.* Ps. xxxiii. 4),
but also admits the article designating the gender (*vid.* at Ps.
xxix. 4). The opposite of צֶדֶק (here in the sense of *veracitas*,
which it means in Arab.) is נִפְתָּל וְעִקֵּשׁ, *dolosum ac perversum.*
עִקֵּשׁ (cf. Gesen. § 84, 9) is that which is violently bent and
twisted, *i.e.* estranged from the truth, which is, so to speak,
parodied or caricatured. Related to it in meaning, but proceeding from a somewhat different idea, is נִפְתָּל. פָּתַל, used primarily
of threads, cords, ropes, and the like, means to twist them, to twine
them over and into one another, whence פָּתִיל, a line or string made
of several intertwisted threads (cf. فَتِيلَة, a wick of a candle or
lamp) ; *Niph.*, to be twisted, specifically *luctari*, of the twisting of
the limbs, and figuratively to bend and twist oneself, like the
crafty (*versutus*) liars and deceivers, of words and thoughts which
do not directly go forth, but by the crafty twistings of truth and
rectitude, *opp.* יָשָׁר, נָכוֹן (Fl.). There is nothing of deception or
error in the utterances of wisdom ; much rather they are all נְכֹחִים,
straight out from her (cf. Isa. lvii. 2), going directly out, and
without circumlocution directed to the right end for the intelligent,
the knowing (cf. Neh. x. 29) ; and יְשָׁרִים, straight or even, giving
no occasion to stumble, removing the danger of erring for those
who have obtained knowledge, *i.e.* of good and evil, and thus the
ability of distinguishing between them (Gesen. § 134, 1),—briefly,
for those who know how to estimate them.

Her self-commendation is continued in the resumed address :

10 " Receive my instruction, and not silver,
   And knowledge rather than choice gold !
11 For wisdom is better than corals,
   And all precious jewels do not equal her.
12 I, Wisdom, inhabit prudence,
   And the knowledge of right counsels is attainable by me."

Instead of וְלֹא־כָסֶף influenced by קְחוּ, is וְאַל־כסף with תִּקְחוּ to be supplied; besides, with most Codd. and older editions, we are to accentuate קְחוּ מוּסָרִי with the erasure of the *Makkeph*. " Such negations and prohibitions," Fleischer remarks, " are to be understood comparatively: instead of acquiring silver, rather acquire wisdom. Similar is the old Arabic النار, ولا العار, the fire, and not the disgrace ! Also among the modern Arabic proverbs collected by Burckhardt, many have this form, *e.g.* No. 34, *alhajamat balafas wala alhajat alanas,* Better to let oneself be cut with the axe than to beg for the favour of another " 10*b* is to be translated, with Jerome, Kimchi, and others: and knowledge is more precious than fine gold (נִבְחָר, neut.: *auro pretiosius*); and in view of xvi. 16, this construction appears to be intended. But Fleischer has quite correctly affirmed that this assertatory clause is unsuitably placed as a parallel clause over against the preceding imperative clause, and, what is yet more important, that then ver. 11 would repeat *idem per idem* in a tautological manner. We therefore, after the Aramaic and Greek translators, take כסף נבחר together here as well as at ver. 19, inasmuch as we carry forward the קחו: *et scientiam præ auro lectissimo,* which is also according to the accentuation. Equally pregnant is the מן in מֵחָרוּץ of the passage iii. 14, 15, which is here varied.

Ver. 12 follows ver. 11 = iii. 15 as a justification of this estimating of wisdom above all else in worth. Regarding אֲנִי with *Gaja, vid.* the rule which the accentuation of this word in the three so-called metrical books follows in Merx' *Archiv,* 1868, p. 203 (cf. Baer's *Torath Emeth,* p. 40). We translate: *ego sapientia incolo sollertiam,* for the verb שָׁכֵן is construed with the accuastive of the object, ii. 21, x. 30, Ps. xxxvii. 3 (cf. גוּר, Ps. v. 5), as well as with בְ, Gen. xxvi. 2, Ps. lxix. 37. Wisdom inhabits prudence, has settled down, as it were, and taken up her residence in it, is at home in its whole sphere, and rules it. Bertheau not unsuitably compares οἰκῶν with μόνος ἔχων, 1 Tim. vi. 16. Regarding מְזִמּוֹת, *vid.* i. 4, v. 2. It denotes well-considered, carefully thought out designs, plans, conclusions, and דַעַת is here the knowledge that is so potent. This intellectual power is nothing beyond wisdom, it is in her possession on every occasion; she strives after it not in vain, her knowledge is defined according to her wish. Wisdom describes herself here personally with regard to that which she bestows on men who receive her.

Far remote is the idea that 13*a* is dependent on אֶמְצָא (I acquire) (Löwenstein, Bertheau). With this verse begins a new series of thoughts raising themselves on the basis of the fundamental clause 13*a*. Wisdom says what she hates, and why she hates it:

> 13 " The fear of Jahve is to hate evil ;
>   Pride and arrogancy, and an evil way
>   And a deceitful mouth, do I hate."

If the fear of God is the beginning of wisdom (ix. 10, i. 7), then wisdom, personally considered, stands before all else that is to be said of her in a relation of homage or reverence toward God corresponding to the fear of God on the part of man ; and if, as the premiss 13*a* shows, the fear of God has as its reverse side the hatred of evil, then there arises what Wisdom says in שָׂנֵאתִי (I hate) of herself. Instead of the *n. actionis* שִׂנְאַת (hatred), formed in the same way with יִרְאַת, which, admitting the article, becomes a substantive, the author uses, in order that he might designate the predicate as such (Hitzig), rather the *n. actionis* שְׂנֹאת, which is indeed also a noun, but is not used substantively ; שְׂנֹאת as מְלֹאת, Jer. xxix. 10. קְרֹאת, Judg. viii. 1, is equivalent to שְׂנֹאת like יְבֹשֶׁת, the becoming dry, יְכֹלֶת, the being able ; cf. (Arab.) *shanat*, hating, *malât*, well-being, *karât*, reading (Fl.). The evil which Wisdom hates is now particularized as, vi. 16–19, the evil which Jahve hates. The virtue of all virtues is humility ; therefore Wisdom hates, above all, self-exaltation in all its forms. The *paronomasia* גֵּאָה וְגָאֹון (pride and haughtiness) expresses the idea in the whole of its contents and compass (cf. Isa. xv. 6, iii. 1, and above at i. 27). גֵּאָה (from גֵּאֶה, the nominal form), that which is lofty = pride, stands with גָאֹון, as Job iv. 10, נֹבַהּ, that which is high = arrogance. There follows the *viam mali*, representing the sins of walk, *i.e.* of conduct, and *os fallax* (*vid.* at ii. 12), the sins of the mouth. Hitzig rightly rejects the interpunctuation רַע, and prefers רָע. In consequence of this *Dechî* (*Tiphcha init.*), וּפִי תַהְפֻּכֹת have in Codd. and good editions the servants *Asla* and *Illuj* (*vid.* Baer's *Torath Emeth*, p. 11) ; Aben-Ezra and Moses Kimchi consider the *Asla* erroneously as disjunctive, and explain וּפִי by *et os* = *axioma meum*, but *Asla* is conjunctive, and has after it the ה *raphatum*.

After Wisdom has said what she hates, and thus what she is not, she now says what she is, has, and promises:

14 " Mine is counsel and promotion ;
   I am understanding, mine is strength.
15 By me kings reign,
   And rulers govern justly.
16 By me princes rule, and nobles—
   All judges of the earth."

Whoever gives anything must himself possess it ; in this sense Wisdom claims for herself counsel, promotion (in the sense of offering and containing that which is essentially and truly good; vid. concerning תּוּשִׁיָה, ii. 7), and energy (vid. Eccles. vii. 19). But she does not merely possess בִּינָה ; this is much rather her peculiar nature, and is one with her. That ver. 14 is formed after Job xii. 13, 16 (Hitzig) is possible, without there following thence any argument against its genuineness. And if ver. 15 f., and Isa. xxxii. 1, x. 1, stand in intentional reciprocal relation, then the priority is on the side of the author of the Proverbs. The connection gives to the laconic expression its intended comprehensiveness. It is not meant that Wisdom has the highest places in the state to give, but that she makes men capable of holding and discharging the duties of these.

Ver. 15b. Here we are led to think of legislation, but the usage of the language determines for the *Po.* חֹקֵק only the significations of commanding, decreeing, or judging; צֶדֶק is the object. accus., the opposite of חִקְקֵי־אָוֶן (decrees of unrighteousness), Isa. x. 1. רֹזֵן is a poetic word, from רָזַן = Arab. *razuna*, to be heavy, weighty, then to be firm, incapable of being shaken, figuratively of majestic repose, dignity (cf. وقار, and כָּבוֹד) in the whole external *habitus*, in speech and action such as befits one invested with power (Fl.).

Ver. 16a. We may not explain the second clause of this verse : *et ad ingenua impelluntur quicunque terrœ imperant,* for נָדִיב is adj. without such a verbal sense. But besides, נדיבים is not pred., for which it is not adapted, because, with the obscuring of its ethical signification (from נָדַב, to impel inwardly, viz. to noble conduct, particularly to liberality), it also denotes those who are noble only with reference to birth, and not to disposition (Isa. xxxii. 8). Thus נדיבים is a fourth synonym for the highly exalted, and כָּל־שֹׁפְטֵי אָרֶץ is the summary placing together of all kinds of dignity; for שָׁפַט unites in itself references to government, administration of justice, and rule. כֹּל is used, and not וְכֹל—a so-called *asyndeton summativum*.

Instead of אֶרֶץ (LXX.) there is found also the word צֶדֶק (Syr., Targ., Jerome, *Græc. Venet.*, adopted by Norzi after Codd. and Neapol. 1487). But this word, if not derived from the conclusion of the preceding verse, is not needed by the text, and gives a summary which does not accord with that which is summed up (מלכים, רוזנים, שׂרים, נדיבים); besides, the Scripture elsewhere calls God Himself שׁופט צדק (Ps. ix. 5; Jer. xi. 20). The Masoretic reading[1] of most of the editions, which is also found in the Cod. Hillel (ספר הללי[2]), merits the preference.

The discourse of Wisdom makes a fresh departure, as at ver. 13: she tells how, to those who love her, she repays this love:

17 " I love them that love me,
      And they that seek me early find me.
18 Riches and honour are with me,
      Durable riches and righteousness.
19 Better is my fruit than pure and fine gold,
      And my revenue (better) than choice silver.
20 In the way of righteousness do I walk,
      In the midst of the paths of justice.
21 To give an inheritance to them that love me
      And I fill their treasuries."

The Chethîb אֹהֲבֶיהָ (*ego hos qui eam amant redamo*), Gesenius, *Lehrgeb.* § 196, 5, regards as a possible synallage (*eam = me*), but one would rather think that it ought to be read (יהוה =) ה' אֹהֲבֵי. The ancients all have the reading אֹהֲבַי. אֱהַב (=אֶאֱהַב, with the change of the *ĕĕ* into *ê*, and the compression of the radical א; cf. הֹבֵא, אֹמַר, i. 10) is the form of the *fut. Kal*, which is inflected תֶּאֱהֲבוּ, i. 22. Regarding שִׁחַר (the *Græc. Venet.* well: οἱ ὀρθρίζοντές μοι), *vid.* i. 28, where the same *epenthet. fut.* form is found.

Ver. 18. In this verse part of iii. 16 is repeated, after which אִתִּי is meant of possession (*mecum* and *penes me*). Regarding הוֹן, *vid.* i. 13; instead of the adjective יָקָר there, we have here עָתֵק. The verb עָתַק signifies *promoveri*, to move forwards, whence are derived the meanings old (cf. *ætas provecta*, advanced age), venerable for age, and noble, free (cf. עָתִיק, Isa. xxviii. 9, and Arab. 'atyk, manu-

[1] If the Masoretes had read שפטי צדק, then would they have added the remark לית ("it does not further occur"), and inserted the expression in their Register of Expressions, which occurs but once, *Masora finalis*, p. 62.
[2] [One of the most ancient and celebrated Codd. of the Heb. Scriptures, called Hillel from the name of the man who wrote it. *Vid.* Strack's *Prolegomena*, p. 112 It was written about A.D. 600.]

missus), unbound, the bold. Used of clothing, עָרִיק (Isa. xxiii. 18) expresses the idea of venerable for age. עָתֵק used of possessions and goods, like the Arab. '*âtak*, denotes such goods as increase during long possession as an inheritance from father to son, and remain firm, and are not for the first time gained, but only need to be inherited, *opes perennes et firmæ* (Schultens, Gesenius' *Thesaur.*, Fleischer), although it may be also explained (which is, however, less probable with the form עָתֵק) of the idea of the venerable from *opes superbæ* (Jerome), splendid opulence. צְדָקָה is here also a good which is distributed, but properly the distributing goodness itself, as the Arab. *sadakat*, influenced by the later use of the Hebrew צדקה (δικαιοσύνη = ἐλεημοσύνη), denotes all that which God of His goodness causes to flow to men, or which men bestow upon men (Fl.). Righteousness is partly a recompensative goodness, which rewards, according to the law of requital, like with like; partly communicative, which, according to the law of love without merit, and even in opposition to it, bestows all that is good, and above all, itself; but giving itself to man, it assimilates him to itself (*vid.* Ps. xxiv. 7), so that he becomes צדיק, and is regarded as such before God and men, ver. 19.

The fruit and product of wisdom (the former a figure taken from the trees, iii. 18; the latter from the sowing of seed, iii. 9) is the gain and profit which it yields. With חרוץ, viii. 10, iii. 14, פֶּז is here named as the place of fine gold, briefly for זָהָב מוּפָז, solid gold, gold separated from the place of ore which contains it, or generally separated gold, from פָּז, violently to separate metals from base mixtures; Targ. דַּהֲבָא אוֹבְרִיזִין, gold which has stood the fire-test, *obrussa*, of the crucible, Greek ὄβρυζον, Pers. *ebríz*, Arab. *ibríz*. In the last clause of this verse, as also in 10*b*, נִבְחָר is to be interpreted as pred. to תְּבוּאָתִי, but the balance of the meaning demands as a side-piece to the מֵחָרוּץ וּמִפָּז (19*a*) something more than the mere כֶּסֶף. In 20 f. the reciprocal love is placed as the answer of love under the point of view of the requiting righteousness. But recompensative and communicative righteousness are here combined, where therefore the subject is the requital of worthy pure love and loving conduct, like with like. Such love requires reciprocal love, not merely cordial love, but that which expresses itself outwardly.

Vers. 20, 21. In this sense, Wisdom says that she acts strictly according to justice and rectitude, and adds (21) wherein this her

conduct manifests itself. The *Piel* הֵלֵךְ expresses firm, constant
action ; and בְּתוֹךְ means that she turns from this line of conduct
on no side. לְהַנְחִיל is distinguished from בְּהַנְחִיל, as *ut possidendam
tribuam* from *possidendam tribuendo;* the former denotes the
direction of the activity, the latter its nature and manner ; both
combine if we translate *ita ut* . . .[1] Regarding the origin of יֵשׁ,
vid. at ii. 7 ; it denotes the being founded, thus *substantia,* and
appears here, like the word in mediæval Latin and Romanic (Ital.
sustanza, Span. *substancia*), and like οὐσία and ὕπαρξις (τὰ ὑπάρ-
χοντα) in classic Greek, to denote possessions and goods. But since
this use of the word does not elsewhere occur (therefore Hitzig
explains יֵשׁ = לִי יֵשׁ, I have it [= *presto est*]), and here, where
Wisdom speaks, יֵשׁ connects itself in thought with תּוּשִׁיָּה, it will at
least denote real possession (as we also are wont to call not every
kind of property, but only landed property, *real* possession), such
possession as has real worth, and that not according to commercial
exchange and price, but according to sound judgment, which applies a higher than the common worldly standard of worth. The
Pasek between אֹהֲבַי and יֵשׁ is designed to separate the two *Jods*
from each other, and has, as a consequence, for לְהַנְחִיל אֹהֲבַי the
accentuation with *Tarcha* and *Mercha* (*vid. Accentssystem,* vi. § 4 ;
cf. *Torath Emeth,* p. 17, § 3). The carrying forward of the inf.
with the finite, 21*b*, is as i. 27, ii. 2, and quite usual.

Ver. 22. Wisdom takes now a new departure, in establishing
her right to be heard, and to be obeyed and loved by men. As
the Divine King in Ps. ii. opposes to His adversaries the self-
testimony: "I will speak concerning a decree ! Jahve said unto
me: Thou art my Son ; this day have I begotten Thee;" so
Wisdom here unfolds her divine patent of nobility : she originates
with God before all creatures, and is the object of God's love and
joy, as she also has the object of her love and joy on God's earth,
and especially among the sons of men :

> " Jahve brought me forth as the beginning of His way,
>   As the foremost of His works from of old."

The old translators render קָנָנִי (with *Kametz* by *Dechî; vid.* under
Ps. cxviii. 5) partly by verbs of creating (LXX. ἔκτισε, Syr.

---

[1] Biesenthal combines the etymologically obscure הנחיל with נָחַל : to make
to flow into, so that נַחַל denotes inheritance in contradistinction to acquisition;
while נַחֲלָה, in contradistinction to יְרֻשָּׁה, denotes the inheritance rather of
many than of the individual.

Targ. בְּרָאָנִי), partly by verbs of acquiring (Aquila, Symmachus, Theodotion, Venet. ἐκτήσατο; Jerome, *possedit*); Wisdom appears also as created, certainly not without reference to this passage, Sir. i. 4, προτέρα πάντων ἔκτισται σοφία; i. 9, αὐτὸς ἔκτισεν αὐτήν; xxiv. 8, ὁ κτίσας με. In the christological controversy this word gained a dogmatic signification, for they proceeded generally on the identity of σοφία ὑποστατική (*sapientia substantialis*) with the *hypostasis* of the Son of God. The Arians used the ἔκτισέ με as a proof of their doctrine of the *filius non genitus, sed factus, i.e.* of His existence before the world began indeed, but yet not from eternity, but originating in time; while, on the contrary, the orthodox preferred the translation ἐκτήσατο, and understood it of the co-eternal existence of the Son with the Father, and agreed with the ἔκτισε of the LXX. by referring it not to the actual existence, but to the position, place of the Son (Athanasius: *Deus me creavit regem* or *caput operum suorum;* Cyrill.: *non condidit secundum substantiam, sed constituit me totius universi principium et fundamentum*). But (1) Wisdom is not God, but is God's; she has personal existence in the Logos of the N. T., but is not herself the Logos; she is the world-idea, which, once projected, is objective to God, not as a dead form, but as a living spiritual image; she is the archetype of the world, which, originating from God, stands before God, the world of the idea which forms the medium between the Godhead and the world of actual existence, the communicated spiritual power in the origination and the completion of the world as God designed it to be. This wisdom the poet here personifies; he does not speak of the personal Logos, but the further progress of the revelation points to her actual personification in the Logos. And (2) since to her the poet attributes an existence preceding the creation of the world, he thereby declares her to be eternal, for to be before the world is to be before time. For if he places her at the head of the creatures, as the first of them, so therewith he does not seek to make her a creature of this world having its commencement in time; he connects her origination with the origination of the creature only on this account, because that *à priori* refers and tends to the latter; the power which was before heaven and earth were, and which operated at the creation of the earth and of the heavens, cannot certainly fall under the category of the creatures around and above us. Therefore (3) the translation with ἔκτισεν has nothing against it, but it is different from the κτίσις of the

heavens and the earth, and the poet has intentionally written not
בְּרָאַנִי, but קֹנֵנִי. Certainly קנה, Arab. *knâ*, like all the words used
of creating, refers to one root-idea : that of forging (*vid.* under
Gen. iv. 22), as ברא does to that of cutting (*vid.* under Gen. i. 1) ;
but the mark of a commencement in time does not affix itself to קנה
in the same way as it does to ברא, which always expresses the
divine production of that which has not hitherto existed. קנה comprehends in it the meanings to create, and to create something for
oneself, to prepare, *parare* (*e.g.* Ps. cxxxix. 13), and to prepare
something for oneself, *comparare*, as κτίζειν and κτᾶσθαι, both
from *kshi*, to build, the former expressed by *struere*, and the latter
by *sibi struere*. In the קֹנֵנִי, then, there are the ideas, both that
God produced wisdom, and that He made Himself to possess it ;
not certainly, however, as a man makes himself to possess wisdom
from without, iv. 7. But the idea of the bringing forth is here
the nearest demanded by the connection. For רֵאשִׁית דַּרְכּוֹ is not
equivalent to בְּרֵאשִׁית דרכו (Syr., Targ., Luther), as Jerome also
reads : *Ita enim scriptum est :* ADONAI CANANI BRESITH DERCHO
(*Ep.* cxl. *ad Cyprian.*) ; but it is, as Job xl. 19 shows, the second
accusative of the object (LXX., Aquila, Symmachus, Theodotion).
But if God made wisdom as the beginning of His way, *i.e.* of His
creative efficiency (cf. Rev. iii. 14 and Col. i. 15), the making is
not to be thought of as acquiring, but as a bringing forth, revealing this creative efficiency of God, having it in view ; and this is
also confirmed by the חוֹלָלְתִּי (*genita sum;* cf. Gen. iv. 1, קָנִיתִי,
genui) following. Accordingly, קֶדֶם מִפְעָלָיו (foremost of His works)
has to be regarded as a parallel second object. accusative. All the
old translators interpret קדם as a preposition [before], but the
usage of the language before us does not recognise it as such ; this
would be an Aramaism, for קֳדָם, Dan. vii. 7, frequently מִן־קֳדָם
(Syr., Targ.), is so used. But as קֶדֶם signifies previous existence
in space, and then in time (*vid.* Orelli, *Zeit und Ewigkeit*, p. 76),
so it may be used of the object in which the previous existence
appears, thus (after Sir. i. 4): προτέραν τῶν ἔργων αὐτοῦ (Hitzig).

Ver. 23. A designation of the When ? expressed first by מֵאָז
(Isa. xlviii. 8, cf. xl. 21), is further unfolded :

> " From everlasting was I set up,
> From the beginning, from the foundations of the earth."

That נִסַּכְתִּי cannot be translated : I was anointed = consecrated,
vid. at Ps. ii. 6. But the translation also : I was woven = wrought

(Hitzig, Ewald, and previously one of the Greeks, ἐδιάσθην), does not commend itself, for רֻקַּם (Ps. cxxxix. 15), used of the embryo, lies far from the metaphorical sense in which נָסַךְ = Arab. *nasaj*, *texere*, would here be translated of the origin of a person, and even of such a spiritual being as Wisdom ; נִסַּכְתִּי, as the LXX. reads (ἐθεμελίωσέ με), is not once used of such. Rightly Aquila, κατεστάθην ; Symmachus, προκεχείρισμαι; Jerome, *ordinata sum*. Literally, but unintelligibly, the *Gr. Venet.* κέχυμαι, according to which (cf. Sir. i. 10) Böttcher: I was poured forth = formed, but himself acknowledging that this figure is not suitable to personification ; nor is it at all likely that the author applied the word, used in this sense of idols, to the origin of Wisdom. The fact is, that נָסַךְ, used as seldom of the anointing or consecration of kings as סוּךְ, passes over, like הִצִּיק (הֵצִיק), מָצוּק צוּק (a pillar), and יַצַּג (הִצִּיג), from the meaning of pouring out to that of placing and appointing ; the mediating idea appears to be that of the pouring forth of the metal, since נָסִיךְ, Dan. xi. 8, like נֶסֶךְ, signifies a molten image. The Jewish interpreters quite correctly remark, in comparing it with the princely name נָסִיךְ [cf. Ps. lxxxiii. 12] (although without etymological insight), that a placing in princely dignity is meant. Of the three synonyms of *æternitas a parte ante*, מֵעוֹלָם points backwards into the infinite distance, מֵרֹאשׁ into the beginning of the world, מִקַּדְמֵי־אָרֶץ not into the times which precede the origin of the earth, but into the oldest times of its gradual arising ; this קַדְמֵי it is impossible to render, in conformity with the Hebr. use of language : it is an extensive plur. of time, Böttcher, § 697. The מִן repeated does not mean that the origin and greatness of Wisdom are contemporaneous with the foundation of the world; but that when the world was founded, she was already an actual existence.

This her existence before the world began is now set forth in yet more explicit statements :

24 " When there were as yet no floods was I brought forth,
    When as yet there were no fountains which abounded with water ;
25 For before the mountains were settled,
    Before the hills was I brought forth,
26 While as yet He had not made land and plains,
    And the sum of the dust of the earth."

The description is poetical, and affords some room for imagination. By תְּהוֹמוֹת are not intended the unrestrained primeval waters, but, as also iii. 20, the inner waters, treasures of the earth ; and consequently by מַעְיְנוֹת, not the fountains of the sea on this earth (Ewald, after Job xxxviii. 16), but the springs or places of springs (for מַעְיָן is *n. loci* to עַיִן, a well as an eye of the earth; *vid.* Gen. xvi. 7), by means of which the internal waters of the earth communicate themselves to the earth above (cf. Gen. vii. 11 with xlix. 25). נִכְבַּדֵּי־מָיִם (abounding with water) is a descriptive *epitheton* to מַעְיָנוֹת, which, notwithstanding its fem. plur., is construed as masc. (cf. v. 16). The Masora does not distinguish the thrice-occurring נכבדי according to its form as written (Isa. xxiii. 8, 9). The form נְכְבְּדֵי (which, like בָּתִּים, would demand *Metheg*) is to be rejected; it is everywhere to be written נִכְבַּדֵּי (Ewald, § 214*b*) with *Pathach*, with *Dagesh* following; *vid.* Kimchi, *Michlol* 61*b*. Kimchi adds the gloss מעיני מים רבים, which the *Gr. Venet.*, in accordance with the meaning of נכבד elsewhere, renders by πηγαῖς δεδοξασμένων ὑδάτων (as also Böttcher: the most honoured = the most lordly); but Meîri, Immanuel, and others rightly judge that the adjective is here to be understood after Gen. xiii. 2, Job xiv. 21 (but in this latter passage כבד does not mean "to be numerous"): loaded = endowed in rich measure.

Ver. 25. Instead of בְּאַיִן, in (yet) non-existence (24), we have here טֶרֶם, a subst. which signifies cutting off from that which already exists (*vid.* at Gen. ii. 5), and then as a particle *nondum* or *antequam*, with בְּ always *antequam*, and in ver. 26 עַד־לֹא, so long not yet (this also originally a substantive from עֲדָה, in the sense of progress). With הָטְבָּעוּ (were settled) (as Job xxxviii. 6, from טָבַע, to impress into or upon anything, *imprimere, infigere*) the question is asked: wherein? Not indeed: in the depths of the earth, but as the Caraite Ahron b. Joseph answers, אֶל קרקע הים, in the bottom of the sea; for out of the waters they rise up, Ps. civ. 8 (cf. at Gen. i. 9).

Ver. 26. אֶרֶץ וְחוּצוֹת is either, connecting the whole with its part: *terra cum campis*, or ארץ gains by this connection the meaning of land covered with buildings, while חוצות the expanse of unoccupied land, or the free field outside the towns and villages (cf. בַּר, Arab. *barrytt*) (Fl.), *vid.* Job v. 10, xviii. 17 (where we have translated " in the steppe far and wide"); and regarding the fundamental idea, *vid.* above at v. 16. Synonymous with ארץ, as contrast to חוצות, is תֵּבֵל, which like יְבוּל (produce, wealth) comes from יָבַל, and thus denotes the earth as fruit-bearing (as אֲדָמָה properly denotes the *humus* as the covering of earth). Accordingly,

with Ewald, we may understand by רֹאשׁ עָפְרוֹת, "the heaps of the
many clods of the fertile arable land lying as if scattered on the
plains." Hitzig also translates : " the first clods of the earth." We
do not deny that עפרות may mean clods of earth, *i.e.* pieces of earth
gathered together, as Job xxviii. 6, עַפְרֹת זהב, gold ore, *i.e.* pieces
of earth or ore containing gold. But for clods of earth the Heb.
language has the nouns רֶגֶב and מְגְרָפָה; and if we read together
עָפְרוֹת, plur. of the collective עָפָר (dust as a mass), which comes as
from a *n. unitatis* עֲפָרָה, and רֹאשׁ, which, among its meanings in
poetry as well as in prose, has also that of the sum, *i.e.* the chief
amount or the total amount (cf. the Arab. *râs âlmâl*, the capital, τὸ
κεφάλαιον), then the two words in their mutual relation yield the
sense of the sum of the several parts of the dust, as of the atoms
of dust (Cocceius ; Schultens, *summam pulverum orbis habitabilis*) ;
and Fleischer rightly remarks that other interpretations, as *ab initio
pulveris orbis*, *præcipua quæque orbis terrarum*, *caput orbis terrarum*
(*i.e.* according to Rashi, the first man ; according to Umbreit, man
generally), leave the choice of the plur. עפרות unintelligible. Before these creatures originated, Wisdom was, as she herself says,
and emphatically repeats, already born ; חוֹלָלְתִּי is the passive of
the *Pilel* חוֹלֵל, which means to whirl, to twist oneself, to bring
forth with sorrow (Aquila, Theodotion, ὠδινήθην; *Græc. Venet.*
24*a*, πέπλασμαι, 25*b*, ὠδίνημαι), then but poet. generally to beget,
to bring forth (xxv. 23, xxvi. 10).

Ver. 27. But not only did her existence precede the laying of
the foundation of the world; she was also actively taking part in
the creative work:

" When He prepared the heavens, I was there,
    When He measured out a circle for the mirror of the multitude of waters."

Again a sentence clothed with two designations of time. The
adv. of place שָׁם is used, chiefly poetically, for אָז, *eo tempore* (Arab.
thumm, in contradistinction to *thamm, eo loco*) ; but here it has the
signification of place, which includes that of time : Wisdom was
there when God created the world, and had then already long
before that come into existence, like as the servant of Jahve, Isa.
xlviii. 16, with just such a שָׁם אָנִי, says that He is there from the
time that the history of nations received a new direction, beginning
with Cyrus. הֵכִין signifies to give a firm position or a definite
direction. Thus Job xxviii. 27 of Wisdom, whom the Creator
places before Himself as a pattern (ideal) ; here, as Jer. x. 12, Ps.

lxv. 7, of the setting up, restoring throughout the whole world. In the parallel member, חוג, corresponding to שָׁמַיִם, appears necessarily to designate the circle or the vault of the heavens (Job xxii. 14), which, according to the idea of the Hebrews, as in Homer, rests as a half-globe on the outermost ends of the disc of the earth surrounded with water, and thus lies on the waters. *Vid.* Hupfeld under Ps. xxiv. 2. This idea of the ocean girdling the earth is introduced into the O. T. without its being sanctioned by it. The LXX. (καὶ ὅτε ἀφώριζε τὸν ἑαυτοῦ θρόνον ἐπ' ἀνέμων) appears to understand תהום of the waters above; but תהום never has this meaning, יָם (Job ix. 8, xxxvi. 30) might rather be interpreted of the ocean of the heavens. The passage in accordance with which this before us is to be expounded is Job xxvi. 10 : He has set a limit for the surface of the waters, *i.e.* describing over them a circle setting bounds to their region. So here, with the exchange of the functions of the two words : when He marked out a circle over the surface of the multitude of waters, viz. to appoint a fixed region (מִקְוֶה, Gen. i. 10) for them, *i.e.* the seas, fountains, rivers, in which the waters under the heavens spread over the earth. חָקַק signifies *incidere, figere,* to prescribe, to measure off, to consign, and directly to mark out, which is done by means of firm impressions of the graver's tools. But here this verb is without the *Dagesh*, to distinguish between the infinitive and the substantive חֻקּוֹ (his statute or limit) ; for correct texts have בְּחֻקּוֹ (*Michlol* 147a); and although a monosyllable follows, yet there is no throwing back of the tone, after the rule that words terminating in o in this case maintain their ultima accentuation (*e.g.* אל מִשְׁמוֹ, Num. xxiv. 23). Fleischer also finally decides for the explanation : *quum delinearet circulum super abysso,* when He marked out the region of the sea as with the circle.

In 28, 29, these two features of the figure of the creation of the world return (the beginning of the firmament, and the embankment of the under waters) ; hence we see that the discourse here makes a fresh start with a new theme :

28 " When He made firm the ether above,
       When He restrained the fountains of the waters;
29 When He set to the sea its bounds,
       That the waters should not pass their limits ;
       When He settled the pillars of the earth ;
30 Then was I with Him as director of the work,
       And was delighted day by day,
       Rejoic ng always before Him,

31 Rejoicing in His earth,
And having my delight in the children of men."

We have, with Symmachus, translated שְׁחָקִים (from שָׁחַק, Arab. shak, to grind, to make thin) by αἰθέρα, for so the fine transparent strata of air above the hanging clouds are called—a poetic name of the firmament רָקִיעַ. The making firm אַמֵּץ is not to be understood locally, but internally of the spreading out of the firmament over the earth settled for continuance (an expression such as Ps. lxxviii. 23). In 28b the Masora notices the plur. עִינוֹת instead of עֲיָנוֹת with לִית as unicum (cf. Michlol 191a); the transition of the sound is as in גָּלִית from galajta. The inf. עֲזוֹז appears on the first look to require a transitive signification, as the LXX. and the Targ., the Græc. Venet. and Luther (da er festiget die Brünnen der tieffen = when He makes firm the fountains of the deep) have rendered it. Elster accordingly believes that this signification must be maintained, because בְּ here introduces creative activity, and in itself is probably the transitive use of עֵז, as the Arab. 'azz shows: when He set His עֹז against the מַיִם עַזִּים (Isa. xliii. 16). But the absence of the subject is in favour of the opinion that here, as everywhere else, it is intransitive; only we may not, with Hitzig, translate : when the fountains of the flood raged wildly ; but, since 28b, if not a creative efficiency, must yet express a creative work, either as Ewald, with reference to מָעוֹז, fortress : when they became firm, or better as Fleischer, with reference to מַיִם עַזִּים : when they broke forth with power, with strong fulness. Whether the suff. of חֻקּוֹ, 29a, refers back to the sea or to Jahve, is decided after the parallel פִּיו. If this word is equivalent to its coast (cf. Ps. civ. 9), then both suffixes refer to the sea ; but the coast of the sea, or of a river, is called שָׂפָה, not פֶּה, which only means ostium (mouth), not ora. Also Isa. xix. 7 will require to be translated: by the mouth of the Nile ; and that פִּי, Ps. cxxxiii. 2, may denote the under edge, arises from this, that a coat has a mouth above as well as below, i.e. is open. Thus both suff. are to be referred to God, and פִּיו is to be determined after Job xxiii. 12. The clause beginning with וּמִים corresponds in periodizing discourse to a clause with ut, Ewald, § 338. בְּחוּקּוֹ is the same form, only written plene, as ver. 27, בְּחֻקּוֹ = בְּחֻקּוֹ = בְּחֻקְקוֹ.[1]

---

[1] One might regard it as modified from בחקקו ; but that שֻׂגְּרִי, Ps. xcii. 12, is modified from שֻׂרְרִי, or הוֹרִי, Gen. xlix. 26, from הֲרָרִי, is by no means certain.

Ver. 30. In this sentence, subordinating to itself these designations of time, the principal question is as to the meaning of אָמוֹן.
Hofmann's interpretation (*Schriftbew.* i. 97) " continually " (*inf.
absol.* in an adverbial sense) is a judicious idea, and אָמֵן, to endure,
remains indeed in אֱמֶת (stability); but in this sense, which נֶאֱמָן
represents, it is not otherwise used.   Also מְהֵימַנְתָּא (believing, trusting) of the Targ. (*Grœc. Venet.* πίστις, as if the word used were אֵמוּן)
is linguistically inadmissible; the Hebr. הָאֱמִין corresponds to the
Aram. *haimēn.*   One of these two only is possible: אָמוֹן means
either *opifex* or *alumnus.*   The meaning *alumnus* (Aquila, τιθηνου-
μένη; Meîri and Malbim, אמון בחיק האל, ἐν τῷ κόλπῳ τοῦ Θεοῦ)
would derive the word from אָמַן, to support, make firm, take care of;
the form ought to have a passive sense (Symm. Theod. ἐστηριγ-
μένη), as גָּדוֹל, twined, pressed, strong, great, and be pointed נָקֹד
(with a moveable *ā*, different from the form בָּגוֹד, חָמוֹץ, Isa. i. 17);
and אָמוֹן, in the meaning nursling, foster-child, favourite (Schultens,
Euchel, Elster, and others, also Rashi and Kimchi, who all find in
אמון the meaning of education, נידול), would place itself with אָמוּן,
fostered, Lam. iv. 5, אֹמֵן, fosterer, אֹמֶנֶת, foster-mother.   This is
the meaning of the word according to the connection, for Wisdom
appears further on as the child of God; as such she had her joy
before Him; and particularly God's earth, where she rejoiced with
the sons of men, was the scene of her mirth.   But on this very
account, because this is further said, we also lose nothing if אמון
should be interpreted otherwise.   And it is otherwise to be interpreted, for Wisdom is, in consequence of קנני (viii. 22), and הוללתי,
which is twice used (viii. 24, 25), God's own child; but the designation אמון would make Him to be the אֹמֵן of Wisdom; and the child
which an אֹמֵן bears, Num. xi. 12, and fosters, Esth. ii. 7, is not
his own.   Hence it follows that אמון in this signification would be
an ἅπαξ λεγόμενον; on the other hand, it really occurs elsewhere,
Jer. lii. 15 (*vid.* Hitzig *l.c.*), in the sense of *opifex.*   This sense,
which recommends itself to Ewald, Hitzig, Bertheau, and Zöckler,
lies also at the foundation of the ἁρμόζουσα of the LXX., מתקנא
of the Syr., the *cuncta componens* of Jerome, and the designation
of Wisdom as ἡ τῶν πάντων τεχνῖτις of the Book of Wisdom vii.
21.   The workmaster is called אָמוֹן, for which, Cant. vii. 2, אָמָן, or
rather אָפָּן (*ommán*), Aram. and Mishn. אוּמָן; not, perhaps, as he
whom one entrusts with something in whom one confides or may
confide in a work (*vid.* Fleischer, *loc.*), but from אָמַן, to be firm, as

one who is strong in his art, as perhaps also the right hand, which has the name יָמִין as being the *artifex* among the members. The word occurs also as an adjective in the sense of "experienced, skilful," and does not form a fem. according to the use of the word in this case before us, only because handicraft (אוּמָנוּת) belongs to men, and not to women; also in the Greek, δημιουργός, in the sense of τὰ δημόσια (εἰς τὸ δημόσιον) ἐργαζόμενος, has no fem.; and in Lat., *artifex* is used as a substantive (*e.g.* in Pliny: *artifex omnium natura*), like an adj. of double gender. It is thus altogether according to rule that we read אָמוֹן and not אֲמוֹנָה (after the form בְּגוֹדָה); also we would make a mistake if we translated the word by the German "*Werkmeisterin*" [work-mistress, directress] (Hitzig), for it is intended to be said that she took up the place of a workmaster with Him, whereby chiefly the artistic performances of a חָרָשׁ [artificer] are thought of. This self-designation of Wisdom is here very suitable; for after she has said that she was brought forth by God before the world was, and that she was present when it was created, this אמון now answers the question as to what God had in view when He gave to Wisdom her separate existence, and in what capacity she assisted in the creation of the world: it was she who transferred the creative thoughts originally existing in the creative will of God, and set in motion by His creative order, from their ideal into their real effectiveness, and, as it were, artistically carried out the delineations of the several creatures; she was the mediating cause, the demiurgic power which the divine creative activity made use of, as is said, iii. 19, "Jahve has by Wisdom founded the earth," and as the Jerusalem Targ. Gen. i. 1, in connection with Prov. viii. 22, translates: בְּחוּכְמָא בְּרָא יְיָ יַת שְׁמַיָא וְיַת אַרְעָא.

But—this is now the question—does the further unfolding of the thoughts here agree with this interpretation of אמון? That we may not misunderstand what follows, we must first of all represent to ourselves, that if אמון meant the foster-child, Wisdom could not yet, in what follows, be thought of as a little child (Num. xi. 12), for that would be an idea without any meaning; to rejoice [*spielen* = play] is certainly quite in accordance with youth, as 2 Sam. ii. 14 shows (where שַׂחֵק לִפְנֵי is said of the sportive combat of youthful warriors before the captain), not exclusively little children. So, then, we must guard against interpreting שַׁעֲשׁוּעִים, with the LXX. and Syr., in the sense of שַׁעֲשׁוּעַי,—an interpretation which the

Targ., Jerome, the *Græc. Venet.*, and Luther have happily avoided;
for mention is not made here of what Wisdom is for Jahve, but of
what she is in herself. The expression is to be judged after Ps.
cix. 4 (cf. Gen. xii. 2), where Hitzig rightly translates, "I am
wholly prayer;" but Böttcher, in a way characteristic of his mode
of interpretation, prefers, "I am ointment" (*vid. Neue Aehrenlese,*
No. 1222). The delight is meant which this mediating participation in God's creating work imparted to her—joy in the work in
which she was engaged. The pluralet. שַׁעֲשֻׁעִים is to be understood
here, not after Jer. xxxi. 20, but after Isa. xi. 8, Ps. cxix. 70,
where its root-word, the *Pilpel* שִׁעֲשַׁע (proceeding from the primary
meaning of caressing, *demulcere*), signifies intransitively: to have his
delight somewhere or in anything, to delight oneself,—a synonym
to the idea of play (cf. Aram. שְׁעָא, *Ethpe.* to play, *Ethpa.* to chatter);
for play is in contrast to work, an occupation which has enjoyment in view. But the work, *i.e.* the occupation, which aims to do
something useful, can also become a play if it costs no strenuous
effort, or if the effort which it costs passes wholly into the background in presence of the pleasure which it yields. Thus Wisdom
daily, *i.e.* during the whole course of creation, went forth in pure
delight; and the activity with which she translated into fact the
creative thoughts was a joyful noise in the sight of God, whose
commands she obeyed with childlike devotion; cf. 2 Sam. vi. 21,
where David calls his dancing and leaping before the ark of the
covenant a שִׂחֵק לִפְנֵי ה'. But by preference, her delight was in the
world, which is illustrated from the Persian *Minokhired*, which
personifies Wisdom, and, among other things, says of her: "The
creation of the earth, and its mingling with water, the springing up
and the growth of the trees, all the different colours, the odour, the
taste, and that which is pleasing in everything—all that is chiefly
the endowment and the performance of Wisdom."[1] She also there
says that she was before all celestial and earthly beings, the first
with Ormuzd, and that all that is celestial and earthly arose and
also remains in existence by her. But the earth was the dearest
object of her delight in the whole world; to help in establishing it
(iii. 19) was her joyful occupation; to fashion it, and to provide it
with the multiplicity of existences designed for it, was the most
pleasant part of her creative activity. For the earth is the abode
of man, and the heart-pleasure of Wisdom was with (אֶת־, prep.)

[1] *Vid.* Spiegel's *Grammatik der Pârsisprache,* p. 162, cf. 182.

the children of men; with them she found her high enjoyment, these were her peculiar and dearest sphere of activity.

Ver. 31. Since the statements of Wisdom, as to her participation in the creation of the world, are at this point brought to a close, in this verse there is set forth the intimate relation into which she thus entered to the earth and to mankind, and which she has continued to sustain to the present day. She turned her love to the earth for the sake of man, and to man not merely as a corporeal, but especially as a spiritual being, to whom she can disclose her heart, and whom, if he receives her, she can bring back to God (Book of Wisdom vii. 27). There are not here express references to Gen. i. or ii. In יוֹם יוֹם (day for day, as Gen. xxxix. 10, cf. Esth. ii. 4, יוֹם וָיוֹם) we have not to think of the six days of creation. But inasmuch as the whole description goes down to בְּנֵי אָדָם as its central-point, it denotes that creation came to its close and its goal in man. The connection of תֵּבֵל אֶרֶץ is as Job xxxvii. 12, where אַרְצָה for אֶרֶץ is wholly, as לַיְלָה, חָרְסָה, and the like, an original accusative.

Ver. 32. After that Wisdom has shown in vers. 22–31 how worthy her fellowship is of being an object of desire from her mediating place between God and the world, she begins with this verse (as vii. 24, v. 7) the hortatory (*paränetische*) concluding part of her discourse:

"And now, ye sons, hearken unto me,
And salvation to those who keep my ways!"

The LXX. omits ver. 33, and obviates the disturbing element of וְאַשְׁרֵי, 32b, arising from its וְ, by a transposition of the stichs. But this ואשרי is the same as the καὶ μακάριος, Matt. xi. 6; the organic connection lies hid, as Schleiermacher (*Hermeneutik*, p. 73) well expresses it, in the mere sequence; the clause containing the proof is connected by וְ with that for which proof is to be assigned, instead of subordinating itself to it with כִּי. Such an exclamatory clause has already been met with in iii. 13; there אָדָם follows as the governed genitive, here a complete sentence (instead of the usual participial construction, שֹׁמְרֵי דרכי) forms this genitive, Gesen. § 123, 3, Anm. 1.

The summons 32a, and its reason 32b, are repeated in these verses which follow:

33 " Hear instruction, and be wise,
And withdraw not.

34 Blessed is the man who hears me,
　　Watching daily at my gates,
　　Waiting at the posts of my doors!
35 For whosoever findeth me has found life,
　　And has obtained favour from Jahve;
36 And whosoever misseth me doeth wrong to himself;
　　All they who hate me love death."

The *imper.* וַחֲכָמוּ, 33a (*et sapite*), is to be judged after iv. 4,
וֶחְיֵה, cf. the *Chethîb*, xiii. 20; one sees this from the words
וְאַל־תִּפְרָעוּ which follow, to which, after xv. 32, as at iv. 13, to
מוּסָר, אַל־תֶּרֶף is to be placed as object: and throw not to the winds
(*ne missam faciatis; vid.* regarding פרע at i. 25), viz. instruction
(*disciplinam*).

Ver. 34. The אַשְׁרֵי here following שִׁמְעוּ is related to it as assigning a motive, like the וְאַשְׁרֵי (ver. 32b) following שׁמעו; according to
the Masora, we have to write אַשְׁרֵי with *Mercha*, and on the first
syllable *Gaja* (*vid.* Baer's *Torath Emeth*, pp. 26, 29; cf. under Ps.
i. 1). לִשְׁקֹד signifies to watch, not in the sense of *ad vigilandum,*
but *vigilando*, as Isa. v. 22, xxx. 1; Ewald, § 380d. In contradistinction to הֵעִיר and הֵקִיץ, which denote watching as the consequence
of wakefulness or an interruption of sleep, שָׁקַד signifies watching
as a condition, and that as one which a person willingly maintains
(*Psychol.* p. 275), the intentional watching (cf. Arab. *shakidha*, to
fix penetrating eyes upon anything), with עַל of the place and object
and aim (Jer. v. 6; cf. הֵעִיר עַל, Job viii. 6). The plurals דְּלָתוֹת
(*fores*, as חֹמוֹת, Jer. i. 18, *mœnia*) and פְּתָחִים are amplifying plurs.
of extension, suggesting the idea of a palace or temple; מְזוּזֹת (*postes
portœ, in quibus cardines ejus moventur*, from זוז, to move hither and
thither) is intended to indicate that he to whom the discourse refers
holds himself in closest nearness to the entrance, that he might not
miss the moment when it is opened, or when she who dwells there
presents herself to view. " The figure is derived from the service
of a court : Wisdom is honoured by her disciples, as a queen
or high patroness; cf. Samachschari's *Golden Necklaces*, Pr. 35 :
Blessed is the man who knocks only at God's door, and who
departs not a nail's breadth from God's threshold " (Fl.).

Ver. 35. This verse gives the reason for pronouncing those
happy who honour Wisdom. The *Chethîb* is כִּי מֹצְאִי מֹצְאֵי חַיִּים, but
the passing over into the sing. 35b is harsh and objectionable; the
Kerî rightly regards the second מצא as a mistaken repetition of the
first, and substitutes כִּי מֹצְאִי מָצָא חַיִּים, with which the וְחֹטְאִי (ver.

36a) of the antithesis agrees. Regarding מֹצָאִי, for which, less accurately, מֹצְאִי (only with the *Dechî* without *Metheg*) is generally written, vid. *Accentuationssystem*, vii. § 2. הֵפִיק, to get out = reach, exchanged with מָצָא, iii. 13 (*vid.* there); according to its etymon, it is connected with מִן, of him from or by whom one has reached anything; here, as xii. 2, xviii. 22, God's favour, *favorem a Jova impetravit*.

Ver. 36. חֹטְאִי may, it is true, mean "my sinning one = he who sins against me (חֹטֵא לִי)," as קָמַי is frequently equivalent to קָמִים עָלַי; but the contrast of מֹצְאִי places it beyond a doubt that חטא stands here in its oldest signification : to miss something after which one runs (xix. 2), seeks (Job v. 24), at which one shoots (*Hiph.* Judg. xx. 16), etc., *id non attingere quod petitur*, Arab. *âkhta*, to miss, opposite to *âṣab*, to hit (Fl.). Just because it is the idea of missing, which, ethically applied, passes over into that of sin and guilt (of fault, mistake, false step, "*Fehls, Fehlers, Fehltritts*"), חטא can stand not only with the accusative of the subject in regard to which one errs, Lev. v. 16, but also with the accusative of the subject which one forfeits, *i.e.* misses and loses, xx. 2, cf. Hab. ii. 10; so that not only מֹאֵס נַפְשׁוֹ, xv. 32 (*animam suam nihili facit*), but also חוֹטֵא נַפְשׁוֹ, xx. 2 (*animam suam pessumdat*), is synonymous with חֹמֵס נַפְשׁוֹ (*animæ suæ h. e. sibi ipsi injuriam facit*). Whoever misses Wisdom by taking some other way than that which leads to her, acts suicidally: all they who wilfully hate (*Piel*) wisdom love death, for wisdom is the tree of life, iii. 18; wisdom and life are one, 35a, as the Incarnate Wisdom saith, John viii. 51, "If a man keep my sayings, he shall never see death." In the Logos, Wisdom has her self-existence; in Him she has her personification, her justification, and her truth.

FIFTEENTH INTRODUCTORY MASHAL DISCOURSE, IX.

A DOUBLE INVITATION : THAT OF WISDOM, AND THAT OF HER RIVAL, FOLLY.

The preceding discourse pronounces those happy who, having taken their stand at the portal of Wisdom, wait for her appearance and her invitation. There is thus a house of Wisdom as there is a

house of God, Ps. lxxxiv. 11; and if now the discourse is of a house
of Wisdom, and of an invitation to a banquet therein (like that in
the parable, Matt. xxii., of the invitation to the marriage feast of
the king's son), it is not given without preparation:

> 1 Wisdom hath builded for herself an house,
>   Hewn out her seven pillars;
> 2 Hath slaughtered her beasts, mingled her wine;
>   Hath also spread her table;
> 3 Hath sent out her maidens; she waiteth
>   On the highest points of the city.

Regarding חָכְמוֹת, vid. at i. 20. It is a plur. excellentiæ, which is a
variety of the plur. extensivus. Because it is the expression of a
plural unity, it stands connected (as for the most part also אלהים,
Deus) with the sing. of the predicate. The perfects enumerate all
that Wisdom has done to prepare for her invitation. If we had a
parable before us, the perf. would have run into the historical וַתִּשְׁלַח;
but it is, as the תִּקְרָא shows, an allegorical picture of the arrangement and carrying out of a present reality. Instead of בָּנְתָה לָהּ בַּיִת
there is בָּנְתָה בֵיתָהּ, for the house is already in its origin represented as hers, and 1b is to be translated: she has hewn out her
seven pillars (Hitzig); more correctly: her pillars, viz. seven (after
the scheme דִּבָּתָם רָעָה, Gen. xxxvii. 2); but the construction is closer.
שבעה is, altogether like Ex. xxv. 37, the accusative of the second
object, or of the predicate after the species of verba, with the idea:
to make something, turn into something, which take to themselves
a double accusative, Gesen. § 139, 2: excidit columnas suas ita ut
septem essent. Since the figure is allegorical, we may not dispense
with the interpretation of the number seven by the remark, "No
emphasis lies in the number" (Bertheau). First, we must contemplate architecturally the house with seven pillars: "They are,"
as Hitzig rightly remarks, "the pillars of the מִסְדְּרוֹן (porch) [vid.
Bachmann under Judg. iii. 23, and Wetstein under Ps. cxliv. 12,
where חָטַב is used of the cutting out and hewing of wood, as
חָצַב of the cutting out and hewing of stone] in the inner court,
which bore up the gallery of the first (and second) floors: four of
these in the corners and three in the middle of three sides; through
the midst of these the way led into the court of the house-floor [the
area]." But we cannot agree with Hitzig in maintaining that, with
the seven pillars of viii. and ix., the author looks back to the first
seven chapters (Arab. âbwab, gates) of this book; we think other-

wise of the component members of this Introduction to the Book of
Proverbs; and to call the sections of a book " gates, שְׁעָרִים," is a late
Arabico-Jewish custom, of which there is found no trace whatever
in the O. T. To regard them also, with Heidenheim (cf. Dante's
Prose Writings, translated by Streckfuss, p. 77), as representing the
seven liberal arts (שֶׁבַע חכמות) is impracticable ; for this division of
the *artes liberales* into seven, consisting of the *Trivium* (Grammar,
Rhetoric, and Dialectics) and *Quadrivium* (Music, Arithmetic,
Geometry, and Astronomy), is not to be looked for within the old
Israelitish territory, and besides, these were the sciences of this
world which were so divided; but wisdom, to which the discourse
here refers, is wholly a religious-moral subject. The Midrash
thinks of the seven heavens (שֹׁבעה רקיעים), or the seven climates or
parts of the earth (שֹׁבעה ארצות), as represented by them; but both
references require artificial combinations, and have, as also the reference to the seven church-eras (Vitringa and Chr. Ben. Michaelis),
this against them, that they are rendered probable neither from
these introductory proverbial discourses, nor generally from the
O. T. writings. The patristic and middle-age reference to the seven
sacraments of the church passes sentence against itself ; but the
old interpretation is on the right path, when it suggests that the
seven pillars are the seven gifts of the Holy Ghost. The seven-
foldness of the manifestation of the Spirit, already brought near
by the seven lamps of the sacred candelabra (the מְנוֹרָה), is established by Isa. xi. 2 (*vid. l.c.*); and that Wisdom is the possessor and
dispenser of the Spirit she herself testifies, i. 23. Her Spirit is the
" Spirit of wisdom;" but at the same time, since, born of God, she
is mediatrix between God and the world, also the "Spirit of Jahve."
He is the " spirit of understanding," the " spirit of counsel,"
and the "spirit of might" (Isa. xi. 2); for she says, viii. 14,
" Counsel is mine, and reflection; I am understanding, I have
strength." He is also the "spirit of knowledge," and the "spirit
of the fear of the Lord" (Isa. xi. 2); for fear and the knowledge
of Jahve are, according to ix. 14, the beginning of wisdom, and
essentially wisdom itself.

Ver. 2. If thus the house of Wisdom is the place of her fellowship with those who honour her, the system of arrangements made
by her, so as to disclose and communicate to her disciples the
fulness of her strength and her gifts, then it is appropriate to
understand by the seven pillars the seven virtues of her nature

communicating themselves (apocalyptically expressed, the ἑπτὰ πνεύματα), which bear up and adorn the dwelling which she establishes among men. Flesh and wine are figures of the nourishment for the mind and the heart which is found with wisdom, and, without asking what the flesh and the wine specially mean, are figures of the manifold enjoyment which makes at once strong and happy. The segolate *n. verbale* טֶבַח, which vii. 22 denoted the slaughtering or the being slaughtered, signifies here, in the concrete sense, the slaughtered ox; Michaelis rightly remarks that טבח, in contradistinction to זבח, is the usual word for *mactatio extrasacrificialis*. Regarding מָסַךְ יַיִן, *vid.* under Isa. v. 22 ; it is not meant of the mingling of wine with sweet scents and spices, but with water (warm or cold), and signifies simply to make the wine palatable (as κεραννύναι, *temperare*) ; the LXX. ἐκέρασεν εἰς κρατῆρα, κρατήρ is the name of the vessel in which the mixing takes place ; they drank not ἄκρατον, but κεκερασμένον ἄκρατον, Rev. xiv. 10. The frequently occurring phrase עָרַךְ שֻׁלְחָן signifies to prepare the table (from שֶׁלַּח, properly the unrolled and outspread leather cover), viz. by the placing out of the dishes (*vid.* regarding עָרַךְ, under Gen. xxii. 9).

Ver. 3. The verb קָרָא, when a feast is spoken of, means to invite ; קְרֻאִים, ver. 18 (cf. 1 Sam. ix. 13, etc.), are the guests. נַעֲרוֹתֶיהָ the LXX. translates τοὺς ἑαυτῆς δούλους, but certainly here the disciples are meant who already are in the service of Wisdom ; but that those who are invited to Wisdom are thought of as feminine, arises from the tasteful execution of the picture. The invitation goes forth to be known to all far and wide, so that in her servants Wisdom takes her stand in the high places of the city. Instead of בְּרֹאשׁ, viii. 2, i. 21, there is used here the expression עַל־גַּפֵּי. We must distinguish the Semitic גַּף (= *ganf*), wings, from גנף = כנף, to cover, and גַּף (= *gaff* or *ganf*), the bark, which is derived either from נָפַף or גָּנַף, جنف, *convexus, incurvus et extrinsecus gibber fuit*, hence originally any surface bent outwards or become crooked (cf. the roots *cap, caf*, קב כף גף גב, etc.), here the summit of a height (Fl.); thus not *super alis* (after the analogy of πτερύγιον, after Suidas = ἀκρωτήριον), but *super dorsis* (as in Lat. we say *dorsum montis*, and also *viæ*).

Now follows the street-sermon of Wisdom inviting to her banquet:

4 " Who is simple? let him come hither!"
  Whoso wanteth understanding, to him she saith:
5 " Come, eat of my bread,
  And drink of the wine which I have mingled!
6 Cease, ye simple, and live,
  And walk straight on in the way of understanding."

The question מִי פֶתִי (thus with *Munach*, not with *Makkeph*, it is to be written here and at ver. 16; *vid.* Baer's *Torath Emeth*, p. 40), *quis est imperitus*, is, as Ps. xxv. 12, only a more animated expression for *quisquis est*. The retiring into the background of the נַעֲרוֹת (servants), and the immediate appearance of Wisdom herself, together with the interruption, as was to be expected, of her connected discourses by the אָמְרָה לּוֹ, are signs that the pure execution of the allegorical representation is here at an end. Hitzig seeks, by the rejection of vers. 4, 5, 7-10, to bring in a logical sequence; but these interpolations which he cuts out are yet far more inconceivable than the proverbial discourses in the mouth of Wisdom, abandoning the figure of a banquet, which besides are wholly in the spirit of the author of this book. That Folly invites to her, ver. 16, in the same words as are used by Wisdom, ver 4, is not strange; both address themselves to the simple (*vid.* on פְתִי at i. 4) and those devoid of understanding (as the youth, vii. 7), and seek to bring to their side those who are accessible to evil as to good, and do not fully distinguish between them, which the emulating *devertat huc* of both imports. The fourth verse points partly backwards, and partly forwards; 4a has its introduction in the תקרא of ver. 3; on the contrary, 4b is itself the introduction of what follows. The setting forth of the *nom. absolutus* חֲסַר־לֵב is conditioned by the form of 4a; the מִי (cf. 4a) is continued (in 4b) without its needing to be supplied: *excors* (= *si quis est excors*) *dicit ei* (not *dixit*, because syntactically subordinating itself to the תקרא). It is a nominal clause, whose virtual predicate (the devoid of understanding is thus and thus addressed by her) is in ver. 16.

Ver. 5. The plur. of the address shows that the simple (inexperienced) and the devoid of understanding are regarded as essentially one and the same class of men. The בְּ after לָחֶם and שָׁתָה proceeds neither from the idea of eating into (hewing into) anything, nor from the eating with anything, *i.e.* inasmuch as one makes use of it, nor of pampering oneself with anything (as רָאָה בְ); Michaelis at last makes a right decision (cf. Lev. xxii. 11, Judg.

xiii. 16, Job xxi. 25, and particularly בְּ לֶחֶם, Ps. cxli. 4) : *communicationem et participationem in re fruenda denotat ;* the LXX. φάγετε τῶν ἐμῶν ἄρτων. The attributive מְסָכְתִּי stands with backward reference briefly for מְסַכְתִּיו. That Wisdom, ver. 2, offers flesh and wine, but here presents bread and wine, is no contradiction, which would lead us, with Hitzig, critically to reject vers. 4 and 5 as spurious ; לֶחֶם is the most common, all-comprehensive name for nourishment. Bertheau suitably compares Jahve's invitation, Isa lv. 1, and that of Jesus, John vi. 35.

Ver. 6. That פְּתָאִים is a plur. with abstract signification (according to which the four Greek and the two Aramæan translations render it ; the *Græc. Venet.*, however, renders τοὺς νηπίους) is improbable; the author forms the abstr. ver. 13 otherwise, and the expression here would be doubtful. For פתאים is here to be rendered as the object-accus. : leave the simple, *i.e.* forsake this class of men (Ahron b. Joseph; Umbreit, Zöckler); or also, which we prefer (since it is always a singular thought that the "simple" should leave the "simple"), as the vocative, and so that עִזְבוּ means not absolutely "leave off" (Hitzig), but so that the object to be thought of is to be taken from פתאים : give up, leave off, viz. the simple (Immanuel and others ; on the contrary, Rashi, Meîri, and others, as Ewald, Bertheau, decide in favour of פתאים as *n. abstr.*). Regarding וְחְיוּ, for *et vivetis, vid.* iv. 4. The LXX., paraphrasing : ἵνα εἰς τὸν αἰῶνα βασιλεύσητε. אֲשֵׁר is related to אֲשׁוּר (אַשּׁוּר) as דֶּרֶךְ to דָּרַךְ ; the *Piel,* not in its intrans. (*vid.* iv. 14) but in its trans. sense (Isa. i. 17, iii. 12, etc.), shows that the idea of going straight out and forwards connects itself therewith. The peculiarity of the פתי is just the absence of character.

In what now follows the discourse of Wisdom is continued; wherefore she directs her invitation to the simple, *i.e.* those who have not yet decided, and are perhaps susceptible of that which is better :

> 7 " He who correcteth a scorner draweth upon himself insult ;
>   And he who communicateth instruction to a scorner, it is a dishonour
>   to him.
> 8 Instruct not a scorner, lest he hate thee ;
>   Give instruction to the wise, so he will love thee.
> 9 Give to the wise, and he becomes yet wiser ;
>   Give knowledge to the upright, and he gains in knowledge."

Zöckler thinks that herewith the reason for the summons to the "simple" to forsake the fellowship of men of their own sort, is

assigned (he explains Ga as Ahron b. Joseph : הפרדו מן הפתאים); but
his remark that, under the term " simple," mockers and wicked persons are comprehended as belonging to the same category, confounds
two sharply distinguished classes of men. לֵץ is the freethinker
who mocks at religion and virtue (vid. i. 22), and רָשָׁע the godless
who shuns restraint by God and gives himself up to the unbridled
impulse to evil. The course of thought in ver. 7 and onwards
shows why Wisdom, turning from the wise, who already are hers,
directs herself only to the simple, and those who are devoid of
understanding : she must pass over the לֵץ and רָשָׁע, because she
can there hope for no receptivity for her invitation ; she would,
contrary to Matt. vii. 6, " give that which is holy to the dogs, and
cast her pearls before swine." יָסַר, παιδεύειν (with the prevailing
idea of the bitter lesson of reproof and punishment), and הוֹכִיחַ,
ἐλέγχειν, are interchangeable conceptions, Ps. xciv. 10 ; the לְ is
here exponent of the object (to bring an accusation against any
one), as ver. 8, xv. 12 (otherwise as Isa. ii. 4, xi. 4, where it is the
dat. commodi : to bring unrighteousness to light, in favour of the
injured). יֹסֵר לֵץ is pointed with Mahpach of the penultima, and
thus with the tone thrown back. The Pasek, placed in some
editions between the two words, is masoretically inaccurate. He
who reads the moral to the mocker brings disgrace to himself ; the
incorrigible replies to the goodwill with insult. Similar to the לֹקֵחַ
here, is מֵרִים tollit = reportat, iii. 35, iv. 27. In 7b מוּמוֹ is by no
means the object governed by וּמוֹכִיחַ : and he who shows to the
godless his fault (Meîri, Arama, Löwenstein : מוּמוֹ = עַל־מוּמוֹ, and
thus also the Græc. Venet. μῶμον ἑαυτῷ, scil. λαμβάνει) ; plainly
מוּמוֹ is parallel with קלון. But מוּמוֹ does not also subordinate itself
to לֹקֵחַ as to the object. parallel קלון : maculam sibimet scil. acquirit ;
for, to be so understood, the author ought at least to have written
מוּם לוֹ. Much rather מוּמוֹ is here, as at Deut. xxxii. 5, appos., thus
pred. (Hitzig), without needing anything to be supplied : his blot
it is, viz. this proceeding, which is equivalent to מוּמָא הוּא לֵיהּ
(Targ.), opprobrio ipsi est. Zöckler not incorrectly compares Ps.
cxv. 7 and Eccles. v. 16, but the expression (macula ejus = ipsi)
lies here less remote from our form of expression. In other words :
Whoever correcteth the mockers has only to expect hatred (אֶל־תּוֹכַח
with the tone thrown back, according to rule ; cf., on the contrary,
Judg. xviii. 25), but on the other hand, love from the wise.

Ver. 8. The וּ in וְיֶאֱהָבֶךָ is that of consequence (*apodosis imperativi*): so he will love thee (as also Ewald now translates), not : that he may love thee (Syr., Targ.), for the author speaks here only of the consequence, not of something else, as an object kept in view. The exhortation influences the mocker less than nothing, so much the more it bears fruit with the wise. Thus the proverb is confirmed *habenti dabitur*, Matt. xiii. 12, xxv. 29.

Ver. 9. If anything is to be supplied to תֵּן, it is לֶקַח (iv. 2) ; but תֵן , *tradere*, παραδιδόναι, is of itself correlat. of לקח, *accipere* (post-bibl. קבֵּל), παραλαμβάνειν, e.g. Gal. i. 9. הוֹדִיעַ לְ = to communi-cate knowledge, דַעַת, follows the analogy of הוֹכִיחַ לְ, to impart instruction, תּוֹכַחַת. Regarding the jussive form וְיוֹסֶף in the *apod. imper.*, *vid.* Gesen. § 128, 2. Observe in this verse the inter-change of חכם and צדיק ! Wisdom is not merely an intellectual power, it is a moral quality ; in this is founded her receptivity of instruction, her embracing of every opportunity for self-improve-ment. She is humble ; for, without self-will and self-sufficiency, she makes God's will her highest and absolutely binding rule (iii. 7).

These words naturally follow :

> 10 "The beginning of wisdom is the fear of Jahve,
> And the knowledge of the Holy One is understanding."

This is the highest principle of the Chokma, which stands (i. 7) as a motto at the beginning of the Book of Proverbs. The LXX. translate רֵאשִׁית there (i. 7), and תְּחִלַּת here, by ἀρχή. Gusset dis-tinguishes the two synonyms as *pars optima* and *primus actus ;* but the former denotes the fear of God as that which stands in the uppermost place, to which all that Wisdom accomplishes subordi-nates itself; the latter as that which begins wisdom, that which it proposes to itself in its course. With יהוה is interchanged, ii. 5, אלהים, as here קְדֹשִׁים, as the internally multiplicative plur. (Dietrich, *Abhandlungen*, pp. 12, 45), as xxx. 3, Josh. xxiv. 9, Hos. xii. 1, of God, the "Holy, holy, holy" (Isa. vi. 3), *i.e.* Him who is abso-lutely Holy. Michaelis inaccurately, following the ancients, who understood not this non-numerical plur.: *cognitio quæ sanctos facit et sanctis propria est*. The דַעַת, parallel with יִרְאַת, is meant of lively practical operative knowledge, which subordinates itself to this All-holy God as the normative but unapproachable pattern.

Ver. 11. The singular reason for this proverb of Wisdom is now given :

> " For by me will thy days become many,
> And the years of thy life will be increased."

Incorrectly Hitzig : " and years of life will increase to thee ;'
הוֹסִיף is always and everywhere (*e.g.* also Job xxxviii. 11) transitive.
In the similar passage, iii. 2, יוסיפו had as its subject the doctrine
of Wisdom ; here חכמה and בינה it is not practicable to interpret as
subj., since 11*a* Wisdom is the subject discoursing—the expression
follows the scheme, *dicunt eos* = *dicuntur*, as *e.g.* Job vii. 3 ; Gesen.
§ 137—a concealing of the operative cause, which lies near, where,
as ii. 22, the discourse is of severe judgment, thus: they (viz. the
heavenly Powers) will grant to thee years of life (חַיִּים in a pregnant sense, as iii. 2) in rich measure, so that constantly one span
comes after another. But in what connection of consequence does
this stand with the contents of the proverb, ver. 10 ? The ancients
say that the clause with כִּי refers back to ver. 5 f. The vers. 7–10
(according also to Fl.) are, as it were, parenthetic. Hitzig rejects
these verses as an interpolation, but the connection of ver. 11 with
5 f. retains also something that is unsuitable : " steps forward on the
way of knowledge, for by me shall thy days become many ;" and if,
as Hitzig supposes, ver. 12 is undoubtedly genuine, whose connection with ver. 11 is in no way obvious, then also will the difficulty of
the connection of vers. 7–10 with the preceding and the succeeding be no decisive mark of the want of genuineness of this course
of thought. We have seen how the progress of ver. 6 to 7 is
mediated : the invitation of Wisdom goes forth to the receptive,
with the exclusion of the irrecoverable. And ver. 11 is related to
ver. 10, as the proof of the cause from the effect. It is the fear of
God with which Wisdom begins, the knowledge of God in which
above all it consists, for by it is fulfilled the promise of life which
is given to the fear of God, x. 27, xiv. 27, xix. 23, cf. Deut. iv.
40, and to humility, which is bound up with it, x. 17.

Ver. 12. This wisdom, resting on the fear of God, is itself a
blessing to the wise :

> " If thou art wise, thou art wise for thyself ;
> And if thou mockest, thou alone shalt bear it."

The LXX., with the Syr., mangle the thought of 12*a*, for they
translate: if thou art wise for thyself, so also thou wilt be wise for
thy neighbour. The *dat. commodi* לָךְ means that it is for the personal advantage of the wise to be wise. The contrast expressed

by Job xxii. 2 f.: not profitable to God, but to thyself (Hitzig), is scarcely intended, although, so far as the accentuation is antithetic, it is the nearest. The perf. וְלָצְתָ is the hypothetical; Gesen. § 126, 1. To bear anything, viz. anything sinful (חֵטְא or עָוֹן), is equivalent to, to atone for it, Job xxxiv. 2, cf. Num. ix. 13, Ezek. xxiii. 35. Also 12b is a contrast scarcely aimed at. Wisdom is its own profit to man; libertinism is its own disgrace. Man decides, whenever he prefers to be wise, or to be a mocker of religion and of virtue, regarding his own weal and woe. With this *nota bene* the discourse of Wisdom closes.

The poet now brings before us another figure, for he personifies Folly working in opposition to Wisdom, and gives her a feminine name, as the contrast to Wisdom required, and thereby to indicate that the seduction, as the 13th proverbial discourse (chap. vii.) has shown, appears especially in the form of degraded womanhood:

> 13 The woman Folly [*Frau Thorheit*] conducts herself boisterously,
>   Wantonness, and not knowing anything at all ;
> 14 And hath seated herself at the door of her house,
>   On a seat high up in the city,
> 15 To call to those who walk in the way,
>   Who go straight on their path.

The connection of אֵשֶׁת כְּסִילוּת is genitival, and the genitive is not, as in אֵשֶׁת רָע, vi. 24, specifying, but appositional, as in בַּת־צִיּוֹן (*vid.* under Isa. i. 8). הוֹמִיָּה [boisterous] is pred., as vii. 11: her object is sensual, and therefore her appearance excites passionately, overcoming the resistance of the mind by boisterousness. In 13b it is further said who and how she is. פְּתַיּוּת she is called as wantonness personified. This abstract פְּתַיּוּת, derived from פֶּתִי, must be vocalized as אַכְזְרִיּוּת; Hitzig thinks it is written with *a* on account of the following *u* sound, but this formation always ends in *ijjûth*, not *ajjûth*. But as from חָזָה as well חִזָּיוֹן = חֶזְיוֹן as חָזוֹן is formed, so from פָּתָה as well פָּתוּת like חָזוּת, or פְּתוּת like לְווּת, רְעוּת, as פְּתַיּוּת (instead of which פְּתִיּוּת is preferred) can be formed; Kimchi rightly (*Michlol* 181a) presents the word under the form פְּעָלוּת. With וּבַל (xiv. 7) poetic, and stronger than וְלֹא, the designation of the subject is continued; the words וּבַל־יָדְעָה מָּה (thus with *Mercha* and without *Makkeph* following, יָדְעָה is to be written, after Codd. and old editions) have the value of an adjective: and not knowing anything at all (מָה = *τὶ*, as Num. xxiii. 3, Job xiii. 13, and here in the negative clause, as in prose מְאוּמָה), *i.e.* devoid of

all knowledge. The Targ. translates explanatorily : not recognising מַבְתָּא, the good ; and the LXX. substitutes : she knows not
shame, which, according to Hitzig, supposes the word כְּלִמָּה, approved of by him ; but כלמה means always *pudefactio*, not *pudor*.
To know no כלמה would be equivalent to, to let no shaming from
without influence one; for shamelessness the poet would have made
use of the expression וּבְל־יָדְעָה בֹּשֶׁת. In וְיָשְׁבָה the declaration regarding the subject beginning with הומיה is continued : Folly also
has a house in which works of folly are carried on, and has set herself down by the door (לְפֶתַח as לְפִי, viii. 3) of this house ; she sits
there עַל־כִּסֵּא. Most interpreters here think on a throne (LXX.
ἐπὶ δίφρου, used especially of the *sella curulis*) ; and Zöckler, as
Umbreit, Hitzig, and others, connecting genitiv. therewith מְרֹמֵי
קָרֶת, changes in 14*b* the scene, for he removes the " high throne of
the city " from the door of the house to some place elsewhere.
But the sitting is in contrast to the standing and going on the part
of Wisdom on the streets preaching (Evagrius well renders : *in
molli ignavaque sella*) ; and if כסא and house-door are named along
with each other, the former is a seat before the latter, and the
accentuation rightly separates by *Mugrash* כסא from מרמי קרת.
" According to the accents and the meaning, מרמי קרת is the *acc.
loci* : on the high places of the city, as viii. 2 f." (Fl.) They are
the high points of the city, to which, as Wisdom, ver. 3, viii. 2, so
also Folly, her rival (wherefore Eccles. x. 6 does not appertain
to this place), invites followers to herself. She sits before her
door to call לְעֹבְרֵי דָרֶךְ (with *Munach*, as in Cod. 1294 and old
editions, without the *Makkeph*), those who go along the way
(genitive connection with the supposition of the accusative construction, *transire viam*, as ii. 7), to call (invite) הַמְיַשְּׁרִים (to be
pointed with מ *raphatum* and *Gaja* going before, according to
Ben-Asher's rule; *vid. Methegsetz.* § 20), those who make straight
their path, *i.e.* who go straight on, directly before them (cf Isa.
lvii. 2). The participial construction (the schemes *amans Dei* and
amans Deum), as well as that of the verb קרא (first with the dat.
and then with the accus.), interchange.

The woman, who in her own person serves as a sign to her
house, addresses those who pass by in their innocence (לְתֻמָּם, 2
Sam. xv. 11):

16 " Whoso is simple, let him turn in hither ! "
    And if any one is devoid of understanding, she saith to him :

> 17 " Stolen waters taste sweet,
> And the bread of secrecy is pleasant."

פֶּתִי (folly, simplicity) has a side accessible to good and its contrary: Wisdom is connected with the one side, and Folly with the other. And as the חֲסַר־לֵב offers a *vacuum* to Wisdom which may perhaps be filled with the right contents, so is this *vacuum* welcome to Folly, because it meets there no resistance. In this sense, ver. 16 is like ver. 4 (excepting the addition of a connecting and of a concluding ו: *et si quis excors, tum dicit ei*) ; the word is the same in both, but the meaning, according to the two speakers, is different. That to which they both invite is the pleasure of her fellowship, under the symbol of eating and drinking; in the one case it is intellectual and spiritual enjoyment, in the other sensual. That Wisdom offers (ix. 5) bread and wine, and Folly water and bread, has its reason in this, that the particular pleasure to which the latter invites is of a sensual kind; for to drink water out of his own or out of another fountain is (iii. 15–20) the symbol of intercourse in married life, or of intercourse between the unmarried, particularly of adulterous intercourse. מַיִם גְּנוּבִים (correct texts have it thus, without the *Makkeph*) is sexual intercourse which is stolen from him who has a right thereto, thus carnal intercouse with אֵשֶׁת אִישׁ ; and לֶחֶם סְתָרִים fleshly lust, which, because it is contrary to the law, must seek (cf. *furtum*, secret love intrigue) concealment (סְתָרִים, extensive plur., as מְעֲמַקִּים; Böttcher, § 694). Just such pleasure, after which one wipes his mouth as if he had done nothing (xxx. 20), is for men who are without wisdom sweet (מָתַק, Job xx. 12) and pleasant ; the prohibition of it gives to such pleasure attraction, and the secrecy adds seasoning; and just such enjoyments the כְּסִילוּת, personified carnality, offers. But woe to him who, befooled, enters her house !

He goes within :

> 18 And he knows not that the dead are there;
> In the depths of Hades, her guests.

How near to one another the house of the adulteress and Hades are, so that a man passes through the one into the other, is already stated in ii. 18, vii. 28. Here, in the concluding words of the introduction to the Book of Proverbs, addressed to youth, and for the most part containing warnings against sinful pleasures, these two further declarations are advanced : the company assembled in the house of lewdness consists of רְפָאִים, *i.e.* (cf. p. 83) the old, worn-out, who are only in appearance living, who have gone down to the seeming life of the shadowy existence of the kingdom of the dead; her (כְּסִילוֹת) invited ones (cf. vii. 26, her slaughtered ones) are in the depths of Hades (not in the valleys, as Umbreit, Löwenstein, and Ewald translate, but in the depths, Aquila, Symmachus, Theodotion, ἐπὶ τοῖς βαθέσι; for עִמְקֵי is not only plur. to עֵמֶק, but also *per metaplasmum* to עֹמֶק, xxv. 3, as אָמְרֵי to אֹמֶר), thus in שְׁאוֹל תַּחְתִּית (Deut. xxxii. 22); they have forsaken the fellow-ship of the life and of the love of God, and have sunk into the deepest destruction. The house of infamy into which Folly allures does not only lead to hell, it is hell itself; and they who permit themselves to be thus befooled are like wandering corpses, and already on this side of death are in the realm of wrath and of the curse.[1]

FIRST COLLECTION OF SOLOMONIC PROVERBS, X.–XXII. 16.

The superscription, מִשְׁלֵי שְׁלֹמֹה, here shows that now we have reached that which the title of the book, i. 1–6, presented to view. Here we have the commencement of that collection of Solomonic Proverbs which under this title forms, together with the introduc-tion, i. 7–ix., the Older Book of Proverbs. The introduction is disproportionately long. It is the manner of the editor to extend himself in length and breadth; and besides, an educational zeal in behalf of youth, and his aim, which was without doubt to put them on their guard against certain prevailing moral evils of his time, make him thus persuasive; and if he detains his readers so long from the proper Solomonic Proverbs, yet this might be excused from the circumstance, that though his introduction does not strictly consist of Proverbs of Solomon, yet it consists of proverbs after the manner of Solomon, *i.e.* of proverbs which, as to their contents and form, take their structure from the pattern of those of Solomonic authorship.

In this introduction, i.–ix., there are larger sections of intercon-nected thoughts having one common aim. Even in vi. 1–19 there are manifestly three proverbial discourses distinguished from one another, shorter indeed, yet containing one fundamental thought.

---

[1] The LXX. has considerable additions introduced after ver. 18, as also after ver. 12, of which we shall elsewhere speak.

Such proverbs as are primarily designed to form one completed little whole of themselves, are not here to be met with. On the contrary, the Solomonic collection which now follows consists of pure distichs, for the most part antithetical, but at the same time going over all the forms of the technical proverb, as we have already shown; *vid*. p. 16. Accordingly the exposition must from this point onward renounce reproduced combinations of thought. The succession of proverbs here is nevertheless not one that is purely accidental or without thought; it is more than a happy accident when three of the same character stand together; the collector has connected together proverb with proverb according to certain common characteristics (Bertheau). And yet more than that: the mass separates itself into groups, not merely succeeding one another, but because a certain connection of ideas connects together a number of proverbs, in such a way that the succession is broken, and a new point of departure is arrived at (Hitzig). There is no comprehensive plan, such as Oetinger in his summary view of its contents supposes; the progressive unfolding follows no systematic scheme, but continuously wells forth. But that the editor, whom we take also to be the arranger of the contents of the book, did not throw them together by good chance, but in placing them together was guided by certain reasons, the very first proverb here shows, for it is chosen in conformity with the design of this book, which is specially dedicated to youth :

> 1 A wise son maketh glad his father ;
> A foolish son is his mother's grief.

One sees here quite distinctly (cf. Hos. xiii. 13) that חָכָם (from חָכַם, properly to be thick, stout, solid, as πυκνός = σοφός) is primarily a practical and ethical conception. Similar proverbs are found further on, but consisting of synonymous parallel members, in which either the father both times represents the parents, as xvii. 21, xxiii. 24, or father and mother are separated, each being named in different members, as xvii. 25, xxiii. 25, and particularly xv. 20, where $20a = 1a$ of the above proverb. It is incorrect to say, with Hitzig, that this contrast draws the division after it : the division lies nearer in the synonymous distichs, and is there less liable to be misunderstood then in the antithetic. Thus, from this proverb before us, it might be concluded that grief on account of a befooled son going astray in bypaths, and not coming to the right way, falls principally on the mother, as (Sir. iii. 9) is often the case in unfortunate marriages. The idea of the parents is in this way only separated, and the two members stand in suppletive interchangeable relationship. יְשַׁמֵּחַ is the middle of the clause, and is the usual form in connection; יְשַׂמַּח is the pausal form. תּוּנָה, from הוּנָה (יגה), has pass. û, as תּוֹרָה, act. ô. "The expression of the pred. 1b is like iii. 17, viii. 6, x. 14 f.; cf. e.g. Arab. âlastaksa furkat, oversharpening is dividing, i.e. effects it [inquiries become or lead to separation] (cf. our proverb, Allzuscharf macht schartig = too much sharpening makes full of notches); Burckhardt, Sprüchw. Nr. 337" (Fl.).

Ver. 2. There follows now a series of proverbs which place possessions and goods under a moral-religious point of view :

> Treasures of wickedness bring no profit ;
> But righteousness delivers from death.

The LXX. and Aquila translate ἀνόμους (ἀσεβεῖς). הוֹעִיל (to profit) with the accus. is possible, Isa. lvii. 12, but אוֹצָרוֹת one does not use by itself; it requires a genitive designating it more closely. But also דְּרָשִׁיעָא of the Targ., παρανόμων of Symmachus, fails; for the question still remains, to whom? Rightly Syr., Jerome, Theodotion, and the Quinta: ἀσεβείας, cf. iv. 17, Mic. iv. 10; Luke xvi. 9, μαμωνᾶς τῆς ἀδικίας. Treasures to which wickedness cleaves profit not, viz. him who has collected them through wickedness. On the contrary, righteousness saves from death (2b = xi. 4b, where the parallelism makes it clear that death as a judgment is meant). In Deut. xxiv. 13 it had been already said that compassionate love is "righteousness before the Lord," the cardinal virtue of the righteousness of life. Faith (Hab. ii. 4) is its soul, and love its life. Therefore δικαιοσύνη and ἐλεημοσύνη are interchangeable ideas; and it ought not to be an objection against the Apocrypha that it repeats the above proverb, ἐλεημοσύνη ἐκ θανάτου ῥύεται, Tob. iv. 10, xii. 9, Sir. iii. 30, xxix. 12, for Dan. iv. 24 also says the very same thing, and the thought is biblical, in so far as the giving of alms is understood to be not a dead work, but (Ps. cxii. 9) the life-activity of one who fears God, and of a mind believing in Him and resting in His word.

Ver. 3. Another proverb, the members of which stand in chiastic relation to those of the preceding :

> Jahve does not suffer the soul of the righteous to hunger ;
> But the craving of the godless He disappointeth.

The thought is the same as xiii. 25. There, as also at vi. 30, the

soul is spoken of as the faculty of desire, and that after nourishment, for the lowest form of the life of the soul is the impulse to
self-preservation. The parallel הַוָּה, in which LXX. and Ar.
erroneously find the meaning of חַיָּה, life, the Syr. Targ. the
meaning of הוֹן, possession, means the desire, without however
being related to אַוָּה (Berth.); it is the Arab. *hawan*, from הַוָּה,
Arab. *haway*, which, from the fundamental meaning χαίνειν, *hiare*,
to gape, yawn, signifies not only unrestrained driving along, and
crashing overthrow (cf. xi. 6, xix. 13), but also the breaking forth,
ferri in aliquid, whence הַוָּה, Arab. *hawan*, violent desire, in Hebr.
generally (here and Ps. lii. 9, Mic. vii. 3) of desire without limits
and without restraint (cf. the plur. *áhawá*, arbitrary actions,
caprices); the meanings deduced from this important verbal stem
(of which also הָיָה הָוָה, *accidere*, and then *esse*, at least after the
Arabic conception of speech, is an offshoot) are given by Fleischer
under Job xxxvii. 6, and after Fleischer by Ethé, *Schlafgemach der
Phantasie*, ii. p. 6 f. The verb הָדַף signifies to push in the most manifold shades, here to push forth, *repellere*, as 2 Kings iv. 27 (cf. Arab.
hadhaf, to push off = to discharge); the fut. is invariably יֶהְדֹּף, like
יֶהְמֶּה. God gives satisfaction to the soul of the righteous, viz. in
granting blessings. The desire of the wicked He does not suffer to
be accomplished; it may appear for a long time as if that which
was aimed at was realized, but in the end God pushes it back, so
that it remains at a distance, because contrary to Him. Instead of
וְהַוַּת רְשָׁעִים, some editions (Plantin 1566, Bragadin 1615) have וְהַוַּת
בְּגֹדִים, but, in opposition to all decided testimony, only through a
mistaken reference to xi. 6.

Ver. 4. There follow two proverbs which say how one man fails
and another succeeds:

> He becomes poor who bears a sluggish hand;
> But the hand of the diligent maketh rich.

These three proverbs, xix. 15, xii. 24, 27, are similar. From the last
two it is seen that רְמִיָּה is a subst., as also from Ps. cxx. 2 f.
(לְשׁוֹן רְמִיָּה, from a crafty tongue) that it is an adject., and from
Lev. xiv. 15 f. (where כַּף is fem.) that it may be at the same time
an adject. here also. The masc. is רָמִי, like טְרִי to טְרִיָּה, but neither
of these occur; "the fundamental idea is that of throwing oneself
down lazily, when one with unbent muscles holds himself no longer
erect and stretched, Arab. *taramy*" (Fl.). The translation: deceitful balances (Löwenstein after Rashi), is contrary to biblical usage,

which knows nothing of כַּף in this Mishnic meaning. But if כַּף is here regarded as fem., then it cannot be the subject (Jerome, *egestatem operata est manus remissa*), since we read עָשָׂה, not עָשְׂתָה. But רָאשׁ also is not suitable as the subject (LXX., Syr., Targ.), for poverty is called רִישׁ, רֵישׁ, רָאשׁ; on the contrary, רָשׁ, plur. רָשִׁים or רָאשִׁים, is used adjectively. Since now the adject. רָשׁ, 1 Sam. xii. 14, is also written רָאשׁ, it may be translated: Poor is he who . . . (Bertheau) ; but we much rather expect the statement of that which happens to such an one, thus : Poor will he be . . . רָאשׁ, 3 *præt.* = רָשׁ, Ps. xxxiv. 11, with the same (grammatically incorrect) full writing as קָאם, Hos. x. 14. In the conception of the subject, כַּף־רְמִיָּה, after Jer. xlviii. 10, is interpreted as the accus. of the manner (Berth.: whoever works with sluggish hand); but since עָשָׂה רְמִיָּה (in another sense indeed : to practise cunning) is a common phrase, Ps. lii. 4, ci. 7, so also will כַּף־רְמִיָּה be regarded as the object : *qui agit manum remissam*, whoever carries or moves such a hand (Hitzig). In 4*b* working is placed opposite to bearing: the diligent hand makes rich, *ditat* or *divitias parit;* but not for itself (Gesen. and others: becomes rich), but for him who bears it. The diligent man is called חָרוּץ, from חָרַץ, to sharpen, for, as in ὀξύς, *acer,* sharpness is transferred to energy ; the form is the same as חַלּוּק, smooth (for the *ā* is unchangeable, because recompensative), a kindred form to קָטוֹל like חָמוֹץ, and Arab. *fa'ûl* as *fashawsh,* a boaster, wind-bag, either of active (as חַנּוּן) or (as חָרוּץ, חַלּוּק, עַמּוּד, שַׁכּוּל) of passive signification.

Ver. 5. There is now added a proverb which, thus standing at the beginning of the collection, and connecting itself with ver. 1, stamps on it the character of a book for youth:

> He that gathereth in summer is a wise son ;
> But he that is sunk in sleep in the time of harvest is a son that causeth shame.

Von Hofmann (*Schriftb.* ii. 2. 403) rightly interprets בֵּן מַשְׂכִּיל and בֵּן מֵבִישׁ, with Cocceius and others, as the subject, and not with Hitzig as predicate, for in nominal clauses the rule is to place the predicate before the subject; and since an accurate expression of the inverted relation would both times require הוּא referring to the subject, so we here abide by the usual syntax : he that gathers in summer time is . . . Also the relation of the members of the sentence, xix. 26, is a parallel from which it is evident that the misguided son is called מֵבִישׁ as causing shame, although in הֵבִישׁ

the idea to put to shame (=to act so that others are ashamed) and to act shamefully (disgracefully), as in הִשְׂכִּיל the ideas to have insight and to act intelligently, lie into one another (cf. xiv. 35); the root-meaning of הִשְׂכִּיל is determined after שֵׂכֶל, which from שָׂכַל, *complicare*, designates the intellect as the faculty of intellectual configuration. בּוֹשׁ, properly *disturbari*, proceeds from a similar conception as the Lat. *confundi* (*pudore*). קַיִץ and קָצִיר fall together, for קַיִץ (from קוץ = קָיַץ, to be glowing hot) is just the time of the קָצִיר; *vid.* under Gen. viii. 22. To the activity of a thoughtful ingathering, אָגַר, for a future store (*vid.* vi. 7), stands opposed deep sleep, *i.e.* the state of one sunk in idleness. נִרְדָּם means, as Schultens has already shown, *somno penitus obrui, omni sensu obstructo et oppilato quasi*, from רָדַם, to fill, to shut up, to conclude; the derivation (which has been adopted since Gesenius) from the Arab. word having the same sound, ردم, *stridere*, to shrill, to rattle (but not *stertere*, to snore), lies remote in the *Niph.*, and also contradicts the usage of the word, according to which it designates a state in which all free activity is bound, and all reference to the external world is interrupted; cf. תַּרְדֵּמָה, xix. 15, of dulness, apathy, somnolency in the train of slothfulness. The LXX. has here one distich more than the Hebr. text.

Ver. 6. There now follow two proverbs regarding the blessings and the curses which come to men, and which flow forth from them. Here, however, as throughout, we take each proverb by itself, that it might not appear as if we had a tetrastich before us. The first of these two antithetic distichs is:

> Blessings (come) on the head of the just;
> But violence covereth the mouth of the godless.

Blessings are, without being distinguished, bestowed as well as prayed for from above. Regarding the undistinguished uses of לְרֹאשׁ (of a recompense of reward), בְּרֹאשׁ (of penal recompense), and עַל־רֹאשׁ (especially of punishment), *vid.* under Gen. xlix. 26. If we understand, with Ewald, Bertheau, Elster, Zöckler, and others, the two lines after ver. 11, xix. 28, cf. x. 18: the mouth of the wicked covers (hides under a mask) violence, inasmuch as he speaks words of blessing while thoughts of malediction lurk behind them (Ps. lxii. 5), then we renounce the sharpness of the contrast. On the contrary, it is preserved if we interpret וּפִי as object: the violence that has gone out from it covereth the mouth of the wicked, *i.e.* it falls back upon his foul mouth; or as Fleischer (and Oetinger almost the same) paraphrases it: the deeds of violence that have gone forth from them are given back to them in curses and maledictions, so that going back they stop, as it were, their mouth, they bring them to silence; for it is unnecessary to take פִּי synecdochically for פְּנֵי (cf. *e.g.* Ps. lxix. 8), since in בְּרָכוֹת 6*a* are perhaps chiefly meant blessings of thankful acknowledgment on the part of men, and the giving prominence to the mouth of the wicked from which nothing good proceeds is well accounted for. The parallels do not hinder us thus to explain, since parts of proverbs repeating themselves in the Book of Proverbs often show a change of the meaning (*vid.* p. 24 f.). Hitzig's conjecture, יְפַסֶּה (better יְכַסֶּה), is unnecessary; for elsewhere we read, as here, that חמס (violence), *jure talionis*, covers, יְכַסֶּה, the wicked, Hab. ii. 17, or that he, using "violence," therewith covers the whole of his external appearance, *i.e.* gives to it the branded impress of the unrighteousness he has done (*vid.* Köhler under Mal. ii. 16).

Ver. 7. Thus, as ver. 6 says how it goes with the righteous and the wicked in this life, so this verse tells how it fares with them after death:

> The memory of the righteous remains in blessings,
> And the name of the godless rots.

The tradition regarding the writing of זכר with five (זֵכֶר) or six points (זֶכֶר) is doubtful (*vid.* Heidenheim in his ed. of the Pentateuch, *Meôr Enajim*, under Ex. xvii. 14); the Cod. 1294 and old printed copies have here זֵכֶר. Instead of לְבְרָכָה, יֵבֹרַךְ might be used; the phrase היה לברכה (*opp.* הָיָה לִקְלָלָה, often used by Jeremiah), subordinate to the substantival clause, paraphrases the passive, for it expresses a growing to something, and thus the entrance into a state of endurance. The remembrance of the righteous endures after his death, for he is thought of with thankfulness (צל"ז = זכר צדיק לברכה, the usual appendix to the name of an honoured, beloved man who has died), because his works, rich in blessing, continue; the name of the godless, on the contrary, far from continuing fresh and green (Ps. lxii. 17) after his departure, becomes corrupt (רקב, from רק, to be or to become thin, to dissolve in fine parts, *tabescere*), like a worm-eaten decayed tree (Isa. xl. 20). The Talmud explains it thus, *Joma* 38*b*: foulness comes over their name, so that we call no one after their name. Also the idea suggests itself, that his name becomes corrupt, as it were, with his bones; the Mishna, at least *Ohaloth* ii. 1, uses רְקַב of the dust of corruption.

Ver. 8. There follows now a series of proverbs in which reference to sins of the mouth and their contrary prevails:

> He that is wise in heart receives precepts;
> But he that is of a foolish mouth comes to ruin.

A חֲכַם־לֵב, wise-hearted, is one whose heart is חָכָם, xxiii. 15; in a word, a נָבוֹן, a person of understanding or judgment, xvi. 21. Such an one does not make his own knowledge the *ne plus ultra*, nor does he make his own will the *noli me tangere*; but he takes commands, *i.e.* instructions directing or prohibiting, to which he willingly subordinates himself as the outflow of a higher knowledge and will, and by which he sets bounds and limits to himself. But a fool of the lips, *i.e.* a braggart blunderer, one pleasing himself with vain talk (xiv. 23), falls prostrate, for he thinks that he knows all things better, and will take no pattern; but while he boasts himself from on high, suddenly all at once—for he offends against the fundamental principle of common life and of morality—he comes to lie low down on the ground. The Syr. and Targ. translate יִלָּבֵט by, he is caught (Bertheau, ensnared); Aquila, Vulgate, Luther, δαρή-σεται, he is slain; Symmachus, βασανισθήσεται; but all without any support in the usage of the language known to us. Theodotion, φυρήσεται, he is confounded, is not tenable; Joseph Kimchi, who after David Kimchi, under Hos. iv. 14, appeals in support of this meaning (יִשְׁתַּבֵּשׁ, similarly Parchon: יתבלבל) to the Arabic, seems to think on *iltibâs*, confusion. The demonstrable meanings of the verb לבט are the following: 1. To occasion trouble. Thus *Mechilta*, under Ex. xvii. 14, לבטוהו, one has imposed upon him trouble; *Sifri*, under Num. xi. 1, נתלבטנו, we are tired, according to which Rashi: he fatigues himself, but which fits neither to the subj. nor to the contrast, which is to be supposed. The same may be said of the meaning of the Syr. ܠܒܛ, to drive on, to press, which without doubt accords with the former meaning of the word in the language of the Midrash. 2. In Arab. *labat* (R. *lab*, *vid.* Wünsche's *Hos.* p. 172), to throw any one down to the earth, so that he falls with his whole body his whole length; the passive נלבט, to be thus thrown down by another, or to throw oneself thus down, figuratively of one who falls hopelessly into evil and destruction (Fl.). The Arabic verb is also used of the springing run of the animal ridden on (to gallop), and of the being lame (to hop), according to which in the Lex. the explanations, he hurries, or he wavers hither and thither, are offered by Kimchi (*Græc. Venet.* πλανηθήσεται). But the former of these explanations, *corruit* (=*in calamitatem ruit*), placed much nearer by the Arabic, is confirmed by the LXX. ὑποσκελισθήσεται, and by the *Berêshith rabba,* c. 52, where לבט is used in the sense to be ruined (=נכשל). Hitzig changes the passive into the active : " he throws the offered לֶקַח scornfully to the ground," but the contrast does not require this. The wanton, arrogant boasting lies already in the designation of the subj. אֱוִיל שְׂפָתִים ; and the sequel involves, as a consequence, the contrasted consequence of ready reception of the limitations and guidance of his own will by a higher.

Ver. 9. The form of this verse is like the eighth, word for word :

> He that walketh in innocence walketh securely ;
> But he that goeth in secret ways is known.

The full form of בַּתּוֹם does not, as Hitzig supposes, stand in causal connection with the *Dechî*, for the consonant text lying before us is at least 500 years older than the accentuation. For הֹלֵךְ תֹּם at ii. 7, there is here הֹלֵךְ בַּתּוֹם = הֹלֵךְ בְּדַרְכֵּי תֹם ; so מְעַקֵּשׁ דְּרָכָיו denotes, after ii. 15, such an one אֲשֶׁר דְּרָכָיו עִקְּשִׁים. Expressed in the language of the N. T., תֹם is the property of the ἁπλοῦς or ἀκέραιος, for the fundamental idea of fulness is here referred to full submission, full integrity. Such an one goes בֶּטַח (Aquila, ἀμερίμνως), for there is nothing designedly concealed by him, of which he has reason to fear that it will come to the light ; whoever, on the contrary, makes his ways crooked, *i.e.* turns into crooked ways, is perceived, or, as we might also explain it (*vid.* under Gen. iv. 15) : if one (*qui* = *si quis*) makes his ways crooked, then it is known—nothing, however, stands opposed to the reference of יִוָּדֵעַ. to the person : he is finally known, *i.e.* unmasked (LXX. Jerome, γνωσθήσεται, *manifestus fiet*). Usually it is explained : he is knowing, clever, with the remark that נוֹדָע is here the passive of הוֹדִיעַ (Gesen., Ewald, Hitzig) ; *Hiph.* to give to feel ; *Niph.* to become to feel, properly to be made to know (Luth. : made wise) ; but the passive of the *Hiph.* is the *Hoph.* Such a *Niph.* in which the causative (not simply transitive) signification of the *Hiph.* would be applied passively is without example (*vid.* Ewald, § 133*a*); the meaning of Jer. xxxi. 19 also is : after I have become known, *i.e.* been made manifest, uncovered, drawn into the light.

Ver. 10. This verse contains another proverb, similarly formed, parallel with the half of ver. 8 :

> He that winketh with the eye causeth trouble ;
> And a foolish mouth comes to ruin.

Regarding the winking or nipping, *i.e.* the repeated nipping of the eyes (cf. *nictare*, frequent. of *nicĕre*), as the conduct of the malicious or malignant, which aims at the derision or injury of him to whom it refers, *vid.* under vi. 13; there קְרַץ was connected with בְּ of the means of the action ; here, as Ps. xxxv. 19, cf. Prov. xvi. 30, it is connected with the object accus. He who so does produces trouble (heart-sorrow, xv. 13), whether it be that he who is the butt of this mockery marks it, or that he is the victim of secretly concerted injury ; יִתֵּן is not here used impersonally, as xiii. 10, but as xxix. 15, cf. Lev. xix. 28, xxiv. 20, in the sense of the cause. 10*b* forms a striking contrast to 10*a*, according to the text of the LXX. : ὁ δὲ ἐλέγχων μετὰ παῤῥησίας εἰρηνοποιεῖ. The Targ., however, abides, contrary to the Syr., by the Hebrew text, which certainly is older than this its correction, which Ewald and Lagarde unsuccessfully attempt to translate into Hebrew. The foolish mouth, here understood in conformity with 10*a*, is one who talks at random, without examination and deliberation, and thus suddenly stumbles and falls over, so that he comes to lie on the ground, to his own disgrace and injury.

Ver. 11. Another proverb, similar to the half of ver. 6 :

> A fountain of life is the mouth of the righteous ;
> But the mouth of the godless hideth violence.

If we understand 11*b* wholly as 6*b* : *os improborum obteget violentia*, then the meaning of 11*a* would be, that that which the righteous speaks tends to his own welfare (Fl.). But since the words spoken are the means of communication and of intercourse, one has to think of the water as welling up in one, and flowing forth to another ; and the meaning of 11*b* has to accommodate itself to the preceding half proverb, whereby it cannot be mistaken that חָמָס (violence), which was 6*b* subj., bears here, by the contrast, the stamp of the obj.; for the possibility of manifold windings and turnings is a characteristic of the Mashal. In the Psalms and Prophets it is God who is called מְקוֹר חַיִּים, Ps. xxxvi. 10, Jer. ii. 13, xvii. 13 ; the proverbial poetry plants the figure on ethical ground, and understands by it a living power, from which wholesome effects accrue to its possessor, xiv. 27, and go forth from him to others,

xiii. 14.. Thus the mouth of the righteous is here called a fountain of life, because that which he speaks, and as he speaks it, is morally strengthening, intellectually elevating, and inwardly quickening in its effect on the hearers; while, on the contrary, the mouth of the godless covereth wrong (*violentiam*), *i.e.* conceals with deceitful words the intention, directed not to that which is best, but to the disadvantage and ruin of his neighbours; so that words which in the one case bring to light a ground of life and of love, and make it effectual, in the other case serve for a covering to an immoral, malevolent background.

Ver. 12. Another proverb of the different effects of hatred and of love:

> Hate stirreth up strife,
> And love covereth all transgressions.

Regarding מְדָנִים, for which the *Keri* elsewhere substitutes מִדְיָנִים, *vid.* under vi. 14. Hatred of one's neighbour, which is of itself an evil, has further this bad effect, that it calls forth hatred, and thus stirreth up strife, feuds, factions, for it incites man against man (cf. עֹרֵר, Job iii. 8); on the contrary, love covers not merely little errors, but also greater sins of every kind (כָּל־פְּשָׁעִים), viz. by pardoning them, concealing them, excusing them, if possible, with mitigating circumstances, or restraining them before they are executed. All this lies in the covering. James, however, gives it, v. 20, another rendering: love covers them, viz. from the eyes of a holy God; for it forgives them to the erring brother, and turns him from the error of his way. The LXX. improperly translate πάντας δὲ τοὺς μὴ φιλονεικοῦντας καλύπτει φιλία; but Peter (1 Pet. iv. 8) as well as James, but none of the Greek versions: ἡ ἀγάπη καλύψει πλῆθος ἁμαρτιῶν. The Romish Church makes use of this passage as a proof for the introduction of the *fides formata*, viz. *caritate*, in justification, which is condemned in the *Apology of the Augsburg Confession*; and, indeed, the *multitudo peccatorum* is not meant of the sins of him who cherishes love, but of the sins of the neighbour. Sin stirs up hatred in men in their relation to one another; but love covers the already existing sins, and smooths the disturbances occasioned by them.

Ver. 13. There follow now two other proverbs on the use and abuse of speech:

> On the lips of the man of understanding wisdom is found;
> And the rod for the back of the fool.

With Löwenstein, Hitzig. and others, it is inadmissible to regard וְשֵׁבֶט as second subject to תִּמָּצֵא. The mouth itself, or the word of the mouth, may be called a rod, viz. a rod of correction (Isa. xi. 4); but that wisdom and such a rod are found on the lips of the wise would be a combination and a figure in bad taste. Thus 13b is a clause by itself, as Luther renders it : " but a rod belongs to the fool's back;" and this will express a contrast to 13a, that while wisdom is to be sought for on the lips of the man of understanding (cf. Mal. ii. 7), a man devoid of understanding, on the contrary, gives himself to such hollow and corrupt talk, that in order to educate him to something better, if possible, the rod must be applied to his back ; for, according to the Talmudic proverb : that which a wise man gains by a hint, a fool only obtains by a club.   The rod is called שֵׁבֶט from שָׁבַט, to be smooth, to go straight down (as the hair of the head); and the back גֵּו, from גָּוָה, to be rounded, i.e. concave or convex.

> Ver. 14 Wise men store up knowledge ;
>   But the mouth of the fool is threatening destruction.

Ewald, Bertheau, Hitzig, Oetinger : " The mouth of the fool blunders out, and is as the sudden falling in of a house which one cannot escape from."   But since מְחִתָּה is a favourite *Mishle*-word to denote the effect and issue of that which is dangerous and destructive, so the sense is perhaps further to be extended: the mouth of the fool is for himself (xiii. 3) and others a near, i.e. an always threatening and unexpectedly occurring calamity; unexpectedly, because suddenly he blunders out with his inconsiderate shame-bringing talk, so that such a fool's mouth is to every one a *præsens periculum*.   As to יִצְפֹּן, it is worthy of remark that in the Beduin, ضفن, *fut. i*, signifies to be still, to be thoughtful, to be absorbed in oneself (*vid.* Wetstein on Job, p. 281).   According to Codd. and editions, in this correct, וּפִי־ is to be written instead of וּפִי אֱוִיל; *vid.* the law concerning the *Makkeph* in the three poetical books, Baer's *Torath Emeth*, p. 40.

A pair of proverbs regarding possession and gain.

Ver. 15. Regarding possession:

> The rich man's wealth is his strong city ;
>   The destruction of the poor is their poverty.

The first line=xviii. 11.   One may render the idea according to that which is internal, and according to that which is external; and the proverb remains in both cases true.   As עֹז may mean, of itself alone,

CHAP. X. 16.   219

power, as means of protection, or a bulwark (Ps. viii. 3), or the consciousness of power, high feeling, pride (Judg. v. 21); so קִרְיַת עֻזּוֹ
may be rendered as an object of self-confidence, and מְחִתָּה, on the
contrary, as an object of terror (Jer. xlviii. 39): the rich man, to
whom his estate (vid. on הוֹן, p. 63) affords a sure reserve and an
abundant source of help, can appear confident and go forth ener-
getically; on the contrary, the poor man is timid and bashful, and
is easily dejected and discouraged.   Thus e.g. Oetinger and Hitzig.
But the objective interpretation is allowable, and lies also much
nearer: the rich man stands thus independent, changes and adversities cannot so easily overthrow him, he is also raised above
many hazards and temptations; on the contrary, the poor man
is overthrown by little misfortunes, and his despairing endeavours
to save himself, when they fail, ruin him completely, and perhaps make him at the same time a moral outlaw.   It is quite an
experienced fact which this proverb expresses, but one from which
the double doctrine is easily derived: (1) That it is not only
advised, but also commanded, that man make the firm establishing
of his external life-position the aim of his endeavour; (2) That
one ought to treat with forbearance the humble man; and if he
always sinks deeper and deeper, one ought not to judge him with
unmerciful harshness and in proud self-exaltation.

    Ver. 16. Regarding gain:

> The gain of the righteous tendeth to life;
> The income of the godless to sin.

Intentionally, that which the righteous receives is called פְּעֻלָּה (as
Lev. xix. 13), as a reward of his labour; that which the godless
receives is called תְּבוּאָה, as income which does not need to be the
reward of labour, and especially of his own immediate labour.
And with לְחַטָּאת, לְחַיִּים runs parallel, from the supposition that sin
carries the germ of death in itself.   The reward of his labour serves
to the righteous to establish his life, i.e. to make sure his life-
position, and to elevate his life-happiness.   On the contrary, the
income of the godless serves only to ruin his life; for, made thereby
full and confident, he adds sin to sin, whose wages is death.
Hitzig translates: for expiation, i.e. to lose it again as atonement
for past sins; but if חיים and חטאת are contrasted with each other,
then חטאת is death-bringing sin (viii. 35 f.).

    The group of proverbs now following bring again to view the

good and bad effects of human speech. The seventeenth verse introduces the transition :

Ver. 17 There is a way to life when one gives heed to correction ;
And whoever disregards instruction runs into error.

Instead of אֹרַח חַיִּים (v. 6), there is here אֹרַח לְחַיִּים; and then this proverb falls into rank with ver. 16, which contains the same word לְחַיִּים. The accentuation denotes אֹרַח as subst.; for אֹרַח [way, road]= אֹרַח [a wayfarer, part. of אֹרֵחַ] would, as שֹׁסַע, Lev. xi. 7, נֹטַע, Ps. xciv. 9, have the tone on the ultima. It is necessary neither to change the tone, nor, with Ewald, to interpret אֹרַח as *abstr. pro concreto*, like הֵלֶךְ, for the expression " wanderer to life " has no support in the *Mishle*. Michaelis has given the right interpretation : *via ad vitam est si quis custodiat disciplinam*. The syntactical contents, however, are different, as *e.g.* 1 Sam. ii. 13, where the participle has the force of a hypothetical clause ; for the expression : " a way to life is he who observes correction," is equivalent to : he is on the way to life who . . ; a variety of the manner of expression : "the porch was twenty cubits," 2 Chron. iii. 4, particularly adapted to the figurative language of proverbial poetry, as if the poet said : See there one observant of correction— that (viz. the שֹׁמֵר [שָׁמַר, to watch] representing itself in this שֹׁמֵר) is the way to life. מוּסָר and תּוֹכַחַת are related to each other as παιδεία and ἔλεγχος ; עֹזֵב [עָזַב, to leave, forsake] is equivalent to בִּלְתִּי שֹׁמֵר. מַתְעֶה would be unsuitable as a contrast in the causative sense : who guides wrong, according to which Bertheau understands 17a, that only he who observes correction can guide others to life. We expect to hear what injuries he who thinks to raise himself above all reproach brings on himself. Hitzig, in his Commentary (1858), for this reason places the *Hithpa.* מִתְעֶה (rather write מַתְעֶה) in the place of the *Hiph.*; but in the *Comm. on Jeremiah* (1866), xlii. 20, he rightly remarks : "To err, not as an involuntary condition, but as an arbitrary proceeding, is suitably expressed by the *Hiph.*" In like manner הוֹסִיף, הִגִּיעַ (to touch), הִרְחִיק (to go to a distance), denote the active conduct of a being endowed with reason ; Ewald, § 122, c. Jewish interpreters gloss מתעה by supplying נַפְשׁוֹ; but it signifies only as inwardly transitive, to accomplish the action of the תְּעוּת.

Ver. 18 He that hideth hatred is a mouth of falsehood ;
And he that spreadeth slander is a fool.

The LXX., καλύπτουσιν ἔχθραν χείλη δίκαια, which Ewald pre-

fers, and which has given occasion to Hitzig to make a remarkable
conjecture (" He who conceals hatred, close lips," which no one
understands without Hitzig's comment. to this his conjecture).
But (1) to hide hatred (cf. ver. 11, xxvi. 24) is something altogether
different from to cover sin (ver. 12, xvii. 9), or generally to keep
anything secret with discretion (x. 13); and (2) that δίκαια is a
corrupt reading for ἄδικα (as Grabe supposes, and Symmachus
translates) or δόλια (as Lagarde supposes, and indeed is found in
Codd.). Michaelis well remarks: *odium tectum est dolosi, mani-
festa sycophantia stultorum.* Whoever conceals hateful feelings
behind his words is שִׂפְתֵי־שָׁקֶר, a mouth of falsehood (cf. the mouth
of the fool, ver. 14); one does not need to supply אִישׁ, but much
rather has hence to conclude that a false man is simply so named,
as is proved by Ps. cxx. 3. There is a second moral judgment,
18*b* : he who spreadeth slander (וּמוֹצִא, according to the Masoretic
writing: he who divulges it, the correlate to הבִיא, to bring to, Gen.
xxxvii. 2) is a *Thor* [fool, stupid, dull], כְּסִיל (not a *Narr* [fool,
godless person], אֱוִיל); for such slandering can generally bring no
advantage; it injures the reputation of him to whom the דִּבָּה, *i.e.*
the secret report, the slander, refers; it sows discord, has incalculable consequences, and finally brings guilt on the tale-bearer
himself.

Ver. 19 In a multitude of words transgression is not wanting;
But he who restrains his lips shows wisdom.

We do not, with Bertheau, understand 19*a* : by many words a
transgression does not cease to be what it is; the contrast 19*b* requires a more general condemnation of the multitude of words, and
חָדַל not only means to cease from doing (to leave off), and to cease
from being (to take away), but also not at all to do (to intermit,
Ezek. iii. 11; Zech. xi. 12), and not at all to be (to fail, to be
absent), thus : *ubi verborum est abundantia non deest peccatum*
(Fl.). Michaelis suitably compares πολυλογία πολλὰ σφάλματα
ἔχει by Stobäus, and כל המרבה דברים מביא חטא in the tractate *Aboth*
i. 17, wherewith Rashi explains the proverb. פֶּשַׁע is not here, as
elsewhere, *e.g.* Ps. xix. 14, with special reference to the sin of
falling away from favour, apostasy, but, like the post-biblical עֲבֵרה,
generally with reference to every kind of violation (פשע = فسق
dirumpere) of moral restraint; here, as Jansen remarks, *peccatum
sive mendacii, sive detractionis, sive alterius indiscretæ læsionis, sive*

vanitatis, sive denique verbi otiosi. In 19*b* it is more appropriate to regard מַשְׂכִּיל as the present of the internal transitive (*intelligenter agit*) than to interpret it in the attributive sense (*intelligens*).

> Ver. 20 Choice silver is the tongue of the righteous;
> But the heart of the godless is little worth.

Choice silver is, as viii. 19, cf. 10, pure, freed from all base mixtures. Like it, pure and noble, is whatever the righteous speaks; the heart, *i.e.* the manner of thought and feeling, of the godless is, on the contrary, like little *instar nihili, i.e.* of little or no worth, Arab. *yasway kâlyla* (Fl.). LXX.: the heart of the godless ἐκλείψει, *i.e.* יִמְעַט, at first arrogant and full of lofty plans, it becomes always the more dejected, discouraged, empty. But 20*a* leads us to expect some designation of its worth. The Targ. (according to which the Peshito is to be corrected; *vid.* Levy's *Wörterbuch*, ii. 26): the heart of the godless is מַחְתָא (from נְחַת), refuse, dross. The other Greek versions accord with the text before us.

> Ver. 21 The lips of the righteous edify many;
> But fools die through want of understanding.

The LXX. translate 21*a*: the lips of the righteous ἐπίσταται ὑψηλά, which would at least require ידעו רבות. רָעָה is, like the postbibl. פרנס (*vid.* the Hebr. *Römerbrief*, p. 97), another figure for the N. T. οἰκοδομεῖν: to afford spiritual nourishment and strengthening, to which Fleischer compares the ecclesiastical expressions: *pastor, ovile ecclesiæ, les ouailles;* רֹעֶה means leader, Jer. x. 21, as well as teacher, Eccles. xii. 11, for it contains partly the prevailing idea of leading, partly of feeding. יִרְעוּ stands for תִּרְעֶינָה, as ver. 32, v. 2. In 21*b*, Bertheau incorrectly explains, as Euchel and Michaelis: *stulti complures per dementem unum moriuntur;* the fool has truly enough in his own folly, and needs not to be first drawn by others into destruction. חֲסַר is not here the connective form of חָסֵר (Jewish interpreters: for that reason, that he is such an one), nor of חֶסֶר (Hitzig, Zöckler), which denotes, as a concluded idea, *penuria*, but like רְחַב, xxi. 4, שְׁכַב, vi. 10, and שְׁפַל, xvi. 19, *infin.*: they die by want of understanding (cf. v. 23); this *amentia* is the cause of their death, for it leads fools to meet destruction without their observing it (Hos. iv. 6).

Three proverbs which say that good comes from above, and is as a second nature to the man of understanding:

Ver. 22 Jahve's blessing—it maketh rich;
And labour addeth nothing thereto

Like 24a, הִיא limits the predicate to this and no other subject: "all depends on God's blessing." Here is the first half of the *ora et labora*. The proverb is a compendium of Ps. cxxvii. 1, 2. 22b is to be understood, according to ver. 2 of this Solomonic psalm, not that God adds to His blessing no sorrow, much rather with the possession grants at the same time a joyful, peaceful mind (LXX., Targ., Syriac, Jerome, Aben-Ezra, Michaelis, and others), which would require the word עָלֶיהָ; but that trouble, labour, *i.e.* strenuous self-endeavours, add not (anything) to it, *i.e.* that it does not associate itself with the blessing (which, as the Jewish interpreters rightly remark, is, according to its nature, תוספת, as the curse is חסרון) as the *causa efficiens*, or if we supply *quidquam*, as the complement to עִמָּהּ [along with it]: nothing is added thereto, which goes along with that which the blessing of God grants, and completes it. Thus correctly Rashi, Luther, Ziegler, Ewald, Hitzig, Zöckler. The now current accentuation, וְלֹא יוֹסִף עֶצֶב עִמָּהּ, is incorrect. Older editions, as Venice 1525, 1615, Basel 1618, have ולא־יוסף עצב עמה, the transformation of ולא־יוסף עצב. Besides, עצב has double Segol (*vid.* Kimchi's *Lex.*), and יוסף is written, according to the Masora, in the first syllable *plene,* in the last *defective.*

Ver. 23 Like sport to a fool is the commission of a crime;
And wisdom to a man of understanding.

Otherwise Löwenstein: to a fool the carrying out of a plan is as sport; to the man of understanding, on the contrary, as wisdom. זִמָּה, from זָמַם, to press together, mentally to think, as Job xvii. 11, and according to Gesenius, also Prov. xxi. 27, xxiv. 9. But זִמָּה has the prevailing signification of an outrage against morality, a sin of unchastity; and especially the phrase עָשָׂה זִמָּה is in Judg. xx. 6 and in Ezekiel not otherwise used, so that all the old interpreters render it here by *patrare scelus;* only the Targum has the equivocal עבד עֲבִידְתָּא; the Syriac, however, ܒܕ ܚܣܖ ܐ. Sinful conduct appears to the fool, who places himself above the solemnity of the moral law, as sport; and wisdom, on the contrary, (appears as sport) to a man of understanding. We would not venture on this acceptation of בִּשְׂחוֹק if שָׂחֵק were not attributed, viii. 30 f., to wisdom itself. This alternate relationship recommends itself by the indetermination of וְחָכְמָה, which is not favourable to the interpretation:

sed sapientiam colit vir intelligens, or as Jerome has it : *sapientia autem est viro prudentia*. The subjects of the antithesis chiastically combine within the verse : חכמה, in contrast to wicked conduct, is acting in accordance with moral principles. This to the man of understanding is as easy as sporting, just as to the fool is shame-less sinning ; for he follows in this an inner impulse, it brings to him joy, it is the element in which he feels himself satisfied.

> Ver. 24 That of which the godless is afraid cometh upon him,
> And what the righteous desires is granted to him.

The formation of the clause 24*a* is like the similar proverb, xi. 27*b* ; the subject-idea has there its expression in the genitival *annexum*, of which Gen. ix. 6*b* furnishes the first example ; in this passage before us it stands at the beginning, and is, as in ver. 22, emphati-cally repeated with הִיא. מְגוֹרָה, properly the turning oneself away, hence shrinking back in terror ; here, as Isa. lxvi. 4, of the object of fear, parallel to תַּאֲוָה, wishing, of the object of the wish. In 24*b* Ewald renders יִתֵּן as adj. from יָתָן (whence אֵיתָן), after the form פֶּקַח, and translates : yet to the righteous desire is always green. But whether יִתֵּן is probably formed from יתן, and not from נתן, is a question in xii. 12, but not here, where wishing and giving (fulfil-ling) are naturally *correlata*. Hitzig corrects יִתֵּן, and certainly the supplying of ה' is as little appropriate here as at xiii. 21. Also a "one gives" is scarcely intended (according to which the Targ., Syr., and Jerome translate passively), in which case the Jewish interpreters are wont to explain יתן, *scil.* הנותן ; for if the poet thought of יתן with a personal subject, why did he not rescue it from the dimness of such vague generality ? Thus, then, יתן is, with Böttcher, to be interpreted as impersonal, like xiii. 10, Job xxxvii. 10, and perhaps also Gen. xxxviii. 28 (Ewald, § 295*a*) : what the righteous wish, that there is, *i.e.* it becomes actual, is fulfilled. In this we have not directly and exclusively to think of the destiny at which the godless are afraid (Heb. x. 27), and toward which the desire of the righteous goes forth ; but the clause has also truth which is realized in this world : just that which they greatly fear, *e.g.* sickness, bankruptcy, the loss of reputation, comes upon the godless ; on the contrary, that which the righteous wish realizes itself, because their wish, in its intention, and kind, and content, stands in harmony with the order of the moral world.

There now follows a series of proverbs, broken by only one dis-similar proverb, on the immoveable continuance of the righteous :

Ver. 25 When the storm sweeps past, it is no more with the wicked;
But the righteous is a building firm for ever.

How ver. 25 is connected with ver. 24 is shown in the Book of
Wisdom v. 15 (the hope of the wicked like chaff which the wind
pursues). The Aram., Jerome, and *Græc. Venet.* interpret כ of
comparison, so that the destruction of the godless is compared in
suddenness and rapidity to the rushing past of a storm; but then רוּחַ
ought to have been used instead of סוּפָה; and instead of וְאֵין רָשָׁע
with the ו *apodosis*, a disturbing element in such a comparison,
would have been used יַחֲלֹף רָשָׁע, or at least רָשָׁע אָיִן. The thought
is no other than that of Job xxi. 18: the storm, which is called סוּפָה,
from סוּף, to rush forth, is meant, as sweeping forth, and כ the
temporal, as Ex. xi. 4 (LXX. παραπορευομένης καταιγίδος), with
ו *apod.* following, like *e.g.,* after a similar member of a temporal
sentence, Isa. x. 25. סוּפָה is a figure of God-decreed calamities,
as war and pestilence, under which the godless sink, while the
righteous endure them; cf. with 25*a*, i. 27, Isa. xxviii. 18; and
with 25*b*, iii. 25, Hab. ii. 4, Ps. xci. "An everlasting foundation,"
since עוֹלָם is understood as looking forwards, not as at Isa. lviii. 12,
backwards, is a foundation capable of being shaken by nothing,
and synecdoch. generally a building. The proverb reminds us of
the close of the Sermon on the Mount, and finds the final confirmation of its truth in this, that the death of the godless is a penal
thrusting of them away, but the death of the righteous a lifting
them up to their home. The righteous also often enough perish in
times of war and of pestilence; but the proverb, as it is interpreted,
verifies itself, even although not so as the poet, viewing it from his
narrow O. T. standpoint, understood it; for the righteous, let him
die when and how he may, is preserved, while the godless perishes.

Ver. 26. This proverb stands out of connection with the series:

As vinegar to the teeth, and as smoke to the eyes,
So is the sluggard to them who give him a commission.

A parabolic proverb (*vid.* p. 9), *priamel*-like in its formation
(p. 13). Here and there לַשְׁלְחָיו is found with *Mugrash*, but in
correct texts it has *Rebia-magnum;* the verse is divided into two by
Athnach, whose subordinate distributive is (*Accentssystem,* xi. § 1)
Rebia-magnum. Smoke makes itself disagreeably perceptible to
the sense of smell, and particularly to the eyes, which it causes to
smart so that they overflow with tears; wherefore Virgil speaks of
it as *amarus,* and Horace *lacrimosus.* הֹמֶץ (from חָמֵץ, to be sour,

harsh) signifies properly that which is sour, as *acetum*, ὄξος; here, after the LXX. ὄμφαξ, the unripe grapes, but which are called בֹּסֶר (בֶּסֶר) (*vid.* under Job xv. 33), by which the Syr., here following the LXX., translates, and which also in the Talmud, *Demaï* i. 1, is named חֹמֶץ, after a doubtful meaning (*vid.* Aruch, and on the other side Rashi), thus: vinegar, which the word commonly means, and which also accords with the object of the comparison, especially if one thinks of the sharp vinegar-wine of the south, which has an effect on the teeth denoted by the Hebr. verb כהה, as the effect of smoke is by כהה (Fl.). The plur. לְשֹׁלְחָיו is that of the category, like xxii. 21, xxv. 13 ; the parallel אֲדֹנָיו of the latter passage does not at least make it necessary to regard it, like this, as a *plur. excellentiæ* (Bertheau, Hitzig, Ewald). They who send a sluggard, *i.e.* who make him their agent, do it to their own sorrow ; his slothfulness is for them, and for that which they have in view, of dull, *i.e.* slow and restrained, of biting, *i.e.* sensibly injurious operation.

From this point the proverbs fall into the series connecting themselves with ver. 25:

> Ver. 27 The fear of Jahve multiplies the days of life;
> But the years of the godless are shortened.

This parable, like ver. 25, also corresponds with the O. T. standpoint, having in view the present life. The present-life history confirms it, for vice destroys body and soul ; and the fear of God, which makes men contented and satisfied in God, is truly the right principle of longevity. But otherwise also the pious often enough die early, for God carries them away מפני הרעה [from the face of the evil], Isa. lvii. 1 f. ; or if they are martyrs for the truth (Ps. xliv. 23, cf. lx. 6), the verification of the above proverb in such cases moves forward (Wisd. iv. 7 ff.) into eternity, in which the life of the pious continues for ever, while that of the godless loses itself with his death in the state of everlasting death. ix. 11, cf. iii. 2, resembles 27a. Instead of תִּקְצֹרְנָה, תִּקְצַרְנָה was to be expected; but the flexion does not distinguish the transitive קָצַר (Arab. *kaṣara*) and intransitive קָצֵר (Arab. *kaṣura*) as it ought.

> Ver. 28 The expectation of the righteous is gladness,
> And the hope of the godless comes to nothing.

תּוֹחֶלֶת as well as תִּקְוָה proceed on the fundamental idea of a strained earnest looking back upon something, the same fundamental idea which in another view gives the meaning of strength (חַיִל, Arab. *ḥayl; kuwwat, kawiyy,* cf. גָּדַל, Arab. *jdl, plectere,* and גָּדוֹל, *strong* and *strength*). The substantival clause 28*a* denotes nothing more than : it is gladness (cf. iii. 17, all their steps are gladness), but which is equivalent to, it is that in its issue, *in gaudium desinit.* Hitzig's remark that תּוֹחֶלֶת is the chief idea for hope and fear, is not confirmed by the usage of the language; it always signifies joyful, not anxious, expectation; cf. the interchange of the same two synonyms xiii. 7, and תַּאֲוַת, Ps. cxii. 10, instead of תִּקְוַת (here and Job viii. 13). While the expectation of the one terminates in the joy of the fulfilment, the hope of the other (אבד, R. בד, to separate) perishes, *i.e.* comes to nothing.

Ver. 29 Jahve's way is a bulwark to the righteous;
But ruin to those that do evil.

Of the two meanings which מָעוֹז (מָעוֹן) has : a stronghold from עֵז, and asylum (=Arab. *m'adz*) from עוּן, the contrast here demands the former. דֶּרֶךְ ה' and יִרְאַת ה', understood objectively, are the two O. T. names of true religion. It means, then, the way which the God of revelation directs men to walk in (Ps. cxliii. 8), the way of His precepts, Ps. cxix. 27, His way of salvation, Ps. lxvii. 3 (4); in the N. T. ἡ ὁδὸς τοῦ Θεοῦ, Matt. xxii. 16, Acts xviii. 25 f.; cf. ἡ ὁδός simply, Acts ix. 2, xxiv. 14. This way of Jahve is a fortress, bulwark, defence for innocence, or more precisely, a disposition wholly, *i.e.* unreservedly and without concealment, directed toward God and that which is good. All the old interpreters, also Luther, but not the *Græc. Venet.*, translate as if the expression were לַתָּם; but the punctuation has preferred the *abstr. pro concreto*, perhaps because the personal תָּם nowhere else occurs with any such prefix; on the contrary, תֹּם is frequently connected with ב, כ, ל. לתם דרך, *integro viæ* (*vitæ*), are by no means to be connected in one conception (Ziegler, Umbr., Elster), for then the poet ought to have written מעז יהוה לתם־דרך. 29*b* cannot be intrepreted as a thought by itself: and ruin (*vid.* regarding מְחִתָּה, *ruina*, and subjectively *consternatio*, ver. 16) comes to those who do evil; but the thought, much more comprehensive, that religion, which is for the righteous a strong protection and safe retreat, will be an overthrow to those who delight only in wickedness (*vid.* on אָוֶן, p. 143), is confirmed by the similarly formed distich, xxi. 15. Also almost all the Jewish interpreters, from Rashi to Malbim, find here expressed the operation of the divine revelation set over against the conduct of men,— essentially the same as when the Tora or the Chokma present to men for their choice life and death; or the gospel of salvation, according to 2 Cor. ii. 15, is to one the savour of life unto life, to another the savour of death unto death.

Ver. 30 The righteous is never moved;
But the godless abide not in the land.

Love of home is an impulse and emotion natural to man; but to no people was fatherland so greatly delighted in, to none was exile and banishment from fatherland so dreadful a thought, as it was to the people of Israel. Expatriation is the worst of all evils with which the prophets threatened individuals and the people, Amos vii. 17, cf. Isa. xxii. 17 f.; and the history of Israel in their exile, which was a punishment of their national apostasy, confirms this proverb and explains its form; cf. ii. 21 f., Ps. xxxvii. 29. בַּל is, like ix. 13, the emphatic No of the more elevated style; נְמוֹט, the opposite of נָכוֹן, xii. 3; and שָׁכַן signifies to dwell, both inchoative: to come to dwell, and consecutive: to continue to dwell (e.g. Isa. lvii. 15, of God who inhabiteth eternity). In general, the proverb means that the righteous fearlessly maintains the position he takes; while, on the contrary, all they who have no hold on God lose also their outward position. But often enough this saying is fulfilled in this, that they, in order that they may escape disgrace, became wanderers and fugitives, and are compelled to conceal themselves among strangers.

Ver. 31. For the third time the favourite theme already handled in three appendixes is taken up:

The mouth of the righteous bringeth forth wisdom,
And the tongue of falsehood shall be rooted up.

Regarding the biblical comparison of thoughts with branches, and of words with flowers and fruits, vid. my Psychol. p. 181; and regarding the root נב (with its weaker אב), to swell up and to spring up (to well, grow, etc.), vid. what is said in the Comm. on Genesis on נביא, and in Isaiah on אוב. We use the word נוב of that which sprouts or grows, and נבב of that which causes that something sprout; but also נוב may, after the manner of verbs of being full (iii. 10), of flowing (Gesen. § 138, 1, Anm. 2), take the object accus. of that from which anything sprouts (xxiv. 31), or which sprouting, it raises up and brings forth (cf. Isa. lvii. 19). The mouth of the righteous sprouts, brings forth (in Ps. xxxvii. 30, without a figure, יֶהְגֶּה, i.e. utters) wisdom, which in all relations knows how to find out that which is truly good, and suitable for the end intended, and happily to unriddle difficult complications.

The conception of wisdom, in itself practical (from חכם, to be thick = solid, firm), here gains such contents by the contrast: the tongue—whose character and fruit is falsehood, which has its delight in intentional perversions of fact, and thus increaseth complications (*vid.* regarding תַּהְפֻּכוֹת, ii. 12)—is rooted up, whence it follows as regards the mouth of the righteous, that it continues for ever with that its wholesome fruit.

> Ver. 32 The lips of the righteous know what is acceptable;
> But the mouth of the godless is mere falsehood.

Hitzig, instead of יֵדְעוּן, reads יַבִּעוּן; the ἀποστάζει [they distil or send forth] of the LXX. does not favour this, for it is probably only a corruption of ἐπίσταται, which is found in several MSS. The *Græc. Venet.*, which translates ποιμανοῦσι, makes use of a MS. which it sometimes misreads. The text does not stand in need of any emendations, but rather of a corrected relation between the clauses, for the relation of 31*a* with 32*b*, and of 32*a* with 31*b*, strongly commends itself (Hitzig); in that case the explanation lies near: the lips of the righteous find what is acceptable, viz. to God. But this thought in the Mashal language is otherwise expressed (xii. 2 and paral.); and also 32*a* and 32*b* fit each other as contrasts, if by רָצוֹן, as xi. 27, xiv. 9, is to be understood that which is acceptable in its widest generality, equally then in relation to God and man. It is a question whether יֵדְעוּן means that they have knowledge of it (as one *e.g.* says יָדַע סֵפֶר, to understand writing, *i.e.* the reading of it), or that they think thereupon (cf. xxvii. 23). Fundamentally the two ideas, according to the Hebrew conception of the words, lie in each other; for the central conception, perceiving, is biblically equivalent to a delighted searching into or going towards the object. Thus: the lips of the righteous think of that which is acceptable (רָצוֹן, cogn. to חֵן, gracefulness; χάρις, Col. iv. 6); while the mouth of the godless is mere falsehood, which God (the wisdom of God) hates, and from which discord on all sides arises. We might transfer יֵדְעוּן to 32*b*; but this line, interpreted as a clause by itself, is stronger and more pointed (Fl.)

The next three proverbs treat of honesty, discretion, and innocence or dove-like simplicity:

> xi. 1 Deceitful balances are an abomination to Jahve;
> But a full weight is His delight.

The very same proverb, with slightly varied expression, is found in xx. 23; and other such like proverbs, in condemnation of false

and in approbation of true balances, are found, xx. 10, xvi. 11;
similar predicates, but connected with other subjects, are found at
xii. 22, xv. 8. "An abomination to Jahve" is an expression we
have already twice met with in the introduction, iii. 32, vi. 16,
cf. viii. 7; תּוֹעֵבָה is, like תּוֹעָה, a participial noun, in which the
active conception of abhorring is transferred to the action accomplished. רָצוֹן is in post-biblical Hebr. the designation of the
arbitrium and the *voluntas*; but here רְצוֹנוֹ signifies not that which
God wishes, but that which He delights in having. " מִרְמָה (here
for the first time in Proverbs), from רָמָה, the *Piel* of which means
(xxvi. 19) *aliquem dolo et fraude petere.* אֶבֶן, like the Pers. *sanak,*
sanakh, Arab. *ṣajat,* a stone for weight; and finally, without any
reference to its root signification, like Zech. v. 8, אבן העופרת, a
leaden weight, as when we say: a horseshoe of gold, a chess-man
of ivory."

Ver. 2. Now follows the Solomonic "Pride goeth before a fall."

> There cometh arrogance, so also cometh shame;
> But with the humble is wisdom.

Interpreted according to the Hebr.: if the former has come, so
immediately also comes the latter. The general truth as to the
causal connection of the two is conceived of historically; the fact,
confirmed by many events, is represented in the form of a single
occurrence as a warning example; the preterites are like the Greek
aoristi gnomici (*vid.* p. 32); and the perf., with the *fut. consec.*
following, is the expression of the immediate and almost simultaneous consequence (*vid.* at Hab. iii. 10): has haughtiness (זָדוֹן
after the form צָצוֹן, from זִיד, to boil, to run over) appeared, then
immediately also disgrace appeared, in which the arrogant behaviour
is overwhelmed. The harmony of the sound of the Hebr. זָדוֹן and
קָלוֹן cannot be reproduced in German [nor in English]; Hitzig
and Ewald try to do so, but such a *quid pro quo* as " *Kommt Un-*
glimpf kommt an ihn Schimpf" [there comes arrogance, there comes
to him disgrace] is not a translation, but a distortion of the text.
If, now, the antithesis says that with the humble is wisdom, wisdom
is meant which avoids such disgrace as arrogance draws along with
it; for the צָנוּעַ thinks not more highly of himself than he ought to
think (R. צנע, *subsidere, demitti, Deutsch. Morgenl. Zeitsch.* xxv. 185).

Ver. 3 The integrity of the upright guideth them;
> But the perverseness of the ungodly destroyeth them.

To the upright, יְשָׁרִים, who keep the line of rectitude without turn-

ing aside therefrom into devious paths (Ps. cxxv. 4 f.), stand opposed (as at ii. 21 f.) the ungodly (faithless), בֹּגְדִים, who conceal
(from בָּגַד, to cover, whence כְּסוּת = בֶּגֶד) malicious thoughts and
plans. And the contrast of תֻּמָּה, integrity = unreserved loving submission, is סֶלֶף, a word peculiar to the Solomonic Mashal, with its
verb סִלֵּף (vid. p. 32). Hitzig explains it by the Arab. saraf, to
step out, to tread over; and Ewald by lafat, to turn, to turn about
(" treacherous, false step"), both of which are improbable. Schultens compares salaf in the meaning to smear (R. לף, לב, ἀλεί-
φειν; cf. regarding such secondary formations with שׁ preceding,
Hupfeld on Ps. v. 7), and translates here, lubricitas. But this
rendering is scarcely admissible. It has against it lexical tradition
(Menahem : מוטה, wavering; Parchon : זיוף, falsifying; Kimchi :
עוות, misrepresentation, according to which the Græc. Venet. σκο-
λιότης), as well as the methodical comparison of the words. The
Syriac has not this verbal stem, but the Targum has סַלֵּף in the
meaning to distort, to turn the wrong way (σκολιοῦν, στρεβλοῦν),
Prov. x. 10, and Esth. vi. 10, where, in the second Targum, פּוּמֵּהּ
אֶסְתְּלִף means " his mouth was crooked." With justice, therefore,
Gesenius in his Thesaurus has decided in favour of the fundamental idea pervertere, from which also the Peshito and Saadia
proceed; for in Ex. xxiii. 8 they translate (Syr.) mhapêk (it, the
gift of bribery, perverts) and (Arab.) tazyf (= תְּזַיֵּף, it falsifies).
Fl. also, who at xv. 4 remarks, " סֶלֶף, from סָלַף, to stir up, to turn
over, so that the lowermost becomes the uppermost," gives the preference to this primary idea, in view of the Arab. salaf, invertere
terram conserendi causa. It is moreover confirmed by salaf, præ-
cedere, which is pervertere modified to prævertere. But how does
סֶלֶף mean perversio (Theod. ὑποσκελισμός), in the sense of the
overthrow prepared for thy neighbour? The parallels demand
the sense of a condition peculiar to the word and conduct of
the godless (treacherous), xxii. 12 (cf. Ex. xxiii. 8), xix. 3, thus
perversitas, perversity; but this as contrary to truth and rectitude (opp. תֻּמָּה), " perverseness," as we have translated it, for we
understand by it want of rectitude (dishonesty) and untruthfulness. While the sincerity of the upright conducts them, and, so
to say, forms their salvus conductus, which guards them against the
danger of erring and of hostile assault, the perverseness of the
treacherous destroys them; for the disfiguring of truth avenges
itself against them, and they experience the reverse of the proverb,

"*das Ehrlich währt am längsten*" (honesty endures the longest).
The *Chethib* וישדם (וְשַׁדֵּם) is an error of transcription; the *Keri* has
the proper correction, יְשָׁדֵּם = יְשָׁדְדֵם, Jer. v. 6. Regarding שָׁדַד
(whence שַׁדַּי), which, from its root-signification of making close and
fast, denotes violence and destruction, *vid.* under Gen. xvii.

Three proverbs in praise of צדקה:

> Ver. 4 Possessions are of no profit in the day of wrath;
> But righteousness delivereth from death.

That which is new here, is only that possessions and goods (*vid.* regarding הוֹן, p. 63) are destitute of all value in the day of the μέλλουσα
ὀργή; for יוֹם עֶבְרָה, the day of wrath breaking through the limits (of
long-suffering), has the same meaning as in the prophets; and
such prophetic words as Isa. x. 3, Zeph. i. 18, and, almost in the
same words, Ezek. vii. 19, are altogether similar to this proverb.
The LXX., which translates ἐν ἡμέρᾳ ἐπαγωγῆς, harmonizes in
expression with Sir. v. 8, cf. ii. 2. Theodotion translates אֵיד, xxvii.
10, by ἐπαγωγή (providence, fate).

> Ver. 5 The righteousness of the blameless smootheth his way,
> And by his own wickedness doth the wicked fall.

With the תָּמִים (cf. i. 12), formed after the passive, more than with
תָּם, is connected the idea of the perfected, but more in the negative
sense of moral spotlessness than of moral perfection. The rectitude of a man who seeks to keep his conscience and his character
pure, maketh smooth (יִשֵּׁר, as iii. 6, not of the straightness of the
line, but of the surface, evenness) his life's path, so that he can
pursue his aim without stumbling and hindrance, and swerving
from the direct way; while, on the contrary, the godless comes to
ruin by his godlessness—that by which he seeks to forward his
interests, and to make a way for himself, becomes his destruction.

> Ver. 6 The rectitude of the upright saveth them,
> And in their own covetousness are the faithless taken.

The integrity of those who go straight forward and straight through,
without permitting themselves to turn aside on crooked ways, delivers them from the snares which are laid for them, the dangers
they encounter; while, on the contrary, the faithless, though they
mask their intentions ever so cunningly, are ensnared in their
passionate covetousness: the mask is removed, they are convicted,
and are caught and lost. Regarding הַוָּה, abyss, overthrow, also
stumbling against anything = covetousness, *vid.* at x. 3, and under
Ps. v. 10. The form of the expression 6b follows the scheme, " in

the image of God created He man," Gen. ix. 6. The subject is to be taken from the genitive, as is marked by the accentuation, for it gives *Mugrash* to the וּבְחַת, as if it were the principal form, for וּבְהֵוֹ.

Three proverbs regarding destruction and salvation :

Ver. 7 When a godless man dies, his hope cometh to nought,
 And the expectation of those who stand in fulness of strength
 is destroyed.

We have already remarked in the Introduction that אדם is a favourite word of the Chokma, and the terminological distinction of different classes and properties of men (*vid.* pp. 40, 42); we read, vi. 12, אָדָם בְּלִיַּעַל, and here, as also Job xx. 29, xxvii. 13, אָדָם רָשָׁע, cf. xxi. 29, אִישׁ רָשָׁע, but generally only רָשָׁע is used. A godless man, to whom earthly possessions and pleasure and honour are the highest good, and to whom no means are too base, in order that he may appease this his threefold passion, rocks himself in unbounded and measureless hopes ; but with his death, his hope, *i.e.* all that he hoped for, comes to nought. The LXX. translate τελευτήσαντος ἀνδρὸς δικαίου οὐκ ὄλλυται ἐλπίς, which is the converse of that which is here said, 7*a* : the hope of the righteous expects its fulfilment beyond the grave. The LXX. further translate, τὸ δὲ καύχημα (וּתְהֶלֶת) τῶν ἀσεβῶν ὄλλυται; but the distich in the Hebr. text is not an antithetic one, and whether אוֹנִים may signify the wicked (thus also the Syr., Targ., Venet., and Luther), if we regard it as a brachyology for אַנְשֵׁי אוֹנִים, or as the plur. of an adj. אָן, after the form טוֹב (Elazar b. Jacob in Kimchi), or wickedness (Zöckler, with Hitzig, " the wicked expectation "), is very questionable. Yet more improbable is Malbim's (with Rashi's) rendering of this אוֹנִים, after Gen. xlix. 3, Ps. lxxviii. 51, and the Targ. on Job xviii. 12, of the children of the deceased ; children *gignuntur ex robore virili*, but are not themselves the *robur virile*. But while אוֹנִים is nowhere the plur. of אֶן in its ethical signification, it certainly means in Ps. lxxviii. 51, as the plur. of אֹן, manly strength, and in Isa. xl. 26, 29 the fulness of strength generally, and once, in Hos. ix. 4, as plur. of אֶן in its physical signification, derived from its root-meaning *anhelitus* (Gen. xxxv. 18, cf. Hab. iii. 7), deep sorrow (a heightening of the אָן, Deut. xxvi. 14). This latter signification has also been adopted : Jerome, *expectatio solicitorum ;* Bertheau, " the expectation of the sorrowing ;" Ewald, " continuance of sorrow ;" but the meaning of this

in this connection is so obscure, that one must question the translators what its import is. Therefore we adhere to the other rendering, "fulness of strength," and interpret אונים as the opposite of
אין אונים, Isa. xl. 29, for it signifies, *per metonymiam abstracti pro
concr.*, those who are full of strength; and we gain the meaning
that there is a sudden end to the expectation of those who are in
full strength, and build their prospects thereon. The two synonymous lines complete themselves, in so far as אונים gains by אדם רשע
the associated idea of self-confidence, and the second strengthens
the thought of the first by the transition of the expression from
the fut. to the preterite (Fl.). ותוחלת has, for the most part in
recent impressions, the *Mugrash;* the correct accentuation, according to codices and old impressions, is ותוחלת אונים (*vid.* Baer's *Torath
Emeth,* p. 10, § 4).

> Ver. 8 The righteous is delivered from trouble,
>   And the godless comes in his stead.

The succession of the tenses gives the same meaning as when,
periodizing, we say: while the one is delivered, the other, on the contrary, falls before the same danger. נחלץ (*vid.* under Isa. lviii. 11)
followed by the historical tense, the expression of the principal fact,
is the perfect. The statement here made clothes itself after the
manner of a parable in the form of history. It is true there are not
wanting experiences of an opposite kind (from that here stated),
because divine justice manifests itself in this world only as a prelude, but not perfectly and finally; but the poet considers this, that
as a rule destruction falls upon the godless, which the righteous
with the help of God escapes; and this he realizes as a moral
motive. In itself תחתיו may also have only the meaning of the exchange of places, but the LXX. translate ἀντ' αὐτοῦ, and thus
in the sense of representation the proverb appears to be understood
in connection with xxi. 18 (cf. the prophetico-historical application, Isa. xliii. 4). The idea of atonement has, however, no
application here, for the essence of atonement consists in the
offering up of an innocent one in the room of the guilty, and its
force lies in the offering up of self; the meaning is only, that if
the divinely-ordained linking together of cause and effect in the
realms of nature and of history brings with it evil, this brings to
the godless destruction, while it opens the way of deliverance for
the righteous, so that the godless becomes for the righteous the

כֹּפֶר, or, as we might say in a figure of similar import, the lightning conductor.

Ver. 9 The wicked with his mouth prepareth destruction for his neighbour;
But by knowledge the righteous are delivered from it.

The LXX. translate, ἐν στόματι ἀσεβῶν παγὶς (רֹשַׁח?) πολίταις, αἴσθησις δὲ δικαίοις εὔοδος (יצלחו). There is no reason for changing (with Hitzig and Ewald) the text, which in the form in which it is here translated was before all other translators (Aq., Symmachus, Theodotion, Syr., Targ., Jerome). The accentuation, which separates the two instrumental statements by greater disjunctives from that which follows, is correct. The "three" Greek versions [viz. of Aquila, Theodotion, and Symmachus] translate חָנֵף by ὑποκριτής, which it means in the modern idiom; but in the ancient Hebr. it signifies, him who is resolved upon evil, as in Arab. hanyf, him who is resolved upon that which is right: he who turns aside to evil enters on a path far removed from that which is right. In יַשְׁחִית one is reminded (without any etymological reason) of שַׁחַת (pit), and so in יַחְלְצוּ of מִשְּׁחִיתוֹתָם (Ps. cvii. 20) or a similar word; but בְּדַעַת contains the reference, in this connection not easy to be mistaken, to the hostile purposes of the wicked masked by the words of the mouth, which are seen through by the righteous by virtue of knowledge which makes them acquainted with men. This penetrating look is their means of deliverance.

Three proverbs follow relating to the nature of city and national life, and between them two against mockery and backbiting:

Ver. 10 In the prosperity of the righteous the city rejoiceth;
And if the wicked come to ruin, there is jubilation.

The בְּ of בְּטוּב denotes the ground but not the object, as elsewhere, but the cause of the rejoicing, like the ב, 10b, and in the similar proverb, xxix. 2, cf. xxviii. 12. If it goes well with the righteous, the city has cause for joy, because it is for the advantage of the community; and if the wicked (godless) come to an end, then there is jubilation (substantival clause for תָּרֹן), for although they are honoured in their lifetime, yet men breathe freer when the city is delivered from the tyranny and oppression which they exercised, and from the evil example which they gave. Such proverbs, in which the city (civitas) represents the state, the πόλις the πολιτεία, may, as Ewald thinks, be of earlier date than the days of an Asa or Jehoshaphat; for "from the days of Moses and Joshua to the days of David and Solomon, Israel was a great nation, divided indeed into many branches and sections, but bound together by covenant, whose life did not at all revolve around one great city alone." We value such critical judgments according to great historical points of view, but confess not to understand why קִרְיָה must just be the chief city and may not be any city, and how on the whole a language which had not as yet framed the conception of the state (post-bibl. מְדִינָה), when it would describe the community individually and as a whole, could speak otherwise than of city and people.

> Ver. 11 By the blessing of the upright a city is exalted,
> But by the mouth of the godless it is broken down.

This verse is related, in the way of confirming it, to ver. 10. The LXX., which omits ver. 4, here omits 10b and 11a, and combines 10a and 11b into one proverb (vid. Lagarde). The meaning is clear : " by the benedictions and pious prayers of the upright a city rises always to a higher eminence and prosperity ; while, on the contrary, the deceitful, arrogant, blasphemous talk of the godless brings ruin to it " (Fl.). The nearest contrast to " by the blessing of the upright " would be " by the cursing of the wicked," but not in the sense of the poet, who means to say that the city raises itself by the blessing of the upright, and on the contrary, when godless men are exalted, then by their words (whose blessing is no better than their curse) it comes to ruin. קֶרֶת (= קִרְיָה) occurs only four times in Proverbs, and in Job xxix. 7.

Ver. 12. There now follow two proverbs which refer to the intercourse of private life.

> He who mocketh his neighbour is devoid of understanding;
> But the intelligent man remaineth silent.

xiv. 21 is a proverb similarly beginning with בָּז לְרֵעֵהוּ ; xiii. 13 is another beginning with בָּז לְדָבָר. From this one sees that בּוּז לְ (cf. בָּזָה לְ, Isa. xxxvii. 22) does not mean a speaking contemptuously in one's presence ; as also from vi. 30, that contemptuous treatment, which expresses itself not in mockery but in insult, is thus named ; so that we do not possess a German [nor an English] expression which completely covers it. Whoever in a derisive or insulting manner, whether it be publicly or privately, degrades his neighbour, is unwise (חֲסַר־לֵב as pred., like vi. 32) ; an intelligent man, on the contrary, keeps silent, keeps his judgment to himself, abstains from arrogant criticisms, for he knows that he is not infallible, that he is not acquainted with the heart, and he possesses too much self-knowledge to raise himself above his neighbour as a judge, and thinks that contemptuous rejection, unamiable, reckless condemnation, does no good, but on the contrary does evil on all sides.

> Ver. 13 He who goeth about tattling revealeth secrets ;
> But he who is of a faithful spirit concealeth a matter.

The tattler is called רָכִיל (intensive form of רֹכֵל), from his going hither and thither. אַנְשֵׁי רָכִיל, Ezek. xxii. 9, are men given to tattling, backbiters; הוֹלֵךְ רָכִיל (cf. Lev. xix. 16), one of the tattlers or backbiters goes, a divulger of the matter, a tell-tale. It is of such an one that the proverb speaks, that he reveals the secret (סוֹד, properly the being close together for the purpose of private intercourse, then that intercourse itself, vid. at Ps. xxv. 14) ; one has thus to be on his guard against confiding in him. On the contrary, a נֶאֱמַן־רוּחַ, firmus (fidus) spiritu, properly one who is established, or reflexively one who proves himself firm and true (vid. at Gen. xv. 6), conceals a matter, keeps it back from the knowledge and power of another. Zöckler rightly concludes, in opposition to Hitzig, from the parallelism that the הולך רכיל is subject ; the arrangement going before also shows that this is the " ground-word " (Ewald) ; in xx. 19a the relation is reversed : the revealer of secrets is rightly named (cf. Sir. xxvii. 16, ὁ ἀποκαλύπτων μυστήρια, κ.τ.λ.).

> Ver. 14 Where there is no direction a people fall ;
> But where there is no want of counsellors there is safety.

Regarding תַּחְבֻּלוֹת, vid. at i. 5. There it means rules of self-government; here, rules for the government of the people, or, since the pluralet. denotes a multiplicity in unity, circumspect κυβέρνησις. With 14b, xxiv. 6b (where direction in war, as here in peace, is spoken of, and the meaning of the word specializes itself accordingly) agrees ; cf. also xv. 22b. Hitzig criticises the proverb, remarking, " we who have the longest resorted to many counsellors, as a consequence of the superabundance have learned to say, 'Too many cooks spoil the broth,' and, 'He who asks long, errs.' " But the truth of the clause 14b is in modern times more fully illustrated in the region of ecclesiastical and political affairs; and in general it is found to be true that it is better with a people when they are governed according to the laws and conclusions which have resulted from the careful deliberation of many competent and authorized men, than when their fate is entrusted unconditionally to one or to a few. The proverb, it must be acknowledged, refers not to counsellors such as in Isa. iii. 3, but as in Isa. i. 26.

Ver. 15. There follow now two proverbs regarding kindness which brings injury and which brings honour:

It fares ill, nothing but ill, with one who is surety for another;
But he who hateth suretyship remaineth in quietness.

More closely to the original: It goes ill with him; for the proverb is composed as if the writer had before his eyes a definite person, whom one assails when he for whom he became security has not kept within the limits of the performance that was due. Regarding עָרַב with the accus. of the person: to represent one as a surety for him, and זָר as denoting the other (the stranger), *vid.* at vi. 1. The meaning of רַע יֵרוֹעַ is seen from xx. 16*a*. יֵרוֹעַ is, like xiii. 20, the *fut. Niph.* of רָעַע, or of רוֹעַ = רָעַע, after the forms יִמּוֹל, יֵעוֹר (Olsh. § 265*e*). The added רַע has, like עֶרְיָה, Hab. iii. 9, the same function as the *inf. absol.* (*intensivus*); but as the infin. form רַע could only be *inf. constr.* after the form שֵׁד, Jer. v. 26, the *infinitive absol.* must be רוֹעַ: thus רַע is an accus., or what is the same, an adverbial adj.: he is badly treated (maltreated) in a bad way, for one holds him to his words and, when he cannot or will not accomplish that which is due in the room of him for whom he is bail, arrests him. He, on the contrary, who hates תּוֹקְעִים has good rest. The persons of such as become surety by striking the hands cannot be meant, but perhaps people thus becoming surety by a hand-stroke,—such sureties, and thus such suretyship, he cannot suffer; תּוֹקְעִים approaches an abstract ["striking hands," instead of "those who strike hands"] in connection with this שֹׂנֵא, expressing only a strong impossibility, as חֹבְלִים, Zech. ii. 7, 14, means uniting together in the sense of combination.

Ver. 16 A gracious woman retaineth honour,
And strong men retain riches.

The LXX. had אֵשֶׁת חֵן (not אֵשֶׁת חַיִל) in view: γυνὴ εὐχάριστος ἐγείρει ἀνδρὶ δόξαν,—this ἀνδρί is an interpolation inserted for the sake of the added line, θρόνος δὲ ἀτιμίας γυνὴ μισοῦσα δίκαια. The proverb thus expanded is on both sides true: an amiable woman (*gratiosa*) brings honour to her husband, gives him relief, while one who hates the right (that which is good, gentle) is a disgraceful vessel (*opp.* כִּסֵּא כָבוֹד, Isa. xxii. 23), which disfigures the household, makes the family unloved, and lowers it. But the commencing line, by which 16b is raised to an independent distich, is so much the more imperfect : πλούτου ὀκνηροὶ ἐνδεεῖς γίνονται ; for that the negligent (idle) bring it not to riches, is, as they are wont in Swabia to call such truisms, a *Binsenwahrheit.* But it is important that the translation of 16b, οἱ δὲ ἀνδρεῖοι ἐρείδονται πλούτῳ (the Syr. has "knowledge" for riches), presupposes the phrase וְחָרוּצִים (cf. x. 4, LXX.), and along with it this, that יתמכו עשׁר is so rendered as if the words were יִפָּמְכוּ בעשׁר, is to be regarded as unhistorical. If we now take the one proverb as it is found in the Hebr. text, then the repetition of the תמך in the two lines excites a prejudice in favour of it. The meaning of this otherwise difficult תמך is missed by Löwenstein and Zöckler : a gracious woman re-taineth honour (Symm. ἀνθέξεται δόξης) ; for (1) תמך חיל would better agree with this predicate, and (2) it is evident from xxix. 23 that תמך כבוד is not to be understood in the sense of *firmiter tenere,* but in the inchoative sense of *consequi honorem,* whence also the ἐγείρει ἀνδρί of the LXX. It is true that xxxi. 30 states that "grace (חֵן) is nothing," and that all depends on the fear of God ; but here the poet thinks on "grace" along with the fear of God, or he thinks on them as not separated from each other ; and since it is doubly true, which is moreover besides this true, that a wife of gracious outward appearance and demeanour obtains honour, her company is sought, she finds her way into the best society, they praise her attractive, pleasant appearance, and that the husband also of such a wife participates to some extent in this honour. Experience also confirms it, that the עָרִיצִים, strong men, obtain riches (cf. Isa. xlix 25) ; and this statement regarding the עריצים fits better as a contrast to 16a, as a like statement regarding the חרוצים, diligent, for the עָרִיץ (from עָרַץ, to place in terror, Ps. x. 18), whose power consists in terrorism or violence, is the most direct contrast of a wife, this σκεῦος ἀσθενέστερον, who by heart-winning attraction makes yet better conquests : she thereby obtains a higher good, viz. honour, while the former gains only riches, for "a name" (viz. a good one) "is better than great riches," xxii. 1. If we read חרוצים, this thoughtful contrast is lost.

Three proverbs regarding benevolence :

> Ver. 17 The benevolent man doeth good to his own soul,
> And the violent man brings trouble on his own flesh.

Many interpreters reverse the relation of subject and predicate

(Targ. only in 17*b*, after the phrase וְדמוביד, for which the Syr. has
only וּמוֹבד): *qui sibi ipsi benefacit, is quidem erga alios quoque
benignus præsumitur, quum caritas ordinata a se ipsa incipiat; qui
vero carnem suam male habet, est crudelis erga alios* (Michaelis).
But this cannot be established; for certainly it occurs that whoever does good to himself does good also to others, and that whoever
is hard against himself also judges and treats others harshly; but in
by far the greatest number of cases the fact is this, that he who
does not deny anything to himself is in relation to others an egoist,
and this is not a " benevolent man;" and, on the contrary, that he
who denies to himself lawful enjoyments is in relation to others
capable of self-denial and self-sacrifice, and thus is the contrast of
a " violent man." The word of Sirach, xiv. 5, ὁ πονηρὸς ἑαυτῷ
τίνα ἀγαθὸς ἔσται, to which Bertheau appeals, alludes to the
niggard, and it is true indeed that this עֹבֵר שְׁאֵרוֹ, but not every עבר
שארו, is a niggard. Thus the " benevolent man " and the " violent
man " will be the two subject conceptions, and as it is said of the
benevolent (חֶסֶד as *e.g.* Hos. vi. 6, of a more restricted sense, as
Isa. lvii. 1) that he does good (גָּמַל, viz. טוֹב, xxxi. 12), so of the
violent (unmerciful) (אַכְזָרִי as xii. 20, Jer. vi. 23, l. 42) that he
brings evil on his own flesh (LXX. αὐτοῦ σῶμα); for שְׁאֵרוֹ as
a parallel word to נַפְשׁוֹ (cf. p. 195) signifies not blood-relations
(Symm., Jerome, Luther, and Grotius), but it has here, as at
Mic. iii. 2, its nearest signification, from which it then comes to
signify those who are of our flesh and blood. But for that reason
the meaning of the poet cannot be that given by Elster: " he
who exercises benevolence toward others creates within himself a
determination which penetrates his whole being with generous
and fruitful warmth, as on the other hand the feeling of hatred
deprives the heart of him who cherishes it of the true fountain of
life." If this were meant, then soul and spirit, not soul and flesh,
would stand in parallelism. The weal and woe refers thus to the
divine retribution which requites the conduct of a man toward his
neighbours, according to its character, with reward or punishment
(Hitzig, Zöckler).

Ver. 18. Man consists of body and soul. In regard to both,
benevolence brings its reward, and hatred its punishment.

> The godless acquires deceptive gain;
> But he that soweth righteousness, a true reward.

Jerome makes 18*b* an independent clause, for he translates it as if

the word were written וּלְזֹרֵעַ ; the Syr. and Targ. also, as if שְׂכָרוֹ
אֱמֻנָתוֹ (his fidelity is his reward). But according to the text as it
stands, עֹשֶׂה extends its regimen to both parts of the verse; to
make is here equivalent to, to work out, to acquire, περιποιεῖσθαι,
as Gen. xxxi. 1, Jer. xvii. 11, etc. The labour of the godless has
selfishness as its motive, and what he acquires by his labour is
therefore " delusive gain,"—it is no blessing, it profits him not
(x. 2), and it brings him no advantage (x. 16). He, on the contrary, acquires truth, i.e. a truly profitable and enduring reward,
who sows right-doing, or better : good-doing, by which we also, as
the biblical moral in צדקה, think principally of well-doing, unselfish
activity and self-sacrificing love. Hos. x. 12 speaks of sowing
which has only צדקה as the norm; and how צדקה is understood is
seen from the parallel use of חסד [piety]. The " true reward " is
just the harvest by which the sowing of the good seed of noble
benevolent actions is rewarded.

> Ver. 19 Genuine righteousness reaches to life,
> And he who pursues evil does it to his death.

The LXX. translate υἱὸς δίκαιος, and the Syrian follows this
unwarrantable *quid pro quo;* the Bible uses the phrase בֶּן־עַוְלָה
and the like, but not בֶּן־צְדָקָה. The *Græc. Venet.* (translating
οὕτω) deprives the distich of its supposed independence. The
Targ. renders כֵּן with the following וֹ as correlates, *sic . . . uti ;*
but כֵּן in comparative proverbs stands naturally in the second, and
not in the first place (*vid.* p. 10). Without doubt כֵּן is here a
noun. It appears to have a personal sense, according to the
parallel וּמְרַדֵּף, on which account Elster explains it : he who is
firm, stedfast in righteousness, and Zöckler : he who holds fast
to righteousness; but כֵּן cannot mean " holding fast," nor does
מְכוֹנֵן ;—"fast" does not at all agree with the meaning of the word,
it means upright, and in the ethical sense genuine ; thus Ewald
better : " he who is of genuine righteousness," but " genuine in (of)
righteousness " is a tautological connection of ideas. Therefore
we must regard כֵּן as a substantival neuter, but neither the *rectum*
of Cocceius nor the *firmum* of Schultens furnishes a naturally
expressed suitable thought. Or is כֵּן a substantive in the sense of
2 Kings vii. 31 ? The word denotes the pedestal, the pillar, the
standing-place; but what can the basis refer to here (Euchel) ?
Rather read "aim" (Oetinger) or "direction" (Löwenstein); but כֵּן
does not take its meaning from the *Hiph.* הֵכִין. One might almost

assume that the *Chokma*-language makes כֵּ, *taliter*, a substantive, and has begun to use it in the sense of *qualitas* (like the post-bibl. אֵיכוּת), so that it is to be explained: the quality of righteousness tendeth to life. But must we lose ourselves in conjectures or in modifications of the text (Hitzig, כַּנֵּס, as a banner), in order to gain a meaning from the word, which already has a meaning? We say דִּבֶּר כֵּן, to speak right (Num. xxvii. 7), and עָשׂוֹת כֵּן, to do right (Eccles. viii. 10); in both cases כֵּן means standing = consisting, stedfast, right, *recte.* The contrast is לֹא־כֵן, 2 Kings vii. 9, which is also once used as a substantive, Isa. xvi. 6 : the unrighteousness of his words. So here כֵן is used as a substantive connected in the genitive, but not so that it denotes the right holding, retaining of righteousness, but its right quality,—אֲמִתָּה שֶׁל־צְדָקָה, as Rashi explains it, *i.e.*, as we understand it: genuineness, or genuine showing of righteousness, which is not mere appearance without reality. That כֵּנִים denotes such people as seek to appear not otherwise than what they truly are, is in favour of this interpretation. Such genuine righteousness as follows the impulse of the heart, and out of the fulness of the heart does good, has life as its result (xix. 23), an inwardly happy and externally a prosperous life; on the other hand, he who wilfully pursues evil, and finds in it satisfaction, brings death upon himself : he does it to his death, or if we make (which is also possible) רֹדֵף the subject: it tends to his death. Thus in other words : Love is life; hatred destroys life.

The following proverbs are especially directed, as connected with this כֵן, against the contradiction of the external appearance and of the masked internal nature.

Ver. 20 An abomination to Jahve are the crookedly dishonest of heart,
        And they who are of honest walk are His delight.

We read, ii. 15, viii. 8, עִקֵּשׁ (the form of the transgressions) ; but here, where the "crookedness" is transferred to the heart, we require another word, which renders the idea of falseness, the contrary of directness, lying in it, without any mixture of the fundamental conception *flexuosus* or *tortuosus.* תְּמִימֵי דָרֶךְ are not only those whose walk is externally without offence and blameless, but, in conformity with the contrast, those whose manner of conduct proceeds from a disposition that is pure, free from deception and concealment. Jerome, *et voluntas ejus in iis qui simpliciter ambulant.* But the word is not בְּתְמִימֵי ; they [the upright] are themselves His רָצוֹן (xi. 1) [delight] : He regards them, and only them, with satisfaction.

Ver. 21 Assuredly [the hand to it] the wicked remaineth not unpunished,
But the seed of the righteous is delivered.

The LXX. render here, as xvi. 5, where the יָד לְיָד repeats itself, χειρὶ χεῖρας ἐμβαλὼν ἀδίκως, which is not to be understood, as Evagrius supposes, of one that can be bribed, but only of a violent person ; the Syr. and Targ. have the same reference ; but the subject is certainly רָע, and a governing word, as נִשָּׂא (2 Sam. xx. 21), is wanting, to say nothing of the fact that the phrase "one hand against the other" would require the words to be יד ביד. Jerome and the *Grœc. Venet.*, without our being able, however, to see their meaning. The translation of the other Greek versions is not given. The Jewish interpreters offer nothing that is worthy, as *e.g.* Immanuel and Meîri explain it by "immediately," which in the modern Hebr. would require מִיָּד, and besides is not here suitable. The Midrash connects with 21a the earnest warning that he who sins with the one hand and with the other does good, is nevertheless not free from punishment. Schultens has an explanation to give to the words which is worthy of examination : hand to hand, *i.e.* after the manner of an inheritance *per posteros* (Ex. xx. 5), resting his opinion on this, that Arab. *yad* (cf. יָד, Isa. lvi. 5) is used among other significations in that of authorizing an inheritance. Gesenius follows him, but only urging the idea of the sequence of time (cf. Pers. *dest bedest*, hand to hand = continuing after one another), and interprets יד ביד as Fleischer does : *ab œtate in œtatem non* (*i.e. nullo unquam tempore futuro*) *erit impunis scelestus, sed posteri justorum salvi erunt.* According to Böttcher, "hand to hand" is equivalent to from one hand to another, and this corresponds to the thought expressed in Plutarch's *de sera numinis vindicta :* if not immediately, yet at last. We may refer in vindication of this to the fact that, as the Arab. lexicographers say, *yad,* used of the course of time, means the extension (*madd*) of time, and then a period of time. But for the idea expressed by *nunquam,* or *neutiquam,* or *tandem aliquando,* the language supplied to the poet a multitude of forms, and we do not see why he should have selected just this expression with its primary meaning *alternatim* not properly agreeing with the connection. Therefore we prefer with Ewald to regard יד ליד as a formula of confirmation derived from the common speech of the people: hand to hand (לְ as in לְיָדִי, Job xvii. 3), *i.e.* the hand for it [I pledge it, guarantee it] (Bertheau, Hitzig, Elster, Zöckler). But if 21*a* assures by the pledge of the hand, and as it were lays a wager to it, that the wicked shall not go unpunished, then the genitive in זֶרַע צַדִּיקִים is not that of dependence by origin, but, as Isa. lxv. 23, i. 4, the genitive of apposition, for זרע here, as דּוֹר, Ps. xxiv. 6, cxii. 2, denotes a oneness of like origin and of like kind, but with a preponderance of the latter. נִמְלָט is the 3d *pret.*, which by the preceding fut. retains the reference to the future: the merited punishment comes on the wicked, but the generation of the righteous escapes the judgment. רָע has the ר dagheshed (*Michlol* 63*b*) according to the rule of the דחיק, according to which the consonant first sounded after a word terminating in an accented *a* or *é* is doubled, which is here, as at xv. 1, done with the ר.

> Ver. 22 A golden ring in a swine's snout,—
> A fair woman and without delicacy.

This is the first instance of an emblematical proverb in which the first and second lines are related to each other as figure and its import, *vid.* p. 9. The LXX. translates rhythmically, but by its ὥσπερ . . . οὕτως it destroys the character of this picture-book proverbial form. The nose-ring, נֶם, generally attached to the right nostril and hanging down over the mouth (*vid.* Lane's *Manners*, etc.) is a female ornament that has been in use since the time of the patriarchs (Gen. xxiv. 47). If one supposes such a ring in a swine's snout, then in such a thing he has the emblem of a wife in whom beauty and the want of culture are placed together in direct contrast. מַעַם is taste carried over into the intellectual region, the capability of forming a judgment, Job xii. 20, and particularly the capability of discovering that which is right and adapted to the end in view, 1 Sam. xxv. 33 (of Abigail), here in accordance with the figure of a beast with which the ideas of uncleanness, shamelessness, and rudeness are associated, a mind for the noble, the fine, the fitting, that which in the higher and at the same time intellectual and ethical sense we call tact (fine feeling); סָרַת (*alienata*) denotes the want of this capacity, not without the accompanying idea of self-guilt.

> Ver. 23 The desire of the righteous is nothing but good,
> The expectation of the godless is presumption.

This is usually explained with Fleischer: If the righteous wish for anything, their wish reaches to no other than a fortunate issue; but if the godless hope for anything, then there is to them in the end as their portion, not the good they hoped for, but wrath (x. 28, cf. xi. 4). However, that עֶבְרָה is at once to be understood thus, as in יוֹם עברה, and that the phrase is to be rendered: the hope of the godless is God's wrath, is doubtful. But עברה denotes also want of moderation, and particularly in the form of presumption, xxi. 24, Isa. xvi. 6; and thus we gain the thought that the desire of the righteous is directed only to that which is good, and thus to an object that is attainable because well-pleasing to God, while on the contrary the hope of the godless consists only in the suggestions of their presumption, and thus is vain self-deceit. The punctuation תַאֲוַת צַדִּיקִים is contrary to rule; correct texts have תַאֲוַת צַדִּיקִים, for *Dechî* stands before *Athnach* only if the *Athnach*-word has two syllables (*Torath Emeth*, p. 43; *Accentssystem*, xviii. § 4).

Three proverbs regarding giving which is not loss but gain.

Ver. 24 There is one who giveth bounteously, and he increaseth still more;
And (there is) one who withholdeth what is due, only to his loss.

The first of the proverbs with יֵשׁ (there is), which are peculiar to the first collection (*vid.* p. 32). The meaning is, that the possessions of the liberal giver do not decrease but increase, and that, on the contrary, the possessions of the niggardly do not increase but decrease. מְפַזֵּר is not to be understood after Ps. cxii. 9. Instead of וְנוֹסָף עוֹד the three Erfurt codd. have וְנוֹסַף (with retrogression of the tone?), which Hitzig approves of; but the traditional phrase which refers (*et qui augetur insuper*) וְנוֹסָף not to the possession of him who scattereth, but to himself, is finer in the expression. In the characteristic of the other, מִיֹּשֶׁר is commonly interpreted comparatively: *plus æquo* (Cocceius) or *justo* (Schelling). But מִן after חָשַׂךְ is to be regarded as governed by it, and יֹשֶׁר denotes not competence, riches, as Arab. *yusr* (Bertheau, Zöckler), also not uprightness = beneficence (Midrash, מִן הצדקה), but duty, uprightness, as Job xxxiii. 23, where it denotes that which is advantageous to man, as here that which befits him: he who holds back, namely himself, from that which is due to himself, and thus should permit to himself, such an one profits nothing at all by this ἀφειδία (17*b*, Col. ii. 23), but it tends only to loss to him, only to the lessening of that which he possesses. We shall meet with this אַךְ לְמַחְסוֹר (לְמַחְסוֹר) xiv. 23, and frequently again—it is a common Mashal formula (cf. καὶ τόσῳ μᾶλλον ὑστερεῖται, Sir. xi. 11). The

cause of the strange phenomenon that the liberal gains and the
niggardly loses is not here expressed, but the following proverb
gives the explanation of it:

> Ver. 25 A liberal soul [soul of blessing] is made fat,
> And he that watereth others is also watered.

A synonymous distich (*vid.* p. 7). A soul of blessing is one from
whom blessings go out to others, who is even a blessing to all with
whom he comes into fellowship; בְּרָכָה denotes also particularly the
gifts of love, 1 Sam. xxv. 27, בְּרֵךְ denotes, if the Arab. is right,
which derives it from the fundamental idea " to spread out:" to
cause to increase and prosper by means of word and deed. The
blessing which goes out from such a soul comes back again to
itself: תְּדֻשָּׁן (as xiii. 4, xxviii. 25), it is made fat, gains thereby sap
and strength in fulness; the *Pual* refers to the ordinance of God;
xxii. 9 is kindred in meaning to this *anima benefica pinguefiet.*
In 25*b* יוֹרֵא is the Aramaic form of writing, but without the
Aramaic vocalization (cf. i. 10 תֹּבֵא, Isa. xxi. 12 וַיֵּתָא). Perhaps
the א makes it noticeable that here a different word from יוֹרֶה,
morning rain, is used; however, Symm. translates πρωϊνός, and
the *Græc. Venet.* (Kimchi following it) ὑετός. As a rule, we do not
derive יוֹרֵא from יָרָה, of which it would be the *Hophal* (=יוֹרֶה, as
הוֹרַע, Lev. iv. 23, =הֹרַע) (Ewald, § 131 f.); for the idea *consper-*
gitur, which the *Ho.* of the *Hiph.* יוֹרֶה, Hos. vi. 3, expresses, is, as
correlate to מַרְוֶה, as a parallel word to תְּדֻשָּׁן, one not of equal force.
Jerome was guided by correct feeling, for he translates: *et qui*
inebriat ipse quoque inebriabitur. The stem-word is certainly רָוָה,
whether it is with Hitzig to be punctuated יְרֻוֶּה=יָרְוֶה, or with
Fleischer we are to regard יוֹרֵא as derived *per metathesin* from
יָרְוֶה, as for Arab. *âráy* (to cause to see) is used[1] the vulgar Arab.
ârway (in the Syr. Arab.) and *âwray* (in the Egypt. Arab.). We
prefer the latter, for the passing of יָרְוֶה (from יְרָוֶה) into יוֹרֶה is
according to rule, *vid.* at xxiii. 21.

> Ver. 26 Whoso withholdeth corn, him the people curse;
> But blessing is on the head of him that selleth it.

This proverb is directed against the corn-usurer, whose covetousness and deceitful conduct is described Amos viii. 4–8. But
whilst it is there said that they cannot wait till the burdensome

---

[1] Hitzig's comparison of *rawaâ, finem respicere,* as transposed from *waray* is
incorrect; the former verb, which signifies to consider, thus appears to be
original.

interruption of their usurious conduct on account of the sacred days come to an end, the figure here is of a different aspect of their character: they hold back their stores of corn in the times of scarcity, for they speculate on receiving yet higher prices for it. בַּר (from בָּרַר, to purify, to be pure) is thrashed grain, cf. Arab. *burr*, wheat, and *nakky* of the cleaning of the grain by the separation from it of the tares, etc. (Fl.); the word has *Kametz*, according to the Masora, as always in pause and in the history of Joseph. מֹנֵעַ has *Munach* on the syllable preceding the last, on which the tone is thrown back, and *Metheg* with the *Tsere* as the sign of a pause, as i. 10 בְּצַע (vid. p. 67). מַשְׁבִּיר, *qui annonam vendit*, is denom. of שֶׁבֶר, properly that which is crushed, therefore grain (Fl.). לְאֻמִּים, which we would understand in the Proph. of nations, are here, as at xxiv. 24, the individuals of the people. The בְּרָכָה which falls on the head of the charitable is the thanks of his fellow-citizens, along with all good wishes.

That self-sacrificing endeavour after the good of others finds its reward in the thought encircling the following proverbs.

Ver. 27 He that striveth after good, seeketh that which is pleasing;
And he that searcheth after evil, it shall find him.

Here we have together three synonyms of seeking: בָּקֵשׁ (R. בק, *findere*), which has the general meaning *quærere*, from the root-idea of penetrating and pressing forwards; דָּרַשׁ (R. דר, *terere*), which from the root-idea of trying (proving) corresponds to the Lat. *studere*; and שָׁחַר (whence here שֹׁחֵר instead of מְשַׁחֵר, as דֹּבֵר instead of מְדַבֵּר), which means *mane*, and thus *sedulo quærere* (vid. at i. 28). From 27b, where by רָעָה is meant evil which one prepares for another, there arises for טוֹב the idea of good thoughts and actions with reference to others. He who applies himself to such, seeks therewith that which is pleasing, *i.e.* that which pleases or does good to others. If that which is pleasing to God were meant, then this would have been said (cf. xii. 2); the idea here is similar to x. 32, and the word יְבַקֵּשׁ is used, and not יִמְצָא, because reference is not made to a fact in the moral government of the world, but a description is given of one who is zealously intent upon good, and thus of a noble man. Such an one always asks himself (cf. Matt. vii. 12): what will, in the given case, be well-pleasing to the neighbour, what will tend to his true satisfaction? Regarding the punctuation here, שֹׁחֵר, vid. at ver. 26. The subject to תְּבוֹאֶנּוּ, which, x. 24, stands as the fundamental idea, here follows

from the governed רֵעֶה, which may be the gen. (Ps. xxxviii. 13)
as well as the accus.

Ver. 28 He that trusteth in his riches shall fall,
            And the righteous shall flourish like the green leaf.

יִפּוֹל (plene after the Masora) as well as the figure וְבֶעָלֶה (cf. for the
punctuation וְבֶעָשִׁן, x. 26) are singular, but are understood if one
observes that in 28a a withered tree, and in 28b a tree with leaves
ever green, hovers before the imagination of the poet (cf. Ps. i. 3,
Jer. xvii. 8). The proud rich man, who on the ground of his
riches appears to himself to be free from danger, goes on to his
ruin (יפול as xi. 5, and frequently in the Book of Proverbs), while
on the contrary the righteous continues to flourish like the leaf—
they thus resemble the trees which perennially continue to flourish
anew. Regarding עָלֶה as originally collective (Symm. θάλλος),
vid. at Isa. i. 30, and regarding פָּרַח (R. פר, to break), here of the
continual breaking forth of fresh-growing leaf-buds, vid. at Isa.
xi. 1. The apostolic word names this continual growth the meta-
morphosis of believers, 2 Cor. ii. 18. The LXX. has read וּמַעֲלֶה
(approved by Hitzig): and he who raiseth up the righteous.

Ver. 29 He that troubleth his own household shall inherit the wind,
            And a fool becomes servant to the wise in heart.

Jerome well translates: qui conturbat domum suam, for עכר closely
corresponds to the Lat. turbare; but with what reference is the
troubling or disturbing here meant? The Syr. translates 29a
doubly, and refers it once to deceit, and the second time to the
contrary of avarice; the LXX., by ὁ μὴ συμπεριφερόμενος τῷ
ἑαυτοῦ οἴκῳ, understands one who acts towards his own not un-
sociably, or without affability, and thus not tyrannically. But עכר
שְׁאֵרוֹ xi. 17, is he who does not grudge to his own body that which
is necessary; עכר יִשְׂרָאֵל is applied to Elijah, 1 Kings xviii. 17, on
account of whose prayer there was a want of rain; and at xv. 27
it is the covetous who is spoken of as עֹכֵר בֵּיתוֹ. The proverb has,
accordingly, in the man who "troubles his own house" (Luth.),
a niggard and sordid person (Hitzig) in view, one who does not
give to his own, particularly to his own servants, a sufficiency of
food and of necessary recreation. Far from raising himself by his
household arrangements, he shall only inherit wind (יִנְחַל, not as
the Syr. translates, יַנְחִיל, in the general signification to inherit, to
obtain, as iii. 35, xxviii. 10, etc.), i.e. he goes always farther and
farther back (for he deprives his servants of all pleasure and love

for their work in seeking the prosperity of his house), till in the end the reality of his possession dissolves into nothing. Such conduct is not only loveless, but also foolish; and a foolish person (*vid.* regarding אֱוִיל at i. 7) has no influence as the master of a house, and generally is unable to maintain his independence: "and the servant is a fool to him who is wise of heart." Thus the LXX. (cf. also the LXX. of x. 5), Syr., Targ., Jerome, *Græc. Venet.*, Luth. construe the sentence. The explanation, *et servus stulti cordato (sc. addicitur), i.e.* even the domestics of the covetous fool are at last partakers in the wise beneficence (Fl.), places 29*b* in an unnecessary connection with 29*a*, omits the verb, which is here scarcely superfluous, and is not demanded by the accentuation (cf. *e.g.* xix. 22*b*).

<blockquote>
Ver. 30 The fruit of the righteous is a tree of life,
And the wise man winneth souls.
</blockquote>

The LXX. translate, ἐκ καρποῦ δικαιοσύνης φύεται δένδρον ζωῆς; Hitzig takes thence the word צֶדֶק; but this translation discredits itself by the unnatural reversal of the relation of fruit and tree. The fruit of the righteous is here not the good which his conduct brings to him, as Isa. iii. 10, Jer. xxxii. 19, but his activity itself proceeding from an internal impulse. This fruit is a tree of life. We need to supplement פְּרִי [fruit] as little here as אֹרַח [a traveller] at x. 17; for the meaning of the proverb is, that the fruit of the righteous, *i.e.* his external influence, itself is a tree of life (*vid.* p. 32), namely for others, since his words and actions exert a quickening, refreshing, happy influence upon them. By this means the wise (righteousness and wisdom come together according to the saying of the *Chokma*, i. 7*a*) becomes a winner of souls (לקח as vi. 25, but taken *in bonam partem*), or, as expressed in the N. T. (Matt. iv. 19), a fisher of men, for he gains them not only for himself, but also for the service of wisdom and righteousness.

<blockquote>
Ver. 31 Lo, the righteous findeth on earth his reward;
How much more the godless and the sinner!
</blockquote>

The particles אַף כִּי signify properly, interrogatively: Shall it yet be said that . . .; it corresponds to the German "*geschweige denn*" [*nedum*] (Fl.). הֵן is already in bibl. Hebr. in the way of becoming a conditional particle; it opens, as here, the antecedent of a *gradatio a minori ad majus* introduced by אַף כִּי, Job xv. 15 f., xxv. 5 f., cf. הֵן (הנה) with וְאֵיךְ following, Gen. xliv. 8, 2 Sam. xii. 18. xiii. 13 presents itself as the nearest parallel to שֻׁלָּם, where it means, to be rewarded. It is a *vocabulum anceps*, and denotes full requital, *i.e.*, according to the reference, either righteous reward or righteous punishment. If 30*a* is understood of reward, and 30*b* of punishment, then the force of the argument in the conclusion consists in this, that the righteous can put forth no claim to a recompense, because his well-doing is never so perfect as not to be mingled with sin (Eccles. vii. 20; Ps. cxliii. 2); while, on the contrary, the repression of the wicked, who, as רָשָׁע as to his intention, and חוֹטֵא as to his conduct, actually denies his dependence on God, is demanded by divine holiness. But the conclusion is not stringent, since in the relation of God to the righteous His dispensation of grace and faithfulness to promises also come into view, and thus in both cases יְשֻׁלָּם appears to require the same interpretation: if the righteous does not remain unrevenged, so much more shall not the godless and the sinner remain . . ., or how much less shall the godless and the sinner remain so. Thus the *Græc. Venet.*, Θεῷ ὁ δίκαιος ἐν τῇ γῇ ἀποτιθήσεται; thus also Luther, and among the moderns Löwenstein and Elster. Of the proverb so understood the LXX. version, εἰ ὁ μὲν δίκαιος μόλις (μόγις) σώζεται, ὁ ἀσεβὴς καὶ ἁμαρτωλὸς ποῦ φανεῖται (cf. 1 Pet. iv. 18) may be a free translation, for in the יְשֻׁלָּם there certainly lies, according to the sense, a כְּמְעַט יֻשַׁע. Also יֻשַׁלָּם has the principal tone, not בָאָרֶץ. The thought: even on this side (on earth), lies beyond the sphere of the O. T. consciousness. The earth is here the world of man.

Three proverbs on knowledge, the favour of God, firmness and the means thereto.

> xii. 1 He loveth correction who loveth knowledge,
> And he hateth instruction who is without reason.

It is difficult in such cases to say which is the relation of the ideas that is intended. The sequence of words which lies nearest in the Semitic substantival clause is that in which the predicate is placed first; but the subject may, if it is to be made prominent, stand at the head of the sentence. Here, 1*b*, the placing of the subject in advance recommends itself: one who hates instruction is devoid of reason. But since we have no reason in 1*a* to invert the order of the words as they lie together, we take the conceptions placed first in both cases as the predicates. Thus: he who loves knowledge shows and proves that he does so by this, that he willingly puts himself in the place of a learner; and devoid of reason is he who with aversion rejects reproof, which is designed to guard him from future mistakes and false steps. Regarding the punctuation אֹהֵב דָּעַת (with *Mercha* on the ante-penult. and the העמדה-sign on the penult.), *vid.* at xi. 26 f., i. 19. In 1*b* the *Munach* in תּוכחת is transformed from *Mugrash* (*Accentssystem*, xviii. § 2), as in xv. 10*b*. בַּעַר (cf. xxx. 2) is a being who is stupid as the brute cattle (בְּעִיר, from בָּעַר, to graze, cattle of all kinds; Arab. *b'ayr*, the beast κατ᾽ ἐξ., *i.e.* the camel); as a *homo brutus* is compared to a בְּהֵמָה (Ps. xlix. 21, lxxiii. 22), and is called Arab. *behymt*, from *bahym*, "shut up" (spec. *dabb*, a bear; *thwr*, an ox; *ḥamâr*, an ass) (Fl.).

> Ver. 2 A good man obtaineth favour with Jahve,
> But the man of wicked devices He condemns.

He who is an אִישׁ מְזִמּוֹת (xiv. 17, cf. Ps. xxxvii. 7) is defined in xxiv. 8 (cf. p. 39): he is a man of devices (*vid.* regarding the etymon, p. 56), namely, that are wicked, one who contrives evil against his neighbour. The meaning of the subject-conception טוב is defined according to this, although in itself also it is clear, for טוב, used of God (*e.g.* Ps. lxxiii. 1, lxxxvi. 5) and of men (xiii. 22, xiv. 14), denotes the good (*bonus*) in the sense of the benevolent (*benignus*); the Scripture truths, that God is love, that love is the essence of goodness and is the fulfilling of the law, are so conformed to reason, that they stamp themselves as immediate component parts of the human consciousness. A טוב is thus a man who acts according to the ruling motive of self-sacrificing love; such an one obtains (*vid.* on יָפִיק, *educit* = *adipiscitur*, at iii. 13) the favour of God, He is and shows Himself kind to him, while on the contrary He condemns the wicked intriguer. Hitzig translates: the former of intrigues is punishable (as the Syr.: is condemned; Targ.: his contrivance is shattered to pieces); but to become a רָשָׁע = *reus* הִרְשִׁיע does not denote, but either to practise רֶשַׁע, Job xxxiv. 12, or to set forth as רָשָׁע = to condemn, Isa. l. 9. Taken in the former signification (Jerome, *impie agit*), a declaration is made which is not needed, since the moral badness already lies in the reference of the subject: thus ירשיע will be used also of Jahve. In proof that the poet did not need to say וְאֶת־אִישׁ, Zöckler rightly points to x. 6, Job xxii. 29.

> Ver. 3 A man does not stand by wickedness,
> But the root of the righteous remains unmoved.

In רֶשַׁע there lies the idea of want of inward stay (*vid.* at Ps. i. 1); in a manner of thought and of conduct which has no stay in God and His law, there can be expected no external endurance, no solidity.

The righteous, on the contrary, have their root in God; nothing can tear them from the ground in which they are rooted, they are as trees which no storm outroots. The very same thought is clothed in other words in x. 25, and another statement regarding the root of the righteous is found at xii. 12.

We now place together vers. 4–12. One proverb concerning the house-wife forms the beginning of this group, and four regarding the management of the house and business form the conclusion.

> Ver. 4 A good [brave] wife is the crown of her husband,
> But as rottenness in his bones is one that causeth shame.

As xi. 16 says of אֵשֶׁת חֵן, the pleasant wife (חֵן = χάρις), that she obtaineth honour, so this proverb of אֵשֶׁת חַיִל, the good wife (חַיִל = ἀρετή, virtus), that she raises her husband to higher honour: she is for his self-consciousness στέφανος καυχήσεως (1 Thess. ii. 19), and is also to him such a crown of honour before the world (cf. xxxi. 23). On the contrary, a מְבִישָׁה, conducting herself shamefully (cf. regarding the double meaning of this Mishle word, which only here occurs in the fem., at x. 5), is to her husband instar cariei in ossibus. רָקָב (רְקַב, x. 7) denotes both the caries and the worm-hole (cf. Job xli. 19, עֵץ רִקָּבוֹן, worm-eaten wood). Like as the caries slowly but continuously increases, till at last the part of the body which the bone bears and the whole life of the man falls to ruin; so an unhappy marriage gnaws at the marrow of life, it destroys the happiness of life, disturbs the pursuit, undermines the life of the husband.

> Ver. 5 The thoughts of the righteous are justice,
> The counsels of the godless are deceit.

They are so, that is, in their contents and their aim. To the righteous are ascribed מַחֲשָׁבוֹת, namely, simple and clear; to the godless, תַּחְבֻּלוֹת, carefully thought out, prudently thought through schemes and measures (regarding the word and the idea, vid. p. 57), but on that very account not simple, because with a tendency; for the righteous have an objective rule, namely, that which is right in the sight of God and of men, but the godless have only a selfish purpose, which they seek to attain by deceiving, and at the cost of, their neighbour.

> Ver. 6 The word of the godless is to lie in wait for the blood of others,
> But the mouth of the upright delivereth them.

Our editions have דִּבְרֵי רְשָׁעִים, but the right sequence of the accents
(in Cod. 1294 and elsewhere) is דִּבְרֵי רְשָׁעִים; the logical relation in
this transformation, which is only rhythmically conditioned, remains
the same. The vocalization wavers between אֱרָב־, which would
be imper., and אֱרָב־, which is infin., like אֱמָר־, xxv. 7, עֲנֹשׁ, xxi. 11,
אֲכָל־, Gen. iii. 11. However one punctuates it, the infin. is intended in any case, in which the expression always remains
sketchy enough : the words of the godless are lying in wait for
blood, i.e. they are calculated to bring others to this, into the
danger of their lives, e.g. before the tribunal by false charges
and false witness. דָּם is the accus. of the object ; for instead
of ארב לְדָם (i. 11), to lurk for blood, a shorter expression, ארב דָּם,
is used (Ewald, § 282a). The suffix of יַצִּילֵם [1] might appear, after
xi. 6a, to refer back to the יְשָׁרִים; but the thought that their mouth
saves the upright, that they thus know to speak themselves out of
the danger, is by far less appropriate (vid., on the contrary, בדעת,
xi. 9) than the thought that the mouth of the upright delivereth
from danger those whose lives are threatened by the godless, as
is rightly explained by Ewald, Bertheau, Elster. The personal
subject or object is in the Mashal style often to be evolved from
the connection, e.g. xiv. 26, xix. 23.

Ver. 7 The godless are overturned and are no more,
But the house of the righteous stands.

Bertheau and Zöckler explain : The wicked turn about, then are
they no more; i.e. as we say : it is over with them " in the turning
of a hand." The noun in the inf. absol. may certainly be the
subject, like xvii. 12, as well as the object (Ewald, § 328c), and
הָפֹךְ may be used of the turning about of oneself, Ps. lxxviii. 9,
2 Kings v. 26, 2 Chron. ix. 12. That explanation also may claim
for itself that הפך nowhere occurs with a personal object, if we
except one questionable passage, Isa. i. 7. But here the interpretation of the רשעים as the object lies near the contrast of בית, and
moreover the interpretation of the הפך, not in the sense of στρέ-
φεσθαι (LXX.), but of καταστρέφειν (Syr., Targ., Jerome, Græc.
Venet., Luther), lies near the contrast of יַעֲמֹד. The inf. absol.
thus leaves the power from which the catastrophe proceeds indefinite, as the pass. יֵהָפְכוּ would also leave it, and the act de-

---

[1] Elias Levita, in his note to the root פה in Kimchi's Wörterbuch, reads הַצִּילֵם,
and so also do 6 codd. in Kennicot. But פֶּה is masculine.

signedly presented in a vague manner to connect with ו the certain consequences therewith, as xxv. 4 f., as if to say: there comes only from some quarter an unparalleled overthrow which overwhelms the godless; thus no rising up again is to be thought on, it is all over with them; while, on the contrary, the house of the righteous withstands the storm which sweeps away the godless.

Ver. 8 According to the measure of his intelligence is a man praised,
And whoever is of a perverse mind is despised.

Everywhere in the *Mishle* שֵׂכֶל has no other meaning than *intellectus* (*vid.* p. 87). The praise which is given to a man measures itself לְפִי שִׂכְלוֹ (punctuate לְפִי־שִׂכְלוֹ, according to *Torath Emeth*, p. 41, *Accentssystem*, xx. § 1), *i.e.* according to the measure (so לְפִי is used in the oldest form of the language) of his intelligence, or as we may also say, of his culture; for in these proverbs, which make the fear of God the highest principle, שֵׂכֶל means also understanding of moral excellence, not merely the intellectual superiority of natural gifts. הֻלָּל is here a relative conception of manifold gradations, but it does not mean renown in general, but good renown. Parallel with שִׂכְלוֹ, לֵב refers to the understanding (νοῦς); the rendering of Löwenstein, "who is of false heart," is defective. נַעֲוֵה (synon. of נִפְתָּל and עִקֵּשׁ, but nowhere else interchanging with it) means here *a vero et recto detortus et aversus* (Fl.). Such a man who has not a good understanding, nor any certain rule of judgment, falls under contempt (*Græc. Venet.* τῷ ὄντωτῇ εἰς μυσαγμόν, after the false reading of יהוה instead of יהיה), *i.e.* he defames himself by his crooked judgment of men, of things and their relations, and is on this account in no position rightly to make use of them.

Ver. 9 Better is he who is lowly and has a servant,
Than he that makes himself mighty and is without bread.

This proverb, like xv. 17, commends the middle rank of life with its quiet excellences. נִקְלֶה (like 1 Sam. xviii. 23), from קָלָה, cognate with קָלַל, Syr. *'kly*, to despise, properly *levi pendere, levem habere* (whence קָלוֹן, scorn, disgrace), here of a man who lives in a humble position and does not seek to raise himself up. Many of the ancients (LXX., Symmachus, Jerome, Syr., Rashi, Luther, Schultens) explain וְעֶבֶד לוֹ by, and is a servant to himself, serves himself; but in that case the words would have been וְעֹבֵד לְנַפְשׁוֹ (Syr. דִּמְשַׁמֵּשׁ נַפְשֵׁהּ), or rather וְעַבְדּוֹ הוּא. וְעֹבֵד לוֹ would be more appropriate, as thus pointed by Ziegler, Ewald, and Hitzig. But if one adheres to the traditional reading, and interprets this, as it must be interpreted: *et cui servus* (Targ., *Græc. Venet.*), then that supplies a better contrast to וְחֲסַר־לָחֶם, for "the first necessity of an oriental in only moderate circumstances is a slave, just as was the case with the Greeks and Romans" (Fl.). A man of lowly rank, who is, however, not so poor that he cannot support a slave, is better than one who boasts himself and is yet a beggar (2 Sam. iii. 29). The *Hithpa.* often expresses a striving to be, or to wish to appear to be, what the adj. corresponding to the verb states, *e.g.* הִתְגַּדֵּל, הִתְעַשֵּׁר; like the Greek middles, εὔξεσθαι, αὔξεσθαι, cf. הִתְחַכֵּם and σοφίζεσθαι. So here, where with Fleischer we have translated: who makes himself mighty, for כבד, *gravem esse*, is etymologically also the contrast of קלה. The proverb, Sirach x. 26: κρείσσων ἐργαζόμενος καὶ περισσεύων ἐν πᾶσιν, ἢ δοξαζόμενος καὶ ἀπορῶν ἄρτων (according to the text of Fritzsche), is a half remodelling, half translation of this before us.

> Ver. 10 The righteous knows how his cattle feel,
> And the compassion of the godless is cruel.

The explanation: the righteous taketh care for the life of his beast (Fl.), fails, for 10a is to be taken with Ex. xxiii. 9; נֶפֶשׁ signifies also the state of one's soul, the frame of mind, the state of feeling; but ידע has, as in the related proverb, xxvii. 23, the meaning of careful cognizance or investigation, in conformity with which one acts. If the *Torá* includes in the law of the Sabbath (Ex. xx. 10, xxiii. 12) useful beasts and cattle, which are here especially meant, and secures to them the reward of their labour (Deut. xxv. 4); if it forbids the mutilation, and generally the giving of unnecessary pain, to beasts; if it enjoins those who take a bird's nest to let the dam escape (Deut. xxii. 6 f.),—these are the prefigurations of that דעת נפש בהמה, and as the God of the *Torá* thus appears at the close of the Book of Jonah, this wonderful apology (*defensio*) of the all-embracing compassion, the God also of the world-history in this sympathy for the beasts of the earth as the type of the righteous.

In 10b most interpreters find an oxymoron: the compassion of the godless is compassionless, the direct opposite of compassion; *i.e.* he possesses either altogether no compassion, or he shows such as in its principle, its expression, and in its effects is the opposite of what it ought to be (Fl.). Bertheau believes that in the sing. of the predicate אַכְזָרִי he is justified in translating: the compassion of the wicked is a tyranny. And as one may speak of a loveless love, *i.e.* of a love which in its principle is nothing else than selfishness, so also of a compassionless compassion, such as consists only in gesture and speech, without truth of feeling and of active results. But how such a compassionless compassion toward the cattle, and one which is really cruel, is possible, it may be difficult to show. Hitzig's conjecture, רַחֲמֵי, sprang from this thought: the most merciful among sinners are cruel—the sinner is as such not רָחוּם. The LXX. is right in the rendering, τὰ δὲ σπλάγχνα τῶν ἀσεβῶν ἀνελεήμονα. The noun רַחֲמִים means here not compassion, but, as in Gen. xliii. 30 (LXX. ἔντερα or ἔγκατα) and 1 Kings iii. 26 (LXX. μήτρα), has the meaning the bowels (properly tender parts, cf. Arab. *rakhuma*, to be soft, tender, with *rḥm*), and thus the interior of the body, in which deep emotions, and especially strong sympathy, are wont to be reflected (cf. Hos. x. 8). The singular of the predicate אכזרי arises here from the unity of the subject-conception : the inwards, as Jer. l. 12, from the reference of the expression to each individual of the many.

Ver. 11 He that tilleth his own ground is satisfied with bread,
    And he that followeth after vain pursuits is devoid of understanding.

Yet more complete is the antithetic parallelism in the *doublette*, xxviii. 19 (cf. also Sir. xx. 27*a*). The proverb recommends the cultivation of the field as the surest means of supporting oneself honestly and abundantly, in contrast to the grasping after vain, *i.e.* unrighteous means of subsistence, windy speculations, and the like (Fl.). רֵיקִים are here not persons (Bertheau), but things without solidity and value (LXX. μάταια; Aquila, Theodotion, κενά), and, in conformity with the contrast, not real business. Elsewhere also the mas. plur. discharges the function of a neut. noun of multitude, *vid.* נְגִידִים, *principalia*, viii. 6, and זֵדִים, Ps. xix. 14—one of the many examples of the imperfect use of the gender in Hebr.; the speaker has in ריקים, *vana et inania*, not אנשים (Judg. ix. 4), but דברים (Deut. xxxii. 47) in view. The LXX. erroneously at xxviii. 19, and Symmachus and Jerome at both places understand ריקים of slothfulness.

Ver. 12 The godless lusteth after the spoil of evil-doers ;
    But the root of the righteous shoots forth.

This translation is at the same time an explanation, and agrees with Fleischer's " the godless strives by unrighteous gain like the wicked (iv. 14) to enrich himself, namely, as must be understood from the antithetic members of the parallelism, in vain, without thereby making progress and gaining anything certain. The preterite, as

xi. 2, 8, etc., places the general true proposition as a separate historic principle derived from experience. In 12*b* יִתֵּן stands elliptically or pregnantly : *edet, scil. quod radix edere solet, sobolem stirpis, ramorum, etc.*, as in the Arab. *natan* and *ánatan* are specially used without an obj. of the spontaneousness of an odour." מָצוֹד (from צוּד, to spy, to hunt) is elsewhere the instrument of the hunt (a net), here the object and end of it. If the words had been מְצוֹדֵי רָעִים, then we would explain after מַלְאֲכֵי רָעִים, Ps. lxxviii. 49 (*vid.* comm. on), and אֶשֶׁת רַע, vi. 24; but in the difference of number, רָעִים will not be the qualitative but the subjective personal genitive : *capturam qualem mali captant.* Ewald, who understands רֵיקִים, 11*b*, of good-for-nothing-fellows, interprets רָעִים here, on the contrary, as neuter (§ 172*b*) : the desire of the wicked is an evil net, *i.e.* wherein he catches all manner of evil for himself. The LXX. has here two proverbs, in which מָצוֹד occurs in the plur. and in the sense of ὀχυρώματα; 12*b* of the Hebr. text is rendered : αἱ δὲ ῥίζαι τῶν εὐσεβῶν ἐν ὀχρυώμασι, which Schleusner explains *immotœ erunt.* The Hebr. text can gain nothing from this variation. That the LXX. read וְשֹׁרֶשׁ צַדִּיקִים אֵיתָן is not probable, since they nowhere thus translate אֵיתָן. But Reiske and Ziegler have, like Ewald and Hitzig, combined יִתֵּן of this proverb with יֵתֵן from אִיתָן (Arab. *wâtin*), *firmum, perennem esse.* Hitzig translates the distich, after emending the text of 12*a* by the help of the LXX. and the Arab. : the refuge of the wicked is crumbling clay, but the root of the righteous endures (יֵתֵן from יתן). Böttcher also reads חֹמֶר instead of חֶמֶד, and translates (*vid.* p. 192, l. 11) : the refuge of the wicked is miry clay, but the root of the righteous holdeth fast (יֵתֵן = Arab. *wâtin*). But this derivation of a verb יתן is not necessary. The *Grœc. Venet.* rightly, ῥίζα δὲ δικαίων δώσει. The obj. is self-evident. Rashi reads מה שהוא ראוי ליתן והוא הפרי. So also Schultens. The root giveth, is equivalent to, it is productive in bringing forth that which lies in its nature. That the root of the righteous endures (Targ. נִתְקַיַּם) is otherwise expressed, xii. 3.

Proverbs regarding injurious and beneficial words, wise hearing and prudent silence.

Ver. 13 In the transgression of the lips there lies a dangerous snare ;
The righteous escapeth from trouble.

The consecutive *modus* (וַיֵּצֵא) is here of greater weight than *e.g.* at xi. 8, where the connection follows without it (וַיָּבֹא) from the idea of the change of place. The translation : but the right-

eous . . . restores יְצֵא (וַיֵּצֵא), and ignores the syllogistic relation of the
members of the proverb, which shows itself here (cf. the contrary,
xi. 9) to a certain degree by וַיֵּצֵא. Ewald displaces this relation,
for he paraphrases : " any one may easily come into great danger
by means of inconsiderate words ; yet it is to be hoped that the
righteous may escape, for he will guard himself against evil from
the beginning." He is right here in interpreting צָרָה and מוֹקֵשׁ רָע
as the designation of danger into which one is betrayed by the
transgressions of his lips, but " inconsiderate words " are less than
פֶּשַׁע שְׂפָתַיִם. One must not be misled into connecting with פֶּשַׁע the
idea of missing, or a false step, from the circumstance that פֶּשַׂע
means a step ; both verbs have, it is true, the common R. פש with
the fundamental idea of placing apart or separating, but פֶּשַׁע has
nothing to do with פֶּשַׂע (step = placing apart of the legs), but
denotes (as Arab. *fusuwk fisk*, from the primary meaning *diruptio,
diremtio*) a sinning, breaking through and breaking off the relation
to God (cf. *e.g.* xxviii. 24), or even the restraints of morality (x. 19).
Such a sinning, which fastens itself to, and runs even among the
righteous, would not be called פֶּשַׁע, but rather חַטָּאת (xx. 9). According to this the proverb will mean that sinful words bring into
extreme danger every one who indulges in them—a danger which
he can with difficulty escape; and that thus the righteous, who
guards himself against sinful words, escapes from the distress (cf.
with the expression, Eccles. vii. 18) into which one is thereby
betrayed. רָע is the descriptive and expressive epithet to מוֹקֵשׁ (cf.
Eccles. ix. 12) : a bad false trap, a malicious snare, for מוֹקֵשׁ is the
snare which closes together and catches the bird by the feet. This
proverb is repeated at xxix. 6, peculiarly remodelled. The LXX.
has after ver. 13 another distich:

> He who is of mild countenance findeth mercy;
> He who is litigious oppresseth souls.

(נפשות, or rather, more in accordance with the Hebrew original :
oppresseth himself, נפשו.)

Ver. 14 From the fruit which the mouth of the man bringeth forth is he
            satisfied with good,
      And what the hands of the man accomplish returns back to him.

The proverb finds its final verification in the last judgment (cf.
Matt. xii. 37), but it is also illustrated in the present life. If the
mouth of a man bringeth forth fruit,—namely, the fruit of wholesome doctrine, of right guidance, of comforting exhortation, of

peace-bringing consolation for others,—this fruit is also to his own advantage, he richly enjoys the good which flows out of his own mouth, the blessing he bestows is also a blessing for himself. The same also is the case with the actions of a man. That which is done, or the service which is rendered by his hands, comes back to him as a reward or as a punishment. גְּמוּל signifies primarily accomplishment, execution, and is a twofold, double-sided conception : a rendering of good or evil, and merit on the side of men (whether merited reward or merited punishment), as well as recompense, requital on the side of God. The first line is repeated, somewhat altered, at xiii. 2, xviii. 20. The whole proverb is prophetically echoed in Isa. iii. 10 f. The *Keri* יָשִׁיב has Jahve as the subject, or rather the subject remains undefined, and " one requites him " is equivalent to : it is requited to him. The *Chethîb* seems to us more expressive ; but this use of the active with the undefined subject, instead of the passive, is certainly as much in the *Mishle* style (cf. xiii. 21) as the development of the subject of the clause from a foregoing genitive.

Ver. 15 The way of the fool is right in his own eyes,
But the wise listeneth to counsel.

Other proverbs, like xvi. 2, say that generally the judgment of a man regarding his character does not go beyond a narrow subjectivity ; but there are objective criteria according to which a man can prove whether the way in which he walks is right ; but the fool knows no other standard than his own opinion, and however clearly and truly one may warn him that the way which he has chosen is the wrong way and leads to a false end, yet he obstinately persists ;[1] while a wise man is not so wise in his own eyes (iii. 7) as not to be willing to listen to well-meant counsel, because, however careful he may be regarding his conduct, yet he does not regard his own judgment so unerring as not to be inclined ever anew to try it and let it stand the test. Ewald has falsely construed : yet whoever hears counsel is wise. In consequence of the contrast, אֱוִיל and חָכָם are the subject ideas, and with וְשֹׁמֵעַ לְעֵצָה is brought forward that which is in contrast to the self-complacency of the fool, the conduct of the wise man.

---

[1] *Vid.* kindred proverbs by Carl Schulze, *Die bibl. Sprichwörter der deutschen Sprache* (1860), p. 50, and M. C. Wahl's *Das Sprichwort in der heb.-aram. Literatur, u.s.w.* (1871), p. 31.

Ver. 16. The relations of the subject and the predicate are the same as in the preceding verse.

> The fool makes known his vexation on the same day [at once],
> On the contrary, the prudent man hideth the offence.

Very frequently in these proverbs the first line is only defined by the adducing of the second, or the second holds itself in the light of the first. A post-bibl. proverb says that a man is known by three things: by his כוס (his behaviour in drinking), his כיס (his conduct in money transactions), and his כעס (his conduct under deep inward excitement). So here: he is a fool who, if some injury is done to him, immediately shows his vexation in a passionate manner; while, on the contrary, the prudent man maintains silence as to the dishonour that is done to him, and represses his displeasure, so as not to increase his vexation to his own injury. Passionless retaliation may in certain cases be a duty of self-preservation, and may appear to be necessary for the protection of truth, but passionate self-defence is always of evil, whether the injury which is inflicted be justifiable or unjustifiable. Regarding עָרוּם, *callidus*, *vid.* p. 56; Schultens' comparison of the Greek γεγυμνασμένος is only a conceit in want of better knowledge. Regarding כָּסָה (only here and at ver. 23) with מִכַסֶּה, as שָׁחַר (only xi. 27) with מְשַׁחֵר, *vid.* Ewald, § 170a. בַּיּוֹם signifies on the self-same day = without delay, immediately, and is well translated by the LXX. αὐθήμερον. With another object, 16b is repeated in 23a.

Most of the remaining parables of this section refer to the right use and the abuse of the tongue.

> Ver. 17 He that breathes the love of truth, utters that which is right;
> But a lying tongue, deceit.

This verse is similar in meaning to xiv. 5 (where 5b = vi. 19a); the second line of the distich = xiv. 25b. Everywhere else יָפִיחַ כְּזָבִים stand together, only here יפיח is joined to אֱמוּנָה; *vid.* regarding this יפיח forming an attributive clause, and then employed as an adjective, but with distinct verbal force, at vi. 19. Viewed superficially, the proverb appears tautological; it is not so, however, but places in causal connection the internal character of men and their utterances: whoever breathes אֱמוּנָה, truth or conscientiousness (the property of the אָמוּן, *vid.* at Ps. xii. 2), i.e. lets the voice of this be heard in his utterances, such an one speaks צֶדֶק, i.e. uprightness, integrity, that which is correct, right (Isa. xlv. 19, cf. xli. 26), in relation to truth in general, and to the present case in particular;

but he who עֵד שְׁקָרִים, *i.e.* he who, against better knowledge and the consciousness of untruth, confirms by his testimony (from עוּד, *revertere*, to say again and again), therewith gives utterance to his impure character, his wicked intention, proceeding from delight in doing evil or from self-interest, and diverted towards the injury of his neighbour.   As אמונה and מרמה correspond as statements of the contents of the utterances, so צדק and שקרים as statements of their motive and aim.   מִרְמָה is obj. accus. of the יַגִּיד (from הִגִּיד, to bring to light, cf. נֶגֶד, visibility) to be supplied, not the pred. nom. *dolorum structor*, as Fleischer poetically finds.

> Ver. 18 There is that babbleth like the thrusts of a sword,
> But the tongue of the wise is healing.

The second (cf. xi. 24) of the proverbs beginning with יֵשׁ.   The verb בָּטָה (בָּטָא), peculiar to the Hebr., which in the modern Hebr. generally means " to speak out " (מִבְטָא in the grammar : the pronunciation) (according to which the LXX., Syr., and Targ. translate it by אמר), means in biblical Hebr., especially with reference to the binding of oneself by an oath (Lev. v. 4), and to solemn protestations (Num. xxx. 7, 9, according to which Jerome, *promittit*) : to utter incautiously in words, to speak without thought and at random, referred erroneously by Gesenius to the R. בט, to be hollow, probably a word imitative of the sound, like the Greek βατταρίζειν, to stammer, and βαττολογεῖν, to babble, which the lexicographers refer to a talkative person of the name of *Βάττος*, as our " *salbadern* " [=to talk foolishly] owes its origin to one Jenaer Bader on the Saal.   Theod. and the *Græc. Venet.* give the false reading· בֹּטֵחַ (πεποιθώς).   כְּמַדְקְרוֹת חָרֶב stands *loco accusativi*, the כְּ being regarded as a noun : (*effutiens verba*) *quæ sunt instar confossionum gladii* (Fl.).   We also call such a man, who bridles his loquacity neither by reflection nor moderates it by indulgent reference to his fellow-men, a *Schwertmaul* (sword-mouth) or a *Schandmaul* (a mouth of shame = slanderer), and say that he has a tongue like a sword.   But on the other hand, the tongue of the wise, which is in itself pure gentleness and a comfort to others, since, far from wounding, rather, by means of comforting, supporting, directing exhortation, exercises a soothing and calming influence.   Regarding רָפָא, whence מַרְפֵּא, Dietrich in Gesenius' *Lex.* is right.   The root-meaning of the verb רָפָא (cognate רָפָה, to be loose, *Hiph.* to let go, *Hithpa.* xviii. 9, to show oneself slothful) is, as the Arab. kindred word *rafâ, rafa, raf, rawf (râf)* shows, that of stilling, softening, soothing, whence arises the meaning of healing (for which the Arab. has *tabb* and *'alkh*) ; the meaning to repair, to mend, which the Arab. *rafâ* and *rafa* have, does not stand in a prior relation to to heal, as might appear from Job xiii. 4, but is a specializing of the general idea of *reficere* lying in *mitigare*, just as the patcher is called ἀκέστρια = ἠπήτρια,[1] from ἀκέομαι, which means equally to still and to heal. Since thus in רפא the meanings of mitigating and of healing are involved, it is plain that מרפא, as it means healing (the remedy) and at the same time (cf. θεραπεία, Rev. xxii. 2) the preservation of health, iv. 22, vi. 15, xvi. 24, xxix. 1, so also may mean mildness (here and xv. 4), tranquillity (xiv. 30 ; Eccles. x. 4, calm patience in contrast to violent passion), and refreshing (xiii. 17). Oetinger and Hitzig translate here "medicine;" our translation, "healing (the means of healing)," is not essentially different from it.

> Ver. 19 The lip of truth endures for ever,
> But the lying tongue only while I wink with the eye.

None of the old translators understood the phrase וְעַד־אַרְגִּיעָה ; the *Venet.* also, which follows Kimchi's first explanation, is incorrect : ἕως ῥήξεως, till I split (shatter) it (the tongue). Abulwalîd is nearer the correct rendering when he takes ארגיעה as a noun = רֶגַע with *He parag.* Ahron b. Joseph is better in rendering the phrase by : until I make a רגע, and quite correct if רגע (from רָגַע = Arab. *raj*', which is used of the swinging of the balance) is taken in the sense of a twinkling of the eye (Schultens: *vibramen*); cf. Orelli's *Die hebr. Synonyme der Zeit und Ewigkeit*, p. 27 f., where the synonyms for a twinkling of the eye, a moment, are placed together. עַד (properly progress) has in this phrase the meaning, while, so long as, and the cohortative signifies, in contradistinction to ארגיע, which may also denote an unwilling movement of the eyelids, a movement proceeding from a free determination, serving for the measurement of a short space of time, Ewald, § 228a. ארגיעה, Jer. xlix. 19, l. 44, where Ewald takes כי ארגיעה (when I . . .) in the same sense as אד־ארגיעה here, which is more appropriate than the explanation of Hitzig, who regards כי as opening the principal clause, and attaches to הרגיע the quite too pregnant signification " to need (for an action) only a moment." The lip of truth, *i.e.* the lip which speaketh truth, endures for ever

---

[1] Whether ῥάπτειν, explained neither by Curtius nor by Flick, stands in a relation to it, we leave out of view.

(for truth, אֱמֶת = אֲמָנְתְּ, is just the enduring); but the tongue of falsehood is only for a moment, or a wink of the eye, for it is soon convicted, and with disgrace brings to silence; for a post-bibl. Aram. proverb says: קוּשְׁטָא קָאֵי שִׁקְרָא לָא קָאֵי, the truth endures, the lie endures not (Schabbath 104a), and a Hebrew proverb: הַשֶּׁקֶר אֵין לוֹ רַגְלַיִם, the lie has no feet (on which it can stand).[1]

Ver. 20 Deceit is in the heart of him who deviseth evil,
But those who devise peace cause joy.

Regarding the figure of forging, fabricating (LXX., Aquila, Symmachus, and Theodotion, τεκταίνειν), or of ploughing, which underlies the phrase חָרַשׁ רָע, moliri malum, vid. at iii. 29. That deceit is in the heart of him who deviseth evil (בְּלֶב־חֹרְשֵׁי רָע, as is correctly punctuated e.g. by Norzi) appears to be a platitude, for the חֹרֵשׁ רע is as such directed against a neighbour. But in the first place, 20a in itself says that the evil which a man hatches against another always issues in a fraudulent, malicious deception of the same; and in the second place, it says, when taken in connection with 20b, where שִׂמְחָה is the parallel word to מִרְמָה, that with the deception he always at the same time prepares for him sorrow. The contrast to חרשי רע is יוֹעֲצֵי שָׁלוֹם, and thus denotes not those who give counsel to contending parties to conclude peace, but such as devise peace, viz. in reference to the neighbour, for יעץ means not merely to impart counsel, but also mentally to devise, to resolve upon, to decree, 2 Chron. xxv. 16, Isa. xxxii. 7 f.; cf. יעץ על, Jer. xlix. 30. Hitzig and Zöckler give to שלום the general idea of welfare (that which is salutary), and interpret the שמחה as the inner joy of the good conscience. Certainly שלום (R. שׁל, extrahere, in the sense of deliverance from trouble) means not only peace as to the external relationship of men with each other, but also both internal and external welfare. Thus it is here meant of external welfare; Hitzig rightly compares Jer. xxix. 11 with Nahum i. 11 to the contrast between שלום and רע. But as מרמה is not self-deception, but the deception of another, so also שמחה is not the joy of those who devise the device in their hearts for the deception of others, but the joy they procure for others. Thoughts of peace for one's neighbour are always thoughts of procuring joy for him, as thoughts of evil are thoughts of deceit, and thus of procuring sorrow for him. Thus וליועצי is an abbreviated expression for ובלב יועצי.

---

[1] Vid. Duke's Rabbin. Blumenlese (1844), p. 231.

Ver. 21 No evil befalls the righteous,
But the godless are full of evil.

Hitzig translates אָוֶן "sorrow," and Zöckler "injury;" but the
word signifies evil as ethical wickedness, and although it may be
used of any misfortune in general (as in בֶּן־אוֹנִי, opp. בִּנְיָמִין); thus
it denotes especially such sorrow as is the harvest and product of
sin, xxii. 8, Job iv. 8, Isa. lix. 4, or such as brings after it punishment, Hab. iii. 7, Jer. iv. 15. That it is also here thus meant the
contrast makes evident. The godless are full of evil, for the moral
evil which is their life-element brings out of itself all kinds of
evil; on the contrary, no kind of evil, such as sin brings forth and
produces, falls upon the righteous. God, as giving form to human
fortune (Ex. xxi. 13), remains in the background (cf. Ps. xci. 10
with v. 1 f.); vid. regarding אנה, the weaker power of ענה, to go
against, to meet, to march against, Fleischer, Levy's Chald. Wört-
buch, 572.

Ver. 22 Lying lips are an abhorrence to Jahve,
And they that deal truly are His delight.

The frame of the distich is like xi. 1, 20. אֱמוּנָה is probity as the
harmony between the words and the inward thoughts. The
LXX., which translates ὁ δὲ ποιῶν πίστεις, had in view עשה אמונים
(עֹשֵׂה אֱמוּנִים, cf. Isa. xxvi. 2); the text of all other translations
agrees with that commonly received.

Ver. 23 A prudent man conceals knowledge,
And a heart-fool proclaims imbecility.

In 23a ver. 16b is repeated, only a little changed; also 16a corresponds with 23a, for, as is there said, the fool knows not how to
keep his anger to himself, as here, that a heart-fool (cf. the lying
mouth, 22a) proclaims (trumpets forth), or as xiii. 16 says, displays
folly without referring to himself the si tacuisses. To this forward
charalatan blustering, which intends to preach wisdom and yet
proclaims in the world mere folly, i.e. nonsense and imbecility, and
thereby makes itself troublesome, and only to be laughed at and
despised, stands in contrast the relation of the אָדָם עָרוּם, homo
callidus, who possesses knowledge, but keeps it to himself without
bringing it forth till an occasion presents itself for setting it forth
at the right place, at the right time, and to the right man. The
right motive also regulates such silence as well as modesty. But
this proverb places it under the point of view of prudence.

We take verses 24–28 together as a group. In these verses

the subject is the means of rising (in the world), and the two ways, the one of which leads to error, and the other to life.

> Ver. 24 The hand of the diligent attains to dominion,
> But slothfulness will become tributary.

In x. 4 רְמִיָּה was adj., but to כַּף standing beside it; here it is to be regarded as adj. to יַד (sluggish hand) supplied from 24*a*, but may be equally regarded as a subst. (slothfulness) (*vid.* at ver. 27). Regarding חָרוּץ, *vid.* p. 211. מַס signifies tribute and service, *i.e.* tributary service rendered to a master. In xi. 29*b* עֶבֶד stands for it. It is still the experience of to-day, as it was of Solomon's time, that slothfulness (indolence) brings down to a state of servitude, if not even deeper, but that vigorous activity raises to dominion or to the position of a master, *i.e.* to independence, wealth, respect, and power.

> Ver. 25 Trouble in the heart of a man boweth it down,
> And a friendly word maketh it glad.

The twofold anomaly that דְּאָגָה is construed as masc. and לֵב as fem. renders the text doubtful, but the LXX., Syr., Targum, which introduce another subject, φοβερὸς λόγος (דְּבַר מַדְאִיג?), do not improve it; Theodotion's is preferable, who translates μέριμνα ἐν καρδίᾳ ἀνδρὸς κατίσχει αὐτόν, and thus reads יָשְׁחֶנּוּ. But the rhyme is thereby lost. As כָּבוֹד, Gen. xlix. 6, so also may לֵב be used as fem., for one thereby thinks on נפשׁ; the plur. לִבּוֹת (לְבָבוֹת), according to which in Ezek. xvi. 30 we find the sing. לִבָּה, may also conform to this. And ישׁחנה as pred. to דאגה follows the scheme ii. 10*b*, perhaps not without attractional co-operation after the scheme קֶשֶׁת גִּבֹּרִים חַתִּים, 1 Sam. ii. 4, הִשְׁחָה, from שָׁחָה, occurs only here; but הֵשַׁח, from שָׁחַח, occurs only twice. דְּבַר טוֹב designates in the book of Joshua and in Kings (1 Kings viii. 56) the divine promise; here it is of the same meaning as 1 Kings xii. 7: an appeasing word. Who has not in himself had this experience, how such a word of friendly encouragement from a sympathizing heart cheers the sorrowful soul, and, if only for a time, changes its sorrow into the joy of confidence and of hope!

> Ver. 26 The righteous looketh after his pastures,
> But the way of the godless leadeth them into error.

In 26*a* no acceptable meaning is to be gained from the traditional mode of vocalization. Most of the ancients translate יָתֵר as part. to יָתַר, as it occurs in post-bib. Hebr., *e.g.* חִבָּה יְתֵרָה, prevailing, altogether peculiar love. Thus the Targum, טַב מִן הַבְרֵיהּ; *Venet.*

πεπερίττευται (after Kimchi); on the other hand, Aquila, active:
περισσεύων τὸν πλησίον (making the neighbour rich), which the
meaning of the *Kal* as well as the form יֶתֶר oppose; Luther, "The
righteous man is better than his neighbour," according to which
Fleischer also explains, " Probably יֶתֶר from יָתַר, πλεονάζειν, has
the meaning of πλέον ἔχων, πλεονεκτῶν, he gains more honour,
respect, riches, etc., than the other, viz. the unrighteous." Yet
more satisfactory Ahron b. Joseph : not the nobility and the
name, but this, that he is righteous, raises a man above others.
In this sense we would approve of the *præstantior altero justus*, if
only the two parts of the proverb were not by such a rendering
wholly isolated from one another.   Thus יֶתֶר is to be treated as the
fut. of הֵתִיר. The Syr. understands it of right counsel; and in like
manner Schultens explains it, with Cocceius, of intelligent, skilful
guidance, and the moderns (*e.g.* Gesenius) for the most part of
guidance generally.   Ewald rather seeks (because the proverb-
style avoids the placing of a fut. verb at the commencement of the
proverb [but cf. xvii. 10]) to interpret יֶתֶר as a noun in the sense
of director, but his justification of the fixed *ā* is unfounded.   And
generally this sense of the word is exposed to many objections.
The verb תּוּר signifies, after its root, to go about, " to make to go
about," but is, however, not equivalent to, to lead (wherefore
Böttcher too ingeniously derives יֶתֶר = יָאתֵר from אתר = אֹשֶׁר); and
wherefore this strange word, since the Book of Proverbs is so rich
in synonyms of leading and guiding!   The *Hiph.* הֵתִיר signifies to
send to spy, Judg. i. 23, and in this sense the poet ought to have
said יָתֵר לְרֵעֵהוּ : the righteous spies out (the way) for his neighbour,
he serves him, as the Targum-Talmud would say, as תַּיָּר.   Thus
connected with the obj. accus. the explanation would certainly be :
the righteous searches out his neighbour (Löwenstein), he has
intercourse with men, according to the maxim, "*Trau schau wem.*"
But why not רֵעֵהוּ, but מֵרֵעֵהוּ, which occurs only once, xix. 7, in the
Mishle, and then for an evident reason ?   Therefore, with Döderlein,
Dathe, J. D. Michaelis, Ziegler, and Hitzig, we prefer to read מֵרֵעֵהוּ;
it is at least not necessary, with Hitzig, to change יֶתֶר into יָתֵר,
since the *Hiphil* may have the force of the intens. of the *Kal,* but
יֶתֶר without the jussive signification is a poetic licence for יָתִיר.
That תּוּר can quite well be used of the exploring of the pasture, the
deriv. יתוּר, Job xxxix. 18, shows.   Thus altered, 26*a* falls into an
appropriately contrasted relation to 26*b*.   The way of the godless

leads them into error; the course of life to which they have given
themselves up has such a power over them that they cannot set
themselves free from it, and it leads the enslaved into destruction :
the righteous, on the contrary, is free with respect to the way which
he takes and the place where he stays; his view (regard) is directed
to his true advancement, and he looketh after his pasture, *i.e.*
examines and discovers, where for him right pasture, *i.e.* the
advancement of his outer and inner life, is to be found. With
מִרְעֵהוּ there is a combination of the thought of this verse with the
following, whose catch-word is צֵידוֹ, his prey.

> Ver. 27 The slothful pursues not his prey ;
> But a precious possession of a man is diligence.

The LXX., Syr., Targ., and Jerome render יַחֲרֹךְ in the sense of
obtaining or catching, but the verbal stem חרך nowhere has this
meaning. When Fleischer remarks, חָרַךְ, *ἄπ. λεγ.*, probably like
לְכַד, properly to entangle in a noose, a net, he supports his opinion
by reference to חֲרַכִּים, which signifies lattice-windows, properly,
woven or knitted like a net. But חֶרֶךְ, whence this חרכים, appears
to be equivalent to the Arab. *khark, fissura*, so that the plur. gives
the idea of a manifoldly divided (lattice-like, trellis-formed) window.
The Jewish lexicographers (Menahem, Abulwalîd, Parchon, also
Juda b. Koreish) all aim at that which is in accord with the meaning of the Aram. חֲרַךְ, to singe, to roast (=Arab. *hark*): the slothful
roasteth not his prey, whether (as Fürst presents it) because he is too
lazy to hunt for it (Berth.), or because when he has it he prepares
it not for enjoyment (Ewald). But to roast is צלה, not דרך, which is
used only of singeing, *e.g.* the hair, and roasting, *e.g.* ears of corn,
but not of the roasting of flesh, for which reason Joseph Kimchi
(*vid.* Kimchi's *Lex.*) understands צידו of wild fowls, and יחרך of the
singeing of the tips of the wings, so that they cannot fly away,
according to which the *Venet.* translates οὐ μενεῖ . . . ἡ θήρα αὐτοῦ.
Thus the Arab. must often help to a right interpretation of the *ἄπ.*
λεγ. Schultens is right: *Verbum harak,* חרך, *apud Arabes est movere,*
ciere, excitare, κινεῖν *generatim, et speciatim excitare prœdam e cubili,*
κινεῖν τὴν θήραν. The Lat. *agitare*, used of the frightening up and
driving forth of wild beasts, corresponds with the idea here, as *e.g.*
used by Ovid, *Metam.* x. 538, of Diana :

> *Aut pronos lepores aut celsum in cornua cervum*
> *Aut agitat damas.*

Thus יחרך together with צידו gains the meaning of hunting, and

generally of catching the prey. רְמִיָּה is here incarnate slothfulness, and thus without ellipse equivalent to אִישׁ רמיה. That in the
contrasted clause חרוץ does not mean ἀποτόμως, decreed (Löwenstein), nor gold (Targ., Jerome, *Venet.*), nor that which is excellent
(Syr.), is manifest from this contrast as well as from x. 4, xii. 24.
The clause has from its sequence of words something striking about
it. The LXX. placed the words in a different order: κτῆμα δὲ
τίμιον ἀνὴρ καθαρὸς (חלוץ in the sense of Arab. *khâlaṣ*). But
besides this transposition, two others have been tried : הון אדם חרוץ
יקר, the possession of an industrious man is precious, and הון יקר אדם
חרוץ, a precious possession is that (supply הון) of an industrious man.
But the traditional arrangement of the words gives a better meaning
than these modifications. It is not, however, to be explained, with
Ewald and Bertheau : a precious treasure of a man is one who is
industrious, for why should the industrious man be thought of as
a worker for another and not for himself ? Another explanation
advanced by Kimchi : a valuable possession to men is industry, has
the twofold advantage that it is according to the existing sequence
of the words, and presents a more intelligible thought. But can
חָרוּץ have the meaning of חֲרִיצוּת (the being industrious) ? Hitzig
reads חָרוֹץ, to make haste (to be industrious). This is unnecessary,
for we have here a case similar to x. 17, where שָׁמֹר for שׁוֹמֵר is to
be expected : a precious possession of a man is it that, or when, he
is industrious, חָרוּץ briefly for חָרוּץ הֱיוֹתוֹ. The accentuation fluctuates between וְהוֹן־אָדָם יָקָר (so *e.g.* Cod. 1294), according to which
the Targum translates, and וְהוֹן־אָדָם יָקָר, which, according to our
explanation, is to be preferred.

Ver. 28 In the path of righteousness is life,
And the way of its path is immortality.

All the old versions to the *Venet.* give אֶל־ instead of אַל־, and are
therefore under the necessity of extracting from וְדֶרֶךְ נְתִיבָה a
meaning corresponding to this, εἰς θάνατον, in which they are
followed by Hitzig : " a devious way leadeth to death." But נָתִיב
(נְתִיבָה) signifies step, and generally way and street (*vid.* at i. 15),
not "devious way," which is expressed, Judg. v. 6, by ארחות עקלקלות.
And that אַל is anywhere punctuated thus in the sense of אֶל is
previously improbable, because the Babylonian system of punctuation distinguishes the negative אל with a short *Pathach*, and the
prepositional אל‎. (Arab. *ilâ*) with a short *Chirek*, from each other

(*vid.* Pinsker, *Einl.* p. xxii. f.); the punctuation 2 Sam. xiii. 16, Jer. li. 3, gives no support to the opinion that here אַל is vocalized thus in the sense of אֵל, and it is not to be thus corrected. Nothing is more natural than that the Chokma in its constant contrast between life and death makes a beginning of expressing the idea of the ἀθανασία (*vid.* p. 42), which Aquila erroneously read from the אַל-מוּת, Ps. xlviii. 15. It has been objected that for the formation of such negative substantives and noun-adjectives לֹא (*e.g.* לֹא-עָם, לֹא-אֵל) and not אַל is used; but that אַל also may be in close connection with a noun, 2 Sam. i. 13 shows. There אַל-טַל is equivalent to אַל יְהִי טַל, according to which it may also be explained in the passage before us, with Luther and all the older interpreters, who accepted אַל in its negative signification : and on (the בְּ governing) the way . . . is no death. The negative אַל frequently stands as an intensifying of the objective לֹא; but why should the Chokma, which has already shown itself bold in the coining of new words, not apply itself to the formation of the idea of immortality?: the idol name אֱלִיל is the result of a much greater linguistic boldness. It is certain that אַל is here not equivalent to אֵל; the Masora is therefore right in affirming that נְתִיבָה is written with *He raphatum pro mappicato* (*vid.* Kimchi, *Michlol* 31*a*, and in the *Lex.*), cf. 1 Sam. xx. 20, *vid.* Böttcher, § 418. Thus: the way of their step is immortality, or much rather, since דֶּרֶךְ is not a fixed idea, but also denotes the going to a distance (*i.e.* the journey), the behaviour, the proceeding, the walk, etc.: the walking (the stepping over and passing through) of their way is immortality. Rich in synonyms of the way, the Hebrew style delights in connecting them with picturesque expressions ; but דֶּרֶךְ always means the way in general, which divides into אֳרָחוֹת or נְתִיבוֹת (Job vi. 18, Jer. xviii. 5), and consists of such (Isa. iii. 16). The distich is synonymous : on the path of righteousness (accentuate בְּאֹרַח צְדָקָה) is life meeting him who walks in it, and giving itself to him as a possession, and the walking in its path is immortality (cf. iii. 17, x. 28); so that to go in it and to be immortal, *i.e.* to be delivered from death, to be exalted above it, is one and the same thing. If we compare with this, xiv. 32*b*, it is obvious that the Chokma begins (*vid. Psychol.* p. 410) to break through the limits of this present life, and to announce a life beyond the reach of death.

The proverb xii. 28 is so sublime, so weighty, that it manifestly

forms a period and conclusion. This is confirmed from the following proverb, which begins like x. 1 (cf. 5), and anew stamps the
collection as intended for youth :

> xiii. 1 A wise son is his father's correction ;
> But a scorner listens not to rebuke.

The LXX., which the Syr. follows, translate Υἱὸς πανοῦργος
ὑπήκοος πατρί, whence it is not to be concluded with Lagarde
that they read נוֹסָר in the sense of a *Ni. tolerativum ;* they correctly
understood the text according to the Jewish rule of interpretation,
" that which is wanting is to be supplied from the context." The
Targ. had already supplied יִשְׁמַע from 1b, and is herein followed by
Hitzig, as also by Glassius in the *Philologia sacra.* But such an
ellipse is in the Hebr. style without an example, and would be comprehensible only in passionate, hasty discourse, but in a language
in which the representation *filius sapiens disciplinam patris audit*
numbers among the anomalies is not in general possible, and has
not even its parallel in Tacitus, *Ann.* xiii. 56 : *deesse nobis terra,
in qua vivamus—in qua moriemur, non potest,* because here the primary idea, which the one expression confirms, the other denies, and
besides no particle, such as the ן of this passage before us, stands
between them. Böttcher therefore maintains the falling out of
the verb, and writes יָבִין before בֵּן ; but one says not בִּין מוּסר, but
שְׁמַע מוּסר, i. 8, iv. 1, xix. 27. Should not the clause, as it thus
stands, give a sense complete in itself ? But מוּסָר can hardly, with
Schultens and Ewald, be taken as *part. Hoph.* of יסר : one brought
up by his father, for the usage of the language knows מוּסר only
as *part. Hoph.* of סוּר. Thus, as Jerome and the *Venet.* translate :
a wise son is the correction of his father, *i.e.* the product of the
same, as also Fleischer explains, " Attribution of the cause, the
ground, as elsewhere of the effect." But we call that which one
has trained (vegetable or animal) his *Zucht* (=παιδεία in the sense of
παίδευμα). To the wise son (x. 1) who is indebted to the מוּסר אב
(iv. 1), stands opposed the לֵץ (*vid.* i. 22), the mocker at religion
and virtue, who has no ear for גְּעָרָה, strong and stern words
which awaken in him a wholesome fear (cf. xvii. 10, Jude 23 : ἐν
φόβῳ).

> Ver. 2 From the fruit of the mouth of a man he himself enjoys good ;
> But the delight of the godless is violence.

2a = xii. 14a, where יִשְׂבַּע for יֹאכַל. A man with a fruit-bringing
mouth, himself enjoys also the blessing of his fruit-producing

speech; his food (cf. βρῶμα, John iv. 34) is the good action in words, which in themselves are deeds, and are followed by deeds; this good action affords enjoyment not merely to others, but also to himself. Ewald and Bertheau attract יאכל to 2*b*; so also does Fleischer: " the violence which the בֹּגְדִים wish to do to others turns back upon themselves; they must eat it also, *i.e.* bear its evil consequences." The thought would then be like x. 6 : *os impro-borum obteget violentia,* and " to eat violence" is parallel to " to drink (xxvi. 6) violence (injury)." But wherefore then the naming of the soul, of which elsewhere it is said that it hungers or satiates itself, but never simply (but cf. Luke xii. 19) that it eats ? On the contrary, נֶפֶשׁ means also *appetitus,* xxiii. 2, and particularly wicked desire, Ps. xxvii. 12; here, as Ps. xxxv. 25, the object of this desire (*Psychol.* p. 202). Regarding בֹּגְדִים, *vid.* above, p. 85. There are such as do injury in a cunning deceitful manner to their neighbour to their own advantage. While the former (the righteous) distri-butes to his neighbour from the inner impulse without having such a result in view, yet according to God's direction he derives enjoyment himself therefrom : the desire of the latter goes to חָמָס, ἀδικία, and thus to the enjoyment of good unrighteously and violently seized.

Ver. 3 He that guardeth his mouth keepeth his soul;
He that openeth wide his lips, to him it is destruction.

3*a* is extended in xxi. 23 to a distich. Mouth and soul stand in closest interchangeable relation, for speech is the most immediate and continuous expression of the soul; thus whoever guards his mouth keeps his soul (the *Venet.,* with excellent rendering of the synonym, ὁ τηρῶν τὸ στόμα ἑαυτοῦ φυλάσσει τὴν ψυχὴν ἑαυτοῦ), for he watches that no sinful vain thoughts rise up in his soul and come forth in words, and because he thus keeps his soul, *i.e.* himself, safe from the destructive consequences of the sins of the tongue. On the contrary, he who opens wide his lips, *i.e.* cannot hold his mouth (LXX. ὁ δὲ προπετὴς χείλεσιν), but expresses unexamined and unconsidered whatever comes into his mind and gives delight, he is destruction to himself (supply הוּא), or to him it is destruction (supply זֹאת); both interpretations are possible, the parallelism brings nearer the former, and the parallel xviii. 7 brings nearer the latter. פָּשַׂק means to spread (Schultens: *diducere cum ruptura vel ad rupturam usque*), here the lips, *Pih.* Ezek. xvi. 25, the legs, Arab. *fashkh, farshkh; vid.* regarding the R. פש, to extend, to spread out, Fleischer in the supplements to the *A. L. Z.* 1843, col. 116. Regarding the *Mishle* word מִחְתָּה, *vid.* under x. 14.

Ver. 4. The three proverbs (1-3) which refer to hearing and speaking are now followed by a fourth which, like vers. 2 and 3, speaks of the נֶפֶשׁ.

> The soul of the sluggard desires, yet has not;
> But the soul of the industrious is richly satisfied.

The view that the *o* in נַפְשׁוֹ עָצֵל is the *cholem compaginis*, Böttcher, § 835, meets with the right answer that this would be the only example of a vocal *casus* in the whole of gnomic poetry; but when on his own part (*Neue Aehrenlese*, § 1305) he regards נפשׁ as the accus. of the nearer definition (=בְּנַפְשׁוֹ), he proceeds inadvertently on the view that the first word of the proverb is מִתְאַוֶּה, while we read מִתְאַוָּה, and נפשׁו is thus the nom. of the subject. נַפְשׁוֹ עָצֵל means "his (the sluggard's) soul" (for עָצֵל occurs as explanatory permutative briefly for נפשׁ עצל), as פֹּרִיָּה סְעִיפֶיהָ means "its branches (*i.e.* of the fruitful tree)," Isa. xvii. 6. One might, it is true, add ה to the following word here, as at xiv. 13; but the similar expression appertaining to the *syntax ornata* occurs also 2 Sam. xxii. 33, Ps. lxxi. 7, and elsewhere, where this is impracticable. Meîri appropriately compares the scheme Ex. ii. 6, she saw him, viz. the boy. With reference to the וָאַיִן here violently (cf. xxviii. 1) introduced, Böttcher rightly remarks, that it is an adverb altogether like *necquidquam*, xiv. 6, xx. 4, Ps. lxviii. 21, etc., thus: *appetit necquidquam anima ejus, scilicet pigri.* 4b shows the meaning of the desire that has not, for there תְּדֻשָּׁן occurs, a favourite strong *Mishle* word (xi. 25, xxviii. 25, etc.) for abundant satisfaction (the LXX. here, as at xxviii. 25, ἐν ἐπιμελείᾳ, *sc.* ἔσονται, instead of which, Montfaucon supposed πιμελείᾳ, which is, however, a word not authenticated). The slothful wishes and dreams of prosperity and abundance (cf. xxi. 25 f., a parallel which the Syr. has here in view), but his desire remains unsatisfied, since the object is not gained but only lost by doing nothing; the industrious gain, and that richly, what the slothful wishes for, but in vain.

Ver. 5. Two proverbs of the character of the righteous and of the effect of righteousness:

> A deceitful thing the righteous hateth;
> But the godless disgraceth and putteth to shame.

With דְּבַר in the sphere of an intelligible generality (as here of falsehood, or Ps. xli. 9 of worthlessness) a concrete event is in view, as with דִּבְרֵי in the following plur. a general fact is separated into its individual instances and circumstances (*vid.* at Ps. lxv. 4); for דבר means not only the word in which the soul reveals itself, but also any fact in which an inner principle or a general fact or a whole comes forth to view. The righteous hateth all that bears in it the character of a falsehood (punctuate דְּבַר־שֶׁקֶר with *Gaja,* cf. xii. 19), but the godless . . . Should we now, with Bertheau, Hitzig, and others, translate "acteth basely and shamefully"? It is true that both *Hiphs.* may be regarded as transitive, but this expression gives no right contrast to 5*a*, and is pointless. We have seen at x. 5 that הֵבִישׁ, like הִשְׂכִּיל, has also a causative signification: to put to shame, *i.e.* bring shame upon others, and that xix. 26, where מֵבִישׁ וּמַחְפִּיר are connected, this causative signification lies nearer than the intrinsically transitive. Thus it will also here be meant, that while the righteous hateth all that is false or that is tainted by falsehood, the godless on the contrary loves to disgrace and to put to shame. But it is a question whether יַבְאִישׁ is to be derived from בָּאַשׁ = בּוּשׁ, and thus is of the same meaning as יָבִישׁ; הבאישׁ, Isa. xxx. 5, which there signifies *pudefactum esse,* is pointed הֹבאישׁ, and is thus derived from a יָבֵשׁ = בּוּשׁ, *vid.* 2 Sam. xix. 6. But הִבְאִישׁ occurs also as *Hiph.* of בָּאַשׁ, and means transitively to make of an evil savour, Gen. xxxiv. 30, cf. Ex. v. 21, as well as intransitively to come into evil savour, 1 Sam. xxvii. 12. In this sense of *putidum faciens,* bringing into evil savour, יבאישׁ occurs here as at xix. 26, suitably along with יחפיר; xix. 26 is the *putidum facere* by evil report (slander), into which the foolish son brings his parents, here by his own evil report, thus to be thought of as brought about by means of slander. The old translators here fall into error; Luther renders both *Hiphils* reflexively; only the *Venet.* (after Kimchi) is right: ὀζώσει (from an ὀζοῦν as trans. to ὀζεῖν) καὶ ἀτιμώσει, he makes to be of ill odour and dishonours.

Ver. 6 Righteousness protecteth an upright walk,
And godlessness bringeth sinners to destruction.

The double thought is closely like that of xi. 5, but is peculiarly and almost enigmatically expressed. As there, צְדָקָה and רִשְׁעָה are meant of a twofold inner relation to God, which consists of a ruling influence over man's conduct and a determination of his walk. But instead of naming the persons of the תְּמִימֵי דֶרֶךְ and חַטָּאִים as the objects of this influence, the proverb uses the abstract expression, but with personal reference, תָּם־דֶּרֶךְ and חַטָּאת, and

274 THE BOOK OF PROVERBS.

designates in two words the connection of this twofold character
with the principles óf their conduct. What is meant by תִּצֹּר and
תְּסַלֵּף proceeds from the contrasted relationship of the two (cf.
xxii. 12). נצר signifies *observare*, which is not suitable here, but
also *tueri* (τηρεῖν), to which סַלֵּף (*vid.* at xi. 3, and in Gesen.
Thesaurus), not so much in the sense of "to turn upside down,"
pervertere (as xi. 3, Ex. xxiii. 8), as in the sense of "to overthrow,"
evertere (as *e.g.* xxi. 12), forms a fitting contrast. He who walks
forth with an unfeigned and untroubled pure mind stands under
the shield and the protection of righteousness (cf. with this proso-
popœia Ps. xxv. 21), from which such a walk proceeds, and at the
same time under the protection of God, to whom righteousness
appertains, is well-pleasing; but he who in his conduct permits
himself to be determined by sin, godlessness (cf. Zech. v. 8) from
which such a love for sin springs forth, brings to destruction; in
other words : God, from whom the רשע, those of a perverse disposition, tear themselves away, makes the sin their snare by virtue of
the inner connection established by Him between the רשעה and
the destruction (Isa. ix. 17). In the LXX. this 6th verse was
originally wanting; the translation in the version of Aquila, in
the Complut. and elsewhere, which the Syr. follows, falsely makes
חטאת the subj. : τοὺς δὲ ἀσεβεῖς φαύλους ποιεῖ ἁμαρτία.

Ver. 7. Two proverbs of riches and poverty :—

There is one who maketh himself rich and hath nothing ;
There is another who representeth himself poor amid great riches.

A sentence which includes in itself the judgment which xii. 9
expresses. To the *Hithpa.* הִתְכַּבֵּד (to make oneself of importance)
there are associated here two others, in the meaning to make oneself something, without anything after it, thus to place oneself
so or so, Ewald, § 124*a*. To the clauses with וְ there is supplied a
self-intelligible לוֹ.

Ver. 8 A ransom for a man's life are his riches ;
But the poor heareth no threatening.

Bertheau falls into error when he understands גְּעָרָה of warning ;
the contrast points to threatening with the loss of life. The
wealth of the rich before the judgment is not here to be thought
of ; for apart from this, that the *Torâ* only in a single case
permits, or rather ordains (Ex. xxi. 29 f.), ransom from the punishment of death, and declares it in all other cases inadmissible,
Num. xxxv. 31 f. (one might indeed think of an administration of

justice not strictly in accordance with the Mosaic law, or altogether accessible to bribery), 8b does not accord therewith, since the poor in such cases would fare ill, because one would lay hold on his person. But one may think *e.g.* on waylayers as those introduced as speaking i. 11–14. The poor has no room to fear that such will threateningly point their swords against his breast, for there is nothing to be got from him: he has nothing, one sees it in him and he is known as such. But the rich is a valuable prize for them, and he has to congratulate himself if he is permitted to escape with his life. Also in the times of war and commotion it may be seen that riches endanger the life of their possessor, and that in fortunate cases they are given as a ransom for his life, while his poverty places the poor man in safety. To שָׁמַע לֹא Hitzig fittingly compares Job iii. 18, xxxix. 7: he does not hear, he has no need to hear. Michaelis, Umbreit, Löwenstein (who calls to remembrance the state of things under despotic governments, especially in the East) also explain 8b correctly; and Fleischer remarks: *pauper minas hostiles non audit, i.e. non minatur ei hostis.* Ewald's syntactic refinement: " Yet he became poor who never heard an accusation," presents a thought not in harmony with 8a.

The three following proverbs in vers. 9–11 have at least this in common, that the two concluding words of each correspond with one another almost rhythmically.

Ver. 9 The light of the righteous burneth joyously,
And the lamp of the godless goeth out.

The second line = xxiv. 20b, cf. xx. 20. In the Book of Job xviii. 5 f., אור רשעים ידעך and נרו עליו ידעך (cf. xxi. 17) stand together, and there is spoken of (xxix. 3) a divine נֵר as well as a divine אור which enlightens the righteous; however, one must say that the poet, as he, vi. 3, deliberately calls the *Torâ* אור, and the commandment, as derived from it and separated, נר, so also here designedly calls the righteous אור, viz. אור היום (iv. 18, cf. 2 Pet. i. 19), and the godless נר, viz. נר דלוק,—the former imparts the sunny daylight, the latter the light of tapers set in darkness. The authentic punctuation is אוֹר־צַדִּיקִים; Ben-Naphtali's is אוֹר צ׳ without *Makkeph*. To יִשְׂמָח. Hitzig compares the " laughing tongue of the taper" of Meidâni, iii. 475; Kimchi also the " laughing, *i.e.* amply measured span, טפח שׂוֹהק," of the Talmud; for the light laughs when it brightly shines, and increases rather than decreases; in Arab. *samuḥa* has in it the idea of joy directly related to that of liberality. The

LXX. translates יִשְׂמַח incorrectly by διαπαντός, and has a distich following ver. 9, the first line of which is ψυχαὶ δόλιαι (נֶפֶשׁ רְמִיָּה?) πλανῶνται ἐν ἁμαρτίαις, and the second line is from Ps. xxxvii. 21b.

Ver. 10 Nothing comes by pride but contention ;
But wisdom is with those who receive counsel.

The restrictive רַק (only) does not, according to the sense, belong to בְּזָדוֹן (by pride), but to מַצָּה, vid. under Ps. xxxii. 6 and Job ii. 10. Of יִתֵּן = there is, vid. under x. 24. Bertheau's " one causes " is not exact, for "one" [man] is the most general personal subject, but יתן is in such cases to be regarded as impersonal : by pride is always a something which causes nothing but quarrel and strife, for the root of pride is egoism. Line second is a variant to xi. 2b. *Bescheidenheit* (modesty) is in our old [German] language exactly equivalent to *Klugheit* (prudence). But here the צנועים are more exactly designated as permitting themselves to be advised ; the elsewhere reciprocal נוֹעָץ has here once a tolerative signification, although the reciprocal is also allowable : with such as reciprocally advise themselves, and thus without positiveness supplement each his own knowledge by means of that of another. Most interpreters regard 10b as a substantival clause, but why should not יתן be carried forward? With such as permit themselves to be advised, or are not too proud to sustain with others the relation of giving and receiving, there is wisdom, since instead of hatred comes wisdom—the peaceful fruit resulting from an interchange of views.

Ver. 11 Wealth by means of fraud always becomes less ;
But he that increaseth it by labour gains always more.

We punctuate הוֹן־מֵהֶבֶל (with *Makkeph*, as in Ven. 1521, Antw. 1582, Frank.-on-the-Oder 1595, Gen. 1618, Leyden 1662), not הוֹן מֵהֶבֶל (as other editions, and e.g. also Löwenstein); for the meaning is not that the wealth becomes less by הבל (Targ., but not the Syr.), or that it is less than הבל (Umbreit), but הון־מהבל is one idea : wealth proceeding from הבל; but הבל, properly a breath (Theod. ἀπὸ ἀτμοῦ or ἀτμίδος), then appearance without reality (Aquila, ἀπὸ ματαιότητος), covers itself here by that which we call swindle, i.e. by morally unrestrained fraudulent and deceitful speculation in contrast to solid and real gain. The translations: ἐπισπουδαζομένη μετὰ ἀνομίας (LXX.), ὑπερσπουδαζομένη (Symmachus, *Quinta*[1]),

---

[1] [A fragment of an anonymous translation, so called from the place it holds in Origen's *Hexapla*.]

festinata (Jerome), do not necessarily suppose the phrase מְהֻבָּל = מִבֹּהָל, xx. 21 *Kerî*, for wealth which comes מהבל is obtained in a windy (unsubstantial) manner and as if by storm, of which the proverb holds good : "*so gewonnen so zerronnen*" (= quickly come, quickly go). מְהֻבָּל needs neither to be changed into that un-hebraic מְהֻבָּל (Hitzig) nor into the cognate מִבֹּהָל (Ewald), but yet inferior to מהבל in the content of its idea. The contrast of one who by fraud and deception quickly arrives at wealth is one who brings it together in his hand, ἐπὶ χειρός (*Venet.*), *i.e.* always as often as he can bear it in his hand and bring it forth (Ewald, Bertheau, Elster, and Lagarde), or according to the measure of the hand, κατὰ χεῖρα (which means "according to external ability"), so that עַל, which is applied to the formation of adverbs, *e.g.* Ps. xxxi. 24 (Hitzig),—by both explanations עַל־יִד has the meaning of "gradually,"—is used as in the post-bib. Hebr. יד על יד על = מעט מעט, *e.g. Schabbath* 156a (*vid.* Aruch under עַל) (distinguish from ביד = with thought, intentionally, *Berachoth* 52b). There is scarcely a word having more significations than יד. Connected with עַל, it means at one time side or place, at another mediation or direction; that which is characteristic here is the omission of the pronoun (עַל־יָדָיו, עַל־יָדָיו). The LXX. translates עַל יד with the unrestrained freedom which it allows to itself by μετ᾽ εὐσεβείας, and has following πληθυνθήσεται another line, δίκαιος οἰκτείρει καὶ κιχρᾷ (from Ps. xxxvii. 26).

The figures of paradise in vers. 12 and 14 require us to take along with them the intermediate verse (13).

Ver. 12 Deferred waiting maketh the heart sick,
　　　　And a tree of life is a wish accomplished.

Singularly the LXX. Κρείσσων ἐναρχόμενος βοηθῶν καρδίᾳ, fol-lowed by the Syr. (which the Targ. transcribes[1]) : Better is he who begins to help than he who remains in hesitating expectation, by which תחלת is doubled, and is derived once from הוחיל, to wait, and the second time from החל, to begin. If the LXX., with its imitators, deteriorates to such a degree proverbs so clear, beautiful, and inviolable, what may one expect from it in the case of those not easily understood ! מָשַׁךְ signifies also, Isa. xviii. 2, to be widely extended (cf. Arab. *meshak*), here in the sense of time, as נִמְשַׁךְ, to prolong, Isa. xiii. 22, and post-bib. מֶשֶׁךְ הַזְּמָן, the course of time.

[1] That the Targum of the Proverbs is a Jewish elaboration of the Peshito text, *vid.* Nöldeke in Merx' *Archiv*, Bd. ii. pp. 246–49.

Regarding תּוֹחֶלֶת, *vid.* at x. 28, where as xi. 27 תִּקְוַת, here תַּאֲוָה, as also Ps. lxxviii. 29 of the object of the wish, and with בוא in the sense of being fulfilled (cf. Josh. xxi. 43), as there with הביא in the sense of accomplishing or performing. Extended waiting makes the heart sick, causes heart-woe (מְחַלָּה, *part. fem. Hiph.* of חָלָה, to be slack, feeble, sick; R. חל, to loosen, to make loose); on the contrary, a wish that has been fulfilled is a tree of life (cf. p. 32), of a quickening and strengthening influence, like that tree of paradise which was destined to renew and extend the life of man.

Ver. 13 Whoever despiseth the word is in bonds to it,
And he that feareth the commandment is rewarded.

The word is thought of as ordering, and thus in the sense of the commandment, *e.g.* 1 Sam. xvii. 19, Dan. ix. 23, 25. That which is here said is always true where the will of a man has subordinated itself to the authoritative will of a superior, but principally the proverb has in view the word of God, the מִצְוָה κατ' ἐξ. as the expression of the divine will, which (vi. 3) appears as the secondary, with the תורה, the general record of the divine will. Regarding בּוּז לְ of contemptuous, despiteful opposition, *vid.* at vi. 30, cf. xi. 12. Joël (*vid.* p. 136, *note*) records the prevailing tradition, for he translates: "Whoever despises advice rushes into destruction; whoever holds the commandment in honour is perfect." But that יְשֻׁלָּם is to be understood neither of perfection nor of peace (LXX. and Jerome), but means *compensabitur* (here not in the sense of punishment, but of reward), we know from xi. 31. The translation also of יֵחָבֶל לּוֹ by " he rushes into destruction " (LXX. καταφθαρήσεται, which the Syr.-Hexap. repeats; Luther, " he destroys himself;" the *Venet.* οἰχήσεται οἱ, *periet sibi*) fails, for one does not see what should have determined the poet to choose just this word, and, instead of the ambiguous *dat. ethicus*, not rather to say יְחַבֵּל נַפְשׁוֹ. So also this יחבל is not with Gesenius to be connected with חבל = Arab. *khabl, corrumpere*, but with חבל = Arab. *habl, ligare, obligare*. Whoever places himself contemptuously against a word which binds him to obedience will nevertheless not be free from that word, but is under pledge until he redeem the pledge by the performance of the obedience refused, or till that higher will enforce payment of the debt withheld by visiting with punishment. Jerome came near the right interpretation: *ipse se in futurum obligat;* Abulwalîd refers to Ex. xxii. 25; and Parchon, Rashi, and others paraphrase: מַשְׁכֵּן יִתְמַשְׁכֵּן עָלָיו,

he is confiscated as by mortgage. Schultens has, with the correct reference of the לֹ not to the contemner, but to the word, well established and illustrated this explanation: he is pledged by the word, Arab. *marhwan* (*rahyn*), viz. *pigneratus pœnœ* (Livius, xxix. 36). Ewald translates correctly: he is pledged to it; and Hitzig gives the right explanation: "A חֲבֹלָה [a pledge, cf. xx. 16] is handed over to the offended law with the חֲבוּלָה [the bad conduct] by the despiser himself, which lapses when he has exhausted the forbearance, so that the punishment is inflicted." The LXX. has another proverb following ver. 13 regarding υἱὸς δόλιος and οἰκέτης σοφός; the Syr. has adopted it; Jerome has here the proverb of the *animœ dolosœ* (*vid.* at ver. 9).

Ver. 14 The doctrine of the wise man is a fountain of life,
To escape the snares of death.

An *integral* distich, *vid.* p. 8 of the Introduction. Essentially like 14a, x. 11 says, "a fountain of life is the mouth of the righteous." The figure of the fountain of life with the teleological לָסוּר וגו (the לֹ of the end and consequence of the action) is repeated xiv. 27. The common non-biblical figure of the *laquei mortis* leads also to the idea of death as יָקוּשׁ [a fowler], Ps. xci. 3. If it is not here a mere formula for the dangers of death (Hitzig), then the proverb is designed to state that the life which springs from the doctrine of the wise man as from a fountain of health, for the disciple who will receive it, communicates to him knowledge and strength, to know where the snares of destruction lie, and to hasten with vigorous steps away when they threaten to entangle him.

Four proverbs follow, whose connection appears to have been occasioned by the sound of their words (שֵׂכֶל . . . כֹּל, בְּדַעַת . . . בְּרַע, רִישׁ . . . רֶשַׁע).

Ver. 15 Fine prudence produceth favour;
But the way of the malicious is uncultivated.

Regarding שֵׂכֶל טוֹב (thus to be punctuated, without *Makkeph* with *Munach*, after Codd. and old editions), *vid.* p. 84; for the most part it corresponds with that which in a deep ethical sense we call fine culture. Regarding יִתֵּן, *vid.* at x. 10: it is not used here, as there, impersonally, but has a personal subject: he brings forth, causes. Fine culture, which shows men how to take the right side and in all circumstances to strike the right key, exercises a kindly heart-winning influence, not merely, as would be expressed by יִמְצָא חֵן, to the benefit of its possessor, but, as is expressed by

יִתֵּן חֵן, such as removes generally a partition wall and brings men closer to one another. The אֵיתָן [*perennis*], touching it both for the eye and the ear, forms the contrast to יתן חן. This word, an elative formation from יתן = وَتَن, denotes that which stretches itself far, and that with reference to time : that which remains the same during the course of time. " That which does not change in time, continuing the same, according to its nature, strong, firm, and thus איתן becomes the designation of the enduring and the solid, whose quality remains always the same." Thus Orelli, *Die hebr. Synonyme der Zeit u. Ewigkeit*, 1871. But that in the passage before us it denotes the way of the בגדים as " endlessly going forward," the explanation of Orelli, after Böttcher (*Collectanea*, p. 135), is with-drawn by the latter in the new *Aehrenlese* (where he reads ריב איתן, " constant strife"). And נחל איתן (Deut. xxi. 4) does not mean " a brook, the existence of which is not dependent on the weather and the season of the year," at least not in accordance with the traditional meaning which is given *Sota* ix. 5 (cf. the Gemara), but a stony valley; for the Mishna says : איתן כמשמעו קשה, *i.e.* איתן is here, according to its verbal meaning, equivalent to קשה (hard). We are of the opinion that here, in the midst of the discussion of the law of the עגלה ערופה (the ritual for the atonement of a murder perpetrated by an unknown hand), the same meaning of the איתן is certified which is to be adopted in the passage before us. Maimuni[1] (in *Sota* and *Hilchoth Rozeach* ix. 2) indeed, with the Mishna and Gemara, thinks the meaning of a " strong rushing wâdy" to be compatible ; but קשה is a word which more naturally denotes the property of the ground than of a river, and the description, Deut. xxi. 4 : in a נחל איתן, in which there is no tillage and sowing, demands for נחל here the idea of the valley, and not primarily that of the valley-brook. According to this tradition, the Targum places a תַּקִּיפָא in the Peshito translation of 15*b*, and the *Venet.* translates, after Kimchi, ὁδὸς δὲ ἀνταρτῶν (of ἀνταρτής from ἀνταίρειν) ἰσχυρά. The fundamental idea of remaining like itself, continuing, passes over into the idea of the firm, the hard, so that איתן is a word that interchanges with סלע, Num. xxiv. 21, and serves as a figurative designation of the rocky mountains, Jer. xlix. 19, and the rocky framework of the earth, Mic. vi. 2. Thus the meaning of hardness (πετρῶδες, Matt. xiii. 5) connects itself with

[1] [= R. Moses b. Maimun=Rambam, so called by the Jews from the initial letters of his name=Maimonides, d. 1204.]

the word, and at the same time, according to Deut. xxi. 4, of the uncultivable and the uncultivated. The way of the בֹּגְדִים, the treacherous (vid. p. 84), i.e. the manner in which they transact with men, is stiff, as hard as stone, and repulsive; they follow selfish views, never placing themselves in sympathy with the condition of their neighbour; they are without the tenderness which is connected with fine culture; they remain destitute of feeling in things which, as we say, would soften a stone. It is unnecessary to give a catalogue of the different meanings of this אֵיתָן, such as *vorago* (Jerome), a standing bog (Umbreit), an ever trodden way (Bertheau), etc.; Schultens offers, as frequently, the relatively best: *at via perfidorum pertinacissime tensum;* but יְתָן does not mean to strain, but to extend. The LXX. has between 15*a* and 15*b* the interpolation: τὸ δὲ γνῶναι νόμον διανοίας ἐστὶν ἀγαθῆς.

Ver. 16 Every prudent man acteth with understanding;
But a fool spreadeth abroad folly.

Hitzig reads, with the Syr. (but not the Targ.) and Jerome, כֹּל (*omnia agit*), but contrary to the Hebr. syntax. The כָּל־ is not feeble and useless, but means that he always acts בְּדַעַת, *mit Bedacht* [with judgment] (*opp.* בְּבְלִי דַעַת, *inconsulto*, Deut. iv. 42, xix. 4), while on the contrary the fool displays folly. xii. 23 and xv. 2 serve to explain both members of the verse. *Bedächtigkeit* [judgment] is just knowledge directed to a definite practical end, a clear thought concentrated on a definite point. יִקְרָא, he calls out, and יַבִּיעַ, he sputters out, are parallels to יִפְרֹשׂ. Fleischer: פָּרַשׂ, *expandit* (*opp.* Arab. *tawy, intra animum cohibuit*), as a cloth or paper folded or rolled together, cf. Schiller's[1]—

" He spreads out brightly and splendidly
The enveloped life."

There lies in the word something derisive: as the merchant unrolls and spreads out his wares in order to commend them, so the fool does with his foolery, which he had enveloped, *i.e.* had the greatest interest to keep concealed within himself—he is puffed up therewith.

Ver. 17 A godless messenger falls into trouble;
But a faithful messenger is a cordial.

The traditional text, which the translations also give (except Jerome, *nuntius impii*, and leaving out of view the LXX., which

[1] [" Er breitet es heiter und glänzend aus,
Das zusammengewickelte Leben."]

makes of ver. 17 a history of a foolhardy king and a wise messenger), has not מַלְאָךְ, but מַלְאָךְ; the Masora places the word along
with הַמַּלְאָךְ, Gen. xlviii. 16. And יִפֹּל is likewise testified to by all
translators; they all read it as *Kal*, as the traditional text punctuates
it; Luther alone departs from this and translates the *Hiph.*: " a
godless messenger bringeth misfortune." Indeed, this conj. יַפֵּל
presses itself forward; and even though one read יִפֹּל, the sense
intended by virtue of the parallelism could be no other than that
a godless messenger, because no blessing rests on his godlessness,
stumbles into disaster, and draws him who gave the commission
along with him. The connection מַלְאָךְ רֵשׁע is like אדם רשע, xi. 7
(cf. the fem. of this adj., Ezek. iii. 18). Instead of בְּרָע is בְּרָעָה,
xvii. 20, xxviii. 14, parallels (cf. also xi. 5) which the punctuators
may have had in view in giving the preference to *Kal*. With
מַלְאָךְ, from לָאַךְ, R. לך, to make to go = to send, is interchanged
צִיר, from צור, to turn, whence to journey (cf. Arab. *sar*, to become,
to be, as the vulg. "to be to Dresden = to journey" is used). The
connection צִיר אֱמוּנִים (cf. the more simple צִיר נֶאֱמָן, xxv. 13) is
like xiv. 15, עֵד אמונים; the *pluralet.* means faithfulness in the full
extent of the idea. Regarding מַרְפֵּא, the means of healing, here of
strength, refreshment, *vid.* iv. 22, xii. 18.

Ver. 18 Poverty and shame (to him) who rejecteth correction ;
But he who regardeth reproof is honoured.

We are neither to supply אִישׁ before רֵישׁ וְקָלוֹן (or more correctly,
abstr. pro concr., as רְמִיָּה, xii. 27), nor לְ before פּוֹרֵעַ, as Gesenius
(*Lehrgeb.* § 227a) does; nor has the *part.* פּוֹרֵעַ the value of a
hypothetical clause like xviii. 13, Job xli. 18, although it may
certainly be changed into such without destroying the meaning
(Ewald, Hitzig) ; but " poverty and shame is he who is without
correction," is equivalent to, poverty and shame is the conclusion
or lot of him who is without correction ; it is left to the hearer to
find out the reference of the predicate to the subject in the sense
of the quality, the consequence, or the lot (cf. *e.g.* x. 17, xiii. 1,
xiv. 35).[1] Regarding פרע, *vid.* p. 73. The Latin expression
corresponding is : *qui detrectat disciplinam.* He who rejects the
admonition and correction of his parents, his pastor, or his friend,
and refuses every counsel to duty as a burdensome moralizing, such
an one must at last gather wisdom by means of injury if he is at

---

[1] *Vid.* regarding the strong demand which the Hebr. style makes on hearer
and reader, my *Gesch. der jüdischen Poesie* (1863), p. 189.

all wise : he grows poorer in consequence of missing the right rule
of life, and has in addition thereto to be subject to disgrace through
his own fault. On the contrary, to him who has the disgrace to
deserve reproof, but who willingly receives it, and gives it effect,
the disgrace becomes an honour, for not to reject reproof shows
self-knowledge, humility, and good-will; and these properties in
the judgment of others bring men to honour, and have the effect
of raising them in their position in life and in their calling.

Two pairs of proverbs regarding fools and wise men, ranged
together by catchwords.

> Ver. 19 Quickened desire is sweet to the soul,
> And it is an abomination to fools to avoid evil.

A synthetic distich (vid. p. 8), the first line of which, viewed by itself,
is only a feebler expression of that which is said in 12b, for תַּאֲוָה נִהְיָה
is essentially of the same meaning as תַּאֲוָה בָאָה, not the desire that
has just arisen and is not yet appeased (Umbreit, Hitzig, Zöckler),
which when expressed by a *part*. of the same verb would be הֹוֶה
(=אֲשֶׁר הָיְתָה), but the desire that is appeased (Jerome, Luther,
also *Venet*. ἔφεσις γενομένη, *i.e.* after Kimchi : in the fulfilling of
past desire; on the contrary, the Syr., Targ. render the phrase נָאוֶה
of becoming desire). The *Niph*. נִהְיָה denotes not the passing into
a state of being, but the being carried out into historical reality,
e.g. Ezek. xxi. 12, xxxix. 8, where it is connected with באה ; it is
always the expression of the completed fact to which there is a
looking back, *e.g.* Judg. xx. 3 ; and this sense of the *Niph*. stands
so fast, that it even means to be done, finished (brought to an end),
to be out, to be done with anything, *e.g.* Dan. ii. 1.[1] The sentence,
that fulfilled desire does good to the soul, appears commonplace
(Hitzig) ; but it is comprehensive enough on the ground of Heb.
xi. to cheer even a dying person, and conceals the ethically significant truth that the blessedness of vision is measured by the degree
of the longing of faith. But the application of the clause in its

[1] We have said, p. 215, that a *Niph*. in which the peculiar causative meaning of the *Hiph*. would be rendered passively is without example ; we must
here with נהיה add, that the *Niph*. of intransitive verbs denotes the entrance
into the condition expressed by the *Kal*, and may certainly be regarded, according to our way of thinking, as passive of the *Hiphil* (Gesen. § 51, 2). But the
old language shows no הֲוָה to which נִהְיָה (Arab. *âinhaway*, in Mutenebbi)
stood as passive ; in the Arab. also the seventh form, rightly regarded, is always
formed from the first, vid. Fleischer's *Beiträge*, u.s.w., in the *Sitzungs-Bericht*.
d. Sächs. Gesellschaft d. Wiss. 1863, p. 172 f.

pairing with 19*b* acquires another aspect. On this account, because the desire of the soul is pleasant in its fulfilment, fools abhor the renouncing of evil, for their desire is directed to that which is morally worthless and blameworthy, and the endeavour, which they closely and constantly adhere to, is to reach the attainment of this desire. This subordinate proposition of the conclusion is unexpressed. The pairing of the two lines of the proverb may have been occasioned by the resemblance in sound of תּוֹעֲבַת and תִּֽאֲוָה. סוּר is *n. actionis*, like xvi. 17, cf. 6. Besides, it is to be observed that the proverb speaks of fools and not of the godless. Folly is that which causes that men do not break free from evil, for it is the deceit of sinful lust which binds them fast thereto.

> Ver. 20 Whoever goes with wise men, becomes wise;
> And whoever has intercourse with fools, becomes base.

Regarding the significance of this proverb in the history of the religion and worship of Israel, *vid.* p. 39. We have translated 20*a* after the *Kerî;* the translation according to the *Chethîb* is: " go with wise men and become wise" (cf. viii. 33), not הָלוֹךְ, for the connection of the (meant imperatively) *infin. absol.* with an imper. (meant conclusively) is not tenable ; but הֲלוֹךְ is an imper. form established by הִלְכוּ, Jer. li. 50 (cf. הָלוֹךְ=לֶכְת, Num. xxii. 14), and appears to have been used with such shades of conception as here of intercourse and companionship for לְ. Regarding יֵרוֹעַ, *vid.* at xi. 15 ; there it meant *malo afficietur*, here it means *malus* (*pejor*) *fiet*. The *Venet.* (contrary to Kimchi, who explains by *frangetur*) rightly has κακωθήσεται. There is here a play upon words ; רָעָה means to tend (a flock), also in general to be considerate about anything (xv. 14, Isa. xliv. 20), to take care of anything with the accusative of the person (xxviii. 7, xxix. 3), to hold intercourse with any one : he who by preference seeks the society of fools, himself becomes such (Jerome, *similis efficietur*), or rather, as ירוע expresses, he comes always morally lower down. " A wicked companion leads his associate into hell."

> Ver. 21 Evil pursueth sinners,
> And the righteous is repaid with good.

To תְּרַדֵּף of the punishment which follows after sinners at their heels, cf. Nah. i. 8. Greek art gives wings to Nemesis in this sense. To translate 21*b*, with Löwenstein, " The pious, the good rewards them," is untenable, for טוֹב, the good (*e.g.* xi. 27), never appears personified, only טוֹב, goodness, Ps. xxiii. 6, according to

which the LXX. τοὺς δὲ δικαίους καταλήψεται (יֵשִׂיג) ἀγαθά. Still
less is טוב meant personally, as the *Venet.* τὰ δὲ δίκαια ἀποδώσει
χρηστός, which probably means: righteous conduct will a good
one, viz. God, reward. טוב is an attribute of God, but never the
name of God. So the verb יַשְׁלֵם, after the manner of verbs of
educating and leading (גמל, עשׂה, עבד), is connected with a double
accusative. The Syr., Targum, and Jerome translate passively,
and so also do we ; for while we must think of God in the *retribuet,*
yet the proverb does not name Him any more than at xii. 14, cf.
x. 24 ; it is designedly constructed, placing Him in the background,
with vague generality : the righteous will one, will they, reward
with good—this expression, with the most general personal subject,
almost coincides with one altogether passive.

Ver. 22 The good man leaveth behind him for his children's children,
And the wealth of the sinner is laid up for the just.

As a commencing word, טוב signifies in the *Mishle* for the most part
bonum (præ) ; but here, as at xii. 2, cf. xxii. 9, xiv. 4, it signifies
bonus. As the expression that God is טוב (Ps. xxv. 8, etc.) of the
O. T. is equivalent to the N. T. that He is ἀγάπη, so that man who
in his relation to others is determined by unselfish love is טוב for
the good man [*der Gütige*], *i.e.* the man who is willing to communicate all good is truly good, because the essence of צדקה, righteousness of life, is love. Such an one suffers no loss by his liberality,
but, according to the law, xi. 25, by which a dispenser of blessings
is at the same time also a recipient of blessings, he has only gain,
so that he makes his children's children to inherit, *i.e.* leaves behind
him an inheritance extending even to his grandchildren (*vid.* regarding הִנְחִיל, p. 182 ; here trans. as containing its object in itself,
as at Deut. xxxii. 8 : to make to inherit, to place in possession
of an inheritance). The sinner, on the contrary (חוֹטֵא sing. to
חַטָּאִים, ἁμαρτωλοί), loses his wealth, it is already destined to pass
over to the righteous who is worthy of it, and makes use (cf. Job
xxvii. 17) of that which he possesses in accordance with the will
and appointment of God—a revelation of justice appertaining to
time, the exceptions to which the old limited doctrine of requital
takes no notice of. חַיִל, strength, then like our " *Vermögen* " (cf.
opes, facultates), that by means of which one is placed in circumstances to accomplish much (Fl.) ; cf. regarding the fundamental
idea *contorquere, compingere,* p. 226, also regarding צפן, properly
condensare, then *condere,* p. 61.

Connected with ver. 22 there now follow two proverbs regarding sustenance, with one intervening regarding education.

Ver. 23 The poor man's fresh land gives food in abundance,
    And many are destroyed by iniquity.

The Targ. and Theodotion (μέγας) translate רָב, but the Masora has רִב־ with short *Kametz*, as xx. 6, Eccles. i. 8 (cf. Kimchi under רבב). The rendering: *multitudo cibi est ager pauperum*, makes the produce the property of the field (=*frugum fertilis*). נִיר is the new field (*novale* or *novalis*, viz. *ager*), from נָיר, to make arable, fruitful; properly to raise up, viz. by grubbing and freeing of stones (סַקֵּל). But why, asks Hitzig, just the new field? As if no answer could be given to this question, he changes ניר into נִיב, and finds in 23*a* the description of a *rentier*, " a great man who consumes the income of his capital." But how much more intelligible is the new field of the poor man than these capitals (ראֹשִׁים) with their *per cents* (נִיב)! A new field represents to us severe labour, and as belonging to a poor man, a moderate field, of which it is here said, that notwithstanding its freshly broken up fallow, it yet yields a rich produce, viz. by virtue of the divine blessing, for the proverb supposes the *ora et labora*. Regarding רָאשִׁים=רָשִׁים, *vid.* at x. 4. Jerome's translation, *patrum* (properly, heads), follows a false Jewish tradition. In the antithesis, 23*b*, one is tempted to interpret יֵשׁ in the sense of viii. 21 [substance, wealth], as Schultens, *opulentia ipsa raditur quum non est moderamen*, and Euchel: that which is essentially good, badly managed, goes to ruin. But יֵשׁ and וְישׁ at the beginning of a proverb, or of a line of a proverb, in every case means *est qui*. That a wealthy person is meant, the contrast shows. נִסְפֶּה, which denotes anything taken away or gathered up, has the same meaning here as at 1 Sam. xxvii. 1: *est qui* (Fl. *quod*, but the parallel does not demand this) *abripiatur, i.e. quasi turbine auferatur et perdatur;* the word reminds us of סוּפָה, whirlwind, but in itself it means only something smooth and altogether carried off. The בְּ is here as at Gen. xix. 15; elsewhere בְּלֹא מִשְׁפָּט means with injustice (properly, not-right), xvi. 8, Jer. xxii. 13, Ezek. xxii. 29; here it is not the ב of the means, but of the mediate cause. While the (industrious and God-fearing) poor man is richly nourished from the piece of ground which he cultivates, many a one who has incomparably more than he comes by his unrighteousness down to a state of beggary, or even lower: he is not only in poverty, but along with this his honour, his freedom, and the very life of his person perish.

Ver. 24 He that spareth his rod hateth his son,
And he who loveth him visits him early with correction.

The pædagogic rule of God, iii. 12, avails also for men, xxiii. 13 f.,
xxix. 15. The rod represents here the means of punishment, the
patria potestas. He who spareth or avoideth this, and who does this
even from love, has yet no true right love for his son; he who loveth
him correcteth him early. With ἐπιμελῶς παιδεύει of the LXX.
(cf. Sir. xxx. 1, ἐνδελεχήσει μάστιγας) the thought is in general
indicated, but the expression is not explained. Many erroneously
regard the suffix of שִׁחֲרוֹ as referring to the object immediately following (de Dieu, Ewald, Bertheau, Zöckler); Hitzig, on the contrary, rightly remarks, that in this case we should expect the words
to be, after v. 22 (cf. Ex. ii. 6), אֶת־הַמּוּסָר. He himself, without any
necessity, takes שִׁחֵר in the sense of the Arab. *skhar, compescere.*
Hofmann (*Schriftbew.* ii. 2. 402) is right in saying that "שִׁחֵר is
connected with a double accusative as elsewhere קִדֵּם occurs; and
the meaning is, that one ought much more to anticipate correction
than restrain it where it is necessary." שִׁחֵר means to go out early
to anything (*vid.* p. 73), according to which a Greek rendering is
ὀρθρίζει (*Venet.* ὀρθριεῖ) αὐτῷ παιδείαν : *maturat ei castigationem =
mature eum castigat* (Fl.). שִׁחַר does not denote the early morning
of the day (as Rashi, לבקרים), but the morning of life (as Euchel,
בשחר ימיו). "The earlier the fruit, the better the training." A
father who truly wishes well to his son keeps him betimes under
strict discipline, to give him while he is yet capable of being
influenced the right direction, and to allow no errors to root themselves in him; but he who is indulgent toward his child when he
ought to be strict, acts as if he really wished his ruin.

Ver. 25 The righteous has to eat to the satisfying of his soul;
But the body of the godless must suffer want.

Jerome translates תחסר freely by *insaturabilis* (he has want = has
never enough), but in that case we would have expected תֶּחְסַר תָּמִיד;
also in 25a עַד־שֹּׂבַע would have been used. We have thus before
us no commendation of temperance and moderation in contrast to
gluttony, but a statement regarding the diversity of fortune of the
righteous and the godless—another way of clothing the idea of
x. 3. שֹׂבַע is a segolate form, thus an infin. formation, formally
different from the similar שָׂבָע, iii. 10. Regarding בֶּטֶן, *vid. Psychol.*
p. 265 f.; it is a nobler word than "*Bauch*" [belly], for it denotes
not the external arch, but, like κοιλία (R. בט, *concavus*), the inner

body, here like xviii. 20, as that which receives the nourishment and changes it *in succum et sanguinem*. That God richly nourishes the righteous, and on the contrary brings the godless to want and misery, is indeed a rule with many exceptions, but understood in the light of the N. T., it has deep inward everlasting truth.

Chap. xiv. The division of chapters here corresponds to a new commencement made in ver. 1. This proverb reminds us of the allegorical conclusion of the Introduction, and appears, since it is older, to have suggested it (*vid.* p. 34). The three proverbs 1–3 form a beautiful *trifolium*: wise mangement, God-fearing conduct, and wise silence, with their threefold contraries.

> Ver. 1 The wisdom of the woman buildeth her house,
> And folly teareth it down with its own hands.

Were it חַכְמוֹת נָשִׁים, after. Judg. v. 29, cf. Isa. xix. 11, then the meaning would be : the wise among women, each of them buildeth her house. But why then not just אִשָּׁה חֲכָמָה, as 2 Sam. xiv. 2, cf. Ex. xxxv. 25 ? The Syr., Targum, and Jerome write *sapiens mulier*. And if the whole class must be spoken of, why again immediately the individualizing in בֵּיתָהּ? The LXX. obliterates that by its ᾠκοδόμησαν. And does not אִוֶּלֶת [folly] in the contrasted proverb (1*b*) lead us to conclude on a similar abstract in 1*a*? The translators conceal this, for they translate אולת personally. Thus also the *Venet.* and Luther; אִוֶּלֶת is, says Kimchi, an adj. like עִוֶּרֶת, *cœca*. But the linguistic usage does not point אֱוִיל with אֱוִילְי to any אֱוִל. It is true that a fem. of אֱוִיל does not occur; there is, however, also no place in which אולת may certainly present itself as such. Thus also חכמות must be an abstr.; we have shown at i. 20 how חַכְמוֹת, as neut. plur., might have an abstr. meaning. But since it is not to be perceived why the poet should express himself so singularly, the punctuation חַכְמוֹת is to be understood as proceeding from a false supposition, and is to be read חָכְמוֹת, as at ix. 1 (especially since this passage rests on the one before us). Fleischer says : " to build the house is figuratively equivalent to, to regulate well the affairs of a house, and to keep them in a good condition ; the contrary, to tear down the house, is the same contrast as the Arab. '*amârat âlbyt* and *kharab albyt*. Thus *e.g.* in Burckhardt's *Sprüchw.* 217, *harrt ṣabrt bythâ 'amârat*, a good woman (*ein braves Weib*) has patience (with her husband), and thereby she builds up her house (at the same time an example of the use of the preterite in like general sentences for individual-

izing); also No. 430 of the same work: *'amârat âlbyt wla kharâbt,*
it is becoming to build the house, not to destroy it; cf. in the
Thousand and One Nights, where a woman who had compelled her
husband to separate from her says: *âna âlty 'amalt hadhâ barwhy
wâkhrnt byty bnfsy.* Burckhardt there makes the remark: *'amârat
âlbyt* denotes the family placed in good circumstances—father,
mother, and children all living together happily and peacefully."
This conditional relation of the wife to the house expresses itself
in her being named as house-wife (cf. *Hausehre* [= honour of a
house] used by Luther, Ps. lxviii. 13), to which the Talmudic דְּבֵיתִי
(= *uxor mea*) answers; the wife is noted for this, and hence is called
עִיקַר הבית, the root and foundation of the house; *vid.* Buxtorf's *Lex.*
col. 301. In truth, the oneness of the house is more dependent on
the mother than on the father. A wise mother can, if her husband
be dead or neglectful of his duty, always keep the house together;
but if the house-wife has neither understanding nor good-will for
her calling, then the best will of the house-father cannot hinder
the dissolution of the house, prudence and patience only conceal
and mitigate the process of dissolution—folly, viz. of the house-
wife, always becomes more and more, according to the degree in
which this is a caricature of her calling, the ruin of the house.

> Ver. 2 He walketh in his uprightness who feareth Jahve,
> And perverse in his ways is he that despiseth Him.

That which syntactically lies nearest is also that which is intended;
the ideas standing in the first place are the predicates. Wherein it
shows itself, and whereby it is recognised, that a man fears God,
or stands in a relation to Him of indifference instead of one of
fear and reverence, shall be declared: the former walketh in his
uprightness, *i.e.* so far as the consciousness of duty which animates
him prescribes; the latter in his conduct follows no higher rule than
his own lust, which drives him sometimes hither and sometimes
thither. הֹלֵךְ בְּיֻשְׁרוֹ (cf. יֻשַׁר הֹלֵךְ, Mic. ii. 7) is of kindred meaning
with הוֹלֵךְ בְּתֻמּוֹ, xxviii. 6 (הֹלֵךְ בַּתּוֹם, x. 9), and הֹלֵךְ נְכֹחוֹ, Isa. lvii. 2.
The connection of נְלוֹז דְּרָכָיו follows the scheme of 2 Kings xviii.
37, and not 2 Sam. xv. 32, Ewald, § 288*c*. If the second word,
which particularizes the idea of the first, has the reflexive suff. as
here, then the accusative connection, or, as ii. 15, the prepositional,
is more usual than the genitive. Regarding לז, *flectere, inclinare*
(a word common to the author of i.–ix.), *vid.* at ii. 15. With

בּוֹזְהוּ, cf. 1 Sam. ii. 30; the suffix without doubt refers to God, for בוזהו is the word that stands in parallel contrast to יְרֵא ה'.

Ver. 3 In the mouth of the fool is a switch of pride;
But the lips of the wise preserve them.

The noun חֹטֶר (Aram. חוּטְרָא, Arab. khitr), which besides here occurs only at Isa. xi. 1, meaning properly a brandishing (from חָטַר=Arab. khatr, to brandish, to move up and down or hither and thither, whence âlkhttâr, the brandisher, poet. the spear), concretely, the young elastic twig, the switch, i.e. the slender flexible shoot. Luther translates, "fools speak tyrannically," which is the briefer rendering of his earlier translation, "in the mouth of the fool is the sceptre of pride;" but although the Targum uses חוטרא of the king's sceptre and also of the prince's staff, yet here for this the usual Hebr. שֵׁבֶט were to be expected. In view of Isa. xi. 1, the nearest idea is, that pride which has its roots in the heart of the fool, grows up to his mouth. But yet it is not thus explained why the representation of this proceeding from within stops with חֹטֶר (cf. xi. 30). The βακτηρία ὕβρεως (LXX., and similarly the other Greek versions) is either meant as the rod of correction of his own pride (as e.g. Abulwalîd, and, among the moderns, Bertheau and Zöckler) or as chastisement for others (Syr., Targum: the staff of reviling). Hitzig is in favour of the former idea, and thinks himself warranted in translating: a rod for his back; but while גֵּוָה is found for גַּאֲוָה, we do not (cf. under Job xli. 7: a pride are the, etc.) find גאוה for גוה, the body, or גַּו, the back. But in general it is to be assumed, that if the poet had meant חטר as the means of correction, he would have written גַּאֲותוֹ. Rightly Fleischer: "The tongue is often compared to a staff, a sword, etc., in so far as their effects are ascribed to it; we have here the figure which in Rev. i. 16 passes over into plastic reality." Self-exaltation (R. גא, to strive to be above) to the delusion of greatness is characteristic of the fool, the אֱוִיל [godless], not the כְּסִיל [stupid, dull]—Hitzig altogether confounds these two conceptions. With such self-exaltation, in which the mind, morally if not pathologically diseased, says, like Nineveh and Babylon in the prophets, I am alone, and there is no one with me, there is always united the scourge of pride and of disgrace; and the meaning of 3b may now be that the lips of the wise protect those who are exposed to this injury (Ewald), or that they protect the wise themselves against such assaults (thus most interpreters).

But this reference of the *eos* to others lies much more remote than
at xii. 6; and that the protection of the wise against injury inflicted
on them by words is due to their own lips is unsatisfactory, as in
this case, instead of *Bewahrung* [*custodia*], we would rather expect
Vertheidigung [*defensio*], *Dämpfung* [damping, extinguishing], *Nie-
derduckung* [stooping down, accommodating oneself to circum-
stances]. But also it cannot be meant that the lips of the wise
preserve them from the pride of fools, for the thought that the
mouth preserves the wise from the sins of the mouth is without
meaning and truth (cf. the contrary, xiii. 3). Therefore Arama
interprets the verb as jussive : the lips = words of the wise mayest
thou keep, *i.e.* take to heart. And the *Venet.* translates : χείλη δὲ
σοφῶν φυλάξεις αὐτά, which perhaps means : the lips of the wise
mayest thou consider, and that not as a prayer, which is foreign to
the gnome, but as an address to the hearer, which *e.g.* xx. 19 shows
to be admissible. But although in a certain degree of similar con-
tents, yet 3*a* and 3*b* clash. Therefore it appears to us more probable that the subject of 3*b* is the חכמה contained in חכמים; in vi.
22 wisdom is also the subject to תשמר עליך without its being
named. Thus: while hurtful pride grows up to the throat of the
fool, that, viz. wisdom, keeps the lips of the wise, so that no word
of self-reflection, especially none that can wound a neighbour,
escapes from them. The form תִּשְׁמוּרֵם is much more peculiar than
יִשְׁפּוּטוּ, Ex. xviii. 26, and תַעֲבוּרִי, Ruth ii. 8, for the latter are obscured forms of יִשְׁפֹּטוּ and תַעֲבְרִי, while on the contrary the former
arises from תִּשְׁמְרֵם.[1] If, according to the usual interpretation, we
make שפתי the subject, then the construction follows the rule,
Gesen. § 146, 2. The LXX. transfers it into Greek : χείλη δὲ
σοφῶν φυλάσσει αὐτούς. The probable conjecture, that תשמורם is
an error in transcription for תִּשְׁמֹרֵנָה אֹתָם = תִּשְׁמְרוּם (this is found
also in Luzzatto's *Gramm.* § 776; and Hitzig adduces as other
examples of such transpositions of the ו Jer. ii. 25, xvii. 23, Job
xxvi. 12, and Josh ii. 4, ותצפנו for ותצפון), we do not acknowledge,
because it makes the lips the subject with an exclusiveness the
justification of which is doubtful to us.

---

[1] *Vid.* regarding these forms with *ŏ* instead of the simple *Sheva*, Kimchi,
Michlol 20*ab*. He also remarks that these three forms with *û* are all *Milra*;
this is the case also in a remarkable manner with יִשְׁפּוּטוּ, *vid. Michlol* 21*b*;
Livjath Chen ii. 9; and particularly Heidenheim, in his edition of the Pentateuch entitled *Meôr Enajim*, under Ex. xviii. 26.

Ver. 4. The switch and the preserving, ver. 3, may have given occasion to the collector, amid the store of proverbs before him, now to present the agricultural figure:

> Without oxen the crib is empty;
> But rich increase is by the strength of the plough-ox.

This is a commendation of the breeding of cattle, but standing here certainly not merely as useful knowledge, but as an admonition to the treatment in a careful, gentle manner, and with thankful recompense of the ox (xii. 10), which God has subjected to man to help him in his labour, and more generally, in so far as one seeks to gain an object, to the considerate adoption of the right means for gaining it. אֲלָפִים (from אָלַף, to cling to) are the cattle giving themselves willingly to the service of men (poet. equivalent to בְּקָרִים). שׁוֹר (תּוֹר, Arab. *thwr*), Ved. *sthûras*, is the Aryan-Semitic name of the plough-ox. The noun אֵבוּס (= אֲבוּס like אֵטוּן, אֵמוּן) denotes the fodder-trough, from אָבַס, to feed, and thus perhaps as to its root-meaning related to φάτνη (πάτνη), and may thus also designate the receptacle for grain where the corn for the provender or feeding of the cattle is preserved—מֵאֲבוּס, Jer. l. 26, at least has this wider signification of the granary; but there exists no reason to depart here from the nearest signification of the word: if a husbandman is not thoughtful about the care and support of the cattle by which he is assisted in his labour, then the crib is empty—he has nothing to heap up; he needs not only fodder, but has also nothing. בַּר (in pause בָּר), clean (synon. נָקִי, cf. at xi. 26), corresponds with our *baar* [bare] = *bloss* [*nudus*]. Its derivation is obscure. The בְּ, 4*b*, is that of the mediating cause: by the strength of the plough-ox there is a fulness of grain gathered into the barn (תְּבוּאוֹת, from בּוֹא, to gather in, anything gathered in). רַב־ is the inverted בַּר. Striking if also accidental is the frequency of the א and ב in ver. 4. This is continued in ver. 5, where the collector gives two proverbs, the first of which commences with a word beginning with א, and the second with one beginning with ב:

> Ver. 5 A faithful witness does not speak untruth;
> But a lying witness breathes out falsehoods.

The right vocalization and sequence of the accents is בִּקֶּשׁ־לֵץ חָכְמָה (ק with *Tsere* and the servile *Mahpach*, חכמה with *Munach*, because the following *Athnach*-word has not two syllables before the tone). As in 5*a* עֵד אֱמוּנִים, so in 5*b* עֵד שֶׁקֶר is the subject. Different is the relation of subject and predicate in the second line of the

parallel proverbs, ver. 25, xix. 5. With 5a cf. צִיר אֱמוּנִים, xiii. 17 ;
and regarding יָפִיחַ (one who breathes out), vid. at vi. 19, xii. 17.

Ver. 6 In vain the scorner seeketh wisdom ;
But to the man of understanding knowledge is easy.

The general sentence is concrete, composed in the common historical
form. Regarding וָאַיִן, necquidquam, vid. at xiii. 4. The participle
נָקֵל is here neut. for נְקַלָּה, something which makes itself easy or
light. The frivolous man, to whom truth is not a matter of conscience, and who recognises no authority, not even the Supreme,
never reaches to truth notwithstanding all his searching, it remains
veiled to him and far remote ; but to the man of understanding,
who knows that the fear of God and not estrangement from God
leads to truth, knowledge is an easy matter—he enters on the right
way to this end, he brings the right receptivity, brings to bear on
it the clear eye, and there is fulfilled to him the saying, " To him
that hath it is given."

Three proverbs regarding fools :

Ver. 7 Go from the presence of a foolish man,
And surely thou hast not known lips of knowledge ;

i.e. surely hast not brought into experience that he possesses lips
which express experimental knowledge, or : surely thou must confess
on reflection that no prudent word has come forth from his mouth.
If 7b were intended to assign a motive, then the expression would
be כִּי בַל־תֵּדַע or וּבַל־תֵּדַע (Isa. xliv. 9), according to which Aquila
and Theodotion translate, καὶ οὐ μὴ γνῷς. נֶגֶד is the sphere of
vision, and מִנֶּגֶד denotes either away from the sphere of vision, as
e.g. Isa. i. 16, or, inasmuch as מִן is used as in מֵעַל, מִתַּחַת, and the
like : at a certain distance from the sphere of vision, but so that
one keeps the object in sight, Gen. xxi. 16. נֶגֶד לְ denotes, as the
inverted expression Deut. xxviii. 66 shows, over against any one,
so that he has the object visibly before him, and מִנֶּגֶד לְ ?, Judg. xx.
34, from the neighbourhood of a place where one has it in view.
So also here : go away from the vis-à-vis (vis = visûs) of the foolish
man, if thou hast to do with such an one ; whence, 7b, follows what
he who has gone away must on looking back say to himself. בל
(with the pret. as e.g. Isa. xxxiii. 23) expresses a negative with
emphasis. Nolde and others, also Fleischer, interpret 7b relatively :
et in quo non cognoveris labia scientiæ. If וּבַל־יָדַע were the expression used, then it would be explained after ix. 13, for the idea of
the foolish man is extended : and of such an one as absolutely

knows not how to speak anything prudent. But in וּבַל־יָדַעְתָּ the
relative clause intended must be indicated by the added בּוֹ : and of
such an one in whom ... Besides, in this case וְלֹא (vid. Ps. xxxv. 15)
would have been nearer than וּבַל. The LXX. has modified this
proverb, and yet has brought out nothing that is correct; not only
the Syr., but also Hitzig follows it, when he translates, " The foolish
man hath everything before him, but lips of knowledge are a
receptacle of knowledge" (וּכְלִי דַעַת). It racks one's brains to find
out the meaning of the first part here, and, as Böttcher rightly
says, who can be satisfied with the " lips of knowledge" as the
"receptacle of knowledge"?

Ver. 8 The wisdom of the prudent is to observe his way,

And the folly of fools is deceit.

The nearest idea is that of self-deceit, according to which the
LXX., Syr., and Jerome render the word error (" Irrsal"). But
מִרְמָה is nowhere else used of self-deception, and moreover is not
the suitable word for such an idea, since the conception of the *dolus
malus* is constantly associated with it. Thus the contrast will be
this: the wisdom of the prudent shows itself in this, that he considers
his conduct (הָבִין as vii. 7, cf. Ps. v. 2), *i.e.* regulates it carefully,
examining and considering (xiii. 16) it according to right and duty ;
and that on the contrary the folly of fools shows itself in this, that
they aim at the malevolent deception of their neighbour, and try
all kinds of secret ways for the gaining of this end. The former
is wisdom, because from the good only good comes; the latter is
folly or madness, because deception, however long it may sneak in
darkness, yet at last comes to light, and recoils in its destructive
effects upon him from whom it proceeds.

Ver. 9 The sacrificial offering of fools mocketh ;

But between upright men there is good understanding.

We may not give to the *Hiph.* יָלִיץ any meaning which it nowhere
has, as, to excuse (Kimchi), or to come to an agreement by mediation (Schultens). So we may not make אֱוִילִים the subject (Targ.,
Symmachus, Jerome, Luther, " fools make sport with sin "), for
one is persuaded that אוילים is equivalent to כל אחד מן האוילים
(Immanuel, Meiri, and others), which would be more admissible if
we had מֵלִיץ (vid. iii. 35), or if יָלִיץ did not immediately follow (vid.
xxviii. 1). Aquila and Theodotion rightly interpret the relation of
the component parts of the sentence: ἄφρονας χλευάζει πλημμέλεια ;
and this translation of אָשָׁם also is correct if we take πλημμέλεια in

the sense of a θυσία περὶ πλημμελείας (Sir. vii. 31), in which the Judæo-Hellenic actually uses it (*vid.* Schleusner's *Lex.*). The idea of sacrificial offering is that of expiation: it is a penitential work, it falls under the prevailing point of view of an ecclesiastical punishment, a *satisfactio* in a church-disciplinary sense; the forgiveness of sins is conditioned by this, (1) that the sinner either abundantly makes good by restitution the injury inflicted on another, or in some other way bears temporal punishment for it, and (2) that he willingly presents the sacrifices of rams or of sheep, the value of which the priest has to determine in its relation to the offence (by a tax-scale from 2 shekels upwards). The *Torâ* gives accurately the offences which are thus to be atoned for. Here, with reference to 9b, there particularly comes into view the offence against property (Lev. v. 20 ff.) and against female honour (Lev. xix. 20–22). Fools fall from one offence into another, which they have to atone for by the presentation of sacrificial offerings; the sacrificial offering mocketh them (הליץ with *accus.-object*, as xix. 28, Ps. cxix. 51), for it equally derides them on account of the self-inflicted loss, and on account of the efforts with which they must make good the effects of their frivolity and madness; while on the contrary, among men of upright character, רָצוֹן, a relation of mutual favour, prevails, which does not permit that the one give to the other an indemnity, and apply the *Asham-* [אָשָׁם = trespass-offering] *Torâ*. Symmachus rightly: καὶ ἀνάμεσον εὐθέων εὐδοκία. But the LXX. confuses this proverb also. Hitzig, with the Syr., follows it and translates:

> The tents of the foolish are in punishment overthrown [*verfällt*];
> The house of the upright is well-pleasing [*wolgefällt*].

Is not this extravagant [*ungereimt* = not rhymed] in spite of the rhyme? These אהלי [tents] extracted from אוילים, and this בית [house] formed out of בין, are nothing but an aimless and tasteless flourish.

Four proverbs of joy and sorrow in the present and the future:

> Ver. 10 The heart knoweth the trouble of its soul,
> And no stranger can intermeddle with its joy.

The accentuation לֵב יֹודֵעַ seems to point out יודע as an adjective (Löwenstein: a feeling heart), after 1 Kings iii. 9, or genit. (of a feeling heart); but Cod. 1294 and the Jemen Cod., and others, as well as the editions of Jablonsky and Michaelis, have לֵב with *Rebia*, so that this is by itself to be taken as the subject (cf. the accentuation xv. 5a and under at 16a). מָרַת has the ר with *Dagesh*, and consequently the short *Kametz* (*Michlol* 63*b*), like שָׁרֵךְ iii. 8, cf. בִּרְתָה, Judg. vi. 28, and on the contrary כַּתַּת, Ezek. xvi. 4 ; it is the fem. of *mōr* = *morr*, from מָרַר, *adstringere, amarum esse*. Regarding לֵב, in contradistinction to נֶפֶשׁ, *vid. Psychol.* p. 251. " All that is meant by the Hellenic and Hellenistic νοῦς, λόγος, συνεί-δησις, θυμός, is comprehended in καρδία, and all by which the בָּשָׂר and נֶפֶשׁ are affected comes in לֵב into the light of consciousness."

The first half of the proverb is clear : the heart, and only it, *i.e.* the man in the centre of his individuality, knows what brings bitterness to his soul, *i.e.* what troubles him in the sphere of his natural life and of the nearest life-circle surrounding him. It thus treats of life experiences which are of too complex a nature to be capable of being fully represented to others, and, as we are wont to say, of so delicate a nature that we shrink from uncovering them and making them known to others, and which on this account must be kept shut up in our own hearts, because no man is so near to us, or has so fully gained our confidence, that we have the desire and the courage to pour out our hearts to him from their very depths. Yet the saying, " Every one knows where the shoe pinches him" (1 Kings viii. 38), stands nearer to this proverb ; here this expression receives a psychological, yet a sharper and a deeper expression, for the knowledge of that which grieves the soul is attributed to the heart, in which, as the innermost of the soul-corporeal life, it reflects itself and becomes the matter-of-fact of the reflex consciousness in which it must shut itself up, but also for the most part without external expression. If we now interpret לֹא־יִתְעָרַב as prohibitive, then this would stand (with this exception, that in this case אַל instead of לֹא is to be expected) in opposition, certainly not intended, to the exhortation, Rom. xii. 15, " Rejoice with them that do rejoice," and to the saying, " Distributed joy is doubled joy, distributed sorrow is half sorrow ; " and an admonition to leave man alone with his joy, instead of urging him to distribute it, does not run parallel with 10*a*. Therefore we interpret the fut. as *potentialis*. As there is a soul-sorrow of the man whose experience is merely a matter of the heart, so there is also a soul-joy with which no other (*vid.* regarding זָר, p. 135, and cf. here particularly Job xix. 27) intermeddleth (התערב בְּ like Ps. cvi. 35), in which no other can intermeddle, because his experience, as *e.g.* of blessed spiritual affection or of benevolent feeling, is purely of a personal nature, and admits of no participation (cf. on ἔκρυψε, Matt. xiii. 44), and thus of no communication to others. Elster well observes: " By this thought, that the innermost feelings of a man are never fully imparted to another man, never perfectly cover themselves with the feelings of another, yea, cannot at all be fully understood by another, the worth and the significance of each separate human personality is made conspicuous, not one of which is the example of a species, but each has its own peculiarity, which no one of countless individuals possesses. At the same time the proverb has the significance, that it shows the impossibility of a perfect fellow-ship among men, because one never wholly understands another. Thereby it is indicated that no human fellowship can give true salvation, but only the fellowship with God, whose love and wisdom are capable of shining through the most secret sanctuary of human personality." Thus also Dächsel (but he interprets 10b admoni-torily) : " Each man is a little world in himself, which God only fully sees through and understands. His sorrow appertaining to his innermost life, and his joy, another is never able fully to transfer to himself. Yea, the most sorrowful of all experiences, the most inward of all joys, we possess altogether alone, without any to participate with us."

Ver. 11 The house of the wicked is overthrown ;
But the tent of the upright flourishes.

In the cogn. proverb, xii. 7, line 2 begins with וּבֵית, but here the apparently firmly-founded house is assigned to the godless, and on the contrary the tent, easily destroyed, and not set up under the delusion of lasting for ever, is assigned to the righteous. While the former is swept away without leaving a trace behind (Isa. xiv. 23), the latter has blossoms and shoots (הַפְרִיחַ as inwardly transi-tive, like Job xiv. 9, Ps. xcii. 14) ; the household of such remains not only preserved in the same state, but in a prosperous, happy manner it goes forward and upward.

Ver. 12 There is a way that seemeth right to one,
But the end thereof are the ways of death.

This is literally repeated in xvi. 25. The rightness is present only as a phantom, for it arises wholly from a terrible self-deception ; the man judges falsely and goes astray when, without regard to God and His word, he follows only his own opinions. It is the way of estrangement from God, of fleshly security; the way of vice, in which the blinded thinks to spend his life, to set himself to fulfil his purposes ; but the end thereof (אַחֲרִיתָהּ with neut.

fem.: the end of this intention, that in which it issues) are the ways of death. He who thus deceives himself regarding his course of life, sees himself at last arrived at a point from which every way which now further remains to him leads only down to death. The self-delusion of one ends in death by the sentence of the judge, that of another in self-murder; of one in loathsome disease, of another in a slow decay under the agony of conscience, or in sorrow over a henceforth dishonoured and distracted life.

Ver. 13 Even in the midst of laughter the heart experiences sadness;
And to it, joy, the end is sorrow.

Every human heart carries the feeling of disquiet and of separation from its true home, and of the nothingness, the transitoriness of all that is earthly; and in addition to this, there is many a secret sorrow in every one which grows out of his own corporeal and spiritual life, and from his relation to other men; and this sorrow, which is from infancy onward the lot of the human heart, and which more and more deepens and diversifies itself in the course of life, makes itself perceptible even in the midst of laughter, in spite of the mirth and merriment, without being able to be suppressed or expelled from the soul, returning always the more intensely, the more violently we may have for a time kept it under and sunk it in unconsciousness. Euchel cites here the words of the poet, according to which 13a is literally true:

" No, man is not made for joy;
Why weep his eyes when in heart he laughs?"[1]

From the fact that sorrow is the fundamental condition of humanity, and forms the background of laughter, it follows, 13b, that in general it is not good for man to give himself up to joy, viz. sensual (worldly), for to it, joy, the end (the issue) is sorrow. That is true also of the final end, which according to that saying, μακάριοι οἱ κλαίοντες νῦν ὅτι γελάσετε, changes laughter into weeping, and weeping into laughter. The correction אַחֲרִית הַשִּׂמְחָה (Hitzig) presses upon the Mishle style an article in such cases rejected, and removes a form of expression of the Hebr. syntaxis ornata, which here, as at Isa. xvii. 6, is easily obviated, but which is warranted by a multitude of other examples, vid. at xiii. 4 (also v. 22), and cf. Philippi's Status Const. p. 14 f., who regards the second word, as here שׂמחה, after the Arab., as accus. But in cases like שְׂנֵאִי

---

[1] " Nein, der Mensch ist zur Freude nicht gemacht,
Darum weint sein Aug' wenn er herzlich lacht."

שֶׁקֶּר, although not in cases such as Ezra ii. 62, the accus. rendering is tenable, and the Arab. does not at all demand it.[1] In the old Hebr. this *solutio* of the *st. constr.* belongs to the elegances of the language; it is the precursor of the vulgar post-bibl. אַחֲרִיתָהּ שֶׁל־שִׂמְחָה. That the Hebr. may also retain a gen. where more or fewer parts of a sentence intervene between it and its governing word, is shown by such examples as Isa. xlviii. 9, xlix. 7, lxi. 7.[2]

There follows a series of proverbs which treat of the wicked and the good, and of the relation between the foolish and the wise:

> Ver. 14 He that is of a perverse heart is satisfied with his own ways;
> And a good man from himself.

We first determine the subject conception. סוּג לֵב (one turning aside τῆς καρδίας or τὴν καρδίαν) is one whose heart is perverted, נָסוֹג, turned away, viz. from God, Ps. xliv. 19. The Book of Proverbs contains besides of this verb only the name of dross (*recedanea*) derived from it; סוּג, separated, drawn away, is such a half passive as סוּר, Isa. xlix. 21, שׁוּב, Mic. ii. 8, etc. (Olsh. § 245a). Regarding אִישׁ טוֹב, *vid.* at xii. 2, cf. xiii. 22: a man is so called whose manner of thought and of action has as its impulse and motive self-sacrificing love. When it is said of the former that he is satisfied with his own ways, viz. those which with heart turned away from God he enters upon, the meaning is not that they give him peace or bring satisfaction to him (Löwenstein), but we see from i. 31, xviii. 20, that this is meant recompensatively: he gets, enjoys the reward of his wandering in estrangement from God. It is now without doubt seen that 14b expresses that wherein the benevolent man finds his reward. We will there-

---

[1] Regarding the supplying (*ibdâl*) of a foregoing genitive or accus. pronoun of the third person by a definite or indefinite following, in the same case as the substantive, Samachschari speaks in the *Mufassal*, p. 94 ss., where, as examples, are found: *raeituhu Zeidan*, I have seen him, the Zeid; *marartu bihi Zeidin*, I have gone over with him, the Zeid; *saraftu wugûhahâ awwalihâ*, in the flight I smote the heads of the same, their front rank. *Vid.* regarding this anticipation of the definite idea by an indefinite, with explanations of it, Fleischer's *Makkari*, *Additions et Corrections*, p. xl. col. 2, and Dieterici's *Mutanabbi*, p. 341, l. 13.

[2] These examples moreover do not exceed that which is possible in the Arab., *vid.* regarding this omission of the *mudâf*, where this is supplied from the preceding before a genitive, Samachschari's *Mufassal*, p. 34, l. 8–13. Perhaps לְחֻמֶךָ, Obad. ver. 7, of thy bread = the (men) of thy bread, is an example of the same thing.

fore not explain (after iv. 15, cf. Num. xvi. 26, 2 Sam. xix. 10) :
the good man turns himself away from him, or the good man
stands over him (as Jerome, *Venet.*, after Eccles. v. 7) ;—this rendering gives no contrast, or at least a halting one. The מִן of מֵעֲלָיו
must be parallel with that of מִדְּרָכָיו. From the LXX., ἀπὸ δὲ
τῶν διανοημάτων αὐτοῦ, the Syr. rightly : from the fruit (religiousness) of his soul ; the Targ. : from his fruit. Buxtorf, against
Cappellus, has already perceived that here no other phrase but
the explanation of מעליו by *ex eo quod penes se est* lies at the foundation. We could, after vii. 14, also explain : from that which he
perceives as his obligation (duty) ; yet that other explanation lies
proportionally nearer, but yet not so that we refer the suffix to the
blackslider of 14*a* : in it (his fate) the good man is satisfied, for
this contrast also halts, the thought is not in the spirit of the
Book of Proverbs (for xxix. 16*b* does not justify it) ; and in how
totally different a connection of thought מֵעֲלָיו is used in the Book of
Proverbs, is shown by xxiv. 17*b* ; but generally the Scripture does
not use שׂבע of such satisfaction, it has, as in 14*a*, also in 14*b*, the
recompensative sense, according to the fundamental principle, ὃ ἐὰν
σπείρῃ ἄνθρωπος τοῦτο καὶ θερίσει (Gal. vi. 7). The suffix refers
back to the subject, as we say : נַפְשִׁי עָלַי, רוּחִי עָלַי (*Psychol.* p. 152).
But considerations of an opposite kind also suggest themselves.
Everywhere else מעל refers not to that which a man has within
himself, but that which he carries without ; and also that מֵעֲלָיו can
be used in the sense of מִשֶּׁעָלָיו, no evidence can be adduced : it
must be admitted to be possible, since the writer of the Chronicles
(2 Chron. i. 4) ventures to use בְּהָכִין. Is מעליו thus used substantively : by his leaves (Aben Ezra and others) ? If one compares xi. 28 with Ps. i. 3, this explanation is not absurd ; but why
then did not the poet rather use מִפִּרְיוֹ ? We come finally to the
result, that וּמֵעָלָיו, although it admits a connected interpretation, is
an error of transcription. But the correction is not וּמֵעַלָיו (Elster)
nor וּמֵעֲלָלָיו (Cappellus), for עַלִּים and עֲלִּים, deeds, are words which do
not exist ; nor is it וּמִפְעָלָיו (Bertheau) nor וּמִגְּמֻלָיו (Ewald), but
וּמִמַּעֲלָלָיו (which Cappellus regarded, but erroneously, as the LXX.
phrase) ; for (1) throughout almost the whole O. T., from Judg. ii.
19 to Zech. i. 18, דרכים and מעללים are interchangeable words, and
indeed almost an inseparable pair, cf. particularly Jer. xvii. 10 ; and
(2) when Isaiah (iii. 10) says, אִמְרוּ צַדִּיק כִּי־טוֹב כִּי־פְרִי מַעַלְלֵיהֶם יֹאכֵלוּ,
this almost sounds like a prophetical paraphrase of the second line

of the proverb, which besides by this emendation gains a more
rhythmical sound and a more suitable compass.[1]

Ver. 15 The simple believeth every word ;
But the prudent takes heed to his step.

We do not translate, " every thing," for " word " and faith are
correlates, Ps. cvi. 24, and פְּתִי is the non-self-dependent who lets
himself be easily persuaded by the talk of another (vid. p. 56) : he
believes every word without proving it, whether it is well-meant,
whether it is true, whether it is salutary and useful, so that he is
thus, without having any firm principle, and without any judgment
of his own, driven about hither and thither; the prudent, on the
other hand, considers and marks his step, that he may not take a false
step or go astray, he proves his way (8a), he takes no step without
thought and consideration (בִּין or הֵבִין with לְ, to consider or reflect
upon anything, Ps. lxxiii. 17, cf. xxxiii. 15)—he makes sure steps
with his feet (Heb. xii. 13), without permitting himself to waver
and sway by every wind of doctrine (Eph. iv. 14).

Ver. 16 The wise feareth and departeth from evil ;
But the fool loseth his wits and is regardless.

Our editions have יָרֵא with Munach, as if חָכָם יָרֵא were a substantive
with its adjective; but Cod. 1294 has חָכָם with Rebia, and thus it
must be : חכם is the subject, and what follows is its complex predicate. Most interpreters translate 16b : the fool is over-confident
(Zöckler), or the fool rushes on (Hitzig), as also Luther : but a fool
rushes wildly through, i.e. in a daring, presumptuous manner. But
הִתְעַבֵּר denotes everywhere nothing else than to fall into extreme
anger, to become heated beyond measure, xxvi. 17 (cf. xx. 2),
Deut. iii. 26, etc. Thus 16a and 16b are fully contrasted. What
is said of the wise will be judged after Job i. 1, cf. Ps. xxxiv. 15,
xxxvii. 27 : the wise man has fear, viz. fear of God, or rather, since
האלהים is not directly to be supplied, that careful, thoughtful, self-
mistrusting reserve which flows from the reverential awe of God ;
the fool, on the contrary, can neither rule nor bridle his affections,
and without any just occasion falls into passionate excitement.
But on the other side he is self-confident, regardless, secure ; while
the wise man avoids the evil, i.e. carefully goes out of its way, and
in N. T. phraseology " works out his own salvation with fear and
trembling."

[1] As here an לְ too few is written, so at Isa. xxxii. 1 (וּלְשָׂרִים) and Ps. lxxiv.
14 (לְצִיִּים) one too many.

Ver. 17. This verse, as if explanatory of מתעבר, connects itself
with this interpretation of the contrasts, corresponding to the general
usus loquendi, and particularly to the *Mishle* style.

> One who is quick to anger worketh folly,
> And a man of intrigues is hated.

Ewald finds here no right contrast. He understands אִישׁ מְזִמָּה in a
good sense, and accordingly corrects the text, substituting for יִשְׂנָא,
יְשֵׁוֶּא (יְשַׁוֶּא), for he translates : but the man of consideration bears
(properly smooths, viz. his soul). On the other hand it is also to be
remarked, that אִישׁ מְזִמָּה, when it occurs, is not to be understood
necessarily in a good sense, since מְזִמָּה is used just like מְזִמּוֹת, at one
time in a good and at another in a bad sense, and that we willingly
miss the "most complete sense" thus arising, since the proverb,
as it stands in the Masoretic text, is good Hebrew, and needs only
to be rightly understood to let nothing be missed in completeness.
The contrast, as Ewald seeks here to represent it (also Hitzig, who
proposes יִשָּׁאֵ : the man of consideration remains quiet ; Syr. *ramys*,
circumspect), we have in ver. 29, where the μακρόθυμος stands over
against the ὀξύθυμος (אַף or אַפַּיִם of the breathing of anger through
the nose, cf. Theocritus, i. 18 : καὶ οἱ ἀεὶ δριμεῖα χολὰ ποτὶ ῥινὶ
κάθηται). Here the contrast is different : to the man who is quick
to anger, who suddenly gives expression to his anger and displeasure,
stands opposed the man of intrigues, who contrives secret vengeance
against those with whom he is angry. Such a deceitful man, who
contrives evil with calculating forethought and executes it in cold
blood (cf. Ps. xxxvii. 7), is hated ; while on the contrary the noisy
lets himself rush forward to inconsiderate, mad actions, but is not
hated on that account ; but if in his folly he injures or disgraces
himself, or is derided, or if he even does injury to the body and
the life of another, and afterwards with terror sees the evil done
in its true light, then he is an object of compassion. Theodotion
rightly : (ἀνὴρ δὲ) διαβουλιῶν μισηθήσεται, and Jerome : *vir versutus
odiosus est* (not the *Venet.* ἀνὴρ βδελυγμῶν, for this signification has
only מְזָה, and that in the sing.); on the contrary, the LXX., Syr.,
Targum, and Symmachus incorrectly understand אִישׁ מְזִמּוֹת *in bonum
partem*.

> Ver. 18 The simple have obtained folly as an inheritance ;
> But the prudent put on knowledge as a crown.

As a parallel word to נְחֲלוּ, יַכְתִּרוּ (after the Masora defective), also
in the sense of Arab. *ákthar*, *multiplicare*, *abundare* (from Arab.

kathura, to be much, perhaps[1] properly comprehensive, encompass-
ing), would be appropriate, but it is a word properly Arabic. On
the other hand, inappropriate is the meaning of the Heb.-Aram.
כַּתֵּר, to wait (properly waiting to surround, to go round any one, cf.
manere aliquem or *aliquod*), according to which Aquila, ἀναμενοῦσιν,
and Jerome, *expectabunt*. Also הִכְתִּיר, to encompass in the sense of
to embrace (LXX. κρατήσουσιν), does not suffice, since in the
relation to נחלו one expects an idea surpassing this. Certainly
there is a heightening of the idea in this, that the *Hiph.* in contradistinction to נחל would denote an object of desire spontaneously
sought for. But far stronger and more pointed is the heightening
of the idea when we take יכתרו as the denom. of כֶּתֶר (Gr. κίταρις,
κίδαρις, Babyl. כדר, *cudur*, cf. כַּדּוּר, a rounding, *sphœra*). Thus
Theodotion, στεφθήσονται. The *Venet*. better actively, ἐστέψαντο
(after Kimchi : ישׂימו הדעת ככתר על ראשׁם), the Targ., Jerome, Luther
(but not the Syr., which translates נחלו by " to inherit," but יכתרו
by μεριοῦνται, which the LXX. has for נחלו). The bibl. language
has also (Ps. cxlii. 8) הכתיר in the denom. signification of to place
a crown, and that on oneself ; the non-bibl. has מכתיר (like the bibl.
מֵעֲטִיר) in the sense of distributor of crowns,[2] and is fond of the
metaphor כתר הדעת, crown of knowledge. With those not self-
dependent (*vid.* regarding the plur. form of פֶּתִי, p. 56), who are
swayed by the first influence, the issue is, without their willing it,
that they become habitual fools : folly is their possession, *i.e.* their
property. The prudent, on the contrary, as ver. 15 designates
them, have thoughtfully to ponder their step to gain knowledge
as a crown (cf. הֶעֲשׁיר, to gain riches, הִפְרִיחַ, 11*b*, to gain flowers,
Gesen. § 53, 2). Knowledge is to them not merely an inheritance,
but a possession won, and as such remains with them a high and
as it were a kingly ornament.

Ver. 19 The wicked must bow before the good,
And the godless stand at the doors of the righteous.

The good, viz. that which is truly good, which has love as its principle, always at last holds the supremacy. The good men who manifest love to men which flows from love to God, come finally forward,
so that the wicked, who for a long time played the part of lords,

---

[1] According to rule the Hebr. שׁ becomes in Arab. ث, as in Aram. ת ;
but *kthar* might be from *ktar*, an old verb rarely found, which *derivata* with
the idea of encircling (wall) and of rounding (bunch) point to.

[2] *Vid. Wissenschaft, Kunst, Judenthum* (1838), p. 240.

bow themselves willingly or unwillingly before them, and often
enough it comes about that godless men fall down from their
prosperity and their places of honour so low, that they post themselves at the entrance of the stately dwelling of the righteous
(xiii. 22), waiting for his going out and in, or seeking an occasion of presenting to him a supplication, or also as expecting gifts
to be bestowed (Ps. xxxvii. 25). The poor man Lazarus πρὸς τὸν
πυλῶνα of the rich man, Luke xvi. 20, shows, indeed, that this is
not always the case on this side of the grave. שָׁחֽוּ has, according
to the Masora (cf. Kimchi's *Wörterbuch* under שׁחח), the ultima
accented; the accentuation of the form סַבּוּ wavers between the
ult. and the *penult.* Olsh. p. 482 f., cf. Gesen. 68, *Anm.* 10.
The substantival clause 19*b* is easily changed into a verbal clause :
they come (Syr.), appear, stand (incorrectly the Targ.: they are
judged in the gates of the righteous).

Three proverbs on the hatred of men :

> Ver. 20 The poor is hated even by his neighbour ;
> But of those who love the rich there are many.

This is the old history daily repeating itself. Among all people is
the saying and the complaint:

> *Donec eris felix multos numerabis amicos,*
> *Tempora si fuerint nubilia solus eris.*[1]

The Book of Proverbs also speaks of this lamentable phenomenon.
It is a part of the dark side of human nature, and one should take
notice of it, so that when it goes well with him, he may not regard
his many friends as all genuine, and when he becomes poor, he
may not be surprised by the dissolution of earlier friendship, but
may value so much the higher exceptions to the rule. The connection of the passive with לְ of the subject (cf. xiii. 13), as in the
Greek with the dative, is pure Semitic; sometimes it stands with
מִן, but in the sense of ἀπό, Cant. iii. 10, before the influence of
the West led to its being used in the sense of ὑπό (Ges. § 143, 2) ;
יִשָּׂנֵא, is hated (Cod. 1294 : יִשָּׂנֵא), connects with the hatred which is
directed against the poor also the indifference which makes him
without sympathy, for one feels himself troubled by him and
ashamed.

> Ver. 21 Whoever despiseth his neighbour committeth sin ;
> But whoever hath compassion on the suffering—blessings on him!

One should regard every human being, especially such as God has

[1] Ovid, *Trist.* i. 8.

placed near to him, as a being having the same origin, as created
in the image of God, and of the same lofty destination, and should
consider himself as under obligation to love him. He who despiseth
his neighbour (write בָּד with *Metheg*, and *vid.* regarding the
constr. with dat. object. vi. 30, cf. xi. 12, xiii. 13) sins in this
respect, that he raises himself proudly and unwarrantably above
him; that the honour and love he shows to him he measures not
by the rule of duty and of necessity, but according to that which
is pleasing to himself; and in that he refuses to him that which
according to the ordinance of God he owes him. In ver. 21*b* the
Chethîb עֲנָיִים and the *Kerî* עֲנָיִם (*vid.* at Ps. ix. 13) interchange in
an inexplicable way; עָנִי is the bowed down (cf. Arab. *ma'nuww*,
particularly of the prisoner, from 'ana, fut. *ya'nw*, to bow, bend), עָנָו
(Arab. 'anin, with the art. *ál'niy*, from the intrans. 'aniya, to be
bowed down) the patient bearer who in the school of suffering has
learned humility and meekness. One does not see why the *Kerî*
here exchanges that passive idea for this ethical one, especially
since, in proving himself to be מְחוֹנֵן (compassionate) (for which
elsewhere the *part. Kal* חוֹנֵן, xiv. 31, xix. 17, xxviii. 8), one must
be determined only by the needy condition of his neighbour, and
not by his (the neighbour's) moral worthiness, the want of which
ought to make him twofold more an object of our compassion.
All the old translators, from the LXX. to the *Venet.* and Luther,
on this account adopt the *Chethîb*.

Ver. 22. The proverb terminating (ver. 21) with אַשְׁרָיו (cf. xvi.
20) is now followed by one not less singularly formed, commencing
with הֲלֹא (cf. viii. 1).

> Will they not go astray who devise evil,
> And are not mercy and truth to those who devise good?

The part. חֹרֵשׁ signifies both the plougher and the artisan; but on
this account to read with Hitzig both times חָרָשֵׁי, *i.e. machinatores*,
is nothing less than advisable, since there is connected with this
metaphorical חָרַשׁ, as we have shown at iii. 29, not only the idea of
fabricating, but also that of ploughing. Just so little is there any
reason for changing with Hitzig, against all old translators, יִתְעוּ into
יֵרְעוּ: will it not go ill with them . . .; the fut. יתעו (cf. Isa. lxiii.
17) is not to be touched; the perf. תעו (*e.g.* Ps. lviii. 4) would denote that those who contrive evil are in the way of error, the fut. on
the contrary that they will fall into error (cf. xii. 26 with Job
xii. 24). But if הלא יתעו is the expression of the result which shall

certainly come to such, then 22*b* stands as a contrast adapted thereto: and are not, on the contrary, mercy and truth those who contrive that which is good, *i.e.* (for that which befalls them, as xiii. 18*a*, cf. xiv. 35*b*, is made their attribute) are they not an object of mercy and truth, viz. on the part of God and of men, for the effort which proceeds from love and is directed to the showing forth of good is rewarded by this, that God and men are merciful to such and maintain truth to them, stand in truth to them; for חֶסֶד וֶאֱמֶת is to be understood here, as at iii. 3, neither of God nor of men exclusively, but of both together: the wicked who contrive evil lose themselves on the way to destruction, but grace and truth are the lot of those who aim at what is good, guarded and guided by which, they reach by a blessed way a glorious end.

There now follows a considerable series of proverbs (vers. 23–31) which, with a single exception (ver. 24), have all this in common, that one or two key-words in them begin with מ.

> Ver. 23 In all labour there is gain,
> But idle talk leadeth only to loss.

Here the key-words are מוֹתָר and מַחְסוֹר (parallel xxi. 5, cf. with xi. 24), which begin with מ. עֶצֶב is labour, and that earnest and unwearied, as at x. 22. If one toils on honestly, then there always results from it something which stands forth above the endeavour as its result and product, *vid.* at Job xxx. 11, where it is shown how יָתַר, from the primary meaning to be stretched out long, acquires the meaning of that which hangs over, shoots over, copiousness, and gain. By the word of the lips, on the contrary, *i.e.* purposeless and inoperative talk (דְּבַר שְׂפָתַיִם as Isa. xxxvi. 5, cf. Job xi. 2), nothing is gained, but on the contrary there is only loss, for by it one only robs both himself and others of time, and wastes strength, which might have been turned to better purpose, to say nothing of the injury that is thereby done to his soul; perhaps also he morally injures, or at least discomposes and wearies others.

> Ver. 24 It is a crown to the wise when they are rich;
> But the folly of fools remains folly.

From xii. 4, 31, xvii. 6, we see that עֲטֶרֶת חֲכָמִים is the predicate. Thus it is the riches of the wise of which it is said that they are a crown or an ornament to them. More than this is said, if with Hitzig we read, after the LXX., עָרְמָם, their prudence, instead of עָשְׁרָם. For then the meaning would be, that the wise need no other crown than that which they have in their prudence. But yet far more appropriately "riches" are called the crown of a wise man when they come to his wisdom ; for it is truly thus that riches, when they are possessed along with wisdom, contribute not a little to heighten its influence and power, and not merely because they adorn in their appearance like a crown, or, as we say, surround as with a golden frame, but because they afford a variety of means and occasions for self-manifestation which are denied to the poor. By this interpretation of 24a, 24b comes out also into the light, without our requiring to correct the first אִוֶּלֶת, or to render it in an unusual sense. The LXX. and Syr. translate the first אולת by διατριβή (by a circumlocution), the Targ. by *gloria*, fame—we know not how they reach this. Schultens in his *Com.* renders: *crassa opulentia elumbium crassities*, but in his *Animadversiones* he combines the first אולת with the Arab. *awwale*, precedence, which Gesen. approves of. But although the meaning to be thick (properly *coalescere*) appertains to the verbal stem אול as well as the meaning to be before (Arab. *ál, âwila, wâl*), yet the Hebr. אִוֶּלֶת always and everywhere means only folly,[1] from the fundamental idea *crassities* (thickness). Hitzig's אִוֶּלֶת (which denotes the consequence with which the fool invests himself) we do not accept, because this word is Hitzig's own invention. Rather לִוְיַת is to be expected: the crown with which fools adorn themselves is folly. But the sentence : the folly of fools is (and remains) folly (Symmachus, Jerome, *Venet.*, Luther), needs the emendation as little as xvi. 22b, for, interpreted in connection with 24a, it denotes that while wisdom is adorned and raised up by riches, folly on the other hand remains, even when connected with riches, always the same, without being either thereby veiled or removed,—on the contrary, the fool, when he is rich, exhibits his follies always more and more. C. B. Michaelis compares Lucian's *simia est simia etiamsi aurea gestet insignia.*

Ver. 25 A witness of truth delivereth souls ;
But he who breathes out lies is nothing but deception.

When men, in consequence of false suspicions or of false accusations, fall into danger of their lives (דיני נפשות is the designation in the later language of the law of a criminal process), then a tongue

---

[1] Ewald's derivation of אויל from אָוֶן=אָוִין, null, vain, is not much better than Heidenheim's from אולי : one who says " perhaps " = a sceptic, *vid.* p. 59, *note.*

which, pressed by conscientiousness and not deterred by cowardice, will utter the truth, saves them. But a false tongue, which as such (*vid.* 5*b*) is a יָפֵחַ כְּזָבִים (after the Masora at this place וְיָפֵחַ *defective*), *i.e.* is one who breathes out lies (*vid.* regarding יפיח at vi. 19), is mere deception (LXX., without reading מִרְמָה [as Hitzig does]: δόλιος). In xii. 17 מִרְמָה is to be interpreted as the object. accus. of יָגִיד carried forward, but here to carry forward מַצִּיל (Arama, Löwenstein) is impracticable—for to deliver deceit = the deceiver is not expressed in the Hebr.—מרמה is, as possibly also xii. 16 (LXX. δόλιος), without אִישׁ or עֵד being supplied, the pred. of the substantival clause : such an one is deception (in bad Latin, *dolositas*), for he who utters forth lies against better knowledge must have a malevolent, deceitful purpose.

> Ver. 26 In the fear of Jahve lies a strong ground of confidence,
> And the children of such an one have a refuge.

The so-called בְּ *essentiæ* stands here, as at Ps. lxviii. 5, lv. 19, Isa. xxvi. 4, before the subject idea ; the clause : in the fear of God exists, *i.e.* it is and proves itself, as a strong ground of confidence, does not mean that the fear of God is something in which one can rely (Hitzig), but that it has (xxii. 19, Jer. xvii. 7, and here) an inheritance which is enduring, unwavering, and not disappointing in God, who is the object of fear ; for it is not faith, nor anything else subjective, which is the rock that bears us, but this Rock is the object which faith lays hold of (cf. Isa. xxviii. 16). Is now the וּלְבָנָיו to be referred, with Ewald and Zöckler, to ה'? It is possible, as we have discussed at Gen. vi. 1 f.; but in view of parallels such as xx. 7, it is not probable. He who fears God entails in the Abrahamic way (Gen. xviii. 19) the fear of God on his children, and in this precious paternal inheritance they have a מַחְסֶה (not מַחֲסֶה, and therefore to be written with Masoretic exactness מַחְסֶה), a fortress or place of protection, a refuge in every time of need (cf. Ps. lxxi. 5–7). Accordingly, וּלְבָנָיו refers back to the ה' יְרֵא, to be understood from בִּיִרְאַת ה' (LXX., Luther, and all the Jewish interpreters), which we find not so doubtful as to regard on this account the explanation after Ps. lxxiii. 15, cf. Deut. xiv. 1, as necessary, although we grant that such an introduction of the N. T. generalization and deepening of the idea of sonship is to be expected from the Chokma.

> Ver. 27 The fear of Jahve is a fountain of life,
> To escape the snares of death.

There springs up a life which makes him who carries in himself (cf. John iv. 14, ἐν αὐτῷ) this welling life, penetrating and strong of will to escape the snares (write after the Masora מִמֹּקְשֵׁי *defective*) which death lays, and which bring to an end in death—a repetition of xiii. 4 with changed subject.

Ver. 28 In the multitude of the people lies the king's honour ;
And when the population diminishes, it is the downfall of his glory.

The honour or the ornament (*vid.* regarding הָדַר, *tumere, ampliari*, the root-word of הָדָר and הֲדָרָה at Isa. lxiii. 1) of a king consists in this, that he rules over a great people, and that they increase and prosper ; on the other hand, it is the ruin of princely greatness when the people decline in number and in wealth. Regarding מְחִתָּה, *vid.* at x. 14. בְּאֶפֶס signifies prepositionally " without " (properly, by non-existence), *e.g.* xxvi. 20, or adverbially " groundless " (properly, for nothing), Isa. lii. 4 ; here it is to be understood after its contrast בְּרָב־ : in the non-existence, but which is here equivalent to in the ruin (cf. אֶפֶס, the form of which in conjunction is אֶפֶס, Gen. xlvii. 15), lies the misfortune, decay, ruin of the princedom. The LXX. ἐν δὲ ἐκλείψει λαοῦ συντριβὴ δυνάστου. Certainly רָזוֹן (from רַז, Arab. *razuna*, to be powerful) is to be interpreted personally, whether it be after the form בָּגוֹד with a fixed, or after the form יְקוֹשׁ with a changeable *Kametz;* but it may also be an abstract like שָׁלוֹם (= Arab. *selâm*), and this we prefer, because in the personal signification רָן, viii. 15, xxxi. 4, is used. We have not here to think of רָזוֹן (from רָזָה), consumption (the *Venet.* against Kimchi, πενίας) ; the choice of the word also is not determined by an intended amphibology (Hitzig), for this would be meaningless.

Ver. 29 He that is slow to anger is rich in understanding ;
But he that is easily excited carries off folly.

אֶרֶךְ אַפַּיִם (constr. of אָרֵךְ) is he who puts off anger long, viz. the outbreak of anger, הַאֲרִיךְ, xix. 11, *i.e.* lets it not come in, but shuts it out long (μακρόθυμος = βραδὺς εἰς ὀργήν, Jas. i. 19) ; and קְצַר־רוּחַ, he who in his spirit and temper, viz. as regards anger (for רוּחַ denotes also the breathing out and snorting, Isa. xxv. 4, xxxiii. 11), is short, *i.e.* (since shortness of time is meant) is rash and suddenly (cf. quick to anger, *præceps in iram*, 17a) breaks out with it, not ὀλιγόψυχος (but here ὀξύθυμος), as the LXX. translate 17a. The former, who knows how to control his affections, shows himself

herein as "great in understanding" (cf. 2 Sam. xxiii. 20), or as a
"man of great understanding" (Lat. *multus prudentiâ*); the contrary is he who suffers himself to be impelled by his affections
into hasty, inconsiderate action, which is here expressed more
actively by מֵרִים אִוֶּלֶת. Does this mean that he bears folly to the
view (Luther, Umbreit, Bertheau, Elster, and others)? But for
that idea the *Mishle* style has other expressions, xii. 23, xiii. 16,
xv. 2, cf. xiv. 17. Or does it mean that he makes folly high, *i.e.*
shows himself highly foolish (LXX., Syr., Targum, Fleischer, and
others)? But that would be expressed rather by הִגְדִּיל or הִרְבָּה.
Or is it he heightens folly (Löwenstein, Hitzig)? But the remark
that the angry ebullition is itself a gradual heightening of the
foolish nature of such an one is not suitable, for the choleric man,
who lets the evenness of his disposition be interrupted by a breaking
forth of anger, is by no means also in himself a fool. Rashi is
right when he says, מפרישה לחלקו, *i.e.* (to which also Fleischer
gives the preference) *aufert pro portione sua stultitiam.* The only
appropriate parallel according to which it is to be explained, is iii.
35. But not as Ewald: he lifts up folly, which lies as it were
before his feet on his life's path; but: he takes off folly, in the
sense of Lev. vi. 8, *i.e.* he carries off folly, receives a portion of
folly; for as to others, so also to himself, when he returns to calm
blood, that which he did in his rage must appear as folly and
madness.

> Ver. 30 A quiet heart is the life of the body,
>   But covetousness is rottenness in the bones.

Heart, soul, flesh, is the O. T. trichotomy, Ps. lxxxiv. 3, xvi. 9;
the heart is the innermost region of the life, where all the rays of
the bodily and the soul-life concentrate, and whence they again
unfold themselves. The state of the heart, *i.e.* of the central,
spiritual, soul-inwardness of the man, exerts therefore on all sides
a constraining influence on the bodily life, in the relation to the
heart the surrounding life. Regarding לֵב מַרְפֵּא, *vid.* at xii. 18,
p. 262. Thus is styled the quiet heart, which in its symmetrical
harmony is like a calm and clear water-mirror, neither interrupted
by the affections, nor broken through or secretly stirred by passion.
By the close connection in which the corporeal life of man stands
to the moral-religious determination of his intellectual and mediately his soul-life—this threefold life is as that of one personality,
essentially one—the body has in such quiet of spirit the best means

of preserving the life which furthers the well-being, and co-operates to the calming of all its disquietude; on the contrary, passion, whether it rage or move itself in stillness, is like the disease in the bones (xii. 4), which works onward till it breaks asunder the framework of the body, and with it the life of the body. The plur. בְּשָׂרִים occurs only here ; Böttcher, § 695, says that it denotes the whole body; but בָּשָׂר also does not denote the half, בשרים is the surrogate of an *abstr.*: the body, *i.e.* the bodily life in the totality of its functions, and in the entire manifoldness of its relations. Ewald translates bodies, but בשׂר signifies not the body, but its material, the animated matter ; rather cf. the Arab. *âbshâr*, " corporeal, human nature," but which (leaving out of view that this plur. belongs to a later period of the language) has the parallelism against it. Regarding קִנְאָה (jealousy, zeal, envy, anger) Schultens is right : *affectus inflammans æstuque indignationis fervidus,* from קָנָא, Arab. *kanâ*, to be high red.

Ver. 31 He who oppresseth the poor reproacheth his Maker;
And whosoever is merciful to the poor, it is an honour to him.

Line first is repeated in xvii. 5*a* somewhat varied, and the relation of the idea in 31*b* is as xix. 17*a*, according to which וּמְכַבְּדוֹ is the predicate and חֹנֵן אֶבְיוֹן the subject (Symmachus, Targ., Jerome, *Venet.*, Luther), not the reverse (Syr.); חֹנֵן is thus not the 3 per. *Po.* (LXX.), but the *part. Kal* (for which 21*b* has the *part. Po.* מְחוֹנֵן). The predicates חֵרֵף עֹשֵׂהוּ (*vid.* regarding the perf. Gesen. § 126, 3) and ומכבדו follow one another after the scheme of the *Chiasmus.* עֹשֵׁק has *Munach* on the first syllable, on which the tone is thrown back, and on the second the העמדה sign (*vid. Torath Emeth,* p. 21), as *e.g.* פּוֹטֵר, xvii. 14, and אֹהֵב, xvii. 19. The showing of forbearance and kindness to the poor arising from a common relation to one Creator, and from respect towards a personality bearing the image of God, is a conception quite in the spirit of the Chokma, which, as in the Jahve religion it becomes the universal religion, so in the national law it becomes the human (*vid.* p. 41). Thus also Job xxxi. 15, cf. iii. 9 of the Epistle of James, which in many respects has its roots in the Book of Proverbs. Matt. xxv. 40 is a New Testament side-piece to 31*b*.

Ver. 32. This verse also contains a key-word beginning with מ, but pairs acrostically with the proverb following :

When misfortune befalls him, the godless is overthrown ;
But the righteous remains hopeful in his death.

312   THE BOOK OF PROVERBS.

When the subject is רָעָה connected with רָשָׁע (the godless), then it
may be understood of evil thought and action (Eccles. vii. 15) as well
as of the experience of evil (*e.g.* xiii. 21). The LXX. (and also the
Syr., Targ., Jerome, and *Venet.*) prefers the former, but for the sake
of producing an exact parallelism changes בְּמוֹתוֹ [in his death] into
בְּתֻמּוֹ [in his uprightness], reversing also the relation of the subject
and the predicate : ὁ δὲ πεποιθὼς τῇ ἑαυτοῦ ὁσιότητι (the Syr.: in
this, that he has no sin; Targ.: when he dies) δίκαιος. But no
Scripture word commends in so contradictory a manner self-righteousness, for the verb חסה never denotes self-confidence, and with
the exception of two passages (Judg. ix. 15, Isa. xxx. 2), where it is
connected with בְּצֵל, is everywhere the exclusive (*vid.* Ps. cxviii. 8 f.)
designation of confidence resting itself in God, even without the
בה', as here and at Ps. xvii. 7. The parallelism leads us to translate ברעתו, not on account of his wickedness, but with Luther, in
conformity with במותו, in his misfortune, *i.e.* if it befall him. Thus
Jeremiah (xxiii. 12) says of the sins of his people : בָּאֲפֵלָה יִדַּחוּ, in
the deep darkness they are driven on (*Niph.* of דחה = דחח), and
xxiv. 16 contains an exactly parallel thought : the godless stumble
ברעה, into calamity. Ewald incorrectly : in his calamity the wicked
is overthrown—for what purpose then the pronoun ? The verb דחה
frequently means, without any addition, " to stumble over heaps,"
e.g. Ps. xxxv. 5, xxxvi. 13. The godless in his calamity is overthrown, or he fears in the evils which befall him the intimations of
the final ruin ; on the contrary, the righteous in his death, even in
the midst of extremity, is comforted, viz. in God in whom he confides. Thus understood, Hitzig thinks that the proverb is not
suitable for a time in which, as yet, men had not faith in immortality and in the resurrection. Yet though there was no such
revelation then, still the pious in death put their confidence in
Jahve, the God of life and of salvation—for in Jahve [1] there was
for ancient Israel the beginning, middle, and end of the work of
salvation—and believing that they were going home to Him, committing their spirit into His hands (Ps. xxxi. 6), they fell asleep,
though without any explicit knowledge, yet not without the hope
of eternal life. Job also knew that (xxvii. 8 ff.) between the death
of those estranged from God and of those who feared God there
was not only an external, but a deep essential distinction ; and now

[1] *Vid.* my *Bibl.-prophet. Theol.* (1845), p. 268, cf. *Bibl. Psychologie* (1861),
p. 410, and *Psalmen* (1867), p. 52 f., and elsewhere.

the Chokma opens up a glimpse into the eternity heavenwards, xv. 24, and has formed, xii. 28, the expressive and distinctive word אַל־מָוֶת, for immortality, which breaks like a ray from the morning sun through the night of the *Sheol.*

> Ver. 33 Wisdom rests in the heart of the man of understanding ;
> But in the heart of fools it maketh itself known.

Most interpreters know not what to make of the second line here. The LXX. (and after it the Syr.), and as it appears, also Aquila and Theodotion, insert *οὐ*; the Targ. improves the Peshito, for it inserts אוּלֶת (so that xii. 23, xiii. 16, and xv. 2 are related). And Abulwalîd explains : in the heart of fools it is lost; Euchel : it reels about ; but these are imaginary interpretations resting on a misunderstanding of the passages, in which ידע means to come to feel, and הודיע to give to feel (to punish, correct). Kimchi rightly adheres to the one ascertained meaning of the words, according to which the *Venet.* μέσον δὲ ἀφρόνων γνωσθήσεται. So also the translation of Jerome : *et indoctos quosque (quoque) erudiet,* is formed, for he understands the "and is manifest among fools" (Luther) not merely, as C. B. Michaelis, after the saying : *opposita juxta se posita magis elucescunt,* but of a becoming manifest, which is salutary to these. Certainly בְּקֶרֶב can mean among = in the circle of, xv. 31 ; but if, as here and *e.g.* Jer. xxxi. 31, בקרב is interchanged with בלב, and if חכמה בקרב is the subject spoken of, as 1 Kings iii. 28, then בקרב does not mean among (in the midst of), but in the heart of the fool. According to this, the Talmud rightly, by comparison with the current proverb (*Mezîa* 85*b*) : אסתירא בלגינא קיש קיש קריא, a stater in a flaggon cries *Kish, Kish, i.e.* makes much clatter. In the heart of the understanding wisdom rests, *i.e.* remains silent and still, for the understanding feels himself personally happy in its possession, endeavours always the more to deepen it, and lets it operate within ; on the contrary, wisdom in the heart of the fools makes itself manifest : they are not able to keep to themselves the wisdom which they imagine they possess, or the portion of wisdom which is in reality theirs ; but they think, as it is said in Persius : *Scire tuum nihil est nisi scire hoc te sciat alter.* They discredit and waste their little portion of wisdom (instead of thinking on its increase) by obtrusive ostentatious babbling.

Two proverbs follow regarding the state and its ruler :

> Ver. 34 Righteousness exalteth a nation,
> And sin is a disgrace to the people.

The Hebr. language is richer in synonyms of "the people" than the German. גּוֹי (formed like the non-bibl. מוֹ, water, and נוֹ, corporealness, from גֵּוָה, to extend itself from within outward; cf. ix. 3, גֵּפִי, x. 13, גֵּו) is, according to the *usus loq.*, like *natio* the people, as a mass swollen up from a common origin, and עַם, 28a (from עָמַם, to bind), the people as a confederation held together by a common law ; לְאֹם (from לָאַם, to unite, bind together) is the mass (multitude) of the people, and is interchanged sometimes with גּוֹי, Gen. xxv. 23, and sometimes with עַם, ver. 28. In this proverb, לְאֻמִּים stands indeed intentionally in the plur., but not גּוֹי, with the plur. of which גּוֹיִם, the idea of the non-Israelitish nations, too easily connects itself. The proverb means all nations without distinction, even Israel (cf. under Isa. i. 4) not excluded. History everywhere confirms the principle, that not the numerical, nor the warlike, nor the political, nor yet the intellectual and the so-called civilized greatness, is the true greatness of a nation, and determines the condition of its future as one of progress; but this is its true greatness, that in its private, public, and international life, צְדָקָה, *i.e.* conduct directed by the will of God, according to the norm of moral rectitude, rules and prevails. Righteousness, good manners, and piety are the things which secure to a nation a place of honour, while, on the contrary, חַטָּאת, sin, viz. prevailing, and more favoured and fostered than contended against in the consciousness of the moral problem of the state, is a disgrace to the people, *i.e.* it lowers them before God, and also before men who do not judge superficially or perversely, and also actually brings them down. רוֹמֵם, to raise up, is to be understood after Isa. i. 2, cf. xxiii. 4, and is to be punctuated תְּרוֹמֵם, with *Munach* of the penult., and the הַעֲמָדָה-sign with the *Tsere* of the last syllable. Ben-Naphtali punctuates thus : תְּרוֹמֵם. In 34b all the artifices of interpretation (from Nachmani to Schultens) are to be rejected, which interpret חֶסֶד as the *Venet.* (ἔλεος δὲ λαῶν ἁμαρτία) in its predominant Hebrew signification. It has here, as at Lev. xx. 17 (but not Job vi. 14), the signification of the Syr. *chesdho, opprobrium;* the Targ. חִסְדָּא, or more frequently חִסּוּדָא, as among Jewish interpreters, is recognised by Chanan'el and Rashbam. That this חֶסֶד is not foreign to the *Mishle* style, is seen from the fact that חִפֵּר, xxv. 10, is used in the sense of the Syr. *chasedh.* The synon. Syr. *chasam, invidere, obtrectare,* shows that these verbal stems are formed from the R. חם, *stringere,* to strike. Already it is in some measure perceived how חָסַד, Syr. *chasadh*, Arab. *hasada*, may acquire the meaning of violent love, and by the mediation of the jealousy which is connected with violent love, the signification of grudging, and thus of reproach and of envy; yet this is more manifest if one thinks of the root-signification *stringere*, in the meaning of loving, as referred to the subject, in the meanings of disgrace and envy, as from the subject directed to others. Ewald (§ 51*c*) compares חָכַל and חָסַר, Ethiop. *chasra*, in the sense of *carpere*, and on the other side חָסָה in the sense of " to join ; " but חסה does not mean to join (*vid*. Ps. ii. 12), and instead of *carpere*, the idea more closely connected with the root is that of *stringere*, cf. *stringere folia ex arboribus* (Cæsar), and *stringere* (to diminish, to squander, strip) *rem ingluvie* (Horace, Sat. i. 2. 8). The LXX. has here read חֶסֶר (xxviii. 22), diminution, decay, instead of חֶסֶר (shame); the *quid pro quo* is not bad, the Syr. accepts it, and the *miseros facit* of Jerome, and Luther's *verderben* (destruction) corresponds with this phrase better than with the common traditional reading which Symmachus rightly renders by ὄνειδος.

> Ver. 35 The king's favour is towards a prudent servant,
> And his wrath visits the base.

Regarding the contrasts מַשְׂכִּיל and מֵבִישׁ, *vid*. at x. 5 ; cf. xii. 4. The substantival clause 35*a* may mean : the king's favour has (possesses) . . ., as well as : it is imparted to, an intelligent servant ; the arrangement of the words is more favourable to the latter rendering. In 35*b* the gender of the verb is determined by attraction after the pred., as is the case also at Gen. xxxi. 8, Job xv. 31, Ewald, § 317*c*. And "his wrath" is equivalent to is the object of it, cf. 22*b*, xiii. 18, and in general, p. 282. The syntactical character of the clause does not permit the supplying of לְ from 35*a*. Luther's translation proceeds only apparently from this erroneous supposition.

Chap. xv. 1-6. We take these verses together as forming a group which begins with a proverb regarding the good and evil which flows from the tongue, and closes with a proverb regarding the treasure in which blessing is found, and that in which no blessing is found.

> Ver. 1 A soft answer turneth away wrath,
> And a bitter word stirreth up anger.

In the second line, the common word for anger (אַף, from the breathing with the nostrils, xiv. 17) is purposely placed, but in the first, that which denotes anger in the highest degree (חֵמָה from יָחַם, cogn. חָמַם, Arab. *hamiya*, to glow, like שֵׁנָה from יָשֵׁן) : a mild, gentle word turns away the heat of anger (*excandescentiam*), puts it back, cf. xxv. 15. The *Dagesh* in רַךְ follows the rule of the דחיק, *i.e.* of the close connection of a word terminating with the accented ◌ָה, ◌ֶה, ◌ֶה with the following word (*Michlol* 63*b*). The same is the meaning of the Latin proverb :

> *Frangitur ira gravis*
> *Quando est responsio suavis.*

The דְּבַר־עֶצֶב produces the contrary effect. This expression does not mean an angry word (Ewald), for עֶצֶב is not to be compared with the Arab. *ghadab*, anger (Umbreit), but with Arab. '*adb*, cutting, wounding, paining (Hitzig), so that דָּבָר מַעֲצִיב is meant in the sense of Ps. lxxviii. 40 : a word which causes pain (LXX. λυπηρός, Theod. πονικός), not after the meaning, a word provoking to anger (Gesenius), but certainly after its effect, for a wounding word " makes anger arise." As one says of anger שָׁב, " it turns itself " (*e.g.* Isa. ix. 11), so, on the other hand, עָלָה, " it rises up," Eccles. x. 4. The LXX. has a third line, ὀργὴ ἀπόλλυσι καὶ φρονίμους, which the Syr. forms into a distich by the repetition of xiv. 32*b*, the untenableness of which is at once seen.

Ver. 2. The πραΰτης σοφίας (Jas. iii. 13) commended in ver. 1 is here continued :

> The tongue of the wise showeth great knowledge,
> And the mouth of fools poureth forth folly.

As הֵיטִיב נַגֵּן, Isa. xxiii. 16, means to strike the harp well, and הֵיטִיב לֶכֶת, xxx. 29, to go along merrily, so הֵיטִיב דַּעַת, to know in a masterly manner, and here, where the subject is the tongue, which has only an instrumental reference to knowledge : to bring to light great knowledge (cf. 7*a*). In 2*b* the LXX. translate στόμα δὲ ἀφρόνων ἀναγγέλλει κακά. From this Hitzig concludes that they read רָעוֹת as 28*b*, and prefers this phrase ; but they also translated in xiii. 16, xiv. 28, xxvi. 11, אִוֶּלֶת by κακίαν, for they interpreted the unintelligible word by combination with עַוְלָת, and in xii. 23 by ἀραῖς, for they thought they had before them אלות (from אָלָה).

Ver. 3 The eyes of Jahve are in every place,
Observing the evil and the good.

The connection of the *dual* עֵינַיִם with the plur. of the adjective, which does not admit of a dual, is like vi. 17, cf. 18. But the first line is a sentence by itself, to which the second line gives a

closer determination, as showing how the eyes of God are everywhere (cf. 2 Chron. xvi. 9, after Zech. iv. 10) abroad over the
whole earth, viz. beholding with penetrating look the evil and the
good (צָפָה, to hold to, to observe, cf. ἐπιβλέποντες, Sir. xxiii. 19),
i.e. examining men whether they are good or evil, and keeping
them closely before His eyes, so that nothing escapes him. This
universal inspection, this omniscience of God, has an alarming but
also a comforting side. The proverb seeks first to warn, therefore
it speaks first of the evil.

> Ver. 4 Gentleness of the tongue is a tree of life ;
> But falseness in it is a wounding to the spirit.

Regarding מַרְפֵּא, *vid.* at xii. 18, and regarding סֶלֶף, at xi. 3 ; this
latter word we derive with Fleischer from סלף, to subvert, overthrow, but not in the sense of " violence, *asperitas*, in as far as
violent speech is like a stormy sea," but of perversity, *perversitas*
(*Venet.* λοξότης), as the contrast to truthfulness, rectitude, kindness. Gentleness characterizes the tongue when all that it says to
a neighbour, whether it be instruction or correction, or warning
or consolation, it says in a manner without rudeness, violence, or
obtrusiveness, by which it finds the easiest and surest acceptance,
because he feels the goodwill, the hearty sympathy, the humility
of him who is conscious of his own imperfection. Such gentleness
is a tree of life, whose fruits preserve life, heal the sick, and raise
up the bowed down. Accordingly, שֶׁבֶר בְּרוּחַ is to be understood
of the effect which goes forth from perversity or falseness of the
tongue upon others. Fleischer translates : *asperitas autem in ea
animum vulnerat*, and remarks, " שבר ברוח, *abstr. pro concreto*. The
verb שבר, and the *n. verbale* שֶׁבֶר derived from it, may, in order
to render the meaning tropical, govern the prep. בְּ, as the Arab.
kaser baklby, he has broken my heart (opp. Arab. *jabar baklaby*),
cf. בְּפָנָיו, xxi. 29, *vid. De Glossis Habichtianis*, p. 18 ; yet it also
occurs with the accus., Ps. lxix. 21, and the corresponding gen.
שֶׁבֶר רוּחַ, Isa. lxv. 14." In any case, the breaking (deep wounding)
is not meant in regard to his own spirit, but to that of the neighbour.
Rightly Luther : but a lying (tongue) makes heart-sorrow (elsewhere, a false one troubles the cheerful) ; Euchel : a false tongue is
soul-wounding ; and the translation of the year 1844 : falsehood
is a breach into the heart. Only for curiosity's sake are two other
intepretations of 4*a* and 4*b* mentioned : the means of safety to the
tongue is the tree of life, *i.e.* the *Tôra* (*Erachin* 15*b*) ; and : per-

versity suffers destruction by a breath of wind, after the proverb,
כל שיש בו נסות רוח רוח קימעא שוברתו, a breath of wind breaks a man
who is puffed up [1] (which Meîri presents for choice, *vid.* also Rashi,
who understands רוח of the storm of judgment). The LXX. translates, in 4*b*, a different text : ὁ δὲ συντηρῶν αὐτὴν πλησθήσεται
πνεύματος ; but the רוּחַ יִשְׂבַּע here supposed cannot mean " to be
full of spirit," but rather " to eat full of wind." Otherwise the
Syr. and Targ. : and he who eateth of his own fruit is satisfied (Heb.
וְאֹכֵל מִפְרִיו יִשְׂבַּע),—an attempt to give to the phrase יִשְׂבַּע a thought
correct in point of language, but one against which we do not give
up the Masoretic text.

> Ver. 5 A fool despiseth his father's correction ;
> But he that regardeth reproof is prudent.

We may with equal correctness translate : he acts prudently (after
1 Sam. xxiii. 22) ; and, he is prudent (after xix. 25). We prefer,
with Jerome, *Venet.*, and Luther, the latter, against the LXX.,
Syr., and Targ., because, without a doubt, the יַעְרִם is so thought of
at xix. 25 : the contrast is more favourable to the former. It is
true that he who regardeth reproof is not only prudent, but also
that he is prudent by means of observing it. With line first cf. i.
7 and i. 30, and with line second, xii. 1. Luther translates : the
fool calumniates . . . ; but of the meanings of abuse (properly
pungere) and scorn, the second is perhaps here to be preferred.

> Ver. 6 The house of the righteous is a great treasure-chamber ;
> But through the gain of the wicked comes trouble.

The constrast shows that הֹסֶן does not here mean force or might
(LXX., Syr., Targ., Jerome, and *Venet.*), which generally this
derivative of the verb חָסַן never means, but store, fulness of
possession, prosperity (Luther : in the house of the righteous are
goods enough), in this sense (cf. xxvii. 24) placing itself, not with
the Arab. *hasuna*, to be firm, fastened (Aram. ܚܣܝܢ, חֲסַן), but
with Arab. *khazan*, to deposit, to lay up in granaries, whence our
" *Magazin*." הֹסֶן may indeed, like חַיִל, have the meaning of riches,
and חֲסַן does actually mean, in the Jewish-Aram., to possess, and
the *Aphel* אַחְסֵן, to take into possession (κρατεῖν) ; but the constant
use of the noun הֹסֶן in the sense of store, with the kindred idea of
laying up, *e.g.* Jer. xx. 5, and of the *Niph.* נֶחְסַן, which means, Isa.
xxiii. 18, with נֶאֱצָר, " to be magazined," gives countenance to the

---

[1] *Vid.* Duke's *Rabbinische Blumenlese*, p. 176, where the rendering is somewhat different.

idea that חֹסֶן goes back to the primary conception, *recondere*, and is to be distinguished from חָסִין, חַסִין, and other derivatives after the fundamental conception. We may not interpret בֵּית, with Fleischer, Bertheau, and Zöckler, as accus.: in the house (cf. בֵּית, viii. 2), nor prepositionally as *chez = casa;* but: " the house of the righteous is a great store," equivalent to, the place of such. On the contrary, destruction comes by the gain of the wicked. It is impossible that נֶעְכָּרֶת can have the house as the subject (Löwenstein), for בַּיִת is everywhere mas. Therefore Abulwalîd, followed by Kimchi and the *Venet.* (ὄλεθρος), interprets נעכרת as subst., after the form of the Mishnic נִבְרֶכֶת, a pool, cf. נֶחֶרְצָה, peremptorily decided, decreed; and if we do not extinguish the ב of וּבְתבוּאַת (the LXX. according to the second translation of this doubly-translated distich, Syr., and Targ.), there remains then nothing further than to regard נעכרת either as subst. neut. overturned = overthrow (cf. such part. nouns as מוּעָקָה, מוּסָדָה, but particularly נְסִבָּה, 2 Chron. x. 15), or as impers. neut. pass: it is overthrown = there is an overthrow, like נִשְׁעָרָה, Ps. l. 3: it is stormed = a storm rages. The gain of the wicked has overthrow as its consequence, for the greed of gain, which does not shrink from unrighteous, deceitful gain, destroys his house, עֹכֵר בֵּיתוֹ, ver. 27 (*vid.* regarding עכר, xi. 29). Far from enriching the house, such gain is the cause of nothing but ruin. The LXX., in its first version of this distich, reads, in 6*a*, בְּרֹבוֹת צֶדֶק (ἐν πλεοναζούσῃ δικαιοσύνῃ), and in 6*b*, וּבְתבוּאַת רֶשַׁע נֶעְכָּר (and together with the fruit the godless is rooted out, ὀλόρριζοι ἐκ γῆς ἀπολοῦνται); for, as Lagarde has observed, it confounds עכר with עקר (to root, *privativ :* to root up).

Vers. 7-17. A second series which begins with a proverb of the power of human speech, and closes with proverbs of the advantages and disadvantages of wealth.

Ver. 7 The lips of the wise spread knowledge;
  But the direction is wanting to the heart of fools.

It is impossible that לֹא־כֵן can be a second object. accus. dependent on יְזָרוּ (*dispergunt*, not יִצְּרוּ, xx. 28; φυλάσσουσι, as Symmachus translates): but the heart of fools is unrighteous (error or falsehood) (Hitzig after Isa. xvi. 6); for then why were the lips of the wise and the heart of the fools mentioned? לֹא־כֵן also does not mean οὐχ οὕτως (an old Greek anonymous translation, Jerome, Targ., *Venet.*, Luther): the heart of the fool is quite different from the heart of the wise man, which spreads abroad knowledge

(Zöckler), for it is not heart and heart, but lip and heart, that are placed opposite to each other. Better the LXX. οὐκ ἀσφαλεῖς, and yet better the Syr. *lo kinîn* (not right, sure). We have seen, at xi. 19, that כֵּן as a participial adj. means standing = being, continuing, or also standing erect = right, *i.e.* rightly directed, or having the right direction ; כְּצְדָקָה means there conducting one-self rightly, and thus genuine rectitude. What, after 7*a*, is more appropriate than to say of the heart of the fool, that it wants the receptivity for knowledge which the lips of the wise scatter abroad ? The heart of the fool is not right, it has not the right direction, is crooked and perverse, has no mind for wisdom ; and that which proceeds from the wise, therefore, finds with him neither estimation nor acceptance.

Ver. 8 The sacrifice of the godless is an abhorrence to Jahve ;
But the prayer of the upright is His delight.

Although the same is true of the prayer of the godless that is here said of their sacrifice, and of the sacrifice of the righteous that is here said of their prayer (*vid.* xxviii. 9, and cf. Ps. iv. 6 with Ps. xxvii. 6), yet it is not by accident that here (line first = xxi. 27) the sacrifice is ascribed to the godless and the prayer to the upright. The sacrifice, as a material and legally-required perform-ance, is much more related to dead works than prayer freely com-pleting itself in the word, the most direct expression of the person-ality, which, although not commanded by the law, because natural to men, as such is yet the soul of all sacrifices ; and the Chokma, like the Psalms and Prophets, in view of the ceremonial service which had become formal and dead in the *opus operatum*, is to such a degree penetrated by the knowledge of the incongruity of the offering up of animals and of plants, with the object in view, that a proverb like " the sacrifice of the righteous is pleasing to God" never anywhere occurs ; and if it did occur without being ex-pressly and unavoidably referred to the legal sacrifice, it would have to be understood rather after Ps. li. 18 f. than Ps. li. 20 f., rather after 1 Sam. xv. 22 than after Ps. lxvi. 13–15. זֶבַח, which, when it is distinguished from עֹלָה, means (cf. vii. 14) the sacrifice only in part coming to the altar, for the most part applied to a sacrificial feast, is here the common name for the bloody, and, *per synecdochen*, generally the legally-appointed sacrifice, consist-ing in external offering. The לְרָצוֹן, Lev. i. 3, used in the *Tôra* of sacrifices, is here, as at Ps. xix. 15, transferred to prayer. The fundamental idea of the proverb is, that sacrifices well-pleasing to God, prayers acceptable to God (that are heard, xv. 29), depend on the relations in which the heart and life of the man stand to God.

Ver. 9. Another proverb with the key-word תּוֹעֲבַת:

> An abomination to Jahve is the way of the godless;
> But He loveth him who searcheth after righteousness.

The manner and rule of life is called the way. מְרַדֵּף is the heightening of רֹדֵף, xxi. 21, and can be used independently *in bonam*, as well as *in malam partem* (xi. 19, cf. xiii. 21). Regarding the form יֶאֱהָב, *vid.* Fleischer in *Deutsch. Morgenl. Zeitsch.* xv. 382.

Ver. 10 Sharp correction is for him who forsaketh the way;
> Whoever hateth instruction shall die.

The way, thus absolute, is the God-pleasing right way (ii. 13), the forsaking of which is visited with the punishment of death, because it is that which leadeth unto life (x. 17). And that which comes upon them who leave it is called מוּסָר רָע, *castigatio dura*, as much as to say that whoever does not welcome instruction, whoever rejects it, must at last receive it against his will in the form of peremptory punishment. The sharp correction (cf. Isa. xxviii. 28, 19b) is just the death under which he falls who accepts of no instruction (v. 23), temporal death, but that as a token of wrath which it is not for the righteous (xiv. 32).

Ver. 11 The underworld [Sheol] and the abyss are before Jahve;
> But how much more the hearts of the children of men!

A syllogism, *a minori ad majus*, with אַף כִּי (LXX. πῶς οὐχὶ καί, *Venet.* μᾶλλον οὖν), like xii. 32.[1] אֲבַדּוֹן has a meaning analogous to that of τάρταρος (cf. ταρταροῦν, 2 Pet. ii. 4, to throw down into the τάρταρος), which denotes the lowest region of Hades (שְׁאוֹל תַּחְתִּיָּה or תַּחְתִּית '(שׁ), and also in general, Hades. If אבדון and מָוֶת are connected, Job xxxvii. 22, and if אבדון is the parallel word to קֶבֶר, Ps. lxxxviii. 12, or also to שְׁאוֹל, as in the passage similar to this proverb, Job xxvi. 6 (cf. xxxviii. 17): "Sheôl is naked before

[1] In Rabbin. this concluding form is called קַל וָחֹמֶר (light and heavy over against one another), and דִּין (judgment, viz. from premisses, thus conclusion), κατ' ἐξ. Instead of the biblical אַף כִּי, the latter form of the language has כָּל־שֶׁכֵּן (all speaks for it that it is so), עַל־אַחַת כַּמָּה וְכַמָּה (so much the more), אֵינוֹ דִין, or also קל וחמר (*a minori ad majus* = *quanto magis*); *vid.* the Hebr. *Römerbrief*, p. 14.

Him, and Abaddon has no covering;" since אבדן is the general
name of the underworld, including the grave, i.e. the inner place
of the earth which receives the body of the dead, as the kingdom
of the dead, lying deeper, does the soul. But where, as here and
at xxvii. 10, שאול and אבדן stand together, they are related to each
other, as ᾅδης and ταρταρος or ἄβυσσος, Rev. ix. 11 : אבדן is the
lowest hell, the place of deepest descent, of uttermost destruction.
The conclusion which is drawn in the proverb proceeds from the
supposition that in the region of creation there is nothing more
separated, and by a wide distance, from God, than the depth, and
especially the undermost depth, of the realm of the dead. If now
God has this region in its whole compass wide open before Him,
if it is visible and thoroughly cognisable by Him (נֶגֶד, acc. adv. : in
conspectu, from נגד, eminere, conspicuum esse),—for He is also present
in the underworld, Ps. cxxxix. 8,—then much more will the hearts
of the children of men be open, the inward thoughts of men living
and acting on the earth being known already from their expressions. Man sees through man, and also himself, never perfectly;
but the Lord can try the heart and prove the reins, Jer. xvii. 10.
What that means this proverb gives us to understand, for it places
over against the hearts of men nothing less than the depths of the
underworld in eternity.

Ver. 12 The scorner liketh not that one reprove him,
To wise men he will not go.

The inf. absol., abruptly denoting the action, may take the place of
the object, as here (cf. Job ix. 18, Isa. xlii. 24), as well as of the
subject (xxv. 27, Job vi. 25). Thus הוכיח is (ix. 7) construed
with the dat. obj. Regarding the probable conclusion which presents itself from passages such as xv. 12 and xiii. 20, as to the
study of wisdom in Israel, vid. p. 39. Instead of אֶל, we read,
xiii. 20 (cf. xxii. 24), אֶת־; for לֶכֶת אֶת־ means to have intercourse
with one, to go a journey with one (Mal. ii. 6, cf. Gen. v. 24,
but not 2 Sam. xv. 22, where we are to translate with Keil),
according to which the LXX. has here μετὰ δὲ σοφῶν οὐχ
ὁμιλήσει. The mocker of religion and of virtue shuns the circle
of the wise, for he loves not to have his treatment of that which is
holy reproved, nor to be convicted of his sin against truth; he
prefers the society where his frivolity finds approbation and a
response.

Ver. 13 A joyful heart maketh the countenance cheerful ;
But in sorrow of the heart the spirit is broken.

The expression of the countenance, as well as the spiritual *habitus*
of a man, is conditioned by the state of the heart. A joyful
heart maketh the countenance טוב, which means friendly, but
here happy-looking = cheerful (for טוב is the most general designation of that which makes an impression which is pleasant to
the senses or to the mind) ; on the contrary, with sorrow of
heart (עַצֶּבֶת, constr. of עַצֶּבֶת, x. 10, as חַטָּאת = חַטָּאת, from חֲטָאָה)
there is connected a stricken, broken, downcast heart ; the spiritual
functions of the man are paralyzed ; self-confidence, without which
energetic action is impossible, is shattered ; he appears discouraged,
whereby רוּחַ is thought of as the power of self-consciousness and
of self-determination, but לֵב, as our " *Gemüt* " [*animus*], as the
oneness of thinking and willing, and thus as the seat of determination, which decides the intellectual-corporeal life-expression of the
man, or without being able to be wholly restrained, communicates
itself to them. The בְ of וּבְעַצְּבַת is, as xv. 16 f., xvi. 8, xvii. 1,
meant in the force of being together or along with, so that רוּחַ
נְכֵאָה do not need to be taken separate from each other as subject
and predicate : the sense of the noun-clause is in the בְ, as *e.g.* also
vii. 23 (it is about his life, *i.e.* it concerns his life). Elsewhere the
crushed spirit, like the broken heart, is equivalent to the heart
despairing in itself and prepared for grace. The heart with a
more clouded mien may be well, for sorrow has in it a healing
power (Eccles. vii. 3). But here the matter is the general psychological truth, that the corporeal and spiritual life of man has its
regulator in the heart, and that the condition of the heart leaves
its stamp on the appearance and on the activity of the man. The
translation of the רוח נכאה by " oppressed breath " (Umbreit,
Hitzig) is impossible ; the breath cannot be spoken of as broken.

Ver. 14 The heart of the understanding seeketh after knowledge,
And the mouth of fools practiseth folly.

Luther interprets רעה as metaphor. for to govern, but with such
ethical conceptions it is metaphor. for to be urgently circumspect
about anything (*vid.* xiii. 20), like Arab. *ra'y* and *r'áyt*, intentional,
careful, concern about anything. No right translation can be
made of the *Chethib* פני, which Schultens, Hitzig, Ewald, and
Zöckler prefer ; the predicate can go before the פְּנֵי, after the
Semitic rule in the fem. of the sing., 2 Sam. x. 9, cf. Job xvi. 16,

Chethib, but cannot follow in the masc. of the sing.; besides, the operations of his look and aspect are ascribed to his face, but not spiritual functions as here, much more to the mouth, *i.e.* to the spirit speaking through it. The heart is within a man, and the mouth without; and while the former gives and takes, the latter is always only giving out. In xviii. 15, where a synonymous distich is formed from the antithetic distich, the ear, as hearing, is mentioned along with the heart as appropriating. נָבוֹן is not an adj., but is gen., like צדיק, 28a (opp. וּפִי). חכם, xvi. 23. The φιλοσοφία of the understanding is placed over against the μωρολογία of the fools. The LXX. translates καρδία ὀρθὴ ζητεῖ αἴσθησιν (cf. xiv. 10, καρδία ἀνδρὸς αἰσθητική); it uses this word after the Hellenistic *usus loq.* for דעת, of experimental knowledge.

> Ver. 15 All the days of the afflicted are evil;
> But he who is of a joyful heart hath a perpetual feast.

Regarding עָנִי (the afflicted), *vid.* 21b. They are so called on whom a misfortune, or several of them, press externally or internally. If such an one is surrounded by ever so many blessings, yet is his life day by day a sad one, because with each new day the feeling of his woe which oppresses him renews itself; whoever, on the contrary, is of joyful heart (gen. connection as xi. 13, xii. 8), such an one (his life) is always a feast, a banquet (not מִשְׁתֶּה, as it may be also pointed, but מִשְׁתֶּה and תָּמִיד thus *adv.*, for it is never adj.; the post-bib. usage is תְּמִידִין for עוֹלוֹת תָּמִיד). Hitzig (and also Zöckler) renders 15b: And (the days) of one who is of a joyful heart are . . . Others supply לוֹ (cf. xxvii. 7b), but our rendering does not need that. We have here again an example of that attribution (Arab. *isnâd*) in which that which is attributed (*musnad*) is a condition (*hal*) of a logical subject (the *musnad ilêhi*), and thus he who speaks has this, not in itself, but in the sense of the condition; the inwardly cheerful is feasts evermore, *i.e.* the condition of such an one is like a continual festival. The true and real happiness of a man is thus defined, not by external things, but by the state of the heart, in which, in spite of the apparently prosperous condition, a secret sorrow may gnaw, and which, in spite of an externally sorrowful state, may be at peace, and be joyfully confident in God.

> Ver. 16 Better is little with the fear of Jahve,
> Than great store and trouble therewith.

The בְּ in both cases the LXX. rightly renders by μετά. How

מְהוּמָה (elsewhere of wild, confused disorder, extreme discord) is meant of store and treasure, Ps. xxxix. 7 shows: it is restless, covetous care and trouble, as the contrast of the quietness and contentment proceeding from the fear of God, the noisy, wild, stormy running and hunting about of the slave of mammon. Theodotion translates the word here, as Aquila and Symmachus elsewhere, by words which correspond (φαγέδαινα = φάγαινα or ἀχορτασία) with the Syr. יענותא, greed or insatiability.

> Ver. 17 Better a dish of cabbage, and love with it,
> Than a fatted ox together with hatred.

With בו is here interchanged שָׁם, which, used both of things and of persons, means to be there along with something. Both have the *Dag. forte conj.*, cf. to the contrary, Deut. xxx. 20, Mic. i. 11, Deut. xi. 22; the punctuation varies, if the first of the two words is a *n. actionis* ending in הָ‎ָ. The dish (portion) is called אֲרֻחָה, which the LXX. and other Greek versions render by ξενισμός, entertainment, and thus understand it of that which is set before a guest, perhaps rightly so, for the Arab. *ârrakh* (to date, to determine), to which it is compared by Gesenius and Dietrich, is equivalent to *warrh*, a denom. of the name of the moon. Love and hatred are, according to circumstances, the disposition of the host, or of the participant, the spirit of the family:

> Cum dat oluscula mensa minuscula pace quietâ,
> Ne pete grandia lautaque prandia lite repleta.

Two proverbs of two different classes of men, each second line of which terminates with a catchword having a similar sound (וארך, וארה).

> Ver. 18 A passionate man stirreth up strife,
> And one who is slow to anger allayeth contention.

xxviii. 25a and xxix. 22a are variations of the first line of this proverb. The *Pih.* גֵּרֶה occurs only these three times in the phrase גֵּרֶה מָדוֹן, R. גר, to grind, thus to strike, to irritate, cogn. to (but of a different root from) the verb עוֹרֵר, to excite, x. 12, and חִרְחַר, to set on fire, xxvi. 21, cf. שָׁלַח, vi. 14. Regarding חֵמָה, *vid.* xv. 1; we call such a man a "hot-head;" but the biblical conception nowhere (except in the Book of Daniel) places the head in connection with spiritual-psychical events (*Psychologie*, p. 254). Regarding אֶרֶךְ אַפַּיִם, *vid.* xiv. 29; the LXX. (which contains a translation of this proverb, and after it of a variation) translates μακρόθυμος δὲ καὶ τὴν μέλλουσαν καταπραΰνει, *i.e.* (as the Syr. render it) he suppresses the strife in its origin, so that it does not break out. But both are true : that he who is slow to anger, who does not thus easily permit himself to become angry, allayeth the strife which one enters into with him, or into which he is drawn, and that he prevents the strife, for he places over against provoking, injurious conduct, patient gentleness (מַרְפֵּא, Eccles. x. 4).

Ver. 19 The way of the slothful is as hedged with thorns;
But the path of the righteous is paved.

Hitzig misses the contrast between עָצֵל (slothful) and יְשָׁרִים (upright), and instead of the slothful reads עָרִיץ, the tyrannical. But is then the slothful יָשָׁר ? The contrast is indeed not that of contradiction, but the slothful is one who does not act uprightly, a man who fails to fulfil the duty of labour common to man, and of his own special calling. The way of such an one is כִּמְשֻׂכַת חָדֶק, like a fencing with thorns (from חדק, R. חד, to be pointed, sharp, distinguished from Arab. ḥadk, to surround, and in the meaning to fix with the look, denom. of khadakt, the apple of the eye), so that he goes not for-wards, and sees hindrances and difficulties everywhere, which frighten him back, excusing his shunning his work, his remissness of will, and his doing nothing ; on the contrary, the path of those who wait truly and honestly on their calling, and prosecute their aim, is raised up like a skilfully made street, so that unhindered and quickly they go forward (סְלִילָה, R. סל, aggerare, cf. Jer. xviii. 15 with Isa. xlix. 11, and iv. 8, סִלְסֵל, which was still in use in the common language of Palestine in the second cent., Rosch haschana, 26b).

This collection of Solomonic proverbs began, x. 1, with a pro-verb having reference to the observance of the fourth command-ment,[1] and a second chief section, xiii. 1, began in the same way. Here a proverb of the same kind designates the beginning of a third chief section. That the editor was aware of this is shown by the homogeneity of the proverbs, xv. 19, xii. 28, which form the conclusion of the first and second sections. We place together first in this new section, vers. 20–23, in which (with the exception of ver. 25) the יִשְׂמַח [maketh glad] of the first (x. 1) is continued.

Ver. 20 A wise son maketh a glad father,
And a fool of a man despiseth his mother.

---

[1] [The fifth commandment of the Westminster Shorter Catechism is named as the fourth in Luther's catechism.]

Line first = x. 1.   The gen. connection of אָדָם כְּסִיל (here and at
xxi. 20) is not superlative [the most foolish of men], but like פֶּרֶא
אָדָם, Gen. xvi. 12; the latter: a man of the wild ass kind; the
former: a man of the fool kind, who is the exemplar of such a sort
among men.   Piety acting in willing subordination is wisdom, and
the contrary exceeding folly.

Ver. 21 Folly is joy to him that is devoid of understanding;
But a man of understanding goeth straight forward.

Regarding חֲסַר־לֵב, *vid.* at vi. 32 (cf. *libîb*, which in the Samaritan
means "dearly beloved," in Syr. "courageous," in Arab. and
Aethiop. *cordatus*); אִישׁ תְּבוּנָה, x. 23, and יְשֶׁר, with the accus. of
the way, here of the going, iii. 6 (but not xi. 5, where the going
itself is not the subject).   In consequence of the contrast, the
meaning of 21a is different from that of x. 23, according to which
sin is to the fool as the sport of a child.   Here אִוֶּלֶת is folly and
buffoonery, drawing aside in every kind of way from the direct
path of that which is good, and especially from the path of one's
duty.   This gives joy to the fool; he is thereby drawn away from
the earnest and faithful performance of the duties of his calling,
and thus wastes time and strength; while, on the contrary, a man
of understanding, who perceives and rejects the vanity and un-
worthiness of such trifling and such nonsense, keeps the straight
direction of his going, *i.e.* without being drawn aside or kept back,
goes straight forward, *i.e.* true to duty, prosecutes the end of his
calling.   לָכֶת is accus., like xxx. 29, Mic. vi. 8.

Ver. 22 A breaking of plans where no counsel is;
But where many counsellors are they come to pass.

On the other side it is also true according to the proverbs, " *so viel
Köpfe so viel Sinne*" [*quot homines, tot sententiæ*], and " *viel Rath
ist Unrath*" [*ne quid nimis*], and the like.   But it cannot become
a rule of morals not to accept of counsel that we may not go
astray; on the contrary, it is and remains a rule of morals: not
stubbornly to follow one's own heart (head), and not obstinately
to carry out one's own will, and not in the darkness of wisdom to
regard one's own plans as unimproveable, and not needing to be
examined; but to listen to the counsel of intelligent and honest
friends, and, especially where weighty matters are in hand, not
affecting one's own person, but the common good, not to listen
merely to one counsellor, but to many.   Not merely the organism
of the modern state, but also of old the Mosaic arrangement of

the Israelitish community, with its representative organization, its courts and councils, rested on the acknowledged justice and importance of the saying uttered in xi. 14, and here generalized. הָפֵר, *infin. abs. Hiph.* of פָּרַר, to break, with the accus. following, stands here, like הָפוֹךְ, xii. 7, instead of the finite: the thoughts come to a fracture (failure), *irrita fiunt consilia.* סוֹד (= יְסוֹד, cf. נוֹסָד, Ps. ii. 2) means properly the being brought close together for the purpose of secret communication and counsel (cf. Arab. *sâwada*, to press close together = to walk with one privately). The LXX.: their plans are unexecuted, οἱ μὴ τιμῶντες συνέδρια, literally Symmachus, διασκεδάζονται λογισμοὶ μὴ ὄντος συμβουλίου. תָּקוּם has, after Jer. iv. 14, li. 29, מַחֲשָׁבוֹת as subject. The LXX. (besides perverting ברב [by a multitude] into בלב [ἐν καρδίαις]), the Syr., and Targ. introduce עֵצָה (xix. 21) as subject.

> Ver. 23 A man has joy by the right answer of his mouth;
> And a word in its season, how fair is it!

If we translate מַעֲנֵה only by "answer," then 23a sounds as a praise of self-complaisance; but it is used of true correspondence (xxix. 19), of fit reply (Job xxxii. 3, 5), of appropriate answer (cf. 28a, xvi. 1). It has happened to one in his reply to hit the nail on its head, and he has joy from that (שִׂמְחָה בְּ after שָׂמַח בְּ, *e.g.* xxiii. 24), and with right; for the reply does not always succeed. A reply like this, which, according to circumstances, stops the mouth or bringeth a kiss (xxiv. 26), is a fortunate throw, is a gift from above. The synonymous parallel line measures that which is appropriate, not to that which is to be answered, but from a general point of view as to its seasonableness; עֵת (= עֵדֶת from יָעַד) is here "the ethically right, becoming time, determined by the laws of wisdom (moral)" (*vid.* Orelli, *Synonyma der Zeit u. Ewigkeit*, p. 48), cf. עַל־אָפְנָיו (translated by Luther "in its time"), xxv. 11. With מַה־טּוֹב, cf. xvi. 16; both ideas lie in it: that such a word is in itself well-conditioned and successful, and also that it is welcome, agreeable, and of beneficial influence.

Four proverbs of fundamentally different doctrines:

> Ver. 24 The man of understanding goeth upwards on a way of life,
> To depart from hell beneath.

The way of life is one, v. 6, Ps. xvi. 11 (where, notwithstanding the want of the article, the idea is logically determined), although in itself forming a plurality of אֹרְחוֹת, ii. 19. "A way of life," in the translation, is equivalent to a way which is a way of life.

לְמַעְלָה, upwards (as Eccles. iii. 21, where, in the doubtful question whether the spirit of a man at his death goes upwards, there yet lies the knowledge of the alternative), belongs, as the parallel מִשְּׁאוֹל מַטָּה shows, to אֹרַח חַיִּים as virtual adj.: a way of life which leads upwards. And the לְ of לְמַשְׂכִּיל is that of possession, but not as of quiet possession (such belongs to him), but as personal activity, as in דֶּרֶךְ לוֹ, he has a journey = he makes a journey, finds himself on a journey, 1 Kings xviii. 27; for לְמַעַן סוּר is not merely, as לָסוּר, xiii. 14, xiv. 27, the expression of the end and consequence, but of the subjective object, *i.e.* the intention, and thus supposes an activity corresponding to this intention. The O. T. reveals heaven, *i.e.* the state of the revelation of God in glory, yet not as the abode of saved men ; the way of the dying leads, according to the O. T. representation, downwards into Sheôl ; but the translations of Enoch and Elijah are facts which, establishing the possibility of an exception, break through the dark monotony of that representation, and, as among the Greeks the mysteries encouraged ἡδυστέρας ἐλπίδας, so in Israel the Chokma appears pointing the possessor of wisdom upwards, and begins to shed light on the darkness of Sheôl by the new great thoughts of a life of immortality, thus of a ζωὴ αἰώνιος (xii. 28) (*Psychologie*, p. 407 ff.), now for the first time becoming prominent, but only as a foreboding and an enigma. The idea of the Sheôl opens the way for a change : the gathering place of all the living on this side begins to be the place of punishment for the godless (vii. 27, ix. 18) ; the way leading upwards, εἰς τὴν ζωὴν, and that leading downwards, εἰς τὴν ἀπώλειαν (Matt. vii. 13 f.), come into direct contrast.

Ver. 25 The house of the proud Jahve rooteth out,
And He establisheth the landmark of the widow.

The power unnamed in יִפְּחוּ, ii. 22 (cf. xiv. 11a), is here named יִפַּח | יְהֹוָה (thus to be pointed with *Mercha* and *Pasek* following). יַצֵּב is the abbreviated fut. form which the elevated style, *e.g.* Deut. xxxii. 8, uses also as indic.,—a syntactical circumstance which renders Hitzig's correction וַיַּצֵּב superfluous. It is the border of the land-possession of the widows, removed by the גֵּאִים (LXX. ὑβριστῶν), that is here meant. The possession of land in Israel was secured by severe punishment inflicted on him who removed the " landmark " (Deut. xix. 14, xxvii. 17), and the Chokma (xxii. 28 ; Job xxiv. 2) as well as the prophets (*e.g.* Hos. v. 10) inculcate the inviolability of the borders of the possession, as the guardian of which Jahve here Himself appears.

> Ver. 26 An abomination to Jahve are evil thoughts ;
> But gracious words are to Him pure.

Not personally (Luther: the plans of the wicked) but neutrally is רָע here meant as at ii. 14, and in אֶשֶׁת רָע, vi. 24 (cf. Pers. *merdi nîku*, man of good = good man), *vid.* Friedr. Philippi's *Status Constr.* p. 121. Thoughts which are of a bad kind and of a bad tendency, particularly (what the parallel member brings near) of a bad disposition and design against others, are an abomination to God ; but, on the contrary, pure, viz. in His eyes, which cannot look upon iniquity (Hab. i. 13), are the אִמְרֵי־נֹעַם, words of compassion and of friendship toward men, which are (after 26a) the expression of such thoughts, thus sincere, benevolent words, the influence of which on the soul and body of him to whom they refer is described, xvi. 24. The Syr., Targ., Symmachus, Theodotion, and the *Venet.* recognise in וּטְהוֹרִים the pred., while, on the contrary, the LXX., Jerome, and Luther (who finally decided for the translation, " but the pure speak comfortably ") regard it as subject. But that would be an attribution which exceeds the measure of possibility, and for which אֹמְרִים or דִּבְרֵי must be used ; also the parallelism requires that טהורים correspond with תּוֹעֲבַת ה'. Hence also the reference of וטהורים to the judgment of God, which is determined after the motive of pure untainted law; that which proceeds from such, that and that only, is pure, pure in His sight, and thus also pure in itself.

> Ver. 27 Whoever does service to [*servit*] avarice troubleth his own house;
> But he that hateth gifts shall live.

Regarding בֹּצֵעַ בֶּצַע, *vid.* at i. 19, and regarding עֹכֵר בֵּיתוֹ, xi. 29, where it is subject, but here object.; xxviii. 16b is a variation of 27b. מַתָּנוֹת are here gifts in the sense of Eccles. vii. 7, which pervert judgment, and cause respect of persons. The LXX. from this point mingles together a series of proverbs with those of the following chapter.

Two proverbs regarding the righteous and the wicked :

> Ver. 28 The heart of the righteous considereth how to answer right,
> And the mouth of the godless poureth forth evil.

Instead of לַעֲנוֹת, the LXX. (Syr. and Targ.) imagines אֱמוּנוֹת, πίστεις ;. Jerome translates, but falsely, *obedientiam* (from עָנָה, to bend oneself) ; Meîri thinks on לַעֲנָה, wormwood, for the heart of the righteous revolves in itself the misery and the vanity of this present life; Hitzig corrects this verse as he does the three preceding: the heart of the righteous thinks on עֲנוֹת, a plur. of verb עָנָה, which, except in this correction, does not exist. The proverb, as it stands, is, in fineness of expression and sharpness of the contrast, raised above such manglings. Instead of the righteous, the wise might be named, and instead of the godless, fools (cf. 2b); but the poet places the proverb here under the point of view of duty to neighbours. It is the characteristic of the righteous that he does not give the reins to his tongue; but as Luther has translated: the heart of the righteous considers [*tichtet* from *dictare*, frequently to speak, here carefully to think over] what is to be answered, or rather, since מַהדְּלַעֲנוֹת is not used, he thinks thereupon to answer rightly, for that the word עֲנוֹת is used in this pregnant sense is seen from 23a. The godless, on the contrary, are just as rash with their mouth as the righteous are of a thoughtful heart: their mouth sputters forth (*effutit*) evil, for they do not first lay to heart the question what may be right and just in the case that has arisen.

Ver. 29 Jahve is far from the godless;
But the prayer of the righteous He heareth.

Line second is a variation of 8b. God is far from the godless, viz. as Polychronius remarks, *non spatii intercapedine, sed sententiæ diversitate*; more correctly: as to His gracious presence—חָלַץ מֵהֶם, He has withdrawn Himself from them, Hos. x. 6, so that if they pray, their prayer reaches not to Him. The prayer of the righteous, on the contrary, He hears, He is graciously near to them, they have access to Him, He listens to their petitions; and if they are not always fulfilled according to their word, yet they are not without an answer (Ps. cxlv. 18).

Two proverbs regarding the eye and the ear:

Ver. 30 The light of the eye rejoiceth the heart,
And a good message maketh the bones fat.

Hitzig corrects also here: מַרְאֵה עֵינִים, that which is seen with the eyes, viz. after long desire; and certainly מראה עינים can mean not only that which the eyes see (Isa. xi. 3), but also this, that the eyes do see. But is it true what Hitzig says in justification of his correction, that מאור never means light, or ray, or brightness, but lamp (φωστήρ)? It is true, indeed, that מאור עינים cannot mean a cheerful sight (Luther) in an objective sense (LXX. θεωρῶν ὀφθαλμὸς καλά), as a verdant garden or a stream flowing through a landscape (Rashi), for that would be מַרְאֶה מֵאִיר עֵינִים, and "brightness which the eyes see" (Bertheau); the genitive connection certainly does not mean: the מאור is not the light from without presenting itself to the eyes, but, like אוֹר עֵינִים (Ps. xxxviii. 11) and similar expressions, the light of the eye itself [bright or joyous eyes]. But מאור does not mean alone the body of light, but also the illumination, Ex. xxxv. 14 and elsewhere, not only that which (ὅ, τι) gives light, but also this, that (ὅτι) light arises and is present, so that we might translate it here as at Ps. xc. 8, either the brightness, or that which gives light. But the clear brightness of one's own eye cannot be meant, for then that were as much as to say that it is the effect, not that it is the cause, of a happy heart, but the brightness of the eyes of others that meet us. That this gladdens the heart of him who has a sight of it is evident, without any interchanging relation of the joy-beaming countenance, for it is indeed heart-gladdening to a man, to whom selfishness has not made the χαίρειν μετὰ χαιρόντων impossible, to see a countenance right joyful in truth. But in connection with xvi. 15, it lies nearer to think on a love-beaming countenance, a countenance on which joyful love to us mirrors itself, and which reflects itself in our heart, communicating this sense of gladness. The ancient Jewish interpreters understand מאור עינים of the enlightening of the eye of the mind, according to which Euchel translates: "clear intelligence;" but Rashi has remarked that that is not the explanation of the words, but the Midrash. That, in line second of this synonymous distich, שְׁמוּעָה טוֹבָה does not mean alloquium humanum (Fl.), nor a good report which one hears of himself, but a good message, is confirmed by xxv. 25; שְׁמוּעָה as neut. part. pass. may mean that which is heard, but the comparison of שְׁבוּעָה, יְשׁוּעָה, stamps it as an abstract formation like גְּדֻלָּה, גְּאֻלָּה (גְּדוּלָה), according to which the LXX. translates it by ἀκοή (in this passage by φήμη). Regarding דִּשֵּׁן, richly to satisfy, or to refresh, a favourite expression in the Mishle, vid. at xi. 25, xiii. 4.

Ver. 31 An ear which heareth the doctrine of life
Keeps itself in the circle of the wise.

As, vi. 33, הוֹכַחַת מוּסָר means instructions aiming at discipline, so here תּוֹכַחַת חַיִּים means instructions which have life as their end, i.e. as showing how one may attain unto true life; Hitzig's חֲכַם, for חַיִּים, is a fancy. Is now the meaning this, that the ear which willingly hears and receives such doctrine of life will come to dwell among the wise, *i.e.* that such an one (for אִוֵּן is *synecdoche partis pro persona*, as Job xxix. 11) will have his residence among wise men, as being one of them, *inter eos sedem firmam habebit iisque annumerabitur* (Fl.)? By such a rendering, one is surprised at the harshness of the synecdoche, as well as at the circumstantiality of the expression (cf. xiii. 20, יֶחְכָּם). On the contrary, this corresponds with the thought that one who willingly permits to be said to him what he must do and suffer in order that he may be a partaker of life, on this account remains most gladly in the circle of the wise, and there has his appropriate place. The "passing the night" (לִין, cogn. לַיִל, Syr. Targ. בּוּת, Arab. *bât*) is also frequently elsewhere the designation of prolonged stay, *e.g.* Isa. i. 21. בְּקֶרֶב is here different in signification from that it had in xiv. 23, where it meant "in the heart." In the LXX. this proverb is wanting. The other Greek translations have οὓς ἀκούων ἐλέγχους ζωῆς ἐν μέσῳ σοφῶν αὐλισθήσεται. Similarly the Syr., Targ., Jerome, Venet., and Luther, admitting both renderings, but, since they render in the fut., bringing nearer the idea of prediction (Midrash : זוכה לישב בישיבת חכמים) than of description of character.

Two proverbs with the catchword מוּסָר :

Ver. 32 He that refuseth correction lightly values his soul ;
But he that heareth reproof getteth understanding.

Regarding פּוֹרֵעַ מוּסָר, *vid.* xiii. 18, cf. i. 25, and מוֹאֵס נַפְשׁוֹ, viii. 36. נַפְשׁוֹ contains more than the later expression עַצְמוֹ, self ; it is equivalent to חַיָּיו (Job ix. 21), for the נפש is the bond of union between the intellectual and the corporeal life. The despising of the soul is then the neglecting, endangering, exposing of the life ; in a word, it is suicide (10*b*). xix. 8*a* is a variation derived from this distich : " He who gains understanding loves his soul," according to which the LXX. translate here ἀγαπᾷ ψυχὴν αὐτοῦ. לֵב the Midrash explains by חכמה שנתונה בלב ; but the correct view is, that לֵב is not thought of as a formal power, but as operative and carried into effect in conformity with its destination.

Ver. 33 The fear of Jahve is a discipline to wisdom,
And before honour is humility.

We may regard יִרְאַת ה' (the fear of Jahve) also as pred. here. The fear of Jahve is an educational maxim, and the end of education of the Chokma ; but the phrase may also be the subject, and by such a rendering Luther's parallelism lies nearer : " The fear

of the Lord is discipline to wisdom ; " the fear of God, viz. continually exercised and tried, is the right school of wisdom, and
humility is the right way to honour. Similar is the connection מוּסָר
הַשְׂכֵּל, discipline binds understanding to itself as its consequence,
i. 3. Line second repeats itself, xviii. 12, " Pride comes before the
fall." Luther's " And ere one comes to honour, he must previously
suffer," renders עָנִי rather than עֲנָוה. But the Syr. reverses the
idea : the honour of the humble goeth before him, as also one of
the anonymous Greek versions : προπορεύεται δὲ ταπεινοῖς δόξα.
But the δόξα comes, as the above proverb expresses it, afterwards.
The way to the height lies through the depth, the depth of humility
under the hand of God, and, as ענוה expresses, of self-humiliation.

Four proverbs of God, the disposer of all things :

Chap. xvi. 1 Man's are the counsels of the heart ;
But the answer of the tongue cometh from Jahve.

Gesen., Ewald, and Bertheau incorrectly understand 1b of hearing,
i.e. of a favourable response to what the tongue wishes ; 1a speaks
not of wishes, and the gen. after מענה (answer) is, as at xv. 23, Mic
iii. 7, and also here, by virtue of the parallelism, the gen. subjecti.
xv. 23 leads to the right sense, according to which a good answer
is joy to him to whom it refers : it does not always happen to one to
find the fitting and effective expression for that which he has in his
mind; it is, as this cog. proverb expresses it, a gift from above (δοθή-
σεται, Matt. x. 19). But now, since מַעֲנה neither means answering,
nor yet in general an expression (Euchel) or report (Löwenstein),
and the meaning of the word at 4a is not here in question, one has
to think of him whom the proverb has in view as one who has to
give a reason, to give information, or generally—since ענה, like
ἀμείβεσθαι, is not confined to the interchange of words—to solve a
problem, and that such an one as requires reflection. The scheme
(project, premeditation) which he in his heart contrives, is here
described as מַעַרְכֵי־לֵב, from עָרַךְ, to arrange, to place together, meta-
phorically of the reflection, i.e. the consideration analyzing and
putting a matter in order. These reflections, seeking at one time
in one direction, and at another in another, the solution of the
question, the unfolding of the problem, are the business of men ;
but the answer which finally the tongue gives, and which here,
in conformity with the pregnant sense of מענה (vid. at xv. 23, 28),
will be regarded as right, appropriate, effective, thus generally the
satisfying reply to the demand placed before him, is from God. It

is a matter of experience which the preacher, the public speaker, the author, and every man to whom his calling or circumstances present a weighty, difficult theme, can attest. As the thoughts pursue one another in the mind, attempts are made, and again abandoned; the state of the heart is somewhat like that of chaos before the creation. But when, finally, the right thought and the right utterance for it are found, that which is found appears to us, not as if self-discovered, but as a gift; we regard it with the feeling that a higher power has influenced our thoughts and imaginings; the confession by us, ἡ ἱκανότης ἡμῶν ἐκ τοῦ Θεοῦ (2 Cor. iii. 5), in so far as we believe in a living God, is inevitable.

Ver. 2 Every way of a man is pure in his own eyes;
But a weigher of the spirits is Jahve.

Variations of this verse are xxi. 2, where יָשָׁר for זַךְ (according to the root-meaning: pricking in the eyes, *i.e.* shining clear, then: without spot, pure, *vid.* Fleischer in Levy's *Chald. Wörterbuch*, i. 424), לְבּוֹת for רוּחוֹת, and כָּל־דֶּרֶךְ for כָּל־דַּרְכֵי, whereupon here without synallage (for כל means the totality), the singular of the pred. follows, as Isa. lxiv. 10, Ezek. xxxi. 15. For the rest, cf. with 2*a*, xiv. 12, where, instead of the subj. בְּעֵינָיו, is used לְפְנֵי, and with 2*b*, xxiv. 12, where God is described by תֹכֵן לִבּוֹת. The verb תָּכַן is a secondary formation from כּוּן (*vid.* Hupfeld on Ps. v. 7), like תָּקַן from Arab. *tyakn* (to be fast, sure), the former through the medium of the reflex. הִתְכּוֹנֵן, the latter of the reflex. Arab. *âitkn*; תָּכַן means to regulate (from *regula*, a rule), to measure off, to weigh, here not to bring into a condition right according to rule (Theodotion, ἑδράζων, *stabiliens*, Syr. Targ. מְתַקֵּן, Venet. καταρτίζει; Luther, "but the Lord maketh the heart sure"), but to measure or weigh, and therefore to estimate rightly, to know accurately (Jerome, *spirituum ponderator est Dominus*). The judgment of a man regarding the cause of life, which it is good for him to enter upon, lies exposed to great and subtle self-deception; but God has the measure and weight, *i.e.* the means of proving, so as to value the spirits according to their true moral worth; his investigation goes to the root (cf. κριτικός, Heb. iv. 12), his judgment rests on the knowledge of the true state of the matter, and excludes all deception, so that thus a man can escape the danger of delusion by no other means than by placing his way, *i.e.* his external and internal life, in the light of the word of God, and desiring for himself the all-penetrating test of the Searcher of hearts (Ps.

cxxxix. 23 f.), and the self-knowledge corresponding to the result of this test.

Ver. 3 Roll on Jahve thy works,
So thy thoughts shall prosper.

The proverbs vers. 1–3 are wanting in the LXX.; their absence is compensated for by three others, but only externally, not according to their worth. Instead of גֹּל, the Syr., Targ., and Jerome read גַּל, *revela*, with which the עַל, Ps. xxxvii. 5, cf. lv. 23, interchanging with אֶל (here and at Ps. xxii. 9), does not agree ; rightly Theodotion, κύλισον ἐπὶ κύριον, and Luther, " commend to the Lord thy works." The works are here, not those that are executed, Ex. xxiii. 16, but those to be executed, as Ps. xc. 17, where כּוֹנֵן, here the active to וְיִכּוֹנוּ, which at iv. 26 as jussive meant to be placed right, here with ו of the consequence in the *apodosis imperativi*: to be brought about, and to have continuance, or briefly : to stand (cf. xii. 3) as the contrast of disappointment or ruin. We should roll on God all matters which, as obligations, burden us, and on account of their weight and difficulty cause us great anxiety, for nothing is too heavy or too hard for Him who can overcome all difficulties and dissolve all perplexities; then will our thoughts, viz. those about the future of our duty and our life-course, be happy, nothing will remain entangled and be a failure, but will be accomplished, and the end and aim be realized.

Ver. 4 Jahve hath made everything for its contemplated end ;
And also the wicked for the day of evil.

Everywhere else מַעֲנֶה means answer (*Venet.* πρὸς ἀπόκρισιν αὐτοῦ), which is not suitable here, especially with the absoluteness of the כֹּל; the Syr. and Targ. translate, *obedientibus ei*, which the words do not warrant; but also *propter semet ipsum* (Jerome, Theodotion, Luther) give to 4b no right parallelism, and, besides, would demand לְמַעֲנוֹ or לְמַעֲנֵהוּ. The punctuation לַמַּעֲנֵהוּ, which is an anomaly (cf. בְּנִבְרָתָהּ, Isa. xxiv. 2, and בְּעֵרִינוּ, Ezra x. 14), shows (Ewald) that here we have, not the prepositional לְמַעַן, but לְ with the subst. מַעֲנֶה, which in derivation and meaning is one with the form מַעַן abbreviated from it (cf. מַעַר, מַעַל), similar in meaning to the Arab. *ma'anyn*, aim, intention, object, and end, and mind, from 'atay, to place opposite to oneself a matter, to make it the object of effort. Hitzig prefers לְמַעֲנֶה, but why not rather לְמַעֲנֵהוּ, for the proverb is not intended to express that all that God has made serve a purpose (by which one is reminded of the arguments for the existence of

God from final causes, which are often prosecuted too far), but that all is made by God for its purpose, *i.e.* a purpose premeditated by Him, that the world of things and of events stands under the law of a plan, which has in God its ground and its end, and that also the wickedness of free agents is comprehended in this plan, and made subordinate to it. God has not indeed made the wicked as such, but He has made the being which is capable of wickedness, and which has decided for it, viz. in view of the " day of adversity" (Eccles. vii. 14), which God will cause to come upon him, thus making His holiness manifest in the merited punishment, and thus also making wickedness the means of manifesting His glory. It is the same thought which is expressed in Ex. ix. 16 with reference to Pharaoh. A *prædestinatio ad malum*, and that in the supralapsarian sense, cannot be here taught, for this horrible dogma (*horribile quidem decretum, fateor,* says Calvin himself) makes God the author of evil, and a ruler according to His sovereign caprice, and thus destroys all pure conceptions of God. What Paul, Rom. ix., with reference to Ex. ix. 16, wishes to say is this, that it was not Pharaoh's conduct that determined the will of God, but that the will of God is always the *antecedens :* nothing happens to God through the obstinacy and rebellion of man which determines Him to an action not already embraced 'in the eternal plan, but also such an one must against his will be subservient to the display of God's glory. The apostle adds ver. 22, and shows that he recognised the factor of human self-determination, but also as one comprehended in God's plan. The free actions of men create no situation by which God would be surprised and compelled to something which was not originally intended by Himself. That is what the above proverb says: the wicked also has his place in God's order of the world. Whoever frustrates the designs of grace must serve God in this, ἐνδείξασθαι τὴν ὀργὴν καὶ γνωρίσαι τὸ δυνατὸν αὐτοῦ (Rom. ix. 22).

Here follow three proverbs of divine punishment, *expiatio* [Versühnung] and *reconciliatio* [Versöhnung].

> Ver. 5 An abomination to Jahve is every one who is haughty ;
> The hand for it [assuredly] he remains not unpunished.

Proverbs thus commencing we already had at xv. 9, 26. גְּבַהּ is a metaplastic connecting form of גָּבֹהַּ ; on the contrary, גֹּבַהּ, 1 Sam. xvi. 7, Ps. ciii. 11, means being high, as גֹּבַהּ, height ; the form underlying גְּבַהּ is not גָּבֵהַּ (as Gesen. and Olshausen write it), but גָּבַהּ. In 5*b*, xi. 21*a* is repeated. The translators are perplexed in their rendering of יָד לְיָד. Fleischer: *ab ætate in ætatem non* (i.e. *nullo unquam tempore futuro*) *impunis erit.*

Ver. 6 By love and truth is iniquity expiated,
And through the fear of Jahve one escapes from evil—

literally, there comes (as the effect of it) the escaping of evil (סוּר, *n. actionis*, as xiii. 19), or rather, since the evil here comes into view as to its consequences (xiv. 27, xv. 24), this, that one escapes evil. By חֶסֶד וֶאֱמֶת are here meant, not the χάρις καὶ ἀλήθεια of God (Bertheau), but, like xx. 28, Isa. xxxix. 8, love and faithfulness in the relation of men to one another. The בּ is both times that of the mediating cause. Or is it said neither by what means one may attain the expiation of his sins, nor how he may attain to the escaping from evil, but much rather wherein the true reverence for Jahve, and wherein the right expiation of sin, consist? Thus von Hofmann, *Schriftbew.* i. 595. But the בּ of בחסד is not different from that of בְּזֹאת, Isa. xxvii. 9. It is true that the article of justification is falsified if good works enter as *causa meritoria* into the act of justification, but we of the evangelical school teach that the *fides quâ justificat* is indeed inoperative, but not the *fides quæ justificat,* and we cannot expect of the O. T. that it should everywhere distinguish with Pauline precision what even James will not or cannot distinguish. As the law of sacrifice designates the victim united with the blood in the most definite manner, but sometimes also the whole transaction in the offering of sacrifice even to the priestly feast as serving לְכַפֵּר, Lev. x. 17, so it also happens in the general region of ethics: the objective ground of reconciliation is the decree of God, to which the blood in the typical offering points, and man is a partaker of this reconciliation, when he accepts, in penitence and in faith, the offered mercy of God; but this acceptance would be a self-deception, if it meant that the blotting out of the guilt of sin could be obtained in the way of imputation without the immediate following thereupon of a blotting of it out in the way of sanctification; and therefore the Scriptures also ascribe to good works a share in the expiation of sin in a wider sense—namely, as the proofs of thankful (Luke vii. 47) and compassionate love (*vid.* at x. 2), as this proverb of love and truth, herein according with the words of the prophets, as Hos. vi. 6, Mic. vi. 6–8. He who is conscious of this, that he is a sinner, deeply guilty before God, who cannot stand before Him if He did not deal with him in mercy instead of justice, according to the purpose of His grace, cannot trust to this mercy if he is not zealous, in his relations to his fellow-men, to practise love and truth; and in view of the fifth petition of the Lord's Prayer, and of the parable of the unmerciful steward rightly understood, it may be said that the love which covers the sins, x. 12, of a neighbour, has, in regard to our own sins, a covering or atoning influence, for "blessed are the merciful, for they shall obtain mercy." That "love and truth" are meant of virtues practised from religious motives, 6b shows; for, according to this line, by the fear of Jahve one escapes evil. The fear of Jahve is subjection to the God of revelation, and a falling in with the revealed plan of salvation.

Ver. 7 If Jahve has pleasure in the ways of a man,
He reconciles even his enemies to him—

properly (for הִשְׁלִים is here the causative of the transitive, Josh. x. 1): He brings it about that they conclude peace with him. If God has pleasure in the ways of a man, i.e. in the designs which he prosecutes, and in the means which he employs, he shows, by the great consequences which flow from his endeavours, that, even as his enemies also acknowledge, God is with him (e.g. Gen. xxvi. 27 f.), so that they, vanquished in heart (e.g. 2 Sam. xix. 9 f.), abandon their hostile position, and become his friends. For if it is manifest that God makes Himself known, bestowing blessings on a man, there lies in this a power of conviction which disarms his most bitter opponents, excepting only those who have in selfishness hardened themselves.

Five proverbs of the king, together with three of righteousness in action and conduct:

Ver. 8 Better is a little with righteousness,
Than rich revenues with unrighteousness.

The cogn. proverb xv. 16 commences similarly. Of רֹב תְּבוּאוֹת, multitude or greatness of income, vid. xiv. 4: "unrighteous wealth profits not." The possessor of it is not truly happy, for sin cleaves to it, which troubles the heart (conscience), and because the enjoyment which it affords is troubled by the curses of those who are injured, and by the sighs of the oppressed. Above all other gains rises ἡ εὐσέβεια μετ' αὐταρκείας (1 Tim. vi. 6).

Ver. 9 The heart of man deviseth his way;
But Jahve directeth his steps.

Similar to this is the German proverb: "Der Mensch denkt, Gott lenkt" [= our "man proposes, God disposes"], and the Arabic

el-'abd (הָעֶבֶד = man) *judebbir wallah jukaddir;* Latin, *homo pro-
ponit, Deus disponit;* for, as Hitzig rightly remarks, 9*b* means,
not that God maketh his steps firm (*Venet.*, Luther, Umbreit,
Bertheau, Elster), but that He gives direction to him (Jerome,
dirigere). Man deliberates here and there (חִשֵּׁב, intens. of חָשַׁב, to
calculate, reflect) how he will begin and carry on this or that; but
his short-sightedness leaves much out of view which God sees;
his calculation does not comprehend many contingencies which
God disposes of and man cannot foresee. The result and issue are
thus of God, and the best is, that in all his deliberations one should
give himself up without self-confidence and arrogance to the
guidance of God, that one should do his duty and leave the rest,
with humility and confidence, to God.

Ver. 10 Oracular decision (belongeth) to the lips of the king;
In the judgment his mouth should not err.

The first line is a noun clause; קֶסֶם, as subject, thus needs a distinctive accent, and that is here, after the rule of the sequence of
accents, and manuscript authority (*vid. Torath Emeth*, p. 49), not
Mehuppach legarme, as in our printed copies, but *Dechi* (קֶ֭סֶם).
Jerome's translation: *Divinatio in labiis regis, in judicio non errabit
os ejus*, and yet more Luther's: "his mouth fails not in judgment," makes it appear as if the proverb meant that the king, in
his official duties, was infallible; and Hitzig (Zöckler agreeing),
indeed, finds here expressed the infallibility of the theocratic
king, and that as an actual testimony to be believed, not only
as a mere political fiction, like the phrase, "the king can do no
wrong." But while this political fiction is not strange even to the
Israelitish law, according to which the king could not be brought
before the judgment, that testimony is only a pure imagination.
For as little as the N. T. teaches that the Pope, as the legitimate
vicarius of Christ, is infallible, *cum ex cathedra docet*, so little does
the O. T. that the theocratic king, who indeed was the legitimate
vicarius Dei, was infallible *in judicio ferendo*. Yet Ewald maintains that the proverb teaches that the word of the king, when on
the seat of justice, is an infallible oracle; but it dates from the first
bright period of the strong uncorrupted kingdom in Israel. One
may not forget, says Dächsel also, with von Gerlach, that these
proverbs belong to the time of Solomon, before it had given to the
throne sons of David who did evil before the Lord. Then it would
fare ill for the truth of the proverb—the course of history would

falsify it. But in fact this was never maintained in Israel. Of the idolizing flattering language in which, at the present day, rulers in the East are addressed, not a trace is found in the O. T. The kings were restrained by objective law and the recognised rights of the people. David showed, not merely to those who were about him, but also to the people at large, so many human weaknesses, that he certainly appeared by no means infallible; and Solomon distinguished himself, it is true, by rare kingly wisdom, but when he surrounded himself with the glory of an oriental potentate, and when Rehoboam began to assume the tone of a despot, there arose an unhallowed breach between the theocratic kingdom and the greatest portion of the people. The proverb, as Hitzig translates and expounds it: " a divine utterance rests on the lips of the king; in giving judgment his mouth deceives not," is both historically and dogmatically impossible. The choice of the word קֶסֶם (from קָסַם, R. קס קש, to make fast, to take an oath, to confirm by an oath, *incantare, vid.* at Isa. iii. 2), which does not mean prediction (Luther), but speaking the truth, shows that 10a expresses, not what falls from the lips of the king in itself, but according to the judgment of the people: the people are wont to regard the utterances of the king as oracular, as they shouted in the circus at Cæsarea of King Agrippa, designating his words as θεοῦ φωνὴ καὶ οὐκ ἀνθρώπων (Acts xii. 22). Hence 10b supplies an earnest warning to the king, viz. that his mouth should not offend against righteousness, nor withhold it. לֹא יִמְעַל is meant as warning (Umbreit, Bertheau), like לֹא תָבֹא, xxii. 24, and ב in מַעַל is here, as always, that of the object; at least this is more probable than that מַעַל stands without object, which is possible, and that ב designates the situation.

Ver. 11 The scale and balances of a right kind are Jahve's;
His work are the weights of the bag.

Regarding פֶּלֶס, *statera,* a level or steelyard (from פָּלַס, to make even), *vid.* iv. 26; מֹאזְנַיִם (from אָזַן, to weigh), *libra,* is another form of the balance: the shop-balance furnished with two scales. אַבְנֵי are here the stones that serve for weights, and כִּיס, which at i. 14 properly means the money-bag, money-purse (cf. vii. 20), is here, as at Mic. vi. 11, the bag in which the merchant carries the weights. The genit. מִשְׁפָּט belongs also to פֶּלֶס, which, in our edition, is pointed with the disjunctive *Mehuppach legarme,* is rightly accented in Cod. 1294 (*vid. Torath Emeth,* p. 50) with the con-

junctive *Mehuppach.* מִשְׁפָּט, as 11*b* shows, is not like מִרְמָה, the
word with the principal tone; 11*a* says that the balance thus, or
thus constructed, which weighs accurately and justly, is Jahve's, or
His arrangement, and the object of His inspection, and 11*b*, that
all the weight-stones of the bag, and generally the means of
weighing and measuring, rest upon divine ordinance, that in the
transaction and conduct of men honesty and certainty might rule.
This is the declared will of God, the lawgiver; for among the few
direct determinations of His law with reference to trade this stands
prominent, that just weights and just measures shall be used, Lev.
xix. 36, Deut. xxv. 13–16. The expression of the poet here frames
itself after this law; yet 'ה is not exclusively the God of positive
revelation, but, as agriculture in Isa. xxviii. 29, cf. Sirach vii. 15,
so here the invention of normative and normal means of commercial intercouse is referred to the direction and institution of God.

> Ver. 12 It is an abomination to kings to commit wickedness,
> For by righteousness the throne is established.

As 10*b* uttered a warning to the king, grounded on the fact of
10*a*, so 12*a* indirectly contains a warning, which is confirmed
by the fact 12*b*. It is a fact that the throne is established by
righteousness (יִכּוֹן as expressive of a rule, like הוּכַן, Isa. xvi. 5, as
expressive of an event); on this account it is an abomination to
kings immediately or mediately to commit wickedness, *i.e.* to place
themselves in despotic self-will above the law. Such wicked conduct shall be, and ought to be, an abhorrence to them, because
they know that they thereby endanger the stability of their throne.
This is generally the case, but especially was it so in Israel, where
the royal power was never absolutistic; where the king as well as
the people were placed under God's law; where the existence of
the community was based on the understood equality of right; and
the word of the people, as well as the word of the prophets, was
free. Another condition of the stability of the throne is, after
xxv. 5, the removal of godless men from nearness to the king.
Rehoboam lost the greater part of his kingdom by this, that he
listened to the counsel of the young men who were hated by the
people.

Ver. 13. History is full of such warning examples, and therefore this proverb continues to hold up the mirror to princes.

> Well-pleasing to kings are righteous lips,
> And whoever speaketh uprightly is loved.

Rightly the LXX. ἀγαπᾷ, individ. plur., instead of the plur. of genus, מְלָכִים ; on the contrary, Jerome and Luther give to the sing. the most general subject (one lives), in which case it must be distinctly said, that that preference of the king for the people who speak out the truth, and just what they think, is shared in by every one. צֶדֶק, as the property of the שְׂפָתֵי, accords with the Arab. ṣidḳ, truth as the property of the lasân (the tongue or speech). יְשָׁרִים, from יָשָׁר, means recta, as נְגִידִים, principalia, viii. 6, and רֵיקִים, inania, xii. 11. יְשָׁרִים, Dan. xi. 10, neut. So neut. וַיִּישַׁר, Ps. cxi. 8; but is rather, with Hitzig and Riehm, to be read וַיֵּשֶׁר. What the proverb says cannot be meant of all kings, for even the house of David had murderers of prophets, like Manasseh and Joiakim; but in general it is nevertheless true that noble candour, united with true loyalty and pure love to the king and the people, is with kings more highly prized than mean flattery, seeking only its own advantage, and that, though this (flattery) may for a time prevail, yet, at last, fidelity to duty, and respect for truth, gain the victory.

Ver. 14 The wrath of the king is like messengers of death;
But a wise man appeaseth him.

The clause: the wrath of the king is many messengers of death, can be regarded as the attribution of the effect, but it falls under the point of view of likeness, instead of comparison: if the king is angry, it is as if a troop of messengers or angels of death went forth to visit with death him against whom the anger is kindled; the plur. serves for the strengthening of the figure: not one messenger of death, but at the same time several, the wrinkled brow, the flaming eye, the threatening voice of the king sends forth (Fleischer). But if he against whom the wrath of the king has thus broken forth is a wise man, or one near the king who knows that ὀργὴ ἀνδρὸς δικαιοσύνην Θεοῦ οὐ κατεργάζεται (Jas. i. 20), he will seek to discover the means (and not without success) to cover or to propitiate, i.e. to mitigate and appease, the king's anger. The Scripture never uses כִּפֶּר, so that God is the object (expiare Deum), because, as is shown in the Comm. zum Hebräerbrief, that were to say, contrary to the decorum divinum, that God's holiness or wrath is covered, or its energy bound, by the offering up of sacrifices or of things in which there is no inherent virtue of atonement, and which are made the means of reconciliation only by the accommodative arrangement of God. On the contrary,

כִּפֶּר is used here and at Gen. xxxii. 21 of covering = reconciling (propitiating) the wrath of a man.

Ver. 15 In the light on the king's countenance there is life,
And his favour is as a cloud of the latter rains.

Hitzig regards אוֹר as the *inf.* (cf. iv. 18), but one says substantively אוֹר פְּנֵי, Job xxix. 24, etc., and in a similar sense מְאוֹר עֵינַיִם, xv. 30; light is the condition of life, and the exhilaration of life, wherefore אוֹר הַחַיִּים, Ps. lvi. 14, Job xxxiii. 30, is equivalent to a fresh, joyous life; in the light of the king's countenance is life, means that life goes forth from the cheerful approbation of the king, which shows itself in his face, viz. in the showing of favour, which cheers the heart and beautifies the life. To speak of liberality as a shower is so common to the Semitic, that it has in Arab. the general name of *nadnâ*, rain. 15*b* conforms itself to this. מַלְקוֹשׁ (cf. Job xxix. 23) is the latter rain, which, falling about the spring equinox, brings to maturity the barley-harvest; on the contrary, יוֹרֶה (מוֹרֶה) is the early rain, which comes at the time of ploughing and sowing; the former is thus the harvest rain, and the latter the spring rain. Like a cloud which discharges the rain that mollifies the earth and refreshes the growing corn, is the king's favour. The noun עָב, thus in the *st. constr.*, retains its *Kametz. Michlol* 191*b.* This proverb is the contrast to ver. 14. xx. 2 has also the anger of the king as its theme. In xix. 12 the figures of the darkness and the light stand together as parts of one proverb. The proverbs relating to the king are now at an end. Ver. 10 contains a direct warning for the king; ver. 12 an indirect warning, as a conclusion arising from 12*b* (cf. xx. 28, where יִצְּרוּ is not to be translated *tueantur;* the proverb has, however, the value of a *nota bene*). Ver. 13 in like manner presents an indirect warning, less to the king than to those who have intercourse with him (cf. xxv. 5), and vers. 14 and 15 show what power of good and evil, of wrath and of blessing, is given to a king, whence so much the greater responsibility arises to him, but, at the same time also, the duty of all to repress the lust to evil that may be in him, and to awaken and foster in him the desire for good.

Five proverbs regarding wisdom, righteousness, humility, and trust in God, forming, as it were, a succession of steps, for humility is the virtue of virtues, and trust in God the condition of all salvation. Three of these proverbs have the word טוֹב in common.

Ver. 16 To gain wisdom, how much better is it than gold :
And to attain understanding to be preferred to silver.

Commendation of the striving after wisdom (understanding) with which all wisdom begins, for one gains an intellectual possession not by inheritance, but by acquisition, iv. 7. A similar " parallel-comparative clause" (Fl.), with the interchange of טוֹב and נִבְחָר, is xxii. 1, but yet more so is xxi. 3, where נבחר, as here, is neut. pred. (not, as at viii. 10 and elsewhere, adj.), and עֲשֹׂה, such an anomalous form of the *inf. constr.* as here קְנֹה, Gesen. § 75, Anm. 2; in both instances it could also be regarded as the *inf. absol.* (cf. xxv. 27) (*Lehrgebäude*, § 109, Anm. 2); yet the language uses, as in the case before us, the form גְּלֹה only with the force of an *abl.* of the gerund, as עֲשׂוֹ occurs Gen. xxxi. 38 ; the *inf.* of verbs ל"ה as *nom.* (as here). *genit.* (Gen. l. 20), and *accus.* (Ps. ci. 3), is always either גְּלוֹת or גְּלֹה. The meaning is not that to gain wisdom is more valuable than gold, but that the gaining of wisdom exceeds the gaining of gold and silver, the common *comparatio decurtata* (cf. Job xxviii. 18). Regarding חָרוּץ, *vid.* at iii. 14.

Ver. 17 The path of the righteous is the avoiding of evil,
And he preserveth his soul who giveth heed to his way.

The meaning of מְסִלָּה, occurring only here in the Proverbs, is to be learned from xv. 19. The attribution denotes that wherein the way they take consists, or by which it is formed; it is one, a straight and an open way, *i.e.* unimpeded, leading them on, because they avoid the evil which entices them aside to the right and the left. Whoever then gives heed to his way, preserveth his soul (שֹׁמֵר נַפְשׁוֹ, as xiii. 3, on the contrary xxv. 5, subj.), that it suffer not injury and fall under death, for סור מרע and סור ממוקשי מות, xiv. 27, are essentially the same. Instead of this distich, the LXX. has three distichs ; the thoughts presented in the four superfluous lines are all already expressed in the one distich. Ewald and Hitzig find in this addition of the LXX. a component part of the original text.

Ver. 18 Pride goeth before destruction,
And haughtiness cometh before a fall.

The contrast is לפני כבוד ענוה, xv. 33, according to which the " haughtiness comes before a fall " in xviii. 22 is expanded into the antithetic distich. שֶׁבֶר means the fracture of the limbs, destruction of the person. A Latin proverb says, " *Magna cadunt, inflata crepant, tumefacta premuntur.*" [1] Here being dashed in pieces and overthrown correspond. שֶׁבֶר means neither bursting (Hitzig) nor shipwreck (Ewald). כִּשָּׁלוֹן (like זִכָּרוֹן, בִּטָּחוֹן, etc.), from כָּשַׁל or נִכְשַׁל, to totter, and hence, as a consequence, to come to ruin, is a *ἅπαξ. λεγ.* This proverb, which stands in the very centre of the Book of Proverbs, is followed by another in praise of humility.

Ver. 19 Better in humility to dwell among sufferers,
Than to divide spoil among the proud.

The form שְׁפַל is here not *adj.* as xxix. 23 (from שָׁפֵל, like חָסֵר, vi. 32, from חָסֵר), but *inf.* (like Eccles. xii. 14, and חֶסַר, *defectio,* x. 21). There existed here also no proper reason for changing עֲנִיִּים (*Chethîb*) into עֲנָוִים; Hitzig is right in saying that עֲנִי may also be taken in the sense of עָנָו [the idea "sufferer" is that which mediates], and that here the inward fact of humility and the outward of dividing spoil, stand opposed to one another. It is better to live lowly, *i.e.* with a mind devoid of earthly pride (*Demut* [humility] comes from *dëo* with the deep *e*, *diu*, servant), among men who have experience of the vanity of earthly joys, than, intoxicated with pride, to enjoy oneself amid worldly wealth and greatness (cf. Isa. ix. 2).

Ver. 20 He that giveth heed to the word will find prosperity ;
And he that trusteth in Jahve, blessed is he !

The " word " here is the word *κατ' ἐξ.*, the divine word, for מַשְׂכִּיל עַל־דָּבָר is the contrast of בָּז לְדָבָר, xiii. 13*a*, cf. Neh. viii. 13. טוֹב is meant, as in xvii. 20, cf. xiii. 21, Ps. xxiii. 6; to give heed to God's word is the way to true prosperity. But at last all depends on this, that one stand in personal fellowship with God by means of faith, which here, as at xxviii. 25, xxix. 25, is designated after its specific mark as *fiducia.* The Mashal conclusion אַשְׁרָיו occurs, besides here, only at xiv. 21, xxix. 18.

Four proverbs of wisdom with eloquence :

Ver. 21 The wise in heart is called prudent,
And grace of the lips increaseth learning.

Elsewhere (i. 5, ix. 9) הוֹסִיף לֶקַח means more than to gain learning, *i.e.* erudition in the ethico-practical sense, for sweetness of the lips (*dulcedo orationis* of Cicero) is, as to learning, without significance, but of so much the greater value for teaching; for grace of

---

[1] An expression of similar meaning is אַחֲרֵי דַרְגָּא תְּבִיר = after *Darga* (to rise up) comes *tebîr* (breaking = destruction) ; cf. Zunz, in Geiger's *Zeitschrift,* vi. 315 ff.

expression, and of exposition, particularly if it be not merely rhetorical, but, according to the saying *pectus disertos facit*, coming out of the heart, is full of mind, it imparts force to the instruction, and makes it acceptable. Whoever is wise of heart, *i.e.* of mind or spirit (לֵב = the N. T. νοῦς or πνεῦμα), is called, and is truly, נָבוֹן [learned, intelligent] (Fleischer compares to this the expression frequent in Isaiah, "to be named" = to be and appear to be, the Arab. *du'ay lah*); but there is a gift which highly increases the worth of this understanding or intelligence, for it makes it fruitful of good to others, and that is grace of the lips. On the lips (x. 13) of the intelligent wisdom is found; but the form also, and the whole manner and way in which he gives expression to this wisdom, is pleasing, proceeding from a deep and tender feeling for the suitable and the beneficial, and thus he produces effects so much the more surely, and beneficently, and richly.

Ver. 22 A fountain of life is understanding to its possessor ;
But the correction of fools is folly.

Oetinger, Bertheau, and others erroneously understand מוּסַר of the education which fools bestow upon others; when fools is the subject spoken of, מוּסַר is always the education which is bestowed on them, vii. 22, i. 7; cf v. 23, xv. 5. Also מוסר does not here mean education, *disciplina*, in the moral sense (Symmachus, ἔννοια; Jerome, *doctrina*) : that which fools gain from education, from training, is folly, for מוסר is the contrast to מְקוֹר חַיִּים, and has thus the meaning of correction or chastisement, xv. 10, Jer. xxx. 14. And that the fruits of understanding (xii. 8, cf. שֵׂכֶל טוֹב, fine culture, xiii. 15) represented by מקור חיים (*vid.* x. 11) will accrue to the intelligent themselves, is shown not only by the contrast, but also by the expression : *Scaturigo vitæ est intellectus præditorum eo*, of those (= to those) who are endowed therewith (the LXX. well, τοῖς κεκτημένοις). The man of understanding has in this intellectual possession a fountain of strength, a source of guidance, and a counsel which make his life secure, deepen, and adorn it ; while, on the contrary, folly punishes itself by folly (cf. to the form, xiv. 24), for the fool, when he does not come to himself (Ps. cvii. 17–22), recklessly destroys his own prosperity.

Ver. 23 The heart of the wise maketh his mouth wise,
And learning mounteth up to his lips.

Regarding הִשְׂכִּיל as causative : to put into the possession of intelligence, *vid.* at Gen. iii. 6. Wisdom in the heart produceth intelli-

gent discourse, and, as the parallel member expresses it, learning
mounteth up to the lips, *i.e.* the learning which the man taketh
into his lips (xxii. 18 ; cf. Ps. xvi. 4) to communicate it to others,
for the contents of the learning, and the ability to communicate it,
are measured by the wisdom of the heart of him who possesses it.
One can also interpret הוֹסִיף as extens. increasing : the heart of the
wise increaseth, *i.e.* spreads abroad learning, but then בִּשְׂפָתָיו (Ps.
cxix. 13) would have been more suitable; עַל־שְׂפָתיו calls up the idea
of learning as hovering on the lips, and thus brings so much nearer,
for הוֹסִיף, the meaning of the exaltation of its worth and impression.

Ver. 24 A honeycomb are pleasant words,
Sweet to the soul, and healing to the bones.

Honeycomb, *i.e.* honey flowing from the צוּף, the comb or cell
(*favus*), is otherwise designated, Ps. xix. 11. מָתוֹק, with מַרְפֵּא (*vid.*
p. 132), is *neut.* אִמְרֵי־נֹעַם are, according to xv. 26, words which love
suggests, and which breathe love. Such words are sweet to the
soul of the hearer, and bring strength and healing to his bones
(xv. 30); for מרפא is not only that which restores soundness, but
also that which preserves and advances it (cf. θεραπεία, Rev.
xxii. 2).

A group of six proverbs follows, four of which begin with אִישׁ,
and five relate to the utterances of the mouth.

Ver. 25 There is a way which appears as right to a man ;
But the end thereof are the ways of death.

This verse = xiv. 12.

Ver. 26 The hunger of the labourer laboureth for him,
For he is urged on by his mouth.

The Syr. translates : the soul of him who inflicts woe itself suffers
it, and from his mouth destruction comes to him ; the Targ. brings
this translation nearer the original text (בִּיְפָא, humiliation, instead of
אבדנא, destruction) ; Luther translates thus also, violently abbrevi-
ating, however. But עָמֵל (from עָמֵל, Arab. 'amila, to exert oneself,
laborare) means, like *laboriosus*, labouring as well as enduring
difficulty, but not, as πονῶν τινα, causing difficulty, or (Euchel)
occupied with difficulty. And labour and the mouth stand together, denoting that man labours that the mouth may have somewhat to eat (cf. 2 Thess. iii. 10 ; נֶפֶשׁ, however, gains in this connection the meaning of ψυχὴ ὀρεκτική, and that of desire after
nourishment, *vid.* at vi. 30, x. 3). אָכֵף also joins itself to this circle

of ideas, for it means to urge (Jerome, *compulit*), properly (related to בָּפַף, *incurvare*, כָּפָה בְּפָא, to constrain, necessitate), to bow down by means of a burden. The Aramæo-Arab. signification, to saddle (Schultens : *clitellas imposuit ei os suum*), is a secondary denom. (*vid.* at Job xxxiii. 7). The *Venet.* well renders it after Kimchi: ἐπεὶ κύπτει ἐπ᾿ αὐτὸν τὸ στόμα αὐτοῦ. Thus: the need of nourishment on the part of the labourer works for him (*dat. commodi* like Isa. xl. 20), *i.e.* helps him to labour, for (not: if, ἐάν, as Rashi and others) it presses upon him ; his mouth, which will have something to eat, urges him. It is God who has in this way connected together working and eating. The curse *in sudore vultus tui comedes panem* conceals a blessing. The proverb has in view this reverse side of the blessing in the arrangement of God.

Ver. 27 A worthless man diggeth evil ;
And on his lips is, as it were, scorching fire.

Regarding אִישׁ בְּלִיַּעַל, *vid.* vi. 12, and regarding בָּרָה, to dig round, or to bore out, *vid.* at Gen. xlix. 5, l. 5 ; here the figure, " to dig for others a pit," xxvi. 27, Ps. vii. 16, etc. : to dig evil is equivalent to, to seek to prepare such for others. צָרֶבֶת Kimchi rightly explains as a form similar to קַשֶּׁבֶת ; as a subst. it means, Lev. xiii. 23, the mark of fire (the healed mark of a carbuncle), here as an adj. of a fire, although not flaming (אֵשׁ לֶהָבָה, Isa. iv. 5, etc); yet so much the hotter, and scorching everything that comes near to it (from צָרֵב, to be scorched, cogn. שָׂרֵב, to which also שָׂרַף is perhaps related as a stronger power, like *comburere* to *adurere*). The meaning is clear : a worthless man, *i.e.* a man whose disposition and conduct are the direct contrast of usefulness and piety, uses words which, like an iron glowing hot, scorches and burns ; his tongue is φλογιζομένη ὑπὸ τῆς γεέννης (Jas. iii. 6).

Ver. 28 A man of falsehood scattereth strife,
And a backbiter separateth confidential friends.

Regarding אִישׁ תַּהְפֻּכוֹת (מדבר), *vid.* ii. 12, and יְשַׁלַּח מָדוֹן, vi. 14 ; the thought of 28*b* is found at vi. 19. נִרְגָּן (with ן *minusculum*, which occurs thrice with the terminal *Nun*) is a *Niphal* formation from רָגַן, to murmur (cf. נָזִיד, from זִיד), and denotes the whisperer, viz. the backbiter, ψίθυρος, Sir. v. 14, ψιθυριστής, *susurro* ; the Arab. *nyrj* is abbreviated from it, a verbal stem of נִרֶג (cf. Aram. *norgo*, an axe, Arab. *naurag*, a threshing-sledge = מוֹרַג) cannot be proved. Aquila is right in translating by τονθρυστής, and Theodotion by γόγγυσος, from רָגַן, *Niph.* נִרְגָּן, γογγύζειν. Regarding

אַלּוּף, confidential friend, *vid.* p. 82 ; the sing., as xviii. 9, is used in view of the mutual relationship, and מַפְרִיד proceeds on the separation of the one, and, at the same time, of the other from it. Luther, in translating by " a slanderer makes princes disagree," is in error, for אַלּוּף, φύλαρχος, is not a generic word for prince.

> Ver. 29 A man of violence enticeth his neighbour,
> And leadeth him in a way which is not good.

Cf. Gen. iv. 8. The subject is not moral enticement, but enticement to some place or situation which facilitates to the violent man the carrying out of his violent purpose (misdemeanour, robbery, extortion, murder). חָמָס (here with אִישׁ at iii. 31) is the injustice of club-law, the conduct of him who puts his superior power in godless rudeness in the place of God, Hab. i. 11, cf. Job xii. 6. "A way not good" (cf. Ps. xxxvi. 5) is the contradictory contrast of the good way : one altogether evil and destructive.

> Ver. 30 He who shutteth his eyes to devise falsehood ;
> He who biteth his lips bringeth evil to pass.

A physiognomical *Caveto.* The ἀπ. λεγ. עָצָה is connected with עָצַם, Isa. xxxiii. 15 (Arab. transp. *ghamd*), *comprimere*, formed from it. Regarding קרץ of lips or eyes, *vid.* p. 144; the biting of the lips is the action of the deceitful, and denotes scorn, malice, knavery. The perf. denotes that he who is seen doing this has some evil as good as accomplished, for he is inwardly ready for it; Hitzig suitably compares 1 Sam. xx. 7, 33. Our editions (also Löwenstein) have כִּלָּה, but the Masora (*vid. Mas. finalis*, p. 1) numbers the word among those which terminate in א, and always writes כִּלָּא.

We now take together a series of proverbs, xvi. 31–xvii. 5, beginning with עֲטֶרֶת.

> Ver. 31 A bright diadem is a hoary head,
> In the way of righteousness it is found—

namely, this bright diadem, this beautiful crown (iv. 8), which silver hair is to him who has it as the result of his advanced age (xx. 29), for " thou shalt rise up before the hoary head," Lev. xix. 32 ; and the contrast of an early death is to die in a good old age, Gen. xv. 15, etc., but a long life is on one side a self-consequence, and on another the promised reward of a course of conduct regulated by God's will, God's law, and by the rule of love to God and love to one's neighbour. From the N. T. standpoint that is also so far true, as in all the world there is no better established means of prolonging life than the avoidance of evil ; but the clause corresponding to the O. T. standpoint, that evil punishes itself by a premature death, and that good is rewarded by long life, has indeed many exceptions arising from the facts of experience against it, for we see even the godless in their life of sin attaining to an advanced old age, and in view of the veiled future it appears only as a one-sided truth, so that the words, Wisd. iv. 9, " discretion is to man the right grey hairs, and an unstained life is the right old age," which is mediated by life experiences, such as Isa. lvii. 1 f., stand opposed to the above proverb as its reversed side. That old Solo-monic proverb is, however, true, for it is not subverted; and, in contrast to self-destroying vice and wickedness; calling forth the judgment of God, it is and remains true, that whoever would reach an honoured old age, attains to it in the way of a righteous life and conduct.

Ver. 32 Better one slow to anger than a hero in war;
      And whoever is master of his spirit, than he who taketh a city.

Regarding אֶרֶךְ אַפַּיִם, *vid.* xiv. 29, where קְצַר־רוּחַ was the parallel of the contrast. The comparison is true as regards persons, with re-ference to the performances expressed, and (since warlike courage and moral self-control may be united in one person) they are pro-perly those in which the טוֹב determines the moral estimate. In *Pirke Aboth* iv. 1, the question, "Who is the hero?" is answered by, " he who overcomes his desire," with reference to this proverb, for that which is here said of the ruling over the passion of anger is true of all affections and passions.

> " Yet he who reigns within himself, and rules
> Passions, desires, and fears, is more a king;
> Which every wise and virtuous man attains." [1]

On the other side, the comparison is suggested:

> Break your head, not so sore;
> Break your will—that is more. [2]

Ver. 33 One casts the lot into the lap;
      But all its decision cometh from Jahve.

The *Tôra* knows only in one instance an ordeal (a judgment of God) as a right means of proof, Num. v. 12–31. The lot is no-where ordained by it, but its use is supported by a custom running parallel with the Mosaic law; it was used not only in private life,

---

[1] Milton's *Paradise Regained*, ii. 466–8.
[2] " *Zerbrich den Kopf dir nicht so sehr;*
    Zerbrich den Willen—das ist mehr."—MATTH. CLAUDIUS.

but also in manifold ways within the domain of public justice, as well as for the detection of the guilty, Josh. vii. 14 f., 1 Sam. xiv. 40–42. So that the proverb xviii. 18 says the same thing of the lot that is said in the Epistle to the Hebrews, vi. 16, of the oath. The above proverb also explains the lot for an ordeal, for it is God who directs and orders it that it fall out thus and not otherwise. A particular sanction of the use of the lot does not lie in this, but it is only said, that where the lot is cast, all the decision that results from it is determined by God. That is in all cases true; but whether the challenging of the divine decision in such a way be right in this or that case is a question, and in no case would one, on the contrary, venture to make the person of the transgressor discoverable by lot, and let it decide regarding human life. But antiquity judged this matter differently, as e.g. the Book of Jonah (chap. i.) shows; it was a practice, animated by faith, in God's government of the world, which, if it did not observe the boundary between faith and superstition, yet stood high above the unbelief of the "Enlightenment." Like the Greek κόλπος, חֵיק (from חוק, Arab. ḥak, khak, to encompass, to stretch out) means, as it is commonly taken, gremium as well as sinus, but the latter meaning is the more sure; and thus also here it is not the lap as the middle of the body, so that one ought to think on him who casts the lot as seated, but also not the lap of the garment, but, like vi. 27, cf. Isa. xl. 11, the swelling, loose, external part of the clothing covering the bosom (the breast), where the lot covered by it is thrown by means of shaking and changing, and whence it is drawn out. The construction of the passive הוּטַל (from טוּל = Arab. tall, to throw along) with the object. accus. follows the old scheme, Gen. iv. 18, and has its reason in this, that the Semitic passive, formed by the change of vowels, has not wholly given up the governing force of the active. מִשְׁפָּט signifies here decision as by the Urim and Thummim, Num. xxvii. 21, but which was no lot-apparatus.

xvii. 1. A comparative proverb with טוב, pairing with xvi. 32 :

> Better a dry piece of bread, and quietness therewith,
> Than a house full of slain beasts with unquietness.

Similar to this in form and contents are xv. 16 f. and xvi. 8. פַּת חֲרֵבָה is a piece of bread (פַּת, fem., as xxiii. 8) without savoury drink (Theodotion, καθ' ἑαυτόν, i.e. nothing with it), cf. Lev. vii. 10, a meat-offering without the pouring out of oil. זְבָחִים are not sacrificial gifts (Hitzig), but, as always, slain animals, i.e. either

offerings or banquets of slain beasts; it is the old name of the
שְׁלָמִים (cf. Ex. xviii. 12, xxiv. 5; Prov. vii. 14), part of which only
were offered on the altar, and part presented as a banquet; and
זֶבַח (in contradist. to טֶבַח, ix. 2, Gen. xliii. 16) denotes generally
any kind of consecrated festival in connection with the worship of
God, 1 Sam. xx. 29; cf. Gen. xxxi. 54. "Festivals of hatred" are
festivals with hatred.   מְלֵא is part. with object.-accus.; in general
מְלֵא forms a constructive, מְלֹא occurs only once (Jer. vi. 11), and
מְלָאֵי not at all. We have already, vii. 14, remarked on the degene-
rating of the *shelamîm* feasts; from this proverb it is to be concluded
that the merriment and the excitement bordering on intoxication
(cf. with Hitzig, 1 Sam. i. 13 and 3), such as frequently at the
Kirmsen merry-makings (*vid.* p. 164), brought quarrels and strife,
so that the poor who ate his dry bread in quiet peace could look on
all this noise and tumult without envy.

> Ver. 2 A prudent servant shall rule over the degenerate son ;
>   And he divides the inheritance among the brethren.

Regarding the contrasts of מַשְׂכִּיל and מֵבִישׁ, *vid.* at x. 5, xiv. 35.
The printed editions present בְּבֶן־מֵבִישׁ in genit. connection : a son
of the scandalous class, which is admissible (*vid.* p. 79 and p. 330);
but Cod. 1294 and Cod. *Jaman,*[1] Erf. No. 2, 3, write בְּבֵן מֵבִישׁ (with
Tsere and *Munach*), and that is perhaps right, after x. 5, xvii. 25.
The futures have here also a fut. signification : they say to what
it will come. Grotius remarks, with reference to this : *manumissus
tutor filiis relinquetur ;* יחלק *tutorio officio.* But if he is a conscientious, unselfish tutor, he will not enrich himself by property which
belongs to another ; and thus, though not without provision, he is
yet without an inheritance. And yet the supplanting of the degenerate is brought about by this, that he loses his inheritance, and the
intelligent servant steps into his place. Has one then to suppose
that the master of the house makes his servant a co-heir with his
own children, and at the same time names him as his executor?
That were a bad anachronism. The idea of the διαθήκη was, at
the time when this proverb was coined, one unknown—Israelitish
antiquity knows only the intestate right of inheritance, regulated
by lineal and gradual succession. Then, if one thinks of the degenerate son, that he is disowned by the father, but that the intelligent servant is not rewarded during the life of his master for his true

[1] The Cod. brought by Sappir from Jemen (*vid.* p. 295), of which there is an
account in the preface to the edition of *Isaiah* by Baer and me.

services, and that, after the death of the master, to such a degree
he possesses the esteem and confidence of the family, that he it is
who divides the inheritance among the brethren, *i.e.* occupies the
place amongst them of distributor of the inheritance, not: takes a
portion of the inheritance, for חָלַק has not the double meaning of
the Lat. *participare;* it means to divide, and may, with בְּ, mean
"to give a part of anything" (Job xxxix. 17); but, with the
accus., nothing else than to distribute, *e.g.* Josh. xviii. 2, where it
is to be translated : " whose inheritance had not yet been distributed
(not yet given to them)." Jerome, *hœreditatem dividet;* and thus
all translators, from the LXX. to Luther.

> Ver. 3 The fining-pot for silver, and the furnace for gold ;
> And a trier of hearts is Jahve.

An emblematical proverb (*vid.* p. 9), which means that Jahve is
for the heart what the smelting-pot (from צָרַף, to change, particularly to melt, to refine) is for silver, and what the smelting furnace (כּוּר, from כּוּר, R. כר, to round, Ex. xxii. 20) is for gold, that
Jahve is for the heart, viz. a trier (בחן, to grind, to try by grinding,
here as at Ps. vii. 10) of their nature and their contents, for which,
of the proof of metals, is elsewhere (xvi. 2, xxi. 2, xxiv. 12) used
the word (cf. בָּחוֹן, the essay-master, Jer. vi. 7) תֹּכֵן, weigher, or
דּוֹרֵשׁ, searcher (1 Chron. xxviii. 9). Wherever the subject spoken
of is God, the searcher of hearts, the plur. לִבּוֹת, once לְבָבוֹת, is used ;
the form לְבָבִים occurs only in the *status conjunctus* with the suffix.
In xxvii. 21 there follow the two figures, with which there is
formed a *priamel* (*vid.* p. 13), as at xxvi. 3, another *tertium com-
parationis*.

> Ver. 4 A profligate person giveth heed to perverse lips ;
> Falsehood listeneth to a destructive tongue.

The meaning, at all events, is, that whoever gives ear with delight
to words which are morally reprobate, and aimed at the destruction
of neighbours, thereby characterizes himself as a profligate. Though
מֵרַע is probably not pred. but subj., yet so that what follows does
not describe the מֵרַע (the profligate hearkens . . .), but stamps
him who does this as a מרע (a profligate, or, as we say : only a profligate . . .). מֵרַע, for מֵרַע, is warranted by Isa. ix. 16, where
מרע (not מֵרַע, according to which the *Venet.* here translates ἀπὸ
κακοῦ) is testified to not only by correct codd. and editions, but
also by the Masora (cf. *Michlol* 116b). הִקְשִׁיב (from קָשַׁב, R. קש, to
stiffen, or, as we say, to prick, viz. the ear) is generally united with לְ

or אַל, but, as here and at xxix. 12, Jer. vi. 19, also with עַל. אָוֶן, wickedness, is the absolute contrast of a pious and philanthropic mind; הַוֹּת, from הַוָּה, not in the sense of eagerness, as x. 3, xi. 6, but of yawning depth, abyss, catastrophe (vid. at Ps. v. 10), is equivalent to entire destruction—the two genitives denote the property of the lips and the tongue (labium nequam, lingua perniciosa), on the side of that which it instrumentally aims at (cf. Ps. xxxvi. 4, lii. 4): practising mischief, destructive plans. שֶׁקֶר beginning the second line is generally regarded as the subj. parallel with מֵרַע, as Luther, after Jerome, " A wicked man gives heed to wicked mouths, and a false man listens willingly to scandalous tongues." It is possible that שֶׁקֶר denotes incarnate falsehood, as רְמִיָּה, xii. 27, incarnate slothfulness, cf. מִרְמָה, xiv. 25, and perhaps also xii. 17 ; צֶדֶק, Ps. lviii. 2, תּוּשִׁיָּה, Mic. vi. 9; יֵצֶר סָמוּךְ, Isa. xxvi. 13, etc., where, without supplying אִישׁ (אַנְשֵׁי), the property stands instead of the person possessing that property. The clause, that falsehood listeneth to a deceitful tongue, means that he who listens to it characterizes himself thereby, according to the proverb, simile simili gaudet, as a liar. But only as a liar ? The punctuation before us, which represents מֵרַע by Dechi as subj., or also pred., takes שֶׁקֶר מֵזִין as obj. with מֵזִין as its governing word, and why should not that be the view intended? The representation of the obj. is an inversion less bold than Isa. xxii. 2, viii. 22, and that עַל here should not be so closely connected with the verb of hearing, as 4a lies near by this, that הִקְשִׁיב עַל is elsewhere found, but not הֶאֱזִין עַל. Jewish interpreters, taking שֶׁקֶר as obj., try some other meaning of מֵזִין than auscultans; but neither זון, to approach, nor זין, to arm (Venet. ψεῦδος ὁπλίζει), gives a meaning suitable to this place. מֵזִין is equivalent to מַאֲזִין. As אַאֲזִין, Job xxxii. 11, is contracted into אָזִין, so must מַאֲזִין, if the character of the part. shall be preserved, become מֵזִין, mediated by מֵיְזִין.

Ver. 5 He that mocketh the poor reproacheth his Maker ;
He that rejoiceth over calamity remains not unpunished.

Line first is a variation of xiv. 31a. God is, according to xxii. 2, the creator of the poor as well as of the rich. The poor, as a man, and as poor, is the work of God, the creator and governor of all things; thus, he who mocketh the poor, mocketh Him who called him into existence, and appointed him his lowly place. But in general, compassion and pity, and not joy (שָׂמֵחַ לְ, commonly

with לְ, of the person, e.g. Obad. ver. 12, the usual formula for
ἐπιχαιρεκακία), is appropriate in the presence of misfortune (אֵיד,
from אוד, to be heavily burdened), for such joy, even if he on
whom the misfortune fell were our enemy, is a *peccatum mortale*,
Job xxxi. 29 f. There is indeed a hallowed joy at the actual
revelation in history of the divine righteousness; but this would
not be a hallowed joy if it were not united with deep sorrow over
those who, accessible to no warning, have despised grace, and, by
adding sin to sin, have provoked God's anger.

Ver. 6. With this verse this series of proverbs closes as it
began:

> A diadem of the old are children's children,
> And the glory of children are their parents.

Children are a blessing from God (Ps. cxxvii., cxxviii.); thus, a
family circle consisting of children and grandchildren (including
great-grandchildren) is as a crown of glory surrounding the grey-
haired patriarch; and again, children have glory and honour in
their parents, for to have a man of an honoured name, or of a
blessed memory, as a father, is the most effective commendation,
and has for the son, even though he is unlike his father, always
important and beneficial consequences. In 6b a fact of experience
is expressed, from which has proceeded the rank of inherited nobility
recognised among men—one may abnegate his social rights, but yet
he himself is and remains a part of the moral order of the world.
The LXX. has a distich after ver. 4 [the Vatican text places it
after ver. 6] : "The whole world of wealth belongs to the faithful,
but to the unfaithful not even an obolus." Lagarde supposes that
ὅλος ὁ κόσμος τῶν χρημάτων is a translation of שִׁפְעַת יֶתֶר, instead of
שְׂפַת יֶתֶר, 7a. But this ingenious conjecture does not amount to the
regarding of this distich as a variation of ver. 7.

The proverbs following, 7–10, appear to be united acrostically
by the succession of the letters שׁ (שׂ, שׁ) and ת.

> Ver. 7 It does not become a fool to speak loftily,
> How much less do lying lips a noble!

As at Isa. xxxii. 5 f., נָבָל and נָדִיב are placed opposite to one another; the latter is the nobly magnanimous man, the former the
man who thinks foolishly and acts profligately, whom it does not
become to use lofty words, who thereby makes the impression of
his vulgarity so much the more repulsive (cf. Job ii. 10). שְׂפַת יֶתֶר
(not יָתֵר, for the word belongs to those which retain their *Pathach*

or *Segol, in pausa*) is neither elevated (soaring) (Ewald) nor diffuse (Jo. Ernst Jungius in Oetinger : *lingua dicax ac sermonem ultra quam decorum verbis extendere solita*), rather imperative (Bertheau), better presumptuous (Hitzig) words, properly words of superfluity, *i.e.* of superabundant self-consciousness and high pretension (cf. the transitive bearing of the Arab. *watr* with ὑβρίζειν, from ὑπέρ, Aryan *upar, Job,* p. 363). Rightly Meîri, שְׂפַת גֵאוּה וְשׁרֵרה. It produces a disagreeable impression, when a man of vulgar mind and of rude conduct, instead of keeping himself in retirement, makes himself of importance, and weighty in a shameless, impudent manner (cf. Ps. xii. 9, where זֻלּוּת, *vilitas,* in a moral sense); but yet more repulsive is the contrast, when a man in whom one is justified in expecting nobility of mind, in accordance with his life-position and calling, degrades himself by uttering deceitful words. Regarding the אַף כִּי, concluding *a minori ad majus,* we have already spoken at xi. 31, xv. 11. R. Ismael, in *Bereschith Rabba,* at xliv. 8, reckons ten such conclusions *a minori ad majus* in the Scriptures, but there are just as many *quanto magis.* The right accentuation (*e.g.* in Cod. 1294) is here אַף כִּי־לְנָדִיב, transformed from אַף כִּי־לְנָדִיב, according to *Accentuationssystem,* xviii. 2.

Ver. 8 The gift of bribery appears a jewel to its receiver ;
Whitherso'er he turneth himself he acteth prudently.

How 8*b* is to be understood is shown by 1 Sam. xiv. 47, cf. Josh. i. 7 ; the *quoque se vertit, prudenter rem agit,* has accordingly in both sentences the person meant by בְּעָלָיו as subject, not the gift (Hitzig), of which יַשְׂכִּיל, " it maketh prosperous," is not said, for הִשְׂכִּיל means, used only of persons, prudent, and therefore successful, fortunate conduct. Such is said of him who has to give (Luther): he presses through with it whithersoever he turns. But the making of בְּעֵינֵי the subj. does not accord with this : this means [gift] to one who has to give, appears to open doors and hearts, not merely as a golden key, it is truly such to him. Thus בעליו, as at iii. 27, will be meant of him to whom the present is brought, or to whom a claim thereto is given. But שֹׁחַד means here not the gift of seasonable liberality (Zöckler), but, as always, the gift of bribery, *i.e.* a gift by which one seeks to purchase for himself (xvii. 23) preference on the part of a judge, or to mitigate the displeasure of a high lord (xxi. 14); here (for one does not let it depend merely on the faithfulness of another to his duty) it is that by which one seeks to secure an advantage to himself. The proverb expresses a fact of experience. The gift of bribery, to which, as to a well-known approved means, הַשֹּׁחַד refers, appears to him who receives and accepts it (Targ.) as a stone of pleasantness, a charming, precious stone, a jewel (*Juwêl* from *joie* = *gaudium*); it determines and impels him to apply all his understanding, in order that he may reach the goal for which it shall be his reward. What he at first regarded as difficult, yea, impossible, that he now prudently carries out, and brings to a successful conclusion, wherever he turns himself, overcoming the seemingly insurmountable hindrances; for the enticement of the gift lifts him, as with a charm, above himself, for covetousness is a characteristic feature of human nature—*pecuniæ obediunt omnia* (Eccles. x. 19, Vulg.).

Ver. 9 He covereth transgressions who seeketh after love,
And he who always brings back a matter separateth friends.

The pred. stands first in the simple clause with the order of the words not inverted. That מכסה פשע is also to be interpreted here as pred. (cf. 19a) is shown by x. 12, according to which love covereth all transgressions. We write מְכַסֶּה־פֶּשַׁע with *Dag. forte conjunctivum* of פ (as of ב in Ezek. xviii. 6), and *Gaja* with the *Sheva*, according to the *Meth.-Setzung*, § 37; the punctuation מְכַסֶּה פֶּשַׁע also occurs. What the expression " to seek love " here means, is to be judged, with Hitzig, after Zeph. ii. 3, 1 Cor. xiv. 1. It is in no case equivalent to seek to gain the love of another, rather to seek to preserve the love of men towards one another, but it is to be understood not after 9b, but after x. 12 : he seeks to prove love who does not strike on the great bell when his neighbour has sinned however grievously against him, does not in a scandal-loving manner make much ado about it, and takes care not thereby to widen the breach between men who stand near to one another, but endeavours by a reconciling, soothing, rectifying influence, to mitigate the evil, instead of making it worse. He, on the contrary, who repeats the matter (שָׁנָה with בְּ of the obj., to come back with something, as xxvi. 11), *i.e.* turns always back again to the unpleasant occurrence (Theodotion, δευτερῶν ἐν λόγῳ; Symmachus, δευτερῶν λόγον, as Sir. vii. 14, xix. 7), divides friends (*vid.* xvi. 28), for he purposely fosters the strife, the disharmony, ill-will, and estrangement which the offence produced ; while the noble man, who has love for his motive and his aim, by prudent silence contributes to bring the offence and the division which it occasioned into forgetfulness.

Ver. 10 One reproof maketh more impression on a wise man
Than if one reckoned a hundred to the fool

One of the few proverbs which begin with a future, vid. xii. 26,
p. 265. It expresses what influence there is in one reproof with a
wise man (מֵבִין, viii. 9) ; גְּעָרָה is the reproof expressed by the post-
bibl. נְזִיפָה, as the lowest grade of disciplinary punishment, ad-
monitio, connected with warning. The verbal form תחת is the
reading of the LXX. and Syr. (συντρίβει ἀπειλὴ καρδίαν φρο-
νίμου) for they read תחת נערה לב מבין, derived from חָתַת, and thus
תֵּחַת (from Hiph. הֵחַת); thus Luther: reproof alarms more the intelligent, but חחת with ב of the obj. is not Hebr. ; on the contrary,
the reading of the LXX. is in accordance with the usage of the
language, and, besides, is suitable. It is, however, first to be seen
whether the traditional text stands in need of this correction. As
fut. Niph. תֵּחַת, apart from the ult. accent. to be expected, gives
no meaning. Also if one derives it from חָתָה, to snatch away, to
take away, it gives no appropriate thought; besides, חתה is construed with the object. accus., and the fut. Apoc., in itself strange
here, must be pointed either תֵּחַת or תֵּחְתְּ (after יַחְדְּ) (Böttcher,
Lehrb. ii. p. 413). Thus יֵחַת, as at Job xxi. 13, Jer. xxi. 13, will
be fut. Kal of יִנְחַת=נָחַת, Ps. xxxviii. 3 (Theodotion, Targ.,
Kimchi). With this derivation, also, תֵּחַת is to be expected; the
reference in the Handwörterbuch to Gesen. Lehrgebäude, § 51, 1,
Anm. 1, where, in an extremely inadequate way, the retrogression
of the tone (נסוג אחור) is spoken of, is altogether inappropriate to
this place ; and Böttcher's explanation of the ult. tone from an
intended expressiveness is ungrammatical ; but why should not תֵּחַת,
from נחת, with its first syllable originating from contraction, and
thus having the tone, be Milel as well as Milra, especially here,
where it stands at the head of the sentence? With ב connected
with it, נחת means : to descend into anything, to penetrate; Hitzig
appropriately compares altius in pectus descendit of Sallust, Jug. 11.
Jerome rightly, according to the sense : plus proficit, and the Venet.
ἀνεῖ (read ὀνεῖ) ἀπειλὴ τῷ συνίοντι. In 10b מַכָּה (cf. Deut. xxv. 3 ;
2 Cor. xi. 24) is to be supplied to מֵאָה, not פְּעָמִים (an hundred
times, which may be denoted correctly by מֵאָה as well as מֵאַת,
Eccles. viii. 12). With the wise (says a Talmudic proverb) a
sign does as much as with the fool a stick does. Zehner, in his
Adagia sacra (1601), cites Curtius (vii. 4): Nobilis equus umbra
quoque virgæ regitur, ignavus ne calcari quidem concitari potest.

Five proverbs of dangerous men against whom one has to be on his guard:

> Ver. 11 The rebellious seeketh only after evil,
> And a cruel messenger is sent out against him.

It is a question what is subj. and what obj. in 11*a*. It lies nearest to look on מְרִי as subj., and this word (from מָרָה, *stringere*, to make oneself exacting against any, to oppose, ἀντιτείνειν) is appropriate thereto; it occurs also at Ezek. ii. 7 as *abstr. pro concreto*. That it is truly subj. appears from this, that בִּקֶּשׁ רָע, to seek after evil (cf. xxix. 10; 1 Kings xx. 7, etc.), is a connection of idea much more natural than בִּקֶּשׁ מְרִי [to seek after rebellion]. Thus אַךְ will be logically connected with רָע, and the reading אַךְ מְרִי will be preferred to the reading אַךְ־מֶרִי; אַךְ (corresponding to the Arab. *áinnama*) belongs to those particles which are placed before the clause, without referring to the immediately following part of the sentence, for they are much more regarded as affecting the whole sentence (*vid.* xiii. 10): the rebellious strives after nothing but only evil. Thus, as neut. obj. רע is rendered by the Syr., Targ., *Venet.*, and Luther; on the contrary, the older Greek translators and Jerome regard רע as the personal subject. If now, in reference to rebellion, the discourse is of a מַלְאָךְ אַכְזָרִי, we are not, with Hitzig, to think of the demon of wild passions unfettered in the person of the rebellious, for that is a style of thought and of expression that is modern, not biblical; but the old unpoetic yet simply true remark remains: *Loquendi formula inde petita quod regis aut summi magistratus minister rebelli supplicium nunciat infligitque.* מלאך is *n. officii*, not *naturæ*. Man as a messenger, and the spiritual being as messenger, are both called מלאך. Therefore one may not understand מלאך אכזרי, with the LXX., Jerome, and Luther, directly and exclusively of an angel of punishment. If one thinks of Jahve as the Person against whom the rebellion is made, then the idea of a heavenly messenger lies near, according to Ps. xxxv. 5 f., lxxviii. 49; but the proverb is so meant, that it is not the less true if an earthly king sends out against a rebellious multitude a messenger with an unlimited commission, or an officer against a single man dangerous to the state, with strict directions to arrest him at all hazards. אַכְזָרִי we had already at xii. 10; the root קשׁ חשׁ means, to be dry, hard, without feeling. The fut. does not denote what may be done (Bertheau, Zöckler), which is contrary to the parallelism, the order of the words, and the style of the proverb, but what is done. And the relation of the clause is not, as Ewald interprets it, " scarcely does the sedition seek out evil when an inexorable messenger is sent." Although this explanation is held by Ewald as " unimprovable," yet it is incorrect, because אַף in this sense demands, e.g. Gen. xxvii. 3, the perf. (strengthened by the infin. intensivus). The relation of the clause is, also, not such as Böttcher has interpreted it : a wicked man tries only scorn though a stern messenger is sent against him, but not because such a messenger is called אכזרי, against whom this "trying of scorn" helps nothing, so that it is not worth being spoken of ; besides, שֻׁלַּח or מְשֻׁלָּח would have been used if this relation had been intended.   We have in 11a and 11b, as also e.g. at xxvi. 24, xxviii. 1, two clauses standing in internal reciprocal relation, but syntactically simply co-ordinated ; the force lies in this, that a messenger who recognises no mitigating circumstances, and offers no pardon, is sent out against such an one.

> Ver. 12 Meet a bear robbed of one of her whelps,
> Only not a fool in his folly.

The name of the bear, as that of the cow, Job xxi. 10, Ps. cxliv. 14, preserves its masculine form, even when used in reference to sexual relationship (Ewald, § 174b); the ursa catulis orbata is proverbially a raging beast.   How the abstract expression of the action פָּגוֹשׁ [to meet], here as e.g. Ps. xvii. 5, with the subj. following, must sound as finite (occurrat, may always meet), follows from וְאַל־יִפְגֹּשׁ = וְאַל (non autem occurrat). פָּגוֹשׁ has on the last syllable Mehuppach, and Zinnorith on the preceding open syllable (according to the rule, Accent-system, vi. § 5d).[1] בְּאִוַּלְתּוֹ, in the state of his folly, i.e. when he is in a paroxysm of his anger, corresponds with the conditional noun-adjective שַׁכּוּל, for folly morbidly heightened is madness (cf. Hos. xi. 7; Psychol. p. 291 f.).

> Ver. 13 He that returneth evil for good,
> From his house evil shall not depart.

If ingratitude appertains to the sinful manifestations of ignoble selfishness, how much more sinful still is black ingratitude, which recompenses evil for good ! (מֵשִׁיב), as 1 Sam. xxv. 21, syn. גָּמַל, to requite, iii. 30, xxxi. 12; שִׁלֵּם, to reimburse, xx. 22).   Instead of חמיש, the Keri reads תָּמוּשׁ; but that this verb, with a middle vowel, may be ע"ו as well as ע"י, Ps. lv. 2 shows.

---

[1] In the Torath Emeth, p. 18, the word is irregularly represented as Milel— a closed syllable with Cholem can suffer no retrogression of the tone.

Ver. 14 As one letteth out water is the beginning of a strife;
But cease thou from such strife ere it comes to showing teeth.

The meaning of this verb פָּטַר is certain: it means to break forth; and transitively, like Arab. *fatṛ*, to bring forth from a cleft, to make to break forth, to let go free (Theodotion, ἀπολύων; Jerome, *dimittit; Venet.* ἀφιείς). The LXX., since it translates by ἐξουσίαν δίδωσι, thinks on the juristic signification, which occurs in the Chronicles: to make free, or to declare so; but here פּוֹטֵר מַיִם (*vid.* regarding the *Metheg* at xiv. 31, p. 311) is, as Luther translates, one who tears away the dam from the waters. And רֵאשִׁית מָדוֹן is not accus. dependent on פּוֹטֵר, to be supplied (Hitzig: he unfetters water who the beginning of strife, viz. unfetters); but the part is used as at x. 17: one who unfetters the water is the beginning of strife, *i.e.* he is thus related to it as when one . . . This is an addition to the free use of the part. in the language of the Mishna, where one would expect the *infin., e.g.* בְּזוֹרֵעַ (= בִּזְרֹעַ), if one sows, בְּמֵזִיד (= בְּזָדוֹן), of wantonness. It is thus unnecessary, with Ewald, to interpret פּוֹטֵר as neut., which lets water go = a water-outbreak; פּוֹטֵר is meant personally; it represents one who breaks through a water-dam, withdraws the restraint of the water, opens a sluice, and then emblematically the proverb says: thus conditioned is the beginning of a strife. Then follows the warning to let go such strife (הָרִיב, with the article used in the more elevated style, not without emphasis), to break from it, to separate it from oneself ere it reach a dangerous height. This is expressed by לִפְנֵי הִתְגַּלַּע, a verb occurring only here and at xviii. 1, xx. 3, always in the *Hithpa.* The Targum (misunderstood by Gesenius after Buxtorf; *vid.* to the contrary, Levy, under the word צדי II.) translates it at xviii. 1, xx. 3, as the Syr., by "to mock," also Aquila, who has at xx. 3, ἐξυβρισθήσεται, and the LXX. at xviii. 1, ἐπονείδιστος ἔσται, and Jerome, who has this in all the three passages, render the *Hithpa.* in this sense, passively. In this passage before us, the Targ., as Hitzig gives it, translates, "before it heats itself," but that is an error occasioned by Buxtorf; *vid.* on the contrary, Levy, under the word קַרְיָא (κύριος); this translation, however, has a representative in Haja Gaon, who appeals for גלע, to glow, to *Nidda* viii. 2.[1] Elsewhere the LXX., at xx. 3, συμπλέκεται (where Jerome, with the amalgamation of the two significations, *miscentur contumeliis*); Kimchi and others gloss it by התערב, and, according to this, the *Venet.* translates, πρὸ τοῦ

[1] *Vid.* Simon Nascher's *Der Gaon Haja u. seine geist. Thätig.* p. 15.

σvγχvθῆναι (τὴν ἔριν); Luther, "before thou art mingled therein."
But all these explanations of the word : *insultare, excandescere,*
and *commisceri,* are etymologically inadmissible. Bertheau's and
Zöckler's "roll itself forth" is connected at least with a meaning
rightly belonging to the R. גל. But the Arab. shows, that not the
meaning *volvere,* but that of *retegere* is to be adopted. Aruch[1] for
Nidda viii. 2 refers to the Arab., where a wound is designated
as יכולה להבלע ולהוציא דם, *i.e.* as breaking up, as it were, when the
crust of that which is nearly healed is broken off (Maimuni glosses
the word by להתקלף, were uncrusted), and blood again comes forth.
The meaning *retegere* requires here, however, another distinction.
The explanation mentioned there by Aruch : before the strife
becomes public to thee, *i.e.* approaches thee, is not sufficient. The
verbal stem גלע is the stronger power of גלה, and means laying bare;
but here, not as there, in the Mishna of a wound covered with a
crust. The Arab. *jal'* means to quarrel with another, properly to
show him the teeth, the *Poël* or the tendency-stem from *jali'a,* to
have the mouth standing open, so that one shows his teeth; and the
Syr. *glas,* with its offshoots and derivatives, has also this meaning
of *ringi,* opening the mouth to show, *i.e.* to make bare the teeth.
Schultens has established this explanation of the words, and
Gesenius further establishes it in the *Thesaurus,* according to
which Fleischer also remarks, "גלע, of showing the teeth, the
exposing of the teeth by the wide opening of the mouth, as
happens in bitter quarrels." But הריב does not agree with this.
Hitzig's translation, "before the strife shows its teeth," is as
modern as in ver. 11 is the passion of the unfettered demon, and
Fleischer's *prius vero quam exacerbetur rixa* renders the *Hithpa.*
in a sense unnecessarily generalized for xviii. 1 and xx. 3. The
accentuation, which separates להתגלע from הָרִיב by *Rebia Mugrash,*
is correct. One may translate, as Schultens, *antequam dentes strin-
gantur,* or, since the *Hithpa.* has sometimes a reciprocal signification,
e.g. Gen. xlii. 1, Ps. xli. 8 : ere one reciprocally shows his teeth.
Hitzig unjustly takes exception to the inversion הָרִיב נְטוֹשׁ. Why
should not the object precede, as at Hos. xii. 15, the נטוש, placed
with emphasis at the end? The same inversion for a like reason
occurs at Eccles. v. 6.

[1] [*Vid.* p. 109, note.]

Ver. 15 He that acquitteth the guilty and condemneth the righteous—
An abomination to Jahve are they both.

The proverb is against the partisan judge who is open to bribery, like xxiv. 24, cf. Isa. v. 23, where, with reference to such, the announcement of punishment is emphatically made. רָשָׁע and צַדִּיק, in a forensic sense, are equivalent to *sons (reus)* and *insons.* גַּם (cf. the Arab. *jmy'na,* altogether, but particularly the Pers. *ham* and the Tuikish *dkhy* standing wholly thus in the numeral) is here, as at Gen. xxvii. 45, equivalent to יַחְדָּיו, Jer. xlvi. 12 (in its unions = united). Whoever pronounces sentence of justification on the guilty, appears as if he must be judged more mildly than he who condemns the guiltless, but both the one and the other alike are an abhorrence to God.

We take vers. 16-21 together. This group begins with a proverb of the heartless, and ends with one of the perverse-hearted; and between these there are not wanting noticeable points of contact between the proverbs that follow one another.

Ver. 16 Why the ready money in the hand of the fool;
To get wisdom when he has yet no heart?

The question is made pointed by זֶה, thus not: why the ready money when . . . ? Is it to obtain wisdom?—the whole is but one question, the reason of which is founded in וְלֶב אָיִן (thus to be accented with *Mugrash* going before).[1] The fool, perhaps, even makes some endeavours, for he goes to the school of the wise, to follow out their admonitions, קְנֵה חָכְמָה (iv. 5, etc.), and it costs him something (iv. 7), but all to no purpose, for he has no heart. By this it is not meant that knowledge, for which he pays his *honorarium,* remains, it may be, in his head, but goes not to his heart, and thus becomes an unfruitful theory; but the heart is equivalent to the understanding (*vid.* p. 174), in the sense in which the heart appears as the previous condition to the attainment of wisdom (xviii. 15), and as something to be gained before all (xv. 32), viz. understanding, as the fitting intellectual and practical *habitus* to the reception, the

[1] If we write וְלֶב־ with *Makkeph,* then we have to accentuate לִקְנוֹת חָכְמָה with *Tarcha Munach,* because the *Silluk* word in this writing has not two syllables before the·tone. This sequence of accents is found in the Codd. Ven. 1521, 1615, Basel 1619, while most editions have לִקְנוֹת חָכְמָה וּלֶב־אָין, which is false. But according to mss. we have וְלֶב without *Makkeph,* and that is right according to the *Makkeph* rules of the metrical *Accentuationssystem; vid. Torath Emeth,* p. 40.

appropriation, and realization of wisdom, the ability rightly to comprehend the fulness of the communicated knowledge, and to adopt
it as an independent possession, that which the Greek called νοῦς,
as in that "golden proverb" of Democrates: πολλοὶ πολυμαθέες
νοῦν οὐκ ἔχουσι, or as in Luke xxiv. 25, where it is said that the
Lord opened τὸν νοῦν of His disciples to understand the Scriptures.
In the LXX. a distich follows ver. 16, which is made up of 19b
and 20b, and contains a varied translation of these two lines.

> Ver. 17 At all times the right friend shows himself loving;
> And as a brother is he born for adversity.

Brother is more than friend, he stands to one nearer than a friend
does, Ps. xxxv. 14; but the relation of a friend may deepen itself
into a spiritual, moral brotherhood, xviii. 24, and there is no name
of friend that sounds dearer than אָחִי, 2 Sam. i. 26.   17a and 17b
are, according to this, related to each other climactically.   The
friend meant in 17a is a true friend.   Of no other is it said that
he loves בְּכָל־עֵת, i.e. makes his love manifest; and also the article
in הָרֵעַ not only here gives to the word more body, but stamps it as
an ideal-word: the friend who corresponds to the idea of such an
one.[1]   The inf. of the Hiph., in the sense "to associate" (Ewald),
cannot therefore be הָרֵעַ, because רֵעַ is not derived from רָעַע, but
from רָעָה.   Thus there exists no contrast between 17a and 17b,
so that the love of a friend is thought of, in contradistinction to
that of a brother, as without permanency (Fl.); but 17b means that
the true friend shows himself in the time of need, and that thus
the friendship becomes closer, like that between brothers.   The
statements do not refer to two kinds of friends; this is seen from
the circumstance that אָח has not the article, as הָרֵעַ has.   It is not
the subj. but pred., as אָדָם, Job xi. 12: sooner is a wild ass born or
born again as a man.   The meaning of הִוָּלֵד there, as at Ps. lxxxvii.
5 f., borders on the notion of regenerari; here the idea is not essentially much less, for by the saying that the friend is born in the time
of need, as a brother, is meant that he then for the first time shows
himself as a friend, he receives the right status or baptism of such
an one, and is, as it were, born into personal brotherly relationship
to the sorely-tried friend.   The translation comprobatur (Jerome)
and erfunden [is found out] (Luther) obliterates the peculiar and

---

[1] The Arab. grammarians say that the article in this case stands, l'astfrâgh
khᵃânas âljnas, as an exhaustive expression of all essential properties of the
genus, i.e. to express the full ideal realization of the idea in that which is named

thus intentional expression, for נוֹלָד is not at all a metaphor used for
passing into the light—the two passages in Proverbs and in Job
have not their parallel. לְצָרָה is not equivalent to בְּצָרָה (cf. Ps. ix.
10, x. 1), for the interchange of the prep. in 17a and 17b would then
be without any apparent reason. But Hitzig's translation also : as
a brother he is born of adversity, is impossible, for ל after נולד and
יֵלֵד always designates that for which the birth is an advantage, not
that from which it proceeds. Thus ל will be that of the purpose :
for the purpose of the need,—not indeed to suffer (Job v. 7) on
account of it, but to bear it in sympathy, and to help to bear it.
Rightly Fleischer : *frater autem ad ærumnam (sc. levandam et re-
movendam) nascitur.* The LXX. gives this sense to the ל: ἀδελφοὶ
δὲ ἐν ἀνάγκαις χρήσιμοι ἔστωσαν, τοῦτο γὰρ χάριν γεννῶνται.

Ver. 18 A man void of understanding is he who striketh hands,
Who becometh surety with his neighbour.

Cf. vi. 1–5, where the warning against suretyship is given at large,
and the reasons for it are adduced. It is incorrect to translate
(Gesen., Hitzig, and others) לִפְנֵי רֵעֵהוּ, with the LXX., Jerome,
the Syr., Targ., and Luther, "for his neighbour;" to become
surety for any one is עָרַב ל, vi. 1, or, with the object. accus., xi.
15, another suitable prep. is בְּעַד ; but לפני never means *pro (ὑπέρ),*
for at 1 Sam. i. 16 it means "to the person," and 2 Sam. iii. 31,
"before Abner's corpse (bier)." רֵעֵהוּ is thus here the person
with whom the suretyship is entered into ; he can be called the
רֵעַ of him who gives bail, so much the more as the reception of the
bail supposes that both are well known to each other. Here also
Fleischer rightly translates : *apud alterum (sc. creditorem pro de-
bitore).*

Ver. 19 He loveth sin who loveth strife ;
He who maketh high his doors seeketh destruction.

A synthetic distich (*vid.* p. 10). Böttcher finds the reason of the
pairing of these two lines in the relationship between a mouth and
a door (cf. Mic. vii. 5, פִּתְחֵי פִיד). Hitzig goes further, and supposes that 19b figuratively expresses what boastfulness brings upon
itself. Against Geier, Schultens, and others, who understand
פִּתְחוֹ directly of the mouth, he rightly remarks that הִגְבִּיהַּ פֶּה is not
heard of, and that הִגְדִּיל פֶּה would be used instead. But the two
lines harmonize, without this interchangeable reference of *os* and
ostium. *Zanksucht* [quarrelsomeness] and *Prunksucht* [ostenta-
tion] are related as the symptoms of selfishness. But both bear

their sentence in themselves. He who has pleasure in quarrelling has pleasure in evil, for he commits himself to the way of great sinning, and draws others along with him; and he who cannot have the door of his house high enough and splendid enough, prepares thereby for himself, against his will, the destruction of his house. An old Hebrew proverb says, כל העוסק בבנין יתמסכן, *ædificandi nimis studiosus ad mendicitatem redigitur.* Both parts of this verse refer to one and the same individual, for the *insanum ædificandi studium* goes only too often hand in hand with unjust and heartless litigation.

> Ver. 20 He that is of a false heart findeth no good;
> And he that goeth astray with his tongue falleth into evil.

Regarding עִקֶּשׁ־לֵב, *vid.* xi. 20. In the parallel member, נֶהְפָּךְ בִּלְשׁוֹנוֹ is he who twists or winds (*vid.* at ii. 12) with his tongue, going about concealing and falsifying the truth. The phrase וְנֶהְפָּךְ (the connecting form before a word with a prep.) is syntactically possible, but the Masora designates the word, in contradistinction to וְנֶהְפַּךְ, pointed with *Pathach*, Lev. xiii. 16, with לית as *unicum*, thus requires וְנֶהְפָּךְ, as is also found in Codd. The contrast of רָעָה is here טוב, also neut., as xiii. 21, cf. xvi. 20, and רָע, xiii. 17.

The first three parts of the old Solomonic Book of Proverbs ((1) x. 1–xii. 28; (2) xiii. 1–xv. 19; (3) xv. 20–xvii. 20) are now followed by the fourth part. We recognise it as striking the same keynote as x. 1. In xvii. 21 it resounds once more, here commencing a part; there, x. 1, beginning the second group of proverbs. The first closes, as it begins, with a proverb of the fool.

> Ver. 21 He that begetteth a fool, it is to his sorrow;
> And the father of a fool hath no joy.

It is admissible to supply יָלַד, developing itself from יֹלֵד, before לְתוּגָה לוֹ (*vid.* regarding this passive formation, at x. 1, cf. xiv. 13), as at Isa. lxvi. 3, מַעֲלֶה (Fl.: *in mœrorem sibi genuit h. e. ideo videtur genuisse ut sibi mœrorem crearet*); but not less admissible is it to interpret לתוגה לו as a noun-clause corresponding to the וְלֹא־יִשְׂמַח (thus to be written with *Makkeph*): it brings grief to him. According as one understands this as an expectation, or as a consequence, ילד, as at xxiii. 24, is rendered either *qui gignit* or *qui genuit*. With נָבָל, seldom occurring in the Book of Proverbs (only here and at ver. 7), כְּסִיל, occurring not unfrequently, is interchanged. Schultens rightly defines the latter etymologically:

marcidus h. e. qui ad virtutem, pietatem, vigorem omnem vitæ spiritualis medullitus emarcuit; and the former : *elumbis et mollitie seg-nitieve fractus,* the intellecually heavy and sluggish (cf. Arab. *kasal,* laziness ; *kaslân,* the lazy).[1]

Ver. 22 A joyful heart bringeth good recovery ;
And a broken spirit drieth the bones.

The heart is the centre of the individual life, and the condition and the tone of the heart communicates itself to this life, even to its outermost circumference ; the spirit is the power of self-consciousness which, according as it is lifted up or broken, also lifts up or breaks down the condition of the body (*Psychol.* p. 199), *vid.* the similar contrasted phrases לֵב שָׂמֵחַ and רוּחַ נְכֵאָה, xv. 13. The ἅπ. λεγ. גֵּהָה (here and there in Codd. incorrectly written גֵּיהָה) has nothing to do with the Arab. *jihat,* which does not mean sight, but direction, and is formed from *wjah* (whence *wajah,* sight), like עֵדָה, congregation, from וָעַד (יָעַד). The Syr., Targ. (perhaps also Symmachus : ἀγαθύνει ἡλικίαν ; Jerome : *ætatem floridam facit;* Luther : makes the life *lüstig* [cheerful]) translate it by body ; but for this גֵּוָה (גְּוִיָּה) is used, and that is a word of an entirely different root from גֵּהָה. To what verb this refers is shown by Hos. v. 13 : וְלֹא־יִגְהֶה מִכֶּם מָזוֹר, and healed not for you her ulcerous wound. מָזוֹר is the compress, *i.e.* the bandage closing up the ulcer, then also the ulcer-wound itself ; and גָּהָה is the contrary of עָלָה, *e.g.* Jer. viii. 22 ; it means the removing of the bandage and the healing of the wound. This is confirmed by the Syr. *gho,* which in like manner is construed with *min,* and means to be delivered from something (*vid.* Bernstein's *Lex. Syr.* to Kirsch's *Chrestomathie*). The Aethiop. quadriliteral *gâhgĕh,* to hinder, to cause to cease, corresponds to the causative Syr. *agahish.* Accordingly גָּהָה means to be in the condition of abatement, mitigation, healing ; and גֵּהָה (as synonym of כֵּהָה, Neh. iii. 19, with which Parchon combines it), *levamen, levatio,* in the sense of bodily healing (LXX. εὐεκτεῖν ποιεῖ ; *Venet.,* after Kimchi, ἀγαθυνεῖ

---

[1] Nöldeke's assertion (Art. *Orion* in Schenkel's *Bibel-Lexicon*) that the Arab. *kasal* corresponds to the Hebr. כָּשַׁל proceeds from the twofold supposition, that the meaning to be lazy underlies the meaning to totter (*vid.* also Dietrich in Gesenius' *Heb. Wörterbuch*), and that the Hebr. ס must correspond with the Arab. ش. The former supposition is untenable, the latter is far removed (cf. *e.g.* כָּסֵּא and *kursî,* סֵפֶר and *sifr,* מִסְכֵּן and *miskin*). The verb כָּשַׁל, Aram. תְּקַל, is unknown in the Arab.

θεραπείαν); and הֵיטִיב גֵּהָה (cf. xv. 2) denotes, to bring good improvement, to advance powerfully the recovery. Schultens compares the Arab. *jahy, nitescere, disserenari*, as Menahem has done נֵגַה, but this word is one of the few words which are explained exclusively from the Syriac (and Æthiop.). גֵּרֶם (here and at xxv. 15) is the word interchanging with עֶצֶם, xv. 30, xvi. 24.

Ver. 23 Bribery from the bosom the godless receiveth,
To pervert the ways of justice.

Regarding שֹׁחַד, *vid.* xvii. 8. The idea of this word, as well as the clause containing the purpose, demand for the רָשָׁע a high judicial or administrative post. The bosom, חֵק (חֵיק), is, as xvi. 23, that of the clothing. From the bosom, מֵחֵק, where it was kept concealed, the gift is brought forth, and is given into the bosom, בַּחֵק, xxi. 14, of him whose favour is to be obtained—an event taking place under four eyes, which purposely withdraws itself from the observation of any third person. Since this is done to give to the course of justice a direction contrary to rectitude, the giver of the bribe has not right on his side; and, under the circumstances, the favourable decision which he purchases may be at once the unrighteous sentence of a צַדִּיק, accusing him, or accused by him, xviii. 5.

Ver. 24 The understanding has his attention toward wisdom ;
But the eyes of a fool are on the end of the earth.

Many interpreters explain, as Euchel :

" The understanding finds wisdom everywhere ;
The eyes of the fool seek it at the end of the world."

Ewald refers to Deut. xxx. 11–14 as an unfolding of the same thought. But although it may be said of the fool (*vid.* on the contrary, xv. 14) that he seeks wisdom, only not at the right place, as at xiv. 6, of the mocker that he seeks wisdom but in vain, yet here the order of the words, as well as the expression, lead us to another thought : before the eyes of the understanding (אֶת־פְּנֵי, as Gen. xxxiii. 18, 1 Sam. ii. 11, 'and frequently in the phrase נראה את־פני ה', *e.g.* 1 Sam. i. 22) wisdom lies as his aim, his object, the end after which he strives ; on the contrary, the eyes of the fool, without keeping that one necessary thing in view, wander *in alia omnia*, and roam about what is far off, without having any fixed object. The fool is everywhere with his thoughts, except where he ought to be. Leaving out of view that which lies nearest, he loses himself in *aliena*. The understanding has an ever present theme in wisdom, which arrests his attention, and on which he concentrates himself; but the fool flutters about fantastically from one thing to another, and that which is to him precisely of least importance interests him the most.

The series of proverbs, ver. 25–xviii. 2, begins and closes in the same way as the preceding, and only ver. 26 stands by itself without apparent connection.

Ver. 25. This verse begins connecting itself with ver. 21:

> A grief to his father is a foolish son,
> And a bitter woe for her that bare him.

The ἅπ. λεγ. מֶמֶר is formed from מָרַר (to be bitter, properly harsh), as מֶכֶס from בָּכַס. The Syr. and Targ. change the subst. into participles; some codd. also have מֵמֵר (after the forms מֵפֵר, מֵסֵב, מֵחֵל, מֵרֵע), but as may be expected in 25a, מַכְעִים. The dat. obj. instead of the accus. may be possible; the verse immediately following furnishes a sufficient example of this.

Ver. 26 Also to inflict punishment on the righteous is not good;
This, that one overthrows the noble on account of his rectitude.

Does the גַּם [also] refer to a connection from which the proverb is separated? or is it tacitly supposed that there are many kinds of worthless men in the world, and that one from among them is brought forward? or is it meant, that to lay upon the righteous a pecuniary punishment is also not good? None of all these. The proverb must have a meaning complete in itself; and if pecuniary punishment and corporeal punishment were regarded as opposed to one another, 26b would then have begun with אַף כִּי (quanto magis percutere ingenuos). Here it is with גם as at xx. 11, and as with אַף at 11a, and רַק at xiii. 10: according to the sense, it belongs not to the word next following, but to לַצַּדִּיק; and עָנַשׁ (whence inf. עֲנוֹשׁ, as xxi. 11, with the ă in ע, cf. also אֲבֹד, xi. 10, for אֱבֹד) means here not specially to inflict a pecuniary fine, but generally to punish, for, as in mulctare, the meaning is generalized, elsewhere with the accus., Deut. xxii. 19, here to give to any one to undergo punishment. The ruler is the servant of God, who has to preserve rectitude, εἰς ὀργὴν τῷ τὸ κακὸν πράσσοντι (Rom. xiii. 14). It is not good when he makes his power to punish to be felt by the innocent as well as by the guilty.

In 26b, instead of הַכּוֹת, the proverb is continued with לְהַכּוֹת; לֹא־טוֹב, which is to be supplied, takes the inf. alone when it precedes, and the inf. with ל when it follows, xviii. 5, xxviii. 21,

xxi. 9 (but cf. xxi. 19). הַכּוֹת is the usual word for punishment by scourging, Deut. xxv. 1–3, cf. 2 Cor. xi. 24, N. T. μαστιγοῦν, δέρειν, Rabb. מַכּוֹת, strokes, or מַלְקוּת מַלְקוֹת from לָקָה, vapulare, to receive stripes. נְדִיבִים are here those noble in disposition. The idea of נדיב fluctuates between *generosus* in an outward and in a moral sense, wherefore עַל־יֹשֶׁר, or rather עֲלֵי־יֹשֶׁר, is added; for the old editions, correct MSS., and *e.g.* also Soncin. 1488, present עֲלֵי (*vid.* Norzi). Hitzig incorrectly explains this, "against what is due" (יֹשֶׁר, as xi. 24); also Ps. xciv. 20, עֲלֵי־חֹק does not mean κατὰ προστάγ- ματος (Symmachus), but ἐπὶ προστάγματι (LXX. and Theod.), on the ground of right = *prætextu juris* (Vatabl.). Thus עלי־יֹשר means here neither against nor beyond what is due, but: on the ground of honourable conduct, making this (of course mistakenly) a lawful title to punishment; Aquila, ἐπὶ εὐθύτητι, cf. Matt. v. 10, ἕνεκεν δικαιοσύνης. Besides, for עַל after הִכָּה, the causal signification lies nearest Num. xxii. 32, cf. Isa. i. 5 (עַל־מֶה, on account of anything). If the power of punishment is abused to the punishing of the righteous, yea, even to the corporeal chastisement of the noble, and their straight, *i.e.* conscientious, firm, open conduct, is made a crime against them, that is not good—it is perversion of the idea of justice, and an iniquity which challenges the penal rectitude of the Most High (Eccles. v. 7 [8]).

Ver. 27 He that keepeth his words to himself hath knowledge,
And the cool of temper is a man of understanding.

The first line here is a variation of x. 19*b*. The phrase יֹדֵעַ דַּעַת (here and at Dan. i. 4) means to possess knowledge (*novisse*); more frequently it is יֹדֵעַ בִּינָה, *e.g.* iv. 1, where ידע has the inchoative sense of *noscere*. In 27*b* the *Kerî* is יְקַר־רוּחַ. Jerome translates it *pretiosi spiritus*, the *Venet.* τίμιος τὸ πνεῦμα. Rashi glosses יקר here, as at 1 Sam. iii. 1, by מנוע (thus to be read after codd.), *retentus spiritu;* most interpreters remark that the spirit here comes into view as expressing itself in words. It is scarcely correct to say that יְקַר דְּבָרִים could designate one who is sparing in his words, but יְקַר־רוּחַ is, according to the fundamental conception of the verb יָקַר, *gravis spiritu* (Schultens), of a dignified, composed spirit ; it is a quiet seriousness proceeding from high conscientiousness, and maintaining itself in self-control, which is designated by this word. But the *Chethîb* וְקַר־רוּחַ presents almost the same descrip- tion of character. קַר from קָרַר (of the same root as יקר) means to be firm, unmoveable, καρτερὸν εἶναι, hence to be congealed, frozen, cold (cf. *frigus* with *rigere, rigor*), figuratively to be cold-blooded, passionless, quiet, composed (Fl.); cf. post-bibl. קֹרַת רוּחַ (Arab. *kurrat ʿain*), cooling = refreshing, ἀνάψυξις (Acts iii. 20).[1] Whether we read יְקַר or קַר, in any case we are not to translate *rarus spiritu*, which, apart from the impossibility of the expression, makes 27*b* almost a tautological repetition of the thought of 27*a*. The first line recommends bridling of the tongue, in contrast to inconsiderate and untimely talk; the second line recommends coldness, *i.e.* equanimity of spirit, in contrast to passionate heat.

Ver. 28 continues the same theme, the value of silence:

> Even a fool, when he keeps silence, is counted wise;
> When he shutteth his mouth, discreet.

The subj. as well as the pred. of the first line avail for the second. אָטַם, *obturare, occludere*, usually of closing the ear, is here transferred to the mouth. The *Hiph.* הֶחֱרִישׁ means *mutum agere* (cf. Arab. *khrs, mutum esse*), from חָרֵשׁ, which, like κωφός, passes from the meaning *surdus* to that of *mutus* (Fl.). The words of Job xiii. 5, and also those of Alexander: *si tacuisses sapiens mansisses*, are applicable to fools. An Arab. proverb says, " silence is the covering of the stupid." In the epigrammatical hexameter,

πᾶς τις ἀπαίδευτος φρονιμώτατός ἐστι σιωπῶν,

the word σιωπῶν has the very same syntactical position as these two participles.[2]

---

[1] " He has made my eye glowing " (*askhn*, cf. שַׁחִין) is in Arab. equivalent to " he has deeply troubled me." The eye of the benevolent is *bârid*, and in the Semitic manner of expression, with deep psychological significance, it is said that the tears of sorrow are hot, but those of joy cold.

[2] Cf. C. Schulze's *Die bibl. Sprichwörter* (1860), p. 60 f.

BIBLICAL COMMENTARY

ON THE

PROVERBS OF SOLOMON

BY

FRANZ DELITZSCH, D.D.,

TRANSLATED FROM THE GERMAN BY

M. G. EASTON, D.D.

TABLE OF CONTENTS.

ABBREVIATIONS.

[THE usual abbreviations of words and phrases are adopted throughout this work, and will readily be understood by the reader. The mark of abbreviation in Hebrew words is a stroke like an acute accent after a letter, as *e.g.* 'תְּר for תְּרוּמוֹת, xxix. 4; and in Hebrew sentences, 'וגו for וְגוֹמַר *et complens* = etc., as *e.g.* at xxx. 4.]

THE BOOK OF PROVERBS

HAP. xviii. 1. This series of proverbs now turns from the fool to the separatist :

> The separatist seeketh after his own pleasure ;
> Against all that is beneficial he showeth his teeth.

The reflexive נִפְרָד has here the same meaning as the Rabbinical פָּרַשׁ מִן־הַצִּבּוּר, to separate oneself from the congregation, *Aboth* ii. 5 ; נִפְרָד denotes a man who separates himself, for he follows his own counsel, Arab. *mnfrd* (*mtfrrd*) *brâyh*, or *jhys almhhl* (*seorsum ab aliis secedens*). Instead of לְתַאֲוָה, Hitzig, after Jerome, adopts the emendation לְתֹאֲנָה, "after an occasion" (a pretext), and by נפרד thinks of one pushed aside, who, thrown into opposition, seeks to avenge himself. But his translation of 1*b*, "against all that is fortunate he gnasheth his teeth," shows how much the proverb is opposed to this interpretation. נִפְרָד denotes one who willingly (Judg. iv. 11), and, indeed, obstinately withdraws himself. The construction of יְבַקֵּשׁ with לְ (also Job x. 6) is explained by this, that the poet, giving prominence to the object, would set it forward : a pleasure (תאוה, as Arab. *hawan*, unstable and causeless direction of the mind to something, pleasure, freak, caprice), and nothing else, he goes after who has separated himself (Fl.) ; the effort of the separatist goes out after a pleasure, *i.e.* the enjoyment and realization of such ; instead of seeking to conform himself to the law and ordinance of the community, he seeks to carry out a separate view, and to accomplish some darling plan : *libidinem sectatur sui cerebri homo.* With this 1*b* accords.

תּוּשִׁיָּה (*vid.* at ii. 7) is concretely that which furthers and profits. Regarding הִתְגַּלָּע, *vid.* at xvii. 14. Thus putting his subjectivity in the room of the common weal, he shows his teeth, places himself in fanatical opposition against all that is useful and profitable in the principles and aims, the praxis of the community from which he separates himself. The figure is true to nature: the polemic of the schismatic and the sectary against the existing state of things, is for the most part measureless and hostile.

Ver. 2 The fool hath no delight in understanding;
But only that his heart may reveal itself therein.

The verb חָפֵץ forms the fut. יֶחְפַּץ as well as יַחְפֹּץ; first the latter from חָפַץ, with the primary meaning, to bow, to bend down; then both forms as intransitive, to bend oneself to something, to be inclined to something, Arab. *'tf.* (Fl.). תְּבוּנָה is here the intelligence which consists in the understanding of one's own deficiency, and of that which is necessary to meet it. The inclination of the fool goes not out after such intelligence, but

(כִּי אִם; according to Ben-Naphtali, כִּי־אָם) only that his heart, *i.e.* the understanding which he thinks that he already possesses, may reveal itself, show itself publicly. He thinks thereby to show himself in his true greatness, and to render a weighty service to the world. This loquacity of the fool, proceeding from self-satisfaction, without self-knowledge, has already, xii. 23, and often, been reprimanded.

The group beginning with ver. 3 terminates in two proverbs (vers. 6 and 7), related to the concluding verse of the foregoing:

Ver. 3 If a godless man cometh, then cometh also contempt;
And together with disgrace, shame.

J. D. Michaelis, and the most of modern critics, read רָשָׁע; then, contempt etc., are to be thought of as the consequences that follow godlessness; for that קָלוֹן means (Hitzig) disgracefulness, *i.e.* disgraceful conduct, is destitute of proof; קלון always means disgrace as an experience. But not only does the Masoretic text punctuate רֶשַׁע, but also all the old translators, the Greek, Aramaic, and Latin, have done so. And is it on this account, because a coming naturally seems to be spoken of a person? The "pride cometh, then cometh shame," xi. 2,

was in their recollection not less firmly, perhaps, than in ours.
They read רָשָׁע, because בּוֹ does not fittingly designate the
first of that which godlessness effects, but perhaps the first of
that which proceeds from it. Therefore we adhere to the
opinion, that the proverb names the fiends which appear in the
company of the godless wherever he goes, viz. first בּוּז, contempt (Ps. xxxi. 19), which places itself haughtily above all
due subordination, and reverence, and forbearance; and then,
with the disgrace [turpitudo], קָלוֹן, which attaches itself to those
who meddle with him (Isa. xxii. 18), there is united the shame,
הֶרְפָּה (Ps. xxxix. 9), which he has to suffer from him who has
only always expected something better from him. Fleischer
understands all the three words in the passive sense, and remarks,
"עַם־קָלוֹן חרפה, a more artificial expression for קלון וחרפה, in the
Turkish quite common for the copula wāw, e.g. swylh tbrâk,
earth and water, 'wrtylh âr, the man and the woman." ' But
then the expression would be tautological; we understand
בּוּז and חרפה of that which the godless does to others by his
words, and קלון of that which he does to them by his conduct.
By this interpretation, עַם is more than the representative of
the copula.

Ver. 4 Deep waters are the words from a man's mouth,
A bubbling brook, a fountain of wisdom.

Earlier, we added to hominis the supplement sc. sapientis, but
then an unnecessary word would be used, and that which is
necessary omitted. Rather it might be said that אִישׁ is meant
in an ideal sense; but thus meant, אִישׁ, like גֶּבֶר, denotes the
valiant man, but not man as he ought to be, or the man of
honour; and besides, a man may be a man of honour without
there being said of him what this proverb expresses. Ewald
comes nearer the case when he translates, " deep waters are the
heart-words of many." Heart-words—what an unbiblical expression! The LXX., which translates λόγος ἐν καρδίᾳ, has
not read דברי לב, but דבר בלב (as xx. 5, עֵצָה בְלֶב־). But that
" of many " is certainly not a right translation, yet right in so
far as אִישׁ (as at xii. 14) is thought of as made prominent: the
proverb expresses, in accordance with the form of narrative
proverbs which present an example, what occurs in actual life,
and is observed. Three different things are said of the words

from a man's mouth: they are deep waters, for their meaning
does not lie on the surface, but can be perceived only by penetrating into the secret motives and aims of him who speaks;
they are a bubbling brook, which freshly and powerfully gushes
forth to him who feels this flow of words, for in this brook
there never fails an always new gush of living water; it is a
fountain or well of wisdom, from which wisdom flows forth, and
whence wisdom is to be drawn.   Hitzig supposes that the distich
is antithetic; מַיִם עֲמֻקִּים, or rather מֵי מַעֲמַקִּים, "waters of the
deep," are cistern waters; on the contrary, "a welling brook is a
fountain of wisdom."   But עָמֹק means deep, not deepened, and
deep water is the contrast of shallow water; a cistern also may
be deep (cf. xxii. 14), but deep water is such as is deep, whether
it be in the ocean or in a ditch.   4b also does not suggest a
cistern, for thereby it would be indicated that the description,
דברי פי־איש, is not here continued; the "fountain of wisdom" does
not form a proper parallel or an antithesis to this subject, since
this much rather would require the placing in contrast of deep
and shallow, of exhausted (drained out) and perennial.   And:
the fountain is a brook, the well a stream—who would thus
express himself!   We have thus neither an antithetic nor a
synonymous (LXX. after the phrase ἀναπηδῶν, Jerome, Venet.,
Luth.), but an integral distich (vid. vol. i. p. 8) before us; and
this leads us to consider what depths of thought, what riches of
contents, what power of spiritual and moral advancement, may
lie in the words of a man.

> Ver. 5 To favour the person of the godless is not good,
>   And to oppress the righteous in judgment.

As ver. 4 has one subject, so ver. 5 has one predicate.   The
form is the same as xvii. 26.   שְׂאֵת פְּנֵי (cf. xxiv. 23), προσω-
πολημψία, acceptio personæ, is this, that one accepts the פְּנֵי, i.e. the
personal appearance of any one (πρόσωπον λαμβάνει), i.e. regards
it as acceptable, respectable, agreeable, which is a thing in itself
not wrong; but in a judge who ought to determine according
to the facts of the case and the law, it becomes sinful partiality.
הַטּוֹת, in a forensic sense, with the accus. of the person, may be
regarded in a twofold way: either as a turning aside, מִדִּין, Isa.
x. 2, from following and attaining unto the right, or as an
oppressing, for the phrase הִטָּה מִשְׁפָּט [to pervert justice] (cf.

xvii. 23) is transferred to the person who experiences the oppression = perversion of the law ; and this idea perhaps always
underlies the expression, wherever, as *e.g.* Mal. iii. 5, no addition
brings with it the other. Under xvii. 15 is a fuller explanation
of לֹא־טוֹב.

Ver. 6 The lips of the fool engage in strife,
And his mouth calleth for stripes.

We may translate : the lips of the fool cause strife, for בּוֹא בְ,
to come with anything, *e.g.* Ps. lxvi. 13, is equivalent to bring
it (to bring forward), as also : they engage in strife; as one
says בּוֹא בְדָמִים : to be engaged in bloodshed, 1 Sam. xxv. 26.
We prefer this *intrant* (*ingerunt se*), with Schultens and
Fleischer. יָבֹאוּ for תְּבֹאנָה, a *synallage generis*, to which, by
means of a "self-deception of the language" (Fl.), the apparent masculine ending of such duals may have contributed.
The stripes which the fool calleth for (קְרָא לְ, like ii. 3) are such
as he himself carries off, for it comes *a verbis ad verbera.* The
LXX.: his bold mouth calleth for death (פִּי הַהֹמֶה מָוֶת יִקְרָא) ;

לְמַהֲלֻמוֹת has, in codd. and old editions, the *Mem raphatum*, as
also at xix. 29; the sing. is thus מַהֲלוּם, like מַנְעִיל מַנְעָלָיו to, for
the *Mem dagessatum* is to be expected in the inflected מַהֲלֻם, by
the passing over of the *ō* into *ŭ*.

Ver. 7 The mouth of the fool is to him destruction,
And his lips are a snare to his soul.

As ver. 6 corresponds to xvii. 27 of the foregoing group, so
this ver. 7 corresponds to xvii. 28. Regarding מְחִתָּה־לּוֹ, *vid.*
xiii. 3. Instead of פִּי כְסִיל, is to be written פִּי־כְסִיל, according to *Torath Emeth*, p. 40, Cod. 1294, and old editions.

A pair of proverbs regarding the flatterer and the slothful :

Ver. 8 The words of the flatterer are as dainty morsels,
And they glide down into the innermost parts.

An " analogy, with an epexegesis in the second member " (Fl.),
which is repeated in xxvi. 22. Ewald, Bertheau, Hitzig, and
others, are constrained to interpret וְהֵם as introducing a contrast, and in this sense they give to מִתְלַהֲמִים all kinds of unwarrantable meanings. Ewald translates : as burning (להם,
cogn. להב), and offers next : as whispering (להם, cogn. רעם, נהם) ;
Ch. B. Michaelis, Bertheau, and others : as sporting (להם, cogn.
להה) ; Hitzig : like soft airs (להם, cogn. Arab. *hillam, flaccus,*

laxus). All these interpretations are without support. The word לָהֶם has none of all these significations; it means, as the Arab. *lahima* warrants, *deglutire*. But Böttcher's explanation also : " as swallowed down, because spoken with reserve," proceeds, like those others, from the supposed syntactically fine yet false supposition, that 8*b* is an antithetic " *dennoch* " [*tamen*]. In that case the poet would have written וְהֵם יֹרְדִים (cf. וְהוּא, as the beginning of a conditional clause, iii. 29, xxiii. 3). But וְהוּא, וְהֵם, with the finite following, introduces neither here nor at Deut. xxxiii. 3, Judg. xx. 34, Ps. xcv. 10, cf. Gen. xliii. 23, a conditional clause. Thus 8*b* continues the clause 8*a* by one standing on the same line ; and thus we do not need to invent a meaning for כְּמִתְלַהֲמִים, which forms a contrast to the penetrating into the innermost parts. The relation of the parts of the proverb is rightly given by Luther :

> The words of the slanderer are stripes,
> And they go through the heart of one.

He interprets לְהֶם as transposed from הֶלֶם (Rashi and others); but stripes cannot be called מִתְלַהֲמִים—they are called, 6*b*, מַהֲלֻמוֹת. This interpretation of the word has always more support than that of Symmachus : ὡς ἀκέραιοι ; Jerome : *quasi simplicia ;* Aquila, xxvi. 22 : γοητικοί ; which last, as also that of Capellus, Clericus, and Schultens : *quasi numine quodam afflata,* seems to support itself on the Arab. *âhm* iv. *inspirare.* But in reality *âhm* does not mean *afflare ;* it means *deglutire,* and nothing else. The Jewish lexicographers offer nothing worth considering ; Kimchi's חֲלָקִים, according to which the *Venet.* translates μαλθακιζόμενοι, is fanciful ; for the Talm. הֶלֶם, striking = hitting, suitable, standing well, furnishes no transition to " smooth " and " soft." Immanuel compares *âhm* = בָּלַע ; and Schultens, who is followed by Gesenius and others, has already, with perfect correctness, explained : *tanquam quæ avidissime in-glutiantur.* Thus also Fleischer : things which offer themselves to be eagerly gulped down, or which let themselves be thus swallowed. But in this way can one be truly just to the *Hithpa.?* The Arab. *âlthm* (stronger form, *âltkm,* according to which van Dyk translates *mthl ukam hlwt,* like sweet morsels) means to swallow into oneself, which is not here appropriate. The *Hithpa.* will thus have here a passive signification : things which are greedily swallowed. Regarding נִרְגָּן from רָגַן, *vid.* at xvi. 28. וְהֵם refers to the words of the flatterer, and is emphatic, equivalent to *æque illa, etiam illa,* or *illa ipsa.* יָרַד is here connected with the obj. accus. (cf. i. 12) instead of with אֶל, vii. 27. חַדְרֵי, *penetralia,* we had already at vii. 27 ; the root-word is (Arab.) *khdr,* to seclude, to conceal, different from *hdr, demittere,* and *hkhr* (cogn. חזר), to finish, *circumire.* בֶּטֶן is the inner part of the body with reference to the organs lying there, which mediate not only the life of the body, but also that of the mind,—in general, the internal part of the per- sonality. The LXX. does not translate this proverb, but has in its stead xix. 15, in a different version, however, from that it gives there ; the Syr. and the Targ. have thereby been drawn away from the Hebr. text.

> Ver. 9 He also who showeth himself slothful in his business,
>   Is a brother to him who proceedeth to destroy.

The *Hithpa.* הִתְרַפָּה signifies here, as at xxiv. 10, to show one- self slack, lazy, negligent. מְלָאכָה is properly a commission for another, as a king has a messenger, ambassador, commissioner to execute it ; here, any business, whether an undertaking in commission from another, or a matter one engages in for him- self. He who shows himself slack therein, produces in his way, viz. by negligence, destruction, as truly as the בַּעַל מַשְׁחִית, who does it directly by his conduct. Thus one is named, who is called, or who has his own delight in it, to destroy or overthrow. Jerome, incorrectly limiting : *sua opera dissipantis.* Hitzig well compares Matt. xii. 30. In the variation, xxviii. 24*b*, the destroyer is called אִישׁ מַשְׁחִית, the connection of the words being adject. ; on the contrary, the connection of בעל משחית is genit. (cf. xxii. 24, xxiii. 2, etc.), for מַשְׁחִית as frequently means that which destroys = destruction. Von Hofmann (*Schriftbew.* ii. 2, 403) understands אִישׁ מ׳ of the street robber, בעל מ׳ of the captain of robbers ; but the designation for the latter must be שַׂר מ׳, though at 1 Kings xi. 24 he is called by the name שַׂר גְּדוּד. The form of the word in the proverb here is more original than at xxviii. 24. There חָבֵר [companion] is used, here אָח [brother], a general Semitic name of him who, or of that which, is in any way related to another, cf. Job xxx. 29. Fleischer compares the Arab. proverb: *álshbht ákht alkhtyât*, scepticism is the sister of sin.

Two proverbs, of the fortress of faith, and of the fortress of presumption:

> Ver. 10 A strong tower is the name of Jahve:
> The righteous runneth into it, and is high.

The name of Jahve is the Revelation of God, and the God of Revelation Himself, the creative and historical Revelation, and who is always continually revealing Himself; His name is His nature representing itself, and therefore capable of being described and named, before all the *Tetragramm*, as the *Anagramm* of the overruling and inworking historical being of God, as the *Chiffre* of His free and all-powerful government in grace and truth, as the self-naming of God the Saviour. This name, which is afterwards interwoven in the name Jesus, is מִגְדַּל־עֹז (Ps. lxi. 4), a strong high tower bidding defiance to every hostile assault. Into this the righteous runneth, to hide himself behind its walls, and is thus lifted (*perf. consec.*) high above all danger (cf. יִשְׂגָּב, xxix. 25). רוּץ אֶל means, Job xv. 26, to run against anything, רוּץ, *seq. acc.*, to invest, blockade anything, רוּץ בְּ, to hasten within; Hitzig's conjecture, יָרוּם [riseth up high], instead of יָרוּץ, is a freak. רוּץ בְּ is speedily בּוֹא בְ, the idea the same as Ps. xxvii. 5, xxxi. 21.

> Ver. 11 The possession of the righteous is his strong fort,
> And is like a high wall in his imagination.

Line first = x. 15*a*. מַשְׂכִּית from שָׂכָה, Chald. סְכָא (whence after *Megilla* 14*a*, יִסְכָּה, she who looks), R. שׂך, cogn. זך, to pierce, to fix, means the image as a medal, and thus also intellectually: image (conception, and particularly the imagination) of the heart (Ps. lxxiii. 7), here the fancy, conceit; Fleischer compares (Arab.) *tswwr*, to imagine something to oneself, French *se figurer*. Translators from the LXX. to Luther incorrectly think on שׂכב (סכך), to entertain; only the *Venet.* is correct in the rendering: ἐν φαντασίᾳ αὐτοῦ; better than Kimchi, who, after Ezra viii. 12, thinks on the chamber where the riches delighted in are treasured, and where he fancies himself in the midst of his treasures as if surrounded by an inaccessible wall.

We place together vers. 12–19, in which the figure of a secure fortress returns:

Ver. 12. This proverb is connected with the preceding of the rich man who trusts in his mammon.

> Before destruction the heart of man is haughty;
> And humility goeth before honour.

Line first is a variation of xvi. 18*a*, and line second is similar to xv. 33*b*.

> Ver. 13 If one giveth an answer before he heareth,
> It is to him as folly and shame.

The *part.* stands here differently from what it does at xiii. 18, where it is subj., and at xvii. 14, where it is pred. of a simple sentence; it is also here, along with what appertains to it in accordance with the Semitic idiom, subj. to 13*b* (one who answers . . . is one to whom this . . .); but, in accordance with our idiom, it becomes a hypothetical antecedent (cf. vol. i. p. 282). For "to answer" one also uses הֵשִׁיב without addition; but the original full expression is הֵשִׁיב דָּבָר, *reddere verbum, referre dictum* (cf. עָנָה דָבָר, Jer. xliv. 20, absol. in the cogn., xv. 28*a*); דבר one may not understand of the word to which, but of the word with which, the reply is made. הִיא לוֹ comprehends the meaning: it avails to him (*ducitur ei*), as well as it reaches to him (*est ei*). In Agricola's *Fünfhundert Sprüchen* this proverb is given thus: *Wer antwortet ehe er höret, der zaiget an sein torhait vnd wirdt ze schanden* [he who answers before he hears shows his folly, and it is to him a shame]. But that would require the word to be יֵבוֹשׁ, *pudefiet;* (הִיא לוֹ) כְּלִמָּה means that it becomes to him a ground of merited disgrace. "כְּלִמָּה, properly wounding, *i.e.* shame (like *atteinte à son honneur*), from כָּלַם (cogn. הָלַם), to strike, hit, wound" (Fl.). Sirach (xi. 8) warns against such rash talking, as well as against the rudeness of interrupting others.

> Ver. 14 The spirit of a man beareth his sickness;
> But a broken spirit, who can bear it?

The breath of the Creator imparting life to man is spoken of as *spiritus spirans*, רוּחַ (רוּחַ חַיִּים), and as *spiritus spiratus*, נֶפֶשׁ (נֶפֶשׁ חַיָּה); the spirit (*animus*) is the primary, and the soul (*anima*) the secondary principle of life; the double gender of רוּחַ is accounted for thus: when it is thought of as the primary, and thus in a certain degree (*vid. Psychol.* p. 103 ff.) the manly principle, it is mas. (Gen. vi. 3; Ps. li. 12, etc.). Here the

change of gender is in the highest degree characteristic, and אִישׁ
also is intentionally used (cf. 1 Sam. xxvi. 15) instead of אָדָם, 16a:
the courageous spirit of a man which sustains or endures (כִּלְכֵּל,
R. כל, *comprehendere, prehendere;* Luther, " who knows how to
contain himself in his sufferings;" cf. Ps. li. 12, " may the free
Spirit hold me ") the sickness [*Siechthum*] (we understand here
" *siech* " in the old meaning = *sick*) with self-control, is *generis
masculini;* while, on the contrary, the רוּחַ נְכֵאָה (as xv. 13, xvii. 22),
brought down from its manliness and superiority to disheartened
passivity, is *genere feminino* (cf. Ps. li. 12 with ver. 19).
Fleischer compares the Arab. proverb, *thbât âlnfs bâlghdhâ
thbât alrwh balghnâ,* the soul has firmness by nourishment, the
spirit by music.[1] The question מִי יִשָּׂאֶנָּה is like Mark ix. 50:
if the salt becomes tasteless, wherewith shall one season it?
There is no seasoning for the spice that has become insipid.
And for the spirit which is destined to bear the life and fortune
of the person, if it is cast down by sufferings, there is no one
to lift it up and sustain it.   But is not God the Most High
the lifter up and the bearer of the human spirit that has been
crushed and broken?   The answer is, that the manly spirit,
14a, is represented as strong in God; the discouraged, 14b, as
not drawing from God the strength and support he ought to
do.   But passages such as Isa. lxvi. 2 do not bring it near
that we think of the רוח נכאה as alienated from God.   The
spirit is נֹשֵׂא, the bearer of the personal and natural life with its
functions, activities, and experiences.   If the spirit is borne
down to powerless and helpless passivity, then within the sphere
of the human personality there is no other sustaining power
that can supply its place.

Ver. 15 The heart of a man of understanding gaineth knowledge,
        And the ear of the wise seeketh after knowledge.

נָבוֹן may be also interpreted as an adj., but we translate it here as
at xiv. 33, because thus it corresponds with the parallelism; cf.
לֵב צַדִּיק, xv. 28, and לֵב חָכָם, xvi. 23, where the adject. interpretation is excluded.   The gaining of wisdom is, after xvii. 16,

---

[1] In the Arab. language, influenced by philosophy, روح, the *anima
vitalis,* and نفس, the *anima rationalis,* are inverted; *vid.* Baudissin's *Trans-
lationis antiquæ Arab. libri Jobi quæ supersunt* (1870), p. 34.

referred to the heart : a heart vigorous in embracing and receiving it is above all necessary, and just such an one possesses
the נבון, which knows how to value the worth and usefulness
of such knowledge. The wise, who are already in possession of such knowledge, are yet at the same time constantly
striving to increase this knowledge : their ear seeks knowledge,
eagerly asking where it is to be found, and attentively listening
when the opportunity is given of מְצֹא, obtaining it.

> Ver. 16 The gift of a man maketh room for him,
> And bringeth him before the great.

That מַתָּן may signify intellectual endowments, Hitzig supposes,
but without any proof for such an opinion. Intellectual ability
as the means of advancement is otherwise designated, xxii. 29.
But Hitzig is right in this, that one mistakes the meaning of
the proverb if he interprets מתן in the sense of שֹׁחַד (vid. at
xvii. 8) : מתן is an indifferent idea, and the proverb means that
a man makes free space, a free path for himself, by a gift, i.e.
by this, that he shows himself to be agreeable, pleasing where it
avails, not niggardly but liberal. As a proverb expresses it :

> *Mit dem Hut in der Hand*
> *Kommt man durchs ganze Land*

[with hat in hand one goes through the whole land], so it
is said here that such liberality brings before the great, i.e.
not : furnishes with introductions to them ; but helps to a
place of honour near the great, i.e. those in a lofty position
(cf. לִפְנֵי, xxii. 29 ; עם, Ps. cxiii. 8). It is an important part of
practical wisdom, that by right liberality, i.e. by liberal giving
where duty demands it, and prudence commends it, one does not
lose but gains, does not descend but rises ; it helps a man over
the difficulties of limited, narrow circumstances, gains for him
affection, and helps him up from step to step. The *â* of מַתָּן
is, in a singular way (cf. מַתְּנַת, מַתָּנָה), treated as unchangeable.

> Ver. 17 He that is first in his controversy is right ;
> But there cometh another and searcheth him thoroughly—

an exhortation to be cautious in a lawsuit, and not to justify
without more ado him who first brings forward his cause, and
supports it by reasons, since, if the second party afterwards
search into the reasons of the first, they show themselves un-

tenable. הָרִאשׁוֹן בְּרִיבוֹ are to be taken together; the words are
equivalent to אֲשֶׁר יָבֹא בְרִיבוֹ בָרִאשֹׁנָה : *qui prior cum causa sua
venit,* i.e. *eam ad judicem defert* (Fl.). הראשון may, however,
also of itself alone be *qui prior venit;* and בריבו will be taken
with צדיק: *justus qui prior venit in causa sua (esse videtur).* The
accentuation rightly leaves the relation undecided. Instead of
יבא (יָבֹא) the *Kerî* has וּבָא, as it elsewhere, at one time, changes
the fut. into the perf. with ו (*e.g.* xx. 4, Jer. vi. 21); and,
at another time, the perf. with ו into the fut. (*e.g.* Ps. x. 10,
Isa. v. 29). But here, where the *perf. consec.* is not so admissible, as vi. 11, xx. 4, the fut. ought to remain unchanged.
רֵעֵהוּ is the other part, synon. with בעל דין חברו, *Sanhedrin*
7b, where the אזהרה לבית־דין (admonition for the court of justice)
is derived from Deut. i. 16, to hear the accused at the same
time with the accuser, that nothing of the latter may be adopted
beforehand. This proverb is just such an *audiatur et altera
pars.* The *status controversiæ* is only brought fairly into the
light by the hearing of the *altera pars :* then comes the other
and examines him (the first) to the very bottom. חָקַר, elsewhere with the accus. of the thing, *e.g.* רִיב, thoroughly to search
into a strife, Job xxix. 16, is here, as at xxviii. 11, connected
with the accus. of the person: to examine or lay bare any
one thoroughly; here, so that the misrepresentations of the state
of the matter might come out to view along with the reasons
assigned by the accuser.

Ver. 18 The lot allayeth contentions,
And separateth between the mighty,

i.e. erects a partition wall between them—those contending
(הַפְרִיד בֵּין, as at 2 Kings ii. 11, cf. Arab. *frk byn*); עֲצוּמִים are
not opponents who maintain their cause with weighty arguments
(עֲצֻמוֹת, Isa. xli. 21), *qui argumentis pollent* (*vid.* Rashi), for
then must the truth appear in the *pro et contra;* but mighty
opponents, who, if the lot did not afford a seasonable means
of reconciliation, would make good their demands by blows and
by the sword (Fl.). Here it is the lot which, as the judgment of God, brings about peace, instead of the *ultima ratio* of
physical force. The proverb refers to the lot what the Epistle
to the Hebrews, vi. 16, refers to the oath, *vid.* at xvi. 33.
Regarding מִדְיָנִים and its altered forms, *vid.* vol. i. p. 145.

Ver. 19 A brother toward whom it has been acted perfidiously resists
more than a strong tower;
And contentions are like the bar of a palace.

Luther rightly regarded the word נּוֹשָׁע, according to which
the LXX., Vulg., and Syr. translated *frater qui adjuvatur a
fratre*, as an incorrect reading; one would rather expect
אָח מוֹשִׁיעַ, "a brother who stands by," as Luther earlier translated; and besides, נוֹשַׁע does not properly mean *adjuvari*, but
salvari. His translation—

Ein verletzt Bruder helt herter denn eine feste Stad,
Und Zanck helt herter, denn rigel am Palast

[a brother wounded resisteth more than a strong city, and
strife resisteth more than bolts in the palace], is one of his
most happy renderings. מִקִּרְיַת־עֹז in itself only means ὑπὲρ
πόλιν ὀχυράν (*Venet.*); the noun-adjective (cf. Isa. x. 10) to
be supplied is to be understood to עַז : הוּא עַז or קָשֶׁה הוּא (Kimchi).
The *Niph.* נפשׁע occurs only here. If one reads נִפְשָׁע, then it
means one who is treated falsely = נִפְשָׁע בּוֹ, like the frequently
occurring קָמַי, my rising up ones = קָמִים עָלַי, those that rise
up against me; but Codd. (also Baer's *Cod. jaman.*) and old
editions have נִפְשָׁע, which, as we have above translated, gives an
impersonal attributive clause; the former: *frater perfidiose
tractatus* (Fl.: *mala fide offensus*); the latter: *perfide actum
est, scil.* בּוֹ *in eum = in quem perfide actum.* אח is, after
xvii. 17, a friend in the highest sense of the word; פּשׁע means
to break off, to break free, with בּ or עַל of him on whom
the action terminates. That the פּשׁע is to be thought of as
אח of the אח נפשׁע is obvious; the translation, "brothers who
break with one another" (Gesen.), is incorrect: אח is not collective, and still less is נפשׁע a *reciprocum*. The relation of
אח is the same as that of אַלּוּף, xvi. 28. The Targum (improv-
ing the Peshito) translates אָחָא דְמִתְעֲוֵי מִן אֲחוּי, which does not
mean: a brother who renounces (Hitzig), but who is treated
wickedly on the part of, his brother. That is correct; on the
contrary, Ewald's "a brother resists more than . . ." proceeds
from a meaning of פּשׁע which it has not; and Bertheau
gives, with Schultens, an untenable[1] reflexive meaning to the

---

[1] Among the whole Heb. synon. for sinning, there exists no reflexive
Niph.; and also the Arab. *fsk* has no ethical signification. נִסְכָּל only, in
the sense of fool, is found.

Niph. (which as denom. might mean "covered with crime," *Venet.* πλημμελ...θείς), and, moreover, one that is too weak, for he translates, "a brother is more obstinate than ..." Hitzig corrects אָחוּ פֶּשַׁע, to shut up sin = to hold it fettered; but that is not correct Heb. It ought to be עָצוּר, כָּבַשׁ, or רָדוּת. In 19*a* the force of the substantival clause lies in the מִן (more than, *i.e.* harder = more difficult to be gained), and in 19*b* in the כְּ; cf. Mic. vii. 4, where they are interchanged. The parallelism is synonymous: strifes and lawsuits between those who had been friends form as insurmountable a hindrance to their reconciliation, are as difficult to be raised, as the great bars at the gate of a castle (Fl.). The point of comparison is not only the weight of the cross-beam (from ברח, crosswise, across, to go across the field), but also the shutting up of the access. Strife forms a partition wall between such as once stood near each other, and so much thicker the closer they once stood.

With ver. 19, the series of proverbs which began with that of the flatterer closes. The catchword אח, which occurred at its commencement, 9*b*, is repeated at its close, and serves also as a landmark of the group following 20-24. The proverb of the breach of friendship and of contentions is followed by one of the reaction of the use of the tongue on the man himself.

Ver. 20 Of the fruit which a man's mouth bringeth is his heart satisfied;
By the revenue of his lips is he filled.

He will taste in rich measure of the consequences not merely of the good (xii. 14, cf. xiii. 2), but of whatever he has spoken. This is an oxymoron like Matt. xv. 11, that not that which goeth into the mouth, but that which cometh out of it, defileth a man. As at John iv. 34 the conduct of a man, so here his words are called his βρῶμα. Not merely the conduct (i. 31, Isa. iii. 10), but also the words are fruit-bringing; and not only do others taste of the fruit of the words as of the actions of a man, whether they be good or bad, but above all he himself does so, both in this life and in that which is to come.

Ver. 21 Death and life are in the power of the tongue;
And whoever loveth it shall eat its fruit.

The hand, יָד, is so common a metaphor for power, that as here a hand is attributed to the tongue, so *e.g.* Isa. xlvii. 14 to the flame, and Ps. xlix. 16 to Hades. Death and life is the great alternative which is placed, Deut. xxx. 15, before man. According as he uses his tongue, he falls under the power of death or attains to life. All interpreters attribute, 21b, וְאֹהֲבֶיהָ to the tongue: *qui eam (linguam) amant vescentur* (יֹאכַל, distrib. sing., as iii. 18, 35, etc.) *fructu ejus.* But "to love the tongue" is a strange and obscure expression. He loves the tongue, says Hitzig, who loves to babble. Euchel: he who guards it carefully, or: he who takes care of it, *i.e.* who applies himself to right discourse. Combining both, Zöckler: who uses it much, as εὐλογῶν or κακολογῶν. The LXX. translates, οἱ δὲ κρατοῦντες αὐτῆς, *i.e.* אֹחֲזֶיהָ; but אחז means *prehendere* and *tenere*, not *cohibere*, and the tongue kept in restraint brings forth indeed no bad fruit, but it brings no fruit at all. Why thus? Does the suffix of ואהביה, perhaps like viii. 17, *Chethîb*, refer to wisdom, which, it is true, is not named, but which lies everywhere before the poet's mind? At xiv. 3 we ventured to make חכמה the subject of 3b. Then 21b would be as a miniature of viii. 17–21. Or is ואהביה a mutilation of וְאֹהֵב יְהֹוָה: and he who loves Jahve (Ps. xcvii. 10) enjoys its (the tongue's) fruit?

Ver. 22 Whoso hath found a wife hath found a good thing,
And hath obtained favour from Jahve.

As ואהביה, 21b, reminds us of viii. 17, so here not only 22b, but also 22a harmonizes with viii. 35 (cf. xii. 2). A wife is such as she ought to be, as ver. 14, אִישׁ, a man is such as he ought to be; the LXX., Syr., Targ., and Vulgate supply *bonam*, but "gnomic brevity and force disdains such enervating adjectives, and cautious limitations of the idea" (Fl.). Besides, אִשָּׁה טוֹבָה in old Hebr. would mean a well-favoured rather than a good-dispositioned wife, which later idea is otherwise expressed, xix. 14, xxxi. 10. The *Venet.* rightly has γυναῖκα, and Luther *ein Ehefrau*, for it is a married woman that is meant. The first מָצָא is *perf. hypotheticum*, Gesen. § 126, Anm. 1. On the other hand, Eccles. vii. 26, "I found, מוֹצֵא אֲנִי, more bitter than death the woman," etc.; wherefore, when in Palestine one married a wife, the question was wont to be asked: מצא או מוצא, has he married happily (after מצא of the book of Proverbs) or unhappily (after מוצא of Ecclesiastes) (*Jebamoth* 63b)?[1]

[1] Cf. Tendlau's *Sprichwörter u. Redensarten deutsch-jüdischer Vorzeit* (1860), p. 235.

The LXX. adds a distich to ver. 22, " He that putteth away a
good wife putteth away happiness; and he that keepeth an
adulteress, is foolish and ungodly." He who constructed this
proverb [added by the LXX.] has been guided by מצא to
מוֹצִיא (Ezra x. 3); elsewhere ἐκβάλλειν (γυναῖκα), Gal. iv. 30,
Sir. xxviii. 15, is the translation of גֵּרֵשׁ. The Syr. has adopted
the half of that distich, and Jerome the whole of it. On the
other hand, vers. 23, 24, and xix. 1, 2, are wanting in the
LXX. The translation which is found in some Codd. is that
of Theodotion (vid. Lagarde).

Ver. 23 The poor uttereth suppliant entreaties;
And the rich answereth rudenesses.

The oriental proverbial poetry furnishes many parallels to this.
It delights in the description of the contrast between a suppliant
poor man and the proud and avaricious rich man; vid. e.g.
Samachschari's *Goldene Halsbänder*, No. 58. תַּחֲנוּנִים, according
to its meaning, refers to the *Hithpa.* הִתְחַנֵּן, *misericordiam alicujus
pro se imploravit;* cf. the old vulgar "*barmen*," i.e. to seek to
move others to *Erbarmen* [compassion] (רחמים). עַזּוֹת, *dura*, from
עַז (synon. קָשֶׁה), hard, fast, of bodies, and figuratively of an un-
bending, hard, haughty disposition, and thence of words of such
a nature (Fl.). Both nouns are accus. of the object, as Job
xl. 27, תחנונים with the parallel רַכּוֹת. The proverb expresses a
fact of experience as a consolation to the poor to whom, if a
rich man insults him, nothing unusual occurs, and as a warning
to the rich that he may not permit himself to be divested of
humanity by mammon. A hard wedge to a hard clod; but
whoever, as the Scripture saith, grindeth the poor by hard
stubborn-hearted conduct, and grindeth his bashful face (Isa.
iii. 15), challenges unmerciful judgment against himself; for
the merciful, only they shall obtain mercy, αὐτοὶ ἐλεηθή-
σονται (Matt. v. 7).

Ver. 24 A man of many friends cometh off a loser;
But there is a friend more faithful than a brother.

Jerome translates the commencing word by *vir*, but the Syr.,
Targ. by אִית, which is adopted by Hitzig, Böttcher, and others.
But will a German poet use in one line " *itzt* " [same as *jetzt* =
now], and in the next "*jetzt*"? and could the Hebrew poet
prefer to יֵשׁ its rarer, and here especially not altogether unam-

biguous form אִישׁ (cf. to the contrary, Eccles. vii. 15)? We write אִישׁ, because the Masora comprehends this passage, with 2 Sam. xiv. 19, Mic. vi. 10, as the יֵשׁ סבירין ג', *i.e.* as the three, where one ought to expect יֵשׁ, and is thus exposed to the danger of falling into error in writing and reading; but erroneously אִישׁ is found in all these three places in the *Masora magna* of the Venetian Bible of 1526; elsewhere the Masora has the *defectiva scriptio* with like meaning only in those two other passages. While יֵשׁ=אִישׁ, or properly יֵשׁ, with equal possibility as אִישׁ,[1] and it makes no material difference in the meaning of 24*a* whether we explain: there are friends who serve to bring one to loss: or a man of many friends comes to loss,—the *inf.* with לְ is used in substantival clauses as the expression of the most manifold relations, Gesen. § 132, Anm. 1 (cf. at Hab. i. 17), here in both cases it denotes the end, as *e.g.* Ps. xcii. 8, to which it hastens with many friends, or with the man of many friends. It is true that אִישׁ (like בַּעַל) is almost always connected only with genitives of things; but as one says אִישׁ אלהים: a man belongs to God, so may one also say אִישׁ רֵעִים: a man belongs to many friends; the common language of the people may thus have named a man, to whom, because he has no definite and decided character, the rule that one knows a man by his friends is not applicable, a so-called every-man's-friend, or all-the-world's-friend. Theodotion translates ἀνὴρ ἑταιριῶν τοῦ ἑταιρεύσασθαι; and thus also the Syr., Targ., and Jerome render (and among the moderns, Hitzig) הִתְרֹעֵעַ as reflexive in the sense of to cherish social intercourse; but this reflexive is הִתְרָעָה, xxii. 24. That הִתְרוֹעֵעַ is either *Hithpa.* of רוּעַ, to exult, Ps. lx. 10, lxv. 14, according to which the *Venet.* translates (contrary to Kimchi) ὥστε ἀλαλάζειν: such an one can exult, but which is not true, since, according to 24*b*, a true friend outweighs the many; or it is *Hithpa.* of רָעַע, to be wicked, sinful (Fl.: *sibi perniciem paraturus est*); or, which we prefer, warranted by Isa. xxiv. 19, of רָעַע, to become brittle (Böttcher and others)—which not only gives a good sense, but also a similar alliteration with רֵעִים, as iii. 29, xiii. 20. In contradistinction to רֵעַ, which is a general,

---

[1] One sees from this interchange how softly the י was uttered; cf. Wellhausen's *Text der Bb. Samuel* (1871) (Preface). Kimchi remarks that we say אֶקְטְל for אֶקְטֹל, because we would otherwise confound it with יִקְטֹל.

and, according to the usage of the language (*e.g.* 17*b*), a familiar idea, the true friend is called, in the antithetical parallel member, אֹהֵב (xxvii. 6); and after xvii. 17, דָּבֵק מֵאָח, one who remains true in misfortune. To have such an one is better than to have many of the so-called friends; and, as appears from the contrast, to him who is so fortunate as to have one such friend, there comes a blessing and safety. Immanuel has given the right explanation : " A man who sets himself to gain many friends comes finally to be a loser (סוֹפוֹ לְהִשָּׁבֵר), for he squanders his means, and is impoverished in favour of others." And Schultens: *At est amicus agglutinatus præ fratre. Rarum et carum esse genus insinuatur, ac proinde intimam illam amicitiam, quæ conglutinet compingatque corda, non per multos spargendam, sed circumspecte et ferme cum uno tantum ineundam.* Thus closes this group of proverbs with the praise of friendship deepened into spiritual brotherhood, as the preceding, ver. 19, with a warning against the destruction of such a relation by a breach of trust not to be made good again.

Chap. xix. The plur. רֵעִים, xviii. 24, is emphatic and equivalent to רֵעִים רַבִּים. The group 1–4 closes with a proverb which contains this catchword. The first proverb of the group comes by שְׂפָתָיו into contact with xviii. 20, the first proverb of the preceding group.

> Ver. 1 Better a poor man walking in his innocence,
> Than one with perverse lips, and so a fool.

The contrast, xxviii. 6, is much clearer. But to correct this proverb in conformity with that, as Hitzig does, is unwarrantable. The Syr., indeed, translates here as there; but the Chald. assimilates this translation to the Heb. text, which Theodotion, and after him the Syro-Hexapl., renders by ὑπὲρ στρεβλόχειλον ἄφρονα. But does 1*a* form a contrast to 1*b*? Fleischer remarks : " From the contrast it appears that he who is designated in 1*b* must be thought of as עָשִׁיר " [rich]; and Ewald, " Thus early the ideas of a rich man and of a fool, or a despiser of God, are connected together." Saadia understands כסיל [a fool], after Job xxxi. 24, of one who makes riches his כֶּסֶל [confidence]. Euchel accordingly translates: the false man, although he builds himself greatly up, viz. on his riches. But כסיל designates the intellectually slothful, in whom the flesh overweighs the mind.

And the representation of the rich, which, for 1*b* certainly arises out of 1*a*, does not amalgamate with כסיל, but with עַקֵּשׁ שְׂפָתָיו. Arama is on the right track, for he translates: the rich who distorts his mouth (cf. vol. i. p. 143), for he gives to the poor suppliant a rude refusal. Better Zöckler: a proud man of perverse lips and haughty demeanour. If one with haughty, scornful lips is opposed to the poor, then it is manifestly one not poor who thinks to raise himself above the poor, and haughtily looks down on him. And if it is said that, in spite of this proud demeanour, he is a fool, then this presents the figure of one proud of his wealth, who, in spite of his emptiness and *nequitia*, imagines that he possesses a greatness of knowledge, culture, and worth corresponding to the greatness of his riches. How much better is a poor man than such an one who walketh (*vid.* on הֹם, vol. i. p. 79) in his innocence and simplicity, with his pure mind wholly devoted to God and to that which is good!—his poverty keeps him in humility which is capable of no malicious conduct; and this pious blameless life is of more worth than the pride of wisdom of the distinguished fool. There is in contrast to עִקְּשׁוּת a simplicity, ἁπλότης, of high moral worth; but, on the other side, there is also a simplicity which is worthless. This is the connecting thought which introduces the next verse.

Ver. 2 The not-knowing of the soul is also not good,
      And he who hasteneth with the legs after it goeth astray.

Fleischer renders נֶפֶשׁ as the subj. and לֹא־טוֹב as neut. pred.: in and of itself sensual desire is not good, but yet more so if it is without foresight and reflection. With this explanation the words must be otherwise accentuated. Hitzig, in conformity with the accentuation, before us: if desire is without reflection, it is also without success. But where נפשׁ denotes desire or sensuality, it is always shown by the connection, as *e.g.* xxiii. 2; here דַּעַת, referring to the soul as knowing (cf. Ps. cxxxix. 14), excludes this meaning. But נפשׁ is certainly *gen. subjecti*; Luzzatto's "self-knowledge" is untenable, for this would require דעת נַפְשׁוֹ; Meîri rightly glosses דעת נפשׁ by שֵׂכֶל. After this Zöckler puts Hitzig's translation right in the following manner: where there is no consideration of the soul, there is no prosperity. But that also is incorrect, for it would require אֵין־טוֹב; לֹא־טוֹב is always pred., not a substantival clause.

Thus the proverb states that בְלֹא־דַעַת נֶפֶשׁ is not good, and that is equivalent to הֱיוֹת בְלֹא־דַעַת נֶפֶשׁ (for the subject to לֹא־טוֹב is frequently, as *e.g.* xvii. 26, xviii. 5, an infinitive); or also: בְלֹא־דַעַת נֶפֶשׁ is a virtual noun in the sense of the not-knowing of the soul; for to say לֹא־דַעַת was syntactically inadmissible, but the expression is בְלֹא־דַעַת, not בְּלִי דַעַת (בִּבְלִי), because this is used in the sense unintentionally or unexpectedly. The גַּם which begins the proverb is difficult. If we lay the principal accent in the translation given above on "not good," then the placing of גם first is a *hyperbaton* similar to that in xvii. 26, xx. 11; cf. אַךְ, xvii. 11; רַק, xiii. 10, as if the words were: if the soul is without knowledge, then also (*eo ipso*) it is destitute of anything good. But if we lay the principal accent on the "also," then the meaning of the poet is, that ignorance of the soul is, like many other things, not good; or (which we prefer without on that account maintaining[1] the original connection of ver. 1 and ver. 2), that as on the one side the pride of wisdom, so on the other ignorance is not good. In this case גם belongs more to the subject than to the predicate, but in reality to the whole sentence at the beginning of which it stands. To hasten with the legs (אָץ, as xxviii. 20) means now in this connection to set the body in violent agitation, without direction and guidance proceeding from the knowledge possessed by the soul. He who thus hastens after it without being intellectually or morally clear as to the goal and the way, makes a false step, goes astray, fails (*vid.* viii. 36, where חֹטֵא is the contrast to מֹצְאִי).

Ver. 3 The foolishness of a man overturneth his way,
And his heart is angry against Jahve.

Regarding סֶלֶף, *vid.* at xi. 3; also the Arab. signification "to go before" proceeds from the root conception *pervertere*, for first a letting precede, or preceding (*e.g.* of the paying before the delivery of that which is paid for: *salaf*, a pre-numbering, and then also: advanced money), consisting in the reversal of the

---

[1] The old interpreters and also the best Jewish interpreters mar the understanding and interpretation of the text, on the one side, by distinguishing between a nearest and a deeper meaning of Scripture (דרך נגלה and דרך נסתר); on the other by this, that they suppose an inward connection of all the proverbs, and expend useless ingenuity in searching after the connection. The former is the method especially adopted by Immanuel and Meïri, the latter has most of all been used by Arama.

natural order, is meant. The way is here the way of life, the walking : the folly of a man overturns, *i.e.* destroys, his life's-course; but although he is himself the fabricator of his own ruin, yet the ill-humour (זַעַף, *œstuare, vid.* at Ps. xi. 6) of his heart turns itself against God, and he blames (LXX. essentially correct : αἰτιᾶται) God instead of himself, viz. his own madness, whereby he has turned the grace of God into lasciviousness, cast to the winds the instruction which lay in His providences, and frustrated the will of God desiring his good. A beautiful paraphrase of this parable is found at Sir. xv. 11–20; cf. Lam. iii. 39.

Ver. 4 Wealth bringeth many friends ;
But the reduced—his friend separateth himself.

The very same contrast, though otherwise expressed, we had at xiv. 20. Regarding הוֹן, *vid.* vol. i. p. 63. דָל is the tottering, or he who has fallen into a tottering condition, who has no resources, possesses no means. The accentuation gives *Mugrash* to the word (according to which the Targ. translates), for it is not the subject of יִפָּרֵד : the reduced is separated (pass. *Niph.*) by his misfortunes, or must separate himself (reflex. *Niph.*) from his friend (מֵרֵעֵהוּ, as Eccles. iv. 4, *præ socio suo*); but subject of the virtual pred. מֵרֵעֵהוּ יִפָּרֵד : the reduced—his friend (מרעהו, as ver. 7) separates himself, *i.e.* (according to the nature of the Semitic substantival clause) he is such (of such a fate) that his friend sets himself free, whereby מִמֶּנּוּ may be omitted as self-obvious ; נִפְרָד means one who separates himself, xviii. 1. If we make דָל the subject of the *separatur*, then the initiative of the separation from the friend is not expressed.

In vers. 5 and 9 we have the introductory proverb of two groups, the former of which, in its close as well as its beginning, cannot be mistaken.

Ver. 5 A lying witness remaineth not unpunished ;
And he who breathes out lies escapeth not.

Regarding יָפִיחַ, *vid.* vol. i. p. 148: as here we read it of false witness at vi. 19, xiv. 5, 25. לֹא יִנָּקֶה occurs four times before, the last of which is at xvii. 5. The LXX. elsewhere translates יפיח כזבים by ἐκκαίειν ψευδῆ, to kindle lies; but here by ὁ δὲ ἐγκαλῶν ἀδίκως, and at ver. 9 by ὃς δ' ἂν ἐκκαύσῃ κακίαν, both times changing only because ψευδής goes before, and instead of ψευδῆ, the choice of a different rendering commended itself.

Ver. 6 Many stroke the cheeks of the noble ;
And the mass of friends belongeth to him who gives.

The phrase חַלּוֹת פְּנֵי פל׳ signifies to stroke the face of any one, from the fundamental meaning of the verb חָלָה, to rub, to stroke, Arab. *khala*, with which the Heb., meaning to be sick, weak (*viribus attritum esse*), and the Arabic : to be sweet (properly *lævem et politum, glabrum esse,* or *palatum demulcere, leniter stringere,* contrast *asperum esse ad gustum*), are connected (Fl.). The object of such insinuating, humble suing for favour is the נָדִיב (from נָדַב, *instigare*), the noble, he who is easily incited to noble actions, particularly to noble-mindedness in bestowing gifts and in doing good, or who feels himself naturally impelled thereto, and spontaneously practises those things ; cf. the Arab. *krym, nobilis* and *liberalis* (Fl.), and at Job xxi. 28; parall. אִישׁ מַתָּן, a man who gives willingly, as אִישׁ חֵמָה, xv. 18, one who is easily kindled into anger. Many (רַבִּים, as Job xi. 19) stroke the face of the liberal (Lat. *caput mulcent* or *demulcent*); and to him who gives willingly and richly belongs כָל־הָרֵעַ, the mass (the totality) of good friends, cf. xv. 17 ; there the art. of הָרֵעַ, according to the manner of expression of the Arab. grammarians, stood for " the exhaustion of the characteristic properties of the genus " : the friend who corresponds to the nature (the idea) of such an one; here it stands for " the comprehension of the individuals of the genus ;" all that is only always friend. It lies near with Ewald and Hitzig to read וְכֻלֹּה רֵעַ (and every one is friend . . .) (כֻּלֹּה = כֻּלּוֹ, as Jer. viii. 10, etc.); but why could not כָל־הָרֵעַ be used as well as כל־האדם, perhaps with the sarcastic appearance which the above translation seeks to express? The LXX. also had וכל הרע in view, which it incorrectly translates πᾶς δὲ ὁ κακός, whereby the Syr. and the Targ. are led into error; but מַתָּן is not one and the same with שֹׁחַד, *vid.* xviii. 6. On the contrary, there certainly lies before us in ver. 7 a mutilated text. The tristich is, as we have shown, vol. i. p. 15, open to suspicion; and the violence which its interpretation needs in order to comprehend it, as a formal part of 7*ab*, places it beyond a doubt, and the LXX. confirms it that 7*c* is the remainder of a distich, the half of which is lost.

Ver. 7*ab.* We thus first confine our attention to these two
lines,—

All the brethren of the poor hate him ;
How much more do his friends withdraw themselves from him ?

Regarding אַף כִּי, *quanto magis, vid.* at xi. 31, xv. 11, xvii. 7.
In a similar connection xiv. 20 spake of hatred, *i.e.* the cooling
of love, and the manifesting of this coldness. The brethren
who thus show themselves here, unlike the friend who has
become a brother, according to xvii. 17, are brothers-german,
including kindred by blood relation. כָּל has *Mercha,* and is
thus without the *Makkeph,* as at Ps. xxxv. 10 (*vid.* the Masora
in Baer's *Liber Psalmorum,* 1861, p. 133). Kimchi (*Michlol*
205*a*), Norzi, and others think that *cāl* (with קמץ רחב) is to be
read as at Isa. xl. 12, where וְכֹל is a verb. But that is incorrect. The case is the same as with אֵת, iii. 12 ; Ps. xlvii. 5,
lx. 2. As here ŏ with *Mercha* remains, so ŏ with *Mercha* in
that twice occurring וְכָל ; that which is exceptional is this, that
the accentuated כל is written thus twice, not as the usual כֹּל, but
as כָל with the *Makkeph.* The ground of the exception lies, as
with other peculiarities, in the special character of metrical
accentuation ; the *Mercha* represents the place of the *Makkeph,*
and ־ָ thus remains in the unchanged force of a *Kametz-
Chatuph.* The plur. רֵחֲקוּ does not stamp מרעהו as the defectively written plur.; the suffix *ēhu* is always sing., and the sing.
is thus, like הָרֵעַ, 6*b*, meant collectively, or better : generally (in
the sense of kind), which is the linguistic usage of these two
words, 1 Sam. xxx. 26 ; Job xlii. 10. But it is worthy of notice
that the Masoretic form here is not מֵרֵעֵהוּ, but מְרֵעֵהוּ, with *Sheva.*
The Masora adds to it the remark לית, and accordingly the word
is thus written with *Sheva* by Kimchi (*Michlol* 202*a* and *Lex.*
under the word רעה), in Codd., and older editions. The *Venet.,*
translating by ἀπὸ τοῦ φίλου αὐτοῦ, has not noticed that. But
how ? Does the punctuation מְרֵעהו mean that the word is here
to be derived from מֵרַע, *maleficus?* Thus understood, it does not
harmonize with the line of thought. From this it is much more
seen that the punctuation of the inflected מֵרַע, *amicus,* fluctuates.
This word מֵרַע is a formation so difficult of comprehension, that
one might almost, with Olshausen, § 210; Böttcher, § 794;
and Lagarde, regard the מ as the partitive מִן, like the French

des amis (cf. Eurip. *Med.* 560 : πένητα φεύγει πᾶς τις ἐκποδὼν φίλος), or : something of friend, a piece of friend, while Ewald and others regard it as possible that מרע is abbreviated from מֵרְעֶה. The punctuation, since it treats the *Tsere* in מרעהו, 4*b*[1] and elsewhere, as unchangeable, and here in מְרֵעהו as changeable, affords proof that in it also the manner of the formation of the word was incomprehensible.

Ver. 7c Seeking after words which are vain.

If now this line belongs to this proverb, then מְרַדֵּף must be used of the poor, and לֹא־הֵמָּה, or לוֹ־הֵמָּה (*vid.* regarding the 15 *Kerîs*, לֹ for לֹא, at Ps. c. 3), must be the attributively nearer designation of the אמרים. The meaning of the *Kerî* would be : he (the poor man) hunts after mere words, which—but no actions correspond-ing to them—are for a portion to him. This is doubtful, for the principal matter, that which is not a portion to him, remains unexpressed, and the לוֹ־הֵמָּה [to him they belong] affords only the service of guarding one against understanding by the אמרים the proper words of the poor. This service is not in the same way afforded by לֹא הֵמָּה [they are not]; but this expression charac-terizes the words as vain, so that it is to be interpreted accord-ing to such parallels as Hos. xii. 2 : words which are not, *i.e.* which have nothing in reality corresponding to them, *verba nihili*, *i.e.* the empty assurances and promises of his brethren and friends (Fl.). The old translators all[2] read לֹא, and the Syr. and Targ. translate not badly : מִלּוֹי לָא שְׁרִיר; Symmachus, ῥήσεσιν ἀνυπάρκτοις. The expression is not to be rejected : לֹא הָיָה sometimes means to come to לֹא, *i.e.* to nothing, Job vi. 21, Ezek. xxi. 32, cf. Isa. xv. 6; and לֹא הוּא, he is not = has no reality, Jer. v. 12, אֲמָרִים לא־המה, may thus mean words which are nothing (vain). But how can it be said of the poor whom everything forsakes, that one dismisses him with words behind which there is nothing, and now also that he pursues such words? The former supposes always a sympathy, though it be a feigned one,

---

[1] In vol. i. p. 266, we have acknowledged מרעהו, from מרע, friend, only for xix. 7 ; but at xix. 4 we have also found *amicus ejus* more probable than *ab amico suo* (=מן רעהו).

[2] Lagarde erroneously calls Theodotion's ῥήσεις οὐκ αὐτῷ a translation of the *Kerî*; οὐκ is, however, לֹא, and instead of αὐτῷ the expression αὐτῶν, which is the translation of המה, is also found.

which is excluded by שְׂנֵאֻהוּ [they hate him] and רָחֵקוּ [with-draw themselves]; and the latter, spoken of the poor, would be unnatural, for his purposed endeavour goes not out after empty talk, but after real assistance. So 7c: pursuing after words which (are) nothing, although in itself not falling under critical suspicion, yet only of necessity is connected with this proverb regarding the poor. The LXX., however, has not merely one, but even four lines, and thus two proverbs following 7b. The former of these distichs is : Ἔννοια ἀγαθὴ τοῖς εἰδόσιν αὐτὴν ἐγγιεῖ, ἀνὴρ δὲ φρόνιμος εὑρήσει αὐτήν; it is translated from the Hebr. (ἔννοια ἀγαθή, v. 2 = מְזִמּוֹת), but it has a meaning complete in itself, and thus has nothing to do with the fragment 7c. The second distich is : Ὁ πολλὰ κακο-ποιῶν τελεσιουργεῖ κακίαν, ὃς δὲ ἐρεθίζει λόγους οὐ σωθήσεται. This ὃς δὲ ἐρεθίζει λόγους is, without doubt, a translation of מרדף אמרים (7c); λόγους is probably a corruption of λόγοις (thus the Complut.), not, he who pursueth words, but he who incites by words, as Homer (Il. iv. 5 f.) uses the expression ἐρεθιζέμεν ἐπέεσσι. The concluding words, οὐ σωθήσεται, are a repetition of the Heb. לא ימלט (cf. LXX. xix. 5 with xxviii. 26), perhaps only a conjectural emendation of the unintelligible לא המה. Thus we have before us in that ὁ πολλὰ κακοποιῶν, κ.τ.λ., the line lost from the Heb. text; but it is difficult to restore it to the Heb. We have attempted it, vol. i. p. 15. Supposing that the LXX. had before them לא המה, then the proverb is—

" He that hath many friends is rewarded with evil,
Hunting after words which are nothing;"

i.e. since this his courting the friendship of as many as possible is a hunting after words which have nothing after them and come to nothing.

Ver. 8 He that getteth understanding loveth his soul,
And he that values reasonableness will acquire good ;

or, more closely, since this would be the translation of יִמְצָא טוֹב, xvi. 20, xvii. 20: so it happens, or it comes to this, that he acquires good (= הָיָה לִמְצֹא); the inf. with ל is here, as at xviii. 24, the expression of a fut. periphrasticum, as in the Lat. con-secuturus est. Regarding קֹנֶה־לֵב, vid. xv. 32, and שֹׁמֵר תְּבוּנָה, vol. i. p. 119. That the deportment of men is either care for

26 THE BOOK OF PROVERBS.

the soul, or the contrary of that, is a thought which runs through
the Book of Proverbs.

The group of proverbs (vers. 9–16) now following begins and
closes in the same way as the preceding.

Ver. 9 A lying witness doth not remain unpunished,
And one who breathes out lies perisheth,

or goeth to ruin, for אָבַד (R. בד, to divide, separate) signifies to
lose oneself in the place of the separated, the dead (Arab. in
the infinite). In ver. 5, instead of this ἀπολεῖται (LXX.), the
negative οὐ σωθήσεται is used, or as the LXX. there more
accurately renders it, οὐ διαφεύξεται.

Ver. 10 Luxury becometh not a fool ;
How much less a servant to rule over princes.

Thus also with לֹא נָאוָה (3 p. Pil. non decet, cf. the adj. xxvi. 1)
xvii. 7 begins. אַף כִּי rises here, as at ver. 7, a minori ad majus :
how much more is it unbecoming = how much less is it seemly.
The contrast in the last case is, however, more rugged, and the
expression harsher. " A fool cannot bear luxury : he becomes
by it yet more foolish ; one who was previously a humble slave,
but who has attained by good fortune a place of prominence and
power, from being something good, becomes at once something
bad : an insolent sceleratus " (Fl.). Agur, xxx. 22 f., describes
such a homo novus as an unbearable calamity ; and the author
of the Book of Ecclesiastes, written in the time of the Persian
domination, speaks, x. 7, of such. The LXX. translates, καὶ
ἐὰν οἰκέτης ἄρξηται μεθ᾽ ὕβρεως δυναστεύειν, rendering the
phrase כְּשָׂרִים by μεθ᾽ ὕβρεως, but all other translators had
בְּשָׂרִים before them.

Ver. 11 The discretion of a man maketh him long-suffering,
And it is a glory for him to be forbearing toward transgression.

The Syr., Targum, Aquila, and Theodotion translate הֶאֱרִיךְ אַפּוֹ
by μακροθυμία, and thus read הַאֲרִיךְ ; but Rashi, Kimchi, and
others remark that הֶאֱרִיךְ is here only another vocalization for
הַאֲרִיךְ, which is impossible. The Venet. also translates : Νοῦς
ἀνθρώπου μηκυνεῖ τὸν θυμὸν ἑαυτοῦ ; the correct word would be
αὐτοῦ : the discretion (intellectus or intelligentia ; vid. regarding
שֵׂכֶל, iii. 4) of a man extends his anger, i.e. brings it about that
it continues long before it breaks out (vid. xiv. 29). One does
not stumble at the perf. in view of ver. 7, xviii. 8, xvi. 26, and

the like; in the proverbial style the fut. or the particip. is more common. In the synonymous parallel member, תִּפְאַרְתּוֹ points to man as such: it is an honour to him to pass by a transgression (particularly that which affects himself), to let it go aside, *i.e.* to forbear revenge or punishment (cf. Arab. *tjâwz 'aly*); thus also the divine πάρεσις (Rom. iii. 25) is designated by Mic. vii. 18; and in Amos vii. 8, viii. 2, עָבַר stands absol. for the divine remission or passing by, *i.e.* unavenging of sin.

> Ver. 12　A murmuring as of a lion is the wrath of the king,
> 　　　And as dew on plants is his favour.

Line 1 is a variation of xx. 2*a;* line 2*a* of xvi. 15*b.* זַעַף is not the being irritated against another, but generally ill-humour, fretfulness, bad humour; the murmuring or growling in which this state of mind expresses itself is compared to that of a lion which, growling, prepares and sets itself to fall upon its prey (*vid.* Isa. v. 29, cf. Amos iii. 4). Opposed to the זעף stands the beneficial effect of the רָצוֹן, *i.e.* of the pleasure, the delight, the satisfaction, the disposition which shows kindness (LXX. τὸ ἱλαρὸν αὐτοῦ). In the former case all are afraid; in the latter, everything lives, as when the refreshing dew falls upon the herbs of the field. The proverb presents a fact, but that the king may mirror himself in it.

> Ver. 13　A foolish son is destruction for his father,
> 　　　And a continual dropping are the contentions of a wife.

Regarding הַוּוֹת, *vid.* at xvii. 4, cf. x. 3. Line 2*a* is expanded, xxvii. 15, into a distich. The dropping is טֹרֵד, properly striking (cf. Arab. *tirad,* from *tarad* III., hostile assault) when it pours itself forth, stroke (drop) after stroke = constantly, or with unbroken continuity. Lightning-flashes are called (*Jer Berachoth,* p. 114, Shitomir's ed.) טורדין, *opp.* מפסיקין, when they do not follow in intervals, but constantly flash; and *b. Bechoroth* 44*a;* דומעות, weeping eyes, דולפות, dropping eyes, and טורדות, eyes always flowing, are distinguished. An old interpreter (*vid.* R. Ascher in *Pesachim* II. No. 21) explains דֶּלֶף טֹרֵד by: "which drops, and drops, and always drops." An Arab proverb which I once heard from Wetzstein, says that there are three things which make our house intolerable: *âltakk* (= *âldhalf*), the trickling through of rain; *âlnakk,* the contention of the wife; and *âlbakk,* bugs.

Ver. 14 House and riches are a paternal inheritance,
But from Jahve cometh a prudent wife.

House and riches (*opulentia*), which in themselves do not make
men happy, one may receive according to the law of inheritance; but a prudent wife is God's gracious gift, xviii. 22.
There is not a more suitable word than מַשְׂכֶּלֶת (fem. of
מַשְׂבִּיל) to characterize a wife as a divine gift, making her
husband happy. שֵׂכֶל (הַשְׂבֵּל) is the property which says: "I
am named modesty, which wears the crown of all virtues." [1]

Ver. 15 Slothfulness sinketh into deep sleep,
And an idle soul must hunger.

Regarding תַּרְדֵּמָה and its root-word רָדַם, *vid.* at x. 5. הִפִּיל, to
befall, to make to get, is to be understood after Gen. iii. 21 ;
the obj. עַל־הָאָדָם, viz. הֶעָצֵל, is naturally to be supplied. In 15*b*
the fut. denotes that which will certainly happen, the inevitable. In both of its members the proverb is perfectly clear ;
Hitzig, however, corrects 15*a*, and brings out of it the meaning, "slothfulness gives tasteless herbs to eat." The LXX.
has two translations of this proverb, here and at xviii. 8. That
it should translate רמיה by ἀνδρόγυνος was necessary, as Lagarde
remarks, for the exposition of the "works of a Hebrew Sotades."
But the Hebrew literature never sunk to such works, wallowing
in the mire of sensuality, and ἀνδρόγυνος is not at all thus enigmatical; the Greek word was also used of an effeminate man, a
man devoid of manliness, a weakling, and was, as the LXX.
shows, more current in the Alexandrine Greek than elsewhere.

Ver. 16 He that keepeth the commandment keepeth his soul ;
He that taketh no heed to his ways dies.

As at vi. 23, cf. Eccles. viii. 5, מִצְוָה is here the commandment
of God, and thus obligatory, which directs man in every case
to do that which is right, and warns him against that which is
wrong. And בּוֹזֶה דְרָכָיו (according to the Masora with *Tsere*,
as in Codd. and old editions, not בֹּזֶה) is the antithesis of
נֹצֵר דַּרְכּוֹ, xvi. 17. To despise one's own way is equivalent to, to
regard it as worth no consideration, as no question of conscience
whether one should enter upon this way or that. Hitzig's

---

[1] The LXX. translates : παρὰ δὲ κυρίου ἁρμόζεται γυνὴ ἀνδρί. Here as
often (*vid.* my *Jesurun*) the Arab. *usus loquendi* makes itself felt in the
idiom of the LXX., for *shâkl* means ἁρμόζειν.

reading, פָּזֵר, "he that scattereth his ways," lets himself be drawn by the manifold objects of sensuality sometimes in one direction and sometimes in another, is supported by Jer. iii. 13, according to which it must be מִפְזֻר; the conj. is not in the style of the Book of Proverbs, and besides is superfluous. The LXX., which is fond of a *quid pro quo*—it makes, 13*b*, a courtesan offering a sacrifice she had vowed of the wages of sin of the quarrelsome woman—has here, as the Heb. text: ὁ καταφρονῶν τῶν ἑαυτοῦ ὁδῶν ἀπολεῖται. Thus after the *Kerî* יֵמָת, as also the Targ., Syro-Hexap., and Luther; on the contrary, the Syr., Jerome, the *Venet.* adopt the *Chethîb* יימָת: he will become dead, *i.e.* dies no natural death. The *Kerî* is more in the spirit and style of the Book of Proverbs (xv. 10, xxiii. 13, x. 21).

Vers. 17–21. These verses we take together. But we have no other reason for making a pause at ver. 21, than that ver. 22 is analogous to ver. 17, and thus presents itself to us as an initial verse.

> Ver. 17 He lendeth to Jahve who is compassionate to the lowly,
> And his bounty He requites to him.

As at xiv. 31, חֹנֵן is *part. Kal.* The Masoretically exact form of the word is חֹנֵן (as וָאֹחֵל, xx. 14) with *Mercha* on the first syllable, on which the tone is thrown back, and the העמדה on the second. The Roman legal phrase, *mutui datione contrahitur obligatio,* serves to explain the fundamental conception of לָוָה, *mutuo accipere,* and הִלְוָה, *mutuum dare (vid.* xxii. 7). The construction, Ex. xxii. 24, "to make any one bound as a debtor, *obligare,*" lies at the foundation of the genitive connection 'מַלְוֵה ה (not מַלְוֶה). With 17*b* cf. xii. 14, where the subject of יָשִׁיב (*Kerî*) remains in the background. גְּמֻלוֹ (not גְּמֻלּוֹ) is here his work done in the sense of good exhibited. "Love," Hedinger once said, "is an imperishable capital, which always bears interest." And the Archbishop Walther: *nam Deo dat qui dat inopibus, ipse Deus est in pauperibus.* Dr. Jonas, as Dächsel relates, once gave to a poor man, and said, "Who knows when God restores it!" There Luther interposed: "As if God had not long ago given it beforehand!" This answer of Luther meets the abuse of this beautiful proverb by the covetous.

Ver. 18. This proverb brings to view once more the pedagogic character of this Older Book of Proverbs:

> Correct thy son, for yet there is hope;
> But go not too far to kill him.

That כִּי is meant relatively, as at xi. 15, is seen from Job xi. 18,
xiv. 7; Jer. xxxi. 16 f.; כִּי־יֵשׁ תִּקְוָה is the usual expression for
etenim spes est. Though a son show obstinacy, and manifest a
bad disposition, yet there is hope in the training of the youth of
being able to break his self-will, and to wean him from his bad
disposition; therefore his education should be carried forward
with rigorous exactness, but in such a way that wisdom and love
regulate the measure and limits of correction: *ad eum interficien-*
dum animam ne tollas (animum ne inducas). נַפְשֶׁךָ is not the
subject, for in that case the word would have been תִּשָּׂאֶךָ (2
Kings xiv. 10). It is the object: To raise the soul to something
is equivalent to, to direct his desire to it, to take delight in it.
The teacher should not seek correction as the object, but only
as the means; he who has a desire after it, to put the child to
death in the case of his guilt, changes correction into revenge,
permits himself to be driven by passion from the proper end of
correction, and to be pushed beyond its limits. The LXX.
translates freely εἰς δὲ ὕβριν, for ὕβρις is unrestrained abuse,
מוסר אכזרי as Immanuel glosses. Besides, all the ancients and
also the *Venet.* translate המיתו as the inf. of הֵמִית. But Oetinger (for he translates: lift not thy soul to his cry, for which
Euchel: let not his complaining move thy compassion) follows
the derivation from הָמָה suggested by Kimchi, Meîri, and Immanuel, and preferred by Ralbag, so that הֲמִיתוֹ after the form
בְּכִית is equivalent to הֲמִיתוֹ. But leaving out of view that המה
means *strepere,* not *lamentari,* and that נשׂא נפשׁ means attention,
not desire, xxiii. 13 points out to us a better interpretation.

Ver. 19. Another proverb with נשׂא:

> A man of excessive wrath must suffer punishment;
> For if thou layest hold of it, hindering it, thou makest it only worse.

The LXX., Syr., and Targ. translate as if the words were
גְּבַר חמה (as בַּעַל חמה, xxix. 22). Theodotion, the *Venet.,* and
Luther render the *Keri* גָּדֹל; Jerome's *impatiens* is colourless.
The *Chethîb* גרל gives no appropriate meaning. The Arab.
jaril means *lapidosus* (whence גּוֹרָל, cf. Aram. פְּסָא = ψῆφος), and
Schultens translates accordingly *aspere scruposus iracundiæ,*
which is altogether after the manner of his own heavy style.

Ewald translates גָּרֶל as derived from the Arab *jazyl, largus, grandis;* but the possibility of the passing over of ר into ז, as maintained by Ewald and also by Hitzig, or the reverse, is physiologically undemonstrable, and is confirmed by no example worthy of mention. Rather it may be possible that the Heb. had an adj. נָּרֶל or גָּרֶל in the sense of stony, gravel-like, hard as gravel, but tow rather than gravel would be appropriate to חֵמָה. Hitzig corrects גֹּמֵל חמה, "who acts in anger;" but he says שִׁלֵּם חמה, to recompense anger, Isa. lix. 18; גמל חמה is without support. This correction, however, is incomparably more feasible than Böttcher's, "moderate inheritance bears expiation;" חֶמָה = חֶמְאָה must mean not only thick [curdled] milk, but also moderation, and Böttcher finds this " sound." From all these instances one sees that גרל is an error in transcription; the *Keri* גְּדָל-חֵמָה rightly improves it, a man is thus designated whose peculiarity it is to fall into a high degree of passionate anger (חֵמָה גְדוֹלָה, Dan. xi. 44): such an one has to bear עֹנֶשׁ, a fine, *i.e.* to compensate, for he has to pay compensation or smart-money for the injury suffered, as *e.g.* he who in strife with another pushes against a woman with child, so that injury befalls her, Ex. xxi. 22. If we compare this passage with 2 Sam. xiv. 6, there appears for הַצִּיל the meaning of taking away of the object (whether a person or a thing) against which the passionate hothead directs himself. Therewith the meaning of וְעוֹד תּוֹסַף accords. The meaning is not that, הַצִּיל, once is not enough, but much rather must be repeated, and yet is without effect; but that one only increases and heightens the חמה thereby. It is in vain to seek to spare such a violent person the punishment into which he obstinately runs; much more advisable is it to let him rage till he ceases; violent opposition only makes the evil the greater. With כִּי אִם, " *denn wenn* " [for then], cf. ii. 3, "*ja wenn*" [yea if], and with וְעוֹד in the conclusion, Job xiv. 7 (a parallelism syntactically more appropriate than Ps. cxxxix. 18).

Ver. 20 Hearken to counsel, and receive instruction,
            That thou mayest become wise afterwards.

The rule of morals, xii. 15*b*, receives here the parænetic tone which is the keynote of the introduction i.-ix. Löwenstein translates: that thou mayest finally become wise. But בְּאַחֲרִיתֶךָ corresponds rather to our " *hinfort* " [*posthac*] than to " *end-*

lich" [finally]. He to whom the warning is directed must break with the self-willed, undisciplined ראשׁית [beginning] of his life, and for the future (τὸν ἐπίλοιπον ἐν σαρκὶ χρόνον, 1 Pet. iv. 2) become wise. The relative contrast between the two periods of life is the same as at Job viii. 7.

> Ver. 21 Many are the thoughts in a man's heart;
> But Jahve's counsel, that stands.

In תָקוּם lies, as at Isa. xl. 8, both: that the counsel of God (His plan of the world and of salvation) is accomplished and comes into actual fact, and that it continues. This counsel is the true reality elevated above the checkered manifoldness of human purposes, aims, and subjectivities, which penetrates and works itself out in history. The thoughts of a man thus gain unity, substance, endurance, only in so far as he subjects himself to this counsel, and makes his thoughts and actions conformable and subordinate to this counsel.

Ver. 22. The series makes a new departure with a proverb regarding the poor (cf. ver. 17) :

> A man's delight is his beneficence ;
> And better is a poor man than a liar.

The right interpretation will be that which presses upon תַּאֲוַת no strange meaning, and which places the two parts of the verse in an inner mutual relation ethically right. In any case it lies nearer to interpret תאות, in relation to man, actively than passively : that which makes man worthy of desire (Rashi), adorns and distinguishes him (Kimchi, Aben-Ezra); or, that which is desired by man, is above all things sought for (Luzzatto); and, in like manner, the Heb. meaning for חַסְדּוֹ lies nearer than the Aram. (*vid.* xiv. 34): the pleasure of a man is his disgrace (Ralbag). Thus Bertheau's translation : the desire of a man is his *charitas*, must mean : that which brings to a man true joy is to act amiably. But is that, thus generally expressed, true ? And if this were the thought, how much more correctly and distinctly would it be expressed by שִׂמְחָה לָאָדָם עֲשׂוֹת חֶסֶד (cf. xxi. 15) ! Hitzig is rightly reminded by חסדו of the Pharisee who thanks God that he is not as other men ; the word ought to have been חסד to remove every trace of self-satisfaction. Hitzig therefore proposes from the LXX. and the Vulgate the text-correction מִתְּבוּאַת, and translates, " from the revenue of a man is his kind gift;" and Ewald, who is satisfied with תְּבוּאַת, "the gain of a man is his pious love." The latter is more judicious: חסד (love) distributed is in reality gain (according to ver. 17); but 22*b* corresponds rather with the former: " better is he who from want does not give תבואה, than he who could give and says he has nothing." But was there then need for that καρπός of the LXX.? If a poor man is better than a lord given to lying,—for אִישׁ with רָשׁ is a man of means and position,—*i.e.* a poor man who would give willingly, but has nothing, than that man who will not give, and therefore lies, saying that he has nothing; then 22*a* means that the will of a man (cf. תאות, xi. 23) is his doing good (*vid.* regarding חֶסֶד, at iii. 3), *i.e.* is its soul and very essence. Euchel, who accordingly translates: the philanthropy of a man consists properly in his goodwill, rightly compares the Rabbinical proverb, אחד המרבה ואחד הממעיט ובלבד שיתכוין, *i.e.* one may give more or less, it all depends on the intention, the disposition.

> Ver. 23 The fear of Jahve tendeth to life;
> Satisfied, one spendeth the night, not visited by evil.

The first line is a variation of xiv. 27*a*. How the fear of God thus reacheth to life, *i.e.* helps to a life that is enduring, free from care and happy, 23*b* says: the promises are fulfilled to the God-fearing, Deut. xi. 15 and Lev. xxvi. 6; he does not go hungry to bed, and needs fear no awakening in terror out of his soft slumber (iii. 24). With ו *explic.*, 23*a* is explained. לִין שָׂבֵעַ means to spend the night (the long night) hungry, as לִין עָרוּם, Job xxiv. 7, to pass the night in nakedness (cold). נִפְקַד, of visitation of punishment, we read also at Isa. xxix. 6, and instead of בְּרָע, as it might be according to this passage, we have here the accus. of the manner placing the meaning of the *Niph.* beyond a doubt (cf. xi. 15, רָע, in an evil manner). All is in harmony with the matter, and is good Heb.; on the contrary, Hitzig's ingenuity introduces, instead of וְשָׂבֵעַ, an unheard of word, וְיִשְׂרַע, " and he stretches himself." One of the Greeks excellently translates: καὶ ἐμπλησθεὶς αὐλισθήσεται ἄνευ ἐπισκοπῆς πονηρᾶς. The LXX., which instead of רע, γνῶσις, translates thus, רֵעַ, discredits itself. The Midrash—Lagarde says of its translation—varies in colour like an opal. In other

34

THE BOOK OF PROVERBS.

words, it handles the text like wax, and forms it according to its own taste, like the Midrash with its " read not so, but so."

Ver. 24 The slothful hath thrust his hand into the dish ;
He bringeth it not again to his mouth.

This proverb is repeated in a different form, xxvi. 15. The figure appears, thus understood, an hyperbole, on which account the LXX. understand by צלחת the bosom or lap, κόλπον; Aquila and Symmachus understand by it the arm-pit, μασχάλην or μάλην; and the Jewish interpreters gloss it by חיק (Kimchi) or קרע החלוק, the slit (Ital. *fenditura*) of the shirt. But the domestic figure, 2 Kings xxi. 13, places before us a dish which, when it is empty, is wiped and turned upside down;[1] and that the slothful when he eats appears too slothful to bring his hand, *e.g.* with the rice or the piece of bread he has taken out of the dish, again to his mouth, is true to nature : we say of such a man that he almost sleeps when he eats. The fut. after the perf. here denotes that which is not done after the former thing, *i.e.* that which is scarcely and only with difficulty done; גם ... לו may have the meaning of " yet not," as at Ps. cxxix. 2; but the sense of " not once " = *ne . . . quidem*, lies here nearer Deut. xxiii. 3.

Ver. 25 The scorner thou smitest, and the simple is prudent;
And if one reprove the man of understanding, he gaineth knowledge

Hitzig translates in a way that is syntactically inexact : • smite the scorner, so the simple becomes prudent; that would have required at least the word וְיֶעְרָם : fut. and fut. connected by ו is one of many modes of expression for the simultaneous, discussed by me at Hab. iii. 10. The meaning of the proverb has a complete commentary at xxi. 11, where its two parts are otherwise expressed with perfect identity of thought. In regard to the לץ, with whom denunciation and threatening bear no fruit (xiii. 1, xv. 12), and perhaps even produce the contrary effect to that intended (ix. 7), there remains nothing

---

[1] While צְפַּחַת, *sahfat*, in the sense of dish, is etymologically clear, for צְלֹחַת, neither *salah* (to be good for), nor *salakh* (to be deaf, mangy), offers an appropriate verbal meaning. The Arab. *zuluh* (large dishes) stands under *zalah* (to taste, of the tasting of food), but is scarcely a derivative from it. Only צלח, which in the meaning of good for, proceeding from the idea of penetrating through, has retained the root-meaning of cleft, furnishes for צְלַּחַת and צְלוֹחִית a root-word in some measure useful.

else than to vindicate the injured truths by means of the private justice of corporal punishment. Such words, if spoken to the right man, in the right spirit, at the right time, may affect him with wholesome terrors; but even though he is not made better thereby, yet the simple, who listens to the mockeries of such not without injury, will thereby become prudent (gain עָרְמָה = הֶעְרִים, prudence, as at xv. 5), *i.e.* either arrive at the knowledge that the mockery of religion is wicked, or guard himself against incurring the same repressive measures. In 25*b* וְהוֹכֵחַ is neither inf. (Umbreit), which after xxi. 11*b* must be וּבְהוֹכֵחַ, nor impr. (Targ., Ewald), which according to rule is הוֹכֵחַ, but the hypothetic perf. (Syr.) with the most general subject (Merc., Hitzig) : if one impart instruction to the (dat. obj. as ix. 7, xv. 2) man of understanding (*vid.* xvi. 21), then he acquires knowledge, *i.e.* gains an insight into the nature and value of that which one wishes to bring him to the knowledge of (הֵבִין דַּעַת, as xxix. 7 ; cf. viii. 5). That which the deterring lesson of exemplary punishment approximately effects with the wavering, is, in the case of the man of understanding, perfectly attained by an instructive word.

We have now reached the close of the third chief section of the older Book of Proverbs. All the three sections begin with בֵּן, חָכַם, x. 1, xiii. 1, xv. 20. The Introduction, i.-ix., dedicates this collection of Solomonic proverbs to youth, and the three beginnings accordingly relate to the relative duties of a son to his father and mother. We are now no longer far from the end, for xxii. 17 resumes the tone of the Introduction. The third principal part would be disproportionately large if it extended from xv. 1 to xxii. 15. But there does not again occur a proverb beginning with the words " son of man." We can therefore scarcely go wrong if we take xix. 26 as the commencement of a fourth principal part. The Masora divides the whole *Mishle* into eight *sedarim*, which exhibit so little knowledge of the true division, that the *parashas* (sections) x. 1, xxii. 17 do not at all find their right place.[1] The MSS., how-

[1] The 915 verses of the *Mishle*, according to the Masora, fall into eight *sedarim*, beginning as follows : i. 1, v. 18, ix. 12, xiv. 4, xviii. 10, xxii. 22, xxv. 13, xxviii. 16.

ever, contain evidences that this Hagiograph was also anciently
divided into *parashas*, which were designated partly by spaces
between the lines (*sethumoth*) and partly by breaks in the lines
(*phethucoth*). In Baer's *Cod. Jamanensis*,[1] after vi. 19, there
is the letter פ written on the margin as the mark of such a
break. With vi. 20 (*vid. l.c.*) there indeed commences a new
part of the introductory Mashal discourses. But, besides, we
only seldom meet with[2] coincidences with the division and
grouping which have commended themselves to us. In the MS.
of the *Græcus Venetus*, xix. 11, 16, and 19 have their initial
letters coloured red ; but why only these verses, is not manifest.
A comparison of the series of proverbs distinguished by such
initials with the *Cod. Jaman.* and Cod. II. of the Leipzig City
Library, makes it more than probable that it gives a traditional
division of the *Mishle*, which may perhaps yet be discovered by
a comparison of MSS.[3] But this much is clear, that a historico-
literary reconstruction of the *Mishle*, and of its several parts,
can derive no help from this comparison.

With xix. 26 there thus begins the fourth principal part of
the Solomonic collection of proverbs introduced by i.–ix.

> He that doeth violence to his father and chaseth his mother,
> Is a son that bringeth shame and disgrace.

The right name is given in the second line to him who acts as
is described in the first. שָׁדַד means properly to barricade
[*obstruere*], and then in general to do violence to, here : to ruin
one both as to life and property. The part., which has the force
of an attributive clause, is continued in the finite : *qui matrem
fugat ;* this is the rule of the Heb. style, which is not φιλομέτοχος, Gesen. § 134, Anm. 2. Regarding מֵבִישׁ, *vid.* at x. 5 ;
regarding the placing together of הֵבִישׁ וְהֶחְפִּיר, *vid.* xiii. 5, where
for הֵבִישׁ, to make shame, to be scandalous, the word הִבְאִישׁ,
which is radically different, meaning to bring into bad odour, is
used. The putting to shame is in בּוּשׁ (kindred with Arab.

---

[1] *Vid.* the *Prefatio* to the Masoretico-Critical Edition of Isaiah by Baer
and myself; Leipzig, 1872.

[2] There are spaces within the lines after i. 7, 9, 33, ii. 22, iii. 18, 35,
v. 17, 23, vi. 4, 11, 15, 19 (here a פ), 35, viii. 21, 31, 35, ix. 18, xvii.
25, xviii. 9, xxii. 19, 27, xxiii. 14, xxiv. 22, 33, xxvi. 21, xxviii. 10,
16, xxix. 17, 27, xxx. 6, 9, 14, 17, 20, 23, 28, 33, xxxi. 9.

[3] *Vid.* Gebhardt's *Prolegomena* to his new edition of the *Versio Veneta.*

bâth) thought of as *disturbatio* (cf. σύγχυσις) (cf. at Ps. vi. 11), in חָפֵר (*khfr*) as *opertio* (cf. Cicero's *Cluent.* 20: *infamia et dedecore opertus*), not, as I formerly thought, with Fürst, as reddening, blushing (*vid.* Ps. xxxiv. 6). Putting to shame would in this connection be too weak a meaning for מַחְפִּיר. The pædagogic stamp which ver. 26 impresses on this fourth principal part is made yet further distinct in the verse that now follows.

> Ver. 27 Cease, my son, to hear instruction,
>> To depart from the words of knowledge.

Oetinger correctly : cease from hearing instruction if thou wilt make no other use of it than to depart, etc., *i.e.* cease to learn wisdom and afterwards to misuse it. The proverb is, as Ewald says, as " bloody irony ;" but it is a dissuasive from hypocrisy, a warning against the self-deception of which Jas. i. 22–24 speaks, against heightening one's own condemnation, which is the case of that servant who knows his lord's will and does it not, Luke xii. 47. חָדַל, in the meaning to leave off doing something further, is more frequently construed with לְ *seq. infin.* than with מִן (cf. *e.g.* Gen. xi. 8 with 1 Kings xv. 21); but if we mean the omission of a thing which has not yet been begun, then the construction is with לְ, Num. ix. 13. Instead of לִשְׁגּוֹת, there might have been also used מִלִּשְׁגּוֹת (omit rather . . . than . . .), and לְמַעַן שְׁגוֹת would be more distinct ; but as the proverb is expressed, לִשְׁגוֹת is not to be mistaken as the subord. infin. of purpose. The LXX., Syr., Targ., and Jerome do violence to the proverb. Luther, after the example of older interpreters : instruction, that which leads away from prudent learning; but *musar* always means either discipline weaning from evil, or education leading to good.

> Ver. 28 A worthless witness scoffeth at right;
>> And the mouth of the godless swalloweth up mischief.

The Mosaic law does not know the oath of witnesses ; but the adjuring of witnesses to speak the truth, Lev. iv. 1, places a false statement almost in the rank of perjury. The מִשְׁפָּט, which legally and morally binds witnesses, is just their duty to state the matter in accordance with truth, and without deceitful and malicious reservation ; but a worthless witness (*vid.* regarding בְּלִיַּעַל, vi. 12) despiseth what is right (יָלִיץ with accus.-

obj. like xiv. 9), *i.e.* scornfully disregards this duty. Under 28*b*
Hitzig remarks that בלע only in *Kal* means to devour, but in
Piel, on the contrary, to absorb = annihilate; therefore he reads
with the LXX. and Syr. דִּין [justice] instead of אָוֶן [mischief]:
the mouth of the wicked murders that which is right, properly,
swallows down his feeling of right.   But בִּלַּע interchanges with
בָּלַע in the sense of swallowing only, without the connected idea
of annihilation; cf. כְּבַלַּע for the continuance [duration] of a
gulp = for a moment, Num. iv. 20 with Job vii. 29; and one
can thus understand 28*b* without any alteration of the text after
Job xv. 16; cf. xx. 12–15, as well as with the text altered
after Isa. iii. 12, by no means so that one makes אָוֶן the subject : mischief swallows up, *i.e.* destroys, the mouth of the
wicked (Rashi); for when "mouth" and "to swallow" stand
connected, the mouth is naturally that which swallows, not that
which is swallowed (cf. Eccles. x. 12 : the mouth of the fool
swallows, *i.e.* destroys, him).   Thus 28*b* means that wickedness,
i.e. that which is morally perverse, is a delicious morsel for the
mouth of the godless, which he eagerly devours; to practise evil
is for him, as we say, "*ein wahrer Genuss*" [a true enjoyment].

Ver. 29 Judgments are prepared for scorners,
And stripes for the backs of fools.

שְׁפָטִים never means punishment which a court of justice inflicts,
but is always used of the judgments of God, even although they
are inflicted by human instrumentality (*vid.* 2 Chron. xxiv. 24);
the singular, which nowhere occurs, is the segolate *n. act.* שֶׁפֶט
= שְׁפוֹט, 2 Chron. xx. 9, plur. שְׁפוּטִים.   Hitzig's remark: "the
judgment may, after ver. 25, consist in stripes," is misleading;
the stroke, הַכּוֹת, there is such as when, *e.g.*, a stroke on the ear
is applied to one who despises that which is holy, which, under
the circumstances, may be salutary; but it does not fall under
the category of *shephuthim*, nor properly under that of מַהֲלֻמוֹת.
The former are providential chastisements with which history
itself, or God in history, visits the despiser of religion; the latter
are strokes which are laid on the backs of fools by one who is
instructing them, in order, if possible, to bring them to thought
and understanding.   נָכוֹן, here inflected as *Niph.*, is used, as
Job xv. 23, as meaning to be placed in readiness, and thus to be
surely imminent.   Regarding *mahalŭmoth, vid.* at xviii. 6.

Chap. xx. 1. This proverb warns against the debauchery with which free-thinking is intimately associated.

> Wine is a mocker, mead boisterous;
> And no one who is overtaken thereby is wise.

The article stands with יָ֑יִן. Ewald maintains that in x.–xxii. 6 the article occurs only here and at xxi. 31, and that it is here, as the LXX. shows, not original. Both statements are incorrect. The article is found, e.g., at xix. 6, xviii. 18, 17, and here the personification of " wine " requires it; but that it is wanting to שֵׁכָר shows how little poetry delights in it; it stands once for twice. The effects of wine and mead (שֵׁכָר from שָׁכַר, to stop, obstruct, become stupid) are attributed to these liquors themselves as their property. Wine is a mocker, because he who is intoxicated with it readily scoffs at that which is holy; mead is boisterous (cf. הוֹמִיָּה, vii. 11), because he who is inebriated in his dissolute madness breaks through the limits of morality and propriety. He is unwise who, through wine and the like, i.e. overpowered by it (cf. 2 Sam. xiii. 28), staggers, i.e. he gives himself up to wine to such a degree that he is no longer master of himself. At v. 19 we read, שָׁגָה בְ, of the intoxication of love; here, as at Isa. xxviii. 7, of the intoxication of wine, i.e. of the passionate slavish desire of wine or for wine. The word " Erpicht " [avidissimus], i.e. being indissolubly bound to a thing, corresponds at least in some degree to the idea. Fleischer compares the French : être fou de quelque chose. Isa. xxviii. 7, however, shows that one has to think on actual staggering, being overtaken in wine.

> Ver. 2 A roaring as of a lion is the terror of the king;
> And he that provoketh him forfeiteth his life.

Line first is a variation of xix. 12. The terror which a king spreads around (מֶלֶךְ, gen. subjecti., as, e.g., at Job ix. 34 and generally) is like the growling of a lion which threatens danger. The thought here suggested is that it is dangerous to arouse a lion. Thus מִתְעַבְּרוֹ does not mean : he who is angry at him (Venet. : χολούμενος αὐτῷ), but he who provokes him (LXX., Syr., Targ., Jerome, Luther). הִתְעַבֵּר signifies, as we saw at xiv. 16, to be in a state of excessive displeasure, extreme anger. Here the meaning must be : he who puts him into a state of anger (LXX., ὁ παροξύνων αὐτόν, in other versions with the addition of καὶ ἐπιμιγνύμενος, who conducts himself familiarly towards him = מִתְעָרְבוֹ). But can *mitharvo* have this meaning? That the *Hithpa.* of transitive stems, *e.g.* הִתְחַנֵּן (1 Kings viii. 59) and הִשְׁתַּמֵּר (Mic. vi. 16), is construed with the accus. of that which any one performs for himself (cf. Ewald's *Gramm. Arab.* § 180), is not unusual; but can the *Hithpa.* of the intrans. עבר, which signifies to fall into a passion, "express with the accusative the passion of another excited thereby" (Ewald, § 282a)? There is no evidence for this; and Hitzig's conjecture, מִתְעַבְּרוֹ (*Tiphel* of the Targ. עֶבְרָה = תִּעֲבוֹר), is thus not without occasion. But one might suppose that הִתְעַבֵּר, as the reflexive of a *Piel* or *Hiphil* which meant to be put into a state of anger, may mean to draw forth the anger of any one, as in Arab., the vIIIth form (*Hithpa.*) of *hadr*, to be present, with the accus. as reflexive of the IVth form, may mean: *sibi aliquid præsens sistere.* Not so difficult is חָטָא with the accus. of that which is missing, *vid.* viii. 36 and Hab. ii. 10.

> Ver. 3 It is an honour to a man to remain far from strife;
> But every fool showeth his teeth.

Or better : whoever is a fool *quisquis amens*, for the emphasis does not lie on this, that every fool, *i.e.* every single one of this sort, contends to the uttermost; but that whoever is only always a fool finds pleasure in such strife. Regarding הִתְגַּלָּע, *vid.* xvii. 14, xviii. 1. On the contrary, it is an honour to a man to be peaceable, or, as it is here expressed, to remain far from strife. The phrase may be translated : to desist from strife; but in this case the word would be pointed שֶׁבֶת, which Hitzig prefers; for שֶׁבֶת from שָׁבַת means, 2 Sam. xxiii. 7, annihilation (the termination of existence); also Ex. xxi. 19, שִׁבְתּוֹ does not mean to be keeping holy day; but to be sitting, viz. at home, in a state of incapability for work. Rightly Fleischer : "יֵשֵׁב מִן, like Arab. *k'ad san*, to remain sitting quiet, and thus to hold oneself removed from any kind of activity." He who is prudent, and cares for his honour, not only breaks off strife when it threatens to become passionate, but does not at all enter into it, keeps himself far removed from it.

> Ver. 4 At the beginning of the harvest the sluggard plougheth not;
> And so when he cometh to the reaping-time there is nothing.

Many translators (Symmachus, Jerome, Luther) and inter-

preters (*e.g.* Rashi, Zöckler) explain : *propter frigus* ; but חֹרֶף
is, according to its verbal import, not a synon. of קֹר and צִנָּה,
but means gathering = the time of gathering (synon. אָסִיף), from
חָרַף, *carpere*,[1] as harvest, the time of the καρπίζειν, the plucking
off of the fruit ; but the harvest is the beginning of the old
Eastern agricultural year, for in Palestine and Syria the time of
ploughing and sowing with the harvest or early rains (יוֹרֶה = חָרִיף,
Neh. vii. 24; Ezra ii. 18) followed the fruit harvest from October
to December.   The מִן is thus not that of cause but of time.
Thus rendered, it may mean the beginning of an event and
onwards (*e.g.* 1 Sam. xxx. 25), as well as its termination and
onwards (Lev. xxvii. 17) : here of the harvest and its ingathering and onwards.   In 4*b*, the *Chethîb* and *Kerî* vary as at
xviii. 17.   The *fut.* יִשְׁאַל would denote what stands before the
sluggard ; the *perf.* וְשָׁאַל places him in the midst of this, and
besides has this in its favour, that, interpreted as *perf. hypotheticum*, it makes the absence of an object to שׁאל more tenable.
The *Chethîb*, יִשְׁאַל, is not to be read after Ps. cix. 10 : he will
beg in harvest—in vain (Jerome, Luther), to which Hitzig
well remarks : Why in vain ?   Amid the joy of harvest people
dispense most liberally ; and the right time for begging comes
later.   Hitzig conjecturally arrives at the translation :

> " A pannier the sluggard provideth not ;
>   Seeketh to borrow in harvest, and nothing cometh of it."

But leaving out of view the " pannier," the meaning " to obtain
something as a loan," which שׁאל from the connection may bear,
is here altogether imaginary.   Let one imagine to himself an
indolent owner of land, who does not trouble himself about the
tilling and sowing of his fields at the right time and with
diligence, but leaves this to his people, who do only as much as
is commanded them : such an one asks, when now the harvest-
time has come, about the ingathering ; but he receives the
answer, that the land has lain unploughed, because he had not
commanded it to be ploughed.   When he asks, there is nothing,
he asks in vain (וָאַיִן, as at xiv. 6, xiii. 4).   Meîri rightly explains מֵהֹרֶף by מתחלת זמן החרישה, and 4*b* by : " so then, when
he asks at harvest time, he will find nothing ; " on the other

---

[1] *Vid.* Fleischer in Levy's *Chald. Wörterbuch*, i. 426.

hand, the LXX. and Aram. think on חרף, *carpere conviciis*, as also in Codd. here and there is found the meaningless מֵחָרֵף.

> Ver. 5 The purpose in the heart of a man is deep water ;
> But a man of understanding draweth it out.

"Still waters are deep." Like such deep waters (xviii. 4) is that which a man hath secretly (Isa. xxix. 15) planned in his heart. He keeps it secret, conceals it carefully, craftily misleads those who seek to draw it out ; but the man of תְּבוּנָה, *i.e.* one who possesses the right criteria for distinguishing between good and bad, true and false, and at the same time has the capacity to look through men and things, draws out (the *Venet.* well, ἀνέλξει) the secret עֵצָה, for he penetrates to the bottom of the deep water. Such an one does not deceive himself with men, he knows how to estimate their conduct according to its last underlying motive and aim ; and if the purpose is one that is pernicious to him, he meets it in the process of realization. What is here said is applicable not only to the subtle statesman and the general, but also to the pragmatical historian and the expositor, as, *e.g.*, of a poem such as the book of Job, the idea of which lies like a pearl at the bottom of deep water.

> Ver. 6 Almost every one meeteth a man who is gracious to him ;
> But a man who standeth the test, who findeth such an one?

As צִיר אֱמוּנִים, xiii. 17, signifies a messenger in whom there is confidence, and עֵד אֱמוּנִים, xiv. 5, a witness who is altogether truthful, so אִישׁ אֱמוּנִים is a man who remains true to himself, and maintains fidelity toward others. Such an one it is not easy to find ; but patrons who make promises and awaken expectations, finally to leave in the lurch him who depends on them—of such there are many. This contrast would proceed from 6a also, if we took קָרָא in the sense of to call, to call or cry out with ostentation : *multi homines sunt quorum suam quisque humanitatem proclamat* (Schelling, Fleischer, Ewald, Zöckler, and also, *e.g.*, Meîri). But אִישׁ חַסְדּוֹ is certainly to be interpreted after xi. 17, Isa. lvii. 1. Recognising this, Hitzig translates : many a man one names his dear friend ; but in point of style this would be as unsuitable as possible. Must יִקְרָא then mean *vocat?* A more appropriate parallel word to מָצָא is קָרָא = קָרָה, according to which, with Oetinger, Heidenheim, Euchel, and Löwenstein, we explain : the greater part of men meet one who shows himself to them (to this or that man) as אִישׁ חֶסֶד, a man well-affectioned and benevolent; but it is rare to find one who in his affection and its fruits proves himself to be true, and actually performs that which was hoped for from him. Luther translates, with the Syr. and Targ. after Jerome: *Viel Menschen werden From gerhümbt* [many men are reputed pious]; but if יִקְרָא were equivalent to יְקָרָא, then אִישׁ חֶסֶד ought to have been used instead of אִישׁ חסדו. The LXX. read רַב אדם יקר איש חסד, man is something great, and a compassionate man is something precious; but it costs trouble to find out a true man. The fundamental thought remains almost the same in all these interpretations and readings: love is plentiful; fidelity, rare; therefore חסד, of the right kind, after the image of God, is joined to אמת.

Ver. 7 He who in his innocence walketh as one upright,
Blessed are his children after him!

We may not take the first line as a separate clause with צַדִּיק, as subject (Van Dyk, Elster) or predicate (Targ.); for, thus rendered, it does not appropriately fall in as parallel to the second line, because containing nothing of promise, and the second line would then strike in at least not so unconnectedly (cf. on the contrary, x. 9, xiv. 25). We have before us a substantival clause, of which the first line is the complex subject. But Jerome, the *Venet.*, and Luther erroneously: the just man walking in his innocence; this placing first of the adj. is in opposition to the Hebr. syntax. We must, if the whole is to be interpreted as nom., regard צדיק as permutative: one walking in his innocence, a righteous one. But, without doubt, *tsedek* is the accus. of the manner; in the manner of one righteous, or in apposition: as one righteous; cf. Job xxxi. 26 with Mic. ii. 7. Thus Hitzig rightly also refers to these two passages, and Ewald also refers to xxii. 11, xxiv. 15. To walk in his innocence as a righteous man, is equivalent to always to do that which is right, without laying claim to any distinction or making any boast on that account; for thereby one only follows the impulse and the direction of his heart, which shows itself and can show itself not otherwise than in unreserved devotion to God and to that which is good. The children after him are not the children after his death (Gen. xxiv. 67); but, according to Deut. iv. 40, cf. Job xxi. 21, those who follow his example, and thus those who come after him; for already in the life-time of such an one, the benediction begins to have its fulfil-ment in his children.

The following group begins with a royal proverb, which expresses what a king does with his eyes. Two proverbs, of the seeing eye and the necessary opening of the eyes, close it.

Ver. 8 A king sitting on the seat of justice,
Scattereth asunder all evil with his eyes.

Excellently the *Venet.* ἐπὶ θρόνου δίκης, for כִּסֵּא־דִין is the name of the seat of rectitude (the tribunal), as the "throne of grace," Heb. iv. 17, is the name of the *capporeth* as the seat of mercy; the seat of the judge is merely called כסא ; on the other hand, כסא־דין is the contrast of כִּסֵּא הַוּוֹת, Ps. xciv. 20 : the seat from which the decision that is in conformity with what is right (cf., *e.g.*, Jer. v. 28) goes forth, and where it is sought. As little here as at ver. 26 is there need for a characterizing adj. to *melek;* but the LXX. hits the meaning for it, understands such to דין: ὅταν βασιλεὺς δίκαιος καθίσῃ ἐπὶ θρόνου. By the "eyes" are we then to understand those of the mind: he sifts, *dignoscit*, with the eyes of the mind all that is evil, *i.e.* distin-guishes it subjectively from that which is not evil? Thus Hitzig by a comparison of Ps. xi. 4, cxxxix. 3 (where Jerome has *eventilasti*, the Vulg. *investigasti*). Scarcely correctly, for it lies nearer to think on the eyes in the king's head (*vid.* xvi. 15); in that case : to winnow (to sift) means to separate the good and the bad, but first mediately : to exclude the bad; finally, ver. 26 leads to the conclusion that מְזָרֶה is to be understood, not of a subjective, but of an actual scattering, or separating, or driving away. Thus the penetrating, fear-inspiring eyes of the king are meant, as Immanuel explains : בראיית עיניו מבריחם מפניו וּמפזר אותם בכל פיאה. But in this explanation the personal ren-dering of כָּל־רָע is incorrect; for *mezareh*, meant of the driving asunder of persons, requires as its object a plur. (cf. 26*a*). *Col-ra* is understood as neut. like v. 14. Before the look of a king to whom it belongs to execute righteousness and justice (Isa. xvi. 5), nothing evil stands ; criminal acts and devices seen through, and so also judged by these eyes, are broken up and scattered to all the winds, along with the danger that thereby threatened

the community. It is the command: "put away the evil"
(Deut. xiii. 6 [5]), which the king carries into effect by the
powerful influence of his look. With *col-ra* there is connected
the thought that in the presence of the heavenly King no one
is wholly free from sin.

Ver. 9 Who can say I have made my heart clean,
I am pure from my sins?

It it the same thought that Solomon expresses in his prayer at
the consecration of the temple, 1 Kings viii. 46 : there is no
man who sinneth not. To cleanse his heart (as Ps. lxxiii. 13),
is equivalent to to empty it, by self-examination and earnest
effort after holiness, of all impure motives and inclinations; *vid.*
regarding זכה, to be piercing, shining brightly, cloudlessly pure,
Fleischer in Levy's *Chald. Wörterbuch,* i. 424. The consequence of זַכּוֹת is, becoming pure; and the consequence of
זַכּוֹת לֵב, *i.e.* of the purifying of the heart, the being pure from
sinful conduct: I have become pure from my sins, *i.e.* from
such as I might fall into by not resisting temptations; the
suffix is not understood as actual, but as potential, like Ps.
xviii. 24. No one can boast of this, for man's knowledge of
himself and of his sins remains always limited (Jer. xvii. 9 f. ;
Ps. xix. 13); and sin is so deeply rooted in his nature (Job
xiv. 4, xv. 14–16), that the remains of a sinful tendency always
still conceal themselves in the folds of his heart, sinful thoughts
still cross his soul, sinful inclinations still sometimes by their
natural force overcome the moral resistance that opposes them,
and stains of all kinds still defile even his best actions.

Ver. 10. This proverb passes sentence of condemnation
against gross sins in action and life.

Diverse stones, diverse measures—
An abomination to Jahve are they both.

The stones are, as at xi. 1, xvi. 11, those used as weights. Stone
and stone, ephah and ephah, means that they are of diverse
kinds, one large and one small (the LXX., in which the
sequence of the proverbs from ver. 10 is different, has μέγα καὶ
μικρόν), so that one may be able deceitfully to substitute the
one for the other. אֵיפָה (from אָפָה, to bake) may originally
have been used to designate such a quantity of meal as supplied
a family of moderate wants; it corresponds to the *bath* (Ezek.

xlv. 11) as a measure for fluids, and stands here synecdochi-cally instead of all the measures, including, *e.g.*, the *cor*, of which the *ephah* was a tenth part, and the *seah*, which was a third part of it. 10*b* = xvii. 5, an echo of Lev. xix. 36; Deut. xxv. 13–16. Just and equal measure is the demand of a holy God; the contrary is to Him an abhorrence.

Ver. 11 Even a child maketh himself known by his conduct,
Whether his disposition be pure and whether it be right.

If מַעֲלָל may be here understood after the use of עוֹלֵל, to play, to pass the time with anything, then גַּם refers thereto: even by his play (Ewald). But granting that מַעֲלָל [children], synon. with נַעַר, had occasioned the choice of the word מַעְלָל (*vid.* Fleischer on Isa. iii. 4), yet this word never means anything else than work, an undertaking of something, and accomplishing it; wherefore Böttcher proposes מַעֲלָלָיו, for מַעֲלוּל may have meant play, in contradistinction to מַעֲלָל. This is possible, but conjectural. Thus *gam* is not taken along with *b'amalalav.* That the child also makes himself known by his actions, is an awkward thought; for if in anything else, in these he must show what one has to expect from him. Thus *gam* is after the syntactical method spoken of at xvii. 26, xix. 2, to be referred to נַעַר (also the child, even the child), although in this order it is referred to the whole clause. The verb נכר is, from its fundamental thought, to perceive, observe from an ἐναντιό-σημον: to know, and to know as strange, to disown (*vid.* under Isa. iii. 9); the *Hithpa.* elsewhere signifies, like (Arab.) *tankkar*, to make oneself unknowable, but here to make one-self knowable; Symmachus, ἐπιγνωρισθήσεται, *Venet.* γνωσθή-σεται. Or does the proverb mean: even the child dissembles in his actions (Oetinger)? Certainly not, for that would be a statement which, thus generally made, is not justified by experience. We must then interpret 11*b* as a direct question, though it has the form of an indirect one: he gives himself to be known, viz. whether his disposition be pure and right. That one may recognise his actions in the conduct of any one, is a platitude; also that one may recognise his conduct in these, is not much better. פֹּעַל is therefore referred by Hitzig to God as the Creator, and he interprets it in the sense of the Arab. *khulk*, being created = *natura.* We also in this way explain יְצָרֵנוּ, Ps.

ciii. 14, as referable to God the יֹצֵר; and that *poal* occurs, *e.g.*
Isa. i. 31, not merely in the sense of action, but also in that of
performance or structure, is favourable to this interpretation.
But one would think that *poal*, if thus used in the sense of
the nature of man, would have more frequently occurred.
It everywhere else means action or work. And thus it is
perhaps also here used to denote action, but regarded as
habitual conduct, and according to the root-meaning, moral
disposition. The N. T. word ἔργον approaches this idea in
such passages as Gal. vi. 4. It is less probable that 11*b* is
understood with reference to the future (Luther and others) ;
for in that case one does not see why the poet did not make use
of the more intelligible phrase אִם זַךְ וְיָשָׁר יִהְיֶה פָעֳלוֹ. It is like
our (Germ.) proverb : *Was ein Haken werden will krümmt sich
bald* [what means to become a hook bends itself early] ; or :
Was ein Dörnchen werden will spitzt sich bei Zeiten [1] [what
means to become a thorn sharpens itself early], and to the
Aram. בּוֹצִין בּוֹצִין מִקַּטְפֵּיהּ יְדִיעַ = that which will become a gourd
shows itself in the bud, *Berachoth* 48*a*.

Ver. 12 The hearing ear and the seeing eye—
Jahve hath created them both.

Löwenstein, like the LXX.: the ear hears and the eye sees—
it is enough to refer to the contrary to ver. 10 and xvii. 15.
In itself the proverb affirms a fact, and that is its *sensus
simplex ;* but besides, this fact may be seen from many points of
view, and it has many consequences, none of which is to be
rejected as contrary to the meaning: (1.) It lies nearest to
draw the conclusion, *viâ eminentiæ*, which is drawn in Ps. xciv.
9. God is thus the All-hearing and the All-seeing, from
which, on the one side, the consolation arises that everything
that is seen stands under His protection and government, xv.
3 ; and on the other side, the warning, *Aboth* ii. 1 : " Know
what is above thee; a Seeing eye and a Hearing ear, and all
thy conduct is marked in His book." (2.) With this also is
connected the sense arising out of the combination in Ps. xl. 7 :
man ought then to use the ear and the eye in conformity with
the design which they are intended to subserve, according to

---

[1] A similar comparison from *Bereschith Rabba*, *vid.* Duke's *Rabbin.
Blumenlese*, p. 126.

the purpose of the Creator (Hitzig compares xvi. 4); it is not first applicable to man with reference to the natural, but to the moral life: he shall not make himself deaf and blind to that which it is his duty to hear and to see; but he ought also not to hear and to see with pleasure that from which he should turn away (Isa. xxxiii. 15),—in all his hearing and seeing he is responsible to the Creator of the ear and the eye. (3.) One may thus interpret "hearing" and "seeing" as commendable properties, as Fleischer suggests from comparison of xvi. 11: an ear that truly hears (the word of God and the lessons of Wisdom) and an eye that truly sees (the works of God) are a gift of the Creator, and are (Arab.) *lillhi*, are to be held as high and precious. Thus the proverb, like a polished gem, may be turned now in one direction and now in another; it is to be regarded as a many-sided fact.

> Ver. 13 Love not sleep, lest thou become poor;
> Open thine eyes, and have enough to eat.

What is comprehended in the first line here is presented in detail in vi. 9–11. The *fut. Niph.* of רוּשׁ, to become poor (cf. x. 4), is formed metaplastically from יָרֵשׁ, xxiii. 21, xxx. 9, as at 1 Sam. ii. 7; Hitzig compares (Arab.) *ryth*, which, however, means to loiter or delay, not to come back or down. The R. רשׁ signifies either to be slack without support (cf. דַּל), or to desire (cf. אֶבְיוֹן, Arab. *fkyr*, properly *hiscens*, R. פק, as in פקח, to open widely, which here follows). Regarding the second imper. 13*b*, *vid.* iii. 4: it has the force of a consequence, *Las deine augen wacker sein, So wirstu brots gnug haben* (Luth.) [Let thine eyes be open, so shalt thou have bread enough]. With these two proverbs of the eyes, the group beginning with ver. 8 rounds itself off.

The following group has its natural limit at the new point of departure at ver. 20, and is internally connected in a diversity of ways.

> Ver. 14 "Bad, bad!" saith the buyer;
> And going his way, he boasteth then.

Luther otherwise:

> "Bad, bad!" saith one if he hath it;
> But when it is gone, then he boasteth of it.

This rendering has many supporters. Geier cites the words
of the Latin poet :

"*Omne bonum præsens minus est, sperata videntur Magna.*"

Schultens quotes the proverbs τὸ παρὸν βαρύ and *Præsentia
laudato*, for with Luther he refers ול ואזל to the present possession (אזל, as 1 Sam. ix. 7 = (Arab.) *zâl*, to cease, to be lost), and
translates : *at dilapsum sibi, tum demum pro splendido celebrat.*
But by this the *Hithpa.* does not receive its full meaning; and
to extract from הַקּוֹנֶה the idea to which ואזל לו refers, if not
unnecessary, is certainly worthless. *Hakkoneh* may also certainly mean the possessor, but the possessor by acquisition
(LXX. and the *Venet.* ὁ κτώμενος) ; for the most part it
signifies the possessor by purchase, the buyer (Jerome, *emptor*),
as correlate of מֹכֵר, Isa. xxiv. 2 ; Ezek. iv. 12. It is customary
for the buyer to undervalue that which he seeks to purchase, so
as to obtain it as cheaply as possible ; afterwards he boasts that
he has bought that which is good, and yet so cheap. That is
an every-day experience ; but the proverb indirectly warns
against conventional lying, and shows that one should not be
startled and deceived thereby. The subject to ואזל לו is thus
the buyer ; אזל with לו denotes, more definitely even than הלך לו,
going from thence, *s'en aller.* Syntactically, the punctuation
וְאָזַל לוֹ [and he takes himself off] (*perf. hypoth.*, Ewald, 357a)
would have been near (Jerome : *et cum recesserit*) ; but yet it is
not necessary, with Hitzig, thus to correct it. The poet means
to say : making himself off, he then boasts. We cannot in
German place the "*alsdann*" [then] as the אז here, and as.
also, *e.g.* at 1 Sam. xx. 12 ; but Theodotion, in good Greek :
καὶ πορευθεὶς τότε καυχήσεται. We may write וְאָזַל לוֹ with
Mercha on the antepenult, on which the accent is thrown back,
cf. חֹנֵן, xix. 17, but not לוֹ ; for the rule for *Dagesh* does not here,
with the retrogression of the tone, come into application, as, *e.g.*,
in אוֹבַל לַחְמִי, Ps. xli. 10. Singularly the Syr. and Targ. do
not read רַע רַע, but רַע לְרֵעַ, and couple ver. 15 with 14. In the
LXX., vers. 14–19 are wanting.

> Ver. 15 There is indeed gold, and many pearls ;
>   But a precious treasure are lips full of knowledge.

In order to find a connection between this proverb and that
which precedes, we need only be reminded of the parable of

the merchantman who sought goodly pearls, Matt. xiii. 45 f.
The proverb rises to a climax: there is gold, and there are
pearls in abundance, the one of which has always a higher
value than the other; but intelligent lips are above all such
jewels—they are a precious treasure, which gold and all pearls
cannot equal. In a similar manner the N. T. places t' ᵌ one
pearl above the many goodly pearls. So might דעת (*chokma*)
be called the pearl above all pearls (iii. 15, viii. 11); but the
lips as the organ of knowledge are fittingly compared with a
precious vessel, a vessel of more precious substance than gold
and pearls are.

> Ver. 16 Take from him the garment, for he hath become surety for
> another;
> And for strangers take him as a pledge.

The same proverb xxvii. 13, where קח, with the usual aphæresis,
here interchanges with it the fuller form לְקַח, which is also
found at Ezek. xxxvii. 16. To this imperative חַבְלֵהוּ is parallel:
take him as a pledge (Theodotion, Jerome, the *Venet.* and
Luther); it is not a substantive: his pledge (Targ.), which
would require the word חֲבֹלְתוֹ (חֲבֹלוֹ); nor is it to be read with
the Syr. חֲבָלֵהוּ, one pledges him; but it is imperative, not
however of the *Piel*, which would be חַבְּלֵהוּ, and would mean
"destroy him;" but, as Aben Ezra rightly, the imperative of
Kal of חָבַל, to take as a pledge, Ex. xxii. 25, for חֲבָלֵהוּ without
any example indeed except חָנֵּנִי, Ps. ix. 14; cf. lxxx. 16. The
first line is clear: take his garment, for he has become good for
another (cf. xi. 15), who has left him in the lurch, so that he
must now become wise by experience. The second line also is
intelligible if we read, according to the *Chethîb*, נָכְרִים (Jerome,
the *Venet.*), not נָכְרִים, as Schultens incorrectly points it, and if
we interpret this plur. like בנים, Gen. xxi. 7, with Hitzig following Luther, as plur. of the category: take him as a pledge, hold
fast by his person, so as not to suffer injury from strange people
for whom he has become surety. But the *Kerî* requires נָכְרִיָּה
(according to which Theodotion and the Syr., and, more distinctly still than these, the Targ. translates), and thus, indeed,
it stands written, xxvii. 13, without the *Kerî*, thus *Bathra* 173*b*
reads and writes also here. Either נָכְרִיָּה is a strange woman,
a prostitute, a *maitresse* for whom the unwise has made himself

surety, or it is neut. for *aliena res* (LXX. xxvii. 13, τὰ
ἀλλότρια), a matter not properly belonging to this unwise
person. We regard נכרים in this passage as original. בעד coincides with vi. 26 : it does not mean ἀντί, but ὑπέρ; " for strange
people" is here equivalent to for the sake of, on account of strange
people (χάριν τῶν ἀλλοτρίων, as the *Venet.* translates it).

Ver. 17 Sweet to a man is the bread of deceit;
Yet at last his mouth is full of gravel.

"Bread of deceit" is not deceit itself, as that after which the
desire of a man goes forth, and that for which he has a relish
(thus, *e.g.*, Immanuel and Hitzig); but that which is not gained
by labour, and is not merited. Possession (*vid.* iv. 17) or
enjoyment (ix. 17) obtained by deceit is thus called, as לֶחֶם כְּזָבִים,
xxiii. 3, denotes bread; but for him who has a relish for it, it
is connected with deceit. Such bread of lies is sweet to a man,
because it has come to him without effort, but in the end not
only will he have nothing to eat, but his tongue, teeth, and
mouth will be injured by small stones; *i.e.* in the end he will
have nothing, and there will remain to him only evil (Fleischer).
Or: it changes itself (Job xx. 14) at last into gravel, of which
his mouth is filled full, as we might say, "it lies at last in his
stomach like lead." חָצָץ is the Arab. *hatny*, gravel (Hitzig, *grien*
= *gries*, coarse sand, grit), R. חץ, *scindere*. Similarly in Arab.
hajar, a stone, is used as the image of disappointed expectations,
e.g. the adulterer finds a stone, *i.e.* experiences disappointment.

Ver. 18 Plans are established by counsel,
And with prudent government make war.

From the conception of a thought, practically influencing the
formation of our own life and the life of the community, to its
accomplishment there is always a long way which does not lead
to the end unless one goes forward with counsel and strength
combined, and considers all means and eventualities. The
Niph. of כון means, in a passive sense: to be accomplished or
realized (Ps. cxli. 2). The clause 18*a* is true for times of
war as well as for times of peace; war is disastrous, unless it
is directed with strategic skill (*vid.* regarding תַחְבֻּלוֹת, i. 5).
Grotius compares the proverb, Γνῶμαι πλέον κρατοῦσιν ἢ σθένος
χειρῶν. In xxiv. 6, the necessity of counsel is also referred
to the case of war. Ewald would read [the infin.] עֲשֹׁה, or

עֹשֶׂה: with management it is that one carries on war. But
why? Because to him the challenge to carry on war appears
to be contrary to the spirit of proverbial poetry. But the
author of the proverb does certainly mean: if thou hast to
carry on war, carry it on with the skill of a general; and the
imper. is protected by xxiv. 6 against that infin., which is,
besides, stylistically incongruous.

> Ver. 19 He that goeth out gossiping revealeth a secret;
> And with the babbler have nothing to do.

Luther otherwise (like Hitzig)—

> Be not complicated with him who revealeth a secret,
> And with the slanderer, and with the false (better: loquacious) mouth,

so that לְ and the warning apply to the threefold description,
a rendering which Kimchi also, and Immanuel, and others at
least suggest. But in connection with xi. 13, the first line
has the force of a *judicium*, which includes the warning to
entrust nothing to a babbler which ought to be kept silent.
Write גּוֹלֶה סּוֹד, as found in Codd. and old Edd., with *Munach* on
the *penultima*, on which the tone is thrown back, and *Dagesh*
to ס, after the rule of the דחיק (Gesen. § 20, 2*a*), altogether
like קוֹנֶה לֵּב, xv. 32. 19*b* the *Venet.* translates after the first
meaning of the word by Kimchi, τῷ ἀπαταιῶνι τοῖς χείλεσι,
to him who slanders and befools, for it thus improves Theodotion's τῷ ἀπατῶντι τὰ χείλη αὐτοῦ. But פֹּתֶה means, Job v. 2,
—cf. Hos. vii. 11,—not him who befools another, but him who is
befooled, is slandered, by another (Aben Ezra: שׂיפתוהו אחרים),
with which שְׂפָתָיו here does not agree. But now he who is
easily befooled is called פֶּתֶה, as being open to influence (susceptible), *patens*; and if this particip. is used, as here, transitively,
and, on account of the object שׂפתיו standing near cannot possibly be equivalent to מְפֻתֶּה, the usage of the language also just
noticed is against it, then it means *patefaciens* or *dilatans*
(cf. הִפְתָּה, Gen. ix. 27, Targ. אַפְתֵּי = הִרְחִיב), and places itself
as synon. to פֹּשֵׂק, xiii. 3; thus one is called who does not
close his mouth, who cannot hold his mouth, who always idly
babbles, and is therefore, because he can keep nothing to himself, a dangerous companion. The Complut. rightly translates:
μετὰ πλατύνοντος τὰ ἑαυτοῦ μὴ μίχθητι χείλη.

The following group begins, for once more the aim of this older Book of Proverbs becomes prominent, with an inculcation of the fourth[1] commandment.

Ver. 20 He that curseth his father and his mother,
His light is extinguished in midnight darkness.

The divine law, Ex. xxi. 17, Lev. xx. 9, condemns such an one to death. But the proverb does not mean this sentence against the criminal, which may only seldom be carried into execution, but the fearful end which, because of the righteousness of God ruling in history, terminates the life of such an unnatural son (xxx. 17). Of the godless, it has already been said that their light is extinguished, xiii. 9, there is suddenly an end to all that brightened, *i.e.* made happy and embellished their life; but he who acts wickedly (קָלַל, R. קל, *levem esse*, synon. הִקְלָה, Deut. xxvii. 16), even to the cursing of his father and mother, will see himself surrounded by midnight darkness (Symmachus, σκοτομήνη, moonless night), not : he will see himself in the greatest need, forsaken by divine protection (Fleischer), for Jansen rightly : *Lux et lucerna in scripturis et vitæ claritatem et posteritatem et prosperitatem significat.* The apple of the eye, אִישׁוֹן, of darkness (*vid.* vii. 9), is that which forms the centre or centralization of darkness. The Syr. renders it correctly by *bobtho*, pupil [of the eye], but the Targ. retains the אִישׁוֹן of the *Kerî*, and renders it in Aram. by אָתוּן, which Rashi regards as an infin., Parchon as a particip. after the form עָרוּף; but it may be also an infin. substantive after the form עֲזוּז, and is certainly nothing else than the abbreviated and vocally obscured אִישׁוֹן. For the Talm. אֲשִׁישׁ, to be hard, furnishes no suitable idea; and the same holds true of אִישׁוּנֵי, times, Lev. xv. 25 of the Jerusalem Targ. ; while the same abbreviation and the same passing over of *o* into *u* represents this as the inflected אִישׁוֹן (=עֵת). There is also no evidence for a verb אָשַׁשׁ, to be black, dark ; the author of Aruch interprets אִישׁוּנָא, *Bereschith Rabba*, c. 33, with reference to the passage before us, of a dark bathing apartment, but only tentatively, and אִישׁוֹן is there quoted as the Targ. of צֵל, Gen. xix. 8, which the text lying before us does not ratify. *Ishon* means the little man (in the eye), and neither the blackness

[1] *i.e.* The *fifth* according to the arrangement of the Westminster Confession.]

(Buxtorf and others) nor the point of strength, the central point (Levy) of the eye.[1]

Ver. 21 An inheritance which in the beginning is obtained in haste,
Its end will not be blessed.

The partic. מְבֹחָל may, after Zech. xi. 8, cf. Syr. ܟܣܕ, *nauseans*, mean "detested," but that affords here no sense; rather it might be interpreted after the Arab. *bajila*, to be avaricious, "gotten by avarice, niggardliness," with which, however, neither נַחֲלָה, inheritance, nor, since avarice is a chronic disease, בָּרִאשֹׁנָה agrees. On the contrary, the *Keri* מְבֹהֶלֶת [hastened] perfectly agrees, both linguistically (*vid.* xxviii. 22; cf. xiii. 11) and actually; for, as Hitzig remarks, the words following ver. 20 fully harmonize with the idea of an inheritance, into the possession of which one is put before it is rightly due to him; for a son such as that, the parents may live too long, and so he violently deprives them of the possession (cf. xix. 26); but on such a possession there rests no blessing. Since the *Piel* may mean to hasten, Esth. ii. 9, so מְבֹהָל may mean hastened = speedy, Esth. viii. 14, as well as made in haste. All the old interpreters adopt the *Keri*; the Aram. render it well by מְסַרְהֲבָא, from מְסַרְהֵב, overturned; and Luther, like Jerome, *hæreditas ad quam festinatur.*

Ver. 22 Say not: I will avenge the evil;
Hope in Jahve, so will He help thee.

Men ought always to act toward their neighbours according to the law of love, and not according to the *jus talionis*, xxiv. 29; they ought not only, by requiting good with evil (xvi. 13; Ps. vii. 5a, xxxv. 12), not to transgress this law of requital, but they ought to surpass it, by also recompensing not evil with evil (*vid.* regarding שִׁלֵּם, and synon. to xvii. 13); and that is what the proverb means, for 22b supposes injustice suffered, which might stir up a spirit of revenge. It does not, however, say that men ought to commit the taking of vengeance to God; but, in the sense of Rom. xii. 17-19, 1 Pet. iii. 9, that, renouncing all dependence on self, they ought to commit their deliverance out of the distress into which they have fallen, and their vindication, into the hands of God; for the promise is not that He will avenge them, but that

[1] *Vid.* Fleischer in Levy's *Chald. Wörterbuch*, i. 419.

He will help them. The jussive וישע (write וְיֵשַׁע, according to *Metheg-setzung*, § 42, with *Gaja* as העמדה, with the ע to secure distinct utterance to the final guttural) states as a consequence, like, *e.g.*, 2 Kings v. 10, what will then happen (Jerome, Luther, Hitzig) if one lets God rule (Gesen. § 128, 2c); equally possible, syntactically, is the rendering: that He may help thee (LXX., Ewald); but, regarded as a promise, the words are more in accordance with the spirit of the proverb, and they round it off more expressively.

> Ver. 23 An abomination to Jahve are two kinds of weights;
>   And deceitful balances are not good.

A variant to ver. 10, xi. 1. The pred. לֹא־טוֹב (xvii. 26, xviii. 5, xix. 3) is conceived of as neut.; they are not good, much rather bad and pernicious, for the deceiver succeeds only in appearance; in reality he fails.

> Ver. 24 The steps of a man depend on Jahve;
>   And a man—how can he understand his way?

Line first is from Ps. xxxvii. 23, but there, where the clause has the verbal predicate כּוֹנָנוּ, the meaning is that it is the gracious assistance of God, by virtue of which a man takes certain steps with his feet, while here we have before us a variation of the proverb " *der Mensch denkt, Gott lenkt* " [= man proposes, God disposes], xvi. 9, Jer. x. 23; for מִן, as at 2 Sam. iii. 37, Ps. cxviii. 23, denotes God in general as conditioning, as the ultimate cause. Man is indeed free to turn himself hither or thither, to decide on this course of conduct or on that, and is therefore responsible for it; but the relations co-operating in all his steps as the possible and defining conditions are God's contrivance and guidance, and the consequences which are connected with his steps and flow therefrom, lie beyond the power of man,— every one of his steps is a link of a chain, neither the beginning nor the end of which he can see; while, on the other hand, God's knowledge comprehends the beginning, middle, and end, and the wisdom of God ruling in the sphere of history, makes all human activity, the free action of man, subservient to his world-plan. The question, which has a negative answer, is applicable to man: what, *i.e.* how shall he understand his way? מה is like, *e.g.*, Ex. x. 26, Job ix. 2, xix. 28, accus., and fluctuates between the functions of a governed accusative: What does he understand . . . (Job xi. 8) and an adv.: how, *i.e.* how so little, how even not, for it is the מה of the negative question which has become in (Arab.) *mâ* a word of negation. The way of a man is his life's-course. This he understands in the present life only relatively, the true unravelling of it remains for the future.

Ver. 25 It is a snare to a man to cry out hastily " holy ; "
And first after vows to investigate.

Two other interpretations of the first line have been proposed. The snare of a man devours, *i.e.* destroys the holy; but then מוֹקֵשׁ אָדָם must be an expression of an action, instead of an expression of an endurance, which is impossible. The same is true against the explanation : the snare of a man devours, *i.e.* consumes, eats up the holy, which as such is withdrawn from common use. Jerome with his *devotare sanctos*, and Luther with his *das Heilige lestern* [to calumniate the holy], give to לוּעַ = בָּלַע a meaning which loses itself in the arbitrary. Accordingly, nothing is to be done with the meaning κατα-πίεται (Aquila, the *Venet.*). But יְלַע will be the abbreviated fut. of לוּעַ (from יִלְוַע), or לָעַע (יִלְע), Job vi. 3 = (Arab.) *laghâ temere loqui* (*proloqui*) ; and קֹדֶשׁ (after Hitzig : consecration, which is contrary to usage) is like κορβᾶν, Mark vii. 11, the exclamation to which one suddenly gives utterance, thereby meaning that this or that among his possessions henceforth no longer belongs to him, but is consecrated to God, and thus ought to be delivered up to the temple. Such a sudden vow and halting deference to the oath that has been uttered is a snare to a man, for he comes to know that he has injured himself by the alienation of his property, which he has vowed beyond that which was due from him, or that the fulfilling of his vow is connected with difficulties, and perhaps also to others, with regard to whom its disposal was not permitted to him, is of evil consequences, or it may be he is overcome by repentance and is constrained to break his oath. The LXX. hits the true meaning of the proverb with rare success : Παγὶς ἀνδρὶ ταχύ τι τῶν ἰδίων ἁγιάσαι, μετὰ δὲ τὸ εὔξασθαι μετανοεῖν γίνεται. נְדָרִים is plur. of the category (cf. 16*b Chethîb*), and בַּקֵּר, as 2 Kings xvi. 15, Arab. *bakr, examinare, inquirere,* means to subject to investigation, viz. whether he ought to observe, and might observe, a vow such as this, or whether he might not and ought not rather to renounce it (Fleischer). Viewed syntactically, 25a is so difficult, that Bertheau, with Hitzig, punctuates יָלַע; but this substantive must be formed from a verb יָלַע (cf. Hab. iii. 13), and this would mean, after (Arab.) wala', " to long eagerly for," which is not suitable here. The punctuation shows ילע as the 3d. fut. What interpreters here say of the doubled accent of the word arises from ignorance : the correct punctuation is יָלַע, with *Gaja* to ע, to give the final guttural more force in utterance. The poet appears to place in the foreground: " a snare for a man," as a *rubrum;* and then continuing the description, he cries out suddenly " holy ! " and after the vow, he proceeds to deliberate upon it. Fleischer rightly : *post vota inquisiturus est* (*in ea*) = יִהְיֶה לְבַקֵּר; *vid.* at Hab. i. 17, which passage Hitzig also compares as syntactically very closely related.

> Ver. 26 A wise king winnoweth the godless,
> And bringeth over them the wheel.

A variant to xx. 8, but here with the following out of the figure of the winnowing. For אוֹפָן with מְזֹרֶה is, without doubt, the wheel of the threshing-cart, עֲגָלָה, Isa. xxviii. 27 f.; and thus with מְזֹרֶה, the winnowing fork, מְזֹרֶה is to be thought of ; *vid.* a description of them along with that of the winnowing shovel, רַחַת, in Wetzstein's *Excursus* to Isa., p. 707 ff. We are not to think of the punishment of the wheel, which occurs only as a terrible custom of war (*e.g.* Amos i. 3). It is only meant that a wise king, by sharp and vigorous procedure, separates the godless, and immediately visits them with merited punishment, as he who works with the winnowing shovel gives the chaff to the wind. Most ancient interpreters think on אוֹפָן (from אָפַן, *vertere*) in its metaphorical meaning : τρόπος (thus also Löwenstein, he deals with them according to merit), or the wheel of fortune, with reference to the constellations; thus, misfortune (Immanuel, Meîri). Arama, Oetinger, and others are, however, on the right track.

With a proverb of a light that was extinguished, ver. 20 began the group ; the proverb of God's light, which here follows, we take as the beginning of a new group.

> Ver. 27 A candle of Jahve is the soul of man,
> Searching through all the chambers of the heart.

If the O. T. language has a separate word to denote the self-conscious personal human spirit in contradistinction to the spirit of a beast, this word, according to the usage of the language, as Reuchlin, in an appendix to Aben Ezra, remarks, is נְשָׁמָה; it is so called as the principle of life breathed immediately by God into the body (vid. at Gen. ii. 7, vii. 22). Indeed, that which is here said of the human spirit would not be said of the spirit of a beast: it is "the mystery of self-consciousness which is here figuratively represented" (Elster). The proverb intentionally does not use the word נֶפֶשׁ, for this is not the power of self-consciousness in man, but the medium of bodily life; it is related secondarily to נשמה (רוח), while נשמת חיים (רוח) is used, נפש חיים is an expression unheard of. Hitzig is in error when he understands by נשמה here the soul in contradistinction to the spirit, and in support of this appeals to an expression in the Cosmography of Kazwini: "the soul (Arab. âl-nefs) is like the lamp which moves about in the chambers of the house;" here also en-nefs is the self-conscious spirit, for the Arab. and post-bibl. Heb. terminology influenced by philosophy reverses the biblical usage, and calls the rational soul נפש, and, on the contrary, the animal soul רוח,נשמה (Psychologie, p. 154). חֹפֵשׂ is the particip. of חָפַשׂ, Zeph. i. 12, without distinguishing the Kal and Piel. Regarding חַדְרֵי־בָטֶן, LXX. ταμιεῖα κοιλίας, vid. at xviii. 8: בֶּטֶן denotes the inner part of the body (R. בט, to be deepened), and generally of the personality; cf. Arab. bâtn âlrwḥ, the interior of the spirit, and xxii. 18, according to which Fleischer explains: "A candle of Jahve, i.e. a means bestowed on man by God Himself to search out the secrets deeply hid in the spirit of another." But the candle which God has kindled in man has as the nearest sphere of illumination, which goes forth from it, the condition of the man himself—the spirit comprehends all that belongs to the nature of man in the unity of self-consciousness, but yet more: it makes it the object of reflection; it penetrates, searching it through, and seeks to take it up into its knowledge, and recognises the problem proposed to it, to rule it by its power. The proverb is thus to be ethically understood: the spirit is that which penetrates that which is within, even into its many secret corners and folds, with its self-testing and self-knowing light

—it is, after Matt. vi. 22, the inner light, the inner eye. Man becomes known to himself according to his moral as well as his natural condition in the light of the spirit; "for what man knoweth the things of a man, save the spirit of man which is in him?" says Paul, 1 Cor. ii. 11. With reference to this Solomonic proverb, the seven-branched candlestick is an ancient symbol of the soul, *e.g.* on the Jewish sepulchral monuments of the Roman *viâ Portuensis*. Our texts present the phrase נֵר יְהוָֹה; but the Talm. *Pesachim 7b, 8a*, the *Pesikta* in part 8, the Midrash *Othijoth de-Rabbi Akiba*, under the letter נ, Alphasi (ר"יף) in *Pesachim*, and others, read נר אֱלֹהִים; and after this phrase the Targum translates, while the Syr. and the other old versions render by the word "Lord" (*Venet.* ὀντωτής), and thus had יהוה before them.

Ver. 28 Love and truth guard the king;
And he supports his throne by love.

We have not in the German [nor in the Eng.] language a couple of words that completely cover חֶסֶד וֶאֱמֶת; when they are used of God, we translate them by grace and truth [*Gnade u. Wahrheit*], Ps. xl. 12 (יִצְּרוּנִי); when of men, by love and truth [*Liebe u. Treue*], xvi. 6; and when of the two-sided divine forces, by kindness and truth, iii. 3. Love and truth are the two good spirits that guard the king. If it is elsewhere said that the king's throne is supported " with judgment and with justice," Isa. ix. 6 [7]; here, on the other side, we see that the exercise of government must have love as its centre; he has not only to act on the line of right, שׁוּרַת הַדִּין; but, as the later proverb says, in such a way, that within this circle his conduct is determined by the central motive of love. In this sense we give the king not only the title of *Grossmächtigster* [most high and mighty], but also that of "*Allergnädigster*" [most gracious], for the king can and ought to exercise grace before other men; the virtue of condescension establishes his throne more than the might of greatness.

Ver. 29 The ornament of young men is their strength;
And the honour of the old is grey hairs.

Youth has the name בַּחוּר (different from בָּחוּר, chosen), of the maturity (R. בחר, cogn. בכר, בגר, whence Mishn. בַּגְרוּת, manhood, in contradistinction to נַעֲרוּת) into which he enters from

the bloom of boyhood; and the old man is called זָקֵן (Arab.
dhikn, as Schultens says, *a mento pendulo,* from the hanging
chin זָקָן, (Arab.) *dhakan,* chin, beard on the chin). To stand in
the fulness of fresh unwasted strength is to youth, as such, an
ornament (תִּפְאֶרֶת, cf. פָּארוּר, blooming colour of the countenance);
on the contrary, to the old man who has spent his strength in
the duties of his office, or as it is said at xvi. 31, " in the way
of righteousness," grey hairs (שֵׂיבָה, from שָׂב, Arab. *shâb, canescere*)
give an honourable appearance (הָדָר, from הָדַר, *turgidum, amplum
esse, vid.* at Isa. lxiii. 1).

Ver. 30 Cutting wounds cleanse away evil,
And reach the inner parts of the body.

The two words for wounds in line first stand in the *st. constr.;*
חַבֻּרָה (from חָבַר, to be bound around with stripes, to be striped)
is properly the streak, the stripe; but is here heightened by
פֶּצַע (from פָּצַע, to cleave, split, tear open), beyond the idea of
the stripe-wound : tearing open the flesh, cuts tearing into the
flesh. The pred. is after the *Kerî* תַּמְרוּק; but this substantive,
found in the Book of Esther, where it signifies the purification
of the women for the harem (according to which, *e.g.,* Ahron
B. Joseph explains כמו תמרוק לנשים שהוא יפה להם, is syntactically
hard, and scarcely original. For if we explain with Kimchi :
wounds of deep incision find their cleansing (cure) by evil, *i.e.*
by means which bring suffering (according to which, probably
the *Venet.* μώλωπες τραύματος λάμψουσιν ἐν κακῷ), then
תמרוק, with the pronoun pointing back, one would have expected.
But the interpretation of בְּרָע, of severe means of cure, is constrained; that which lies nearest, however, is to understand
רע of evil. But if, with this understanding of the word, we
translate: *Vibices plagarum sunt lustratio quæ adhibetur malo*
(Fleischer), one does not see why בְּרָע, and not rather gen. רָע,
is used. But if we read after the *Chethîb* תַּמְרִיק, then all is
syntactically correct; for (1.) that the word יַמְרִיקוּ, or תַּמְרִקְנָה, is
not used, is in accordance with a well-known rule, Gesen. §
146, 3; and (2.) that הִמְרִיק is connected, not directly with an
accus. obj., but with בְּ, has its analogy in הִתְעָה בְ, Jer. xlii. 2,
הִשְׁרִישׁ בְּ, Job xxxi. 12, and the like, and besides has its special ground in the metaphorical character of the cleansing.
Thus, *e.g.,* one uses Syr. ܐܛܥܝ of external misleading; but with

כ of moral misleading (Ewald, § 217, 2); and Arab. اشاك of erecting a building; but with ب of the intellectual erection of a memorial (monument). It is the so-called *Bâ-âlmojâz; vid.* de Sacy's *Chrest. Arab.* i. 397. The verb מָרַק means in Talm. also, " to take away" (a metaph. of *abstergere;* cf. Arab. *marak,* to wipe off [1]); and that meaning is adopted, *Schabbath* 33a, for the interpretations of this proverb: stripes and wounds a preparedness for evil carries away, and sorrow in the innermost part of the body, which is explained by דרוקן (a disease appearing in diverse forms; cf. " *Drachenschuss,*" as the name of an animal disease); but granting that the biblical מרק may bear this meaning, the ב remains unaccountable; for we say מרק עצמו לַעֲבֵרָה, for to prepare oneself for a transgression (sin of excess), and not בָּעֲבֵרָה. We have thus to abide by the primary meaning, and to compare the proverb, *Berachoth* 5a : " afflictive providences wash away all the transgressions of a man." But the proverb before us means, first at least, not the wounds which God inflicts, but those which human educational energy inflicts: deep-cutting wounds, *i.e.* stern discipline, leads to the rubbing off of evil, *i.e.* rubs it, washes it, cleanses it away. It may now be possible that in 30b the subject idea is permutatively continued : *et verbera penetralium corporis* (thus the *Venet.: πληγαὶ τῶν ταμιείων τοῦ γαστρός*), *i.e. quorum vis ad intimos corporis et animi recessus penetrat* (Fleischer). But that is encumbered, and חַדְרֵי־בָטֶן (cf. ver. 27, xviii. 8), as referring to the depths to which stern corporal discipline penetrates, has not its full force. וּמַכּוֹת is either a particip.: and that as touching (*ferientes*) the inner chambers of the body, or חדרי־בטן is with the ב, or immediately, the second object of תמריק to be supplied : and strokes (rub off, cleanse, make pure) the innermost part. Jerome and the Targ. also supply ב, but erroneously, as designating place : *in secretioribus ventris,* relatively better the LXX. and Syr.: *εἰς ταμεῖα κοιλίας.* Luther hits the sense at least, for he translates :

> One must restrain evil with severe punishment,
> And with hard strokes which one feels.

---

[1] *Vid.* Dozy's *Lettre à M. Fleischer* (1871), p. 198.

Chap. xxi. 1. The group, like the preceding one, now closes with a proverb of the king.

A king's heart in Jahve's hand is like brooks of water;
He turneth it whithersoever He will.

Brook and canal (the *Quinta*: ὑδραγωγοί) are both called פֶּלֶג, or פֶּלֶג, Job xx. 17, Arab. *falaj* (from פָּלַג, to divide, according to which Aquila, Symmachus, and Theodotion, διαιρέσεις; *Venet.* διανομαί; Jerome, *divisiones*); *Jâkût* has the explanation of the word: "*falaj* is the name given to flowing water, particularly the brook from a spring, and every canal which is led from a spring out over flat ground." Such brooks of water are the heart of a king, *i.e.* it is compared to such, in Jahve's hand. The second line contains the point of comparison: He inclines it, gives to it the direction (הִטָּה, causat. of נָטָה, Num. xxi. 15) toward whatever He will (חָפֵץ denotes willing, as a bending and inclining, viz. of the will; *vid.* at xviii. 2). Rightly Hitzig finds it not accidental that just the expression "brooks of water" is chosen as the figure for tractableness and subjection to government. In Isa. xxxii. 2, the princes of Judah are compared to "rivers of water in a dry place" with reference to the exhaustion of the land during the oppression of the Assyrian invasion; the proverb has specially in view evidences of kindness proceeding from the heart, as at xvi. 15 the favour of the king is compared to clouds of latter rain emptying themselves in beneficent showers, and at xix. 12 to the dew refreshing the plants. But the speciality of the comparison here is, that the heart of the king, however highly exalted above his subjects, and so removed from their knowledge he may be, has yet One above it by whom it is moved by hidden influences, *e.g.* the prayer of the oppressed; for man is indeed free, yet he acts under the influence of divinely-directed circumstances and divine operations; and though he reject the guidance of God, yet from his conduct nothing results which the Omniscient, who is surprised by nothing, does not make subservient to His will in the world-plan of redemption. Rightly the Midrash: God gives to the world good or bad kings, according as He seeks to bless it or to visit it with punishment; all decisions that go forth from the king's mouth come לכתחלה, *i.e.* in their

first commencement and their last reason they come from the
Holy One.

The next group extends from ver. 2 to ver. 8, where it closes
as it began.

> Ver. 2 Every way of a man is right in his own eyes;
> But a weigher of hearts is Jahve.

A proverb similar to xvi. 2 (where דַּרְכֵי for דֶּרֶךְ, זַּ for יָשָׁר,
רוּחוֹת for לְבּוֹת). God is also, xvii. 3, called a trier, בֹּחֵן, of
hearts, as He is here called a weigher, תֹּכֵן. The proverb
indirectly admonishes us of the duty of constant self-examination, according to the objective norm of the revealed will of
God, and warns us against the self-complacency of the fool, of
whom xii. 15 says (as Trimberg in "*Renner*"): "all fools live
in the pleasant feeling that their life is the best," and against
the self-deception which walks in the way of death and dreams
of walking in the way of life, xiv. 12 (xvi. 25).

> Ver. 3 To practise justice and right
> Hath with Jahve the pre-eminence above sacrifice.

We have already (vol. i. p. 42) shown how greatly this depreciation of the works of the ceremonial *cultus*, as compared
with the duties of moral obedience, is in the spirit of the
Chokma ; cf. also at xv. 8. Prophecy also gives its testimony,
e.g. Hos. vi. 7, according to which also here (cf. xx. 8*b* with
Isa. ix. 8) the practising of צְדָקָה וּמִשְׁפָּט (sequence of words
as at Gen. xviii. 19, Ps. xxxiii. 5, elsewhere צֶדֶק וּמִשְׁפָט, and yet
more commonly מִשְׁפָט וּצְדָקָה) does not denote legal rigour, but
the practising of the *justum et æquum*, or much rather the
æquum et bonum, thus in its foundation conduct proceeding
from the principle of love. The *inf.* עֲשׂה (like קְנֹה, xvi. 16)
occurs three times (here and at Gen. l. 20; Ps. ci. 3); once עֲשׂוֹ is
written (Gen. xxxi. 18), as also in the *infin. absol.* the form עָשׂה
and עָשׂוֹ interchange (*vid.* Norzi at Jer. xxii. 4) ; once עֲשׂהוּ for
עֲשׂוֹתוֹ (Ex. xviii. 18) occurs in the *status conjunctus*.

> Ver. 4 Loftiness of eyes and swelling of heart—
> The husbandry of the godless is sin.

If נֵר, in the sense of light, gives a satisfactory meaning, then
one might appeal to 1 Kings xi. 36 (cf. 2 Sam. xxi. 17), where נִיר
appears to signify lamp, in which meaning it is once (2 Sam.
xxii. 29) written נֵיר (like חֵיק); or since נֵר = נִיר (ground-form,

nawir, lightening) is as yet certainly established neither in the Heb. nor Syr., one might punctuate נֵר instead of נִר, according to which the Greeks, Aram., and Luther, with Jerome, translate. But of the lamp of the godless we read at xiii. 9 and elsewhere, that it goeth out. We must here understand by נר the brilliant prosperity (Bertheau and others) of the wicked, or their "proud spirit flaming and flaring like a bright light" (Zöckler), which is contrary to the use of the metaphor as found elsewhere, which does not extend to a prosperous condition. We must then try another meaning for נִר; but not that of yoke, for this is not Heb., but Aram.-Arab., and the interpretation thence derived by Lagarde: "Haughtiness and pride; but the godless for all that bear their yoke, viz. sin," seeks in vain to hide behind the "for all that" the breaking asunder of the two lines of the verse. In Heb. נֵר means that which lightens (burning) = lamp, נוּר, the shining (that which burns) = fire, and נִיר, xiii. 23, from נִיר, to plough up (Targ. 1 Sam. viii. 12, יְמֵנַר = לַחֲרֹשׁ) the fresh land, *i.e.* the breaking up of the fallow land; according to which the *Venet.* as Kimchi: νέωμα ἀσεβῶν ἁμαρτία, which as Ewald and Elster explain: "where a disposition of wicked haughtiness, of unbridled pride, prevails, there will also sin be the first-fruit on the field of action; נִר, *novale*, the field turned up for the first time, denotes here the first-fruits of sin." But why just the first-fruits, and not the fruit in general? We are better to abide by the field itself, which is here styled נִר, not שָׂדֶה (or as once in Jer. xxxix. 10, יָגֵב); because with this word, more even than with שָׂדֶה, is connected the idea of agricultural work, of arable land gained by the digging up or the breaking up of one or more years' fallow ground (cf. *Pea* ii. 1, נִיר, Arab. *sikâk*, opp. בּוּר, Arab. *bûr*, *Menachoth* 85a, שדות מְנִירוֹת, a fresh broken-up field, *Erachin* 29b, נִר, opp. הֵבִיר, to let lie fallow), so that נִר רְשָׁעִים may mean the cultivation of the fields, and generally the husbandry, *i.e.* the whole conduct and life of the godless. נִר is here ethically metaph., but not like Hos. x. 12, Jer. iv. 3, where it means a new moral commencement of life; but like חרש, *arare*, Job iv. 8, Hos. x. 13; cf. Prov. iii. 29. רְחַב is not adj. like xxviii. 25, Ps. ci. 5, but infin. like חֲסַר, x. 21; and accordingly also רוּם is not adj. like חוּם, or past like סוּג, but infin. like Isa. x. 12. And חַטָּאת is the pred. of the complex subject, which consists of רוּם עֵינַיִם, a haughty looking down with the eyes, רְחַב־לֵב, breadth of heart, *i.e.* excess of self-consciousness, and נִר רְשָׁעִים taken as an *asyndeton summativum*: pride of look, and making oneself large of heart, in short, the whole husbandry of the godless, or the whole of the field cultivated by them, with all that grows thereon, is sin.

Ver. 5 The striving of the diligent is only to advantage.
And hastening all [excessive haste] only to loss;

or in other words, and agreeably to the Heb. construction:

The thoughts of the industrious are (reach) only to gain,
And every one who hastens—it (this his hastening) is only to loss.

Vid. at xvii. 21. At x. 4, Luther translates "the hand of the diligent," here "the plans of an expert [*endelichen*]," *i.e.* of one actively striving (xxii. 29, *endelich* = מָהִיר) to the end. The אָץ, hastening overmuch, is contrasted with the diligent; Luther well: but he who is altogether too precipitant. Everywhere else in the Proverbs אץ has a closer definition with it, wherefore Hitzig reads אֹצֵר, which must mean: he who collects together; but אץ along with חרוץ is perfectly distinct. The thought is the same as our " *Eile mit Weile* " [= *festina lente*], and Goethe's

Wie das Gestirn ohne Hast,
Aber ohne Rast
Drehe sich jeder
Um die eigne Last.

" Like the stars, without haste but without rest, let every one carry about his own burden," viz. of his calling that lies upon him. The fundamental meaning of אוץ is to throng, to urge (Ex. v. 13), here of impatient and inconsiderate rashness. While on the side of the diligent there is nothing but gain, such haste brings only loss; over-exertion does injury, and the work will want care, circumspection, and thoroughness. In the Book of Proverbs, the contrasts " gain " and " loss " frequently occur, xi. 24, xiv. 23, xxii. 16: profit (the increase of capital by interest), opp. loss (of capital, or of part thereof), as commercial terms.

Ver. 6 The gaining of treasures by a lying tongue
Is a fleeting breath of such as seek death.

One may, at any rate, after the free manner of gnomic resem-

blances and comparisons, regard " fleeting breath " and " such
as seek death" as two separated predicates : such gain is fleeting
breath, so those who gain are seeking death (Caspari's *Beiträge
zu Jes.* p. 53). But it is also syntactically admissible to interpret the words rendered " seekers of death " as gen. ; for such
interruptions of the *st. constr.*, as here by נִדָּף [fleeting], frequently occur, *e.g.* Isa. xxviii. 1, xxxii. 13 ; 1 Chron. ix. 13 ;
and that an idea, in spite of such interruption, may be thought
of as gen., is seen from the Arab.[1] But the text is unsettled.
Symmachus, Syr., Targ., the *Venet.*, and Luther render the
phrase מבקשׁי [seekers] ; but the LXX. and Jerome read מוֹקְשֵׁי
[snares] (cf. 1 Tim. vi. 9) ; this word Rashi also had before
him (*vid.* Norzi), and Kennicott found it in several Codd.
Bertheau prefers it, for he translates: . . . is fleeting breath,
snares of death ; Ewald and Hitzig go further, for, after the
LXX., they change the whole proverb into : הֶבֶל רֹדֵף אֶל־מוֹקְשֵׁי
מָוֶת (בְּמוֹקְשֵׁי), with פֹּעַל in the first line. But διώκει of the
LXX. is an incorrect rendering of נדף, which the smuggling in
of the ἐπὶ (παγίδας θανάτου) drew after it, without our concluding therefrom that אֶל־מוּקְשׁי, or לְמוּקְשׁי (Lagarde), lay before
the translators ; on the contrary, the word which (Cappellus)
lay before them, מוּקְשׁי, certainly deserves to be preferred to
מבקשׁי : the possession is first, in view of him who has gotten it,
compared to a fleeting (נִדָּף, as Isa. xlii. 2) breath (cf. *e.g.*
smoke, Ps. lxviii. 3), and then, in view of the inheritance itself
and its consequences, is compared to the snares of death (xiii.
14, xiv. 27) ; for in פֹּעַל (here equivalent to עֲשׂוֹת, *acquisitio*, Gen.
xxxi. 1 ; Deut. viii. 17) lie together the ideas of him who procures and of the thing that is procured or effected (*vid.* at
xx. 11).

> Ver. 7 The violence of the godless teareth them away,
> For they have refused to do what is right.

The destruction which they prepare for others teareth or
draggeth them away to destruction, by which wicked conduct
brings punishment on itself ; their own conduct is its own
executioner (cf. i. 19) ; for refusing to practise what is right,

---

[1] *Vid.* Friedr. Philippi's *Status constructus*, p. 17, Anm. 3 ; and cf. therewith such constructions as (Arab.) *mân'u fadlah âlmahtâji*, *i.e.* a refuser
of the needy, his beneficence=one who denies to the needy his beneficence.

they have pronounced judgment against themselves, and fallen under condemnation. Rightly Jerome, *detrahent*, with Aquila, κατασπάσει = *j*ʿ*gurrem* (as Hab. i. 15), from גָּרַר; on the contrary, the LXX. incorrectly, ἐπιξενωθήσεται, from גּוּר, to dwell, to live as a guest; and the *Venet.*, as Luther, in opposition to the *usus loq.*: δεδίξεται (fut. of δεδίσσεσθαι, to terrify), from גּוּר, to dread, fear, which also remains intrans., with the accus. following, Deut. xxxii. 27. The Syr. and the Targ. freely: robbery (Targ. רְבוּנָא, perhaps in the sense of usury) will seize them, viz. in the way of punishment. In Arab. *jarr* (*jariyratn*) means directly to commit a crime; not, as Schultens explains, *admittere crimen poenam trahens*, but *attrahere* (*arripere*), like (Arab.) *jany* (*jináyatn*), *contrahere crimen*; for there the crime is thought of as violent usurpation, here as wicked accumulation.

> Ver. 8 Winding is the way of a man laden with guilt;
> But the pure—his conduct is right.

Rightly the accentuation places together "the way of a man" as subject, and "winding" as predicate: if the poet had wished to say (Schultens, Bertheau) "one crooked in his way" (*quoad viam*), he would have contented himself with the phrase נְהֶפֶּךְ דָּרֶךְ. But, on the other hand, the accentuation is scarcely correct (the second *Munach* is a transformed *Mugrash*), for it interprets וָזָר as a second pred.; but וָזָר is adj. to אִישׁ. As הֲפַכְפַּךְ (synon. עֲקַלְקַל, פְּתַלְתֹּל) is a *hapax leg.*, so also *vazar*, which is equivalent to (Arab.) *mawzwr, crimine onustus*, from *wazira, crimen committere*, properly to charge oneself with a crime. The ancient interpreters have, indeed, no apprehension of this meaning before them; the LXX. obtain from the proverb a thought reminding us of Ps. xviii. 27, in which *vazar* does not at all appear; the Syr. and Targ. translate as if the *vav* of *vazar* introduces the conclusion: he is a barbarian (*nuchrojo*); Luther: he is crooked; Jerome also sets aside the syntax: *perversa via viri aliena est;* but, syntactically admissible, the *Venet.* and Kimchi, as the Jewish interpreters generally, διαστροφωτάτη ὁδὸς ἀνδρὸς καὶ ἀλλόκοτος. Fleischer here even renounces the help of the Arab., for he translates: *Tortuosa est via viri criminibus onusti, qui autem sancte vivit, is recte facit;* but he adds thereto the remark that "*vazar* thus explained, with Cappellus, Schultens, and Gesenius, would, it is true, corresponding to the Arab. *wazar*, have first the abstract meaning of a verbal noun from *wazira;*[1] the old explanation is therefore perhaps better : *tortuosa est via viri et deflectens* (*scil. a recta linea*, thus *devia est*), when the '*viri*' is to be taken in the general sense of 'many, this and that one;' the closer definition is reflected from the זַךְ of the second clause." But (1) זָר as an adj. signifies *peregrinus;* one ought thus rather to expect סָר, degenerated, corrupt, although that also does not rightly accord ; (2) the verbal noun also, *e.g.* *'all,* passes over into a subst. and adj. signification (the latter without distinction of number and gender) ; (3) זָר, after its adj. signification, is related to (Arab.) *wazyr*, as חָכָם is to *hakym*, רָחָב to *rahyb ;* it is of the same form as עָנָו, with which it has in common its derivation from a root of similar meaning, and its ethical signification. In 8*b*, וְזַךְ is rightly accented as subj. of the complex pred. זַךְ is the pure in heart and of a good conscience. The laden with guilt (guilty) strikes out all kinds of crooked ways; but the pure needs no stealthy ways, he does not stand under the pressure of the bondage of sin, the ban of the guilt of sin; his conduct is straightforward, directed by the will of God, and not by cunning policy. Schultens : *Integer vitæ scelerisque purus non habet cur vacillet, cur titubet, cur sese contorqueat.* The choice of the designation זַךְ [and the pure] may be occasioned by זֵר (Hitzig) ; the expression 8*b* reminds us of xx. 11.

The group now following extends to ver. 18, where a new one begins with a variation of its initial verse.

Ver. 9 Better to sit on the pinnacle of a house-roof,
 Than a contentious wife and a house in common.

We have neither to supplement the second line : than with a contentious wife . . . (Symmachus, Theodotion, Jerome, Luther), nor: than that one have a contentious . . . ; but the meaning is, that sitting on the roof-top better befits one, does better than a quarrelsome wife and a common house (rightly the Targ. and *Venet.*), *i.e.* in a common house; for the connecting together of the wife and the house by *vav* is a Semitic

---

[1] The *n. act* formed from *wazara* is *wazr, wizr, wizat.* These three forms would correspond to the Heb. vĕzĕr, vēzĕr, and zĕrĕth (z'rāh, cf. rĕdĕth, r'dah, Gen. xlvi. 3).

hendiadys, a juxtaposition of two ideas which our language
would place in a relation of subordination (Fleischer). This
hendiadys would, indeed, be scarcely possible if the idea of the
married wife were attached to אֵשֶׁת; for that such an one has
with her husband a " house of companionship, *i.e.* a common
house," is self-evident. But may it not with equal right be
understood of the imperious positive mother-in-law of a widower,
a splenetic shrewish aunt, a sickly female neighbour disputing
with all the world, and the like? A man must live together
with his wife in so far as he does not divorce her; he must then
escape from her; but a man may also be constrained by circumstances to live in a house with a quarrelsome mother-in-law, and
such an one may, even during the life of his wife, and in spite
of her affection, make his life so bitter that he would rather, in
order that he might have rest, sit on the pinnacle or ridge of a
house-roof. פִּנָּה is the battlement (Zeph. i. 16) of the roof, the
edge of the roof, or its summit; he who sits there does so not
without danger, and is exposed to the storm, but that in contrast with the alternative is even to be preferred; he sits alone.
Regarding the *Chethîb* מִדְוֹנִים, *Kerî* מִדְיָנִים, *vid.* at vi. 14; and
cf. the figures of the " continual dropping" for the continual
scolding of such a wife, embittering the life of her husband,
xix. 13.

> Ver. 10 The soul of the godless hath its desire after evil ;
>   His neighbour findeth no mercy in his eyes.

The interchange of perf. and fut. cannot be without intention.
Löwenstein renders the former as *perf. hypotheticum* : if the
soul of the wicked desires anything evil . . . ; but the רָשָׁע wishes
evil not merely now and then, but that is in general his nature
and tendency. The perf. expresses that which is actually the
case : the soul of the wicked has its desire directed (write אִוְּתָה
with *Munach*, after Codd. and old Ed., not with *Makkeph*) toward
evil, and the fut. expresses that which proceeds from this : he
who stands near him is not spared. יֻחַן is, as at Isa. xxvi.
10, *Hoph.* of חָנַן, to incline, viz. oneself, compassionately toward
any one, or to bend to him. But in what sense is בְּעֵינָיו added?
It does not mean, as frequently, *e.g.* ver. 2, according to his
judgment, nor, as at xx. 8, vi. 13 : with his eyes, but is to be
understood after the phrase מָצָא חֵן בְּעֵינֵי : his neighbour finds no

mercy in his eyes, so that in these words the sympathy ruling
within him expresses itself : " his eyes will not spare his friends,"
vid. Isa. xiii. 18.

> Ver. 11 When the scorner is punished, the simple is made wise ;
>   And when insight is imparted to a wise man, he receives
>   knowledge.

The thought is the same as at xix. 25. The mocker at religion
and virtue is incorrigible, punishment avails him nothing, but
yet it is not lost ; for as a warning example it teaches the simple,
who might otherwise be easily drawn into the same frivolity.
On the other hand, the wise man needs no punishment, but
only strengthening and furtherance : if " instruction " is imparted to him, he embraces it, makes it his own דַּעַת; for, being
accessible to better insight, he gains more and more knowledge.
De Dieu, Bertheau, and Zöckler make " the simple " the subject also in 11*b* : and if a wise man prospers, he (the simple)
gains knowledge. But לְ הַשְׂכִּיל, used thus impersonally, is unheard of ; wherefore Hitzig erases the לְ before חָכָם : if a wise
man has prosperity. But השׂכיל does not properly mean to have
prosperity, but only mediately : to act with insight, and on that
account with success. The thought that the simple, on the one
side, by the merited punishment of the mocker ; on the other,
by the intelligent prosperous conduct of the wise, comes to
reflection, to reason, may indeed be entertained, but the traditional form of the proverb does not need any correction. הַשְׂכִּיל
may be used not only transitively : to gain insight, Gen. iii. 6,
Ps. ii. 10, and elsewhere, but also causatively : to make intelligent, with the accus. following, xvi. 23, Ps. xxxii. 8, or : to
offer, present insight, as here with the dat.-obj. following (cf.
xvii. 26). Instead of בַּעֲנָשׁ־, the *Kametz* of which is false, Codd.
and good Edd. have, rightly, בַּעֲנשׁ־. Hitzig, making " the wise "
the subject to בהשׂכיל (and accordingly " the scorner " would
be the subject in 11*a*), as a correct consequence reads בַּעֲנָשׁ =
בְּהֵעָנֵשׁ. For us, with that first correction, this second one also
fails. " Both *infinitivi constr.*," Fleischer remarks, " are to be
taken passively ; for the Semitic infin., even of transitive form,
as it has no designation of gender, time, and person, is an indeterminate *modus*, even in regard to the *generis verbi* (Act. and

Pass.)" [1] To this proverb with *u-behaskil* there is connected
the one that follows, beginning with *maskil.*

Ver. 12 A righteous One marketh the house of the godless;
He hurleth the godless to destruction.

If we understand by the word צַדִּיק a righteous man, then 12*a*
would introduce the warning which he gives, and the unexpressed subject of 12*b* must be God (Umbreit). But after
such an *introitus*, יהוה ought not to be wanting. If in 12*a* " the
righteous man " is the subject, then it presents itself as such
also for the second parallel part. But the thought that the
righteous, when he takes notice of the house of the godless,
shows attention which of itself hurls the godless into destruction
(Löwenstein), would require the sing. רשע in the conclusion ;
also, instead of מְסַלֵּף the fut. יְסַלֵּף would have been found ; and
besides, the judicial סָלֵף (*vid.* regarding this word at xi. 3, xix.
3) would not be a suitable word for this confirmation in evil.
Thus by צדיק the proverb means God, and מסלף has, as at xxii.
12, Job xii. 19, this word as its subject. " A righteous One "
refers to the All-righteous, who is called, Job xxxiv. 17, "the All-
just One," and by Rashi, under the passage before us, צַדִּיקוֹ שֶׁל
עוֹלָם. Only do not translate with Bertheau and Zöckler : The
Righteous One (All-righteous), for (1) this would require הַצַּדִּיק,
and (2) הצדיק is never by itself used as an attributive designation of God. Rightly, Fleischer and Ewald : a Righteous One,
viz. God. It is the indetermination which seeks to present
the idea of the great and dreadful : a Righteous One, and
such a Righteous One ! [2] הִשְׂכִּיל with עַל, xvi. 20, or אֶל, Ps.
xli. 2, Neh. viii. 13, here with לְ, signifies to give attention to
anything, to look attentively on it. The two participles stand
in the same line : *animum advertit . . . evertit.* Hitzig changes

---

[1] The Arab. National Grammarians, it is true, view the matter otherwise.
When *ḳatlu zydn*, the putting to death of Zeid, is used in the sense of
Zeid's becoming dead, according to their view the *fâ'l* (the *gen. subjecti*) is
omitted ; the full expression would be *ḳatlu 'amrn zaydnâ.* Since now *'amrn*
is omitted, *zaydn* has in the gen. form taken the place of the *fâ'l*, but this
gen. is the representative of the *acc. objecti.* Without thus going round
about, we say : it is the *gen. objecti.*

[2] The Arabs call this indetermination *âlnkrt lalt'zym wallthwyl. Vid.*
under Ps. ii. 12.

רֶשַׁע לְבֵית into לְבֵיתוֹ, and makes רֶשַׁע the subject of 12*b*; but the proverb as it lies before us is far more intelligible.

Ver. 13 He that stoppeth his ear at the cry of the poor—
He also calls and is not heard.

Only the merciful find mercy, Matt. v. 7 ; the unmerciful rich man, who has no ear for the cry of the דָּל, *i.e.* of him who is without support and means of subsistence, thus of one who is needing support, will also remain unheard when he himself, in the time of need, calls upon God for help. Cf. the parable of the unmerciful servant of the merciful king, Matt. xviii. 23 ff. מִן in מִזְּעַקַת, as Isa. xxiii. 15, Gen. iv. 13, xxvii. 1 ; no preposition of our [German] language [nor English] expresses, as Fleischer here remarks, such a fulness of meaning as this מִן does, to which, after a verb of shutting up such as אטם (cf. xvii. 28), the Arab. ع would correspond, *e.g. a'my 'n âltryk* : blind, so that he does not see the way.

Ver. 14 A gift in secret turneth away anger ;
And a bribe into the bosom violent wrath.

Hitzig reads with Symmachus, the Targ., and Jerome, יְכַבֶּה, and translates : "extinguishes anger ;" but it does not follow that they did read יכבה ; for the Talm. Heb. כְּפָה signifies to cover by turning over, *e.g.* of a vessel, *Sanhedrin* 77*a*, which, when it is done to a candle or a fire, may mean its extinction. But כפה of the post-bibl. Heb. also means to bend, and thence to force out (Aram. כְּפָא, כְּפֵי), according to which Kimchi hesitates whether to explain : overturns = smothers, or : bends = forces down anger. The *Venet.* follows the latter signification : κάμψει (for Villoison's καλύψει rests on a false reading of the ms.). But there is yet possible another derivation from the primary signification, *curvare, flectere, vertere,* according to which the LXX. translates ἀνατρέπει, for which ἀποτρέπει would be yet better : כפה, to bend away, to turn off, ἀρκεῖν, *arcere,* altogether like the Arab. (compared by Schultens) *kfâ,* and *kfy,* ἀρκεῖν, to prevent, whence, *e.g., ikfini hada:* hold that away from me, or : spare me that (Fleischer); with the words *hafika sharran* (Lat. *defendaris semper a malo*) princes were anciently saluted; *kfy* signifies "to suffice," because enough is there, where there is a keeping off of want. Accordingly we translate : *Donum clam acceptum avertit iram,* which also the

Syr. meant by *mephadka* (מְפָרֵק). This verb is naturally to be supplied to 14*b*, which the LXX. has recognised (it translates: but he who spares gifts, excites violent anger). Regarding שֹׁחַד, *vid.* at xvii. 8 ; and regarding בַּחֵק, at xvii. 23. Also here חֵק (חֵיק = חַיִק), like Arab. *jayb*, *'ubb*, חֹב, denotes the bosom of the garment; on the contrary, (Arab.) *hijr*, *hidn*, הֹצֶן, is more used of that of the body, or that formed by the drawing together of the body (*e.g.* of the arm in carrying a child). A present is meant which one brings with him concealed in his bosom ; perhaps 13*b* called to mind the judge that took gifts, Ex. xxiii. 8 (Hitzig).

> Ver. 15 It is a joy to the just to do justice,
> And a terror for them that work iniquity.

To act according to the law of rectitude is to these as unto death ; injustice has become to them a second nature, so that their heart strives against rectitude of conduct; it also enters so little into their plan of life, and their economy, that they are afraid of ruining themselves thereby. So we believe, with Hitzig, Elster, Zöckler, and Luther, this must be explained in accordance with our interpretation of x. 29. Fleischer and others supplement the second parallel member from the first : וּפֹעַל אָוֶן מְחִתָּה לְפֹעֲלֵי אָוֶן ; others render 15*b* as an independent sentence : ruin falls on those who act wickedly. But that ellipsis is hard and scarcely possible ; but in general מחתה, as contrasted correlate to שִׂמְחָה, can scarcely have the pure objective sense of ruin or destruction. It must mean a revolution in the heart. Right-doing is to the righteous a pleasure (cf. x. 23) ; and for those who have אָוֶן, and are devoid of moral worth, and thus simply immoral as to the aim and sphere of their conduct, right-doing is something which alarms them : when they act in conformity with what is right, they do so after an external impulse only against their will, as if it were death to them.

> Ver. 16 A man who wanders from the way of understanding,
> Shall dwell in the assembly of the dead.

Regarding הִשְׂכֵּל, *vid.* i. 3 ; and regarding רְפָאִים, ii. 18. The verb נוּחַ means to repose, to take rest, Job iii. 13, and to dwell anywhere, xiv. 33 ; but originally like (Arab.) *nâkh* and *hadd*, to lay oneself down anywhere, and there to come to rest ; and that is the idea which is here connected with יָנוּחַ, for the figura-

tive description of יֹאבֵד or יָמוּת is formed after the designation
of the subject, 16a : he who, forsaking the way of understanding, walks in the way of error, at length comes to the assembly
of the dead ; for every motion has an end, and every journey
a goal, whether it be one that is self-appointed or which is
appointed for him. Here also it is intimated that the way of
the soul which loves wisdom and follows her goes in another
direction than earthwards down into hades; hades and death,
its background appear here as punishments, and it is true that
as such one may escape them.

> Ver. 17 He who loveth pleasure becometh a man of want;
> He who loveth wine and oil doth not become rich.

In Arab. *samh* denotes the joyful action of the " cheerful
giver," 2 Cor. ix. 7 ; in Heb. the joyful affection ; here, like
farah, pleasure, delight, festival of joy. Jerome: *qui diligit
epulas.* For feasting is specially thought of, where wine was
drunk, and oil and other fragrant essences were poured (cf.
xxvii. 9 ; Amos vi. 6) on the head and the clothes. He who
loves such festivals, and is commonly found there, becomes a
man of want, or suffers want (cf. Judg. xii. 2, אִישׁ רִיב, a man of
strife) ; such an one does not become rich (הֶעָשִׁיר, like x. 4, =
עָשָׂה עֹשֶׁר, Jer. xvii. 11) ; he does not advance, and thus goes
backwards.

> Ver. 18 The godless becometh a ransom for the righteous ;
> And the faithless cometh into the place of the upright.

The thought is the same as at xi. 8. An example of this is,
that the same world - commotion which brought the nations
round Babylon for its destruction, put an end to Israel's exile :
Cyrus, the instrument in God's hands for inflicting punishment
on many heathen nations, was Israel's liberator, Isa. xliii. 3.
Another example is in the exchange of places by Haman and
Mordecai, to which Rashi refers. כֹּפֶר is equivalent to λύτρον,
ransom; but it properly signifies price of atonement, and generally, means of reconciliation, which covers or atones for the
guilt of any one; the poll-tax and " oblations " also, Ex. xxx.
15 f., Num. xxxi. 50, are placed under this point of view, as
blotting out guilt : if the righteousness of God obtains satisfaction, it makes its demand against the godless, and lets the
righteous go free; or, as the substantival clause 18b expresses,

the faithless steps into the place of the upright, for the wrath passes by the latter and falls upon the former. Regarding בּוֹגֵד, *vid.* ii. 22. Thus, in contrast to the יָשָׁר, he is designated, who keeps faith neither with God nor man, and with evil intention enters on deceitful ways,—the faithless, the malicious, the assassin.

Ver. 19. With this verse, a doublet to ver. 9 (xxv. 24), the collector makes a new addition; in ver. 29 he reaches a proverb which resembles the closing proverb of the preceding group, in its placing in contrast the רשׁע and ישׁר ;—

> It is better to dwell in a waste land,
> Than a contentious wife and vexation.

The corner of the roof, Hitzig remarks, has been made use of, and the author must look further out for a lonely seat. But this is as piquant as it is devoid of thought; for have both proverbs the same author, and if so, were they coined at the same time? Here also it is unnecessary to regard מֵאֵשֶׁת as an abbreviation for מִשֶּׁבֶת עִם אֵשֶׁת. Hitzig supplies שֵׁבֶת, by which אֵשֶׁת, as the accus.-obj., is governed; but it is not to be supplied, for the proverb places as opposite to one another dwelling in a waste land (read שֶׁבֶת בְּאֶרֶץ־מִדְבָּר, with Codd. and correct Ed.) and a contentious wife (*Chethîb*, מְדוֹנִים; *Kerî*, מִדְיָנִים) and vexation, and says the former is better than the latter. For וָכַעַס [and vexation] is not, as translated by the ancients, and generally received, a second governed genitive to אֵשֶׁת, but dependent on מִן, follows "contentious woman" (cf. 9*b*): better that than a quarrelsome wife, and at the same time vexation.

Ver. 20 Precious treasure and oil are in the dwelling of the wise;
And a fool of a man squanders it.

The wise spares, the fool squanders; and if the latter enters on the inheritance which the former with trouble and care collected, it is soon devoured. The combination אוֹצָר נֶחְמָד וָשֶׁמֶן [desirable treasure and oil] has something inconcinnate, wherefore the accentuation places אוֹצָר by itself by *Mehuppach Legarmeh;* but it is not to be translated "a treasure of that which is precious, and oil," since it is punctuated אוֹצָר, and not אוֹצַר; and besides, in that case מַחֲמַדִּים would have been used instead of נֶחְמָד. Thus by אוֹצָר נחמד, a desirable and splendid capital in gold and things of value (Isa. xxiii. 18; Ps. xix. 11); and by שׁמן, mentioned by

way of example, stores in kitchen and cellar are to be thought
of, which serve him who lives luxuriously, and afford noble
hospitality,—a fool of a man (כְּסִיל אָדָם, as at xv. 20), who finds
this, devours it, *i.e.* quickly goes through it, makes, in short, a
tabula rasa of it; cf. בַּלַּע, Isa. xxviii. 4, with בִּלַּע, 2 Sam. xx.
26, and Prov. xix. 28. The suffix of יְבַלְּעֶנּוּ refers back to
אוֹצָר as the main idea, or distributively also both to the treasure
and the oil. The LXX. (θησαυρὸς ἐπιθυμητὸς) ἀναπαύσεται
ἐπὶ στόματος σοφοῦ, *i.e.* ישׁכֹן בפה חכם, according to which Hitzig
corrects; but the fool, he who swallows down "the precious
treasure with a wise mouth," is a being we can scarcely conceive
of. His taste is not at all bad; why then a fool? Is it perhaps because he takes more in than he can at one time digest?
The reading of the LXX. is corrected by 20*b*.

> Ver. 21 He that followeth after righteousness and kindness
> Will obtain life, righteousness, and honour.

How we are to render צְדָקָה וָחֶסֶד is seen from the connection of
xxi. 3 and Hos. vi. 7: *tsedakah* is conduct proceeding from the
principle of self-denying compassionate love, which is the
essence of the law, Mic. vi. 8; and *hĕsĕd* is conduct proceeding
from sympathy, which, placing itself in the room of another,
perceives what will benefit him, and sets about doing it (cf.
e.g. Job vi. 14: to him who is inwardly melted [disheartened]
חֶסֶד is due from his neighbour). The reward which one
who strives thus to act obtains, is designated 21*b* by חַיִּים and
כָּבוֹד. Honour and life stand together, xxii. 4, when עֹשֶׁר precedes, and here צְדָקָה stands between, which, viii. 18, Ps. xxiv. 5,
is thought of as that which is distributed as a gift of heaven,
Isa. xlv. 8, which has glory in its train, Isa. lviii. 8; as Paul
also says, "Whom He justified, them He also glorified." The
LXX. has omitted *tsedakah*, because it can easily appear as
erroneously repeated from 21*a*. But in reality there are three
good things which are promised to those who are zealous in the
works of love: a prosperous life, enduring righteousness, true
honour. Life as it proceeds from God, the Living One, righteousness as it avails the righteous and those doing righteously
before God, honour or glory (Ps. xxix. 3) as it is given (Ps.
lxxxiv. 12) by the God of glory. Cf. with חיים צדקה, x. 2, and
with צדקה, especially Jas. ii. 13, κατακαυχᾶται ἔλεος κρίσεως.

Ver. 22 A wise man scaleth a city of the mighty ;
And casteth down the fortress in which they trusted.

Eccles. ix. 14 f. is a side-piece to this, according to which a single wise man, although poor, may become the deliverer of a city besieged by a great army, and destitute of the means of defence. עָלָה, *seq. acc.*, means to climb up, Joel ii. 7 ; here, of the scaling of a fortified town, viz. its fortress. עֹז is that which makes it עִיר עֹז, Isa. xxvi. 1 : its armour of protection, which is designated by the genit. מבטחה, as the object and ground of their confidence. The vocalization מִבְטָחָה, for *mibtachcha* (cf. Jer. xlviii. 13 with Job xviii. 14), follows the rule Gesen. § 27,

Anm. 2*b.* The suff., as in לְאֶתְנַנָּה, Isa. xxiii. 17, is lightened, because of its *mappik, Michlol* 30*b* ; *vid.* regarding the various grounds of these *formæ raphatæ pro mappicatis*, Böttcher, § 418. If a city is defended by ever so many valiant men, the wise man knows the point where it may be overcome, and knows how to organize the assault so as to destroy the proud fortress. With וַיֹּרֶד, he brings to ruin, cf. עַד רִדְתָּהּ, Deut. xx. 20.

Ver. 23 He that guardeth his mouth and his tongue,
Keepeth his soul from troubles.

xiii. 3 resembles this. He guardeth his mouth who does not speak when he does better to be silent; and he guardeth his tongue who says no more than is right and fitting. The troubles comprehend both external and internal evils, hurtful incidents and (נפש) צרות לבב, Ps. xxv. 17, xxxi. 8, *i.e.* distress of conscience, self-accusation, sorrow on account of the irreparable evil which one occasions.

Ver. 24 A proud and arrogant man is called mocker (free-spirit) ;
One who acteth in superfluity of haughtiness.

We have thus translated (vol. i. p. 39) : the proverb defines almost in a formal way an idea current from the time of Solomon : לֵץ (properly, the distorter, *vid.* i. 7) is an old word; but as with us in the west since the last century, the names of *free-thinkers* and *esprits forts* (cf. Isa. xlvi. 12) have become current for such as subject the faith of the Church to destructive criticism, so then they were called לֵצִים, who mockingly, as men of full age, set themselves above revealed religion and prophecy (Isa. xxviii. 9) ; and the above proverb gives the meaning of this name, for it describes in his moral character such a man. Thus we call one זֵד, haughty, and זֵד יָהִיר, *i.e.* destroying himself, and thus thoughtlessly haughty, who בְּעֶבְרַת זָדֹן acts in superfluity or arrogance (*vid.* at xi. 23) of haughtiness; for not only does he inwardly raise himself above all that is worthy of recognition as true, of faith as certain, of respect as holy; but acting as well as judging frivolously, he shows reverence for nothing, scornfully passing sentence against everything. Abulwalîd (*vid.* Gesen. *Thes.*) takes יהיר in the sense of obstinate; for he compares the Arab. *jahr* (*jahar*), which is equivalent to *lijâj*, constancy, stubbornness. But in the Targ. and Talm. (*vid.* at Hab. ii. 5, Levy's Chald. *Wörterb.* under יָהִיר) יהר in all its offshoots and derivations has the sense of pride; we have then rather to compare the Arab.*istaihara,* to be insane (= *dhahb 'aklh, mens ejus alienata est*), perhaps also to *hajjir, mutahawwir,* being overthrown, *præceps,* so that יהיר denotes one who by his ὑπερφρονεῖν is carried beyond all σωφρονεῖν (*vid.* Rom. xii. 3), one who is altogether mad from pride. The Syr. *madocho* (Targ. מְרִיחָא), by which יהיר (Targ. יָהִיר) is rendered here and at Hab. ii. 5, is its synonym; this word also combines in itself the ideas foolhardy, and of one acting in a presumptuous, mad way; in a word, of one who is arrogant. Schultens is in the right way; but when he translates by *tumidus mole cava ruens,* he puts, as it is his custom to do, too much into the word; *tumidus,* puffed up, presents an idea which, etymologically at least, does not lie in it. The *Venet.*: ἀκρατὴς θρασὺς βωμολόχος τοὔνομά οἱ, which may be translated: an untractable reckless person we call a fool [*homo ineptus*], is not bad.

Ver. 25 The desire of the slothful killeth him;
For his hands refuse to be active.

The desire of the עָצֵל, Hitzig remarks, goes out first after meat and drink; and when it takes this direction, as hunger, it kills him indeed. But in this case it is not the desire that kills him, but the impossibility of satisfying it. The meaning is simply: the inordinate desire after rest and pleasure kills the slothful; for this always seeking only enjoyment and idleness brings him at last to ruin. תַּאֲוָה means here, as in *Kibroth ha-tava,* Num. xi. 34, inordinate longing after enjoyments. The proverb is connected by almost all interpreters (also Ewald,

Bertheau, Hitzig, Elster, Zöckler) as a tetrastich with ver. 25:
he (the slothful) always eagerly desires, but the righteous giveth
and spareth not.   But (1) although צַדִּיק, since it designates one
who is faithful to duty, might be used particularly of the industrious (cf. xv. 19), yet would there be wanting in 26a וְאֵין,
xiii. 4, cf. xx. 4, necessary for the formation of the contrast;
(2) this older Book of Proverbs consists of pure distichs; the
only tristich, xix. 7, appears as the consequence of a mutilation
from the LXX.   Thus the pretended tetrastich before us is
only apparently such.

> Ver. 26 One always desireth eagerly;
> But the righteous giveth and holdeth not back.

Otherwise Fleischer: *per totum diem avet avidus, i.e. avarus;*
but that in הִתְאַוָּה תַאֲוָה the verb is connected with its inner
obj. is manifest from Num. xi. 4; it is the mode of expression
which is called in the Greek syntax *schema etymologicum,* and
which is also possible without an adj. joined to the obj., as in
the ὕβριν θ'ὑβρίζεις (Eurip. *Herc. fur.* 706), the Arab. *marâhu
miryatn:* he had a strife with him.   Euchel impossibly: necessities
will continually be appeased, which would have required תִּתְאַוֶּה
or מִתְאַוֶּה.   The explanation also cannot be: each day presents
its special demand, for כָּל־הַיּוֹם does not mean each day, but the
whole day, *i.e.* continually.   Thus we render התאוה with the
most general subject (in which case the national grammarians
supply הַמִּתְאַוֶּה): continually one longs longing, *i.e.* there are
demands, solicitations, wishes, importunate petitions; but still
the righteous is not embarrassed in his generosity, he gives as
unceasingly (cf. Isa. xiv. 6, lviii. 1) as one asks.   Thus the
pref. is explained, which is related hypothetically to the fut.
following: though one, etc.

> Ver. 27 The sacrifice of the godless is an abomination;
> How much more if it is brought for evil!

Line first = xv. 8a.   Regarding the syllogistic אַף כִּי, *vid.* xii.
31, xv. 11; regarding זִמָּה, crime, particularly the sin of lewdness (from זָמַם, to press together, to collect the thoughts upon
something, to contrive, cf. *raffinement de la volupté*), at x. 23.
בְּזִמָּה is too vaguely rendered in the LXX. by παρονόμως,
falsely by Jerome, *ex scelere* (cf. ἐξ ἀδίκου, Sir. xxxi. 18, with
Mal. i. 13).   The בּ is not meant, as at Ezek. xxii. 11, of the

way and manner; for that the condition of life of the רשע is not
a pure one, is not to be supposed. It is as Hitzig, rightly, that
of price: for a transgression, *i.e.* to atone for it; one is hereby
reminded, that he who had intercourse with a betrothed bond-
maid had to present an *ascham* [trespass-offering], Lev. xix.
20–22. But frequently enough would it occur that rich
sensualists brought trespass-offerings, and other offerings, in
order thereby to recompense for their transgressions, and to
purchase for themselves the connivance of God for their dissolute life. Such offerings of the godless, the proverb means,
are to God a twofold and a threefold abomination; for in this
case not only does the godless fail in respect of repentance and
a desire after salvation, which are the conditions of all sacrifices
acceptable to God, but he makes God directly a minister of
sin.

Ver. 28 A false witness shall perish;
But he who heareth shall always speak truth.

The LXX. translate 28*b* by ἀνὴρ δὲ φυλασσόμενος λαλήσει.
Cappellus supposes that they read לנצר for לנצח, which, however, cannot mean "taking care." Hitzig further imagines
שמח for שמע, and brings out the meaning: "the man that
rejoiceth to deliver shall speak." But where in all the world
does נצר mean "to deliver"? It means, "to guard, preserve;"
and to reach the meaning of "to deliver," a clause must be
added with מן, as מֵרָע. When one who speaks lies (עֵד כְּזָבִים),
and a man who hears (אִישׁ שׁוֹמֵעַ, *plene*, and with the orthophonic
Dagesh), are contrasted, the former is one who fancifully or
malevolently falsifies the fact, and the latter is one who before
he speaks hears in order that he may say nothing that he has
not surely heard. As לֵב שֹׁמֵעַ, 1 Kings iii. 9, means an obedient
heart, so here אִישׁ שׁוֹמֵעַ means a man who attentively hears,
carefully proves. Such an one will speak לָנֶצַח, *i.e.* not: according to the truth, and not: for victory (Aquila, Symmachus,
Theodotion, εἰς νῖκος), *i.e.* so that accomplishes it (Oetinger);
for the Heb. נֶצַח has neither that Arab. nor this Aram. signification; but, with the transference of the root meaning of
radiating or streaming over, to time, continuous existence (*vid.*
Orelli, *Synonyma der Zeit und Ewigkeit*, pp. 95–97), thus: he
will speak for continuance, *i.e.* either: without ever requiring

to be silent, or, which we prefer: so that what he says stands; on the contrary, he who testifies mere fictions, *i.e.* avers that they are truth, is destroyed (28*a*=xix. 9*b*, cf. 5) : he himself comes to nothing, since his testimonies are referred to their groundlessness and falsity; for שֶׁקֶר אֵין לוֹ רַגְלִים, the lie has no feet on which it can· stand, it comes to nothing sooner or later.

Ver. 29. Another proverb with אִישׁ :—

> A godless man showeth boldness in his mien;
> But one that is upright—he proveth his way.

The *Chethîb* has יָכִין; but that the upright directeth, *dirigit,* his way, *i.e.* gives to it the right direction (cf. 2 Chron. xxvii. 6), is not a good contrast to the boldness of the godless; the *Kerî,* יָבִין דַּרְכּוֹ, deserves the preference. Aquila, Symmachus, the Syr., Targ., and *Venet.* adhere to the *Chethîb,* which would be suitable if it could be translated, with Jerome, by *corrigit;* Luther also reads the verb with בּ, but as if it were יָכּוֹן (whoever is pious, his way will stand)—only the LXX. render the *Kerî* (συνιεῖ) ; as for the rest, the ancients waver between the *Chethîb* דְּרָכָיו and the *Kerî* דַּרְכּוֹ : the former refers to manner of life in general ; the latter (as at iii. 31 and elsewhere) to the conduct in separate cases; thus the one is just as appropriate as the other. In the circumstantial designation אִישׁ רָשָׁע (cf. xi. 7) we have the stamp of the distinction of different classes of men peculiar to the Book of Proverbs. הֵעֵז (to make firm, defiant) had, vii. 13, פָּנִים as accus.; the בּ here is not that used in metaphoristic expressions instead of the accus. obj., which we have spoken of at xv. 4, xx. 30, but that of the means ; for the face is thought of, not as the object of the action, but, after Gesen. § 138. 1, as the means of its accomplishment: the godless makes (shows) firmness, *i.e.* defiance, accessibility to no admonition, with his countenance ; but the upright considers, *i.e.* proves (xiv. 8), his way. (הֵבִין) בִּין means a perceiving of the object in its specific peculiarity, an understanding of its constituent parts and essential marks; it denotes knowing an event analytically, as הִשְׂכִּיל, as well as synthetically (cf. Arab. *shakl*), and is thus used as the expression of a perception, which apprehends the object not merely immediately, but closely examines into its circumstances.

If we further seek for the boundaries, the proverbs regarding the rich and the poor, xxii. 2, 7, 16, present themselves as such, and this the more surely as xxii. 16 is without contradiction the terminus. Thus we take first together xxi. 30–xxii. 2.

Ver. 30 No wisdom and no understanding,
And no counsel is there against Jahve.

The expression might also be ה' לִפְנֵי; but the predominating sense would then be, that no wisdom appears to God as such, that He values none as such. With לְנֶגֶד the proverb is more objective: there is no wisdom which, compared with His, can be regarded as such (cf. 1 Cor. iii. 19), none which can boast itself against Him, or can at all avail against Him (לנגד, as Dan. x. 12; Neh. iii. 37); whence it follows (as Job xxviii. 28) that the wisdom of man consists in the fear of God the Alone-wise, or, which is the same thing, the All-wise. Immanuel interprets חָכְמָה of theology, תְּבוּנָה of worldly science, עֵצָה of politics; but חכמה is used of the knowledge of truth, i.e. of that which truly is and continues; תבונה of criticism, and עצה of system and method; vid. at i. 2, viii. 14, from which latter passage the LXX. has substituted here נבורה instead of תבונה. Instead of לנגד ה' it translates πρὸς τὸν ἀσεβῆ, i.e. for that which is נגד ה' against Jahve.

Ver. 31 The horse is harnessed for the day of battle;
But with Jahve is the victory,

i.e. it remains with Him to give the victory or not, for the horse is a vain means of victory, Isa. xxxiii. 17; the battle is the Lord's, 1 Sam. xvii. 47, i.e. it depends on Him how the battle shall issue; and king and people who have taken up arms in defence of their rights have thus to trust nothing in the multitude of their war-horses (סוס, horses, including their riders), and generally in their preparations for the battle, but in the Lord (cf. Ps. xx. 8, and, on the contrary, Isa. xxxi. 1). The LXX. translates הַתְּשׁוּעָה by ἡ βοήθεια, as if the Arab. name of victory, naṣr, proceeding from this fundamental meaning, stood in the text; תשועה (from ישע, Arab. wsʾ, to be wide, to have free space for motion) signifies properly prosperity, as the contrast of distress, oppression, slavery, and victory (cf. e.g. Ps. cxliv. 10, and יִשְׁעָה, 1 Sam. xiv. 45). The post-bibl. Heb. uses נָצַח

(נִצָּחוֹן) for victory; but the O. T. Heb. has no word more fully covering this idea than תְּשׁוּעָה (יְשׁוּעָה).[1]

Chap. xxii. 1 A good name has the preference above great riches;
For more than silver and gold is grace.

The proverb is constructed chiastically; the commencing word נִבְחָר (cf. xxi. 3), and the concluding word טוֹב, are the parallel predicates; rightly, none of the old translators have been misled to take together חֵן טוֹב, after the analogy of שֵׂכֶל טוֹב, iii. 14, xiii. 15. שֵׁם also does not need טוֹב for nearer determination; the more modern idiom uses שֵׁם טוֹב,[2] the more ancient uses שֵׁם alone (e.g. Eccles. vii. 1), in the sense of ὄνομα καλόν (thus here LXX.); for being well known (renowned) is equivalent to a name, and the contrary to being nameless (Job xxx. 8); to make oneself a name, is equivalent to build a monument in honour of oneself; possibly the derivation of the word from שָׁמָה, to be high, prominent, known, may have contributed to this meaning of the word sensu eximio, for שֵׁם has the same root word as שָׁמַיִם. Luther translates שֵׁם by Das Gerücht [rumour, fame], in the same pregnant sense; even to the present day, renom, renommée, riputazione, and the like, are thus used. The parallel חֵן signifies grace and favour (being beloved); grace, which brings favour (xi. 16); and favour, which is the consequence of a graceful appearance, courtesy, and demeanour (e.g. Esth. ii. 15).

Ver. 2 The rich and the poor meet together;
The creator of them all is Jahve.

From this, that God made them all, i.e. rich and poor in the totality of their individuals, it follows that the meeting together is His will and His ordinance; they shall in life push one against another, and for what other purpose than that this relation-

---

[1] In the old High German, the word for war is urlag (urlac), fate, because the issue is the divine determination, and nôt (as in "der Nibelunge Not"), as binding, confining, restraint; this nôt is the correlate to תְּשׁוּעָה, victory; מִלְחָמָה corresponds most to the French guerre, which is not of Romanic, but of German origin: the Werre, i.e. the Gewirre [complication, confusion], for נִלְחַם signifies to press against one another, to be engaged in close conflict; cf. the Homeric κλόνος of the turmoil of battle.

[2] e.g. Aboth iv. 17: there are three crowns: the crown of the Tôra, the crown of the priesthood, and the crown of royalty; but כֶּתֶר שֵׁם טוֹב, the crown of a good name, excels them all.

ship of mutual intercourse should be a school of virtue: the poor shall not envy the rich (iii. 31), and the rich shall not despise the poor, who has the same God and Father as himself (xiv. 31, xvii. 5 ; Job xxxi. 15) ; they shall remain conscious of this, that the intermingling of the diversities of station is for this end, that the lowly should serve the exalted, and the exalted should serve the lowly. xxix. 13 is a variation ; there also for both, but particularly for the rich, lies in the proverb a solemn warning.

The group of proverbs beginning here terminates at ver. 7, where, like the preceding, it closes with a proverb of the rich and the poor.

> Ver. 3 The prudent seeth the evil, and hideth himself ;
> But the simple go forward, and suffer injury.

This proverb repeats itself with insignificant variations, xxvii. 12. The *Kerí* וְנִסְתָּר makes it more conformable to the words there used. The *Chethíb* is not to be read וַיִּסְתֹּר, for this *Kal* is *inusit.*, but וַיִּסָּתֵר, or much rather וַיִּסְתֵּר, since it is intended to be said what immediate consequence on the part of a prudent man arises from his perceiving an evil standing before him ; he sees, *e.g.*, the approaching overthrow of a decaying house, or in a sudden storm the fearful flood, and betimes betakes himself to a place of safety ; the simple, on the contrary, go blindly forward into the threatening danger, and must bear the punishment of their carelessness. The *fut. consec.* 3*a* denotes the hiding of oneself as that which immediately follows from the being observant ; the two *perf.* 3*b*, on the other hand, with or without וְ, denote the going forward and meeting with punishment as occurring contemporaneously (cf. Ps. xlviii. 6, and regarding these diverse forms of construction, at Hab. iii. 10). " The interchange of the sing. and plur. gives us to understand that several or many simple ones are found for one prudent man " (Hitzig). The *Niph.* of עָנַשׁ signifies properly to be punished by pecuniary fine (Ex. xxi. 22) (cf. the post-bibl. קְנָס, קְנַס, to threaten punishment, which appears to have arisen from *censere*, to estimate, to lay on taxes) ; here it has the general meaning of being punished, viz. of the self-punishment of want of foresight.

Ver. 4 The reward of humility is the fear of Jahve,
Is riches, and honour, and life.

As עֲנָוָה־צֶדֶק, Ps. xlv. 5, is understood of the two virtues, meekness and righteousness, so here the three Göttingen divines
(Ewald, Bertheau, and Elster), as also Dunasch, see in עֲנָוָה יִרְאַת ה׳
an asyndeton; the poet would then have omitted *vav*, because
instead of the copulative connection he preferred the appositional (Schultens : *præmium mansuetudinis quæ est reverentia
Jehovæ*) or the permutative (the reward of humility; more
accurately expressed : the fear of God). It is in favour of this
interpretation that the verse following (ver. 5) also shows an
asyndeton. Luther otherwise : where one abides in the fear of
the Lord ; and Oetinger : the reward of humility, endurance,
calmness in the fear of the Lord, is . . .; Fleischer also interprets
יִרְאַת ה׳ as xxi. 4, חטאת (*lucerna impiorum vitiosa*), as the accus. of
the nearer definition. But then is the nearest-lying construction : the reward of humility is the fear of God, as all old
interpreters understand 4*a* (*e.g.* Symmachus, ὕστερον πραΰτητος
φόβος κυρίου), a thought so incomprehensible, that one must
adopt one or other of these expedients ? On the one side, we
may indeed say that the fear of God brings humility with it ;
but, on the other hand, it is just as comfortable to experience
that the fear of God is a consequence of humility ; for actually
to subordinate oneself to God, and to give honour to Him alone,
one must have broken his self-will, and come to the knowledge
of himself in his dependence, nothingness, and sin ; and one
consequence by which humility is rewarded, may be called the
fear of God, because it is the root of all wisdom, or as is here
said (cf. iii. 16, viii. 18), because riches, and honour, and life
are in its train. Thus 4*a* is a concluded sentence, which in
4*b* is so continued, that from 4*a* the predicate is to be continued : the reward of humility is the fear of God ; it is at the
same time riches . . . Hitzig conjectures רְאוּת ה׳, the beholding
Jahve ; but the *visio Dei* (*beatifica*) is not a dogmatic idea thus
expressed in the O. T. עֵקֶב denotes what follows a thing, from
עָקַב, to tread on the heels (Fleischer) ; for עָקֵב (Arab. *'akib*) is
the heels, as the incurvation of the foot ; and עֵקֶב, the consequence (cf. Arab. *'akb, 'ukb, posteritas*), is mediated through the
v. *denom.* עָקַב, to tread on the heels, to follow on the heels (cf.

denominatives, such as Arab. *batn, zahr, 'ân,* עַיִן, to strike the body, the back, the eye).

> Ver. 5 Thorns, snares, are on the way of the crooked;
> He that guardeth his soul, let him keep far from them.

Rightly the *Venet.* ἄκανθαι παγίδες ἐν ὁδῷ στρεβλοῦ. The meaning of צִנִּים (plur. of צֵן, or צִנָּה, the same as צְנִינִים) and פַּחִים (from פַּח, Arab. *fah*), stands fast, though it be not etymologically verified; the placing together of these two words (the LXX. obliterating the asyndeton: τρίβολος καὶ παγίδες) follows the scheme שְׁמֵשׁ יָרֵחַ, Hab. iii. 11. The עִקֵּשׁ־לֵב (perverse of heart, crooked, xvii. 20, xi. 20) drives his crooked winding way, corresponding to his habit of mind, which is the contrast and the perversion of that which is just, a way in which there are thorns which entangle and wound those who enter thereon, snares which unexpectedly bring them down and hold them fast as prisoners; the hedge of thorns, xv. 19, was a figure of the hindrances in the way of the wicked themselves. The thorn and snares here are a figure of the hindrances and dangers which go forth from the deceitful and the false in the way of others, of those who keep their souls, *i.e.* who outwardly and morally take heed to their life (xvi. 17, xiii. 3, pred. here subj.), who will keep, or are disposed to keep, themselves from these thorns, these snares into which the deceitful and perverse-hearted seek to entice them.

> Ver. 6 Give to the child instruction conformably to His way;
> So he will not, when he becomes old, depart from it.

The first instruction is meant which, communicated to the child, should be עַל־פִּי, after the measure (Gen. xliii. 7 = postbibl. לְפִי and כְּפִי) of his way, *i.e.* not: of his calling, which he must by and by enter upon (Bertheau, Zöckler), which דַּרְכּוֹ of itself cannot mean; also not: of the way which he must keep in during life (*Kidduschin* 30a); nor: of his individual nature (Elster); but: of the nature of the child as such, for דֶּרֶךְ נַעַר is the child's way, as *e.g. derek col-haarets,* Gen. xix. 31, the general custom of the land; *derek Mitsrâyim,* Isa. x. 24, the way (the manner of acting) of the Egyptians. The instruction of youth, the education of youth, ought to be conformed to the nature of youth; the matter of instruction, the manner of instruction, ought to regulate itself according to the stage of

life, and its peculiarities; the method ought to be arranged
according to the degree of development which the mental and
bodily life of the youth has arrived at. The verb חֲנֹךְ is a de-
nominative like עָקַב, ver. 4; it signifies to affect the taste, חֵךְ
(= חִנֵּךְ), in the Arab. to put date syrup into the mouth of the
suckling; so that we may compare with it the saying of Horace,
[Ep. i. 2, 69]: *Quo semel est imbuta recens servabit odorem
Testa diu.* In the post-bibl. Heb. חִנּוּךְ denotes that which in
the language of the Church is called *catechizatio;* ספר (לנער)
חנוך is the usual title of the catechisms. It is the fundamental
and first requisite of all educational instruction which the proverb formulates, a suitable motto for the lesson-books of peda-
gogues and catechists. מִפֶּנָּה [from it] refers to that training of
youth, in conformity with his nature, which becomes a second
nature, that which is imprinted, inbred, becomes accustomed.
Ver. 6 is wanting in the LXX.; where it exists in MSS. of
the LXX., it is supplied from Theodotion; the Complut. translates independently from the Heb. text.

Ver. 7 A rich man will rule over the poor,
And the borrower is subject to the man who lends.

" This is the course of the world. As regards the sing. and plur.
in 7a, there are many poor for one rich; and in the Orient the
rule is generally in the hands of one" (Hitzig). The fut.
denotes how it will and must happen, and the substantival
clause 7b, which as such is an expression of continuance (Arab.
thabât, i.e. of the remaining and continuing), denotes that contracting of debt brings naturally with it a slavish relation of
dependence. לֹוֶה, properly he who binds himself to one *se ei
obligat,* and מַלְוֶה, as xix. 17 (*vid. l.c.*), *qui alterum (mutui datione)
obligat,* from לָוָה, Arab. *lwy,* to wind, turn, twist round (*cog.* root
laff), whence with Fleischer is also to be derived the Aram. לְוָת,
"into connection;" so אֶל, properly "pushing against," refers
to the radically related אָלָה (= ולה), *contiguum esse.* אִישׁ מַלְוֶה is
one who puts himself in the way of lending, although not
directly in a professional manner. The pred. precedes its subject according to rule. Luther rightly translates: and he who
borrows is the lender's servant, whence the pun on the proper
names: " Borghart [= the borrower] is Lehnhart's [= lender's]
servant."

The group now following extends to the end of this first
collection of Solomon's proverbs; it closes also with a proverb
of the poor and the rich.

> Ver. 8 He that soweth iniquity shall reap calamity;
> And the rod of his fury shall vanish away.

"Whatsoever a man soweth, that shall he also reap " (Gal. vi.
7); he that soweth good reapeth good, xi. 18; he that soweth
evil reapeth evil, Job iv. 8; cf. Hos. x. 12 f. עַוְלָה is the direct
contrast of צְדָקָה or יֹשֶׁר (e.g. Ps. cxxv. 3, cvii. 42), proceeding
from the idea that the good is right, i.e. straight, rectum; the
evil, that which departs from the straight line, and is crooked.
Regarding אָוֶן, which means both perversity of mind and conduct,
as well as destiny, calamity, vid. xii. 21. That which the poet
particularly means by עַוְלָה is shown in 8b, viz. unsympathizing
tyranny, cruel misconduct toward a neighbour. שֵׁבֶט עֶבְרָתוֹ is
the rod which he who soweth iniquity makes another to feel in
his anger. The saying, that an end will be to this rod of his
fury, agrees with that which is said of the despot's sceptre, Isa.
xiv. 5 f.; Ps. cxxv. 3. Rightly Fleischer: *baculus insolentiae
ejus consumetur h. e. facultas qua pollet alios insolenter tractandi
evanescet.* Hitzig's objection, that a rod does not vanish away,
but is broken, is answered by this, that the rod is thought of as
brandished; besides, one uses כָּלָה of anything which has an end,
e.g. Isa. xvi. 4. Other interpreters understand " the rod of his
fury" of the rod of God's anger, which will strike the עַוָּל and
יִכְלֶה, as at Ezek. v. 13; Dan. xii. 7: " and the rod of His punishment will surely come" (Ewald, and similarly Schultens,
Euchel, Umbreit). This thought also hovers before the LXX.:
πληγὴν δὲ ἔργων αὐτοῦ (עֲבֹדָתוֹ) συντελέσει (וִיכַלֶּה). But if the rod
of punishment which is appointed for the unrighteous be meant,
then we would have expected וְכִלָּה. Taken in the future, the כְּלוֹת
of the שֵׁבֶט is not its *confectio* in the sense of completion, but its
termination or annihilation; and besides, it lies nearer after 8a
to take the suffix of עֶבְרָתוֹ subjectively (Isa. xiv. 6, xvi. 6)
than objectively. The LXX. has, after ver. 8, a distich:—

> ἄνδρα ἱλαρὸν καὶ δότην εὐλογεῖ ὁ θεός,
> ματαιότητα δὲ ἔργων αὐτοῦ συντελέσει.

The first line (2 Cor. ix. 7) is a variant translation of 9a (cf.
xxi. 17), the second (וְשֹׁא עֲבֹדָתוֹ) is a similar rendering of 8b.

Ver. 9 He who is friendly is blessed ;
  Because he giveth of his bread to the poor.

The thought is the same as at xi. 25. עַיִן טוֹב (thus to be written without *Makkeph*, with *Munach* of the first word, with correct Codd., also 1294 and *Jaman*), the contrast of עַיִן רַע, xxiii. 6, xxii. 22, *i.e.* the envious, evil-eyed, ungracious (post-bibl. also צַר עַיִן), is one who looks kindly, is good-hearted, and as ἱλαρὸς δότης, shows himself benevolent. Such gentleness and kindness is called in the Mishna עַיִן טוֹבָה (*Aboth* ii. 13), or עַיִן יָפֶה. Such a friend is blessed, for he has also himself scattered blessings (cf. גַּם־הוּא, xi. 25, xxi. 13); he has, as is said, looking back from the blessing that has happened to him, given of his bread (Luther, as the LXX., with partitive genitive: *seines brots* [= of his bread]) to the poor; cf. the unfolding of this blessing of self-denying love, Isa. viii. The LXX. has also here another distich :

  Νίκην καὶ τιμὴν περιποιεῖται ὁ δῶρα δούς,
  Τὴν μέντοι ψυχὴν ἀφαιρεῖται τῶν κεκτημένων.

The first line appears a variant translation of xix. 6b, and the second of i. 19b, according to which selfishness, in contrast to liberality, is the subject to be thought of. Ewald translates the second line :

  And he (who distributes gifts) conquers the soul of the recipients.

But κεκτημένος = בַּעַל (בְּעָלִים) signifies the possessor, not the recipient of anything as a gift, who cannot also be here meant because of the μέντοι.

Ver. 10 Chase away the scorner, and contention goeth out,
  And strife and reproach rest.

If in a company, a circle of friends, a society (LXX. ἔκβαλε ἐκ συνεδρίου), a wicked man is found who (*vid.* the definition of לֵץ, xxi. 24) treats religious questions without respect, moral questions in a frivolous way, serious things jestingly, and in his scornful spirit, his passion for witticism, his love of anecdote, places himself above the duty of showing reverence, veneration, and respect, there will arise ceaseless contentions and conflicts. Such a man one ought to chase away; then there will immediately go forth along with him dispeace (מָדוֹן), there will then be rest from strife and disgrace, viz. of the strife which such a one draws forth, and the disgrace which it brings on the

society, and continually prepares for it. קָלוֹן is commonly
understood of the injury, abuse, which others have to suffer
from the scoffer, or also (thus Fleischer, Hitzig) of the *opprobria*
of the contentious against one another.   But קָלוֹן is not so used ;
it means always disgrace, as something that happens, an experience, *vid.* at xviii. 3.   The praise of one who is the direct contrast of a לֵץ is celebrated in the next verse.

Ver. 11 He that loveth heart-purity,
Whose is grace of lips, the king is his friend.

Thus with Hitzig, it is to be translated not: he who loveth
with a pure heart,—we may interpret טְהוֹר־לֵב syntactically in
the sense of *puritate cordis* or *purus corde* (Ralbag, Ewald,
after xx. 7), for that which follows אהב and is its supplement has to stand where possible as the accus. of the object;
thus not: *qui amat puritatem cordis, gratiosa erunt labia ejus*
(de Dieu, Geier, Schultens, C. B. Michaelis, Fleischer), for
between heart-purity and graciousness of speech there exists a
moral relation, but yet no necessary connection of sequence;
also not: he who loves purity of heart, and grace on his lips
(Aben Ezra, Schelling, Bertheau), for " to love the grace of
one's own lips" is an awkward expression, which sounds more
like reprehensible self-complacency than a praiseworthy endeavour after gracious speech.   Excellently Luther :

" He who has a true heart and amiable speech,
The king is his friend."

טְהוֹר־לֵב is not adjectival, but substantival ; טְהָר־ is thus not the
constr. of the mas. טָהוֹר, as Job xvii. 10, but of the segolate
טֹהַר, or (since the ground-form of גֻּבַהּ, 1 Sam. xvi. 7, may be
גָּבַהּ as well as גֹּבַהּ) of the neut. טָהוֹר, like קֹדֶשׁ, Ps. xlvi. 5, lxv.
5: that which is pure, the being pure = purity (Schultens).
חֵן שְׂפָתָיו (gracefulness of his lips) is the second subject with the
force of a relative clause, although not exactly thus thought of,
but: one loving heart-purity, gracefulness on his lips—the
king is his friend.   Ewald otherwise : " he will be the king's
friend," after the scheme xiii. 4 ; but here unnecessarily refined.
A counsellor and associate who is governed by a pure intention,
and connects therewith a gentle and amiable manner of speech
and conversation, attaches the king to himself ; the king is the
רֵעֵהוּ (רֵעַ), the friend of such an one, and he also is " the friend

of the king," 1 Kings iv. 5. It is a Solomonic proverb, the same in idea as xvi. 13. The LXX., Syr., and Targ. introduce after אהב the name of God; but 11b does not syntactically admit of this addition. But it is worth while to take notice of an interpretation which is proposed by Jewish interpreters: the friend of such an one is a king, *i.e.* he can royally rejoice in him and boast of him. The thought is beautiful; but, as the comparison of other proverbs speaking of the king shows, is not intended.

> Ver. 12 The eyes of Jahve preserve knowledge;
> So He frustrateth the words of the false.

The phrase " to preserve knowledge " is found at v. 2; there, in the sense of to keep, retain ; here, of protecting, guarding; for it cannot possibly be said that the eyes of God keep themselves by the rule of knowledge, and thus preserve knowledge; this predicate is not in accord with the eyes, and is, as used of God, even inappropriate. On the other hand, after " to preserve," in the sense of watching, guarding a concrete object is to be expected, cf. Isa. xxvi. 3. We need not thus with Ewald supply יוֹדֵעַ; the ancients are right that דַעַת, knowledge, stands metonymically for אִישׁ (Meîri), or אנשי (Aben Ezra), or יודעי דעת (Arama); Schultens rightly: *Cognitio veritatis ac virtutis practica fertur ad homines eam colentes ac præstantes.* Where knowledge of the true and the good exists, there does it stand under the protection of God. 12b shows how that is meant, for there the perf. is continued in the second *consec. modus* (*fut. consec.*): there is thus protection against the assaults of enemies who oppose the knowledge which they hate, and seek to triumph over it, and to suppress it by their crooked policy. But God stands on the side of knowledge and protects it, and consequently makes vain the words (the outspoken resolutions) of the deceitful. Regarding סָלַף (סֶלֶף), *vid.* xi. 3 and xix. 3. The meaning of כִּלֵּף דִּבְרֵי is here essentially different from that in Ex. xxiii. 8, Deut. xvi. 19: he perverteth their words, for he giveth them a bearing that is false, *i.e.* not leading to the end. Hitzig reads רעות [wickedness] for דעת, which Zöckler is inclined to favour : God keeps the evil which is done in His eyes, and hinders its success; but "to observe wickedness" is an ambiguous, untenable expression; the only passage that can be quoted in favour of this " to observe " is Job vii. 20. The word רַעַת, handed down without variation, is much rather justified.

> Ver. 13 The sluggard saith, " A lion is without,
> I shall be slain in the midst of the streets."

Otherwise rendered, xxvi. 13. There, as here, the perf. אָמַר has the meaning of an abstract present, Gesen. § 126. 3. The activity of the industrious has its nearest sphere at home; but here a work is supposed which requires him to go forth (Ps. civ. 3) into the field (Prov. xxiv. 27). Therefore חוּץ stands first, a word of wide signification, which here denotes the open country outside the city, where the sluggard fears to meet a lion, as in the streets, *i.e.* the rows of houses forming them, to meet a רֹצֵחַ (מְרַצֵּחַ), *i.e.* a murder from motives of robbery or revenge. This strong word, properly to destroy, crush, Arab. *radkh*, is intentionally chosen: there is designed to be set forth the ridiculous hyperbolical pretence which the sluggard seeks for his slothfulness (Fleischer). Luther right well: "I might be murdered on the streets." But there is intentionally the absence of אוּלַי [perhaps] and of פֶּן [lest]. Meîri here quotes a passage of the moralists: ממופתי העצל הנבואה (prophesying) belongs to the evidences of the sluggard; and Euchel, the proverb העצלים מתנבאים (the sluggard's prophecy), *i.e.* the sluggard acts like a prophet, that he may palliate his slothfulness.

> Ver. 14 A deep pit is the mouth of a strange woman;
> He that is cursed of God falleth therein.

The first line appears in a different form as a synonymous distich, xxiii. 27. The LXX. translate στόμα παρανόμου without certainly indicating which word they here read, whether רָע (iv. 14), or רִשע (xxix. 12), or נלוז (iii. 32). xxiii. 27 is adduced in support of זָרוֹת (*vid.* ii. 16); זנות (harlots) are meant, and it is not necessary thus to read with Ewald. The mouth of this strange woman or depraved Israelitess is a deep ditch (שׁוּחָה עֲמֻקָּה, otherwise עֲמֻקָּה, as xxiii. 27a, where also occurs עֲמוּקָה [1]), namely, a snare-pit into which he is enticed by her wanton words; the man who stands in fellowship with God is

---

[1] The text to Immanuel's *Comment.* (Naples 1487) has in both instances עֲמוּקָה.

armed against this syren voice; but the זֵעוּם ה', *i.e.* he who is an object of the divine זָעַם (*Venet.* κεχολωμένος τῷ ὀντωτῇ), indignation, punishing evil with evil, falls into the pit, yielding to the seduction and the ruin. Schultens explains זעום ה' by, *is in quem despumat indignabundus;* but the meaning *despumat* is not substantiated; זַעַם, cf. Arab. *zaghm,* is probably a word which by its sound denoted anger as a hollow roaring, and like pealing thunder. The LXX. has, after ver. 14, three tedious moralizing lines.

Ver. 15 Folly is bound to the heart of a child;
The rod of correction driveth it forth.

Folly, *i.e.* pleasure in stupid tricks, silly sport, and foolish behaviour, is the portion of children as such; their heart is as yet childish, and folly is bound up in it. Education first driveth forth this childish, foolish nature (for, as Menander says:

ʹΟ μὴ δαρεὶς ἄνθρωπος οὐ παιδεύεται),

and it effects this when it is unindulgently severe: the שֵׁבֶט מוּסָר (*vid.* xxiii. 13) removeth אִוֶּלֶת from the heart, for it imparts intelligence and makes wise (xxix. 15). The LXX. is right in rendering 16*a*: ἄνοια ἐξῆπται (from ἐξάπτειν) καρδίας νέου; but the Syr. has " here mangled the LXX., and in haste has read ἀνοία ἐξίπταται: folly makes the understanding of the child fly away" (Lagarde).

Ver. 16 Whosoever oppresseth the lowly, it is gain to him;
Whosoever giveth to the rich, it is only loss.

It is before all clear that לְהַרְבּוֹת and לְמַחְסוֹר, as at xxi. 5, לְמוֹתַר and למחסור, are contrasted words, and form the conclusions to the participles used, with the force of hypothetical antecedents. Jerome recognises this: *qui calumniatur pauperem, ut augeat divitias suas, dabit ipse ditiori et egebit.* So Rashi, who by עָשִׁיר thinks on heathen potentates. Proportionally better Euchel, referring עֹשֵׁק and נֹתֵן, not to one person, but to two classes of men: he who oppresses the poor to enrich himself, and is liberal toward the rich, falls under want. The antithetic distich thus becomes an integral one,—the antithesis manifestly intended is not brought out. This may be said also against Bertheau, who too ingeniously explains: He who oppresses the poor to enrich himself gives to a rich man, *i.e.* to himself, the enriched, only to want, *i.e.* only to lose again that which he gained unrighteously.   Ralbag is on the right track, for he suggests the explanation : he who oppresses the poor, does it to his gain, for he thereby impels him to a more energetic exercise of his strength; he who gives to the rich man does it to his own loss, because the rich man does not thank him for it, and still continues to look down on him.   But if one refers לֹו to the poor, then it lies nearer to interpret אַךְ לְמַחְסוֹר of the rich : he who gives presents to the rich only thereby promotes his sleepy indolence, and so much the more robs him of activity (Elster); for that which one gives to him is only swallowed up in the whirlpool of his extravagance (Zöckler).   Thus Hitzig also explains, who remarks, under 17*a* : " Oppression produces reaction, awakens energy, and thus God on the whole overrules events " (Ex. i. 12).   Similarly also Ewald, who thinks on a mercenary, unrighteous rich man : God finally lifts up the oppressed poor man ; the rich man always becoming richer, on the contrary, is " punished for all his wickedness only more and more."   But with all these explanations there is too much read between the lines.   Since אַךְ לְמַחְסוֹר (xi. 24, xxi. 5) refers back to the subject : himself to mere loss, so also will it be here; and the LXX., Symmachus, Jerome (cf. also the Syr. *auget malum suum*) are right when they also refer לֹו, not to the poor man, but to the oppressor of the poor.   We explain : he who extorts from the poor enriches himself thereby ; but he who gives to the rich has nothing, and less than nothing, thereby—he robs himself, has no thanks, only brings himself by many gifts lower and lower down.   In the first case at least, 17*a*, the result corresponds to the intention; but in this latter case, 17*b*, one gains only bitter disappointment.

FIRST APPENDIX TO THE FIRST COLLECTION OF SOLOMONIC PROVERBS.—XXII. 17–XXIV. 22.

The last group of distiches, beginning with x. 1, closed at xxii. 16 with a proverb of the poor and the rich, as that before the last, *vid.* at xxii. 7. In xxii. 17 ff., the law of the distich form is interrupted, and the tone of the introductory Mashals is again perceptible. Here begins an appendix to the older Book of Proverbs, introduced by these Mashals. *Vid.* regarding the style and proverbial form of this introduction, at pages 4 and 16 of vol. i.

xxii. 17-21, forming the introduction to this appendix, are these Words of the Wise:

Ver. 17 Incline thine ear and hear the words of the wise,
And direct thine heart to my knowledge!
18 For it is pleasant if thou keep them in thine heart;
Let them abide together on thy lips.
19 That thy trust may be placed in Jahve,
I have taught thee to-day, even thee!
20 Have not I written unto thee choice proverbs,
Containing counsels and knowledge,
21 To make thee to know the rule of the words of truth,
That thou mightest bring back words which are truth to them
that send thee?

From x. 1 to xxii. 16 are the "Proverbs of Solomon," and not "The Words of the Wise;" thus the above παραίνεσις is not an epilogue, but a prologue to the following proverbs. The perfects הוֹדַעְתִּיךָ and כָתַבְתִּי refer, not to the Solomonic proverbial discourses, but to the appendix following them; the preface commends the worth and intention of this appendix, and uses perfects because it was written after the forming of the collection. The author of this preface (*vid.* pp. 23, 36, vol. i.) is no other than the author of i.–ix. The הַט (with *Mehuppach*, after *Thorath Emeth*, p. 27) reminds us of iv. 20, v. 1. The phrase שִׁית לֵב, *animum advertere*, occurs again in the second appendix, xxiv. 32. נָעִים is repeated at xxiii. 8, xxiv. 4; but נָעֵם with נֹעַם is common in the preface, i.–ix. כִּי־נָעִים contains, as at Ps. cxxxv. 3, cxlvii. 1, its subject in itself. כִּי־תִשְׁמְרֵם is not this subject: this that thou preservest them, which would have required rather the infin. שָׁמְרָם (Ps. cxxxiii. 1) or לְשָׁמְרֵם; but it supposes the case in which appears that which is amiable and praiseworthy : if thou preservest them in thy heart, *i.e.* makest them thoughtfully become thy mental possession. The suffix ם— refers to the Words of the Wise, and mediately also to לְדַעְתִּי, for the author designates his practical wisdom דַעְתִּי, which is laid down in the following proverbs, which, although not composed by him, are yet penetrated by his subjectivity. Regarding בֶּטֶן, which, from meaning the inner parts of the body, is transferred to the inner parts of the mind, *vid.* under xx. 27. The clause 18*b*, if not dependent on כי, would begin with וְיִכֹּנוּ. The absence of the copula and the antecedence of the verb bring the optative rendering nearer. Different is the syntactical relation of v. 2, where the infin. is continued in the fin. The *fut. Niph.* יִכֹּנוּ, which, iv. 27, meant to be rightly placed, rightly directed, here means : to stand erect, to have continuance, *stabilem esse.* In ver. 19, the fact of instruction precedes the statement of its object, which is, that the disciple may place his confidence in Jahve, for he does that which is according to His will, and is subject to His rule. מִבְטַחֶךָ, in Codd. and correct editions with *Pathach* (*vid. Michlol* 184*b*) ; the ה is as virtually doubled ; *vid.* under xxi. 22. In 19*b* the accentuation הוֹדַעְתִּיךָ הַיּוֹם is contrary to the syntax ; Codd. and old editions have rightly הוֹדַעְתִּיךָ הַיּוֹם, for אַף־אַתָּה is, after Gesen. § 121. 3, an emphatic repetition of the " thee ;" אַף, like גַּם, xxiii. 15 ; 1 Kings xxi. 19. Hitzig knows of no contrast which justifies the emphasis. But the prominence thus effected is not always of the nature of contrast (cf. Zech. vii. 5, have ye truly fasted to me, *i.e.* to serve me thereby), here it is strong individualizing ; the *te etiam te* is equivalent to, thee as others, and thee in particular. Also that, as Hitzig remarks, there does not appear any reason for the emphasizing of " to-day," is incorrect : הַיּוֹם is of the same signification as at Ps. xcv. 7 ; the reader of the following proverbs shall remember later, not merely in general, that he once on a time read them, but that he to-day, that he on this definite day, received the lessons of wisdom contained therein, and then, from that time forth, became responsible for his obedience or his disobedience.

In 20*a* the *Chethîb* שלשום denotes no definite date ; besides, this word occurs only always along with תְּמוֹל (אֶתְמוֹל). Umbreit, Ewald, Bertheau, however, accept this "formerly (lately)," and suppose that the author here refers to a "Book for Youths," composed at an earlier period, without one seeing what this reference, which had a meaning only for his contemporaries, here denotes. The LXX. reads כָּתְבָּה, and finds in 20a, contrary to the syntax and the *usus loq.*, the exhortation that he who is addressed ought to write these good doctrines thrice (τρισσῶς) on the tablet of his heart; the Syr. and Targ. suppose the author to say that he wrote them three times; Jerome, that he wrote them threefold—both without any visible meaning, since threefold cannot be equivalent to *manchfeltiglich* (Luther) [= several times, in various ways]. Also the *Keri* שָׁלִישִׁים, which without doubt is the authentic word, is interpreted in many unacceptable ways; Rashi and Elia Wilna, following a Midrash explanation, think on the lessons of the Law, the Prophets, and the Hagiographa; Arama, on those which are referable to three classes of youth; Malbim (as if here the author of the whole Book of Proverbs, from i. to xxxi., spake), on the supposed three chief parts of the *Mishle;* Dächsel better, on i.–ix., as the product of the same author as this appendix. Schultens compares Eccles. iv. 12, and translates *triplici filo nexa.* Kimchi, Meîri, and others, are right, who gloss שלישים by דברים נכבדים, and compare נגידים, viii. 6; accordingly the *Veneta,* with the happy *quid pro quo,* by τρισμέγιστα. The LXX. translates the military שָׁלִישׁ by τριστάτης; but this Greek word is itself obscure, and is explained by Hesychius (as well as by Suidas, and in the *Etymologicum*) by *Regii satellites qui ternas hastas manu tenebant,* which is certainly false. Another Greek, whom Angellius quotes, says, under Ex. xv. 4, that τριστάτης was the name given to the warriors who fought from a chariot, every three of whom had one war-chariot among them; and this appears, according to Ex. xiv. 7, xv. 4, to be really the primary meaning. In the period of David we meet with the word שלישים as the name of the heroes (the *Gibbôrim*) who stood nearest the king. The *shalish*-men form the *élite* troops that stood highest in rank, at whose head stood two triads of heroes, —Jashobeam at the head of the first trias, and thus of the *shalish*-men generally; Abishai at the head of the second trias,

who held an honourable place among the *shalish*-men, but yet
reached not to that first trias, 2 Sam. xxiii. 8 ff. (=1 Chron. xi.
11 ff.). The name הַשָּׁלִשִׁים (*Apoc.* 2 Sam. xxiii. 8, הִשָּׁלִשִׁי, and
ver. 13, 1 Chron. xxvii. 6, incorrectly הַשִּׁלְשִׁים) occurs here with
reference to the threefold division of this principal host; and
in regard to the use of the word in the time of Pharaoh, as
well as in the time of the kings, it may be granted that *shalish*
denoted the Three-man (*triumvir*), and then generally a high
military officer; so that שָׁלִשִׁים here has the same relation to
נְגִידִים, viii. 6, as *ducalia* to *principalia*. The name of the chief
men (members of the chief troop) is transferred to the chief
proverbs, as, Jas. ii. 8, that law which stands as a king at the
head of all the others is called the " royal law;" or, as Plato
names the chief powers of the soul, μέρη ἡγεμόνες. As in this
Platonic word-form, so *shalishim* here, like *negidim* there, is
understood neut., cf. under viii. 6, and רֵיקִים, xii. 11 ; יְשָׁרִים, xvi.
13. The ב of בְּמֹעֵצוֹת (occurring at i. 31 also) Fleischer rightly
explains as the ב of uniting or accompanying: chief proverbs
which contain good counsels and solid knowledge.

In the statement of the object in ver. 21, we interpret that
which follows לְהוֹדִיעֲךָ not permutat. : *ut te docerem recta, verba
vera* (Fleischer); but קֹשְׁטְ (ground-form to קֹשֶׁט, Ps. lx. 6) is the
bearer of the threefold idea : *rectitudinem*, or, better, *regulam
verborum veritatis*. The (Arab.) verb *kasiṭa* means to be straight,
stiff, inflexible (synon. צדק, to be hard, tight, proportionately
direct) ; and the name *kist* denotes not only the right conduct,
the right measure (*quantitas justa*), but also the balance, and
thus the rule or the norm. In 21*b*, אֲמָרִים אֱמֶת (as *e.g.* Zech. i.
13; *vid.* Philippi, *Status Constr.* p. 86 f.) is equivalent to אִמְרֵי
אֱמֶת; the author has this second time intentionally chosen the
appositional relation of connection : words which are truth ; the
idea of truth presents itself in this form of expression more
prominently. Impossible, because contrary to the *usus loq.*, is
the translation : *ut respondeas verba vera iis qui ad te mittunt*
(Schultens, Fleischer), because שׁלח, with the accus. following,
never means " to send any one." Without doubt הֵשִׁיב and
שׁלח stand in correlation to each other: he who lets himself be
instructed must be supposed to be in circumstances to bring
home, to those that sent him out to learn, doctrines which are

truth, and thus to approve himself. The subject spoken of
here is not a right answer or a true report brought back to one
giving a commission; and it lies beyond the purpose and power
of the following proverbs to afford a universal means whereby
persons sent out are made skilful. The שְׁלְחִים [senders] are here
the parents or guardians who send him who is to be instructed to
the school of the teacher of wisdom (Hitzig). Yet it appears
strange that he who is the learner is just here not addressed as
" my son," which would go to the support of the expression,
" to send to school," which is elsewhere unused in Old Hebrew,
and the שֹׁלְחֵי of another are elsewhere called those who make
him their *mandatar*, x. 26, xxv. 13; 2 Sam. xxiv. 13. The reference to the parents would also be excluded if, with Norzi
and other editors, לְשֹׁלְחֶךָ were to be read instead of לְשֹׁלְחֶיךָ (the
Venet. 1521, and most editions). Therefore the phrase לְשֹׁאֲלֶיךָ,
which is preferred by Ewald, recommends itself, according to
which the LXX. translates, τοῖς προβαλλομένοις σοι, which
the Syro-Hexap. renders [1] by להנון דאחדין לך אוחדתא, *i.e.* to those
who lay problems before thee (*vid.* Lagarde). The teacher of
wisdom seeks to qualify him who reads the following proverbs,
and permits himself to be influenced by them, to give the
right answer to those who question him and go to him for
counsel, and thus to become himself a teacher of wisdom.

After these ten lines of preliminary exhortation, there now
begins the collection of the " Words of the Wise" thus introduced. A tetrastich which, in its contents, connects itself with
the last proverb of the Solomonic collection, xxii. 16, forms the
commencement of this collection:

> Ver. 22 Rob not the lowly because he is lowly;
>   And oppress not the humble in the gate.
>   23 For Jahve will conduct their cause,
>   And rob their spoilers of life.

Though it may bring gain, as said xxii. 16a, to oppress the דָּל,
the lowly or humble, yet at last the oppressor comes to ruin.
The poet here warns against robbing the lowly because he

---

[1] The Syr. *n. fem.* awchda (אוּחְדָּא, Ps. xlix. 5, Targ.) is equivalent to
Heb. חִירָה, from (Syr.) achd, אֲחַר = אֲחַז, Neh. vii. 3, to shut up, properly,
to lay hold on and retain; the Arab. *akhdhat* means magic, incantation;
as seizing and making fast.

is lowly, and thus without power of defence, and not to be feared; and against doing injustice to the עָנִי, the bowed down, and therefore incapable of resisting in the gate, *i.e.* in the court of justice. These poor men have not indeed high human patrons, but One in heaven to undertake their cause: Jahve will conduct their cause (יָרִיב רִיבָם, as at xxiii. 10), *i.e.* will undertake their vindication, and be their avenger. דִּכָּא (דִּכָּה), Aram. and Arab. *dakk* (cf. דָּקַק, (Arab.) *dakk*), signifies to crush anything so that it becomes broad and flat, figuratively to oppress, synon. עָשַׁק (Fleischer). The verb קבע has, in Chald. and Syr., the signification to stick, to fix (according to which Aquila here translates καθηλοῦν, to nail; Jerome, *configere*); and as root-word to קָבַּעַת, the signification to be arched, like (Arab.) *kab'*, to be humpbacked; both significations are here unsuitable. The connection here requires the meaning to rob; and for Mal. iii. 8 also, this same meaning is to be adopted, robbery and taking from one by force (Parchon, Kimchi), not: to deceive (Köhler, Keil), although it might have the sense of robbing by withholding or refraining from doing that which is due, thus of a sacrilege committed by omission or deception. The Talm. does not know the verb קבע in this meaning; but it is variously found as a dialectic word for גזל.[1] Schultens' etymological explanation, *capitium injicere* (after (Arab.) *kab'*, to draw back and conceal the head), is not satisfactory. The construction, with the double accus., follows the analogy of הִכָּהוּ נֶפֶשׁ and the like, Gesen. § 139. 2. Regarding the sing. נפשׁ, even where several are spoken of, *vid.* under i. 19.

Another tetrastich follows:

[1] Thus *Rosch ha-schana* 26*b*: Levi came once to N.N. There a man came to meet him, and cried out קבען פלניא. Levi knew not what he would say, and went into the Madrash-house to ask. One answered him: He is a robber (גזלן) said that one to thee; for it is said in the Scriptures (Mal. iii. 8), "Will a man rob God?" etc. (*vid. Wissenschaft Kunst Judenthum*, p. 243). In the Midrash, שׁוחר טוב, to Ps. lvii., R. Levi says that אתה קיבע קבע is used in the sense of אתה גוזל לי. And in the Midrash *Tanchuma*, P. תרומה, R. Levi answers the question, "What is the meaning of קבע, Mal. iii. 8?"—It is an Arabic expression. An Arabian, when he wishes to say to another מה אתה גוזלני, says instead of it, מה אתה קובעני. Perhaps קבע is cogn. to קבץ; the R. קב coincides in several groups of languages (also the Turkish *kb*) with the Lat. *capere*.

Ver. 24 Have no intercourse with an angry man,
   And with a furious man go thou not;
25 Lest thou adopt his ways,
   And bring destruction upon thy soul.

The *Piel* רֵעָה, Judg. xiv. 20, signifies to make or choose any one
as a friend or companion (רֵעַ, רֵעָה); the *Hithpa.* הִתְרָעָה (cf. at
xviii. 24), to take to oneself (for oneself) any one as a friend,
or to converse with one; אַל־תִּתְרַע sounds like אַל־תִּשְׁתַּע, Isa. xli.
10, with *Pathach* of the closed syllable from the apocope. The
angry man is called בַּעַל אַף, as the covetous man בַּעַל נֶפֶשׁ, xxiii.
2, and the mischievous man בַּעַל מְזִמּוֹת, xxiv. 8; *vid.* regarding
בַּעַל at i. 19 and xviii. 9. אִישׁ חֵמוֹת is related superlat. to אִישׁ
חֵכָה, xv. 18 (cf. xxix. 22), and signifies a hot-head of the
highest degree. לֹא תָבוֹא is meant as warning (cf. xvi. 10b).
בּוֹא אֶת, or בּוֹא עִם, Ps. xxvi. 4, to come along with one, is equivalent to go into fellowship or companionship with one, which
is expressed by הָלַךְ אֶת, xiii. 20, as בּוֹא בְ means, Josh. xxiii. 7,
12, to enter into communion with one, *venire in consuetudinem.*
This בּוֹא אֶת is not a trace of a more recent period of the
language. Also תֶּאְלַף, *discas*, cannot be an equivalent for it:
Heb. poetry has at all times made use of Aramaisms as
elegancies. אֲלַף, Aram. יְלַף אֲלַף, Arab. *álifa*, signifies to be entrusted with anything = to learn (*Piel* אַלַף, to teach, Job xv. 15,
and in Elihu's speeches), or also to become confidential with
one (whence אַלּוּף, companion, confidant, ii. 17); this אָלַף is
never a Heb. prose word; the bibl. אַלּוּף is only used at a later
period in the sense of teacher. אָרְחוֹת are the ways, the conduct
(ii. 20, etc.), or manner of life (i. 19) which any one enters
upon and follows out, thus manners as well as lot, condition.
In the phrase " to bring destruction," לָקַח is used as in our
phrase *Schaden nehmen* [to suffer injury]; the ancient language
also represented the forced entrance of one into a state as a
being laid hold on, *e.g.* Job xviii. 20, cf. Isa. xiii. 8; here מוֹקֵשׁ
is not merely equivalent to danger (Ewald, falsely : that thou
takest not danger for thy soul), but is equivalent to destruction,
sin itself is a snare (xxix. 6); to bring a snare for oneself is
equivalent to suffer from being ensnared. Whosoever comes
into a near relation with a passionate, furious man, easily accommodates himself to his manners, and, hurried forward by

him and like him to outbreaks of anger, which does that which
is not right before God, falls into ruinous complications.
A third distich follows :

> Ver. 26 Be not among those who strike hands,
> Among those who become surety for loans.
> 27 If thou hast nothing to pay,
> Why shall he take away thy bed from under thee?

To strike hands is equivalent to, to be responsible to any one for
another, to stake one's goods and honour for him, vi. 1, xi. 15,
xvii. 18,—in a word, עֲרֹב, *seq. acc.*, to pledge oneself for him
(Gen. xliii. 9), or for the loan received by him, מַשָּׁאָה, Deut.
xxiv. 10 (from הִשָּׁה, with בְּ, of the person and accus. of the
thing: to lend something to one on interest).   The proverb
warns against being one of such sureties (write בַּעֲרֹבִים with
Cod. 1294, and old impressions such as the Venice, 1521),
against acting as they do; for why wouldest thou come to this,
that when thou canst not pay (שַׁלֵּם, to render a full equivalent
reckoning, and, generally, to pay, vi. 31),[1] he (the creditor)
take away thy bed from under thee?—for, as xx. 16 says, thus
improvident suretyships are wont to be punished.

A fourth proverb—a distich—beginning with the warning
אַל :

> Ver. 28 Remove not the perpetual landmark
> Which thy ancestors have set up.

28*a* = xxiii. 10*a*.   Regarding the inviolability of boundaries
established by the law, *vid.* at xv. 25.   גְּבוּל עוֹלָם denotes " the
boundary mark set up from ancient times, the removal of
which were a double transgression, because it is rendered sacred
by its antiquity " (*Orelli*, p. 76).   סוּג = נָסַג signifies to remove
back, *Hiph.* to shove back, to move away.   אֲשֶׁר has the meaning of (ὅριον) ὅ, τι, *quippe quod.*   Instead of עוֹלָם, the *Mishna*
reads, *Pea* v. 6, עוֹלִים, which in the Jerusalem Gemara one Rabbi
understands of those brought up out of Egypt, another of the

---

[1] After Ben-Asher, the pointing is אִם־אֵין־לְךָ ; while, on the contrary,
Ben-Naphtali prefers אִם־אֵין לְךָ ; *vid.* my *Genesis* (1869), pp. 74 (under i.
3) and 81.   So, without any bearing on the sense, Ben-Asher points לָמָּה
with *Tarcha*, Ben-Naphtali with *Mercha.*

poor; for "to rise " (in the world) is a euphemism (כבוד לשׁון) for " to come down " (be reduced in circumstances).[1]

After these four proverbs beginning with אל, a new series begins with the following tristich :

> Ver. 29 Seest thou a man who is expert in his calling—
> Before kings may he stand ;
> Not stand before obscure men ;

i.e., he can enter into the service of kings, and needs not to enter into the service of mean men = he is entitled to claim the highest official post. חָזִיתָ, in xxvi. 12 = xxix. 20, interchanging with רָאִיתָ, is *perf. hypotheticum* (cf. xxiv. 10, xxv. 16): *si videris ;* the conclusion which might begin with דַּע כִּי expresses further what he who sees will have occasion to observe. Rightly Luther: *Sihestu einen Man endelich* (*vid.* at xxi. 5) *in seinem geschefft*, u.s.w. [=seest thou a man expert in his business, etc.]. מָהִיר denotes in all the three chief dialects one who is skilful in a matter not merely by virtue of external artistic ability, but also by means of intellectual mastery of it. הִתְיַצֵּב לִפְנֵי, to enter on the situation of a servant before any one ; cf. Job i. 6, ii. 1. עָמַד לִפְנֵי, 1 Sam. xvi. 21, 1 Kings x. 8. Along with the pausal form יִתְיַצָּב, there is also found in Codd. the form יִתְיַצֵּב (the ground-form to יתיצב, whence that pausal form is lengthened), which Ben-Bileam defends, for he reckons this word among "the pathachized pausal forms." חֲשֻׁכִּים, in contrast to מְלָכִים, are the *obscuri = ignobiles.* The Targ. translate the Heb. דַּל and אֶבְיוֹן by חֲשִׁיךְ and חֲשׁוּךְ. Kimchi compares Jer. xxxix. 10, where הָעָם הַדַּלִּים is translated by חֲשִׁיבַיָּא (cf. 2 Kings xxiv. 14, xxv. 12). חֵלְכָה (חֶלְכָּה) is the old Heb. synonym in Ps. x. The poet seems here to transfer the Aram. *usus loq.* into the Heb.

Ver. 29, which speaks of a high position near the king, is appropriately followed by a hexastich referring to the slipperiness of the smooth ground of the king's court.

> xxiii. 1 When thou sittest to eat with a ruler,
> Consider well whom thou hast before thee.
> 2 And put thy knife to thy throat
> If thou art a man of good appetite.
> 3 Be not lustful after his dainties,
> Because it is deceitful food.

---

[1] As an analogical example, סַנְוֵי נְהוֹר, seeing clearly = blind.

The ל of לְלחֹום is that of end : *ad cibum capiendum*, thus as one invited by him to his table; in prose the expression would be לֶחֶם לֶאֱכֹל לֶחֶם; , to eat, is poet., iv. 17, ix. 5. The fut. תָּבִין clothes the admonition in the form of a wish or counsel ; the *infin. intens.* בִּין makes it urgent: consider well him whom thou hast before thee, viz. that he is not thine equal, but one higher, who can destroy thee as well as be useful to thee. With וְשַׂמְתָּ the jussive construction begun by חבין is continued. Zöckler and Dächsel, after Ewald and Hitzig, translate incorrectly: thou puttest . . ., the *perf. consec.* after an imperf., or, which is the same thing, a fut. meant optatively (*e.g.* Lev. xix. 18 with לֹא, and also ver. 34 without לֹא) continues the exhortation; to be thus understood, the author ought to have used the expression שַׂמְתָּ שַׂבִּין and not וְשַׂמְת שַׂבִין. Rightly Luther: "and put a knife to thy throat," but continuing: "wilt thou preserve thy life," herein caught in the same mistake of the idea with Jerome, the Syr., and Targ., to which נפֹש here separates itself. שַׂבִּין (סַבִּין) (Arab. with the assimilated *a sikkîn*, plur *sekâkîn*, whence *sekâkîni*, cutler) designates a knife (R. סַך שֵׁך, to stick, *vid.* at Isa. ix. 10). לֹעַ, from לוּעַ, to devour, is the throat; the word in Aram. signifies only the cheek, while Lagarde seeks to interpret בִּלְעֶה infinitively in the sense of (Arab.) *bwlw'ak*, if thou longest for (from *wl'a*); but that would make 2b a tautology. The verb לוּעַ (cf. Arab. *l'al'*, to pant for) shows for the substantive the same primary meaning as *glutus* from *glutire*, which was then transferred from the inner organ of swallowing (Kimchi, בֵּית הַבְּלִיעָה, Parchon : חַוֶּשֶׁט, *œsophagus*) to the external. "Put a knife to thy throat, is a proverbial expression, like our : the knife stands at his throat; the poet means to say : restrain thy too eager desire by means of the strongest threatening of danger—threaten as it were death to it" (Fleischer). In בַּעַל נֶפֶשׁ, נפֹש means, as at xiii. 2, desire, and that desire of eating, as at vi. 30. Rightly Rashi: if thou art greedy with hunger, if thou art a glutton; cf. Sir. xxxiv. (xxxi.) 12, "If thou sittest at a great table, then open not widely thy throat (φάρυγγα), and say not : There is certainly much on it !" The knife thus denotes the restraining and moderating of too good an appetite.

In 3a the punctuation fluctuates between תִּתְאָו (*Michlol*

131a) and תִּתְאָו ; the latter is found in Cod. 1294, the Erfurt
2 and 3, the Cod. *Jaman.*, and thus it is also to be written at
ver. 6 and xxiv. 1 ; וַיִּתְאָו, 1 Chron. xi. 17 and Ps. xlv. 12, Codd.
and older Edd. (*e.g.* Complut. 1517, Ven. 1515, 1521) write
with *Pathach.* מַטְעַמּוֹת, from טַעַם, signifies savoury dishes,
dainties, like (Arab.) *dhwâkt*, from *dhâk* (to taste, to relish) ; cf.
sapores, from *sapere*, in the proverb: the tit-bits of the king burn
the lips (*vid.* Fleischer, *Ali's Hundred Proverbs*, etc., pp. 71,
104). With וְהוּא begins, as at iii. 29, a conditioning clause: since
it is, indeed, the bread of deceit (the connection like עַד־כְּזָבִים, xxi.
28), food which, as it were, deceives him who eats it, *i.e.* appears to secure for him the lasting favour of princes, and often
enough herein deceives him ; cf. the proverb by Burckhardt
and Meidani : whoever eats of the sultan's soup burns his lips,
even though it may be after a length of time (Fleischer). One
must come near to a king, says Calovius, hitting the meaning
of the proverb, as to a fire : not too near, lest he be burned ;
nor too remote, so that he may be warmed therewith.

All the forms of proverbs run through these appended proverbs. There now follows a pentastich :

> Ver. 4 Do not trouble thyself to become rich ;
> Cease from such thine own wisdom.
> 5 Wilt thou let thine eyes fly after it, and it is gone?
> For it maketh itself, assuredly it maketh itself wings,
> Like an eagle which fleeth toward the heavens.

The middle state, according to xxx. 8, is the best: he who
troubleth himself (cf. xxviii. 20, hasteth) to become rich, placeth
before himself a false, deceitful aim. יָגַע is essentially one with
(Arab.) *waji'a*, to experience sorrow, *dolere*, and then signifies,
like πονεῖν and κάμνειν, to become or to be wearied, to weary or
trouble oneself, to toil and moil (Fleischer). The בִּינָה (cf. iii.
5) is just wisdom, prudence directed towards becoming rich;
for striving of itself alone does not accomplish it, unless wisdom
is connected with it, which is not very particular in finding out
means in their moral relations ; but is so much the more crafty,
and, as we say, speculative. Rightly Aquila, the *Venet.*, Jerome,
and Luther: take not pains to become rich. On the contrary,
the LXX. reads אַל תִּיגַע לְהַעֲשִׁיר, stretch not thyself (if thou art
poor) after a rich man ; and the Syr. and Targ. אַל תִּתַּע לְהַעֲשִׁיר,

draw not near to the rich man; but, apart from the uncertainty
of the expression and the construction in both cases, poetry, and
proverbial poetry too, does not prefer the article; it never uses
it without emphasis, especially as here must be the case with it
not elided. These translators thought that בּוֹ וגו׳, ver. 5, presupposed a subject expressed in ver. 4; but the subject is not הֶעָשִׁיר,
but the עֹשֶׁר [riches] contained in לְהַעֲשִׁיר. The self-intelligible
it [in " it maketh wings," etc.] is that about which trouble has
been taken, about which there has been speculation. That is a
deceitful possession; for what has been gained by many years
of labour and search, often passes away suddenly, is lost in a
moment. To let the eyes fly after anything, is equivalent to,
to direct a (flying) look toward it: wilt thou let thine eyes rove
toward the same, and it is gone? *i.e.*, wilt thou expose thyself to
the fate of seeing that which was gained with trouble and craft
torn suddenly away from thee? Otherwise Luther, after
Jerome: Let not thine eyes fly after that which thou canst
not have; but apart from the circumstance that בּוֹ וְאֵינֶנּוּ cannot
possibly be understood in the sense of *ad opes quas non potes
habere* (that would have required בַּאֲשֶׁר אֵינֶנּוּ), in this sense after
the analogy of (לְ) נָשָׂא נֶפֶשׁ אֶל, the end aimed at would have been
denoted by לֹ and not by בוּ. Better Immanuel, after Rashi : if
thou doublest, *i.e.* shuttest (by means of the two eyelids) thine
eyes upon it, it is gone, *i.e.* has vanished during the night; but
עוּף, *duplicare*, is Aram. and not Heb. Rather the explanation is
with Chajûg, after Isa. viii. 22 f.: if thou veilest (darkenest)
thine eyes, *i.e.* yieldest thyself over to carelessness; but the
noun עַפְעַפָּה shows that עוּף, spoken of the eyes, is intended to
signify to fly (to rove, flutter). Hitzig too artificially (altering
the expression to לְהַעֲשִׁיר) : if thou faintest, art weary with the
eyes toward him (the rich patron), he is gone,—which cannot
be adopted, because the form of a question does not accord
with it. Nor would it accord if וְאֵינֶנּוּ were thought of as a
conclusion: " dost thou let thy look fly toward it? It is gone ;"
for what can this question imply? The ו of וְאֵינֶנּוּ shows that
this word is a component part of the question; it is a question
lla nakar, i.e. in rejection of the subject of the question : wilt
thou cast thy look upon it, and it is gone? *i.e.*, wilt thou experience instant loss of that which is gained by labour and acquired

by artifice? On בּוֹ, cf. Job vii. 8. עֵינֶיךָ וגו', "thou directest
thine eyes to me: I am no more." We had in xii. 19 another
mode of designating [viz. till I wink again] an instant. The
Chethîb הֲתָעִיף וגו' is syntactically correct (cf. xv. 22, xx. 30),
and might remain. The *Kerî* is mostly falsely accentuated
הֲתָעִיף, doubly incorrectly; for (1) the tone never retreats from a
shut syllable terminating in *î, e.g.* לְהָכִין, Isa. xl. 20; בְּהָכִין,
1 Chron. i. 4; אָבִין, Job xxiii. 8; and (2) there is, moreover,
wanting here any legitimate occasion for the retrogression of

the tone; thus much rather the form הַתָּעִיף (with *Mehuppach*
of the last, and *Zinnorith* of the preceding open syllable) is to
be adopted, as it is given by Opitz, Jablonsky, Michaelis, and
Reineccius.

The subject of 5*b* is, as of 5*a*, riches. That riches take
wings and flee away, is a more natural expression than that the
rich patron flees away,—a quaint figure, appropriate however
at Nah. iii. 16, where the multitude of craftsmen flee out of
Nineveh like a swarm of locusts. עשׂה has frequently the sense
of *acquirere*, Gen. xii. 5, with לוֹ, *sibi acquirere*, 1 Sam.
xv. 1; 1 Kings i. 15; Hitzig compares *Silius Ital.* xvi. 351: *sed
tum sibi fecerat alas.* The *inf. intensivus* strengthens the assertion: it will certainly thus happen.

In 5*c* all unnecessary discussion regarding the *Chethîb* וְעִיף is
to be avoided, for this *Chethîb* does not exist; the *Masora* here
knows only of a simple *Chethîb* and *Kerî*, viz. וָעוּף (read יָעוּף),
not of a double one (וְעִיף), and the word is not among those
which have in the middle a ', which is to be read like ו. The
manuscripts (*e.g.* also the Bragadin. 1615) have וָעוּף, and the
Kerî יָעוּף; it is one of the ten words registered in the *Masora*, at
the beginning of which a ' is to be read instead of the written ו.
Most of the ancients translate with the amalgamation of the
Kerî and the *Chethîb*: and he (the rich man, or better: the
riches) flees heavenwards (Syr., Aquila, Symmachus, Theodotion, Jerome, and Luther). After the *Kerî* the *Venet.*
renders: ὡς ἀετὸς πτήσεται τοῖς οὐρανοῖς (viz. ὁ πλοῦτος).
Rightly the Targ.: like an eagle which flies to heaven (according to which also it is accentuated), only it is not to be translated "*am Himmel*" [to heaven], but "*gen Himmel*" [towards

heaven]: הַשָּׁמַיִם is the accusative of direction—the eagle flies
heavenward. Bochart, in the *Hierozoïcon*, has collected many
parallels to this comparison, among which is the figure in
Lucian's *Timon*, where Pluto, the god of wealth, comes to one
limping and with difficulty ; but going away, outstrips in speed
the flight of all birds.   The LXX. translates ὥσπερ ἀετοῦ καὶ
ὑποστρέφει εἰς τὸν οἶκον τοῦ προεστηκότος αὐτοῦ.   Hitzig
accordingly reads וְשָׁב לְבֵית מְשֻׁגְּבוֹ, and he (the rich patron)
withdraws from thee to his own steep residence.   But ought
not οἶκος τοῦ προεστηκότος αὐτοῦ to be heaven, as the residence
of Him who administers wealth, *i.e.* who gives and again takes
it away according to His free-will ?

There now follows a proverb with unequally measured lines,
perhaps a heptastich :

> Ver. 6 Eat not the bread of the jealous,
>   And let not thyself lust after his dainties ;
>   7 For as one who calculates with himself, so is he :
>   " Eat and drink," saith he to thee ;
>   But his heart is not with thee.
>   8 Thy morsel which thou hast enjoyed wilt thou cast up,
>   And hast lost thy pleasant words.

As טוֹב עַיִן, xxii. 9, *benignus oculo*, denotes the pleasantness and
joy of social friendship; so here (cf. Deut. xv. 9; Matt. xv. 15)
רַע עַיִן, *malignus oculo*, the envy and selfishness of egoism seeking to have and retain all for itself.   The LXX. ἀνδρὶ
βασκάνῳ, for the look of the evil eye, עַיִן רַע, עֵינָא בִישָׁא (*cattivo
occhio*), refers to enchantment; cf. βασκαίνειν, *fascinare*, to
bewitch, to enchant, in modern Greek, to envy, Arab. 'an, to
eye, as it were, whence *ma'jûn, ma'în*, hit by the piercing look
of the envious eye, *invidiæ*, as Apuleius says, *letali plaga percus-
sus* (Fleischer).   Regarding תִּקְאוּ with *Pathach, vid.* the parallel
line 3*a*. 7*a* is difficult. The LXX. and Syr. read שֵׂעָר [hair].
The Targ. renders תִּרְעָא רָמָא, and thus reads שַׂעַר [fool], and
thus brings together the soul of the envious person and a high
portal, which promises much, but conceals only deception behind
(Ralbag). Joseph ha-Nakdan reads [1] שֵׂעָר with *sîn ;* and Rashi,
retaining the *schîn*, compares the " sour figs," Jer. xxix. 17.

---

[1] In an appendix to *Ochla We-Ochla*, in the University Library at Halle,
he reads שֵׂעָר, but with פְלִיגָא [doubtful] added.

According to this, Luther translates : like a ghost (a monster of
lovelessness) is he inwardly; for, as it appears in שָׁעַר, the goat-
like spectre שָׂעִיר hovered before him. Schultens better, because
more in conformity with the text : *quemadmodum suam ipsius
animam abhorret (i.e.* as he does nothing to the benefit of his
own appetite) *sic ille (erga alios multo magis).* The thought is
appropriate, but forced. Hitzig for once here follows Ewald ;
he does not, however, translate : " like as if his soul were
divided, so is it ;" but: " as one who is divided in his soul, so is
he ;" but the verb שָׁעַר, to divide, is inferred from שַׁעַר, gate =
division, and is as foreign to the extra-bibl. *usus loq.* as it is to
the bibl. The verb שָׁעַר signifies to weigh or consider, to value,
to estimate. These meanings Hitzig unites together : *in similitudinem arioli et conjectoris æstimat quod ignorat,* perhaps
meaning thereby that he conjecturally supposes that as it is
with him, so it is with others : he dissembles, and thinks that
others dissemble also. Thus also Jansen explains. The
thought is far-fetched, and does not cover itself by the text.
The translation of the *Venet.* also : ὡς γὰρ ἐμέτρησεν ἐν ψυχῇ
οἱ οὕτως ἐστίν (perhaps : he measures to others as penuriously
as to himself), does not elucidate the text, but obscures it.
Most moderns (Bertheau, Zöckler, Dächsel, etc.) : as he reckons
in his soul, so is he (not as he seeks to appear for a moment
before thee). Thus also Fleischer : *quemadmodum reputat apud
se, ita est (sc. non ut loquitur),* with the remark that שָׁעַר (whence
שַׁעַר, measure, market value, Arab. *si'r),* to measure, to tax so
as to determine the price, to reckon ; and then like חָשַׁב, in
general, to think, and thus also Meîri with the neut. rendering
of *ita est.* But why this circumlocution in the expression?
The poet ought in that case just to have written כִּי לֹא כְמוֹ דִבֶּר
בִּשְׂפָתָיו כֵּן הוּא, for he is not as he speaks with his mouth. If one
read שֹׁעֵר (Symmachus, εἰκάζων), then we have the thought
adapted to the portrait that is drawn; for like one calculating by himself, so is he, *i.e.* he is like one who estimates
with himself the value of an object; for which we use the ex
pression : he reckons the value of every piece in thy mouth.
However, with this understanding the punctuation also of שֹׁעֵר
as finite may be retained and explained after Isa. xxvi. 18 : for
as if he reckoned in his soul, so is he ; but in this the perf. is

inappropriate; by the particip. one reaches the same end[1] by a smoother way. True, he says to thee: eat and drink (Song v. 1*b*), he invites thee with courtly words; but his heart is not with thee (בַּל, like xxiv. 23): he only puts on the appearance of joy if thou partakest abundantly, but there lurks behind the mask of liberal hospitality the grudging niggardly calculator, who poisons thy every bite, every draught, by his calculating, grudging look. Such a feast cannot possibly do good to the guest: thy meal (פַּת, from פָּתַת; cf. κλᾶν τὸν ἄρτον, Aram. פְּרַס לַחְמָא, to divide and distribute bread, whence פְּרֵנָס, to receive aliment, is derived) which thou hast eaten thou wilt spue out, *i.e.* wilt vomit from disgust that thou hast eaten such food, so that that which has been partaken of does thee no good. פִּתְּךָ is also derived from פָּתָה:[2] has he deceived thee (with his courtly words), but with this אָכַלְתָּ, which, as the *Makkeph* rightly denotes, stands in an attributive relation to פתך, does not agree. תְקִיאֶנָּה is *Hiph.* of קוֹא, as transitive: to make vomiting; in Arab. the fut. *Kal* of *ka* terminates in *î*. The fair words which the guest, as the *perf. consec.* expresses, has lavished, are the words of praise and thanks in which he recognises the liberality of the host appearing so hospitable. Regarding the penult. accenting of the *perf. consec.* by *Mugrasch*, as xxx. 9, *vid.* under Ps. xxvii. 1. Pinsker (*Babyl.-Hebr. Punktations-system*, p. 134) conjectures that the line 8*b* originally formed the concluding line of the following proverb. But at the time of the LXX. (which erroneously expresses וְשִׁחֵת) it certainly stood as in our text.

Ver. 9. Another case in which good words are lost:

> Speak not to the ears of a fool,
> For he will despise the wisdom of thy words.

---

[1] We may write כֵּן הוּא: the *Mehuppach* (*Jethîb*) sign of the *Olewejored* standing between the two words represents also the place of the *Makkeph*; *vid. Thorath Emeth*, p. 20.

[2] Immanuel makes so much of having recognised the verb in this פִּתְּךָ (and has he persuaded thee), that in the concluding part of his Divan (entitled *Machberoth Immanuel*), which is an imitation of Dante's *Divina Commedia*, he praises himself on this account in the paradise of King Solomon, who is enraptured by this explanation, and swears that he never meant that word otherwise.

To speak in the ears of any one, does not mean to whisper to him, but so to speak that it is distinctly perceived. כְּסִיל, as we have now often explained, is the intellectually heavy and dull, like *pinguis* and *tardus;* Arab. *balyd,* clumsy, intellectually immoveable (cf. *bld,* the place where one places himself firmly down, which one makes his point of gravity). The heart of such an one is covered over (Ps. cxix. 70), as with grease, against all impressions of better knowledge; he has for the knowledge which the words spoken design to impart to him, no susceptibility, no mind, but only contempt. The construction בּוּז לְ has been frequently met with from vi. 30.

The following proverb forms a new whole from component parts of xxii. 28 and xxii. 22 f. :

> Ver. 10 Remove not ancient landmarks ;
> And into the fields of orphans enter thou not.
> 11 For their Saviour is a mighty one ;
> He will conduct their cause against thee.

בּוֹא בְ separates itself here to the meaning of *injuste invadere et occupare;* French, *empiéter sur son voisin,* advance not into the ground belonging to thy neighbour (Fleischer). If orphans have also no *goel* among their kindred (Aquila, Symmachus, Theodotion, ἀγχιστεύς) to redeem by purchase (Lev. xxv. 25) their inheritance that has passed over into the possession of another, they have another, and that a mighty Saviour, *Re-demptor,* who will restore to them that which they have lost,—viz. God (Jer. l. 34),—who will adopt their cause against any one who has unjustly taken from them.

The following proverb warrants us to pause here, for it opens up, as a compendious echo of xxii. 17–21, a new series of proverbs of wisdom :

> Ver. 12 Apply thine heart to instruction,
> And thine ear to the utterances of knowledge.

We may, according as we accent in לַמּוּסָר the divine origin or the human medium, translate, *offer disciplinæ* (Schultens), or *adhibe ad disciplinam cor tuum* (Fleischer). This general ad-monition is directed to old and young, to those who are to be educated as well as to those who are educated. First to the educator :

Ver. 13 Withhold not correction from the child ;
   For thou will beat him with the rod, and he will not die.
  14 Thou beatest him with the rod,
   And with it deliverest his soul from hell.

The exhortation, 13a, presupposes that education by word and deed is a duty devolving on the father and the teacher with regard to the child. In 13b, כִּי is in any case the relative conjunction. The conclusion does not mean : so will he not fall under death (destruction), as Luther also would have it, after Deut. xix. 21, for this thought certainly follows ver. 14; nor after xix. 18 : so may the stroke not be one whereof he dies, for then the author ought to have written אַל־תְּמִיתֶנּוּ; but : he will not die of it, i.e. only strike if he has deserved it, thou needest not fear ; the bitter medicine will be beneficial to him, not deadly. The אַתָּה standing before the double clause, ver. 14, means that he who administers corporal chastisement to the child, saves him spiritually; for שְׁאוֹל does not refer to death in general, but to death falling upon a man before his time, and in his sins, vid. xv. 24, cf. viii. 26.

The following proverb passes from the educator to the pupil :

Ver. 15 My son, if thine heart becometh wise,
   My heart also in return will rejoice;
  16 And my reins will exult
   If thy lips speak right things.

Wisdom is inborn in no one. A true Arab. proverb says, " The wise knows how the fool feels, for he himself was also once a fool;"[1] and folly is bound up in the heart of a child, according to xxii. 15, which must be driven out by severe discipline. 15b, as many others, cf. xxii. 19b, shows that these " words of the wise " are penetrated by the subjectivity of an author; the author means : if thy heart becomes wise, so will mine in return, i.e. corresponding to it (cf. גַּם, Gen. xx. 6), rejoice. The thought of the heart in ver. 15 repeats itself in ver. 16, with reference to the utterance of the mouth. Regarding מֵישָׁרִים,

---

[1] The second part of the saying is, " But a fool knows not how a wise man feels, for he has never been a wise man." I heard this many years ago, from the mouth of the American missionary Schaufler, in Constantinople.

vid. i. 5. Regarding the "reins," כְּלָיוֹת (perhaps from כָּלָה, to languish, Job xix. 21), with which the tender and inmost affections are connected, *vid. Psychologie*, p. 268 f.

The poet now shows how one attains unto wisdom—the beginning of wisdom is the fear of God:

Ver. 17 Let not thine heart strive after sinners,
But after the fear of Jahve all the day.
18 Truly there is a future,
And thy hope shall not come to naught.

The LXX., Jerome, the *Venet.*, and Luther, and the Arab. interpreters, render 17*b* as an independent clause : "but be daily in the fear of the Lord." That is not a substantival clause (cf. xxii. 7), nor can it be an interjectional clause, but it may be an elliptical clause (Fleischer : from the prohibitive אַל־תְּקַנֵּא is to be taken for the second parallel member the *v. subst.* lying at the foundation of all verbs) ; but why had the author omitted הֱיֵה ? Besides, one uses the expressions, to act (עָשֹׁה), and to walk (הלך) in the fear of God, but not the expression to be (היה) in the fear of God. Thus בְּיִרְאַת, like בַחַטָּאִים, is dependent on אַל־תְּקַנֵּא ; and Jerome, who translates : *Non æmuletur cor tuum peccatores, sed in timore Domini esto tota die,* ought to have continued : *sed timorem Domini tota die ;* for, as one may say in Latin : *æmulari virtutes,* as well as *æmulari aliquem,* so also in Heb. קִנֵּא בְּ, of the envying of those persons whose fortune excites to dissatisfaction, because one has not the same, and might yet have it, iii. 31, xxiv. 1, 19, as well as of emulation for a thing in which one might not stand behind others : envy not sinners, envy much rather the fear of God, *i.e.* let thyself be moved with eager desire after it when its appearance is presented to thee. There is no O. T. parallel for this, but the Syr. *tan* and the Greek ζηλοτυποῦν are used in this double sense. Thus Hitzig rightly, and, among the moderns, Malbim ; with Aben Ezra, it is necessary to take ביראת for באיש יראת, this proverb itself declares the fear of God to be of all things the most worthy of being coveted.

In ver. 18, Umbreit, Elster, Zöckler, and others interpret the כִּי as assigning a reason, and the אִם as conditioning : for when the end (the hour of the righteous judgment) has come ; Bertheau better, because more suitable to the יֵשׁ and the אַחֲרִית : when an

end (an end adjusting the contradictions of the present time)
comes, as no doubt it will come, then thy hope will not be destroyed; but, on the other hand, the succession of words in the
conclusion (vid. at iii. 34) opposes this; also one does not see
why the author does not say directly כי יש אחרית, but expresses
himself thus conditionally.[1] If אם is meant hypothetically, then,
with the LXX. ἐὰν γὰρ τηρήσῃς αὐτὰ ἔσταί σοι ἔκγονα, we
should supply after it תִּשְׁמְרֶנָּה, that had fallen out.   Ewald's:
much rather there is yet a future (Dächsel: much rather be
happy there is . . .), is also impossible; for the preceding clause
is positive, not negative. The particles כִּי אָם, connected thus,
mean: for if (e.g. Lam. iii. 32); or also relatively: that if
(e.g. Jer. xxvi. 15).   After a negative clause they have the
meaning of " unless," which is acquired by means of an ellipsis;
e.g. Isa. lv. 10, it turns not back thither, unless it has watered
the earth (it returns back not before then, not unless this is
done). This "unless" is, however, used like the Lat. nisi, also
without the conditioning clause following, e.g. Gen. xxviii. 17,
hic locus non est nisi domus Dei.   And hence the expression
כי אם, after the negation going before, acquires the meaning of
"but," e.g. 17b: let not thy heart be covetous after sinners, for
thou canst always be zealous for the fear of God, i.e. much
rather for this, but for this. This pleonasm of אם sometimes
occurs where כי is not used confirmatively, but affirmatively:
the "certainly if" forms the transition, e g. 1 Kings xx. 6 (vid.
Keil's Comm. l.c.), whose "if" is not seldom omitted, so that
כי אם has only the meaning of an affirmative "certainly," not
"truly no," which it may also have, 1 Sam. xxv. 34, but "truly
yes." Thus כי אם is used Judg. xv. 7; 2 Sam. xv. 21 (where
אם is omitted by the Kĕrî); 2 Kings v. 20; Jer. li. 14; and thus
it is also meant here, 18a, notwithstanding that כי אם, in its
more usual signification, "besides only, but, nisi," precedes, as
at 1 Sam. xxi. 6, cf. 5. The objection by Hitzig, that with
this explanation : " certainly there is a future," vers. 18 and 17
are at variance, falls to the ground, if one reflects on the Heb.
idiom, in which the affirmative signification of כי is interpene-

[1] The form כִּי אִם- does not contradict the connection of the two particles.
This use of the Makkeph is general, except in these three instances: Gen.
xv. 4; Num. xxxv. 33; Neh. ii. 2.

trated by the confirmative. אַחֲרִית used thus pregnantly, as
here (xxiv. 14), is the glorious final issue; the word in itself
designates the end into which human life issues (cf. Ps. xxxvii.
37 f.); here, the end crowning the preceding course. Jeremiah
(xxix. 11) in this sense connects אחרית ותקוה [end and expecta-
tion]. And what is here denied of the תִּקְוָה, the hope (not as
certain Jewish interpreters dream, the thread of life) of him
who zealously strives after the fear of God, is affirmed, at Ps.
xxxvii. 38, of the godless: the latter have no continuance, but
the former have such as is the fulfilling of his hope.

Among the virtues which flow from the fear of God, temperance is made prominent, and the warning against excess is
introduced by the general exhortation to wisdom :

> Ver. 19 Hear thou, my son, and become wise,
> And direct thy heart straight forward on the way.
> 20 And be not among wine-drinkers,
> And among those who devour flesh ;
> 21 For the drunkard and glutton become poor,
> And sleepiness clotheth in rags.

The אַתָּה, connected with שְׁמַע, imports that the speaker has to
do with the hearer altogether by himself, and that the latter
may make an exception to the many who do not hear (cf. Job
xxxiii. 33; Jer. ii. 31). Regarding אִשֵּׁר, to make to go straight
out, vid. at iv. 14; the Kal, ix. 6, and also the Piel, iv. 14, mean
to go straight on, and, generally, to go. The way merely, is the
one that is right in contrast to the many byways. Fleischer:
" the way sensu eximio, as the Oriental mystics called the way
to perfection merely (Arab.) âlatryk; and him who walked
therein, âlsâlak, the walker or wanderer."[1] אַל־תְּהִי בְ, as at xxii.
26, the " Words of the Wise," are to be compared in point of
style. The degenerate and perverse son is more clearly described, Deut. xxi. 20, as זוֹלֵל וְסֹבֵא. These two characteristics
the poet distributes between 20a and 20b. סָבָא means to drink
(whence סֹבֶא, drink = wine, Isa. i. 22) wine or other intoxicating drinks; Arab. sabâ, vinum potandi causa emere. To the
יַיִן here added, בָּשָׂר in the parallel member corresponds, which

---

[1] Rashi reads בְּדֶרֶךְ לבך (walk), in the way of thy heart (which has
become wise), and so Heidenheim found it in an old MS.; but בדרך is
equivalent to בְּדֶרֶךְ בינה, ix. 6.

consequently is not the fleshly body of the gluttons themselves, but the prepared flesh which they consume at their luxurious banquets. The LXX. incorrectly as to the word, but not contrary to the sense, " be no wine-bibber, and stretch not thyself after *picknicks* (συμβολαῖς), and buying in of flesh (κρεῶν τε ἀγορασμοῖς)," whereby זֹלֵל is translated in the sense of the Aram. זְבְנִי (Lagarde). זָלַל denotes, intransitively, to be little valued (whence זוֹלֵל, *opp.* יָקַר, Jer. xv. 19), transitively to value little, and as such to squander, to lavish prodigally; thus: *qui prodigi sunt carnis sibi;* לָמוֹ is *dat. commodi.* Otherwise Gesenius, Fleischer, Umbreit, and Ewald: *qui prodigi sunt carnis suœ,* who destroy their own body; but the parallelism shows that flesh is meant wherewith they feed themselves, not their own flesh (בָּשָׂר לָמוֹ, like חֲמַת־לָמוֹ, Ps. lviii. 5), which, *i.e.* its health, they squander. זוֹלֵל also, in phrase used in Deut. xxi. 20 (cf. with Hitzig the formula φάγος καὶ οἰνοπότης, Matt. xi. 19), denotes not the dissolute person, as the sensualist, πορνοκόπος (LXX.), but the συμβολοκόπος (Aquila, Symmachus, Theodotion), κρεωβόρος (*Venet.*), זָלֵל בְּסַר (Onkelos), *i.e.* flesheater, ravenous person, glutton, in which sense it is rendered here, by the Syr. and Targ., by אסוט (אסיט), *i.e.* ἄσωτος. Regarding the metaplastic *fut. Niph.* יִוָּרֵשׁ (LXX. πτωχεύσει), *vid.* at xx. 13, cf. xi. 25. נוּמָה (after the form of דּוּגָה, בּוּשָׁה, צוּרָה) is drowsiness, lethargy, long sleeping, which necessarily follows a life of riot and revelry. Such a slothful person comes to a bit of bread (xxi. 17); and the disinclination and unfitness for work, resulting from night revelry, brings it about that at last he must clothe himself in miserable rags. The rags are called קֶרַע and ῥάκος, from the rending (tearing), Arab. *ruk'at,* from the patching, mending. Lagarde, more at large, treats of this word here used for rags.

The *parainesis* begins anew, and the division is open to question. Vers. 22–24 can of themselves be independent distichs; but this is not the case with ver. 25, which, in the resumption of the address and in expression, leans back on ver. 22. The author of this appendix may have met with vers. 23 and 24 (although here also his style, as conformed to that of i. 9, is noticeable, cf. 23*b* with i. 2), but vers. 22 and 25 are the form which he has given to them.

Thus 22-25 are a whole :—

Ver. 22 Hearken to thy father, to him who hath begotten thee,
And despise not thy mother when she has grown old.
23 Buy the truth, and sell it not,
Wisdom and discipline and understanding.
24 The father of a righteous man rejoiceth greatly;
(And) he that is the father of a wise man—he will rejoice.
25 Let thy father and thy mother be glad;
And her that bare thee exult.

The ostastich begins with a call to childlike obedience, for
שְׁמַע לְ, to listen to any one, is equivalent to, to obey him, *e.g.*
Ps. lxxxi. 9, 14 (cf. " hearken to his voice," Ps. xcv. 7). זֶה יְלָדֶךָ
is a relative clause (cf. Deut. xxxii. 18, without זֶה or אֲשֶׁר),
according to which it is rightly accentuated (cf. on the contrary,
Ps. lxxviii. 54). 22*b*, strictly taken, is not to be translated
neve contemne cum senuerit matrem tuam (Fleischer), but *cum
senuerit mater tua*, for the logical object to אַל־תָּבוּז is attracted
as subj. of זָקְנָה (Hitzig). There now follows the exhortation
comprehending all, and formed after iv. 7, to buy wisdom, *i.e.*
to shun no expense, no effort, no privation, in order to attain to
the possession of wisdom; and not to sell it, *i.e.* not to place it
over against any earthly possession, worldly gain, sensual enjoyment; not to let it be taken away by any intimidation,
argued away by false reasoning, or prevailed against by enticements into the way of vice, and not to become unfaithful to it
by swimming with the great stream (Ex. xxiii. 2); for truth,
אֱמֶת, is that which endures and proves itself in all spheres, the
moral as well as the intellectual. In 23*b*, in like manner as
i. 3, xxii. 4, a threefold object is given to קְנֵה instead of אמת :
there are three properties which are peculiar to truth, the
three powers which handle it : חָכְמָה is knowledge solid, pressing into the essence of things; מוּסָר is moral culture; and
בִּינָה the central faculty of proving and distinguishing (*vid.* i.
3-5). Now ver. 24 says what consequences are for the parents
when the son, according to the exhortation of 23, makes truth
his aim, to which all is subordinated. Because in אמת the
ideas of practical and theoretical truth are inter-connected. צַדִּיק
and חָכָם are also here parallel to one another. The *Chethîb* of
24*a* is גּוֹל יָגוּל, which Schultens finds tenable in view of (Arab.)
jal, fut. *jajûlu* (to turn round; Heb. to turn oneself for joy)

118 THE BOOK OF PROVERBS.

but the Heb. *usus loq.* knows elsewhere only יָגֵיל גִּיל, as the *Kerî* corrects. The LXX., misled by the *Chethîb*, translates καλῶς ἐκτρέφει (incorrect ἐκτρυφήσει), *i.e.* יְנַדֵּל גַּ. In 24*b*, וְיִשְׂמַח is of the nature of a pred. of the conclusion (cf. Gen. xxii. 24; Ps. cxv. 7), as if the sentence were : has one begotten a wise man, then (cf. xvii. 21) he has joy of him ; but the *Kerî* effaces this *Vav apodosis*, and assigns it to יוֹלֵד as *Vav copul.*—an unnecessary mingling of the syntactically possible, more emphatic expression. This proverbial whole now rounds itself off in ver. 25 by a reference to ver. 22,—the Optative here corresponding to the Impr. and Prohib. there : let thy father and thy mother rejoice (LXX. εὐφρανέσθω), and let her that bare thee exult (here where it is possible the Optat. form וְתָגֵל).

Vers. 26–28. This hexastich warns against unchastity. What, in i.–ix., extended discourses and representations exhibited to the youth is here repeated in miniature pictures. It is the teacher of wisdom, but by him Wisdom herself, who speaks :

> Ver. 26 Give me, my son, thine heart;
> And let thine eyes delight in my ways.
> 27 For the harlot is a deep ditch,
> And the strange woman a narrow pit.
> 28 Yea, she lieth in wait like a robber,
> And multiplieth the faithless among men

We have retained Luther's beautiful rendering of ver. 26,[1] in which this proverb, as a warning word of heavenly wisdom and of divine love, has become dear to us. It follows, as Symmachus and the *Venet.*, the *Chethîb* תִּרְצֶנָה (for תרצינה, like Ex. ii. 16; Job v. 12), the stylistic appropriateness of which proceeds from xvi. 7, as on the other hand the *Kerî* תִּצֹּרְנָה (cf. 1 Sam. xiv. 27) is supported by xxii. 12, cf. v. 2. But the correction is unnecessary, and the *Chethîb* sounds more affectionate, hence it is with right defended by Hitzig. The ways of wisdom are ways of correction, and particularly of chastity, thus placed over against "the ways of the harlot," vii. 24 ff. Accordingly the exhortation, ver. 26, verifies itself ; warning, by ver. 27, cf. xxii. 14, where עֲמֻקָה was written, here as at Job xii. 22, with the long vowel עֲמוּקָה (עֲמָקָה). בְּאֵר צָרָה interchanges

---

[1] The right punctuation of 26*a* is תְּנָה־בְנִי לִבְּךָ, as it is found in the editions: Ven. 1615 ; Basel 1619 ; and in those of Norzi and Michaelis.

with שׁוּחָה עֲמוּקָה, and means, not the fountain of sorrow (Löwenstein), but the narrow pit. בְּאֵר is fem. gen., xxvi. 21 f., and
צַר means narrow, like *étroit* (old French, *estreit*), from *strictus*.
The figure has, after xxii. 14, the mouth of the harlot in view.
Whoever is enticed by her syren voice falls into a deep ditch,
into a pit with a narrow mouth, into which one can more easily
enter than escape from.   Ver. 28 says that it is the artifice of
the harlot which draws a man into such depth of wickedness
and guilt.   With אַף, which, as at Judg. v. 29, belongs not to
הִיא but to the whole sentence, the picture of terror is completed.
The verb חָתַף (whence Arab. *hataf*, death, natural death)
means to snatch away.   If we take חֶתֶף as *abstr.*: a snatching
away, then it would here stand elliptically for אִישׁ (בַּעַל) חֶתֶף,
which in itself is improbable (*vid.* vii. 22, עֶכֶם) and also unnecessary, since, as הֹלֵךְ, עֶבֶד, מֶלֶךְ, etc. show, such *abstracta* can
pass immediately into *concreta*, so that חֶתֶף thus means the
person who snatches away, *i.e.* the street robber, *latro* (cf. חָטַף,
(Arab.) *khataf*, Ps. x. 9, rightly explained by Kimchi as cogn.).
In 28*b*, תּוֹסִיף cannot mean *abripit* (as LXX., Theodotion, and
Jerome suppose), for which the word תְּסַפֶּה (תֶּאֱסֹף) would have
been used.[1] But this verbal idea does not harmonize with the
connection; תוֹסִיף means, as always, *addit* (*auget*), and that here
in the sense of *multiplicat*.   The same thing may be said of
בּוֹגְדִים as is said (xi. 15) of תּוֹקְעִים. Hitzig's objection, "הוֹסִיף,
to multiply, with the accusative of the person, is not at all
used," is set aside by xix. 4.   But we may translate: the faithless, or: the breach of faith she increases.   Yet it always
remains a question whether בְּאָדָם is dependent on בוגדים, as
Eccles. viii. 9, cf. 2 Sam. xxiii. 3, on the verb of ruling (Hitzig),
or whether, as frequently בָּאָדָם, *e.g.* Ps. lxxviii. 60, it means
inter homines (thus most interpreters).   Uncleanness leads to
faithlessness of manifold kinds: it makes not only the husband
unfaithful to his wife, but also the son to his parents, the
scholar to his teacher and pastor, the servant (cf. the case of
Potiphar's wife) to his master.   The adulteress, inasmuch as
she entices now one and now another into her net, increases the

---

[1] The Targ. translates 28*b* (here free from the influence of the Peshito)
in the Syro-Palestinian idiom by וְצָאֵד אַבְנָא שַׁבְרֵי, *i.e.* she seizes thought-
less sons.

number of those who are faithless towards men. But are they
not, above all, faithless towards God? We are of opinion that
not בוגדים, but תוסיף, has its complement in באדם, and needs it:
the adulteress increases the faithless among men, she makes
faithlessness of manifold kinds common in human society.
According to this, also, it is accentuated; ובוגדים is placed as
object by *Mugrasch*, and באדם is connected by *Mercha* with
תוסיף.

Vers. 29–35. The author passes from the sin of uncleanness
to that of drunkenness; they are nearly related, for drunkenness
excites fleshly lust; and to wallow with delight in the mire of sensuality, a man, created in the image of God, must first brutalize
himself by intoxication. The *Mashal* in the number of its lines
passes beyond the limits of the distich, and becomes a Mashal ode.

Ver. 29 Whose is woe? Whose is grief?
  Whose are contentions, whose trouble, whose wounds
     without cause?
  Whose is dimness of eyes?
30 Theirs, who sit late at the wine,
  Who turn in to taste mixed wine.
31 Look not on the wine as it sparkleth red,
  As it showeth its gleam in the cup,
  Glideth down with ease.
32 The end of it is that it biteth like a serpent,
  And stingeth like a basilisk.
33 Thine eyes shall see strange things,
  And thine heart shall speak perverse things;
34 And thou art as one lying in the heart of the sea,
  And as one lying on the top of a mast.
35 "They have scourged me—it pained me not;
  They have beaten me—I perceived it not.
  When shall I have wakened from sleep?
  Thus on I go, I return to it again."

The repeated לְמִי[1] asks who then has to experience all that;
the answer follows in ver. 30. With אוי, the אֲבוֹי occurring
only here accords; it is not a substantive from אָבָה (whence
אֶבְיוֹן) after the form of צְחִק, in the sense of *egestas*; but, like
the former [אי], an interjection of sorrow (*Venet.* τίνι αἲ,
τίνι φεῦ). Regarding מִדְיָנִים (*Chethîb* מִדוֹנִים), *vid.* at vi. 14.

[1] We punctuate לְמִי אוֹי, for that is Ben Asher's punctuation, while that
of his opponent Ben Naphtali is לְמִי־אוֹי. *Vid. Thorath Emeth*, p. 33.

שִׂיחַ signifies (vid. at vi. 22) meditation and speech, here sorrowful thought and sorrowful complaint (1 Sam. i. 16; Ps. lv. 18 ; cf. הָגִיג, הֶגֶה), e.g. over the exhausted purse, the neglected work, the anticipated reproaches, the diminishing strength. In the connection פְּצָעִים חִנָּם (cf. Ps. xxxv. 19) the accus. adv. חנם (French gratuitement) represents the place of an adjective: strokes which one receives without being in the situation from necessity, or duty to expect them, strokes for nothing and in return for nothing (Fleischer), wounds for a long while (Oetinger). חַכְלִלוּת עֵינַיִם is the darkening (clouding) of the eyes, from חָכַל, to be firm, closed, and transferred to the sensation of light: to be dark (vid. at Gen. xlix. 12; Ps. x. 8); the copper-nose of the drunkard is not under consideration; the word does not refer to the reddening, but the dimming of the eyes, and of the power of vision. The answer, ver. 30, begins, in conformity with the form of the question, with לְ (write לְמְאַחֲרִים, with Gaja to לְ, according to Metheg-Setzung, § 20, Michlol 46b): pain, and woe, and contention they have who tarry late at the wine (cf. Isa. v. 11), who enter (viz. into the wine-house, Eccles. ii. 4, the house of revelry) "to search" mingled drink (vid. at ix. 2; Isa. v. 22). Hitzig: "they test the mixing, as to the relation of the wine to the water, whether it is correct." But לַחְקוֹר is like גִּבֹּרִים, Isa. v. 22, meant in mockery: they are heroes, viz. heroes in drinking; they are searchers, such, namely, as seek to examine into the mixed wine, or also: thoroughly and carefully taste it (Fleischer).

The evil consequences of drunkenness are now registered. That one may not fall under this common sin, the poet, ver. 31, warns against the attraction which the wine presents to the sight and to the sense of taste: one must not permit himself to be caught as a prisoner by this enticement, but must maintain his freedom against it. הִתְאַדֵּם, to make, i.e. to show oneself red, is almost equivalent to הָאֳדִים; and more than this, it presents the wine as itself co-operating and active by its red play of colours (Fleischer). Regarding the antiptosis (antiphonesis): Look not on the wine that is . . ., vid. at Gen. i. 3; yet here, where ראה means not merely "to see," but "to look at," the case is somewhat different. In 31b, one for the most part assumes that עֵינוֹ signifies the eye of the wine, i.e. the pearls which play on the surface of the wine (Fleischer). And, indeed, Hitzig's translation, after Num. xi. 7 : when it presents its appearance in the cup, does not commend itself, because it expresses too little. On the other hand, it is saying too much when Böttcher maintains that עין never denotes the mere appearance, but always the shining aspect of the object. But used of wine, עין appears to denote not merely aspect as such, but its gleam, glance; not its pearls, for which עֵינֵי would be the word used, but shining glance, by which particularly the bright glance, as out of deep darkness, of the Syro-Palestinian wine is thought of, which is for the most part prepared from red (blue) grapes, and because very rich in sugar, is thick almost like syrup. Jerome translates עֵינוֹ well : (*cum splenduerit in vitro*) *color ejus.* But one need not think of a glass; Böttcher has rightly said that one might perceive the glittering appearance also in a metal or earthen vessel if one looked into it. The *Chethîb* בכים is an error of transcription ; the *Midrash* makes the remark on this, that בַּבַּיִם fits the wine merchant, and בַּכּוֹם the wine drinker. From the pleasure of the eye, 31c passes over to the pleasures of the taste : (that, or, as it) goeth down smoothly (Luther) ; the expression is like Eccles. vii. 10. Instead of הלך (like *jâry,* of fluidity) there stands here התהלך, commonly used of pleasant going; and instead of לְמֵישָׁרִים with לְ, the norm בְּמֵישָׁרִים with בְּ of the manner; directness is here easiness, facility (Arab. *jusr*); it goes as on a straight, even way unhindered and easily down the throat.[1]

Ver. 32 shows how it issues with the wine, viz. with those who immoderately enjoy it. Is אַחֲרִיתוֹ [its end] here the subject, as at v. 4 ? We must in that case interpret יִשֵּׁךְ and יַפְרִשׁ as attributives, as the Syr. and Targ. translate the latter, and Ewald both. The issue which it brings with it is like the serpent which bites, etc., and there is nothing syntactically opposed to this (cf. *e.g.* Ps. xvii. 12) ; the future, in contradistinction to the participle, would not express properties, but intimations of facts. But the end of the wine is not like a serpent, but like the bite of a serpent. The wine itself, and

---

[1] The English version is, "when it moveth itself aright," which one has perceived in the phenomenon of the tears of the wine, or of the movement in the glass. *Vid. Ausland,* 1869, p. 72.

independent of its consequences, is in and of itself like a serpent. In accordance with the matter, אחריתו may be interpreted, with Hitzig (after Jerome, *in novissimo*), as *acc. adverb.* = באחריתו, Jer. xvii. 11. But why did not the author more distinctly write this word 'בא? The syntactic relation is like xxix. 21: אחריתו is after the manner of a substantival clause, the subject to that which follows as its virtual predicate: "its end is: like a serpent it biteth = this, that it biteth like a serpent." Regarding צִפְעֹנִי, *serpens regulus* (after Schultens, from צפע = (Arab.) *saf*', to breathe out glowing, scorching), *vid.* at Isa. vii. 8. The *Hiph.* הפריש Schultens here understands of the division of the liver, and Hitzig, after the LXX., Vulgate, and *Venet.*, of squirting the poison; both after the Arab. *farth.* But הפריש, Syr. *afrês*, also signifies, from the root-idea of dividing and splitting, to sting, *poindre, pointer*, as Rashi and Kimchi gloss, whence the Aram. פְּרֵשׁ, an ox-goad, with which the ancients connect פרש (of the spur), the name for a rider, *eques*, and also a horse (cf. on the contrary, Fleischer in Levy, *W. B.* ii. 574); a serpent's bite and a serpent's sting (Lat. *morsus, ictus*, Varro: *cum pepugerit colubra*) are connected together by the ancients.[1]

The excited condition of the drunkard is now described. First, ver. 33 describes the activity of his imagination as excited to madness. It is untenable to interpret זָרוֹת here with Rashi, Aben Ezra, and others, and to translate with Luther: "so shall thine eyes look after other women" (*circumspicient mulieres impudicas*, Fleischer, for the meaning to perceive, to look about for something, to seek something with the eyes, referring to Gen. xli. 33). For זרות acquires the meaning of *mulieres impudicæ* only from its surrounding, but here the parallel תַּהְפֻּכוֹת (perverse things) directs to the neut. *aliena* (cf. xv. 28, רָעוֹת), but not merely in the sense of unreal things (Ralbag, Meîri), but: strange, *i.e.* abnormal, thus bizarre, mad, dreadful things. An old Heb. parable compares the changing circumstances which wine produces with the man-

[1] However, we will not conceal it, that the post-bibl. Heb. does not know הפריש in the sense of to prick, sting (the *Midrash* explains the passage by יפריש בין מיתה לחיים, *i.e.* it cuts off life); and the Nestorian Knanishu of Superghan, whom I asked regarding *aphrish*, knew only of the meanings "to separate" and "to point out," but not "to sting."

ner of the lamb, the lion, the swine, the monkey; here juggles and phantoms of the imagination are meant, which in the view and fancy of the drunken man hunt one another like monkey capers. Moreover, the state of the drunken man is one that is separated from the reality of a life of sobriety and the safety of a life of moderation, 34a : thou act like one who lies in the heart of the sea. Thus to lie in the heart, i.e. the midst, of the sea as a ship goes therein, xxx. 19, is impossible; there one must swim; but swimming is not lying, and to think on a situation like that of Jonah, i. 5, one must think also of the ship; but שׁכב does not necessarily mean " to sleep," and, besides, the sleep of a passenger in the cabin on the high sea is of itself no dangerous matter. Rightly Hitzig : in the depth of the sea (cf. Jonah ii. 4)—the drunken man, or the man overcome by wine (Isa. xxviii. 7), is like one who has sunk down into the midst of the sea ; and thus drowned, or in danger of being drowned, he is in a condition of intellectual confusion, which finally passes over into perfect unconsciousness, cut off from the true life which passes over him like one dead, and in this condition he has made a bed for himself, as שֹׁכֵב denotes. With בְּרֹאשׁ בלב, stands in complete contrast : he is like one who lies on the top of the mast. חִבֵּל, after the forms דִּבֵּר, שִׁלֵּם, is the sail-yard fastened by ropes, חֲבָלִים (Isa. xxxiii. 23). To lay oneself down on the sail-yard happens thus to no one, and it is no place for such a purpose; but as little as one can quarter him who is on the ridge of the roof, in the 'Alija, because no one is able to lie down there, so little can he in the bower [Mastkorb] him who is here spoken of (Böttcher). The poet says, but only by way of comparison, how critical the situation of the drunkard is ; he compares him to one who lies on the highest sail-yard, and is exposed to the danger of being every moment thrown into the sea ; for the rocking of the ship is the greater in proportion to the height of the sail-yard. The drunkard is, indeed, thus often exposed to the peril of his life ; for an accident of itself not great, or a stroke, may suddenly put an end to his life.

Ver. 35. The poet represents the drunken man as now speaking to himself. He has been well cudgelled; but because insensible, he has not felt it, and he places himself now where he will sleep out his intoxication. Far from being made temperate by the strokes inflicted on him, he rejoices in the prospect, when he has awaked out of his sleep, of beginning again the life of drunkenness and revelry which has become a pleasant custom to him. חָלָה means not only to be sick, but generally to be, or to become, affected painfully; cf. Jer. v. 3, where חָלוּ is not the 3d pl. mas. of חִיל, but of חלה. The words מָתַי אָקִיץ are, it is true, a cry of longing of a different kind from Job vii. 4. The sleeping man cannot forbear from yielding to the constraint of nature: he is no longer master of himself, he becomes giddy, everything goes round about with him, but he thinks with himself: Oh that I were again awake! and so little has his appetite been appeased by his sufferings, that when he is again awakened, he will begin where he left off yesterday, when he could drink no more. מָתַי is here, after Nolde, Fleischer, and Hitzig, the relative *quando* (*quum*); but the bibl. *usus loq.* gives no authority for this. In that case we would have expected הֲקִיצוֹתִי instead of אָקִיץ. As the interrog. מתי is more animated than the relat., so also אוֹסִיף אֲבַקְשֶׁנּוּ is more animated (1 Sam. ii. 3) than אוסיף לבקש. The suffix of אבקשנו refers to the wine: raised up, he will seek that which has become so dear and so necessary to him.

After this divergence (in vers. 29-35) from the usual form of the proverb, there is now a return to the tetrastich:

> xxiv. 1 Envy not evil men,
>   And desire not to have intercourse with them.
>   2 For their heart thinketh of violence,
>   And their lips speak mischief.

The warning, not to envy the godless, is also found at iii. 31, xxiii. 17, xxiv. 19, but is differently constructed in each of these passages. Regarding תִּתְאַו with *Pathach*, *vid.* at xxiii. 3. אַנְשֵׁי רָעָה (cf. רָע, xxviii. 5) are the wicked, *i.e.* such as cleave to evil, and to whom evil clings. The warning is grounded in this, that whoever have intercourse with such men, make themselves partners in greater sins and evil: for their heart broodeth (write כִּי שֹׁד, *Munach Dechî*) violence, *i.e.* robbery, plunder, destruction, murder, and the like. With שֹׁד (in the *Mishle* only here and at xxi. 7, cf. שֹׁדֵד, xix. 26) connects itself elsewhere חָמָס, here (cf. Hab. i. 3) עָמָל, *labor, molestia*, viz. those

who prepare it for others by means of slanderous, crafty, uncharitable talk.

Vers. 3, 4. The warning against fellowship with the godless
is followed by the praise of wisdom, which is rooted in the fear
of God.

> Ver. 3 By wisdom is the house builded,
> And by understanding is it established.
> 4 And by knowledge shall the chambers be filled
> With all manner of precious and pleasant goods.

What is meant by the " building of the house " is explained at
xiv. 1. It is wisdom, viz. that which originates from God,
which is rooted in fellowship with Him, by which every household, be it great or small, prospers and attains to a successful
and flourishing state ; כּוֹנֵן, as parallel word to בָּנָה (iii. 19; Hab.
ii. 12), is related to it as *statuere* to *extruere;* the *Hithpal* (as at
Num. xxi. 17) means to keep oneself in a state of continuance,
to gain perpetuity, to become established. That יִמָּלְאוּ by
Athnach has not passed over into the pausal יִמָּלֵאוּ, arises from
this, that the *Athnach*, by the poetical system of accents, has
only the force of the prose accent *Sakef;* the clause completes
itself only by 4*b*; the pausal form on that account also is not
found, and it is discontinued, because the *Athnach* does not
produce any pausal effect (*vid.* at Ps. xlv. 6). The form of
expression in ver. 4 is like i. 13, iii. 10. But the חֲדָרִים, of
storerooms (LXX. as Isa. xxvi. 20, ταμιεῖα), and נָעִים, like xxii.
18, xxiii. 8, is peculiar to this collection.

Vers. 5, 6. The praise of wisdom is continued : it brings
blessings in the time of peace, and gives the victory in war.

> Ver. 5 A wise man is full of strength ;
> And a man of understanding showeth great power.
> 6 For with wise counsel shalt thou carry on successful war ;
> And safety is where counsellors are not wanting.

The ב of בְּעוֹז (thus with *Pathach* in old impressions, Cod. 1294,
Cod. *Jaman.*, and elsewhere with the Masoretic note לִית ומלא)
introduces, as that of בְּכֹחַ, Ps. xxix. 4, the property in which a
person or thing appears; the article (cf. הָעֹזְבִים, ii. 13, Gesen.
§ 35, 2A) is that of gender. The parallel מאמץ כח, a Greek
translates by ὑπὲρ κραταιὸν ἰσχύι = מֵאַמִּיץ בֹּחַ (Job ix. 4;
Isa. xl. 26). But after 5*a* it lies nearer that the poet means

to express the power which lies in wisdom itself (Eccles. vii. 19), and its superiority to physical force (xxi. 22) ; the LXX., Syr., and Targ. also, it is true, translate 5a as if מֵעָז (præ potente) were the words used. אִמֵּץ כֹּחַ means to strengthen the strength, and that is (Nah. ii. 2) equivalent to, to collect the strength (to take courage), here and at Amos ii. 14, to show strong (superior) strength. The reason is gathered from xx. 18b and xi. 14b. The לְךָ here added, Hitzig is determined to read תַּעֲשֶׂה : for with prudent counsel the war shall be carried out by thee. The construction of the passive with ל of the subject is correct in Heb. (vid. at xiv. 20) as well as in Aram.,[1] and עשׂה frequently means, in a pregnant sense : to complete, to carry out, to bring to an end; but the phrase עָשׂה מלחמה means always to carry on war, and nothing further. לְךָ is the dat. commod., as in נִלְחַם ל, to wage war (to contend) for any one, e.g. Ex. xiv. 14. Instead of ברב, the LXX. reads בלב ; regarding γεωργίου μεγάλου for מאמץ כח, without doubt a corrupt reading, vid. Lagarde.

Till now in this appendix we have found only two distichs (vid. vol. i. p. 17); now several of them follow. From this, that wisdom is a power which accomplishes great things, it follows that it is of high value, though to the fool it appears all too costly.

Ver. 7 Wisdom seems to the fool to be an ornamental commodity ;
He openeth not his mouth in the gate.

Most interpreters take רָאמֹות for רָמֹות (written as at 1 Chron. vi. 58 ; cf. Zech. xiv. 10 ; רָאשׁ, Prov. x. 4 ; קָאם, Hos. x. 14), and translate, as Jerome and Luther : " Wisdom is to the fool too high;" the way to wisdom is to him too long and too steep, the price too costly, and not to be afforded. Certainly this thought does not lie far distant from what the poet would say ; but why does he say חָכְמֹות, and not חָכְמָה ? This חכמות is not a numerical plur., so as to be translated with the Venet. : μετέωροι τῷ ἄφρονι αἱ ἐπιστῆμαι ; it is a plur., as Ps. xlix. 4 shows ; but, as is evident from the personification and the construction, i. 20, one inwardly multiplying and heightening, which is related to חכמה as science or the contents of knowledge is to knowledge. That this plur. comes here into view

[1] Vid. Nöldeke's Neusyrische Gram. p. 219, Anm., and p. 416.

as in i.–ix. (*vid.* vol. i. p. 34), is definitely accounted for in
these chapters by the circumstance that wisdom was to be designated, which is the *mediatrix* of all wisdom ; here, to be
designated in intentional symphony with ראמות, whose plur.
ending *ôth* shall be for that very reason, however, inalienable.
Thus ראמות will be the name of a costly foreign *bijouterie*,
which is mentioned in the Book of Job, where the unfathom-
ableness and inestimableness of wisdom is celebrated ; *vid.* Job
xxvii. 18, where we have recorded what we had to say at the
time regarding this word. But what is now the meaning of
the saying that wisdom is to the fool a pearl or precious coral ?
Joël Bril explains : " The fool uses the sciences like a precious
stone, only for ornament, but he knows not how to utter a word
publicly." This is to be rejected, because ראמות is not so usual
a trinket or ornament as to serve as an expression of this
thought. The third of the comparison lies in the rarity, costliness, unattainableness ; the fool despises wisdom, because the
expenditure of strength and the sacrifices of all kinds which are
necessary to put one into the possession of wisdom deter him
from it (Rashi). This is also the sense which the expression
has when רמות = ראמות ; and probably for the sake of this double
meaning the poet chose just this word, and not פנינים, גביש, or
any other name, for articles of ornament (Hitzig). The Syr.
has incorrectly interpreted this play upon words : *sapientia
abjecta stulto;* and the Targumist : the fool grumbles (מִתְרְעֵם)
against wisdom.[1] He may also find the grapes to be sour because they hang too high for him ; here it is only said that
wisdom remains at a distance from him because he cannot soar
up to its attainment ; for that very reason he does not open
his mouth in the gate, where the council and the representatives
of the people have their seats : he has not the knowledge necessary for being associated in counselling, and thus must keep
silent ; and this is indeed the most prudent thing he can do.

Ver. 8. From wisdom, which is a moral good, the following
proverb passes over to a kind of σοφία δαιμονιώδης :

> He that meditateth to do evil,
> We call such an one an intriguer.

---

[1] This explanation is more correct than Levy's : he lifts himself up (boasts)
with wisdom.

A verbal explanation and definition like xxi. 24 (cf. vol. i. p. 40), formed like xvi. 21 from נבון. Instead of בַּעַל־מְזִמּוֹת [lord of mischief] in xii. 2, the expression is אִישׁ מ' (cf. at xxii. 24). Regarding מזמות in its usual sense, *vid.* v. 2. Such definitions have of course no lexicographical, but only a moral aim. That which is here given is designed to warn one against gaining for himself this ambiguous title of a refined (cunning, *versutus*) man; one is so named whose schemes and endeavours are directed to the doing of evil. One may also inversely find the turning-point of the warning in 8*b*: "he who projects deceitful plans against the welfare of others, finds his punishment in this, that he falls under public condemnation as a worthless intriguer" (Elster). But מזמות is a ῥῆμα μέσον, *vid.* v. 2; the title is thus equivocal, and the turning-point lies in the bringing out of his kernel: מְחַשֵּׁב לְהָרַע = meditating to do evil.

Ver. 9. This proverb is connected by זמת with ver. 8, and by אויל with ver. 7; it places the fool and the mocker over against one another.

> The undertaking of folly is sin;
> And an abomination to men is the scorner.

Since it is certain that for 9*b* the subject is "the scorner," so also "sin" is to be regarded as the subject of 9*a*. The special meaning *flagitium*, as xxi. 27, זִמָּה will then not have here, but it derives it from the root-idea "to contrive, imagine," and signifies first only the collection and forthputting of the thoughts towards a definite end (Job xvii. 11), particularly the refined preparation, the contrivance of a sinful act. In a similar way we speak of a sinful beginning or undertaking. But if one regards sin in itself, or in its consequences, it is always a contrivance or desire of folly (*gen. subjecti*), or: one that bears on itself (*gen. qualitatis*) the character of folly; for it disturbs and destroys the relation of man to God and man, and rests, as Socrates in *Plato* says, on a false calculation. And the mocker (the mocker at religion and virtue) is תּוֹעֲבַת לְאָדָם. The form of combination stands here before a word with לְ, as at Job xviii. 2, xxiv. 5, and frequently. But why does not the poet say directly תועבת אָדָם? Perhaps to leave room for the double sense, that the mocker is not only an abomination to men, viz. to the better disposed; but also, for he makes others err as to

their faith, and draws them into his frivolous thoughts, becomes
to them a cause of abomination, *i.e.* of such conduct and of
such thoughts as are an abomination before God (xv. 9, 26).

Ver. 10. The last of these four distichs stands without
visible connection :

> Hast thou shown thyself slack in the day of adversity,
> Then is thy strength small.

The perf. 10*a* is the hypothetic, *vid.* at xxii. 29. If a man
shows himself remiss (xviii. 9), *i.e.* changeable, timorous, incapable of resisting in times of difficulty, then shall he draw
therefrom the conclusion which is expressed in 10*b*. Rightly
Luther, with intentional generalization, " he is not strong who
is not firm in need." But the address makes the proverb an
earnest admonition, which speaks to him who shows himself
weak the judgment which he has to pronounce on himself.
And the *paronomasia* צָרָה and צַר may be rendered, where possible, " if thy strength becomes, as it were, pressed together and
bowed down by the difficulty just when it ought to show itself
(viz. לְהַרְחִיב לְךָ), then it is limited, thou art a weakling." Thus
Fleischer accordingly, translating : *si segnis fueris die angustiœ,
angustœ sunt vires tuœ.* Hitzig, on the contrary, corrects after
Job vii. 11, רוּחֲךָ, " *Klemm* (*klamm*) *ist dein Mut*" [= strait is
thy courage]. And why ? Of כֹּח [strength], he remarks, one
can say כָּשֵׁל [it is weak] (Ps. xxxi. 11), but scarcely צַר [strait,
straitened] ; for force is exact, and only the region of its energy
may be wide or narrow. To this we answer, that certainly of
strength in itself we cannot use the word כֹּח in the sense here
required ; the confinement (limitation) may rather be, as with a
stream, Isa. lix. 19, the increasing (heightening) of its intensity.
But if the strength is in itself anything definite, then on the
other hand its expression is something linear, and the force in
view of its expression is that which is here called צַר, *i.e.* not
extending widely, not expanding, not inaccessible. צַר is all to
which narrow limits are applied. A little strength is limited,
because it is little also in its expression.

Now, again, we meet with proverbs of several lines. The first
here is a hexastich :

> Ver. 11 Deliver them that are taken to death,
> And them that are tottering to destruction, oh stop them !

12 If thou sayest, " We knew not of it indeed,"—
It is not so : The Weigher of hearts, who sees through it,
And He that observeth thy soul, He knoweth it,
And requiteth man according to his work.

If אִם is interpreted as a particle of adjuration, then אִם־תֶּחְשׂוֹךְ
is equivalent to: I adjure thee, forbear not (cf. Neh. xiii. 25
with Isa. lviii. 1), viz. that which thou hast to do, venture all
on it (LXX., Syr., Jerome). But the parallelism requires us
to take together מָטִים לַהֶרֶג (such as with tottering steps are led
forth to destruction) as object along with אִם־תַּחְשׂוֹךְ, as well
as לְקֻחִים לַמָּוֶת (such as from their condition are carried away to
death, cf. Ex. xiv. 11) as object to הַצֵּל, in which all the old
interpreters have recognised the *imper.*, but none the *infin.*
(*eripere . . . ne cesses*, which is contrary to Heb. idiom, both in
the position of the words and in the construction). אִם also is
not to be interpreted as an interrogative ; for, thus expressed, *an
retinetis* ought rather to have for the converse the meaning :
thou shalt indeed not do it! (cf. *e.g.* Isa. xxix. 16.) And אִם
cannot be conditional: *si prohibere poteris* (Michaelis and
others), for the fut. after אִם has never the sense of a potential.
Thus אִם is, like לֻא, understood in the sense of *utinam*, as it is
used not merely according to later custom (Hitzig), but from
ancient times (cf. *e.g.* Ex. xxxii. 32 with Gen. xxiii. 13).
כִּי־תֹאמַר (reminding[1] us of the same formula of the Rabbinical
writings) introduces an objection, excuse, evasion, which is met
by הֲלֹא; introducing " so say I on the contrary," it is of itself a
reply, *vid.* Deut. vii. 17 f. זֶה we will not have to interpret personally (LXX. τοῦτον) ; for, since ver. 11 speaks of several of
them, the neut. rendering (Syr., Targ., *Venet.*, Luther) in itself
lies nearer, and זֶה, *hoc*, after יָדַע, is also in conformity with the
usus loq. ; *vid.* at Ps. lvi. 10. But the neut. זֶה does not refer
to the moral obligation expressed in ver. 11; to save human
life when it is possible to do so, can be unknown to no one,
wherefore Jerome (as if the words of the text were אֵין לְאֵל יָדֵנוּ
זֶה): *vires non suppetunt.* זֶה refers to the fact that men are led
to the tribunal; only thus is explained the change of יָדַעְתִּי,
which was to be expected, into יְדַעֲנוּ : the objection is, that one
certainly did not know, viz. that matters had come to an

---

[1] *Vid.* my *hebräischen Römerbrief,* p. 14 f.

extremity with them, and that a short process will be made
with them.   To this excuse, with pretended ignorance, the reply
of the omniscient God stands opposed, and suggests to him who
makes the excuse to consider : It is not so : the Searcher of
hearts (*vid.* at xvi. 2), He sees through it, viz. what goes on
in thy heart, and He has thy soul under His inspection (נֹצֵר, as
Job vii. 20 ; LXX. καὶ ὁ πλάσας ; וַיֹּצֶר, which Hitzig prefers,
for he thinks that נצר must be interpreted in the sense of to
guard, preserve ; Luther rightly) ; He knows, viz., how it is with
thy mind , He looks through it, He knows (cf. for both, Ps.
cxxxix. 1–4), and renders to man according to his conduct,
which, without being deceived, He judges according to the
state of the heart, out of which the conduct springs.   It is
to be observed that ver. 11 speaks of one condemned to death
generally, and not expressly of one innocently condemned, and
makes no distinction between one condemned in war and in
peace.   One sees from this that the Chokma generally has no
pleasure in this, that men are put to death by men, not even
when it is done legally as punishment for a crime.   For, on the
one side, it is true that the punishment of the murderer by
death is a law proceeding from the nature of the divine holiness and the inviolability of the divine ordinance, and the worth
of man as formed in the image of God, and that the magistrate
who disowns this law as a law, disowns the divine foundation of
his office; but, on the other side, it is just as true that
thousands and thousands of innocent persons, or at least persons
not worthy of death, have fallen a sacrifice to the abuse or the
false application of this law ; and that along with the principle
of recompensative righteousness, there is a principle of grace
which rules in the kingdom of God, and is represented in the
O. T. by prophecy and the Chokma.   It is, moreover, a noticeable fact, that God did not visit with the punishment of death
the first murderer, the murderer of the innocent Abel, his
brother, but let the principle of grace so far prevail instead of
that of law, that He even protected his life against any avenger
of blood.   But after that the moral ruin of the human race
had reached that height which brought the Deluge over the
earth, there was promulgated to the post-diluvians the word of
the law, Gen. ix. 6, sanctioning this inviolable right of putting

to death by the hand of justice. The conduct of God regulates itself thus according to the aspect of the times. In the Mosaic law the greatness of guilt was estimated not externally (cf. Num. xxxv. 31), but internally, a very flexible limitation in its practical bearings. And that under certain circumstances grace might have the precedence of justice, the parable having in view the pardon of Absalom (2 Sam. xiv.) shows. But a word from God, like Ezek. xviii. 23, raises grace to a principle, and the word with which Jesus (John viii. 11) dismisses the adulteress is altogether an expression of this purpose of grace passing beyond the purpose of justice. In the later Jewish common-wealth, criminal justice was subordinated to the principle of predominating compassion; practical effect was given to the consideration of the value of human life during the trial, and even after the sentence was pronounced, and during a long time no sentence of death was passed by the Sanhedrim. But Jesus, who was Himself the innocent victim of a fanatical legal murder, adjudged, it is true, the supremacy to the sword; but He preached and practised love, which publishes grace for justice. He was Himself incarnate Love, offering Himself for sinners, the Mercy which Jahve proclaims by Ezek. xviii. 23. The so-called Christian state [" *Civitas Dei* "] is indeed in manifest opposition to this. But Augustine declares himself, on the supposition that the principle of grace must penetrate the new era, in all its conditions, that began with Christianity, for the suspension of punishment by death, especially because the heathen magistrates had abused the instrument of death, which, according to divine right, they had control over, to the destruction of Christians; and Ambrosius went so far as to impress it as a duty on a Christian judge who had pronounced the sentence of death, to exclude himself from the Holy Supper. The magisterial control over life and death had at that time gone to the extreme height of bloody violence, and thus in a certain degree it destroyed itself. Therefore Jansen changes the proverb (ver. 11) with the words of Ambrosius into the admonition : *Quando indulgentia non nocet publico, eripe inter-cessione, eripe gratia tu sacerdos, aut tu imperator eripe sub-scriptione indulgentiæ.* When Samuel Romilly's Bill to abolish the punishment of death for a theft amounting to the sum of

five shillings passed the English House of Commons, it was
thrown out by a majority in the House of Lords. Among
those who voted against the Bill were one archbishop and
five bishops. Our poet here in the Proverbs is of a different
mind. Even the law of Sinai appoints the punishment of
death only for man-stealing. The Mosaic code is incomparably milder than even yet the *Carolina*. In expressions, however, like the above, a true Christian spirit rules the spirit
which condemns all blood-thirstiness of justice, and calls forth
to a crusade not only against the inquisition, but also against
such unmerciful, cruel executions even as they prevailed in
Prussia in the name of law in the reign of Friedrich Wilhelm i.,
the Inexorable.

Vers. 13, 14. The proverb now following stands in no obvious
relation with the preceding. But in both a commencement is
made with two lines, which contain, in the former, the principal thought; in this here, its reason:

> Ver. 13 My son, eat honey, for it is good,
>   And honeycomb is sweet to thy taste.
>   14 So apprehend wisdom for thy soul:
>   When thou hast found it, there is a future,
>   And thy hope is not destroyed.

After its nearest fundamental thought, טוֹב, Arab. *tejjib*, means
that which smells and tastes well; honey (דְּבַשׁ, from דָּבַשׁ, to be
thick, consistent) has, besides, according to the old idea (*e.g.* in
the Koran), healing virtue, as in general bitterness is viewed as
a property of the poisonous, and sweetness that of the wholesome. וְנֹפֶת is second accus. dependent on אֱכָל-, for honey and
honeycomb were then spoken of as different; נֹפֶת (from
נָפַת, to pour, to flow out) is the purest honey (virgin-honey),
flowing of itself out of the comb. With right the accentuation
takes 13*b* as independent, the substantival clause containing
the reason, "for it is good:" honeycomb is sweet to thy taste,
i.e. applying itself to it with the impression of sweetness; עַל, as
at Neh. ii. 5; Ps. xvi. 6 (Hitzig).

In the כֵּן of 14*a*, it is manifest that ver. 13 is not spoken for
its own sake. To apprehend wisdom, is elsewhere equivalent
to, to receive it into the mind, i. 2, Eccles. i. 17 (cf. דַעַת בִּינָה,
iv. 1, and frequently), according to which Böttcher also here

explains : learn to understand wisdom. But כִּן unfolds itself in
14*bc* : even as honey has for the body, so wisdom has for the
soul, beneficent wholesome effects. דְעָה חכמה is thus not absolute, but is meant in relation to these effects. Rightly
Fleischer : *talem reputa;* Ewald : *sic (talem) scito sapientiam
(esse) animœ tuœ*, know, recognise wisdom as something advantageous to thy soul, and worthy of commendation. Incorrectly Hitzig explains אִם־מָצָאתָ, " if the opportunity presents
itself." Apart from this, that in such a case the words would
rather have been כִּי תְמְצָא, to find wisdom is always equivalent
to, to obtain it, to make it one's own, iii. 13, viii. 35 ; cf. ii. 5,
viii. 9. דְּעֶה [1] stands for דְּעָה, after the form רְדָה; שְׁבָה (after
Böttcher, § 396, not without the influence of the following
commencing sound), cf. the similar transitions of ⟊ into ⟊
placed together at Ps. xx. 4 ; the form דְּעֶה is also found, but
דְּעֶה is the form in the *Cod. Hilleli*,[2] as confirmed by Moses
Kimchi in *Comm.*, and by David Kimchi, *Michlol* 101*b*. With
וְיֵשׁ begins the apodosis (LXX., Jerome, Targ., Luther, Rashi,
Ewald, and others). In itself, ויֵשׁ (cf. Gen. xlvii. 6) might
also continue the conditional clause ; but the explanation, *si
inveneris (eam) et ad postremum ventum erit* (Fleischer, Bertheau,
Zöckler), has this against it, that יֵשׁ אַחֲרִית does not mean : the
end comes, but : there is an end, xxiii. 18 ; cf. xix. 18 ; here :
there is an end for thee, viz. an issue that is a blessed reward.
The promise is the same as at xxiii. 18. In our own language
we speak of the hope of one being cut off ; (Arab.) *jaz'a*, to be
cut off, is equivalent to, to give oneself up to despair.

> Ver. 15 Lie not in wait, oh wicked man, against the dwelling of the
>   righteous ;
>   Assault not his resting-place.
> 16 For seven times doth the righteous fall and rise again,
>   But the wicked are overthrown when calamity falls on them.

The אֹרֵב [lying in wait] and שֹׁדֵד [practising violence], against
which the warning is here given, are not directed, as at i. 11,
xix. 26, immediately against the person, but against the dwell-

---

[1] Write דְּעֶה with *Illuj* after the preceding *Legarmeh*, like 12*b*, הוּא
(*Thorath Emeth*, p. 28).
[2] *Vid.* Strack's *Prolegomena critica in V. T.* (1872), p. 19.

ing-place and resting-place (רְבֵץ, *e.g.* Jer. l. 6, as also נָוֶה, iii. 33) of the righteous, who, on his part, does injustice and wrong to no one; the warning is against coveting his house, Ex. xx. 17, and driving him by cunning and violence out of it. Instead of רָשָׁע, Symmachus and Jerome have incorrectly read רֶשַׁע, and from this misunderstanding have here introduced a sense without sense into ver. 15; many interpreters (Löwenstein, Ewald, Elster, and Zöckler) translate with Luther appositionally: as a wicked man, *i.e.* " with mischievous intent," like one stealthily lurking for the opportunity of taking possession of the dwelling of another, as if this could be done with a good intent: רָשָׁע is the vocative (Syr., Targ., *Venet.*: ἀσεβές), and this address (cf. Ps. lxxv. 5 f.) sharpens the warning, for it names him who acts in this manner by the right name. The reason, 16*a*, sounds like an echo of Job v. 19. שֶׁבַע signifies, as at Ps. cxix. 164, seven times; cf. מֵאָה, xvii. 10. וְקָם (not וָקָם) is *perf. consec.*, as וָחַי, *e.g.* Gen. iii. 22: and he rises afterwards (notwithstanding), but the transgressors come to ruin; בְּרָעָה, if a misfortune befall them (cf. xiv. 32), they stumble and fall, and rise no more.

Vers. 17, 18. Warning against a vindictive disposition, and joy over its satisfaction.

> Ver. 17 At the fall of thine enemy rejoice not,
> And at his overthrow let not thine heart be glad;
> 18 That Jahve see it not, and it be displeasing to Him,
> And He turns away His anger from Him.

The *Chethîb*, which in itself, as the plur. of category, אֹויְבֶיךָ, might be tolerable, has 17*b* against it: with right, all interpreters adhere to the *Kerî* אֹויִבְךָ (with *i* from *ē* in doubled close syllable, as in the like *Kerî*, 1 Sam. xxiv. 5). וּבְכִשְׁלֹו, for וּבְהִכָּשְׁלֹו, is the syncope usual in the *inf. Niph.* and *Hiph.*, which in *Niph.* occurs only once with the initial guttural (as בֵּעָטֵף) or half guttural (לֵרָאֹות). וְרַע is not adj. here as at 1 Sam. xxv. 3, but *perf.* with the force of a *fut.* (Symmachus: καὶ μὴ ἀρέσῃ ἐνώπιον αὐτοῦ). The proverb extends the duty of love even to an enemy; for it requires that we do good to him and not evil, and warns against rejoicing when evil befalls him. Hitzig, indeed, supposes that the noble morality which is expressed in ver. 17 is limited to a moderate extent by the motive assigned in 18*b*. Certainly the poet means to say that God could easily give a gracious turn for the better, as to the punishment of the wicked, to the decree of his anger against his enemy; but his meaning is not this, that one, from joy at the misfortune of others, ought to desist from interrupting the process of the destruction of his enemy, and let it go on to its end; but much rather, that one ought to abstain from this joy, so as not to experience the manifestation of God's displeasure thereat, by His granting grace to him against whom we rejoice to see God's anger go forth.[1]

Vers. 19, 20. Warning against envying the godless for their external prosperity:

> Be not enraged on account of evil-doers,
> Envy not the godless;
> 20 For the wicked men shall have no future,
> The light of the godless is extinguished.

Ver. 19 is a variation of Ps. xxxvii. 1; cf. also iii. 21 (where with בכל־דרכיו following the traditional תבחר is more appropriate than תתחר, which Hupfeld would here insert). תִּתְחַר is *fut. apoc.* of הִתְחָרה, to be heated (to be indignant), distinguished from the *Tiphel* תְּחָרֶה, to be jealous. The ground and occasion of being enraged, and on the other side, of jealousy or envy, is the prosperity of the godless, Ps. lxxiii. 3; cf. Jer. xii. 1. This anger at the apparently unrighteous division of fortune, this jealousy at the success in which the godless rejoice, rest on short-sightedness, which regards the present, and looks not on to the end. אַחֲרִית, merely as in the expression יֵשׁ אח', 14*b* (cf. Ps. xxxvii. 37), always denotes the happy, glorious issue indemnifying for past sufferings. Such an issue the wicked man has not; his light burns brightly on this side, but one day it is extinguished. In 20*b* is repeated xiii. 9; cf. xx. 20.

Vers. 21, 22. A warning against rebellious thoughts against God and the king:

> My son, honour Jahve and the king,
> And involve not thyself with those who are otherwise disposed;
> 22 For suddenly their calamity ariseth,
> And the end of their years, who knoweth it?

---

[1] This proverb, according to *Aboth* iv. 24, was the motto of that Samuel with the surname הקטן, who formulated ברכת המינים (the interpolation in the Schemone-Esre prayer directed against the schismatics): he thus distinguished between private enemies and the enemies of the truth.

The verb שָׁנָה, proceeding from the primary idea of folding
(*complicare, duplicare*), signifies transitively to do twice, to
repeat, xvii. 9, xxvi. 11, according to which Kimchi here inappropriately thinks on relapsing; and intransitively, to change,
to be different, Esth. i. 7, iii. 8. The Syr. and Targ. translate
the word שָׁטֵי, fools; but the *Kal* (טְעֲמוֹ) שָׁנָה occurs, indeed, in
the Syr., but not in the Heb., in the meaning *alienata est (mens
ejus)*; and besides, this meaning, *alieni*, is not appropriate here.
A few, however, with Saadia (cf. *Deutsch-Morgenländische
Zeitschr.* xxi. 616), the dualists (Manichees), understand it in a
dogmatic sense; but then שׁוֹנִים must be denom. of שָׁנַים, while
much more it is its root-word. Either שׁונים means those who
change, *novantes = novarum rerum studiosi*, which is, however,
exposed to this objection, that the Heb. שׁנה, in the transitive
sense to change, does not elsewhere occur; or it means, according to the *usus loq., diversos = diversum sentientes* (C. B.
Michaelis and others), and that with reference to 21*a*: הממרים
דבריהם ומצותם (Meîri, Immanuel), or מֹשנים מנהג החכמה (Ahron
b. Joseph). Thus they are called (for it is a common name of a
particular class of men) dissidents, oppositionists, or revolution-
aries, who recognise neither the monarchy of Jahve, the King
of kings, nor that of the earthly king, which perhaps Jerome
here means by the word *detractoribus* (= *detractatoribus*). The
Venet. incorrectly, σὺν τοῖς μισοῦσι, *i.e.* שׁוֹנְאִים. With בְּ at
xiv. 10, הִתְעָרֵב meant to mix oneself up with something, here
with עַם, to mix oneself with some one, *i.e.* to make common
cause with him.

The reason assigned in ver. 22 is, that although such persons
as reject by thought and action human and divine law may for
a long time escape punishment, yet suddenly merited ruin falls
on them. אֵיד is, according to its primary signification, weighty,
oppressive misfortune, *vid.* i. 27. In יָקוּם it is thought of as
hostile power (Hos. x. 14); or the rising up of God as Judge
(*e.g.* Isa. xxxiii. 10) is transferred to the means of executing
judgment. פִּיד (= פּוּד of פּוד or פִיד, Arab. *fâd*, fut. *jafûdu* or
jafîdu, a stronger power of *bâd*, cogn. אבד) is destruction (Arab.
feid, fîd, death); this word occurs, besides here, only thrice in the
Book of Job. But to what does שְׁנֵיהֶם refer? Certainly not to
Jahve and the king (LXX., Schultens, Umbreit, and Bertheau),

for in itself it is doubtful to interpret the genit. after פִּיד as designating the subject, but improper to comprehend God and man under one cipher. Rather it may refer to two, of whom one class refuse to God, the other to the king, the honour that is due (Jerome, Luther, and at last Zöckler); but in the foregoing, two are not distinguished, and the want of reverence for God, and for the magistrates appointed by Him, is usually met with, because standing in interchangeable relationship, in one and the same persons. Is there some misprint then in this word? Ewald suggests שְׁנֵיהֶם, *i.e.* of those who show themselves as שׁוֹנִים (*altercatores*) towards God and the king. In view of קָמֵיהֶם, Ex. xxxii. 25, this brevity of expression must be regarded as possible. But if this were the meaning of the word, then it ought to have stood in the first member (אִיד שׁניהם), and not in the second. No other conjecture presents itself. Thus שְׁנֵיהֶם is perhaps to be referred to the שׁוֹנִים, and those who engage with them: join thyself not with the opposers; for suddenly misfortune will come upon them, and the destruction of both (of themselves and their partisans), who knows it? But that also is not satisfactory, for after the address שְׁנֵיכֶם was to have been expected, 22*b*. Nothing remains, therefore, but to understand שְׁנֵיהֶם, with the Syr. and Targ., as at Job xxxvi. 11; the proverb falls into rhythms פִּתְאֹם and פִּיד, שׁוֹנִים and שְׁנֵיהֶם. But "the end of their year" is not equivalent to the hour of their death (Hitzig), because for this פִּידָם (cf. Arab. *feid* and *fîd*, death) was necessary; but to the expiring, the vanishing, the passing by of the year during which they have succeeded in maintaining their ground and playing a part. There will commence a time which no one knows beforehand when all is over with them. In this sense, "who knoweth," with its object, is equivalent to "suddenly ariseth," with its subject. In the LXX., after xxiv. 22, there follow one distich of the relations of man to the word of God as deciding their fate, one distich of fidelity as a duty towards the king, and the duty of the king, and one pentastich or hexastich of the power of the tongue and of the anger of the king. The Heb. text knows nothing of these three proverbs. Ewald has, *Jahrb.* xi. 18 f., attempted to translate them into Heb., and is of opinion that they are worthy of being regarded as original component parts of i.–xxix., and that they ought certainly to have come in after xxiv. 22. We doubt this originality, but recognise their translation from the Heb. Then follows in the LXX. the series of Proverbs, xxx. 1–14, which in the Heb. text bear the superscription of "the Words of Agur;" the second half of the "Words of Agur," together with the "Words of Lemuel," stand after xxiv. 34 of the Heb. text. The state of the matter is this, that in the copy from which the Alexandrines translated the Appendix xxx.–xxxi. 9, stood half of it, after the "Words of the Wise" [which extend from xxii. 17 to xxiv. 22], and half after the supplement headed "these also are from wise men" [xxiv. 23–34], so that only the proverbial ode in praise of the excellent matron [xxxi. 10] remains as an appendix to the Book of Hezekiah's collection, xxv.–xxix.

SECOND SUPPLEMENT TO THE FIRST SOLOMONIC COLLECTION.—XXIV. 23–34.

There now follows a brief appendix to the older Book of Proverbs, bearing the superscription, 23a, "*These also are from wise men,*" *i.e.* also the proverbs here following originate from wise men. The old translators (with the exception of Luther) have not understood this superscription; they mistake the *Lamed auctoris,* and interpret the ל as that of address: also these (proverbs) I speak to wise men, *sapientibus* (LXX., Syr., Targ., Jerome, *Venet.*). The formation of the superscription is like that of the Hezekiah collection, xxv. 1, and from this and other facts we have concluded (*vid.* vol. i. pp. 26, 27) that this second supplement originated from the same source as the extension of the older Book of Proverbs, by the appending of the more recent, and its appendices. The linguistic complexion of the proverbs here and there resembles that of the first appendix (cf. 29b with 12d, and ינעם, 25a, with נעים, xxii. 18, xxiii. 8, xxiv. 4); but, on the other hand, 23b refers back to xxviii. 21 of the Hezekiah collection, and in ver. 33 f. is repeated vi. 10 f. This appendix thus acknowledges its secondary character; the poet in minute details stands in the same relation to the Solomonic Mashal as that in which in general he stands to the author of the Introduction, i.–ix. That 23*b* is not in itself a proverb, we have already (vol. i. p. 6) proved; it is the first line of a hexastich (*vid.* vol. i. p. 16).

Vers. 23*b*–25. The curse of partiality and the blessing of impartiality:

> Respect of persons in judgment is by no means good:
> 24 He that saith to the guilty, "Thou art in the right,"
> Him the people curse, nations detest.
> 25 But to them who rightly decide, it is well,
> And upon them cometh blessing with good.

Partiality is either called שְׂאֵת פָּנִים, xviii. 5, respect to the person, for the partisan looks with pleasure on the פְּנֵי, the countenance, appearance, personality of one, by way of preference; or הַכֵּר־פָּנִים, as here and at xxviii. 21, for he places one person before another in his sight, or, as we say, has a regard to him; the latter expression is found in Deut. i. 17, xvi. 19. הִכִּיר (*vid.* xx. 11) means to regard sharply, whether from interest in the object, or because it is strange. בַּל Heidenheim regards as weaker than לֹא; but the reverse is the case (*vid.* vol. i. p. 204), as is seen from the derivation of this negative (= *balj*, from בָּלָה, to melt, to decay); thus it does not occur anywhere else than here with the pred. adj. The two supplements delight in this בל, xxii. 29, xxiii. 7, 35. The thesis 23*b* is now confirmed in vers. 24 and 25, from the consequences of this partiality and its opposite: He that saith (אֹמֵר, with *Mehuppach Legarmeh* from the last syllable, as rightly by Athias, Nissel, and Michaelis, *vid. Thorath Emeth*, p. 32) to the guilty: thou art right, *i.e.* he who sets the guilty free (for רָשָׁע and צַדִּיק have here the forensic sense of the post-bibl. חַיָּב and זַכַּי), him they curse, etc.; cf. the shorter proverb, xvii. 15, according to which a partial, unjust judge is an abomination to God. Regarding נָקַב (קָבַב) here and at xi. 26, Schultens, under Job iii. 8, is right; the word signifies *figere*, and hence to distinguish and make prominent by distinguishing as well as by branding; cf. *defigere*, to curse, properly, to pierce through. Regarding זָעַם, *vid.* at xxii. 14. עַמִּים and לְאֻמִּים (from עָמַם and לְאֹם, which both mean to bind and combine) are plur. of categ.: not merely

individuals, not merely families, curse such an unrighteous
judge and abhor him, but the whole people in all conditions
and ranks of society; for even though such an unjust judge
bring himself and his favourites to external honour, yet among
no people is conscience so blunted, that he who absolves the
crime and ennobles the miscarriage of justice shall escape the
vox populi. On the contrary, it goes well (יִנְעָם, like ii. 10,
ix. 17, but here with neut. indef. subj. as יִטַב, Gen. xii. 13, and
frequently) with those who place the right, and particularly the
wrong, fully to view ; מוֹכִיחַ is he who mediates the right, Job
ix. 33, and particularly who proves, censures, punishes the
wrong, ix. 7, and in the character of a judge as here, Amos
v. 10 ; Isa. xxix. 21. The genitive connection בִּרְכַּת־טוֹב is not
altogether of the same signification as יַיִן הַטּוֹב, wine of a good
sort, Song vii. 10, and אֵשֶׁת רַע, a woman of a bad kind, vi. 24,
for every blessing is of a good kind ; the gen. טוֹב thus, as at
Ps. xxi. 4, denotes the contents of the blessing ; cf. Eph. i. 3,
" with all spiritual blessings," in which the manifoldness of the
blessing is presupposed.

Ver. 26. Then follows a distich with the watchword נְבֹחִים :

> He kisseth the lips
> Who for the end giveth a right answer.

The LXX., Syr., and Targ. translate : one kisseth the lips
who, or : of those who . . . ; but such a meaning is violently
forced into the word (in that case the expression would have
been שְׂפָתַי מֵשִׁיב or שְׂפָתִים מְשִׁיבִים). Equally impossible is Theodotion's χείλεσι καταφιληθήσεται, for יִשָּׁק cannot be the *fut.
Niph.* Nor is it : lips kiss him who . . . (Rashi) ; for, to be
thus understood, the word ought to have been לְמֵשִׁיב. מֵשִׁיב is
naturally to be taken as the subj., and thus it supplies the
meaning : he who kisseth the lips giveth an excellent answer,
viz. the lips of him whom the answer concerns (Jerome, *Venet.*,
Luther). But Hitzig ingeniously, " the words reach from the
lips of the speaker to the ears of the hearer, and thus he kisses
his ear with his lips." But since to kiss the ear is not a custom,
not even with the Florentines, then a welcome answer, if its
impression is to be compared to a kiss, is compared to a kiss on
the lips. Hitzig himself translates : he commends himself with
the lips who . . . ; but נָשַׁק may mean to join oneself, Gen.

xli. 40, as kissing is equivalent to the joining of the lips ; it does
not mean intrans. to cringe.   Rather the explanation : he who
joins the lips together . . .; for he, viz. before reflecting, closed
his lips together (suggested by Meîri) ; but נשׁק, with שׂפתים,
brings the idea of kissing, *labra labris jungere,* far nearer.
This prevails against Schultens' *armatus est (erit) labia,* besides
נשׁק, certainly, from the primary idea of connecting (laying
together) (*vid.* Ps. lxxviii. 9), to equip (arm) oneself therewith ;
but the meaning arising from thence : with the lips he arms
himself . . . is direct nonsense.   Fleischer is essentially right,
*Labra osculatur (i.e. quasi osculum oblatum reddit) qui congrua
respondet.*   Only the question has nothing to do with a kiss ;
but if he who asks receives a satisfactory answer, an enlightening counsel, he experiences it as if he received a kiss.   The
Midrash incorrectly remarks under דְּבָרִים נְכֹחִים, "words of
merited denunciation," according to which the Syr. translates.
Words are meant which are corresponding to the matter and the
circumstances, and suitable for the end (cf. viii. 9).   Such
words are like as if the lips of the inquirer received a kiss from
the lips of the answerer.

Ver. 27. Warning against the establishing of a household
where the previous conditions are wanting :

> Set in order thy work without,
> And make it ready for thyself beforehand in the fields,—
> After that then mayest thou build thine house.

The interchange of בַּחוּץ and בַּשָּׂדֶה shows that by מְלֶאכֶת הַשָּׂדֶה
field-labour, 1 Chron. xxvii. 26, is meant.   הכין, used of arrangement, procuring, here with מלאכה, signifies the setting in
order of the work, viz. the cultivation of the field.   In the
parallel member, עַתְּדָה, carrying also its object, in itself is admissible : make preparations (LXX., Syr.) ; but the punctuation עַתְּדָהּ (Targ., *Venet.;* on the other hand, Jerome and Luther
translate as if the words were וְעַתְּדָה הַשָּׂדֶה) is not worthy of
being contended against : set it (the work) in the fields in
readiness, *i.e.* on the one hand set forward the present necessary work, and on the other hand prepare for that which next
follows; thus : do completely and circumspectly what thy
calling as a husbandman requires of thee,—then mayest thou
go to the building and building up of thy house (*vid.* at ver. 3,

xiv. 1), to which not only the building and setting in order of
a convenient dwelling, but also the bringing home of a house-
wife and the whole setting up of a household belongs ; prosperity
at home is conditioned by this—one fulfils his duty without in
the fields actively and faithfully. One begins at the wrong
end when he begins with the building of his house, which is
much rather the result and goal of an intelligent discharge of
duty within the sphere of one's calling. The *perf.*, with ו
after a date, such as עוֹד, מְעַט אַחַר, and the like, when things
that will or should be done are spoken of, has the fut. signification of a *perf. consec.*, Gen. iii. 5; Ex. xvi. 6 f., xvii. 4;
Ewald, § 344*b*.

Ver. 28. Warning against unnecessary witnessing to the
disadvantage of another :

> Never be a causeless witness against thy neighbour ;
> And shouldest thou use deceit with thy lips ?

The phrase עֵד־חִנָּם does not mean a witness who appears against
his neighbour without knowledge of the facts of the case, but
one who has no substantial reason for his giving of testimony ;
חִנָּם means groundless, with reference to the occasion and
motive, iii. 30, xxiii. 29, xxvi. 2. Other designations stood for
false witnesses (LXX., Syr., Targ.). Rightly Jerome, the
Venet., and Luther, without, however, rendering the gen. connection עֵד־חנם, as it might have been by the adj.

In 28*b*, Chajûg derives וַהֲפִתִּיתָ from פָּתַת, to break in pieces,
to crumble; for he remarks it might stand, with the passing over
of *ô* into *î*, for וַהֲפִתּוֹתָ [and thou wilt whisper]. But the ancients
had no acquaintance with the laws of sound, and therefore
with *naive* arbitrariness regarded all as possible; and Böttcher,
indeed, maintains that the *Hiphil* of פתת may be הֵפִתִּית as well
as הֵפֵתוֹת ; but the former of these forms with *î* could only be
metaplastically possible, and would be הֵפִתִּית (*vid.* Hitzig under
Jer. xi. 20). And what can this *Hiph.* of פתת mean ? " To
crumble " one's neighbours (Chajûg) is an unheard of expression ; and the meanings, to throw out crumbs, viz. crumbs
of words (Böttcher), or to speak with a broken, subdued voice
(Hitzig), are extracted from the rare Arab. *fatâfit* (*fatafit*), for
which the lexicographers note the meaning of a secret, moaning
sound. When we see והפתית standing along with בִּשְׂפָתֶיךָ, then

before all we are led to think of פתח [to open], xx. 19; Ps.
lxxiii. 36. But we stumble at the interrog. הֲ, which nowhere
else appears connected with ו. Ewald therefore purposes to
read וְהִפְתִּיתָ [and will open wide] (LXX. μηδὲ πλατύνου):
" that thou usest treachery with thy lips; " but from הפתה, to
make wide open, Gen. ix. 27, " to use treachery " is, only for
the flight of imagination, not too wide a distance. On וַהֲ, et
num, one need not stumble; וַהֲלֹא, 2 Sam. xv. 35, shows that
the connection of a question by means of ו is not inadmissible;
Ewald himself takes notice that in the Arab. the connection of
the interrogatives أَ and هَل with و and فَ is quite common;[1]
and thus he reaches the explanation : wilt thou befool then by
thy lips, i.e. pollute by deceit, by inconsiderate, wanton testimony against others? This is the right explanation, which
Ewald hesitates about only from the fact that the interrog. הֲ
comes in between the ו consec. and its perf., a thing which is
elsewhere unheard of. But this difficulty is removed by the
syntactic observation, that the perf. after interrogatives has
often the modal colouring of a conj. or optative, e.g. after the
interrog. pronoun, Gen. xxi. 7, quis dixerit, and after the interrogative particle, as here and at 2 Kings xx. 9, iveritne,
where it is to be supplied (vid. at Isa. xxxviii. 8). Thus: et
num persuaseris (deceperis) labiis tuis, and shouldest thou practise slander with thy lips, for thou bringest thy neighbour,
without need, by thy uncalled for rashness, into disrepute?

" It is a question, âl'nakar (cf. xxiii. 5), for which أَ (not هَل),
in the usual Arab. interrogative: how, thou wouldest? one
then permits the inquirer to draw the negative answer: " No, I
will not do it " (Fleischer).

Ver. 29. The following proverb is connected as to its subject with the foregoing: one ought not to do evil to his neighbour without necessity; even evil which has been done to one
must not be requited with evil:

> Say not, " As he hath done to me, so I do to him:
> I requite the man according to his conduct."

---

[1] We use the forms âwa, âba, âthûmm, for we suppose the interrogative
to the copula; we also say fahad, vid. Mufaṣṣal, p. 941.

On the ground of public justice, the *talio* is certainly the nearest form of punishment, Lev. xxiv. 19 f.; but even here the Sinaitic law does not remain in the retortion of the injury according to its external form (it is in a certain manner practicable only with regard to injury done to the person and to property), but places in its stead an atonement measured and limited after a higher point of view. On pure moral grounds, the *jus talionis* ("as thou to me, so I to thee") has certainly no validity. Here he to whom injustice is done ought to commit his case to God, xx. 22, and to oppose to evil, not evil but good; he ought not to set himself up as a judge, nor to act as one standing on a war-footing with his neighbour (Judg. xv. 11); but to take God as his example, who treats the sinner, if only he seeks it, not in the way of justice, but of grace (Ex. xxxiv. 6 f.). The expression 29*b* reminds of xxiv. 12. Instead of לָאָדָם, there is used here, where the speaker points to a definite person, the phrase לָאִישׁ. Jerome, the *Venet.*, and Luther translate: to each one, as if the word were vocalized thus, לְאִישׁ (Ps. lxii. 13).

A Mashal ode of the slothful, in the form of a record of experiences, concludes this second supplement (*vid.* vol. i. p. 17):

> Ver. 30 The field of a slothful man I came past,
> And the vineyard of a man devoid of understanding.
> 31 And, lo! it was wholly filled up with thorns;
> Its face was covered with nettles;
> And its wall of stones was broken down.
> 32 But I looked and directed my attention to it;
> I saw it, and took instruction from it:
> 33 "A little sleep, a little slumber,
> A little folding of the hands to rest.
> 34 Then cometh thy poverty apace,
> And thy want as an armed man."

The line 29*b* with לָאִישׁ is followed by one with אִישׁ. The form of the narrative in which this warning against drowsy slothfulness is clothed, is like Ps. xxxvii. 35 f. The distinguishing of different classes of men by אִישׁ and אדם (cf. xxiv. 20) is common in proverbial poetry. עָבַרְתִּי, at the close of the first parallel member, retains its *Pathach* unchanged. The description: and, lo! (וְהִנֵּה, with *Pazer*, after *Thorath Emeth*, p. 34, Anm. 2) it was . . . refers to the vineyard, for גֶדֶר אֲבָנָיו

(its stone wall, like Isa. ii. 20, "its idols of silver") is, like Num. xxii. 24, Isa. v. 5, the fencing in of the vineyard. עָלָה כֻלּוֹ, *totus excreverat* (*in carduos*), refers to this as subject, cf. in Ausonius: *apex vitibus assurgit;* the Heb. construction is as Isa. v. 6, xxxiv. 13; Gesen. § 133, 1, Anm. 2. The sing. קִמָּשׂוֹן of קִמְּשׂוֹנִים does not occur; perhaps it means properly the weed which one tears up to cast it aside, for (Arab.) *kumâsh* is matter dug out of the ground.[1] The ancients interpret it by *urticæ;* and חָרֻל, plur. חֲרֻלִּים (as from חָרָל), R. חר, to burn, appears, indeed, to be the name of the nettle; the botanical name (Arab.) *khullar* (beans, pease, at least a leguminous plant) is from its sound not Arab., and thus lies remote.[2] The Pual כָּסּוּ sounds like Ps. lxxx. 11 (cf. כָּלּוּ, Ps. lxxii. 20); the position of the words is as this passage of the Psalm; the Syr., Targ., Jerome, and the *Venet.* render the construction actively, as if the word were כִּסּוּ.

In ver. 32, Hitzig proposes to read וָאֶחֱזֶה: and I stopped (stood still); but אחז is trans., not only at Eccles. vii. 9, but also at ii. 15: to hold anything fast; not: to hold oneself still. And for what purpose the change? A contemplating and looking at a thing, with which the turning and standing near is here connected, manifestly includes a standing still; רָאִיתִי, after וָאֶחֱזֶה, is, as commonly after הביט (*e.g.* Job xxxv. 5, cf. Isa. xlii. 18), the expression of a lingering looking at an object after the attention has been directed to it. In modern impressions, וָאֶחֱזֶה אָנֹכִי are incorrectly accentuated; the old editions have rightly וָאֶחֱזֶה with *Rebia;* for not וא' אנכי, but אנכי אשׁית are connected. In viii. 17, this prominence of the personal pronoun serves for the expression of reciprocity; elsewhere, as *e.g.* Gen. xxi. 24, 2 Kings vi. 3, and particularly, frequently in Hosea, this circumstantiality does not make the subject prominent, but the action; here the suitable extension denotes that he rightly makes his comments at leisure (Hitzig). שִׁית לֵב is, as at xxii. 17, the turning of attention and reflection;

---

[1] This is particularly the name of what lies round about on the ground in the Bedouin tents, and which one takes up from thence (from *kamesh*, cogn. קבץ קמץ, *ramasser*, cf. the journal המגיד, 1871, p. 287b); in modern Arab., linen and matter of all kinds; *vid.* Bocthor, under *linge* and *étoffe.*

[2] Perhaps ὄλυρα, vid. Lagarde's *Gesamm. Abhandl.* p. 59.

elsewhere לָקַח מוּסָר, to receive a moral, viii. 10, Jer. vii. 28, is here equivalent to, to abstract, deduce one from a fact, to take to oneself a lesson from it. In vers. 33 and 34 there is a repetition of vi. 9, 10. Thus, as ver. 33 expresses, the sluggard speaks to whom the neglected piece of ground belongs, and ver. 34 places before him the result. Instead of כְּמֵהַלֵּךְ of the original passage [vi. 9, 10], here מִתְהַלֵּךְ, of the coming of poverty like an avenging Nemesis; and instead of וּמַחְסֹרְךָ, here וּמַחְסֹרֶיךָ (the Cod. *Jaman.* has it without the י), which might be the *plene* written pausal form of the sing. (*vid.* at vi. 3, cf. vi. 11), but is more surely regarded as the plur.: thy deficits, or wants; for to thee at one time this, and at another time that, and finally all things will be wanting. Regarding the variants רָאשֶׁךָ and רֵישֶׁךָ (with א in the original passage, here in the borrowed passage with י), *vid.* at x. 4. כְּאִישׁ מָגֵן is translated in the LXX. by ὥσπερ ἀγαθὸς δρομεύς (*vid.* at vi. 11); the Syr. and Targ. make from it a גַּבְרָא טַבְלָרָא, *tabellarius*, a letter-carrier, coming with the speed of a courier.

SECOND COLLECTION OF SOLOMONIC PROVERBS.— XXV.–XXIX.

The older Solomonic Book of Proverbs, with its introduction, i. 9, and its two supplements, (1) xxii. 17–xxiv. 22, (2) xxiv. 23–34, is now followed by a more modern Solomonic Book of Proverbs, a second extensive series of מִשְׁלֵי שְׁלֹמֹה, which the collector has introduced with the superscription:

xxv. 1 These also are proverbs of Solomon,
　　　Which the men of Hezekiah the king of Judah have collected.

Hezekiah, in his concern for the preservation of the national literature, is the Jewish Pisistratos, and the "men of Hezekiah" are like the collectors of the poems of Homer, who were employed by Pisistratos for that purpose. גַּם־אֵלֶּה is the subject, and in Cod. 1294, and in the editions of Bomberg 1515, Hartmann 1595, Nissel, Jablonsky, Michaelis, has *Dechî*. This title is like that of the second supplement, xxiv. 23. The form of the name חִזְקִיָּה, abbreviated from יְחִזְקִיָּהוּ (חִזְקִיָּהוּ), is not favourable to the derivation of the title from the collectors themselves. The LXX. translates: Αὗται αἱ παιδεῖαι Σαλω-μῶντος αἱ ἀδιάκριτοι (cf. Jas. iii. 17), ἃς ἐξεγράψαντο οἱ φίλοι Ἐζεκίου, for which Aquila has ἃς μετῆραν ἄνδρες Ἐζεκίου, Jerome, transtulerunt. הֶעְתִּיק signifies, like (Arab.) nsah, נָסַח, to snatch away, to take away, to transfer from another place; in later Heb.: to transcribe from one book into another, to translate from one language into another: to take from another place and place together; the Whence? remains undetermined: according to the anachronistic rendering of the Midrash מגניותם, i.e. from the Apocrypha; according to Hitzig, from the mouths of the people; more correctly Euchel and others: from their scattered condition, partly oral, partly written. Vid. regarding העתיק, Zunz, in Deutsch - Morgenl. Zeitsch. xxv. 147 f., and regarding the whole title, vol. i. pp. 5, 6; regarding the forms of proverbs in this second collection, vol. i. p. 17; regarding their relation to the first, and their end and aim, vol. i. pp. 25, 26. The first Collection of Proverbs is a Book for Youth, and this second a Book for the People.

Ver. 2. It is characteristic of the purpose of the book that it begins with proverbs of the king:

> It is the glory of God to conceal a thing;
> And the glory of the king to search out a matter.

That which is the glory of God and the glory of the king in itself, and that by which they acquire glory, stand here contrasted. The glory of God consists in this, to conceal a matter, i.e. to place before men mystery upon mystery, in which they become conscious of the limitation and insufficiency of their knowledge, so that they are constrained to acknowledge, Deut. xxix. 28, that " secret things belong unto the Lord our God." There are many things that are hidden and are known only to God, and we must be contented with that which He sees it good to make known to us.[1] The honour of kings, on the contrary, who as pilots have to steer the ship of the state (xi. 14), and as supreme judges to administer justice (1 Kings iii. 9), consists in this, to search out a matter, i.e. to place in the

---

[1] Cf. von Lasaulx, Philosophie der Geschichte, p. 128 f.: " God and Nature love to conceal the beginning of things."

light things that are problematical and subjects of controversy, in conformity with their high position, with surpassing intelligence, and, in conformity with their responsibility, with conscientious zeal. The thought that it is the glory of God to veil Himself in secrecy (Isa. lv. 15; cf. 1 Kings viii. 12), and of the king, on the contrary, not to surround himself with an impenetrable nimbus, and to withdraw into inaccessible remoteness,—this thought does not, immediately at least, lie in the proverb, which refers that which is concealed, and its contrary, not to the person, but to a matter. Also that God, by the concealment of certain things, seeks to excite to activity human research, is not said in this proverb; for 2*b* does not speak of the honour of wise men, but of kings; the searching out, 2*b*, thus does not refer to that which is veiled by God. But since the honour of God at the same time as the welfare of men, and the honour of the king as well as the welfare of his people, is to be thought of, the proverb states that God and the king promote human welfare in very different ways,—God, by concealing that which sets limits to the knowledge of man, that he may not be uplifted ; and the king, by research, which brings out the true state of the matter, and thereby guards the political and social condition against threatening danger, secret injuries, and the ban of offences unatoned for. This proverb, regarding the difference between that which constitutes the honour of God and of the king, is followed by one which refers to that in which the honour of both is alike.

> Ver. 3 The heavens in height, and the earth in depth,
> And the heart of kings are unsearchable.

This is a proverb in the priamel-form, *vid.* p. 13. The *praeambulum* consists of three subjects to which the predicate אֵין חֵקֶר [= no searching out] is common. "As it is impossible to search through the heavens and through the earth, so it is also impossible to search the hearts of common men (like the earth), and the hearts of kings (like the heavens)" (Fleischer). The meaning, however, is simple. Three unsearchable things are placed together : the heavens, with reference to their height, stretching into the impenetrable distance ; the earth, in respect to its depth, reaching down into the immeasurable abyss ; and the heart of kings—it is this third thing which the proverb

particularly aims at—which in themselves, and especially with
that which goes on in their depths, are impenetrable and unsearchable. The proverb is a warning against the delusion of
being flattered by the favour of the king, which may, before
one thinks of it, be withdrawn or changed even into the contrary; and a counsel to one to take heed to his words and acts,
and to see to it that he is influenced by higher motives than by
the fallacious calculation of the impression on the view and
disposition of the king. The לְ in both cases is the expression
of the reference, as *e.g.* at 2 Chron. ix. 22.   וָאָרֶץ, not = וְהָאָרֶץ,
but like Isa. xxvi. 19, lxv. 17, for וָאָרֶץ, which generally occurs
only in the *st. constr.*

There now follows an emblematic (*vid.* vol. i. p. 10)
tetrastich :

> Ver. 4 Take away the dross from silver,
>   So there is ready a vessel for the goldsmith ;
>   5 Take away the wicked from the king,
>   And his throne is established by righteousness.

The form הָגוֹ (cf. the *inf. Poal* הֹגוֹ, Isa. lix. 13) is regarded by
Schultens as showing a ground-form הָגַו; but there is also
found *e.g.* עָשׂוֹ, whose ground-form is עָשׂוֹ; the verb הָגָה, R. הג
(whence Arab. *hajr, discedere*), cf. יָנָה (whence הִגָּה, *semovit*,
2 Sam. xx. 13 = Syr. *âwagy*, cf. Arab. *âwjay*, to withhold, to
abstain from), signifies to separate, withdraw; here, of the separation of the סִיגִים, the refuse, *i.e.* the dross (*vid.* regarding the
plena scriptio, Baer's *krit. Ausg. des Jesaia*, under i. 22); the
goldsmith is designated by the word צֹרֵף, from צָרַף, to turn,
change, as he who changes the as yet drossy metal by means of
smelting, or by purification in water, into that which is pure.
In 5*a* הגה is, as at Isa. xxvii. 8, transferred to a process of moral
purification; what kind of persons are to be removed from the
neighbourhood of the king is shown by Isa. i. 22, 23. Here
also (as at Isa. *l.c.*) the emblem or figure of ver. 4 is followed
in ver. 5 by its moral antitype aimed at. The punctuation of
both verses is wonderfully fine and excellent. In ver. 4, ויצא
is not pointed וַיֵּצֵא, but as the consecutive *modus* וַיֵּצֵא; this first
part of the proverb refers to a well-known process of art: the
dross is separated from the silver (*inf. absol.*, as xii. 7, xv. 22),
and so a vessel (utensil) proceeds from the goldsmith, for he

manufactures pure silver; the ל is here similarly used as the
designation of the subject in the passive, xiii. 13, xiv. 20. In
ver. 5, on the contrary, וַיָּבֹן (וַיָּבֹן) is not the punctuation used,
but the word is pointed indicatively וְיָבֹן; this second part of
the proverb expresses a moral demand (*inf. absol.* in the sense of
the imperative, Gesen. § 131, 4*b* like xvii. 12, or an optative or
concessive conjunction): let the godless be removed, לִפְנֵי מֶלֶךְ,
i.e. not from the neighbourhood of the king, for which the
words are מִלִּפְנֵי מלך; also not those standing before the king,
i.e. in his closest neighbourhood (Ewald, Bertheau); but since,
in the absolute, הֲגֹה, not an act of another in the interest of the
king, but of the king himself, is thought of: let the godless be
removed from before the king, *i.e.* because he administers justice
(Hitzig), or more generally: because after that Psalm (ci.),
which is the "mirror of princes," he does not suffer him to come
into his presence.   Accordingly, the punctuation is בְּצֶדֶק, not
בְּצֶדֶק (xvi. 12); because such righteousness is meant as separates
the רָשָׁע from it and itself from him, as Isa. xvi. 5 (*vid.* Hitzig),
where the punctuation of בַּחֶסֶד denotes that favour towards
Moab seeking protection.   There now follows a second proverb with מלך, as the one just explained was a second with
מלכים: a warning against arrogance before kings and nobles.

> Ver. 6 Display not thyself before the king,
>   And approach not to the place of the great.
>   7 For better that one say to thee, " Come up hither,"
>   Than that they humble thee before a prince,
>   Whom thine eyes had seen.

The גְּדֹלִים are those, like xviii. 16, who by virtue of their
descent and their office occupy a lofty place of honour in the
court and in the state.   נָדִיב (*vid.* under viii. 16) is the noble in
disposition and the nobleman by birth, a general designation
which comprehends the king and the princes.   The *Hithpa.*
הִתְהַדֵּר is like the reflex forms xii. 9, xiii. 7, for it signifies to
conduct oneself as הָדוּר or נֶהְדָּר (*vid.* xx. 29), to play the part of
one highly distinguished.   עָמַד has, 6*b*, its nearest signification:
it denotes, not like נִצַּב, standing still, but approaching to, *e.g.*
Jer. vii. 2.   The reason given in ver. 7 harmonizes with the rule
of wisdom, Luke xiv. 10 f.: better is the saying to thee, *i.e.* that
one say to thee (Ewald, § 304*b*), עֲלֵה הֵנָּה (so the *Olewejored* is

to be placed), προσανάβηθι ἀνώτερον (thus in Luke), than that
one humble thee לִפְנֵי נָדִיב, not : because of a prince (Hitzig),
for לפני nowhere means either *pro* (xvii. 18) or *propter*, but
before a prince, so that thou must yield to him (cf. xiv. 19),
before him whom thine eyes had seen, so that thou art not
excused if thou takest up the place appropriate to him. Most
interpreters are at a loss to explain this relative. Luther :
" which thine eyes must see," and Schultens : *ut videant oculi
tui.* Michaelis, syntactically admissible: *quem videre gestiverunt
oculi tui*, viz. to come near to him, according to Bertheau, with
the request that he receives some high office. Otherwise
Fleischer : before the king by whom thou and thine are seen,
so much the more felt is the humiliation when it comes upon
one after he has pressed so far forward that he can be perceived
by the king. But נדיב is not specially the king, but any distinguished personage whose place he who has pressed forward
has taken up, and from which he must now withdraw when the
right possessor of it comes and lays claim to his place. אֲשֶׁר is
never used in poetry without emphasis. Elsewhere it is equivalent to ὅντινα, *quippe quem*, here equivalent to ὅνπερ, *quem
quidem.* Thine eyes have seen him in the company, and thou
canst say to thyself, this place belongs to him, according to his
rank, and not to thee,—the humiliation which thou endurest is
thus well deserved, because, with eyes to see, thou wert so blind.
The LXX., Syr., Symmachus (who reads 8*a*, לְרֹב, εἰς πλῆθος),
and Jerome, refer the words " whom thine eyes had seen " to
the proverb following ; but אשר does not appropriately belong to
the beginning of a proverb, and on the supposition that the
word לָרִב is generally adopted, except by Symmachus, they are
also heterogeneous to the following proverb :

Ver. 8 Go not forth hastily to strife,
      That it may not be said, " What wilt thou do in the end
        thereof,
      When now thy neighbour bringeth disgrace upon thee ? "
  9 Art thou striving with thy neighbour ? strive with him,
      But disclose not the secret of another ;
 10 That he who heareth it may not despise thee,
      And thine evil name depart no more.

Whether רִיב in לָרִיב is *infin.*, as at Judg. xxi. 22, or *subst.*, as at

2 Chron. xix. 8, is not decided: *ad litigandum* and *ad litem*
harmonize. As little may it be said whether in אַל־תֵּצֵא [go not
forth], a going out to the gate (court of justice), or to the place
where he is to be met who is to be called to account, is to be
thought of; in no respect is the sense metaphorical: let not
thyself transgress the bounds of moderation, *ne te laisse pas em-
porter;* יָצָא לָרִב is correlate to בּוֹא לָרִיב, Judg. xxi. 22. The use of
פֶּן in 8*b* is unprecedented. Euchel and Löwenstein regard it as
an *imper.*: reflect upon it (test it); but פְּנֵה does not signify this,
and the interjectional הַם does not show the possibility of an
imper. Kal פֶּן, and certainly not פֶּן (פֶּ). The conj. פֶּן is the connecting form of an original subst. (= *panj*), which signifies a
turning away. It is mostly connected with the future, according to which Nolde, Oetinger, Ewald, and Bertheau explain מה
indefinite, something, viz. unbecoming. In itself, it may,
perhaps, be possible that פן מה was used in the sense of *ne quid*
(*Venet.* μήποτέ τι); but "to do something," for "to commit
something bad," is improbable; also in that case we would
expect the words to be thus: פֶּן תַּעֲשֶׂה מַה. Thus מה will be an
interrogative, as at 1 Sam. xx. 10 (*vid.* Keil), and the expression is brachylogical: that thou comest not into the situation
not to know what thou oughtest to do (Rashi: פֶּן תָּבֹא לִידֵי לֹא תֵדַע
מַה לַעֲשׂוֹת), or much rather anakoluth.; for instead of saying
פֶּן־לֹא תֵדַע מַה־לַעֲשׂוֹת, the poet, shunning this unusual פֶּן לֹא, adopts
at once the interrogative form: that it may not be said at the
end thereof (viz. of the strife): what wilt thou do? (Umbreit,
Stier, Elster, Hitzig, and Zöckler.) This extreme perplexity
would occur if thy neighbour (with whom thou disputest
so eagerly and unjustly) put thee to shame, so that thou
standest confounded (כלם, properly to hurt, French *blesser*).
If now the summons 9*a* follows this warning against going out
for the purpose of strife: fight out thy conflict with thy neighbour, then רִיבְךָ, set forth with emphasis, denotes not such a
strife as one is surprised into, but that into which one is drawn,
and the *tuam* in *causam tuam* is accented in so far as 9*b* localizes
the strife to the personal relation of the two, and warns against
the drawing in of an אַחֵר, *i.e.* in this case, of a third person:
and expose not the secret of another אַל־תְּגַל (after *Michlol*
130*a*, and Ben-Bileam, who places the word under the פ״בס, פתחין בס,

is vocalized with *Pathach* on נ, as is Cod. 1294, and elsewhere
in correct texts). One ought not to bring forward in a dispute,
as material of proof and means of acquittal, secrets entrusted
to him by another, or secrets which one knows regarding the
position and conduct of another; for such faithlessness and
gossiping affix a stigma on him who avails himself of them, in
the public estimation, ver. 10 ; that he who hears it may not
blame thee (חֵפֶר = Aram. חֲסַד, *vid.* under xiv. 34), and the evil
report concerning thee continue without recall. Fleischer : *ne
infamia tua non recedat i. e. nunquam desinat per ora hominum
propagari*, with the remark, " in דִּבָּה, which properly means a
stealthy creeping on of the rumour, and in שׁוּב lies a (Arab.)
tarshyh," *i.e.* the two ideas stand in an interchangeable relation
with a play upon the words : the evil rumour, once put in circulation, will not again retrace its steps ; but, on the contrary,
as Virgil says :

> *Mobilitate viget viresque acquirit eundo.*

In fact, every other can sooner rehabilitate himself in the public
estimation than he who is regarded as a prattler, who can keep
no secret, or as one so devoid of character that he makes public
what he ought to keep silent, if he can make any use of it in
his own interest. In regard to such an one, the words are continually applicable, *hic niger est, hunc tu, Romane, caveto*, xx. 19.
The LXX. has, instead of ורבתך 10*b*, read וּמְרִיבָתְךָ, and translated it with the addition of a long appendix : " They quarrel,
and hostilities will not cease, but will be to thee like death.
Kindness and friendship deliver, let these preserve thee, that
thou mayest not become one meriting reproaches (Jerome : *ne
exprobrabilis fias*), but guard thy ways, εὐσυναλλάκτως."

The first emblematical distich of this collection now follows:

> Ver. 11 Golden apples in silver salvers.
> A word spoken according to its circumstances.

The Syr. and Jerome vocalize דְּבַר דָּבָר, and the Targ. דְּבַר דֹּבֵר ;
both are admissible, but the figure and that which is represented are not placed in so appropriate a relation as by דָּבָר דְּבַר ;
the wonderfully penetrating expression of the text, which is
rendered by the traditional *nikkud*, agrees here with the often
occurring דֹּבֵר (= מְדַבֵּר), also its passive דָּבוּר. The defective

writing is like, *e.g.*, בְּטַח, Ps. cxii. 7, and gives no authority to prefer דְּבַר = מִדְבָּר (Böttcher). That דְּבָרֵי, corresponding to the plur. תִּפּוּחֵי, is not used, arises from this, that דבר is here manifestly not a word without connection, but a sentence of motive, contents, and aim united. For עַל־אָפְנָיו, the meaning of בְּעִתּוֹ presents itself from xv. 23, according to which, among the old interpreters, Symmachus, Jerome, and Luther render " at its time." Abulwalîd compared the Arab. *âiffan* (*âibban*, also *'iffan*, whence *'aly 'iffanihi, justo tempore*), which, as Orelli has shown in his *Synon. der Zeitbegriffe*, p. 21 f., comes from the roots *af ab*, to drive (from within) going out, time as consisting of individual moments, the one of which drives on the other, and thus denotes time as a course of succession. One may not hesitate as to the prep. עַל, for אפנים would, like עִתּוֹת, denote the circumstances, the relations of the time, and עַל would, as *e.g.* in עַל־פִּי and עַל־דִּבְרָתִי, have the meaning of κατά. But the form אָפְנָיו, which like חָפְנָיו, Lev. xvi. 12, sounds dualistic, appears to oppose this. Hitzig supposes that אָפְנַיִם may designate the time as a circle, with reference to the two arches projecting in opposite directions, but uniting themselves together; but the circle which time describes runs out from one point, and, moreover, the Arab. names for time *âfaf, âifaf*, and the like, which interchange with *âiffan*, show that this does not proceed from the idea of circular motion. Ewald and others take for אפניו the meaning of wheels (the *Venet.*, after Kimchi, ἐπὶ τῶν τροχῶν αὐτῆς), whereby the form is to be interpreted as dual of אֹפֶן = אוֹפָן, " a word driven on its wheels,"—so Ewald explains : as the potter quickly and neatly forms a vessel on his wheels, thus a fit and quickly framed word. But דבר signifies to drive cattle and to speak = to cause words to follow one another (cf. Arab. *syâk*, pressing on = flow of words), but not to drive = to fashion in that artisan sense. Otherwise Böttcher, " a word fitly spoken, a pair of wheels perfect in their motion," to which he compares the common people " in their jesting," and adduces all kinds of heterogeneous things partly already rejected by Orelli (*e.g.* the Homeric ἐπιτροχάδην, which is certainly no commendation). But "jesting" is not appropriate here; for what man conceives of human speech as a carriage, one only sometimes compares that of a babbler to a sledge, or says of him that he

shoves the cart into the mud.[1] Is it then thus decided that אָפְנָיו
is a dual? It may be also like אֲשֵׁרָיו, the plur. especially in the
adverbial expression before us, which readily carried the abbreviation with it (*vid.* Gesen. *Lehrgebr.* § 134, Anm. 17). On this
supposition, Orelli interprets אֹפֶן from אָפַן, to turn, in the sense
of turning about, circumstances, and reminds of this, that in the
post.-bibl. Heb. this word is used as indefinitely as τρόπος, *e.g.*
בְּאוֹפֶן מה, *quodammodo* (*vid.* Reland's *Analecta Rabbinica,* 1723,
p. 126). This late Talm. usage of the word can, indeed, signify
nothing as to the bibl. word; but that אֲפָנִים, abbreviated
אָפְנִים, can mean circumstances, is warranted by the synon.
אֹדוֹת. Aquila and Theodotion appear to have thus understood
it, for their ἐπὶ ἁρμόζουσιν αὐτῷ, which they substitute for
the colourless οὕτως of the LXX., signifies: under the circumstances, in accordance therewith. So Orelli thus rightly
defines: "אפנים denote the *áhwâl,* circumstances and conditions,
as they form themselves in each turning of time, and those
which are ascribed to דבר by the suffix are those to which it is
proper, and to which it fits in. Consequently a word is commended which is spoken whenever the precise time arrives to
which it is adapted, a word which is thus spoken at its time as
well as at its place (van Dyk, *fay mahllah*), and the grace of
which is thereby heightened." Aben Ezra's explanation, עַל פָּנִים
הָרְאוּיִם, in the approved way, follows the opinion of Abulwalîd
and Parchon, that אפניו is equivalent to פָּנָיו (cf. *aly wajhihi, sua
ratione*), which is only so far true, that both words are derived
from R. פ, to turn. In the figure, it is questionable whether
by תַּפּוּחֵי זָהָב, apples of gold, or gold-coloured apples, are meant
(Luther: as pomegranates and citrons); thus oranges are
meant, as at Zech. iv. 12. הַזָּהָב denotes golden oil. Since
כסף, besides, signifies a metallic substance, one appears to be
under the necessity of thinking of apples of gold; cf. the
brazen pomegranates. But (1) apples of gold of natural size
and massiveness are obviously too great to make it probable
that such artistic productions are meant; (2) the material of

[1] It is something different when the weaver's beam, *minwâl* in Arab., is
metaph. for kind and manner: they are 'aly minwâl wâhad, is equivalent to
they are of a like calibre, Arab. *kalib,* which is derived from καλόπους
(καλοπόδιον), a shoemaker's last.

the emblem is usually not of less value than that of which it is
the emblem (Fleischer) ; (3) the Scriptures are fond of comparing words with flowers and fruits, x. 31, xii. 14, xiii. 2,
xviii. 20, and to the essence of the word which is rooted in the
spirit, and buds and grows up to maturity through the mouth
and the lips, the comparison with natural fruits corresponds
better in any case than with artificial. Thus, then, we interpret
" golden apples " as the poetic name for oranges, *aurea mala*,
the Indian name of which with reference to *or* (gold) was
changed into the French name *orange*, as our *pomeranze* is
equivalent to *pomum aurantium.* מַשְׂכִּיּוֹת is the plur. of מַשְׂכִּית,
already explained, xviii. 11; the word is connected neither
with שָׂכַךְ, to twist, wreathe (Ewald, with most Jewish interpreters [1]), nor with שָׂכָה, to pierce, *infigere* (Redslob, *vid.* under
Ps. lxxiii. 7) ; it signifies medal or ornament, from שָׂכָה, to
behold (cf. שְׂכִיָּה, θέα = θέαμα, Isa. ii. 6), here a vessel which is
a delight to the eyes. In general the *Venet.* rightly, ἐν μορφώ-
μασιν ἀργύρου; Symmachus and Theodotion, more in accordance
with the fundamental idea, ἐν περιβλέπτοις ἀργύρου ; the Syr.
and Targ. specially : in vessels of embossed work (נְגּוּדֵי, from
נגד, to draw, to extend) ; yet more specially the LXX., ἐν
ὁρμίσκῳ σαρδίου, on a chain of cornelian stone, for which, perhaps, ἐν φορμίσκῳ (Jäger) ἀργυρίου, in a little silver basket,
is the original phrase. Aquila, after *Bereschith rabba* c. 93,
translates by μῆλα χρύσου ἐν δίσκοις ἀργυφίου. Jerome : *in
lectis argenteis*, appears to have fallen into the error of taking משׂכ
for משכב, *lectus*. Hitzig here emends a self-made ἅπαξ λεγ.
Luther's " golden apples in silver baskets " is to be preferred.[2]
A piece of sculpture which represents fruit by golden little disks
or points within groups of leaves is not meant,—for the proverb
does not speak of such pretty little apples,—but golden oranges
are meant. A word in accordance with the circumstances which

---

[1] On this proceeds also the beautiful interpretation by Maimuni in the
preface to *More Nebuchim: Maskiyyôth sont des ciselures réticulaires*, etc.,
according to Munk's translation from the Arab. text, *vid.* Kohut's *Pers.
Pentateuch-Uebers.* (1871), p. 356. Accordingly Jewish interpreters (*e.g.*
Elia Wilna) understand under אפנין the four kinds of writing : פְּשַׁט, רֶמֶז,
דְּרוֹשׁ, and סוֹד, which are comprehended under the memorial word פרדם.

[2] A favourite expression of Goethe's, *vid.* Büchmann's *Geflügelte Worte*,
1688.

occasion it, is like golden oranges which are handed round in
silver salvers or on silver waiters. Such a word is, as adopting
another figure we might say, like a well-executed picture, and
the situation into which it appropriately fits is like its elegant
frame. The comparison with fruit is, however, more significant; it designates the right word as a delightful gift, in a way
which heightens its impression and its influences.

Ver. 12. Another proverb continues the commendation of
the effective word; for it represents, in emblem, the interchangeable relation of speaker and hearer :

> A golden earring and an ornament of fine gold—
> A wise preacher to an ear that heareth ;

i.e., as the former two ornaments form a beautiful *ensemble*, so
the latter two, the wise preacher of morality and an attentive
ear, form a harmonious whole : עַל, down upon, is explained by
Deut. xxxii. 2. נֶזֶם, at xi. 12, standing along with בָּאָף, meant
a ring for the nose; but here, as elsewhere, it means an earring (LXX., Jerome, *Venet.*), translated by the Syr. and Targ.
by קְדָשָׁא, because it serves as a talisman. A ring for the nose[1]
cannot also be here thought of, because this ornament is an
emblem of the attentive ear : willingly accepted chastisement
or instruction is an ear-ornament to him who hears (Stier).
But the gift of the wise preacher, which consists in rightly
dividing the word of truth, 2 Tim. ii. 15, is as an ornament for
the neck or the breast חֲלִי (= Arab. *khaly*, fem. חֶלְיָה = *hilyt*),
of fine gold (כֶּתֶם, jewel, then particularly precious gold, from
כָּתַם, Arab. *katam, recondere*).[2] The *Venet.* well : κόσμος ἀπυρο-

---

[1] *Vid.* Geiger's *Zeitschrift*, 1872, pp. 45–48, where it is endeavoured to
be shown that נזם, as an earring, is rejected from the later biblical literature, because it had become " an object used in the worship of idols," and
that the word was used only of a ring for the nose as a permissible ornament, while עניל was used for the earring. But that does not apply to
the Solomonic era; for that, in the passage under review, נזם signifies a
ring for the nose, is only a supposition of Geiger's, because it accords with
his construction of history.

[2] Hitzig compares Arab. *kumêt;* but this means bayard, as Lagarde remarks, the Greek κόμαιθος; and if by כתם gold foxes (gold money) are to be
thought of, yet they have nothing whatever to do with bayards (red-brown
horses) ; cf. Boehmer, *de colorum nominibus equinorum*, in his *Roman. Stud.*
Heft 2, 1872, p. 285.

χρύσου (fine gold) ; on the contrary (perhaps in want of another name for gold), כתם is translated, by the LXX. and Syr., by sardine; by the Targ., by emerald ; and by Jerome, by *margaritum*.[1] It looks well when two stand together, the one of whom has golden earrings, and the other wears a yet more precious golden necklace—such a beautiful mutual relationship is formed by a wise speaker and a hearer who listens to his admonitions.

Ver. 13. The following comparative tristich refers to faithful service rendered by words :

> Like the coolness of snow on a harvest day
> Is a faithful messenger to them that send him:
> He refresheth the soul of his master.

The coolness (צִנָּה from צָנַן, צֵן, to be cool) of snow is not that of a fall of snow, which in the time of harvest would be a calamity, but of drink cooled with snow, which was brought from Lebanon or elsewhere, from the clefts of the rocks ; the peasants of Damascus store up the winter's snow in a cleft of the mountains, and convey it in the warm months to Damascus and the coast towns. Such a refreshment is a faithful messenger (*vid.* regarding צִיר, xiii. 17, here following קָצִיר as a kind of echo) to them that send him (*vid.* regarding this plur. at x. 26, cf. xxii. 21); he refreshes, namely (ו *explicativum*, as *e.g.* Ezek. xviii. 19, *etenim filius*, like the ו *et quidem*, Mal. i. 11, different from the ו of conditional clause xxiii. 3), the soul of his master; for the answer which he brings to his master refreshes him, as does a drink of snow-cooled water on a hot harvest day.

Ver. 14. This proverb relates to the word which promises much, but remains unaccomplished :

> Clouds and wind, and yet no rain—
> A man who boasteth with a false gift.

Incorrectly the LXX. and Targ. refer the predicate contained in the concluding word of the first line to all the three subjects ; and equally incorrectly Hitzig, with Heidenheim, interprets מַתַּת שָׁקֶר, of a gift that has been received of which one boasts,

---

[1] Another Greek translates πίνωσις χρυσῆ. This πίνωσις is a philological mystery, the solution of which has been attempted by Bochart, Letronne, and Field.

although it is in reality of no value, because by a lying promise a gift is not at all obtained. But as לחם כזבים, xxiii. 3, is bread which, as it were, deceives him who eats it, so מתת שקר is a gift which amounts to a lie, *i.e.* a deceitful pretence. Rightly Jerome : *vir gloriosus et promissa non complens.* In the Arab. *saliḍ*, which Fleischer compares, the figure 14*a* and its counterpart 14*b* are amalgamated, for this word signifies both a boaster and a cloud, which is, as it were, boastful, which thunders much, but rains only sparsely or not at all. Similar is the Arab. *khullab*, clouds which send forth lightning, and which thunder, but yet give no rain ; we say to one, *magno promissor hiatu :* thou art (Arab.) *kabarakn khullabin, i.e.* as Lane translates it : " Thou art only like lightning with which is no rain." Schultens refers to this proverbial Arabic, *fulmen nubis infecundæ.* Liberality is called (Arab.) *nadnay*, as a watering, cf. xi. 25. The proverb belongs to this circle of figures. It is a saying of the German peasants, " *Wenn es sich wolket, so will es regnen* " [when it is cloudy, then there will be rain]; but according to another saying, "*nicht alle Wolken regnen*" [it is not every cloud that yields rain]. "There are clouds and wind without rain."

Three proverbs follow, which have this in common, that they exhort to moderation :

> Ver. 15 By forbearance is a judge won over,
> And a gentle tongue breaketh the bone.

קָצִין (*vid.* vi. 7) does not denote any kind of distinguished person, but a judge or a person occupying a high official position. And פֻּתָּה does not here mean, to talk over or delude ; but, like Jer. xx. 7, to persuade, to win over, to make favourable to one ; for אֹרֶךְ אַפַּיִם (*vid.* xiv. 29) is dispassionate calmness, not breaking out into wrath, which finally makes it manifest that he who has become the object of accusation, suspicion, or of disgrace, is one who nevertheless has right on his side ; for indecent, boisterous passion injures even a just cause ; while, on the contrary, a quiet, composed, thoughtful behaviour, which is not embarrassed by injustice, either experienced or threatened, in the end secures a decision in our favour. "Patience overcomes" is an old saying. The soft, gentle tongue (cf. רַךְ, xv. 1) is the opposite of a passionate,

sharp, coarse one, which only the more increases the resistance
which it seeks to overcome. " Patience," says a German proverb, " breaks iron ; " another says, " Patience is stronger than
a diamond." So here : a gentle tongue breaketh the bone
(גֶּרֶם = עֶצֶם, as at xvii. 22), it softens and breaks to pieces that
which is hardest. Sudden anger makes the evil still worse;
long-suffering, on the contrary, operates convincingly ; cutting,
immoderate language, embitters and drives away ; gentle words,
on the contrary, persuade, if not immediately, yet by this, that
they remain as it were unchangeable.

Ver. 16. Another way of showing self-control :

> Hast thou found honey? eat thy enough,
> Lest thou be surfeited with it, and vomit it up.

Honey is pleasant, salutary, and thus to be eaten sparingly,
xxiv. 13, but *ne quid nimis*. Too much is unwholesome, 27a :
αὐτοῦ καὶ μέλιτος τὸ πλέον ἐστὶ χολή, *i.e.* even honey enjoyed
immoderately is as bitter as gall; or, as Freidank says : *des
honges süeze erdriuzet sô mans ze viel geniuzet* [the sweetness of
honey offends when one partakes too much of it]. Eat if thou
hast found any in the forest or the mountains, דַּיֶּךָ, thy enough
(LXX. τὸ ἱκανόν; the *Venet.* τὸ ἀρκοῦν σοι), *i.e.* as much as
appeases thine appetite, that thou mayest not become surfeited and vomit it out (וַהֲקֵאתוֹ with *Tsere*, and א quiesc., as
at 2 Sam. xiv. 10; *vid. Michlol* 116a, and Parchon under קוא).
Fleischer, Ewald, Hitzig, and others, place vers. 16 and 17
together, so as to form an emblematic tetrastich ; but he who
is surfeited is certainly, in ver. 16, he who willingly enjoys,
and in 17, he to whom it is given to enjoy without his will;
and is not, then, ver. 16 a sentence complete in itself in meaning? That it is not to be understood in a purely dietetic
sense (although thus interpreted it is a rule not to be despised),
is self-evident. As one can suffer injury from the noblest of
food if he overload his stomach therewith, so in the sphere
of science, instruction, edification, there is an injurious over-
loading of the mind ; we ought to measure what we receive by
our spiritual want, the right distribution of enjoyment and
labour, and the degree of our ability to change it *in succum et
sanguinem*,—else it at last awakens in us dislike, and becomes
an evil to us.

Ver. 17. This proverb is of a kindred character to the foregoing. "If thy comrade eats honey," says an Arabic proverb
quoted by Hitzig, "do not lick it all up." But the emblem of
honey is not continued in this verse:

> Make rare thy foot in thy neighbour's house,
> Lest he be satiated with thee, and hate thee.

To make one's foot rare or dear from a neighbour's house is
equivalent to: to enter it seldom, and not too frequently; הוֹקַר
includes in itself the idea of keeping at a distance (Targ.
בְּלֵה רַגְלָךְ; Symmachus, ὑπόστειλον; and another: φίμωσον πόδα
σου), and מִן has the sense of the Arab. 'an, and is not the comparative, as at Isa. xiii. 12: regard thy visit dearer than the
house of a neighbour (Heidenheim). The proverb also is
significant as to the relation of friend to friend, whose reciprocal
love may be turned into hatred by too much intercourse and
too great fondness. But רֵעֶךָ is including a friend, any one with
whom we stand in any kind of intercourse. "Let him who
seeks to be of esteem," says a German proverb, "come seldom;"
and that may be said with reference to him whom his heart
draws to another, and also to him who would be of use to another
by drawing him out of the false way and guiding on the right
path,—a showing of esteem, a confirming of love by visiting,
should not degenerate into forwardness which appears as
burdensome servility, as indiscreet self-enjoyment; nor into a
restless impetuosity, which seeks at once to gain by force that
which one should allow gradually to ripen.

Vers. 18–22. This group of proverbs has the word רֵעַ in each
of them, connecting them together. The first of the group
represents a false tongue:

> Ver. 18 A hammer, and a sword, and a sharp arrow—
> A man that beareth false witness against his neighbour.

An emblematic, or, as we might also say, an iconological proverb; for 18a is a *quodlibet* of instruments of murder, and 18b
is the subscription under it: that which these weapons of
murder accomplish, is done to his neighbour by a man who
bears false witness against him—he ruins his estate, takes away
his honour, but yet more: he murders him, at one time more
grossly, at another time with more refinement; at one time
slowly, at another time more quickly. מֵפִיץ, from פּוּץ, is equiva-

lent to מַפֵּץ, and מַפֵּץ from נָפַץ; the Syr. and Targ. have instead
(פדיעא) פדועא from פֶּצַע = פְּרַע; the word פְּרִיעָא, on which Hitzig
builds a conjecture, is an error of transcription (vid. Lagarde
and Levy). The expression, 18b, is from the decalogue, Ex.
xx. 16; Deut. v. 17. It is for the most part translated the
same here as there : he who speaks against his neighbour as a
false witness. But rightly the LXX., Jerome, the Venet.,
and Luther: false testimony. As אֵל signifies both that which
is mighty = power, and Him who is mighty = God, so עֵד signifies
both him who bears testimony and the testimony that is borne,
properly that which repeats itself and thereby strengthens itself ;
accordingly we say עָנָה עֵד, to give testimony in reply,—viz. to
the judge who asks,—or generally to offer testimony (even
unasked); as well as ענה לְעֵד, Deut. xxxi. 21, i.e. as evidence
(Jerome, pro testimonio). The prep. ב with this ענה has
always the meaning of contra, also at 1 Sam. xii. 3; Gen.
xxx. 33 is, however, open to question.

> Ver. 19 A worthless tooth and an unsteady foot—
> Trust in a faithless man in the day of need.

The form רֹעָה (with Mercha on the antepenult), Isa. xxix. 19,
takes the place of an inf. absol.; רֹעָה here (about the tone
syllable of which Dechî does not decide, thus without doubt
Milra) is certainly not a subst. : tooth of breaking (Gesen.) ;
for how strange such a designation of a worthless tooth ! שֵׁן is
indeed mas. in 1 Sam. xiv. 5, but it can also be used as fem.,
as רֶגֶל, which is for the most part fem., also occurs as mas.,
Böttch. § 650. Böttcher, in the new Aehrenlese, and in the
Lehrbuch, takes רֹעָה as fem. of an adj. רַע, after the form חֹל ;
but חֹל is not an adj., and does not form a fem., although it
means not merely profanity, but that which is profane; this is
true also of the Aram. חֻל; for חֻלָּתְא, Esth. ii. 9, Targ., is a
female name mistaken by Buxtorf. Are we then to read רָעָה,
with Hitzig, after the LXX.?—an unimportant change. We
interpret the traditional רֹעָה, with Fleischer, as derived from
רֹועֲעָה, from רֹעַע, breaking to pieces (crumbling), in an intransitive sense. The form מוּעֶדֶת is also difficult. Böttcher regards
it as also, e.g. Aben Ezra after the example of Gecatilia as
part. Kal. = מֹעֶדֶת, " only on account of the pausal tone and the
combination of the two letters מע with û instead of ô." But

this vocal change, with its reasons, is merely imaginary. מוּעֶדֶת
is the *part. Pual*, with the preformative מ struck out, Ewald
169*d*. The objection that the *part. Pual* should be מְמֹעָר, after
the form מְבֹעָר, does not prove anything to the contrary; for
מוּעֶדֶת cannot be the fem. so as not to coincide with the fem. of
the *part. Kal.*, cf. besides to the long *û* the form without the
Dagesh יוּקְשִׁים, Eccles. ix. 12 = מְיֻקָּשִׁים (Arnheim, *Gramm.* p.
139). רֶגֶל מוּעֶדֶת is a leg that has become tottering, trembling.
He who in a time of need makes a faithless man his ground of
confidence, is like one who seeks to bite with a broken tooth,
and which he finally crushes, and one who supports himself
on a shaking leg, and thus stumbles and falls. The gen. connection מבטח בוגד signifies either the ground of confidence
consisting in a faithless man, or the confidence placed in one
who is faithless. But, after the Masora, we are to read here,
as at Ps. lxv. 6, מבְטָח, which *Michlol* 184*a* also confirms, and
as it is also found in the Venice 1525, Basel 1619, and in
Norzi. This מִבְטָח is constr. according to Kimchi, notwithstanding the *Ḳametz*; as also מִשְׁקָל, Ezra viii. 30 (after Abulwalîd, Kimchi, and Norzi). In this passage before us, מבטח
בוגד may signify a deceitful ground of confidence (cf. Hab. ii.
5), but the two other passages present a genit. connection of
the words. We must thus suppose that the ־ָ of מבטח and
מִשְׁקָל, in these three passages, is regarded as fixed, like the *â* of
the form (Arab.) *mif'âl.*

The above proverb, which connects itself with ver. 18, not
only by the sound רע, but also by שׂ, which is assonant with
שׁנן, is followed by another with the catchword רע:

Ver. 20 He that layeth aside his coat on a day of frost, vinegar on
　　　nitre,
　　And he who welcomes with songs a dejected heart.

Is not this intelligible, sensible, ingenious? All these three
things are wrong. The first is as wrong as the second, and
the third, which the proverb has in view, is morally wrong,
for one ought to weep with those that weep, Rom. xii. 15; he,
on the contrary, who laughs among those who weep, is, on the
most favourable judgment, a fool. That which is wrong in
20*a*, according to Böttcher in the *Aehrenlese*, 1849, consists in
this, that one in severe cold puts on a fine garment. As if

there were not garments which are at the same time beautiful, and keep warm! In the new *Aehrenlese* he prefers the reading מְשַׁנֶּה : if one changes his coat. But that surely he might well enough do, if the one were warmer than the other! Is it then impossible that מַעֲדֶה, in the connection, means *transire faciens* = *removens?* The *Kal* עָדָה, *transiit,* occurs at Job xxviii. 8. So also, in the poetic style, הֶעֱדָה might be used in the sense of the Aram. אַעְדִּי. Rightly Aquila, Symmachus, περιαιρῶν; the *Venet.* better, ἀφαιρούμενος (Mid.). בֶּגֶד is an overcoat or mantle, so called from covering, as לְבוּשׁ (R. לב, to fasten, fix), the garment lying next the body, *vid.* at Ps. xxii. 19. Thus, as it is foolish to lay off upper clothing on a frosty day, so it is foolish also to pour vinegar on nitre; carbonic acid nitre, whether it be mineral (which may be here thought of) or vegetable, is dissolved in water, and serves diverse purposes (*vid.* under Isa. i. 25); but if one pours vinegar on it, it is destroyed. לְבִ־רָע [1] is, at xxvi. 23 and elsewhere, a heart morally bad, here a heart badly disposed, one inclined to that which is evil; for שָׁר שִׁיר is the contrast of קוֹנֵן קִינָה, and always the consequence of a disposition joyfully excited; the inconsistency lies in this, that one thinks to cheer a sorrowful heart by merry singing, if the singing has an object, and is not much more the reckless expression of an animated pleasure in view of the sad condition of another. שִׁיר עַל signifies, as at Job xxxiii. 27, to sing to any one, to address him in singing; cf. דִּבֶּר עַל, Jer. vi. 10, and particularly עַל־לֵב, Hos. ii. 16; Isa. xl. 2. The ב of בַּשִּׁירִים is neither the partitive, ix. 5, nor the transitive, xx. 30, but the instrumental; for, as *e.g.* at Ex. vii. 20, the obj. of the action is thought of as its means (Gesen. § 138, Anm. 3*); one sings "with songs," for definite songs underlie his singing. The LXX., which the Syr., Targ., and Jerome more or less follow, has formed from this proverb one quite different : "As vinegar is hurtful to a wound, so an injury to the body makes the heart sorrowful; as the moth in clothes, and the worm in wood, so the sorrow of a man injures his heart." The wisdom of this pair of proverbs is not worth much, and after all inquiry little or nothing comes of it. The Targ. at least preserves the

---

[1] The writing wavers between עַל לֶב־רָע (cf. עַל עַם־הָל) and עַל־לֵב רָע.

figure 20*b*: as he who pours vinegar (Syr. *chalo*) on nitre; the Peshito, however, and here and there also the Targum, has *jathro* (arrow-string) instead of *nethro* (nitre). Hitzig adopts this, and changes the tristich into the distich :

> He that meeteth archers with arrow on the string,
> Is like him who singeth songs with a sad heart.

The Hebrew of this proverb of Hitzig's (מֹרִים קְרֶה עַל־יֶתֶר) is unhebraic, the meaning dark as an oracle, and its moral contents *nil.*

> Ver. 21 If thine enemy hunger, feed him with bread ;
> And if he thirst, give him water to drink.
> Ver. 22 For thereby thou heapest burning coals on his head,
> And Jahve will recompense it to thee.

The translation of this proverb by the LXX. is without fault; Paul cites therefrom Rom. xii. 20. The participial construction of 22*a*, the LXX., rightly estimating it, thus renders : for, doing this, thou shalt heap coals on his head. The expression, "thou shalt heap" (σωρεύσεις), is also appropriate; for חָתָה certainly means first only to fetch or bring fire (*vid.* vi. 27); but here, by virtue of the *constructio prægnans* with עַל, to fetch, and hence to heap up,—to pile upon. Burning pain, as commonly observed, is the figure of burning shame, on account of undeserved kindness shown by an enemy (Fleischer). But how burning coals heaped on the head can denote burning shame, is not to be perceived, for the latter is a burning on the cheeks; wherefore Hitzig and Rosenmüller explain : thou wilt thus bring on him the greatest pain, and appease thy vengeance, while at the same time Jahve will reward thy generosity. Now we say, indeed, that he who rewards evil with good takes the noblest revenge; but if this doing of good proceed from a revengeful aim, and is intended sensibly to humble an adversary, then it loses all its moral worth, and is changed into selfish, malicious wickedness. Must the proverb then be understood in this ignoble sense? The Scriptures elsewhere say that guilt and punishment are laid on the head of any one when he is made to experience and to bear them. Chrysostom and others therefore explain after Ps. cxl. 10 and similar passages, but thereby the proverb is morally falsified, and ver. 22 accords with ver. 21, which counsels not to the avenging of oneself,

but to the requital of evil with good. The burning of coals
laid on the head must be a painful but wholesome consequence;
it is a figure of self-accusing repentance (Augustine, Zöckler),
for the producing of which the showing of good to an enemy is
a noble motive. That God rewards such magnanimity may
not be the special motive; but this view might contribute to it,
for otherwise such promises of God as Isa. lviii. 8–12 were
without moral right. The proverb also requires one to show
himself gentle and liberal toward a needy enemy, and present
a twofold reason for this: first, that thereby his injustice is
brought home to his conscience; and, secondly, that thus God
is well-pleased in such practical love toward an enemy, and
will reward it;—by such conduct, apart from the performance
of a law grounded in our moral nature, one advances the
happiness of his neighbour and his own.

The next group of proverbs extends from ver. 23 to ver. 28.

Ver. 23 Wind from the north produceth rain;
And a secret tongue a troubled countenance.

The north is called צָפוֹן, from צָפַן, to conceal, from the firmament
darkening itself for a longer time, and more easily, like the old
Persian *apâkhtara*, as (so it appears) the starless, and, like
aquilo, the north wind, as bringing forward the black clouds.
But properly the "fathers of rain" are, in Syria, the west
and the south-west; and so little can צפון here mean the pure
north wind, that Jerome, who knew from his own experience the changes of weather in Palestine, helps himself, after
Symmachus (διαλύει βροχήν), with a *quid pro quo* out of the
difficulty: *ventus aquilo dissipat pluvias*; the Jewish interpreters (Aben Ezra, Joseph Kimchi, and Meîri) also thus explain, for they connect together תחולל, in the meaning תמנע,
with the unintelligible חלילה (far be it!). But צפון may also,
perhaps like ζόφος (*Deutsch. Morgenl. Zeitsch.* xxi. 600 f.),
standing not without connection therewith, denote the north-
west; and probably the proverb emphasized the northern
direction of the compass, because, according to the intention of
the similitude, he seeks to designate such rain as is associated
with raw, icy-cold weather, as the north wind (xxvii. 16,
LXX., Sir. xliii. 20) brings along with it. The names of
the winds are *gen. fem.*, *e.g.* Isa. xliii. 6. תְּחוֹלֵל (Aquila, ὠδίνει;

cf. viii. 24, ὠδινήθην) has in Codd., *e.g.* the *Jaman.*, the tone on the penult, and with *Tsere Metheg* (*Thorath Emeth*, p. 21) serving as העמדה. So also the Arab. *nataj* is used of the wind, as helping the birth of the rain-clouds. Manifestly פָּנִים נִזְעָמִים, countenances manifesting extreme displeasure (*vid.* the *Kal* זָעַם, xxiv. 24), are compared to rain. With justice Hitzig renders פנים, as *e.g.* John ii. 6, in the plur. sense; because, for the influence which the tongue slandering in secret (Ps. ci. 5) has on the slandered, the "sorrowful countenance" would not be so characteristic as for the influence which it exercises on the mutual relationships of men: the secret babbler, the confidential communication throwing suspicion, now on this one and now on that one, behind their backs, excites men against one another, so that one shows to another a countenance in which deep displeasure and suspicion express themselves.

> Ver. 24 Better to sit on the top of a roof,
> Than a quarrelsome woman and a house in common.

A repetition of xxi. 9.

> Ver. 25 Fresh water to a thirsty soul;
> And good news from a far country.

Vid. regarding the form of this proverb, vol. i. p. 9; we have a similar proverb regarding the influence of good news at xv. 30. Fresh cold water is called at Jer. xviii. 14 מַיִם קָרִים; *vid.* regarding קַר, xviii. 27. "עָיֵף, cogn. יָעֵף and עוּף, properly to become darkened, therefore figuratively like (Arab.) *gushiya 'alyh*, to become faint, to become feeble unto death, of the darkness which spreads itself over the eyes" (Fleischer).

This proverb, with the figure of "fresh water," is now followed by one with the figure of a "fountain":

> Ver. 26 A troubled fountain and a ruined spring—
> A righteous man yielding to a godless man.

For the most part, in מָט one thinks of a yielding in consequence of being forced. Thus *e.g.* Fleischer: as a troubled ruined spring is a misfortune for the people who drink out of it, or draw from it, so is it a misfortune for the surrounding of the righteous, when he is driven from his dwelling or his possession by an unrighteous man. And it is true: the righteous can be compared to a well (מעין, well-spring, from עַיִן, a well, as an eye of the earth, and מקור, fountain, from קוּר, R. קר,

כר, to round out, to dig out), with reference to the blessing which flows from it to its surroundings (cf. x. 11 and John vii. 38). But the words "yielding to" (contrast "stood before," 2 Kings x. 4, or Josh. vii. 12), in the phrase "yielding to the godless," may be understood of a spontaneous as well as of a constrained, forced, wavering and yielding, as the expression in the Psalm בַּל־אֶמּוֹט [non movebor, Ps. x. 6] affirms the certainty of being neither inwardly nor outwardly ever moved or shaken. The righteous shall stand fast and strong in God without fearing the godless (Isa. li. 12 f.), unmoveable and firm as a brazen wall (Jer. i. 17 f.). If, however, he is wearied with resistance, and from the fear of man, or the desire to please man, or from a false love of peace he yields before it, and so gives way,—then he becomes like to a troubled fountain (רָפַשׂ, cogn. רָמַס, Ezek. xxxiv. 18; Isa. xli. 25; Jerome: fons turbatus pede), a ruined spring; his character, hitherto pure, is now corrupted by his own guilt, and now far from being a blessing to others, his wavering is a cause of sorrow to the righteous, and an offence to the weak—he is useful no longer, but only injurious. Rightly Lagarde: "The verse, one of the most profound of the whole book, does not speak of the misfortune, but of the fall of the righteous, whose sin compromises the holy cause which he serves, 2 Sam. xii. 14." Thus also e.g. Löwenstein, with reference to the proverb Sanhedrin 92b: also in the time of danger let not a man disown his honour. Bachja, in his Ethics, referring to this figure, 26a, thinks of the possibility of restoration : the righteous wavers only for the moment, but at last he comes right (מתמומט ועולה). But this interpretation of the figure destroys the point of the proverb.

Ver. 27. This verse, as it stands, is scarcely to be understood. The Venet. translates 27b literally: ἔρευνά τε δόξας αὐτῶν δόξα; but what is the reference of this כְּבֹדָם ? Euchel and others refer it to men, for they translate : "to set a limit to the glory of man is true glory;" but the "glory of man" is denoted by the phrase כְּבֹד אָדָם, not by כְּבֹדָם ; and, besides, חֵקֶר does not mean measure and limit. Oetinger explains: "To eat too much honey is not good; whereas the searching after their glory, viz. of pleasant and praiseworthy things, which are likened to honey, is glory, cannot be too much done, and is never without utility and honour;" but how can כְּבֹדָם be of the same meaning as כְּבֹד הדברים אשר or הַגְּמִשָׁלִים כַּדְּבַשׁ—such an abbreviation of the expression is impossible. Schultens, according to Rashi: *vestigatio gravitatis eorum est gravitas, i.e.* the searching out of their difficulty is a trouble; better Vitringa (since כבוד nowhere occurs in this sense of *gravitas molesta ac pondere oppressura*): *investigatio præstantiæ eorum est gloriosa;* but Vitringa, in order to gain a connection to 27a, needs to introduce *etiamsi*, and in both explanations the reference of the כְּבֹדָם is imaginary, and it by no means lies near, since the Scripture uses the word כבוד of God, and His kingdom and name, but never of His law or His revelation. This also is an argument against Bertheau, who translates : the searching out of their glory (viz. of the divine law and revelation) is a burden, a strenuous occupation of the mind, since חקר does not in itself mean searching out, and is equivocally, even unintelligibly, expressed, since כבוד denotes, it is true, here and there, a great multitude, but never a burden (as כֹּבֶד). The thought which Jerome finds in 27b : *qui scrutator est majestatis opprimetur a gloria*, is judicious, and connects itself synonym. with 27a; but such a thought is unwarranted, for he disregards the suff. of כְּבֹדָם, and renders כבוד in the sense of difficulty (oppression). Or should it perhaps be vocalized כְּבֹדָם (Syr., Targ., Theodotion, δεδοξασμένα = נִכְבָּדוֹת)? Thus vocalized, Umbreit renders it in the sense of *honores;* Elster and Zöckler in the sense of *difficultates (difficilia);* but this plur., neither the biblical, nor, so far as I know, the post-bibl. usage of the word has ever adopted. However, the sense of the proverb which Elster and Zöckler gain is certainly that which is aimed at. We accordingly translate :

> To surfeit oneself in eating honey is not good,
> But as an inquirer to enter on what is difficult is honour.

We read כְּבֵדִם instead of כְּבֹדָם. This change commends itself far more than כָּבֹר מִכָּבוֹד (וחקר), according to which Gesenius explains : *nimium studium honoris est sine honore*—impossible, for חֵקֶר does not signify *nimium studium*, in the sense of striving, but only that of inquiry : one strives after honour, but does not study it. Hitzig and Ewald, after the example of J. D. Michaelis, Arnoldi, and Ziegler, betake themselves therefore to

the Arabic; Ewald explains, for he leaves the text unchanged:
" To despise their honour (that is, of men) is honour (true, real
honour) ; " Hitzig, for he changes the text like Gesenius : " To
despise honour is more than honour," with the ingenious
remark : To obtain an order [*insigne ordinis*] is an honour, but
not to wear it then for the first time is its *bouquet*. Nowhere
any trace either in Hebrew or in Aramaic is to be found of the
verb חקר, to despise (to be despised), and so it must here remain
without example.[1] Nor have we any need of it. The change
of כְּבֹדָם into כְּבֵדָם is enough. The proverb is an antithetic
distich ; 27*a* warns against inordinate longing after enjoyments,
27*b* praises earnest labour. Instead of דְּבַשׁ הַרְבּוֹת, if honey in
the mass were intended, the words would have been דְּבַשׁ הַרְבֵּה
(Eccles. v. 11 ; 1 Kings x. 10), or at least הַרְבּוֹת דְּבַשׁ (Amos
iv. 9) ; הרבות can only be a *n. actionis*, and אֲכֹל דְּבַשׁ its inverted
object (cf. Jer. ix. 4), as Böttcher has discerned : to make much
of the eating of honey, to do much therein is not good (cf. ver.
16). In 27*b* Luther also partly hits on the correct rendering :
" and he who searches into difficult things, to him it is too difficult," for which it ought to be said : to him it is an honour.
כְּבֵדָם, viz. דברים, signifies difficult things, as רֵיקִים, xii. 11, vain
things. The Heb. כָּבֵד, however, never means difficult to be
understood or comprehended (although more modern lexicons
say this),[2] but always only burdensome and heavy, *gravis*, not
difficilis. כבדם are also things of which the חֵקֶר, *i.e.* the fundamental searching into them (xviii. 17, xxv. 2 f.), costs an earnest
effort, which perhaps, according to the first impression, appears
to surpass the available strength (cf. Ex. xviii. 18). To overdo
oneself in eating honey is not good ; on the contrary, the searching into difficult subjects is nothing less than an eating of
honey, but an honour. There is here a *paronomasia*. Fleischer
translates it : *explorare gravia grave est ;* but we render *grave*

---

[1] The Hebrew meaning *investigare*, and the equivalent Arabic ḥakr, *con-
temnere* (*contemtui esse*), are derivations from the primary meaning (R.
חק): to go down from above firmly on anything, and thus to press in (to
cut in), or also to press downward.

[2] Cf. Sir. iii. 20 f. with Ben-Sira's Heb. text in my *Gesch. der jüd. Poesie*,
p. 204 (vers. 30–32) ; nowhere does this adj. כבד appear here in this
warning against meditating over the transcendental.

est not in the sense of *molestiam creat*, but *gravitatem parit* (weight = respect, honour).

Ver. 28. This verse, counselling restraint as to the spirit, is connected with the foregoing, which counsels to self-control as to enjoyment :

> A city broken through, now without walls—
> A man without self-control over his spirit.

A " city broken down " is one whose wall is " broken," 2 Chron. xxxii. 5, whether it has met with breaches (פְּרָצִים), or is wholly broken ; in the former case also the city is incapable of being defended, and it is all one as if it had no wall. Such a city is like a man " who hath no control over his own spirit " (for the accentuation of the Heb. words here, *vid. Thorath Emeth*, p. 10) : *cujus spiritui nulla cohibitio* (Schultens), *i.e. qui animum suum cohibere non potest* (Fleischer : עָצַר, R. צר, to press together, to oppress, and thereby to hold back). As such a city can be plundered and laid waste without trouble, so a man who knows not to hold in check his desires and affections is in constant danger of blindly following the impulse of his unbridled sensuality, and of being hurried forward to outbreaks of passion, and thus of bringing unhappiness upon himself. There are sensual passions (*e.g.* drunkenness), intellectual (*e.g.* ambition), mingled (*e.g.* revenge) ; but in all of these a false *ego* rules, which, instead of being held down by the true and better *ego*, rises to unbounded supremacy.[1] Therefore the expression used is not לְנַפְשׁוֹ, but לְרוּחוֹ ; desire has its seat in the soul, but in the spirit it grows into passion, which in the root of all its diversities is selfishness (*Psychol.* p. 199) ; self-control is accordingly the ruling of the spirit, *i.e.* the restraining (keeping down) of the false enslaved ego-life by the true and free, and powerful in God Himself.

xxvi. 1. There now follows a group of eleven proverbs of the fool ; only the first of the group has after it a proverb of different contents, but of similar form :

> As snow in summer, and rain in harvest ;
> So honour befitteth not a fool.

If there is snow in high summer (קַיִץ, to be glowing hot), it is contrary to nature ; and if there is rain in harvest, it is (accord-

---

[1] *Vid.* Drbal's *Empirische Psychologie,* § 137.

ing to the alternations of the weather in Palestine) contrary to what is usually the case, and is a hindrance to the ingathering of the fruits of the field. Even so a fool and respect, or a place of honour, are incongruous things; honour will only injure him (as according to xix. 10, luxury); he will make unjust use of it, and draw false conclusions from it; it will strengthen him in his folly, and only increase it. נָאוֶה (= נָאוִי) is the adj. to the *Pil.* נֵאוָה, Ps. xciii. 5 (plur. נָאוּוּ); נָאוֶה, xix. 10, and נָאוֶה, xvii. 7, are also masc. and fem. of the adj., according to which, that which is said under xix. 10 is to be corrected. Symmachus and Theodotion have translated οὐκ ἔπρεψεν, and have therefore read נָאוָה. The root word is נָאָה (as שָׁחָה to שְׁחָחָה)=נָוָה, to aim at something (*vid.* Hupfeld under Ps. xxiii. 2).

Ver. 2. This verse is formed quite in the same way as the preceding:

> As the sparrow in its fluttering, as the swallow in its flying,
> So the curse that is groundless: it cometh not.

This passage is one of those fifteen (*vid.* under Ps. c. 3) in which the לֹא of the text is changed by the *Kerî* into לֹו; the Talm., Midrash, and Sohar refer this לֹו partly to him who utters the curse himself, against whom also, if he is a judge, such inconsiderate cursing becomes an accusation by God; partly to him who is cursed, for they read from the proverb that the curse of a private person also (הֶדְיוֹט, ἰδιώτης) is not wont to fall to the ground, and that therefore one ought to be on his guard against giving any occasion for it (*vid.* Norzi). But Aben Ezra supposes that לֹא and לֹו interchange, as much as to say that the undeserved curse falls on him (לֹו) who curses, and does not fall (לֹא) on him who is cursed. The figures in 2*a* harmonize only with לֹא, according to which the LXX., the Syr., Targ., *Venet.*, and Luther (against Jerome) translate, for the principal matter, that the sparrow and the swallow, although flying out (xxvii. 8), return home again to their nest (Ralbag), would be left out of view in the comparison by לֹו. This emphasizes the fluttering and flying, and is intended to affirm that a groundless curse is a פֹּרֵחַ בָּאֲוִיר, aimless, *i.e.* a thing hovering in the air, that it fails and does not take effect. Most interpreters explain the two *Lameds* as declaring the destination: *ut passer (sc. natus est) ad vagandum,* as the sparrow, through necessity of nature, roves about . . . (Fleischer). But from xxv. 3 it is evident that the *Lamed* in both cases declares the reference or the point of comparison : as the sparrow in respect to its fluttering about, etc. The names of the two birds are, according to Aben Ezra, like dreams without a meaning ; but the Romanic exposition explains rightly צִפּוֹר by *passereau*, and דְּרוֹר by *hirondelle*, for צפור (Arab. '*usfuwr*), twitterer, designates at least preferably the sparrow, and דרור the swallow, from its flight shooting straight out, as it were radiating (*vid.* under Ps. lxxxiv. 4) ; the name of the sparrow, *dûrî* (found in court-yards), which Wetstein, after Saadia, compares to דרור, is ety-mologically different.[1] Regarding חִנָּם, *vid.* under xxiv. 28. Rightly the accentuation separates the words rendered, " so the curse undeserved " (קִלְלַת, after Kimchi, *Michlol* 79*b*, קִלֲלַת), from those which follow ; לֹא תָבֹא is the explication of כֵּן : thus hovering in the air is a groundless curse—it does not come (בוא, like *e.g.* Josh. xxi. 43). After this proverb, which is formed like ver. 1, the series now returns to the " fool."

> Ver. 3 A whip for the horse, a bridle for the ass,
> And a rod for the back of fools.

J. D. Michaelis supposes that the order should be reversed : a bridle for the horse, a whip for the ass ; but Arnoldi has here discovered the figure of speech *merismus* (cf. x. 1) ; and Hitzig, in the manner of the division, the rhythmical reason of the combination (cf. שׁם חם ויפת for שׁם יפת וחם): whip and bridle belong to both, for one whips a horse (Neh. iii. 2) and also bridles him ; one bridles an ass (Ps. xxxii. 9) and also whips him (Num. xxii. 28 f.). As whip and bridle are both service-able and necessary, so also serviceable and necessary is a rod, לְגֵו כְּסִילִים, x. 13, xix. 29.

> Ver. 4 Answer not the fool according to his folly,
> Lest thou thyself also become like unto him.

After, or according to his folly, is here equivalent to recognising the foolish supposition and the foolish object of his question, and thereupon considering it, as if, *e.g.*, he asked why the ignorant man was happier than the man who had much know-ledge, or how one may acquire the art of making gold ; for " a

---

[1] It is true that the Gemara to *Negaïm*, xiv. 1, explains the Mishnic צפרים דרור, " house-birds," for it derives דרור דרור from דור, to dwell.

fool can ask more than ten wise men can answer." He who recognises such questions as justifiable, and thus sanctions them, places himself on an equality with the fool, and easily himself becomes one. The proverb that follows affirms apparently the direct contrary:

Ver. 5 Answer the fool according to his folly,
Lest he regard himself as wise.

עֲנֵה־כְסִיל (with *Makkeph*, and *Gaja*, and *Chatef*[1]) here stands opposed to אַל־תַּעַן כְּסִיל. The Gospel of John, *e.g.* v. 31, cf. viii. 31,[2] is rich in such apparently contradictory sayings. The *sic et non* here lying before us is easily explained; after, or according to his folly, is this second time equivalent to, as is due to his folly: decidedly and firmly rejecting it, making short work with it (returning a sharp answer), and promptly replying in a way fitted, if possible, to make him ashamed. Thus one helps him, perhaps, to self-knowledge; while, in the contrary case, one gives assistance to his self-importance. The Talmud, *Schabbath* 30*b*, solves the contradiction by referring ver. 4 to worldly things, and ver. 5 to religious things; and it is true that, especially in the latter case, the answer is itself a duty toward the fool, and toward the truth. Otherwise the Midrash: one ought not to answer when one knows the fool as such, and to answer when he does not so know him; for in the first instance the wise man would dishonour himself by the answer, in the latter case he would give to him who asks the importance appertaining to a superior.

Ver. 6 He cutteth off the feet, he drinketh injury,
Who transacteth business by a fool.

He cutteth off, *i.e.* his own feet, as we say: he breaks his neck, *il se casse le cou;* Lat. *frangere brachium, crus, coxam; frangere navem* (Fleischer). He thinks to supplement his own two legs by those of the messenger, but in reality he cuts them off; for not only is the commission not carried out, but it is even badly carried out, so that instead of being refreshed (xiii.

---

[1] Thus after Ben Asher; while, on the contrary, Ben Naphtali writes עֲנֵה כְסִיל with *Munach, vid. Thorath Emeth*, p. 41.

[2] *Vid.* my dissertation on three little-observed passages in the Gospel of John, and their practical lessons, in the *Evang. luth. Kirchenzeitung*, 1869, Nos. 37, 38.

17, xxv. 13) by the quick, faithful execution of it, he has to
swallow nothing but damage; cf. Job xxxiv. 7, where, however, drinking scorn is meant of another (LXX.), not his own;
on the contrary, חָמָס here refers to injury suffered (as if it were
חֲמָסוֹ, for the suff. of חמס is for the most part objective); cf. the
similar figures x. 26. So שָׁלַח בְּיַד, to accomplish anything by
the mediation of another, cf. Ex. iv. 13; with דבר (דברים),
2 Sam. xv. 36. The reading מְקֻצֶּה (Jerome, Luther, *claudus*)
is unnecessary; since, as we saw, מְקַצֶּה includes it in the *sibi*.
The Syr. reads, after the LXX. (the original text of which
was ἐκ τῶν ποδῶν ἑαυτοῦ), מִקְצֵה, for he errs, as also does the
Targumist, in thinking that מקצה can be used for מקץ; but
Hitzig adopts this reading, and renders: " from the end of the
legs he swallows injury who sends messages by a fool." The
end of the legs are the feet, and the feet are those of the
foolish messenger. The proverb in this form does not want in
boldness, but the wisdom which Hitzig finds in it is certainly
not mother-wit.[1] Böttcher, on his part, also with מְקַצֶּה, renders:
" from the end of his feet he drinks in that which is bitter . . ."
—that also is too artificial, and is unintelligible without the
explanation of its discoverer. But that he who makes a fool
his messenger becomes himself like unto one who cuts off his
own legs, is a figure altogether excellent.

Ver. 7 The hanging down of the legs of a lame man;
And a proverb in a fool's mouth.

With reference to the obscure דַּלְיוּ, the following views have
been maintained :—(1) The form as punctuated appears directly
as an imperative. Thus the LXX. translate, the original text
of which is here: ἀφελοῦ πορείαν κυλλῶν (conj. Lagarde's) καὶ
παροιμίαν ἐκ στόματος ἀφρόνων, which the Syr. (with its
imitator, the Targ.) has rendered positively: " If thou canst
give the power of (sound) going to the lame, then wilt thou
also receive (prudent) words from the mouth of a fool." Since
Kimchi, דַּלְיוּ has been regarded by many as the softening of the
Imp. Piel דַּלּוּ, according to which the *Venet.* translates : ἐπάρατε

---

[1] The *Venet.* translates שֹׁתֶה by ἄνους, so שֹׁטֶה (the post-bibl. designation of a fool)—one of the many indications that this translator is a Jew,
and as such is not confined in his knowledge of language only to the bibl.
Hebrew.

κνήμας χωλοῦ; and Bertheau and Zöckler explain: always
take away his legs from the lame, since they are in reality
useless to him, just as a proverb in the mouth of the fool is
useless,—something that without loss might be never there."
But why did not the poet write הָרִימוּ, or הָסִירוּ, or קְחוּ, or the
like? דְּלִי, to carry away, to dispense with, is Syriac (Targ. Jer.
I., under Deut. xxxii. 50), but not Hebrew. And how meaningless is this expression! A lame man would withstand a
surgeon (as he would a murderer) who would amputate his
legs; for lame legs are certainly better than none, especially
since there is a great distinction between a lame man (פִּסֵּחַ,
from פָּסַח, luxare; cf. (Arab.) fasaḥ, laxare, vid. Schultens) who
halts or goes on crutches (2 Sam. iii. 29), and one who is
maimed (paralytic), who needs to be carried. It comes to this,
that by this rendering of 7a one must, as a consequence, with
the LXX., regard וּמָשָׁל [and a proverb] as object. accus.
parallel to שֹׁקַיִם [legs]; but "to draw a proverb from one's
mouth" is, after xx. 5, something quite different from to
tear a proverb away from him, besides which, one cannot see
how it is to be caught. Rather one would prefer: attollite
crura claudi (ut incedat, et nihil promovebitis); but the מִן of
מִפִּסֵּחַ does not accord with this, and 7b does not connect itself
with it. But the explanation: "take away the legs from a
lame man who has none, at least none to use, and a proverb in
the mouth of fools, when there is none," is shattered against
the "leg-taking-away," which can only be used perhaps of
frogs' legs. (2) Symmachus translates: ἐξέλιπον κνῆμαι ἀπὸ
χωλοῦ; and Chajûg explains דַּלְיוּ as 3 pret. Kal, to which
Kimchi adds the remark, that he appears to have found דָּלְיוּ,
which indeed is noted by Norzi and J. H. Michaelis as a
variant. But the Masoretic reading is דַּלְיוּ, and this, after
Gesenius and Böttcher (who in this, without any reason, sees
an Ephraimitic form of uttering the word), is a softened variation from דָּלְלוּ. Only it is a pity that this softening, while it
is supported by alius = ἄλλος, folium = φύλλον, faillir = fallere,
and the like, has yet not a single Hebrew or Semitic example
in its favour. (3) Therefore Ewald finds, "all things considered," that it is best to read דָּלְיוּ, "the legs are too loose for
the lame man to use them." But, with Dietrich, we cannot

concur in this, nor in the more appropriate translation : " the
legs of the lame hang down loose," to say nothing of the clearly
impossible : " high are the legs of the lame (one higher than
the other)," and that because this form דַּלְיוּ for דָּלְיוּ also occurs
without pause, Ps. lvii. 2, lxxiii. 2, cxxii. 6, Isa. xxi. 12 ; but
although thus, as at Ps. xxxvi. 9, lxviii. 32, at the beginning of
a clause, yet always only in connection, never at the beginning
of an address.   (4) It has also been attempted to interpret דַּלְיוּ
as abstr., e.g. Euchel: " he learns from a cripple to dance, who
seeks to learn proverbs from the mouth of a fool."   דַּלְיוּ שֹׁקַיִם
must mean the lifting up of the legs = springing and dancing.
Accordingly Luther translates :

> " As dancing to a cripple,
>   So does it become a fool to speak of wisdom."

The thought is agreeable, and according to fact; but these
words do not mean dancing, but much rather, as the Arabic
shows (vid. Schultens at xx. 5, and on the passage before us),
a limping, waddling walk, like that of ducks, after the
manner of a well - bucket dangling to and fro.   And דַּלְיוּ,
after the form מַלְכוּ, would be an unheard-of Aramaism.   For
forms such as שָׂחוּ, swimming, and שָׁלוּ, security, Ps. xxx. 7, on
which C. B. Michaelis and others rest, cannot be compared,
since they are modified from sachw, salw, while in דַּלְיוּ the û
ending must be, and besides the Aramaic דַּלְיוּ must in st. constr.
be דַּלְיוּת.   Since none of these explanations are grammatically
satisfactory, and besides דַּלְיוּ = דְּלָלוּ = דַּלּוּ gives a parallel member
which is heterogeneous and not conformable to the nature of
an emblematical proverb, we read דַּלְיוּ after the forms צִפּוּי, שִׁקּוּי
(cf. חִבּוּק, vi. 10, xxiv. 33), and this signifies loose, hanging
down, from דָּלָה, to hang at length and loosely down, or transitively : to hang, particularly of the hanging down at length of
the bucket-rope, and of the bucket itself, to draw water from
the well.   The מן is similar to that of Job xxviii. 4, only that
here the connecting of the hanging down, and of that from
which it hangs down, is clear.   Were we to express the purely
nominally expressed emblematical proverb in the form of a
comparative one, it would thus stand as Fleischer translates it:
*ut laxa et flaccida dependent (torpent) crura a claudo, sic sen-
tentia in ore stultorum (sc. torpet h. e. inutilis est).*   The fool can

as little make use of an intelligent proverb, or moral maxim (*dictum sententiosum*), as a lame man can of his feet; the word, which in itself is full of thought, and excellent, becomes halting, lame, and loose in his mouth (Schultens: *deformiter claudicat*); it has, as spoken and applied by him, neither hand nor foot. Strangely, yet without missing the point, Jerome: *quomodo pulcras frustra habet claudus tibias, sic indecens est in ore stultorum parabola.* The lame man possibly has limbs that appear sound; but when he seeks to walk, they fail to do him service,—so a *bon-mot* comes forth awkwardly when the fool seeks to make use of it. Hitzig's conjecture: as leaping of the legs on the part of a lame man . . ., Böttcher has already shown sufficient reasons for rejecting; leaping on the part of any one, for the leaping of any one, were a court style familiar to no poet.

Ver. 8. This proverb presents to us a new difficulty.

> As one binds a stone in a sling,
> So is he who giveth honour to a fool.

This translation is warranted by tradition, and is in accordance with the actual facts. A sling is elsewhere called קֶלַע; but that מַרְגֵּמָה also in the passage before us signifies a sling (from רָגַם, to throw with stones = to stone or to throw stones = to sling, cf. Targ. Esth. v. 14 רַגֵּם, of David's slinging stones against Goliath), is supported by the LXX., Syr., and Targ. on the one side, and the Jewish Glossists on the other (Rashi: *fronde*, Ital. *frombola*). Rightly the LXX. renders כִּצְרוֹר as a verb: ὡς ἀποδεσμεύει; on the contrary, the Syr. and Targ. regard it as a substantive: as a piece of stone; but צְרוֹר as a substantive does not mean a piece, as one would put into a sling to use as a weapon, but a grain, and thus a little piece, 2 Sam. xvii. 13; cf. Amos ix. 9. Erroneously Ewald: " if one binds to the sling the stone which he yet seeks to throw, then all his throwing and aiming are in vain; so it is in vain to give to a fool honour which does not reach him." If one seeks to sling a stone, he must lay the *lapis missilis* so in the sling that it remains firm there, and goes forth only by the strong force of the slinging; this fitting in (of the stone), so that it does not of itself fall out, is expressed by צְרָר בְּ (cf.

xxx. 4 ; Job xxvi. 8).   The giving is compared to the binding,
the stones to the honour, and the sling to the fool : the fool is
related to the honour which one confers on him, as the stone to
the sling in which one lays it—the giving of honour is a slinging
of honour.   Otherwise (after Kimchi) the *Venet. ὡς συνδεσμὸς
λίθου ἐν λιθάδι*, i.e. as Fleischer translates : *ut qui crumenam
gemmarum plenam in acervum lapidum conjicit.*   Thus also
Ralbag, Ahron b. Josef, and others, and lastly Zöckler.   The
figure is in the form of an address, and מַרְגֵּמָה (from רָגַם,
accumulare, congerere, vid. under Ps. lxvii. 28) might certainly
mean the heaping of stones.   But אֶבֶן is not used in the sense of
אֶבֶן יְקָרָה (precious stone) ; also one does not see why one precious
stone is not enough as the figure of honour, and a whole heap is
named ; but in the third place, כֵּן נוֹתֵן requires for כצרור a verbal
signification.   Therefore Jerome translates : *sicut qui mittit
lapidem in acervum Mercurii ;* in this the echo of his Jewish
teacher, for the Midrash thus explains literally : every one who
gives honour to a fool is like one who throws a stone on a heap
of stones consecrated to Mercury.   Around the Hermes (ἑρμαί),
i.e. pillars with the head of Mercury (*statuæ mercuriales* or
viales), were heaps of stones (ἕρμακες), to which the passer-by
was wont to throw a stone ; it was a mark of honour, and
served at the same time to improve the way, whose patron was
Mercurius (מרקולים).   It is self-evident that this Græco-Roman
custom to which the Talm. make frequent reference, cannot be
supposed to have existed in the times of Solomon.   Luther
translates independently, and apparently rendering into German
that *in acervum Mercurii :* that is as if one threw a precious
stone on the " *Rabenstein,*" *i.e.* the heap of stones raised at the
foot of the gallows.   This heap of stones is more natural and
suitable to the times of Solomon than the heap of stones dedicated to Mercury, if, like Gussetius, one understands מרגמה of
a heap of stones, *supra corpus lapidatum.*   But against this
and similar interpretations it is enough to remark that כצרור
cannot signify *sicut qui mittit.*   Had such a meaning been
intended, the word would have been כְּהַשְׁלִיךְ or כְּמַשְׁלִיךְ.   Still
different is the rendering of Joseph Kimchi, Aben Ezra, and
finally Löwenstein : as when one wraps up a stone in a piece of
purple stuff.   But אַרְגְּמָן, purple, has nothing to do with the verb

רָגַם; it is, as the Aramaic אַרְגִּין shows, a compound word; the supposition of a denom. מַרְגֵּמָה thus proceeds from a false etymological supposition. And Hitzig's combination of מרגמה with (Arab.) *munjam*, handle and beam of a balance (he translates: as a stone on the beam of a balance, *i.e.* lies on it), is nothing but refined ingenuity, since we have no need at all of such an Arab. word for a satisfactory clearing up of מרגמה. We abide by the rendering of the sling. Böttcher translates: a sling that scatters; perhaps מרגמה in reality denotes such a sling as throws many stones at once. Let that, however, be as it may: that he who confers a title of honour, a place of honour, and the like, on a fool, is like one who lays a stone in a sling, is a true and intelligibly formed thought: the fool makes the honour no honour; he is not capable of maintaining it; that which is conferred on him is uselessly wasted.

Ver. 9 A thorn goeth into the hand of a drunkard,
And a proverb in a fool's mouth;

i.e., if a proverb falls into a fool's mouth, it is as if a thorn entered into the hand of a drunken man; the one is as dangerous as the other, for fools misuse such a proverb, which, rightly used, instructs and improves, only to the wounding and grieving of another, as a drunken man makes use of the pointed instrument which he has possession of for coarse raillery, and as a welcome weapon of his strife. The LXX., Syr. (Targ.?), and Jerome interpret עָלָה in the sense of shooting up, *i.e.* of growing; Böttcher also, after xxiv. 31 and other passages, insists that the thorn which has shot up may be one that has not grown to perfection, and therefore not dangerous. But thorns grow not in the hand of any one; and one also does not perceive why the poet should speak of it as growing in the hand of a drunken man, which the use of the hand with it would only make worse. We have here עָלָה בְיָדִי, *i.e.* it has come into my hand, commonly used in the *Mishna*, which is used where anything, according to intention, falls into one's hands, as well as where it comes accidentally and unsought for, *e.g. Nazir* 23a, מי שנתכוון לעלות בידו בשר חזיר ועלה בידו בשר טלה, he who designs to obtain swine's flesh and (accidentally) obtains lamb's flesh. Thus rightly Heidenheim, Löwenstein, and the *Venet.*: ἄκανθα ἀνέβη εἰς χεῖρα μεθύοντος. חוֹחַ signifies a thorn bush, 2 Kings xiv. 9,[1] as well as a thorn, Song ii. 2, but where not the thorns of the rose, and indeed no rose at all, is meant. Luther thinks of the rose with the thorn when he explains: "When a drunkard carries and brandishes in his hand a thorn bush, he scratches more with it than allows the roses to be smelled—so a fool with the Scriptures, or a right saying, often does more harm than good." This paraphrase of Luther's interprets עלה ביד more correctly than his translation does ; on the other hand, the latter more correctly is satisfied with a thorn twig (as a thorn twig which pierces into the hand of a drunken man) ; the roses are, however, assumed contrary to the text. This holds good also against Wessely's explanation : " the Mashal is like a rose not without thorns, but in the mouth of a fool is like a thorn without a rose, as when a drunken man seeks to pluck roses and gains by his effort nothing but being pierced by thorns." The idea of roses is to be rejected, because at the time when this proverb was formed there were no roses in Palestine. The proverb certainly means that a right Mashal, *i.e.* an ingenious excellent maxim, is something more and better than a חוֹחַ (the prick as of the Jewish thorn, *Zizyphus vulgaris*, or the *Christus*-thorn, the *Ziz. spina Christi*) ; but in the mouth of a fool such a maxim becomes only a useless and a hurtful thing ; for the fool so makes use of it, that he only embarrasses others and recklessly does injury to them. The LXX. translates מֹשֵׁל by δουλεία, and the Aram. by שְׁטְיוּתָא ; how the latter reached this " folly " is not apparent; but the LXX. vocalized מֹשֵׁל, according to which Hitzig, at the same time changing שָׂבוּר into שָׂכוּר, translates : "thorns shoot up by the hand of the hireling, and tyranny by the mouth of fools." Although a hired labourer, yet, on this account, he is not devoid of conscience; thus 9*a* so corrected has something in its favour : one ought, as far as possible, to do all with his own hand; but the thought in 9*b* is far-fetched, and if Hitzig explains that want of judgment in the state councils creates despotism, so, on the other hand, xxiv. 7 says that the fool cannot give counsel in the gate, and therefore he holds his mouth.

[1] The plur. חַוְחִים, 1 Sam. xiii. 6, signifies not thorn bushes, but rock-splitting ; in Damascus, *chôcha* means a little gate in the wing of a large door ; *vid.* Wetstein's *Nordarabien*, p. 23.

Ver. 10. All that we have hitherto read is surpassed in obscurity by this proverb, which is here connected because of the resemblance of וׁשכר to שׁכור. We translate it thus, vocalizing differently only one word :

> Much bringeth forth from itself all;
> But the reward and the hirer of the fool pass away.

The LXX. translates πολλὰ χειμάζεται πᾶσα σὰρξ ἀφρόνων (all the flesh of fools suffers much), συντριβήσεται γὰρ ἡ ἔκστασις αὐτῶν, which is in Hebrew :

$$\text{רב מחולל כל בְּשַׂר כסיל}$$
$$\text{יְשֶׁבֶר עָבְרָתָם}$$

An unfortunate attempt so to rectify the words that some meaning might be extracted from them. The first line of this translation has been adopted by the Syr. and Targ., omitting only the כל, in which the self-condemnation of this deciphering lies (for כל בשׂר means elsewhere, humanity, not the whole body of each individual) ; but they translate the second line as if the words were :

$$\text{יְשֹׁבֹּר עֹבֵר יָם}$$

i.e., and the drunken man sails over the sea (עברים is separated into עבר ים, as בבקרים, Amos vi. 12, is to be separated into בַּבָּקָר יָם); but what does that mean ? Does it mean that to a drunkard (but שִׁכּוֹר, the drunken man, and not סֹבֵא, the drunkard, is used) nothing remains but to wander over the sea ? or that the drunken man lets his imagination wander away over the sea, while he neglects the obligation that lies upon him ? Symmachus and Theodotion, with the Midrash (Rashi) and Saadia (Kimchi), take שׁכר in 10b = סגר (like Isa. xix. 10, שֶׂכֶר = embankment, cf. סַכָּרִין, Kelim, xxiii. 5) ; the former translates by καὶ ὁ φράσσων ἄφρονα ἐμφράσσει τὰς ὀργὰς αὐτοῦ, the latter by καὶ φιμῶν ἄφρονα φιμοῖ χόλους, yielding to the imagination that עֲבָרִים, like עֲבָרוֹת, may be the plur. of עֶבְרָה, anger. Jerome punctuates רב as, xxv. 8, רָב, and interprets, as Symmachus and Theodotion, שֶׂכֶר both times = סֹגֵר, translating : Judicium determinat causas, et qui imponit stulto silentium iras mitigat ; but רב does not mean judicium, nor מחולל determinat, nor כל causas. As Gussetius, so also Ralbag (in the first of his three explanations), Meîri, Elia

Wilna interpret the proverb as a declaration regarding quarrelsome persons : he causeth woe to all, and hireth fools, hireth transgressors, for his companions; but in that case we must read רָב for רַב ; מְחוֹלֵל, bringing woe, would be either the *Po.* of חָלַל, to bore through, or *Pilel* of חִיל (חוֹל), to put into distress (as with pangs); but עֹבְרִים, transgressors = sinners, is contrary to the O. T. *usus loq.*, xxii. 3 (xxvii. 12) is falsely cited in its favour; besides, for רַב there should have been at least אִישׁ רָב, and why וְשֹׂכֵר is repeated remains inexplicable. Others take מְחוֹלֵל־כֹּל as the name of God, the creator of all men and things; and truly this is the nearest impression of these two words, for חוֹלֵל is the usual designation for divine production, *e.g.* Ps. xc. 2. Accordingly Kimchi explains : The Lord is the creator of all, and He gives to fools and to transgressors their maintenance; but עֹבְרִים, transgressors, is Mishnic, not bibl.; and שֹׂכֵר means tò hire, but not to supply with food. The proverb is thus incapable of presenting a thought like Matt. v. 45 (He maketh His sun to rise on the evil and on the good). Others translate: " The Lord is creator of all, and takes fools, takes idlers, into His service." Thus rendered, the proverb is offensive; wherefore Rashi, Moses Kimchi, Arama, and others regard the Mashal as in the mouth of fools, and thus they take vers. 9 and 10 together as a tetrastich. Certainly this second collection of proverbs contains also tetrastiches; but vers. 9 and 10 cannot be regarded as together forming a tetrastich, because רַב (which is valid against Kimchi also) cannot mean God the Lord : רַב, Lord, is unheard of in bibl. Heb., and at least the word הָרַב must be used for God. The *Venet.* on this account does not follow Kimchi, but translates, Ἄρχων πλάττει πάντα, καὶ μισθοῦται μωρὸν καὶ μισθοῦται ὡς παραβάτης (ought to have been παραβάτας) ; but who could this cunning man be ? Perhaps the *Venet.* is to be understood, after Gecatilia (in Rashi): a great (rich) man performs all manner of things; but if he hires a fool, it is as if he hired the first best who pass along the way. But that חוֹל is used in the general sense of to execute, to perform, is without example, and improbable. Also the explanation : a ruler brings grief, *i.e.* severe oppression, upon all (Abulwalîd, Immanuel, Aben Ezra, who, in his smaller grammar, explains רַב = רָב after Isa. xlix. 9;

C. B. Michaelis: *dolore afficit omnes*), does not recommend itself; for חולל, whether it be from חלל, Isa. li. 9 (to bore through), or from חיל, Ps. xxix. 9 (to bring on the pangs of birth), is too strong a word for hurting; also the clause, thus generally understood, is fortunately untrue. Translated as by Euchel: "the prominent persons destroy all; they keep fools in pay, and favour vagabonds,"—it sounds as if it had been picked up in an assembly of democrats. On the other hand, the proverb, as translated by Luther:

> A good master maketh a thing right;
> But he who hireth a bungler, by him it is spoiled,

is worthy of the Book of Proverbs. The second line is here freely rendered, but it is also appropriate, if we abide closer by the words of the text, in this connection. Fleischer: *Magister (artifex peritus) effingit omnia* (i.e. *bene perficit quæcunque ei committuntur*); *qui autem stultum conducit, conducit transeuntes* (i.e. *idem facit ac si homines ignotos et forte transeuntes ad opus gravius et difficilius conduceret*). Thus also Gesenius, Böttcher, and others, who all, as Gecatilia above, explain עברים, *τοὺς τυχόντας*, the first best. But we are reluctantly constrained to object to this thought, because רַב nowhere in bibl. Hebrew signifies a master; and the ו of the second וְשֹׂבֵר cannot bear that rendering, *ac si*. And if we leave it out, we nevertheless encounter a difficulty in חולל, which cannot be used of human production. Many Christian interpreters (Cocceius, Schultens, Schelling, Ewald, Bertheau, Stier, Zöckler) give to רב a meaning which is found in no Jewish interpreter, viz. *sagittarius*, from רָבַב (רְבֹב), Gen. xlix. 23 (and perhaps Ps. xviii. 15), after the forms צַר, שַׂר, the plur. of which, רַבִּים, is found at Job xvi. 13, Jer. l. 29, but in a connection which removes all doubt from the meaning of the word. Here also רַב may be more closely defined by מְחוֹלֵל; but how then does the proverb stand? "an archer who wounds everything, and he who hires a fool, and hires passers-by" (Ewald: street-runners), *i.e.* they are alike. But if the archer piercing everything is a comic *Hercules furens*, then, in order to discover the resemblance between the three, there is need of a portion of ingenuity, such as is only particularly assigned to the favoured. But it is also against the form and the usage of the word to interpret עברים simply of rogues and vagabonds. Several interpreters have supposed that רב and כל must stand in a certain interchangeable relation to each other. Thus, *e.g.*, Ahron b. Josef: "Much makes amazement to all, but especially one who hires a fool. . . ." But this "especially" (before all) is an expression smuggled in. Agreeing with Umbreit and Hitzig, we translate line first; but in translating line second, we follow our own method:

> Much bringeth all out of it;

i.e., where there is much, then one has it in his power, if he begins right, to undertake everything. רַב has by כֹּל the definition of a neuter, so as to designate not only many men, Ex. xix. 21, but also much ability in a pecuniary and facultative sense (cf. the subst. רָב, Isa. lxiii. 7; Ps. cxlv. 7); and of the much which bringeth forth all out of itself, effects all by itself, חולל with equal right might be used, as xxv. 23, of the north wind. The antithesis 10*b* takes this form:

> But the reward (read וְשֹׂכֵר) and the master (who hires him for
> wages) of the fool pass away,

i.e. perish; עֹבְרִים, as if עֹבֵר, is used of chaff, Isa. xxix. 5; of stubble, Jer. xiii. 24; of shadow, Ps. cxliv. 4. That which the fool gains passes away, for he squanders it; and he who took him into his service for wages is ruined along with him, for his work is only pernicious, not useful. Although he who possesses much, and has great ability, may be able to effect everything of himself, yet that is not the case when he makes use of the assistance therein of foolish men, who not only do not accomplish anything, but, on the contrary, destroy everything, and are only ruinous to him who, with good intention, associates them with himself in his work. That the word must be more accurately וְשֹׂכֵר, instead of וְשֹׂכְרוֹ, one may not object, since וְשֹׂכֵר is perfectly unambiguous, and is manifestly the object.

Ver. 11. The series of proverbs regarding fools is continued:

> Like a dog which returneth to his vomit,
> Is a fool who cometh again with his folly.

שָׁב is like שׁוֹנֶה, particip.; only if the punctuation were בְּכֶּלֶב, ought "which returneth to his vomit" to be taken as a relative clause (*vid.* under Ps. xxxviii. 14). Regarding עַל as designating the *terminus quo* with verbs of motions, *vid.* Köhler under Mal. iii. 24. On אָק = קִיא, cf. xxiii. 8. Luther rightly: as a dog devours again his vomit. The LXX. translate: ὥσπερ κύων ὅταν ἐπέλθῃ ἐπὶ τὸν ἑαυτοῦ ἔμετον; the reference in 2 Pet. ii. 22: κύων ἐπιστρέψας ἐπὶ τὸ ἴδιον ἐξέραμα, is thus not from the LXX.; the *Venet.* is not connected with this N. T. citation, but with the LXX., if its accordance with it is not merely accidental. To devour again its vomit is common with the dog.[1] Even so, it is the manner of fools to return again in word and in deed to their past folly (*vid.* regarding שׁנה with בּ of the object, xvii. 9); as an Aram. popular saying has it: the fool always falls back upon his foolish conduct.[2] He must needs do so, for folly has become to him a second nature; but this " must " ceases when once a divine light shines forth upon him. The LXX. has after ver. 11 a distich which is literally the same as Sir. iv. 21.

> Ver. 12 Seest thou a man who is wise in his own eyes?
> The fool hath more hope than he.

Regarding the *perf. hypotheticum* רָאִיתָ, *vid.* at xxii. 29. Line second is repeated, xxix. 20, unchanged. מִמֶּנּוּ, *præ eo*, is equivalent to the Mishnic יוֹתֵר מִמֶּנּוּ, *plus quam ei.* As the conversion of a sinner, who does not regard himself as righteous, is more to be expected than that of a self-righteous man (Matt. ix. 12 f.), so the putting right of a fool, who is conscious that he is not wise (cf. xxiv. 7), is more likely to be effected than that of one deeming himself wise; for the greatest hindrance to any turning toward that which is better lies in the delusion that he does not need it.[3] Thus far the group of proverbs regarding fools.

There follows now a group of proverbs regarding the slothful:

> Ver. 13 The slothful saith there is a lion without,
> A lion in the midst of the streets;

---

[1] *Vid.* Schulze's *Die bibl. Sprichwörter der deutschen Sprache*, p. 71 f.

[2] *Vid.* Wahl's *Das Sprichwort der heb.-aram. Literatur*, p. 147; Duke's *Rabbin. Blumenlese*, p. 9.

[3] The Targum has 12b after Codd. פְּקַח סַכְלָא טַב מִנֵּיהּ (= Syr. *pekach, expedit, convenit, melius est*), it is far better circumstanced regarding the fool han regarding him. *Vid.* Geiger's *Zeitschr.* vi. (1868), p. 154.

cf. the original of this proverb, xxii. 13. שׁוּעָל, to say nothing of שַׁחַל, is not the jackal ; שַׁחַל is the bibl. name for the lion. בֵּין is the more general expression for בְּקֶרֶב, Isa. v. 25 ; by the streets he thinks of the rows of houses that form them.

> Ver. 14 The door turneth on its hinges,
> And the sluggard on his bed.

The comparison is clear. The door turns itself on its hinges, on which it hangs, in and out, without passing beyond the narrow space of its motion; so is the fool on his bed, where he turns himself from the one side to the other. He is called עָצֵל, because he is fast glued to the place where he is (Arab. 'azila), and cannot be free (contrast of the active, cf. Arab. hafyf, moving nimbly, agilis). But the door offers itself as a comparison, because the diligent goes out by it to begin his work without (xxiv. 27 ; Ps. civ. 23), while the sluggard rolls himself about on his bed. The hook, the hinge, on which the door is moved, called צִיר, from צוּר, to turn,[1] has thus the name of הַסּוֹב.

> Ver. 15 The slothful has thrust his hand into the dish,
> It is hard for him to bring it back to his mouth again.

A variation of xix. 24 ; the fut. יְשִׁיבֶנָּה there, is here explained by נִלְאָה לַהֲשִׁיבָהּ.

> Ver. 16 The sluggard is wise in his own eyes,
> More than seven men who give an excellent answer.

Between slothfulness and conceit there exists no inward neces- sary mutual relation. The proverb means that the sluggard as such regards himself as wiser than seven, who all together answer well at any examination : much labour—he thinks with himself—only injures the health, blunts men for life and its joys, leads only to over-exertion ; for the most prudent is, as a general rule, crack-brained. Böttcher's " maulfaule " [slow to speak] belongs to the German style of thinking ; עטל לשׁנא in Syr. is not he who is slow to speak, but he who has a

---

[1] The Arab. verb signifies radically : to turn, like the Persian verbs kashatn and kardydan, and like our " werden " [to grow, turn], accords with vertere (Fleischer).

faltering tongue.[1] Seven is the number of manifoldness in completed unfolding (ix. 1). Meîri thinks, after Ezra vii. 14, on the council of seven of the Asiatic ruler. But seven is a round number of plurality, ver. 25, xxiv. 16, vi. 31. Regarding טַעַם, *vid.* at xi. 22.

A series of proverbs which recommend the love of peace, for they present caricatures of the opposite:

> Ver. 17 He seizeth by the ears a dog passing by,
> Who is excited by a strife which concerns him not.

According to the accentuation in the text, the proverb is to be translated with Fleischer: *Qualis est qui prehendit aures canis, talis est qui forte transiens ira abripitur propter rixam alienam* (*eique temere se immiscet*). Since he is cautioned against unwarranted interference, the expression מִתְעָרֵב בְּרִין might have been used (xiv. 10), according to which the Syr. translates; but עַל-רִיב substantiates the originality of מִתְעַבֵּר (*vid.* xiv. 16, xx. 2). On the other hand, the placing together, without any connection of the two participles, is perplexing; why not עֹבֵר וּמִתְעַבֵּר? For it is certainly not meant, that falling into a passion he passes by; but that passing by, he falls into a passion; for he stands to this object. The Targumist, feeling this also, renders עֹבֵר in the sense of being angry, but contrary to the *usus loq.* Wherefore the conjecture of Euchel and Abramsohn commends itself, that עֹבֵר belongs to כלב—the figure thereby becomes more distinct. To seize one's own dog by the ear is not dangerous, but it is not advisable to do this with a strange dog. Therefore עבר belongs as a necessary attribute to the dog. The dog accidentally passing by corresponds to the strife to which one stands in no relation (רִיב לֹא-לֹו, *vid.* regarding the *Makkeph*, Baer's *Genesis*, p. 85, *not.* 9). Whoever is excited to passion about a strife that does not belong to him, is like one who lays hold by the ears (the LXX. arbitrarily: by the tail) of a dog that is passing by—to the one or to the other it happens right when he brings evil upon himself thereby.

Vers. 18, 19. These verses form a tetrastich:

> Ver. 18 As a man who casteth brands,
> And arrows, and death;

---

[1] The Aram. עֲטַל is the Hebr. עָצַל, as עֲטָא=עָצָה; but in Arab. corresponds not to 'atal, but to 'azal.

19 So is the man who deceiveth his neighbour,
   And saith : I only make sport.

The old translations of מתלהלה are very diverse. Aquila has
rendered it by κακοηθιζόμενος ; Symmachus : πειρώμενοι ; the
Syr. : the vainglorious ; the Targ. : מִתַּחַת (from נָחַת), a successor (spiritually) ; Jerome : noxius (injurious ; for which
Luther : secret). There is thus no traditional translation.
Kimchi explains the word by הִשְׁתַּגֵּעַ (Venet. ἐξεστώς) ; Aben
Ezra by הִשְׁתַּטֵּה (from שָׁטָה), to behave thoughtlessly, foolishly ;
but both erroneously, confounding with it וַתֵּלַהּ, Gen. xlvii. 13,
which is formed from לָהָה and not from לָהַהּ, and is related to
לָאָה, according to which מתלהלה would designate him who exerts
himself (Rashi, המתיגע), or who is worn out (Saadia : who does
not know what to do, and in weariness passes his time). The
root לָהַהּ (לָהּ, whence the reflex form הִתְלַהְלַהּ, like הִתְמַהְמֵהַּ, from
מָהַהּ, מַהּ) leads to another primary idea. The root לַהּ presents
in (Arab.) âliha (vid. Fleischer in the Comm. zur Genesis, p.
57), waliha, and taliha, formed from the 8th form of this verb
(aittalah), the fundamental meaning of internal and external
unrest ; these verbs are used of the effect of fear (shrinking
back from fear), and, generally, the want of self-command ;
the Syr. otlahlah, to be terrified, obstupescere, confirms this
primary conception, connecting itself with the R. לה. Accordingly, he who shoots every possible death-bringing arrow, is
thought of as one who is beside himself, one who is of confused
mind, in which sense the passive forms of (Arab.) âlah and
talah are actually used. Schultens' reference to (Arab.) lâh
micare, according to which כמתלהלה must mean sicut ludicram
micationem exercens (Böttcher : one who exerts himself ; Malbim : one who scoffs, from הָתֵל), is to be rejected, because
מתלהלה must be the direct opposite of מְשַׂחֵק ; and Ewald's comparison of (Arab.) wâh and akhkh, to be entangled, distorted,
lâh, to be veiled, confounds together heterogeneous words.
Regarding זִקִּים (from זָנַק), burning arrows, vid. under Isa. 1. 11.
Death stands third, not as comprehensive (that which is deadly
of every kind), but as a climax (yea, even death itself). The כֵּן
of the principal sentence, correlate to כְּ of the contiguous
clause, has the Makkeph in our editions ; but the laws of the
metrical Makkeph require כֵּן אִישׁ (with Munach), as it occurs

e.g. in Cod. 1294. A man who gives vent to his malice against his neighbour, and then says: seest thou not that . . . (הֲלֹא, like Arab. *âlâ*), *i.e.* I am only jesting, I have only a joke with thee: he exhibits himself as being mad, who in blind rage scatters about him deadly arrows.

There now follow proverbs regarding the *nirgán*, the slanderer (*vid.* regarding the formation and import of this word at xvi. 28):

> Ver. 20 Where the wood faileth, the fire goeth out;
>   And where no tale-bearer, discord cometh to silence.

Wood, as material for building or for burning, is called, with the plur. of its product, עֵצִים. Since אֶפֶס is the absolute end of a thing, and thus expresses its no longer existing, so it was more appropriate to wood (Fleischer: *consumtis lignis*) than to the tale-bearer, of whom the proverb says the same thing as xxii. 10 says of the mocker.

> Ver. 21 Black coal to burning coal, and wood to fire;
>   And a contentious man to stir up strife.

The *Venet.* translates פֶּחָם by καρβών, and נֶּחֶלֶת by ἄνθραξ; the former (from פָּחַם, Arab. *fahuma*, to be deep black) is coal in itself; the latter (from נָחַל, *jaham*, to set on fire, and intrans. to burn), coal in a glowing state (*e.g.* xxv. 22; Ezek. i. 13). Black coal is suited to glowing coal, to nourish it; and wood to the fire, to sustain it; and a contentious man is suited for and serves this purpose, to kindle up strife. חָרַר signifies to be hot, and the *Pilpel* חִרְחֵר, to heat, *i.e.* to make hot or hotter. The three—coal, wood, and the contentious man—are alike, in that they are a means to an end.

> Ver. 22 The words of the tale-bearer are like dainty morsels;
>   And they glide down into the innermost parts.

A repetition of xviii. 8.

The proverbs next following treat of a cognate theme, hypocrisy (the art of dissembling), which, under a shining [*gleissen*] exterior,[1] conceals hatred and destruction:

> Ver. 23 Dross of silver spread over an earthen vessel—
>   Lips glowing with love and a base heart.

---

[1] *Vid.* regarding *gleisen* (to give a deceitful appearance) and *gleissen* (to throw a dazzling appearance), Schmitthenner-Weigand's *Deutsches Wörterbuch.*

Dross of silver is the so-called *glätte* (French, *litharge*), a combination of lead and oxygen, which, in the old process of producing silver, was separated (Luther: *silberschaum, i.e.* the silver litharge; Lat. *spuma argenti*, having the appearance of foam). It is still used to glaze over potter's ware, which here (Greek, κέραμος) is briefly called חֶרֶשׂ for כְּלִי חֶרֶשׂ; for the vessel is better in appearance than the mere potsherd. The glossing of the earthenware is called צָפָּה עַל־חָרֶשׂ, which is applicable to any kind of covering (צָפָּה, R. צף, to spread or lay out broad) of a less costly material with that which is more precious. 23a contains the figure, and 23b its subscription: שְׂפָתִים דֹּלְקִים וְלֵב רָע. Thus, with the taking away of the *Makkeph* after Codd., to be punctuated: burning lips, and therewith a base heart; burning, that is, with the fire of love (Meîri, אֵשׁ הַחֵשֶׁק), while yet the assurances of friendship, sealed by ardent kisses, serve only to mask a far different heart. The LXX. translate דלקים [burning] by λεῖα, and thus have read חלקים [smooth], which Hitzig without reason prefers; burning lips (Jerome, incorrectly: *tumentia*; Luther, after Deut. xxxii. 33, חמת: *Gifftiger mund* = a poisonous mouth) are just flattering, and at the same time hypocritical[1] lips. Regarding שפתים as masc., *vid*. vol. i. p. 119; לב רע means, at xxv. 20, *animus mæstus*; here, *inimicus*. The figure is excellent: one may regard a vessel with the silver gloss as silver, and it is still earthen; and that also which gives forth the silver glance is not silver, but only the refuse of silver. Both are suitable to the comparison: the lips only glitter, the heart is false (Heidenheim).

Vers. 24 and 25 form a tetrastich.

> Ver. 24 With his lips the hater dissembleth,
> And in his heart he museth deceit.
> 25 If he maketh his voice agreeable, believe him not,
> For seven abominations are in his heart.

---

[1] Schultens explains the *labia flagrantia* by *volubiliter prompta et diserta*. But one sees from the Arab. *dhaluḳa*, to be loose, lightly and easily moved (*vid*. in Fleischer's *Beiträgen zur arab. Sprachkunde* the explanation of the designation of the liquid expressed with the point of the tongue by *dhalḳiytt*, at i. 26, 27; cf. de Sacy's *Grammar*), and *dalḳ*, to draw out (of the sword from its scabbard), to rinse (of water), that the meaning of the Heb. דלק, to burn, from R. דל, refers to the idea of the flickering, tongue-like movement of the flame.

All the old translators (also the *Venet.* and Luther) give to
יִנָּכֵר the meaning, to become known; but the *Niph.* as well as
the *Hithpa.* (*vid.* at xx. 11; Gen. xlvii. 7) unites with this
meaning also the meaning to make oneself known: to make
oneself unknown, unrecognisable = (Arab.) *tanakkr, e.g.* by
means of clothing, or by a changed expression of countenance.[1]
The contrast demands here this latter signification: *labiis suis
alium se simulat osor, intus in pectore autem reconditum habet
dolum* (Fleischer). This rendering of יְשִׁית מִרְמָה is more correct
than Hitzig's ("in his breast) he prepares treachery;" for שִׁית
מרמה is to be rendered after שִׁית עֵצוֹת, Ps. xiii. 3 (*vid.* Hupfeld's
and also our comm. on this passage), not after Jer. ix. 7; for
one says שִׁית מוֹקְשִׁים, to place snares, שִׁית אֹרֶב, to lay an ambush,
and the like, but not to place or to lay deceit. If such a
dissembler makes his voice agreeable (*Piel* of חָנַן only here, for
the form Ps. ix. 14 is, as it is punctuated, *Kal*), trust not
thyself to him (הַאֲמֵין, with בּ: to put firm trust in anything,
vid. Genesis, p. 312 [2]); for seven abominations, *i.e.* a whole
host of abominable thoughts and designs, are in his heart; he
is, if one may express it, after Matt. xii. 45, possessed inwardly
of seven devils. The LXX. makes a history of 24*a*: an
enemy who, under complaints, makes all possible allowances,
but in his heart τεκταίνεται δόλους. The history is only too
true, but it has no place in the text.

   Ver. 26 Hatred may conceal itself behind deceit:
          Its wickedness shall be exposed in the assembly.

Proverbs which begin with the fut. are rarely to be found, it is

──────────

[1] *Vid.* de Goeje's *Fragmenta Hist. Arab.* ii. (1871), p. 94. The verb
נכר, primarily to fix one's attention, sharply to contemplate anything,
whence is derived the meanings of knowing and of not knowing, disowning. The account of the origin of these contrasted meanings, in
Gesenius-Dietrich's *Lexicon*, is essentially correct; but the Arab. *nakar*
there referred to means, not sharpness of mind, from *nakar* = הִכִּיר, but
from the negative signification prevailing in the Arab. alone, a property by
which one makes himself worthy of being disowned: craftiness, cunning,
and then also *in bonam partem:* sagacity.

[2] The fundamental idea of firmness in הַאֲמִין is always in the subject, not
the object. The Arabic interpreters remark that *âman* with *b* expresses
recognition, and with *l* submission (*vid.* Lane's *Lexicon* under *âman*); but
in Hebr. האמין with בּ *fiducia fidei*, with לֹ *assensus fidei;* the relation is
thus not altogether the same.

true; yet, as we have seen, xii. 26, they are sometimes to be met
with in the collection. This is one of the few that are of such
a character; for that the LXX. and others translate ὁ κρύπ-
των, which gives for רֵעֵתוֹ a more appropriate reference, does
not require us to agree with Hitzig in reading הַפְּסֵה (xii. 16,
23),—the two clauses rendered fut. stand in the same syntactical
relation, as e.g. Job xx. 24. Still less can the rendering of
במשאון by συνίστησι δόλον, by the LXX., induce us to read
with Hitzig אָ֫וֶן חֹרֵשׁ, especially since it is doubtful whether the
Heb. words which floated before those translators (the LXX.)
have been fallen upon. מַשָּׁאוֹן (beginning and ending with a
formative syllable) is certainly a word of rare formation, to be
compared only to מִסְדְּרוֹן, Judg. iii. 23; but since the nearest-
lying formation מַשָּׁא signifies usury (from נָשָׁא, to credit) (according to which Symmachus, διὰ λήμματα, to desire gain), it
is obvious that the language preferred this double formation
for the meaning deceiving, illusion, or, exactly : fraud. It
may also be possible to refer it, like מַשּׁוּאוֹת (vid. under Ps.
xxiii. 18), to שׁוֹא = שָׁאָה, to be confused, waste, as this is done
by Parchon, Kimchi (Venet. ἐν ἐρημίᾳ), Ralbag, and others;
משאון, in this sense of deepest concealment, certainly says not a
little as the contrast of קָהָל [an assembly], but יְשִׁימוֹן [a desert]
stood ready for the poet to be used in this sense; he might
also have expressed himself as Job xxx. 3, xxxviii. 27. The
selection of this rare word is better explained if it denotes the
superlative of deceit,—a course of conduct maliciously directed
toward the deception of a neighbour. That is also the impression which the word has made on Jerome (fraudulenter),
the Targ. (בְּמוּרְסְתָּא, in grinding), Luther (to do injury), and
according to which it has already been explained, e.g. by C. B.
Michaelis and Oetinger (" with dissembled, deceitful nature").
The punctuation of תכסה, Codd. and editions present in three
different forms. Buxtorf in his Concordance (also Fürst), and
the Basel Biblia Rabbinica, have the form תְּכַסֶּה; but this is a
mistake. Either תִּכָּסֶה (Niph.) or תִּכַּסֶּה (Hithpa., with the same
assimilation of the preformative ת as in הֻכַּבֵּס, Lev. xiii. 55 ; נִכַּפֵּר,
Deut. xxi. 8) is to be read; Kimchi, in his Wörterbuch, gives תִּכַּסֶּה,
which is certainly better supported. A surer contrast of במשאון
and בקהל remains in our interpretation; only we translate not

as Ewald: "hatred seeks to conceal itself by hypocrisy," but: in deceitful work. Also we refer רֶעָתוֹ, not to בְּמַשָּׁאוֹן, but to שִׂנְאָה, for hatred is thought of in connection with its personal representative. We see from 26b that hatred is meant which not only broods over evil, but also carries it into execution. Such hatred may conceal itself in cunningly-contrived deception, yet the wickedness of the hater in the end comes out from behind the mask with the light of publicity.

> Ver. 27 He who diggeth a pit falleth therein ;
> And he that rolleth up a stone, upon himself it rolleth back.

The thought that destruction prepared for others recoils upon its contriver, has found its expression everywhere among men in divers forms of proverbial sayings; in the form which it here receives, 27a has its oldest original in Ps. vii. 16, whence it is repeated here and in Eccles. x. 8, and Sir. xxvii. 26. Regarding בֹּרֶה, vid. at xvi. 27. בָּהּ here has the sense of in eam ipsam; expressed in French, the proverb is : celui qui creuse la fosse, y tombera; in Italian : chi cava la fossa, caderà in essa. The second line of this proverb accords with Ps. vii. 17 (vid. Hupfeld and Riehm on this passage). It is natural to think of the rolling as a rolling upwards ; cf. Sir. xxvii. 25, ὁ βάλλων λίθον εἰς ὕψος ἐπὶ κεφαλὴν αὐτοῦ βάλλει, i.e. throws it on his own head. וְגֹלֵל אֶבֶן is to be syntactically judged of like xviii. 13.

> Ver. 28 The lying tongue hateth those whom it bruiseth ;
> And a flattering mouth causeth ruin.

The LXX., Jerome, the Targ., and Syr. render דְבִיו יִשְׂנָא in the sense of non amat veritatem; they appear by דכיו to have thought of the Aram. דָּכְיָא, that which is pure; and thus they gain nothing else but an undeniable plain thought. Many Jewish interpreters gloss : מוכיחיו, also after the Aram. : דַּכְּיוֹ = מְדַכְּיו ; but the Aram. דַּכִּי does not mean pure in the sense of being right, therefore Elia Wilna understands him who desires to justify himself, and this violent derivation from the Aram. thus does not lead to the end. Luther, translating : " a false tongue hates those who punish it," explains, as also Gesenius, conterentes = castigantes ipsam; but דַּךְ signifies, according to the usage of the language before us, " bruised " (vid. Ps. ix. 10), not : bruising ; and the thought that the liar hates him who listens to him, leads ad absurdum; but that he does not love him

who bruises (punishes) him, is self-evident. Kimchi sees in דַּכָּיו
another form of דַּכָּא ; and Meîri, Jona Gerundi in his ethical
work (שַׁעֲרֵי תְשׁוּבָה = The gates of Repentance), and others,
accordingly render דכיו in the sense of עֲנָו (עָנְיָו) : the lying
tongue hates—as Löwenstein translates—the humble [pious] ;
also that for דַּכָּיו, by the omission of ו, זַךְ יְדַּכִּי = זַכִּי may be read, is
supposable ; but this does not harmonize with the second half
of the proverb, according to which לְשׁוֹן שֶׁקֶר must be the subject,
and יִשְׂנָא דכיו must express some kind of evil which proceeds
from such a tongue. Ewald : " the lying tongue hates its
master (אֲדֹנָיו)," but that is not in accordance with the Heb.
style ; the word in that case should have been בְעָלָיו. Hitzig
countenances this אדניו, with the remark that the tongue is
here personified ; but personified, the tongue certainly means
him who has it (Ps. cxx. 3). Böttcher's conjecture יְשַׁנֶּא דְּכָיו,
" confounds their talk," is certainly a curiosity. Spoken of
the sea, those words would mean, " it changes its surge." But
is it then at all necessary to uncover first the meaning of 28a ?
Rashi, Arama, and others refer דַּכָּיו to דַּכִּים = נִדְכָּאִים (מְדֻכִּים).
Thus also perhaps the Venet., which translates τοὺς ἐπιτριμμοὺς
(not : ἐπιτετριμμένους) αὐτῆς. C. B. Michaelis : Lingua falsi-
tatis odio habet contritos suos, h. e. eos quos falsitate ac mendacio
lædit contritosque facit. Hitzig objects that it is more correct to
say : conterit perosos sibi. And certainly this lay nearer, on
which account Fleischer remarks : in 28a there is to be supposed a poetic transposition of the ideas (Hypallage) : homo qui
lingua ad calumnias abutitur conterit eos quos odit. The poet
makes יִשְׂנָא the main conception, because it does not come
to him so readily to say that the lying tongue bruises those
against whom it is directed, as that it is hatred, which is
active in this. To say this was by no means superfluous. There
are men who find pleasure in repeating and magnifying scandal-
ously that which is depreciatory and disadvantageous to their
neighbour unsubstantiated, without being at all conscious of
any particular ill-will or personal enmity against him ; but this
proverb says that such untruthful tongue-thrashing proceeds
always from a transgression of the commandment, " Thou shalt
not hate thy brother," Lev. xix. 17, and not merely from the
want of love, but from a state of mind which is the direct

opposite of love (*vid.* x. 18). Ewald finds it incongruous that
28*a* speaks of that which others have to suffer from the lying
tongue, whereas the whole connection of this proverb requires
that the tongue should here be regarded as bringing ruin upon
its owner himself. But of the destruction which the wicked
tongue prepares for others many proverbs also speak, *e.g.* xii.
13, cf. xvii. 4, לְשׁוֹן הַוֺּת; and 28*b* does not mention that the
smooth tongue (written וּפֶה־חָלָק with *Makkeph*) brings injury upon
itself (an idea which must be otherwise expressed; cf. xiv. 32),
but that it brings injury and ruin on those who have pleasure in
its flatteries (חֲלָקוֹת, Ps. xii. 3; Isa. xxx. 10), and are befooled
thereby: *os blandiloquum* (*blanditiis dolum tegens*) *ad casum
impellit, sc. alios* (Fleischer).

xxvii. In the group 1–6 of this chapter every two proverbs
form a pair. The first pair is directed against unseemly
boasting:

> Ver. 1 Boast not thyself of to-morrow,
>   For thou knowest not what a day bringeth forth.

The בְּ of בְּיוֹם is like, *e.g.* that in xxv. 14, the בְּ of the ground
of boasting. One boasts of to-morrow when he boasts of that
which he will then do and experience. This boasting is foolish
and presumptuous (Luke xii. 20), for the future is God's; not
a moment of the future is in our own power, we know not what
a day, this present day or to-morrow (Jas. iv. 13), will bring
forth, *i.e.* (cf. Zeph. ii. 2) will disclose, and cannot therefore
order anything beforehand regarding it. Instead of לֹא־תֵדַע
(with *Kametz* and *Mugrash*), לֹא־תֵדַע (thus *e.g.* the Cod. *Jaman*)
is to be written; the Masora knows nothing of that pausal
form. And instead of מַה־יֵּלֶד יוֹם, we write מַה יֵּלֶד יוֹם with
Zinnorith. יֵלֶד before יוֹם has the tone thrown back on the
penult., and consequently a shortened *ult.*; the Masora reckons
this word among the twenty-five words with only one *Tsere.*

> Ver. 2 Let another praise thee, and not thine own mouth;
>   A stranger, and not thine own lips.

The negative לֹא is with פִּיךָ, as in (Arab.) *ghyra fyk*, bound into
one compact idea: that which is not thine own mouth
(Fleischer), "not thine own lips," on the other hand, is not to
be interpreted as corresponding to it, like אַל־מָוֶת, xii. 28; since

after the prohibitive אַל, יְהַלֶּלוּךְ [praise thee] easily supplies
itself. זָר is properly the stranger, as having come from a distance, and נָכְרִי he who comes from an unknown country, and is
himself unknown (*vid.* under xxvi. 24); the idea of both words,
however, passes from *advena* and *alienigena* to *alius*. There is
certainly in rare cases a praising of oneself, which is authorized
because it is demanded (2 Cor. xi. 18), which, because it is
offered strongly against one's will, will be measured by truth
(x. 13); but in general it is improper to applaud oneself, because
it is a vain looking at oneself in a glass; it is indecent, because
it places others in the shade; imprudent, because it is of no
use to us, but only injures, for *propria laus sordet*, and as
Stobäus says, οὐδὲν οὕτως ἄκουσμα φορτικὸν ὡς ὁ καθ' αὐτοῦ
ἔπαινος. Compare the German proverb, " *Eigenlob stinkt,*
Freundes Lob hinkt, fremdes Lob klingt " [= self-praise stinks,
a friend's praise is lame, a stranger's praise sounds].

The second pair of proverbs designates two kinds of violent
passion as unbearable :

Ver. 3 The heaviness of a stone, the weight of sand—
A fool's wrath is heavier than both.

We do not translate : *Gravis est petra et onerosa arena*, so that
the substantives stand for strengthening the idea, instead of the
corresponding adjective (Fleischer, as the LXX., Jerome, Syr.,
Targum); the two pairs of words stand, as 4*a*, in genit. relation
(cf. on the contrary, xxxi. 30), and it is as if the poet said :
represent to thyself the heaviness of a stone and the weight of
sand, and thou shalt find that the wrath of a fool compared
thereto is still heavier, viz. for him who has to bear it ; thus
heavier, not for the fool himself (Hitzig, Zöckler, Dächsel), but
for others against whom his anger goes forth. A Jewish proverb (*vid.* Tendlau, No. 901) says, that one knows a man by
his wine-glass (כום), his purse (כים), and his anger (כעם), viz.
how he deports himself in the tumult ; and another says that
one reads what is in a man ביום כעסו, when he is in an ill-
humour. Thus also כעם is to be here understood : the fool in
a state of angry, wrathful excitement is so far not master of
himself that the worst is to be feared ; he sulks and shows
hatred, and rages without being appeased ; no one can calculate

what he may attempt, his behaviour is unendurable.   Sand, חוֹל,[1]
as it appears, as to the number of its grains innumerable, so as
to its mass (in weight) immeasurable, Job vi. 3 ; Sir. xxii. 13.
נֵטֶל the *Venet.* translates, with strict regard to the etymology, by
ἄρμα.

> Ver. 4 The madness of anger, and the overflowing of wrath—
> And before jealousy who keeps his place !

Here also the two pairs of words 4*a* stand in connection ; אַכְזְרִיּוּת
(for which the Cod. *Jaman* has incorrectly אכזריות) is the connecting form; *vid.* regarding אַכְזָרִי, v. 9.   Let one imagine the
blind, relentless rage of extreme excitement and irritation, a
boiling over of anger like a water-flood, which bears everything
down along with it—these paroxysms of wrath do not usually
continue long, and it is possible to appease them ; but jealousy
is a passion that not only rages, but reckons calmly ; it inces-
santly ferments through the mind, and when it breaks forth, he
perishes irretrievably who is its object.   Fleischer generalizes
this idea : " enmity proceeding from hatred, envy, or jealousy,
it is difficult or altogether impossible to withstand, since it puts
into operation all means, both secretly and openly, to injure the
enemy."   But after vi. 34 f., cf. Song viii. 8, there is particularly
meant the passion of scorned, mortified, deceived love, viz. in
the relation of husband and wife.

The third pair of proverbs passes over from this special love
between husband and wife to that subsisting between friends :

> Ver. 5 Better is open accusation
> Than secret love.

An integral distich ; מֵאַהֲבָה has *Munach*, and instead of the
second Metheg *Tarcha*, after *Thorath Emeth*, p. 11.   Zöckler,
with Hitzig, incorrectly : better than love which, from false
indulgence, keeps concealed from his neighbour his faults,
when he ought to tell him of them.   That would require the
phrase אהבה מַסְתֶּרֶת, not מְסֻתֶּרֶת.   Dächsel, in order to accommodate the text to this meaning, remarks : concealed censure is
concealed love ; but it is much rather the neglected duty of
love,—love without mutual discipline is weak, faint-hearted,

---

[1] Sand is called by the name חוּל (חִיל), to change, whirl, particularly to
form sand-wreaths, whence (Arab.) *al-Habil*, the region of moving sand;
vid. Wetzstein's *Nord-arabien*, p. 56.

and, if it is not too blind to remark in a friend what is
worthy of blame, is altogether too forbearing, and essentially
without conscience; but it is not "hidden and concealed love."
The meaning of the proverb is different: it is better to be
courageously and sternly corrected—on account of some fault
committed—by any one, whether he be a foe or a friend, than
to be the object of a love which may exist indeed in the heart,
but which fails to make itself manifest in outward act. There
are men who continually assure us of the reality and depth of
their friendship; but when it is necessary for them to prove
their love to be self-denying and generous, they are like a
torrent which is dry when one expects to drink water from it
(Job vi. 15). Such "secret" love, or, since the word is not
נִסְתֶּרֶת, but מְסֻתֶּרֶת, love confined to the heart alone, is like a fire
which, when it burns secretly, neither lightens nor warms;
and before such a friend, any one who frankly and freely tells
the truth has by far the preference, for although he may pain
us, yet he does us good; while the former deceives us, for he
leaves us in the lurch when it is necessary to love us, not
merely in word and with the tongue, but in deed and in truth
(1 John iii. 18). Rightly Fleischer: *Præstat correptio aperta
amicitiæ tectæ*, i.e. *nulla re probatæ.*

> Ver. 6 Faithful are the wounds of a friend,
> And overloaded [plentiful] the kisses of an enemy.

The contrast to נֶאֱמָנִים, true, *i.e.* honourable and good (with the
transference of the character of the person to his act), would
be *fraudulenta* (Jerome), or נהפכות, *i.e.* false (Ralbag); Ewald
seeks this idea from עתר, to stumble, make a false step;[1]
Hitzig, from עתר ≐ (Arab.) *dadhr*, whence *dâdhir, perfidus*, to
gain from; but (1) the comparison does not lie near, since
usually the Arab. ث corresponds to the Heb. שׁ, and the
Arab. ذ to the Heb. ז; (2) the Heb. עתר has already three
meanings, and it is not advisable to load it with yet another
meaning assumed for this passage, and elsewhere not found.
The three meanings are the following: (*a*) to smoke, Aram. עֲטַר,

---

[1] Thus also Schultens in the *Animadversiones*, which later he fancied
was derived from עתר, *nidor*, from the meaning *nidorosa*, and thence
virulenta.

whence עָתָר, vapour, Ezek. viii. 11, according to which the *Venet.*, with Kimchi's and Parchon's *Lex.*, translates : the kisses of an enemy συνωμίχλωνται, *i.e.* are fog; (*b*) to sacrifice, to worship, Arab. *atar;* according to which Aquila : ἱκετικά (as, with Grabe, it is probably to be read for ἑκούσια of the LXX.); and agreeably to the *Niph.*, but too artificially, Arama : obtained by entreaties = constrained; (*c*) to heap up, whence *Hiph.* הֶעְתִּיר, Ezek. xxxv. 13, cf. Jer. xxxiii. 6, according to which Rashi, Meîri, Gesenius, Fleischer, Bertheau, and most explain, cogn. with עָשַׁר, whose Aram. form is עֲתַר, for עֹשֶׁר is properly a heap of goods or treasures.[1] This third meaning gives to the kisses of an enemy a natural adjective : they are too abundant, so much the more plentiful to veil over the hatred, like the kisses by means of which Judas betrayed his Lord, not merely denoted by φιλεῖν, but by καταφιλεῖν, Matt. xxvi. 49. This, then, is the contrast, that the strokes inflicted by one who truly loves us, although they tear into our flesh (פֶּצַע, from פָּצַע, to split, to tear open), yet are faithful (cf. Ps. cxli. 5); on the contrary, the enemy covers over with kisses him to whom he wishes all evil. Thus also נעתרות forms an indirect contrast to נאמנים.

In 7–10 there is also visible a weaving of the external with the internal. First, there are two proverbs, in each of which there is repeated a word terminating with נ.

Ver. 7 A satisfied soul treadeth honeycomb under foot;
And a hungry soul—everything bitter is (to it) sweet.

It is unnecessary to read תָּבוּז (Hitzig) ; תָּבוּס is stronger; "to tread with the feet" is the extreme degree of scornful despite. That satiety and hunger are applicable to the soul, *vid.* under x. 3. In 7*b*, the adverb לוֹ, relative to the *nomin. absol.*, like xxviii. 7, but not xiii. 18. "Hunger is the best cook," according to a German proverb; the Hebrew proverb is so formed that it is easily transferred to the sphere of the soul. Let the man whom God has richly satisfied with good things guard himself against ingratitude towards the Giver, and against an undervaluing of the gifts received; and if they are spiritual blessings, let him guard himself against self-satisfaction and

[1] *Vid.* regarding this word, Schlottmann in *Deutsch.-Morgenl. Zeitschrift*, xxiv. 665, 668.

self-contentment, which is, in truth, the worst poverty, Rev. iii. 17; for life without God is a constant hunger and thirst. There is in worldly things, even the most pleasing, a dissatisfaction felt, and a dissatisfaction awakening disgust; and in spiritual life, a satiety which supposes itself to be full of life, but which is nothing else than the decay of life, than the changing of life into death.

Ver. 8 As a bird that wandereth from her nest,
　　　So is a man that wandereth from his home.

It is not a flying out that is meant, from which at any moment a return is possible, but an unwilling taking to flight (LXX. 8b: ὅταν ἀποξενωθῇ ; *Venet.*: πλανούμενον . . . πλανούμενος) ; for עוֹף נוֹדֵד, Isa. xvi. 2, cf. Jer. iv. 25, birds that have been frightened ; and נֹדֵד, xxi. 15 f., designates the fugitive ; cf. נָע וָנָד, Gen. iv. 14, and above, xxvi. 2, where נוד designates aimless roving about. Otherwise Fleischer : " warning against unnecessary roaming about, in journeyings and wanderings far from home : as a bird far from its nest is easily wounded, caught, or killed, so, on such excursions, one easily comes to injury and want. One may think of a journey in the East. The Arabs say, in one of their proverbs : *âlsafar kat̊'at man âlklyym* (= journeying is a part of the pains of hell)." But נדד here is not to be understood in the sense of a *libere vagari.* Rightly C. B. Michaelis : *qui vagatur extorris et exul a loco suo sc. natali vel habitationis ordinariæ.* This proverb mediately recommends the love of one's fatherland, *i.e.* " love to the land in which our father has his home ; on which our paternal mansion stands ; in which we have spent the years of our childhood, so significant a part of one's whole life ; from which we have derived our bodily and intellectual nourishment; and in which home we recognise bone of our bone and flesh of our flesh." [1] But next it says, that to be in a strange land must be an unhappiness, because a man never feels better than at home, as the bird in its nest. We say : *Heimat* [home]—this beautiful word becomes the German language, which has also coined the expressive idea of *Heimweh* [longing for home] ; the

---

[1] Gustave Baur's article " Vaterlandsliebe," in Schmid's *Pädagogischer Encyklopädie.*

Heb. uses, to express the idea of home, the word מְקוֹמִי; and of fatherland, the word אֶרֶץ or אַדְמָתִי. The Heb. שְׁבוּת corresponds [1] to the German *Elend*, but = *Ellend, elilenti*, of another land, strange.

The two following proverbs have in common the catchword רֵעַ, and treat of the value of friendship :—

Ver. 9 Oil and frankincense rejoice the heart ;
    And the sweet discourse of a friend from a counselling of soul.

Regarding the perfuming with dry aromas, and sprinkling with liquid aromas, as a mark of honour towards guests, and as a

---

[1] The translators transfer to this place a note from vol. ii. p. 191 f. of the author's larger *Comm. ü. den Psalter*, to which Delitzsch refers the reader :—" The modern High German adj. *elend*, middle High German *ellende*, old High German *alilandi*, *elilendi*, or *elilenti*, is composed of *ali* and *land*. The adj. *ali* occurs only in old High German in composition. In the Gothic it is found as an independent adj., in the sense of *alius* and ἄλλος (*vid.* Ulfilas, Gal. v. 10). The primary meaning of *elilenti* is consequently : of another country, foreign. In glosses and translations it is rendered by the Lat. words *peregrinus, exul, advena*, also *captivus*. In these meanings it occurs very frequently. In the old High German translation of Ammonius, *Diatessaron, sive Harmoniæ in quatuor Evangelica*, the word proselytism, occurring in Matt. xxiii. 15, is rendered by *elilantan*. To the adj. the old High German subst. corresponds. This has the meaning *exilium, transmigratio, captivitas*. The connection *in elilenti* or *elilentes*, used adverbially, is rendered by the Lat. *peregre*. In the middle High German, however, the proper signification of both words greatly predominates. But as, in the old High German, the idea of *miser* is often at the same time comprehended in the proper signification : he who is miserable through banishment, imprisonment, or through sojourning in a strange land ; thus, in several places of the middle High German, this derived idea begins to separate itself from the fundamental conception, so that *ellende* comes in general to be called *miser*. In the new High German this derived conception is almost alone maintained. Yet here also, in certain connections, there are found traces of the original idea, *e.g. in's Elend schicken*, for to banish. Very early also the word came to be used, in a spiritual sense, to denote our present abode, in contrast to paradise or the heavenly kingdom. . . . Thus, *e.g.* in one of Luther's hymns, when we pray to the Holy Ghost :

"   Das er vns behüte, an vnserm ende,
    Wenn wir heim farn aus diesem elende."

[That He guard us to our end
    When we go home from this world.]

—Rud. von Raumer.

means of promoting joyful social fellowship, *vid.* at vii. 16 f.,
xxi. 17. The pred. יְשַׂמַּח comprehends frankincense or oil as the
two sides of one and the same thing; the LXX. introduces,
from Ps. civ. 15, also wine. It also reads ומתק רעה as one
word, וּמִתְקָרְעָה: καταρρήγνυται δὲ ὑπὸ συμπτωμάτων ψυχή,
which Hitzig regards as original; for he translates, understanding מֵעָצַת after Ps. xiii. 3, " but the soul is torn by cares."
But why מתקרעה, this *Hithpa.* without example, for נִקְרָעָה? and
now connected with מִן in the sense of ὑπό! And what does
one gain by this Alexandrian wisdom [of the LXX.]—a contrast to 9*a* which is altogether incongruous? Döderlein's rendering accords far better with 9*a*: " but the sweetness of a
friend surpasses fragrant wood." But although this rendering
of the word [עֵצָה] by " fragrant wood " is found in Gesen. *Lex.*,
from one edition to another, yet it must be rejected; for the
word signifies wood as the contents of trees, the word for
aromatic wood must be עֵצִים; and if the poet had not intentionally aimed at dubiety, he ought to have written עֲצֵי בֹשֶׂם, since
נפשׁ, with the exception of Isa. iii. 20, where it is beyond doubt,
nowhere means fragrance. If we read עצת and נפשׁ together,
then we may suppose that the latter designates the soul, as at
Ps. xiii. 3; and the former, counsel (from the verb יָעַץ). But
to what does the suffix of רֵעֵהוּ refer? One may almost conjecture that the words originally were וּמֶתֶק נֶפֶשׁ מֵעֲצַת רֵעֵהוּ, and
the sweetness of the soul (*i.e.* a sweet relish for it, cf. ver. 7
and xvi. 24) consists in the counsel of a friend, according to
which Jerome translates: *et bonis amici consiliis anima dulcora-
tur.* By this transposition רעהו refers back to נפשׁ; for if *nephesh*
denote a person or a living being, it can be construed *ad sensum*
as masc., *e.g.* Num. xxxi. 28. But the words may remain in
the order in which they are transmitted to us. It is possible
that רֵעֵהוּ is (Böttcher refers to Job xii. 4) of the same meaning
as הָרֵעַ (the friend of one = the friend), as כֻּלּוֹ denotes directly
the whole; חֶצְיוֹ, the half; עִתּוֹ, the right time. Recognising
this, Cocceius, Umbreit, Stier, and Zöckler explain: sweetness,
i.e. the sweet encouragement (מֶתֶק, in the sense of " sweetness
(grace) of the lips," xvi. 21) of a friend, is better than one's
own counsel, than prudence seeking to help oneself, and trusting
merely to one's own resources; thus also Rashi: better than

what one's own soul advises him. But (1) נפש cannot mean
one's own person (oneself) in contrast to another person;
and (2) this does not supply a correct antithesis to 9a. Thus
מן will not express the preference, but the origin. Accordingly
Ewald, e.g., explains: the sweetness of a friend whom one has
proceedeth from the counsel of soul, i.e. from such counsel as
is drawn from a deep, full soul. But no proof can be brought
from the usage of the language that עצת־נפש can be so meant;
these words, after the analogy of דעת נפש, xix. 2, mean ability to
give counsel as a quality of the soul (viii. 14 ; Job xii. 13), i.e.
its ability to advise. Accordingly, with Bertheau, we explain
ישמח־לב as the common predicate for 9a and 9b: ointment and
perfume rejoice the heart, and (the Syr., Targ., well: even so)
the sweet exhortation of a friend, from a soul capable of rendering counsel; also, this and this, more than that fragrance.
This proverb is formed in the same way as xxvi. 9, 14. In
this explanation רעהו is well referred back to לב: and (more
than) the sweet advice of his friend. But not so that רעהו is
equivalent to רע הלב, for one does not thus speak; but the construction is as when we say, in the German language: *Nichts
thut einem Herzen woler als wenn sein Freund es mitfühlend
tröstet* [nothing does more good to a heart than when a friend
sympathizingly comforts it]; or: *Zage nicht, tief betrübtes Herz!
Dein Freund lebt und wird dir bald sich zeigen* [Be not dismayed,
deeply-troubled heart! thy friend lives, and will soon show
himself to thee]. In such cases the word " *Herz* " [heart] does
not designate a distinct part of the person, but, synecdochically,
it denotes the whole person.

Ver. 10. Another proverb, consisting of three lines, in commendation of friendship:

> Thine own friend and the friend of thy father forsake not,
> And into thy brother's house go not in the day of thy misfortune—
> Better is a near neighbour than a far-off brother.

In our editions רעך is incorrectly pointed with *Pasek* after it, so
that the accent is *Asla Legarmeh;* the *Pasek* is, after the
example of older editions, with Norzi, to be cancelled, so that
only the conjunctive *Asla* remains; " thine own and the friend
of thy father" denotes the family friend, like some family

heirloom, descending from father to son. Such an old tried friend one must certainly not give up. The *Kerî* changes the second ורעה into וְרֵעַ, but וְרֵעֶה (which, after the Masora in *st. constr.*, retains its *segol*, Ewald, § 211*e*) is also admissible, for a form of comparison (Hitzig) this רֵעֶה is not, but the fuller form of the abbreviated רֵעַ, from רָעָה, to take care of, to tend, to pasture—an infinitive formation (= רְעִי) like the cogn. רָעִ a participial. Such a proved friend one ought certainly not to give up, and in the time of heavy trial (*vid.* regarding אֵיד, i. 26) one should go to him and not to a brother's house—it is by this supposed that, as xviii. 24 says, there is a degree of friendship (cf. xvii. 17) which in regard to attachment stands above that of mere fraternal relationship, and it is true; blood-relationship, viewed in itself, stands as a relationship of affection on natural grounds below friendship, which is a relationship of life on moral grounds. But does blood-relationship exclude friendship of soul? cannot my brother be at the same time my heart-friend? and is not friendship all the firmer when it has at the same time its roots in the spirit and in natural grounds? The poet seems to have said this, for in 10*c*, probably a popular saying (cf. "*Besser Nachbar an der Wand als Bruder über Land*" [Better a neighbour by one's side than a brother abroad]), he gives to his advice a foundation, and at the same time a limitation which modifies its ruggedness. But Dächsel places (like Schultens) in קָרוֹב and רָחוֹק meanings which the words do not contain, for he interprets them of inward nearness and remoteness; and Zöckler reads between the lines, for he remarks, a "near neighbour" is one who is near to the oppressed to counsel and help them, and a "distant brother" is one who with an unamiable disposition remains far from the oppressed. The state of the matter is simple. If one has a tried friend in neighbourly nearness, so in the time of distress, when he needs consolation and help, he must go to this friend, and not first to the house of a brother dwelling at a distance, for the former certainly does for us what the latter probably may and probably may not do for us.

Ver. 11. This proverb has, in common with the preceding tristich, the form of an address:

> Become wise, my son, and make my heart rejoice,
> That I may give an answer to my accusers.

Better than "be wise" (Luther), we translate "become wise"
(LXX. σοφὸς γίνου); for he who is addressed might indeed be
wise, though not at present so, so that his father is made to
listen to such deeply wounding words as these, "Cursed be he
who begat, and who educated this man" (Malbim). The
cohortative clause 11*b* (cf. Ps. cxix. 42) has the force of a clause
with a purpose (Gesen. § cxxviii. 1): *ut habeam quod iis qui me
convicientur regerere possim ;* it does not occur anywhere in the
Hezekiah collection except here.

Ver. 12. עָרוּם appears to lean on חכם.

> The prudent man seeth the misfortune, hideth himself ;
> The simple pass on, suffer injury.

= xxii. 3, where וּפְתָיִם for פְּתָאִים, וְנִסְתָּר for נִסְתָּר, and וְנֶעֱנָשׁ for
נֶעֱנָשׁוּ ; the three *asyndeta* make the proverb clumsy, as if it
counted out its seven words separately to the hearer. Ewald,
§ 349*a*, calls it a "*Steinschrift*" [an inscription on a stone].
The perfects united in pairs with, and yet more without, *Vav*,
express the coincidence[1] as to time.

Ver. 13. עָרוּם alliterates with עֲרֹב.

> Take from him the garment, for he hath become surety for another,
> And for the sake of a strange matter put him under bonds.

= xx. 16, *vid.* there.   נָכְרִיָּה we interpret neut. (LXX. τὰ
ἀλλότρια; Jerome, *pro alienis*), although certainly the case
occurs that one becomes surety for a strange woman (Aquila,
Theodotion, περὶ ξένης), by whose enticements and flatteries he

---

[1] The second *Munach* is at xxii. 3, as well as here, according to the rule
xviii. 4 of the *Accentuationssystem*, the transformation of the *Dechi*, and pre-
serves its value of interpunction ; the *Legarmeh* of עָרוּם | is, however, a
disjunctive of less force than *Dechi*, so that thus the sequence of the accents
denotes that עָרוּם רָאָה רָעָה is a clause related to וְנִסְתָּר as a hypothetical
antecedent: if the prudent sees the calamity, then he hides himself from it.
This syntactic relation is tenable at xxii. 3, but not here at xxvii. 12. Here,
at least, עָרוּם would be better with *Rebia*, to which the following *Dechi*
would subordinate itself. The prudent seeth the evil, concealeth himself ;
or also, prudent is he who sees the evil, hides himself. For of two disjunctives before *Athnach*, the first, according as it is greater or less than
the second, retains either *Legarmeh* (*e.g.* Ps. i. 5, lxxxvi. 12, lxxxviii. 14,
cix. 14) or *Rebia* (xii. 2 ; Ps. xxv. 2, lxix. 9, cxlvi. 5).

is taken, and who afterwards leaves him in the lurch with the debts for which he had become security, to show her costly favour to another.

Ver. 14. This proverb, passing over the three immediately intervening, connects itself with vers. 9 and 10. It is directed against cringing, noisy complimenting:

> He who blesseth his neighbour with a loud voice, rising early in the
> morning,
> It is reckoned as a curse to him.

The first line is intentionally very heavy, in order to portray the *empressement* of the maker of compliments : he calls out to another his good wishes with a loud voice, so as to make the impression of deep veneration, of deeply felt thankfulness, but in reality to gain favour thereby, and to commend himself to greater acts of kindness ; he sets himself to meet him, having risen up (הַשְׁכֵּים, adverbial *inf. abs.* ; cf. Jer. xliv. 4 with xxv. 4) early in the morning, to offer his *captatio benevolentiæ* as speedily as possible ; but this salutation of good wishes, the affected zeal in presenting which is a sign of a selfish, calculating, servile soul, is reckoned to him as קְלָלָה, viz. before God and every one who can judge correctly of human nature, also before him who is complimented in so ostentatious and troublesome a manner, the true design of which is thus seen. Others understand the proverb after the example of *Berachoth* 14a, that one ought to salute no one till he has said his morning's prayer, because honour is due before all to God (the Book of Wisdom, x. 28) ; and others after *Erachin* 16a, according to which one is meant who was invited as a guest of a generous lord, and was liberally entertained, and who now on the public streets blesses him, *i.e.* praises him for his nobility of mind—such blessing is a curse to him whom it concerns, because this trumpeting of his praise brings upon him a troublesome, importunate crowd. But plainly the particularity of בְּקוֹל וגו' lays the chief emphasis on the servility manifested ; and one calls to mind the case of the clients besieging the doors of their patrons, those *clientes matutini*, each of whom sought to be the first in the *salutatio* of his distinguished wealthy patron.

Ver. 15. This proverb passes from the *complimentarius* to its opposite, a shrewish wife:

A continual dropping in a rainy day
And a contentious woman are alike.

Thus we have already translated (vol. i. p. 9), where, when
treating of the manifold forms of parabolic proverbs, we began
with this least poetic, but at the same time remarked that
vers. 15 and 16 are connected, forming a tetrastich, which is
certainly the case according to the text here lying before us.
In verse 15, xix. 13*b* is expanded into a distich, and made a
complete verse. Regarding טוֹרֵד הֶלֶף, *vid.* the explanation there
given. The noun סַגְרִיר, which the Syr. translates by ܡܛܪܐ,
but the Targumist retains, because it is in common use in the
post.-bibl. Heb. (*Bereschith rabba*, c. 1) and the Jewish Aramaic,
signifies violent rain, after the Jewish interpreters, because then
the people remain shut up in their houses; more correctly, perhaps, from the unbroken continuousness and thickness (cf. the
Arab. *insajara*, to go behind each other in close column) with
which the rain pours down. Regarding מְדוֹנִים, *Keri* מִדְיָנִים, *vid.*
vi. 14; the genit. connection of מ' אֵשֶׁת we had already at xxi.
9. The form נִשְׁתָּוָה is doubtful. If accented, with Löwenstein and others, as *Milra*, then we would have a *Nithkatal*
before us, as at Num. i. 47, or a *Hothkatal* — a passive
form of the *Kal*, the existence of which, however, is not fully
established. Rather this word is to be regarded as נִשְׁתָּוָה
(*Nithpa.* as Deut. xxi. 8; Ezek. xxiii. 48) without the *dagesh*,
and lengthened; the form of the word נִשְׁתָּוָה, as found in the
Cod. *Jaman.*, aims at this. But the form נִשְׁתָּוָה is better established, *e.g.* by Cod. 1294, as *Milel*. Kimchi, *Michlol* 131*a* (cf.
Ewald, § 132*c*), regards it as a form without the *dagesh*, made
up of the *Niph.* and *Hithpa.*, leaving the *penultima* toning unexplained. Bertheau regards it as a voluntative: let us compare
(as נִשְׁתָּעָה, Isa. xli. 23); but as he himself says, the reflexive
form does not accord with this sense. Hitzig has adopted the
right explanation (cf. Olshausen, § 275, and Böttcher, § 1072,
who, however, registers it at random as an Ephraimitism). נִשְׁתָּוָה
is a *Niphal*, with a transposition of consonants for נִשְׁוְתָה, since
נִשְׁוְתָה passes over into נִשְׁתָּוָה. Such is now the *genus* in the
arrangement; the *Milra* form would be as masc. syntactically
inaccurate. "The finite following the subjects is regulated by

the gender and number of that which is next before it, as at
2 Sam. iii. 22, xx. 20 ; Ps. lv. 6 ; Job xix. 15 " (Hitzig).

Ver. 16. This verse stands in close connection with the preceding, for it speaks of the contentious woman:

> He that restraineth her restraineth the wind,
> And oil meeteth his right hand.

The connection of the plur. subject צֹפְנֶיהָ = *quicunque eam
cohibet*, with a sing. predicate, is not to be disputed (*vid.* iii. 18
and xxviii. 16, *Chethîb*) ; but can צפן gain from the meaning of
preserving, laying up, also the meanings of keeping, of confining, and shutting up ?—for these meanings we have כָּלָא
and עָצַר (cf. צָרַר, xxx. 4). In 16*b* it lies nearer to see in
יְמִינוֹ the object of the clause (oil meeteth his right hand)
than the subject (his right hand meeteth oil), for the gender
of ימין directs to יָד (*e.g.* Ezek. xv. 6*b* ; cf. 6*a*, where נֶאְדָּרִי is as
to gender indifferent) : it is fem., while on the contrary שֶׁמֶן is
generally masc. (cf. Song i. 3). There is no reason for regarding ימינו as an adverbial accus. (he meets oil with his right
hand), or, with Hitzig, as a second subject (he meets oil, his
right hand); the latter, in the order of the words lying before us,
is not at all possible. We suppose that יִקְרָא, as at Gen. xlix. 1,
is equivalent to יִקְרֶה (Ewald, § 116*c*), for the explanation *oleum
dexteræ ejus præconem agit* (Cocceius, Schultens) does not
explain, but only darkens ; and *oleum dexterâ suâ legit*, i.e. *colligit*
(Fleischer), is based on an untenable use of the word. As one
may say of person to person, קְרָאֲךָ, *occurrit tibi*, Num. xxv. 18,
so also יִקְרָא (יִקְרֶה), of a thing that meets a man or one of his
members; and if we compare לְקִרְאַת and קְרִי, then for 16*b* the
meaning is possible : oil meets his right hand; the quarrelsome
woman is like oil that cannot be held in the hand, which struggles
against that which holds it, for it always glides out of the hand.
Thus also Luther : " and seeks to hold oil with his hand," as if
he read יְקַמֵּץ. In fact, this word was more commonly used as
the expression of untenableness than the colourless and singular
word יקרא, which, besides, is so ambiguous, that none of the old
translators has thought on any other קרא than that which signifies
" to call," " to name." The Jewish interpreters also adhere to
this nearest lying קרא, and, moreover, explain, as the Syr.,
Targ., Aquila, Symmachus, Jerome, and the *Venet.*, שֶׁמֶן יְמִינוֹ,

according to the accentuation as genit. connected, *e.g.* Rashi : he calls for oil to his right hand, viz. as the means of purifica- tion from leprosy, Lev. viii. 14 [xiv. 16] ; and Aben Ezra : even when he calls for oil to his right hand, *i.e.* would move them to silence with the precious anointing oil. Perhaps ver. 16 was originally an independent proverb as follows :

צפני הון צפן רוח
ושמן ימינו יקרא

> He who layeth up riches in store layeth up the wind,
> And he nameth them the fat of his right hand ;

i.e., he sees in them that which makes his right hand fat and strong (שֶׁמֶן, as at Ps. cix. 24, *opp.* Zech. xi. 17 ; cf. בְּמִשְׁמַנָּיו, Isa. x. 16, and regarding 'Εσμούν, the Phœnican god of health, at Isa. lix. 10), and yet it is only the wind, *i.e.* something that is worthless and transient, which he stored up (צָפַן, as at xiii. 22, and in מַצְפֻנָיו, Obad. ver. 6). הוֹן is used as it frequently occurs in the Book of Proverbs, *e.g.* xi. 4, and the whole proverb expresses by another figure the same as xviii. 11. The fact that צפון (רוח), xxv. 23, and as a contrast thereto in the compass ימין (the south), hovered before the poet, may not have been without its influence on the choice of the words and expression here.

Ver. 17. This proverb expresses the influence arising from the intercourse of man with man :

> Iron is sharpened by iron,
> And a man may sharpen the appearance of another.

When the Masora reads יַחַד, Ewald remarks, it interprets the word as denoting "at the same time," and the further meaning of the proverb must then accord therewith. Accordingly he trans- lates : " iron together with iron ! and one together with the face of another ! " But then the prep. ב or עם is wanting after the second יחד—for יַחַד is, in spite of Ewald, § 217*h,* never a prep. —and the " face," 17*b,* would be a perplexing superfluity. Hitzig already replies, but without doing homage to the tra- ditional text-punctuation, that such a violence to the use of language, and such a darkening of the thought, is not at all to be accepted. He suggests four ways of interpreting יחד: (1) the adverb יַחַד, united, properly (taken accusat.) union ; (2) יַחֵר, Ps. lxxxvi. 11, imper. of the *Piel* יִחֵר, unite ; (3) יַחְדְּ, Job iii. 6,

jussive of the *Kal* חָדָה, *gaudeat;* and (4) as Kimchi, in *Michlol*
126a, jussive of the *Kal* חָדָה (= חָדַד) *acuere,* after the form תַּחַז,
Mic. iv. 11. וַיַּחַז, Gen. xxxii. 8, etc. *in p.* יֵחַד, after the form
אֶחַז, Job xxiii. 9. וַיֵּחַל, 2 Kings i. 2 (= וַיֵּחֲלָא, 2 Chron. xvi. 12).
If we take יחד with בַּרְזֶל, then it is *à priori* to be supposed that
in יחד the idea of sharpening lies; in the Arab. iron is simply
called *hadyda* = חָדוּד, that which is sharpened, sharp; and a
current Arab. proverb says : *alhadyd balhadyd yuflah* = *ferrum
ferro diffinditur* (*vid.* Freytag under the word *falah*). But is
the traditional text-punctuation thus understood to be rightly
maintained ? It may be easily changed in conformity with the
meaning, but not so that with Böttcher we read יֵחַד and יֵחַד,
the *fut. Kal* of חָדַד : "iron sharpeneth itself on iron, and a
man sharpeneth himself over against his neighbour"—for פני
after a verb to be understood actively, has to be regarded as the
object—but since יֵחַד is changed into יֵחַד (*fut. Hiph.* of חָדַד),
and יַחַד into יֵחַד or יַחַד (*fut. Hiph.* of חָדַד, after the form אָחֵל,
incipiam, Deut. ii. 25, or אָחֵל, *profanabo,* Ezek. xxxix. 7; Num.
xxx. 3). The passive rendering of the idea 17a and the active of
17b thus more distinctly appear, and the unsuitable jussive forms
are set aside : *ferrum ferro exacuitur, et homo exacuit faciem amici
sui* (Jerome, Targ., the *Venet.*). But that is not necessary.
As וַיַּעַל may be the *fut.* of the *Hiph.* (he brought up) as well as
of the *Kal* (he went up), so יֵחַד may be regarded as *fut. Kal,*
and יַחַד as *fut. Hiph.* Fleischer prefers to render יֵחַד also as
Hiph. : *aciem exhibet,* like יַעֲשִׁיר, *divitias acquirit,* and the like ;
but the jussive is not favourable to this supposition of an intransitive (inwardly transitive) *Hiph.* It may indeed be said
that the two jussives appear to be used, according to poetic
licence, with the force of indicatives (cf. under xii. 26), but the
repetition opposes it. Thus we explain : iron is sharpened
[*gewetzt,* Luther uses this appropriate word] by iron (ב of the
means, not of the object, which was rather to be expected in
17b after xx. 30), and a man whets פני, the appearance, the
deportment, the nature, and manner of the conduct of his
neighbour. The proverb requires that the intercourse of man
with man operate in the way of sharpening the manner and
forming the habits and character ; that one help another to
culture and polish of manner, rub off his ruggedness, round

his corners, as one has to make use of iron when he sharpens iron and seeks to make it bright. The jussive form is the oratorical form of the expression of that which is done, but also of that which is to be done.

The following three proverbs are connected with 17 in their similarity of form :—

> Ver. 18 Whosoever watcheth the fig-tree will enjoy its fruit;
> And he that hath regard to his master attaineth to honour.

The first member is, as in ver. 17, only the means of contemplating the second; as faithful care of the tree has fruit for a reward, so faithful regard for one's master, honour ; נֹצֵר is used as at Isa. xxvii. 3, שֹׁמֵר as at Hos. iv. 10, etc.—the proverb is valid in the case of any kind of master up to the Lord of lords. The fig-tree presented itself, as Heidenheim remarks, as an appropriate figure; because in the course of several years' training it brings forth its fruit, which the language of the Mishna distinguishes as פגין, unripe, בוחל, half ripe, and צמל, fully ripe. To fruit in the first line corresponds honour in the second, which the faithful and attentive servant attains unto first on the part of his master, and then also from society in general.

> Ver. 19 As it is with water, face correspondeth to face,
> So also the heart of man to man.

Thus the traditional text is to be translated ; for on the supposition that כַּמַּיִם must be used for כְּבַמַּיִם, yet it might not be translated : as in waters face corresponds to face (Jerome : *quomodo in aquis resplendent vultus respicientium*), because כְּ (*instar*) is always only a prep. and never conj. subordinating to itself a whole sentence (*vid.* under Ps. xxxviii. 14). But whether כַּמַּיִם, " like water," may be an abridgment of a sentence: " like as it is with water," is a question, and the translation of the LXX. (Syr., Targ., Arab.), ὥσπερ οὐχ ὅμοια πρόσωπα προσώποις, κ.τ.λ., appears, according to Böttcher's ingenious conjecture, to have supposed כאשר במים, from which the LXX. derived כְּאֵין דֹּמִים, *sicut non pares*. The thought is beautiful: as in the water-mirror each one beholds his own face (Luther : *der Scheme* = the shadow), so out of the heart of another each sees his own heart, *i.e.* he finds in another the dispositions and feelings of his own heart (Fleischer)—the face finds in water its reflection, and the heart of a man finds in man its echo ; men are ὁμοιοπαθεῖς, and it is a fortunate thing that their heart is capable of the same sympathetic feelings, so that one can pour into the heart of another that which fills and moves his own heart, and can there find agreement with it, and a re-echo. The expression with ל is extensive : one corresponds to another, one belongs to another, is adapted to the other, turns to the other, so that the thought may be rendered in manifold ways; the divinely-ordained mutual relationship is always the ground-thought. This is wholly obliterated by Hitzig's conjecture כְּמוֹם, " what a mole on the face is to the face, that is man's heart to man," *i.e.* the heart is the dark spot in man, his *partie honteuse.* But the Scripture nowhere speaks of the human heart after this manner, at least the Book of Proverbs, in which לב frequently means directly the understanding. Far more intelligible and consistent is the conjecture of Mendel Stern, to which Abrahamsohn drew my attention : כַּמַּיִם הַפֹּנִים לְפָנִים, like water (viz. flowing water), which directs its course always forward, thus (is turned) the heart of man to man. This conjecture removes the syntactic harshness of the first member without changing the letters, and illustrates by a beautiful and excellent figure the natural impulse moving man to man. It appears, however, to us, in view of the LXX., more probable that כַּמַּיִם is abbreviated from the original כאשר במים (cf. xxiv. 29).

The following proverb has, in common with the preceding, the catchword האדם, and the emphatic repetition of the same expression :

> Ver. 20 The under-world and hell are not satisfied,
> And the eyes of man are not satisfied.

A *Keri* ואבדון is here erroneously noted by Löwenstein, Stuart, and others. The *Keri* to וַאֲבַדֹּה is here וַאֲבַדּוֹ, which secures the right utterance of the ending, and is altogether wanting[1] in many MSS. (*e.g.* Cod. *Jaman*). The stripping off of the ן from the ending וֹן is common in the names of persons and places (*e.g.* שְׁלֹמֹה, LXX. Σολομών and שְׁלֹה); we write at pleasure either ו or ה— (*e.g.* מִגְדּוֹ), Olsh. § 215*g*. (אֲבַדּוֹן) אֲבַדֹּה of the

---

[1] In Gesen. *Lex.* this אבדה stands to the present day under אֲבֵדָה.

nature of a proper name, is already found in its full form אֲבַדּוֹן
at xv. 11, along with שְׁאוֹל; the two synonyms are, as was there
shown, not wholly alike in the idea they present, as the under-
world and realm of death, but are related to each other almost
the same as Hades and Gehenna; אבדון is what is called[1] in the
Jonathan-Targum בֵּית אֲבְדָנָא, the place of destruction, i.e of the
second death (מוֹתָא תִּנְיָנָא). The proverb places Hades and Hell
on the one side, and the eyes of man on the other, on the same
line in respect of their insatiableness. To this Fleischer adds
the remark: cf. the Arab. al'ayn l'a taml'aha all'a altrab,
nothing fills the eyes of man but at last the dust of the grave—
a strikingly beautiful expression! If the dust of the grave fills
the open eyes, then they are full—fearful irony! The eye is
the instrument of seeing, and consequently in so far as it
always looks out farther and farther, it is the instrument and
the representation of human covetousness. The eye is filled,
is satisfied, is equivalent to: human covetousness is appeased.
But first "the desire of the eye," 1 John ii. 16, is meant in the
proper sense. The eyes of men are not satisfied in looking and
contemplating that which is attractive and new, and no command is more difficult to be fulfilled than that in Isa. xxxiii.
15, "... that shutteth his eyes from seeing evil." There is
therefore no more inexhaustible means, impiæ speculationis, than
the desire of the eyes.

There follow here two proverbs which have in common with
each other the figures of the crucible and the mortar:

> Ver. 21 The crucible for silver and the furnace for gold,
> And a man according to the measure of his praise;

i.e., silver and gold one values according to the result of the
smelting crucible and the smelting furnace; but a man, according to the measure of public opinion, which presupposes that
which is said in xii. 8, "according to the measure of his wisdom
is a man praised." מַהֲלָל is not a ῥῆμα μέσον like our Leumund
[renown], but it is a graduated idea which denotes fame down
to evil Lob [fame], which is only Lob [praise] per antiphrasin.
Ewald otherwise: "according to the measure of his glorying;"
or Hitzig better: "according to the measure with which he
praises himself," with the remark: "מהלל is not the act, the

[1] Vid. Frankel, Zu dem Targum der Propheten (1872), p. 25.

glorifying of self, but the object of the glorying (cf. מבטח,
מדון), *i.e.* that in which he places his glory." Böttcher something further: " one recognises him by that which he is
generally wont to praise in himself and others, persons and
things." Thus the proverb is to be understood ; but in connection with xii. 8 it seems to us more probable that מהלל is
thought of as going forth from others, and not as from himself. In line first, xvii. 3*a* is repeated ; the second line there
is conformable to the first, according to which it should be here
said that the praise of a man is for him what the crucible and
the furnace is for metal. The LXX., Syr., Targ., Jerome,
and the *Venet.* read לְפִי מְהַלֲלוֹ, and thereby obtain more con-
cinnity. Luther accordingly translates :

> A man is tried by the mouth of his praise,
> As silver in the crucible and gold in the furnace.

Others even think to interpret man as the subject examining,
and so they vocalize the words. Thus *e.g.* Fleischer : *Qualis
est catinus argento et fornax auro, talis sit homo ori a quo laudatur,*
so that " mouth of his praise " is equivalent to the man who
praises him with his mouth. But where, as here, the language
relates to relative worth, the supposition for לְפִי, that it denotes,
as at xii. 8, *pro ratione,* is tenable. And that the mouth of him
who praises is a smelting crucible for him who is praised, or
that the praised shall be a crucible for the mouth of him who
praises, would be a wonderful comparison. The LXX. has
here also an additional distich which has no place in the Heb.
text.

Ver. 22 Though thou bruise a fool in a mortar among grit with a
　　　　pestle,
　　　　Yet would not his folly depart from him.

According to the best accredited accentuations, אִם־תִּכְתּוֹשׁ has
Illuj. and בַּמַּכְתֵּשׁ has *Pazer,* not *Rebia,* which would separate
more than the *Dechi,* and disturb the sequence of the thoughts.
The first line is long ; the chief disjunctive in the sphere of the
Athnach is *Dechi* of הר', this disjoins more than the *Pazer* of
בַּמ', and this again more than the *Legarmeh* of אֶת־הָאֱוִיל|. The
ה of הָרִפוֹת does not belong to the stem of the word (Hitzig),
but is the article ; רִפוֹת (from רוּף, to shake, to break ; according

to Schultens, from רָפַת, to crumble, to cut in pieces, after the form קִיטוֹר, which is improbable) are bruised grains of corn (peeled grain, grit), here they receive this name in the act of being bruised; rightly Aquila and Theodotion, ἐν μέσῳ ἐμπτισ-σομένων (grains of corn in the act of being pounded or bruised), and the *Venet.* μέσον τῶν πτισανῶν.[1] In בְּעֱלִי (thus to be written after *Michlol* 43b, not בְּעֱלִי, as Heidenheim writes it without any authority) also the article is contained. מכתש is the vessel, and the ב of בעלי is *Beth instrumenti;* עֱלִי (of lifting up for the purpose of bruising) is the club, pestle (Luther: *stempffel* = pounder); in the Mishna, *Beza* i. 5, this word denotes a pounder for the cutting out of flesh. The proverb interprets itself: folly has become to the fool as a second nature, and he is not to be delivered from it by the sternest discipline, the severest means that may be tried; it is not indeed his substance (Hitzig), but an inalienable accident of his substance.

Vers. 23–27. An exhortation to rural industry, and particularly to the careful tending of cattle for breeding, forms the conclu-sion of the foregoing series of proverbs, in which we cannot always discern an intentional grouping. It is one of the Mashal-odes spoken of vol. i. p. 12. It consists of 11 = 4 + 7 lines.

Ver. 23 Give heed to the look of thy small cattle,
          Be considerate about the herds.
     24 For prosperity continues not for ever;
          And does the diadem continue from generation to generation?
     25 (But) the hay is gone, and the after-growth appears,
          And the grass of the mountains is gathered:
     26 Lambs serve to clothe thee,
          And goats are the price of a field.
     27 And there is plenty of goats' milk for thy nourishment,
          And for the nourishment of thy house,
          And subsistence for thy maidens.

The beginning directs to the fut., as is not common in these proverbs, *vid.* xxvi. 26. With ידע, to take knowledge, which is strengthened by the *inf. intensivus*, is interchanged שִׁית לֵב, which means at xxiv. 32 to consider well, but here, to be careful regarding anything. צֹאן is the small or little cattle, thus sheep and goats. Whether לַעֲדָרִים (here and at Isa. xvii. 2) contains the

──────────

[1] The LXX. translates ἐν μέσῳ συνεδρίου, and has thereby misled the Syr., and mediately the Targum.

article is questionable (Gesen. § 35. 2 *A*), and, since the herds are called הָעֲדָרִים, is not probable; thus : direct thy attention to the herds, that is; to this, that thou hast herds.   פְּנֵי is the external side in general ; here, the appearance which the sheep present; thus their condition as seen externally.   In ver. 24 I formerly regarded נֵזֶר as a synonym of גֵּז, to be understood of the produce of wool, or, with Hitzig, of the shearing of the meadow, and thus the produce of the meadow.   But this interpretation of the word is untenable, and ver. 25 provides for ver. 24, thus understood, no natural continuation of thought.   That הֹסֶן signifies a store, fulness of possessions, property, and abundance, has already been shown under xv. 6 ; but נֵזֶר is always the mark of royal, and generally of princely dignity, and here denotes, *per meton. signi pro re signata*, that dignity itself.   With the negative expression in 24*a* the interrogative in 24*b* is interchanged as at Job xl. 9, with the implied negative answer; וְאִם, of an oath (" and truly not," as at Isa. lxii. 8), presents the same thought, but with a passionate colouring here unnecessary.   Rightly Fleischer : " ready money, moveable property, and on the other hand the highest positions of honour, are far more easily torn away from a man, and secure to him far less of quiet prosperity, than husbandry, viewed particularly with respect to the rearing of cattle."   In other words : the possession of treasures and of a lofty place of power and of honour has not in itself the security of everlasting duration ; but rural economy, and particularly the rearing of cattle, gives security for food and clothing. The *Chethîb* לְדוֹר דוֹר is found, *e.g.* at Ex. iii. 15 ; the *Keri* לְדוֹר וָדוֹר substitutes the more usual form.   If ver. 25 was an independent whole (Hitzig: grass vanishes and fresh green appears, etc.), then the meaning here and onward would be that in the sphere of husbandry it is otherwise than is said in ver. 24 : there that which is consumed renews itself, and there is an enlarging circulation.   But this contrast to ver. 24 must be expressed and formed unambiguously.   The connection is rather this, that ver. 23 commends the rearing of cattle, ver. 24 confirms it, and 25 ff. discuss what real advantages, not dependent on the accidents of public and social life, it brings.

I rejoice to agree with Fleischer in the opinion that the perfects of ver. 25 form a complex hypothetical antecedent to ver.

26: *Quum evanuerit gramen (sc. vetus) et apparuerint herbæ recentes et collecta fuerint pabula montium, agni vestitui tuo (inservient) et pretium agri (sc. a te emendi) erunt hirci, i.e.* then wilt thou nourish thy herds of sheep and goats with the grass on thy fields, and with the dried gathered hay; and these will yield for thee, partly immediately and partly by the money derived therefrom (viz. from the valuable goats not needed for the flocks), all that is needful for thy life. He also remarks, under גָּלָה, that it means to make a place void, empty (viz. to quit the place, *évacuer la forteresse*); hence to leave one's fatherland or home, to wander abroad; thus, rhetorically and poetically of things and possessions: to disappear. חָצִיר (from חָצַר, to be green) is hay, and דֶּשֶׁא the after-growing second crop (after-grass); thus a meadow capable of being mowed a second time is thought of. עִשְּׂבוֹת הָרִים (with *Dag. dirimens*, as *e.g.* עִנְּבֵי, Deut. xxxii. 32) are the herbage of the mountains. The time when one proceeds to sheep-shearing, ver. 25 cannot intend to designate; it sets before us an interesting rural harvest scene, where, after a plentiful ingathering of hay, one sees the meadows again overspread with new grass (Ewald); but with us the shearing of sheep takes place in the month of May, when the warm season of the year is just at hand. The poet means in general to say, that when the hay is mown and now the herbage is grown up, and also the fodder from the mountains (Ps. cvi. 20) has been gathered home, when thus the barns are filled with plenty, the husbandman is guaranteed against the future on all sides by his stock of cattle. חֲלֵב (from חָלָב, Arab. *halyb*, with *halab*) is the usual metaplastic connecting form of חָלָב, milk. דֵּי (from דַּי, like חֵי from חַי), generally connected with the genitive of the person or thing, for which anything is sufficient (*e.g.* xxv. 16, דַּיֶּךָ, to which Fleischer compares Arab. *hasbuha, tassuha kifayuha*), has here the genitive of the thing of which, or in which, one has enough. The complex subject-conception is limited by *Rebia*, and the governing דֵּי has the subordinated disjunctive *Legarmeh*. עִזִּים is a word of two genders (*epicoenum*), Gesen. § 107, 1*d*. In וְחַיִּים the influence of the לְ still continues; one does not need to supply it meanwhile, since all that maintains and nourishes life can be called חַיִּים (*vita = victus*), *e.g.* iii. 22. The LXX. translates בֵּיתֶךָ by

σῶν θεραπόντων, and omits (as also the Syr., but not the Syro-
Hexap.) the last line as now superfluous; but that the maids
attending to the cattle—by whom we particularly think of
milkers—are especially mentioned, intentionally presents the
figure of a well-ordered household, full of varied life and
activity (Job xl. 29).

This Mashal-ode, commending the rearing of cattle, is a
boundary. The series of proverbs beginning with the next
chapter is not, however, a commencement, like that at xxii. 17;
and Hitzig's supposition, that xxviii. 1–16 and xxii. 17 ff. have
one and the same author, stands on a false foundation. The
second proverb of the twenty-eighth chapter shows directly that
this new series of proverbs is subordinated to the aim of the
Hezekiah-collection beginning with xxv., and thus has to be
regarded as an original component part of it. The traces of
the post-exilian period which Hitzig discovers in xxviii. 1–16
are not sufficient to remove the origin of the proverbs so far
down from the times of Hezekiah. We take the first group,
xxviii. 1–11, together; for מבין and יבינו, pervading these eleven
proverbs, gives to them, as a whole, a peculiar colouring; and
xxviii. 12 presents itself as a new beginning, going back to
ver. 2, which ver. 1 precedes as a prelude.

xxviii. 1 The godless flee without any one pursuing them;
   But the righteous are bold like a lion.

We would misinterpret the sequence of the accents if we supposed that it denoted רָשָׁע as obj.; it by no means takes וְאֵין־רֹדֵף
as a parenthesis. רשע belongs thus to נָסוּ as collective sing.
(cf. e.g. Isa. xvi. 4b);[1] in 1b, יִבְטָח, as comprehensive or distributive (individualizing) singular, follows the plur. subject.
One cannot, because the word is vocalized כִּכְפִיר and not כַּכְּפִיר,
regard יבטח as an attributive clause thereto (Ewald, like Jerome,
quasi leo confidens); but the article, denoting the idea of kind,
does not certainly always follow כ. We say, indifferently, כְּאֲרִי
or כַּאֲרִי, כְּלָבִיא or כַּלָּבִיא, and always כְּאַרְיֵה, not כָּאַרְיֵה. In itself,
indeed, יבטח may be used absolutely: he is confident, undis-
mayed, of the lion as well as of the leviathan, Job xl. 23. But

[1] The Targum of xxviii. 1a is, in Bereschith rabba, c. 84, ערק רַשִׁיעָא
וְלָא רְדִיפִין לֵהּ; that lying before us is formed after the Peshito.

it is suitable thus without any addition for the righteous, and נסו
and יבטח correspond to each other as predicates, in accordance
with the parallelism; the accentuation is also here correct. The
perf. נסו denotes that which is uncaused, and yet follows: the
godless flee, pursued by the terrible images that arise in their
own wicked consciences, even when no external danger threatens.
The fut. יבטח denotes that which continually happens: the
righteous remains, even where external danger really threatens,
bold and courageous, after the manner of a young, vigorous
lion, because feeling himself strong in God, and assured of his
safety through Him.

Ver. 2. There now follows a royal proverb, whose key-note
is the same as that struck at xxv. 2, which states how a
country falls into the οὐκ ἀγαθόν of the rule of the many:

> Through the wickedness of a land the rulers become many;
> And through a man of wisdom, of knowledge, authority continues.

If the text presented בְּפֶשַׁע as Hitzig corrects, then one might
think of a political revolt, according to the usage of the word,
1 Kings xii. 19, etc.; but the word is בְּפֶשַׁע,[1] and פֶּשַׁע (from
פָּשַׁע, dirumpere) is the breaking through of limits fixed by God,
apostasy, irreligion, e.g. Mic. i. 5. But that many rulers for a
land arise from such a cause, shows a glance into the Book of
Hosea, e.g. vii. 16: "They return, but not to the Most High
(sursum); they are become like a deceitful bow; their princes
shall then fall by the sword;" and viii. 4: "They set up
kings, but not by me; they have made princes, and I knew it
not." The history of the kingdom of Israel shows that a land
which apostatizes from revealed religion becomes at once the
victim of party spirit, and a subject of contention to many
would-be rulers, whether the fate of the king whom it has
rejected be merited or not. But what is now the contrast
which 2b brings forward? The translation by Bertheau and
also by Zöckler is impossible: "but through intelligent, prudent
men, he (the prince) continueth long." For 2a does not mean
a frequent changing of the throne, which in itself may not be
a punishment for the sins of the people, but the appearance
at the same time of many pretenders to the throne, as was the

[1] Thus to be written with *Gaja* here and at xxix. 6, after the rule of
Metheg-Setzung, § 42.

case in the kingdom of Israel during the interregnum after
the death of Jeroboam II., or in Rome at the time of the thirty
tyrants; יַאֲרִיךְ must thus refer to one of these "many" who
usurp for a time the throne. בְּאָדָם may also mean, xxiii. 28,
inter homines; but אָדָם, with adjective following, *e.g.* xi. 7,
xii. 23, xvii. 18, xxi. 16, always denotes one; and that translation also changes the כֵּן into a "so," "then" introducing
the concluding clause, which it altogether disregards as un-
translatable. But equally impossible is Böttcher's : "among
intelligent, prudent people, one continues (in the government),"
for then the subject-conception on which it depends would be
slurred over. Without doubt כֵּן is here a substantive, and just
this subject-conception. That it may be a substantive has been
already shown at xi. 19. There it denoted integrity (properly that which is right or genuine) ; and accordingly it means
here, not the *status quo* (Fleischer: *idem rerum status*), but
continuance, and that in a full sense : the jurisdiction (properly
that which is upright and right), *i.e.* this, that right continues
and is carried on in the land. Similarly Heidenheim, for he
glosses כן by מכן הארץ ; and Umbreit, who, however, unwarned
by the accent, subordinates this כ [in the sense of "right"] to
יֹדֵעַ as its object. Zöckler, with Bertheau, finds a difficulty in
the *asyndeton* מֵבִין יֹדֵעַ. But these words also, Neh. x. 29, stand
together as a formula ; and that this formula is in the spirit
and style of the Book of Proverbs, passages such as xix. 25,
xxix. 7 [1] show. A practical man, and one who is at the same
time furnished with thorough knowledge, is thus spoken of,
and prudence and knowledge of religious moral character and
worth are meant. What a single man may do under certain
circumstances is shown in xxi. 22 ; Eccles. ix. 15. Here one
has to think of a man of understanding and spirit at the helm
of the State, perhaps as the nearest counsellor of the king. By
means of such an one, right continues long (we do not need to
supply לִהְיוֹת after "continues long"). If, on the one side, the
State falls asunder by the evil conduct of the inhabitants of the

---

[1] The three connected words ובאדם מבין ידע have, in Löwenstein, the
accents *Mercha, Mercha, Mugrash;* but the Venetian, 1515, 20, Athias, v. d.
Hooght, and Hahn, have rightly *Tarcha, Mercha, Mugrash,*—to place two
Merchas is Ben-Naphtali's manner.

land, on the other hand a single man who unites in himself sound understanding and higher knowledge, for a long time holds it together.

Ver. 3. A proverb of a tyrant here connects itself with that of usurpers:

> A poor man and an oppressor of the lowly—
> A sweeping rain without bringing bread.

Thus it is to be translated according to the accents. Fleischer otherwise, but also in conformity with the accents: *Quales sunt vir pauper et oppressor miserorum, tales sunt pluvia omnia secum abripiens et qui panem non habent,* i.e. the relation between a poor man and an oppressor of the needy is the same as that between a rain carrying all away with it and a people robbed thereby of their sustenance; in other words: a prince or potentate who robs the poor of their possessions is like a pouring rain which floods the fruitful fields—the separate members of the sentence would then correspond with each other after the scheme of the chiasmus. But the comparison would be faulty, for גֶּבֶר רָשׁ and אֵין לָחֶם fall together, and then the explanation would be *idem per idem.* A "sweeping rain" is one which has only that which is bad, and not that which is good in rain, for it only destroys instead of promoting the growth of the corn; and as the Arab, according to a proverb compared by Hitzig, says of an unjust sultan, that he is a stream without water, so an oppressor of the helpless is appropriately compared to a rain which floods the land and brings no bread. But then the words, "a poor man and an oppressor of the lowly," must designate one person, and in that case the Heb. words must be accentuated, גבר רשׁ ועשׁק דלים (cf. xxix. 4*a*). For, that the oppressor of the helpless deports himself toward the poor man like a sweeping rain which brings no bread, is a saying not intended to be here used, since this is altogether too obvious, that the poor man has nothing to hope for from such an extortioner. But the comparison would be appropriate if 3*a* referred to an oppressive master; for one who belongs to a master, or who is in any way subordinated to him, has before all to expect from him that which is good, as a requital for his services, and as a proof of his master's condescending sympathy.

It is thus asked whether "a poor man and an oppressor of the lowly" may be two properties united in the person of one master. This is certainly possible, for he may be primarily a poor official or an upstart (Zöckler), such as were the Roman proconsuls and procurators, who enriched themselves by impoverishing their provinces (cf. LXX. xxviii. 15); or a hereditary proprietor, who seeks to regain what he has lost by extorting it from his relatives and workmen. But רִשׁ (poor) is not sufficient to give this definite feature to the figure of the master; and what does this feature in the figure of the master at all mean? What the comparison 3*b* says is appropriate to any oppressive ruler, and one does not think of an oppressor of the poor as himself poor; he may find himself in the midst of shattered possessions, but he is not poor; much rather the oppressor and the poor are, as *e.g.* at xxix. 13, contrasted with each other. Therefore we hold, with Hitzig, that רִשׁ of the text is to be read *rosh*, whether we have to change it into רֹאשׁ, or to suppose that the Jewish transcriber has here for once slipped into the Phœnician writing of the word;[1] we do not interpret, with Hitzig, גֶּבֶר רֹאשׁ in the sense of ἄνθρωπος δυνάστης, Sir. viii. 1, but explain: a man (or master = גְּבִיר) is the head (cf. *e.g.* Judg. xi. 8), and oppresses the helpless. This rendering is probable, because גֶּבֶר רָשׁ, a poor man, is a combination of words without a parallel; the Book of Proverbs does not once use the expression אִישׁ רָשׁ, but always simply רָשׁ (*e.g.* xxviii. 6, xxix. 13); and גֶּבֶר is compatible with חָכָם and the like, but not with רִשׁ. If we stumble at the isolated position of רֹאשׁ, we should consider that it is in a certain measure covered by דַלִּים; for one has to think of the גבר, who is the ראשׁ, also as the ראשׁ of these דלים, as one placed in a high station who numbers poor people among his subordinates. The LXX. translates ἀνδρεῖος ἐν ἀσεβείαις as if the words of the text were גִּבּוֹר רָשָׁע (cf. the interchange of גֶּבֶר and גִּבּוֹר in both texts of Ps. xviii. 26), but what the LXX. read must have been גִּבּוֹר לְהַרְשִׁיעַ (Isa. v. 22); and what can גִּבּוֹר here mean? The statement here made refers to the ruinous conduct of a גֶּבֶר, a man of standing, or גְּבִיר, a high lord, a "wicked ruler," xxviii. 15. On the

---

[1] The Phœn. writes רשׁ (*i.e.* רֹשׁ, *rus*); *vid.* Schröder's *Phönizische Gram.* p. 133; cf. Gesen. *Thes.* under רֹאשׁ.

contrary, what kind of rain the rule of an ideal governor is
compared to, Ps. lxxii. 1–8 tells.

> Ver. 4 They who forsake the law praise the godless;
> But they who keep the law become angry with them,

viz. the godless, for רָשָׁע is to be thought of collectively, as at
ver. 1. They who praise the godless turn away from the
revealed word of God (Ps. lxxiii. 11–15); those, on the contrary, who are true to God's word (xxix. 18) are aroused
against them (vid. regarding גרה, xv. 18), they are deeply moved
by their conduct, they cannot remain silent and let their
wickedness go unpunished; הִתְגָּרָה is zeal (excitement) always
expressing itself, passing over into actions (syn. הִתְעוֹרֵר, Job
xvii. 8).

Ver. 5. A similar antithetic distich:

> Wicked men understand not what is right;
> But they who seek Jahve understand all.

Regarding the gen. expression אַנְשֵׁי־רָע, vid. under ii. 14. He
who makes wickedness his element, falls into the confusion of
the moral conception; but he whose end is the one living God,
gains from that, in every situation of life, even amid the greatest
difficulties, the knowledge of that which is morally right.
Similarly the Apostle John (1 John ii. 20): "ye have an unction
from the Holy One, and ye know all things" (οἴδατε πάντα):
i.e., ye need to seek that knowledge which ye require, and
which ye long after, not without yourselves, but in the new
divine foundation of your personal life; from thence all that
ye need for the growth of your spiritual life, and for the turning away from you of hostile influences, will come into your
consciences. It is a potential knowledge, all-comprehensive in
its character, and obviously a human relative knowledge, that
is here meant.

Ver. 6. What is stated in this proverb is a conclusion from
the preceding, with which it is also externally connected, for רֹשׁ
(= ראשׁ), רָשָׁע, רַע, and now רֹשׁ, follow each other:

> Better a poor man who walketh in his innocence,
> Than a double-going deceiver who is rich thereby.

A variation of xix. 1. Stainlessness, integritas vitæ, as a consequence of unreserved devotion to God, gives to a man with
poverty a higher worth and nobility than riches connected with

falsehood which "halts between two opinions" (1 Kings xviii. 21), and appears to go one way, while in reality it goes another. The two ways דְּרָכַיִם (cf. Sir. ii. 12, οὐαί ἁμαρτωλῷ ... ἐπιβαίνοντι ἐπὶ δύο τρίβους) are, as ver. 18, not ways going aside to the right or to the left of the right way, but the evil way which the deceiver truly walks in, and the good way which he pretends to walk in (Fleischer); the two ways of action placed over against one another, by one of which he masks the other.

> Ver. 7 He who keepeth instruction is a wise son;
> But he that is a companion of profligates bringeth his father
>   into shame.

We have translated תורה at ver. 4 by "law;" here it includes the father's instruction regarding the right way of life. נוֹצֵר תּוֹרָה, according to the nearest lying syntax, has to be taken as pred. זוֹלְלִים are such as squander their means and destroy their health, vid. under xxiii. 20 f. רָעָה signifies, as frequently from the idea of (cf. xxix. 3) pasturing, or properly of tending, to take care of, and to have fellowship with. יַכְלִים [shall put to shame] denotes both that he himself does disgrace to him, and that he brings disgrace to him on the part of others.

Ver. 8. This verse continues a series of proverbs (commencing in ver. 7) beginning with a participle :

> He who increaseth his wealth by interest and usury,
> Gathereth it for one who is benevolent toward the lowly.

Wealth increased by covetous plundering of a neighbour does not remain with him who has scraped it together in so relentless a manner, and without considering his own advantage; but it goes finally into the possession of one who is merciful towards the poor, and thus it is bestowed in a manner that is pleasing to God (cf. xiii. 22, Job xxii. 16 f.). The Kerî, which drops the second ב, appears to wish to mitigate the sharpness of the distinction of the second idea supposed in its repetition. But Lev. xxv. 35–37, where an Israelite is forbidden to take usury and interest from his brother, the two are distinguished; and Fleischer rightly remarks that there נשׁך means usury or interest taken in money, and תרבית usury or interest taken in kind ; i.e., of that which one has received

in loan, such as grain, or oil, etc., he gives back more than he
has received.   In other words : נֶשֶׁךְ is the name of the interest
for the capital that is lent, and מַרְבִּית, or, as it is here called
תרבית, the more, the addition thereto, the increase (Luther:
vbersatz).   This meaning of gain by means of lending on interest remains in נֶשֶׁךְ ; but תרבית, according to the later *usus loq.*,
signifies gain by means of commerce, thus business-profit, *vid.*
Baba Mezia, v. 1.   Instead of יְקַבְּצֶנּוּ, more recent texts have the
Kal [1] יִקְבְּצֶנּוּ.   לְחוֹנֵן also is, as xiv. 31, xix. 17, *part. Kal*, not *inf.*
Poel : ad largiendum pauperibus (Merc., Ewald, Bertheau), for
there the person of him who presents the gift is undefined ; but
just this, that it is another and better-disposed, for whom,
without having it in view, the collector gathers his stores, is the
very point of the thought.

Ver. 9 He who turneth away his ear not to hear of the law,
Even his prayer is an abomination.

Cf. xv. 8 and the argument 1 Sam. xv. 22.   Not only the evil
which such an one does, but also the apparent good is an
abomination, an abomination to God, and *eo ipso* also in itself :
morally hollow and corrupt ; for it is not truth and sincerity, for
the whole soul, the whole will of the suppliant, is not present :
he is not that for which he gives himself out in his prayer, and
does not earnestly seek that which he presents and expresses a
wish for in prayer.

Ver. 10. A tristich beginning with a participle :

He who misleads the upright into an evil way,
He shall fall into his own pit ;
But the innocent shall inherit that which is good.

In the first case, xxvi. 27 is fulfilled : the deceiver who leads
astray falls himself into the destruction which he prepared for
others, whether he misleads them into sin, and thus mediately
prepares destruction for them, or that he does this immediately

---

[1] If, as Hitzig, after J. H. Michaelis, remarks, the word were Ben-Asher's
יְקַבְּצֶנּוּ, then it would be thus rightly punctuated by Clodius and the
moderns.   Kimchi, in the *Wörterbuch* under קבץ, adduces this word as
Ben-Asher's.   But the Masora knows nothing of it.   It marks יְקַבְּצֶנּוּ, Jer.
xxxi. 10, with לית as *unicum*, and thus supposes for the passage before us
יְקַבְּצֶנּוּ, which certainly is found in MSS., and is also marked on the margin
with לית as *unicum*.

by enticing them into this or that danger; for בְּדֶרֶךְ רָע may be understood of the way of wicked conduct, as well as of the experience of evil, of being betrayed, robbed, or even murdered. That those who are misled are called יְשָׁרִים, explains itself in the latter case: that they are such as he ought to show respect towards, and such as deserved better treatment, heightens the measure of his guilt. If we understand being morally led astray, yet may we not with Hitzig here find the "theory" which removes the punishment from the just and lays it on the wicked. The clause xi. 8 is not here applicable. The first pages of the Scripture teach that the deceiver does not by any means escape punishment; but certainly the deceiver of the upright does not gain his object, for his diabolical joy at the destruction of such an one is vain, because God again helps him with the right way, but casts the deceiver so much the deeper down. As the idea of דרך רע has a twofold direction, so the connections of the words may be genitival (via mali) as well as adjectival (via mala). בִּשְׁחוּתוֹ is not incorrectly written for בְּשִׁחְתּוֹ, for שְׁחִית occurs (only here) with שְׁחוּת as its warrant both from שָׁחָה, to bend, to sink; cf. לְווּת under iv. 24. In line third, opposite to "he who misleads," stand "the innocent" (pious), who, far from seeking to entice others into the evil way and bring them to ruin, are unreservedly and honestly devoted to God and to that which is good; these shall inherit good (cf. iii. 35); even the consciousness of having made no man unhappy makes them happy; but even in their external relations there falls to them the possession of all good, which is the divinely ordained reward of the good.

Ver. 11 A rich man deems himself wise;
But a poor man that hath understanding searcheth him out,

or, as we have translated, xviii. 17, goes to the bottom of him, whereby is probably thought of the case that he seeks to use him as a means to an ignoble end. The rich man appears in his own eyes to be a wise man, i.e. in his self-delusion he thinks that he is so; but if he has anything to do with a poor man who has intelligence, then he is seen through by him. Wisdom is a gift not depending on any earthly possession.

We take vers. 12-20 together. A proverb regarding riches

closes this group, as also the foregoing is closed, and its commencement is related in form and in its contents to ver. 2 :

Ver. 12 When righteous men triumph, the glory is great ;
And when the godless rise, the people are searched for.

The first line of this distich is parallel with xxix. 2 ; cf. xi. 10a,
11a : when the righteous rejoice, viz. as conquerors (cf. e.g. Ps.
lx. 8), who have the upper hand, then תִּפְאָרֶת, bright prosperity,
is increased ; or as Fleischer, by comparison of the Arab. yawm
alazynt (day of ornament = festival day), explains : so is there
much festival adornment, i.e. one puts on festival clothes, signum
pro re signata : thus all appears festal and joyous, for prosperity and happiness then show themselves forth.   רַבָּה is adj.
and pred. of the substantival clause ; Hitzig regards it as the
attribute : " then is there great glory ; " this supposition is
possible (vid. vii. 26, and under Ps. lxxxix. 51), but here it is
purely arbitrary.   28a is parallel with 12b : if the godless
arise, attain to power and prominence, these men are spied out,
i.e. as we say, after Zeph. i. 12, they are searched for as with
lamps.   יְחֻפַּשׂ אָדָם is to be understood after Obadiah, ver. 6,
cf. ii. 4 : men are searched out, i.e. are plundered (in which
sense Heidenheim regards חפש as here a transposition from
חשׂף), or, with reference to the secret police of despotism : they
are subjected to an espionage.   But a better gloss is יִפָּתֵר אָדָם
28a : the people let themselves be sought for, they keep themselves concealed in the inside of their houses, they venture not
out into the streets and public places (Fleischer), for mistrust
and suspicion oppress them all ; one regards his person and
property nowhere safer than within the four walls of his house ;
the lively, noisy, variegated life which elsewhere rules without,
is as if it were dead.

Ver. 13 He that denieth his sin shall not prosper ;
But he that acknowledgeth and forsaketh it shall obtain mercy.

Thus is this proverb translated by Luther, and thus it lives in
the mouth of the Christian people.   He who falsely disowns, or
with self-deception excuses, if he does not altogether justify his
sins, which are discernible as פְּשָׁעִים, has no success ; he remains,
after Ps. xxxii., in his conscience and life burdened with a secret
ban ; but he who acknowledges (the LXX. has ἐξηγούμενος

instead of ἐξομολογούμενος, as it ought to be) and forsakes (for
the *remissio* does not follow the *confessio*, if there is not the
accompaniment of *nova obedientia*) will find mercy (ירחם, as
Hos. xiv. 4). In close connection therewith stands the thought
that man has to work out his salvation "with fear and trembling" (Phil. ii. 12).

Ver. 14 Well is it with the man who feareth always :
But he that is stiff-necked shall fall into mischief.

The *Piel* פִּחֵד occurs elsewhere only at Isa. li. 13, where it is
used of the fear and dread of men ; here it denotes the anxious
concern with which one has to guard against the danger of
evil coming upon his soul. Aben Ezra makes God the object ;
but rather we are to regard sin as the object, for while the truly
pious is one that " fears God," he is at the same time one that
" feareth evil." The antithesis extends beyond the nearest
lying contrast of fleshly security ; this is at the same time more
or less one who hardens or steels his heart (מַקְשֶׁה לִבּוֹ), viz. against
the word of God, against the sons of God in his heart, and
against the affectionate concern of others about his soul, and as
such rushes on to his own destruction (יִפּוֹל בְּרָעָה, as at xvii. 20).

This general ethical proverb is now followed by one concerning the king :

Ver. 15 A roaring lion and a ravening bear
Is a foolish ruler over a poor people,

i.e. a people without riches and possessions, without lasting
sources of help,—a people brought low by the events of war and
by calamities. To such a people a tyrant is a twofold terror,
like a ravenous monster. The LXX. translate מוֹשֵׁל רָשָׁע by
ὃς τυραννεῖ πτωχὸς ὤν, as if רָשׁ had been transferred to this
place from ver. 3. But their translation of רָשָׁע, xxix. 7, wavers
between ἀσεβής and πτωχός, and of the bear they make a
wolf זְאֵב, dialectical דֵּיב. שׁוֹקֵק designates a bear as lingering
about, running hither and thither, impelled by extreme hunger
(*Venet.* ἐπιοῦσα), from שָׁקַק = שׁוּק, to drive, which is said of
nimble running, as well as of urging impulses (cf. under Gen.
iii. 16), viz. hunger.

Ver. 16. Another proverb of the king :

O prince devoid of understanding and rich in oppression !
He that hateth unrighteous gain continueth long.

The old interpreters from the LXX. interpret וְרַב מַעֲשֵׁקּוֹת as
pred. (as also Fleischer : *princeps qui intelligentiæ habet parum
idem oppressionis exercet multum*) ; but why did not the author
use the word הוּא or וְהוּא instead of this ambiguous inconvenient
וּ? Hitzig regards the first term as a nominative absolute,
which does not assume a suffix in the second line. But examples
such as 27*a*, xxvii. 7*b*, are altogether of a different sort ; there
occurs a reference that is in reality latent, and only finds not
expression ; the clause following the nominative is related to it
as its natural predicate, but here 15*b* is an independent clause
standing outside of any syntactical relation to 15*a*. Heidenheim
has acknowledged that here there lies before us a proverb not in
the form of a mere declaration, but of a warning address, and thus
also it is understood by Ewald, Bertheau, Elster, and Zöckler.
The accentuation seems to proceed on the same supposition.
It is the only passage in the Book of Proverbs where נָגִיד, of the
supreme ruler of the people, and where the plur. תְּבוּנוֹת, occur ;
it is not therefore at all strange if the proverb also has something strange in its formation. Often enough, proverbs are in
the form of an address to a son, and generally to their reader ;
why not also one at least to the king ? It is a proverb as when
I say : Oh thou reckless, merry fellow ! he who laughs much
will sometimes weep long. Thus here the address is directed to
the prince who is devoid of all wisdom and intelligence, which
are necessary for a prince ; but on this account the more
earnest in exhortation to say to him that only one who hates
defrauding the people attains an old age ; thus that a prince
who plunders the people wantonly shortens his life as a man,
and his position as a ruler (cf. שְׁנֵיהֶם, xxiv. 22). The *Kerî*
שֹׂנֵא has the tone thrown back on the *penult.*, as the *Chethîb*
שֹׂנְאִי would also have it, cf. לִמְצֹאִי, viii. 9. The relation of a
plur. subj. to a sing. pred. is as at xxvii. 16. Regarding בֶּצַע,
vid. under i. 19. A confirmation of this proverb directing itself
to princes is found in Jer. xxii. 13–19, the woe pronounced
upon Jehoiakim. And a glance at the woe pronounced in Hab.
ii. 12, shows how easily ver. 17 presents itself in connection.

> Ver. 17 A man burdened with the guilt of blood upon his soul
> Fleeth to the pit ; let no one detain him.

Luther translates : "A man that doeth violence to the blood

of any one," as if he had read the word עָשֵׁק. Löwenstein persuades himself that עָשֵׁק may mean " having oppressed," and
for this refers to לְבוּשׁ, having clothed, in the Mishna נָשׂוּי, רָכוּב,
Lat. *coenatus, juratus ;* but none of all these cases are of the
same nature, for always the conduct designated is interpreted as
a suffering of that which is done, *e.g.* the drawing on, as a being
clothed ; the riding, as a being ridden, etc. Of עָשֵׁק, in the sense
of the oppression of another, there is no such *part. pass.* as
throws the action as a condition back upon the subject. This
is valid also against Aben Ezra, who supposes that עָשֵׁק means
oppressing after the forms אָגוּר, שָׁדוּד, שָׁכֵן, for of שָׁכֵן, settled =
dwelling, that which has just been said is true ; that אָגוּר is
equivalent to אֹגֵר, cf. regarding it under xxx. 1, and that שָׁדוּד,
Ps. cxxxvii. 8, is equivalent to שֹׁדֵד, is not true. Kimchi adds,
under the name of his father (Joseph Kimchi), also שָׁחוּט, Jer.
ix. 7 = שׁוֹחֵט; but that "slaughtered" can be equivalent to
slaughtering is impossible. Some MSS. have the word עָשֵׁק,
which is not inadmissible, but not in the sense of " accused "
(Löwenstein), but : persecuted, exposed to war ; for עָשֵׁק signifies
to treat hostilely, and post-bibl. generally to aspire after or
pursue anything, *e.g.* עָסוּק בְּדִבְרֵי תוֹרָה, R. עָשׂ (whence *Piel contrectare*, cf. Isa. xxiii. 2, according to which עָשֵׁק appears to be
an intensifying of this עָשָׂה). However, there is no ground for
regarding עָשֵׁק [1] as not original, nor in the sense of " hard
pressed ; " for it is not used of avenging persecution, but :
inwardly pressed, for Isa. xxxviii. 14 עָשְׁקָה also signifies the
anguish of a guilty conscience. Whoever is inwardly bowed
down by the blood of a man whom he has murdered, betakes
himself to a ceaseless flight to escape the avenger of blood, the
punishment of his guilt, and his own inward torment ; he flees
and finds no rest, till at last the grave (בוֹר according to the
Eastern, *i.e.* the Babylonian, mode of writing בֹּר) receives him,
and death accomplishes the only possible propitiation of the
murderer. The exhortation, " let no one detain him," does not
mean that one should not lay hold on the fugitive ; but, since
תָּמַךְ בְּ does not mean merely to hold fast, but to hold right, that

---

[1] Böttcher supposes much rather עָשַׁק עָשֵׁק = מְעֻשָּׁק; also, xxv. 11, דָּבֵר =
מְדֻבָּר; but that does not follow from the *defectiva scriptio*, nor from anything else.

one should not afford him any support, any refuge, any covering
or security against the vengeance which pursues him ; that one
should not rescue him from the arm of justice, and thereby
invade and disturb the public administration of justice, which
rests on moral foundations ; on the other side, the Book of Proverbs, xxiv. 11 f., has uttered its exhortation to save a human
life whenever it is possible to do so. The proverb lying before
us cannot thus mean anything else than that no one should give
to the murderer, as such, any assistance; that no one should
save him clandestinely, and thereby make himself a partaker
of his sin. Grace cannot come into the place of justice till
justice has been fully recognised. Human sympathy, human
forbearance, under the false title of grace, do not stand in contrast to this justice. We must, however, render אל־יתמכרבו not
directly as an admonition against that which is immoral; it may
also be a declaration of that which is impossible : only let no
one support him, let no one seek to deliver him from the unrest
which drives him from place to place. This is, however, in
vain; he is unceasingly driven about to fulfil his lot. But the
translation : *nemine eum sustinente* (Fleischer), is inadmissible ;
a mere declaration of a fact without any subjective colouring is
never אל *seq. fut.*

Ver. 18 He who walketh blamelessly is helped,
And he who is perverse in a double way suddenly perisheth.

The LXX. translate תמים by δικαίως (as the accusative of
manner), Aquila and Theodotion by τέλειος; but it may also
be translated τέλειον or τελειότητα, as the object accus. of
ii. 7. Instead of עֵקֵּשׁ דְּרָכַיִם, ver. 6, there is here נֶעְקַשׁ דְּרָכַיִם,
obliquely directed in a double way, or reflex bending himself.
At ver. 6 we have interpreted the *dual* דְּרָכַיִם rightly, thus
בְּאַחַת cannot refer back to one of these two ways; besides, דֶּרֶךְ
as fem. is an anomaly, if not a solecism. בְּאַחַת signifies, like
the Aram. בְּחֲדָא, either all at once (for which the Mish. כְּאַחַת,
Aram. כַּחֲדָא), or once (= בְּפַעַם אַחַת), and it signifies in the
passage before us, not : once, *aliquando*, as Nolde, with Flacius,
explains, but : all at once, *i.e.* as Geier explains : *penitus, sic
ut pluribus casibus porro non sit opus.* Schultens compares :

" *Procubuit moriens et humum semel ore momordit.*"[1]

─────────────
[1] *Æneid*, xi. 418.

Rightly Fleischer: *repente totus concidet.*

Ver. 19 He who cultivateth his land is satisfied with bread,
And he that graspeth after vanities is satisfied with poverty.

A variation of xii. 11. The pred. here corresponds to its contrast. On רֵישׁ (here and at xxxi. 7), instead of the more frequent רָאשׁ, cf. x. 4.

To this proverb of the cultivation of the land as the sure source of support, the next following stands related, its contents being cognate:

Ver. 20 A strong, upright man is enriched with blessings;
But he that hastens to become rich remains not unpunished.

אִישׁ אֱמוּנִים, xx. 6, as well as א׳ אֱמוּנוֹת, denotes a man *bonæ fidei;* but the former expression refers the description to a constancy and certainty in the relations of favour and of friendship, here to rectitude or integrity in walk and conduct; the plur. refers to the all-sidedness and the ceaselessness of the activity. בְּרָכוֹת is related, as at x. 6: the idea comprehends blessings on the side of God and of man, thus *benedictio rei* and *benedictio voti.* On the contrary, he who, without being careful as to the means, is in haste to become rich, remains not only unblessed, but also is not guiltless, and thus not without punishment; also this לֹא יִנָּקֶה (e.g. vi. 29), frequently met in the Mishle, is, like ברכות, the union of two ideas, for generally the bibl. mode of conception and language comprehends in one, sin, guilt, and punishment.

With a proverb, in the first half of which is repeated the beginning of the second appendix, xxiv. 23, a new group commences:

Ver. 21 Respect of persons is not good;
And for a morsel of bread a man may become a transgressor.

Line first refers to the administration of justice, and line second —the special generalized—to social life generally. The "morsel of bread," as example of a bribe by means of which the favour of the judge is purchased, is too low a conception. Hitzig well: "even a trifle, a morsel of bread (1 Sam. ii. 36), may, as it awakens favour and dislike within us, thus in general call forth in the will an inclination tending to draw one aside from the line of strict rectitude." Geier compares A. Gellius' *Noct.*

Att. i. 15, where Cato says of the Tribune Cœlius: *Frusto panis conduci potest vel ut taceat vel ut loquatur.*

> Ver. 22 The man of an evil eye hasteneth after riches,
> And knoweth not that want shall come upon him.

Hitzig renders אִישׁ וגו' [the man of an evil eye] as appos. of the subject; but in that case the phrase would have been אִישׁ רַע עַיִן נִבְהָל לָהוֹן (cf. *e.g.* xxix. 1). רַע עַיִן (xxiii. 6) is the jealous, envious, grudging, and at the same time covetous man. It is certainly possible that an envious man consumes himself in ill-humour without quietness, as Hitzig objects; but as a rule there is connected with envy a passionate endeavour to raise oneself to an equal height of prosperity with the one who is the object of envy; and this zeal, proceeding from an impure motive, makes men blind to the fact that thereby they do not advance, but rather degrade themselves, for no blessing can rest on it; discontentedness loses, with that which God has assigned to us, deservedly also that which it has. The *pret.* נִבְהַל, the expression of a fact; the *part.* נִבְהָל, the expression of an habitual characteristic action; the word signifies *præceps* (*qui præceps fertur*), with the root-idea of one who is unbridled, who is not master of himself (*vid.* under Ps. ii. 5, and above at xx. 21). The phrase wavers between נִבְהָל (Kimchi, under בהל; and Norzi, after Codd. and old editions) and נְבֶהָל (thus, *e.g.*, Cod. *Jaman*); only at Ps. xxx. 8 נִבְהָל stands unquestioned. חֶסֶר [want] is recognised by Symmachus, Syr., and Jerome. To this, as the authentic reading, cf. its ingenious rendering in *Bereschith Rabba*, c. 58, to Gen. xxiii. 14. The LXX. reads, from 22*b*, that a חָסִיד, ἐλεήμων, will finally seize the same riches, according to which Hitzig reads חֶסֶד, disgrace, shame (cf. xxv. 10).

> Ver. 23 He that reproveth a man who is going backwards,
> Findeth more thanks than the flatterer.

It is impossible that *aj* can be the suffix of אַחֲרַי; the Talmud, *Tamid* 28*a*, refers it to God; but that it signifies: after my (Solomon's) example or precedence (Aben Ezra, Ahron b. Josef, *Venet.*, J. H. Michaelis), is untenable — such a name given by the teacher here to himself is altogether aimless. Others translate, with Jerome: *Qui corripit hominem gratiam postea inveniet apud eum magis, quam ille qui per linguæ blandi-*

menta decipit, for they partly purpose to read אַחֲרֵי־כֵן, partly to
give to 'אַ֫חַ the meaning of *postea*. אחרי, Ewald says, is a
notable example of an adverb. Hitzig seeks to correct this
adv. as at Neh. iii. 30 f., but where, with Keil, אַחֲרָו is to be
read; at Josh. ii. 7, where אחרי is to erased; and at Deut. ii.
30, where the traditional text is accountable. This אחרי may
be formed like אֲנִי and מָתַי; but if it had existed, it would not
be a ἅπαξ λεγ. The accentuation also, in the passage before
us, does not recognise it; but it takes אַחֲרִי and אדם together, and
how otherwise than that it appears, as Ibn-Jachja in his *Grammar*,
and Immanuel [1] have recognised it, to be a noun terminating in
aj. It is a formation, like לִפְנַי, 1 Kings vi. 10 (cf. Olshausen's
Lehrb. p. 428 f.), of the same termination as שַׁדַּי, חַגַּי, and in
the later Aram.-Heb. זַכַּי, and the like. The variant אַחֲרִי,
noticed by Heidenheim, confirms it; and the distinction between different classes of men (*vid*. vol. i. p. 39) which prevails
in the Book of Proverbs favours it. A אדם אחרי is defined, after
the manner of Jeremiah (vii. 24): a man who is directed backwards, and not לְפָנִים, forwards. Not the renegade—for מוכיח,
opp. מחליק לשון, does not lead to so strong a conception—but the
retrograder is thus called in German: *Rückläufige* [one who
runs backwards] or *Rückwendige* [one who turns backwards],
who turns away from the good, the right, and the true, and
always departs the farther away from them (Immanuel: going
backwards in his nature or his moral relations). This centri-
fugal direction, leading to estrangement from the fear of
Jahve, or, what is the same thing, from the religion of revelation, would lead to entire ruin if unreserved and fearless
denunciation did not interpose and seek to restrain it; and
he who speaks [2] so truly, openly, and earnestly home to the
conscience of one who is on the downward course, gains for
himself thereby, on the part of him whom he has directed
aright, and on the part of all who are well disposed, better
thanks (and also, on the part of God, a better reward, James

---

[1] Abulwalîd (*Rikma*, p. 69) also rightly explains אַחֲרִי, as a characterizing
epithet, by אחרני (turned backwards).

[2] Löwenstein writes מוֹכִיחַ, after *Metheg-Setzung*, § 43, not incorrectly;
for the following word, although toned on the first syllable, begins with
guttural having the same sound.

v. 19 f.) than he who, speaking to him, smooths his tongue
to say to him who is rich, or in a high position, only that which
is agreeable. *Laudat adulator, sed non est verus amator.* The
second half of the verse consists, as often (Ps. lxxiii. 8 ; Job
xxxiii. 1; cf. *Thorath Emeth,* p. 51), of only two words, with
Mercha Silluk.

> Ver. 24 He who robbeth his father and mother, and saith : It is no
>   wrong,
>   Is a companion of the destroyer.

The second line is related to xviii. 9*b*. Instead of *dominus
perditionis* there found, there is here אִישׁ מַשְׁחִית, *vir perdens*
(*perditor*) ; the word thus denotes a man who destroys, not
from revenge, but from lust, and for the sake of the life of
men, and that which is valuable for men ; thus the spoiler, the
incendiary, etc. Instead of אָח there, here we have חָבֵר in the
same sense. He who robs his parents, *i.e.* takes to himself
what belongs to them, and regards his doing so as no particular
sin,[1] because he will at last come to inherit it all (cf. xx. 21
with xix. 26), is to be likened to a man who allows himself in
all offences against the life and property of his neighbour ; for
what the deed of such a son wants in external violence, it
makes up in its wickedness, because it is a rude violation of
the tenderest and holiest demands of duty.

> Ver. 25 The covetous stirreth up strife ;
>   But he that trusteth in Jahve is richly comforted.

Line first is a variation of xv. 18*a* ; רְחַב־נֶפֶשׁ is not to be interchanged with רְחַב־לֵב, xxi. 4. He is of a wide heart who
haughtily puffs himself up, of a wide soul (cf. with Schultens הרחיב
נפשׁו, of the opening up of the throat, or of revenge, Isa. v. 14;
Hab. ii. 5) who is insatiably covetous ; for לב is the spiritual,
and נפשׁ the natural, heart of man, according to which the
widening of the heart is the overstraining of self-consciousness,
and the widening of the soul the overstraining of passion.
Rightly the LXX., according to its original text : ἄπληστος
ἀνὴρ κινεῖ (thus with Hitzig for κρινεῖ) νείκη. Line second
is a variation of xvi. 20, xxix. 25. Over against the insatiable
is he who trusts in God (וּב מֵחַ, with *Gaja* to the vocal, concluding

---

[1] Accentuate וְאֹמֶר אֵין פֶּשַׁע without *Makkeph,* as in Codd. 1294 and
old editions.

the word, for it follows a word accented on the first syllable, and beginning with a guttural; cf. 'אַ֫, xxix. 2; 'פֶּ֫, xxix. 18), that He will bestow upon him what is necessary and good for him. One thus contented is easily satisfied (compare with the word xi. 25, xiii. 4, and with the matter, x. 3, xiii. 24), is externally as well as internally appeased; while that other, never contented, has no peace, and creates dispeace around him.

The following proverb assumes the בֹּטֵחַ of the foregoing :[1]

> Ver. 26 He that trusteth in his own heart is a fool;
> But he that walketh in wisdom shall escape.

From the promise in the second line, Hitzig concludes that a courageous heart is meant, but when by itself לב never bears this meaning. He who trusteth in his own heart is not merely one who is guided solely "by his own inconsiderate, defiant impulse to act" (Zöckler). The proverb is directed against a false subjectivity. The heart is that fabricator of thoughts, of which, as of man by nature, nothing good can be said, Gen. vi. 5, viii. 21. But wisdom is a gift from above, and consists in the knowledge of that which is objectively true, that which is normatively godlike. הֹלֵךְ בְּחָכְמָה is he who so walks that he has in wisdom a secure authority, and has not then for the first time, when he requires to walk, need to consider, to reckon, to experiment. Thus walking in the way of wisdom, he escapes dangers to which one is exposed who walks in foolish confidence in his own heart and its changeful feelings, thoughts, imaginations, delusions. One who thoughtlessly boasts, who vainly dreams of victory before the time, is such a person; but confidence in one's own heart takes also a hundred other forms. Essentially similar to this proverb are the words of Jer. ix. 22 f., for the wisdom meant in 26b is there defined at ver. 23.

> Ver. 27 He that giveth to the poor suffereth no want;
> But he that covereth his eyes meeteth many curses.

In the first line the pronoun לֹו, referring back to the subject noun, is to be supplied, as at xxvii. 7 לֹה. He who gives to the poor has no want (מַחְסֹור), for God's blessing reimburses

---

[1] We take the opportunity of remarking that the tendency to form together certain proverbs after one catchword is found also in German books of proverbs; vid. Paul, *Ueber die urspr. Anord. von Freidanks Bescheidenheit* (1870), p. 12.

him richly for what he bestows. He, on the other hand, who veils (מַעְלִים, cf. the *Hithpa.*, Isa. lviii. 7) his eyes so as not to see the misery which calls forth compassion, or as if he did not see the misery which has a claim on his compassion ; he is (becomes) rich in curses, *i.e.* is laden with the curses of those whose wants he cared not for ; curses which, because they are deserved, change by virtue of a divine requital (*vid.* Sir. iv. 5f.; Tob. iv. 7) into all kinds of misfortunes (*opp.* רַב־בְּרָכוֹת, 20a). מְאֵרָה is constructed after the form מְקֵרָה, מְגֵרָה from אָרַר.

The following proverb resembles the beginnings xxviii. 2, 12. The proverbs xxviii. 28, xxix. 1, 2, 3, form a beautiful square grasp, in which the first and third, and the second and fourth, correspond to one another.

> Ver. 28 When the godless rise up, men hide themselves;
> And when they perish, the righteous increase.

Line first is a variation of 12b. Since they who hide themselves are merely called men, people, the meaning of יִרְבּוּ is probably not this, that the righteous then from all sides come out into the foreground (Hitzig), but that they prosper, multiply, and increase as do plants, when the worms, caterpillars, and the like are destroyed (Fleischer) ; Löwenstein glosses יִרְבּוּ by יִגְדְּלוּ, they become great = powerful, but that would be Elihu's style, Job xxxiii. 12, which is not in common use ; the names of masters and of those in authority, רַבָּנוּת, רַבָּן, רִבִּי, רַב, are all derived from רָבַב, not from רָבָה. The increase is to be understood of the prosperous growth (to become great = to increase, as perhaps also Gen. xxi. 10) of the congregation of the righteous, which gains in the overthrow of the godless an accession to its numbers ; cf. xxix. 2, and especially 16.

xxix. 1. A general ethical proverb here follows :

> A man often corrected who hardeneth his neck,
> Shall suddenly go to ruin without remedy.

Line second = vi. 15b. The connection אִישׁ תּוֹכָחוֹת must make the nearest impression on a reader of the Book of Proverbs that they mean a censurer (reprehender), but which is set aside by what follows, for the genit. after אִישׁ is, xvi. 29, xxvi. 21, xxix. 10, xiii. 20, the designation of that which proceeds from the subject treated. And since תּוֹכָחוֹת, Ps. xxxvii. 15, Job xxiii. 4, denotes counter evidence, and generally rejoinders, thus in the first line a reasoner is designated who lets nothing be said to him, and nothing be shown to him, but contradicts all and every one. Thus *e.g.* Fleischer: *vir qui correptus contradicit et cervicem obdurat.* But this interpolated *correptus* gives involuntary testimony of this, that the nearest lying impression of the אִישׁ תּוֹ suffers a change by מַקְשֶׁה עֹרֶף: if we read הַקְשֵׁה (לֵב) עֹרֶף with תּוֹ, the latter then designates the *correptio*, over against which is placed obstinate boldness (Syr., Targ., Jerome, Luther), and תּוֹ shows itself thus to be *gen. objecti*, and we have to compare the gen. connection of אִישׁ, as at xviii. 23, xxi. 17, or rather at 1 Kings xx. 42 and Jer. xv. 10. But it is unnecessary, with Hitzig, to limit תּוֹ to divine infliction of punishment, and after Hos. v. 9, Isa. xxxvii. 3, to read תּוֹכֵחוֹת [punishment], which occurs, Ps. cxlix. 7, in the sense of punishment inflicted by man.[1] Besides, we must think first not of actual punishment, but of chastening, reproving words; and the man to whom are spoken the reproving words is one whose conduct merits more and more severe censure, and continually receives correction from those who are concerned for his welfare. Hitzig regards the first line as a conditional clause: "Is a man of punishment stiff-necked?" . . . This is syntactically impossible. Only מַקְשֶׁה עֹרֶף could have such force : a man of punishment, if he . . . But why then did not the author rather write the words וְהוּא מַקְשֶׁה עֹרֶף? Why then could not מַקְשֶׁה עֹרֶף be a co-ordinated further description of the man? Cf. *e.g.* Ex. xvii. 21. The door of penitence, to which earnest, well-meant admonition calls a man, does not always remain open. He who with stiff-necked persistence in sin and in self-delusion sets himself in opposition to all endeavours to save his soul, shall one day suddenly, and without the prospect and possibility of restoration (cf. Jer. xix. 11), become a wreck. *Audi doctrinam si vis vitare ruinam.* The general ethical proverb is here followed by one that is political:

Ver. 2 When the righteous increase, the people rejoice ;
And when a godless man ruleth, the people mourn.

Regarding בִּרְבוֹת צַדִּ' (Aquila rightly, ἐν τῷ πληθῦναι δικαίους), *vid.* at xxviii. 28. If the righteous form the majority, or are

[1] *Vid.* Zunz, "Regarding the Idea and the Use of *Tokhecha*," in Steinschneider's *Heb. Bibliographia*, entitled הַמַזְכִּיר, 1871, p. 70 f.

in such numbers that they are the party that give the tone, that form the predominant power among the people (Fleischer, *cum incrementa capiunt justi*), then the condition of the people is a happy one, and their voice joyful (xi. 10); if, on the contrary, a godless man or (after xxviii. 1) godless men rule, the people are made to sigh (יֵאָנַח עָם, with the *Gaja*, according to rule). "There is reason," as Hitzig remarks, "why עם should be placed first with, and then without, the article." In the first case it denotes the people as those among whom there is such an increase of the righteous; in the second case, the article is wanting, because it is not generally used in poetry; and, besides, its absence makes the second line consist of nine syllables, like the first. This political proverb is now followed by one of general ethics:

> Ver. 3 A man who loveth wisdom delighteth his father;
> And he who keepeth company with harlots spendeth his
> substance.

Line first is a variation of x. 1. אִישׁ־אֹהֵב has, according to rule, the *Metheg*, cf. 9*a*. אִישׁ is man, without distinction of age, from childhood (Gen. iv. 1) up to ripe old age (Isa. lxvi. 13); love and dutiful relation towards father and mother never cease. Line second reminds of xxviii. 7 (cf. xiii. 20).

A series of six proverbs follows, beginning with a proverb of the king:

> Ver. 4 A king by righteousness bringeth the land to a good condition;
> But a man of taxes bringeth it down.

The *Hiph.* הֶעֱמִיד signifies to make it so that a person or matter comes to stand erect and stand fast (*e.g.* 1 Kings xv. 4); הָרַס, to tear down, is the contrary of building up and extending (Ps. xxviii. 5), cf. נֶהֱרַס, *opp.* רוּם, of the state, xi. 11. By אִישׁ תְּר' is meant the king, or a man of this kind; but it is questionable whether as a man of gifts, *i.e.* one who lets gifts be made to him (Grotius, Fleischer, Ewald, Bertheau, Zöckler), or as a man of taxes, *i.e.* who imposes them (Midrash, Aben Ezra, Ralbag, Rosenmüller, Hitzig). Both interpretations are possible, for תר' means tax (lifting, raising = dedicating), freewill offerings, as well as gifts that are obligatory and required by the laws of nature. Since the word, in the only other place

where it occurs, Ezek. xlv. 13–16, is used of the relation of the
people to the prince, and denotes a legally-imposed tax, so it
appears also here, in passing over from the religious sphere to
the secular, to be meant of taxes, and that according to its
fundamental conception of gifts, *i.e.* such taxes as are given on
account of anything, such as the produce of the soil, manufactures, heritages. Thus also is to be understood Aquila's and
Theodotion's ἀνὴρ ἀφαιρεμάτων, and the rendering also of the
Venet. ἐράνων. A man on the throne, covetous of such gifts,
brings the land to ruin by exacting contributions; on the
contrary, a king helps the land to a good position, and an
enduring prosperity, by the exercise of right, and that in appointing a well-proportioned and fit measure of taxation.

> Ver. 5 A man who flattereth his neighbour
> Spreadeth a net for his steps.

Fleischer, as Bertheau: *vir qui alterum blanditiis circumvenit;*
but in the עַל there does not lie in itself a hostile tendency, an
intention to do injury; it interchanges with אֶל, Ps. xxxvi. 3,
and what is expressed in line second happens also, without any
intention on the part of the flatterer: the web of the flatterer
before the eyes of a neighbour becomes, if he is caught thereby,
a net for him in which he is entangled to his own destruction
(Hitzig). הֶחֱלִיק signifies also, without any external object,
xxviii. 23, ii. 16, as internally transitive: to utter that which is
smooth, *i.e.* flattering. פְּעָמָיו is, as Ps. lvii. 7 = רַגְלָיו, for which
it is the usual Phœnician word.

> Ver. 6 In the transgression of the wicked man lies a snare;
> But the righteous rejoiceth [*jubelt*] and is glad.

Thus the first line is to be translated according to the sequence
of the accents, *Mahpach, Munach, Munach, Athnach,* for the
second *Munach* is the transformation of *Dechi;* אִישׁ רָע thus,
like אַנְשֵׁי־רָע, xxviii. 5, go together, although the connection is
not, like this, genitival, but adjectival. But there is also this
sequence of the accents, *Munach, Dechi, Munach, Athnach,*
which separates רָע and אִישׁ. According to this, Ewald translates: "in the transgression of one lies an evil snare;" but in
that case the word ought to have been מוֹקֵשׁ רע, as at xii. 13;
for although the numeral רבים sometimes precedes its substantive, yet no other adjective ever does; passages such as Isa.

xxviii. 21 and x. 30 do not show the possibility of this position
of the words. In this sequence of accents the explanation
must be : in the wickedness of a man is the evil of a snare, *i.e.*
evil is the snare laid therein (Böttcher) ; but a reason why the
author did not write מוקש רע would also not be seen there, and
thus we must abide by the accentuation אִישׁ רע. The righteous
also may fall, yet he is again raised by means of repentance
and pardon ; but in the wickedness of a bad man lies a snare
into which having once fallen, he cannot again release himself
from it, xxiv. 16. In the second line, the form יָרוּן, for יָרֹן, is
defended by the same metaplastic forms as יָשׂוּד, Ps. xci. 6 ;
יָרוּן, Isa. xlii. 4 ; and also that the order of the words is not
יִשְׂמַח וְרָנֵּן (LXX. ἐν χαρᾷ καὶ ἐν εὐφροσύνῃ ; Luther : *frewet
sich vnd hat wonne* [rejoices and has pleasure]), is supported by
the same sequence of ideas, Zech. ii. 14, cf. Jer. xxxi. 7 : the
Jubeln is the momentary outburst of gladness; the *Freude*
[gladness], however, is a continuous feeling of happiness. To
the question as to what the righteous rejoiceth over [*jubelt*] and
is glad [*freuet*] because of, the answer is not : because of his
happy release from danger (Zöckler), but : because of the
prosperity which his virtue procures for him (Fleischer). But
the contrast between the first and second lines is not clear and
strong. One misses the expression of the object or ground of
the joy. Cocceius introduces into the second line a *si lapsus
fuerit.* Schultens translates, *justus vel succumbens triumphabit,*
after the Arab. *rân f. o.,* which, however, does not mean *succum-
bere,* but *subigere* (*vid.* under Ps. lxxviii. 65). Hitzig compares
Arab. *raym f. i., discedere, relinquere,* and translates : " but the
righteous passeth through and rejoiceth." Böttcher is inclined
to read יִרְאֶה וְשָׂמֵחַ, he sees it (what?) and rejoiceth. All these
devices, however, stand in the background compared with
Pinsker's proposal (*Babylon.-Heb. Punktationssystem,* p. 156) :

> " On the footsteps of the wicked man lie snares,
>   But the righteous runneth and is glad,"

i.e. he runneth joyfully (like the sun, Ps. xix. 6) on the divinely-
appointed way (Ps. cxix. 132), on which he knows himself
threatened by no danger. The change of בפשע into בפשע has
xii. 13 against it ; but ירוץ may be regarded, after iv. 12, cf.
xviii. 10, as the original from which ירון is corrupted.

Ver. 7 The righteous knoweth the cause of the poor,
　　　　But the godless understandeth no knowledge.

The righteous knoweth and recogniseth the righteous claims of
people of low estate, *i.e.* what is due to them as men, and in
particular cases; but the godless has no knowledge from which
such recognition may go forth (cf. as to the expression, xix. 25).
The proverb begins like xii. 10, which commends the just
man's compassion to his cattle; this commends his sympathy
with those who are often treated as cattle, and worse even
than cattle. The LXX. translates 7*b* twice: the second time
reading רֹשׁ instead of רֹשׁע, it makes nonsense of it.

Ver. 8 Men of derision set the city in an uproar,
　　　　But wise men allay anger.

Isa. xxviii. shows what we are to understand by אַנְשֵׁי לָצוֹן:
men to whom nothing is holy, and who despise all authority.
The *Hiphil* יָפִיחוּ does not signify *irretiunt*, from פָּחַח (*Venet.*
παγιδοῦσι, after Kimchi, Aben Ezra, and others), but *sufflant*,
from פוח (Rashi: ילהיבו): they stir up or excite the city, *i.e.* its
inhabitants, so that they begin to burn as with flames, *i.e.* by
the dissolution of the bonds of mutual respect and of piety, by
the letting loose of passion, they disturb the peace and excite
the classes of the community and individuals against each
other; but the wise bring it about that the breathings of anger
that has broken forth, or is in the act of breaking forth, are
allayed. The anger is not that of God, as it is rendered by
Jerome and Luther, and as יפיחו freely translated might mean.
The Aram. err in regard to יפיחו in passages such as vi. 19.

Ver. 9 If a wise man has to contend with a fool,
　　　　He [the fool] rageth and laugheth, and hath no rest.

Among the old translators, Jerome and Luther take the "wise
man" as subject even of the second line, and that in all its
three members: *vir sapiens si cum stulto contenderit, sive iras-
catur sive rideat, non inveniet requiem.* Thus Schultens, C. B.
Michaelis, Umbreit, Ewald, Elster, and also Fleischer: "The
doubled *Vav* is correlative, as at Ex. xxi. 16, Lev. v. 3, and
expresses the perfect sameness in respect of the effect, here of
the want of effect. If the wise man, when he disputes with a
fool, becomes angry, or jests, he will have no rest, *i.e.* he will
never bring it to pass that the fool shall cease to reply; he yields

the right to him, and thus makes it possible for him to end the strife." But the angry passion, and the bursts of laughter alternating therewith, are not appropriate to the wise man affirming his right; and since, after Eccles. ix. 17, the words of the wise are heard בְּנַחַת, the וְאֵין נָחַת [and there is no rest] will cause us to think of the fool as the logical subject. So far correctly, but in other respects inappropriately, the LXX. ἀνὴρ σοφὸς κρινεῖ ἔθνη (after the expression עַם, i.e. עָם, instead of אֵת), ἀνὴρ δὲ φαῦλος (which אִישׁ אֱוִיל does not mean) ὀργιζόμενος καταγελᾶται καὶ οὐ καταπτήσσει (as if the words were וְלֹא יֵחָת).[1] The syntactical relation would be simpler if נִשְׁפָּט in 9a were vocalized as a hypothetical perfect. But we read for it the past נִשְׁפָּט. Ewald designates 9a as a conditional clause, and Hitzig remarks that the Lat. viro sapiente disceptante cum stulto corresponds therewith. It marks, like 1 Sam. ii. 13, Job i. 16, the situation from which there is a departure then with perf. consec.: if a wise man in the right is in contact with a fool, he starts up, and laughs, and keeps not quiet (supply לוֹ as at xxviii. 27), or (without לוֹ): there is no keeping quiet, there is no rest. The figure is in accordance with experience. If a wise man has any controversy with a fool, which is to be decided by reasonable and moral arguments, then he becomes boisterous and laughs, and shows himself incapable of quietly listening to his opponent, and of appreciating his arguments.

We now group together vers. 10–14. Of these, vers. 10 and 11 are alike in respect of the tense used; vers. 12–14 have in common the pronoun pointing back to the first member.

Ver. 10 Men of blood hate the guiltless
And the upright; they attempt the life of such

The nearest lying translation of the second line would certainly be: the upright seek his soul (that of the guiltless). In accordance with the contrasted יִשְׂנְאוּ, the Aram. understand the seeking of earnest benevolent seeking, but disregarding the נפש

---

[1] According to this the Targum וְלָא מִתְחַבַּר (he remains obstinate), according to which the וְלָא מִתְחַפִּיר (he does not lose his wits) of the Peshito is perhaps to be corrected. The distribution of the subjects is obscure.

in לנפשׁו ;[1] Symmachus (ἐπιζητήσουσι), Jerome (quærunt), and
Luther thus also understand the sentence ; and Rashi remarks
that the phrase is here לשׁון חבּה, for he rests ; but mistrusting
himself, refers to 1 Sam. xxi. 23. Ahron b. Josef glosses : to enter
into friendship with him. Thus, on account of the contrast,
most moderns, interpreting the phrase *sensu bono*, also Fleischer:
probi autem vitam ejus conservare student. The thought is, as
xii. 6 shows, correct ; but the *usus loq.* protests against this
rendering, which can rest only on Ps. cxlii. 5, where, however,
the poet does not say אֵין דּוֹרֵשׁ נַפְשִׁי, but, as here also the *usus
loq.* requires, לְנַפְשִׁי. There are only three possible explanations
which Aben Ezra enumerates : (1) they seek his, the bloody
man's, soul, *i.e.* they attempt his life, to take vengeance against
him, according to the meaning of the expressions as generally
elsewhere used, *e.g.* at Ps. lxiii. 10 ; (2) they revenge his, the
guiltless man's, life (LXX. ἐκζητήσουσιν), which has fallen a
victim, after the meaning in which elsewhere only בִּקֵּשׁ דָּם and דָּרַשׁ
נֶפֶשׁ, Gen. ix. 5, occur. This second meaning also is thus not
in accordance with the usage of the words, and against both
meanings it is to be said that it is not in the spirit of the Book
of Proverbs to think of the ישׁרים [the upright, righteous] as
executors of the sentences of the penal judicature. There thus
remains[2] the interpretation (3) : the upright—they (the bloody
men) seek the soul of such an one. The transition from the plur.
to the sing. is individualizing, and thus the arrangement of the
words is like Gen. xlvii. 21 : "And the people (as regards them),
he removed them to the cities," Gesen. § 145. 2. This last
explanation recommends itself by the consideration that תם and
ישׁרים are cognate as to the ideas they represent,—let one call to
mind the common expression תָּם וְיָשָׁר [perfect and upright, *e.g.*
Job i. 1, 8, ii. 3],—that the same persons are meant thereby,
and it is rendered necessary by this, that the thought, " bloody
men hate the guiltless," is incomplete ; for the same thing may
also be said of the godless in general. One expects to hear
that just against the guiltless, *i.e.* men walking in their inno-

---

[1] The Targum translates תם, guiltlessness, and the *Venet.* (μισοῦσι)
γνῶσιν, turning to i. 22.

[2] For εὐθεῖς δὲ συνάξουσιν (will bring away ?) τὴν ψυχὴν αὐτῶν, understood after Jer. xlv. 5, lies linguistically yet further off.

cence, the bloody-mindedness of such men is specially directed, and 10*b* says the same thing; this second clause first brings the contrast to the point aimed at. Lutz is right in seeking to confute Hitzig, but he does so on striking grounds.

> Ver. 11 All his wrath the fool poureth out;
> But the wise man husheth it up in the background.

That רוּחוֹ is not meant here of his spirit (Luther) in the sense of *quæcunque in mente habet* (thus *e.g.* Fleischer) the contrast shows, for יְשַׁבְּחֶנָּה does not signify *cohibet*, for which יְחַשְׁבֶנָּה (LXX. ταμιεύεται) would be the proper word: רוּחַ thus is not here used of passionate emotion, such as at xvi. 31; Isa. xxv. 4, xxxiii. 11. שָׁבַּח is not here equivalent to Arab. *sabbah, αἰνεῖν* (Imman., *Venet.*, and Heidenheim), which does not supply an admissible sense, but is equivalent to Arab. *sabbakh*, to quiet (Ahron b. Josef: קטפיאן = καταπαύειν), the former going back to the root-idea of extending (*amplificare*), the latter to that of going to a distance, putting away: *sabbakh, procul recessit, distitit*, hence שְׁבַּח, Ps. lxxxix. 10, and here properly to drive off into the background, synon. הֵשִׁיב (Fleischer). But בְּאָחוֹר (only here with בְּ) is ambiguous. One might with Rashi explain: but the wise man finally, or afterwards (Symmachus, ἐπ' ἐσχάτων; *Venet.* κατόπιν = κατόπισθε), appeaseth the anger which the fool lets loose; *i.e.*, if the latter gives vent to his anger, the former appeases, subdues, mitigates it (cf. לְאָחוֹר, בְּאַחֲרֹנָה, Isa. xlii. 23). But it lies still nearer to refer the antithesis to the anger of the wise man himself; he does not give to it unbridled course, but husheth it in the background, viz. in his heart. Thus Syr. and Targ. reading בְּרַעְיָנָא, the former, besides יְחַשְׁבֶנָּה (*reputat eam*), so also Aben Ezra: in the heart as the background of the organ of speech. Others explain: in the background, afterward, *retrorsum*, *e.g.* Nolde, but to which *compescit* would be more appropriate than *sedat*. Hitzig's objection, that in other cases the expression would be בְּקִרְבּוֹ, is answered by this, that with באחור the idea of pressing back (of אָחוֹר) is connected. The order of the words also is in favour of the meaning *in recessu (cordis)*. *Iræ dilatio mentis pacatio* (according to an old proverb).

> Ver. 12 A ruler who listens to deceitful words,
> All his servants are godless.

They are so because they deceive him, and they become so ; for instead of saying the truth which the ruler does not wish to hear, they seek to gain his favour by deceitful flatteries, misrepresentations, exaggerations, falsehoods. *Audiat rex quæ præcipit lex.* He does not do this, as the saying is, *sicut rex ita grex* (Sir. x. 2), in the sense of this proverb of Solomon.

> Ver. 13 The poor man and the usurer meet together—
> Jahve lighteneth the eyes of both.

A variation of xxii. 2, according to which the proverb is to be understood in both of its parts. That אִישׁ תְּכָכִים is the contrast of רָשׁ, is rightly supposed in *Temura* 16*b* ; but Rashi, who brings out here a man of moderate learning, and Saadia, a man of a moderate condition (thus also the Targ. גַּבְרָא מַצְעָיָא, after Buxtorf, *homo mediocris fortunæ*), err by connecting the word with תָּוֶךְ. The LXX. δανειστοῦ καὶ χρεωφειλέτου (ἀλλήλοις συνελθόντων), which would be more correct inverted, for אִישׁ תכבים is a man who makes oppressive taxes, high previous payments of interest ; the verbal stem תָּכַךְ, Arab. *tak*, is a secondary to R. *wak*, which has the meanings of pressing together, and pressing firm (whence also the middle is named; cf. Arab. *samym álaklab*, the solid = the middle point of the heart). תֹּךְ, with the plur. תכבים, scarcely in itself denotes interest, τόκος ; the designation אִישׁ תכבים includes in it a sensible reproach (Syr. *afflictor*), and a *rentier* cannot be so called (Hitzig). Luther : *Reiche* [rich men], with the marginal note : " who can practise usury as they then generally all do ?" Therefore Löwenstein understands the second line after 1 Sam. ii. 7 : God enlighteneth their eyes by raising the lowly and humbling the proud. But this line, after xxii. 2*b*, only means that the poor as well as the rich owe the light of life (Ps. xiii. 4) to God, the creator and ruler of all things,—a fact which has also its moral side : both are conditioned by Him, stand under His control, and have to give to Him an account; or otherwise rendered : God maketh His sun to rise on the low and the high, the evil and the good (cf. Matt. v. 45)—an all-embracing love full of typical moral motive.[1]

---

[1] מאיר has, by Löwenstein, *Mehuppach Legarmeh*, but incorrectly, since after *Legarmeh* two conjunctives cannot occur. Also Norzi with *Mehuppach Mercha* is irregular, since Ben-Asher recognises only two examples of

Ver. 14 A king who judgeth the poor with truth,
His throne shall stand for ever.

בֶּאֱמֶת, as at Isa. xvi. 5 (synon. במישׁור‎, במישׁרים‎, באמונה‎), is equivalent to fidelity to duty, or a complete, full accomplishment of
his duty as a ruler with reference to the dispensing of justice; in
other words: after the norm of actual fact, and of the law, and
of his duty proceeding from both together. מֶלֶךְ has in Codd.,
e.g. Jaman., and in the Venetian 1517, 21, rightly Rebia. In
that which follows, שׁופט באמת are more closely related than באמת
דלים, for of two conjunctives standing together the first always
connects more than the second. מֹלך שׁופט באמת דלים is the
truest representation of the logical grammatical relation. To
14b compare the proverb of the king, xvi. 12, xxv. 5.

A proverb with שׁבט, ver. 15, is placed next one with שׁופט,
but it begins a group of proverbs regarding discipline in the
house and among the people:

Ver. 15 The rod and reproof give wisdom;
But an undisciplined son is a shame to his mother.

With שֵׁבֶט [a rod], which xxii. 15 also commends as salutary,
תּוֹכַחַת refers to discipline by means of words, which must
accompany bodily discipline, and without them is also necessary;
the construction of the first line follows in number and gender
the scheme xxvii. 9, Zech. vii. 7; Ewald, § 339c. In the second
line the mother is named, whose tender love often degenerates
into a fond indulgence; such a darling, such a mother's son,
becomes a disgrace to his mother. Our " ausgelassen," by
which Hitzig translates מְשֻׁלָּח, is used of joyfulness unbridled
and without self-restraint, and is in the passage before us too
feeble a word; שֻׁלַּח is used of animals pasturing at liberty,
wandering in freedom (Job xxxix. 5; Isa. xvi. 2); נַעַר מֻשְׁלָח is
accordingly a child who is kept in by no restraint and no
punishment, one left to himself, and thus undisciplined (Luther,
Gesenius, Fleischer, and others).

Ver. 16 When the godless increase, wickedness increaseth;
But the righteous shall see their fall.

---

this double accentuation to which this מָאִיר does not belong; vid. Thorath
Emeth, p. 12. That the penultima toning מָאִיר in several editions is false
scarcely needs to be remarked. Jablonski rightly points with Mehuppach
on the ult., and Zinnorith on the preceding open syllable.

The LXX. translation is not bad: πολλῶν ὄντων ἀσεβῶν πολλαὶ γίνονται ἁμαρτίαι (vid. regarding רָבָה, ver. 2, xxviii. 28); but in the main it is only a *Binsenwahrheit*, as they say in Swabia, *i.e.* a trivial saying. The proverb means, that if among a people the party of the godless increases in number, and at the same time in power, wickedness, *i.e.* a falling away into sins of thought and conduct, and therewith wickedness, prevails. When irreligion and the destruction of morals thus increase, the righteous are troubled; but the conduct of the godless carries the judgment in itself, and the righteous shall with joy perceive, in the righteous retribution of God, that the godless man will be cast down from his power and influence. This proverb is like a motto to Ps. xii.

Ver. 17 Correct thy son, and he will give thee delight,
And afford pleasure to thy soul.

The LXX. well translates וִינִיחֶךָ by καὶ ἀναπαύσει σε;[1] הֵנִיחַ denotes rest properly, a breathing again, ἀνάψυξις; and then, with an obliteration of the idea of restraint so far, generally (like the Arab. *arah*, compared by Fleischer) to afford pleasure or delight. The post.-bibl. language uses for this the words נַחַת רוּחַ, and says of the pious that he makes נחת רוח to his Creator, *Berachoth* 17a; and of God, that He grants the same to them that fear Him, *Berach.* 29b; in the morning prayer of the heavenly spirits, that they hallow their Creator בנחת רוח (with inward delight). Write with Codd. (also *Jaman.*) and older editions וְינִיחֶךָ, not וְינִיחֲךָ; for, except in verbs ל"ה, the suffix of this *Hiphil* form is not dagheshed, *e.g.* אֲמִיתֶךָ, 1 Kings ii. 26; cf. also 1 Kings xxii. 16 and Ps. l. 8. מַעֲדַנִּים the LXX. understands, after 2 Sam. i. 24 (עִם־עֲדָנִים, μετὰ κόσμου), also here, of ornament; but the word signifies dainty dishes—here, high spiritual enjoyment. As in vers. 15 and 16 a transition was made from the house to the people, so there now follows the proverb of the discipline of children, a proverb of the education of the people:

Ver. 18 Without a revelation a people becomes ungovernable;
But he that keepeth the law, happy is he.

---

[1] Their translation of vers. 17 and 18 here is found, in a marred and mutilated form, after xxviii. 17. At that place the words are καὶ ἀγαπήσει σε.

Regarding the importance of this proverb for estimating the relation of the *Chokma* to prophecy, *vid*. vol. i. p. 41. חָזוֹן is, according to the sense, equivalent to נְבוּאָה, the prophetic revelation in itself, and as the contents of that which is proclaimed. Without spiritual preaching, proceeding from spiritual experience, a people is unrestrained (יִפָּרַע, *vid*. regarding the punctuation at xxviii. 25, and regarding the fundamental meaning, at i. 25); it becomes פָּרַע, disorderly, Ex. xxxii. 25; *wild vnd wüst*, as Luther translates. But in the second line, according to the unity of the antithesis, the words are spoken of the people, not of individuals. It is therefore not to be explained, with Hitzig: but whoever, in such a time, nevertheless holds to the law, it is well with him ! Without doubt this proverb was coined at a time when the preaching of the prophets was in vogue; and therefore this, " but whoever, notwithstanding," is untenable; such a thought at that time could not at all arise; and besides this, תורה is in the Book of Proverbs a moveable conception, which is covered at least by the law in contradistinction to prophecy. *Tôra* denotes divine teaching, the word of God; whether that of the Sinaitic or that of the prophetic law (2 Chron. xv. 3, cf. *e.g.* Isa. i. 10). While, on the one hand, a people is in a dissolute condition when the voice of the preacher, speaking from divine revelation, and enlightening their actions and sufferings by God's word, is silent amongst them (Ps. lxxiv. 9, cf. Amos viii. 12); on the other hand, that same people are to be praised as happy when they show due reverence and fidelity to the word of God, both as written and as preached. That the word of God is preached among a people belongs to their condition of life; and they are only truly happy when they earnestly and willingly subordinate themselves to the word of God which they possess and have the opportunity of hearing. אַשְׁרֵהוּ (defective for אַשְׁרֵיהוּ) is the older, and here the poetic kindred form to אַשְׁרֵי, xiv. 21, xvi. 20. From the discipline of the people this series of proverbs again returns to the discipline of home:

> Ver. 19 With words a servant will not let himself be bettered;
>   For he understandeth them, but conformeth not thereto.

The *Niph.* נוֹסָר becomes a so-called tolerative, for it connects with the idea of happening that of reaching its object: to become truly bettered (taught in wisdom, corrected), and thus to let himself be bettered. With mere words this is not reached; the unreasonable servant needs, in order to be set right, a more radical means of deliverance. This assertion demands confirmation; therefore is the view of von Hofmann (*Schriftbew.* ii. 2. 404) improbable, that 19*b* has in view a better-disposed servant: supposing that he is intelligent, in which case he is admonished without cause, then the words are also lost: he will let them pass over him in silence without any reply. This attempted explanation is occasioned by this, that מַעֲנֶה can signify nothing else than a response in words. If this were correct, then without doubt its fundamental meaning would correspond with בְּ׳; for one explains, with Löwenstein, "for he perceives it, and may not answer," *i.e.* this, that a reply cut off frustrates the moral impression. Or also: for he understands it, but is silent,—*in præfractum se silentium configit* (Schultens); and thus it is with the ancients (Rashi). But why should not וְאֵין מַעֲנֶה itself be the expression of this want of any consequences? מענה cannot certainly mean humiliation [1] (Meîri, after Ex. x. 3, הכנעה), but why as an answer in words and not also a response by act (Stuart: a practical answer)? Thus the LXX. ἐὰν γὰρ καὶ νοήσῃ, ἀλλ᾽ οὐχ ὑπακούσεται, according to which Luther: for although he at once understands it, he does not yet take it to himself. That מענה may mean obedience, the Aram. so understood, also at xvi. 4. It denoted a reply in the most comprehensive meaning of the word, *vid.* at xvi. 1. The thought, besides, is the same as if one were to explain: for he understands it, and is silent, *i.e.* lets thee speak; or: he understands it, but that which he perceives finds no practical echo.

Ver. 20 Seest thou a man hasty in his words?
The fool hath more hope than he.

Cf. xxvi. 12. Such an one has blocked up against himself the path to wisdom, which to the fool, *i.e.* to the ingenuous, stands open; the former is perfect, of the latter something may yet be made. In this passage the contrast is yet more precise, for the fool is thought of as the dull, which is the proper meaning

---

[1] The Syr. and Targ. also think on ענה, for they translate: "for he knows that he receives no strokes."

of כְּסִיל, *vid.* under xvii. 24. There is more hope for the fool than for him, although he may be no fool in himself, who overthrows himself by his words. "The προπετὴς ἐν λόγῳ αὐτοῦ (Sir. ix. 18) has, in the existing case, already overleaped the thought; the כסיל has it still before him, and comes at length, perhaps with his slow conception, to it" (Hitzig); for the ass, according to the fable, comes at last farther than the greyhound. Hence, in words as well as in acts, the proverb holds good, "*Eile mit Weile*" [= *festina lente*]. Every word, as well as act, can only be matured by being thought out, and thought over. From this proverb, which finds its practical application to the affairs of a house, and particularly also to the relation to domestics, the group returns to the subject of instruction, which is its ground-tone.

Ver. 21 If one pampers his servant from youth up,
He will finally reach the place of a child.

The LXX. had no answer to the question as to the meaning of מנון. On the other hand, for פִּנֵּק, the meaning to fondle; *delicatius enutrire*, is perfectly warranted by the Aram. and Arab. The Talmud, *Succa* 52*b*, resorts to the alphabet אט״בח in order to reach a meaning for מנון. How the Targ. comes to translate the word by מְנַפַּח (outrooted) is not clear; the rendering of Jerome: *postea sentiet eum contumacem*, is perhaps mediated by the ἔσται γογγυσμός of Symmachus, who combines נון with לֹן, *Niph.* γογγύζειν. The ὀθυνηθήσεται of the LXX., with the Syr., von Hofmann has sought to justify (*Schriftbew.* ii. 2. 404), for he derives מָנוֹן = מַנְהוֹן from נָהָה. We must then punctuate מַנּוֹן; but perhaps the LXX. derived the word from אָנַן = מְאַנוֹן, whether they pronounced it מָנוֹן (cf. מְאַסֹרֶת = מָסֹרֶת) or מַנּוֹן. To follow them is not wise, for the formation of the word is precarious; one does not see what the speaker of this proverb, to whom the language presented a fulness of synonyms for the idea of complaint, meant by using this peculiar word. Linguistically these meanings are impossible: of Jerome, *dominus* = מְמַּה (Ahron b. Josef, Meïri, and others); or: the oppressed = מוּנֶה, from יָנָה (Johlson); or: one who is sick = מוֹנֶה (Euchel). And Ewald's "*undankbar*" [unthankful], derived from the Arabic, is a mere fancy, since (Arab.) *manuwan* does not mean one who is unthankful, but,

on the contrary, one who upbraids good deeds shown.[1] The
ancients are in the right track, who explain מנון after the
verb נון, Ps. lxxii. 17 = נין = בֶּן; the *Venet.*, herein following
Kimchi, also adopts the nominal form, for it translates (but
without perceptible meaning) γόνωσις. Luther's translation is
fortunate:

> " If a servant is tenderly treated from youth up,
> He will accordingly become a *Junker* [squire]."

The ideas represented in modern Jewish translations: that of a
son (*e.g.* Solomon: he will at last be the son) and that of a
master (Zunz), are here united. But how the idea of a son (from
the verb נון), at the same time that of a master, may arise, is not
to be perceived in the same way as with *Junker* and the Spanish
infante and *hidalgo;* rather with מנון, as the ironical naming
of the son (little son), the idea of a weakling (de Wette) may
be connected. The state of the matter appears as follows:—
The verb נון has the meanings of luxuriant growth, numerous
propagation; the fish has from this the Aram. name of נון, like
the Heb. דָּג, from דָּנָה, which also means luxuriant, exuberant
increase (*vid.* at Ps. lxxii. 17). From this is derived נין, which
designates the offspring as a component part of a kindred, as
well as מָנון, which, according as the מ is interpreted infin. or
local, means either this, that it sprouts up luxuriantly, the
abundant growth, or also the place of luxuriant sprouting,
wanton growing, abundant and quick multiplication: thus the
place of hatching, spawning. The subject in יִהְיֶה might be the
fondled one; but it lies nearer, however, to take him who
fondles as the subject, as in 21a. אַחֲרִיתו is either adv. accus.
for בְּאַחֲרִיתו, or, as we preferred at xxiii. 32, it is the subj. in-

---

[1] In *Jahrb.* xi. p 10 f. Ewald compares, in an expressive way, the
Ethiopic *mannána (Piel)* to scorn; *menûn,* a reprobate; and *mannâni,* one
who is despised; according to which מנון could certainly designate " a man
despising scornfully his own benefactors, or an unthankful man." But this
verbal stem is peculiarly Ethiop., and is certainly not once found in Arab.
For *minnat* (which Ewald compares) denotes benefaction, and the duty
laid on one thereby, the dependence thereby produced. The verb (Arab.)
minn (= מָנַן) signifies to divide; and particularly, partly to confer benefaction, partly to attribute benefaction, reckon to, enumerate, and thereby
to bring out the sense of obligation. Thus nothing is to be derived from
this verbal stem for מנון.

troducing, after the manner of a substantival clause, the
following sentence as its virtual predicate : " one has fondled
his servant from his youth up, and his (that of the one who
fondles) end is ꞉ he will become a place of increase." The
master of the house is thought of along with his house ; and
the servant as one who, having become a man, presents his
master with יְלִידֵי בַיִת, who are spoilt scapegraces, as he himself
has become by the pampering of his master. There was
used in the language of the people, נִי for בֵּן, in the sense in
which we name a degenerate son a " *Schönes Früchtchen* "
[pretty little fruit] ; and מָנוֹן is a place (house) where many
נינים are ; and a man (master of a house) who has many of
them is one whose family has increased over his head. One
reaches the same meaning if מָנוֹן is rendered more immediately
as the place or state of growing, increasing, luxuriating. The
sense is in any case : he will not be able, in the end, any more
to defend himself against the crowd which grows up to him
from this his darling, but will be merely a passive part of it.

The following group begins with a proverb which rhymes by
מדון, with מנון of the foregoing, and extends on to the end of
this Hezekiah collection :

> Ver. 22 A man of anger stirreth up strife ;
>   And a passionate man aboundeth in trangression.

Line first is a variation of xv. 18a and xxviii. 25a. אִישׁ and
בַּעַל as here, but in the reverse order at xxii. 24.[1] אַף here
means anger, not the nose, viz. the expanded nostrils (Schultens).
In רַב־פֶּשַׁע the פֶּשַׁע is, after xiv. 29, xxviii. 16, xx. 27, the
governed genitive ; Hitzig construes it in the sense of פֶּשַׁע רב,
Ps. xix. 2, with יגרה, but one does not say גֵּרָה פֶּשַׁע ; and that
which is true of רַבִּים, that, after the manner of a numeral, it
can precede its substantive (*vid.* under Ps. vii. 26, lxxxix. 51),
cannot be said of רַב. Much (great) in wickedness denotes
one who heaps up many wicked actions, and burdens himself
with greater guilt (cf. פֶּשַׁע, ver. 16). The wrathful man stirreth up (*vid.* under xv. 18) strife, for he breaks through the
mutual relations of men, which rest on mutual esteem and

---

[1] For אִישׁ־אַף (Löwenstein after Norzi) is to be written, with Baer
(*Thorath Emeth*, p. 19), אִישׁ אַף. Thus also in *Cod. Jaman.*

love, and by means of his passionate conduct he makes enemies of those against whom he thinks that he has reason for being angry; that on account of which he is angry can be settled without producing such hostility, but passion impels him on, and misrepresents the matter; it embitters hearts, and tears them asunder. The LXX. has, instead of רב, ἐξώρυξεν, of dreaming, כרה (xvi. 27).

Ver. 23 passes from anger to haughtiness:

> A man's pride will bring him low;
> But the lowly attaineth to honour.

Thus we translate תִּתְמֹךְ כָּבוֹד (Lat. *honorem obtinet*) in accord with xi. 16, and שְׁפַל־רוּחַ with xvi. 19, where, however, שָׁפֵל is not adj. as here, but inf. The haughty man obscures the honour which he has by this, that he boasts immeasurably of it, and aspires yet more after it; the lowly man, on the other hand, obtains honour without his seeking it, honour before God and before men, which would be of no worth were it not connected with the honour before God. The LXX.: τοὺς δὲ ταπεινόφρονας ἐρείδει δόξῃ κύριος. This κύριος is indeed not contrary to the sense, but it is opposed to the style. Why the 24th verse should now follow is, as regards the contents and the expression, hard to say; but one observes that vers. 22–27 follow each other, beginning with the successive letters of the alphabet א (ב), ג, ח, ח, ר, ת (ת).

Ver. 24 He that taketh part with a thief hateth himself;
He heareth the oath and confesseth not.

Hitzig renders the first member as the pred. of the second: " he who does not bring to light such sins as require an atonement (Lev. v. 1 ff.), but shares the secret of them with the sinner, is not better than one who is a partner with a thief, who hateth himself." The construction of the verse, he remarks, is not understood by any interpreter. It is not, however, so cross,—for, understood as Hitzig thinks it ought to be, the author should have expressed the subject by שֹׁמֵעַ אָלָה ולֹא יַגִּיד,—but is simple as the order of the words and the verbal form require it. The oath is, after Lev. v. 1, that of the judge who adjures the partner of the thief by God to tell the truth; but he conceals it, and burdens his soul with a crime worthy of

death, for from a concealer he becomes in addition a perjured
man.

Ver. 25 Fear of man bringeth a snare with it;
But he that trusteth in Jahve is advanced.

It sounds strange, Hitzig remarks, that here in the Book of an
Oriental author one should be warned against the fear of man.
It is enough, in reply to this, to point to Isa. li. 12 f.   One of
the two translations in the LXX. (cf. Jerome and Luther)
has found this " strange " thought not so strange as not to
render it, and that in the gnomic aorist: φοβηθέντες καὶ αἰσχυν-
θέντες ἀνθρώπους ὑπεσκελίσθησαν.   And why should not חֶרְדַּת
אָדָם be able to mean the fear of man (cowardice)?   Perhaps
not so that אדם is the *gen. objecti*, but so that חרדת אדם means
to frighten men, as in 1 Sam. xiv. 15.   חרדת אלהים, a trembling
of God; cf. Ps. lxiv. 2; פחד איב, the fear occasioned by the
enemy, although this connection, after Deut. ii. 25, can also
mean fear of the enemy (*gen. objecti*).   To יִתֵּן, occasioned =
brings as a consequence with it, cf. x. 10, xiii. 15; the *synallage generis* is as at xii. 25 a : it is at least strange with fem.
infinit. and infinitival nouns, xvi. 16, xxv. 14; Ps. lxxiii. 28; but
חֲרָדָה (trembling) is such a *nom. actionis*, Ewald, § 238a.   Regarding יְשֻׂגָּב (for which the LXX.[1] σωθήσεται, and LXX.[2]
εὐφρανθήσεται = ישמח), *vid.* at xviii. 10.   He who is put into
a terror by a danger with which men threaten him, so as to do
from the fear of man what is wrong, and to conceal the truth,
falls thereby into a snare laid by himself—it does not help him
that by this means he has delivered himself from the danger,
for he brands himself as a coward, and sins against God, and
falls into an agony of conscience (reproach and anguish of
heart) which is yet worse to bear than the evil wherewith he
was threatened.   It is only confidence in God that truly saves.
The fear of man plunges him into yet greater suffering than
that from which he would escape; confidence in God, on the
other hand, lifts a man internally, and at last externally, above
all his troubles.

Ver. 26. A similar gen. connection to that between חרדת אדם
exists between משפט־איש :

Many seek the countenance of the ruler;
Yet from Jahve cometh the judgment of men.

Line first is a variation of xix. 6a, cf. 1 Kings x. 24. It lies
near to interpret אִישׁ as *gen. obj.* : the judgment regarding any
one, *i.e.* the estimating of the man, the decision regarding him;
and it is also possible, for מִשְׁפָטִי, Ps. xvii. 2, may be understood
of the judgment which I have, as well as of the judgment pronounced regarding me (cf. Lam. iii. 59). But the usage
appears to think of the genit. after משפט always as subjective,
e.g. xvi. 33, of the decision which the lot brings, Job xxxvi. 6,
the right to which the poor have a claim; so that thus in the
passage before us מִשׁפט־אִישׁ means the right of a man, as that
which is proper or fitting to him, the judgment of a man, as
that to which as appropriate he has a claim (LXX. τὸ δίκαιον
ἀνδρί). Whether the genit. be rendered in the one way or the
other, the meaning remains the same: it is not the ruler who
finally decides the fate and determines the worth of a man, as
they appear to think who with eye-service court his favour and
fawn upon him.

Ver. 27 An abomination to a righteous man is a villanous man ;
     And an abomination to the godless is he who walketh uprightly.

In all the other proverbs which begin with תּוֹעֲבַת, *e.g.* xi. 20,
יהוה follows as genit., here צַדִּיקִים, whose judgment is like that
of God. אִישׁ עָוֶל is an abhorrence to them, not as a man,
but just as of such a character; עָוֶל is the direct contrast to
יָשָׁר. The righteous sees in the villanous man, who boldly does
that which is opposed to morality and to honour, an adversary
of his God; on the other hand, the godless sees in the man that
walketh uprightly (יְשַׁר־דָּרֶךְ, as at Ps. xxxvii. 14) his adversary,
and the condemnation of himself.

With this doubled ח the Book of Proverbs, prepared by the
men of Hezekiah, comes to an end. It closes, in accordance
with its intention announced at the beginning, with a proverb
concerning the king, and a proverb of the great moral contrasts
which are found in all circles of society up to the very throne
itself.

FIRST APPENDIX TO THE SECOND SOLOMONIC COLLECTION OF PROVERBS.—CHAP. XXX.

The title of this first appendix, according to the text lying before us, is:

" The words of Agur the son of Jakeh, the utterance."

This title of the following collection of proverbs is limited by *Olewejored;* and הַמַּשָּׂא, separated from the author's name by *Rebia,* is interpreted as a second inscription, standing on one line with דִּבְרֵי, as particularizing that first. The old synagogue tradition which, on the ground of the general title i. 1, regarded the whole Book of Proverbs as the work of Solomon, interpreted the words, " Agur the son of Jakeh," as an allegorical designation of Solomon, who appropriated the words of the *Tôra* to the king, Deut. xvii. 17, and again rejected them, for he said: God is with me, and I shall not do it (viz. take many wives, without thereby suffering injury), *Schemôth rabba,* c. 6. The translation of Jerome: *Verba congregantis filii Vomentis,* is the echo of this Jewish interpretation. One would suppose that if " Agur " were Solomon's name, " Jakeh " must be that of David; but another interpretation in *Midrash Mishle* renders בֵּן (" son ") as the designation of the bearer of a quality, and sees in " Agur " one who girded (חגר = אגר) his loins for wisdom; and in " son of Jakeh " one free from sin (נקי מכל חטא ועון). In the Middle Ages this mode of interpretation, which is historically and linguistically absurd, first began to prevail; for then the view was expressed by several (Aben Ezra, and Meîri the Spaniard) that Agur ben Jakeh was a wise man of the time of Solomon. That of Solomon's time, they thence conclude (blind to xxv. 1) that Solomon collected together these proverbs of the otherwise unknown wise man. In truth, the age of the man must remain undecided; and at all events, the time of Hezekiah is the fixed period from which, where possible, it is to be sought. The name " Agur " means the gathered (vi. 8, x. 5), or, after the predominant meaning of the Arab. *âjar,* the bribed, *mercede conductum;* also the collector (cf. יָקוּשׁ, fowler); or the word might mean, perhaps, industrious in collecting (cf. 'alwaḳ, attached to, and other examples in Mühlau, p. 36).

Regarding בֵּן = *binj* (usual in בִּן־נֻן), and its relation to the Arab. *ibn*, *vid. Genesis*, p. 555. The name *Jakeh* is more transparent. The noun יָקְהָה, xxx. 17, Gen. xlix. 10, means the obedient, from the verb יָקַה; but, formed from this verbal stem, the form of the word would be יֻקָּה (not יָקֶה). The form יָקֶה is the participial adj. from יָקָה, like יָפֶה from יָפָה; and the Arab. *wakay*, corresponding to this יָקָה, viii. *ittakay*, to be on one's guard, particularly before God; the usual word for piety regarded as εὐλάβεια. Mühlau (p. 37) rightly sees in the proper names *Eltekeh* [Josh. xix. 44] and *Eltekon* [Josh. xv. 59]· the secondary verbal stem תָּקָה, which, like *e.g.* תָּוָה (תָּאָה), תָּאַב, עָתַד, has originated from the reflexive, which in these proper names, supposing that אַל is subj., means to take under protection; not: to give heed = *cavere*. All these meanings are closely connected. In all these three forms—תָּקָה, יָקָה, יָקֶה—the verb is a synonym of שָׁמַר; so that יָקֶה denotes[1] the pious, either as taking care, εὐλαβής, or as keeping, *i.e.* observing, viz. that which is commanded by God.

In consequence of the accentuation, הַמַּשָּׂא is the second designation of this string of proverbs, and is parallel with דברי. But that is absolutely impossible. מַשָּׂא (from נָשָׂא, to raise, viz. the voice, to begin to express) denotes the utterance, and according to the usage of the words before us, the divine utterance, the message of God revealed to the prophet and announced by him, for the most part, if not always (*vid.* at Isa. xiii. 1), the message of God as the avenger. Accordingly Jewish interpreters (*e.g.* Meîri and Arama) remark that מַשָּׂא designates what follows, as דבר נבואיי, *i.e.* an utterance of the prophetic spirit. But, on the other hand, what follows begins with the confession of human weakness and short-sightedness; and, moreover, we read proverbs not of a divine but altogether

---

[1] According to the *Lex.* '*Gezerî* (from the Mesopotamian town of '*Geziret ibn* '*Amr*), the word *wakihon* is, in the Mesopotamian language, "the overseer of the house in which is the cross of the Christians;" and accordingly, in Muhammed's letter to the Christians of Negran, after they became subject to him, "a monk shall not be removed from his monastery, nor a presbyter from his presbyterate, (*wakâhtah) wala watah wakahyttah*" (this will be the correct phrase), "nor an overseer from his office." The verbal stem *wak-ah* (יָקָה) is, as it appears, Northern Semitic; the South Arabian lexicographer Neshwan ignores it (Wetzstein in Mühlau).

of a human and even of a decaying spiritual stamp, besides
distinguished from the Solomonic proverbs by this, that the *I*
of the poet, which remains in the background, here comes to
the front. This מַשָּׂא of prophetic utterances does not at all
harmonize with the following string of proverbs. It does not
so harmonize on this account, because one theme does not run
through these proverbs which the sing. מַשָּׂא requires. It comes
to this, that מַשָּׂא never occurs by itself in the sense of a divine, a
solemn utterance, without having some more clearly defining
addition, though it should be only a demonstrative הַזֶּה (Isa. xiv.
28). But what author, whether poet or prophet, would give to
his work the title of מַשָּׂא, which in itself means everything, and
thus nothing ! And now : the utterance—what can the article
at all mean here ? This question has remained unanswered
by every interpreter. Ewald also sees himself constrained to
clothe the naked word ; he does it by reading together הַמַּשָּׂא
נְאֻם, and translating the " sublime saying which he spoke." But
apart from the consideration that Jer. xxiii. 31 proves nothing
for the use of this use of נְאֻם, the form נְאֻם (הַגֶּבֶר) is supported
by 2 Sam. xxiii. 1 (cf. ver. 5 with 2 Sam. xxii. 31) ; and besides,
the omission of the אֲשֶׁר, and in addition of the relative pronoun
(נְאֻמוֹ), would be an inaccuracy not at all to be expected on the
brow of this gnomology (*vid.* Hitzig). If we leave the altogether unsuspected נְאֻם undisturbed, הַמַּשָּׂא will be a nearer definition of the name of the author. The Midrash has a right
suspicion, for it takes together *Hamassa* and *Agur ben Jakeh*,
and explains : of Agur the son of Jakeh, who took upon himself the yoke of the most blessed. The *Græcus Venetus* comes
nearer what is correct, for it translates : λόγοι ᾿Αγούρου υἱέως
᾿Ιακέως τοῦ Μασάου. We connect xxxi. 1, where לְמוּאֵל מֶלֶךְ,
" Lemuel (the) king," is a linguistic impossibility, and thus, according to the accentuation lying before us, מֶלֶךְ מַשָּׂא also are
to be connected together ; thus it appears that מַשָּׂא must be the
name of a country and a people. It was Hitzig who first made
this Columbus-egg to stand. But this is the case only so far
as he recognised in לְמוּאֵל מֶלֶךְ מַשָּׂא a Lemuel, the king of
Massa, and recognised this Massa also in xxx. 1 (*vid.* his dissertation : *Das Königreich Massa* [the kingdom of Massa], in
Zeller's *Theolog. Jahrbb.* 1844, and his *Comm.*), viz. the Israel-

itish *Massa* named in Gen. xxv. 14 (=1 Chron. i. 30) along
with *Dumah* and *Tema.* But he proceeds in a hair-splitting
way, and with ingenious hypothesis, without any valid foundation. That this *Dumah* is the *Dumat el-jendel* (cf. under Isa.
xxi. 11) lying in the north of Nejed, near the southern fron-
tiers of Syria, the name and the founding of which is referred
by the Arabians to *Dûm* the son of Ishmael, must be regarded
as possible, and consequently *Massa* is certainly to be sought
in Northern Arabia. But if, on the ground of 1 Chron. iv.
42 f., he finds there a Simeonitic kingdom, and finds its origin
in this, that the tribe of Simeon originally belonging to the ten
tribes, and thus coming from the north settled in the south of
Judah, and from thence in the days of Hezekiah, fleeing before
the Assyrians, were driven farther and farther in a south-east
direction towards Northern Arabia ; on the contrary, it has been
shown by Graf (*The Tribe of Simeon,* a contribution to the
history of Israel, 1866) that Simeon never settled in the north
of the Holy Land, and according to existing evidences extended their settlement from Negeb partly into the Idumean
highlands, but not into the highlands of North Arabia. Hitzig
thinks that there are found traces of the *Massa* of Agur and
Lemuel in the Jewish town[1] of מילמאס, of Benjamin of Tudela,
lying three days' journey from Chebar, and in the proper name
(Arab.) *Malsā* (smooth), which is given to a rock between Tema
and Wady el-Kora (*vid.* Kosegarten's *Chrestom.* p. 143); but
how notched his ingenuity here is need scarcely be shown. By
means of more cautious combinations Mühlau has placed the
residence of Agur and Lemuel in the Hauran mountain range,
near which there is a *Dumah,* likewise a *Têmâ;* and in the name of
the town *Mismîje,* lying in the Lejâ, is probably found the *Mishma*
which is named along with *Massa,* Gen. xxv. 14; and from this
that is related in 1 Chron. v. 9 f., 18–22, of warlike expeditions
on the part of the tribes lying on the east of the Jordan against
the Hagarenes and their allies *Jetur, Nephish,* and *Nodab,*[2] it

---

[1] Cf. Blau's *Arab. im sechsten Jahrh.* in the *Deutsch. Morgl. Zeits.* xxxiii.
590, and also p. 573 of the same, regarding a family of proselytes among
the Jews in Taima.

[2] Mühlau combines *Nodab* with *Nudêbe* to the south-east of Bosra ;
Blau (*Deut. Morg. Zeit.* xxv. 566), with the Ναβδαίοι of Eupolemos named
along with the Ναβαταίοι. The Kamûs has Nadab as the name of a tribe.

is with certainty concluded that in the Hauran, and in the wilderness which stretches behind the Euphrates towards it, Israelitish
tribes have had their abode, whose territory had been early seized
by the trans-Jordanic tribes, and was held " until the captivity,"
1 Chron. v. 22, *i.e.* till the Assyrian deportation.   This designation of time is almost as unfavourable to Mühlau's theory of
a *Massa* in the Hauran, inhabited by Israelitish tribes from the
other side, as the expression "*to Mount Seir*" (1 Chron. iv. 42) is
to Hitzig's North Arabian *Massa* inhabited by Simeonites.   We
must leave it undecided whether *Dumah* and *Têmâ*, which the
Toledoth of Ismael name in the neighbourhood of *Massa*, are
the east Hauran districts now existing; or as Blau (*Deut. Morgl.
Zeit.* xxv. 539), with Hitzig, supposes, North Arabian districts
(cf. *Genesis*, p. 377, 4th ed.).[1]   " Be it as it may, the contents
and the language of this difficult piece almost necessarily point
to a region bordering on the Syro-Arabian waste.   Ziegler's
view (*Neue Uebers. der Denksprüche Salomo's*, 1791, p. 29),
that Lemuel was probably an emir of an Arabian tribe in the
east of Jordan, and that a wise Hebrew translated those proverbs of the emir into Hebrew, is certainly untenable, but does
not depart so far from the end as may appear at the first
glance" (Mühlau).[2]   If the text-punctuation lying before us
rests on the false supposition that *Massa*, xxx. 1, xxxi. 1, is a
generic name, and not a proper name, then certainly the
question arises whether מִשָּׁא should not be used instead of מַשָּׂא,
much more מֵישָׁא, which is suggested as possible in the article
"Sprüche," in Herzog's *Encycl.* xiv. 694.   Were מֵישָׁא, Gen. x. 30,
the region Μεσήνη, on the northern border of the Persian Gulf,
in which Apamea lay, then it might be said in favour of this,
that as the histories of Muhammed and of Benjamin of Tudela
prove the existence of an old Jewish occupation of North Arabia,
but without anything being heard of a מַשָּׂא, the Talmud
bears testimony[3] to a Jewish occupation of Mesene, and particularly of Apamea; and by the mother of Lemuel, the king

---

[1] Dozy (*Israeliten in Mecca*, p. 89 f.) connects *Massa* with *Mansâh*, a
pretended old name of Mecca.

[2] These German quotations with the name of Mühlau are taken from the
additions to his book, which he placed at my disposal.

[3] *Vid.* Neubauer's *La Géographie du Talmud*, pp. 325, 329, 382.

of *Mesha,* one may think[1] of Helena, celebrated in Jewish
writings, queen of Adiabene, the mother of Monabaz and
Izates. But the identity of the *Mesha* of the catalogue of
nations with Μεσήνη is uncertain, and the Jewish population of
that place dates at least from the time of the Sassanides to the
period of the Babylonian exile. We therefore hold by the
Ishmaelite *Massa,* whether North Arabian or Hauranian; but
we by no means subscribe Mühlau's *non possumus non negare,
Agurum et Lemuëlem proselytos e paganis, non Israelitas fuisse.*
The religion of the tribes descended from Abraham, so far as it
had not degenerated, was not to be regarded as idolatrous. It
was the religion which exists to the present day among the great
Ishmaelite tribes of the Syrian desert as the true tradition of
their fathers under the name of *Dîn Ibrâhîm* (Abraham's religion); which, as from Wetzstein, we have noted in the *Commentary on Job* (p. 387 and elsewhere), continues along with
Mosaism among the nomadic tribes of the wilderness; which
shortly before the appearance of Christianity in the country
beyond the Jordan, produced doctrines coming into contact
with the teachings of the gospel; which at that very time,
according to historic evidences (*e.g.* Mêjâsinî's chronicles of
the *Ka'be*), was dominant even in the towns of Higâz; and in
the second century after Christ, was for the first time during
the repeated migration of the South Arabians again oppressed
by Greek idolatry, and was confined to the wilderness; which
gave the mightiest impulse to the rise of Islam, and furnished
its best component part; .and which towards the end of the
last century, in the country of Neged, pressed to a reform of
Islam, and had as a result the Wahabite doctrine. If we
except xxx. 5 f., the proverbs of Agur and Lemuel contain
nothing which may not be conceived from a non-Israelitish
standpoint on which the author of the Book of Job placed
himself. Even xxx. 5 f. is not there (cf. Job vi. 10, xxiii. 12)
without parallels. When one compares Deut. iv. 2, xiii. 1, and
2 Sam. xxii. 31 = Ps. xviii. 31 (from which ver. 5 of the
proverbs of Agur is derived, with the change of יהוה into
אֱלוֹהַּ), Agur certainly appears as one intimately acquainted with
the revealed religion of Israel, and with their literature. But

---

[1] Derenbourg's *Essai sur l'Hist. et la Géog. de la Palestine,* i. p. 224.

must we take the two Massites therefore, with Hitzig, Mühlau,
and Zöckler, as born Israelites? Since the Bible history knows
no Israelitish king outside of the Holy Land, we regard it as
more probable that King Lemuel and his countryman Agur were
Ishmaelites who had raised themselves above the religion of
Abraham, and recognised the religion of Israel as its completion.

If we now return to the words of xxx. 1a, Hitzig makes
Agur Lemuel's brother, for he vocalizes אָגוּר בִּן־יָקְהָה מַשָּׁא, i.e.
Agur the son of her whom Massa obeys. Ripa and Björck
of Sweden, and Stuart of America, adopt this view. But
supposing that יָקֵה is connected with the accusative of him who
is obeyed, בֵּן, as the representative of such an attributive clause,
as of its virtual genitive, is elsewhere without example; and
besides, it is unadvisable to explain away the proper name יָקֵה,
which speaks for itself. There are two other possibilities of
comprehending הַמַּשָּׂא, without the change, or with the change
of a single letter. Wetzstein, on xxxi. 1, has said regarding
Mühlau's translation "King of Massa:" "I would more
cautiously translate, 'King of the Massans,' since this interpretation is unobjectionable; while, on the contrary, this is not *terra
Massa*, nor *urbs Massa*. It is true that the inhabitants of
Massa were not pure nomads, after xxx. and xxxi., but probably, like the other tribes of Israel, they were half nomads,
who possessed no great land as exclusive property, and whose
chief place did not perhaps bear their name. The latter may
then have been as rare in ancient times as it is in the present
day. Neither the *Sammar*, the *Harb*, the *Muntefik*, nor other
half nomads whom I know in the southern parts of the Syrian
desert, have any place which bears their name. So also, it
appears, the people of Uz (עוּץ), which we were constrained to
think of as a dominant, firmly-settled race, since it had so great
a husbandman as Job, possessed no קִרְיַת עוּץ. Only in certain
cases, where a tribe resided for many centuries in and around
a place, does the name of this tribe appear to have remained
attached to it. Thus from גּוּף דּוּמָה, 'the low-country of the
Dumahns,' or קִרְיַת דּוּמָה, 'the city of Dumahns,' as also from
קִרְיַת תֵּימָא, 'the city of the Temans,' gradually there arose (probably not till the decline and fall of this tribe) a city of *Dumah*,
a haven of *Midian*, and the like, so that the primary meaning of

the name came to be lost." It is clear that, from the existence
of an Ishmaelite tribe מַשָּׁא, there does not necessarily follow a
similar name given to a region. The conj. מִמַּשָּׁא, for הַמַּשָּׁא
(vid. Herzog's Encycl. xiv. 702), has this against it, that although
it is good Heb., it directly leads to this conclusion (e.g. 2 Sam.
xxiii. 20, 29, cf. 1 Kings xvii. 1). Less objectionable is Bunsen's and Böttcher's הַמַּשָּׁאִי. But perhaps המשא may also have
the same signification ; far rather at least this than that which
Malbim, after הֵשׂר הַמַּשָּׁא, 1 Chron. xv. 27, introduced with the
LXX. ἄρχων τῶν ᾠδῶν: "We ought then to compare 2 Sam.
xxiii. 24, דּוֹדוֹ בֵּית לָחֶם, a connection in which, after the analogy
of such Arabic connections as kaysu 'aylana, Kais of the tribe
of 'Ailân (Ibn Coteiba, 13 and 83), or Ma'nu Ṭayyin, Ma'n of
the tribe of Tay, i.e. Ma'n belonging to this tribe, as distinguished from other men and families of this name (Schol.
Hamasæ 144. 3), בֵּית לחם is thought of as genit."[1] (Mühlau).
That בית לחם (instead of בֵּית הַלַּחְמִי) is easily changed, with
Thenius and Wellhausen, after 1 Chron. xi. 26, into מִבֵּית לחם,
and in itself it is not altogether homogeneous, because without
the article. Yet it may be supposed that instead of משׂא, on
account of the appellat. of the proper name (the lifting up,
elatio), the word המשׂא might be also employed. And since
בֻּדִיקה, along with אָגוּר, forms, as it were, one compositum, and
does not at all destroy[2] the regulating force of אָגוּר, the expression is certainly, after the Arabic usus loq., to be thus
explained: The words of Agur the son of Jakeh, of the tribe
(the country) of Massa.

The second line of this verse, as it is punctuated, is to be
rendered :

The saying of the man to Ithîel, to Ithîel and Uchal,

not Ukkal; for, since Athias and van der Hooght, the incorrect
form וְאֻכָל has become current. J. H. Michaelis has the right
form of the word וְאָכָל. Thus, with כ raphatum, it is to be
read after the Masora, for it adds to this word the remark לית

[1] In הָעָם וגו', Jer. viii. 5, יְרוּשׁ' is thought of as genit., although it may
be also nom., after the scheme of apposition instead of annexion. That it
is genit., cf. Philippi's St. Const. pp. 192-195.

[2] We say, in Arab., without any anomaly, e.g. Alîju-bnu-Muḥammadin
Tajjïn, i.e. the Ali son of Muhammed, of the tribe (from the tribe) of Tay ;
cf. Josh. iii. 11 ; Isa. xxviii. 1, lxiii. 11 ; and Deut. iii. 13.

וחסר, and counts it among the forty-eight words sometimes written defectively without‍ ו (vid. this list in the Masora finalis, 27b, Col. 4); and since it only remarks the absence of the letter lengthening the word where no dagesh follows the vocal, it thus supposes that the כ has no dagesh, as it is also found in Codd. (also Jaman.) written with the Raphe. לְאִיתִיאֵל is doubly accentuated; the Tarcha represents the Metheg, after the rule Thorath Emeth, p. 11. The ל after נְאֻם is, in the sense of the punctuation, the same dat. as in לַאדֹנִי, Ps. cx. 1, and has an apparent right in him who asks כִּי חָדָע in the 4th verse. Ithîel and Uchal must be, after an old opinion, sons, or disciples, or contemporaries, of Agur. Thus, e.g., Gesenius, in his Lex. under אִיתִיאֵל, where as yet his reference to Neh. xi. 7 is wanting. אִיתִיאֵל is rendered by Jefet and other Karaites, "there is a God" = אִיתִי אֵל; but it is perhaps equivalent to אִתִּי אֵל, "God is with me;" as for אִתִּי, the form אִיתִי is also found. אֻכָל (אֲכָל) nowhere occurs as a proper name; but in the region of proper names, everything, or almost everything, is possible.[1] Ewald sees in 1b–14 a dialogue: in vers. 2–4 the הַגֶּבֶר, i.e. as the word appears to him, the rich, haughty mocker, who has worn out his life, speaks; and in 5–14 the "Mitmirgott" [= God with me], or, more fully, "Mitmirgott-sobinichstark" [= God with me, so am I strong], i.e. the pious, humble man answers. "The whole," he remarks, "is nothing but poetical; and it is poetical also that this discourse of mockery is called an elevated strain." But (1) גֶּבֶר is a harmless word; and in נְאֻם הַגֶּבֶר, Num. xxiv. 3, 15, 2 Sam. xxiii. 1, it is a solemn, earnest one; (2) a proper name, consisting of two clauses connected by Vav, no matter whether it be an actual or a symbolical name, is not capable of being authenticated; Ewald, § 274b, recognises in וּדַלְתִּי וגו', 1 Chron. xxv. 4, the naming, not of one son of Heman, but of two; and (3) it would be a very forced, inferior poetry if the poet placed one half of the name in one line, and then, as if constrained to take a new breath, gave the other half of it in a second line. But, on the other hand, that אִיתִיאֵל and אכל are the names of two different persons, to whom the address of the man is directed, is attested by the, in this

---

[1] Vid. Wetzstein's Inschriften aus den Trachonen und dem Haurangebirge (1864), p. 336 f.

case aimless, *anadiplosis*, the here unpoetical parallelism with reservation. The repetition, as Fleischer remarks, of the name Ithîel, which may rank with Uchal, as the son or disciple of Agur, has probably its reason only in this, that one placed a second more extended phrase simply along with the shorter. The case is different; but Fleischer's supposition, that the poet himself cannot have thus written, is correct. We must not strike out either of the two לְאִיתִיאֵל; but the supposed proper names must be changed as to their vocalization into a declaratory clause. A principal argument lies in ver. 2, beginning with כִּי: this כִּי supposes a clause which it established; for, with right, Mühlau maintains that כִּי, in the affirmative sense, which, by means of *aposiopesis*, proceeds from the confirmative, may open the conclusion and enter as confirmatory into the middle of the discourse (*e.g.* Isa. xxxii. 13), but cannot stand abruptly at the commencement of a discourse (cf. under Isa. xv. 1 and vii. 9). But if we now ask how it is to be vocalized, there comes at the same time into the sphere of investigation the striking phrase נְאֻם הַגֶּבֶר. This phrase all the Greek interpreters attest by their rendering, τάδε λέγει ὁ ἀνήρ (*Venet.* φησὶν ἀνήρ); besides, this is to be brought forward from the wilderness of the old attempts at a translation, that the feeling of the translators strives against the recognition in וְאֻכָל of a second personal name: the Peshito omits it; the Targ. translates it, after the Midrash, by וְאוּכַל (I may do it); as Theodotion, καὶ δυνήσομαι, which is probably also meant by the καὶ συνήσομαι (from συνιέναι, to be acquainted with) of the *Venet.*; the LXX. with καὶ παύομαι; and Aquila, καὶ τέλεσον (both from the verb כלה). As an objection to נְאֻם הַגֶּבֶר is this, that it is so bald without being followed, as at Num. xxiv. 3, 15, 2 Sam. xxiii. 1, with the attributive description of the man. Luther was determined thereby to translate: discourse of the man Leithiel . . . And why could not לְאִיתִיאֵל be a proper-name connection like שְׁאַלְתִּיאֵל (שְׁלַתִּיאֵל)? Interpreted in the sense of "I am troubled concerning God," it might be a symbolical name of the φιλόσοφος, as of one who strives after the knowledge of divine things with all his strength. But (1) לָאָה, with the accus. obj., is not established, and one is rather inclined to think of a name such as פְּלִיתִיאֵל, after Ps. lxxxiv. 3; (2) moreover, לְאִיתִיאֵל cannot be at one

time a personal name, and at another time a declarative sentence
—one must both times transform it into לְאִיתִי אֵל; but אֵל has to be
taken as a vocative, not as accus., as is done by J. D. Michaelis,
Hitzig, Bunsen, Zöckler, and others, thus: I have wearied
myself, O God! . . . The nakedness of הגבר is accordingly not
covered by the first *Leithiel.* Mühlau, in his work, seeks to introduce המשא changed into ממשא: " The man from Massa," and
prefers to interpret הגבר generically:[1] " proverb (confession)
of the man (*i.e.* the man must confess): I have wearied myself, O God! . . ." Nothing else in reality remains. The
article may also be retrospective: the man just now named,
whose " words" are announced, viz. Agur. But why was not
the expression נאם אגור then used? Because it is not poetical
to say: " the (previously named) man." On the other hand,
what follows applies so that one may understand, under הגבר,
any man you choose. There are certainly among men more
than too many who inquire not after God (Ps. xiv. 2 f.). But
there are also not wanting those who feel sorrowfully the
distance between them and God. Agur introduces such a man
as speaking, for he generalizes his own experience. Ps. xxxvi.
2 (*vid.* under this passsge) shows that a proper name does not
necessarily follow נאם. With נאם הגבר Agur then introduces
what the man has to confess—viz. a man earnestly devoted to
God; for with נאם the ideas of that which comes from the
heart and the solemnly earnest are connected. If Agur so far
generalizes his own experience, the passionate *anadiplosis* does
not disturb this. After long contemplation of the man, he
must finally confess: I have troubled myself, O God! I have
troubled myself, O God! . . . That the trouble was directed
toward God is perhaps denoted by the alliteration of לְאִיתִי with
אֵל. But what now, further? ואבל is read as וָאֵכַל, וָאֵכֶל,
וְאֵכֶל, וָאֵכֶל, and it has also been read as וָאֵכֶל. The reading
וָאֵכֶל no one advocates; this that follows says the direct contrary, *et potui* (*pollui*). Geiger (*Urschrift*, p. 61) supports the
reading וָאֵכֶל, for he renders it interrogatively: " I wearied my-

---

[1] Thus, viz., that הגבר denotes, not the man as he ought to be, but the
man as he usually is (the article, as the Arabic grammarians say, " not
for the exhaustion of the characteristic marks of the genus," but for the
expression of " the quality *mâhîje* of the genus ").

self in vain about God, I wearied myself in vain about God;
why should I be able to do it?" But since one may twist any
affirmative clause in this way, and from a *yes* make a *no*, one
should only, in cases of extreme necessity, consent to such a question in the absence of an interrogative word. Böttcher's אַל לְאִיתִי,
I have wearied myself out in vain, is not Hebrew. But at any
rate the expression might be אַל־אֻכָל, if only the *Vav* did not
stand between the words! If one might transpose the letters,
then we might gain וְלֹא אֻכָל, according to which the LXX.
translates: οὐ δυνήσομαι. At all events, this despairing as to
the consequence of further trouble, " I shall be able to do
nothing (shall bring it to nothing)," would be better than וָאֻכָל
(and I shall withdraw—become faint), for which, besides, וָאֶכְלֶה
should be used (cf. xxii. 8 with Job xxxiii. 21). One expects,
after לְאִיתִי, the expression of that which is the consequence of
earnest and long-continued endeavour. Accordingly Hitzig
reads וָאֵכַל, and I have become dull—suitable to the sense, but
unsatisfactory on this account, because כָּלַל, in the sense of the
Arab. *kall, hebescere,* is foreign to the Heb. *usus loq.* Thus ואכל
will be a *fut. consec.* of בלה. J. D. Michaelis, and finally
Böttcher, read it as *fut. consec. Piel* וָאֲכַל or וָאֶכַל (*vid.* regarding
this form in pause under xxv. 9), " and I have made an end ;"
but it is not appropriate to the inquirer here complaining,
when dissatisfaction with his results had determined him to
abandon his research, and let himself be no more troubled.
We therefore prefer to read with Dahler, and, finally, with
Mühlau and Zöckler, וָאֶכַל, and I have withdrawn. The form
understood by Hitzig as a pausal form is, in the unchangeableness of its vocals, as accordant with rule as those of יָחַד, xxvii.
17, which lengthen the ⸗ of their first syllables in pause. And
if Hitzig objects that too much is said, for one of such meditation
does not depart, we answer, that if the inquiry of the man who
speaks here has completed itself by the longing of his spirit and
his soul (Ps. lxxxiv. 3, cxliii. 7), he might also say of himself,
in person, כָּלִיתִי or וָאֶכַל. An inquiry proceeding not merely
from intellectual, but, before all, from practical necessity, is
meant—the doubled לְאִיתִי means that he applied thereto the
whole strength of his inner and his outer man; and ואכל, that
he nevertheless did not reach his end, but wearied himself in

vain.   By this explanation which we give to 1*a*, no change of
its accents is required; but 1*b* has to be written :

נְאֻם הַגֶּבֶר לְאִיתִי אֵל

לְאִיתִי אֵל וָאֻכָל: ¹

Vers. 2, 3. The כִּי now following confirms the fruitlessness
of the long zealous search :

> For I am without reason for a man,
> And a man's understanding I have not.
> 3 And I have not learned wisdom,
> That I may possess the knowledge of the All-Holy.

He who cannot come to any fixed state of consecration, inasmuch as he is always driven more and more back from the
goal he aims at, thereby brings guilt upon himself as a sinner
so great, that every other man stands above him, and he is
deep under them all.   So here Agur finds the reason why in
divine things he has failed to attain unto satisfying intelligence,
not in the ignorance and inability common to all men—he
appears to himself as not a man at all, but as an irrational
beast, and he misses in himself the understanding which a
man properly might have and ought to have.   The מִן of
מֵאִישׁ is not the partitive, like Isa. xliv. 11, not the usual comparative : than any one (Böttcher), which ought to be expressed
by מִכָּל־אִישׁ, but it is the negative, as Isa. lii. 14 ; Fleischer :
rudior ego sum quam ut homo appeller, or : *brutus ego, hominis
non similis.*   Regarding בַּעַר, *vid.* under xii. 1.²   Ver. 3 now
says that he went into no school of wisdom, and for that reason
in his wrestling after knowledge could attain to nothing, because the necessary conditions to this were wanting to him.
But then the question arises : Why this complaint ?   He must
first go to school in order to obtain, according to the word
" To him who hath is given," that for which he strove.
Thus לָמַדְתִּי refers to learning in the midst of wrestling ; but

¹ The *Munach* is the transformation of *Mugrash*, and this sequence of
accents—*Tarcha, Munach, Silluk*—remains the same, whether we regard
אֵל as the accusative or as the vocative.

² According to the Arab. בָּעַיר is not a beast as grazing, but as dropping
stercus (*ba'r*, camel's or sheep's droppings) ; to the R. בר, Mühlau rightly
gives the meanings of separating, whence are derived the meanings of
grazing as well as of removing (cleansing) (cf. Pers. *thak karadn*, to make
clean = to make clean house, *tabula rasa*).

למד, spiritually understood, signifies the acquiring of a *kennens*
[knowledge] or *können* [knowledge = ability] : he has not
brought it out from the deep point of his condition of knowledge to make wisdom his own, so that he cannot adjudge to
himself knowledge of the all-holy God (for this knowledge is
the kernel and the star of true wisdom). If we read 3b לֹא אֵדָע,
this would be synchronistic, *nesciebam*, with למדתי standing on
the same line. On the contrary, the positive אדע subordinates
itself to ולא־למדתי, as the Arab. *fáa' lama*, in the sense of (*ita*)
ut scirem scientiam Sanctissimi, thus of a conclusion, like Lam.
i. 19, a clause expressive of the intention, Ewald, § 347a.
קְדֹשִׁים is, as at ix. 10, the name of God in a superlative sense,
like the Arab. *el-kuddûs*.

> Ver. 4 Who hath ascended to the heavens and descended?
> Who hath grasped the wind in his fists?
> Who hath bound up the waters in a garment?
> Who hath set right all the ends of the earth?
> What is his name, and what his son's name, if thou knowest?

The first question here, מִי וגו', is limited by *Pazer*; עלה־שמים
has *Metheg* in the third syllable before the tone. The second
question is at least shut off by *Pazer*, but, contrary to the rule,
that *Pazer* does not repeat itself in a verse; Cod. Erfurt. 2,
and several older editions, have for בחפניו more correctly בחפניו
with *Rebia*. So much for the interpunction. חָפְנַיִם are properly not the two fists, for the fist—that is, the hand gathered
into a ball, *pugnus*—is called אֶגְרֹף; while, on the contrary,
הֹפֶן (in all the three dialects) denotes the palm of the hand, *vola*
(*vid*. Lev. xvi. 12); yet here the hands are represented after
they have seized the thing as shut, and thus certainly as fists.
The dual points to the dualism of the streams of air produced
by the disturbance of the equilibrium; he who rules this movement has, as it were, the north or east wind in one fist, and the
south or west wind in the other, to let it forth according to his
pleasure from this prison (Isa. xxiv. 22). The third question
is explained by Job xxvi. 8; the שִׂמְלָה (from שמל, *comprehendere*) is a figure of the clouds which contain the upper waters,
as Job xxxviii. 37, the bottles of heaven. " All the ends of
the earth " are as at five other places, *e.g.* Ps. xxii. 28, the most
distant, most remote parts of the earth; the setting up of all

these most remote boundaries (*margines*) of the earth is equivalent to the making fast and forming the limits to which the
earth extends (Ps. lxxiv. 17), the determining of the compass of
the earth and the form of its figures. כִּי תֵדָע is in symphony
with Job xxxviii. 5, cf. 18. The question is here formed as it
is there, when Jahve brings home to the consciousness of Job
human weakness and ignorance. But there are here two possible significations of the fourfold question. Either it aims at
the answer: No man, but a Being highly exalted above all
creatures, so that the question מַה־שְּׁמוֹ [what his name?] refers
to the name of this Being. Or the question is primarily meant
of men: What man has the ability?—if there is one, then name
him! In both cases מִי עָלָה is not meant, after xxiv. 28, in the
modal sense, *quis ascenderit*, but as the following וַיֵּרַד requires, in
the nearest indicative sense, *quis ascendit*. But the choice
between these two possible interpretations is very difficult. The
first question is historical: Who has gone to heaven and (as a
consequence, then) come down from it again? It lies nearest
thus to interpret it according to the *consecutio temporum*. By
this interpretation, and this representation of the going up
before the descending again, the interrogator does not appear
to think of God, but in contrast to himself, to whom the divine
is transcendent, of some other man of whom the contrary is
true. Is there at all, he asks, a man who can comprehend and
penetrate by his power and his knowledge the heavens and
the earth, the air and the water, *i.e.* the nature and the inner
condition of the visible and invisible world, the quantity and
extent of the elements, and the like? Name to me this man, if
thou knowest one, by his name, and designate him to me exactly
by his family—I would turn to him to learn from him what I
have hitherto striven in vain to find. But there is no such an
one. Thus: as I feel myself limited in my knowledge, so there
is not at all any man who can claim limitless *können* and *kennen*
[ability and knowledge]. Thus casually Aben Ezra explains,
and also Rashi, Arama, and others, but without holding fast to
this in its purity; for in the interpretation of the question, "Who
hath ascended?" the reference to Moses is mixed up with it,
after the Midrash and Sohar (Parasha, ויקהל, to Ex. xxxv. 1),

to pass by other obscurities and difficulties introduced. Among the moderns, this explanation, according to which all aims at the answer, " there is no man to whom this appertains," has no exponent worth naming. And, indeed, as favourable as is the *quis ascendit in cœlos ac rursus descendit*, so unfavourable is the *quis constituit omnes terminos terræ*, for this question appears not as implying that it asks after the man who has accomplished this; but the thought, according to all appearance, underlies it, that such an one must be a being without an equal, after whose name inquiry is made. One will then have to judge עלה and וירד after Gen. xxviii. 12; the ascending and descending are compared to our German "*auf und nieder*" [up and down], for which we do not use the phrase "*nieder und auf*," and is the expression of free, expanded, unrestrained presence in both regions; perhaps, since וירד is historical, as Ps. xviii. 10, the speaker has the traditional origin of the creation in mind, according to which the earth arose into being earlier than the starry heavens above.

Thus the four questions refer (as *e.g.* also Isa. xl. 12) to Him who has done and who does all that, to Him who is not Himself to be comprehended as His works are, and as He shows Himself in the greatness and wonderfulness of these, must be exalted above them all, and mysterious. If the inhabitant of the earth looks up to the blue heavens streaming in the golden sunlight, or sown with the stars of night; if he considers the interchange of the seasons, and feels the sudden rising of the wind; if he sees the upper waters clothed in fleecy clouds, and yet held fast within them floating over him; if he lets his eye sweep the horizon all around him to the ends of the earth, built up upon nothing in the open world-space (Job xxvi. 7): the conclusion comes to him that he has before him in the whole the work of an everywhere present Being, of an all-wise omnipotent Worker—it is the Being whom he has just named as אֵל, the absolute Power, and as the קְדֹשִׁים, exalted above all created beings, with their troubles and limitations; but this knowledge gained *viâ causalitatis, viâ eminentiæ,* and *viâ negationis*, does not satisfy yet his spirit, and does not bring him so near to this Being as is to him a personal necessity, so that if he can in some measure answer the fourfold מִי, yet there always

presses upon him the question מה־שמו, what is his name, *i.e.* the
name which dissolves the secret of this Being above all beings,
and unfolds the mystery of the wonder above all wonders. That
this Being must be a person the fourfold מי presupposes; but
the question, " What is his name? " expresses the longing to
know the name of this supernatural personality, not any kind of
name which is given to him by men, but the name which covers
him, which is the appropriate personal immediate expression
of his being. The further question, " And what the name of
his son?" denotes, according to Hitzig, that the inquirer strives
after an adequate knowledge, such as one may have of a human
being. But he would not have ventured this question if he did
not suppose that God was not a *monas* [unity] who was without
manifoldness in Himself. The LXX. translates: ἢ τί ὄνομα
τοῖς τέκνοις αὐτοῦ (בָּנָו), perhaps not without the influence of the
old synagogue reference testified to in the Midrash and Sohar
of בנו to Israel, God's first-born ; but this interpretation is
opposed to the spirit of this חידה (intricate speech, enigma).
Also in general the interrogator cannot seek to know what man
stands in this relation of a son to the Creator of all things, for
that would be an ethical question which does not accord with this
metaphysical one. Geier has combined this ומה־שם־בנו with viii. ;
and that the interrogator, if he meant the חכמה, ought to have
used the phrase ומה־שם־בתו, says nothing against this, for also
in אמון, viii. 30, whether it means foster-child or *artifex*, workmaster, the feminine determination disappears. Not Ewald
alone finds here the idea of the Logos, as the first-born Son of
God, revealing itself, on which at a later time the Palestinian
doctrine of מימרא דיהוה imprinted itself in Alexandria;[1] but
also J. D. Michaelis felt himself constrained to recognise here
the N. T. doctrine of the Son of God announcing itself from afar.
And why might not this be possible? The Rig-Veda contains
two similar questions, x. 81, 4 : " Which was the primeval forest,
or what the tree from which one framed the heavens and the
earth ? Surely, ye wise men, ye ought in your souls to make
inquiry whereon he stood when he raised the wind!" And i.
164, 4 : " Who has seen the first-born? Where was the life,
the blood, the soul of the world ? Who came thither to ask

[1] *Vid. Apologetik* (1869), p. 432 ff.

this from any one who knew it?"[1] Jewish interpreters also interpret בנו of the *causa media* of the creation of the world. Arama, in his work עקדת יצחק, *sect.* xvi., suggests that by בנו we are to understand the primordial element, as the Sankhya-philosophy understands by the first-born there in the Rig, the *Prakriti, i.e.* the primeval material. R. Levi b. Gerson (Ralbag) comes nearer to the truth when he explains בנו as meaning the cause caused by the supreme cause, in other words: the *principium principiatum* of the creation of the world. We say : the inquirer meant the demiurgic might which went forth from God, and which waited on the Son of God as a servant in the creation of the world; the same might which in chap. viii. is called Wisdom, and is described as God's beloved Son. But with the name after which inquiry is made, the relation is as with the "more excellent name than the angels," Heb. i. 4.[2] It is manifestly not the name בן, since the inquiry is made after the name of the בן ; but the same is the case also with the name חכמה, or, since this does not harmonize, according to its grammatical gender, with the form of the question, the name דבר (מֵימַר) ; but it is the name which belongs to the first and only-begotten Son of God, not merely according to creative analogies, but according to His true being. The inquirer would know God, the creator of the world, and His Son, the mediator in the creation of the world, according to their natures. If thou knowest, says he, turning himself to man, his equal, what the essential names of both are, tell them to me! But who can name them! The nature of the Godhead is hidden, as from the inquirer, so from every one else. On this side of eternity it is beyond the reach of human knowledge.

The solemn confession introduced by נאם is now closed.

---

[1] Cited by Lyra in *Beweis des Glaubens Jahrg.* 1869, p. 230. The second of these passages is thus translated by Wilson (*Rig-Veda-Sanhitá,* London, 1854, vol. ii. p. 127) : "Who has seen the primeval (being) at the time of his being born? What is that endowed with substance which the unsubstantial sustains? From earth are the breath and blood, but where is the soul? Who may repair to the sage to ask this?"

[2] The *Comm.* there remarks : It is the heavenly whole name of the highly exalted One, the שם המפורש, *nomen explicitum,* which here on this side has entered into no human heart, and can be uttered by no human tongue, the ὄνομα ὃ οὐδεὶς οἶδεν εἰ μὴ ὁ αὐτός, Rev. xix. 12.

Ewald sees herein the discourse of a sceptical mocker at religion; and Elster, the discourse of a meditating doubter; in ver. 5, and on, the answer ought then to follow, which is given to one thus speaking: his withdrawal from the standpoint of faith in the revelation of God, and the challenge to subordinate his own speculative thinking to the authority of the word of God. But this interpretation of the statement depends on the symbolical rendering of the supposed personal names איתיאל and אכל, and, besides, the dialogue is indicated by nothing; the beginning of the answer ought to have been marked, like the beginning of that to which it is a reply. The confession, 1b–4, is not that of a man who does not find himself in the right condition, but such as one who is thirsting after God must renounce: the thought of a man does not penetrate to the essence of God (Job xi. 7–9); even the ways of God remain inscrutable to man (Sir. xviii. 3; Rom. xi. 33); the Godhead remains, for our thought, in immeasurable height and depth; and though a relative knowledge of God is possible, yet the dogmatic thesis, *Deum quidem cognoscimus, sed non comprehendimus*, i.e. *non perfecte cognoscimus quia est infinitus*,[1] even over against the positive revelation, remains unchanged. Thus nothing is wanting to make 1–4 a complete whole; and what follows does not belong to that section as an organic part of it.

> Ver. 5 Every word of *Eloah* is pure;
> A shield is He for those who hide themselves in Him.
> 6 Add thou not to His words,
> Lest He convict thee and thou becomest a liar.

Although the tetrastich is an independent proverb, yet it is connected to the foregoing *Neûm* [utterance, ver. 1]. The more limited a man is in his knowledge of God,—viz. in that which presents itself to him *lumine naturæ*,—so much the more thankful must he be that God has revealed Himself in history, and so much the more firmly has he to hold fast by the pure word of the divine revelation. In the dependent relation of ver. 5 to Ps. xviii. 31 (2 Sam. xxii. 31), and of ver. 6 to Deut. iv. 2, there is no doubt the self-testimony of God given to Israel, and recorded in the book of the Tôra, is here meant. כָּל־אִמְרַת

---

[1] *Vid.* Luthardt's *Kompendium der Dogmatik*, § 27.

is to be judged after πᾶσα γραφή, 2 Tim. iii. 16, not : every
declaration of God, wherever promulgated, but : every declaration within the revelation lying before us.   The primary
passage [Ps. xviii. 31] has not כל here, but, instead of it,
לְכֹל הַחֹסִים, and instead of אִמְרַת אֱלוֹהַּ it has אמ' יהוה ; his change
of the name of Jahve is also not favourable to the opinion that
ver. 5 f. is a part of the Nᵉûm, viz. that it is the answer thereto.
The proverb in this contains traces of the Book of Job, with
which in many respects that Nᵉûm harmonizes; in the Book
of Job, אֱלוֹהַּ (with שַׁדַּי) is the prevailing name of God; whereas
in the Book of Proverbs it occurs only in the passage before
us.   Mühlau, p. 41, notes it as an Arabism.   צָרַף (Arab. ṣaraf,
to turn, to change) is the usual word for the changing process
of smelting ; צָרוּף signifies solid, pure, i.e. purified by separating:
God's word is, without exception, like pure, massive gold.   Regarding חָסָה, to hide oneself, vid. under Ps. ii. 12 : God is a
shield for those who make Him, as revealed in His word, their
refuge.   The part. חֹסֶה occurs, according to the Masora, three
times written defectively,—xiv. 32 ; 2 Sam. xxii. 31 ; Neh. i.
7 ; in the passage before us it is to be written לַחֹסִים ; the proverbs of Agur and Lemuel have frequently the *plena scriptio*
of the *part. act. Kal*, as well as of the *fut. Kal*, common to the
Book of Job (vid. Mühlau, p. 65).

In 6a, after Aben Ezra's *Moznajim* 2b (11b of Heidenheim's edition), and *Zachoth* 53a (cf. Lipmann's ed.), and
other witnesses (vid. Norzi), t sp (the פ with *dagesh*) is to be
written,—the Cod. *Jaman.* and others *defect.* without ו,—not
tôsf ; for, since תּוֹסֵף (Ex. x. 28) is yet further abbreviated in
this way, it necessarily loses[1] the aspiration of the *tenuis*, as in יֵלְדְתְּ
(= יֵלְדְתְּ).   The words of God are the announcements of His holy
will, measured by His wisdom ; they are then to be accepted as
they are, and to be recognised and obeyed.   He who adds anything to them, either by an overstraining of them or by repress-
ing them, will not escape the righteous judgment of God : God
will convict him of falsifying His word (הוֹכִיחַ, Ps. l. 21 ; only

---

[1] That both *Shevas* in *tôsp* are quiesc., vid. Kimchi, *Michlol* 155 a b, who
is finally decided as to this.   That the word should be read *tôspᵉal* is the
opinion of Chajûg in הנוח 'ס (regarding the quiesc. letters), p. 6 of the
Ed. by Dukes-Ewald.

here with ב of the obj.), and expose him as a liar—viz. by the dispensations which unmask the falsifier as such, and make manifest the falsehood of his doctrines as dangerous to souls and destructive to society. An example of this is found in the kingdom of Israel, in the destruction of which the curse of the human institution of its state religion, set up by Jeroboam, had no little share. Also the Jewish traditional law, although in itself necessary for the carrying over of the law into the *praxis* of private and public life, falls under the Deuteron. prohibition,—which the poet here repeats,—so far as it claimed for itself the same divine authority as that of the written law, and so far as it hindered obedience to the law—by the straining-at-a-gnat policy—and was hostile to piety. Or, to adduce an example of an addition more dogmatic than legal, what a fearful impulse was given to fleshly security by that overstraining of the promises in Gen. xvii., which were connected with circumcision by the tradition, " the circumcised come not into hell," or by the overstraining of the prerogative attributed by Paul, Rom. ix. 4 f., to his people according to the Scriptures, in the principle, " All Israelites have a part in the future world!" Regarding the accentuation of the *perf. consec.* after פֶּן, *vid.* at Ps. xxviii. 1. The penultima accent is always *in pausa* (cf. vers. 9 and 10).

In what now follows, the key-note struck in ver. 1 is continued. There follows a prayer to be kept in the truth, and to be preserved in the middle state, between poverty and riches. It is a Mashal-ode, *vid.* vol. i. p. 12. By the first prayer, " vanity and lies keep far from me," it is connected with the warning of ver. 6.

> Ver. 7 Two things I entreat from Thee,
>   Refuse them not to me before I die.
>   8 Vanity and lies keep far away from me
>   Poverty and riches give me not :
>   Cause me to eat the bread which is allotted to me,
>   9 Lest in satiety I deny,
>   And say : Who is Jahve?
>   And lest, in becoming poor, I steal,
>   And profane the name of my God.

We begin with the settlement and explanation of the traditional punctuation. A monosyllable like שָׁוְא receives, if *Legarmeh,*

always *Mehuppach Legarmeh*, while, on the contrary, the poly-
syllable אֱשָׂבַּע has *Asla Legarmeh*. אַל־תִּתֶּן־לִי, with double
Makkeph and with *Gaja* in the third syllable before the tone
(after the *Metheg-Setzung*, § 28), is Ben-Asher's; whereas Ben-
Naphtali prefers the punctuation לִ אַל־תִּתֶּן (*vid.* Baer's *Genesis*,
p. 79, note 3).   Also פֶּן־אֶשְׂבַּע has (cf. פֶּן־יִשְׁתֶּה, xxxi. 5) *Makkeph*,
and on the antepenultima *Gaja* (*vid. Thorath Emeth*, p. 32).

The *perf. consec.* וְכִחַשְׁתִּי has on the *ult.* the disjunctive *Zinnor*
(*Sarka*), which always stands over the final letter; but that the
ult. is also to be accented, is shown by the counter-tone *Metheg*,
which is to be given to the first syllable.   Also וְאָמַרְתִּי has in
correct Codd., *e.g.* Cod. 1294, the correct ultima toning of a
perf. consec.; Kimchi in the *Michlol* 6*b*, as well as Aben Ezra
in both of his *Grammars*, quotes only וְגָנַבְתִּי וְתָפַשְׂתִּי as toned on
the *penult*.   That וְגָנַבְתִּי cannot be otherwise toned on account
of the pausal accent, has been already remarked under 6*b*; the
word, besides, belongs to the פתחין בא״סף, *i.e.* to those which preserve their *Pathach* unlengthened by one of the greater disjunctives; the *Athnach* has certainly in the three so-called metrical
books only the disjunctive form of the *Zakeph* of the prose
books.   So much as to the form of the text.

As to its artistic form, this prayer presents itself to us as the
first of the numerical proverbs, under the "Words" of Agur, who
delighted in this form of proverb.   The numerical proverb is
a brief discourse, having a didactic end complete in itself, which
by means of numerals gives prominence to that which it seeks
to bring forward.   There are two kinds of these.   The more
simple form places in the first place only one numeral, which is
the sum of that which is to be brought forth separately: the
numerical proverb of one cipher; to this class belong, keeping
out of view the above prayer, which if it did not commence a
series of numerical proverbs does not deserve this technical name
on account of the low ciphers: vers. 24–28, with the cipher 4;
Sir. xxv. 1 and 2, with the cipher 3.   Similar to the above
prayer are Job xiii. 20 f., Isa. li. 19; but these are not numerical proverbs, for they are not proverbs.   The more artistic
kind of numerical proverb has two ciphers: the two-ciphered
numerical proverb we call the sharpened (pointed) proverb.

Of such two-ciphered numerical proverbs the "words" of
Agur contain four, and the whole Book of Proverbs, reckoning vi. 16–19, five—this ascending numerical character belongs
to the popular saying, 2 Kings ix. 32, Job xxxiii. 29, Isa.
xvi. 6, and is found bearing the stamp of the artistic distich
outside of the Book of Proverbs, Ps. lxii. 12, Job xxxiii. 14,
xl. 5; Job v. 19, and particularly Amos i. 3–ii. 6. According
to this scheme, the introduction of Agur's prayer should be :

אַחַת שָׁאַלְתִּי מֵאִתָּךְ

וּשְׁתַּיִם אַל־תִּמְנַע מִמֶּנִּי בְּטֶרֶם אָמוּת

and it could take this form, for the prayer expresses two requests, but dwells exclusively on the second. A twofold
request he presents to God, these two things he wishes to be
assured of on this side of death ; for of these he stands in need,
so as to be able when he dies to look back on the life he has
spent, without the reproaches of an accusing conscience. The
first thing he asks is that God would keep far from him vanity
and lying words. שָׁוְא (= שָׁוְא, from שׁוֹא = שָׁאָה, to be waste, after
the form מָוֶת) is either that which is confused, worthless, untrue,
which comes to us from without (e.g. Job xxxi. 5), or dissolute-
ness, hollowness, untruthfulness of disposition (e.g. Ps. xxvi. 4) ;
it is not to be decided whether the suppliant is influenced by
the conception thus from within or from without, since דְּבַר־כָּזָב
[a word of falsehood] may be said by himself as well as to him,
a falsehood can intrude itself upon him. It is almost more
probable that by שָׁוְא he thought of the misleading power of
God-estranged, idolatrous thought and action; and by דבר־כזב,
of lying words, with which he might be brought into sympathy,
and by which he might ruin himself and others. The second
petition is that God would give him neither poverty (רֵאשׁ, vid.
x. 4) nor riches, but grant him for his sustenance only the
bread of the portion destined for him. The *Hiph.* הַטְרִיף (from
טָרַף, to grind, viz. the bread with the teeth) means to give[1]
anything, as טֶרֶף, with which, xxxi. 15, נָתַן חֹק is parallel : to
present a fixed piece, a definite portion of sustenance. חֹק,
Gen. xlvii. 22, the portion assigned as nourishment; cf. Job

---

[1] The *Venet.* translates, according to Villoison, θέρψον με ; but the MS.
has, according to Gebhardt, θρέψον.

xxiii. 14 חֻקִּי, the decree determined regarding me. Accordingly, לֶחֶם חֻקִּי does not mean the bread appropriately measured out for me (like ἄρτος ἐπιούσιος, that which is required for οὐσία, subsistence), but the bread appropriate for me, determined for me according to the divine plan. Fleischer compares (Arab.) *ratab* and *marsaum*, which both in a similar way designate a fixed sustentation portion. And why does he wish to be neither poor nor rich? Because in both extremes lie moral dangers: in riches, the temptation to deny God (which כִּחֵשׁ בְּה' signifies, in the later Heb. כָּפַר בְּעִקָּר, to deny the fundamental truth; cf. (Arab.) *kafar*, unbelieving), whom one flowing in superabundance forgets, and of whom one in his self-indulgence desires to know nothing (Job xxi. 14–16, xxii. 16 f.); in poverty, the temptation is to steal and to blaspheme the name of God, viz. by murmuring and disputing, or even by words of blasphemy; for one who is in despair directs the outbreaks of his anger against God (Isa. viii. 21), and curses Him as the cause of His misfortune (Rev. xvi. 11, 21). The question of godless haughtiness, מִי יהוה, the LXX. improperly change into מִי יְרָאֶה, τίς με ὁρᾷ. Regarding נוֹרַשׁ, to grow poor, or rather, since only the *fut. Niph.* occurs in this sense, regarding יִוָּרֵשׁ, *vid.* at xx. 13.

That the author here, by blaspheming (grasping at) the name of God, especially thinks on that which the *Tôra* calls " cursing (קִלֵּל) God," and particularly " blaspheming the name of the Lord," Lev. xxiv. 15, 16, is to be concluded from the two following proverbs, which begin with the catchword קלל:

Ver. 10 Calumniate not a servant with his master,
Lest he curse thee, and thou must atone for it.

Incorrectly Ewald: entice not a servant to slander against his master; and Hitzig: "Make not a servant tattle regarding his master." It is true that the *Poel* לוֹשֵׁן (to pierce with the tongue, *linguâ petere*) occurs twice in the sense of to calumniate; but that הִלְשִׁין means nothing else, is attested by the post.-bibl. Hebrew; the proverb regarding schismatics (בִּרְכַּת הַמִּינִים) in the Jewish *Schemone-Esre* (prayer of the eighteen benedictions) began with וְלַמַּלְשִׁינִים, "and to the calumniators" (*delatoribus*). Also in the Arab. *âlsana* signifies *pertulit verba alicujus ad alterum*, to make a babbler, *rapporteur* (Fleischer). That the word also here is not to be otherwise interpreted, is to be concluded from אֶל with the causative rendering. Rightly Symmachus, μὴ διαβάλῃς; Theodotion, μὴ καταλαλήσῃς; and according to the sense also, Jerome, *ne accuses;* the *Venet.* μὴ καταμηνύσῃς (give not him) ; on the contrary, Luther, *verrate nicht* [betray not], renders הלשׁין with the LXX., Syr. in the sense of the Aram. אַשׁלֶם and the Arab. *âslam* (*tradere, prodere*). One should not secretly accuse (Ps. ci. 5) a servant with his master, and in that lies the character of slander (לְשׁוֹן הָרָע) when one puts suspicion upon him, or exaggerates the actual facts, and generally makes the person suspected—one thereby makes a man, whose lot in itself is not a happy one, at length and perhaps for ever unhappy, and thereby he brings a curse on himself. But it is no matter of indifference to be the object of the curse of a man whom one has unrighteously and unjustly overwhelmed in misery : such a curse is not without its influence, for it does not fruitlessly invoke the righteous retribution of God, and thus one has sorrowfully to atone for the wanton sins of the tongue (*ve-aschâmta,* for *ve-aschamtá* as it is would be without pause).

There now follows a *Priamel,*[1] the first line of which is, by יקלל, connected with the יקלל of the preceding distich :

> Ver. 11 A generation that curseth their father,
>   And doth not bless their mother ;
>   12 A generation pure in their own eyes,
>   And yet not washed from their filthiness;
>   13 A generation—how haughty their eyes,
>   And their eyelids lift themselves up ;
>   14 A generation whose teeth are swords and their jaw teeth
>   knives
>   To devour the poor from the earth and the needy from
>   the midst of men.

Ewald translates : O generation ! but that would have required the word, 13a, הֲדוֹר (Jer. ii. 31), and one would have expected

---

[1] [Cf. vol. i. p. 13. The name (from *præambulum*) given to a peculiar form of popular gnomic poetry which prevailed in Germany from the 12th (*e.g.* the Meistersinger or Minstrel Sparvogel) to the 16th century, but was especially cultivated during the 14th and 15th centuries. Its peculiarity consisted in this, that after a series of antecedents or subjects, a briefly-expressed consequent or predicate was introduced as the epigrammatic point applicable to all these antecedents together. *Vid.* Erschenburg's *Denkmälern altdeutscher Dichtkunst,* Bremen 1799.]

to have found something mentioned which the generation addressed were to take heed to; but it is not so. But if "O
generation!" should be equivalent to "O regarding the generation!" then הוי ought to have introduced the sentence. And if
we translate, with Luther: There is a generation, etc., then יֵשׁ
is supplied, which might drop out, but could not be omitted.
The LXX. inserts after ἔκγονον the word κακόν, and then
renders what follows as pred.—a simple expedient, but worthless.
The *Venet.* does not need this expedient, for it renders γενεὰ
τὸν πατέρα αὐτοῦ βλασφημήσει; but then the order of the
words in 11a would have been דור יקלל אביו; and in 12a, after
the manner of a subst. clause, דור טהור בעיניו הוא, one sees distinctly, from 13 and 14, that what follows דור is to be understood, not as a pred., but as an attributive clause. As little can
we interpret ver. 14, with Löwenstein, as pred. of the three
subj., "it is a generation whose teeth are swords;" that would
at least have required the words דור הוא; but ver. 14 is not at
all a judgment valid for all the three subjects. The Targ.
and Jerome translate correctly, as we above;[1] but by this
rendering there are four subjects in the preamble, and the
whole appears, since the common pred. is wanting, as a mutilated Priamel. Perhaps the author meant to say: it is such
a generation that encompasses us; or: such is an abomination
to Jahve; for דור is a *Gesamtheit* = totality, generation of men
who are bound together by contemporary existence, or homogeneity, or by both, but always a totality; so that these verses,
11–14, might describe *quatuor detestabilia genera hominum* (C.
B. Michaelis), and yet one *generatio*, which divide among
themselves these four vices, of blackest ingratitude, loathsome
self-righteousness, arrogant presumption, and unmerciful covetousness. Similar is the description given in the Mishna *Sota*
ix. 14, of the character of the age in which the Messiah appeared. "The appearance of this age," thus it concludes, "is
like the appearance of a dog; a son is not ashamed before his
father; to whom will we then look for help? To our Father
in heaven!"[2] The undutifulness of a child is here placed

---

[1] The Syr. begins 11a as if הוי were to be supplied.

[2] Cf. also Ali b. Abi Tâleb's dark description, beginning with *hadha
alzman* (this age), *Zur allg. Char. der arab. Poesie* (1870), p. 54 f

first. To curse one's parents is, after Ex. xxi. 17, cf. Prov. xx. 10, a crime worthy of death; "not to bless," is here, *per litoten*, of the same force as קַלֵּל [to curse]. The second characteristic, ver. 12, is wicked blindness as to one's judgment of himself. The LXX. coarsely, but not bad : τὴν δ' ἔξοδον αὐτοῦ οὐκ ἀπένιψεν. Of such darkness one says : *sordes suas putat olere cinnama.* רֻחַץ is not the abbreviated part. (Stuart), as *e.g.* Ex. iii. 2, but the finite, as *e.g.* Hos. i. 6.

In 13*a* the attributive clause forms itself, so as to express the astonishing height of arrogance, into an exclamation : a generation, how lofty are their eyes (cf. *e.g.* vi. 17, עֵינַיִם רָמוֹת)! to which, as usual, it is simply added : and his eyelids (*palpebræ*) lift themselves up; in Lat., the lifting up of the eyebrow as an expression of haughtiness is described by *elatum* (*superbum*) *supercilium.*

The fourth characteristic is insatiable covetousness, which does not spare even the poor, and preys upon them, the helpless and the defenceless : they devour them as one eats bread, Ps. xiv. 4. The teeth, as the instruments of eating, are compared to swords and knives, as at Ps. lvii. 4 to spears and arrows. With שִׁנָּיו there is interchanged, as at Job xxix. 17,

Jonah i. 6, מְתַלְּעֹתָיו (not מְתַ, as Norzi writes, contrary to *Metheg-Setzung*, § 37, according to which *Gaja*, with the servant going before, is inadmissible), transposed from מַלְתְּעוֹתָיו, Ps. lviii. 7, from לָתַע, to strike, pierce, bite. The designation of place, מֵאֶרֶץ, " from the earth " (which also, *in pausa*, is not modified into מֵאָרֶץ), and מֵאָדָם, " from the midst of men," do not belong to the obj.: those who belong to the earth, to mankind (*vid.* Ps. x. 18), for thus interpreted they would be useless; but to the word of action : from the earth, out from the midst of men away, so that they disappear from thence (Amos viii. 4). By means of fine but cobweb combinations, Hitzig finds Amalek in this fourfold proverb. But it is a portrait of the times, like Ps. xiv., and certainly without any national stamp.

With the characteristic of insatiableness it closes, and there follows an *apophthegma de quatuor insatiabilibus quæ ideo comparantur cum sanguisuga* (C. B. Michaelis). We translate the text here as it lies before us :

Ver. 15 The 'Alûka hath two daughters : Give! Give!
Three of these are never satisfied ;
Four say not : Enough !
16 The under-world and the closing of the womb;
The earth is not satisfied with water ;
And the fire saith not: Enough !

We begin with Masoretic externalities. The first ב in הַב is
Beth minusculum; probably it had accidentally this diminutive
form in the original MSS., to which the Midrash (cf. *Sepher
Taghin ed. Bargès,* 1866, p. 47) has added absurd conceits.
This first וַהַב has *Pasek* after it, which in this case is servant
to the *Olewejored* going before, according to the rule *Thorath
Emeth,* p. 24, here, as at Ps. lxxxv. 9, *Mehuppach.* The second
הַב, which of itself alone is the representative of *Olewejored,* has
in Hutter, as in the Cod. Erfurt 2, and Cod. 2 of the Leipzig
Public Library, the pausal punctuation הָב (cf. קָח, 1 Sam. xxi.
10), but which is not sufficiently attested. Instead of לֹא־אָמְרוּ,
15b, לֹא אָמְרוּ, and instead of לֹא־אָמְרָה, 16b, לֹא אָמְרָה are to be
written; the *Zinnorith* removes the *Makkeph,* according to
Thorath Emeth, p. 9, *Accentuationssystem,* iv. § 2. Instead of
מַיִם, 16a, only Jablonski, as Mühlau remarks, has מָיִם; but incorrectly, since *Athnach,* after *Olewejored,* has no pausal force
(*vid. Thorath Emeth,* p. 37). All that is without any weight
as to the import of the words. But the punctuation affords
some little service for the setting aside of a view of Rabbenu
Tam (*vid. Tosaphoth* to *Aboda zara* 17a, and *Erubin* 19a),
which has been lately advocated by Löwenstein. That view
is, that '*Alûka* is the name of a wise man, not Solomon's,
because the Pesikta does not reckon this among the names of
Solomon, nor yet a name of hell, because it is not, in the
Gemara, numbered among the names of Gehinnom. Thus
לַעֲלוּקָה would be a superscription, like לְדָוִד and לִשְׁלֹמֹה, Ps. xxvi.
1, lxxii. 1, provided with *Asla Legarmeh.* But this is not
possible, for the *Asla Legarmeh,* at Ps. xxvi. 1 and lxxii. 1, is
the transformation of *Olewejored,* inadmissible on the first word
of the verse (*Accentuationssystem,* xix. § 1); but no *Olewejored*
can follow such an *Asla Legarmeh,* which has the force of an
Olewejored, as after this לעלוקה, which the accentuation then does
not regard as the author's name given as a superscription.

עֲלוּקָה is not the name of a person, and generally not a proper
name, but a generic name of certain traditional signification.
"One must drink no water"—says the Gemara *Aboda zara*
12b—"out of a river or pond, nor (immediately) with his
mouth, nor by means of his hand; he who, nevertheless, does
it, his blood comes on his own head, because of the danger.
What danger? סַכָּנַת עֲלוּקָה," *i.e.* the danger of swallowing a
leech. The Aram. also designates a leech by עֲלוּקָא (cf. *e.g.*
Targ. Ps. xii. 9: hence the godless walk about like the leech,
which sucks the blood of men), and the Arab. by *'alak* (*n. unit.*
'alakat), as the word is also rendered here by the Aram. and Arab.
translators. Accordingly, all the Greeks render it by βδέλλη;
Jerome, by *sanguisuga* (Rashi, *sangsue*); also Luther's *Eigel*
is not the *Igel erinaceus* [hedgehog], but the *Egel*, *i.e.*, as we
now designate it, the *Blutegel* [leech], or (less correctly) *Blutigel*.
עֲלוּקָה is the fem. of the adj. עָלוּק, attached to, which meaning, together with the whole verbal stem, the Arab. has preserved (*vid.*
Mühlau's *Mittheilung des Art. 'aluka aus dem Kamus*, p. 42).[1]
But if, now, the *'Alûka* is the leech,[2] which are then its two
daughters, to which is here given the name הב הב, and which at
the same time have this cry of desire in their mouths? Grotius
and others understand, by the two daughters of the leech,
the two branches of its tongue; more correctly: the double-
membered overlip of its sucker. C. B. Michaelis thinks that
the greedy cry, "Give! Give!" is personified: *voces istæ con-
cipiuntur ut hirudinis filiæ, quas ex se gignat et velut mater
sobolem impense diligat.* But since this does not satisfy, symbolical interpretations of *'Aluka* have been resorted to. The
Talmud, *Aboda zara* 17a, regards it as a name of hell. In
this sense it is used in the language of the Pijut (synagogue

---

[1] Nöldeke has remarked, with reference to Mühlau's *Monographie*, that
'aluka, in the sense of tenacious (*tenax*), is also found in Syr. (*Geopon.*
xiii. 9, xli. 26), and that generally the stem עלק, to cleave, to adhere, is
more common in Aram. than one would suppose. But this, however
common in Arab., is by no means so in Syr.; and one may affirm that,
among other Arabisms found in the Proverbs of Agur, the word *'Alûka*
has decidedly an Arab. sound.

[2] In Sanscrit the leech is called *galaukas* (masc.) or *galaukâ* (fem.), *i.e.*
the inhabitant of the water (from *gala*, water, and *ôkas*, dwelling). Ewald
regards this as a transformation of the Semitic name.

poetry).[1] If 'Alûka is hell, then fancy has the widest room for
finding an answer to the question, What are the two daughters?
The Talmud supposes that רשות (the worldly domination) and
מינות (heresy) are meant. The Church-fathers also, understanding by 'Alûka the power of the devil, expatiated in such
interpretations. Of the same character are Calmet's interpretation, that *sanguisuga* is a figure of the *mala cupiditas*, and its
twin-daughters are *avaritia* and *ambitio*. The truth lying in
all these is this, that here there must be some kind of symbol.
But if the poet meant, by the two daughters of the 'Alûka, two
beings or things which he does not name, then he kept the
best of his symbol to himself. And could he use 'Alûka, this
common name for the leech, without further intimation, in any
kind of symbolical sense? The most of modern interpreters
do nothing to promote the understanding of the word, for
they suppose that 'Alûka, from its nearest signification, denotes
a demoniacal spirit of the character of a vampire, like the
Ḍakinî of the Indians, which nourish themselves on human
flesh; the *ghouls* of the Arabs and Persians, which inhabit
graveyards, and kill and eat men, particularly wanderers in the
desert; in regard to which it is to be remarked, that (Arab.)
'awlak̲ is indeed a name for a demon, and that al'aluwak, according to the Kamus, is used in the sense of *alghwal*. Thus
Dathe, Döderlein, Ziegler, Umbreit; thus also Hitzig, Ewald,
and others. Mühlau, while he concurs in this understanding
of the word, and now throwing open the question, Which,
then, are the two daughters of the demoness 'Alûka? finds no
answer to it in the proverb itself, and therefore accepts of the
view of Ewald, since 15b–16, taken by themselves, form a fully
completed whole, that the line לעלוקה וגו' is the beginning of a
numerical proverb, the end of which is wanting. We acknowledge, because of the obscurity—not possibly aimed at by the
author himself—in which the two daughters remain, the fragmentary characters of the proverb of the 'Alûka; Stuart also
does this, for he regards it as brought out of a connection in
which it was intelligible,—but we believe that the line שלוש וגו'

---

[1] So says *e.g.* Salomo ha-Babli, in a *Zulath* of the first *Chanukka-Sabbats*
(beginning אֵין צוּר חֶלֶף : (אֵין צוּר חֶלֶף), יֵקְדוּ כְּהַבְהֲבֵי עֶלֶק, they burn like the flames of
hell.

is an original formal part of this proverb. For the proverb forming, according to Mühlau's judgment, a whole rounded off :

שָׁלוֹשׁ הֵנָּה לֹא תִשְׂבַּעְנָה
אַרְבַּע לֹא אָמְרוּ הוֹן:
שְׁאוֹל וְעֹצֶר רָחַם
אֶרֶץ לֹא שָׂבְעָה מַיִם
וְאֵשׁ לֹא אָמְרָה הוֹן:

contains a mark which makes the original combination of these five lines improbable. Always where the third is exceeded by the fourth, the step from the third to the fourth is taken by the connecting *Van:* ver. 18, וְאַרְבַּע ; 21, וְתַחַת אַרְבַּע ; 29, וְאַרְבָּעָה. We therefore conclude that אַרְבַּע לֹא וגו׳ is the original commencement of independent proverb. This proverb is :

> Four things say not: Enough!
> The under-world and the closing of the womb [*i.e.* unfruitful womb]—
> The earth is not satisfied with water,
> And the fire says not: Enough!

a tetrastich more acceptable and appropriate than the Arab. proverb (Freytag, *Provv.* iii. p. 61, No. 347) : "three things are not satisfied by three : the womb, and wood by fire, and the earth by rain ;" and, on the other hand, it is remarkable to find it thus clothed in the Indian language,[1] as given in the Hitopadesa (p. 67 of Lassen's ed.), and in Pantschatantra, i. 153 (ed. of Kosegarten) :

> *nâgnis tṛpjati kâshṭhânân nâpagânân mahôdadhih*
> *nântakah sarvabhûtânân na puṅsân vâmalocanâh.*

> Fire is not sated with wood, nor the ocean with the streams,
> Nor death with all the living, nor the beautiful-eyed with men.

As in the proverb of Agur the 4 falls into 2 + 2, so also in this Indian *sloka*. In both, fire and the realm of death (*ántaka* is death as the personified "end-maker") correspond ; and as there the

[1] That not only natural productions, but also ideas and literary productions (words, proverbs, knowledge), were conveyed from the Indians to the Semites, and from the Semites to the Indians, on the great highways by sea and land, is a fact abundantly verified. There is not in this, however, any means of determining the situation of Massa.

womb and the earth, so here *feminarium cupiditas* and the ocean.
The parallelizing of ארץ and רחם is after passages such as Ps.
cxxxix. 15, Job i. 21 (cf. also Prov. v. 16; Num. xxiv. 7; Isa.
xlviii. 1); that of שאול and אש is to be judged of [1] after passages
such as Deut. xxxii. 22, Isa. lvi. 24.   That לא אמרו הון repeats
itself in לא אמרה הון is now, as we render the proverb independently, much more satisfactory than if it began with שלוש וגו':
it rounds itself off, for the end returns into the beginning.
Regarding הון, *vid.* i. 13.   From הון, to be light, it signifies
living lightly; ease, superabundance, in that which renders life
light or easy.   "Used accusatively, and as an exclamation, it is
equivalent to plenty! enough!   It is used in the same sense
in the North African Arab. *brrakat* (spreading out, fulness).
Wetzstein remarks that in Damascus *lahôn, i.e.* hitherto, is used
in the sense of *hajah,* enough; and that, accordingly, we may
attempt to explain הון of our [Heb.] language in the sense of
(Arab.) *hawn haddah, i.e.* here the end of it!"   (Mühlau.)
   But what do we now make of the two remaining lines of the
proverb of the *'Alûka?*   The proverb also in this division of two
lines is a fragment.   Ewald completes it, for to the one line, of
which, according to his view, the fragment consists, he adds two:

> The bloodsucker has two daughters, "Hither! hither!"
> Three saying, "Hither, hither, hither the blood,
> The blood of the wicked child."

A proverb of this kind may stand in the O. T. alone: it sounds
as if quoted from Grimm's *Mährchen,* and is a side-piece to
Zappert's *altdeutsch. Schlummerliede.*   Cannot the mutilation of
the proverb be rectified in a less violent way without any self-
made addition?   If this is the case, that in vers. 15 and 16, which
now form one proverb, there are two melted together, only the
first of which lies before us in a confused form, then this
phenomenon is explained by supposing that the proverb of the
'Alûka originally stood in this form:

> The *'Alûka* has two daughters: Give! give!—
> The under-world and the closing of the womb;
> There are three that are never satisfied.

Thus completed, this tristich presents itself as the original side-

---

[1] The parallelizing of רחם and שאול, *Berachoth* 15*b,* is not directly aimed
at by the poet.

piece of the lost tetrastich, beginning with ארבע. One might
suppose that if שְׁאוֹל and עֹצֶר רֶחֶם have to be regarded as the
daughters of the 'Alûka, which Hitzig and also Zöckler have
recognised, then there exists no reason for dividing the one
proverb into two. Yet the taking of them as separate is necessary, for this reason, because in the fourth, into which it
expands, the 'Alûka is altogether left out of account. But in
the above tristich it is taken into account, as was to be expected,
as the mother with her children. This, that sheol (שְׁאוֹל is for
the most part fem.), and the womb (רֶחֶם = רַחַם, which is fem.,
Jer. xx. 17) to which conception is denied, are called, on account
of their greediness, the daughters of the 'Alûka, is to be understood in the same way as when a mountain height is called,
Isa. v. 1, a horn of the son of oil. In the Arab., which is
inexhaustibly rich in such figurative names, a man is called
" a son of the clay (limi) ;" a thief, " a son of the night ; " a
nettle, " the daughter of fire." The under-world and a closed
womb have the 'Alûka nature; they are insatiable, like the
leech. It is unnecessary to interpret, as Zöckler at last does,
'Alûka as the name of a female demon, and the לִילִית,
" daughters," as her companions. It may be adduced in favour
of this view that לַעֲלוּקָה is without the article, after the manner
of a proper name. But is it really without the article? Such
a doubtful case we had before us at xxvii. 23. As yet only
Böttcher, § 394, has entered on this difficulty of punctuation.
We compare Gen. xxix. 27, בַּעֲבֹדָה ; 1 Kings xii. 32, לָעֲגָלִים ; 1
Chron. xiii. 7, בַּעֲגָלָה ; and consequently also Ps. cxlvi. 7, לָעֲשׁוּקִים ;
thus the assimilating force of the Chateph appears here to have
changed the syntactically required לְ and בְּ into לַ and בַּ. But
also supposing that עֲלוּקָה in לַעֲלוּקָה is treated as a proper name,
this is explained from the circumstance that the leech is not
meant here in the natural history sense of the word, but as
embodied greediness, and is made a person, one individual
being. Also the symbol of the two daughters is opposed to the
mythological character of the 'Alûka. The imper. הַב, from יהב,
occurs only here and at Dan. vii. 17 (= יְהַב), and in the bibl.
Heb. only with the intentional הָ—, and in inflection forms.
The insatiableness of sheol (xxvii. 20a) is described by Isaiah,
v. 14; and Rachel, Gen. xxx. 1, with her " Give me children,"

is an example of the greediness of the " closed-up womb "
(Gen. xx. 18).   The womb of a childless wife is meant, which,
because she would have children, the *nuptiæ* never satisfy; or
also of one who, because she does not fear to become pregnant,
invites to her many men, and always burns anew with lust.
" In Arab. *'aluwaḳ* means not only one fast bound to her
husband, but, according to Wetzstein, in the whole of Syria
and Palestine, the prostitute, as well as the κίναιδοι, are called
'ulaḳ (plur. *'alwaḳ*), because they obtrude themselves and hold
fast to their victim" (Mühlau).   In the third line, the three :
the leech, hell, and the shut womb, are summarized : *tria sunt
quæ non satiantur.*   Thus it is to be translated with Fleischer,
not with Mühlau and others, *tria hæc non satiantur.*   " These
three " is expressed in Heb. by שְׁלָשׁ־אֵלֶּה, Ex. xxi. 11, or שְׁלֹשֶׁת
אֵלֶּה(הָ), 2 Sam. xxi. 22 ; הֵנָּה (which, besides, does not signify
hæc, but *illa*) is here, taken correctly, the pred., and represents
in general the verb of being (Isa. li. 19), *vid.* at vi. 16.
Zöckler finds the point of the proverb in the greediness of the
unfruitful womb, and is of opinion that the poet purposely
somewhat concealed this point, and gave to his proverb thereby
the enhanced attraction of the ingenious.   But the tetrastich
ארבע וגו' shows that hell, which is compared to fire, and the unfruitful womb, to which the parched and thirsty earth is compared, were placed by the poet on one and the same line ; it is
otherwise with vers. 18–20, but where that point is nothing less
than concealed.

The proverb of the *'Alúka* is the first of the proverbs
founded on the figure of an animal among the " words" of
Agur.   It is now followed by another of a similar character :

> Ver. 17 An eye that mocketh at his father,
>   And despiseth obedience to his mother :
>   The ravens of the brook shall pluck it out,
>   And the young eagles shall eat it.

If " an eye," and not " eyes," are spoken of here, this is
accounted for by the consideration that the duality of the
organ falls back against the unity of the mental activity and
mental expression which it serves (cf. *Psychol.* p. 234).   As
haughtiness reveals itself (ver. 13) in the action of the eyes, so
is the eye also the mirror of humble subordination, and also of

malicious scorn which refuses reverence and subjection to father and mother. As in German the verbs [*verspotten, spotten, höhnen, hohnsprechen*] signifying to mock at or scorn may be used with the accus., genit., or dat., so also לָעַג [to deride] and בּוּז [to despise] may be connected at pleasure with either an accusative object or a dative object. Ben-Chajim, Athias, van der Hooght, and others write תִּלְעַג; Jablonski, Michaelis, Löwenstein, תְּלְעַג; Mühlau, with Norzi, accurately, תִּלְעַג, with *Munach*, like תְּבִחַר, Ps. lxv. 5; the writing of Ben-Asher [1] is תִּלְעַג, with *Gaja, Chateph*, and *Munach*. The punctuation of לִיקֲהַת is more fluctuating. The word לְקֲהַת (*e.g.* Cod. *Jaman.*) may remain out of view, for the *Dag. dirimens* in ק stands here as firmly as at Gen. xlix. 10, cf. Ps. xlv. 10. But it is a question whether one has to write לִיקֲהַת with *Yod quies.* (regarding this form of writing, preferred by Ben-Naphtali, the *Psalmen-Comm.* under Ps. xlv. 10, in both Edd.; Luzzatto's *Gramm.* § 193; Baer's *Genesis*, p. 84, note 2; and Heidenheim's *Pentateuch*, with the text-crit. *Comm.* of Jekuthiël ha-Nakdans, under Gen. xlvii. 17, xlix. 10), as it is found in Kimchi, *Michlol 45a*, and under יקה, and as also Norzi requires, or לִקֲהַת (as *e.g.* Cod. Erfurt 1), which appears to be the form adopted by Ben-Asher, for it is attested[2] as such by Jekuthiël under Gen. xlix. 10, and also expressly as such by an old Masora-Cod. of the Erfurt Library. Löwenstein translates, "the weakness of the mother." Thus after Rashi, who refers the word to קָהָה, to draw together, and explains it, Gen. xlix. 10, "collection;" but in the passage before us, understands it of the wrinkles on the countenance of the aged mother. Nachmani (Ramban) goes still further, giving to the word, at Gen. xlix. 10, everywhere the meaning of weakness and frailty. Aben Ezra also, and Gersuni (Ralbag), do not go beyond the meaning of a drawing together; and the LXX., with the

---

[1] The *Gaja* has its reason in the *Zinnor* that follows, and the *Munach* in the syllable beginning with a moveable *Sheva*; תִּלְעַג with *Scheva quiesc.* must, according to rule, receive *Mercha*, vid. *Thorath Emeth*, p. 26.

[2] Kimchi is here no authority, for he contradicts himself regarding such word-forms. Thus, regarding וַיְלֲלַת, Jer. xxv. 36, in *Michlol 87b*, and under ילל. The form also wavers between כִּיתְרוֹן and כִּיתְרוֹן, Eccles. ii. 13. The Cod. *Jaman.* has here the *Jod* always *quiesc.*

Aram., who all translate the word by *senectus*, have also קָהָה in
the sense of to become dull, infirm (certainly not the Æthiopic
leh^eka, to become old, weak through old age).   But Kimchi,
whom the *Venet.* and Luther[1] follow, is informed by Abulwalîd, skilled in the Arab., of a better : יְקָהָה (or יִקְהָה, cf. נִצְּרָה,
Ps. cxli. 3) is the Arab. *wakhat,* obedience (*vid.* above יְקֵה,
under 1*a*).   If now it is said of such a haughty, insolent eye,
that the ravens of the brook (cf. 1 Kings xvii. 4) will pluck it
out, and the בְּנֵי־נָשֶׁר eat it, they, the eagle's children, the unchild-
like human eye : it is only the description of the fate that is
before such an one, to die a violent death, and to become a prey
to the fowls of heaven (cf. *e.g.* Jer. xvi. 3 f., and Passow's *Lex.*
under κόραξ) ; and if this threatening is not always thus literally
fulfilled, yet one has not on that account to render the future
optatively, with Hitzig; this is a false conclusion, from a too
literal interpretation, for the threatening is only to be understood after its spirit, viz. that a fearful and a dishonourable
end will come to such an one.   Instead of יִקְּרוּהָ, as Mühlau
reads from the Leipzig Cod., יקרוה, with *Mercha* (Athias and
Nissel have it with *Tarcha*), is to be read, for a word between
Olewejored and *Athnach* must always contain a conjunctive
accent (*Thorath Emeth*, p. 51 ; *Accentuationssystem*, xviii. § 9).
ערבי־נָחַל is also irregular, and instead of it ערבי־נַחַל is to be
written, for the reason given above under ver. 16 (מֵיִם).

The following proverb, again a numerical proverb, begins
with the eagle, mentioned in the last line of the foregoing :

Ver. 18 Three things lie beyond me,
     And four I understand not :
   19 The way of the eagle in the heavens,
     The way of a serpent over a rock,
     The way of a ship on the high sea,
     And the way of a man with a maid.
   20 Thus is the way of the adulterous woman :
     She eateth and wipeth her mouth, and saith :
     I have done no iniquity.

---

[1] Jerome translates, *et qui despicit partum matris suæ.* To *partus* there
separates itself to him here the signification *expectatio*, Gen. xlix. 10,
resting on a false combination with קוה. To think of *pareo, parui, paritum*
(Mühlau), was not yet granted to him.

THE BOOK OF PROVERBS.

נִפְלְאוּ מִמֶּנִּי, as relative clause, like 15*b* (where Aquila, Symmachus, Theodotion rightly : τρία δέ ἐστιν ἃ οὐ πλησθήσεται), is joined to שְׁלֹשָׁה הֵמָּה. On the other hand, ארבע (τέσσαρα, for which the *Kerî*, conforming to 18*a*, אַרְבָּעָה, τέσσαρας) has to be interpreted as object. accus. The introduction of four things that are not known is in expressions like Job xlii. 3; cf. Ps. cxxxix. 6. The turning-point lies in the fourth; to that point the other three expressions gravitate, which have not an object in themselves, but are only as *folie* to the fourth. The articles wanting after הַנֶּשֶׁר : they would be only the marks of the gender, and are therefore unnecessary; cf. under xxix. 2. And while בַּשָּׁמַיִם, in the heavens, and בְלֵב־יָם, in the sea, are the expressions used, עֲלֵי צוּר is used for on the rock, because here " on " is not at the same time " in," " within," as the eagle cleaves the air and the ship the waves. For this same reason the expression, " the way of a man בְּעַלְמָה," is not to be understood of love unsought, suddenly taking possession of and captivating a man toward this or that maid, so that the principal thought of the proverb may be compared to the saying, " marriages are made in heaven;" but, as in *Kidduschin* 2*b*, with reference to this passage, is said *coitus via appellatur*. The בְ refers to *copula carnalis*. But in what respect did his understanding not reach to this? " Wonderful," thus Hitzig explains as the best interpreter of this opinion elsewhere (cf. *Psychol.* p. 115) propounded, " appeared to him the flying, and that how a large and thus heavy bird could raise itself so high in the air (Job xxxix. 27); then how, over the smooth rock, which offers no hold, the serpent pushes itself along; finally, how the ship on the trackless waves, which present nothing to the eye as a guide, nevertheless finds its way. These three things have at the same time this in common, that they leave no trace of their pathway behind them. But of the fourth way that cannot be said; for the trace is left on the *substrat*, which the man דַּרְכּוֹ, and it becomes manifest, possibly as pregnancy, keeping out of view that the עלמה may yet be בתולה. That which is wonderful is consequently only the coition itself, its mystical act and its incomprehensible consequences." But does not this interpretation carry in itself its own refutation? To the three wonderful ways which leave no traces behind them, there

cannot be compared a fourth, the consequences of which are
not only not trackless, but, on the contrary, become manifest as
proceeding from the act in an incomprehensible way. The
point of comparison is either the wonderfulness of the event or
the tracklessness of its consequences. But now " the way of a
man בתולה " is altogether inappropriate to designate the wonderful event of the origin of a human being. How altogether
differently the *Chokma* expresses itself on this matter is seen
from Job x. 8–12; Eccles. xi. 5 (cf. *Psychol.* p. 210). That
"way of a man with a maid" denotes only the act of coition, which
physiologically differs in nothing from that of the lower animals,
and which in itself, in the externality of its accomplishment,
the poet cannot possibly call something transcendent. And why
did he use the word בעלמה, and not rather בִּנְקֵבָה [with a female]
or בְּאִשָּׁה [*id.*]? For this reason, because he meant the act of
coition, not as a physiological event, but as a historical occurrence, as it takes place particularly in youth as the goal of love,
not always reached in the divinely-appointed way. The point
of comparison hence is not the secret of conception, but the
tracelessness of the carnal intercourse. Now it is also clear
why the way of the serpent עֲלֵי צוּר was in his eye : among grass,
and still more in sand, the trace of the serpent's path would
perhaps be visible, but not on a hard stone, over which it has
glided. And it is clear why it is said of the ship בְלֶב־יָם [in the
heart of the sea]: while the ship is still in sight from the land,
one knows the track it follows; but who can in the heart of the
sea, *i.e.* on the high sea, say that here or there a ship has ploughed
the water, since the water-furrows have long ago disappeared?
Looking to the heavens, one cannot say that an eagle has
passed there ; to the rock, that a serpent has wound its way
over it; to the high sea, that a ship has been steered through it;
to the maid, that a man has had carnal intercourse with her.
That the fact might appear on nearer investigation, although
this will not always guide to a certain conclusion, is not kept in
view ; only the outward appearance is spoken of, the intentional
concealment (Rashi) being in this case added thereto. Sins
against the sixth [= the seventh] commandment remain concealed from human knowledge, and are distinguished from
others by this, that they shun human cognition (as the proverb

says: אין אפיטרופוס לעריות, there is for sins of the flesh no ἐπί-
τροπος)—unchastity can mask itself, the marks of chastity are
deceitful, here only the All-seeing Eye (עֵין רֹאָה כֹּל, *Aboth* ii. 1)
perceives that which is done. Yet it is not maintained that
" the way of a man with a maid " refers exclusively to external
intercourse ; but altogether on this side the proverb gains
ethical significance. Regarding עַלְמָה (from עלם, *pubes esse et
cœundi cupidus*, not from עלם, to conceal, and not, as Schultens
derives it, from עלם, *signare*, to seal) as distinguished from
בְּתוּלָה, *vid.* under Isa. vii. 14. The mark of maidenhood belongs
to עלמה not in the same way as to בתולה (cf. Gen. xxiv. 43
with 16), but only the marks of puberty and youth; the wife אִשָּׁה
(viz. אֵשֶׁת אִישׁ) cannot as such be called עלמה. Ralbag's gloss
עלמה שהיא בעולה is incorrect, and in Arama's explanation (*Akeda*,
Abschn. 9) : the time is not to be determined when the sexual
love of the husband to his wife flames out, ought to have been ודרך
אִישׁ בְּאִשְׁתּוֹ. One has therefore to suppose that ver. 20 explains
what is meant by " the way of a man with a maid " by a strong
example (for " the adulterous woman " can mean only an old
adulteress), there not inclusive, for the tracklessness of sins of
the flesh in their consequences.

This 20th verse does not appear to have been an original part
of the numerical proverb, but is an appendix thereto (Hitzig).
If we assume that כֵּן points forwards : thus as follows is it with
the . . . (Fleischer), then we should hold this verse as an independent cognate proverb; but where is there a proverb
(except xi. 19) that begins with כֵּן ? כן, which may mean
eodem modo (for one does not say כֵּן גַּם) as well as *eo modo*,
here points backwards in the former sense. Instead of וּמָחֲתָה
פֶּיהָ (not פִּיהָ ; for the attraction of that which follows, brought
about by the retrogression of the tone of the first word, requires
dageshing, *Thorath Emeth*, p. 30) the LXX. has merely ἀπονι-
ψαμένη, i.e. as Immanuel explains : מְקַנְּחָה עצמה, *abstergens semet
ipsam*, with Grotius, who to *tergens os suum* adds the remark :
σεμνολογία (*honesta elocutio*). But eating is just a figure, like
the " secret bread," ix. 17, and the wiping of the mouth belongs
to this figure. This appendix, with its כן, confirms it, that the
intention of the four ways refers to the tracklessness of the
consequences.

It is now not at all necessary to rack one's brains over the grounds or the reasons of the arrangement of the following proverb (*vid.* Hitzig). There are, up to this point, two numerical proverbs which begin with שְׁתַּיִם, ver. 7, and שְׁתֵּי, ver. 15 ; after the cipher 2 there then, ver. 18, followed the cipher 3, which is now here continued :

Ver. 21 Under three things doth the earth tremble,
And under four can it not stand :
22 Under a servant when he becomes king,
And a profligate when he has bread enough ;
23 Under an unloved woman when she is married,
And a maid-servant when she becomes heiress to her mistress.

We cannot say here that the 4 falls into 3 + 1; but the four consists of four ones standing beside one another. אֶרֶץ is here without pausal change, although the *Athnach* here, as at ver. 24, where the modification of sound occurs, divides the verse into two ; מֵאֶרֶץ, 14*b* (cf. Ps. xxxv. 2), remains, on the other hand, correctly unchanged. The " earth " stands here, as frequently, instead of the inhabitants of the earth. It trembles when one of the four persons named above comes and gains free space for acting ; it feels itself oppressed as by an insufferable burden (an expression similar to Amos vii. 10);—the arrangement of society is shattered ; an oppressive closeness of the air, as it were, settles over all minds. The first case is already designated, xix. 10, as improper : under a slave, when he comes to reign (*quum rex fit*) ; for suppose that such an one has reached the place of government, not by the murder of the king and by the robbery of the crown, but, as is possible in an elective monarchy, by means of the dominant party of the people, he will, as a rule, seek to indemnify himself in his present highness for his former lowliness, and in the measure of his rule show himself unable to rise above his servile habits, and to pass out of the limited circle of his earlier state. The second case is this : a נָבָל, one whose mind is perverted and whose conduct is profligate,—in short, a low man (*vid.* xvii. 17), —יִשְׂבַּע־לָחֶם (cf. *Metheg-Setzung*, § 28), *i.e.* has enough to eat (cf. to the expression xxviii. 19, Jer. xliv. 17) ; for this undeserved living without care and without want makes him only so much the more arrogant, and troublesome, and dangerous. The שְׂנוּאָה, in the second case, is not thought of as a spouse, and that, as in supposed polygamy, Gen. xxix. 31, Deut. xxi. 15–17, as fallen into disfavour, but who again comes to favour and honour (Dathe, Rosenmüller); for she can be שְׂנוּאָה without her own fault, and as such she is yet no גְּרוּשָׁה; and it is not to be perceived why the re-assumption of such an one should shatter social order. Rightly Hitzig, and, after his example, Zöckler: an unmarried lady, an old spinster, is meant, whom no one desired because she had nothing attractive, and was only repulsive (cf. Grimm, under Sir. vii. 26b). If such an one, as כִּי תִבְעֵל says, at length, however, finds her husband and enters into the married relation, then she carries her head so much the higher; for she gives vent to ill-humour, strengthened by long restraint, against her subordinates; then she richly requites her earlier and happily married companions for their depreciation of her, among whom she had to suffer, as able to find no one who would love her. In the last case it is asked whether כִּי־תִירַשׁ is meant of inheriting as an heiress (Aquila, Symmachus, Theodotion, the Targ., Jerome, the *Venet.*, and Luther), or supplanting (Euchel, Gesenius, Hitzig), i.e. an entering into the inheritance of the dead, or an entering into the place of a living mistress. Since יִרַשׁ, with the accus. of the person, Gen. xv. 3, 4, signifies to be the heir of one, and only with the accus. of peoples and lands signifies, "to take into possession (to seize) by supplanting," the former is to be preferred; the LXX. (Syr.), ὅταν ἐκβάλῃ, appear to have read כִּי־תְגָרֵשׁ. This גָּרֵשׁ would certainly be, after Gen. xxi. 10, a piece of the world turned upside down; but also the entering, as heiress, into the inheritance, makes the maid-servant the reverse of that which she was before, and brings with it the danger that the heiress, notwithstanding her want of culture and dignity, demean herself also as heiress of the rank. Although the old Israelitish law knew only intestate succession to an inheritance, yet there also the case might arise, that where there were no natural or legal heirs, the bequest of a wife of rank passed over to her servants and nurses.

Vers. 24–28. Another proverb with the cipher 4, its first line terminating in אֶרֶץ:

Ver. 24 Four are the little things of the earth,
　　　And yet they are quick of wit—wise:
　25 The ants—a people not strong,
　　　And yet they prepare in summer their food ;
　26 Conies—a people not mighty,
　　　And yet set their dwelling on the rocks ;
　27 No king have the locusts,
　　　And yet they go forth in rank and file, all of them together ;
　28 The lizard thou canst catch with the hands,
　　　And yet it is in the king's palaces.

By the disjunctive accent, אַרְבָּעָה, in spite of the following word toned on the beginning, retains its *ultima*-toning, 18*a;* but here, by the conjunctive accent, the tone retrogrades to the *penult.*, which does not elsewhere occur with this word. The connection קְטַנֵּי־אֶרֶץ is not superlat. (for it is impossible that the author could reckon the שְׁפַנִּים, conies, among the smallest of beasts), but, as in the expression נִכְבַּדֵּי־אֶרֶץ, the honoured of the earth, Isa. xxiii. 8. In 24*b*, the LXX., Syr., Jerome, and Luther see in מ the comparative: σοφώτερα τῶν σοφῶν (מֵחֲכָמִים), but in this connection of words it could only be partitive (wise, reckoning among the wise) ; the *part. Pual* מְחֻכָּמִים (Theodotion, the *Venet.* σεσοφισμένα) was in use after Ps. lviii. 6, and signified, like בָּשֵׁל מְבֻשָּׁל, Ex. xii. 9, boiled well ; thus חכמים מחכמים, taught wit, wise, cunning, prudent (cf. Ps. lxiv. 7, a planned plan = a cunningly wrought out plan ; Isa. xxviii. 16, and Vitringa thereto: grounded = firm, grounding), Ewald, § 313*c.* The reckoning moves in the contrasts of littleness to power, and of greatness to prudence. The unfolding of the ארבעה [four] begins with the הַנְּמָלִים [the ants] and שְׁפַנִּים [conies], subject conceptions with apposit. joined ; 26*a*, at least in the indetermination of the subject, cannot be a declaration. Regarding the *fut. consec.* as the expression, not of a causal, but of a contrasted connection, *vid.* Ewald, § 342, 1*a.* The ants are called עַם, and they deserve this name, for they truly form communities with well-ordered economy; but, besides, the ancients took delight in speaking of the various classes of animals as peoples and states.[1] That which is said, 25*b*, as also vi. 8, is not to be understood of stores laid up for the winter. For the ants are torpid for the most part in winter; but certainly the summer is their time

[1] *Vid. Walter von der Vogelweide*, edited by Lachmann, p. 8 f.

for labour, when the labourers gather together food, and feed
in a truly motherly way the helpless. שָׁפָן, translated arbitrarily
in the *Venet.* by ἐχῖνοι, in the LXX. by χοιρογρύλλιοι, by
the Syr. and Targ. here and at Ps. civ. by חֲנַם, and by
Jerome by *lepusculus* (cf. λαγίδιον), both of which names, here
to be understood after a prevailing Jewish opinion, denote the
Caninichen [1] (Luther), Latin *cuniculus* (κόνικλος), is not the
kaninchen [rabbit], nor the marmot, χοιρογρύλλιος (C. B.
Michaelis, Ziegler, and others); this is called in Arab. *yarbuw';*
but שׁפן is the *wabr*, which in South Arab. is called *thufun*, or
rather *thafan*, viz. the *klippdachs* (*hyrax syriacus*), like the
marmot, which lives in societies and dwells in the clefts of the
mountains, *e.g.* at the Kedron, the Dead Sea, and at Sinai (*vid.*
Knobel on Lev. xi. 5; cf. Brehm's *Thierleben*, ii. p. 721 ff., the
Illustrirte Zeitung, 1868, Nr. 1290). The *klippdachs* are a
weak little people, and yet with their weakness they unite the
wisdom that they establish themselves among the rocks. The
ants show their wisdom in the organization of labour, here in
the arranging of inaccessible dwellings.

Ver. 27. Thirdly, the locusts belong to the class of the wise
little folk: these have no king, but notwithstanding that, there
is not wanting to them guidance; by the power and foresight of
one sovereign will they march out as a body, חֹצֵץ, dividing, viz.
themselves, not the booty (Schultens); thus: dividing themselves into companies, *ordine dispositæ*, from חָצַץ, to divide, to
fall into two (cogn. חָצָה, *e.g.* Gen. xxxii. 7) or more parts;
Mühlau, p. 59–64, has thoroughly investigated this whole wide
range of roots. What this חֹצֵץ denotes is described in Joel ii. 7:
" Like mighty men they hunt; like men of war they climb the
walls; they march forward every one on his appointed way,
and change not their paths." Jerome narrates from his own
observation: *tanto ordine ex dispositione jubentis* (LXX. at
this passage before us: ἀφ' ἑνὸς κελεύσματος εὐτάκτως) *volitant,
ut instar tesserularum, quæ in pavimentis artificis figuntur manu,*

---

[1] The *kaninchen* as well as the *klippdachs* [cliff-badgers] may be meant,
Lev. xi. 5 (Deut. xiv. 7); neither of these belong to the *bisulca*, nor yet,
it is true, to the ruminants, though to the ancients (as was the case also
with hares) they seemed to do. The *klippdach* is still, in Egypt and Syria,
regarded as unclean.

*suum locum teneant et ne puncto quidem 'et ut ita dicam ungue
transverso declinent ad alterum.* Aben Ezra and others find in
חצץ the idea of gathering together in a body, and in troops,
according to which also the Syr., Targ., Jerome, and Luther
translate; Kimchi and Meîri gloss חצץ by חותך and כורת, and
understand it of the cutting off, *i.e.* the eating up, of plants and
trees, which the *Venet.* renders by ἐκτέμνουσα.

Ver. 28. In this verse the expression wavers in a way that is
with difficulty determinable between שְׂמָמִית and שְׁמָמִית. The
Edd. of Opitz Jablonski and Van der Hooght have 'שׂמ, but the
most, from the Venetian 1521 to Nissel, have 'שׁמ (*vid* Mühlau,
p. 69). The Codd. also differ as to the reading of the word :
thus the Codd. Erfurt 2 and 3 have 'שׂמ, but Cod. 1294 has
'שׁמ. Isaak Tschelebi and Moses Algazi, in their writings
regarding words with שׂ and שׁ (Constant. 1723 and 1799),
prefer 'שׂמ, and so also do Mordecai Nathan in his *Concordance*
(1563–4), David de Pomis (1587), and Norzi. An important
evidence is the writing סממית, *Schabbath* 77*b*, but it is as little
decisive as סריון [coat of mail], used by Jeremiah [xlvi. 4], is
decisive against the older expression שִׁרְיוֹן. But what kind of a
beast is meant here is a question. The swallow is at once to be
set aside, as the *Venet.* translates (χελιδών) after Kimchi, who
explains after Abulwalîd, but not without including himself,
that the Heb. word for (Arab.) *khuttaf* (which is still the name
given to the swallow from its quickness of motion), according
to Haja's testimony, is much rather סנונית, a name for the
swallow; which also the Arab. (Freytag, ii. p. 368) and the
modern Syriac confirm; besides, in old Heb. it has the name
of סוס or סים (from Arab. *shash*, to fly confusedly hither and
thither). In like manner the ape (Aben Ezra, Meîri, Immanuel) is to be set aside, for this is called קוף (Indian *kapi,
kap, kamp,* to move inconstantly and quickly up and down),[1]
and appears here admissible only on the ground that from
בידים תתפש they read that the beast had a resemblance to man.
There remains now only the lizard (LXX. Jerome) and the
spider (Luther) to be considered. The Talmud, *Schabbath* 77*b*,
reckons five instances in which fear of the weaker pursues the
stronger : one of these instances is אימת סנונית על הנשר, another

---

[1] *Vid.* A. Weber's *Indische Studien,* i. pp. 217, 343.

אימת סממית על העקרב. The swallow, thus Rashi explains, creeps under the wings of the eagle and hinders it from spreading them out in its flight; and the spider (*araigne*) creeps into the ear of the scorpion; or also: a bruised spider applied heals the scorpion's sting. A second time the word occurs, *Sanhedrin* 103b, where it is said of King Amon that he burnt the Tôra, and that over the altar came a שממית (here with שׁ), which Rashi explains of the spider (a spider's web). But Aruch testifies that in these two places of the Talmud the explanation is divided between *ragnatelo* (spider) and (Ital.) *lucêrta* (lizard). For the latter, he refers to Lev. xi. 30, where לטאה (also explained by Rashi by *lézard*) in the Jerus. Targ. is rendered[1] by שממיתא (the writing here also varies between שׁ and שׂ or ס). Accordingly, and after the LXX. and Jerome, it may be regarded as a confirmed tradition that שממית means not the spider, for which the name עַכָּבִישׁ is coined, but the lizard, and particularly the stellion (spotted lizard). Thus the later language used it as a word still living (plur. סְמָמִיּוֹת, *Sifre*, under Deut. xxxiii. 19). The Arab. also confirms this name as applicable to the lizard.[2] "To this day in Syria and in the Desert it is called *samawiyyat*, probably not from poison, but from *samawah* = שְׁמָמָה, the wilderness, because the beast is found only in the stony heaps of the *Kharab*" (Mühlau after Wetzstein). If this derivation is correct, then שממית is to be regarded as an original Heb. expression; but the lizard's name, *samm*, which, without doubt, designates the animal as poisonous (cf. סם, *samam, samm*, vapour, poisonous breath, poison), favours Schultens' view: שממית = (Arab.) *samamyyat, afflatu interficiens*, or generally *venenosa*. In the expression בְּיָדִים תְּתַפֵּשׂ, Schultens, Gesenius, Ewald, Hitzig, Geier, and others, understand ידים of the two fore-feet of the lizard: "the lizard feels (or: seizes) with its two hands;" but granting that ידים is used of the fifteen feet of the *stellio*, or of the climbing feet of any other animal (LXX. καλα-

---

[1] The Samaritan has, Lev. xi. 30, שממית for אנקה, and the Syr. translates the latter word by אמקתא, which is used in the passage before us (cf. Geiger's *Urschrift*, p. 68 f.) for שממית; *omakto* (Targ. *aḳmetha*) appears there to mean, not a spider, but a lizard.

[2] Perhaps also the modern Greek, σαμιάμινθος (σαμιάμιδος, σαμιαμίδιον), which Grotius compares.

βώτης = ἀσκαλαβώτης), yet it is opposed by this explanation, that in line first of this fourth distich an expression regarding the smallness or the weakness of the beast is to be expected, as at 25a, 26a, and 27a. And since, besides, חפש with יד or בכף always means "to catch" or "seize" (Ezek. xxi. 16, xxix. 7; Jer. xxxviii. 23), so the sense according to that explanation is: the lizard thou canst catch with the hand, and yet it is in kings' palaces, i.e. it is a little beast, which one can grasp with his hand, and yet it knows how to gain an entrance into palaces, by which in its nimbleness and cunning this is to be thought of, that it can scale the walls even to the summit (Aristoph. Nubes 170). To read תִּתְפֵּשׂ with Mühlau, after Böttcher, recommends itself by this, that in תְּתַפֵּשׂ one misses the suff. pointing back (תְתַפְּשֶׂנָה); also why the intensive of חפש is used, is not rightly comprehended. Besides, the address makes the expression more animated; cf. Isa. vii. 25, תָּבוֹא. In the LXX. as it lies before us, the two explanations spoken of are mingled together: καὶ καλαβώτης (= ἀσκαλαβώτης) χερσὶν ἐρειδόμενος καὶ εὐάλωτος ὤν . . . This εὐάλωτος ὤν (Symmachus, χερσὶν ἐλλαμβανόμενος) hits the sense of 28a. In הֵיכְלֵי מֶלֶךְ, מלך is not the genit. of possession, as at Ps. xlv. 9, but of description (Hitzig), as at Amos vii. 13.

Vers. 29-31. Another numerical proverb with the cipher 4 = 3 + 1 :

> Three things are of stately walk,
> And four of stately going :
> 30 The lion, the hero among beasts,
> And that turneth back before nothing ;
> 31 The swift-loined, also the goat ;
> And a king with whom is the calling out of the host.

Regarding הֵיטִיב with inf. following (the segolated n. actionis צַעַד is of equal force with an inf.), vid. under xv. 2.[1] The relation of the members of the sentence in 30a is like that in 25a and 26a : subj. and apposit., which there, as here, is continued in a verbal clause which appears to us as relative. It deserves to be here remarked that לַיִשׁ, as the name for a

---

[1] In 29a, after Norzi, מֵיטִיבֵי, and in 29b, מֵיטְבֵי, is to be written, and this is required by the little Masora to 1 Sam. xxv. 31, the great, to Ezek. xxxiii. 33, and also the Erfurt little Masora to the passage before us.

lion, occurs only here and at Job iv. 11, and in the description
of the Sinai wilderness, Isa. xxx. 6 ; in Arab. it is *layth*, Aram.
לַיְת, and belongs to the Arameo-Arab. dialect of this language ;
the LXX. and Syr. translate it " the young lion ;" the *Venet.*
excellently, by the epic λῖς. בַּבְּהֵמָה has the article only to
denote the genus, viz. of the beasts, and particularly the four-
footed beasts. What is said in 30*b* (cf. with the expression,
Job xxxix. 22) is described in Isa. xxx. 4. The two other
beasts which distinguish themselves by their stately going are
in 31*a* only briefly named. But we are not in the condition of
the readers of this Book of Proverbs, who needed only to hear
the designation זַרְזִיר מָתְנַיִם at once to know what beast was meant.
Certainly זַרְזִיר, as the name for a beast, is not altogether unknown in the post-bibl. Heb. "In the days of Rabbi Chija
(the great teacher who came from Babylon to the Academy of
Sepphoris), as is narrated in *Bereschith rabba*, sect. 65, a *zarzir*
flew to the land of Israel, and it was brought to him with the
question whether it were eatable. Go, said he, place it on the
roof ! Then came an Egyptian raven and lighted down beside
it. See, said Chija, it is unclean, for it belongs to the genus of
the ravens, which is unclean (Lev. xi. 15). From this circumstance there arose the proverb : The raven goes to the *zarzir*
because it belongs to his own tribe."[1] Also the *Jer. Rosch ha-
schane*, Halacha 3 : "It is the manner of the world that one seeks
to assist his *zarzir*, and another his *zarzir*, to obtain the victory ;"
and *Midrash Echa* v. 1, according to which it is the custom of
the world, that one who has a large and a little *zarzir* in his
house, is wont to treat the little one sparingly, so that in the case
of the large one being killed, he might not need to buy another.
According to this, the *zarzir* is a pugnacious animal, which also
the proverb *Bereschith rabba*, c. 75, confirms : two *zarzir* do
not sleep on one board ; and one makes use of his for contests
like cock-fights. According to this, the זַרְזִיר is a bird, and that
of the species of the raven ; after Rashi, the *étourneau*, the
starling, which is confirmed by the Arab. *zurzur* (vulgar Arab.

---

[1] This " like draws to like" in the form : "not in vain goes the raven to
the *zarzir*, it belongs just to its own tribe," came to be often employed,
Chullin 65*a*, *Baba Kamma* 92*b*. Plantavitius has it, Tendlau more at large,
Sprichwörter, u.s.w., Nr. 577.

zarzur), the common name of starlings (cf. Syr. *zarzizo*, under *zrz* of Castelli). But for the passage before us, we cannot regard this as important, for why is the starling fully named זַרְזִיר מָתְנָיִם? To this question Kimchi has already remarked that he knows no answer for it. Only, perhaps, the grave magpie (*corvus pica*), strutting with upraised tail, might be called *succinctus lumbos*, if מתנים can at all be used here of a bird. At the earliest, this might possibly be used of a cock, which the later Heb. named directly גֶּבֶר, because of its manly demeanour; most old translators so understand it. The LXX. translates, omitting the loins, by ἀλέκτωρ ἐμπεριπατῶν θηλείαις εὔψυχος, according to which the Syr. and Targ.: like the cock which struts about proudly among the hens;[1] Aquila and Theodotion: ἀλέκτωρ (ἀλεκτρυὼν) νώτου; the Quinta: ἀλέκτωρ ὀσφύος; Jerome: *gallus succinctus lumbos*. *Sarsar* (not *sirṣir*, as Hitzig vocalizes) is in Arab. a name for a cock, from *ṣarṣara*, to crow, an *onomatopœia*. But the Heb. זַרְזִיר, as the name of a bird, signifies, as the Talmud proves on the ground of that history, not a cock, but a bird of the raven order, whether a starling, a crow, or a magpie. And if this name of a *corvinus* is formed from the *onomatopœia* זרזר, the weaker form of that (Arab.) *sarsar*, then מתנים, which, for זרזיר, requires the verbal root זרן, to girdle, is not wholly appropriate; and how strangely would the three animals be mingled together, if between לַיִשׁ and תַּיִשׁ, the two four-footed animals, a bird were placed! If, as is to be expected, the "*Lendenumgürtete*" [the one girded about the loins = זַרְזִיר מָתְנָיִם] be a four-footed animal, then it lies near, with C. B. Michaelis and Ziegler, after Ludolf's[2] example, to

---

[1] Regarding the Targum Text, *vid.* Levy under אַבְּבָא and זְרִבֵּל. The expression דִּמְזָדְּרָז (who is girded, and shows himself as such) is not unsuitable.

[2] Ludolf gave, in his *Hist. Æthiop.* i. 10, and *Commentarius*, p. 150, only a description of the *Zecora*, without combining therewith זרזיר; but *vid.* Joh. Dietr. Winckler's *Theol. u. Philol. Abhand.* i. (1755) p. 33 ff.: "A nearer explanation of what is to be understood by זרזיר מתנים, Prov. xxx. 31, along with a statement from a hitherto unpublished correspondence between the learned philologists Hiob Ludolf and Matthai Leydecker, a Reformed preacher in Batavia." With Ludolf, Joh. Simonis also, in the *Arcanum Formarum* (1735), p. 687 sq., decides in favour of the zebra.

think of the zebra, the South African wild ass. But this
animal lay beyond the sphere of the author's observation, and
perhaps also of his knowledge, and at the same time of that of
the Israelitish readers of this Book of Proverbs; and the dark-
brown cross stripes on a white ground, by which the zebra is
distinguished, extend not merely to its limbs, but over the
whole body, and particularly over the front of the body. It
would be more tenable to think of the leopard, with its black
round spots, or the tiger, with dark stripes ; but the name זרזיר
מתנים scarcely refers to the colour of the hair, since one has to
understand it after the Aram. שַׁנֵּס מָתְנָיו = זְרֵז חַרְצֵיה, 1 Kings
xviii. 46, or אֱזָר חֲלָצָיו, Job xxxviii. 3, and thus of an activity,
i.e. strength and swiftness, depending on the condition of the
loins. Those who, with Kimchi, think that the נָמֵר [leopard]
is thus named, ground their view, not on this, that it has
rings or stripes round its legs, but on this, that it דק מתנים וחזק
במתניו. But this beast has certainly its definite name ; but a
fundamental supposition entering into every attempt at an explanation is this, that זרזיר מתנים, as well as לַיִשׁ and תַּיִשׁ, is the
proper name of a beast, not a descriptive attribute. Therefore
the opinion of Rosse, which Bochart has skilfully established
in the *Hierozoicon*, does not recommend itself, for he only
suggests, for choice, to understand the name, " the girded
about the loins," in the proper sense of straps and clasps
around and on the loins (thus *e.g.* Gesenius, Fleischer, Hitzig),
or of strength, in the sense of the Arab. *habuwk*, the firmly-
bound = compact, or *samm alslab*, the girded loin (thus *e.g.*
Muntinghe). Schultens connects together both references :
Utrumque jungas licet. That the by-name fits the horse,
particularly the war-horse, is undeniable ; one would have to
refer it, with Mühlau, to the slender structure, the thin flanks,
which are reckoned among the requisites of a beautiful horse.[1]
But if *succinctus lumbos* were a by-name of a horse, why did
not the author at once say סום זרזיר מתנים ? We shall give the
preference to the opinion, according to which the expression,
" girt about the loins " = " with strong loins," or " with slender
limbs," is not the by-name, but the proper name of the animal.

[1] *Vid.* Ahlwardt, *Chalef elahmar's Qasside* (1859), and the interpretation of the description of the horse contained therein, p. 201 ff.

This may be said of the hunting-hound, *lévrier* (according to which the *Venet.*, incorrectly translating מתנים: λαγῷοκύων ψοιῶν),[1] which Kimchi ranks in the first place. Luther, by his translation, *Ein Wind = Windhund* [greyhound], of good limbs, has given the right direction to this opinion. Melanchthon, Lavater, Mercier, Geier, and others, follow him ; and, among the moderns, so also do Ewald and Böttcher (also Bertheau and Stuart), which latter supposes that before זרזיר מתנים there originally stood כלב, which afterwards disappeared. But why should the greyhound not at once be called זרזיר מתנים ? We call the smaller variety of this dog the *Windspiel* [greyhound] ; and by this name we think on a hound, without saying *Windspielhund*. The name זרזיר מתנים (Symmachus excellently : περιεσφιγμένος, not περιεσφραγισμένος, τὴν ὀσφύν, *i.e.* strongly bound in the limbs) is fitted at once to suggest to us this almost restless, slender animal, with its high, thin, nimble limbs. The verbal stem זָרַר, (Arab.) *zarr*, signifies to press together, to knit together ; the reduplicative form זִרְזֵר, to bind firmly together, whence זַרְזִיר, firmly bound together, referred to the limbs as designating a natural property (Ewald, § 158a) : of straight and easily-moveable legs.[2] The hunting-hound (*saláki* or *salúki, i.e.* coming from Seleucia) is celebrated by the Arab. poets as much as the hunting-horse.[3] The name כֶּלֶב, though not superfluous, the author ought certainly to have avoided, because it does not sound well in the Heb. collocation of words.

There now follows תַּיִשׁ, a goat, and that not the ram (Jerome, Luther), which is called אַיִל, but the he-goat, which bears this name, as Schultens has already recognised, from its pushing, as it is also called עַתּוּד, as *paratus ad pugnam ;* the two names appear to be only provincially different ; שָׂעִיר, on the contrary, is the old he-goat, as shaggy ; and צָפִיר also perhaps denotes it, as Schultens supposes, with twisted, *i.e.* curled hair (*tortipilus*).

---

[1] Thus reads Schleusner, *Opusc. Crit.* p. 318, and refers it to the horse: *nam solebant equos figuris quibusdam notare et quasi sigillare.*

[2] The Aram. זָרַן is shortened from זַרְזֵר, as כְּרַךְ from כַּרְכֵּב ; the particip. adj. זָרִין signifies nimble, swift, eager, *e.g. Pesachim* 4a : " the zealous obey the commandment—as soon as possible hasten to fulfil it."

[3] *Vid.* Ahlwardt, *Chalef elahmar's Qasside,* p. 205 f.

In Arab. *tays* denotes the he-goat as well as the roebuck and the gazelle, and that at full growth. The LXX. (the Syr. and Targ., which is to be emended after the Syr.) is certainly right, for it understands the leading goat : καὶ τράγος ἡγούμενος αἰπολίου. The text, however, has not וְתָיִשׁ, but אוֹ תַיִשׁ, ἢ τράγος (Aquila, Theodotion, Quinta, and the *Venet.*). Böttcher is astonished that Hitzig did not take hold of this אוֹ, and conjectures תְּאוֹ־תַיִשׁ, which should mean a "gazelle-goat" (Mühlau: *dorcas mas*). But it is too bold to introduce here תְּאוֹ (תּוֹא), which is only twice named in the O. T., and תּאו־תיש for תְּאוֹ זָכָר is not the Heb. style; and besides, the setting aside of אוֹ has a harsh *asyndeton* for its consequence, which bears evidence to the appearance that תאו and תיש are two different animals. And is the אוֹ then so objectionable ? More wonderful still must Song ii. 9 appear to us. If the author enumerated the four of stately going on his fingers, he would certainly have said וְתָיִשׁ. By אוֹ he communicates to the hearer, setting before him another figure, how there in the Song Sulamith's fancy passed from one object to another.

To the lion, the king of the animal world, the king אַלְקוּם עִמּוֹ corresponds. This אַלְקוּם Hitzig regards as mutilated from אֱלֹהִים (which was both written and pronounced as אֱלֹקִים by the Jews, so as to conceal the true sound of the name of God),— which is untenable, for this reason, that this religious conclusion ["A king with whom God is"] accords badly with the secular character of this proverb. Geiger (*Urschrift*, p. 62 ff.) translates : " and King Alkimos corresponding to it (the lustful and daring goat) "—he makes the harmless proverb into a *ludibrium* from the time of the Maccabeo-Syrian war. The LXX., which the Syr. and Targ. follow, translates καὶ βασιλεὺς δημηγορῶν ἐν ἔθνει ; it appears to have changed אלקום עמו into קם אל עמו (standing with his people and haranguing them), like the Quinta : καὶ βασ. ἀναστὰς (ὃς ἀνέστη) ἐν τῷ λαῷ αὐτοῦ. Ziegler and Böttcher also, reading עִמּוֹ and אֶל without any transposition, get וּמֶלֶךְ אֶל־קוּם עַמּוֹ, which the former translates : " a king with the presence of his people ;" the latter, " a king with the setting up of his people,"—not accordant with the thought, for the king should be brought forward as מֵיטִיב לֶכֶת. For the same reason, Kimchi's explanation is not suitable : a king with whom is no resistance, *i.e.* against whom no one can rank himself (thus *e.g.* also Immanuel) ; or more specially, but not better : who has no successor of his race (according to which the *Venet.* ἀδιάδεκτος ξὺν ἑαυτῷ). Rather this explanation commends itself : a king with whom (*i.e.* in war with whom) is no resistance. Thus Jerome and Luther : against whom no one dare place himself ; thus Rashi, Aben Ezra, Ralbag (שׁאין תקומה עמו), Ahron b. Josef (קום = ἀντίστασις), Arama, and others ; 'thus also Schultens, Fleischer (*adversus quem nemo consistere audet*), Ewald, Bertheau, Elster, Stuart, and others. But this connection of אל with the infin. is not Heb. ; and if the *Chokma,* xii. 28, has coined the expression אל־מָוֶת for the idea of " immortality," then certainly it does not express the idea of resistlessness by so bold a *quasi compositum.* But this boldness is also there mitigated, for יְהִי is supplied after אל, which is not here practicable with קום, which is not a subst. like מָוֶת. Pocock in the *Spec. historiæ Arabum,* and Castellus in the *Lex. Heptaglotton* (not Castellio, as the word is printed by Zöckler), have recognised in אלקום the Arab. *âlkawm ;* Schultens gives the LXX. the honour of this recognition, for he regards their translation as a paraphrase of ὁ δῆμος μετ' αὐτοῦ. Bertheau thinks that it ought to be in Arab. *kawmuhu,* but אלקום עמו = *âlkawhu ma'ahu* is perfectly correct, *âlkawhu* is the summons or the *Heerbann* = *arriere-ban ;*[1] in North Africa they speak in their language in the same sense of the *Gums.* This explanation of אלקום, from the Arab. Dachselt (*rex cum satellitio suo*), Diedrichs in his Arab.-Syr. *Spicilegium* (1777), Umbreit, Gesenius, and Vaihinger, have recognised, and Mühlau has anew confirmed it at length. Hitzig, on the contrary, remarks that if Agur wrote on Arab. territory, we could be contented with the Arab. appellative, but not with the article, which in words like אלגביש and אלמנים is no longer of force as an art., but is an integ. component part of the word. We think that it is with אלקום exactly as with other words descriptive of lordship, and the many similar that have passed over into the Spanish

[1] Wetzstein's *Ausgewählte Inschriften,* p. 355 : "The word *kawm* signifies people, not in the sense of *populus,* but in the sense of the Heb. קים (Job xxiv. 17) = *mukawim abrajul,* he who breaks with or against any one." Incorrect in Gesenius-Dietrich's *Heb. Wörterbuch.*

language ; the word is taken over along with the article, without requiring the Heb. listener to take the art. as such, although
he certainly felt it better than we do, when we say " *das Al-
koran*" [the Alcoran], " *das Alcohol*," and the like.   Blau also,
in his *Gesch. der Arab. Substantiv-Determ.*,[1] regards it as certain
that Agur borrowed this אלקום from the idiom of the Arabians,
among whom he lived, and heard it constantly spoken.   By
this explanation we first reach a correspondence between what
is announced in lines first and second and line sixth.   A king
as such is certainly not " comely in going;" he can sit upon his
throne, and especially as δημηγορῶν will he sit (Acts xii. 21)
and not stand.   But the majesty of his going shows itself
when he marches at the head of those who have risen up at his
summons to war.   Then he is for the army what the תיש [he-
goat] is for the flock.   The או, preferred to ו, draws close
together the תיש and the king (cf. *e.g.* Isa. xiv. 9).

Vers. 32, 33. Another proverb, the last of Agur's " Words "
which exhorts to thoughtful, discreet demeanour, here follows
the proverb of self-conscious, grave deportment :

> If thou art foolish in that thou exaltest thyself,
> Or in devising,—put thy hand to thy mouth !
> 33 For the pressure on milk bringeth forth butter,
> And pressure on the nose bringeth forth blood,
> And pressure on sensibility bringeth forth altercation.

Löwenstein translates ver. 32 :

> Art thou despicable, it is by boasting ;
> Art thou prudent, then hold thy hand on thy mouth.

But if זמם denotes reflection and deliberation, then נבל, as its
opposite, denotes unreflecting, foolish conduct.   Then בהתנשׂא
[by boasting] is not to be regarded as a consequent (thus it
happens by lifting thyself up; or : it is connected with boasting) ; by this construction also, אם־נבלתּ must be accented with
Dechi, not with *Tarcha*.   Otherwise Euchel :

> Hast thou become offensive through pride,
> Or seems it so to thee,—lay thy hand to thy mouth.

---

[1] In the " *Alt-arab. Sprachstudien*," *Deutsch. Morgenl. Zeitschr.* xxv.
539 f.

The thought is appropriate,[1] but נָבַלְתָּ for נִבַּלְתָּ is more than improbable; נָבָל, thus absolutely taken in an ethical connection, is
certainly related to נָבֵל, as כָּסַל, Jer. x. 8, to כְּסִיל. The prevailing mode of explanation is adopted by Fleischer: *si stulta
arrogantia elatus fueris et si quid durius (in alios) mente con-
ceperis, manum ori impone;* i.e., if thou arrogantly, and with
offensive words, wilt strive with others, then keep thyself back,
and say not what thou hast in thy mind. But while מְזִמָּה and
מְזִמּוֹת denote intrigues, xiv. 17, as well as plans and considerations, זָמַם has never by itself alone the sense of *meditari mala;*
at Ps. xxxvii. 12, also with לְ of the object at which the evil
devices aim. Then for וְאִם . . . אִם (Arab. *án . . . wân*) there
is the supposition of a correlative relation, as *e.g.* 1 Kings xx.
18, Eccles. xi. 3, by which at the same time זַמּוֹתָ is obviously
thought of as a contrast to נָבַלְתָּ. This contrast excludes[2] for
זמות not only the sense of *mala moliri* (thus *e.g.* also Mühlau),
but also the sense of the Arab. *zamm, superbire* (Schultens).
Hitzig has the right determination of the relation of the members of the sentence and the ideas: if thou art irrational in
ebullition of temper and in thought—thy hand to thy mouth!
But הִתְנַשֵּׂא has neither here nor elsewhere the meaning of
הִתְעַבֵּר (to be out of oneself with anger); it signifies everywhere
to elevate or exalt oneself, *i.e.* rightly or wrongly to make much
of oneself. There are cases where a man, who raises himself
above others, appears as a fool, and indeed acts foolishly; but
there are also other cases, when the despised has a reason and an
object for vindicating his superiority, his repute, his just claim:
when, as we say, he places himself in his right position, and
assumes importance; the poet here recommends, to the one as
well as to the other, silence. The rule that silence is gold has
its exceptions, but here also it is held valid as a rule. Luther
and others interpret the *perfecta* as looking back: " hast thou be-

---

[1] Yet the Talmud, *Nidda* 27a, derives another moral rule from this proverb, for it interprets זָמַם in the sense of זָמַם = חָסַם, to tie up, to bridle,
to shut up, but אם נבלת in the sense of " if thou hast made thyself
despicable," as Löwenstein has done.

[2] The Arab. signification, to become proud, is a *nüance* of the primary
signification, to hold erect—viz. the head,—as when the rider draws up
the head of a camel by means of the halter (Arab. *zamam*).

come a fool and ascended too high and intended evil, then lay thy
hand on thy mouth." But the reason in ver. 33 does not accord
with this rendering, for when that has been done, the occasion
for hatred is already given; but the proverb designs to warn
against the stirring up of hatred by the reclaiming of personal
pretensions. The *perfecta*, therefore, are to be interpreted as
at Deut. xxxii. 29, Job ix. 15, as the expression of the abstract
present; or better, as at Job ix. 16, as the expression of the
fut. *exactum*: if thou wouldest have acted foolishly, since thou
walkest proudly, or if thou hadst (before) thought of it (Aquila,
Theodotion: καὶ ἐὰν ἐννοηθῇς)—the hand on thy mouth, *i.e.*
let it alone, be silent rather (expression as xi. 24; Judg. xviii.
19; Job xl. 4). The *Venet.* best: εἴπερ ἐμώρανας ἐν τῷ ἐπαί-
ρεσθαι καὶ εἴπερ ἐλογίσω, χεὶρ τῷ στόματι. When we have
now interpreted התנשא, not of the rising up of anger, we do not
also, with Hitzig, interpret the dual of the two snorting noses—
viz. of the double anger, that of him who provokes to anger, and
that of him who is made angry,—but אַפַּיִם denotes the two nostrils
of one and the same person, and, figuratively, snorting or anger.
Pressure against the nose is designated מִיץ־אַף, ἐκμύζησις (ἐκπί-
εσις) μυκτῆρος (write וּמִיץ־אַף, with *Metheg*, with the long tone,
after *Metheg-Setzung*, § 11, 9, 12), and מִיץ אַפַּיִם, ἐκμύζησις
θυμοῦ (Theodotion), with reference to the proper meaning of
אפים, pressure to anger, *i.e.* to the stirring up and strengthening
of anger. The nose of him who raises himself up comes into
view, in so far as, with such self-estimation, sneering, snuffling
scorn (μυκτηρίζειν) easily connects itself; but this view of
מתנשא is not here spoken of.

SECOND APPENDIX TO THE SECOND SOLOMONIC COLLECTION OF PROVERBS.—XXXI. 1-9.

Superscription :

> Ver. 1 Words of Lemuel the king,
> The utterance wherewith his mother warned him.

Such would be the superscription if the interpunction of the
text as it lies before us were correct. But it is not possibly

right. For, notwithstanding the assurance of Ewald, § 277*b*, למואל מלך, nevertheless, as it would be here used, remains an impossibility. Certainly under circumstances an indeterminate apposition can follow a proper name. That on coins we read מתתיה כהן גדול or נרון קיסר is nothing strange; in this case we also use the words " Nero, emperor," and that we altogether omit the article shows that the case is singular : the apposition wavers between the force of a generic and of a proper name. A similar case is the naming of the proper name with the general specification of the class to which this or that one bearing the name belongs in lists of persons, as *e.g.* 1 Kings iv. 2–6, or in such expressions as, *e.g.*, " Damascus, a town," or " *Tel Hum,* a castle," and the like; here we have the indefinite article, because the apposition is a simple declaration of the class.[1] But would the expression, " The poem of Oscar, a king," be proper as the title of a book? Proportionally more so than " Oscar, king;" but also that form of indeterminate apposition is contrary to the *usus loq.*, especially with a king with whom the apposition is not a generic name, but a name of honour. We assume that " Lemuel " is a symbolical name, like " Jareb " in " King Jareb," Hos. v. 13, x. 6 ; so we would expect the phrase to be (ה)מלך למואל rather than למואל מלך. The phrase " Lemuel, king," here in the title of this section of the book, sounds like a double name, after the manner of עֵבֶר מֶלֶךְ in the book of Jeremiah. In the Greek version also the phrase Λεμουέλου βασιλέως (*Venet.*) is not used as syntactically correct without having joined to the βασιλέως a dependent genitive such as τῶν Ἀράβων, while none of the old translators, except Jerome, take the words למואל מלך together in the sense of *Lamuelis regis.* Thus מֶלֶךְ מַשָּׂא are to be taken together, with Hitzig, Bertheau, Zöckler, Mühlau, and Dächsel, against Ewald and Kamphausen; מַשָּׂא, whether it be a name of a tribe or a country, or of both

---

[1] Thus it is also with the examples of indeterminate *gentilicia*, which Riehm makes valid for למואל מלך (for he translates למואל symbolically, which, however, syntactically makes no difference) : "As analogous to ' Lemuel, a king,' one may adduce ' Jeroboam, son of Nebat, an Ephrathite,' 1 Kings xi. 26, instead of the usual form ' the Ephrathite ; ' " and בן־ימיני, Ps. vii. 1, for בן הימיני ; on the contrary, כהן, 1 Kings iv. 5, does not belong to the subject, but is the pred.

at the same time, is the region ruled over by Lemuel, and since
this proper name throws back the determination which it has in
itself on מלך, the phrase is to be translated : " Words of Lemuel
the king of Massa" (*vid.* under xxx. 1). If Aquila renders
this proper name by Δεμμοῦν, Symmachus by ʾΙαμουήλ, Theodotion by Ρεβουήλ, the same arbitrariness prevails with reference to the initial and terminal sound of the word, as in the
case of the words ʾΑμβακούμ, Βεελζεβούλ, Βελίαρ. The name
למואל sounds like the name of Simeon's first-born, ימואל, Gen.
xlvi. 10, written in Num. xxvi. 12 and 1 Chron. iv. 24 as נמואל ;
יאל also appears, 1 Chron. iv. 35, as a Simeonite name, which
Hitzig adduces in favour of his view that משא was a North
Arab. Simeonite colony. The interchange of the names ימואל
and נמואל is intelligible if it is supposed that ימואל (from ימה =
ימא) designates the sworn (sworn to) of God, and נמואל (from
נם Mishnic = נאם)[1] the expressed (addressed) of God; here the
reference of ימו and נמו to verbal stems is at least possible, but a
verb למה is found only in the Arab., and with significations *inus.*
But there are two other derivations of the name : (1) The verb
(Arab.) *waála* signifies to hasten (with the infin. of the *onoma-
top.* verbs *waniyal*, like *rahyal*, walking, because motion, especially that which is tumultuous, proceeds with a noise), whence
mawnil, the place to which one flees, retreat. Hence למואל or
למואל, which is in this case to be assumed as the ground-form,
might be formed from אל מואל, God is a refuge, with the rejection of the א. This is the opinion of Fleischer, which Mühlau
adopts and has established, p. 38–41 ; for he shows that the
initial א is not only often rejected where it is without the support of a full vocal, *e.g.* נחנו = אנחנו, *lalah* = *ilalah* (*Deus*), but
that this aphaeresis not seldom also occurs where the initial
has a full vocal, *e.g.* לעזר = אלעזר, *lahmaru* = *állahmaru* (*ruber*),
lahsâ = *ál-lahsâ* (the name of a town); cf. also Blau in *Deutsch.
Morgenl. Zeitschr.* xxv. 580. But this view is thus acceptable
and tenable; a derivation which spares us by a like certainty
the supposition of such an abbreviation established only by the
late Palestinian לעזר, Λάζαρος, might well desire the preference.
(2) Fleischer himself suggests another derivation : " The signi-

---

[1] In the *Midrash Koheleth* to i. 1, the name Lemuel (as a name of
Solomon) is explained : he who has spoken to God in his heart.

fication of the name is *Deo consecratus*, לְמוֹ, poetic for לְ, as also in ver. 4 it is to be vocalized לְמוֹאֵל after the Masora." The form לְמוֹאֵל is certainly not less favourable to that first derivation than to this second; the *û* is in both cases an obscuration of the original . But that "Lemuel" may be explained in this second way is shown by "Lael," Num. iii. 24 (Olshausen, § 277*d*).[1] It is a beautiful sign for King Lemuel, and a verification of his name, that it is he himself by whom we receive the admonition with which his mother in her care counselled him when he attained to independent government. אֲשֶׁר connects itself with דברי, after we have connected מַשָּׂא with מלך; it is accus. of the manner to יִפַּרְתּוּ = יִסַּרְתּוּ; cf. הַמַּתּוּ, vii. 21, with גִּמַלָתְהוּ, xxxi. 12 : wherewith (with which words) she earnestly and impressively admonished him. The Syr. translates : words of Muel, as if לְ were that of the author. "Others as inconsistently : words to Lemuel—they are words which he himself ought to carry in his mouth as received from his mother" (Fleischer).

The name "Massa," if it here means *effatum*, would be proportionally more appropriate for these "Words" of Lemuel than for the "Words" of Agur, for the maternal counsels form an inwardly connected compact whole. They begin with a question which maternal love puts to itself with regard to the beloved son whom she would advise :

Ver. 2 What, my son? and what the son of my womb?
And what, O son of my vows ? !

The thrice repeated מה is completed by תֶּעֱשֶׂה (cf. Köhler under Mal. ii. 15), and that so that the question is put for the purpose of exciting attention : Consider well, my son, what thou wilt do as ruler, and listen attentively to my counsel (Fleischer). But the passionate repetition of מה would be only affectation if thus interpreted; the underlying thought must be of a subjective nature: what shall I say, אֲדַבֵּר (*vid.* under Isa. xxxviii. 15), what advise thee to do ? The question, which is at the same time a call, is like a deep sigh from the heart of the mother concerned for the welfare of her son, who would say to him what is beneficial, and say it in words which strike and remain fixed. He

[1] Simonis has also compared Æthiopic proper names, such as *Zakrestos, Zaiasus. Zamikaël, Zamariam.*

is indeed her dear son, the son whom she carries in her heart,
the son for whom with vows of thanksgiving she prayed to
God ; and as he was given her by God, so to His care she commits him.   The name "Lemuel" is, as we interpret it, like the
anagram of the fulfilment of the vows of his mother.   בְּרִי bears
the Aramaic shade in the Arameo-Arab. colouring of these
proverbs from Massa ; בְּרֵיהּ is common in the Aram., and
particularly in the Talmudic, but it can scarcely be adduced in
support of ברי.   וּמֶה belongs to the 24, מֶה, with ה or ע not following ; *vid.* the Masora to Ex. xxxii. 1, and its correction by
Norzi at Deut. xxix. 23.   We do not write וּמַה־בַּר ; מַה, with
Makkeph and with *Metheg*, exclude one another.

Ver. 3. The first admonition is a warning against effeminat-
ing sensuality :

> Give not thy strength to women,
> Nor thy ways to them that destroy kings.

The punctuation לַמְחוֹת sees in this form a syncopated *inf.*
Hiph. = לְהַמְחוֹת (*vid.* at xxiv. 17), according to which we are
to translate : *viasque tuas ad perdendos reges* (*ne dirige*), by
which, as Fleischer formulates the twofold possibility, it may
either be said : direct not thy effort to this result, to destroy
neighbouring kings,—viz. by wars of invasion (properly, to
wipe them away from the table of existence, as the Arabs say),
—or : do not that by which kings are overthrown ; *i.e.*, with
special reference to Lemuel, act not so that thou thyself must
thereby be brought to ruin.   But the warning against vengeful,
rapacious, and covetous propensity to war (thus Jerome, so the
Venet. after Kimchi : ἀπομάττειν βασιλέας, C. B. Michaelis,
and earlier, Gesenius) does not stand well as parallel with the
warning against giving his bodily and mental strength to
women, *i.e.* expending it on them.   But another explanation : direct not thy ways to the destruction of kings, *i.e.*
toward that which destroys kings (Elster) ; or, as Luther
translates : go not in the way wherein kings destroy themselves,—puts into the words a sense which the author cannot
have had in view ; for the individualizing expression would
then be generalized in the most ambiguous way.   Thus למחות
מלכין will be a name for women, parallel to לַנָּשִׁים.   So far the
translation of the Targum : לִבְנָת מַלְכִין, *filiabus* (לַאֲמָהֹת?) *regum,*

lies under a right supposition. But the designation is not thus general. Schultens explains *catapultis regum* after Ezek. xxvi. 9; but, inasmuch as he takes this as a figure of those who lay siege to the hearts of men, he translates: *expugnatricibus regum*, for he regards מחות as the plur. of מָחָה, a particip. noun, which he translates by *deletor*. The connecting form of the fem. plur. of this מָחָה might certainly be מְחוֹת (cf. מְזֵי, from מְזֶה), but לִמְחוֹת מלכין ought to be changed into לְמ' וגו'; for one will not appeal to anomalies, such as לְמ', xvi. 4; בַּג, Isa. xxiv. 2; לְמ', Lam. i. 19; or הַת' וגו', 1 Kings xiv. 24, to save the *Pathach* of לְמְחוֹת, which, as we saw, proceeds from an altogether different understanding of the word. But if לְמ' is to be changed into לְמ', then one must go further, since for מָחָה not an active but a conditional meaning is to be assumed, and we must write לִמְחוֹת, in favour of which Fleischer as well as Gesenius decides: *et ne committe consilia factaque tua iis quæ reges perdunt, regum pestibus.* Ewald also favours the change לְמְחוֹת, for he renders מָחָה as a denom. of מֹחַ, marrow: those who enfeeble kings, in which Kamphausen follows him. Mühlau goes further; he gives the privative signification, to enfeeble, to the *Piel* מִחָה = *makhakha* (cf. Herzog's *Real-Wörterb.* xiv. 712), which is much more probable, and proposes לְמְמַחוֹת: *iis quæ vires enervant regum.* But we can appropriately, with Nöldeke, adhere to לְמֹחוֹת, *deletricibus* (*perditricibus*), for by this change the parallelism is satisfied; and that מָחָה may be used, with immediate reference to men, of entire and total destruction, is sufficiently established by such passages as Gen. vi. 7, Judg. xxi. 17, if any proof is at all needed for it. Regarding the LXX. and those misled by it, who, by מלכין and מלכים, 4*a*, think on the Aram. מִלְכִּין, βουλαί, vid. Mühlau, p. 53.[1] But the Syr. has an idea worthy of the discourse, who translates *epulis regum* without our needing, with Mühlau, to charge him with dreaming of לְחֶם in למחות. Perhaps that is true; but perhaps by למחות he thought of לְמְחוֹת (from מֵחַ, the particip. adj. of מֵחַ): do not direct thy ways to rich food (morsels), such as kings love and can have. By this reading,

---

[1] Also Hitzig's *Blinzlerinnen* [women who ogle or leer = seductive courtesans] and Böttcher's *Streichlerinnen* [caressers, viz. of kings] are there rejected, as they deserve to be.

3*b* would mediate the transition to ver. 4; and that the mother
refers to the immorality, the unseemliness, and the dangers of a
large harem, only in one brief word (3*a*), cannot seem strange,
much rather it may be regarded as a sign of delicacy. But so
much the more badly does וּדְרָכֶיךָ accord with לְמֵהוֹת. Certainly
one goes to a banquet, for one finds leisure for it; but of one
who himself is a king, it is not said that he should not direct
his ways to a king's dainties. But if לְמֹחוֹת refers to the whole
conduct of the king, the warning is, that he should not regulate
his conduct in dependence on the love and the government of
women. But whoever will place himself amid the revelry of
lust, is wont to intoxicate himself with ardent spirits; and he
who is thus intoxicated, is in danger of giving reins to the
beast within him. Hence there now follows a warning against
drunkenness, not unmediated by the reading לְמֹחוֹת:

Ver. 4 It is not for kings, O Lemuel,
   Not for kings to drink wine,
   Not for rulers to ask for intoxicating drink;
   5 Lest he drink, and forget what is prescribed,
   And pervert the right of all the children of want.

The usual translation of 4*a* is: *non decet reges* ... (as *e.g.* also
Mühlau); but in this אַל is not rightly rendered, which indeed
is at times only an οὐ, spoken with close interest, but yet first
of all, especially in such paraenetic connection as here, it is a
dissuasive μή. But now לֹא לַמְלָכִים לִשְׁתּוֹת or לֹא לַמְלָכִים שְׁתוֹת,
after 2 Chron. xxvi. 18, Mic. iii. 1, signifies: it is not the
part of kings, it does not become them to drink, which may also
be turned into a dissuasive form: let it not be the part of kings
to drink, let them not have any business therewith, as if it belonged to their calling; according to which Fleischer renders:
Absit a regibus, Lemuel, absit a regibus potare vinum. The
clearer expression לְמוֹאֵל, instead of לְמוּאֵל, is, after Böttcher,
occasioned by this, that the name is here in the vocative; perhaps rather by this, that the meaning of the name: consecrated
to God, belonging to God, must be placed in contrast to the
descending to low, sensual lust. Both times we write אַל לַמְלָכִים
with the orthophonic *Dagesh*[1] in the ל following ל, and with-

[1] *Vid. Luth. Zeitschrift*, 1863, p. 413. It is the rule, according to
which, with Ben-Asher, it is to be written בֶּן־נּוּן

out the recompensative *Dagesh*, the want of which is in a certain measure covered by the *Metheg* (*vid.* Norzi). Regarding the *inf. constr.* שְׁתוֹ (cf. קְנֹה, xvi. 16), *vid.* Gesen. § 75, Anm. 2 ; and regarding the sequence of accents here necessary, אַל לַמְלָכִים שְׁתוֹ־יַיִן (not *Mercha, Dechi, Athnach,* for *Dechi* would be here contrary to rule), *vid. Thorath Emeth,* p. 22 § 6, p. 43 § 7. In 4b nothing is to be gained from the *Chethîb* או. There is not a substantive אָו, desire, the *constr.* of which would here have to be read, not אִו (Umbreit, Gesenius), but אַו, after the form קַו (Maurer) ; and why did the author not write תַּאֲוַת שֵׁכָר? But the particle או does not here also fall in with the connection ; for if אוֹ שֵׁכָר connect itself with יַיִן (Hitzig, Ewald, and others), then it would drag disagreeably, and we would have here a spiritless classification of things unadvisable for kings. Böttcher therefore sees in this או the remains of the obliterated סְבוֹא ; a corrector must then have transformed the או which remained into או. But before one ventures on such conjectures, the *Kerî* אֵי [where ?] must be tried. Is it the abbreviated אַיִן (Herzog's *Real-Wörterbuch,* xiv. 712) ? Certainly not, because וּלְרוֹזְנִים אֵין שֵׁכָר would mean : and the princes, or rulers (*vid.* regarding רוֹזְנִים at viii. 15), have no mead, which is inconsistent. But אַיִן does not abbreviate itself into אֵי, but into אַי. Not אֵי, but אִי, is in Heb., as well as in Ethiop., the word with which negative adjectives such as אִי נָקִי, not innocent, Job xxii. 30, and in later Heb. also, negative sentences, such as אִי אֶפְשָׁר : it is not possible, are formed.[1] Therefore Mühlau vocalizes אִי, and thinks that the author used this word for אַל, so as not to repeat this word for the third time. But how is that possible ? אִי שֵׁכָר signifies either : not mead, or : there is not mead ; and both afford, for the passage before us, no meaning. Is, then, the *Kerî* אֵי truly so unsuitable ? Indeed, to explain : how came intoxicating drink to rulers ! is inadmissible, since אֵי always means only *ubi* (*e.g.* Gen. iv. 9) ; not, like the Ethiop. *aitê,* also *quomodo.* But the

[1] The author of the Comm. עטרת זקנים to the ארח חיים, c. 6, Geiger and others would read אֵי, because אִי is abbreviated from אַיִן. But why not from אַיִן, 1 Sam. xxi. 9 ? The traditional expression is אֵי ; and Elias Levita in the *Tishbi,* as also Baer in the Siddur *Abodath Jisrael,* are right in defending it against that innovation.

question *ubi temetum*, as a question of desire, fits the connection, whether the sentence means: *non decet principibus dicere* (Ahron b. Josef supplies שיאמרו) *ubi temetum*, or: *absit a principibus quærere ubi temetum* (Fleischer), which, from our view of 4*a*, we prefer. There is in reality nothing to be supplied; but as 4*a* says that the drinking of wine ought not to characterize kings, so 4*b*, that "Where is mead?" (*i.e.* this eager inquiry after mead) ought not to characterize rulers.[1] Why not? ver. 5 says. That the prince, being a slave to drink, may not forget the מְחֻקָּק, *i.e.* that which has been made and has become חֹק, thus that which is lawfully right, and may not alter the righteous cause of the miserable, who cry against their oppressors, *i.e.* may not handle falsely the facts of the case, and give judgment contrary to them. שַׁנֶּה דִין (Aquila, Theodotion, Quinta, ἀλλοιοῦν κρίσιν) is elsewhere equivalent to הִטָּה מִשְׁפָּט (עִוֵּת). בְּנֵי־עֹנִי are those who are, as it were, born to oppression and suffering. This mode of expression is a Semitism (Fleischer), but it here heightens the impression of the Arab. colouring. In כל (*Venet.* ὡντινοῦν) it is indicated that, not merely with reference to individual poor men, but in general to the whole class of the poorer people, suffering humanity, sympathy and a regard for truth on the part of a prince given to sensuality are easily thrown aside. Wine is better suited for those who are in a condition to be timeously helped over which, is a refreshment to them.

> Ver. 6 Give strong drink to him that is perishing,
>   And wine to those whose soul is in bitter woe;
> 7 Let him drink and forget his poverty,
>   And let him think of his misery no more.

The preparation of a potion for malefactors who were condemned to death was, on the ground of these words of the proverb, cared for by noble women in Jerusalem (נשים יקרות שבירושלים), *Sanhedrin* 43*a*; Jesus rejected it, because He wished, without becoming insensible to His sorrow, to pass away from the earthly life freely and in full consciousness, Mark xv. 23.

---

[1] The translation of Jerome, *quia nullum secretum est ubi regnat ebrietas* (as if the words were לֵית רָזָא אֵי שֵׁכָר), corresponds to the proverb: נכנס יין יצא סוד, when the wine goes in the secret comes out; or, which is the same thing: if one adds יין (= 70), סוד (= 70) comes out.

The transition from the plur. to the sing. of the subject is in ver. 7 less violent than in ver. 5, since in ver. 6 singular and plur. already interchange. We write תְּנוּ־שֵׁכָר with the counter-tone *Metheg* and *Mercha*. אוֹבֵד designates, as at Job xxix. 13, xxxi. 19, one who goes to meet destruction : it combines the present signification *interiens*, the fut. signif. *interiturus*, and the perf. *perditus* (hopelessly lost). מָרֵי נָפֶשׁ (those whose minds are filled with sorrow) is also supported from the Book of Job, iii. 20, cf. xxi. 25, the language and thought and mode of writing of which notably rests on the Proverbs of Agur and Lemuel (*vid.* Mühlau, pp. 64–66). The *Venet.* τοῖς πικροῖς (not ψυχροῖς) τὴν ψυχήν. וָרִישׁ (poverty) is not, however, found there, but only in the Book of Proverbs, in which this word-stem is more at home than elsewhere. Wine rejoices the heart of man, Ps. civ. 15, and at the same time raises it for the time above oppression and want, and out of anxious sorrow, wherefore it is soonest granted to them, and in sympathizing love ought to be presented to them by whom this its beneficent influence is to be wished for. The ruined man forgets his poverty, the deeply perplexed his burden of sorrow ; the king, on the contrary, is in danger from this cause of forgetting what the law required at his hands, viz. in relation to those who need help, to whom especially his duty as a ruler refers.

> Ver. 8 Open thy mouth for the dumb,
>   For the right of all the children of leaving ;
>   9 Open thy mouth, judge righteously,
>   And do right to the poor and needy.

He is called dumb who suffers the infirmity of dumbness, as עִוֵּר and פִּסֵּחַ, Job xxix. 15, is he who suffers the infirmity of blind-ness or lameness, not here figuratively ; at the same time, he who, on account of his youth, or on account of his ignorance, or from fear, cannot speak before the tribunal for himself (Fleischer). With לְ the *dat. commodi* (LXX. after Lagarde, μογιλάλῳ ; Aquila, Symmachus, Theodotion, ἀλάλῳ ; the *Venet.* after Gebhardt, βωβῷ) אֶל, of the object aimed at, interchanges, as *e.g.* 1 Kings xix. 3, 2 Kings vii. 7, אֶל־נַפְשָׁם, for the preserva-tion of their life, or for the sake of their life, for it is seldom that it introduces the object so purely as here. And that an infin. such as חֲלוֹף should stand as a subst. occurs proportionally

seldomer in Heb. (Isa. iv. 4 ; Ps. xxii. 7 ; cf. with ה of the
artic., Num. iv. 12 ; Ps. lxvi. 9) than it does in Arab. בְּנֵי חֲלוֹף
in the same way as בְּנֵי־עֹנִי, 5b, belongs to the Arab. complexion
of this proverb, but without its being necessary to refer to the
Arab. in order to fix the meaning of these two words. Hitzig
explains after *khalf*, to come after, which further means " to
have the disadvantage," in which Zöckler follows him ; but this
verb in Arab. does not mean ὑστερεῖν (ὑστερεῖσθαι), we must
explain " sons of him that remains behind," *i.e.* such as come
not forward, but remain behind (*'an*) others. Mühlau goes
further, and explains, with Schultens and Vaihinger : those
destitute of defence, after (Arab.) *khalafahu* he is ranked next
to him, and has become his representative—a use of the word
foreign to the Heb. Still less is the rendering of Gesenius
justified, " children of inheritance " = children left behind,
after *khallafa*, to leave behind ; and Luther, " for the cause of
all who are left behind," by the phrase (Arab.) *khallfany 'an
'awnih*, he has placed me behind his help, denied it to me, for
the *Kal* of the verb cannot mean to abandon, to leave. And
that בני חלוף means the opposers of the truth, or of the poor, or
the litigious person, the quarrelsome, is perfectly inadmissible,
since the *Kal* חלוף cannot be equivalent to (Arab.) *khilaf*, the
inf. of the 3d conj., and besides, the gen. after דִּין always
denotes those in whose favour, not those against whom it is
passed ; the latter is also valid against Ralbag's "sons of
change," *i.e.* who say things different from what they think ;
and Ahron b. Josef's " sons of changing," viz. the truth into
lies. We must abide by the meaning of the Heb. חָלַף, " to
follow after, to change places, pass away." Accordingly,
Fleischer understands by חֲלוֹף, the going away, the dying, viz.
of parents, and translates : *eorum qui parentibus orbati sunt*.
In another way Rashi reaches the same sense : orphans deprived of their helper. But the connection בני חלף requires
that we make those who are intended themselves the subject of
חלוף. Rightly Ewald, Bertheau, Kamphausen, compare Isa.
ii. 18 (and Ps. xc. 5 f., this with questionable right), and understand by the sons of disappearance those whose inherited lot,
whose proper fate, is to disappear, to die, to perish (Symmachus:
πάντων υἱῶν ἀποιχομένων ; Jerome: *omnium filiorum qui per-*

transeunt). It is not men in general as children of frailty that are meant (Kimchi, Meïri, Immanuel, Euchel, and others), after which the *Venet.* τῶν υἱῶν τοῦ μεταβάλλειν (*i.e.* those who must exchange this life for another), but such as are on the brink of the abyss. צֶדֶק in שְׁפָט־צֶדֶק is not equivalent to בְּצֶדֶק, but is the accus. of the object, as at Zech. viii. 16, decide justice, *i.e.* so that justice is the result of thy judicial act; cf. Knobel on Deut. i. 16. וְדִין is imper., do right to the miserable and the poor; cf. Ps. liv. 3 with Jer. xxii. 16, v. 28. That is a king of a right sort, who directs his high function as a judge, so as to be an advocate [*procurator*] for the helpless of his people.

THIRD APPENDIX TO THE SECOND COLLECTION OF SOLOMONIC PROVERBS.—XXXI. 10 ff.

The admonitions of a faithful mother are followed by words in praise of a virtuous wife; the poet praises them through all the *prædicamenta*, *i.e.* all the twenty-two letters of the Hebrew alphabet. The artificialness of the order, says Hitzig, proves that the section belongs to a proportionally late age. But if, as he himself allows, even a Davidic psalm, viz. Ps. ix.–x., is constructed acrostically, then from this, that there the acrostic design is not so purely carried out as it is here in this ode, no substantial proof can be drawn for the more recent origin of the latter. Yet we do not deny that it belongs to an earlier time than the earliest of the era of Hezekiah. If Hitzig carries it back to the times subsequent to Alexander on account of the *scriptio plena*, without distinctive accents, vers. 17, 25, it is, on the other hand, to be remarked that it has the *scriptio plena* in common with the "utterance from Massa," which he places forward in the times of Hezekiah, without being influenced to such clear vision by writings such as יִמְלֹוךְ, xxx. 22, אוּבַד, xxxi. 6, רוֹזְנִים, xxxi. 4. Besides, the *plene* written עֹז, ver. 25, is incorrect, and בְּעֹז, ver. 17, which has its parallel in עֹז־, Ps. lxxxiv. 6, is in its form altogether dependent on the *Munach*, which was added some thousand years after.

In the LXX. this section forms the concluding section of the Book of Proverbs. But it varies from the Heb. text in that the פ (στόμα) goes before the ע (ἰσχύν). The very same sequence of letters is found in the Heb. text of Ps. xxxiv. and Lam. ii. iii. and iv.

Stier has interpreted allegorically the matron here commended. He understands thereby the Holy Ghost in His regenerating and sanctifying influence, as the *Midrash* does the *Tôra;* Ambrosius, Augustine, and others, the Church; Immanuel, the soul in covenant with God, thirsting after the truth. As if it were not an invaluable part of Biblical moral instruction which is here presented to us! Such a woman's mirror is nowhere else found. The housewife is depicted here as she ought to be; the poet shows how she governs and increases the wealth of the house, and thereby also advances the position of her husband in the common estimation, and he refers all these, her virtues and her prudence, to the fear of God as their root (Von Hofmann's *Schriftbeweis,* ii. 2. 404 f.). One of the most beautiful expositions of this section is that of Luis de Leon, *La perfecta casada* (Salamanca, 1582), which has been revived in a very attractive way by Wilkens.[1]

A wife, such as she ought to be, is a rare treasure, a good excelling all earthly possession :

> Ver. 10 א A virtuous woman, who findeth her!
> She stands far above pearls in worth.

In the connection אֵשֶׁת חַיִל and the like, the idea of bodily vigour is spiritualized to that of capacity, ability, and is generalized; in *virtus* the corresponding transition from manliness, and in the originally Romanic " *Bravheit,*" valour to ability, is completed; we have translated as at xii. 4, but also Luther, " a virtuous woman," is suitable, since *Tugend* (virtue) has with *Tüchtigkeit* [ability] the same root-word, and according to our linguistic [German] usage designates the property of moral goodness and propriety, while for those of former times, when they spoke of the *tugend* (*tugent*) of a woman, the word combined with it the idea of fine manners (cf. חֵן, xi. 16) and culture (cf. שֵׂכֶל טוֹב, xiii. 15). The question מִי יִמְצָא, *quis inveniat,* which,

---

[1] C. A. Wilkens' *Fray Luis de Leon.* A biography from the History of the Spanish Inquisition and Church of the 16th cent. (1866), pp. 322–327.

Eccles. vii. 24, proceeds from the supposition of the impossibility of finding, conveys here only the idea of the difficulty of
finding. In ancient Jerusalem, when one was married, they were
wont to ask : מצא או מוצא, *i.e.* has he found ? thus as is said at
Prov. xviii. 22, or at Eccles. vii. 26. A virtuous woman [*braves
Weib*] is not found by every one, she is found by comparatively
few. In 10*b* there is given to the thought which underlies the
question a synonymous expression. Ewald, Elster, and Zöckler
incorrectly render the ו by "although" or "and yet." Fleischer
rightly : the second clause, if not in form yet in sense, runs
parallel to the first. מֶכֶר designates the price for which such a
woman is sold, and thus is purchasable, not without reference
to this, that in the Orient a wife is obtained by means of מֹהַר.
מֶכֶר, synon. מְחִיר, for which a wife of the right kind is gained,
is רָחוֹק, placed further, *i.e.* is more difficult to be obtained, than
pearls (*vid.* regarding "pearls" at iii. 15), *i.e.* than the price for
such precious things. The poet thereby means to say that such
a wife is a more precious possession than all earthly things
which are precious, and that he who finds such an one has to
speak of his rare fortune. The reason for this is now given :

> Ver. 11 ב The heart of her husband doth trust her,
> And he shall not fail of gain.

If we interpret שָׁלָל, after Eccles. ix. 8, as subject, then we miss
לוֹ; it will thus be object., and the husband subj. to לֹא יֶחְסָר: *nec
lucro carebit*, as *e.g.* Fleischer translates it, with the remark that
שָׁלָל denotes properly the spoil which one takes from an enemy,
but then also, like the Arab. *ḍanymat*, can mean profit and gain
of all kinds (cf. Rödiger in Gesenius' *Thes.*). Thus also in
our " *kriegen* " = to come into possession, the reference to war
disappears. Hitzig understands by שׁלי, the continual prosperity
of the man on account of his fortunate possession of such a
wife; but in that case the poet should have said שִׂמְחַת שׁלל; for
שׁלל is gain, not the feeling that is therewith connected. There
is here meant the gain, profit, which the housewife is the
means of bringing in (cf. Ps. lxviii. 13). The heart of her
husband (בַּעְלָהּ) can be at rest, it can rest on her whom it loves
—he goes after his calling, perhaps a calling which, though
weighty and honourable, brings in little or nothing; but the
wife keeps the family possessions scrupulously together, and

increases them by her laborious and prudent management, so that there is not wanting to him gain, which he properly did not acquire, but which the confidence he is justified in reposing in his wife alone brings to him. She is to him a perpetual spring of nothing but good.

Ver. 12 נ She doeth good to him, and not evil,
All the days of her life;

or, as Luther translates:

"*Sie thut jm liebs vnd kein leids.*"
[She does him good, and no harm.]

She is far from ever doing him evil, she does him only good all her life long; her love is not dependent on freaks, it rests on deep moral grounds, and hence derives its power and purity, which remain ever the same. גָּמַל signifies to accomplish, to perform. To the not assimilated form גְּמָלַתְהוּ, cf. יִפְרָתוּ, 1*b*. The poet now describes how she disposes of things:

Ver. 13 ד She careth for wool and flax,
And worketh these with her hands' pleasure.

The verb דָּרַשׁ proceeds, as the Arab. shows,[1] from the primary meaning *terere*; but to translate with reference thereto: *tractat lanam et linum* (LXX., Schultens, Dathe, Rosenmüller, Fleischer), is inadmissible. The Heb. דרש does not mean the external working at or manufacturing of a thing; but it means, even when it refers to this, the intention of the mind purposely directed thereto. Thus wool and flax come into view as the material of work which she cares to bring in; and וַתַּעַשׂ signifies the work itself, following the creation of the need of work. Hitzig translates the second line: she works at the business of her hands. Certainly בְּ after עָשָׂה may denote the sphere of activity, Ex. xxxi. 4; 1 Kings v. 30, etc.; but if חֵפֶץ had here the weakened signification business, πρᾶγμα,—which it gains in the same way as we say business, affair, of any object of care,—the scarcely established meaning presents itself, that she shows herself active in that which she has made the business of her hands. How much more beautiful, on the contrary, is the thought: she is active with her hands' pleasure! חֵפֶץ is, as Schultens rightly explains, *inclinatio flexa et propensa in aliquid*, and *pulchre manibus diligentissimis attribuitur lubentia cum ob-*

---

[1] The inquirer is there called (Arab.) *daras*, as *libros terens*.

lectatione et per oblectationem sese animans. עָשָׂה, without obj. accus., signifies often: to accomplish, *e.g.* Ps. xxii. 32; here it stands, in a sense, complete in itself, and without object. accus., as when it means " *handeln* " [*agere*], xiii. 16, and particularly to act in the service of God = to offer sacrifice, Ex. x. 25; it means here, and at Ruth ii. 19, Hag. ii. 4, to be active, as at Isa. xix. 15, to be effective; וַתַּעַשׂ is equivalent to ותעשׂ בִּמְלָאכָה or וְתֵעֵשׂ מְלַאכְתָּהּ (cf. under x. 4). And pleasure and love for the work, חֵפֶץ, can be attributed to the hands with the same right as at Ps. lxxviii. 72, discretion. The disposition which animates a man, especially his inner relation to the work devolving upon him, communicates itself to his hands, which, according as he has joy or aversion in regard to his work, will be nimble or clumsy. The Syr. translates: " and her hands are active after the pleasure of her heart;" but בחפץ is not equivalent to בְּחֶפְצָהּ; also בְּחֵפֶץ, in the sense of *con amore* (Böttcher), is not used. The following proverb praises the extent of her housewifely transactions:

> Ver. 14 ה She is like the ships of the merchant—
> Bringeth her food from afar.

She is (LXX. ἐγένετο) like merchant ships (כָּאֳנִיּוֹת, indeterminate, and thus to be read *kŏŏnîjoth*), *i.e.* she has the art of such ships as sail away and bring wares from a distance, are equipped, sent out, and managed by an enterprising spirit; so the prudent, calculating look of the brave wife, directed towards the care and the advancement of her house, goes out beyond the nearest circle; she descries also distant opportunities of advantageous purchase and profitable exchange, and brings in from a distance what is necessary for the supply of her house, or, mediately, what yields this supply (מִמֶּרְחָק, Cod. *Jaman.* ממרחק, cf. under Isa. x. 6), for she finds that source of gain she has espied. With this diligence in her duties she is not a long sleeper, who is not awakened till the sun is up; but

> Ver. 15 ו She riseth up while it is yet night,
> And giveth food to her house,
> And the fixed portion to her maidens.

The *fut. consec.* express, if not a logical sequence of connection, yet a close inner binding together of the separate features of the character here described. Early, ere the morning dawns,

such a housewife rises up, because she places care for her
house above her own comfort; or rather, because this care is to
her a satisfaction and a joy. Since now the poet means without doubt to say that she is up before the other inmates of the
house, especially before the children, though not before the
maids: we have not, in וַתִּתֵּן, to think that the inmates of
the house, all in the morning night-watch, stand round about
her, and that each receives from her a portion for the approaching day; but that she herself, early, whilst yet the most
are asleep, gives out or prepares the necessary portions of food
for the day (cf. וַיִּתֵּן, Isa. liii. 9). Regarding טֶרֶף, food, from
טָרַף (to tear in pieces, viz. with the teeth), and regarding חֹק, a
portion decreed, vid. at xxx. 8. It is true that חֹק also means
the appointed labour (pensum), and thus the day's work
(דְּבַר יוֹם); but the parallelism brings it nearer to explain after
xxx. 8, as is done by Gesenius and Hitzig after Ex. v. 14.
This industry,—a pattern for the whole house,—this punctu-
ality in the management of household matters, secures to her
success in the extension of her household wealth :

> Ver. 16 ? She seeketh a field and getteth possession of it ;
>   Of the fruit of her hands she planteth a vineyard.

The field which she considereth, towards which her wish and
her effort are directed, is perhaps not one beyond those which
she already possesses, but one which has hitherto been wanting
to her family; for the poet has, after ver. 23, an inhabitant of
a town in his eye,—a woman whose husband is not a landlord,
but has a business in the city. The perf. זָמְמָה precedes and
gives circumstantiality to the chief factum expressed by וַתִּקָּחֵהָ.
Regarding זָמַם, vid. xxi. 27. "לָקַח is the general expression
for purchasing, as נָתַן, 24b, for selling. Thus the Aram. and
Arab. אֲחַד, while, (Arab.) akhadh w'ta, Turk. alisch werisch
(from elmek, to take, and wirmek, to give—viz. sâtün, in the
way of selling; Lat. venum), post.-bibl. מַשָּׂא וּמַתָּן or מִקָּח וּמִמְכָּר,
denotes giving and taking = business in general" (Fleischer).
In 16b the Chethîb is, with Ewald and Bertheau, to be read נֶטַע,
and, with Hitzig, to be made dependent on ותקחה, as parallel
obj.: " of her hands' fruit (she gaineth) a planting of vines."
But a planting of vines would be expressed by מַטַּע כרם (Mic.
i. 6); and the Kerî נָטְעָה is more acceptable. The perf., as a

fundamental verbal form, is here the expression of the abstract
present: she plants a vineyard, for she purchases vines from
the profit of her industry (Isa. vii. 23, cf. v. 2). The poet has
this augmented household wealth in his eye, for he continues:

> Ver. 17 ח She girdeth her loins with strength,
> And moveth vigorously her arms.

Strength is as the girdle which she wraps around her body (Ps.
xciii. 1). We write חָגְרָה בְעוֹז; both words have *Munach*, and
the ב of בעוז is aspirated. Thus girded with strength, out of
this fulness of strength she makes firm or steels her arms (cf.
Ps. lxxxix. 22). The produce of the field and vineyard extend
far beyond the necessity of her house; thus a great portion is
brought to sale, and the gain thence arising stimulates the
industry and the diligence of the unwearied woman.

> Ver. 18 ט She perceiveth that her gain is good;
> And her light goeth not out at night.

The perf. and fut. are related to each other as antecedent and
consequent, so that 18*a* can also be rendered as an hypothetical
antecedent. She comes to find (taste) how profitable her
industry is by the experience resulting from the sale of its product: the corn, the grapes, and the wine are found to be good,
and thus her gain (cf. iii. 14) is better, this opened new source
of nourishment productive.

This spurs on her active industry to redoubled effort, and at
times, when she is not fully occupied by the oversight of her
fields and vineyard, she has another employment over which
her light goes not out till far in the night. בַּלַּיְלָה is, as at Lam.
ii. 19, a needless *Kerî* for the poetic בַּלֵּיל (Isa. xvi. 3). What
other business it is to which she gives attention till in the
night, is mentioned in the next verse.

> Ver. 19 י She putteth her hand to the rock [*Spinnrocken*];
> And her fingers lay hold on the spindle.

She applies herself to the work of spinning, and performs it with
skill. The phrase שִׁלַּח יָד בְּ (שָׁלַח, Job xxviii. 9) signifies to take
up an object of work, and תָּמַךְ, with obj. accus. (cf. Amos i. 5),
the handling of the instrument of work necessary thereto. כַּפִּים
denotes the hands when the subject is skilful, successful work;
we accordingly say יָגִיע כפים, not יניע ידים; cf. vers. 13 and 16,

Ps. lxxviii. 72. What פֶּלֶךְ means is shown by the Arab. *falakat*, which, as distinguished from *mighzal*, *i.e. fuseau* (Lat. *fusus*), is explained by *bout arrondi et conique au bas du fuseau*, thus: the whorl, *i.e.* the ring or knob fastened on the spindle below, which gives it its necessary weight and regulates its movement, Lat. *verticellus*, post-bibl. פִּיקָה (which Bartenora glosses by the Ital. *fusajuolo*) or צִנּוֹרָה, *e.g. Kelim* ix. 6, כּוֹשׁ שֶׁבָּלַע אֶת הַצִּנּוֹרָה, a spindle which holds the whorl hidden (*vid.* Aruch under כּשׁ, iii.). But the word then also signifies *per synecdochen partis pro toto*, the spindle, *i.e.* the cylindrical wood on which the thread winds itself when spinning (cf. 2 Sam. iii. 29, where it means the staff on which the infirm leans); Homer gives to Helen and the goddesses golden spindles (χρυσηλάκατοι). Accordingly it is not probable that כִּישׁוֹר also denotes the whorl, as Kimchi explains the word: " כישור is that which one calls by the name *verteil*, viz. that which one fixes on the spindle (פלך) above to regulate the spinning (מטוה)," according to which the *Venet.* renders כישור by σφόνδυλος, whorl, and פלך by ἄτρακτος, spindle. The old interpreters have not recognised that כישור denotes a thing belonging to the spinning apparatus; the LXX., Aquila, Symmachus, Theodotion, Syr., and Jerome see therein an ethical idea (from כָּשֵׁר, to be capable, able); but Luther, not misled thereby, translates with unusual excellence:

> She stretches her hand to the rock,
> And her fingers grasp the spindle.

He has in this no predecessors, except only the Targumists, whose כּוּנְשָׁרָא (*vid.* Levy) appears also to denote the spinning-rock. The Syriac and Talmudic כּוּשׁ, which is compared by Gesenius-Dietrich, is another word, and denotes, not the rock, but the spindle. Immanuel also, who explains פלך as the מֵעֲזָל, *i.e.* the spindle, understands (as perhaps also Parchon) by כישור the rock. And why should not the rock (*wocken* = distaff), *i.e.* the stock to which the tuft of flax, hemp, or wool is fixed for the purpose of being spun, Lat. *colus*, not be named כִּישׁוֹר, from כשׁר, to be upright as a stick, upright in height, or perhaps more correctly as מכשׁיר, *i.e.* as that which prepares or makes fit the flax for spinning? Also in צִינֹק, Jer. xxix. 26, there are united the meanings of the close and the confining dungeon, and שִׁילוֹן = שָׁלֹה

signifies[1] the place which yields rest. The spinning-wheel is a German invention of the 16th century, but the rock standing on the ground, or held also in the hands, the spindle and the whorl, are more ancient.[2] With the spindle תמך stands in fit relation, for it is twirled between the fingers, as Catullus says of Fate:

Libratum tereti versabat pollice fusum.[3]

That which impels the housewife to this labour is not selfishness, not a narrow-hearted limitation of her care to the circle of what is her own, but love, which reaches out far beyond this circle:

Ver. 20 כ She holdeth out her hand to the unfortunate,
And stretcheth forth her hands to the needy.

With כַּפֶּיהָ, 19b, is connected the idea of artistic skilfulness; with כַּפָּהּ, here that of offering for counsel (*vid.* at Isa. ii. 6); with sympathy and readiness to help, she presents herself to those who are oppressed by the misfortunes of life as if for an alliance, as if saying: place confidence in me, I shall do whatever I can—there thou hast my hand! Hitzig erroneously thinks of the open hand with a gift lying in it: this ought to be named, for כף in itself is nothing else than the half-opened

---

[1] Otherwise, but improbably, Schultens: *colus a* בשר = *katr kathr, necti in orbem, circumnecti in globum.* In פֶּלֶך, whence פֶּלֶךְ, he rightly finds the primary meaning of *circumvolutio sive gyratio.*

[2] A view of the ancient art of spinning is afforded by the figures of the 12th Dynasty (according to Lepsius, 2380–2167 B.C.) in the burial chamber of *Beni Hassan* (270 kilometres above Bulak, on the right bank of the Nile). M. J. Henry, in his work *L'Egypte Pharaonique* (Paris 1846), Bd. 2, p. 431, mentions that there are figures there which represent " *toutes les opérations de la fabrication des tissus depuis le filage jusqu au tissage.*" Then he continues : *Lex fuseaux dont se servent les fileuses sont exactement semblables aux nôtres, et on voit même ces fileuses imprimer le mouvement de rotation à ces fuseaux, en en froissant le bout inferieur entre leur main et leur cuisse.*

[3] In the "marriage of Peleus and Thetis," Catullus describes the work of the Fates : " Their hands are ceaselessly active at their never-ending work ; while the left holds the rock, surrounded with a soft fleece, the right assiduously draws the thread and forms it with raised fingers ; then it swiftly turns the spindle, with the thumb stretched down, and swings it away in whirling circles." Then follows the refrain of the song of the Fates:

Currite ducentes subtegmina, currite, fusi.

(After HERTZBERG'S *Translation.*)

hand. Also in 20*b* we are not to think of alms. Here Hitzig rightly: she stretches out to him both of her hands, that he might grasp them, both of them, or whichever he may. She does not throw to him merely a gift from a distance, but above all she gives to him to experience her warm sympathy (cf. Ezek. xvi. 49). Here, as at 19*a*, שלחה is punctuated (with *Dagesh*) as *Piel*. The punctuation supposes that the author both times not unintentionally made use of the intensive form. This one verse (20) is complete in itself as a description of character; and the author has done well in choosing such strong expressions, for, without this sympathy with misery and poverty, she, so good and trustworthy and industrious, might indeed be pleasing to her husband, but not to God. One could almost wish that greater expansion had been given to this one feature in the picture. But the poet goes on to describe her fruitful activity in the nearest sphere of her calling:

> Ver. 21 ל She is not afraid of the snow for her house;
> For her whole house is clothed in scarlet.

A fall of snow in the rainy season of winter is not rare in Palestine, the Hauran, and neighbouring countries, and is sometimes accompanied with freezing cold.[1] She sees approaching the cold time of the year without any fear for her house, even though the season bring intense cold; for her whole house, *i.e.* the whole of the members of her family, are לְבֻשׁ שָׁנִים. The connection is accusatival (*Venet.* ἐνδεδυμένος ἐρυθρά), as at 2 Sam. xv. 32; Ezek. ix. 2, 3. שָׁנִי, from שָׁנָה, to shine, glance clear, or high red, and is with or without תּוֹלַעַת the name of the colour of the *Kermes* worm, crimson or scarlet, perhaps to be distinguished from אַרְגָּמָן, the red-purple shell colour; and תְּכֵלֶת, the blue. שָׁנִים are clothing or material coloured with such שָׁנִי (bright red) (*vid.* at Isa. i. 18). The explanation of the word by *dibapha* is inadmissible, because the doubled colouring, wherever it is mentioned, always refers to the purple, particularly that of Tyre (*dibapha Tyria*), not to the scarlet.[2] But why does the poet name scarlet-coloured clothing? On

---

[1] *Vid.* regarding a fall of snow in Jerusalem, the journal *Saat auf Hoffnung Jahrg.* 3, Heft 3; and in the Hauran Comm. to Job xxxviii. 22.

Vid. Blümner's *Die gewerbliche Thätigkeit der Völker des klassischen Alterthums* (1869), p. 21 f.

account of the contrast to the white snow, says Hitzig, he clothes the family in crimson. But this contrast would be a meaningless freak. Rather it is to be supposed that there is ascribed to the red material a power of retaining the heat, as there is to the white that of keeping off the heat; but evidences for this are wanting. Therefore Rosenmüller, Vaihinger, and Böttcher approve of the translation *duplicibus* (Jerome, Luther) [= with double clothing], because they read, with the LXX., שְׁנַיִם.[1] But, with right, the Syr., Targ. abide by וְהוֹרִיתָא, scarlet. The scarlet clothing is of wool, which as such preserves warmth, and, as high-coloured, appears at the same time dignified (2 Sam. i. 24). From the protecting, and at the same time ornamental clothing of the family, the poet proceeds to speak of the bed-places, and of the attire of the housewife:

> Ver. 22 מ She prepareth for herself pillows;
> Linen and purple is her raiment.

Regarding מַרְבַדִּים (with ב *raphatum*), *vid*. at vii. 16. Thus, pillows or mattresses (Aquila, Theodotion, περιστρώματα; Jerome, *stragulatam vestem;* Luther, *Decke* = coverlets) to make the bed soft and to adorn it (Kimchi: לִפּוֹת עַל המטות, according to which *Venet.* κόσμια); Symmachus designates it as ἀμφιτάπους, *i.e.* τάπητες (*tapetæ, tapetia,* carpets), which are hairy (shaggy) on both sides.[2] Only the LXX. makes out of it δισσὰς χλαίνας, lined overcoats, for it brings over שנים. By עָשְׂתָה־לָּהּ it is not meant that she prepares such pillows for her own bed, but that she herself (*i.e.* for the wants of her house) prepares them. But she also clothes herself in costly attire. שֵׁשׁ (an Egyptian word, not, as Heb., derived from שֵׁשׁ, cogn. שׁוּשׁ, to be white) is the old name for linen, according to which the Aram. translates it by בּוּץ, the Greek by βύσσος, *vid.* *Genesis*, pp. 470, 557, to which the remark is to be added, that

---

[1] The LXX. reads together שנים מרבדים, δισσὰς χλαίνας, and brings into vers. 21 (her husband remains without care for the members of the family if it does not snow χιονίζῃ, as it is to be read for χρονίζῃ) and 22 the husband, who appears to the translator too much kept in the background.

[2] *Vid.* Lumbroso, *Recherches sur l'Economie politique de l'Egypte sous les Lagides* (Turin, 1870), p. 111; *des tapis de laine de première qualité, pourpres, laineux des deux côtés* (ἀμφίταποι).

the linen [Byssus], according to a prevailing probability, was
not a fine cotton cloth, but linen cloth.   Luther translates שֵׁשׁ,
here and elsewhere, by *weisse Seide* [white silk] (σηρικόν, *i.e.*
from the land of the Σῆρες, Rev. xviii. 12) ; but the silk is first
mentioned by Ezekiel under the name of מֶשִׁי ; and the ancients
call the country where silk - stuff (*bombycina*) was woven,
uniformly Assyria.   אַרְגָּמָן (Aram. אַרְגְּוָן, derived by Benfey,
with great improbability, from the rare Sanscrit word *rága-
vant*, red-coloured ; much rather from רָגֻם = רָקַם, as stuff of
variegated colour) is red purple ; the most valuable purple
garments were brought from Tyre and Sidon.

Now, first, the description turns back to the husband, of the
woman who is commended, mentioned in the introduction :

> Ver. 23 ג Well known in the gates is her husband,
> Where he sitteth among the elders of the land.

Such a wife is, according to xii. 4, עֲטֶרֶת בַּעְלָהּ,—she advances
the estimation and the respect in which her husband is held.
He has, in the gates where the affairs of the city are de-
liberated upon, a well-known, reputable name ; for there he
sits, along with the elders of the land, who are chosen into the
council of the city as the chief place of the land, and has a
weighty voice among them.   The phrase wavers between נוֹדָע
(LXX. περίβλεπτος γίνεται ; *Venet.* ἔλνωσται) and נוֹדָע.   The
old Venetian edd. have in this place (like the Cod. *Jaman.*),
and at Ps. ix. 17, נוֹדָע ; on the contrary, Ps. lxxvi. 2, Eccles.
vi. 10, נוֹדָע, and that is correct ; for the Masora, at this place
and at Ps. lxxvi. 2 (in the *Biblia rabb.*), is disfigured.   The
description, following the order of the letters, now directs attention to the profitable labour of the housewife :

> Ver. 24 ד She prepareth body-linen and selleth it,
> And girdles doth she give to the Phœnicians.

It is a question whether סָדִין signifies σινδών, cloth from
Sindhu, the land of India (*vid.* at Isa. iii. 23) ; the Arab. *sadn*
(*sadl*), to cause to hang down, to descend (for the purpose of
covering or veiling), offers an appropriate verbal root.   In the
Talmud, סדין is the sleeping linen, the curtain, the embroidered
cloth, but particularly a light smock-frock, as summer costume,
which was worn on the bare body (cf. Mark xiv. 51 f.).
Kimchi explains the word by night-shirt ; the *Edictum Diocle-*

tiani, xviii. 16, names σινδόνες κοιταρίαι, as the *Papyrus Louvre,* ὀθόνια ἐγκοιμήτρια; and the connection in the Edict shows that linen attire (ἐκ λίνου) is meant, although—as with שֵׁשׁ, so also with סדין—with the ancients and the moderns, sometimes linen and sometimes cotton is spoken of without any distinction. Æthicus speaks of costly girdles, *Cosmogr.* 84, as fabricated at Jerusalem : *baltea regalia . . . ex Hierosolyma allata;* Jerusalem and Scythopolis were in later times the chief places in Palestine for the art of weaving. In Galilee also, where excellent flax grew, the art of weaving was carried on ; and the ὀθόναι, which, according to Clemens Alex. *Pædag.* ii. 10, p. 239, were exported ἐκ γῆς Ἑβραίων, are at least in their material certainly synon. with σινδόνες. Regarding נָתַן, syn. מָכַר, opp. לָקַח, syn. נָשָׂא = קָנָה, *vid.* at 16*a.* There is no reason to interpret כְּנַעֲנִי here, with the obliteration of the ethnographical meaning, in the general sense of סֹחֵר, trader, merchant ; for purple, 22*b,* is a Phœnician manufacture, and thus, as an article of exchange, can be transferred to the possession of the industrious wife. The description is now more inward :

> Ver. 25 ע Strength and honour is her clothing ;
> Thus she laugheth at the future day.

She is clothed with עֹז, strength, *i.e.* power over the changes of temporal circumstances, which easily shatter and bring to ruin a household resting on less solid foundations; clothed with הָדָר, glory, *i.e.* elevation above that which is low, little, common, a state in which they remain who propose to themselves no high aim after which they strive with all their might : in other words, her raiment is just pride, true dignity, with which she looks confidently into the future, and is armed against all sorrow and care. The connection of ideas, עֹז והדר (defectively written, on the contrary, at Ps. lxxxiv. 6, Masora, and only there written *plene,* and with *Munach*), instead of the frequent הוֹד והדר, occurs only here. The expression 25*b* is like Job xxxix. 7, wherefore Hitzig rightly compares Job xxiv. 14 to 25*a.* יוֹם אַחֲרוֹן, distinguished from אַחֲרִית, and incorrectly interpreted (Rashi) of the day of death, is, as at Isa. xxx. 8, the future, here that which one at a later period may enter upon.

The next verse presents one of the most beautiful features in the portrait :

Ver. 26 פ She openeth her mouth with wisdom,
And amiable instruction is on her tongue.

The ב of בְּחָכְמָה is, as also at Ps. xlix. 5, lxxviii. 2, that of means : when she speaks, then it is wisdom pressing itself from her heart outward, by means of which she breaks the silence of her mouth. With עַל, in the expression 26*b*, elsewhere תַּחַת interchanges : under the tongue, Ps. x. 7, one has that which is ready to be spoken out, and on the tongue, Ps. xv. 3, that which is in the act of being spoken out. תּוֹרַת־חֶסֶד is a genitive connection after the manner of *tôrath* אֱמֶת, Mal. ii. 6. The gen. is not, as at Lev. vi. 2, in *tôrath* הָעֹלָה, the gen. of the object (thus *e.g.* Fleischer's *institutio ad humanitatem*), but the gen. of property, but not so that חסד denotes grace (Symmachus, νόμος ἐπίχαρις; Theodotion, νόμος χάριτος), because for this meaning there is no example except Isa. xl. 6; and since חסד in the O. T. is the very same as in the N. T., love, which is the fulfilling of the law, Hos. vi. 6, cf. 1 Kings xx. 31,[1] it is supposed that the poet, since he writes תורת חֶסֶד, and not תורת חֵן, means to designate by חֶסֶד this property without which her love for her husband, her industry, her high sentiment, would be no virtues, viz. unselfish, sympathizing, gentle love. Instruction which bears on itself the stamp of such amiability, and is also gracious, *i.e.* awakening love, because going forth from love (according to which Luther, translating *holdselige Lere* = pleasing instructions, thus understands it)—such instruction she carries, as house-mother (i. 8), in her mouth. Accordingly the LXX. translate (*vid.* Lagarde regarding the mistakes of this text before us) θεσμοὶ ἐλεημοσύνης, and Jerome *lex clementiæ*. חֶסֶד is related to אַהֲבָה as grace to love; it denotes love showing itself in kindness and gracefulness, particularly condescending love, proceeding from a compassionate sympathy with the sufferings and wants of men. Such graceful instruction she communicates

---

[1] Immanuel remarks that *Tôrath* חסד probably refers to the *Tôra*, and שכולה חסד, *i.e.* which is wholly love, which goes forth in love, to the *Gesetz* = statute.

now to this and now to that member of her household, for nothing that goes on in her house escapes her observation.

Ver. 27 צ   She looketh well to the ways of her house,
         And eateth not the bread of idleness.

Although there exists an inner relation between 27*a* and ver. 26, yet 27*a* is scarcely to be thought of (Hitzig) as appos. to the suffix in לִשׁוֹנָהּ.   Participles with or without determination occur in descriptions frequently as predicates of the subject standing in the discourse of the same force as abstr. present declarations, *e.g.* Isa. xl. 22 f., Ps. civ. 13 f.   צוֹפִיָּה is connected with the accus. of the object of the intended warning, like xv. 3, and is compared according to the form with הֹמִיָּה, vii. 11. הֲלִיכָה signifies elsewhere things necessary for a journey, Job vi. 19, and in the *plur. magnificus* it denotes show (*pompa*), Hab. iii. 6 : but originally the walk, conduct, Nah. ii. 6; and here in the plur. walks = comings and goings, but not these separately, but in general, the *modi procedendi* (LXX. διατριβαι).   The *Chethîb* has הילכות, probably an error in writing, but possibly also the plur. of הֲלָכָה, thus found in the post.-bibl. Heb. (after the form צְדָקוֹת), custom, viz. appointed traditional law, but also like the Aram. הִלְכָא (*emph.* הִלְכְתָא), usage, manner, common practice.   Hitzig estimates this *Chethîb,* understood Talmudically, as removing the section into a late period ; but this Talmudical signification is not at all appropriate (Hitzig translates, with an incorrect rendering of צוֹפִיה, " for she sees after the ordering of the house "), and besides the Aram. הִלְכָא, *e.g.* Targ. Prov. xvi. 9, in the first line, signifies only the walk or the manner and way of going, and this gives with the *Kerî* essentially the same signification.   Luther well : *Sie schawet wie es in jrem Hause zugeht* [= she looks how it goes in her house].   Her eyes are turned everywhere ; she is at one time here, at another there, to look after all with her own eyes ; she does not suffer the day's work, according to the instructions given, to be left undone, while she folds her own hands on her bosom ; but she works, keeping an oversight on all sides, and does not eat the bread of idleness (עַצְלוּת = עַצְלָה, xix. 15), but bread well deserved, for εἴ τις οὐ θέλει ἐργάζεσθαι, μηδὲ ἐσθιέτω, 2 Thess. iii. 10.

Now begins the finale of this song in praise of the virtuous woman :

> Ver. 28 ק Her sons rise up and bless her,
> Her husband (riseth up) and praiseth her.

The *Piel* אִשֵּׁר in such a connection is denom. of אֹשֶׁר (אַשְׁרֵי). Her children rise up (קוּם, like *e.g.* Jer. xxvi. 17, but here, perhaps, with the associated idea of reverential honour) and bless her, that she has on her part brought the house and them to such prosperity, such a position of respect, and to a state where love (חסד) reigns, and her husband rises up and sings her praise.

> Ver. 29 ר " Many are the daughters who have done bravely,
> But thou hast surpassed them all together."

We have already often remarked, last time under xxix. 6, that רַב, not indeed in its sing., but in its plur. רַבִּים and רַבּוֹת, can precede, after the manner of a numeral, as attribute ; but this syntactical licence, xxviii. 12, by no means appears, and needs to be assumed as little here as at viii. 26, although there is no reason that can be adduced against it. עָשָׂה חַיִל signifies here not the gaining of riches (the LXX., Syr., Targ., Jerome, Luther, Gesenius, Böttcher, and others), which here, where the encomium comes to its height, would give to it a mercenary mammon-worship note—it indeed has this signification only when connected with לְ of the person : *Sibi opes acquirere*, Deut. vi. 17; Ezek. xxviii. 4—but: bravery, energy, and, as the reference to אֵשֶׁת חַיִל demands, moral activity, capacity for activity, in accordance with one's calling, ποιεῖν ἀρετήν, by which the *Venet.* translates it. בָּנוֹת is, as in the primary passages, Gen. xxx. 13, Song vi. 9, a more delicate, finer name of women than נָשִׁים : many daughters there have always been who have unfolded ability, but thou my spouse hast raised thyself above them all, *i.e.* thou art excellent and incomparable. Instead of עָלִית, there is to be written, after Chajug, Aben Ezra (*Zachoth* 7a), and Jekuthiel under Gen. xvi. 11, עָלִיתְ; the Spanish *Nakdanim* thus distinguish the forms מָצָאתְ, thou hast found, and מָצָאת, she has found. כִּלְּנָה, for כֻּלָּן, Gen. xlii. 36. What now follows is not a continuation of the husband's words of praise (Ewald, Elster, Löwenstein), but an *epiphonema auctoris*

(Schultens) ; the poet confirms the praise of the husband by referring it to the general ground of its reason :

> Ver. 30 שׁ Grace is deceit; and beauty, vanity.—
>
>   A wife that feareth Jahve, she shall be praised.

Grace is deceit, because he who estimates the works of a wife merely by the loveliness of her external appearance, is deceived by it; and beauty is vanity, *vanitas,* because it is nothing that remains, nothing that is real, but is subject to the law of all material things—transitoriness. The true value of a wife is measured only by that which is enduring, according to the moral background of its external appearance ; according to the piety which makes itself manifest when the beauty of bodily form has faded away, in a beauty which is attractive.[1] יִרְאַת (with *Makkeph* following)[2] is here the connective form of יְרֵאָה (fem. of יָרֵא). The *Hithpa.* תִּתְהַלֵּל is here manifestly (xxvii. 2) not reflexive, but representative of the passive (cf. xii. 8, and the frequently occurring מְהֻלָּל, *laudatus = laudandus*), nowhere occurring except in the passage before us. In itself the fut. may also mean : she will be praised = is worthy of praise, but the jussive rendering (Luther : Let her be praised) is recommended by the verse which follows :

> Ver. 31 ת Give to her of the fruit of her hands ;
>
>   And let her works praise her in the gates!

The fruit of her hands is the good which, by her conduct, she has brought to maturity,—the blessing which she has secured for others, but, according to the promise (Isa. iii. 10), has also secured for her own enjoyment. The first line proceeds on the idea that, on account of this blessing, she herself shall rejoice. תְּנוּ־לָהּ (with *Gaja,* after *Metheg-Setzung,* § 37) is not equivalent to give to her honour because of . . .; for in that case, instead of the ambiguous מִן, another preposition—such *e.g.* as עַל —would have been used ; and so תְּנוּ, of itself, cannot be equi-

---

[1] *Vid.* the application of ver. 30 in *Taanith* 26b: " Young man," say the maidens, " lift up thine eyes and behold that which thou choosest for thyself ! Direct thine eyes not to beauty (נוֹי), direct thine eyes to the family (מִשְׁפָּחָה) ; pleasantness is a deception, etc."

[2] The writing יְרָאַת־ is that of Ben Asher, יִרְאַת that of Ben Naphtali ; Norzi, from a misunderstanding, claims יְרָאַת־ (with *Gaja*) as Ben Asher's manner of writing.

valent to חַנּוּ (sing the praise of), as Ziegler would read, after Judg. xi. 40. It must stand with כבוד, or instead of מִפְּרִי an accus. obj. is to be thought of, as at Ps. lxviii. 35, Deut. xxxii. 3, which the necessity of the case brings with it,—the giving, as a return in the echo of the song of praise. Immanuel is right in explaining תנו־לה by תגמלו לה חסד or עשׂו עתה חסד וכבוד, cf. Ps. xxviii. 4. The מִן, as is not otherwise to be expected, after תנו is partitive : give to her something of the fruit of her hands, *i.e.* recompense it to her, render it thankfully, by which not exclusively a requital in the form of honourable recognition, but yet this specially, is to be thought of. Her best praise is her works themselves. In the gates, *i.e.* in the place where the representatives of the people come together, and where the people are assembled, her works praise her ; and the poet desires that this may be right worthily done, full of certainty that she merits it, and that they honour themselves who seek to praise the works of such a woman, which carry in themselves their own commendation.

NOTE.

The Proverbs peculiar to the Alexandrine Translation.

In the LXX. there are not a few proverbs which are not found in the Heb. text, or, as we may express it, are peculiar to the Egyptian Text Recension, as distinguished from the Palestinean. The number is not so great as they appear to be on a superficial examination ; for many of these apparently independent proverbs are duplicate translations. In many places there follows the Greek translation of the Heb. proverbs another translation, *e.g.* at i. 14, 27, ii. 2, iii. 15, iv. 10, vi. 25*b*, x. 5, xi. 16, xiv. 22, xv. 6, xvi. 26, xxiii. 31, xxix. 7*b*, 25, xxxi. 29*a*. These duplicate translations are found sometimes at different places, *e.g.* xvii. 20*b* is duplicate to xvii. 16*d*; xix. 15 is duplicate to xviii. 8 ; xxii. 9*cd* = xix. 6*b*, i. 19*b*; xxix. 17 is duplicate to xxviii. 17*cd* ; or, according to the enumeration of the verses as it lies before us, not within the compass of one verse to which they belong : xxii. 8, 9 is a duplicate translation of ver. 8*b* and 9*a* of the Heb. text; xxiv. 23, xxx. 1, a duplicate translation of xxx. 1; and xxxi. 26, 27*b*, of xxxi. 26 of the Heb. text.[1] Everywhere, here, along with the translated proverb of our Heb. text, there is not an independent one. Also one has to be on his guard against seeing independent proverbs where the translator only, at his own will, modified one of the Heb. proverbs lying before us, as *e.g.* at x. 10, xiii. 23, xix. 7, as he here and there lets his Alexandrine exegesis influence him, ii. 16 f., v. 5, ix. 6, and adds explanatory clauses, ii. 19, iii. 18, v. 3, ix. 12; seldom fortunate in this, oftener, as at i. 18, 22, 28, ix. 12, xxviii. 10, showing by these interpolations his want of knowledge. There are also, in the translation, here and there passages introduced from some other part of Scripture, *e.g.*: i. 7*ab* = Ps. cxi. 10, LXX.; iii. 22*cd* = iii. 8; iii. 28*c* = xxvii. 1*b*, xiii. 5*c*, from Ps. cxii. 5, cf. xxxvii. 21; xvi. 1 ($\H{o}\sigma\varphi$ $\mu\acute{\epsilon}\gamma\alpha\varsigma$ $\kappa.\tau.\lambda.$) = Sir. iii. 18; xxvi. 11*cd* = Sir. iv. 21. A free reminiscence, such as xvi. 17, may speak a certain independence, but not those borrowed passages.

Keeping out of view all this only apparent independence, we place together the independent proverbs contained in the LXX., and, along with them, we present a translation of them into Heb. Such a translation has already been partly attempted by Ewald, Hitzig, and Lagarde; perhaps we have been here and there more fortunate in our rendering. It is certainly doubtful whether the translator found all these proverbs existing in Heb. Many of them appear to be originally Greek. But the rendering of them into Hebrew is by no means useless. It is of essential importance in forming a judgment regarding the original language.[2]

[1] One must suppose that here translations of other Greeks, which were placed alongside of the LXX. in Origen's *Hexapla*, were taken up into the LXX. But this is not confirmed : these duplicates were component parts of the LXX., which Origen and the Syriac translators found already existing.

[2] These the translator has not printed, because, however interesting it may be to the student of the Hebrew language as such, to compare Delitzsch's renderings into Hebrew with the Greek original, as placed before him, they may be here omitted, inasmuch as all that is of importance on the subject, in an exegetical point of view, has been already embodied in the Commentary.]

There are a few grains of wheat, and, on the other hand, much chaff, in these proverbs that are peculiar to the LXX. They are not, in the most remote way, fit to supply the place of the many proverbs of our Heb. text which are wanting in the LXX. One must also here be cautious in examining them. Thus, *e.g.*, xvii. 19 stands as a proverb of only one line ; the second forms a part of ver. 16. As true defects, we have noticed the following proverbs and parts of proverbs : i. 16, vii. 25*b*, viii. 32*b*, 33, xi. 3*b*, 4, 10*b*, xviii. 8, 23, 24, xix. 1, 2, 15, xxi. 5, xxii. 6, xxiii. 23, xxv. 20*a*. All these proverbs and parts of proverbs of the Heb. text are wanting in the LXX.

It is difficult to solve the mystery of this Alexandrine translation, and to keep separate from each other the Text Recension which the translator had before him, the transformations and corrections which, of his own authority, he made on the corruptions which the text of the translation, as it came from the first translator and the later revisers of it, has suffered in the course of time. They appear in Egypt to have been as arbitrary as incompetent in handling the sacred Scriptures. The separating from each other of the proverbs of Agur and Lemuel, xxx.–xxxi. 9, has its side-piece in the separation of Jeremiah's procemiums of the prophecies concerning the people, Jer. xxv.

INDEXES

I.—WORDS ETYMOLOGICALLY EXPLAINED.

אָבַד, x. 28, xix. 9.

אֲבוֹי, xxiii. 29.

אֵבוּס, xiv. 4.

אָגוּר, *pr. n.*, xxx. 1.

אֲהָלִים, vii. 17.

אוּל, xiv. 24.

אִוֶּלֶת, v. 23, xiv. 24.

אָזַל, xx. 14.

אָטוּן, vii. 16.

אֵיפָה, xx. 10.

אִישׁוֹן, vii. 2.

אֵיתָן, xiii. 15.

אַכְזָרִי, xvii. 12.

אָכַף, xvi. 26.

אֵל, xxii. 7.

אַלּוּף, ii. 17.

אַלְקוּם, xxx. 31.

אָלַף, xxii. 24.

אֶלֶף, xiv. 4.

אָמוֹן, viii. 30.

אמן, *Hiphil*, xxvi. 25, *note*, cf. viii. 30.

אָנָה, xii. 21.

אָסַם, iii. 10.

אַף כִּי, xi. 31, cf. xv. 11.

אֹפֶן, xxv. 11.

אֵצֶל, vii. 8.

אַרְגָּמָן, xxxi. 22.

אֲרֻחָה, xv. 17.

אָרַר, iii. 33.

אִשּׁוּן, xx. 20.

אֶשְׁנָב, vii. 6.

אָשָׁר, iv. 14.

בֶּגֶד, ii. 19, xi. 3.

R. בד, x. 28, xix. 9.

בָּהַל, xxviii. 22.

בֶּהֱמָה, xii. 1.

בּוֹשׁ, xxix. 26.

בָּחוּר, xx. 30.

בָּחַן, xvii. 3.

בָּטָה (בָּטָא), xii. 18.

בָּטַח, iii. 5.

בֶּטֶן, xiii. 25, xx. 27.

בִּין, i. 2.

בַּל, xxiv. 23.

בְּלִיַּעַל, vi. 12.

בְּעַד, vi. 25.

בָּעַר בְּעִיר, xii. 1, xxx. 2, *note*.

בָּקָר, i. 28.

בָּקַשׁ, xi. 27.

R. בר, xxx. 2, *note*.

בַּר, xi. 26.

בְּרִיחַ, xviii. 19.

בֶּרֶךְ, בָּרַךְ, v. 18, xi. 23.

בָּשָׂר, xiv. 30.

גַּאֲוָה, xiv. 3.

גֶּבֶר, vi. 34.

גָּדוֹל, x. 28.

גֵּהָה, גָּהָה, xvii. 22.

גֵּו, x. 13.

גּוֹי, xiv. 34.

נַחֲלַת, xxvi. 21.

גָּלַע, xvii. 14.

גַּם, xvii. 15.

גָּמוּל, xii. 14.

גַּף, ix. 3.

R. גר, גֵּרָה, xv. 18.

גֶּרֶל, גּוֹרָל, xix. 19.

גָּרַר, xxi. 7.

דִּבָּה, xxv. 9.

דַּד, v. 18.

דָּכָא, xxii. 22.

R. דל, xxvi. 23, *note*.

דָּלַק, *id.*

דְּרוֹר, xxvi. 2.

דָּרַשׁ, xi. 27, xxxi. 13.

הֶבֶל, xiii. 11.

הָגָה, R. הג, xxv. 4.

הָדַף, x. 3.

הֹוֶה, הֹוָה, x. 3, xvii. 4.

הוֹבִיחַ, xxiv. 26, *note*.

הוֹן, i., xxx. 15.

הָיָה, x. 3, *Niph.* xiii. 19

Wâla (Arab.), *confu-gere*, xxxi. 1.
זוּר, xxi. 8.
R. *wk* (Arab.), xxix. 13.
Wakiha,wakay(Arab.), xxx. 1.

זָדוֹן, xi. 2.
R. זך, זכה, xviii. 11, xx. 9.
זַךְ, xvi. 2.
זִמָּה, זָמַם, i. 4, x. 23, xxi. 27, xxx. 32, *note*.
זַעַם, זַעַף, xxii. 14.
זָקֵן, xx. 29.
זָרַר, *canere*, xxx. 31.
זָרַר, *eingere*, xxx. 31.

חֹב, xxi. 14.
חַבּוּרָה, xx. 30.
חָבַל, xiii. 13.
חָדָה, xxvii. 17.
חֶדֶק, xv. 19.
חָדַר, vii. 27, xviii. 8.
חוֹחַ, חֲוִים, xxvi. 9.
חוּל, xxvii. 3, *note*.
חוּץ, v. 16.
חָטָא, viii. 36.
חָטַב, vii. 16.
חֹטֶר, xiv. 3.
חִידָה, i. 6, xxii. 21, *note*.
חַיִל, x. 28, xiii. 22.
חָק חַיִק, v. 20, xvi. 33, xxi. 14.
חֵךְ, v. 3.
חַכְלִלוּת, xxiii. 29.
חָכְמָה, חָכַם, i. 2, x. 1.
R. חל, חלה, xiii. 12, xix. 6.
חֲלִי, xxv. 12.
חָלַף, xxxi. 8.
חֵמָה, xv. 1.

חָמַס, iv. 17.
חָנַךְ, xxii. 6.
חָנֵף, xi. 9.
R. חס, iii. 3, xiv. 34.
חָפֵד, חֶסֶד, *id.*, xxv. 10.
חֹסֶן, חָסַן, xv. 6.
חֹפֶן, xxx. 4.
חֵפֶץ, חָפֵץ, iii. 15, xviii. 2, xxxi. 13.
חָפַר, xix. 26.
חָפֵשׂ, ii. 4.
חָצִיר, xxvii. 25.
חֹצֶן, xxi. 14.
R. חץ, חָצַץ, חָצָץ, xx. 17, xxx. 27.
חֵק, *vid.* חֵיק, v. 20, xvi. 33, xxi. 14.
R. חץ, חָקַר, xxv. 27.
חָקַק, viii. 29.
חֲרֻלִּים, חרגל, xxiv. 31.
חָרַץ, חָרוּץ, iii. 14, x. 4.
חָרִיף, xx. 4.
חָרַךְ, xii. 27.
חֹרֶף, xx. 4.
חָרֵץ, *vid.* חָרוּץ.
חָרֵשׁ, iii. 29.
הֶחֱרִישׁ חרשׁ, xvii. 28.
R. חשׁ, xvii. 11.
חָתָה, vi. 27.
חָתֵף, חָתַף, xxiii. 28.

טוֹב, xv. 13, xxiv. 13.
טוּג, xvi. 33.
R. טם, טַם, צם, צוּף, ii. 1.
טָרַד, xix. 13.

יָגַע, xxiii. 4.
יָדַע, i. 2.
יָהִיר, xxi. 24.
יָמִין, viii. 30.

יָסַד, iii. 19.
יַעֲלָה, v. 19.
יָקֵב, iii. 10.
יָקֶה, *pr. n.*, xxx. 1.
יְקָהָה, xxx. 17.
יָקוֹשׁ, vi. 5.
יָקַר, יָקָר, i. 13, xvii. 27.
יֵשׁ, ii. 7. viii. 21.
יֹשֶׁר, xi. 24.
יתן (?), xii. 12, xiii. 15.
יֶתֶר, יָתַר, ii. 21, xiv. 13, xvii. 7.

כָּבֵד, xxv. 27.
כֵּן, iii. 19.
בֻּגַּר, xvii. 3.
R. (Arab.) *kz*, חֹשׁ, קֹשׁ, xvii. 11.
R. כח, xxiv. 26, *note*.
כִּפֵּר, vi. 25.
R. כל, xviii. 14.
כִּלְמָה, כָּלַם, xviii. 13, xxv. 8.
כֵּן, as substantive, xi. 19, xv. 7.
כֵּסֶא, vii. 17.
כְּסִיל, i. 18, viii. 5, xvii. 21, xxiii. 9.
כֶּסֶל, iii. 26.
כִּפָּה, xiv. 30.
R. כר, vi. 25, xxv. 26.
כָּשֵׁר, xxxi. 19.
כֶּתֶם (also Egypt.*ketem*), xxv. 12.
כָּתַר, *Hiph.*, xiv. 18.

לֵב, iv. 23, viii. 5.
R. לבושׁ לב, xxv. 20.
לְבַט, x. 8.
R. להה לה, xxvi. 18.
לָהַם, xviii. 8.

II.—SYNONYMS EXPLAINED.

רֵאשִׁית ,תְּחִלָּה, ix. 10.

נֶפֶשׁ, vid. רוּחַ.

שָׂעִיר, vid. תַּיִשׁ.

שְׁאוֹל, vid. אֲבַדּוֹן.

בָּשָׂר, vid. שְׁאָר.

אֶלֶף, vid. שׁוֹר.

שְׁחָקִים, vid. עֲרִיפִים.

שַׁחַר, vid. בֹּקֶשׁ.

מֹשֵׁל, vid. שֹׁטֵר.

הֵעִיר, vid. שָׁקַד.

כְּזָבִים, vid. שֶׁקֶר.

תְּבוּאָה, vid. פְּעֻלָּה.

תְּבוּנָה, vid. בִּינָה.

תֵּבֵל, vid. אֲדָמָה.

תְּחִלָּה, vid. רֵאשִׁית.

שָׂעִיר ,צְפִיר, עַתּוּד ,תַּיִשׁ, xxx. 31.

כֶּסֶל, vid. תִּקְוָה.

תַּרְבִּית, vid. נֶשֶׁךְ.

COMMENTARY

ON

THE SONG OF SONGS

AND

ECCLESIASTES

BY

FRANZ DELITZSCH, D.D.,

PROFESSOR OF OLD AND NEW TESTAMENT EXEGESIS, LEIPSIC.

Translated from the German

BY

REV. M. G. EASTON, D.D.,

THE TRANSLATOR'S PREFACE

THE volume now offered to students of the Bible completes the Keil and Delitzsch series of Commentaries on the Old Testament. Like those which have preceded, it is intended exclusively for theological students and scholars, with whom it cannot but gain a welcome reception, as a most important contribution to the right interpretation of those difficult portions of the sacred canon, whether the reader may agree with the conclusions of the learned author or not.

At the end of the original volume there are added three dissertations by Wetzstein. But as the commentary is in itself complete without those, they have been omitted with Dr. Delitzsch's concurrence. I content myself by merely indicating here their import. In the first of them, Wetzstein aims at showing that the words פֶּלַח הָרִמּוֹן, Song iv. 3, vi. 7, signify the slice (*Spalt, Ritz*) of a pomegranate = the inner surface of a sliced pomegranate. In the second, he argues that the *Dudaim* plant, Song vii. 13, is not the *mandragora vernalis* of botanists, but the *mandr. autumnalis*, which begins to bud and blossom, as is the case with most of the Palestinian flora, about the time of the first winter rains in the month of November. The passage, הד' . . . ריח־, he accordingly translates : " Already the mandragora apples give forth their fragrance," *i.e.* are already ripe ; because it is only the ripe apples that are fragrant. In the third dissertation, on Eccles. xii. 5, he seeks to establish the translation of החנב . . . ויסתבל by " And the almond tree flourisheth, and the locusts creep forth, and the wretched life is brought to dissolution." The first two of these clauses, he holds, denote the season of the year [the beginning of the meteorological spring. The seven days from 25th February to 3d March are called the *eijam el-'agaiz*, *i.e.* the (seven death-) days for old people], in which that which is said in the third (the death of the old man) takes place.

I cannot send forth this volume without expressing the deep obligation I am under to Dr. Delitzsch for his kindness in forwarding to me various important corrections and additions which I have incorporated in the translation, and for valuable suggestions with reference to it. This English edition may, from these circumstances, be almost regarded as a second edition of the original. I have done my best to verify the references, and to present a faithful rendering of the original, and in such a form as to allow the author to express himself in his own way, without violating the idiomatic structure of the language.

ABBREVIATIONS.

THE abbreviations and technical forms common to such critical works as this have been retained. These require no explanation. The colon (:) has been used, as in the original, to introduce a translation or a quotation. In the text criticisms, the following abbreviations have been used :—

F. = *Cod. Francofurtensis* of 1294, described by Delitzsch in his Preface to Baer's edition of the *Psalter* of 1861 and 1874.

H. = *Cod. Heidenheimii*, a MS.

J. = *Cod. Jamanensis*, which was brought from South Arabia by Jacob Sappir, and passed into Baer's possession. *Vid.* Delitzsch's Preface to Baer's edition of *Isaiah*, 1872.

P. = *Cod. Petropolitanus* of the year 1010, now in St. Petersburg. *Vid.* Pinner's *Prospectus*, pp. 81–88.

D. = A parchment MS. of the Song placed at Delitzsch's disposal by Baer.

E^1, E^2, E^3, E^4 = The four Erfurt Manuscripts.

TABLE OF CONTENTS

I. THE SONG OF SONGS.

II. THE BOOK OF ECCLESIASTES.

CONTENTS.

THE SONG AND ECCLESIASTES.

INTRODUCTION TO THE SONG OF SONGS.

HE *Song* is the most obscure book of the Old Testament. Whatever principle of interpretation one may adopt, there always remains a number of inexplicable passages, and just such as, if we understood them, would help to solve the mystery. And yet the interpretation of a book presupposes from the beginning that the interpreter has mastered the idea of the whole. It has thus become an ungrateful task; for however successful the interpreter may be in the separate parts, yet he will be thanked for his work only when the conception as a whole which he has decided upon is approved of.

It is a love-poem. But why such a *minne*-song in the canon? This question gave rise in the first century, in the Jewish schools, to doubts as to the canonicity of the book. Yet they firmly maintained it; for they presupposed that it was a spiritual and not a secular love-poem. They interpreted it allegorically. The Targum paraphrases it as a picture of the history of Israel from the Exodus to the coming of the Messiah. The bride is the congregation of Israel; and her breasts, to quote one example, are interpreted of the Messiah in His lowliness and the Messiah in His glory. But "Solomon" is an anthropomorphic representation of Jahve Himself. And all the instances of the occurrence of the name, with one exception, are therefore regarded as an indirect allegorical designation of the God of peace (*vid.* Norzi under i. 1). And because of its apparently erotic, but in truth mysterious contents, it was a Jewish saying, as Origen and Jerome mention, that the Song should not be studied by any one till he was thirty years of age (*nisi quis ætatem sacerdotalis ministerii, id est, tricesimum annum impleverit*). Because, according to the traditional Targ. interpretation, it begins with the departure out of Egypt, it forms a part of the liturgy for the eighth day of the Passover.   The five Megilloths are arranged in the calendar according to their liturgical use.[1]

In the church this synagogal allegorizing received a new turn. They saw represented in the Song the mutual love of Christ and His church, and it thus became a mine of sacred mysticism in which men have dug to the present day.   Thus Origen explains it in twelve volumes.   Bernhard of Clairvaux died (1153) after he had delivered eighty-six sermons on it, and had only reached the end of the second chapter;[2] and his disciple Gilbert Porretanus carried forward the interpretation in forty-eight sermons only to v. 10, when he died.   Perluigi de Palestrina gained by his twenty-nine motettoes on the Song (1584) the honoured name of *Principe della Musica*. In modern times this allegorico-mystical interpretation is represented in the department of exegesis (Hengst.), sermon (F. W. Krummacher), and poetry (Gustav Jahn), as well as of music (Neukomm's duet: *Er und sie*), and even of painting (Ludw. von Maydell).

If the Song is to be understood allegorically, then Shulamith is the personification of the congregation of Israel, and mediately of the church.   All other interpretations fall below this.   Hug (1813) understands by the "beloved" the kingdom of the ten tribes longing after a reunion with the house of David; and Heinr. Aug. Hahn (1852), the Japhetic heathendom.   Ludw. Noack (1869) has even changed and modified the readings of the Heb. text, that he might find therein the ballads of a Tirhâka romance, *i.e.* a series of pictures of the events occurring between Samaria and her Aethiopian lover Tirhâka, of the years (B.C.) 702, 691, and 690.   These are the aberrations of individuals.   Only one other interpretation recommends itself.   Solomon's *charisma* and aim was the Chokma.   The Peshito places over the Song the superscription חכמת דחכמתא.   Is Shulamith, then, the personification of wisdom, like Dante's Beatrice ? Rosenmüller (1830) is the most recent representative of this view ; we ought then to have in Dante's *Convito* the key to the allegorical interpretation.   He there sings sweet songs of love of his mistress Philosophy.   But there is nothing in the description here to show that Shulamith is Wisdom.   The one expression, "Thou shalt teach me " (viii. 2), warns us against attempting to put Wisdom in the place of the church, as a reversal of the facts of the case.

[1] The *Song* was read on the 8th day of the Passover; *Ruth*, on the second Shabuoth [Pentecost] ; *Lamentations*, on the 9th Ab ; *Ecclesiastes*, on the 3d Succoth [Tabernacles] ; *Esther*, between the 11th and 16th Adar [feast of Purim].

[2] *Vid.* Fernbacher's *Die Reden des. h. Bernhard über das Hohelied*, prefaced by Delitzsch.   Leipzig 1862.

But if one understands the church to be meant, there yet remains much that is inexplicable. Who are the sixty queens and the eighty concubines (vi. 8) ? And why are the heroes just sixty (iii. 7) ? The synagogal and church interpretation, in spite of two thousand years' labour, has yet brought to light no sure results, but only numberless absurdities, especially where the Song describes the lovers according to their members from head to foot and from foot to head. But notwithstanding all this, it is certain that the " great mystery " (Eph. v. 32) mirrors itself in the Song. In this respect it resembles the love of Joseph and Zuleikha, often sung by the Arabian poets, which is regarded by the mystics[1] as a figure of the love of God toward the soul longing for union with Him. Shulamith is a historic personage ; not the daughter of Pharaoh, as has been often maintained since the days of Theodore of Mopsuestia (died 429) and Abulfaraj (died 1286), but a country maiden of humble rank, who, by her beauty and by the purity of her soul, filled Solomon with a love for her which drew him away from the wantonness of polygamy, and made for him the primitive idea of marriage, as it is described in Gen. iii. 23 ff., a self-experienced reality. This experience he here sings, idealizing it after the manner of a poet ; *i.e.*, removing the husk of that which is accidental, he goes back to its kernel and its essential nature. We have before us six dramatic figures, each in two divisions, which represent from within the growth of this delightful relation to its conclusion. This sunny glimpse of paradisaical love which Solomon experienced, again became darkened by the insatiableness of passion ; but the Song of Songs has perpetuated it, and whilst all other songs of Solomon have disappeared, the providence of God has preserved this one, the crown of them all. It is a protest against polygamy, although only in the measure one might expect from the Mosaic standpoint. For the *Tôra* recognises, indeed, in its primitive history monogamy as the original form (Matt. xix. 4-6) ; but in its legislation, giving up the attempt to abolish polygamy, it is satisfied with its limitation (Deut. xvii. 17).

The Song celebrates paradisaical, but yet only natural love (*minne*). It stands, however, in the canon of the church, because Solomon is a type of Him of whom it can be said, " a greater than Solomon is here " (Matt. xii. 12). Referred to Him the antitype, the earthly contents receive a heavenly import and glorification. We see therein the mystery of the love of Christ and His church shadowed forth, not, however, allegorically, but typically. The allegory has to coincide throughout with that which is represented ; but

[1] *Vid.* Hammer-Purgstall's *Das hohe Lied der Liebe der Araber*, 1854.

the type is always only a type *subtractis subtrahendis*, and is exceedingly surpassed by the antitype. In this sense Jul. Sturm (1854) has paraphrased the Song under the title of "*Zwei Rosen*" (two roses) (the typical and the antitypical). When my monograph on the Song appeared (1851), a notice of it in Colani's *Revue de Theologie* (1852) began with the frivolous remark: "*Ce n'est pas la première rêverie de ce genre sur le livre en question; plût à Dieu que ce fût la dernière;*" and Hitzig (1855) judged that "such a work might properly have remained unprinted; it represents nothing but a perverse inconsiderate literature which has no conception of scientific judgment and industry." But this work (long since out of print and now rare) was the fruit of many years of study. The commentary here given is based on it, but does not put it out of date. It broke with the allegorizing interpretation, the untenableness of which appears against his will in Hengstenberg's commentary (1853); it broke also with the theory which regards the poem as a history of Solomon's unsuccessful seductive efforts to gain the Shulamite's affections, a theory which Hitzig (1855) tries to exempt from the necessity of doing violence to the text by arbitrarily increasing the number of speakers and actors in the plot. I certainly succeeded in finding the right key to the interpretation of this work. Zöckler has recognised my book[1] as presenting "the only correct interpretation of its design and contents." Kingsbury, author of the notes on the Song in *The Speaker's Commentary*, has expressed the same judgment. Poets such as Stadelmann (*Das Hohelied, ein dramatisches Gedicht =* The Song of Songs: a dramatic poem, 1870) and J. Koch, late pastor of St. Mary's in Parchim (died 1873), have recognised in their beautiful German paraphrases my interpretation as natural and in conformity with the text; and for twenty years I have constantly more and more seen that the solution suggested by me is the right and only satisfactory one.

Shulamith is not Pharaoh's daughter. The range of her thoughts is not that of a king's daughter, but of a rustic maiden; she is a stranger among the daughters of Jerusalem, not because she comes from a foreign land, but because she is from the country; she is dark-complexioned, not from the sun of her more southern home, but from the open sunshine to which she has been exposed as the keeper of a vineyard; in body and soul she is born to be a princess, but in reality she is but the daughter of a humble family in a remote part of Galilee; hence the child-like simplicity and the rural character of her thoughts, her joy in the open fields, and her longing after the

[1 *Das Hohelied untersucht u. ausg.* Leipzig 1851.]

quiet life of her village home. Solomon appears here in loving fellowship with a woman such as he had not found among a thousand (Eccles. vii. 28); and although in social rank far beneath him, he raises her to an equality with himself. That which attached her to him is not her personal beauty alone, but her beauty animated and heightened by nobility of soul. She is a pattern of simple devotedness, naive simplicity, unaffected modesty, moral purity, and frank prudence,—a lily of the field, more beautifully adorned than he could claim to be in all his glory. We cannot understand the Song of Songs unless we perceive that it presents before us not only Shulamith's external attractions, but also all the virtues which make her the ideal of all that is gentlest and noblest in woman. Her words and her silence, her doing and suffering, her enjoyment and self-denial, her conduct as betrothed, as a bride, and as a wife, her behaviour towards her mother, her younger sister, and her brothers,—all this gives the impression of a beautiful soul in a body formed as it were from the dust of flowers. Solomon raises this child to the rank of queen, and becomes beside this queen as a child. The simple one teaches the wise man simplicity; the humble draws the king down to her level; the pure accustoms the impetuous to self-restraint. Following her, he willingly exchanges the bustle and the outward splendour of court life for rural simplicity, wanders gladly over mountain and meadow if he has only her; with her he is content to live in a lowly cottage. The erotic external side of the poem has thus an ethical background. We have here no "song of loves" (Ezek. xxxiii. 32) having reference to sensual gratification. The rabbinical proverb is right when it utters its threat against him who would treat this Song, or even a single verse of it, as a piece of secular literature.[1] The Song transfigures natural but holy love. Whatever in the sphere of the divinely-ordered marriage relation makes love the happiest, firmest bond uniting two souls together, is presented to us here in living pictures. "The Song," says Herder, "is written as if in Paradise. Adam's song: Thou art my second self! Thou art mine own! echoes in it in speech and interchanging song from end to end." The place of the book in the canon does not need any further justification; that its reception was favoured also by the supposition that it represented the intercourse between Jahve and the congregation of Israel, may be conjectured indeed, but is not established. The supposition, however, would have been false; for the book is not an allegory, and Solomon is by no means an *Alle-*

---

[1] Cf. *Tosefta Sanhedrin* xii., *Sanhedrin* iii.*a*, and the commencement of the tract *Kalla*.

gorumenon of God. But the congregation is truly a bride (Jer. ii. 2; Isa. lxii. 5), and Solomon a type of the Prince of peace (Isa. ix. 5 ; Luke xi. 31), and marriage a mystery, viz. as a pattern of the loving relation of God and His Christ to the church (Eph. v. 32). The Song has consequently not only a historico-ethical, but also a typico-mystical meaning. But one must be on his guard against introducing again the allegorical interpretation as Soltz (1850) has done, under the misleading title of the typical interpretation. The typical interpretation proceeds on the idea that the type and the antitype do not exactly coincide ; the mystical, that the heavenly stamps itself in the earthly, but is yet at the same time immeasurably different from it. Besides, the historico-ethical interpretation is to be regarded as the proper business of the interpreter. But because Solomon is a type (*vaticinium reale*) of the spiritual David in his glory, and earthly love a shadow of the heavenly, and the Song a part of sacred history and of canonical Scripture, we will not omit here and there to indicate that the love subsisting between Christ and His church shadows itself forth in it.

But the prevailing view which Jacobi (1771) established, and which has predominated since Umbreit (1820) and Ewald (1826), is different from ours. According to them, the Song celebrates the victory of the chaste passion of conjugal love. The beloved of Shulamith is a shepherd, and Solomon acts toward her a part like that of Don Juan with Anna, or of Faust with Gretchen. Therefore, of course, his authorship is excluded, although Anton (1773), the second oldest representative of this so-called shepherd hypothesis, supposes that Solomon at a later period of his life recognised his folly, and now here magnanimously praises the fidelity of Shulamith, who had spurned his enticements away from her ; and a Jewish interpreter, B. Holländer (1871), following Hezel (1780), supposes that Solomon represents himself as an enticer, only to exhibit the ideal of female virtue as triumphing over the greatest seduction. Similarly also Godet (1867),[1] who, resting on Ewald, sees here a very complicated mystery presented by Solomon himself, and pointing far beyond him : Solomon, the earthly Messiah ; Shulamith, the true Israel ; the shepherd, Jahve, and as Jahve who is about to come, the heavenly Solomon ; the little sisters, heathenism——it is the old allegory, able for everything, only with changed names and a different division of the parts which here comes in again by the back-door of the seduction-history.[2]

---

[1] *Vid.* Jahrg. i. No. 22–24 of the Berne *Kirchenfreund.*

[2] And in this Godet stands not alone. The Jewish interpreter Malbim (1850) accepts also this seduction-history : Solomon = the sensual impulse ; Shulamith =

Thus this seduction-history has not put an end to the over-ingenious allegorizing. In one point, however, at least, it has aided in the understanding of the Song. Herder saw in the Song a collection of Solomonic songs of love, which he translated (1778), as the oldest and the most beautiful, from the Orient. But Goethe, who in the *Westöst. Divan* (1819) praises the Song as the most divine of all love-songs, recognised, after the appearance of Umbreit's Comm., the unity also of the "inexplicably mysterious."

We are not conscious of any prejudice which makes it impossible for us to do justice to the interpretation to which Umbreit and Ewald gave currency. It abundantly accounts for the reception of the book into the canon, for so interpreted it has a moral motive and aim. And the personality of Solomon has certainly not merely a bright side, which is typical, but also a dark side, which is pregnant with dark issues for his kingdom; it may perhaps be possible that in the Song the latter, and not the former, is brought to view. Then, indeed, the inscription would rest on an error; for that in this case also the Solomonic authorship could be maintained, is an idea which, in the traditional-apologetical interest, mounts up to a faith in the impossible. But the truth goes beyond the tradition; the inscription would then indicate a traditional interpretation which, as is evident from the book itself, does not correspond with its original meaning and aim. "It is clear to every unprejudiced mind," says Gustav Baur,[1] "that in ii. 10–15, iv. 8–15, a different person speaks from the royal wooer; for (1) Solomon only says, 'my friend' [i. 15, etc.]; while, on the other hand, the shepherd heaps up flattering words of warmest love; (2) Solomon praises only the personal beauty of the woman; the shepherd, the sweet voice, the enchanting look, the warm love, the incorruptible chastity of his beloved;—in short, the former reveals the eye and the sensuousness of the king; the latter, the heart of a man who is animated by the divine flame of true love." We only ask, meanwhile, whether words such as iv. 13 are less sensuous than iv. 5, and whether the image of the twin gazelles is not more suitable in the mouth of the shepherd than the comparison of the attractions of Shulamith with the exotic plants of Solomon's garden? "In three passages," says Godet, "lies open the slender thread which Ewald's penetrating eye discovered under the flowers and leaves which adorn the poem: 'The king has brought me into his palace' (i. 4); 'I knew not how my heart has

the spirit-soul; the little sister = the natural soul; and Shulamith's beloved = the heavenly Friend, the Shepherd of the universe.

[1] *Literaturb. der Darmst. Kirchenzeitung*, 1851, pp. 114–146, and 1854, No. 11.

brought me to the chariots of a princely people' (vi. 12); 'I was a wall, and have found peace before his eyes' (viii. 10)." The same critic also finds in several passages an apparent contrariety between Solomon and the shepherd. "Observe," says he, "*e.g.* i. 12, 13, where the shepherd—whom Shulamith calls her spikenard, and compares to a bunch of flowers on her breast—is placed over against the king, who sits on his divan; or vii. 9 f., where, suddenly interrupting the king, she diverts the words which he speaks concerning herself to her beloved; or viii. 7, where, leaning on the arm of her beloved, she expresses her disregard for riches, with which Solomon had sought to purchase her love." But spikenard is not the figure of the shepherd, not at all the figure of a man; and she who is praised as a " prince's daughter " (vii. 2) cannot say (vi. 12) that, enticed by curiosity to see the royal train, she was taken prisoner, and now finds herself, against her will, among the daughters of Jerusalem; and he whom she addresses (viii. 12) can be no other than he with whom she now finds herself in her parents' home. The course of the exposition will show that the shepherd who is distinguished from Solomon is nothing else than a shadow cast by the person of Solomon.

The Song is a dramatic pastoral. The ancients saw in it a *carmen bucolicum mimicum*. Laurentius Peträus, in his Heb.-Danish Paraphrase (1640), calls it *carmen bucolicum, ἀμοιβαῖον* (δραματι- κόν); George Wachter (1722), an "opera divided into scenic parts." It acquires the character of a pastoral poem from this, that Shula- mith is a shepherdess, that she thinks of Solomon as a shepherd, and that Solomon condescends to occupy the sphere of life and of thought of the shepherdess. It is not properly an idyll, nor yet pro- perly a drama. Not an idyll, because the life-image which such a miniature drawn from life—such, *e.g.*, as the Adon. of Theocritus presents to us—unfolds itself within a brief time without inter- ruption ; in the Song, on the other hand, not merely are the places and persons interchanged, but also the times. The whole, how- ever, does not fall into little detached pictures ; but there runs through this wreath of figures a love-relation, which embodies itself externally and internally before our eyes, and attains the end of its desire, and shows itself on the summit of this end as one that is not merely sensuous, but moral. The Song is certainly not a theatrical piece :[1] the separate pieces would necessarily have been longer if the

[1] " Shulamith," says E. F. Friedrich (1855 and 1866), " is the oldest theatrical piece in existence." Ewald and Böttcher, who find not fewer than twelve persons mentioned in it, think that it was represented on an actual stage. Then, indeed, it

poet had had in view the changes of theatrical scenery. But at all events the theatre is not a Semitic institution, but is of Indo-Persian Greek origin. Jewish poetry attempted the drama only after it began in Alexandrinism[1] to emulate Greece. Grätz' (1871) polemic against the dramatists is so far justified. But yet we see, as in the Book of Job, so in the Song, the drama in process of formation from the lyric and narrative form of poetry, as it has developed among the Greeks from the lyric, and among the Indians from the epic. In the Book of Job the colloquies are all narrative. In the Song this is never the case;[2] for the one expression, "answered my beloved, and said to me" (ii. 10), is not to be compared with, "and Job answered and said:" the former expression indicates a monologue. And in the "Daughters of Jerusalem" (i. 5, etc.) we have already something like the chorus of the Greek drama. The ancient Greek MSS. bear involuntary testimony to this dramatic character of the Song. There are several of them which prefix to the separate addresses the names of the persons speaking, as ἡ νύμφη, ὁ νυμφίος.[3] And the Aethiopic translation makes five separate pieces, probably, as the *Cod. Sinait.* shows, after the example of the LXX., which appear as divisions into Acts.

The whole falls into the following six Acts:—

(1.) The mutual affection of the lovers, i. 2–ii. 7, with the conclusion, "I adjure you, ye daughters of Jerusalem."

(2.) The mutual seeking and finding of the lovers, ii. 8–iii. 5, with the conclusion, "I adjure you, ye daughters of Jerusalem."

(3.) The fetching of the bride, and the marriage, iii. 6–v. 1, beginning with, "Who is this . . .?" and ending with, "Drink and be drunken, beloved."

(4.) Love scorned, but won again, v. 2–vi. 9.

(5.) Shulamith the attractively fair but humble princess, vi. 10–viii. 4, beginning with, "Who is this . . .?" and ending with, "I adjure you, ye daughters of Jerusalem."

would be the oldest drama—older than Thespis and Kalîdasa. For the Sakuntâla and the drama *Der Kaufmann und die Bajadere* belong to the first century of our era.

[1] *Vid.* my *Prolegomena* to Luzzatto's עגדל עי (Heb Paraphrase of the *Pastors fido* of Guarini), 1837, pp. 24–32.

[2] Similar is the relation between Homer, where the speakers are introduced with narrative, and our national epics, the *Nibelungen* and *Gudrun*, which become dramatic when the action and the feeling rise to a higher elevation: the words of the different persons follow each other without introduction, so that here the manner of the singer had to become dramatic.

[3] *Vid. Repert. für bibl. u. morgenl. Lit.* viii. (1781), p. 180. The Archimandrite Porphyrios describes such a MS. in his (Russian) *Reisewerk* (1856).

(6.) The ratification of the covenant of love in Shulamith's home, viii. 5–14, beginning with, " Who is this . . . ? "

Zöckler reckons only five acts, for he comprehends v. 2–viii. 4 in one; but he himself confesses its disproportionate length; and the reasons which determine him are invalid; for the analogy of the Book of Job, which, besides, including the prologue and the epilogue, falls into seven formal parts, can prove nothing; and the question, " Who is this ? " vi. 10, which he interprets as a continuation of the encomium in vi. 9, is rather to be regarded, like iii. 8, viii. 5, as a question with reference to her who is approaching, and as introducing a new act; for the supposition that vi. 9 requires to be further explained by a statement of what was included in the " blessing " and the " praising " is unwarranted, since these are ideas requiring no supplement to explain them (Gen. xxx. 13 ; Ps. xli. 3, cvii. 32), and the poet, if he had wished to explain the praise as to its contents, would have done this otherwise (cf. Prov. xxxi. 28 f.) than in a way so fitted to mislead. Rightly, Thrupp (1862) regards vi. 10 as the chorus of the daughters of Jerusalem. He divides as follows: (1) the Anticipation, i. 2–ii. 7 ; (2) the Awaiting, ii. 8– iii. 5 ; (3) the Espousal and its Results, iii. 6–v. 1 ; (4) the Absence, v. 2–8 ; (5) the Presence, v. 9–viii. 4 ; (6) Love's Triumph, viii. 5–12, with the Conclusion, viii. 13, 14. But how can v. 9 begin a new formal part ? It is certainly the reply to Shulamith's adjuration of the daughters of Jerusalem, and not at all the commencement of a new scene, much less of a new act.

In our division into six parts, the separate acts, for the most part necessarily, and in every case without any violence, divide themselves into two scenes each, thus :—

Act I. i. 2–ii. 7.	Scene 1. i. 2–8.	Scene 2. i. 9–ii. 7.
„ II. ii. 8–iii. 5.	„ ii. 8 ff.	„ iii. 1–5.
„ III. iii. 6–v. 1.	„ iii. 6 ff.	„ iv. 1–v. 1.
„ IV. v. 2–vi. 9.	„ v. 2–vi. 3.	„ vi. 4–9.
„ V. vi. 10–viii. 4.	„ vi. 10–vii. 6.	„ vii. 7–viii. 4.
„ VI. viii. 5–14.	„ viii. 5–7.	„ viii. 8–14.

The first scene of the first act I formerly (1851) extended to i. 17, but it reaches only to i. 8 ; for up to this point Solomon is absent, but with i. 9 he begins to converse with Shulamith, and the chorus is silent—the scene has thus changed. Kingsbury in his translation (1871) rightly places over i. 9 the superscription, " The Entrance of the King."

The change of scenery is not regulated in accordance with stage decoration, for the Song is not a theatrical piece.[1] The first act is played both in the dining-room and in the wine-room appertaining to the women of the royal palace. In the second act, Shulamith is again at home. In the third act, which represents the marriage, the bride makes her entrance into Jerusalem from the wilderness, and what we further then hear occurs during the marriage festival. The locality of the fourth act is Jerusalem, without being more particularly defined. That of the fifth act is the park of Etam, and then Solomon's country house there. And in the sixth act we see the newly - married pair first in the way to Shulem, and then in Shulamith's parental home. In the first half of the dramatic pictures, Shulamith rises to an equality with Solomon; in the second half, Solomon descends to an equality with Shulamith. At the close of the first, Shulamith is at home in the king's palace; at the close of the second, Solomon is at home with her in her Galilean home.

. . . .

In our monograph on the Song (1851), we believe we have proved that it distinctly bears evidences of its Solomonic origin. The familiarity with nature, the fulness and extent of its geographical and artistic references, the mention made of so many exotic plants and foreign things, particularly of such objects of luxury as the Egyptian horses, point to such an authorship; in common with Ps. lxxii., it has the multiplicity of images taken from plants; with the Book of Job, the dramatic form; with the Proverbs, manifold allusions to Genesis. If not the production of Solomon, it must at least have been written near his time, since the author of Prov. i.-ix., the introduction to the older Book of Proverbs, for the origin of which there is no better defined period than that of Jehoshaphat (909–883 B.C.), and the author or authors of the supplement (Prov. xxii. 17– xxiv. 22), reveal an acquaintance with the Song. Ewald also, and Hitzig, although denying that Solomon is the author because it is directed against him, yet see in it a product of the most flourishing state of the language and of the people; they ascribe it to a poet of the northern kingdom about 950 B.C. Modern Jewish criticism surpasses, however, on the field of O. T. history, the anachronisms of the Tübingen school. As Zunz has recently (*Deut. Morgenl. Zeitsch.*

---

[1] Ephr. Epstein, surgeon in Cincinnati, in a review of Von Grätz' *Comm.* in *The Israelite* (1872), calls the Song quite in our sense, "a dramatic poem, though not a complete scenic drama." But the bridal procession in the third act is not of this character—he sees in it a return from a hunting expedition.

xxvii.) sought to show that the Book of Leviticus was written about
a thousand years after Moses, that there never was a prophet Ezekiel,
that the dates of this book are fictitious, etc.; so Grätz attempts
to prove that the Song in its Graecising language and Greek customs and symbols bears evidences of the Syro-Macedonian age;[1]
that the poet was acquainted with the idylls of Theocritus and
the Greek erotic poets, and, so far as his Israelitish standpoint
admitted, imitates them; and that he placed an ideal picture of
pure Jewish love over against the immorality of the Alexandrine
court and its Hellenistic partisans, particularly of Joseph b. Tobia,
the collector of taxes in the time of Ptolemy Euergetes (247–
221 B.C.),—a picture in which " the Shepherd,"[2] now grown into
a fixed idea, renders welcome service, in contrast to Solomon, in
whom the poet glances at the court of Alexandria. One is thus
reminded of Kirschbaum (1833), who hears in Ezek. xxxiii. 5 an
echo of Cicero's *dixi et salvavi animam,* and in the Song ii. 17, a
reference to the Bethar of Barcochba. We do not deny the penetration which this chief of Jewish historians has expended on the
establishment of his hypothesis; but the same penetration may prove
that the Babylon.-Assyr. " *syllabaries*" of the time of Asurbanipal
(667–626) belong to the Greek era, because there occurs therein
the word *azamillav* (knife), and this is the Greek σμίλη; or that the
author of Prov. i.-ix. alludes in vii. 23 to Eros and his quivers, and
in ix. 1 betrays a knowledge of the seven *artes liberales.* Parallels
to the Song are found wherever sensuous love is sung, also in the
Pastoralia of Longus, without the least dependence of one author
upon another. And if such a relation is found between Theocritus
and the Song, then it might rather be concluded that he became
acquainted with it in Alexandria from Jewish literates,[3] than that the
author of the Song has imitated Greek models, as Immanuel Romi,
the Arabians and Dante; besides, it is not at all the Song lying before
us which Grätz expounds, but the Song modified by violent corrections of all kinds, and fitted to the supposed tendency. Thus he
changes (i. 3) שְׁמָנֶיךָ (thine unguent) into בִּשָׂמָיִךְ, and שֶׁמֶן תּוּרַק (ointment
poured forth) into שֶׁמֶן תַּמְרוּק. — Shulamith says this of her beautiful
shepherd, and what follows (i. 4) the damsels say to him; he changes

---

[1] So also, on linguistic grounds, Ant. Theod. Hartmann in Winer's *Zeitschr.* 1829.
[2] Epstein, in true American style, calls him " the bogus shepherd."
[3] *Vid.* my *Gesch. der jud. Poesie,* p. 205 ff. Not as Joh. Gott. Lessing (*Eclogae regis Salomonis,* 1777), the brother of Gotthold Ephraim Lessing, supposes: through the LXX. translation; for the Song was among the books latest in being translated.

משכני into משכנו, הביאני into הביאנו, and then remarks: " Shulamith mentions it as to the praise of her beloved, that the damsels, attracted by his beauty, love him, and say to him, 'Draw us, we will run after thee; though the king brought us into his chambers, we would rejoice only with thee, and prefer thee to the king.'" His too confident conjectural criticism presents us with imaginary words, such as (iii. 10) אֲהָבִים (ebony); with unfortunate specimens of style, such as (vi. 10), "Thou hast made me weak, O daughter of Aminadab;" and with unheard-of renderings, such as (viii. 5), "There where thy mother has wounded thee;" for he supposes that Shulamith is chastised by her mother because of her love. *This* Song is certainly not written by Solomon, nor yet does it date from the Syro-Macedonian time, but was invented in Breslau in the 19th century of our era!

Grätz (1871) has placed yet farther down than the Song the Book of Ecclesiastes, in which he has also found Graecisms; the tyrannical king therein censured is, as he maintains, Herod the Great, and the last three verses (xii. 12–14) are not so much the epilogue of the book as that of the Hagiographa which closes with it. Certainly, if this was first formed by the decision of the conference in Jerusalem about 65, and of the synod in Jabne about 90, and the reception of the Books of Ecclesiastes and the Song was carried not without controversy, then it lies near to regard these two books as the most recent, originating not long before. But the fact is this: We learn from *Jud-ajim* iii. 5, iv. 6, cf. *Edujoth* v. 3, that in the decade before the destruction of Jerusalem the saying was current among the disciples of Hillel and Shammai, that " all Holy Scriptures (*Kethubîm*) pollute the hands;"[1] but that the question whether Ecclesiastes is included was answered in the negative by the school of Shammai, and in the affirmative by the school of Hillel—of the Song nothing is here said. But we learn further, that several decades later the Song also was comprehended in this controversy along with Ecclesiastes; and in an assembly of seventy-two doctors of the law in Jabne, that decree, " all Holy Scriptures (*Kethubîm*) pollute the hands," was extended to Ecclesiastes and the Song. R. Akiba

[1] *Vid.* for the explanation of this, my essay, " Das Hohelied verunreinigt die Hände," in the *Luth. Zeitsch.* 1854. [The *Tôra* and the *Theruma*-food, as being both reckoned holy, were usually placed together in the temple. It was discovered that the sacred books were thereby exposed to damage by mice; and hence, to prevent their being brought any longer into contact with the *Theruma*, the Rabbins decided that they were henceforth to be regarded as unclean, and they gave forth the decree, " All Holy Scriptures pollute the hand." This decree was applicable only to *holy* or *inspired* books. *Vid.* Ginsburg on the Song, p. 3, *note*.]

(or some one else) asserted, in opposition to those who doubted the
canonicity of the Song, "No day in the whole history of the world
is so much worth as that in which the Song of Songs was given;
for all the *Kethubim* are holy, but the Song of Songs is most holy."
From this Grätz draws the conclusion that the Hagiographa was
received as canonical for the first time about 65, and that its canon
was finally fixed so as to include Ecclesiastes and the Song, not till
about 90; but this conclusion rests on the false supposition that
"Holy Scriptures" (*Kethubim*) is to be understood exclusive of the
Hagiographa, which is just as erroneous as that *Sephârim* designates
the prophets, with the exclusion of the Hagiographa. Holy *Kethubim*
is a general designation, without distinction, of all the canonical
books, *e.g. Bathra* i. 6, and *Sepharim* in like manner, with the
exception only of the Tôra, *Megilla* i. 8, iii. 1, *Shabbath* 115*b*. And
it rests on a misapprehension of the question discussed: the question
was not whether Ecclesiastes and the Song should be admitted, but
whether they had been justly admitted, and whether the same
sacred character should be ascribed to them as to the other holy
writings; for in *Bathra* 14*b*–15*a* (without a parallel in the Palest.
Talmud) the enriching of the canon by the addition of the Books of
Isaiah, Proverbs, the Song, and Ecclesiastes, is ascribed to the
Hezekiah-*Collegium* (Prov. xxi. 5), and thus is dated back in the
period before the rise of the great synagogue. That Philo does not
cite the Song proves nothing; he cites none of the five Megilloth. But
Josephus (*C. Ap.* 1, § 8; cf. Euseb. *H. E.* iii. 10), since he enumerates
five books of the Mosaic law, thirteen books of prophetic history
and prediction, and four books of a hymno-ethical character, certainly means by these four the Psalms, Proverbs, Ecclesiastes, and
the Song, which in the Alexandrine canon stand thus connected.
His work, *Cont. Apion,* was not indeed written till about 100 A.D.;
but Josephus there speaks of a fact which had existed for centuries.
The Song and Ecclesiastes formed part of the sacred books among
the Hellenists as well as among the Palestinian Jews of the first
Christian century; but, as those Talmud notices show, not without
opposition. The Old Testament canon, as well as that of the New
Testament, had then also its *Antilegomena*. These books were opposed
not because of their late origin, but because their contents apparently
militated against the truth of revelation and the spiritual nature
of revealed religion. Similar doubts, though not so strong and
lasting, were also uttered with reference to Proverbs, Esther, and
Ezekiel.

The history of the exposition of this book is given in detail by

Christian D. Ginsburg in *The Song of Songs*, London 1857; and by Zöckler in "The Song," forming part of Lange's *Bibelwerk*, 1868, and supplemented by an account of the English interpretations and translations in the Anglo-American translation of this work by Green. Zunz, in the preface to Rebenstein's (Bernstein's) *Lied der Lieder*, 1834, has given an historical account of the Jewish expositors. Steinschneider's המזכיר (*Heb. Bibliograph.* 1869, p. 110 ff.) presents a yet fuller account of the Jewish commentaries. The Münich royal library contains a considerable number of these,—*e.g.* by Moses b. Tibbon, Shemariah, Immanuel Romi, Moses Calais (who embraced Christianity). Our commentary presents various new contributions to the history of the interpretation of this book. No other book of Scripture has been so much abused, by an unscientific spiritualizing, and an over-scientific unspiritual treatment, as this has. Luther says, at the close of his exposition : *Quodsi erro, veniam meretur primus labor, nam aliorum cogitationes longe plus absurditatis habent.* To inventory the *maculatur* of these absurdities is a repulsive undertaking, and, in the main, a useless labour, from which we absolve ourselves.

EXPOSITION OF THE SONG OF SONGS

HE title of the book at once denotes that it is a connected whole, and is the work of one author.—Ch. i. 1. *The Song of Songs, composed by Solomon.* The genitival connection, " Song of Songs," cannot here signify the Song consisting of a number of songs, any more than calling the Bible " The Book of books " leads us to think of the 24 + 27 canonical books of which it consists. Nor can it mean " one of Solomon's songs;" the title, as it here stands, would then be the paraphrase of שִׁיר שִׁירֵי ', chosen for the purpose of avoiding the redoubled genitives; but " one of the songs " must rather have been expressed by שִׁיר מִשִּׁירֵי. It has already been rightly explained in the *Midrash:* [1] " the most praiseworthy, most excellent, most highly-treasured among the songs." The connection is superl. according to the sense (cf. ἄρρητα ἀρρήτων of Sophocles), and signifies that song which, as such, surpasses the songs one and all of them; as " servant of servants," Gen. ix. 25, denotes a servant who is such more than all servants together. The plur. of the second word is for this superl. sense indispensable (*vid.* Dietrich's *Abhand. zur hebr. Gramm.* p. 12), but the article is not necessary: it is regularly wanting where the complex idea takes the place of the predicate, Gen. ix. 25, Ex. xxix. 37, or of the inner member of a genitival connection of words, Jer. iii. 19; but it is also wanting in other places, as Ezek. xvi. 7 and Eccles. i. 2, xii. 8, where the indeterminate plur. denotes not totality, but an unlimited number; here it was necessary, because a definite Song—that, namely, lying before us—must be designated as the paragon of songs. The relative clause, " *asher lishlōmō,*" does not refer to the single word " Songs " (Gr. Venet. τῶν τοῦ), as it would if the expression were שִׁיר מֵחַשׁ ', but to the whole idea of " the Song of Songs." A relative clause of similar formation and reference occurs at 1 Kings iv. 2 : " These are the princes, *asher lo,* which belonged

[1] *Vid.* Fürst's *Der Kanon des A. T.* (1868), p. 86.

to him (Solomon)." They who deny the Solomonic authorship
usually explain : The Song of Songs which concerns or refers to
Solomon, and point in favour of this interpretation to LXX. B. ὅ
ἐστι Σαλ., which, however, is only a latent genit., for which LXX. A.
τῷ Σαλ. *Lamed* may indeed introduce the reference of a writing,
as at Jer. xxiii. 9 ; but if the writing is more closely designated as
a " Song," " Psalm," and the like, then *Lamed* with the name of a
person foll. is always the *Lamed auctoris ;* in this case the idea of
reference to, as *e.g.* at Isa. i. 1, cf. 1 Kings v. 13, is unequivocally
expressed by עַל. We shall find that the dramatized history which
we have here, or as we might also say, the fable of the melodrama
and its dress, altogether correspond with the traits of character, the
favourite turns, the sphere of vision, and the otherwise well-known
style of authorship peculiar to Solomon. We may even suppose
that the superscription was written by the author, and thus by
Solomon himself. For in the superscription of the Proverbs he is
surnamed " son of David, king of Israel," and similarly in Ecclesiastes. But he who entitles him merely " Solomon " is most probably himself. On the other hand, that the title is by the author
himself, is not favoured by the fact that instead of the שׁ, everywhere
else used in the book, the fuller form *asher* is employed. There is the
same reason for this as for the fact that Jeremiah in his prophecies
always uses *asher*, but in the Lamentations interchanges שׁ with
asher. This original demonstrative שׁ is old-Canaanitish, as the
Phoenician אשׁ, arrested half-way toward the form *asher*, shows.[1] In
the Book of Kings it appears as a North Palest. provincialism, to the
prose of the pre-exilian literature it is otherwise foreign ;[2] but
the pre-exilian *shir* and *kinah* (cf. also Job xix. 29) make use of it
as an ornament. In the post-exilian literature it occurs in poetry
(Ps. cxxii. 3, etc.) and in prose (1 Chron. v. 20, xxvii. 27); in
Ecclesiastes it is already a component part of the rabbinism in full
growth. In a pre-exilian book-title שׁ in place of *asher* is thus not
to be expected. On the other hand, in the Song itself it is no sign
of a post-exilian composition, as Grätz supposes. The history of
the language and literature refutes this.

[1] From this it is supposed that *asher* is a pronom. root-cluster equivalent to
אֲשֶׁל. Fleischer, on the contrary, sees in *asher* an original substantive *athar* =
(Arab.) *ithr*, Assyr. *asar*, track, place, as when the vulgar expression is used,
" The man where (*wo* instead of *welcher*) has said."

[2] We do not take into view here Gen. vi. 3. If בְּשֻׁגַּם is then to be read, then
there is in it the pronominal שׁ, as in the old proper name *Mishael* (who is what
God is ?).

FIRST ACT.

THE MUTUAL AFFECTION OF THE LOVERS.—CHAP. I. 2–II. 7.

FIRST SCENE OF THE ACT, I. 2–8.

The first act of the melodrama, which presents the loving relationship in the glow of the first love, now opens. i. 5, 6, are evidently the words of Shulamith. Here one person speaks of herself throughout in the singular. But in vers. 2–4 one and several together speak. Ewald also attributes vers. 2–4 to Shulamith, as words spoken by her concerning her shepherd and to him. She says, "Draw me after thee, so will we run," for she wishes to be brought by him out of Solomon's court. But how can the praise, "an ointment poured forth is thy name,"—an expression which reminds us of what is said of Solomon, 1 Kings v. 11 [1 Kings iv. 31], " and his fame was in all nations round about,"—be applicable to the shepherd? How could Shulamith say to the shepherd, "virgins love thee," and including herself with others, say to him also, "we will exult and rejoice in thee"? on which Ewald remarks: it is as if something kept her back from speaking of herself alone. How this contradicts the psychology of love aiming at marriage! This love is jealous, and does not draw in rivals by head and ears. No; in vers. 2–4 it is the daughters of Jerusalem, whom Shulamith addresses in ver. 5, who speak. The one who is praised is Solomon. The ladies of the palace are at table (*vid.* under ver. 12), and Solomon, after whom she who is placed amid this splendour which is strange to her asks longingly (ver. 7), is not now present. The two pentastichal strophes, vers. 2–4, are a scholion, the table song of the ladies; the solo in both cases passes over into a chorus.

Ver. 2. From these words with which as a solo the first strophe begins :

Let him kiss me with kisses of his mouth,

we at once perceive that she who here speaks is only one of many among whom Solomon's kisses are distributed; for *min* is partitive, as *e.g.* Ex. xvi. 27 (cf. Jer. xlviii. 32 and Isa. xvi. 9), with the underlying phrase נָשַׁק נְשִׁיקָה, *osculum osculari = figere, jungere, dare. Nashak* properly means to join to each other and to join together, particularly mouth to mouth. פִּיהוּ is the parallel form of פִּיו, and is found in prose as well as in poetry; it is here preferred for the sake of the rhythm. Böttcher prefers, with Hitzig, יַשְׁקֵנִי ("let him give me to drink"); but "to give to drink with kisses" is an expression unsupported.

In line 2 the expression changes into an address:

For better is thy love than wine.

Instead of " thy love," the LXX. render "thy breasts," for they had before them the word written defectively as in the traditional text, and read דַּדֶּיךָ. Even granting that the dual דַּדַּיִם or דַּדִּים could be used in the sense of the Greek μαστοί (Rev. i. 13),[1] of the breasts of a man (for which Isa. xxxii. 12, Targ., furnishes no sufficient authority); yet in the mouth of a woman it were unseemly, and also is itself absurd as the language of praise. But, on the other hand, that דִּרַיֶךָ is not the true reading ("for more lovely—thus he says to me—are," etc.), R. Ismael rightly says, in reply to R. Akiba, *Aboda zara* 29b, and refers to שְׁמָנֶיךָ following (ver. 3), which requires the mas. for דֹּדֶיךָ. Rightly the Gr. Venet. οἱ σοὶ ἔρωτες, for דּוֹדִים is related to אַהֲבָה, almost as ἔρως to ἀγάπη, *Minne* to *Liebe*. It is a plur. like חַיִּים, which, although a *pluraletantum*, is yet connected with the plur. of the pred. The verbal stem דּוּד is an abbreviated reduplicative stem (Ewald, § 118. 1); the root דו appears to signify "to move by thrusts or pushes" (*vid.* under Ps. xlii. 5); of a fluid, "to cause to boil up," to which the word דּוּד, a kitchen-pot, is referred.[2] It is the very same verbal stem from which דָּוִד (David), the beloved, and the name of the foundress of Carthage, דִּידֹה (= דִּידוֹן) *Minna*, is derived. The adj. *tov* appears here and at 3a twice in its nearest primary meaning, denoting that which is pleasant to the taste and (thus particularly in Arab.) to the smell.

This comparison *suaves prae vino*, as well as that which in line 3 of the pentastich, ver. 3,

To the smell thy ointments are sweet,

shows that when this song is sung wine is presented and perfumes are sprinkled; but the love of the host is, for those who sing, more excellent than all. It is maintained that רֵיחַ signifies fragrance emitted, and not smell. Hence Hengst., Hahn, Hölem., and Zöck. explain: in odour thy ointments are sweet. Now the words can certainly, after Josh. xxii. 10, Job xxxii. 4, 1 Kings x. 23, mean " sweet in (of) smell;" but in such cases the word with *Lamed* of reference naturally stands after that to which it gives the nearer reference, not as here before it. Therefore Hengst.: *ad odorem unguentorum tuorum quod attinet bonus est,* but such giving prominence to the subject and

---

[1] *Vid.* my *Handsch. Funde*, Heft 2 (1862).

[2] Yet it is a question whether דד, to love, and דד, the breast (Arab. *thady*, with a verb *thadiyi*, to be thoroughly wet), are not after their nearest origin such words of feeling, caressing, prattling, as the Arab. *dad*, sport (also *dadad*, the only Arab. word which consists of the same three letters); cf. Fr. *dada*, hobby-horse.

attraction (cf. 1 Sam. ii. 4a; Job xv. 20) exclude one another; the
accentuation correctly places לְרֵיחַ out of the gen. connection. Certainly
this word, like the Arab. *ryḥ*, elsewhere signifies *odor*, and the *Hiph.*
הֵרִיחַ (*araḥ*) *odorari*; but why should not רִיחַ be also used in the
sense of *odoratus*, since in the post-bibl. Heb. חֹשׁ הֵרִיחַ means the
sense of smell, and also in Germ. "*riechen*" means to emit fragrance
as well as to perceive fragrance? We explain after Gen. ii. 9, where
Lamed introduces the sense of sight, as here the sense of smell.
Zöckl. and others reply that in such a case the word would have
been לָרֵיחַ; but the art. is wanting also at Gen. ii. 9 (cf. iii. 6), and
was not necessary, especially in poetry, which has the same relation
to the art. as to *asher*, which, wherever practicable, is omitted.

Thus in line 4:

An ointment poured forth is thy name.

By " thy ointments," line 3, spices are meant, by which the palace
was perfumed; but the fragrance of which, as line 4 says, is surpassed by the fragrance of his name. שֵׁם (name) and שֶׁמֶן (fragrance)
form a paranomasia by which the comparison is brought nearer Eccles.
vii. 1. Both words are elsewhere mas.; but sooner than שֵׁם, so
frequently and universally mas. (although its plur. is שֵׁמוֹת, but cf.
אָבוֹת), שֶׁמֶן may be used as fem., although a parallel example is
wanting (cf. *d⁽e⁾vash*, *mōr*, *nōphĕth*, *kĕmāh*, and the like, which are
constantly mas.). Ewald therefore translates שֶׁמֶן תּוּרַק as a proper
name: " O sweet *Salbenduft*" [Fragrance of Ointment]; and Böttcher
sees in *turăk* a subst. in the sense of " sprinkling" [*Spreng-Oel*]; but
a name like " *Rosenoel*" [oil of roses] would be more appropriately
formed, and a subst. form תּוּרַק is, in Heb. at least, unexampled (for
neither תּוּגָה nor תּוּבַל, in the name Tubal-Cain, is parallel). Fürst
imagines " a province in Palestine where excellent oil was got,"
called *Turak*; " Turkish" *Rosenöl* recommends itself, on the contrary,
by the fact of its actual existence. Certainly less is hazarded
when we regard *shĕmĕn*, as here treated exceptionally, as fem.; thus,
not: *ut unguentum nomen tuum effunditur*, which, besides, is unsuitable, since one does not empty out or pour out a name; but: *unguentum quod effunditur* (Hengst., Hahn, and others), an ointment
which is taken out of its depository and is sprinkled far and wide,
is thy name. The harsh expression שֶׁמֶן מוּרָק is intentionally avoided;
the old Heb. language is not φιλομέτοχος (fond of participles); and,
besides, מוּרָק sounds badly with מרק, to rub off, to wash away. Perhaps, also, שֶׁמֶן יוּרַק is intentionally avoided, because of the collision
of the weak sounds *n* and *j*. The name *Shĕm* is derived from the
verb *shāmā*, to be high, prominent, remarkable: whence also the

name for the heavens (*vid.* under Ps. viii. 2). That attractive charm
(lines 2, 3), and this glory (line 4), make him, the praised, an object
of general love, line 5, ver. 3*b*:

Therefore virgins love thee.

This "therefore" reminds us of Ps. xlv. עֲלָמוֹת (sing. Isa. vii. 14),
from עָלַם (Arab.), *ghalima, pubescere,* are maidens growing to maturity.
The intrans. form אֲהֵבוּךְ, with transitive signification, indicates a
pathos. The perf. is not to be translated *dilexerunt,* but is to be
judged of according to Gesen. § 126. 3 : they have acquired love to
thee (= love thee), as the ἠγάπησάν σε of the Greek translators is
to be understood. The singers themselves are the evidence of the
existence of this love.

With these words the first pentastich of the table-song terminates. The mystical interpretation regards it as a song of praise
and of loving affection which is sung to Christ the King, the fairest
of the children of men, by the church which is His own. The
Targum, in line first, thinks of the "mouth to mouth" [Num. xii. 8]
in the intercourse of Moses with God. Evidence of divine love is
also elsewhere thought of as a kiss : the post-bibl. Heb. calls the
gentlest death the death בנשׁיקה, *i.e.* by which God takes away the
soul with a kiss.

The second pentastich also begins with a solo :

Ver. 4 Draw me, so will we run after thee.

All recent interpreters (except Böttcher) translate, like Luther,
"Draw me after thee, so we run." Thus also the Targ., but doubt-
fully : *Trahe nos post te et curremus post viam bonitatis tuae.* But the
accentuation which gives *Tiphcha* to מָשְׁ requires the punctuation to
be that adopted by the Peshito and the Vulg., and according to which
the passage is construed by the Greeks (except, perhaps, by the
Quinta) : Draw me, so will we, following thee, run (*vid.* Dachselt,
Biblia Accentuata, p. 983 *s.*). In reality, this word needs no complement : of itself it already means, one drawing towards, or to himself ; the corresponding (Arab.) *masak* signifies, *prehendere prehen-
sumque tenere;* the root is משׁ, *palpare, contrectare.* It occurs also
elsewhere, in a spiritual connection, as the expression of the gentle
drawing of love towards itself (Hos. xi. 4 ; Jer. xxxi. 3) ; cf. ἑλκύειν,
John vi. 44, xii. 32. If one connects "after thee" with "draw me,"
then the expression seems to denote that a certain violence is needed
to bring the one who is drawn from her place ; but if it is connected with "we will run," then it defines the desire to run expressed
by the cohortative, more nearly than a willing obedience or following.
The whole chorus, continuing the solo, confesses that there needs

only an indication of his wish, a direction given, to make those who here speak eager followers of him whom they celebrate.

In what follows, this interchange of the *solo* and the *unisono* is repeated:

> Ver. 4*b* If the king has brought me into his chambers,
> So will we exult and rejoice in thee.
> We will praise thy love more than wine!
> Uprightly have they loved thee.

The cohortative נָרוּצָה (we will run) was the *apodosis imperativi;* the cohortatives here are the *apodosis perfecti hypothetici.* "Suppose that this has happened," is oftener expressed by the perf. (Ps. lvii. 7; Prov. xxii. 29, xxv. 16); "suppose that this happens," by the fut. (Job xx. 24; Ewald, § 357*b*). חֲדָרִים are the *interiora domus;* the root word *hhādăr,* as the Arab. *khadar* shows, signifies to draw oneself back, to hide; the *hhĕdĕr* of the tent is the back part, shut off by a curtain from the front space. Those who are singing are not at present in this innermost chamber. But if the king brings one of them in (הֵבִיא, from בּוֹא, *introire,* with *acc. loci*), then—they all say—we will rejoice and be glad in thee. The cohortatives are better translated by the fut. than by the conjunctive (*exultemus*); they express as frequently not what they then desire to do, but what they then are about to do, from inward impulse, with heart delight. The sequence of ideas, " exult" and " rejoice," is not a *climax descendens,* but, as Ps. cxviii. 24, etc., an advance from the external to the internal,—from jubilation which can be feigned, to joy of heart which gives it truth; for שָׂמַח —according to its root signification: to be smoothed, unwrinkled, to be glad[1]—means to be of a joyful, bright, complaisant disposition; and גִּיל, cogn. חִיל, to turn (wind) oneself, to revolve, means conduct betokening delight. The prep. בּ in verbs of rejoicing, denotes the object on account of which, and in which, one has joy. Then, if admitted into the closest neighbourhood of the king, they will praise his love more than wine. זָכַר denotes to fix, viz. in the memory; *Hiph.*: to bring to remembrance, frequently in the way of praise, and thus directly equivalent to *celebrare, e.g.* Ps. xlv. 18. The wine represents the gifts of the king, in contradistinction to his person. That in inward love he gives himself to them, excels in their esteem all else he gives. For, as the closing line expresses, " uprightly they love thee,"—viz. they love thee, *i.e.* from a right heart, which seeks nothing besides, and nothing with thee; and a right mind, which is pleased with thee, and with nothing but thee. Heiligstedt, Zöckler, and others translate: with right they love thee. But the *pluralet.*

---

[1] *Vid.* Friedr. Delitzsch's *Indo-german.-sem. Studien* (1873), p. 99 f.

מֵישָׁרִים (from מִישָׁר, for which the sing. מִישׁוֹר occurs) is an ethical conception (Prov. i. 3), and signifies, not: the right of the motive, but:
the rightness of the word, thought, and act (Prov. xxiii. 16 ; Ps.
xvii. 2, lviii. 2) ; thus, not: *jure ;* but : *recte, sincere, candide.* Hengst.,
Thrupp, and others, falsely render this word like the LXX., Aquil.,
Symm., Theod., Targ., Jerome, Venet., and Luther, as subject : recti-
tudes [abstr. for concr.] = those who have rectitude, the upright.
Hengstenberg's assertion, that the word never occurs as an adv., is
set aside by a glance at Ps. lviii. 2, lxxv. 3 ; and, on the other hand,
there is no passage in which it is used as *abstr. pro concr.* It is
here, as elsewhere, an adv. acc. for which the word בְּמֵישָׁרִים might
also be used.

The second pentastich closes similarly with the first, which
ended with "love thee." What is there said of this king, that the
virgins love him, is here more generalized; for *diligunt te* is
equivalent to *diligeris* (cf. viii. 1, 7). With these words the table-
song ends. It is erotic, and yet so chaste and delicate,—it is sensuous,
and yet so ethical, that here, on the threshold, we are at once
surrounded as by a mystical cloudy brightness. But how is it to be
explained that Solomon, who says (Prov. xxvii. 2), "Let another
praise thee, and not thine own mouth," begins this his Song of Songs
with a song in praise of himself ? It is explained from this, that
here he celebrates an incident belonging to the happy beginning of
his reign ; and for him so far fallen into the past, although not to
be forgotten, that what he was and what he now is are almost as
two separate persons.

After this choral song, Shulamith, who has listened to the
singers not without being examined by their inquisitive glances as
a strange guest not of equal rank with them, now speaks:

> Ver. 5 Black am I, yet comely, ye daughters of Jerusalem,
> As the tents of Kedar, as the hangings of Solomon.

From this, that she addresses the ladies of the palace as " daughters of
Jerusalem " (*Kerî* יְרוּשָׁלַיִם, a *du. fractus ;* like עֶפְרַיִן for עֶפְרוֹן, 2 Chron.
xiii. 19), it is to be concluded that she, although now in Jerusalem,
came from a different place. She is, as will afterwards appear, from
Lower Galilee ;—and it may be remarked, in the interest of the
mystical interpretation, that the church, and particularly her first
congregations, according to the prophecy (Isa. viii. 23), was also
Galilean, for Nazareth and Capernaum are their original seats ;—and
if Shulamith is a poetico-mystical Mashal or emblem, then she represents the synagogue one day to enter into the fellowship of Solomon
—*i.e.* of the son of David, and the daughters of Jerusalem, *i.e.* the

congregation already believing on the Messiah. Yet we confine ourselves to the nearest sense, in which Solomon relates a self-experience.
Shulamith, the lightly esteemed, cannot boast that she is so ruddy
and fair of countenance as they who have just sung how pleasant it
is to be beloved by this king; but yet she is not so devoid of
beauty as not to venture to love and hope to be loved: "Black am
I, yet comely." These words express humility without abjectness.
She calls herself "black," although she is not so dark and unchangeably black as an "Ethiopian" (Jer. xiii. 23). The verb שָׁחַר has
the general primary idea of growing dark, and signifies not necessarily
soot-blackness (modern Arab. shuhwar, soot), but blackness more or less
deep, as שַׁחַר, the name of the morning twilight, or rather the morning
grey, shows; for (Arab.) sahar[1] denotes the latter, as distinguished
from (Arab.) fajr, the morning twilight (vid. under Isa. xiv. 12,
xlvii. 11). She speaks of herself as a Beduin who appears to
herself as (Arab.) sawda, black, and calls[2] the inhabitants of the
town (Arab.) hawaryyat (cute candidas). The Vav we have translated "yet" ("yet comely"); it connects the opposite, which exists
along with the blackness. נָאוָה is the fem. of the adj. נָאוֶה = נָאוֶה = נָאוִי,
which is also formed by means of the doubling of the third stem-
letter of נָאָה = נָאוּ, נָאִי (to bend forward, to aim; to be corresponding
to the aim, conformable, becoming, beautiful), e.g. like רַעֲנָן, to be full
of sap, green. Both comparisons run parallel to nigra et bella; she
compares on the one hand the tents of Kedar, and on the other the
tapestry of Solomon. אֹהֶל signifies originally, in general, the dwelling-
place, as בַּיִת the place where one spends the night; these two
words interchange: ohel is the house of the nomad, and bäith is the
tent of him who is settled. קֵדָר (with the Tsere, probably from
(Arab.) kadar, to have ability, be powerful, thought of after the
Heb. manner, as Theodoret explains and Symm. also translates:
σκοτασμός, from (Heb.) Kadar, atrum esse) is the name of a tribe of
North. Arab. Ishmaelites (Gen. xxv. 13) whom Pliny speaks of
(Cedraei in his Hist. Nat. v. 11), but which disappeared at the era
of the rise of Islam; the Karaite Jefeth uses for it the word (Arab.)
Karysh, for he substitutes the powerful Arab tribe from which
Muhammed sprung, and rightly remarks: "She compares the colour
of her skin to the blackness of the hair tents of the Koreishites,"—

---

[1] After an improbable etymology of the Arab., from sahar, to turn, to depart,
"the departure of the night" (Lane). Magic appears also to be called sihar, as
nigromantia (Mediaev. from nekromantia), the black art.
[2] The houri (damsel of paradise) is thus called hawaryyt, adj. relat. from hawra,
from the black pupil of the eye in the centre of the white eyeball.

even to the present day the Beduin calls his tent his "hair-house" (bêt wabar, or, according to a more modern expression, bêt sa‘r, בֵּית שֵׂעָר); for the tents are covered with cloth made of the hair of goats, which are there mostly black-coloured or grey. On the one hand, dark-coloured as the tents of the Kedarenes, she may yet, on the other hand, compare herself to the beautiful appearance of the יְרִיעוֹת of Solomon. By this word we will have to think of a pleasure-tent or pavilion for the king; *pavillon* (softened from Lat. *papilio*) is a pleasure-tent spread out like the flying butterfly. This Heb. word could certainly also mean curtains for separating a chamber; but in the tabernacle and the temple the curtains separating the Most Holy from the Holy Place were not so designated, but are called פָּרֹכֶת and מָסָךְ; and as with the tabernacle, so always else-where, יְרִיעוֹת (from יָרַע, to tremble, to move hither and thither) is the name of the cloths or tapestry which formed the sides of the tent (Isa. liv. 2); of the tent coverings, which were named in parall. with the tents themselves as the clothing of their framework (Hab. iii. 7; Jer. iv. 20, x. 20, xlix. 29). Such tent hangings will thus also be here meant; precious, as those described Ex. xxvi. and xxxvi., and as those which formed the tabernacle on Zion (2 Sam. vii.; cf. 1 Chron. xvii. 1) before the erection of the temple. Those made in Egypt[1] were particularly prized in ancient times.

Shulamith now explains, to those who were looking upon her with inquisitive wonder, how it is that she is swarthy:

> Ver. 6a Look not on me because I am black,
> Because the sun has scorched me.

If the words were אַל־תִּרְאוּ (תִּרְאֶינָה) בִי, then the meaning would be: look not at me, stare not at me. But אַל־תִּרְאֻנִי, with שׁ (elsewhere כִּי) following, means: Regard me not that I am blackish (*subnigra*); the second שׁ is to be interpreted as co-ordin. with the first (that ... that), or assigning a reason, and that objectively (for). We prefer, with Böttch., the former, because in the latter case we would have had שֶׁהַשֶּׁמֶשׁ. The *quinqueliterum* שְׁחַרְחֹרֶת signifies, in contra-distinction to שָׁחוֹר, that which is black here and there, and thus not altogether black. This form, as descriptive of colour, is diminutive; but since it also means *id quod passim est*, if the accent lies on *passim*, as distinguished from *raro*, it can be also taken as increasing instead of diminishing, as in הֲפַכְפַּךְ, יְפֵיפָה. The LXX. trans. παρέβλεψέ (Symm. παρανέβλεψέ) με ὁ ἥλιος: the sun has looked askance on me. But why only askance? The Venet. better: κατεῖδέ με; but that is too little. The look is thought of as scorching; wherefore

<hr/>

[1] *Vid.* Wetzstein's *Isaiah* (1869), p. 698.

Aquila: συνέκαυσέ με, it has burnt me; and Theodotion: περιέφρυξέ με, it has scorched me over and over. שָׁזַף signifies here not *adspicere* (Job iii. 9, xli. 10) so much as *adurere*. In this word itself (cogn. שָׁדַף; Arab. *sadaf*, whence *asdaf*, black; cf. רָעֵף and עֵיף, Job xvii. 1), the looking is thought of as a scorching; for the rays of the eye, when they fix upon anything, gather themselves, as it were, into a focus. Besides, as the Scriptures ascribe twinkling to the morning dawn, so it ascribes eyes to the sun (2 Sam. xii. 11), which is itself as the eye of the heavens.[1] The poet delicately represents Shulamith as regarding the sun as fem. Its name in Arab. and old Germ. is fem., in Heb. and Aram. for the most part mas. My lady the sun, she, as it were, says, has produced on her this swarthiness.

She now says how it has happened that she is thus sunburnt:

> 6b My mother's sons were angry with me,
> Appointed me as keeper of the vineyards—
> Mine own vineyard have I not kept.

If " mother's sons " is the parallel for " brothers " (אַחַי), then the expressions are of the same import, *e.g.* Gen. xxvii. 29; but if the two expressions stand in apposition, as Deut. xiii. 7 [6], then the idea of the natural brother is sharpened; but when " mother's sons " stands thus by itself alone, then, after Lev. xviii. 9, it means the relationship by one of the parents alone, as " father's wife " in the language of the O. T. and also 1 Cor. v. 5 is the designation of a step-mother. Nowhere is mention made of Shulamith's father, but always, as here, only of her mother, iii. 4, viii. 2, vi. 9; and she is only named without being introduced as speaking. One is led to suppose that Shulamith's own father was dead, and that her mother had been married again; the sons by the second marriage were they who ruled in the house of their mother. These brothers of Shulamith appear towards the end of the melodrama as rigorous guardians of their youthful sister; one will thus have to suppose that their zeal for the spotless honour of their sister and the family proceeded from an endeavour to accustom the fickle or dreaming child to useful activity, but not without step-brotherly harshness. The form נִחֲרוּ, Ewald, § 193c, and Olsh. p. 593, derive from חָרַר, the *Niph.* of which is either נָחַר or נִחַר (= נִחְרַר), Gesen. § 68, An. 5; but the plur. of this נִחַר should, according to rule, have been נִחֲרוּ (cf. how-

---

[1] According to the Indian idea, it is the eye of Varuna; the eye (also after Plato: ἡλιοειδέστατον τῶν περὶ τὰς αἰσθήσεις ὀργάνων) is regarded as taken from the sun, and when men die returning to the sun (Muir in the *Asiatic Journal*, 1865, p. 294, S. 309).

ever, נֶחֱלוּ, *profanantur*, Ezek. vii. 24); and what is more decisive, this נִחַר from חָרַר everywhere else expresses a different passion from that of anger; Böttch. § 1060 (2, 379). חָרָה is used of the burning of anger; and that נִחֲרוּ (from נִחֲרָה = נִחֲרָה) can be another form for נֶחֱרוּ, is shown, *e.g.*, by the interchange of אֶחֱרוּ and אֶחֱרוּ ; the form נֶחֱרוּ, like נֶחֱלוּ, Amos vi. 6, resisted the bringing together of the ח and the half guttural ר. *Něhěrā* (here as Isa. xli. 11, xlv. 24) means, according to the original, mid. signif. of the *Niph.*, to burn inwardly, ἀναφλέγεσθαι = ὀργίζεσθαι. Shulamith's address consists intention-ally of clauses with perfects placed together : she speaks with childlike artlessness, and not " like a book;" in the language of a book, וַיִּשְׁמוּנִי would have been used instead of שָׂמֻנִי. But that she uses נֹטֵרָה (from נטר, R. טר = τηρεῖν ; cf. Targ. Gen. xxxvii. 11 with Luke ii. 51), and not נֹצְרָה, as they were wont to say in Judea, after Prov. xxvii. 18, and after the designation of the tower for the protection of the flocks by the name of " the tower of the *nōtsrīm* " [the watchmen], 2 Kings xvii. 9, shows that the maid is a Galilean, whose manner of speech is Aramaiz-ing, and if we may so say, platt-Heb. (= Low Heb.), like the Lower Saxon *plattdeutsch*. Of the three forms of the particip. נֹטְרָה, נֹטֵרָה, נֹטֶרֶת, we here read the middle one, used subst. (Ewald, § 188*b*), but retaining the long *ē* (ground-form, *nâṭir*). The plur. אֶת־הֲפִּ does not necessarily imply that she had several vineyards to keep, it is the categ. plur. with the art. designating the genus ; *custodiens vineas* is a keeper of a vineyard. But what kind of vineyard, or better, vine-garden, is that which she calls כַּרְמִי שֶׁלִּי, *i.e. meam ipsius vineam ?* The personal possession is doubly expressed ; *shělli* is related to *cărmī* as a nearer defining apposition : my vineyard, that which belongs to me (*vid.* Fr. Philippi's *Status constr.* pp. 112–116). Without doubt the figure refers to herself given in charge to be cared for by her-self : vine-gardens she had kept, but her own vine-garden, *i.e.* her own person, she had not kept. Does she indicate thereby that, in connection with Solomon, she has lost herself, with all that she is and has ? Thus in 1851 I thought; but she certainly seeks to explain why she is so sunburnt. She intends in this figurative way to say, that as the keeper of a vineyard she neither could keep nor sought to keep her own person. In this connection *cărmī*, which by no means = the colourless *memet ipsam*, is to be taken as the figure of the person in its external appearance, and that of its fresh-blooming attractive appearance which directly accords with כֶּרֶם, since from the stem-word כָּרַם (Arab.), *karuma*, the idea of that which is noble and distinguished is connected with this designation of the planting of vines (for כֶּרֶם, (Arab.) *karm*, cf. *karmat*, of a single vine-stock, denotes not so much the soil in which the vines are planted, as rather the vines themselves): her *kĕrĕm* is her (Arab.) *karamat*, *i.e.* her stately attractive appearance. If we must interpret this mystically then, supposing that Shulamith is the congregation of Israel moved at some future time with love to Christ, then by the step-brothers we think of the teachers, who after the death of the fathers threw around the congregation the fetters of their human ordinances, and converted fidelity to the law into a system of hireling service, in which all its beauty disappeared. Among the allegorists, Hengstenberg here presents the extreme of an interpretation opposed to what is true and fine.

These words (vers. 5–6) are addressed to the ladies of the palace, who look upon her with wonder. That which now follows is addressed to her beloved:

> Ver. 7 O tell me, thou whom my soul loveth : where feedest thou ?
>   Where causest thou it (thy flock) to lie down at noon ?
>   For why should I appear as one veiled
>   Among the flocks of thy companions !

The country damsel has no idea of the occupation of a king. Her simplicity goes not beyond the calling of a shepherd as of the fairest and the highest. She thinks of the shepherd of the people as the shepherd of sheep. Moreover, Scripture also describes governing as a tending of sheep ; and the Messiah, of whom Solomon is a type, is specially represented as the future Good Shepherd. If now we had to conceive of Solomon as present from the beginning of the scene, then here in ver. 7 would Shulamith say that she would gladly be alone with him, far away from so many who are looking on her with open eyes ; and, indeed, in some country place where alone she feels at home. The entreaty " O tell me" appears certainly to require (cf. Gen. xxxvii. 19) the presence of one to whom she addresses herself. But, on the other hand, the entreaty only asks that he should let her know where he is ; she longs to know where his occupation detains him, that she may go out and seek him. Her request is thus directed toward the absent one, as is proved by ver. 8. The vocat., " O thou whom my soul loveth," is connected with אַתָּה, which lies hid in הַגִּידָה (" inform thou"). It is a circumlocution for " beloved " (cf. Neh. xiii. 26), or " the dearly beloved of my soul " (cf. Jer. xii. 7). The entreating request, *indica quaeso mihi ubi pascis*, reminds one of Gen. xxxvii. 16, where, however, *ubi* is expressed by אֵיפֹה, while here by אֵיכָה, which in this sense is ἅπ. λεγ. For *ubi* = אֵיפֹה, is otherwise denoted only by אֵיכֹה (אֵיכוֹ), 2 Kings vi. 13, and usually אַיֵּה, North Palest., by Hosea אֱהִי. This אֵיכָה elsewhere means *quo-*

modo, and is the key-word of the *Kina*, as אֵיךְ is of the *Mashal* (the satire) ; the Song uses for it, in common with the Book of Esther, אֵיכָכָה. In themselves כֹּה and כָּה, which with אֵי preceding, are stamped as interrog. in a sense analogous to *hic, ecce, κεῖνος*, and the like ; the local, temporal, polite sense rests only on a conventional *usus loq.*, Böttch. § 530. She wishes to know where he feeds, viz. his flock, where he causes it (viz. his flock) to lie down at mid-day. The verb רָבַץ (R. רב, with the root signif. of condensation) is the proper word for the lying down of a four-footed animal : *complicatis pedibus procumbere (cubare)* ; *Hiph.* of the shepherd, who causes the flock to lie down ; the Arab. *rab'a* is the name for the encampment of shepherds. The time for encamping is the mid-day, which as the time of the double-light, *i.e.* the most intense light in its ascending and descending, is called צָהֳרַיִם. שַׁלָּמָה, occurring only here, signifies *nam cur*, but is according to the sense = *ut ne*, like אֲשֶׁר לָמָה, Dan. i. 10 (cf. Ezra vii. 23) ; לָמָה, without *Dag. forte euphon.*, is, with the single exception of Job vii. 20, always *milra*, while with the *Dag.* it is *milel*, and as a rule, only when the following word begins with אהע״ר carries forward the tone to the *ult.* Shulamith wishes to know the place where her beloved feeds and rests his flock, that she might not wander about among the flocks of his companions seeking and asking for him. But what does כְּעֹטְיָה mean ? It is at all events the *part. act. fem.* of עָטִי which is here treated after the manner of the strong verb, the kindred form to the equally possible עָטָה (from 'átaja) and עֹטְיָה. As for the meaning, *instar errabundae* (Syr., Symm., Jerome, Venet., Luther) recommends itself ; but עטה must then, unless we wish directly to adopt the reading כְּטֹעֲיָה (Böttch.), have been transposed from טעה (תעה), which must have been assumed if עטה, in the usual sense of *velare* (cf. עָטַף), did not afford an appropriate signification. Indeed, *velans*, viz. *sese*, cannot denote one whom consciousness veils, one who is weak or fainting (Gesen. *Lex.*), for the *part. act.* expresses action, not passivity. But it can denote one who covers herself (the LXX., perhaps, in this sense ὡς περιβαλλομένη), because she mourns (Rashi) ; or after Gen. xxxviii. 14 (cf. Martial, ix. 32) one who muffles herself up, because by such affected apparent modesty she wishes to make herself known as a Hierodoule or harlot. The former of these significations is not appropriate ; for to appear as mourning does not offend the sense of honour in a virtuous maiden, but to create the appearance of an immodest woman is to her intolerable ; and if she bears in herself the image of an only beloved, she shrinks in horror from such a base appearance, not only as a debasing of herself, but also as a desecration of this sanctuary in her heart.

Shulamith calls entreatingly upon him whom her soul loveth to tell her how she might be able directly to reach him, without feeling herself wounded in the consciousness of her maidenhood and of the exclusiveness of her love. It is thereby supposed that the companions of her only beloved among the shepherds might not treat that which to her is holy with a holy reserve,—a thought to which Hattendorff has given delicate expression in his exposition of the Song, 1867. If Solomon were present, it would be difficult to understand this entreating call. But he is not present, as is manifest from this, that she is not answered by him, but by the daughters of Jerusalem.

> Ver. 8 If thou knowest not, thou fairest of women,
> Go after the footprints of the flock,
> And feed thy kids beside the shepherds' tents.

הַיָּפָה, standing in the address or call, is in the voc.; the art. was indispensable, because " the beautiful one among women " = the one distinguished for beauty among them, and thus is, according to the meaning, superlative; cf. Judg. vi. 15, Amos ii. 16, with Judg. v. 24; Luke i. 28; Ewald, § 313c. The verb יָפָה refers to the fundamental idea: *integrum, completum esse*, for beauty consists in well-proportioned fulness and harmony of the members. That the ladies of the court are excited to speak thus may arise from this, that one often judges altogether otherwise of a man, whom one has found not beautiful, as soon as he begins to speak, and his countenance becomes intellectually animated. And did not, in Shulamith's countenance, the strange external swarthiness borrow a brightness from the inner light which irradiated her features, as she gave so deep and pure an expression to her longing? But the instruction which her childlike, almost childish, *naïvete* deserved, the daughters of Jerusalem do not feel disposed to give her. לֹא ידע signifies, often without the obj. supplied, *non sapere, e.g.* Ps. lxxxii. 5; Job viii. 9. The לָךְ subjoined guards against this inclusive sense, in which the phrase here would be offensive. This *dat. ethicus* (*vid.* ii. 10, 11, 13, 17, iv. 6, viii. 14), used twice here in ver. 8 and generally in the Song, reflects that which is said on the will of the subject, and thereby gives to it an agreeable cordial turn, here one bearing the colour of a gentle reproof: if thou knowest not to thee,—*i.e.* if thou, in thy simplicity and retirement, knowest it not, viz. that he whom thou thinkest thou must seek for at a distance is near to thee, and that Solomon has to tend not sheep but people,—now, then, so go forth, viz. from the royal city, and remain, although chosen to royal honours, as a shepherdess beside thine own sheep and kids. One misapprehends the answer if he supposes that they in reality point out the

way to Shulamith by which she might reach her object; on the
contrary, they answer her ironically, and, entering into her confusion
of mind, tell her that if she cannot apprehend the position of
Solomon, she may just remain what she is. עָקֵב (Arab. 'akib), from
עָקַב, to be convex, arched, is the heel; to go in the heels (the reading
fluctuates between the form, with and without *Dag. dirimens* in ק)
of one = to press hard after him, to follow him immediately.   That
they assign to her not goats or kids of goats, but kids, גְּדִיֹּת, is an involuntary fine delicate thought with which the appearance of the
elegant, beautiful shepherdess inspires them.   But that they name
kids, not sheep, may arise from this, that the kid is a near-lying
erotic emblem; cf. Gen. xxxviii. 17, where it has been fittingly remarked that the young he-goat was the proper courtesan-offering in
the worship of Aphrodite (Movers' *Phönizier*, I. 680).   It is as if they
said: If thou canst not distinguish between a king and shepherds,
then indulge thy love-thoughts beside the shepherds' tents,—remain
a country maiden if thou understandest not how to value the fortune
which has placed thee in Jerusalem in the royal palace.

SECOND SCENE OF THE FIRST ACT, I. 9—II. 7.

Solomon, while he was absent during the first scene, is now present.   It is generally acknowledged that the words which follow
were spoken by him:

> Ver. 9 To a horse in the chariot of Pharaoh
>   Do I compare thee, my love.
> 10 Beautiful are thy cheeks in the chains,
>   Thy neck in the necklaces.
> 11 Golden chains will we make for thee,
>   With points of silver.

Till now, Shulamith was alone with the ladies of the palace in the
banqueting-chamber.   Solomon now comes from the banquet-hall of
the men (ver. 12); and to ii. 7, to which this scene extends, we
have to think of the women of the palace as still present, although
not hearing what Solomon says to Shulamith.   He addresses her,
" my love:" she is not yet his bride.   רַעְיָה (female friend), from
רָעָה (רָעִי), to guard, care for, tend, ethically: to delight in something
particularly, to take pleasure in intercourse with one, is formed in
the same way as נַעֲרָה; the mas. is רֵעֶה (= ra'j), abbreviated רֵעַ,
whence the fem. *ra'yāh* (Judg. xi. 37 ; *Chethîb*), as well as *rē'āh*, also
with reference to the ground-form.   At once, in the first words used

by Solomon, one recognises a Philip, *i.e.* a man fond of horses,—an important feature in the character of the sage (*vid.* Sur. 38 of the Koran),—and that, one fond of Egyptian horses: Solomon carried on an extensive importation of horses from Egypt and other countries (2 Chron. ix. 28); he possessed 1400 war-chariots and 12,000 horsemen (1 Kings x. 26); the number of stalls of horses for his chariots was still greater (1 Kings v. 6) [iv. 26]. Horace (Ode iii. 11) compares a young sprightly maiden to a nimble and timid *equa trima;* Anacreon (60) addresses such an one: "thou Thracian filly;" and Theocritus says (Idyl xviii. 30, 31):

> " As towers the cypress mid the garden's bloom,
> As in the chariot proud Thessalian steed,
> Thus graceful rose-complexioned Helen moves."

But how it could occur to the author of the Song to begin the praise of the beauty of a shepherdess by saying that she is like a horse in Pharaoh's chariot, is explained only by the supposition that the poet is Solomon, who, as a keen hippologue, had an open eye for the beauty of the horse. Egyptian horses were then esteemed as afterwards the Arabian were. Moreover, the horse was not native to Egypt, but was probably first imported thither by the Hyksos: the Egyptian name of the horse, and particularly of the mare, *ses-t, sesmut*, and of the chariot, *markabuta*, are Semitic.[1] סוּסָה is here not *equitatus* (Jerome), as Hengst. maintains: "*Susah* does not denote a horse, but is used collectively;" while he adds, "Shulamith is compared to the whole Egyptian cavalry, and is therefore an ideal person." The former statement is untrue, and the latter is absurd. *Sûs* means *equus*, and *susâ* may, indeed, collectively denote the stud (cf. Josh. xix. 5 with 1 Chron. iv. 31), but obviously it first denotes the *equa*. But is it to be rendered, with the LXX. and the Venet., "to my horse"? Certainly not; for the chariots of Pharaoh are just the chariots of Egypt, not of the king of Israel. The *Chirek* in which this word terminates is the *Ch. compag.*, which also frequently occurs where, as here and Gen. xlix. 11, the second member of the word-chain is furnished with a prep. (*vid.* under Ps. cxiii.). This *i* is an old genitival ending, which, as such, has disappeared from the language; it is almost always accented as the suff. Thus also here, where the *Metheg* shows that the accent rests on the *ult.* The plur. רִכְבֵי, occurring only here, is the amplificative poetic, and denotes state equipage. דִּמָּה is the trans. of דָּמָה, which combines the meanings *aequum* and *aequalem esse*. Although not allegorizing, yet, that

---

[1] Eber's *Aegypten u. die B. Mose's*, Bd. I. pp. 221 f. 226; cf. *Aeg. Zeitschr.* 1864, p. 26 f.

we may not overlook the judiciousness of the comparison, we must remark that Shulamith is certainly a "daughter of Israel;" a daughter
of the people who increased in Egypt, and, set free from the bondage
of Pharaoh, became the bride of Jahve, and were brought by the
law as a covenant into a marriage relation to Him.

The transition to ver. 10 is mediated by the effect of the comparison; for the head-frame of the horse's bridle, and the poitral,
were then certainly, just as now, adorned with silken tassels, fringes,
and other ornaments of silver (vid. Lane's Modern Egypt, I. 149).
Jerome, absurdly, after the LXX.: pulchrae sunt genae tuae sicut
turturis. The name of the turtle, תֹּר, redupl. turtur, is a pure onomatopoeia, which has nothing to do with תּוּר, whence דּוּר, to go round
about, or to move in a circle; and turtle-dove's cheeks — what
absurdity! Birds have no cheeks; and on the sides of its neck the
turtle-dove has black and white variegated feathers, which also
furnishes no comparison for the colour of the cheeks. תּוֹרִים are the
round ornaments which hang down in front on both sides of the
head-band, or are also inwoven in the braids of hair in the forehead;
תּוּר, circumire, signifies also to form a circle or a row; in Aram. it thus
denotes, e.g., the hem of a garment and the border round the eye.
In נָאווּ (vid. at 5a) the Aleph is silent, as in אָכַל, לֵאמֹר. חֲרוּזִים are
strings of pearls as a necklace; for the necklace (Arab. kharaz) consists of one or more, for the most part, of three rows of pearls. The
verb חָרַז signifies, to bore through and to string together; e.g. in the
Talm., fish which one strings on a rod or line, in order to bring them
to the market. In Heb. and Aram. the secondary sense of stringing
predominates, so that to string pearls is expressed by חרז, and to
bore through pearls, by קדח; in Arab., the primary meaning of
piercing through, e.g. michraz, a shoemaker's awl.

After ver. 11, one has to represent to himself Shulamith's
adorning as very simple and modest; for Solomon seeks to make her
glad with the thought of a continued residence at the royal court by
the promise of costly and elegant ornaments. Gold and silver were
so closely connected in ancient modes of representation, that in the
old Aegypt. silver was called nub het, or white gold. Gold derived
its name of זָהָב from its splendour, after the witty Arab. word zahab,
to go away, as an unstable possession; silver is called כֶּסֶף, from כָּסַף,
scindere, abscindere, a piece of metal as broken off from the mother-
stone, like the Arab. dhukrat, as set free from the lump by means of
the pickaxe (cf. at Ps. xix. 11, lxxxiv. 3). The name of silver
has here, not without the influence of the rhythm (cf. viii. 9), the
article designating the species; the Song frequently uses this, and

is generally in using the art. not so sparing as poetry commonly is.[1] עַם makes prominent the points of silver as something particular, but not separate. In נַעֲשֶׂה, Solomon includes himself among the other inhabitants, especially the women of the palace; for the *plur. majest.* in the words of God of Himself (frequently in the Koran), or persons of rank of themselves (general in the vulgar Arab.), is unknown in the O. T. They would make for her golden globules or knobs with (*i.e.* provided with . . .; cf. Ps. lxxxix. 14) points of silver sprinkled over them,—which was a powerful enticement for a plain country damsel.

Now for the first time Shulamith addresses Solomon, who is before her. It might be expected that the first word will either express the joy that she now sees him face to face, or the longing which she had hitherto cherished to see him again. The verse following accords with this expectation:

Ver. 12 While the king is at his table,
My nard has yielded its fragrance.

עַד שֶׁ or עַד אֲשֶׁר, with fut. foll., usually means: *usque eo*, until this and that shall happen, ii. 7, 17; with the perf. foll., until something happened, iii. 4. The idea connected with "until" may, however, be so interpreted that there comes into view not the end of the period as such, but the whole length of the period. So here in the subst. clause following, which in itself is already an expression of continuance, *donec = dum* (*erat*); so also עַד alone, without *asher*, with the part. foll. (Job i. 18), and the infin. (Judg. iii. 26; Ex. xxxiii. 22; Jonah iv. 2; cf. 2 Kings ix. 22); seldomer with the

---

[1] The art. denoting the idea of species in the second member of the *st. const.* standing in the sing. without a determining reference to the first, occurs in i. 13, "a bundle of (*von*) myrrh;" i. 14, "a cluster of (*von*) the cyprus-flower;" iv. 3, "a thread of (*von*) scarlet," "a piece of pomegranate;" v. 13, "a bed of balm" (but otherwise, vi. 2); vii. 9, "clusters of the vine;" vii. 3, "a bowl of roundness" (which has this property); vii. 10, "wine (of the quality) of goodness;" cf. viii. 2, "wine the (= of the) spicing." It also, in cases where the defined species to which the first undefined member of the *st. const.* belongs, stands in the pl.: ii. 9, 17, viii. 14, "like a young one of the hinds;" iv. 1, vi. 5, "a herd of goats;" iv. 2, "a flock of shorn sheep;" vi. 6, "a flock of lambs," *i.e.* consisting of individuals of this kind. Also, when the second member states the place where a thing originates or is found, the first often remains indeterminate, as one of that which is there found, or a part of that which comes from thence: ii. 1, "a meadow-saffron of Sharon," "a lily of the valleys;" iii. 9, "the wood of Lebanon." The following are doubtful: iv. 4, "a thousand bucklers;" and vii. 5, "a tower of ivory;" less so vii. 1, "the dance of Mahanaim." The following are examples of a different kind: Gen. xvi. 7, "a well of water;" Deut. xxii. 19, "a damsel of Israel;" Ps. cxiii. 9, "a mother of children;" cf. Gen. xxi. 28.

fin. foll., once with the perf. foll. (1 Sam. xiv. 19), once (for Job
viii. 21 is easily explained otherwise) with the fut. foll. (Ps. cxli. 10,
according to which Gen. xlix. 10 also is explained by Baur and
others, but without עד כי in this sense of limited duration: " so long
as," being anywhere proved). מְסִבּוֹ is the inflected מֵסַב, which, like
the post-bibl. מְסִבָּה, signifies the circuit of the table ; for סָבַב signifies
also, after 1 Sam. xvi. 11 (the LXX. rightly, after the sense οὐ μὴ
κατακλιθῶμεν), to seat themselves around the table, from which
it is to be remarked that not till the Greek-Roman period was the
Persian custom of reclining at table introduced, but in earlier times
they sat (1ˢ Sam. xx. 5 ; 1 Kings xiii. 20 ; cf. Ps. cxxviii. 3).   Reclining and eating are to be viewed as separate from each other, Amos
vi. 4 ; הֵסַב, " three and three they recline at table," is in matter as
in language *mishnic* (*Berachoth* 42b; cf. *Sanhedrin* ii. 4, of the
king: if he reclines at table, the Tôra must be opposite him).
Thus : While (*usque eo*, so long as), says Shulamith, the king was
at his table, my nard gave forth its fragrance.

נֵרְדְּ is an Indian word : *naladâ*, *i.e.* yielding fragrance, Pers.
nard (*nârd*), Old Arab. *nardîn* (*nârdîn*), is the aromatic oil of an
Indian plant *valeriana*, called *Nardostachys* '*Gatâmânsi* (hair-tress
nard).   Interpreters are wont to represent Shulamith as having a stalk
of nard in her hand.   Hitzig thinks of the nard with which she who
is speaking has besprinkled herself, and he can do this because he
regards the speaker as one of the court ladies.   But that Shulamith
has besprinkled herself with nard, is as little to be thought of as
that she has in her hand a sprig of nard (*spica nardi*), or, as the
ancients said, an ear of nard ; she comes from a region where no
nard grows, and nard-oil is for a country maiden unattainable.[1]
Horace promises Virgil a *cadus* (= 9 gallons) of the best wine for a
small onyx-box full of nard; and Judas estimated at 300 denarii
(about £8, 10s.) the genuine nard (how frequently nard was
adulterated we learn from Pliny) which Mary of Bethany poured
from an alabaster box on the head of Jesus, so that the whole house
was filled with the odour of the ointment (Mark xiv. 5 ; John xii. 2).
There, in Bethany, the love which is willing to sacrifice all expressed
itself in the nard ; here, the nard is a figure of the happiness of love,
and its fragrance a figure of the longing of love.   It is only in the
language of flowers that Shulamith makes precious perfume a figure
of the love which she bears in the recess of her heart, and which, so

[1] The nard plant grows in Northern and Eastern India; the hairy part of the
stem immediately above the root yields the perfume.   *Vid.* Lassen's *Indische
Alterthumskunde*, I. 338 f., III. 41 f.

long as Solomon was absent, breathed itself out and, as it were, cast forth its fragrance [1] (cf. ii. 13, vii. 14) in words of longing. She has longed for the king, and has sought to draw him towards her, as she gives him to understand. He is continually in her mind.

> Ver. 13 A bundle of myrrh is my beloved to me,
>   Which lieth between my breasts.
>   14 A bunch of cypress-flowers is my beloved to me,
>   From the vine-gardens of Engedi.

Most interpreters, ignoring the lessons of botany, explain 13a of a little bunch of myrrh; but whence could Shulamith obtain this? Myrrh, מֹר (מָרַר, to move oneself in a horizontal direction hither and thither, or gradually to advance; of a fluid, to flow over the plain [2]), belongs, like the frankincense, to the amyrids, which are also exotics [3] in Palestine; and that which is aromatic in the *Balsamodendron myrrha* are the leaves and flowers, but the resin (*Gummi myrrhae*, or merely *myrrha*) cannot be tied in a bunch. Thus the myrrh here can be understood in no other way than as at v. 5; in general צְרוֹר, according to Hitzig's correct remark, properly denotes not what one binds up together, but what one ties up—thus *sacculus*, a little bag. It is not supposed that she carried such a little bag with her (cf. Isa. iii. 20), or a box of frankincense (Luth. musk-apple); but she compares her beloved to a myrrh-repository, which day and night departs not from her bosom, and penetrates her inwardly with its heart-strengthening aroma. So constantly does she think of him, and so delightful is it for her to dare to think of him as her beloved.

The 14th verse presents the same thought. כֹּפֶר is the cypress-cluster or the cypress-flowers, κύπρος (according to Fürst, from כפר= עפר, to be whitish, from the colour of the yellow-white flowers), which botanists call *Lawsonia*, and in the East *Alhennâ*; its leaves yield the orange colour with which the Moslem women stain [4] their hands and feet. אֶשְׁכֹּל (from שָׁכַל, to interweave) denotes that which is woven, tresses, or a cluster or garland of their flowers. Here also we

---

[1] In Arab. نتن = נתן, to give an odour, has the specific signification, to give an ill odour (*mintin, foetidus*), which led an Arab. interpreter to understand the expression, "my nard has yielded, etc.," of the stupifying savour which compels Solomon to go away (*Mittheilung*, Goldziher's)

[2] *Vid.* Schlotmann in the *Stud. u. Krit.* (1867), p. 217.

[3] They came from Arabia and India; the better Arabian was adulterated with Indian myrrh.

[4] *Vid.* the literature of this subject in Defrémery's notice of Dozy-Engelmann's work in the *Revue Critique*, III. 2 (1868), p. 408.

have not to suppose that Shulamith carried a bunch of flowers; in her imagination she places herself in the vine-gardens which Solomon had planted on the hill-terraces of Engedi lying on the west of the Dead Sea (Eccles. ii. 4), and chooses a cluster of flowers of the cypress growing in that tropical climate, and says that her beloved is to her internally what such a cluster of cypress-flowers would be to her externally. To be able to call him her beloved is her ornament; and to think of him refreshes her like the most fragrant flowers.

In this ardour of loving devotion, she must appear to the king so much the more beautiful.

> Ver. 15 Lo, thou art fair, my love.
> Lo, thou art fair; thine eyes are doves.

This is a so-called *comparatio decurtata*, as we say: feet like the gazelle, *i.e.* to which the swiftness of the gazelle's feet belongs (Hab. iii. 19); but instead of "like doves," for the comparison mounts up to equalization, the expression is directly, " doves." If the pupil of the eye were compared with the feathers of the dove (Hitz.), or the sprightliness of the eye with the lively motion hither and thither of the dove (Heiligst.), then the eulogium would stand out of connection with what Shulamith has just said. But it stands in reference to it if her eyes are called doves; and so the likeness to doves' eyes is attributed to them, because purity and gentleness, longing and simplicity, express themselves therein. The dove is, like the myrtle, rose, and apple, an attribute of the goddess of love, and a figure of that which is truly womanly; wherefore יְמִימָה (the Arab. name of a dove), *Columbina*, and the like names of women, *columba* and *columbari*, are words of fondness and caressing. Shulamith gives back to Solomon his eulogium, and rejoices in the prospect of spending her life in fellowship with him.

> Ver. 16 Behold, thou art comely, my beloved; yea, charming;
> Yea, our couch is luxuriously green.
> 17 The beams of our house are cedars,
> Our wainscot of cypresses.

If ver. 16 were not the echo of her heart to Solomon, but if she there-with meant some other one, then the poet should at least not have used הִנָּךְ, but הִנֵּה. Hitzig remarks, that up to "my beloved" the words appear as those of mutual politeness—that therefore נָעִים (charming) is added at once to distinguish her beloved from the king, who is to her insufferable. But if a man and a woman are together, and he says הִנָּךְ and she says הִנְּךָ, that is as certainly an interchange of address as that one and one are two and not three.

He praises her beauty; but in her eyes it is rather he who is beautiful, yea charming: she rejoices beforehand in that which is assigned to her. Where else could her conjugal happiness find its home but among her own rural scenes? The city with its noisy display does not please her; and she knows, indeed, that her beloved is a king, but she thinks of him as a shepherd. Therefore she praises the fresh green of their future homestead; cedar tops will form the roof of the house in which they dwell, and cypresses its wainscot. The bed, and particularly the bridal-bower (*D. M. Z.* xxii. 153),—but not merely the bed in which one sleeps, but also the cushion for rest, the divan (Amos vi. 4),—has the name עֶרֶשׂ, from עָרַשׂ, to cover over; cf. the "network of goats' hair" (1 Sam. xix. 13) and the κωνωπεῖον of Holofernes (Judith x. 21, xiii. 9), (whence our *kanapee* = canopy), a bed covered over for protection against the κώνωπες, the gnats. רַעֲנָן, whence here the fem. adj. accented on the *ult.*, is not a word of colour, but signifies to be extensible, and to extend far and wide, as *lentus* in *lenti salices;* we have no word such as this which combines in itself the ideas of softness and juicy freshness, of bending and elasticity, of looseness, and thus of overhanging ramification (as in the case of the weeping willow). The beams are called קֹרוֹת, from קָרָה, to meet, to lay crosswise, to hold together (cf. *contingere* and *contignare*). רְחִיטֵנוּ (after another reading, רָח, from רָחִיט, with *Kametz* immutable, or a virtual *Dag.*) is North Palest. = רהִיט (*Kerî*), for in place of רְהָטִים, troughs (Ex. ii. 16), the Samarit. has רחטים (cf. *sahar* and *sahhar, circumire, zahar* and *zahhar,* whence the Syr. name of scarlet); here the word, if it is not defect. plur. (Heiligst.), is used as collect. sing. of the hollows or panels of a wainscoted ceiling, like φάτναι, whence the LXX. φατνώματα (Symm. φατνώσεις), and like *lacunae,* whence *lacunaria,* for which Jerome has here *laquearia,* which equally denotes the wainscot ceiling Abulwalîd glosses the word rightly by מרזבים, gutters (from רָהַט, to run); only this and οἱ διάδρομοι of the Gr. Venet. is not an architectural expression, like רהיטים, which is still found in the Talm. (*vid.* Buxtorf's *Lex.*). To suppose a transposition from חריטנו, from חָרַט, to turn, to carve (Ew. Heiligst. Hitz.), is accordingly not necessary. As the ת in בְּרוֹתִים belongs to the North Palest. (Galilean) form of speech,[1] so also ח for ה in this word: an exchange of the gutturals was characteristic of the Galilean idiom (*vid.* Talm. citations by Frankel, *Einl. in d. jerus. Talm.*

[1] Pliny, *H. N.* xxiv. 102, ed. Jan., notes *brathy* as the name of the savin-tree *Juniperus sabina.* Wetstein is inclined to derive the name of Beirut from ברות, as the name of the sweet pine, the tree peculiar to the Syrian landscape, and which,

1870, 7b). Well knowing that a mere hut was not suitable for the king, Shulamith's fancy converts one of the magnificent nature-temples of the North Palest. forest-solitudes into a house where, once together, they will live each for the other. Because it is a large house, although not large by art, she styles it by the poet. plur. *bāttenu.* The mystical interpretation here finds in Isa. lx. 13 a favourable support.

What Shulamith now further says confirms what had just been said. City and palace with their splendour please her not ; forest and field she delights in ; she is a tender flower that has grown up in the quietness of rural life.

Ch. ii. 1 I am a meadow-flower of Sharon,

A lily of the valleys.

We do not render : " the wild-flower," " the lily," . . . for she seeks to represent herself not as the one, but only as one of this class ; the definiteness by means of the article sometimes belongs exclusively to the second number of the genit. word-chain. מלאך ה' may equally (*vid.* at i. 11, Hitz. on Ps. cxiii. 9, and my *Comm.* on Gen. ix. 20) mean " an angel " or " the angel of Jahve ;" and בת ישׂ' " a virgin," or " the virgin of Israel " (the personification of the people). For *hhăvatsĕlĕth* (perhaps from *hhivtsĕl,* a denom. quadril. from *bĕtsĕl,* to form bulbs or bulbous knolls) the Syr. Pesh. (Isa. xxxv. 1) uses *chamsaljotho,* the meadow-saffron, *colchicum autumnale ;* it is the flesh-coloured flower with leafless stem, which, when the grass is mown, decks in thousands the fields of warmer regions. They call it *filius ante patrem,* because the blossoms appear before the leaves and the seed-capsules, which develope themselves at the close of winter under the ground. Shulamith compares herself to such a simple and common flower, and that to one in Sharon, *i.e.* in the region known by that name. *Sharon* is *per aphaer.* derived from יָשָׁרוֹן. The most celebrated plain of this name is that situated on the Mediterranean coast between Joppa and Caesarea ; but there is also a trans-Jordanic Sharon, 1 Chron. v. 16 ; and according to Eusebius and Jerome, there is also another district of this name between Tabor and the Lake of Tiberias,[1] which is the one here intended, because Shulamith is a Galilean : she calls herself a flower from the neighbourhood of Nazareth. Aquila translates : " A rosebud of Sharon ; " but שׁוֹשַׁנָּה (designedly here the fem. form of the name, which is also

---

growing on the sandy hills, prevents the town from being filled with flying sand. The cypress is now called (Arab.) *sanawbar;* regarding its old names, and their signification in the figurative language of love, *vid.* under Isa. xli. 19.

[1] *Vid.* Lagarde, *Onomastica,* p. 296 ; cf. Neubauer, *Géographie du Talm.* p. 47.

the name of a woman) does not mean the Rose which was brought at a later period from Armenia and Persia, as it appears,[1] and cultivated in the East (India) and West (Palestine, Egypt, Europe). It is nowhere mentioned in the canonical Scriptures, but is first found in Sir. xxiv. 14, xxxix. 13, l. 8; Wisd. ii. 8; and Esth. i. 6, LXX. Since all the *rosaceae* are five-leaved, and all the *liliaceae* are six-leaved, one might suppose, with Aben Ezra, that the name *sosan* (*susan*) is connected with the numeral שֵׁשׁ, and points to the number of leaves, especially since one is wont to represent to himself the Eastern lilies as red. But they are not only red, or rather violet, but also white: the Moorish-Spanish *azucena* denotes the white lily.[2] The root-word will thus, however, be the same as that of שֵׁשׁ, *byssus*, and שַׁיִשׁ, white marble. The comparison reminds us of Hos. xiv. 6 [5], " I shall be as the dew unto Israel: he shall grow as the lily." הָעֲמָקִים are deep valleys lying between mountains. She thinks humbly of herself; for before the greatness of the king she appears diminutive, and before the comeliness of the king her own beauty disappears—but he takes up her comparison of herself, and gives it a notable turn.

> Ver. 2 As a lily among thorns,
> So is my love among the daughters.

By הַחֹחִים are not meant the thorns of the plant itself, for the lily has no thorns, and the thorns of the rose are, moreover, called *kotsim*, and not *hhohhim*;[3] besides, *ben* (among) contradicts that idea, since the thorns are on the plant itself, and it is not among them— thus the *hhohhim* are not the thorns of the flower-stem, but the thorn-plants that are around. חוֹחַ designates the thorn-bush, *e.g.* in the allegorical answer of King Josiah to Amaziah, 2 Kings xiv. 9. Simplicity, innocence, gentleness, are the characteristics in which Shulamith surpasses all בָּנוֹת, *i.e.* all women (*vid.* vi. 9), as the lily of the valley surpasses the thorn-bushes around it. "Although thorns surround her, yet can he see her; he sees her quiet life, he finds her beautiful." But continuing this reciprocal rivalry in the praise of mutual love, she says:

---

[1] *Vid.* Ewald, *Jahrbuch*, IV. p. 71; cf. Wüstemann, *Die Rose*, etc., 1854.

[2] *Vid.* Fleischer, *Sitzungs-Berichten d. Sächs. Gesell. d. Wissensch.* 1868, p. 305. Among the rich flora on the descent of the Hauran range, Wetstein saw (*Reisebericht*, p. 148) a dark-violet magnificent lily (*susan*) as large as his fist. We note here Rückert's "Bright lily! The flowers worship God in the garden: thou art the priest of the house."

[3] An Aramaic proverb: "from thorns sprouts the rose" (*i.e.* bad fathers have often pious children), in Heb. is קוֹץ מוֹצִיא שׁוֹשָׁן; *vid. Jalkut Samuel*, § 134.

Ver. 3*a* As an apple-tree among the trees of the wood,
So is my beloved among the sons.

The apple-tree, the name of which, תַּפּוּחַ, is formed from נָפַח, and denominates it from its fragrant flower and fruit, is as the king among fruit trees, in Shulamith's view. יַעַר (from יָעַר, to be rough, rugged, uneven) is the wilderness and the forest, where are also found trees bearing fruit, which, however, is for the most part sour and unpalatable. But the apple-tree unites delicious fruit along with a grateful shade; and just such a noble tree is the object of her love.

3*b* Under his shadow it delighted me to sit down;
And his fruit is sweet to my taste.

In *concupivi et consedi* the principal verb completes itself by the co-ordinating of a verb instead of an adv. or inf. as Isa. xlii. 21; Esth. viii. 7; Ewald, § 285. However, *concupivi et consedi* is yet more than *concupivi considere*, for thereby she not only says that she found delight in sitting down, but at the same time also in sitting down in the shadow of this tree. The *Piel* חִמַּד, occurring only here, expresses the intensity of the wish and longing. The shadow is a figure of protection afforded, and the fruit a figure of enjoyment obtained. The taste is denoted by חֵךְ = חִנֵּךְ, from חָנַךְ, to chew, or also *imbuere*; and that which is sweet is called מָתוֹק, from the smacking connected with an agreeable relish. The *usus loq.* has neglected this image, true to nature, of physical circumstances in words, especially where, as here, they are transferred to the experience of the soul-life. The taste becomes then a figure of the soul's power of perception (αἰσθητικόν); a man's fruit are his words and works, in which his inward nature expresses itself; and this fruit is sweet to those on whom that in which the peculiar nature of the man reveals itself makes a happy, pleasing impression. But not only does the person of the king afford to Shulamith so great delight, he entertains her also with what can and must give her enjoyment.

Ver. 4 He has brought me into the wine-house,
And his banner over me is love.

After we have seen the ladies of the palace at the feast, in which wine is presented, and after Solomon, till now absent, has entered the banqueting-chamber (Arab. *meǵlis*), by בֵּית הַיַּיִן we are not to understand the vineyard, which would be called *bêth hăggephānim* or *bêth hā'ănāvim*, as in Acts i. 12, Pesh. the Mount of Olives, *bêth zaite.*[1] He has introduced her to the place where he royally entertains his friends. Well knowing that she, the poor and sunburnt

[1] In Heb. יין does not denote the vine as a plant, as the Aethiop. *wain*, whence *asada wain*, wine-court = vineyard, which Ewald compares; Dillmann, however,

maiden, does not properly belong to such a place, and would rather escape away from it, he relieves her from her fear and bashfulness, for he covers her with his fear-inspiring, awful, and thus surely protecting, banner; and this banner, which he waves over her, and under which she is well concealed, is "love." דֶּגֶל (from דָּגַל, to cover) is the name of the covering of the shaft or standard, *i.e. pannus*, the piece of cloth fastened to a shaft. Like a pennon, the love of the king hovers over her; and so powerful, so surpassing, is the delight of this love which pervades and transports her, that she cries out:

> Ver. 5 Support me with grape-cakes,
> Refresh me with apples:
> For I am sick with love.

She makes use of the intensive form as one in a high degree in need of the reanimating of her almost sinking life: סַמֵּךְ is the intens. of סָמַךְ, to prop up, support, or, as here, to under-prop, uphold; and רַפֵּד, the intens. of רָפַד (R. רף), to raise up from beneath (*vid.* at Prov. vii. 16), to furnish firm ground and support. The apple is the Greek attribute of Aphrodite, and is the symbol of love; but here it is only a means of refreshing; and if thoughts of love are connected with the apple-tree (ii. 3, viii. 5), that is explained from Shulamith's rural home. Böttcher understands quinces; Epstein, citrons; but these must needs have been more closely denoted, as at Prov. xxv. 11, by some addition to the expression. אֲשִׁישׁוֹת (from אָשַׁשׁ, to establish, make firm) are (cf. Isa. xvi. 7; Hos. iii. 1) grapes pressed together like cakes; different from צִמּוּקִים, dried grapes (cf. וּדְבֵלָה), fig-cakes (Arab. *dabbûle*, a mass pressed together), and πλακοῦς, *placenta*, from the pressed-out form. A cake is among the gifts (2 Sam. vi. 19) which David distributed to the people on the occasion of the bringing up of the ark; date-cakes, *e.g.* at the monastery at Sinai, are to the present day gifts for the refreshment of travellers. If Shulamith's cry was to be understood literally, one might, with Noack, doubt the correctness of the text; for "love-sickness, even in the age of passion and sentimentality, was not to be cured with roses and apples." But (1) sentimentality, *i.e.* susceptibility, does not belong merely to the Romantic, but also to Antiquity, especially in the Orient, as *e.g.* is shown by the symptoms of sympathy with which the prophets were affected when uttering their threatenings of judgment; let one read such outbreaks of sorrow as Isa. xxi. 3, which, if one is disposed to scorn, may be derided as hysterical fits. Moreover, the Indian, Persian, and Arabic erotic ineptly cites "vine-arbour," and South-Germ. "*kamerte*" = *vinea camerata*; in Heb. בֵּית הַיַּיִן is the house in which wine is drunk.

(*vid. e.g.* the Romance *Siret 'Antar*) is as sentimental as the German has at any time been. (2) The subject of the passage here is not the curing of love-sickness, but bodily refreshment : the cry of Shulamith, that she may be made capable of bearing the deep agitation of her physical life, which is the consequence, not of her love-sickness, but of her love-happiness. (3) The cry is not addressed (although this is grammatically possible, since סַמְּכוּנִי is, according to rule, = סַמְּכְנָה אֹתִי) to the daughters of Jerusalem, who would in that case have been named, but to some other person ; and this points to its being taken not in a literal sense. (4) It presupposes that one came to the help of Shulamith, sick and reduced to weakness, with grapes and apple-scent to revive her fainting spirit. The call of Shulamith thus means : hasten to me with that which will revive and refresh me, for I am sick with love. This love-sickness has also been experienced in the spiritual sphere. St. Ephrem was once so overcome by such a joy that he cried out : " Lord, withdraw Thine hand a little, for my heart is too weak to receive so great joy." And J. R. Hedinger († 1704) was on his deathbed overpowered with such a stream of heavenly delight that he cried : " Oh, how good is the Lord ! Oh, how sweet is Thy love, my Jesus ! Oh, what a sweetness ! I am not worthy of it, my Lord ! Let me alone ; let me alone ! " As the spiritual joy of love, so may also the spiritual longing of love consume the body (cf. Job xix. 27 ; Ps. lxiii. 2, lxxxiv. 3) ; there have been men who have actually sunk under a longing desire after the Lord and eternity. It is the state of love-ecstasy in which Shulamith calls for refreshment, because she is afraid of sinking. The contrast between her, the poor and unworthy, and the king, who appears to her as an ideal of beauty and majesty, who raises her up to himself, was such as to threaten her life. Unlooked for, extraordinary fortune, has already killed many. Fear, producing lameness and even death, is a phenomenon common in the Orient.[1] If Pharaoh's daughter, if the Queen of Sheba, finds herself in the presence of Solomon, the feeling of social equality prevents all alarm. But Shulamith is dazzled by the splendour, and disconcerted;

---

[1] " *Ro'b* (רְעַב, thus in Damascus), or *ra'b* (thus in the Hauran and among the Beduins), is a state of the soul which with us is found only in a lower degree, but which among the Arabians is psychologically noteworthy. The *wahm, i.e.* the idea of the greatness and irresistibility of a danger or a misfortune, overpowers the Arabian ; all power of body and of soul suddenly so departs from him, that he falls down helpless and defenceless. Thus, on the 8th July 1860, in a few hours, about 6000 Christian men were put to death in Damascus, without one lifting his hand in defence, or uttering one word of supplication. That the *ro'b*

and it happens to her in type as it happened to the seer of Patmos, who, in presence of the ascended Lord, fell at His feet as one dead, Rev. i. 17. If beauty is combined with dignity, it has always, for gentle and not perverted natures, something that awakens veneration and tremor; but if the power of love be superadded, then it has, as a consequence, that combination of awe and inward delight, the psychological appearance of which Sappho, in the four strophes which begin with "Φαίνεταί μοι κῆνος ἴσος θεοῖσιν ἔμμεν ὠνήρ," has described in a manner so true to nature. We may thus, without carrying back modern sentimentality into antiquity, suppose that Shulamith sank down in a paroxysm caused by the rivalry between the words of love and of praise, and thus thanking him,—for Solomon supports and bears her up,—she exclaims:

Ver. 6 His left hand is under my head,
And his right hand doth embrace me.

With his left hand he supports her head that had fallen backwards, and with his right he embraces her [herzet], as Luther rightly renders it (as he also renders the name Habakkuk by "der Herzer" = the embracer); for חִבֵּק signifies properly to enfold, to embrace; but then generally, to embrace lovingly, to fondle, of that gentle stroking with the hand elsewhere denoted by חִלָּה, mulcere. The situation here is like that at Gen. xxix. 13, xlviii. 10; where, connected with the dat., it is meant of loving arms stretched out to embrace. If this sympathetic, gentle embracing exercises a soothing influence on her, overcome by the power of her emotions; so love mutually kindled now celebrates the first hour of delighted enjoyment, and the happy Shulamith calls to those who are witnesses of her joy:

Ver. 7 I adjure you, ye daughters of Jerusalem,
By the gazelles or the hinds of the field,
That ye arouse not and disturb not love
Till she pleases.

It is permitted to the Israelites to swear, נִשְׁבַּע, only by God (Gen. xxi. 23); but to adjure, הִשְׁבִּיעַ, by that which is not God, is also admissible, although this example before us is perhaps the only

kills in Arabia, European and native physicians have assured me; and I myself can confirm the fact. Since it frequently produces a stiffening of the limbs, with chronic lameness, every kind of paralysis is called ro'b, and every paralytic mar'ûb. It is treated medically by applying the 'terror-cup' (tâset er-ro'b), covered over with sentences engraved on it, and hung round with twenty bells; and since, among the Arabians, the influence of the psychical on the physical is stronger and more immediate than with us, the sympathetic cure may have there sometimes positive results."—Wetstein.

direct one in Scripture. צְבִי (= צְבִי, dialect. טַבְי), fem. צְבִיָה (Aram. טַבְיְתָא, Acts ix. 36), plur. *tsebaim* or *tsebajim*, fem. *tsabaōth* (according with the pl. of צְבָא), softened from *tsebajōth*, is the name for the gazelle, from the elegance of its form and movements. אַיְלוֹת is the connecting form of אַיָּלוֹת, whose consonantal *Yod* in the Assyr. and Syr. is softened to the diphthong *ailuv*, *ailā*; the gen. "of the field," as not distinguishing but describing, belongs to both of the animals, therefore also the first is without the article. אוֹ (after the etymon corresponding to the Lat. *vel*) proceeds, leaving out of view the repetition of this so-called Slumber-Song (iii. 5; cf. viii. 4, as also ii. 9), from the endeavour to give to the adjuration the greatest impression; the expression is varied, for the representations flit from image to image, and the one, wherever possible, is surpassed by the other (*vid.* at Prov. xxx. 31). Under this verse Hengst. remarks: "The bride would not adjure by the hinds, much more would she adjure by the stags." He supposes that Solomon is here the speaker; but a more worthless proof for this could not be thought of. On the contrary, the adjuration by the gazelles, etc., shows that the speaker here is one whose home is the field and wood; thus also not the poet (Hitz.) nor the queen-mother (Böttch.), neither of whom is ever introduced as speaking. The adjuration is that love should not be disturbed, and therefore it is by the animals that are most lovely and free, which roam through the fields. Zöckler, with whom in this one point Grätz agrees, finds here, after the example of Böttch. and Hitz., the earnest warning against wantonly exciting love in themselves (cf. Lat. *irritamenta veneris, irritata voluptas*) till God Himself awakens it, and heart finds itself in sympathy with heart. But the circumstances in which Shulamith is placed ill accord with such a general moralizing. The adjuration is repeated, iii. 5, viii. 4, and wherever Shulamith finds herself near her beloved, as she is here in his arms. What lies nearer, then, than that she should guard against a disturbance of this love-ecstasy, which is like a slumber penetrated by delightful dreams? Instead of תְּעִירוּ אֶתְכֶם, and תְּעוֹרְרוּ, should be more exactly the words תְּעֵרְנָה אֶתְכֶן, and תְּעוֹרֵרְנָה; but the gram. distinction of the *genera* is in Heb. not perfectly developed. We meet also with the very same *synallage generis*, without this adjuration formula, at v. 8, vii. 1, iv. 2, vi. 8, etc.; it is also elsewhere frequent; but in the Song it perhaps belongs to the foil of the vulgar given to the highly poetic. Thus also in the vulgar Arab. the fem. forms *jaktulna, taktulna*, corresponding to תִּקְטֹלְנָה, are fallen out of use. With הֵעִיר, *expergefacere*, there is connected the idea of an interruption of sleep; with עוֹרֵר,

excitare, the idea, which goes further, of arousing out of sleep, placing in the full activity of awakened life.[1] The one adjuration is, that love should not be awakened out of its sweet dream; the other, that it should not be disturbed from its being absorbed in itself. The *Pasek* between תעירו and the word following has, as at Lev. x. 6, the design of keeping the two *Vavs* distinct, that in reading they might not run together; it is the *Pasek* which, as Ben Asher says, serves "to secure to a letter its independence against the similar one standing next it." הָאַהֲבָה is not *abstr. pro concreto*, but love itself in its giving and receiving. Thus closes the second scene of the first act: Shulamith lies like one helpless in the arms of Solomon; but in him to expire is her life; to have lost herself in him, and in him to find herself again, is her happiness.

SECOND ACT.

THE MUTUAL SEEKING AND FINDING OF THE LOVERS.—
CHAP. II. 8–III. 5.

FIRST SCENE OF THE SECOND ACT, II. 8–17.

With ii. 8 the second act begins. The so-callèd slumber-song (iii. 5) closes it, as it did the first act; and also the refrain-like summons to hasten to the mountains leaves no doubt regarding the close of the first scene. The locality is no longer the royal city. Shulamith, with her love-sickness, is once more at home in the house which she inhabits along with her own friends, of whom she has already (i. 6) named her brothers. This house stands alone among the rocks, and deep in the mountain range; around are the vineyards which the family have planted, and the hill-pastures on which they feed their flocks. She longingly looks out here for her distant lover.

> Ver. 8 Hark, my beloved! lo, there he comes!
> Springs over the mountains,
> Bounds over the hills.

---

[1] The distinction between these words is well explained by Lewisohn in his *Investigationes Linguae* (Wilna, 1840), p. 21: "The מעיר את־הישן is satisfied that the sleeper wakes, and it is left to him fully to overcome the influence of sleep; the מעורר, however, arouses him at once from sleepiness, and awakes him to such a degree that he is secured against falling asleep again."

9 My beloved is like a gazelle,
  Or a young one of the harts.
  Lo, there he stands behind our wall!
  He looks through the windows,
  Glances through the lattices.

The word קוֹל, in the expression קוֹל דּוֹדִי, is to be understood of the call of the approaching lover (Böttch.), or only of the sound of his footsteps (Hitz.); it is an interjectional clause (sound of my beloved!), in which *kōl* becomes an interjection almost the same as our "*horch*" ["hear!"]. *Vid.* under Gen. iv. 10. זֶה after הִנֵּה sharpens it, as the demonst. *ce* in *ecce* = *en ce*. בָּא is thought of as partic., as is evident from the accenting of the fem. בָּאָה, *e.g.* Jer. x. 22. דִּלֵּג is the usual word for springing; the parallel קָפַץ (קִפֵּץ), Aram. קְפַץ, קַפֵּץ, signifies properly *contrahere* (cogn. קָמַץ, whence *Kametz*, the drawing together of the mouth, more accurately, of the muscles of the lips), particularly to draw the body together, to prepare it for a spring. In the same manner, at the present day, both in the city and in the Beduin Arab. *kamaz*, for which also *famaz*, is used of the springing of a gazelle, which consists in a tossing up of the legs stretched out perpendicularly. 'Antar says similarly, as Shulamith here of the swift-footed *schébûb* (*D. M. Zeitung*, xxii. 362): *wahu jeǵmiz ǵamazât el-ǵazâl*, it leaps away with the springing of a gazelle.

The figure used in ver. 8 is continued in ver. 9. צְבִי is the gazelle, which is thus designated after its Arab. name *ghazāl*, which has reached us probably through the Moorish-Spanish *gazela* (distinct from "ghasele," after the Pers. *ghazal*, love-poem). עֹפֶר is the young hart, like the Arab. *ghufar* (*ghafar*), the young chamois, probably from the covering of young hair; whence also the young lion may be called כְּפִיר. Regarding the effect of אוֹ passing from one figure to another, *vid.* under ii. 7*a*. The meaning would be plainer were ver. 9*a* joined to ver. 8, for the figures illustrate quick-footed speed (2 Sam. ii. 18; 1 Chron. xii. 8; cf. Ps. xviii. 34 with Hab. iii. 19 and Isa. xxxv. 6). In ver. 9*b* he comes with the speed of the gazelle, and his eyes seek for the unforgotten one. כֹּתֶל (from כָּתַל, *compingere, condensare*; whence, *e.g.*, Arab. *mukattal*, pressed together, rounded, *ramassé*; *vid.* regarding R. כת at Ps. lxxxvii. 6), Aram. כּוּתַל (Josh. ii. 15; Targ. word for קִיר), is meant of the wall of the house itself, not of the wall surrounding it. Shulamith is within, in the house: her beloved, standing behind the wall, stands without, before the house (Tympe: *ad latus aversum parietis*, viz. out from it), and looks through the windows,—at one time through this one, at another through that one,—that he might see her and feast his eyes on her. We have here two verbs from the fulness of Heb. synon. for one idea of seeing. הִשְׁגִּיחַ, from שָׁגַח, occurring only three times in the O. T., refers, in respect of the roots שג, שך, שע, to the idea of piercing or splitting (whence also שָׁגַע, to be furious, properly pierced, *percitum esse;* cf. *oestrus*, sting of a gadfly = madness, Arab. transferred to hardiness = madness), and means fixing by reflection and meditation; wherefore הַשְׁגָּחָה in post-bibl. Heb. is the name for Divine Providence. הֵצִיץ, elsewhere to twinkle and to bloom, appears only here in the sense of seeing, and that of the quick darting forward of the glance of the eye, as *blick* [glance] and *blitz* [lightning] (*blic*) are one word; "he saw," says Goethe in *Werther*, "the glance of the powder" (Weigand).[1] The plurs. *fenestrae* and *transennae* are to be understood also as *synechdoche totius pro parte*, which is the same as the plur. of categ.; but with equal correctness we conceive of him as changing his standing place. חַלּוֹן is the window, as an opening in the wall, from חָלַל, *perforare.* חֲרַכִּים we combine most certainly (*vid.* Prov. xii. 27) with (Arab.) *khark, fissura,* so that the idea presents itself of the window broken through the wall, or as itself broken through; for the window in the country there consists for the most part of a pierced wooden frame of a transparent nature,—not (as one would erroneously conclude, from the most significant name of a window שְׂבָכָה, now *schubbâke,* from שָׂבַךְ, to twist, to lattice, to close after the manner of our Venetian blinds) of rods or boards laid crosswise. הֵצִיץ accords with the looking out through the pierced places of such a window, for the glances of his eye are like the penetrating rays of light.

When now Shulamith continues:

> Ver. 10a My beloved answered and said to me,
> Arise, my love, my fair one, and go forth!

the words show that this first scene is not immediately dramatic, but only mediately; for Shulamith speaks in monologue, though in a dramatic manner narrating an event which occurred between the commencement of their love-relation and her home-bringing.[2] She does not relate it as a dream, and thus it is not one. Solomon

---

[1] In this sense: to look sharply toward, is הֵצִיץ (Talm.)—for Grätz alone a proof that the Song is of very recent date; but this word belongs, like סמדר, to the old Heb. still preserved in the Talm.

[2] Grätz misinterprets this in order by the supplement of similar ones to make the whole poem a chain of narrative which Shulamith declaims to the daughters of Jerusalem. Thereby it certainly ceases to be dramatic, but so much more tedious does it become by these interposed expressions, " I said," " he said," " the sons of my mother said."

again once more passes, perhaps on a hunting expedition into the
northern mountains after the winter with its rains, which made them
inaccessible, is over ; and after long waiting, Shulamith at length
again sees him, and he invites her to enjoy with him the. spring
season. עָנָה signifies, like ἀποκρίνεσθαι, not always to answer to
the words of another, but also to speak on the occasion of a person
appearing before one ; it is different from עָנָה, the same in sound,
which signifies to sing, properly to sing through the nose, and has
the root-meaning of replying (of the same root as עָנָן, clouds, as that
which meets us when we look up toward the heavens); but taking
speech in hand in consequence of an impression received is equivalent to an answer. With קוּמִי he calls upon her to raise herself from
her stupor, and with וּלְכִי־לָךְ, French va-t-en, to follow him.

> Ver. 11 For, lo ! the winter is past,
> The rain is over, is gone.
> 12 The flowers appear in the land;
> The time of song has come,
> And the voice of the turtle makes itself heard in our land.
> 13 The fig-tree spices her green figs,
> And the vines stand in bloom, they diffuse fragrance ;—
> Rise up, my love, my fair one, and go forth !

The winter is called סְתָו, perhaps from a verb סָתָה (of the same root
as סָתַר, סָתַם, without any example, since סוּת, Gen. xlix. 11, is certainly not derived from a verb סוּת), to conceal, to veil, as the time of
being overcast with clouds, for in the East winter is the rainy season ;
(Arab.) *shataā* is also used in the sense of rain itself (vid. *D. M.
Zeitsch.* xx. 618) ; and in the present day in Jerusalem, in the
language of the people, no other name is used for rain but *shataā*
(not *metar*). The word סְתָיו, which the *Keri* substitutes, only means
that one must not read סְתָו, but סְתָו with long *a ;* in the same way
עָנָיו, humble, from עָנָה, to be bowed down, and שְׂלָיו, a quail, from שָׁלָה,
to be fat, are formed and written. Rain is here, however, especially
mentioned : it is called *gĕshĕm*, from *gāshăm*, to be thick, massy (cf.
revīvīm, of density). With עָבַר, to pass by, there is interchanged
חָלַף, which, like (Arab.) *khalaf*, means properly to press on, and then
generally to move to another place, and thus to remove from the
place hitherto occupied. In הָלַךְ לוֹ, with the *dat. ethicus*, which
throws back the action on the subject, the winter rain is thought of
as a person who has passed by. נִצָּן, with the noun-ending *ăn*, is the
same as נִיסָן, and signifies the flower, as the latter the flower-month,
floréal ; in the use of the word, נִצָּן is related to נֵץ and נִצָּה, probably
as little flower is to flower. In *hăzzāmīr* the idea of the song of
birds (Arab. *gharad*) appears, and this is not to be given up. The

LXX., Aquila, Symm., Targ., Jerome, and the Venet. translate *tempus putationis:* the time of the pruning of vines, which indeed corresponds to the *usus loq.* (cf. זָמַר, to prune the vine, and מַזְמֵרָה, a pruning-knife), and to similar names, such as אָסִיף [ingathering of fruit], but supplies no reason for her being invited out into the open fields, and is on this account improbable, because the poet further on speaks for the first time of vines.   זָמַר (זִמֵּר) is an onomatopoeia, which for the most part denotes song and music; why should זָמִיר thus not be able to denote singing, like זִמְרָה,—but not, at least not in this passage, the singing of men (Hengst.), for they are not silent in winter; but the singing of birds, which is truly a sign of the spring, and as a characteristic feature, is added[1] to this lovely picture of spring? Thus there is also suitably added the mention of the turtle-dove, which is a bird of passage (*vid.* Jer. viii. 7), and therefore a messenger of spring.   נִשְׁמַע is 3d pret.: it makes itself heard.

The description of spring is finished by a reference to the fig-tree and the vine, the standing attributes of a prosperous and peaceful homestead, 1 Kings v. 5; 2 Kings xviii. 31.   פַּג (from פָּנַג, and thus named, not from their hardness, but their delicacy) are the little fruits of the fig-tree which now, when the harvest-rains are over, and the spring commences with the equinox of Nisan, already begin to assume a red colour; the verb חָנַט does not mean " to grow into a bulb," as Böttch. imagines; it has only the two meanings, *condire (condiri,* post-bibl. syn. of בָּשַׁל) and *rubescere.* From its colour, wheat has the name חִנְטָה = חִטָּה; and here also the idea of colour has the preference, for becoming fragrant does not occur in spring,—in the history of the cursing of the fig-tree at the time of the Passover, Mark (xi. 13) says, " for the time of figs was not yet."   In fig-trees, by this time the green of the fruit-formation changes its colour, and the vines are סְמָדַר, blossom, *i.e.* are in a state of bloom (LXX. κυπρίζουσαι; cf. vii. 13, κυπρισμός)—it is a clause such as Ex. ix. 31, and to which " they diffuse fragrance " (ver. 13) is parallel. This word סמדר is usually regarded as a compound word, consisting of סם, scent, and הָדָר, brightness = blossom (*vid.* Gesen. *Thes.*); it is undeniable that there are such compound formations, *e.g.* שַׁלְאֲנָן, from שָׁלָה and שָׁאַן; הַלְמִישׁ, from (Arab.) *ḥams,* to be hard, and *ḥals,* to be dark-brown.[2]   But the

---

[1] It is true that besides in this passage *zāmăr,* of the singing of birds, is not demonstrable, the Arab. *zamar* is only used of the shrill cry of the ostrich, and particularly the female ostrich.

[2] In like manner as (Arab.) *karbsh, corrugare,* is formed of *karb,* to string, and *karsh,* to wrinkle, combined; and another extension of *karsh* is *kurnash,* wrinkles, and *mukarnash,* wrinkled. " One day," said Wetstein to me, " I asked an

traditional reading סְמָדַר (not סְמָדָר) is unfavourable to this view; the middle *ā* accordingly, as in צְלָצַל, presents itself as an *ante*-tone vowel (Ewald, § 154*a*), and the stem-word appears as a quadril. which may be the expansion of סָדַר, to range, put in order in the sense of placing asunder, unfolding. Symm. renders the word by οἰνάνθη, and the Talm. idiom shows that not only the green five-leaved blossoms of the vine were so named, but also the fruit-buds and the first shoots of the grapes. Here, as the words "they diffuse fragrance" (as at vii. 14 of the mandrakes) show, the vine-blossom is meant which fills the vineyard with an incomparably delicate fragrance. At the close of the invitation to enjoy the spring, the call "Rise up," etc., with which it began, is repeated. The *Chethîb* לכי, if not an error in writing, justly set aside by the *Kerî*, is to be read לְכִי (cf. Syr. *bechi*, in thee, *l'votechi*, to thee, but with occult *i*)—a North Palestinism for לָךְ, like 2 Kings iv. 2, where the *Kerî* has substituted the usual form (*vid.* under Ps. ciii. introd.) for this very dialectic form, which is there undoubtedly original.

Ver. 14. Solomon further relates how he drew her to himself out of her retirement:

> My dove in the clefts of the rock,
> In the hiding-place of the cliff;
> Let me see thy countenance,
> Let me hear thy voice!
> For thy voice is sweet and thy countenance comely.

"Dove" (for which Castellio, *columbula*, like *vulticulum, voculam*) is a name of endearment which Shulamith shares with the church of God, Ps. lxxiv. 19; cf. lvi. 1; Hos. vii. 11. The wood-pigeon builds its nest in the clefts of the rocks and other steep rocky places, Jer. xlviii. 28.[1] That Shulamith is thus here named, shows that, far removed from intercourse with the world, her home was among the mountains. חֲגָוִי, from חֲגָו, or also חָגוּ, requires a verb חָגָה = (Arab.)

Arab the origin of the word *karnasa*, to wrinkle, and he replied that it was derived from a sheep's stomach that had lain over night, *i.e.* the stomach of a slaughtered sheep that had lain over night, by which its smooth surface shrinks together and becomes wrinkled. In fact, we say of a wrinkled countenance that it is *mathal alkarash albayt.*" With right Wetstein gathers from this curious fact how difficult it is to ascertain by purely etymological considerations the view which guided the Semites in this or that designation. *Samdor* is also a strange word; on the one side it is connected with *sadr*, of the veiling of the eyes, as the effect of terror; and on the other with *samd*, of stretching oneself straight out. E. Meier takes סמדר as the name of the vine-blossom, as changed from סמסר, bristling. Just as unlikely as that סָמַד is cogn. to חָמַד, *Jesurun*, p. 221.

[1] Wetstein's *Reisebericht*, p. 182: "If the Syrian wood-pigeon does not find a

khajja, findere. סֶלַע, as a Himyar. lexicographer defines it, is a cleft into the mountains after the nature of a defile; with צוּר, only the ideas of inaccessibility and remoteness are connected; with סֶלַע, those of a secure hiding-place, and, indeed, a convenient, pleasant residence. מַדְרֵגָה is the stairs; here the rocky stairs, as the two chalk-cliffs on the Rügen, which sink perpendicularly to the sea, are called "*Stubben-kammer*," a corruption of the Slavonic *Stupnykamen, i.e.* the Stair-Rock. "Let me see," said he, as he called upon her with enticing words, "thy countenance;" and adds this as a reason, "for thy countenance is lovely." The word מַרְאַיִךְ, thus pointed, is sing.; the *Jod otians* is the third root letter of רָאַי, retained only for the sake of the eye. It is incorrect to conclude from *ashrêch*, in Eccles. x. 17, that the *ech* may be also the plur. suff., which it can as little be as *êhu* in Prov. xxix. 18; in both cases the sing. *êshĕr* has substituted itself for *ashrê*. But, inversely, *mărāĭch* cannot be sing.; for the sing. is simply *marêch*. Also *mărāv*, Job xli. 1, is not sing.: the sing. is *marêhu*, Job iv. 16; Song v. 15. On the other hand, the determination of such forms as מַרְאֵיהֶם, מַרְאֵינוּ, is difficult: these forms may be sing. as well as plur. In the passage before us, מַרְאִים is just such a non-numer. plur. as פָּנִים. But while *panîm* is an extensive plur., as Böttcher calls it: the countenance, in its extension and the totality of its parts,—*marîm*, like *marôth*, vision, a stately term, Ex. xl. 2 (*vid.* Dietrich's *Abhand.* p. 19), is an amplificative plur.: the countenance, on the side of its fulness of beauty and its overpowering impression.

There now follows a *cantiuncula*. Shulamith comes forward, and, singing, salutes her beloved. Their love shall celebrate a new spring. Thus she wishes everything removed, or rendered harmless, that would disturb the peace of this love:

> Ver. 15 Catch us the foxes, the little foxes,
> The spoilers of the vineyards;
> For our vineyards are in bloom!
> 16 My beloved is mine, and I am his;
> Who feeds [his flock] among the lilies.

If the king is now, on this visit of the beloved, engaged in hunting, the call: "Catch us," etc., if it is directed at all to any definite persons, is addressed to those who follow him. But this is a vine-dresser's ditty, in accord with Shulamith's experience as the keeper

pigeon-tower, περιστερεῶνα, it builds its nest in the hollows of rocky precipices, or in the walls of deep and wide fountains." See also his *Nord-arabien*, p. 58: "A number of scarcely accessible mountains in Arabia are called *alkunnat*, a rock-nest."

of a vineyard, which, in a figure, aims at her love-relation. The
vineyards, beautiful with fragrant blossom, point to her covenant of
love; and the foxes, the little foxes, which might destroy these united
vineyards, point to all the great and little enemies and adverse circumstances which threaten to gnaw and destroy love in the blossom,
ere it has reached the ripeness of full enjoyment. שְׁעָלִים comprehends both foxes and jackals, which " destroy or injure the vineyards; because, by their holes and passages which they form in the
ground, loosening the soil, so that the growth and prosperity of the
vine suffers injury" (Hitzig). This word is from שָׁעַל (R. שֹׁל), to go
down, or into the depth. The little foxes are perhaps the jackals,
which are called *tănnīm*, from their extended form, and in height are
seldom more than fifteen inches. The word "jackal" has nothing to
do with שׁוּעָל, but is the Persian-Turkish *shaghal*, which comes from the
Sanscr. *crgâla*, the howler (R. *krag*, like *kap-âla*, the skull; R. *kap*, to
be arched). Moreover, the mention of the foxes naturally follows 14*a*,
for they are at home among rocky ravines. Hitzig supposes Shulamith to address the foxes: hold for us = wait, ye rascals! But אָחַז,
Aram. אֲחַד, does not signify to wait, but to seize or lay hold of
(synon. לָכַד, Judg. xv. 4), as the lion its prey, Isa. v. 29. And the
plur. of address is explained from its being made to the king's
retinue, or to all who could and would give help. Fox-hunting is
still, and has been from old times, a sport of rich landowners; and
that the smaller landowners also sought to free themselves from
them by means of snares or otherwise, is a matter of course,—they
are proverbially as destroyers, Neh. iii. 35 [iv. 3], and therefore
a figure of the false prophets, Ezek. xiii. 4. מְחַבְּ׳ כְּרָמ׳ are here
instead of מְחַבְּלֵי הַכְּרָמ׳. The articles are generally omitted, because
poetry is not fond of the article, where, as here (cf. on the other
hand, i. 6), the thoughts and language permit it; and the fivefold
im is an intentional mere *verborum sonus*. The clause וּכְר׳ סְמָדַר is an
explanatory one, as appears from the *Vav* and the subj. preceding, as
well as from the want of a *finitum*. סְמָדַר maintains here also, *in
pausa*, the sharpening of the final syllable, as חַצ׳, Deut. xxviii. 42.

The 16th verse is connected with the 15th. Shulamith, in the
pentast. song, celebrates her love-relation; for the praise of it extends
into ver. 15, is continued in ver. 16, and not till ver. 17 does she
address her beloved. Luther translates:

> My beloved is mine, and I am his;
> He feeds [his flock] among the roses.

He has here also changed the " lilies " of the Vulgate into " roses; "
for of the two queens among the flowers, he gave the preference to the

popular and common rose; besides, he rightly does not translate הָרֹעֶה, in the mid. after the *pascitur inter lilia* of the Vulgate: who feeds himself, *i.e.* pleases himself; for רעה has this meaning only when the object expressly follows, and it is evident that בַּשּׁ׳ cannot possibly be this object, after Gen. xxxvii. 2,—the object is thus to be supplied. And which? Without doubt, *gregem;* and if Heiligst., with the advocates of the shepherd-hypothesis, understands this feeding (of the flock) among the lilies, of feeding on a flowery meadow, nothing can be said against it. But at vi. 2 f., where this saying of Shulamith is repeated, she says that her beloved בַּנְּנִים feeds and gathers lilies. On this the literal interpretation of the *qui pascit (gregem) inter lilia* is wrecked; for a shepherd, such as the shepherd-hypothesis supposes, were he to feed his flock in a garden, would be nothing better than a thief; such shepherds, also, do not concern themselves with the plucking of flowers, but spend their time in knitting stockings. It is Solomon, the king, of whom Shulamith speaks. She represents him to herself as a shepherd; but in such a manner that, at the same time, she describes his actions in language which rises above ordinary shepherd-life, and, so to speak, idealizes. She, who was herself a shepherdess, knows from her own circle of thought nothing more lovely or more honourable to conceive and to say of him, than that he is a shepherd who feeds among lilies. The locality and the surroundings of his daily work correspond to his nature, which is altogether beauty and love. Lilies, the emblem of unapproachable highness, awe-inspiring purity, lofty elevation above what is common, bloom where the lily-like (king) wanders, whom the Lily names her own. The mystic interpretation and mode of speaking takes "lilies" as the figurative name of holy souls, and a lily-stalk as the symbol of the life of regeneration. Mary, who is celebrated in song as the *rosa mystica,* is rightly represented in ancient pictures with a lily in her hand on the occasion of the Annunciation; for if the people of God are called by Jewish poets "a people of lilies," she is, within this lily-community, this *communio sanctorum,* the lily without a parallel.

Shulamith now further relates, in a dramatic, lively manner, what she said to her beloved after she had saluted him in a song:

> Ver. 17 Till the day cools and the shadows flee away,
> Turn; make haste, my beloved,
> Like a gazelle or a young one of the hinds
> On the craggy mountains.

With the perf., עַד שֶׁ (cf. עַד אִם, Gen. xxiv. 33) signifies, till something is done; with the fut., till something will be done. Thus: till the

evening comes—and, therefore, before it comes—may he do what she
requires of him.   Most interpreters explain סב, *verte te*, with the
supplement *ad me;* according to which Jerome, Castell., and others
translate by *revertere*.   But Ps. lxxi. 21 does not warrant this rendering ; and if Shulamith has her beloved before her, then by סב she
can only point him away from herself; the parall. viii. 14 has בְּרַח
instead of סב, which consequently means, "turn thyself from here
away."   Rather we may suppose, as I explained in 1851, that she
holds him in her embrace, as she says, and, inseparable from him, will
wander with him upon the mountains.   But neither that *ad me* nor
this *mecum* should have been here (cf. on the contrary viii. 14) unexpressed.   We hold by what is written.   Solomon surprises Shulamith,
and invites her to enjoy with him the spring-time ; not alone, because he is on a hunting expedition, and—as denoted by "catch us"
(ver. 15)—with a retinue of followers.   She knows that the king has
not now time to wander at leisure with her ; and therefore she asks
him to set forward his work for the day, and to make haste on the
mountains till "the day cools and the shadows flee."   Then she will
expect him back ; then in the evening she will spend the time with
him as he promised her.   The verb פּוּחַ, with the guttural letter *Hheth*
and the labial *Pe*, signifies *spirare*, here of being able to be breathed,
i.e. cool, like the expression רוּחַ הַ׳, Gen. iii. 8 (where the guttural *Hheth*
is connected with *Rêsh*).   The shadows flee away, when they become
longer and longer, as if on a flight, when they stretch out (Ps. cix. 23,
cii. 12) and gradually disappear.   Till that takes place—or, as we say,
will be done—he shall hasten with the swiftness of a gazelle on the
mountains, and that on the mountains of separation, *i.e.* the riven
mountains, which thus present hindrances, but which he, the "swift as
the gazelle" (*vid.* ii. 9), easily overcomes.   Rightly, Bochart : *montes
scissionis, ita dicti propter,* ῥωχμούς *et* χάσματα.   Also, Luther's
"*Scheideberge*" are "mountains with peaks, from one of which to the
other one must spring."   We must not here think of *Bithron*
(2 Sam. ii. 29), for that is a mountain ravine on the east of Jordan ;
nor of Bar-Cochba's ביתר (Kirschbaum, Landau), because this mountain (whether it be sought for to the south of Jerusalem or to the
north of Antipatris) ought properly to be named ביתתר (*vid.* Aruch).
It is worthy of observation, that in an Assyrian list of the names of
animals, along with *ṣabi* (gazelle) and *apparu* (the young of the
gazelle or of the hind), the name *bitru* occurs, perhaps the name of
the *rupicapra*.   At the close of the song, the expression "mountain
of spices" occurs instead of "mountain of separation," as here.
There no more hindrances to be overcome lie in view, the rock-cliffs

have become fragrant flowers. The request here made by Shulamith breathes self - denying humility, patient modesty, inward joy in the joy of her beloved. She will not claim him for herself till he has accomplished his work. But when he associates with her in the evening, as with the Emmaus disciples, she will rejoice if he becomes her guide through the new-born world of spring. The whole scene permits, yea, moves us to think of this, that the Lord already even now visits the church which loves Him, and reveals Himself to her; but that not till the evening of the world is His *varousia* to be expected.

SECOND SCENE OF THE SECOND ACT, III. 1–5.

In the first scene, Shulamith relates what externally happened to her one day when the evening approached. In this second scene, she now relates what she inwardly experienced when the night came. She does not indeed say that she dreamed it; but that it is a dream is seen from this, that that which is related cannot be represented as an external reality. But it at once appears as an occurrence that took place during sleep.

> Chap. iii. 1 On my bed in the nights
> I sought him whom my soul loveth:
> I sought him, and found him not.

She does not mean to say that she sought him beside herself on her couch; for how could that be of the modest one, whose home-bringing is first described in the next act—she could and might miss him there neither waking nor sleeping. The commencement is like Job xxxiii. 15. She was at night on her couch, when a painful longing seized her: the beloved of her soul appeared to have forsaken her, to have withdrawn from her; she had lost the feeling of his nearness, and was not able to recover it. לֵילוֹת is neither here nor at iii. 8 necessarily the categ. plur. The meaning may also be, that this pain, arising from a sense of being forgotten, always returned upon her for several nights through : she became distrustful of his fidelity ; but the more she apprehended that she was no longer loved, the more ardent became her longing, and she arose to seek for him who had disappeared.

> Ver. 2 So I will arise, then, and go about the city,
> The markets, and the streets ;
> I will seek him whom my soul loveth !—
> I sought him, and found him not.

How could this night-search, with all the strength of love, be consistent with the modesty of a maiden? It is thus a dream which she relates. And if the beloved of her soul were a shepherd, would she seek him in the city, and not rather without, in the field or in some village? No; the beloved of her soul is Solomon; and in the dream, Jerusalem, his city, is transported close to the mountains of her native home. The resolution expressed by "I will arise, then," is not introduced by "then I said," or any similar phrase: the scene consists of a monologue which dramatically represents that which is experienced. Regarding the second *Chatef-Pathach* of 'וָאֵס, *vid.* Baer's *Genesis*, p. 7. שְׁוָקִים is the plur. of שׁוּק (= *shavk*), as שְׁוָרִים of שׁוּר (= *shavr*); the root-word שׁוּק (Arab. *shaḳ*) signifies to press on, to follow after continuously; (Arab.) *suwaḳ* designates perhaps, originally, the place to which one drives cattle for sale, as in the desert; (Arab.) *sawaḳ* designates the place to which one drives cattle for drink (Wetzst.). The form אֲבַקְשָׁה is without the *Daghesh*, as are all the forms of this verb except the imper.; the semi-guttural nature of the *Koph* has something opposing the simple *Sheva*.

Shulamith now relates what she further experienced when, impelled by love-sorrow, she wandered through the city:

Ver. 3 The watchmen who go about in the city found me:
"Have ye seen him whom my soul loveth?"

Here also (as in ver. 2) there is wanting before the question such a phrase as, "and I asked them, saying:" the monologue relates dramatically. If she described an outward experience, then the question would be a foolish one; for how could she suppose that the watchmen, who make their rounds in the city (Epstein, against Grätz, points for the antiquity of the order to Ps. cxxvii. 1; Isa. lxii. 6; cf. xxi. 11), could have any knowledge of her beloved! But if she relates a dream, it is to be remembered that feeling and imagination rise higher than reflection. It is in the very nature of a dream, also, that things thus quickly follow one another without fixed lineaments. This also, that having gone out by night, she found in the streets him whom she sought, is a happy combination of circumstances formed in the dreaming soul; an occurrence without probable external reality, although not without deep inner truth:

Ver. 4 Scarcely had I passed from them,
When I found him whom my soul loveth.
I seized him, and did not let him go
Until I brought him into the house of my mother,
And into the chamber of her that gave me birth.

כִּמְעַט = *paululum,* here standing for a sentence: it was as a little that I passed, etc. Without שֶׁ, it would be *paululum transii;* with it, *paululum fuit quod transii,* without any other distinction than that in the latter case the *paululum* is more emphatic. Since Shulamith relates something experienced earlier, אֲחַזְתִּי is not fitly rendered by *teneo,* but by *tenui;* and וְלֹא אַרְפֶּנּוּ, not by *et non dimittam eum,* but, as the neg. of וָאַרְפֵּנוּ, *et dimisi eum,*—not merely *et non dimittebam eum,* but *et non dimisi eum.* In Gen. xxxii. 27 [26], we read the cogn. שַׁלַּח, which signifies, to let go ("let me go"), as הִרְפָּה, to let loose, to let free. It is all the same whether we translate, with the subjective colouring, *donec introduxerim,* or, with the objective, *donec introduxi;* in either case the meaning is that she held him fast till she brought him, by gentle violence, into her mother's house. With בַּיִת there is the more definite parallel חֶדֶר, which properly signifies (*vid.* under i. 4), *recessus, penetrale;* with אִמִּי, the seldom occurring (only, besides, at Hos. ii. 7) הוֹרָה, *part. f. Kal* of הָרָה, to conceive, be pregnant, which poetically, with the accus., may mean *parturire* or *parere.* In Jacob's blessing, Gen. xlix. 26, as the text lies before us, his parents are called הוֹרַי; just as in Arab. *ummâni,* properly "my two mothers," may be used for "my parents;" in the Lat. also, *parentes* means father and mother zeugmatically taken together.

The closing words of the monologue are addressed to the daughters of Jerusalem.

> Ver. 5 I adjure you, O ye daughters of Jerusalem,
> By the gazelles or the hinds of the field,
> That ye awake not and disturb not love
> Till she pleases.

We are thus obliged apparently to think of the daughters of Jerusalem as being present during the relation of the dream. But since Shulamith in the following Act is for the first time represented as brought from her home to Jerusalem, it is more probable that she represented her experience to herself in secret, without any auditors, and feasting on the visions of the dream, which brought her beloved so near, that she had him by herself alone and exclusively, that she fell into such a love-ecstasy as ii. 7; and pointing to the distant Jerusalem, deprecates all disturbance of this ecstasy, which in itself is like a slumber pervaded by pleasant dreams. In two monologues dramatically constructed, the poet has presented to us a view of the thoughts and feelings by which the inner life of the maiden was moved in the near prospect of becoming a bride and being married. Whoever reads the Song in the sense in which it is incor-

porated with the canon, and that, too, in the historical sense fulfilled in
the N. T., will not be able to read the two scenes from Shulamith's
experience without finding therein a mirror of the intercourse of
the soul with God in Christ, and cherishing thoughts such, *e.g.*, as
are expressed in the ancient hymn:

> *Quando tandem venies, meus amor?*
> *Propera de Libano, dulcis amor!*
> *Clamat, amat sponsula: Veni, Jesu,*
> *Dulcis veni Jesu!*

THIRD ACT.

THE BRINGING OF THE BRIDE AND THE MARRIAGE.
CHAP. III. 6–V. I.

FIRST SCENE OF THE THIRD ACT, III. 6–11.

In this third Act the longing of the loving one after her beloved
is finally appeased. The first scene [1] represents her home-bringing
into the royal city. A gorgeous procession which marches towards
Jerusalem attracts the attention of the inhabitants of the city.

> Ver. 6 Who is this coming up from the wilderness
>   Like pillars of smoke,
>   Perfumed with myrrh and frankincense,
>   With all aromatics of the merchants?

It is possible that זאת and עָלָה may be connected; but זֶה עָנִי, Ps.
xxxiv. 7 (this poor man, properly, this, a poor man), is not analogous,
it ought to be זאת הָעלה. Thus *zoth* will either be closely connected
with מִי, and make the question sharper and more animated, as is
that in Gen. xii. 18, or it will be the subject which then, as in Isa.
lxiii. 1, Job xxxviii. 2, cf. below vii. 5b, Jonah iv. 17, Amos ix. 12,
is more closely written with indeterminate participles, according to
which it is rightly accented. But we do not translate with Heiligst.
quid est hoc quod adscendit, for *mî* asks after a person, *mâ* after a
thing, and only *per attract.* does *mî* stand for *mâ* in Gen. xxxiii. 8;
Judg. xiii. 17; Mic. i. 5; also not *quis est hoc* (Vaih.), for *zoth* after
mi has a personal sense, thus: *quis (quaenam) haec est.* That it is

---

[1] *Vid.* Schlottmann in the *Stud. u. Kritiken,* 1867, pp. 209–243. Rejecting the
dramatic arrangement of this section, he interprets it throughout as a song of the
chorus of the daughters of Jerusalem, which is already contradicted by 10b.

a woman that is being brought forward those who ask know, even if she is yet too far off to be seen by them, because they recognise in the festal gorgeous procession a marriage party. That the company comes up from the wilderness, it may be through the wilderness which separates Jerusalem from Jericho, is in accordance with the fact that a maiden from Galilee is being brought up, and that the procession has taken the way through the Jordan valley (Ghôr); but the scene has also a typical colouring; for the wilderness is, since the time of the Mosaic deliverance out of Egypt, an emblem of the transition from a state of bondage to freedom, from humiliation to glory (*vid.* under Isa. xl. 3; Hos. i. 16; Ps. lxviii. 5). The pomp is like that of a procession before which the censer of frankincense is swung. Columns of smoke from the burning incense mark the line of the procession before and after. תִּימְרוֹת (תִּימְ') here and at Job iii. (*vid.* Norzi) is formed, as it appears, from יָמַר, to strive upwards, a kindred form to אָמַר; cf. Isa. lxi. 6 with xvii. 6, Ps. xciv. 4; the verb תָּמַר, whence the date-palm receives the name תָּמָר, is a secondary formation, like תָּאַב to אָבָה. Certainly this form תִּימָרָה (cf. on the contrary, תּוֹלֵדָה) is not elsewhere to be supported; Schlottm. sees in it תִּמְרוֹת, from תִּמְרָה; but such an expansion of the word for *Dag. dirimens* is scarcely to be supposed. This naming of the pillars of smoke is poet., as Jonah iii. 3; cf. "a pillar of smoke," Judg. xx. 40. She who approaches comes from the wilderness, brought up to Jerusalem, placed on an elevation, "like pillars of smoke," *i.e.* not herself likened thereto, as Schlottm. supposes it must be interpreted (with the *tertium comp.* of the slender, precious, and lovely), but encompassed and perfumed by such. For her whom the procession brings this lavishing of spices is meant; it is she who is incensed or perfumed with myrrh and frankincense. Schlottm. maintains that מְקֻטֶּרֶת cannot mean anything else than "perfumed," and therefore he reads מִקְטֹרֶת (as Aq. ἀπὸ θυμιάματος, and Jerome). But the word *mekuttĕrĕth* does not certainly stand alone, but with the genit. foll.; and thus as "rent in their clothes," 2 Sam. xiii. 31, signifies not such as are themselves rent, but those whose clothes are rent (Ewald, § 288b, compare also de Sacy, II. § 321), so מקט' וגו' can also mean those for whom (for whose honour) this incense is expended, and who are thus fumigated with it. מֹר, myrrh, (Arab.) *murr* (*vid.* above under i. 13), stands also in Ex. xxx. 23 and Ps. xlv. 9 at the head of the perfumes; it came from Arabia, as did also frankincense *levōnā*, Arab. *lubán* (later referred to benzoin); both of the names are Semitic, and the circumstance that the *Tôra* required myrrh as a component part of the holy oil, Ex. xxx. 23, and frank-

incense as a component part of the holy incense, Ex. xxx. 34, points
to Arabia as the source whence they were obtained.   To these two
principal spices there is added מִכֹּל (cf. Gen. vi. 20, ix. 2) as an
et cetera. רוֹכֵל denotes the travelling spice merchants (traders in
aromatics), and traders generally.   אֲבָקָה, which is related to אָבָק as
powder to dust (cf. *abacus*, a reckoning-table, so named from the
sand by means of which arithmetical numbers were reckoned), is the
name designating single drugs (*i.e.* dry wares; cf. the Arab. *elixir*
= ξηρόν).

The description of the palanquin now following, one easily
attributes to another voice from the midst of the inhabitants of
Jerusalem.

> Ver. 7 Lo! Solomon's palanquin,
>   Threescore heroes are around it,
>   Of the heroes of Israel,
>   8 All of them armed with the sword, expert in war.
>   Each with his sword on his thigh,
>   Against fear in the nights.

Since אַפִּרְיוֹן, 9*a*, is not by itself a word clearly intelligible, so as to
lead us fully to determine what is here meant by מִטָּה as distinguished
from it, we must let the connection determine.   We have before us
a figure of that which is called in the post-bibl. Heb. הַכְנָסַת כַּלָּה (the
bringing-home of the bride).   The bridegroom either betook himself
to her parents' house and fetched his bride thence, which appears to
be the idea lying at the foundation of Ps. xlv., if, as we believe, the
ivory-palaces are those of the king of Israel's house; or she was
brought to him in festal procession, and he went forth to meet her,
1 Macc. ix. 39—the prevailing custom, on which the parable of the
ten virgins (Matt. xxv.) is founded.[1] Here the bride comes from a
great distance; and the difference in rank between the Galilean maid
and the king brings this result, that he does not himself go and fetch
her, but that she is brought to him.   She comes, not as in old times
Rebecca did, riding on a camel, but is carried in a *mittā*, which is
surrounded by an escort for protection and as a mark of honour.
Her way certainly led through the wilderness, where it was necessary,
by a safe convoy, to provide against the possibility (*min* in *mippahad*,
cf. Isa. iv. 6, xxv. 4) of being attacked by robbers; whereas it would
be more difficult to understand why the marriage-bed in the palace
of the king of peace (1 Chron. xxii. 9) should be surrounded by such

---

[1] Weigand explains the German word *Braut* (bride) after the Sanscr. *praudha*,
"she who is brought in a carriage;" but this particip. signifies nothing more
than (*aetate*) *provecta*.

an armed band for protection. That Solomon took care to have his chosen one brought to him with royal honours, is seen in the lavish expenditure of spices, the smoke and fragrance of which signalized from afar the approach of the procession,—the *mittā*, which is now described, can be no other than that in which, sitting or reclining, or half sitting, half reclining, she is placed, who is brought to him in such a cloud of incense. Thus *mittā* (from *nāthā*, to stretch one-self out), which elsewhere is also used of a bier, 2 Sam. iii. 21 (like the Talm. עֶרֶס = עָרֶשׂ), will here signify a portable bed, a sitting cushion hung round with curtains after the manner of the Indian palanquin, and such as is found on the Turkish caiques or the Venetian gondolas. The appositional nearer definition שֶׁלִּשְׁ, "which belonged to Solomon" (*vid.* under i. 6*b*), shows that it was a royal palanquin, not one belonging to one of the nobles of the people. The bearers are unnamed persons, regarding whom nothing is said; the sixty heroes form only the guard for safety and for honour (*sauvegarde*), or the *escorte* or *convoie*. The sixty are the tenth part (the *élite*) of the royal body-guard, 1 Sam. xxvii. 2, xxx. 9, etc. (Schlottm.). If it be asked, Why just 60 ? we may perhaps not unsuitably reply: The number 60 is here, as at vi. 8, the number of Israel multiplied by 5, the fraction of 10 ; so that thus 60 distin-guished warriors form the half of the escort of a king of Israel. אֲחֻזֵי חֶרֶב properly means, held fast by the sword so that it does not let them free, which, according to the sense = holding fast [= practised in the use of the sword] ; the Syr. translation of the Apoc. renders παντοκράτωρ by "he who is held by all," *i.e.* holding it (cf. Ewald, § 149*d*).[1]

Another voice now describes the splendour of the bed of state which Solomon prepared in honour of Shulamith :

> Ver. 9 A bed of state hath King Solomon made for himself
> Of the wood of Lebanon.
> 10 Its pillars hath he made of silver,
> Its support of gold, its cushion of purple ;
> Its interior is adorned from love
> By the daughters of Jerusalem.

The sound of the word, the connection and the description, led the Greek translators (the LXX., Venet., and perhaps also others) to render אַפִּרְיוֹן by φορεῖον, litter, palanquin (Vulg. *ferculum*). The *appiryon* here described has a silver pedestal and a purple cushion —as we read in Athenaeus v. 13 (II. p. 317, ed. Schweigh.) that the

---

[1] This deponent use of the *part. pass.* is common in the Mishna ; *vid.* Geiger's *Lehrbuch zur Sprache der Mishna*, § 16. 5.

philosopher and tyrant Athenion showed himself "on a silver-legged
φορεῖον, with purple coverlet;" and the same author, v. 5 (II. p. 253),
also says, that on the occasion of a festal procession by Antiochus
Epiphanes, behind 200 women who sprinkled ointments from golden
urns came 80 women, sitting in pomp on golden-legged, and 500 on
silver-legged, φορεῖα—this is the proper name for the costly women's-
litter (Suidas: φορεῖον γυναικεῖον), which, according to the number
of bearers (Mart. VI. 77: six Cappadocians and, ix. 2, eight Syrians),
was called ἐξάφορον (hexaphorum, Mart. II. 81) or ὀκτώφορον (octo-
phorum, Cicero's Verr. v. 10). The Mishna, Sota ix. 14, uses
appiryon in the sense of phoreion: "in the last war (that of
Hadrian) it was decreed that a bride should not pass through the
town in an appiryon [on account of the danger], but our Rabbis
sanctioned it later [for modesty's sake];" as here, "to be carried in
an appiryon," so in Greek, προιέναι (καταστείχειν) ἐν φορείῳ. In
the Midrash also, Bamidbar rabba c. 12, and elsewhere, appiryon of
this passage before us is taken in all sorts of allegorical significations, in most of which the identity of the word with φορεῖον is
supposed, which is also there written פּוּרְיוֹן (after Aruch), cf. Isa.
xlix. 22, Targ., and is once interchanged with פָּאפְלִיּן, papilio (pavillon),
pleasure-tent. But a Greek word in the Song is in itself so improbable, that Ewald describes this derivation of the word as a frivolous
jest; so much the more improbable, as φορεῖον as the name of a
litter (lectica) occurs first in such authors (of the κοινή) as Plutarch,
Polybius, Herodian, and the like, and therefore, with greater right,
it may be supposed that it is originally a Semitic word, which the
Greek language adopted at the time when the Oriental and Graeco-
Roman customs began to be amalgamated. Hence, if mittā, 7a,
means a portable bed,—as is evident from this, that it appears as
the means of transport with an escort,—then appiryon cannot also
mean a litter; the description, moreover, does not accord with a
litter. We do, not read of rings and carrying-poles, but, on the
contrary, of pillars (as those of a tent-bed) instead, and, as might be
expected, of feet. Schlottm., however, takes mittā and appiryon as
different names for a portable bed; but the words, " an appiryon
has King Solomon made," etc., certainly indicate that he who thus
speaks has not the appiryon before him, and also that this was
something different from the mittā. While Schlottm. is inclined to
take appiryon, in the sense of a litter, as a word borrowed from the
Greek (but in the time of the first king?), Gesen. in his Thes. seeks
to derive it, thus understood, from פָּרָה, cito ferri, currere; but this
signification of the verb is imaginary. We expect here, in accord-

ance with the progress of the scene, the name of the bridal couch; and on the supposition that *appiryon*, *Sota* 12*a*, as in the Mishna, means the litter (Aruch) of the bride, Arab. *maziffat*, and not *torus nuptialis* (Buxt.), then there is a possibility that *appiryon* is a more dignified word for *'ĕrĕs*, i. 17, yet sufficient thereby to show that פּוּרְיָא is the usual Talm. name of the marriage-bed (*e.g. Mezia* 23*b*, where it stands, *per meton.*, for *concubitus*), which is wittily explained by שְׁפָרִין וּרבִין עֲלֵיה (*Kethuboth* 10*b*, and elsewhere). The Targ. has for it the form פּוּרְיָן (*vid.* Levy). It thus designates a bed with a canopy (a tent-bed), Deut. xxxii. 50, *Jerus;* so that the ideas of the bed of state and the palanquin (cf. כִּילָה, canopy, and כִּילַת חתנים, bridal-bed, *Succa* 11*a*) touch one another. In general, פּוּרִין (פּוּרִיָא), as is also the case with *appiryon*, must have been originally a common designation of certain household furniture with a common characteristic; for the Syr. *parautha*, plur. *parjevatha* (Wiseman's *Horae*, p. 255), or also *parha* (Castell.), signifies a cradle. It is then to be inquired, whether this word is referable to a root-word which gives a common characteristic with manifold applications. But the Heb. פָּרָה, from the R. פָּר, signifies to split,[1] to tear asunder, to break forth, to bring fruit, to be fruitful, and nothing further. *Pārā* has nowhere the signification to run, as already remarked; only in the Palest.-Aram. פְּרָא is found in this meaning (*vid.* Buxt.). The Arab. *farr* does not signify to run, but to flee; properly (like our "*ausreissen*" = to tear out, to break out), to break open by flight the rank in which one stands (as otherwise turned by horse-dealers: to open wide the horse's mouth). But, moreover, we do not thus reach the common characteristic which we are in search of; for if we may say of the litter that it runs, yet we cannot say that of a bed or a cradle, etc. The Arab. *farfâr*, *species vehiculi muliebris*, also does not help us; for the verb *farfar*, to vacillate, to shake, is its appropriate root-word.[2] With better results shall we compare the Arab. *fary*, which, in *Kal* and *Hiph.*, signifies to break open, to cut out (*couper, tailler une étoffe*), and also, figuratively, to bring forth something strange, something not yet existing (*yafry alfaryya*, according to the Arab. *Lex.* = *yaty bal'ajab fy 'amalh*, he accomplishes something wonderful); the primary

---

[1] *Vid.* Friedr. Delitzsch's *Indogerman.-semit. Studien*, p. 72.

[2] The Turkish *Kâmûs* says of *farfâr:* "it is the name of a vehicle (*merkeb*), like the camel-litter (*haudej*), destined merely for women." This also derives its name from rocking to and fro. So *farfâr*, for *farfara* is to the present day the usual word for *agiter*, *sécouer les ailes; farfarah*, for *légèreté; furfûr*, for butterfly (cf. Ital. *farfalla*); generally, the ideas of that which is light and of no value—*e.g.* a babbler—connect themselves with the root *far* in several derivatives.

meaning in Conj. viii. is evidently: *yftarra kidban*, to cut out lies,
to meditate and to express that which is calumnious (a similar
metaphor to *khar'a, findere*, viii. *fingere*, to cut out something in the
imagination; French, *inventer, imaginer*). With this *fary*, however,
we do not immediately reach אַפִּרְיָא, פִּרְיוֹן; for *fary*, as well as *fara*
(*farw*), are used only of cutting to pieces, cutting out, sewing
together of leather and other materials (cf. Arab. *farwat*, fur; *farrā*,
furrier), but not of cutting and preparing wood. But why should
not the Semitic language have used פָּרָה, פְּרָא, also, in the sense of
the verb בְּרָא, which signifies[1] to cut and hew, in the sense of forming
(cf. *Pih.* בֵּרֵא, *sculpere*, Ezek. xxi. 24), as in the Arab. *bara* and *bary*,
according to Lane, mean, "be formed or fashioned by cutting (a
writing-reed, stick, bow), shaped out, or pared,"—in other words:
Why should פרה, used in the Arab. of the cutting of leather, not be
used, in the Heb. and Aram., of the preparing of wood, and thus of
the fashioning of a bed or carriage? As חֶשְׁבּוֹן signifies a machine,
and that the work of an engineer, so פִּרְיוֹן signifies timber-work,
carpenter-work, and, lengthened especially by *Aleph prosthet.*, a product of the carpenter's art, a bed of state. The *Aleph prosth.* would
indeed favour the supposition that *appiryon* is a foreign word; for
the Semitic language frequently forms words after this manner,—
e.g. אַמְגּוּשָׁא, a magician; אַסְתֵּרָא, a stater.[2] But apart from such words
as אַגַּרְטֵל, oddly sounding in accord with κάρταλλος as *appiryon*
with φορεῖον, אַבְטִיחַ and אֲבַעְבֻּעָה are examples of genuine Heb. words
with such a prosthesis, *i.e.* an *Aleph* added at the beginning of the
word; not a formative *Aleph*, as in אַכְזָב and the like. אַפֶּדֶן, palace,
Dan. xi. 45, is, for its closer amalgamation by means of *Dag.*, at
least an analogous example; for thus it stands related to the Syr.
opadna, as, *e.g.* (Syr.), *oparsons*, net, Ewald, § 163*c*, to the Jewish-
Aram. אַפְּרַסְנָא or אַפַּדְסְנָא; cf. also אַפְּתֹם, "finally," in relation to the
Pehlv. אַפְדּוּם (Spiegel's *Literatur der Parsen*, p. 356).[3] We think
we have thus proved that אַפִּרְיוֹן is a Heb. word, which, coming from
the verb פָּרָה, to cut right, to make, frame, signifies[4] a bed, and that,
as Ewald also renders, a bed of state.

[1] *Vid.* Friedr. Delitzsch's *Indogerm.-sem. Stud.* p. 50. We are now taught by
the Assyr. that as בֶּן goes back to בנה, so בר (Assyr. *nibru*) to ברה = בְּרָא, to
bring forth.

[2] *Vid.* Merx's *Gramm. Syr.* p. 115.

[3] אַפּוּרְיָא, quoted by Gesen. in his *Thes.*, *Sanhedrin* 109*b*, is not applicable
here; it is contracted from אַדְּ־פּוּרְיָא (on the bed).

[4] This derivation explains how it comes that *appiryon* can mean, in the Karaite
Heb., a bird-cage or aviary, *vid.* Gottlober's בקרת ס', p. 208. We have left out
of view the phrase אפריון נמטיי ליה, which, in common use, means: we present

רְפִידָה (from רָפַד, R. רפ, to lift from beneath, *sublevare*, then *sternere*) is the head of the bed; LXX. ἀνάκλιτον; Jerome, *reclinatorium*, which, according to Isidore, is the Lat. vulgar name for the *fulchra*, the reclining (of the head and foot) of the bedstead. Schlottmann here involuntarily bears testimony that *appiryon* may at least be understood of a bed of state as well as of a litter of state; for he remarks: "The four sides of the bed were generally adorned with carved work, ivory, metal, or also, as in the case of most of the Oriental divans, with drapery." "*Nec mihi tunc*," says Propertius, ii. 10, 11, "*fulcro lectus sternatur eburno*." Here the *fulcrum* is not of ivory, but of gold.

מֶרְכָּב (from רָכַב, to lie upon anything; Arab. II. *componere;* Aethiop. *adipisci*) is that which one takes possession of, sitting or lying upon it, the cushion, *e.g.* of a saddle (Lev. xv. 9); here, the divan (*vid.* Lane, *Mod. Egypt*, I. 10) arranged on an elevated frame, serving both as a seat and as a couch. Red purple is called אַרְגָּמָן, probably from רָגַם = רָקַם, as material of variegated colour. By the interior תּוֹךְ of the bed, is probably meant a covering which lay above this cushion. רָצַף, to arrange together, to combine (whence רִצְפָּה, pavement; Arab. *rusafat*, a paved way), is here meant like στορέννυμι, στόρνυμι, στρώννυμι, whence στρῶμα. And רָצוּף אַהֲ' is not equivalent to רָצוּף אַהֲ' (after the construction 1 Kings xxii. 10; Ezek. ix. 2), inlaid with love, but is the adv. accus. of the manner; "love" (cf. *hhesed*, Ps. cxli. 5) denotes the motive: laid out or made up as a bed from love on the part of the daughters of Jerusalem, *i.e.* the ladies of the palace—these from love to the king have procured a costly tapestry or tapestries, which they have spread over the purple cushion. Thus rightly Vaihinger in his *Comm.*, and Merx, *Archiv.* Bd. II. 111–114. Schlottmann finds this interpretation of מִן "stiff and hard;" but although מִן in the pass. is not used like the Greek ὑπό, yet it can be used like ἀπό (Ewald, sec. 295b); and if there be no actual example of this, yet we point to Ps. xlv. in illustration of the custom of presenting gifts to a newly - married pair. He himself understands אהבה personally, as do also Ewald, Heiligst., Böttcher; "the voice of the people," says Ewald, "knows that the finest ornament with which the in-

to him homage (of approbation or thanks). It occurs first, as uttered by the Sassanidean king, Shabur I., *Mezia* 119a, *extr.;* and already Rapoport, in his *Erech Millin*, 1852, p. 183, has recognised this word *appiryon* as Pers. It is the Old Pers. *âfrîna* or *âfrivana* (from *frî*, to love), which signifies blessing or benediction (*vid.* Justi's *Handb. d. Zendsprache*, p. 51). Rashi is right in glossing it by חן שלנו (the testimony of our favour).

visible interior of the couch is adorned, is a love from among the
daughters of Jerusalem,—*i.e.* some one of the court ladies who
was raised, from the king's peculiar love to her, to the rank of a
queen-consort.   The speaker thus ingeniously names this newest
favourite ' a love,' and at the same time designates her as the only
thing with which this elegant structure, all adorned on the outside
is adorned within."   Relatively better Böttcher: with a love
(beloved one), *prae filiis Hierus.*   But even though אהבה, like *amor*
and *amores*, might be used of the beloved one herself, yet רצוף does
not harmonize with this, seeing we cannot speak of being paved or
tapestried with persons.   Schlottm. in vain refers for the personal
signification of אהבה to ii. 7, where it means love and nothing else,
and seeks to bring it into accord with רצוף ; for he remarks, " as the
stone in mosaic work fills the place destined for it, so the bride the
interior of the litter, which is intended for just one person filling
it."   But is this not more comical, without intending to be so, than
Juvenal's (i. 1. 32 s.) :

> *Causidici nova cum veniat lectica Mathonis*
> *Plena ipso* . . . .

But Schlottm. agrees with us in this, that the marriage which is
here being prepared for was the consummation of the happiness of
Solomon and Shulamith, not of another woman, and not the consummation of Solomon's assault on the fidelity of Shulamith, who
hates him to whom she now must belong, loving only one, the shepherd
for whom she is said to sigh (i. 4*a*), that he would come and take her
away.   " This triumphal procession," says Rocke,[1] " was for her a
mourning procession, the royal litter a bier ; her heart died within
her with longing for her beloved shepherd."   Touching, if it were
only true !   Nowhere do we see her up to this point resisting ; much
rather she is happy in her love.   The shepherd-hypothesis cannot comprehend this marriage procession without introducing incongruous
and imaginary things ; it is a poem of the time of Gellert.   Solomon
the seducer, and Shulamith the heroine of virtue, are figures as from
Gellert's Swedish Countess ; they are moral commonplaces personified, but not real human beings.   In the litter sits Shulamith,
and the *appiryon* waits for her.   Solomon rejoices that now the
reciprocal love-bond is to find its conclusion ; and what Shulamith,
who is brought from a lowly to so lofty a station, experiences, we
shall hear her describe in the sequel.

---

[1] *Das Hohelied, Erstlingsdrama, u.s.w.* [The Song, a Primitive Drama from the
East ; or, Family Sins and Love's Devotion.   A Moral Mirror for the Betrothed
and Married], 1851.

At the close of the scene, the call now goes forth to the daughters of Zion, *i.e.* the women of Jerusalem collectively, to behold the king, who now shows himself to the object of his love and to the jubilant crowd, as the festal procession approaches.

> Ver. 11 Come out, ye daughters of Zion, and see
> King Solomon with the crown
> With which his mother crowned him
> On the day of his espousal,
> And on the day of the gladness of his heart.

The women of the court, as distinguished from the Galilean maiden, are called "daughters of Jerusalem;" here, generally, the women of Zion or Jerusalem (Lam. v. 11) are called "daughters of Zion." Instead of צֶאֶנָה (since the verb *Lamed Aleph* is treated after the manner of verbs *Lamed He*, cf. Jer. l. 20 ; Ezek. xxiii. 49), צְאֶינָה, and that defect. צֶאֶנָה,[1] is used for the sake of assonance with וּרְאֶינָה ;[2] elsewhere also, as we have shown at Isa. xxii. 13, an unusual form is used for the sake of the sound. It is seen from the *Sota* (ix. 14) that the old custom for the bridegroom to wear a "crown" was abolished in consequence of the awful war with Vespasian. Rightly Epstein, against Grätz, shows from Job xxxi. 36, Isa. xxviii. 1, Ps. ciii. 4, that men also crowned themselves. בַּעֲטָרָה (with the crown) is, according to the best authorities, without the art., and does not require it, since it is determined by the relat. clause following. חֲתֻנָּה is the marriage (the word also used in the post.-bibl. Heb., and interchanging with חֻפָּה, properly νυμφών, Matt. ix. 15), from the verb חָתַן, which, proceeding from the root-idea of cutting into (Arab. *khatn*, to circumcise ; R. חת, whence חָתַם, חָתַךְ, חָתַר), denotes the pressing into, or going into, another family ; חָתָן is he who enters into such a relation of affinity, and חֹתֵן the father of her who is taken away, who also on his part is related to the husband.[3] Here also the seduction fable is shattered. The marriage with Shulamith takes place with the joyful consent of the queen-mother. In order to set aside this fatal circumstance, the "crown"

---

[1] Without the *Jod* after *Aleph* in the older ed. Thus also in J and H with the note לית וחסר [= *nonnisi h. l. et defective*] agreeing with the MS. Masora Parna. Thus also Kimchi, *Michlol* 108*b*.

[2] The *Resh* has in H *Chatef-Pathach*, with *Metheg* preceding. This, according to Ben-Asher's rule, is correct (cf. Ps. xxviii. 9. וּרְ). In the punctuation of the *Aleph* with Tsere or Segol the Codd. vary, according to the different views of the punctuation. J has Segol; D H, Tsere, which latter also Kimchi, *Michlol* 109*a*.

[3] L. Geiger (*Ursprung der Sprache*, 1869, p. 88) erroneously finds in R. חת (חתם, etc.) the meaning of binding. The (Arab.) noun *Khatan* means first a

is referred back to the time when Solomon was married to Pharaoh's daughter. *Cogitandus est Salomo*, says Heiligst., *qui cum Sulamitha pompa sollemni Hierosolyma redit, eadem corona nuptiali ornatus, qua quum filiam regis Aegyptiorum uxorem duxeret ornatus erat.* But was he then so poor or niggardly as to require to bring forth this old crown? and so basely regardless of his legitimate wife, of equal rank with himself, as to wound her by placing this crown on his head in honour of a rival? No; at the time when this youthful love-history occurred, Pharaoh's daughter was not yet married. The mention of his mother points us to the commencement of his reign. His head is not adorned with a crown which had already been worn, but with a fresh garland which his mother wreathed around the head of her youthful son. The men have already welcomed the procession from afar; but the king in his wedding attire has special attractions for the women—they are here called upon to observe the moment when the happy pair welcome one another.

SECOND SCENE OF THE THIRD ACT, IV. 1–V. 1.

This scene contains a conversation between Solomon and his beloved, whom he at first calls friend, and then, drawing always nearer to her, bride. The place of the conversation is, as v. 1 shows, the marriage hall. That the guests there assembled hear what Solomon says to Shulamith, one need not suppose; but the poet has overheard it from the loving pair. Fairer than ever does Shulamith appear to the king. He praises her beauty, beginning with her eyes.

> Chap. iv. 1*a* Lo, thou art fair, my friend! yes, thou art fair!
> Thine eyes are doves behind thy veil.

The Gr. Venet. translates, after Kimchi, "looking out from behind, thy hair flowing down from thy head like a mane." Thus also Schultens, *capillus plexus;* and Hengst., who compares πλέγμα, 1 Tim. ii. 9, and ἐμπλοκὴ τριχῶν, 1 Pet. iii. 3, passages which do not accord with the case of Shulamith; but neither צָמָם, ـمـ, nor ـلـ signifies to plait; the latter is used of the hair when it is too abundant, and ready for the shears. To understand the hair as

---

married man, and then any relation on the side of the wife (Lane); the fundamental idea must be the same as that of *Khatn, circumcidere* (cf. Ex. iv. 25), viz that of penetrating, which חָתַת, *percellere*, and נָחַת, *descendere* (cf. *e.g. ferrum descendit haud alte in corpus*, in Livy, and Prov. xvii. 1), also exhibit.

denoted here, is, moreover, inadmissible, inasmuch as מבעד cannot be used of the eyes in relation to the braids of hair hanging before them. Symm. rightly translates צמה by κάλυμμα [veil] (in the Song the LXX. erroneously renders by σιωπήσεως [behind thy silence]), Isa. xlvii. 2. The verb צָמַם, (Arab.) *ṣamm*, to make firm, solid, massive, impenetrable; whence *e.g.* (Arab.) *ṣimam*, a stopper, and (Arab.) *alṣamma*, a plaid in which one veils himself, when he wraps it around him.[1] The veil is so called, as that which closely hides the face. In the Aram. צְמַם, *Palp.* צִמְצֵם, means directly to veil, as *e.g. Bereshith rabba* c. 45, *extr.*, of a matron whom the king lets pass before him it is said, צימצמה פניה. Shulamith is thus veiled. As the Roman bride wore the *velum flammeum*, so also the Jewish bride was deeply veiled; cf. Gen. xxiv. 65, where Rebecca veiled herself (Lat. *nubit*) before her betrothed. בַּעַד, constr. בְּעַד, a segolate noun, which denotes separation, is a prep. in the sense of *pone*, as in Arab. in that of *post*. Ewald, sec. 217*m*, supposes, contrary to the Arab., the fundamental idea of covering (cogn. בגד); but that which surrounds is thought of as separating, and at the same time as covering, the thing which it encompasses. From behind her veil, which covered her face (*vid.* Bachmann, under Judg. iii. 23), her eyes gleam out, which, without needing to be supplemented by עֵינֵי, are compared, as to their colour, motion, and lustre, to a pair of doves.

From the eyes the praise passes to the hair.

Ver. 1*b* Thy hair is like a flock of goats
Which repose downwards on Mount Gilead.

The hair of the bride's head was uncovered. We know from later times that she wore in it a wreath of myrtles and roses, or also a 'golden city " (עיר של זהב), *i.e.* an ornament which emblematically represented Jerusalem. To see that this comparison is not incongruous, we must know that sheep in Syria and Palestine are for the most part white; but goats, for the most part, black, or at least dark coloured, as *e.g.* the brown *gedi Mamri*.[2] The verb גָּלַשׁ is the Arab. جلس, which signifies, to rest upon; and is distinguished from

---

[1] Regarding this verbal stem and its derivatives, see Ethé's *Schlafgemach der Phantasie*, pp. 102–105.

[2] Burns, the Scottish poet, thinking that goats are white, transfers the comparison from the hair to the teeth:

> " Her teeth are like a flock of sheep,
> With fleeces newly washen clean,
> That slowly mount the rising steep;
> And she's twa glancin', sparklin' een."

the synon. تعد in this, that the former is used of him who has previously lain down; the latter, of one who first stands and then sits down.[1] The *nejd* bears also the name *jals*, as the high land raising itself, and like a dome sitting above the rest of the land. One has to think of the goats as having lain down, and thus with the upper parts of their bodies as raised up. מִן in מֵהַר is used almost as in מַר מִדְּלִי, Isa. xl. 15. A flock of goats encamped on a mountain (rising up, to one looking from a distance, as in a steep slope, and almost perpendicularly), and as if hanging down lengthwise on its sides, presents a lovely view adorning the landscape. Solomon likens to this the appearance of the locks of his beloved, which hang down over her shoulders. She was till now a shepherdess, therefore a second rural image follows:

> Ver. 2 Thy teeth are like a flock of shorn sheep
> Which come up from the washing
> All bearing twins,
> And a bereaved one is not among them.

The verb קָצַב is, as the Arab. shows, in the sense of *tondere oves*, the synon. of גָּזַז. With shorn (not to be shorn) sheep, the teeth in regard to their smoothness, and with washed sheep in regard to their whiteness, are compared—as a rule the sheep of Palestine are white; in respect of their full number, in which in pairs they correspond to one another, the one above to the one below, like twin births in which there is no break. The parallel passage, vi. 6, omits the point of comparison of the smoothness. That some days after the shearing the sheep were bathed, is evident from Columella vii. 4. Regarding the incorrect exchange of mas. with fem. forms, *vid.* under ii. 7. The part. *Hiph.* מַתְאִימוֹת (cf. διδυματόκος, Theocr. i. 25) refers to the mothers, none of which has lost a twin of the pair she had borne. In "which come up from the washing," there is perhaps thought of, at the same time with the whiteness, the *saliva dentium*. The moisture of the saliva, which heightens the glance of the teeth, is frequently mentioned in the love-songs of Mutenebbi, Hariri, and Deschami. And that the saliva of a clean and sound man is not offensive, is seen from this, that the Lord healed a blind man by means of His spittle.

The mouth is next praised:

> Ver. 3a Like a thread of crimson thy lips,
> And thy mouth is lovely.

---

[1] *K'ad* cannot be used of one who sits on the bed *farash*; in *jalas* lies the direction from beneath to above; in *k'ad* (properly, to heap together, to cower down), from above to beneath.

As distinguished from red-purple, אַרְגָּמָן ,שָׁנִי (properly, shining, glistening; for this form has an active signification, like נָקִי, as well as a passive, like עָנִי)—fully, תּוֹלַעַת שָׁנִי—signifies the *kermes* or worm-colour; the *karmese*, the red juice of the cochineal. מִדְבָּרֵךְ (מִדְבְּרֵיךְ) is translated by the LXX. "thy speech;" Jerome, *eloquium;* and the Venet. "thy dialogue;" but that would be expressed, though by a ἅπ. λεγ., by דִּבּוּרֵךְ. מִדְבָּר is here the name of the mouth, the naming of which one expects; the preform. is the *mem instrumenti:* the mouth, as the instrument of speech, as the organ by which the soul expresses itself in word and in manner of speech. The poet needed for פִּין a fuller, more select word; just as in Syria the nose is not called *anf*, but *minchâr* (from *nachara*, to blow, to breathe hard).

Praise of her temples.

Ver. 3*b* Like a piece of pomegranate thy temples
Behind thy veil.

רַקָּה is the thin piece of the skull on both sides of the eyes; Lat., mostly in the plur., *tempora;* German, *schläfe*, from *schlaff*, loose, slack, *i.e.* weak = רַק. The figure points to that soft mixing of colours which makes the colouring of the so-called carnation one of the most difficult accomplishments in the art of painting. The half of a cut pomegranate (Jer. *fragmen mali punici*) is not meant after its outer side, as Zöckler supposes, for he gives to the noun *râkkâ*, contrary to Judg. iv. 21, v. 26, the meaning of cheek, a meaning which it has not, but after its inner side, which presents[1] a red mixed and tempered with the ruby colour,—a figure so much the more appropriate, since the ground-colour of Shulamith's countenance is a subdued white.[2] Up to this point the figures are borrowed from the circle of vision of a shepherdess. Now the king derives them from the sphere of his own experience as the ruler of a kingdom. She who has eyes like doves is in form like a born queen.

Ver. 4 Like the tower of David thy neck,
Built in terraces;
Thereon a thousand shields hang,
All the armour of heroes.

---

[1] The interior of a pomegranate is divided by tough, leather-like white or yellow skins, and the divisions are filled with little berries, in form and size like those of the grape, in the juicy inside of which little, properly, seed-corns, are found. The berries are dark red, or also pale red. The above comparison points to the mixing of these two colours.

[2] The Moslem erotic poets compare the division of the lips to the dividing cleft into a pomegranate.

The tower of David is, as it appears, "the tower of the flock,"
Mic. iv. 4, from which David surveyed the flock of his people.
In Neh. iii. 25 f. it is called the "tower which lieth out from the
king's high house," *i.e.* not the palace, but a government house
built on Zion, which served as a court of justice. But what is the
meaning of the ἀπ. λεγ. תַּלְפִּיּוֹת? Grätz translates: for a prospect;
but the Greek τηλωπός, of which he regards 'לת as the Heb. abstr.,
is a word so rare that its introduction into the Semitic language is
on that account improbable. Hengst. translates: built for hanging
swords; and he sees in the word a compound of 'תַל (from תֵּלָה, with
which forms such as יָד = *jadj*, שַׁד = *shadj*, שַׁל, 2 Sam. vi. 7, are
compared) and פִּיּוֹת; but this latter word signifies, not swords, but
edges of the (double-edged) sword; wherefore Kimchi (interpreting תַל
as the constr. of תֵל, as אֵל, in בְּצַלְאֵל, is of צֵל) explains: an erection of
sharp-cornered stones; and, moreover, the Heb. language knows no
such *nmm. comp. appellativa*: the names of the frog, צְפַרְדֵּעַ, and the
bat, עֲטַלֵּף (cf. the *Beth* in (Arab.) *sa'lab*, fox, with the added *Pe*), are not
such; and also *tsalmâveth*, the shadow of death, is at a later period,
for the first time, restamped [1] as such from the original *tsalmuth* (cf.
Arab. *zalumat = tenebrae*). Gesen. obtains the same meanings; for
he explains 'לתל by *exitialibus* (*sc. armis*), from an adj. תִּלְפִּי, from
תָּלֵף = Arab. *talifa*, to perish, the inf. of which, *talaf*, is at the present
day a word synon. with *halak* (to perish); (Arab.) *matlaf* (place of
going down) is, like יְשִׁימוֹן, a poetic name of the wilderness. The
explanation is acceptable but hazardous, since neither the Heb. nor
the Aram. shows a trace of this verb; and it is thus to be given up,
if 'תלפ can be referred to a verbal stem to be found in the Heb. and
Aram. This is done in Ewald's explanation, to which also Böttcher
and Rödig. give the preference: built for close (crowded) troops (so,
viz., that many hundreds or thousands find room therein); the
(Arab.) verb *aff*, to wrap together (opp. *nashar*, to unfold), is used of
the packing together of multitudes of troops (*liff*, plur. *lufuf*), and
also of warlike hand-to-hand conflicts; 'תלפ would be traced to a
verb לָפָה synon. therewith, after the form תַּאֲנִיָּה. But if 'תלפ were
meant of troops, then they would be denoted as the garrison found
therein, and it would not be merely said that the tower was built for
such; for the point of comparison would then be, the imposing look
of the neck, overpowering by the force of the impression proceeding
from within. But now, in the Aram., and relatively in the Talm.
Heb., not only לָפַף and לוּף occur, but also לְפִי (Af. אַלְפִּי), and that in

---

[1] Cf. regarding such double words belonging to the more modern Semitic
language, *Jesurun*, pp. 232–236.

the sense of enclosure, *i.e.* of joining together, the one working into the
other,—*e.g.* in the Targ. : of the curtain of the tabernacle (בֵּית לוֹפֵי, place
of the joining together = חֹבֶרֶת or מַחְבֶּרֶת of the Heb. text) ; and in the
Talm. : of the roofs of two houses (*Bathra* 6*a*, לוּפְתָּא, the joining[1]).
Accordingly 'לְתַלְפּ, if we interpret the *Lamed* not of the definition,
but of the norm, may signify, " in ranks together." The *Lamed* has
already been thus rendered by Döderl. : " in turns " (cf. לָפַת, to turn,
to wind) ; and by Meier, Mr. : " in gradation ;" and Aq. and Jerome
also suppose that 'תלפ refers to component parts of the building
itself, for they understand [2] pinnacles or parapets (ἐπάλξεις, *propugnacula*) ; as also the Venet. : εἰς ἐπάλξεις χιλίας. But the name for
pinnacles is פִּנָּה, and their points, שְׁמָשׁוֹת ; while, on the contrary,
'תלפ is the more appropriate name for terraces which, connected
together, rise the one above the other. Thus to build towers like
terraces, and to place the one, as it were, above the other, was a
Babylonian custom.[3] The comparison lies in this, that Shulamith's
neck was surrounded with ornaments so that it did not appear as a
uniform whole, but as composed of terraces. That the neck is
represented as hung round with ornaments, the remaining portion of
the description shows.

מָגֵן signifies a shield, as that which protects, like *clupeus* (*clypeus*),
perhaps connected with καλύπτειν and שֶׁלֶט, from שָׁלַט = (Arab.)
shalita, as a hard impenetrable armour. The latter is here the more
common word, which comprehends, with מָגֵן, the round shield ; also
צִנָּה, the oval shield, which covers the whole body ; and other forms
of shields. אֶלֶף הַמָּגֵן, " the thousand shields," has the indicative, if
not (*vid.* under i. 11) the generic article. The appositional כֹּל שִׁלְטֵי
הַגִּ is not intended to mean : all shields of (*von*) heroes, which it would
if the article were prefixed to *col* and omitted before *gibborim*, or if
כֻּלָּם, iii. 8, were used ; but it means : all the shields of heroes, as
the accentuation also indicates. The article is also here significant.
Solomon made, according to 1 Kings x. 16 f., 200 golden targets
and 300 golden shields, which he put in the house of the forest of
Lebanon. These golden shields Pharaoh Shishak took away with
him, and Rehoboam replaced them by " shields of brass," which the
guards bore when they accompanied the king on his going into the
temple (1 Kings xiv. 26–28 ; cf. 2 Chron. xii. 9–11) ; these

---

[1] The Arab. *lafa*, vi., proceeding from the same root-idea, signifies to bring in
something again, to bring in again, to seek to make good again.

[2] *Vid.* also Lagarde's *Onomastica*, p. 202 : Θαλπιὼθ ἐπάλξη (read εἰς) ἡ
ὑψηλά.

[3] *Vid.* Oppert's *Grundzüge der Assyr. Kunst* (1872), p. 11.

"shields of David," *i.e.* shields belonging to the king's house, were given to the captains of the guard on the occasion of the raising of Joash to the throne, 2 Kings xi. 10; cf. 2 Chron. xxiii. 9. Of these brazen shields, as well as of those of gold, it is expressly said how and where they were kept, nowhere that they were hung up outside on a tower, the tower of David. Such a display of the golden shields is also very improbable. We will perhaps have to suppose that 4*b* describes the tower of David, not as it actually was, but as one has to represent it to himself, that it might be a figure of Shulamith's neck. This is compared to the terraced tower of David, if one thinks of it as hung round by a thousand shields which the heroes bore, those heroes, namely, who formed the king's body-guard. Thus it is not strange that to the 200 + 300 golden shields are here added yet 500 more; the body-guard, reckoned in companies of 100 each, 2 Kings xi. 4, is estimated as consisting of 1000 men. The description, moreover, corresponds with ancient custom. The words are תְּלוּי עָלָיו, not תְּלוּי בּוֹ; the outer wall of the tower is thought of as decorated with shields hung upon it. That shields were thus hung round on tower-walls, Ezekiel shows in his prophecy regarding Tyre, xxvii. 11; cf. 1 Macc. iv. 57, and *supra foris Capitolinae aedis*, Pliny, *Hist. Nat.* xxxv. 3; and although we express the presumption that Solomon's imagination represented David's tower as more gorgeous than it actually was, yet we must confess that we are not sufficiently acquainted with Solomon's buildings to be able to pass judgment on this. These manifold inexplicable references of the Song to the unfolded splendour of Solomon's reign, are favourable to the Solomonic authorship of the book. This grandiose picture of the distinguished beauty of the neck, and the heightening of this beauty by the ornament of chains, is now followed by a beautiful figure, which again goes back to the use of the language of shepherds, and terminates the description:

> Ver. 5 Thy two breasts are like two fawns,
> Twins of a gazelle,
> Which feed among lilies.

The dual, originating in the inner differ. of the plur., which denotes in Heb. not two things of any sort, but two paired by nature or by art, exists only in the principal form; שָׁדַיִם, as soon as inflected, is unrecognisable, therefore here, where the pair as such is praised, the word שְׁנֵי is used. The breasts are compared to a twin pair of young gazelles in respect of their equality and youthful freshness, and the bosom on which they raise themselves is compared to a meadow covered with lilies, on which the twin-pair of young gazelles feed.

With this tender lovely image the praise of the attractions of the chosen one is interrupted. If one counts the lips and the mouth as a part of the body, which they surely are, there are seven things here praised, as Hengst. rightly counts (the eyes, the hair, teeth, mouth, temples, neck, breasts); and Hahn speaks with right of the sevenfold beauty of the bride.

Shulamith replies to these words of praise:

> Ver. 6 Until the day cools and the shadows flee,
> I will go forth to the mountain of myrrh
> And to the hill of frankincense.

All those interpreters who suppose these to be a continuation of Solomon's words, lose themselves in absurdities. Most of them understand the mountain of myrrh and the hill of frankincense of Shulamith's attractions, praised in ver. 5, or of her beauty as a whole; but the figures would be grotesque (cf. on the other hand v. 13), and אֵלֶךְ לִי prosaic, wherefore it comes that the idea of betaking oneself away connects itself with הֶלֶךְ לִי (Gen. xii. 1; Ex. xviii. 27), or that it yet preponderates therein (Gen. xxii. 2; Jer. v. 5), and that, for אֵלֶךְ לִי in the passage before us in reference to ii. 10, 11, the supposition holds that it will correspond with the French je m'en irai. With right Louis de Leon sees in the mountain of myrrh and the hill of frankincense names of shady and fragrant places; but he supposes that Solomon says he wishes to go thither to enjoy a siesta, and that he invites Shulamith thither. But we read nothing of this invitation; and that a bridegroom should sleep a part of his marriage-day is yet more unnatural than that, e.g., Wilh. Budäus, the French philologist, spent a part of the same at work in his study. That not Solomon but Shulamith speaks here is manifest in the beginning, "until the day," etc., which at ii. 17 are also Shulamith's words. Anton (1773) rightly remarks, "Shulamith says this to set herself free." But why does she seek to make herself free? It is answered, that she longs to be forth from Solomon's too ardent eulogies; she says that, as soon as it is dark, she will escape to the blooming aromatic fields of her native home, where she hopes to meet with her beloved shepherd. Thus, e.g., Ginsburg (1868). But do myrrh and frankincense grow in North Palestine? Ginsburg rests on Florus' Epitome Rerum Rom. iii 6, where Pompey the Great is said to have passed over Lebanon and by Damascus "per nemora illa odorata, per thuris et balsami sylvas." But by these thuris et balsami sylvae could be meant only the gardens of Damascus; for neither myrrh nor frankincense is indigenous to North Palestine, or generally to any part of Palestine.

Friedrich (1866) therefore places Shulamith's home at Engedi, and supposes that she here once more looks from the window and dotes on the mountain of myrrh and the hill of frankincense, "where, at the approach of twilight, she was wont to look out for her betrothed shepherd." But Shulamith, as her name already denotes, is not from the south, but is a Galilean, and her betrothed shepherd is from Utopia! That myrrh and frankincense were planted in the gardens of Engedi is possible, although (i. 14) mention is made only of the *Al-henna* there. But here places in the neighbourhood of the royal palace must be meant; for the myrrh tree, the gum of which, prized as an aroma, is the Arab. *Balsamodendron Myrrha*, and the frankincense tree, the resin of which is used for incense, is, like the myrrh tree, an Arab. amyrid. The *Boswellia serrata*,[1] indigenous to the East Indies, furnishes the best frankincense; the Israelites bought it from Sheba (Isa. lx. 6; Jer. vi. 20). The myrrh tree as well as the frankincense tree were thus exotics in Palestine, as they are in our own country; but Solomon, who had intercourse with Arabia and India by his own mercantile fleet, procured them for his own garden (Eccles. ii. 5). The modest Shulamith shuns the loving words of praise; for she requests that she may be permitted to betake herself to the lonely places planted with myrrh and frankincense near the king's palace, where she thinks to tarry in a frame of mind befitting this day till the approaching darkness calls her back to the king. It is the importance of the day which suggests to her this אֵלֶךְ לִי, a day in which she enters into the covenant of her God with Solomon (Prov. ii. 17). Without wishing to allegorize, we may yet not omit to observe, that the mountain of myrrh and the hill of frankincense put us in mind of the temple, where incense, composed of myrrh, frankincense, and other spices, ascended up before God every morning and evening (Ex. xxx. 34 ff.). הַר הַמּוֹר is perhaps a not unintentional accord to הַר הַמּוֹרִיָּה (2 Chron. iii. 1), the mountain where God appeared; at all events, "mountain of myrrh" and "hill of frankincense" are appropriate names for places of devout meditation, where one holds fellowship with God.

This childlike modest disposition makes her yet more lovely in the eyes of the king. He breaks out in these words:

> Ver. 7 Thou art altogether fair, my love,
> And no blemish in thee.

Certainly he means, no blemish either of soul or body. In vers. 1–5 he has praised her external beauty; but in ver. 6 her soul has disclosed itself: the fame of her spotless beauty is there extended to

[1] Lassen's *Ind. Alterthumskunde*, I. 334.

her soul no less than to her external appearance. And as to her longing after freedom from the tumult and bustle of court life, he thus promises to her:

> Ver. 8 With me from Lebanon, my bride,
> With me from Lebanon shalt thou come;
> Shalt look from the top of Amana,
> From the top of Shenir and Hermon,
> From dens of lions,
> From mountains of leopards.

Zöckl. interprets אִתִּי in the sense of אֵלַי, and תָּשׁוּרִי in the sense of journeying to this definite place: "he announces to her in overflowing fulness of expression, that from this time forth, instead of the lonely mountainous regions, and the dangerous caves and dens, she shall inhabit with him the royal palace." Thus also Kingsbury. But the interpretation, however plausible, cannot be supported. For (1) such an idea ought to be expressed either by אֵלַי תב' or by תב' וְאִתִּי חֵשֵׁבִי, instead of אִתִּי הָב'; (2) Shulamith is not from Lebanon, nor from the Anti-Libanus, which looks toward Damascus; (3) this would be no answer to Shulamith's longing for lonely quietness. We therefore hold by our explanation given in 1851. He seeks her to go with him up the steep heights of Lebanon, and to descend with him from thence; for while ascending the mountain one has no view before him, but when descending he has the whole panorama of the surrounding region lying at his feet. Thus חשׁ' is not to be understood as at Isa. lvii. 9, where it has the meaning of *migrabas*, but, as at Num. xxiii. 9, it means *spectabis*. With מֵר' the idea of prospect lies nearer than that of descending; besides, the meaning *spectare* is secondary, for שׁוּר signifies first "to go, proceed, journey," and then "going to view, to go in order to view." *Sêr* in Arab. means "the scene," and *sêr etmek* in Turkish, "to contemplate" (cf. Arab. *tamashy*, to walk, then, to contemplate). *Lebanon* is the name of the Alpine range which lies in the N.-W. of the Holy Land, and stretches above 20 (German) miles from the Leontes (*Nahr el-Kasmie*) northwards to the Eleutheros (*Nahr el-Kebîr*). The other three names here found refer to the Anti-Libanus separated from the Lebanon by the Coelo-Syrian valley, and stretching from the Banias northwards to the plain of Hamâth.

Amana denotes that range of the Anti-Libanus from which the springs of the river Amana issue, one of the two rivers which the Syrian captain (2 Kings v. 12) named as better than all the waters of Israel. These are the *Amana* and *Pharpar*, *i.e.* the *Baradâ* and *A'wadsh*; to the union of the Baradâ (called by the Greeks *Chry-*

sorrhoas, i.e. "golden stream") with the *Feidshe,* the environs of Damascus owe their *ghuwdat,* their paradisaical beauty.

Hermon (from חָרַם, to cut off; cf. Arab. *kharom* and *makhrim,* the steep projection of a mountain) is the most southern peak of the Anti-Libanus chain, the lofty mountains (about 10,000 feet above the level of the sea) which form the north-eastern border of Palestine, and from which the springs of the Jordan take their rise.

Another section of the Anti-Libanus range is called *Senîr,* not *Shenîr.* The name, in all the three places where it occurs (Deut. iii. 9 ; 1 Chron. v. 23), is, in accordance with tradition, to be written with *Sin.* The Onkelos Targum writes סריון ; the Jerusalem paraphrases, טורא דמסרי פירוי (the mountain whose fruits become putrid, viz. on account of their superabundance); the Midrash explains otherwise : שהוא שונא הניר (the mountain which resists being broken up by the plough),—everywhere the writing of the word with the letter *Sin* is supposed. According to Deut. iii. 9, this was the Amorite name of Hermon. The expression then denotes that the Amorites called Hermon—*i.e.* the Anti-Libanus range, for they gave the name of a part to the whole range—by the name *Senîr;* Abulfeda uses سنير as the name of the part to the north of Damascus, with which the statement of Schwarz (*Das h. Land,* p. 33) agrees, that the Hermon (Anti-Libanus) to the north-west of Damascus is called *Senîr.*

נְמֵרִים, panthers, to the present day inhabit the clefts and defiles of the Lebanon, and of the Anti-Libanus running parallel to it; whereas lions have now altogether disappeared from the countries of the Mediterranean. In Solomon's time they were to be met with in the lurking-places of the Jordan valley, and yet more frequently in the remote districts of the northern Alpine chains. From the heights of these Alps Solomon says Shulamith shall alone with him look down from where the lions and panthers dwell. Near these beasts of prey, and yet inaccessible by them, shall she enjoy the prospect of the extensive pleasant land which was subject to the sceptre of him who held her safe on these cliffs, and accompanied her over these giddy heights. If "mountain of myrrh," so also "the top of Amana" is not without subordinate reference. *Amana,* proceeding from the primary idea of firmness and verification, signifies fidelity and the faithful covenant as it is established between God and the congregation, for He betrothes it to Himself באמונה ("in faithfulness"), Hos. ii. 22 [20]; the congregation of which the apostle (Eph. v. 27) says the same as is here said by

Solomon of Shulamith. Here for the first time he calls her כַּלָּה,
not כַּלָּתִי; for that, according to the *usus loq.*, would mean "my
daughter-in-law." Accordingly, it appears that the idea of "daughter-
in-law" is the primary, and that of "bride" the secondary one.
כַּלָּה, which is = כְּלִלָה, as חַלָּה, a cake, is = חֲלִלָה, that which is pierced
through (cf. בְּלִלוֹת, being espoused ; Jer. ii. 2), appears to mean [1]
(cf. what was said regarding חָתָן under iii. 11*b*) her who is comprehended with the family into which, leaving her parents' house,
she enters; not her who is embraced = crowned with a garland
(cf. Arab. تَكَلَّلَ, to be garlanded ; *tĕklîl*, garlanding ; *iklîl*, Syr. k*e*lilo,
a wreath), or her who is brought to completion (cf. the verb, Ezek.
xxvii. 4, 11), *i.e.* has reached the goal of her womanly calling.
Besides, כַּלָּה, like "*Braut*" in the older German (*e.g.* Gudrun), means
not only her who is betrothed, but also her who has been lately
married.

All that the king calls his, she now can call hers; for she has
won his heart, and with his heart himself and all that is his.

> Ver. 9 Thou hast taken my heart, my sister-bride ;
>   Thou hast taken my heart with one of thy glances,
>   With a little chain of thy necklace.

The *Piel* לִבֵּב may mean to make courageous, and it actually has this
meaning in the Aram., wherefore the Syr. retains the word ; Symm.
renders it by ἐθάρσυνάς με. But is it becoming in a man who is no
coward, especially in a king, to say that the love he cherishes gives
him heart, *i.e.* courage ? It might be becoming, perhaps, in a warrior
who is inspired by the thought of his beloved, whose respect and
admiration he seeks to gain, to dare the uttermost. But Solomon is
no Antar, no wandering knight.[2] Besides, the first effect of love is
different : it influences those whom it governs, not as encouraging, in
the first instance, but as disarming them ; love responded to encourages,
but love in its beginning, which is the subject here, overpowers. We
would thus more naturally render : "thou hast unhearted me ;" but
"to unheart," according to the Semitic and generally the ancient
conception of the heart (*Psychol.* p. 254), does not so much mean to

---

[1] L. Geiger's *Ursprung d. Sprach.* p. 227 ; cf. 88.

[2] A specimen of Böttcher's interpretation : "What is more natural than to
suppose that the keeper of a vineyard showed herself with half of her head and
neck exposed at the half-opened window to her shepherd on his first attempt to
set her free, when he cried, ' my dove in the clefts of the rocks,' etc., and animated
him thereby to this present bold deliverance of her from the midst of robbers ? "
We pity the Shulamitess, that she put her trust in this moonshiny coward.

captivate the heart, as rather to deprive of understanding or of judgment (cf. Hos. iv. 11). Such denomin. *Pi.* of names of corporeal members signify not merely taking away, but also wounding, and generally
any violent affection of it, as זָנַב, גֵּרֵם, Ewald, § 120*c;* accordingly the
LXX., Venet., and Jerome: ἐκαρδίωσάς με, *vulnerasti cor meum.*
The meaning is the same for "thou hast wounded my heart" =
"thou hast subdued my heart" (cf. Ps. xlv. 6*b*). With one of her
glances, with a little chain of her necklace, she has overcome him
as with a powerful charm: *veni, visa sum, vici.* The *Kerî* changes
באחד into בְּאַחַת; certainly עַיִן is mostly fem. (*e.g.* Judg. xvi. 28), but
not only the non-bibl. *usus loq.*, which *e.g.* prefers רָעָה or עַיִן רָע, of a
malignant bewitching look, but also the bibl. (*vid.* Zech. iii. 9,
iv. 10) treats the word as of double gender. עֲנָק and צַוְּרֹנִים are
related to each other as a part is to the whole. With the subst.
ending *ôn,* the designation of an ornament designed for the neck is
formed from צַוָּאר, the neck; cf. שַׂהֲרֹן, the "round tires like the
moon" of the women's toilet, Isa. iii. 18 ff. עֲנָק (connected with
עוּנַק עֲנָק, *cervix*) is a separate chain (Aram. עוּנְקְתָא) of this necklace.
In the words עֲנָק אַחַד אֶחָד, אֶחָד is used instead of אֶחָד, occurring also out
of genit. connection (Gen. xlviii. 22; 2 Sam. xvii. 22), and the
arrangement (*vid.* under Ps. lxxxix. 51) follows the analogy of the
pure numerals as שָׁלשׁ נָשִׁים; it appears to be transferred from the
vulgar language to that used in books, where, besides the passage
before us, it occurs only in Dan. viii. 13. That a glance of the eye
may pierce the heart, experience shows; but how can a little chain
of a necklace do this? That also is intelligible. As beauty becomes
unlike itself when the attire shows want of taste, so by means of
tasteful clothing, which does not need to be splendid, but may even
be of the simplest kind, it becomes mighty. Hence the charming
attractive power of the impression one makes communicates itself to
all that he wears, as, *e.g.,* the woman with the issue of blood touched
with joyful hope the hem of Jesus' garment; for he who loves feels
the soul of that which is loved in all that stands connected therewith, all that is, as it were, consecrated and charmed by the beloved
object, and operates so much the more powerfully if it adorns it,
because as an ornament of that which is beautiful, it appears so
much the more beautiful. In the preceding verse, Solomon has for
the first time addressed Shulamith by the title "bride." Here with
heightened cordiality he calls her "sister-bride." In this change in
the address the progress ofthe story is mirrored. Why he does not
say כַּלָּתִי (my bride), has already been explained, under 8*a*, from the
derivation of the word. Solomon's mother might call Shulamith

callathi, but he gives to the relation of affinity into which Shulamith has entered a reference to himself individually, for he says *ăhhothi callā* (my sister-bride) : she who as *callā* of his mother is to her a kind of daughter, is as *callā* in relation to himself, as it were, his sister.

He proceeds still further to praise her attractions.

> Ver. 10 How fair is thy love, my sister-bride!
> How much better thy love than wine!
> And the fragrance of thy unguents than all spices!
> 11 Thy lips drop honey, my bride ;
> Honey and milk are under thy tongue ;
> And the fragrance of thy garments is like the fragrance of Lebanon.

Regarding the connection of the *pluralet*. דּוֹדִים with the plur. of the pred., *vid.* at i. 2*b*. The pred. יָפוּ praises her love in its manifestations according to its impression on the sight ; טֹבוּ, according to its experience on nearer intercourse. As in ver. 9 the same power of impression is attributed to the eyes and to the necklace, so here is intermingled praise of the beauty of her person with praise of the fragrance, the odour of the clothing of the bride ; for her soul speaks out not only by her lips, she breathes forth odours also for him in her spices, which he deems more fragrant than all other odours, because he inhales, as it were, her soul along with them. נֹפֶת, from נָפַח, *ebullire* (*vid.* under Prov. v. 3, also Schultens), is virgin honey, ἄκοιτον (*acetum*, Pliny, xi. 15), *i.e.* that which of itself flows from the combs (צוּפִים). Honey drops from the lips which he kisses ; milk and honey are under the tongue which whispers to him words of pure and inward joy ; cf. the contrary, Ps. cxl. 4. The last line is an echo of Gen. xxvii. 27. שַׂלְמָה is שִׂמְלָה (from שָׂמַל, *complicare*, *complecti*) transposed (cf. עַלְוָה from עַוְלָה, כַּשְׂבָּה from כִּבְשָׂה). As Jacob's raiment had for his old father the fragrance of a field which God had blessed, so for Solomon the garments of the faultless and pure one, fresh from the woods and mountains of the north, gave forth a heart-strengthening savour like the fragrance of Lebanon (Hos. iv. 7), viz. of its fragrant herbs and trees, chiefly of the balsamic odour of the apples of the cedar.

The praise is sensuous, but it has a moral consecration.

> Ver. 12 A garden locked is my sister-bride ;
> A spring locked, a fountain sealed.

גַּן (according to rule masc. Böttch. § 658) denotes the garden from its enclosure ; גַּל (elsewhere גֻּלָּה), the fountain (synon. מַבּוּעַ), the waves bubbling forth (cf. Amos v. 24) ; and מַעְיָן, the place, as it were an eye of the earth, from which a fountain gushes forth. Luther distinguishes rightly between *gan* and *gal* ; on the contrary, all the old translators (even the Venet.) render as if the word in both cases were *gan*. The *Pasek* between *gan* and *nā'ul*, and between *gal* and *nā'ul*, is designed to separate the two *Nuns*, as *e.g.* at 2 Chron. ii. 9, Neh. ii. 2, the two *Mems*; it is the orthophonic *Pasek*, already described under ii. 7, which secures the independence of two similar or organically related sounds. Whether the sealed fountain (*fons signatus*) alludes to a definite fountain which Solomon had built for the upper city and the temple place,[1] we do not now inquire. To a locked garden and spring no one has access but the rightful owner, and a sealed fountain is shut against all impurity. Thus she is closed against the world, and inaccessible to all that would disturb her pure heart, or desecrate her pure person.[2] All the more beautiful and the greater is the fulness of the flowers and fruits which bloom and ripen in the garden of this life, closed against the world and its lust.

> Ver. 13 What sprouts forth for thee is a park of pomegranates,
>   With most excellent fruits ;
>   Cypress flowers with nards ;
>   14 Nard and crocus ; calamus and cinnamon,
>   With all kinds of incense trees ;
>   Myrrh and aloes,
>   With all the chief aromatics.

The common subject to all down to ver. 15 inclusive is שְׁלָחַיִךְ (" what sprouts for thee " = " thy plants "), as a figurative designation, borrowed from plants, of all the " phenomena and life utterances " (Böttch.) of her personality. " If I only knew here," says Rocke, " how to disclose the meaning, certainly all these flowers and fruits, in the figurative language of the Orient, in the flower-language of love, had their beautiful interpretation." In the old German poetry, also, the phrase *bluomen brechen* [to break flowers] was equivalent to : to enjoy love ; the flowers and fruits named are figures of all that the *amata* offers to the *amator*. Most of the plants here named are exotics ; פַּרְדֵּם (heaping around, circumvallation, enclosing) is a garden or park, especially with foreign ornamental and fragrant plants—an old Persian word, the explanation of which, after Spiegel, first given in our exposition of the Song, 1851 (from *pairi* = περί, and *dêz*, R. *diz*, a heap), has now become common property (Justi's *Handb. der Zendsprache*, p. 180). פְּרִי מְגָדִים (from מֶגֶד, which corresponds to

---

[1] *Vid.* Zschocke in the *Tübinger Quartalschrift*, 1867, 3.

[2] Seal, חוֹתָם, pers. *muhr*, is used directly in the sense of maiden-like behaviour ; *vid.* Perles' *etymol. Studien* (1871), p. 67.

the Arab. *mejd*, praise, honour, excellence; *vid.* Volck under Deut. xxxiii. 13) are *fructus laudum*, or *lautitiarum*, excellent precious fruits, which in the more modern language are simply called מְגָדִים (*Shabbath* 127*b*, מיני מגדים, all kinds of fine fruits); cf. Syr. *magdo*, dried fruit. Regarding כֹּפֶר, *vid.* under i. 14; regarding מֹר, under i. 13; also regarding נֵרְדְּ, under i. 12. The long vowel of נֵרְדְּ corresponds to the Pers. form *nârd*, but near to which is also *nard*, Indian *nalada* (fragrance-giving); the *ê* is thus only the long accent, and can therefore disappear in the plur. For נרדים, Grätz reads יְרָדִים, roses, because the poet would not have named nard twice. The conjecture is beautiful, but for us, who believe the poem to be Solomonic, is inconsistent with the history of roses (*vid.* under ii. 1), and also unnecessary. The description moves forward by steps rhythmically.

כַּרְכֹּם is the *crocus stativus*, the genuine Indian *safran*, the dried flower-eyes of which yield the safran used as a colour, as an aromatic, and also as medicine; *safran* is an Arab. word, and means yellow root and yellow colouring matter. The name כַּרְכֹּם, Pers. *karkam*, Arab. *karkum*, is radically Indian, Sanscr. *kuṅkuma*. קָנֶה, a reed (from קָנָה, R. קנ, to rise up, viewed intrans.),[1] viz. sweet reed, *acorus calamus*, which with us now grows wild in marshes, but is indigenous to the Orient.

קִנָּמוֹן is the *laurus cinnamomum*, a tree indigenous to the east coast of Africa and Ceylon, and found later also on the Antilles. It is of the family of the *laurineae*, the inner bark of which, peeled off and rolled together, is the cinnamon-bark (*cannella*, French *cannelle*); Aram. קוּנְמָא, as also the Greek κιννάμωμον and κίνναμον, Lat. (*e.g.* in the 12th book of Pliny) *cinnamomum* and *cinnamum*, are interchanged, from קְנַם, probably a secondary formation from קָנָה (like בָּם, whence בָּמָה, from בָּא), to which also ܩܘܡܐ, ὑπόστασις, and the Talm.-Targ. קוּנָם קוֹנָם, an oath (cf. קְיָם), go back, so that thus the name which was brought to the west by the Phoenicians denoted not the tree, but the reed-like form of the rolled dried bark. As "nards" refer to varieties of the nard, perhaps to the Indian and the Jamanic spoken of by Strabo and others, so "all kinds of incense trees" refers definitely to Indo-Arab. varieties of the incense tree and its fragrant resin; it has its name from the white and transparent seeds of this its resin (cf. Arab. *lubân*, incense and benzoin, the resin of

---

[1] In this general sense of "reed" (Syn. *arundo*) the word is also found in the Gr. and Lat.: χάνναι (χάναι), reed-mats, χάνεον, χάναστρον, a wicker basket, *canna*, *canistrum*, without any reference to an Indo-Germ. verbal stem, and without acquiring the specific signification of an aromatic plant.

the storax tree, לְבֹנֶה); the Greek λίβανος, λιβανωτός (Lat. *thus*, frankincense, from θύω), is a word derived from the Phoenicians.

אֲהָלִים or אֲהָלוֹת (which already in a remarkable way was used by Balaam, Num. xxiv. 6, elsewhere only since the time of Solomon) is the Semitized old Indian name of the aloe, *agaru* or *aguru;* that which is aromatic is the wood of the aloe-tree (*aloëxylon agallochum*), particularly its dried root (*agallochum* or *lignum aloës*, ξυλαλόη, according to which the Targ. here : אכסיל אלואין, after the phrase in Aruch) mouldered in the earth, which chiefly came from farther India.[1] עַם, as everywhere, connects things contained together or in any way united (v. 1 ; cf. i. 11, as Ps. lxxxvii. 4 ; cf. 1 Sam. xvi. 12). The concluding phrase עִם כָּל־רָ' וגו', *cum praestantissimis quibusque aromatibus*, is a poet. *et cetera*. רֹאשׁ, with the gen. of the object whose value is estimated, denotes what is of *meilleure qualité ;* or, as the Talm. says, what is אלפא, άλφα, *i.e.* number one.   Ezekiel, xxvii. 22, in a similar sense, says, " with chief (רֹאשׁ) of all spices."

The panegyric returns now once more to the figure of a fountain.

> Ver. 15 A garden-fountain, a well of living water,
>   And torrents from Lebanon.

The *tertium compar.* in ver. 12 was the collecting and sealing up ; here, it is the inner life and its outward activity.   A fountain in gardens (גַּנִּים, categ. pl.) is put to service for the benefit of the beds of plants round about, and it has in these gardens, as it were, its proper sphere of influence.   A well of living water is one in which that which it distributes springs up from within, so that it is indeed given to it, but not without at the same time being its own true property.   נָזַל is related, according to the Semitic *usus loq.*, to אָזַל, as " *niedergehen* " (to go down) to " *weggehen* " (to go away) (*vid.* Prov. v. 15) ; similarly related are (Arab.) *sar*, to go, and *sal* (in which

---

[1] *Vid.* Lassen's *Ind. Alterthumsk.* I. 334 f.   Furrer, in Schenkel's *Bib. Lex.*, understands אהלות of the *liliaceae*, indigenous to Palestine as to Arabia, which is also called *aloë*.   But the drastic purgative which the succulent leaves of this plant yield is not aromatic, and the verb אהל " to glisten," whence he seeks to derive the name of this aloe, is not proved.   Cf. besides, the Petersburg *Lex.* under *aguru* (" not difficult "), according to which is this name of the *amyris agallocha*, and the *aquilaria agallocha*, but of no *liliaceae*.   The name *Adlerholz* (" eaglewood ") rests on a misunderstanding of the name of the Agila tree.   It is called " *Paradiesholz*," because it must have been one of the paradise trees (*vid. Bereshith rabba* under Gen. ii. 8).   Dioskorides says of this wood : θυμιᾶται ἀντὶ λιβανωτοῦ ; the Song therefore places it along with myrrh and frankincense.   That which is common to the lily-aloe and the wood-aloe, is the bitter taste of the juice of the former and of the resinous wood of the latter.   The Arab. name of the aloe, *ṣabir*, is also given to the lily-aloe.   The proverbs : *amarru min eṣ-ṣabir*, bitterer than the aloe, and *es-sabr ṣabir*, patience is the aloe, refer to the aloe-juice.

the letter *ra* is exchanged for *lam*, to express the softness of the liquid), to flow, whence *syl* (*sêl*), impetuous stream, rushing water, kindred in meaning to נֹזְלִים. Streams which come from Lebanon have a rapid descent, and (so far as they do not arise in the snow region) the water is not only fresh, but clear as crystal. All these figures understood sensuously would be insipid ; but understood ethically, they are exceedingly appropriate, and are easily interpreted, so that the conjecture is natural, that on the supposition of the spiritual interpretation of the Song, Jesus has this saying in His mind when He says that streams of living water shall flow " out of the belly " of the believer, John vii. 38.

The king's praise is for Shulamith proof of his love, which seeks a response. But as she is, she thinks herself yet unworthy of him; her modesty says to her that she needs preparation for him, preparation by that blowing which is the breath of God in the natural and in the spiritual world.

> Ver. 16 Awake, thou North (wind), and come, thou South !
> Blow through my garden, cause its spices to flow—
> Let my beloved come into his garden,
> And eat the fruits which are precious to him.

The names of the north and south, denoting not only the regions of the heavens, but also the winds blowing from these regions, are of the fem. gender, Isa. xliii. 6. The east wind, קָדִים, is purposely not mentioned ; the idea of that which is destructive and adverse is connected with it (*vid.* under Job xxvii. 21). The north wind brings cold till ice is formed, Sir. xliii. 20 ; and if the south wind blow, it is hot, Luke xii. 55. If cold and heat, coolness and sultriness, interchange at the proper time, then growth is promoted. And if the wind blow through a garden at one time from this direction and at another from that,—not so violently as when it shakes the trees of the forest, but softly and yet as powerfully as a garden can bear it,—then all the fragrance of the garden rises in waves, and it becomes like a sea of incense. The garden itself then blows, *i.e.* emits odours ; for (פֵּחַ = the Arab. *fakh, fah,* cf. *fawh,* pl. *afwâh,* sweet odours, fragrant plants) as in רוּחַ הַיּוֹם, Gen. iii. 8, the idea underlies the expression, that when it is evening the day itself blows, *i.e.* becomes cool, the causative הֵפִיחִי, connected with the object-accus. of the garden, means to make the garden breezy and fragrant. נָזַל is here used of the odours which, set free as it were from the plants, flow out, being carried forth by the waves of air. Shulamith wishes that in her all that is worthy of love should be fully realized. What had to be done for Esther (Esth. ii. 12) before she could be brought in to the king, Shulamith calls on the winds to accomplish for her, which are, as it were, the breath of the life of all nature, and as such, of the life-spirit, which is the sustaining background of all created things. If she is thus prepared for him who loves her, and whom she loves, he shall come into his garden and enjoy the precious fruit belonging to him. With words of such gentle tenderness, childlike purity, she gives herself to her beloved.

She gives herself to him, and he has accepted her, and now celebrates the delight of possession and enjoyment.

> Chap. v. 1 I am come into my garden, my sister-bride ;
> Have plucked my myrrh with my balsam ;
> Have eaten my honeycomb with my honey ;
> Have drunk my wine with my milk—
> Eat, drink, and be drunken, ye friends !

If the exclamation of Solomon, 1a, is immediately connected with the words of Shulamith, iv. 16, then we must suppose that, influenced by these words, in which the ardour of love and humility express themselves, he thus in triumph exclaims, after he has embraced her in his arms as his own inalienable possession. But the exclamation denotes more than this. It supposes a union of love, such as is the conclusion of marriage following the betrothal, the God-ordained aim of sexual love within the limits fixed by morality. The poetic expression בָּאתִי לְגַנִּי points to the בּוֹא אֶל, used of the entrance of a man into the woman's chamber, to which the expression (Arab.) dakhal bihā (he went in with her), used of the introduction into the bride's chamber, is compared. The road by which Solomon reached this full and entire possession was not short, and especially for his longing it was a lengthened one. He now triumphs in the final enjoyment which his ardent desire had found. A pleasant enjoyment which is reached in the way and within the limits of the divine order, and which therefore leaves no bitter fruits of self-reproach, is pleasant even in the retrospect. His words, beginning with "I am come into my garden," breathe this pleasure in the retrospect. Ginsburg and others render incorrectly, "I am coming," which would require the words to have been (הִנֵּה אֲנִי בָא). The series of perfects beginning with בָאתִי cannot be meant otherwise than retrospectively. The "garden" is Shulamith herself, iv. 12, in the fulness of her personal and spiritual attractions, iv. 16 ; cf. כְּרָמִי, i. 6. He may call her " my sister-bride ; " the garden is then his by virtue of divine and human right, he has obtained possession of this garden, he has broken its costly rare flowers.

אָרָה (in the Mishna dialect the word used of plucking figs) signifies to pluck; the Aethiop. trans. *ararku karbé*, I have plucked myrrh ; for the Aethiop. has *arara* instead of simply ארה. בְּשָׂמִי is here בְּשָׂם deflected. While בֶּשֶׂם, with its plur. *b'sâmim*, denotes fragrance in general, and only balsam specially, *bāsām* = (Arab.) *bashâm* is the proper name of the balsam-tree (the Mecca balsam), *amyris opobalsamum*, which, according to Forskal, is indigenous in the central mountain region of Jemen (S. Arabia) ; it is also called (Arab.) *balsaman;* the word found its way in this enlarged form into the West, and then returned in the forms בַּלְסְמוֹן, אַפּוֹפַלְסָמוֹן, אַפַּרְסְמָא (Syr. *afrusomo*), into the East.   Balsam and other spices were brought in abundance to King Solomon as a present by the Queen of Sheba, 1 Kings x. 10 ; the celebrated balsam plantations of Jericho (*vid.* Winer's *Real-W.*), which continued to be productive till the Roman period, might owe their origin to the friendly relations which Solomon sustained to the south Arab. princess.   Instead of the Indian aloe, iv. 14, the Jamanic balsam is here connected with myrrh as a figure of Shulamith's excellences.   The plucking, eating, and drinking are only interchangeable figurative descriptions of the enjoyment of love.

   " Honey and milk," says Solomon, iv. 11, " is under thy tongue." יַעַר is like יַעְרָה, 1 Sam. xiv. 27, the comb (*favus*) or cells containing the honey,—a designation which has perhaps been borrowed from porous lava.[1] With honey and milk " under the tongue " wine is connected, to which, and that of the noblest kind, vii. 10, Shulamith's palate is compared.   Wine and milk together are οἰνόγαλα, which Chloe presents to Daphnis (Longus, i. 23).   Solomon and his Song here hover on the pinnacle of full enjoyment ; but if one understands his figurative language as it interprets itself, it here also expresses that delight of satisfaction which the author of Ps. xix. 6*a* transfers to the countenance of the rising sun, in words of a chaste purity which sexual love never abandons, in so far as it is connected with esteem for a beloved wife, and with the preservation of mutual personal dignity.   For this very reason the words of Solomon, 1*a*, cannot be thought of as spoken to the guests.   Between iv. 16 and v. 1*a* the bridal night intervenes.   The words used in 1*a* are Solomon's morning salutation to her who has now wholly become his own.   The call addressed to the guests at the feast is given forth on the second day of the marriage, which, according to ancient custom, Gen. xxix. 28, Judg. xiv. 12, was wont to be celebrated for seven days, Tob. xi. 18.   The dramatical character of the Song leads to this result, that the pauses are passed over, the scenes are quickly changed, and the times appear to be continuous.

   [1] *Vid.* Wetstein in the *Zeitsch. für allgem. Erdkunde*, 1859, p. 123.

The plur. דּוֹדִים Hengst. thinks always designates "love" (*Liebe*);
thus, after Prov. vii. 28, also here: Eat, friends, drink and intoxicate
yourselves in love.   But the summons, *inebriamini amoribus*, has a
meaning if regarded as directed by the guests to the married pair,
but not as directed to the guests.   And while we may say רוה דֹדִים,
yet not 'שכר דו, for *shakar* has always only the accus. of a spirituous
liquor after it.   Therefore none of the old translators (except only
the Venet. : μεθύσθητε ἔρωσιν) understood *dodim*, notwithstanding
that elsewhere in the Song it means love, in another than a personal
sense ; רֵעִים and 'דו are here the plur. of the elsewhere parallels
רֵע and דּוֹד, *e.g.* v. 16*b*, according to which also (cf. on the contrary,
iv. 16*b*) they are accentuated.   Those who are assembled are, as sympathizing friends, to participate in the pleasures of the feast.   The Song
of Songs has here reached its climax.   A Paul would not hesitate,
after Eph. v. 31 f., to extend the mystical interpretation even to this.
Of the antitype of the marriage pair it is said : "For the marriage
of the Lamb is come, and His wife hath made herself ready" (Rev.
xix. 7); and of the antitype of the marriage guests : "Blessed are they
which are called unto the marriage supper of the Lamb" (Rev.
xix. 9).

FOURTH ACT.

LOVE DISDAINED BUT WON AGAIN.—Chap. V. 2–VI. 9.

FIRST SCENE OF THE FOURTH ACT, V. 2–VI. 3.

In this fourth Act we are not now carried back to the time when
Solomon's relation to Shulamith was first being formed.   We are not
placed here amid the scenes of their first love, but of those of their
married life, and of their original ardour of affection maintaining
itself not without trial.   This is evident from the circumstance that
in the first two Acts the beloved is addressed by the title רעיתי (my
friend, beloved), and that the third Act rises [1] to the title כלה (bride)
and אחתי כלה (my sister-bride) ; in the fourth Act, on the other hand,
along with the title *ra'yaihi*, we hear no longer *calla*, nor *ahhothi*

---

[1] Among the Slovacs a bride is called *malducha*, "virgin-bride," before she has
a cap placed on her head ; and after that, *nevesta*, "bride-spouse."   In England,
bride does not designate the betrothed as such, but the betrothed when near her
marriage.

calla, but simply *ahhothi,*[1]—a title of address which contributes to heighten the relation, to idealize it, and give it a mystical background. We have here presented to us pictures from the life of the lovers after their marriage has been solemnized. Shulamith, having reached the goal of her longing, has a dream like that which she had (iii. 1–4) before she reached that goal. But the dreams, however they resemble each other, are yet also different, as their issues show; in the former, she seeks him, and having found him holds him fast; here, she seeks him and finds him not. That that which is related belongs to the dream-life in ch. iii., was seen from the fact that it was inconceivable as happening in real life; here that which is related is expressly declared in the introductory words as having occurred in a dream.

> Ver. 2 I sleep, but my heart keeps waking—
> Hearken! my beloved is knocking:
> Open to me, my sister, my love,
> My dove, my perfect one;
> For my head is filled with dew,
> My locks (are) full of the drops of the night.

The partic. subst. clauses, 2*a,* indicate the circumstances under which that which is related in 2*b* occurred. In the principal sentence in hist. prose וַיִּדְפֹּק would be used; here, in the dramatic vivacity of the description, is found in its stead the interject. *vocem = ausculta* with the gen. foll., and a word designating[2] state or condition added, thought of as accus. according to the Semitic syntax (like Gen. iv. 10; Jer. x. 22; cf. 1 Kings xiv. 6). To sleep while the heart wakes signifies to dream, for sleep and distinct consciousness cannot be co-existent; the movements of thought either remain in obscurity or are projected as dreams. עֵר = *'awir* is formed from עוּר, to be awake

---

[1] There is scarcely any other example of the husband calling his spouse "sister" than that found in Esth. v. 9 (Apocr.), where Ahasuerus says to Esther: "What is it, Esther? I am thy brother." Still more analogous are the words of Tob. vii. 12: "From this time forth thou art her brother, and she is thy sister;" but here the relation of affinity blends itself with the marriage relationship. In Lat. *soror* frequently denotes a lover, in contrast to *uxor.* But here in the Song *ahhothi calla* comes in the place of *callathi,* which is ambiguous ("my daughter-in-law").

[2] דּוֹפֵק [is knocking] is not an attribute to the determinate דּוֹדִי [my beloved] which it follows, but a designation of state or condition, and thus acc., as the Beirut translation renders it: "hear my beloved in the condition of one knocking." On the other hand, דּוֹד דּוֹפֵק signifies "a beloved one knocking." But "hear a beloved one knocking" would also be expressed acc. In classical language, the designation of state, if the subst. to which it belongs is indeterminate, is placed before it, *e.g.* "at the gate stood a beloved one knocking."

(in its root cogn. to the Aryan *gar*, of like import in γρηγορεῖν, ἐγείρειν), in the same way as מֵת = *mawith* from מוּת. The שׁ has here the conj. sense of "*dieweil*" (because), like *asher* in Eccles. vi. 12, viii. 15. The ר *dag.*, which occurs several times elsewhere (*vid.* under Prov. iii. 8, xiv. 10), is one of the inconsistencies of the system of punctuation, which in other instances does not double the ר; perhaps a relic of the Babylonian idiom, which was herein more accordant with the lingual nature of the ר than the Tiberian, which treated it as a semi-guttural. קְוֻצָּה, a lock of hair, from קָץ = קְוַץ, *abscîdit*, follows in the formation of the idea, the analogy of קָצִיר, in the sense of branch, from קְצַר, *desecuit*; one so names a part which is removed without injury to the whole, and which presents itself conveniently for removal; cf. the oath sworn by Egyptian women, *laḥajât muksûsi*, "by the life of my separated," *i.e.* "of my locks" (Lane, *Egypt*, etc., I. 38). The word still survives in the Talmud dialect. Of a beautiful young man who proposed to become a Nazarite, *Nedarim* 9a says the same as the *Jer. Horajoth* iii. 4 of a man who was a prostitute in Rome: his locks were arranged in separate masses, like heap upon heap; in *Bereshith rabba* c. lxv., under Gen. xxvii. 11, קְוָץ, curly-haired, is placed over against קֵרֵחַ, bald-headed, and the Syr. also has *kauṣoto* as the designation of locks of hair,—a word used by the Peshito as the rendering of the Heb. קְוֻצּוֹת, as the Syro-Hexap. Job xvi. 12, the Greek κόμη. טַל, from טָלַל (ﻃﻞ, to moisten, viz. the ground; to squirt, viz. blood), is in Arabic drizzling rain, in Heb. dew; the drops of the night (רְסִיסֵי, from רָסַס, to sprinkle, to drizzle)[1] are just drops of dew, for the precipitation of the damp air assumes this form in nights which are not so cold as to become frosty. Shulamith thus dreams that her beloved seeks admission to her. He comes a long way and at night. In the most tender words he entreats for that which he expects without delay. He addresses her, "my sister," as one of equal rank with himself, and familiar as a sister with a brother; "my love" (רַעְיָ), as one freely chosen by him to intimate fellowship; "my dove," as beloved and prized by him on account of her purity, simplicity, and loveliness. The meaning of

[1] According to the primary idea: to break that which is solid or fluid into little pieces, wherefore רסיסים means also broken pieces. To this root appertains also the Arab. *rashh*, to trickle through, to sweat through, II. to moisten (*e.g.* the mouth of a suckling with milk), and the Aethiop. *raseḥa*, to be stained. Drops scattered with a sprinkling brush the Arabs call *rashaḥât*; in the mystical writings, *rashaḥât el-uns* (dew-drops of intimacy) is the designation of sporadic gracious glances of the deity.

the fourth designation used by him, תֻּמָּתִי, is shown by the Arab. *tam* to be " wholly devoted," whence *teim*, " one devoted " = a servant, and *mutajjam*, desperately in love with one.   In addressing her חמתי, he thus designates this love as wholly undivided, devoting itself without evasion and without reserve.   But on this occasion this love did not approve itself, at least not at once.

> Ver. 3 I have put off my dress,
>   How shall I put it on again?
>   I have washed my feet,
>   How shall I defile them again?

She now lies unclothed in bed. כֻּתֹּנֶת is the χιτών worn next the body, from כתן, linen (diff. from the Arab. *kutun*, cotton, whence French *coton*, calico = cotton-stuff).   She had already washed her feet, from which it is supposed that she had throughout the day walked barefooted,—how (אֵיכָכָה, how? both times with the tone on the *penult.;*[1] cf. אֵיכָה, where? i. 7) should she again put on her dress, which she had already put off and laid aside (פָּשַׁט)? why should she soil (אֲטַנְּפֵם, relating to the fem. רַגְלַי, for אטנפן) again her feet, that had been washed clean?   Shulamith is here brought back to the customs as well as to the home of her earlier rural life; but although she should thus have been enabled to reach a deeper and more lively consciousness of the grace of the king, who stoops to an equality with her, yet she does not meet his love with an equal requital.   She is unwilling for his sake to put herself to trouble, or to do that which is disagreeable to her.   It cannot be thought that such an interview actually took place; and yet what she here dreamed had not only inward reality, but also full reality.   For in a dream, that which is natural to us or that which belongs to our very constitution becomes manifest, and much that is kept down during our waking hours by the power of the will, by a sense of propriety, and by the activities of life, comes to light during sleep; for fancy then stirs up the ground of our nature and brings it forth in dreams, and thus exposes us to ourselves in such a way as oftentimes, when we waken, to make us ashamed and alarmed.   Thus it was with Shulamith.   In the dream it was inwardly manifest that she had

---

[1] That it has the tone on the *penult.*, like בָּכָה, *e.g.*, v. 9, is in conformity with the paragog. nature of ה. The tone, however, when the following word in close connection begins with א, goes to the *ult.*, Esth. vii. 6. That this does not occur in אֵיכָ׳ אֵל, is explained from the circumstance that the word has the disjunctive *Tifcha*. But why not in אֵיכָ׳ אֵט? I think it is for the sake of the rhythm. Pinsker, *Einl.* p. 184, seeks to change the accentuation in order that the *penult.* accent might be on the second אֵיכָ׳, but that is not necessary. Cf. Ps. cxxxvii. 7.

lost her first love.   She relates it with sorrow; for scarcely had she rejected him with these unworthy deceitful pretences when she comes to herself again.

> Ver. 4 My beloved stretched his hand through the opening,
> And my heart was moved for him.

חֹר,[1] from the verb חוּר, in the sense of to break through (R. חר, whence also חָרַי, i. 10, and חָרֻם, Arab. *kharam*, part. broken through, *e.g.* of a lattice-window), signifies *foramen*, a hole, also *caverna* (whence the name of the Troglodytes, חֹרִי, and the Haurân, חַוְרָן), here the loophole in the door above (like *khawkht*, the little door for the admission of individuals in the street or house-door). It does not properly mean a window, but a part of the door pierced through at the upper part of the lock of the door (the door-bolt). מִן־הַחוֹר is understood from the standpoint of one who is within; "by the opening from without to within," thus "through the opening;" stretching his hand through the door-opening as if to open the door, if possible, by the pressing back of the lock from within, he shows how greatly he longed after Shulamith.   And she was again very deeply moved when she perceived this longing, which she had so coldly responded to: the interior of her body, with the organs which, after the bibl. idea, are the seat of the tenderest emotions, or rather, in which they reflect themselves, both such as are agreeable and such as are sorrowful, groaned within her,—an expression of deep sympathy so common, that "the sounding of the bowels," Isa. lxiii. 15, an expression used, and that anthropopathically of God Himself, is a direct designation of sympathy or inner participation.   The phrase here wavers between עָלָיו and עָלָי (thus, *e.g.* Nissel, 1662).   Both forms are admissible.   It is true we say elsewhere only *naphshi 'ālāi, ruhi 'ālāi, libbi 'ālāi*, for the *Ego* distinguishes itself from its substance (cf. *System d. bibl. Psychologie*, p.151 f.); *meäi 'alāi*, instead of *bi* (בְּקִרְבִּ), would, however, be also explained from this, that the bowels are meant, not anatomically, but as *psychical* organs.   But the old translators (LXX., Targ., Syr., Jerome, Venet.) rendered עָלָיו, which rests on later MS. authority (*vid.* Norzi and de Rossi), and is also more appropriate: her bowels are stirred, viz. over him, *i.e.* on account of him (Alkabez: בעבורו).   As she will now open to him, she is inwardly more ashamed, as he has come so full of love and longing to make her glad.

---

[1] Cf. the Arab. *ghawr (ghôr)*, as a sinking of the earth, and *khawr (khôr)*, as a breaking through, and, as it were, a piercing.   The mouth of a river is also called *khôr*, because there the sea breaks into the river.

Ver. 5 I arose to open to my beloved,
   And my hands dropped with myrrh,
   And my fingers with liquid myrrh,
   On the handle of the bolt.

The personal pron. אֲנִי stands without emphasis before the verb which already contains it; the common language of the people delights in such particularity. The Book of Hosea, the Ephraimite prophet's work, is marked by such a style. מוֹר עֹבֵר, with which the parallel clause goes beyond the simple *mōr*, is myrrh flowing over, dropping out of itself, *i.e.* that which breaks through the bark of the *balsamodendron myrrha*, or which flows out if an incision is made in it; *myrrha stacte*, of which Pliny (xii. 35) says: *cui nulla praefertur*, otherwise מֹר דְּרוֹר, from דָּרַר, to gush out, to pour itself forth in rich jets. He has come perfumed as if for a festival, and the costly ointment which he brought with him has dropped on the handles of the bolts (מַנְעוּל, keeping locked, after the form מַלְבּוּשׁ, drawing on), viz. the inner bolt, which he wished to withdraw. A classical parallel is found in Lucretius, iv. 1171:

  " At lacrimans exclusus amator limina saepe
   Floribus et sertis operit postesque superbos
   Unguit amaracĭno " . . .

Böttch. here puts to Hitzig the question, "Did the shepherd, the peasant of Engedi, bring with him oil of myrrh?" Rejecting this reasonable explanation, he supposes that the Shulamitess, still in Solomon's care, on rising up quickly dipped her hand in the oil of myrrh, that she might refresh her beloved. She thus had it near her before her bed, as a sick person her decoction. The right answer was, that the visitant by night is not that imaginary personage, but it is Solomon. She had dreamed that he stood before her door and knocked. But finding no response, he again in a moment withdrew, when it was proved that Shulamith did not requite his love and come forth to meet it in its fulness as she ought.

   Ver. 6 I opened to my beloved;
    And my beloved had withdrawn, was gone:
    My soul departed when he spake—
    I sought him, and found him not;
    I called him, and he answered me not.

As the disciples at Emmaus, when the Lord had vanished from the midst of them, said to one another : Did not our heart burn within us when He spake with us ? so Shulamith says that when he spake, *i.e.* sought admission to her, she was filled with alarm, and almost terrified to death. Love-ecstasy (ἐκστῆναι, as contrast to γενέσθαι ἐν ἑαυτῷ) is not to be here understood, for in such a state she would have flown to meet him; but a sinking of the soul, such as is described by Terence (*And.* I. 5. 16):

"*Oratio haec me miseram exanimavit metu.*"

The voice of her beloved struck her heart; but in the consciousness that she had estranged herself from him, she could not openly meet him and offer empty excuses. But now she recognises it with sorrow that she had not replied to the deep impression of his loving words; and seeing him disappear without finding him, she calls after him whom she had slighted, but he answers her not. The words: "My soul departed when he spake," are the reason why she now sought him and called upon him, and they are not a supplementary remark (Zöckl.); nor is there need for the correction of the text בְּדָבְרוֹ, which should mean: (my soul departed) when he turned his back (Ewald), or, behind him (Hitz., Böttch.), from דִּבֵּר = (Arab.) *dabara, tergum vertere, praeterire,*—the Heb. has the word דְּבִיר, the hinder part, and as it appears, דִּבֵּר, to act from behind (treacherously) and destroy, 2 Chron. xxii. 10; cf. under Gen. xxxiv. 13, but not the *Kal* דָּבַר, in that Arab. signification. The meaning of חָמַק has been hit upon by Aquila (ἔκλινεν), Symmachus (ἀπονεύσας), and Jerome (*declinaverat*); it signifies to turn aside, to take a different direction, as the *Hithpa.* Jer. xxxi. 22: to turn oneself away; cf. חַמּוּקִים, turnings, bendings, vii. 2. חָבַק and אָבַק (cf. Gen. xxxii. 25), Aethiop. *ḥakafa,* Amhar. *akafa* (reminding us of נָקַף, *Hiph.* הִקִּיף), are usually compared; all of these, however, signify to "encompass;" but חָמַק does not denote a moving in a circle after something, but a half circular motion away from something; so that in the Arab. the prevailing reference to fools, *aḥamḳ,* does not appear to proceed from the idea of closeness, but of the oblique direction, pushed sideways. Turning himself away, he proceeded farther. In vain she sought him; she called without receiving any answer. עֲנָנִי is the correct pausal form of עֲנָנִי, *vid.* under Ps. cxviii. 5. But something worse than even this seeking and calling in vain happened to her.

> Ver. 7 The watchmen who go about in the city found me,
>   They beat me, wounded me;
>   My upper garment took away from me,
>   The watchmen of the walls.

She sought her beloved, not "in the *midbar*" (open field), nor "in the *kepharim*" (villages), but בעיר, "in the city,"—a circumstance which is fatal to the shepherd-hypothesis here, as in the other dream. There in the city she is found by the watchmen who patrol the city, and have their proper posts on the walls to watch those who approach the city and depart from it (cf. Isa. lxii. 6). These rough, regardless men,—her story returns at the close like a palindrome to those previously named,—who judge only according to that which is external, and have neither an eye nor a heart for the sorrow of a loving soul, struck (הִכָּה, from נָכָה, to pierce, hit, strike) and wounded (פָּצַע, R. פְּ, to divide, to inflict wounds in the flesh) the royal spouse as a common woman, and so treated her, that, in order to escape being made a prisoner, she was constrained to leave her upper robe in their hands (Gen. xxxix. 12). This upper robe, not the veil which at iv. 1, 3 we found was called *tsammā*, is called רְדִיד. Aben Ezra compares with it the Arab. *ridâ*, a plaid-like over-garment, which was thrown over the shoulders and veiled the upper parts of the body. But the words have not the same derivation. The *ridâ* has its name from its reaching downward,—probably from the circumstance that, originally, it hung down to the feet, so that one could tread on it; but the (Heb.) *rᵉdid* (in Syr. the *dalmatica* of the deacons), from רָדַד, *Hiph.*, 1 Kings vi. 32, Targ., Talm., Syr., רְדַד, to make broad and thin, as *expansum*, *i.e.* a thin and light upper robe, viz. over the *cuttonĕth*, 3*a*. The LXX. suitably translates it here and at Gen. xxiv. 65 (*hatstsäiph*, from *tsa'aph*, to lay together, to fold, to make double or many-fold) by θέριστρον, a summer overdress. A modern painter, who represents Shulamith as stripped naked by the watchmen, follows his own sensual taste, without being able to distinguish between *tunica* and *pallium*; for neither Luther, who renders by *schleier* (veil), nor Jerome, who has *pallium* (cf. the saying of Plautus: *tunica propior pallio est*), gives any countenance to such a freak of imagination. The city watchmen tore from off her the upper garment, without knowing and without caring to know what might be the motive and the aim of this her nocturnal walk.

All this Shulamith dreamed; but the painful feeling of repentance, of separation and misapprehension, which the dream left behind, entered as deeply into her soul as if it had been an actual external experience. Therefore she besought the daughters of Jerusalem:

> Ver. 8 I adjure you, ye daughters of Jerusalem,
> If ye find my beloved,—
> What shall ye then say to him?
> " That I am sick of love."

That אִם is here not to be interpreted as the negative particle of adjuration (Böttch.), as at ii. 7, iii. 5, at once appears from the absurdity arising from such an interpretation. The *or. directa*, following " I adjure you," can also begin (Num. v. 19 f.) with the usual אִם, which is followed by its conclusion. Instead of " that ye say to him I am sick of love," she asks the question : What shall ye say to him ? and adds the answer : *quod aegra sum amore*, or, as Jerome rightly renders, in conformity with the root-idea of חלה : *quia amore langueo ;* while, on the other hand, the LXX. : ὅτι τετρωμένη (*saucia*) ἀγάπης ἐγώ εἰμι, as if the word were חֲלָלַת, from חָלָל. The question proposed, with its answer, inculcates in a naive manner that which is to be said, as one examines beforehand a child who has to order something. She turns to the daughters of Jerusalem, because she can presuppose in them, in contrast with those cruel watchmen, a sympathy with her love-sorrow, on the ground of their having had similar experiences. They were also witnesses of the origin of this covenant of love, and graced the marriage festival by their sympathetic love. When, therefore, they put to her the question :

> Ver. 9 What is thy beloved before another (beloved),
> Thou fairest of women ?
> What is thy beloved before another (beloved),
> That thou dost adjure us thus ?

the question thus asked cannot proceed from ignorance ; it can only have the object of giving them the opportunity of hearing from Shulamith's own mouth and heart her laudatory description of him, whom they also loved, although they were not deemed worthy to stand so near to him as she did who was thus questioned. Böttch. and Ewald, secs. 325*a*, 326*a*, interpret the מָן in מִדּוֹד partitively : *quid amati* (as in Cicero : *quod hominis*) *amatus tuus ;* but then the words would have been מַה־מִדּוֹד דּוֹדֵךְ, if such a phrase were admissible ; for מַה־דּוֹד certainly of itself alone means *quid amati*, what kind of a beloved. Thus the מִן is the comparative (*prae amato*), and דּוֹד the sing., representing the idea of species or kind ; מִדּוֹדִים, here easily misunderstood, is purposely avoided. The use of the form הִשְׁבַּעְתָּנוּ for הִשְׁבַּעְתִּינוּ is one of the many instances of the disregard of the generic distinction occurring in this Song, which purposely, after the manner of the vulgar language, ignores pedantic regularity.

Hereupon Shulamith describes to them who ask what her beloved is. He is the fairest of men. Everything that is glorious in the kingdom of nature, and, so far as her look extends, everything in the sphere of art, she appropriates, so as to present a picture of his external appearance. Whatever is precious, lovely, and grand, is

all combined in the living beauty of his person.[1] She first praises
the mingling of colours in the countenance of her beloved,

Ver. 10 My beloved is dazzlingly white and ruddy,
Distinguished above ten thousand.

The verbal root צח has the primary idea of purity, i.e. freedom from
disturbance and muddiness, which, in the stems springing from it,
and in their manifold uses, is transferred to undisturbed health
(Arab. ṣaḥḥ, cf. baria, of smoothness of the skin), a temperate stomach
and clear head, but particularly to the clearness and sunny brightness of the heavens, to dazzling whiteness (צָחַח, Lam. iv. 7; cf.
צָחַר), and then to parched dryness, resulting from the intense and
continued rays of the sun; צַח is here adj. from צָחַח, Lam. iv. 7,
bearing almost the same relation to לָבָן as λαμπρός to λευκός, cogn.
with lucere. אָדוֹם, R. דם, to condense, is properly dark-red, called by
the Turks kuju kirmesi (from kuju, thick, close, dark), by the French
rouge foncé, of the same root as דָּם, the name for blood, or a thick
and dark fluid. White, and indeed a dazzling white, is the colour
of his flesh, and redness, deep redness, the colour of his blood tinging
his flesh. Whiteness among all the race-colours is the one which
best accords with the dignity of man; pure delicate whiteness is
among the Caucasian races a mark of high rank, of superior training,
of hereditary nobility; wherefore, Lam. iv. 7, the appearance of the
nobles of Jerusalem is likened in whiteness to snow and milk, in
redness to corals; and Homer, Il. iv. 141, says of Menelaus that he
appeared stained with gore, " as when some woman tinges ivory with
purple colour." In this mingling of white and red, this fulness of
life and beauty, he is דָּגוּל, distinguished above myriads. The old
translators render dagul by " chosen " (Aquila, Symm., Syr., Jerome,
Luther), the LXX. by ἐκλελοχισμένος, e cohorte selectus; but it means
"bannered " (degel, ii. 4), as the Venet.: σεσημαιωμένος, i.e. thus
distinguished, as that which is furnished with a degel, a banner, a
pennon. Grätz takes dagul as the Greek σημειωτός (noted). With
רְבָבָה, as a designation of an inconceivable number, Rashi rightly
compares Ezek. xvi. 7. Since the " ten thousand " are here thought
of, not in the same manner as דְּגוּלִים, the particle min is not the
compar. magis quam, but, as at Gen. iii. 14, Judg. v. 24, Isa. lii. 14,
prae, making conspicuous (cf. Virgil, Aen. v. 435, prae omnibus

---

[1] Hengstenberg finds in this eulogium, on the supposition that Solomon is the
author, and is the person who is here described, incomprehensible self-praise. But
he does not certainly say all this immediately of himself, but puts it into the mouth
of Shulamith, whose love he gained. But love idealizes; she sees him whom she
loves, not as others see him,—she sees him in her own transforming light.

unum). After this praise of the bright blooming countenance, which in general distinguished the personal appearance of her beloved, so far as it was directly visible, there now follows a detailed description, beginning with his head.

Ver. 11 His head is precious fine gold,
His locks hill upon hill,
Black as the raven.

The word-connection כֶּתֶם פָּז, occurring only here, serves as a designation of the very finest pure gold; for כֶּתֶם (hiding, then that which is hidden), from כתם, R. כת (*vid.* concerning the words appertaining to this root, under Ps. lxxxvii. 6), is the name of fine gold, which was guarded as a jewel (cf. Prov. xxv. 12), and פָּז (with long *ā*) is pure gold freed from inferior metals, from פָּזַז, to set free, and generally violently to free (cf. *zahav muphaz,* 1 Kings x. 18, with *zahav tahor,* 2 Chron. ix. 17). The Targ. to the Hagiog. translate פז by אוֹבְרִיזָא (*e.g.* Ps. cxix. 127), or אוֹבְרִיזִין (*e.g.* Ps. xix. 11), ὄβρυζον, *i.e.* gold which has stood the fire-proof (*obrussa*) of the cupel or the crucible. Grammatically regarded, the word-connection *kethem paz* is not genit., like *kethem ophir,* but appositional, like *naarah bᵉthulah,* Deut. xxii. 28, *zᵉvahim shᵉlamim,* Ex. xxiv. 5, etc. The point of comparison is the imposing nobility of the fine form and noble carriage of his head. In the description of the locks of his hair the LXX. render תלתלים by ἐλάται, Jerome by *sicut elatae palmarum,* like the young twigs, the young shoots of the palm. Ewald regards it as a harder parall. form of זַלְזַלִּים, Isa. xviii. 15, vine-branches; and Hitzig compares the *Thousand and One Nights,* iii. 180, where the loose hair of a maiden is likened to twisted clusters of grapes. The possibility of this meaning is indisputable, although (Arab.) *taltalat,* a drinking-vessel made of the inner bark of palm-branches, is named, not from *taltalah,* as the name of the palm-branch, but from *taltala,* to shake down, viz. in the throat. The palm-branch, or the vine-branch, would be named from תִּלְתֵּל, *pendulum esse,* to hang loosely and with a wavering motion, the freq. of תָּלָה, *pendere.* The Syr. also think on תלה, for it translates "spread out," *i.e.* waving downward; and the Venet., which translates by ἀπαιωρήματα. The point of comparison would be the freshness and flexibility of the abundant long hair of the head, in contrast to motionless close-lying smoothness. One may think of Jupiter, who, when he shakes his head, moves heaven and earth. But, as against this, we have the fact: (1) That the language has other names for palm-branches and vine-branches; the former are called in the Song vii. 9, *sansinnim.* (2) That תלתלים, immediately referred to the hair, but not in the sense of "hanging locks" (Böttch.), is still in use in the post-bibl. Heb. (*vid.* under v. 2*b*) ; the Targ. also, in translating דְּגוּרִין דְּגוּרִין, *cumuli cumuli*, thinks תִּלִּין תִּלִּין = תלחלים, Menachoth 29*b*. A hill is called תֵּל, (Arab.) *tall*, from תָּלַל, *prosternere*, to throw along, as of earth thrown out, sand, or rubbish ; and תַּלְתַּל, after the form גַּלְגַּל, in use probably only in the plur., is a hilly country which rises like steps, or presents an undulating appearance. Seen from his neck upwards, his hair forms in undulating lines, hill upon hill. In colour, these locks of hair are black as a raven, which bears the Semitic name עוֹרֵב from its blackness (עָרַב), but in India is called *kârava* from its croaking. The raven-blackness of the hair contrasts with the whiteness and redness of the countenance, which shines forth as from a dark ground, from a black border. The eyes are next described.

Ver. 12 His eyes like doves by the water-brooks,
Bathing in milk, stones beautifully set

The eyes in their glancing moistness (cf. ὑγρότης τῶν ὀμμάτων, in Plutarch, of a languishing look), and in the movement of their pupils, are like doves which sip at the water-brooks, and move to and fro beside them. אָפִיק, from אָפַק, *continere*, is a watercourse, and then also the water itself flowing in it (*vid.* under Ps. xviii. 16), as (Arab.) *wadin*, a valley, and then the river flowing in the valley, *bahr*, the sea-basin (properly the cleft), and then also the sea itself. The pred. "bathing" refers to the eyes (cf. iv. 9), not to the doves, if this figure is continued. The pupils of the eyes, thus compared with doves, seem as if bathing in milk, in that they swim, as it were, in the white in the eye. But it is a question whether the figure of the doves is continued also in יֹשְׁבוֹת עַל־מִלֵּאת. It would be the case if *milleth* meant "fulness of water," as it is understood, after the example of the LXX., also by Aquila (ἐκχύσεις), Jerome (*fluenta plenissima*), and the Arab. (*piscinas aqua refertas*); among the moderns, by Döpke, Gesen., Hengst., and others. But this pred. would then bring nothing new to 12*a;* and although in the Syr. derivatives from ܡܶܠܳܐ signify flood and high waters, yet the form *milleth* does not seem, especially without מַיִם, to be capable of bearing this significa- tion. Luther's translation also, although in substance correct : *vnd stehen in der fülle* (and stand in fulness) (*milleth*, like שַׁלְמוּתָא of the Syr., πληρώσεως of the Gr. Venet., still defended by Hitz.), yet does not bring out the full force of *milleth*, which, after the analogy of כַּפָּא, רִצְפָּה, appears to have a concrete signification which is seen from a comparison of Ex. xxv. 7, xxvii. 17, 20, xxxix. 13. There מִלֻּאָה and מִלֻּאִים signify not the border with precious stones, but, as rightly maintained by Keil, against Knobel, their filling in, *i.e.* their bordering, setting. Accordingly, *milleth* will be a synon. technical expression : the description, passing from the figure of the dove, says further of the eyes, that they are firm on (in) their setting ; עַל is suitable, for the precious stone is laid within the casket in which it is contained. Hitzig has, on the contrary, objected that מִלֵּאָה and מִלֵּאִים denote filling up, and thus that *milleth* cannot be a filling up, and still less the place thereof. But as in the Talm. מוּלְיָתָא signifies not only fulness, but also stuffed fowls or pies, and as πλήρωμα in its manifold aspects is used not only of that with which anything is filled, but also of that which is filled (*e.g.* of a ship that is manned, and Eph. i. 23 of the church in which Christ, as in His body, is immanent),—thus also *milleth*, like the German " *Fassung*," may be used of a ring-casket (*funda* or *pala*) in which the precious stone is put. That the eyes are like a precious stone in its casket, does not merely signify that they fill the sockets,—for the *bulbus* of the eye in every one fills the *orbita*,—but that they are not sunk like the eyes of one who is sick, which fall back on their supporting edges in the *orbita,* and that they appear full and large as they press forward from wide and open eyelids. The cheeks are next described.

> Ver. 13*a* His cheeks like a bed of sweet herbs,
> Towers of spicy plants.

A flower-bed is called עֲרוּגָה, from עָרַג, to be oblique, inclined. His cheeks are like such a soft raised bed, and the impression their appearance makes is like the fragrance which flows from such a bed planted with sweet-scented flowers. *Mig°daloth* are the tower-like or pyramidal mounds, and *merkahhim* are the plants used in spicery. The point of comparison here is thus the soft elevation ; perhaps with reference to the mingling of colours, but the word chosen (*merkahhim*) rather refers to the lovely, attractive, heart-refreshing character of the impression. The Venet., keeping close to the existing text : αἱ σιαγόνες αὐτοῦ ὡς πρασιὰ τοῦ ἀρώματος, πύργοι ἀρωμα-τισμῶν (thus (not ἀρωματιστῶν) according to Gebhardt's just conjecture). But is the punctuation here correct? The sing. כַּעֲרוּנַת is explained from this, that the bed is presented as sloping from its height downward on two parallel sides ; but the height would then be the nose dividing the face, and the plur. would thus be more suitable ; and the LXX., Symm., and other ancient translators have, in fact, read כַּעֲרוּנוֹת. But still less is the phrase *migd°loth merkah-him* to be comprehended ; for a tower, however diminutive it may be, is not a proper figure for a soft elevation, nor even a gradu-ated flowery walk, or a terraced flowery hill, — a tower always presents, however round one may conceive it, too much the idea of a natural chubbiness, or of a diseased tumour. Therefore the expression used by the LXX., φύουσαι μυρεψικά, i.e. 'מַנְדִּלוֹת מרק, commends itself. Thus also Jerome : *sicut areolae aromatum consitae a pigmentariis*, and the Targ. (which refers לְחָיַם allegorically to the לוּחֵי of the law, and *merkahhim* to the refinements of the Halacha): "like the rows of a garden of aromatic plants which produce (*gignentes*) deep, penetrating sciences, even as a (magnificent) garden, aromatic plants." Since we read כָּערוֹגת מַנְדִּלוֹת, we do not refer *migadloth*, as Hitzig, who retains כָּערוּנַת, to the cheeks, although their name, like that of the other members (*e.g.* the ear, hand, foot), may be fem. (Böttch. § 649), but to the beds of spices; but in this carrying forward of the figure we find, as he does, a reference to the beard and down on the cheeks. גָּדֵל is used of suffering the hair to grow, Num. vi. 5, as well as of cultivating plants; and it is a similar figure when Pindar, *Nem.* v. 11, compares the milk-hair of a young man to the fine woolly down of the expanding vine-leaves (*vid.* Passow). In *merkahhim* there scarcely lies anything further than that this *flos juventae* on the blooming cheeks gives the impression of the young shoots of aromatic plants; at all events, the *merkahhim*, even although we refer this feature in the figure to the fragrance of the unguents on the beard, are not the perfumes themselves, to which *m'gadloth* is not appropriate, but fragrant plants, so that in the first instance the growth of the beard is in view with the impression of its natural beauty.

Ver. 13*b* His lips lilies,
> Dropping with liquid myrrh.

Lilies, viz. red lilies (*vid.* under ii. 1), unless the point of comparison is merely loveliness associated with dignity. She thinks of the lips as speaking. All that comes forth from them, the breath in itself, and the breath formed into words, is מוֹר עֹבֵר, most precious myrrh, viz. such as of itself wells forth from the bark of the *balsamodendron*. עֹבֵר, the running over of the eyes (cf. *myrrha in lacrimis*, the most highly esteemed sort, as distinguished from *myrrha in granis*), with which Dillmann combines the Aethiop. name for myrrh, *karbê* (*vid.* under v. 5).

Ver. 14*a* His hands golden cylinders,
> Filled in with stones of Tarshish.

The figure, according to Gesen., *Heb. Wörterbuch*, and literally also Heilgst., is derived from the closed hand, and the stained nails are compared to precious stones. Both statements are incorrect; for (1) although it is true that then Israelitish women, as at the present day Egyptian and Arabian women, stained their eyes with *stibium* (*vid.*

under Isa. liv. 11), yet it is nowhere shown that they, and particularly men, stained the nails of their feet and their toes with the
orange-yellow of the Alhenna (Lane's *Egypt*, I. 33–35); and (2)
the word used is not כַּפָּיו, but יָדָיו; it is thus the outstretched hands
that are meant; and only these, not the closed fist, could be compared
to "lilies," for גָּלִיל signifies not a ring (Cocc., Döpke, Böttch., etc.),
but that which is rolled up, a roller, cylinder (Esth. i. 6), from גָּלַל,
which properly means not κυκλοῦν (Venet., after Gebhardt: κεκυκλω-
μέναι), but κυλίνδειν. The hands thus are meant in respect of the
fingers, which on account of their noble and fine form, their full,
round, fleshy mould, are compared to bars of gold formed like rollers,
garnished (מְמֻלָּאִים, like מִלֵּא, Ex. xxviii. 17) with stones of Tarshish,
to which the nails are likened. The transparent horn-plates of the
nails, with the *lunula*, the white segment of a circle at their roots, are
certainly, when they are beautiful, an ornament to the hand, and,
without our needing to think of their being stained, are worthily
compared to the gold-yellow topaz. *Tarshish* is not the onyx, which
derives its Heb. name שֹׁהַם from its likeness to the finger-nail, but
the χρυσόλιθος, by which the word in this passage before us is
translated by the Quinta and the Sexta, and elsewhere also by the
LXX. and Aquila. But the chrysolite is the precious stone which
is now called the topaz. It receives the name *Tarshish* from Spain,
the place where it was found. Pliny, xxxviii. 42, describes it as
aureo fulgore tralucens. Bredow erroneously interprets *Tarshish* of
amber. There is a kind of chrysolite, indeed, which is called *chrys-
electron*, because *in colorem electri declinans*. The comparison of the
nails to such a precious stone (Luther, influenced by the consonance,
and apparently warranted by the *plena hyacinthis* of the Vulg., has
substituted golden rings, *vol Türkissen*, whose blue-green colour is
not suitable here), in spite of Hengst., who finds it insipid, is as true
to nature as it is tender and pleasing. The description now proceeds from the uncovered to the covered parts of his body, the
whiteness of which is compared to ivory and marble.

Ver. 14b His body an ivory work of art,
Covered with sapphires.

The plur. מֵעִים or מֵעַיִם, from מֵעָה or מְעִי (*vid.* under Ps. xl. 9), signifies properly the tender parts, and that the inward parts of the body,
but is here, like the Chald. מְעִין, Dan. ii. 32, and the בְּטֵן, vii. 3,
which also properly signifies the inner part of the body, κοιλία,
transferred to the body in its outward appearance. To the question
how Shulamith should in such a manner praise that which is for
the most part covered with clothing, it is not only to be answered

that it is the poet who speaks by her mouth, but also that it is not
the bride or the beloved, but the wife, whom he represents as thus
speaking. עָשָׂה (from the peculiar Hebraeo-Chald. and Targ. עֲשַׁת,
which, after Jer. v. 28, like *khalak*, *creare*, appears to proceed from
the fundamental idea of smoothing) designates an artistic figure.
Such a figure was Solomon's throne, made of שֵׁן, the teeth of
elephants, ivory,[1] 1 Kings x. 18. Here Solomon's own person,
without reference to a definite admired work of art, is praised as
being like an artistic figure made of ivory, — like it in regard
to its glancing smoothness and its fine symmetrical form. When,
now, this work of art is described as covered with sapphires
(מְעֻלֶּפֶת, referred to עָשָׂה, as apparently gramm., or as ideal, fem.),
a sapphire-coloured robe is not meant (Hitzig, Ginsburg); for עלף,
which only means to disguise, would not at all be used of such a
robe (Gen. xxxviii. 14; cf. xxiv. 65), nor would the one uniform
colour of the robe be designated by sapphires in the plur. The choice
of the verb עלף (elsewhere used of veiling) indicates a covering
shading the pure white, and in connection with סַפִּירִים, thought of
as accus., a moderating of the bright glance by a soft blue. For
ספיר (a genuine Semit. word, like the Chald. שַׁפִּיר; cf. regarding
שָׁפַר = סָפַר, under Ps. xvi. 6) is the sky-blue sapphire (Ex. xxiv. 10),
including the *Lasurstein* (*lapis lazuli*), sprinkled with golden, or
rather with gold-like glistening points of pyrites, from which, with the
l omitted, sky-blue is called *azur* (azure) (*vid.* under Job xxviii. 6).
The work of art formed of ivory is quite covered over with sapphires
fixed in it. That which is here compared is nothing else than the
branching blue veins under the white skin.

> Ver. 15a His legs white marble columns,
> Set on bases of fine gold.

If the beauty of the living must be represented, not by colours, but
in figurative language, this cannot otherwise be done than by the
selection of minerals, plants, and things in general for the comparison, and the comparison must more or less come short, because dead
soulless matter does not reach to a just and full representation of
the living. Thus here, also, the description of the lower extremity,
which reaches from the thighs and the legs down to the feet, of which
last, in the words of an anatomist,[2] it may be said that "they form
the pedestal for the bony pillars of the legs." The comparison is
thus in accordance with fact; the שׁוֹקַיִם (from שׁוּק = (Arab.) *sak*, to

---

[1] Ivory is fully designated by the name שֶׁנְהַבִּים, Lat. *ebur*, from the Aegypt.
ebu, the Aegypto-Indian *ibha*, elephant.

[2] Hyrtl's *Lehrbuch der Anat. des Menschen*, sec. 155.

drive : the movers forward), in the structure of the human frame, take
in reality the place of "pillars," and the feet the place of "pedes-
tals," as in the tabernacle the wooden pillars rested on small supports
in which they were fastened, Ex. xxvi. 18 f.   But in point of
fidelity to nature, the symbol is inferior to a rigid Egyptian figure.
Not only is it without life ; it is not even capable of expressing the
curvilinear shape which belongs to the living.   On the other hand,
it loses itself in symbol; for although it is in conformity with
nature that the legs are compared to pillars of white (according to
Aquila and Theod., Parian) marble,—שֵׁשׁ = שֵׁישׁ, 1 Chron. xxix. 2
(material for the building of the temple), Talm. מַרְמְרָא, of the same
verbal root as שׁוֹשָׁן, the name of the white lily,—the comparison of
the feet to bases of fine gold is yet purely symbolical.   Gold is a
figure of that which is sublime and noble, and with white marble
represents greatness combined with purity.   He who is here praised
is not a shepherd, but a king.   The comparisons are thus so grand
because the beauty of the beloved is in itself heightened by his
kingly dignity.[1]

Ver. 15. His aspect like Lebanon,
Distinguished as the cedars.

By בָּחוּר the Chald. thinks of "a young man" (from בָּחַר = בָּגַר, to be
matured, as at Ps. lxxxix. 20); but in that case we should have
expected the word כָּאֶרֶז instead of כָּאֲרָזִים.   Luther, with all other
translators, rightly renders "chosen as the cedars."   His look, i.e.
his appearance as a whole, is awe-inspiring, majestic, like Lebanon,
the king of mountains ; he (the praised one) is chosen, i.e. presents
a rare aspect, rising high above the common man, like the cedars,
those kings among trees, which as special witnesses of creative
omnipotence are called " cedars of God," Ps. lxxx. 11 [10].   בָּחוּר,
electus, everywhere else an attribute of persons, does not here refer
to the look, but to him whose the look is ; and what it means in
union with the cedars is seen from Jer. xxii. 7 ; cf. Isa. xxxvii. 24.
Here also it is seen (what besides is manifest), that the fairest of the
children of men is a king.   In conclusion, the description returns
from elevation of rank to loveliness.

[1] Dillmann proposes the question, the answer to which he desiderates in Ewald,
how the maiden could be so fluent in speaking of the new glories of the Solomonic
era (plants and productions of art).   Böttcher answers, that she had learned to know
these whilst detained at court, and that the whole description has this ground-
thought, that she possessed in her beloved all the splendour which the women of the
harem value and enjoy.   But already the first words of the description, " white
and ruddy," exclude the sunburnt shepherd.   To refer the gold, in the figurative
description of the uncovered parts of the body, to this bronze colour is insipid.

Ver. 16*a* His palate is sweets [sweetnesses],
And he is altogether precious [lovelinesses].

The palate, חֵךְ, is frequently named as the organ of speech, Job vi. 30, xxxi. 30, Prov. v. 3, viii. 7 ; and it is also here used in this sense. The meaning, "the mouth for kissing," which Böttch. gives to the word, is fanciful ; חֵךְ (=*hink,* Arab. *ḥanak*) is the inner palate and the region of the throat, with the *uvula* underneath the chin. Partly with reference to his words, his lips have been already praised, 13*b ;* but there the fragrance of his breath came into consideration, his breath both in itself and as serving for the formation of articulate words. But the naming of the palate can point to nothing else than his words. With this the description comes to a conclusion; for, from the speech, the most distinct and immediate expression of the personality, advance is made finally to the praise of the person. The *pluraliatant.* מַמְתַקִּים and מַחֲמַדִּים designate what they mention in richest fulness. His palate, *i.e.* that which he speaks and the manner in which he speaks it, is true sweetness (cf. Prov. xvi. 21 ; Ps. lv. 15), and his whole being true loveliness. With justifiable pride Shulamith next says :

Ver. 16*b* This is my beloved and this my friend,
Ye daughters of Jerusalem !

The emphatically repeated "this" is here pred. (Luth.: "such an one is " . . .); on the other hand, it is subj. at Ex. iii. 15 (Luth.: "that is " . . .).

The daughters of Jerusalem now offer to seek along with Shulamith for her beloved, who had turned away and was gone.

Chap. vi. 1. Whither has thy beloved gone,
Thou fairest of women ?
Whither has thy beloved turned,
That we may seek him with thee ?

The longing remains with her even after she has wakened, as the after effect of her dream. In the morning she goes forth and meets with the daughters of Jerusalem. They cause Shulamith to describe her friend, and they ask whither he has gone. They wish to know the direction in which he disappeared from her, the way which he had probably taken (פנה, R. פן, to drive, to urge forward, to turn from one to another), that with her they might go to seek him (*Vav* of the consequence or the object, as at Ps. lxxxiii. 17). The answer she gives proceeds on a conclusion which she draws from the inclination of her beloved.

> Ver. 2 My beloved has gone down into the garden,
> To the beds of sweet herbs,
> To feed in the gardens
> And gather lilies.

He is certainly, she means to say, there to be found where he
delights most to tarry. He will have gone down—viz. from the
palace (vi. 11 ; cf. 1 Kings xx. 43 and Esth. vii. 7)—into his garden,
to the fragrant beds, there to feed in his garden and gather lilies
(cf. Old Germ. "to collect *rôsen*") ; he is fond of gardens and flowers.
Shulamith expresses this in her shepherd-dialect, as when Jesus
says of His Father (John xv. 1), " He is the husbandman." Flower-
beds are the feeding place (*vid.* regarding לְרָעוֹת under ii. 16) of her
beloved. Solomon certainly took great delight in gardens and
parks, Eccles. ii. 5. But this historical fact is here idealized ; the
natural flora which Solomon delighted in with intelligent interest
presents itself as a figure of a higher Loveliness which was therein
as it were typically manifest (cf. Rev. vii. 17, where the " Lamb,"
" feeding," and " fountains of water," are applied as anagogics, *i.e.*
heavenward-pointing types). Otherwise it is not to be comprehended why it is lilies that are named. Even if it were supposed
to be implied that lilies were Solomon's favourite flowers, we must
assume that his taste was determined by something more than by
form and colour. The words of Shulamith give us to understand
that the inclination and the favourite resort of her friend corre-
sponded to his nature, which is altogether thoughtfulness and depth
of feeling (cf. under Ps. xcii. 5, the reference to Dante : the beautiful
women who gather flowers representing the paradisaical life) ; lilies,
the emblems of unapproachable grandeur, purity inspiring reverence,
high elevation above that which is common, bloom there wherever
the lily-like one wanders, whom the lily of the valley calls her own.
With the words :

> Ver. 3 I am my beloved's, and my beloved is mine,
> Who feeds among the lilies,

Shulamith farther proceeds, followed by the daughters of Jerusalem, to
seek her friend lost through her own fault. She always says, not אִישׁ,
but דּוֹדִי and רֵעִי ; for love, although a passion common to mind and
body, is in this Song of Songs viewed as much as possible apart
from its basis in the animal nature. Also, that the description
hovers between that of the clothed and the unclothed, gives to it an
ideality favourable to the mystical interpretation. Nakedness is
עֶרְוָה. But at the cross nakedness appears transported from the
sphere of sense to that of the supersensuous.

SECOND SCENE OF THE FOURTH ACT, VI. 4–9.

With ver. 4 Solomon's address is resumed, and a new scene opens. Shulamith had found him again, and she who is beautiful in herself appears now so much the more beautiful, when the joy of seeing him again irradiates her whole being.

> Ver. 4 Beautiful art thou, my friend, as Tirzah,
> Comely as Jerusalem,
> Terrible as a battle-array.

In the praise of her beauty we hear the voice of the king. The cities which are the highest ornament of his kingdom serve him as the measure of her beauty, which is designated according to the root conceptions by יָפֶה, after the quality of completeness; by נָאוָה, after the quality of that which is well-becoming, pleasing. It is concluded, from the prominence given to Tirzah, that the Song was not composed till after the division of the kingdom, and that its author was an inhabitant of the northern kingdom; for Tirzah was the first royal city of this kingdom till the time of Omri, the founder of Samaria. But since, at all events, it is Solomon who here speaks, so great an historical judgment ought surely to be ascribed to a later poet who has imagined himself in the exact position of Solomon, that he would not represent the king of the undivided Israel as speaking like a king of the separate kingdom of Israel. The prominence given to Tirzah has another reason. Tirzah was discovered by Robinson on his second journey, 1852, in which Van de Velde accompanied him, on a height in the mountain range to the north of Nablûs, under the name *Tullûzah*. Brocardus and Breydenbach had already pointed out a village called *Thersa* to the east of Samaria. This form of the name corresponds to the Heb. better than that Arab. *Tullûzah*; but the place is suitable, and if Tullûzah lies high and beautiful in a region of olive trees, then it still justifies its ancient name, which means pleasantness or sweetness. But it cannot be sweetness on account of which Tirzah is named before Jerusalem, for in the eye of the Israelites Jerusalem was " the perfection of beauty " (Ps. l. 2; Lam. ii. 15). That there is gradation from Tirzah to Jerusalem (Hengst.) cannot be said; for נָאוָה (*decora*) and יפה (*pulchra*) would be reversed if a climax were intended. The reason of it is rather this, that Shulamith is from the higher region, and is not a daughter of Jerusalem, and that therefore a beautiful city situated in the north toward Sunem must serve as a comparison of her beauty. That Shulamith is both beautiful and terrible (אֲיֻמָּה from אָיֹם) is no contradiction : she is terrible in the irresistible power of the impression of her personality, terrible as *nidgaloth, i.e.* as troops going forth with their banners unfurled (cf. the *Kal* of this *v. denom.*, Ps. xx. 6). We do not need to supply מַחֲנוֹת, which is sometimes fem., Ps. xxv. 3, Gen. xxxii. 9, although the attribute would here be appropriate, Num. ii. 3, cf. x. 5 ; still less צְבָאוֹת, which occurs in the sense of military service, Isa. xl. 2, and a war-expedition, Dan. viii. 12, but not in the sense of war-host, as fem. Much rather *nidgaloth*, thus neut., is meant of bannered hosts, as אֳרָחוֹת (not אֹרַח), Isa. xxi. 13, of those that are marching. War-hosts with their banners, their standards, go forth confident of victory. Such is Shulamith's whole appearance, although she is unconscious of it—a *veni, vidi, vici.* Solomon is completely vanquished by her. But seeking to maintain himself in freedom over against her, he cries out to her:

> Ver. 5*a* Turn away thine eyes from me,
>   For overpoweringly they assail me.

Döpke translates, *ferocire me faciunt ;* Hengst. : they make me proud; but although הִרְהִיב, after Ps. cxxxviii. 3, may be thus used, yet that would be an effect produced by the eyes, which certainly would suggest the very opposite of the request to turn them away. The verb רָהַב means to be impetuous, and to press impetuously against any one; the *Hiph.* is the intens. of this trans. signification of the *Kal :* to press overpoweringly against one, to infuse terror, *terrorem incutere.* The LXX. translates it by ἀναπτεροῦν, which is also used of the effect of terror ("to make to start up"), and the Syr. by *afred,* to put to flight, because *arheb* signifies to put in fear, as also *arhab = khawwaf, terrefacere;* but here the meaning of the verb corresponds more with the sense of رعَب, to be placed in the state of *ro'b, i.e.* of paralyzing terror. If she directed her large, clear, penetrating eyes to him, he must sink his own : their glance is unbearable by him. This peculiar form the praise of her eyes here assumes; but then the description proceeds as at iv. 1*b,* ii. 3*b.* The words used there in praise of her hair, her teeth, and her cheeks, are here repeated.

> Ver. 5*b* Thy hair is like a flock of goats
>   Which repose downwards on Gilead.
>   6 Thy teeth like a flock of lambs
>   Which come up from the washing,
>   All of them bearing twins,
>   And a bereaved one is not among them.
>   7 Like a piece of pomegranate thy temples
>   Behind thy veil.

The repetition is literal, but yet not without change in the expression,—there, 'לֵ מֵהַר, here, מִן־הַגַּל; there, הַקֵּץ, *tonsarum*, here, הָרְחֵ, *agnarum* (Symm., Venet. τῶν ἀμνάδων); for רָחֵל, in its proper signification, is like the Arab. *rachil, richl, richleh,* the female lamb, and particularly the ewe. Hitzig imagines that Solomon here repeats to Shulamith what he had said to another *donna* chosen for marriage, and that the flattery becomes insipid by repetition to Shulamith, as well as also to the reader. But the romance which he finds in the Song is not this itself, but his own palimpsest, in the style of Lucian's transformed ass. The repetition has a morally better reason, and not one so subtle. Shulamith appears to Solomon yet more beautiful than on the day when she was brought to him as his bride. His love is still the same, unchanged; and this both she and the reader or hearer must conclude from these words of praise, repeated now as they were then. There is no one among the ladies of the court whom he prefers to her,—these must themselves acknowledge her superiority.

> Ver. 8 There are sixty queens,
>   And eighty concubines,
>   And virgins without number.
>   9 One is my dove, my perfect one,—
>   The only one of her mother,
>   The choice one of her that bare her.
>   The daughters saw her and called her blessed,—
>   Queens and concubines, and they extolled her.

Even here, where, if anywhere, notice of the difference of gender was to be expected, הֵמָּה stands instead of the more accurate הֵנָּה (*e.g.* Gen. vi. 2). The number of the women of Solomon's court, 1 Kings xi. 3, is far greater (700 wives and 300 concubines); and those who deny the Solomonic authorship of the Song regard the poet, in this particular, as more historical than the historian. On our part, holding as we do the Solomonic authorship of the book, we conclude from these low numbers that the Song celebrates a love-relation of Solomon's at the commencement of his reign: his luxury had not then reached the enormous height to which he, the same Solomon, looks back, and which he designates, Eccles. ii. 8, as *vanitas vanitatum.* At any rate, the number of 60 מְלָכוֹת, *i.e.* legitimate wives of equal rank with himself, is yet high enough; for, according to 2 Chron. xi. 21, Rehoboam had 18 wives and 60 concubines. The 60 occurred before, at iii. 7. If it be a round number, as sometimes, although rarely, *sexaginta* is thus used (Hitzig), it may be reduced only to 51, but not further, especially here, where 80 stands along with it. פִּילֶגֶשׁ (פִּלֶגֶשׁ), Gr. πάλλαξ, παλλακή (Lat. *pellex*), which in the form פִּלַקְתָּא

(פִּלַקְתָא) came back from the Greek to the Aramaic, is a word as yet unexplained. According to the formation, it may be compared to חֶרְמֵשׁ, from חָרַם, to cut off; whence also the harem bears the (Arab.) name *haram*, or the separated *gynaeconitis*, to which access is denied. An ending in *is* (שׁ) is known to the Assyr., but only as an adverbial ending, which, as *'istinis* = לְבַדּו, alone, *solus*, shows is connected with the pron. *su*. These two nouns appear as thus requiring to be referred to *quadrilitera*, with the annexed שׁ; perhaps פלשׁ, in the sense of to break into splinters, from פָּלַל, to divide (whence a brook, as dividing itself in its channels, has the name of פֶּלֶג), points to the polygamous relation as a breaking up of the marriage of one; so that a concubine has the name *pillĕgĕsh*, as a representant of polygamy in contrast to monogamy.

In the first line of ver. 9 אַחַת is subj. (one, who is my dove, my perfect one); in the second line, on the contrary, it is pred. (one, *unica*, is she of her mother). That Shulamith was her mother's only child does not, however, follow from this; אַחַת, *unica*, is equivalent to *unice dilecta*, as יָחִיד, Prov. iv. 3, is equivalent to *unice dilectus* (cf. Keil's *Zech.* xiv. 7). The parall. בָּרָה has its nearest signification *electa* (LXX., Syr., Jerome), not *pura* (Venet.); the fundamental idea of cutting and separating divides itself into the ideas of choosing and purifying. The Aorists, 9*b*, are the only ones in this book; they denote that Shulamith's look had, on the part of the women, this immediate result, that they willingly assigned to her the good fortune of being preferred to them all,—that to her the prize was due. The words, as also at Prov. xxxi. 28, are an echo of Gen. xxx. 13,—the books of the *Chokma* delight in references to Genesis, the book of pre-Israelitish origin. Here, in vers. 8, 9, the distinction between our typical and the allegorical interpretation is correctly seen. The latter is bound to explain what the 60 and the 80 mean, and how the wives, concubines, and "virgins" of the harem are to be distinguished from each other; but what till now has been attempted in this matter has, by reason of its very absurdity or folly, become an easy subject of wanton mockery. But the typical interpretation regards the 60 and the 80, and the unreckoned number, as what their names denote,—viz. favourites, concubines, and serving-maids. But to see an allegory of heavenly things in such a herd of women—a kind of thing which the Book of Genesis dates from the degradation of marriage in the line of Cain—is a profanation of that which is holy. The fact is, that by a violation of the law of God (Deut. xvii. 17), Solomon brings a cloud over the typical representation, which is not at all to be thought of in connection with the Antitype. Solomon, as Jul. Sturm rightly remarks, is not to be considered by himself, but only in his relation to Shulamith. In Christ, on the contrary, is no imperfection; sin remains in the congregation. In the Song, the bride is purer than the bridegroom; but in the fulfilling of the Song this relation is reversed: the bridegroom is purer than the bride.

FIFTH ACT.

SHULAMITH, THE ATTRACTIVELY FAIR BUT HUMBLE PRINCESS.— CHAP. VI. 10–VIII. 4.

FIRST SCENE OF THE FIFTH ACT, VI. 10–VII. 6.

The fourth Act, notwithstanding little disturbances, gives a clear view of the unchanging love of the newly-married pair. This fifth shows how Shulamith, although raised to a royal throne, yet remains, in her childlike disposition and fondness for nature, a lily of the valley. The first scene places us in the midst of the royal gardens. Shulamith comes to view from its recesses, and goes to the daughters of Jerusalem, who, overpowered by the beauty of her heavenly appearance, cry out:

> Ver. 10 Who is this that looketh forth like the morning-red,
> Beautiful as the moon, pure as the sun,
> Terrible as a battle-host?

The question, "Who is this?" is the same as at iii. 6. There, it refers to her who was brought to the king; here, it refers to her who moves in that which is his as her own. There, the "this" is followed by עֹלָה appositionally; here, by הַנִּשְׁקָ֫פָה [looking forth] determ., and thus more closely connected with it; but then indeterm., and thus apposit. predicates follow. The verb שָׁקַף signifies to bend forward, to overhang; whence the *Hiph.* הִשְׁקִיף and *Niph.* נִשְׁקַף, to look out, since in doing so one bends forward (*vid.* under Ps. xiv. 2). The LXX. here translates it by ἐκκύπτουσα, the Venet. by παρακύπτουσα, both of which signify to look toward something with the head inclined forward. The point of comparison is, the rising up from the background: Shulamith breaks through the shades of the garden-grove like the morning-red, the morning dawn; or, also: she comes nearer and nearer, as the morning-red rises behind the mountains, and then fills always the more widely the whole horizon. The Venet. translates ὡς ἑωσφόρος; but the morning star is not שַׁחַר, but בֶּן־שַׁחַר, Isa. xiv. 12; *shaḥar*, properly, the morning - dawn, means, in Heb., not only this, like the Arab. *shahar*, but rather, like the Arab. *fajr*, the morning-red,—*i.e.* the red tinge of the morning mist.   From the morning-red the description proceeds to the moon, yet visible in the morning sky, before the sun has risen.   It is usually called יָרֵחַ, as being yellow; but here it is called לְבָנָה, as being white; as also the sun, which here is spoken of as having risen (Judg. v. 31), is designated not by the word שֶׁמֶשׁ, as the unwearied (Ps. xix. 6*b*, 6*a*), but, on account of the intensity of its warming light (Ps. xix. 7*b*), is called חַמָּה.   These, in the language of poetry, are favourite names of the moon and the sun, because already the primitive meaning of the two other names had disappeared from common use; but with these, definite attributive ideas are immediately connected.   Shulamith appears like the morning-red, which breaks through the darkness; beautiful, like the silver moon, which in soft still majesty shines in the heavens (Job xxxi. 26); pure (*vid.* regarding בָּרוּר, בַּר in this signification: smooth, bright, pure, under Isa. xlix. 2) as the sun, whose light (cf. טָהוֹר with the Aram. טִיהֲרָא, mid-day brightness) is the purest of the pure, imposing as war-hosts with their standards (*vid.* vi. 4*b*).   The answer of her who was drawing near, to this exclamation, sounds homely and childlike:

> Ver. 11 To the nut garden I went down
> To look at the shrubs of the valley,
> To see whether the vine sprouted,
> The pomegranates budded.
> Ver. 12 I knew it not that my soul lifted me up
> To the royal chariots of my people, a noble (one).

In her loneliness she is happy; she finds her delight in quietly moving about in the vegetable world; the vine and the pomegranate, brought from her home, are her favourites.   Her soul—viz. love for Solomon, which fills her soul—raised her to the royal chariots of her people, the royal chariots of a noble (one), where she sits beside the king, who drives the chariot; she knew this, but she also knew it not for what she had become without any cause of her own, that she is without self-elation and without disavowal of her origin.   These are Shulamith's thoughts and feelings, which we think we derive from these two verses without reading between the lines and without refining.   I went down, she says, viz. from the royal palace, cf. vi. 2. Then, further, she speaks of a valley; and the whole sounds rural, so that we are led to think of Etam as the scene. This Etam, romantically (*vid.* Judg. xv. 8 f.) situated, was, as Josephus (*Antt.* viii. 7. 3) credibly informs us, Solomon's Belvedere. " In the royal stables," he says, " so great was the regard for beauty and swiftness, that nowhere else could horses of greater beauty or greater fleetness be found. All had to acknowledge that the appearance of the king's horses was wonderfully pleasing, and that their swiftness was incomparable. Their riders also served as an ornament to them. They were young men in the flower of their age, and were distinguished by their lofty stature and their flowing hair, and by their clothing, which was of Tyrian purple. They every day sprinkled their hair with dust of gold, so that their whole head sparkled when the sun shone upon it. In such array, armed and bearing bows, they formed a body-guard around the king, who was wont, clothed in a white garment, to go out of the city in the morning, and even to drive his chariot. These morning excursions were usually to a certain place which was about sixty stadia from Jerusalem, and which was called Etam ; gardens and brooks made it as pleasant as it was fruitful." This Etam, from whence (the עיטם עֵין [1]) a watercourse, the ruins of which are still visible, supplied the temple with water, has been identified by Robinson with a village called *Artas* (by Lumley called *Urtas*), about a mile and a half to the south of Bethlehem. At the upper end of the winding valley, at a considerable height above the bottom, are three old Solomonic pools,—large, oblong basins of considerable compass placed one behind the other in terraces. Almost at an equal height with the highest pool, at a distance of several hundred steps there is a strong fountain, which is carefully built over, and to which there is a descent by means of stairs inside the building. By it principally were the pools, which are just large reservoirs, fed, and the water was conducted by a subterranean conduit into the upper pool. Riding along the way close to the aqueduct, which stills exists, one sees even at the present day the valley below clothed in rich vegetation ; and it is easy to understand that here there may have been rich gardens and pleasure-grounds (Moritz Lüttke's *Mittheilung*). A more suitable place for this first scene of the fifth Act cannot be thought of ; and what Josephus relates serves remarkably to illustrate not only the description of ver. 11, but also that of ver. 12.

אֱגוֹז is the walnut, *i.e.* the Italian nut tree (*Juglans regia L.*), originally brought from Persia ; the Persian name is *keuz,* Aethiop. *gûz,* Arab. Syr. *gauz* (*gôz*), in Heb. with א prosth., like the Armen. *engus.* גִּנַּת אֱגוֹז is a garden, the peculiar ornament of which is the

[1] According to *Sebachim* 54*b*, one of the highest points of the Holy Land.

fragrant and shady walnut tree; גִּנַּת אֱגוֹזִים would not be a nut
garden, but a garden of nuts, for the plur. signifies, Mishn. *nuces*
(viz. *juglandes = Jovis glandes*, Pliny, xvii. 136, ed. Jan.), as תְּאֵנִים,
figs, in contradistinction to תְּאֵנָה, a fig tree, only the Midrash uses
אֱגוֹזָה here, elsewhere not occurring, of a tree. The object of her
going down was one, viz. to observe the state of the vegetation; but
it was manifold, as expressed in the manifold statements which
follow יָרַדְתִּי. The first object was the nut garden. Then her intention was to observe the young shoots in the valley, which one has
to think of as traversed by a river or brook; for נַחַל, like *Wady*,
signifies both a valley and a valley-brook. The nut garden might
lie in the valley, for the walnut tree is fond of a moderately cool,
damp soil (Joseph. *Bell.* iii. 10. 8). But the אִבֵּי are the young shoots
with which the banks of a brook and the damp valley are usually
adorned in the spring-time. אֵב, shoot, in the Heb. of budding and
growth, in Aram. of the fruit-formation, comes from R. אב, the
weaker power of נב, which signifies to expand and spread from
within outward, and particularly to sprout up and to well forth.
רָאָה בְ signifies here, as at Gen. xxxiv. 1, attentively to observe
something, looking to be fixed upon it, to sink down into it. A
further object was to observe whether the vine had broken out, or
had budded (this is the meaning of פָּרַח, breaking out, to send forth,
R. פר, to break),[1]—whether the pomegranate trees had gained flowers
or flower-buds הֵנֵצוּ, not as Gesen. in his *Thes.* and *Heb. Lex.* states, the
Hiph. of נוץ, which would be הֵנִיצוּ, but from נָצַץ instead of הֵנֵצּוּ, with
the same omission of *Dagesh*, after the forms הֵפֵרוּ, הֵרֵעוּ, cf. Prov. vii. 13,
R. נס נץ, to glance, bloom (whence *Nisan* as the name of the flower-
month, as *Ab* the name of the fruit-month).[2] Why the pomegranate
tree (*Punica granatum L.*), which derives this its Latin name from
its fruit being full of grains, bears the Semitic name of רִמּוֹן, (Arab.)
rummân, is yet unexplained; the Arabians are so little acquainted
with it, that they are uncertain whether *ramm* or *raman* (which,
however, is not proved to exist) is to be regarded as the root-word.
The question goes along with that regarding the origin and signification of *Rimmon*, the name of the Syrian god, which appears to denote[3]
" sublimity;" and it is possible that the pomegranate tree has its
name from this god as being consecrated to him.[4]

---

[1] *Vid.* Fried. Delitzsch, *Indo-Germ. Sem. Studien*, p. 72.

[2] Cf. my *Jesurun*, p. 149.

[3] An old Chald. king is called *Rim-Sin; rammu* is common in proper names, as *Ab-rammu.*

[4] The name scarcely harmonizes with רִמָּה, worm, although the pomegranate

In ver. 12, Shulamith adds that, amid this her quiet delight in contemplating vegetable life, she had almost forgotten the position to which she had been elevated. לֹא יָדַעְתִּי may, according to the connection in which it is used, mean, " I know not," Gen. iv. 9, xxi. 26, as well as " I knew not," Gen. xxviii. 16, Prov. xxiii. 35 ; here the latter (LXX., Aquila, Jerome, Venet., Luther), for the expression runs parallel to ירדתי, and is related to it as verifying or circumstantiating it. The connection לֹא יד' נפשי, whether we take the word נפשי as permut. of the subject (Luther: My soul knew it not) or as the accus. of the object : I knew not myself (after Job ix. 21), is objectionable, because it robs the following שָׂמַתְנִי of its subject, and makes the course of thought inappropriate. The accusative, without doubt, hits on what is right, since it gives the *Rebia*, corresponding to our colon, to יָד' ; for that which follows with נַפְשִׁי שָׂמ' is just what she acknowledges not to have known or considered. For the meaning cannot be that her soul had placed or brought her in an unconscious way, *i.e.* involuntarily or unexpectedly, etc., for " I knew not," as such a declaration never forms the principal sentence, but, according to the nature of the case, always a subordinate sentence, and that either as a conditional clause with *Vav*, Job ix. 5, or as a relative clause, Isa. xlvii. 11 ; cf. Ps. xlix. 21. Thus " I knew not " will be followed by what she was unconscious of ; it follows in *oratio directa* instead of *obliqua*, as also elsewhere after כִּי יֵדַע, elsewhere introducing the object of knowledge, is omitted, Ps. ix. 21 ; Amos v. 12. But if it remains unknown to her, if it has escaped her consciousness that her soul placed her, etc., then *naphshi* is here her own self, and that on the side of desire (Job xxiii. 13 ; Deut. xii. 15) ; thus, in contrast to external constraint, her own most inward impulse, the leading of her heart. Following this, she has been placed on the height on which she now finds herself, without being always mindful of it. It would certainly now be most natural to regard מַרְכְּבוֹת, after the usual constr. of the verb שׂוּם with the double accus., *e.g.* Gen. xxviii. 22, Isa. l. 2, Ps. xxxix. 9, as pred. accus. (Venet. ἔθετό με ὀχήματα), as *e.g.* Hengst. : I knew not, thus my soul brought me (*i.e.* brought me at unawares) to the chariots of my people, who are noble. But what does this mean ? He adds the remark : " Shulamith stands in the place of the war-chariots of her people as their powerful protector, or by the heroic spirit residing in her." But apart from the syntactically false rendering of לֹא ידעתי, and the unwarrantable allegorizing, this interpretation suffers from worm-holes ; the worm which pierces it bears the strange name הה (דרימוני), *Shabbath* 90a.

wrecks itself on this, that "chariots" in themselves are not for
protection, and thus without something further, especially in this
designation by the word מרכבות, and not by רכב (2 Kings vi. 17;
cf. 2 Kings ii. 12, xiii. 14), are not war-chariots. מר' will thus
be the accus. of the object of motion. It is thus understood,
e.g., by Ewald (sec. 281d): My soul brought me to the chariots,
etc. The shepherd-hypothesis finds here the seduction of Shulamith. Holländer translates: "I perceived it not; suddenly, it can
scarcely be said unconsciously, I was placed in the state-chariots
of Amminadab." But the Masora expressly remarks that עמי נדיב are
not to be read as if forming one, but as two words, תרין מלין.[1] Hitzig
proportionally better, thus: without any apprehension of such a
coincidence, she saw herself carried to the chariots of her noble
people, i.e. as Gesen. in his Thes.: inter currus comitatus principis.
Any other explanation, says Hitzig, is not possible, since the accus.
מרכ' in itself signifies only in the direction whither, or in the neighbourhood whence. And certainly it is generally used of the aim
or object toward which one directs himself or strives, e.g. Isa.
xxxvii. 23. Kodĕsh, "toward the sanctuary," Ps. cxxxiv. 2; cf.
hashshā'rā, "toward the gate," Isa. xxii. 7. But the accus. mārom can
also mean "on high," Isa. xxii. 16, the accus. hashshāmaīm "in the
heavens," 1 Kings viii. 32; and as hishlic häiōrah is used, Ex. i. 22,
of being cast into the Nile, and shalahh hāărĕts of being sent into
the land, Num. xiii. 27, thus may also sīm mĕrkāvāh be used for sim
bĕmĕrkāvāh, 1 Sam. viii. 11, according to which the Syr. (bĕmercabto)
and the Quinta (εἰς ἅρματα) translate; on the contrary, Symm. and
Jerome destroy the meaning by adopting the reading שָׂמְתְנִי (my soul
placed me in confusion). The plur. markĕvoth is thus meant amplifi.,
like richvē, i. 9, and battĕnu, i. 17. As regards the subject, 2 Sam.
xv. 1 is to be compared; it is the king's chariot that is meant,
yoked, according to i. 9, with Egypt. horses. It is a question
whether nadiv is related adject. to ammi: my people, a noble
(people),—a connection which gives prominence to the attribute
appositionally, Gen. xxxvii. 2; Ps. cxliii. 10; Ezek. xxxiv. 12,—or
permutat., so that the first gen. is exchanged for one defining more
closely: to the royal chariot of my people, a prince. The latter
has the preference, not merely because (leaving out of view the
proper name Amminadab) wherever עם and נדיב are used together

---

[1] עַמִּי־נָדִיב, thus in D F: עַמִּי, without the accent and connected with נָדִיב
by Makkeph. On the contrary, P has עַמִּינָדִיב as one word, as also the Masora
parva has here noted חדה מלה. Our Masora, however, notes לית ותרתין כתיבין,
and thus Rashi and Aben Ezra testify.

they are meant of those who stand prominent above the people, Num. xxi. 18, Ps. xlvii. 10, cxiii. 8, but because this נדיב and בַּת־נָדִיב evidently stand in interchangeable relation. Yet, even though we take נדיב and עַמִי together, the thought remains the same. Shulamith is not one who is abducted, but, as we read at iii. 6 ff., one who is honourably brought home; and she here expressly says that no kind of external force but her own loving soul raised her to the royal chariots of her people and their king. That she gives to the fact of her elevation just this expression, arises from the circumstance that she places her joy in the loneliness of nature, in contrast to her driving along in a splendid chariot. Designating the chariot that of her noble people, or that of her people, and, indeed, of a prince, she sees in both cases in Solomon the concentration and climax of the people's glory.

Encouraged by Shulamith's unassuming answer, the daughters of Jerusalem now give utterance to an entreaty which their astonishment at her beauty suggests to them.

> Chap. vii. 1 Come back, come back, O Shulamith!
>
> Come back, come back, that we may look upon thee!

She is now (vi. 10 ff.) on the way from the garden to the palace. The fourfold "come back" entreats her earnestly, yea, with tears, to return thither with them once more, and for this purpose, that they might find delight in looking upon her; for חָזָה בְ signifies to sink oneself into a thing, looking at it, to delight (feast) one's eyes in looking on a thing. Here for the first time Shulamith is addressed by name. But הַשׁוּ cannot be a pure proper name, for the art. is vocat., as e.g. הַבַּת ירו׳, "O daughter of Jerusalem!" Pure proper names like שׁלמה are so determ. in themselves that they exclude the article; only such as are at the same time also nouns, like יַרְדֵן and לְבָנוֹן, are susceptible of the article, particularly also of the vocat., Ps. cxiv. 5; but cf. Zech. xi. 1 with Isa. x. 34. Thus הַשׁוּ will be not so much a proper name as a name of descent, as generally nouns in î (with a few exceptions, viz. of ordinal number, הֲרָרִי, יְמָנִי, etc.) are all *gentilicia*. The LXX. render השׁו׳ by ἡ Σουναμῖτις, and this is indeed but another form for הַשּׁוּנַמִּית, *i.e.* she who is from Sunem. Thus also was designated the exceedingly beautiful Abishag, 1 Kings i. 3, Elisha's excellent and pious hostess, 2 Kings iv. 8 ff. *Sunem* was in the tribe of Issachar (Josh. xix. 18), near to Little Hermon, from which it was separated by a valley, to the south-east of Carmel. This lower Galilean Sunem, which lies south from Nain, south-east from Nazareth, south-west from Tabor, is also called *Shulem*. Eusebius in his *Onomasticon* says regarding it: Σουβήμ (*l.* Σουλήμ) κλήρου

Ἰσσάχαρ. καὶ νῦν ἐστὶ κώμη Σουλὴμ κ.τ.λ., *i.e.* as Jerome translates it: *Sunem in tribu Issachar. et usque hodie vicus ostenditur nomine Sulem in quinto miliario montis Thabor contra australem plagam.* This place is found at the present day under the name of *Suwlam* (*Sôlam*), at the west end of *Jebel ed-Duhi* (Little Hermon), not far from the great plain (*Jisre'el,* now *Zer'în*), which forms a convenient way of communication between Jordan and the sea-coast, but is yet so hidden in the mountain range that the Talmud is silent concerning this Sulem, as it is concerning Nazareth. Here was the home of the Shulamitess of the Song. The ancients interpret the name by εἰρηνεύουσα, or by ἐσκυλευμένη (*vid.* Lagarde's *Onomastica*), the former after Aquila and the Quinta, the latter after Symm. The Targum has the interpretation: הַשְּׁלֵמָה בֶּאֱמוּנָתָהּ עִם ה׳ (*vid.* Rashi). But the form of the name (the Syr. writes שִׁילוּמִיתָא) is opposed to these allegorical interpretations. Rather it is to be assumed that the poet purposely used, not הַשּׁוּנַ׳, but הַשּׁוּלַ׳, to assimilate her name to that of Solomon; and that it has the parallel meaning of one devoted to Solomon, and thus, as it were, of a passively-applied שְׁלוּמִית = Σαλώμη, is the more probable, as the daughters of Jerusalem would scarcely venture thus to address her who was raised to the rank of a princess unless this name accorded with that of Solomon.

Not conscious of the greatness of her beauty, Shulamith asks,—

1b α   What do you see in Shulamith?

She is not aware that anything particular is to be seen in her; but the daughters of Jerusalem are of a different opinion, and answer this childlike, modest, but so much the more touching question,—

1b β   As the dance of Mahanāïm!

They would thus see in her something like the dance of Mahanāïm. If this be here the name of the Levitical town (now *Mahneh*) in the tribe of Gad, north of Jabbok, where Ishbosheth resided for two years, and where David was hospitably entertained on his flight from Absalom (Luthr.: "the dance to Mahanāïm"), then we must suppose in this trans-Jordanic town such a popular festival as was kept in Shiloh, Judg. xxi. 19, and we may compare *Abel-Meholah* [= meadow of dancing], the name of Elisha's birth-place (cf. also Herod. i. 16: "To dance the dance of the Arcadian town of Tegea"). But the Song delights in retrospective references to Genesis (cf. iv. 11b, vii. 11). At xxxii. 3, however, by *Mahanāïm*[1] is meant the double encampment of angels who protected Jacob's two companies

---

[1] Böttcher explains *Mahanāïm* as a plur.; but the plur. of מַחֲנֶה is מַחֲנוֹת and מַחֲנִים; the plur. termination *ajim* is limited to מַיִם and שָׁמַיִם.

(xxxii. 8). The town of Mahanāïm derives its name from this vision of Jacob's. The word, as the name of a town, is always without the article; and here, where it has the article, it is to be understood appellatively. The old translators, in rendering by "the dances of the camps" (Syr., Jerome, *choros castrorum*, Venet. θίασον στρατοπέδων), by which it remains uncertain whether a war-dance or a parade is meant, overlook the dual, and by exchanging מַחֲנַיִם with מְחוֹלֹת, they obtain a figure which in this connection is incongruous and obscure. But, in truth, the figure is an angelic one. The daughters of Jerusalem wish to see Shulamith dance, and they designate that as an angelic sight. *Mahanāïm* became in the postbibl. dialect a name directly for angels. The dance of angels is only a step beyond the responsive song of the seraphim, Isa. vi. *Engelkoere* [angel-choir] and "heavenly host" are associated in the old German poetry.[1] The following description is undeniably that (let one only read how Hitzig in vain seeks to resist this interpretation) of one dancing. In this, according to biblical representation and ancient custom, there is nothing repulsive. The women of the ransomed people, with Miriam at their head, danced, as did also the women who celebrated David's victory over Goliath (Ex. xv. 20; 1 Sam. xviii. 66). David himself danced (2 Sam. vi.) before the ark of the covenant. Joy and dancing are, according to Old Testament conception, inseparable (Eccles. iii. 4); and joy not only as the happy feeling of youthful life, but also spiritual holy joy (Ps. lxxxvii. 7). The dance which the ladies of the court here desire to see, falls under the point of view of a play of rival individual *artistes* reciprocally acting for the sake of amusement. The play also is capable of moral nobility, if it is enacted within the limits of propriety, at the right time, in the right manner, and if the natural joyfulness, penetrated by intelligence, is consecrated by a spiritual aim. Thus Shulamith, when she dances, does not then become a Gaditanian (Martial, xiv. 203) or an *Alma* (the name given in Anterior Asia to those women who go about making it their business to dance mimic and partly lascivious dances); nor does she become a *Bajadere* (Isa. xxiii. 15 f.),[2] as also Miriam, Ex. xv. 20, Jephthah's daughter, Judg. xi. 34, the "daughters of Shiloh," Judg.

---

[1] Vid. *Walther von der Vogelweide*, 173. 28. The Indian mythology goes farther, and transfers not only the original of the dance, but also of the drama, to heaven; vid. *Götting. Anzeigen*, 1874, p. 106.

[2] *Alma* is the Arab. *'ualmah* (one skilled, viz. in dancing and *jonglerie*), and *Bajadere* is the Portug. softening of *baladera*, a dancer, from *balare* (*ballare*), mediaev. Lat., and then Romanic: to move in a circle, to dance.

xxi. 21, and the women of Jerusalem, 1 Sam. xviii. 6, did not dishonour themselves by dancing; the dancing of virgins is even a feature of the times after the restoration, Jer. xxxi. 13. But that Shulamith actually danced in compliance with the earnest entreaty of the daughters of Jerusalem, is seen from the following description of her attractions, which begins with her feet and the vibration of her thighs.

After throwing aside her upper garments, so that she had only the light clothing of a shepherdess or vinedresser, Shulamith danced to and fro before the daughters of Jerusalem, and displayed all her attractions before them. Her feet, previously (v. 3) naked, or as yet only shod with sandals, she sets forth with the deportment of a prince's daughter.

Ver. 2a How beautiful are thy steps in the shoes, O prince's daughter!

The noun נָדִיב, which signifies noble in disposition, and then noble by birth and rank (cf. the reverse relation of the meanings in *generosus*), is in the latter sense synon. and parallel to מֶלֶךְ and שַׂר; Shulamith is here called a prince's daughter because she was raised to the rank of which Hannah, 1 Sam. ii. 8, cf. Ps. cxiii. 8, speaks, and to which she herself, vi. 12, points. Her beauty, from the first associated with unaffected dignity, now appears in native princely grace and majesty. פַּעַם (from פָּעַם, *pulsare*, as in *nunc pede libero pulsanda tellus*) signifies step and foot,—in the latter sense the poet. Heb. and the vulgar Phoen. word for רֶגֶל; here the meanings *pes* and *passus* (Fr. *pas*, dance-step) flow into each other. The praise of the spectators now turns from the feet of the dancer to her thighs:

Ver. 2b The vibration of thy thighs like ornamental chains,
　　　　The work of an artist's hands.

The double-sided thighs, viewed from the spine and the lower part of the back, are called מָתְנַיִם; from the upper part of the legs upwards, and the breast downwards (the lumbar region), thus seen on the front and sidewise, חֲלָצַיִם or יְרֵכַיִם. Here the manifold twistings and windings of the upper part of the body by means of the thigh-joint are meant; such movements of a circular kind are called חַמּוּקִים, from חָמַק, v. 6. חֲלָאִים is the plur. of חֲלִי = (Arab.) ḥaly, as צְבָאִים (gazelles) of צְבִי = zaby. The sing. חֲלִי (or חֶלְיָה = (Arab.) ḥulyah) signifies a female ornament, consisting of gold, silver, or precious stones, and that (according to the connection, Prov. xxv. 2; Hos. ii. 15) for the neck or the breast as a whole; the plur. 'חל, occurring only here, is therefore chosen because the bendings of the loins, full of life and beauty, are compared to the free swingings to and fro of such an ornament, and thus to a connected ornament of chains; for 'חמ

are not the beauty-curves of the thighs at rest,—the connection here requires movement. In accordance with the united idea of חֵל, the appos. is not מַעֲשֵׂי, but (according to the Palestin.) מַעֲשֵׂה (LXX., Targ., Syr., Venet.). The artist is called אָמָּן (ommân) (the forms אָמָן and אָמֵן are also found), Syr. avmon, Jewish-Aram. אוּמָן; he has, as the master of stability, a name like יָמִין, the right hand: the hand, and especially the right hand, is the *artifex* among the members.[1] The eulogists pass from the loins to the middle part of the body. In dancing, especially in the Oriental style of dancing, which is the mimic representation of animated feeling, the breast and the body are raised, and the forms of the body appear through the clothing.

> Ver. 3 Thy navel is a well-rounded basin—
> Let not mixed wine be wanting to it
> Thy body is a heap of wheat,
> Set round with lilies.

In interpreting these words, Hitzig proceeds as if a "voluptuary" were here speaking. He therefore changes שָׁרְרֵךְ into שִׁרְרֵךְ, "thy *pudenda*." But (1) it is no voluptuary who speaks here, and particularly not a man, but women who speak; certainly, above all, it is the poet, who would not, however, be so inconsiderate as to put into the mouths of women immodest words which he could use if he wished to represent the king as speaking. Moreover (2) שֵׁר = (Arab.) *surr*, secret (that which is secret; in Arab. especially referred to the *pudenda*, both of man and woman), is a word that is[2] foreign to the Heb. language, which has for "*Geheimnis*" [secret] the corresponding word סוֹד (*vid.* under Ps. ii. 2, xxv. 14), after the root-signification of its verbal stem (viz. to be firm, pressed together); and (3) the reference—preferred by Döpke, Magnus, Hahn, and others, also without any change of punctuation—of שֵׁר to the *interfeminium mulieris*, is here excluded by the circumstance that the attractions of a woman dancing, as they unfold themselves, are here described. Like the Arab. *surr*, שֵׁר (= *shurr*), from שָׁרַר, to bind fast, denotes properly the umbilical cord, Ezek. xvi. 4, and then the umbilical scar. Thus, Prov. iii. 8, where most recent critics prefer, for לְשָׁרֶךָ, to read, but without any proper reason, לִשְׁאֵרֶךָ = לְשָׁרֶךָ, "to thy flesh," the navel comes there into view as the centre of the body,—which it always is with new-born infants, and is almost so with grown-up persons in respect of the length of the body,—and as, indeed, the centre, whence the pleasurable feeling of health diffuses its rays of heat. This middle and prominent point of the

---

[1] *Vid.* Ryssel's *Die Syn. d. Wahren u. Guten in d. Sem. Spr.* (1873), p. 12.

[2] *Vid.* Tebrizi, in my work entitled *Jud.-Arab. Poesien, u.s.w.* (1874), p. 24.

abdomen shows itself in one lightly clad and dancing when she breathes deeply, even through the clothing; and because the navel commonly forms a little funnel-like hollow (Böttch.: in the form almost of a whirling hollow in the water, as one may see in nude antique statues), therefore the daughters of Jerusalem compare Shulamith's navel to a "basin of roundness," *i.e.* which has this general property, and thus belongs to the class of things that are round. אַגָּן does not mean a *Becher* (a cup), but a *Bechen* (basin), *pelvis;* properly a washing basin, *ijjanah* (from אָגַן = *ajan*, to full, to wash = כִּבֵּם); then a sprinkling basin, Ex. xxiv. 6; and generally a basin, Isa. xxii. 24; here, a mixing basin, in which wine was mingled with a proportion of water to render it palatable (κρατήρ, from κεραννύναι, *temperare*),—according to the Talm. with two-thirds of water. In this sense this passage is interpreted allegorically, *Sanhedrin* 14*b*, 37*a*, and elsewhere (*vid.* Aruch under מזג). מֶזֶג is not spiced wine, which is otherwise designated (viii. 2), but, as Hitzig rightly explains, mixed wine, *i.e.* mixed with water or snow (*vid.* under Isa. v. 22). מֶזֶג is not borrowed from the Greek μίσγειν (Grätz), but is a word native to all the three chief Semitic dialects,— the weaker form of מָסַךְ, which may have the meaning of "to pour in;" but not merely "to pour in," but, at the same time, "to mix" (*vid.* under Isa. v. 22; Prov. ix. 2). סַהַר, with אַגָּן, represents the circular form (from סָהַר = סָחַר), corresponding to the navel ring; Kimchi thinks that the moon must be understood (cf. שַׁהֲרוֹן, *lunula*): a moon-like round basin; according to which the Venet., also in Gr., choosing an excellent name for the moon, translates: ῥάντιστρον τῆς ἑκάτης. But "moon-basin" would be an insufficient expression for it; Ewald supposes that it is the name of a flower, without, however, establishing this opinion. The "basin of roundness" is the centre of the body a little depressed; and that which the clause, "may not mixed wine be lacking," expresses, as their wish for her, is soundness of health, for which no more appropriate and delicate figure can be given than hot wine tempered with fresh water.

The comparison in 3*b* is the same as that of R. Johanan's of beauty, *Mezîa* 84*a*: "He who would gain an idea of beauty should take a silver cup, fill it with pomegranate flowers, and encircle its rim with a garland of roses."[1] To the present day, winnowed and sifted corn is piled up in great heaps of symmetrical half-spherical form,

---

[1] See my *Gesch. d. Jüd. Poesie*, p. 30 f. Hoch (the German Solomon) reminds us of the Jewish marriage custom of throwing over the newly-married pair the contents of a vessel wreathed with flowers, and filled with wheat or corn (with money underneath), accompanied with the cry, פְּרוּ וּרְבוּ [be fruitful and multiply].

which are then frequently stuck over with things that move in the wind, for the purpose of protecting them against birds. " The appearance of such heaps of wheat," says Wetstein (*Isa.* p. 710), " which one may see in long parallel rows on the thrashing-floors of a village, is very pleasing to a peasant; and the comparison of the Song, vii. 3, every Arabian will regard as beautiful." Such a corn-heap is to the present day called *ṣubbah*, while *'aramah* is a heap of thrashed corn that has not yet been winnowed; here, with עֲרֵמָה, is to be connected the idea of a *ṣubbah, i.e.* of a heap of wheat not only thrashed and winnowed, but also sifted (riddled). סוּג, enclosed, fenced about (whence the post-bibl. סְיָג, a fence), is a part. pass. such as פִּזֵּר, scattered (*vid.* under Ps. xcii. 12). The comparison refers to the beautiful appearance of the roundness, but, at the same time, also to the flesh-colour shining through the dress; for fancy sees more than the eyes, and concludes regarding that which is veiled from that which is visible. A wheat-colour was, according to the Moslem Sunna, the tint of the first created man. Wheat-yellow and lily-white is a subdued white, and denotes at once purity and health; by πυρός [wheat] one thinks of πῦρ—heaped up wheat develops a remarkable heat, a fact for which Biesenthal refers to Plutarch's *Quaest.* In accordance with the progress of the description, the breasts are now spoken of:

Ver. 4 Thy two breasts are like two fawns,
Twins of a gazelle.

iv. 5 is repeated, but with the omission of the attribute, " feeding among lilies," since lilies have already been applied to another figure. Instead of תְּאוֹמֵי there, we have here תָּאֳמֵי (*taŏme*), the former after the ground-form *ti'âm*, the latter after the ground-form *to'm* (cf. גָּאֳלִי, Neh. xiii. 29, from גָּאַל = גְּאָל).

Ver. 5*a* Thy neck like an ivory tower.

The article in הַשֵּׁן may be that designating species (*vid.* under i. 11); but, as at vii. 5 and iv. 4, it appears to be also here a definite tower which the comparison has in view: one covered externally with ivory tablets, a tower well known to all in and around Jerusalem, and visible far and wide, especially when the sun shone on it; had it been otherwise, as in the case of the comparison following, the locality would have been more definitely mentioned. So slender, so dazzlingly white, so imposing, and so captivating to the eye did Shulamith's neck appear. These and the following figures would be open to the objection of being without any occasion, and mon-strous, if they referred to an ordinary beauty; but they refer to Solomon's spouse, they apply to a queen, and therefore are derived from that which is most splendid in the kingdom over which, along with him, she rules; and in this they have the justification of their grandeur.

Ver. 5b α Thine eyes pools in Heshbon,
At the gate of the populous (city).

Heshbon, formerly belonging to the Amorites, but at this time to the kingdom of Solomon, lay about $5\frac{1}{2}$ hours to the east of the northern point of the Dead Sea, on an extensive, undulating, fruitful, high table-land, with a far-reaching prospect. Below the town, now existing only in heaps of ruins, a brook, which here takes it rise, flows westward, and streams towards the Ghôr as the *Nahr Hesbán.* It joins the Jordan not far above its entrance into the Dead Sea. The situation of the town was richly watered. There still exists a huge reservoir of excellent masonry in the valley, about half a mile from the foot of the hill on which the town stood. The comparison here supposes two such pools, but which are not necessarily together, though both are before the gate, *i.e.* near by, outside the town. Since שַׁעַר, except at Isa. xiv. 31, is fem., בַּת־רַבִּים, in the sense of רַבָּתִי עָם, Lam. i. 1 (cf. for the non-determin. of the adj., Ezek. xxi. 25), is to be referred to the town, not to the gate (Hitz.); Blau's[1] conjectural reading, *bath-'akrabbim,* does not recommend itself, because the craggy heights of the " ascent of Akrabbim" (Num. xxxiv. 4; Josh. xv. 3), which obliquely cross[2] the Ghôr to the south of the Dead Sea, and from remote times formed the southern boundary of the kingdom of the Amorites (Judg. i. 36), were too far off, and too seldom visited, to give its name to a gate of Heshbon. But generally the crowds of men at the gate and the topography of the gate are here nothing to the purpose; the splendour of the town, however, is for the figure of the famed cisterns like a golden border. בְּרֵכָה (from בָּרַךְ, to spread out, *vid. Genesis,* p. 98; Fleischer in *Levy,* I. 420b) denotes a skilfully built round or square pool. The comparison of the eyes to a pool means, as Wetstein[3] remarks, " either thus glistening like a water-mirror, or thus lovely in appearance, for the Arabian knows no greater pleasure than to look upon clear, gently rippling water." Both are perhaps to be taken together; the mirroring glance of the moist eyes (cf. Ovid, *De Arte Am.* ii. 722:

" *Adspicies oculos tremulo fulgore micantes,
Ut sol a liquida saepe refulget aqua* "),

and the spell of the charm holding fast the gaze of the beholder.

[1] In Merx' *Archiv.* III. 355.
[2] *Vid.* Robinson's *Phys. Geogr.* p. 51.
[3] *Zeitschr. für allgem. Erdkunde,* 1859, p. 157 f.

Ver. 5b β Thy nose like the tower of Lebanon,
Which looks towards Damascus.

This comparison also places us in the midst of the architectural
and artistic splendours of the Solomonic reign. A definite town is
here meant; the art. determines it, and the part. following appositionally without the art., with the expression "towards Damascus"
defining it more nearly (vid. under iii. 6), describes it. הַלְּבָנוֹן designates here "the whole Alpine range of mountains in the north of
the land of Israel" (Furrer); for a tower which looks in the direction
of Damascus (פְּנֵי, accus., as אֶת־פְּנֵי, 1 Sam. xxii. 4) is to be thought
of as standing on one of the eastern spurs of Hermon, or on the top
of Amana (iv. 8), whence the Amana (Barada) takes its rise, whether
as a watch-tower (2 Sam. viii. 6), or only as a look-out from which
might be enjoyed the paradisaical prospect. The nose gives to the
face especially its physiognomical expression, and conditions its
beauty. Its comparison to a tower on a lofty height is occasioned
by the fact that Shulamith's nose, without being blunt or flat, formed
a straight line from the brow downward, without bending to the
right or left (Hitzig), a mark of symmetrical beauty combined with
awe-inspiring dignity. After the praise of the nose it was natural
to think of Carmel; Carmel is a promontory, and as such is called
anf el-jebel (" nose of the mountain-range ").

Ver. 6a α Thy head upon thee as Carmel.

We say that the head is " on the man " (2 Kings vi. 31; Judith xiv.
18), for we think of a man ideally as the central unity of the
members forming the external appearance of his body. Shulamith's
head ruled her form, surpassing all in beauty and majesty, as Carmel
with its noble and pleasing appearance ruled the land and sea
at its feet. From the summit of Carmel, clothed with trees (Amos
ix. 3; 1 Kings xviii. 42), a transition is made to the hair on the
head, which the Moslem poets are fond of comparing to long leaves, as
vine leaves and palm branches; as, on the other hand, the thick leafy
wood is called (vid. under Isa. vii. 20) comata silva (cf. Oudendorp's
Apuleii Metam. p. 744). Grätz, proceeding on the supposition of the
existence of Persian words in the Song, regards כרמל as the name of
a colour; but (1) crimson is designated in the Heb.-Pers. not כַּרְמֶל,
but כַּרְמִיל, instead of תּוֹלַעַת שָׁנִי (vid. under Isa. i. 18; Prov. xxxi. 21);
(2) if the hair of the head (if רֹאשׁ might be directly understood of
this) may indeed be compared to the glistening of purple, not, however, to the glistening of carmese or scarlet, then red and not black
hair must be meant. But it is not the locks of hair, but the hair in

locks that is meant. From this the eulogium finally passes to the
hair of the head itself.

> Ver. 6a β The flowing hair of thy head like purple—
> A king fettered by locks.

Hitzig supposes that כַּרְמֶל reminded the poet of כַּרְמִיל (carmese), and
that thus he hit upon אַרְגָּמָן (purple); but one would rather think
that *Carmel* itself would immediately lead him to purple, for near
this promontory is the principal place where purple shell-fish are
found (Seetzen's *Reisen*, IV. 277 f.). דַּלָּה (from דָּלַל, to dangle, to hang
loose, Job xxviii. 4, Arab. *tadladal*) is *res pendula*, and particularly
coma pendula. Hengst. remarks that the " purple " has caused much
trouble to those who understand by דלה the hair of the head. He
himself, with Gussetius, understands by it the temples, *tempus
capitis;* but the word רַקָּה is used (iv. 3) for " temples," and " purple-
like " hair hanging down could occasion trouble only to those who
know not how to distinguish purple from carmese. Red purple,
אַרְגָּמָן (Assyr. *argamannu*, Aram., Arab., Pers., with departure from
the primary meaning of the word, אַרְגָּמָן), which derives this name
from רָגַם = רָקַם, material of variegated colour, is dark-red, and
almost glistening black, as Pliny says (*Hist. Nat.* ix. 135): *Laus ei*
(the Tyrian purple) *summa in colore sanguinis concreti, nigricans
adspectu idemque suspectu* (seen from the side) *refulgens, unde et Homero
purpureus dicitur sanguis.* The purple hair of Nisus does not play
a part in myth alone, but beautiful shining dark black hair is elsewhere also called purple, *e.g.* πυρφύρεος πλόκαμος in Lucian,
πορφυραῖ χαῖται in Anacreon. With the words " like purple," the
description closes; and to this the last characteristic distinguishing
Shulamith there is added the exclamation : " A king fettered by
locks !" For רְהָטִים, from רָהַט, to run, flow, is also a name of flowing
locks, not the ear-locks (Hitz.), *i.e.* long ringlets flowing down in front ;
the same word (i. 17) signifies in its North Palest. form רָחִיט (*Chethîb*),
a water-trough, *canalis.* The locks of one beloved are frequently
called in erotic poetry " the fetters " by which the lover is held fast,
for " love wove her net in alluring ringlets " (Deshâmi in *Joseph and
Zuleika*).[1] Goethe in his *Westöst. Divan* presents as a bold yet moderate example : " There are more than fifty hooks in each lock of thy
hair ;" and, on the other hand, one offensively extravagant, when it is
said of a Sultan : " In the bonds of thy locks lies fastened the neck of
the enemy." אָסוּר signifies also in Arab. frequently one enslaved by

---

[1] Compare from the same poet: " Alas ! thy braided hair, a heart is in every curl,
and a dilemma in every ring " (*Deut. Morg. Zeit.* xxiv. 581).

love : *astruha* is equivalent to her lover.[1]   The mention of the king
now leads from the imagery of a dance to the scene which follows,
where we again hear the king's voice.   The scene and situation are
now manifestly changed.   We are transferred from the garden to
the palace, where the two, without the presence of any spectators,
carry on the following dialogue.

SECOND SCENE OF THE FIFTH ACT, VII. 7–VIII. 4.

It is the fundamental thought forming the motive and aim of the
Song which now expresses itself in the words of Solomon.

> Ver. 7 How beautiful art thou, and how charming,
>   O love, among delights !

It is a truth of all-embracing application which is here expressed.
There is nothing more admirable than love, *i.e.* the uniting or mingling
together of two lives, the one of which gives itself to the other, and
so finds the complement of itself; nor than this self-devotion, which
is at the same time self-enrichment.   All this is true of earthly love,
of which Walther v. d. Vogelweide says : " *minne ist zweier herzen
wünne* " [love is the joy of two hearts], and it is true also of heavenly
love; the former surpasses all earthly delights (also such as are purely
sensuous, Eccles. ii. 8), and the latter is, as the apostle expresses
himself in his spiritual " Song of Songs," 1 Cor. xiii. 13, in relation
to faith and hope, " greater than these," greater than both of them,
for it is their sacred, eternal aim.   In יָפִית it is indicated that the ideal,
and in נָעַמְתְּ that the eudaemonistic feature of the human soul attains
its satisfaction in love.   The LXX., obliterating this so true and
beautiful a promotion of love above all other joys, translate ἐν ταῖς
τρυφαῖς σου (in the enjoyment which thou impartest).   The Syr.,
Jerome, and others also rob the Song of this its point of light and of
elevation, by reading אֲהֻבָה (O beloved !) instead of אַהֲבָה.   The words
then declare (yet contrary to the spirit of the Hebrew language,
which knows neither אֲהוּבָה nor אֲהוּבְתִי as vocat.) what we already
read at iv. 10 ; while, according to the traditional form of the text,
they are the prelude of the love-song, to love as such, which is continued in viii. 6 f.

When Solomon now looks on the wife of his youth, she stands
before him like a palm tree with its splendid leaf-branches, which
the Arabians call *ucht insân* (the sisters of men); and like a vine

[1] Samachshari, *Mufaṣṣal*, p. 8.

which climbs up on the wall of the house, and therefore is an emblem of the housewife, Ps. cxxviii. 3.

> Ver. 8 Thy stature is like the palm tree;
> And thy breasts clusters.
> 9 I thought: I will climb the palm,
> Grasp its branches;
> And thy breasts shall be to me
> As clusters of the vine,
> And the breath of thy nose like apples,
> 10a α And thy palate like the best wine.

Shulamith stands before him. As he surveys her from head to foot, he finds her stature like the stature of a slender, tall date-palm, and her breasts like the clusters of sweet fruit, into which, in due season, its blossoms are ripened. That קוֹמָתֵךְ (thy stature) is not thought of as height apart from the person, but as along with the person (cf. Ezek. xiii. 18), scarcely needs to be remarked. The palm derives its name, *tāmār*, from its slender stem rising upwards (*vid.* under Isa. xvii. 9, lxi. 6). This name is specially given to the *Phoenix dactylifera*, which is indigenous from Egypt to India, and which is principally cultivated (*vid.* under Gen. xiv. 7), the female flowers of which, set in panicles, develope into large clusters of juicy sweet fruit. These dark-brown or golden-yellow clusters, which crown the summit of the stem and impart a wonderful beauty to the appearance of the palm, especially when seen in the evening twilight, are here called אַשְׁכֹּלוֹת (connecting form at Deut. xxxii. 32), as by the Arabians *'ithkal*, plur. *'ithakyl* (*botri dactylorum*). The perf. דִּמְתָה signifies *aequata est = aequa est*; for דָּמָה, R. דם, means, to make or to become plain, smooth, even. The perf. אָמַרְתִּי, on the other hand, will be meant retrospectively. As an expression of that which he just now purposed to do, it would be useless; and thus to notify with emphasis anything beforehand is unnatural and contrary to good taste and custom. But looking back, he can say that in view of this august attractive beauty the one thought filled him, to secure possession of her and of the enjoyment which she promised; as one climbs (עָלָה with בְּ, as Ps. xxiv. 3) a palm tree and seizes (אָחַז, fut. אֹחֵז, and אֵאָחֹז with בְּ, as at Job xxiii. 11) its branches (סַנְסִנִּים, so called, as it appears,[1] after the feather-like pointed leaves proceeding from the mid-rib on both sides), in order to break off the fulness of the sweet fruit under its leaves. As the cypress (*sarwat*), so also the palm is with the Moslem poets the figure of a loved one, and with the mystics, of God;[2]

---

[1] Also that סנסן is perhaps equivalent to סלסל (תלתל, זלזל), to wave hither and thither, comes here to view.

[2] *Vid.* Hâfiz, ed. Brockhaus, II. p. 46.

and accordingly the idea of possession is here particularly intended. וִיהִי־נָא denotes what he then thought and aimed at. Instead of בְּתְמָר, 9a, the punctuation בַּתָּמָר is undoubtedly to be preferred. The figure of the palm tree terminates with the words, "will grasp its branches." It was adequate in relation to stature, but less so in relation to the breasts; for dates are of a long oval form, and have a stony kernel. Therefore the figure departs from the date clusters to that of grape clusters, which are more appropriate, as they swell and become round and elastic the more they ripen. The breath of the nose, which is called אַף, from breathing hard, is that of the air breathed, going in and out through it; for, as a rule, a man breathes through his nostrils with closed mouth. Apples present themselves the more naturally for comparison, that the apple has the name תַּפּוּחַ (from נָפַח, after the form תַּמְכוּף), from the fragrance which it exhales.

יֵין הַטּוֹב. is wine of the good kind, i.e. the best, as אֵשֶׁת רָע, Prov. vi. 24, a woman of a bad kind, i.e. a bad woman; the neut. thought of as adject. is both times the gen. of the attribute, as at Prov. xxiv. 25 it is the gen. of the *substratum*. The punctuation כַּיֵּין הַטּוֹב (Hitz.) is also possible; it gives, however, the common instead of the delicate poetical expression. By the comparison one may think of the expressions, *jungere salivas oris* (Lucret.) and *oscula per longas jungere pressa moras* (Ovid). But if we have rightly understood iv. 11, v. 16, the palate is mentioned much rather with reference to the words of love which she whispers in his ears when embracing her. Only thus is the further continuance of the comparison to be explained, and that it is Shulamith herself who continues it.

The dramatic structure of the Song becomes here more strongly manifest than elsewhere before. Shulamith interrupts the king, and continues his words as if echoing them, but again breaks off.

Ver. 10a β b Which goes down for my beloved smoothly,
Which makes the lips of sleepers move.

The LXX. had here לְדוֹדִי in the text. It might notwithstanding be a spurious reading. Hitzig suggests that it is erroneously repeated, as if from ver. 11. Ewald also (*Hohesl.* p. 137) did that before,— Heiligstedt, as usual, following him. But, as Ewald afterwards objected, the line would then be "too short, and not corresponding to that which follows." But how shall לְדוֹדִי now connect itself with Solomon's words? Ginsburg explains: "Her voice is not merely compared to wine, because it is sweet to everybody, but to such wine as would be sweet to a friend, and on that account is more valuable and pleasant." But that furnishes a thought digressing εἰς ἄλλο γένος; and besides, Ewald rightly remarks that Shulamith always uses the word דּוֹדִי of her beloved, and that the king never uses it in a similar sense. He contends, however, against the idea that Shulamith here interrupts Solomon; for he replies to me (*Jahrb*. IV. 75): "Such interruptions we certainly very frequently find in our ill-formed and dislocated plays; in the Song, however, not a solitary example of this is found, and one ought to hesitate in imagining such a thing." He prefers the reading לְדוֹדִים [beloved ones], although possibly לְדוֹדִי, with *i*, abbreviated after the popular style of speech from *im*, may be the same word. But is this *l*ᵉ*dodim* not a useless addition? Is excellent wine good to the taste of friends merely; and does it linger longer in the palate of those not beloved than of those loving? And is the circumstance that Shulamith interrupts the king, and carries forward his words, not that which frequently also occurs in the Greek drama, as *e.g.* Eurip. *Phoenissae*, v. 608? The text as it stands before us requires an interchange of the speakers, and nothing prevents the supposition of such an interchange. In this idea Hengstenberg for once agrees with us. The *Lamed* in *l*ᵉ*dodi* is meant in the same sense as when the bride drinks to the bridegroom, using the expression *l*ᵉ*dodi*. The *Lamed* in לְמֵישָׁרִים is that of the defining norm, as the *Beth* in בְּמִי, Prov. xxiii. 31, is that of the accompanying circumstance: that which tastes badly sticks in the palate, but that which tastes pleasantly glides down directly and smoothly. But what does the phrase דּוֹבֵב שִׂפְתֵי וגו' mean? The LXX. translate by ἱκανούμενος χείλεσί μου καὶ ὀδοῦσιν, "accommodating itself (Sym. προστιθέμενος) to my lips and teeth." Similarly Jerome (omitting at least the false μου), *labiisque et dentibus illius ad ruminandum*, in which דִּבָּה, *rumor*, for דּוֹבֵב, seems to have led him to *ruminare*. Equally contrary to the text with Luther's translation: "which to my friend goes smoothly down, and speaks of the previous year;" a rendering which supposes יְשֵׁנִים (as also the Venet.) instead of יָשָׁנִים (good wine which, as it were, tells of former years), and, besides, disregards שִׂפְתֵי. The translation: "which comes at unawares upon the lips of the sleepers," accords with the language (Heiligst., Hitz.). But that gives no meaning, as if one understood by יְשֵׁנִים, as Gesen. and Ewald do, *una in eodem toro cubantes;* but in this case the word ought to have been שֹׁכְבִים. Since, besides, such a thing is known as sleeping through drink or speaking in sleep, but not of drinking in sleep, our earlier translation approves itself: which causes the lips of sleepers to speak. This interpretation is also supported by a proverb in the Talm. *Jebamoth* 97a, *Jer. Moëd Katan*, iii. 7, etc., which, with reference to the passage under review, says that if any one in this world adduces the saying of a righteous man in his name (רוחשות or מרחשות), שפתותיו דובבות בקבר. But it is an error inherited from Buxtorf, that דובבות means there *loquuntur*, and, accordingly, that דובב of this passage before us means *loqui faciens*. It rather means (*vid.* Aruch), *bullire*, *stillare*, *manare* (cogn. זב, טף, Syn. רחש), since, as that proverb signifies, the deceased experiences an after-taste of his saying, and this experience expresses itself in the smack of the lips; and דּוֹבֵב, whether it be part. *Kal* or *Po.* = מְדוֹבֵב, thus: brought into the condition of the overflowing, the after-experience of drink that has been partaken of, and which returns again, as it were, *ruminando.* The meaning "to speak" is, in spite of Parchon and Kimchi (whom the Venet., with its φθεγγό-μενος, follows), foreign to the verb; for דִּבָּה also means, not discourse, but sneaking, and particularly sneaking calumny, and, generally, *fama repens.* The calumniator is called in Arab. *dabûb*, as in Heb. רָכִיל. We now leave it undecided whether in דובב, of this passage before us, that special idea connected with it in the Gemara is contained; but the roots דב and זב are certainly cogn., they have the fundamental idea of a soft, noiseless movement generally, and modify this according as they are referred to that which is solid or fluid. Consequently דָּבַב, as it means in *lente incedere* (whence the bear has the name דֹּב), is also capable of being interpreted *leniter se movere*, and trans. *leniter movere*, according to which the Syr. here translates, *quod commovet labia mea et dentes meos* (this absurd bringing in of the teeth is from the LXX. and Aq.), and the Targ. allegorizes, and whatever also in general is the meaning of the Gemara as far as it exchanges דובבות for רוחשות (*vid.* Levy under רְחַשׁ). Besides, the translations *qui commovet* and *qui loqui facit* fall together according to the sense. For when it is said of generous wine, that it makes the lips of sleepers move, a movement is meant expressing itself in the sleeper speaking. But generous wine is a figure of the love-responses of the beloved, sipped in, as it were, with pleasing satisfaction, which hover still around the sleepers in delightful dreams, and fill them with hallucinations.

It is impossible that לדודי in ver. 10 has any other reference than it has in ver. 11, where it is without doubt Shulamith who speaks.

Ver. 11 I am my beloved's,
And to me goeth forth his desire.

After the words "I am my beloved's," we miss the "and my beloved is mine" of vi. 3, cf. ii. 16, which perhaps had dropped out. The second line here refers back to Gen. iii. 16, for here, as there, תְּשׁוּקָה, from שׁוּק, to impel, move, is the impulse of love as a natural power.

When a wife is the object of such passion, it is possible that, on the one side, she feels herself very fortunate therein; and, on the other side, if the love, in its high commendations, becomes excessive, oppressed, and when she perceives that in her love-relation she is the observed of many eyes, troubled. It is these mingled feelings which move Shulamith when she continues the praise so richly lavished on her in words which denote what she might be to the king, but immediately breaks off in order that, as the following verse now shows, she might use this superabundance of his love for the purpose of setting forth her request, and thus of leading into another path; her simple, child-like disposition longs for the quietness and plainness of rural life, away from the bustle and display of city and court life.

> Ver. 12 Up, my lover; we will go into the country,
> 　　　　 Lodge in the villages.

Hitzig here begins a new scene, to which he gives the superscription: "Shulamith making haste to return home with her lover." The advocate of the shepherd-hypothesis thinks that the faithful Shulamith, after hearing Solomon's panegyric, shakes her head and says: "I am my beloved's." To him she calls, "Come, my beloved;" for, as Ewald seeks to make this conceivable: the golden confidence of her near triumph lifts her in spirit forthwith above all that is present and all that is actual; only to him may she speak; and as if she were half here and half already there, in the midst of her rural home along with him, she says, "Let us go out into the fields," etc. In fact, there is nothing more incredible than this Shulamitess, whose dialogue with Solomon consists of Solomon's addresses, and of answers which are directed, not to Solomon, but in a monologue to her shepherd; and nothing more cowardly and more shadowy than this lover, who goes about in the moonlight seeking his beloved shepherdess whom he has lost, glancing here and there through the lattices of the windows and again disappearing. How much more justifiable is the drama of the Song by the French Jesuit C. F. Menestrier (born in Sion 1631, died 1705), who, in his two little works on the opera and the ballet, speaks of Solomon as the creator of the opera, and regards the Song as a shepherd-play, in which his love-relation to the daughter of the king of Egypt is set forth under the allegorical figures of the love of a shepherd and a shepherdess![1] For Shulamith is thought of as a רֹעָה [shepherdess], i. 8, and she thinks of Solomon

---

[1] *Vid.* Eugène Despris in the *Revue politique et litteraire* 1873. The idea was not new. This also was the sentiment of Fray Luis de Leon; *vid.* his *Biographie* by Wilkens (1866), p. 209.

as a רֹעָה [shepherd]. She remains so in her inclination even after her elevation to the rank of a queen. The solitude and glory of external nature are dearer to her than the bustle and splendour of the city and the court. Hence her pressing out of the city to the country. הַשָּׂדֶה is local, without external designation, like *rus* (to the country). כְּפָרִים (here and at 1 Chron. xxvii. 25) is plur. of the unused form כְּפָר (const. כְּפַר, Josh. xviii. 24) or כְּפָר, Arab. *kafar* (cf. the Syr. dimin. *kafrûno*, a little town), instead of which it is once pointed כֹּפֶר, 1 Sam. vi. 18, of that name of a district of level country with which a multitude of later Palest. names of places, such as כְּפַר נַחוּם, are connected. Ewald, indeed, understands *k͑phārim* as at iv. 13 : we will lodge among the fragrant Al-henna bushes. But yet בַּכְּפ' cannot be equivalent to תַּחַת הכפרים; and since לִין (probably changed from לִיל) and הִשְׁכִּים, 13*a*, stand together, we must suppose that they wished to find a bed in the henna bushes; which, if it were conceivable, would be too gipsy-like, even for a pair of lovers of the rank of shepherds (*vid.* Job xxx. 7). No. Shulamith's words express a wish for a journey into the country : they will there be in freedom, and at night find shelter (בכפ', as 1 Chron. xxvii. 25 and Neh. vi. 2, where also the plur. is similarly used), now in this and now in that country place. Spoken to the supposed shepherd, that would be comical, for a shepherd does not wander from village to village; and that, returning to their home, they wished to turn aside into villages and spend the night there, cannot at all be the meaning. But spoken of a shepherdess, or rather a vine-dresser, who has been raised to the rank of queen, it accords with her relation to Solomon,—they are married,—as well as with the inexpressible impulse of her heart after her earlier homely country-life. The former vine-dresser, the child of the Galilean hills, the lily of the valley, speaks in the verses following.

> Ver. 13 In the morning we will start for the vineyards,
> See whether the vine is in bloom,
> Whether the vine-blossoms have opened,
> The pomegranates budded—
> There will I give thee my love.
> 14 The mandrakes breathe a pleasant odour,
> And over our doors are all kinds of excellent fruits,
> New, also old,
> Which, my beloved, I have kept for thee.

As the rising up early follows the tarrying over night, the description of that which is longed for moves forward. As הִשְׁכִּים is denom. of שְׁכֶם, and properly signifies only to shoulder, *i.e.* to rise, make oneself ready, when early going forth needs to be designated it has generally בַּבֹּקֶר (cf. Josh. vi. 15) along with it; yet this word may also be wanting, 1 Sam. ix. 26, xvii. 16. נָשַׁב׳ לַבֹּקֶר = נֵשֵׁב׳ וְנֵלֵךְ לְבָקָר, an abbreviation of the expression which is also found in hist. prose, Gen. xix. 27; cf. 2 Kings xix. 9. They wished in the morning, when the life of nature can best be observed, and its growth and progress and striving upwards best contemplated, to see whether the vine had opened, *i.e.* unfolded (thus, vi. 11), whether the vine-blossom (*vid.* at ii. 13) had expanded (LXX. ἤνθησεν ὁ κυπρισμός), whether the pomegranate had its flowers or flower-buds (הֵנֵצוּ, as at vi. 11); פְּתַח is here, as at Isa. xlviii. 8, lx. 11, used as internally transitive: to accomplish or to undergo the opening, as also (Arab.) *fattah* [1] is used of the blooming of flowers, for (Arab.) *tafttah* (to unfold). The vineyards, inasmuch as she does not say כְּרָמֵינוּ, are not alone those of her family, but generally those of her home, but of *her* home; for these are the object of her desire, which in this pleasant journey with her beloved she at once in imagination reaches, flying, as it were, over the intermediate space. There, in undisturbed quietness, and in a lovely region consecrating love, will she give herself to him in the entire fulness of her love. By דֹּדַי she means the evidences of her love (*vid.* under iv. 10, i. 2), which she will there grant to him as thankful responses to his own. Thus she speaks in the spring-time, in the month Ijjar, corresponding to our *Wonnemond* (pleasure-month, May), and seeks to give emphasis to her promise by this, that she directs him to the fragrant " mandragoras," and to the precious fruits of all kinds which she has kept for him on the shelf in her native home.

דּוּדָי (after the form לוּלָי), love's flower, is the *mandragora offici-nalis,* L., with whitish green flowers and yellow apples of the size of nutmegs, belonging to the Solanaceae; its fruits and roots are used as an aphrodisiac, therefore this plant was called by the Arabs *abd al-sal'm,* the servant of love, *postillon d'amour;* the son of Leah found such mandrakes (LXX. Gen. xxx. 14, μῆλα μανδραγορῶν) at the time of the vintage, which falls in the month of Ijjar; they have a strong but pleasant odour. In Jerusalem mandrakes are rare; but so much the more abundantly are they found growing wild in Galilee, whither Shulamith is transported in spirit. Regarding the מְגָדִים (from מֶגֶד, occurring in the sing. exclusively in the blessing of Moses, Deut. xxxiii.), which in the Old Testament is peculiar to the Song, *vid.* iv. 13, 16. From " over our doors," down to " I have kept for thee," is, according to the LXX., Syr., Jerome, and others, one sentence, which in itself is not inadmissible; for the object can precede

---

[1] *Vid.* Fleischer, *Makkari,* 1868, p. 271.

its verb, iii. 3b, and can stand as the subject between the place mentioned and the verb, Isa. xxxii. 13a, also as the object, 2 Chron. xxxi. 6, which, as in the passage before us, may be interpunctuated with *Athnach* for the sake of emphasis; in the bibl. Chald. this inverted sequence of the words is natural, *e.g.* Dan. ii. 17b. But such a long-winded sentence is at least not in the style of the Song, and one does not rightly see why just " over our doors " has the first place in it. I therefore formerly translated it as did Luther, dividing it into parts: " and over our doors are all kinds of precious fruits; I have," etc. But with this departure from the traditional division of the verse nothing is gained; for the "keeping" (laying up) refers naturally to the fruits of the preceding year, and in the first instance can by no means refer to fruits of this year, especially as Shulamith, according to the structure of the poem, has not visited her parental home since her home-bringing in marriage, and now for the first time, in the early summer, between the barley harvest and the wheat harvest, is carried away thither in her longing. Therefore the expression, "my beloved, I have kept for thee," is to be taken by itself, but not as an independent sentence (Böttch.), but is to be rendered, with Ewald, as a relative clause; and this, with Hitz., is to be referred to יְשָׁנִים (old). *Col* refers to the many sorts of precious fruits which, after the time of their ingathering, are divided into " new and old " (Matt. xiii. 52). The plur. " our doors," which as amplif. poet. would not be appropriate here, supposes several entrances into her parents' home; and since " I have kept " refers to a particular preserving of choice fruits, *al* does not (Hitzig) refer to a floor, such as the floor above the family dwelling or above the barn, but to the shelf above the inner doors, a board placed over them, on which certain things are wont to be laid past for some particular object. She speaks to the king like a child; for although highly elevated, she yet remains, without self-elation, a child.

If Solomon now complies with her request, yields to her invitation, then she will again see her parental home, where, in the days of her first love, she laid up for him that which was most precious, that she might thereby give him joy. Since she thus places herself with her whole soul back again in her home and amid its associations, the wish expressed in these words that follow rises up within her in the childlike purity of her love:

> Chap. viii. 1 O that thou wert like a brother to me,
> Who sucked my mother's breasts!
> If I found thee without, I would kiss thee;
> They also could not despise me.

> 2 I would lead thee, bring thee into my mother's house;
>   Thou wouldest instruct me—
>   I would give thee to drink spiced wine,
>   The must of my pomegranates.

Solomon is not her brother, who, with her, hung upon the same
mother's breast; but she wishes, carried away in her dream into
the reality of that she wished for, that she had him as her
brother, or rather, since she says, not אָח, but כְּאָח (with כְּ, which
here has not, as at Ps. xxxv. 14, the meaning of *tanquam*, but of
instar, as at Job xxiv. 14), that she had in him what a brother is
to a sister.   In that case, if she found him without, she would
kiss him (hypoth. fut. in the protasis, and fut. without *Vav* in the
apodosis, as at Job xx. 24; Hos. viii. 12; Ps. cxxxix. 18)—she
could do this without putting any restraint on herself for the sake
of propriety (cf. the kiss of the wanton harlot, Prov. vii. 13), and
also (גַּם) without needing to fear that they who saw it would treat
it scornfully (בּוּז ל, as in the reminiscence, Prov. vi. 30).   The close
union which lies in the sisterly relationship thus appeared to her to
be higher than the near connection established by the marriage
relationship, and her childlike feeling deceived her not: the sisterly relationship is certainly purer, firmer, more enduring than that
of marriage, so far as this does not deepen itself into an equality
with the sisterly, and attain to friendship, yea, brotherhood (Prov.
xvii. 17), within.   That Shulamith thus feels herself happy in the
thought that Solomon was to her as a brother, shows, in a characteristic manner, that " the lust of the flesh, the lust of the eye, and
the pride of life," were foreign to her.   If he were her brother, she
would take him by the hand,[1] and bring him into her mother's house,
and he would then, under the eye of their common mother, become
her teacher, and she would become his scholar.   The LXX. adds,
after the words "into my mother's house," the phrase, καὶ εἰς ταμεῖον
τῆς συλλαβούσης με, cf. iii. 4.   In the same manner also the Syr.,
which has not read the words διδάξεις με following, which are found
in some Codd. of the LXX.   Regarding the word *t⁰lammᵉdēne* (thou
wouldest instruct me) as incongruous, Hitzig asks: What should he
then teach her ?   He refers it to her mother: " who would teach me,"
namely, from her own earlier experience, how I might do everything
rightly for him.   " Were the meaning," he adds, " *he* should do it,
then also it is she who ought to be represented as led home by him

---

[1] Ben-Asher punctuates אֶנְהָגְךָ. Thus also P. rightly. Ben-Naphtali, on the
contrary, punctuates אַנְהָגְךָ.   Cf. *Genesis* (1869), p. 85, note 3.

into his house, the bride by the bridegroom." But, correctly, Jerome, the Venet., and Luther: "Thou wouldest (shouldest) instruct me;" also the Targ.: "I would conduct thee, O King Messiah, and bring Thee into the house of my sanctuary; and Thou wouldest teach me (וּתְאַלֵּף יָתִי) to fear God and to walk in His ways." Not her mother, but Solomon, is in possession of the wisdom which she covets; and if he were her brother, as she wishes, then she would constrain him to devote himself to her as her teacher. The view, favoured by Leo Hebraeus (*Dialog. de amore*, c. III.), John Pordage (*Metaphysik*, III. 617 ff.), and Rosenmüller, and which commends itself, after the analogy of the Gîtagovinda, Boethius, and Dante, and appears also to show itself in the Syr. title of the book, "Wisdom of the Wise," that Shulamith is wisdom personified (cf. also viii. 2 with Prov. ix. 2, and viii. 3, ii. 6 with Prov. iv. 8), shatters itself against this תלמדני; the fact is rather the reverse: Solomon is wisdom in person, and Shulamith is the wisdom-loving soul,[1]—for Shulamith wishes to participate in Solomon's wisdom. What a deep view the "Thou wouldest teach me" affords into Shulamith's heart! She knew how much she yet came short of being to him all that a wife should be. But in Jerusalem the bustle of court life and the burden of his regal duties did not permit him to devote himself to her; but in her mother's house, if he were once there, he would instruct her, and she would requite him with her spiced wine and with the juice of the pomegranates. יֵין הָרֶקַח, *vinum conditura*, is appos. = genitiv. יֵין הרקח, *vinum conditurae* (ἀρωματίτης in Dioscorides and Pliny), like יֵין תַּר׳, Ps. vi. 5, מַיִם לַחַץ, 1 Kings xxii. 27, etc., vid. Philippi's *Stat. Const.* p. 86. אַשְׁקְךָ carries forward אֶשָּׁקְךָ in a beautiful play upon words. עָסִים designates the juice as pressed out: the Chald. עֲפִי corresponds to the Heb. דָּרַךְ, used of treading the grapes. It is unnecessary to render רִמֹּנִי as apoc. plur., like מֵנִי, Ps. xlv. 9 (Ewald, § 177a); *rimmoni* is the name she gives to the pome-granate trees belonging to her,—for it is true that this word, *rimmon*, can be used in a collective sense (Deut. viii. 8); but the connection with the possessive suff. excludes this; or by *'asis rimmoni* she means the pomegranate must (cf. ῥοίτης = *vinum e punicis*, in Dioscorides and Pliny) belonging to her. Pomegranates are not to be thought of as an erotic symbol;[2] they are named as something beautiful and precious. "O Ali," says a proverb of

[1] Cf. my *Das Hohelied unter. u. ausg.* (1851), pp. 65–73.
[2] *Vid.* Porphyrius, *de Abstin.* iv. 16, and Inman in his smutty book, *Ancient Faiths*, vol. I. 1868, according to which the pomegranate is an emblem of "a full womb."

Sunna, " eat eagerly only pomegranates (Pers. *anâr*), for their grains are from Paradise." [1]

Resigning herself now dreamily to the idea that Solomon is her brother, whom she may freely and openly kiss, and her teacher besides, with whom she may sit in confidential intercourse under her mother's eye, she feels herself as if closely embraced by him, and calls from a distance to the daughters of Jerusalem not to disturb this her happy enjoyment:

> Ver. 3 His left hand is under my head,
> And his right doth embrace me :
> 4 I adjure you, ye daughters of Jerusalem,
> That ye awake not and disturb not love
> Till she please !

Instead of תַּחַת לְ, " underneath," there is here, as usual, תַּחַת (cf. 5*b*). Instead of אִם . . . אִם in the adjuration, there is here the equivalent וּמַה . . . מַה; the interrogative מַה, which in the Arab. *má* becomes negat., appears here, as at Job xxxi. 1, on the way toward this change of meaning. The *per capreas vel per cervas agri* is wanting, perhaps because the natural side of love is here broken, and the ἔρως strives up into ἀγάπη. The daughters of Jerusalem must not break in upon this holy love-festival, but leave it to its own course.

SIXTH ACT.

THE RATIFICATION OF THE COVENANT OF LOVE IN SHULAMITH'S NATIVE HOME.—CHAP. VIII. 5-14.

FIRST SCENE OF THE SIXTH ACT, VIII. 5-7.

Shulamith's longing wish attains its satisfaction. Arm in arm with Solomon, she comes forth and walks with him on her native ground. Sunem (Sulem), at the west end of Little Hermon ('*Gebel ed-Duhî*), lay something more than $1\frac{1}{2}$ hour[2] to the north of Jezreel (*Zera'în*), which also lay at the foot of a mountain, viz. on a N.-W. spur of Gilboa. Between the two lay the valley of Jezreel in the " great plain," which was called, 2 Chron. xxxv. 22, Zech. xii. 11, " the valley of *Megiddo*" [Esdraelon], now *Merj ibn 'Amir*—an extensive level plain, which, seen from the south Galilean hills in the spring-

----

[1] *Vid.* Fleischer's *Catal. Codd. Lips.* p. 428.
[2] *Vid.* " Jisreel" in Schenkel's *Bib. Lex.*

time, appears "like a green sea encompassed by gently sloping banks." From this we will have to suppose that the loving pair from the town of Jezreel, the highest point of which afforded a wide, pleasant prospect, wandered on foot through the "valley of Jezreel," a beautiful, well-watered, fruitful valley, which is here called מדבר, as being uncultivated pasture land. They bend their way toward the little village lying in the valley, from which the dark sloping sides of Little Hermon rise up suddenly. Here in this valley are the countrymen (*populares*) of these wanderers, as yet unrecognised from a distance, into whose mouth the poet puts these words:

> Ver. 5a Who is this coming up out of the wilderness,
> Leaning on her beloved?

The third Act, iii. 6, began with a similar question to that with which the sixth here commences. The former closed the description of the growth of the love-relation, the latter closes that of the consummated love-relation. Instead of "out of the wilderness," the LXX. has "clothed in white" (λελευκανθισμένη); the translator has gathered מִתְחַוֶּרֶת from the illegible consonants of his MS. before him. On the contrary, he translates מתרפקת correctly by ἐπιστηριζομένη (Symm. ἐπερειδομένη, Venet. κεκμηκυῖα ἐπί, wearily supporting herself on . . .), while Jerome renders it unsuitably by *deliciis affluens*, interchanging the word with מִתְפַּנֶּקֶת. But הִתְרַפֵּק, common to the Heb. with the Arab. and Aethiop., signifies to support oneself, from רָפַק, *sublevare* (French, *soulager*), Arab. *rafaḳa*, *rafuḳa*, to be helpful, serviceable, compliant, viii. *irtafaḳa*, to support oneself on the elbow, or (with the elbow) on a pillow (cf. *rafîḳ*, fellow-traveller, *rufḳa*, a company of fellow-travellers, from the primary idea of mutually supporting or being helpful to each other); Aethiop. *rafaḳa*, to encamp for the purpose of taking food, ἀνακλίνεσθαι (cf. John xiii. 23). That Shulamith leant on her beloved, arose not merely from her weariness, with the view of supplementing her own weakness from his fulness of strength, but also from the ardour of the love which gives to the happy and proud Solomon, raised above all fears, the feeling of his having her in absolute possession. The road brings the loving couple near to the apple tree over against Shulamith's parental home, which had been the witness of the beginning of their love.

> Ver. 5b Under the apple tree I waked thy love:
> There thy mother travailed with thee;
> There travailed she that bare thee.

The words, "under the apple tree I waked thee," עוֹרַרְתִּיךָ, might be regarded as those of Shulamith to Solomon : here, under this apple tree, where Solomon met with her, she won his first love ; for the words cannot mean that she wakened him from sleep under the apple tree, since עוֹרֵר has nowhere the meaning of הֵקִיץ and הֵעִיר here given to it by Hitzig, but only that of " to stir, to stir up, to arouse ;" and only when sleep or a sleepy condition is the subject, does it mean " to shake out of sleep, to rouse up " (*vid.* under ii. 7). But it is impossible that " there " can be used by Shulamith even in the sense of the shepherd hypothesis ; for the pair of lovers do not wander to the parental home of the lover, but of his beloved. We must then here altogether change the punctuation of the text, and throughout restore the fem. suffix forms as those originally used : עוֹרַרְתִּיךְ, אִמֶּךְ חִבְּלָתֶךְ,[1] and יְלָדָתֶךְ (cf. שִׁי', Isa. xlvii. 10), in which we follow the example of the Syr. The allegorizing interpreters also meet only with trouble in regarding the words as those of Shulamith to Solomon. If התפוח were an emblem of the Mount of Olives, which, being wonderfully divided, gives back Israel's dead (Targ.), or an emblem of Sinai (Rashi), in both cases the words are more appropriately regarded as spoken to Shulamith than by her. Aben-Ezra correctly reads them as the words of Shulamith to Solomon, for he thinks on prayers, which are like golden apples in silver bowls ; Hahn, for he understands by the apple tree, Canaan, where with sorrow his people brought him forth as their king ; Hengstenberg, rising up to a remote-lying comparison, says, " the mother of the heavenly Solomon is at the same time the mother of Shulamith." Hoelemann thinks on Sur. xix. 32 f., according to which 'Isa, Miriam's son, was born under a palm tree ; but he is not able to answer the question, What now is the meaning here of the apple tree as Solomon's birthplace ? If it were indeed to be interpreted allegorically, then by the apple tree we would rather understand the " tree of knowledge " of Paradise, of which Aquila, followed by Jerome, with his ἐκεῖ διεφθάρη, appears to think,—a view which recently Godet approves of ;[2] there Shulamith, *i.e.* poor humanity,

---

[1] חִבְּלָתֶךְ, penult. accented, and *Lamed* with *Pathach* in P. This is certainly right. *Michlol* 33a adduces merely יְלָדָתֶךְ of the verse as having Kametz, on account of the pause, and had thus in view חֶבְ', with the *Pathach* under *Lamed*. But P. has also 'לְי, with *Pathach* under *Daleth*, and so also has H, with the remark ב' פתחין (viz. here and Jer. xxii. 26). The *Biblia Rabbinica* 1526 and 1615 have also the same pointing, *Pathach* under *Daleth*. In the printed list of words having *Pathach* in pause, this word is certainly not found. But it is found in the MS. list of the *Ochla veochla*, at Halle.

[2] Others, *e.g.* Bruno von Asti († 1123) and the Waldensian Exposition, edited

awakened the compassionate love of the heavenly Solomon, who
then gave her, as a pledge of this love, the *Protevangelium,* and in
the neighbourhood of this apple tree, *i.e.* on the ground and soil
of humanity fallen, but yet destined to be saved, Shulamith's
mother, *i.e.* the pre-Christian O. T. church, brought forth the
Saviour from itself, who in love raised Shulamith from the depths to
regal honour.   But the Song of Songs does not anywhere set before
us the task of extracting from it by an allegorizing process such far-
fetched thoughts.   If the masc. suff. is changed into the fem., we
have a conversation perfectly corresponding to the situation.   Solomon
reminds Shulamith by that memorable apple tree of the time when
he kindled within her the fire of first love ; עוֹרֵר elsewhere signifies
energy (Ps. lxxx. 3), or passion (Prov. x. 12), put into a state of
violent commotion; connected with the accus. of the person, it signifies, Zech. ix. 13, excited in a warlike manner; here, placed in a
state of pleasant excitement of love that has not yet attained its
object.   Of how many references to contrasted affections the reflex.
התע is capable, is seen from Job xvii. 8, xxxi. 29 ; why not thus
also עוֹרֵר ?

With שָׁמָּה Solomon's words are continued, but not in such a
way as that what follows also took place under the apple tree.   For
Shulamith is not the child of Beduins, who in that case might even
have been born under an apple tree.   Among the Beduins, a maiden
accidentally born at the watering-place (*menhîl*), on the way (*rahîl*),
in the dew (*ṭall*) or snow (*thelg*), is called from that circumstance
Munêhil, Ruhêla, Talla, or *Thelga.*[1]   The birthplace of her love is
not also the birthplace of her life.   As התפוח points to the apple
tree to which their way led them, so שמה points to the end of their
way, the parental home lying near by (Hitzig).   The LXX. translates well : ἐκεῖ ὠδίνησέ σε ἡ μήτηρ σου, for while the Arab. *ḥabida*
means *concipere,* and its *Pi., ḥabbada,* is the usual word for *gravidam
facere,* חִבֵּל in the passage before us certainly appears to be[2] a denom.

by Herzog in the *Zeit. für hist. Theol.* 1861 : *malum = crux dominica.*   Th. Harms
(1870) quotes ii. 3, and remarks : The church brings forth her children under the
apple tree, Christ.   Into such absurdities, in violation of the meaning of the words,
do the allegorizing interpreters wander.

[1] *Vid.* Wetstein's *Inschriften* (1864), p. 336.

[2] The Arab. *ḥabilat,* she has conceived, and is in consequence pregnant, accords
in the latter sense with *ḥamilat,* she bears, *i.e.* is pregnant, without, however, being,
as Hitzig thinks, of a cognate root with it.   For *ḥamal* signifies to carry ; *ḥabal,* on
the contrary, to comprehend and to receive (whence also the cord, figuratively, the
tie of love, *liaison,* as enclosing, embracing, is called *ḥabl,* חֶבֶל), and like the Lat.
concipere and *suscipere,* is used not only in a sexual, but also in an ethical sense, to

Pi. in the sense of "to bring forth with sorrow" (חֶבְלֵי הַיֹּלֵדָה).
The LXX. further translates : ἐκεῖ ὠδίνησέ σε ἡ τεκοῦσά σε, in
which the σε is inserted, and is thus, as also by the Syr., Jerome,
and Venet., translated, with the obliteration of the finite יְלָדַתֶךְ, as if
the reading were יֹלַדְתֵּךְ. But not merely is the name of the mother
intentionally changed, it is also carried forward from the labour, *eniti*,
to the completed act of birth.

After Solomon has thus called to remembrance the commencement of their love-relation, which receives again a special consecration by the reference to Shulamith's parental home, and to her
mother, Shulamith answers with a request to preserve for her this love.

> Ver. 6 Place me as a signet-ring on thy heart,
>   As a signet-ring on thine arm !
>   For strong as death is love ;
>   Inexorable as hell is jealousy :
>   Its flames are flames of fire,
>   A flame of Jah.
>   7 Mighty waters are unable
>   To quench such love,
>   And rivers cannot overflow it.
>   If a man would give
>   All the wealth of his house for love,—
>   He would only be contemned.

The signet-ring, which is called חוֹתָם (חָתַם, to impress), was carried
either by a string on the breast, Gen. xxxviii. 18, or also, as that
which is called טַבַּעַת denotes (from טָבַע, to sink into), on the hand,
Jer. xxii. 24, cf. Gen. xli. 42, Esth. iii. 12, but not on the arm,
like a bracelet, 2 Sam. i. 10 ; and since it is certainly permissible to
say "hand" for "finger," but not "arm" for "hand," so we may
not refer "on thine arm" to the figure of the signet-ring, as if
Shulamith had said, as the poet might also introduce her as saying :
Make me like a signet-ring (כְּחוֹתָם) on thy breast; make me like a
signet-ring "on thy hand," or "on thy right hand." The words,
"set me on thy heart," and "(set me) on thine arm," must thus
also, without regard to "as a signet-ring," express independent
thoughts, although שִׂימֵנִי is chosen (*vid.* Hag. ii. 23) instead of
קָחֵנִי, in view of the comparison.[1] Thus, with right, Hitzig finds the

---

conceive anger, to take up and cherish sorrow. The Assyr. *habal*, corresponding to
the Heb. בֵּן, is explained from this Arab. *habl, concipere.* On the supposition
that the Heb. had a word, חבל, of the same meaning as the Arab. *habl*, then
חֵבֶל might mean *concipiendo generare ;* but the Heb. sentence lying before us leads
to the interpretation *eniti.*

[1] Of the copy of the *Tôra,* which was to be the king's *vade-mecum,* it is said,

thought therein expressed: "Press me close to thy breast, enclose me in thine arms." But it is the first request, and not the second, which is in the form עַל־זְרוֹעֶךָ, and not (שִׂימֵנִי) עַל־זְרוֹעֹתֶיךָ, which refers to embracing, since the subject is not the relation of person and thing, but of person and person. The signet-ring comes into view as a jewel, which one does not separate from himself; and the first request is to this effect, that he would bear her thus inalienably (the art. is that of the specific idea) on his heart (Ex. xxviii. 29); the meaning of the second, that he would take her thus inseparably as a signet-ring on his arm (cf. Hos. xi. 3 : "I have taught Ephraim also to go, taking them by their arms"), so that she might lie always on his heart, and have him always at her side (cf. Ps. cx. 5) : she wishes to be united and bound to him indissolubly in the affection of love and in the community of life's experience.

The reason for the double request following פִּי, abstracted from the individual case, rises to the universality of the fact realized by experience, which specializes itself herein, and celebrates the praise of love; for, assigning a reason for her "set me," she does not say, "my love," nor "thy love," but אַהֲבָה, "love" (as also in the address at vii. 7). She means love undivided, unfeigned, entire, and not transient, but enduring; thus true and genuine love, such as is real, what the word denotes, which exhausts the conception corresponding to the idea of love.

קִנְאָה, which is here parallel to "love," is the jealousy of love asserting its possession and right of property; the reaction of love against any diminution of its possession, against any reserve in its response, the "self-vindication of angry love."[1] Love is a passion, *i.e.* a human affection, powerful and lasting, as it comes to light in "jealousy." *Zelus*, as defined by Dav. Chyträus, *est affectus mixtus ex amore et ira, cum videlicet amans aliquid irascitur illi, a quo laeditur res amata*, wherefore here the adjectives עַזָּה (strong) and קָשָׁה (hard, inexorable, firm, severe) are respectively assigned to "love" and "jealousy," as at Gen. xlix. 7 to "anger" and "wrath." It is much more remarkable that the energy of love, which, so to say, is the life of life, is compared to the energy of death and Hades; with at least equal right מָוֶת and שְׁאוֹל might be used, for love scorns both, outlasts both, triumphs over both (Rom. viii. 38 f.; 1 Cor. xv. 54 f.). But the text does not speak of surpassing, but of equality; not of love and jealousy that they surpass death and Hades,

Sanhedrin 21b: עֲשָׂה אוֹתָהּ כְּמִין קָמֵיעַ וְתוֹלָהּ בִּזְרוֹעַ, but also there the amulet is thought of not as fastened to the finger, but as wound round the arm.

[1] *Vid.* my *Prolegomena* to Weber's *Vom Zorne Gottes* (1862), p. 35 ss.

but that they are equal to it. The point of comparison in both cases is to be obtained from the predicates. עז, powerful, designates the person who, being assailed, cannot be overcome (Num. xiii. 28), and, assailing, cannot be withstood (Judg. xiv. 18). Death is obviously thought of as the assailer (Jer. ix. 20), against which nothing can hold its ground, from which nothing can escape, to whose sceptre all must finally yield (*vid.* Ps. xlix.). Love is like it in this, that it also seizes upon men with irresistible force (Böttcher: "He whom Death assails must die, whom Love assails must love"); and when she has once assailed him, she rests not till she has him wholly under her power; she kills him, as it were, in regard to everything else that is not the object of his love. קָשָׁה, hard (opposed to רַךְ, 2 Sam. iii. 39), σκληρός, designates one on whom no impression is made, who will not yield (Ps. xlviii. 4, xix. 4), or one whom stern fate has made inwardly stubborn and obtuse (1 Sam. i. 15). Here the point of comparison is inflexibility; for *Sheol*, thought of with שָׁאַל, to ask (*vid.* under Isa. v. 14), is the God-ordained messenger of wrath, who inexorably gathers in all that are on the earth, and holds them fast when once they are swallowed up by him. So the jealousy of love wholly takes possession of the beloved object not only in arrest, but also in safe keeping; she holds her possession firmly, that it cannot be taken from her (Wisd. ii. 1), and burns relentlessly and inexorably against any one who does injury to her possession (Prov. vi. 34 f.). But when Shulamith wishes, in the words, "set me," etc., to be bound to the heart and to the arm of Solomon, has she in the clause assigning a reason the love in view with which she loves, or that with which she is loved? Certainly not the one to the exclusion of the other; but as certainly, first of all, the love with which she wishes to fill, and believes that she does fill, her beloved. If this is so, then with "for strong as death is love," she gives herself up to this love on the condition that it confesses itself willing to live only for her, and to be as if dead for all others; and with "inexorable as hell is jealousy," in such a manner that she takes shelter in the jealousy of this love against the occurrence of any fit of infidelity, since she consents therein to be wholly and completely absorbed by it.

To קנאה, which proceeds from the primary idea of a red glow, there is connected the further description of this love to the sheltering and protecting power of which she gives herself up: "its flames, רְשָׁפֶיהָ, are flames of fire;" its sparkling is the sparkling of fire. The verb רשף signifies, in Syr. and Arab., to creep along, to make short steps; in Heb. and Chald., to sparkle, to flame, which in Samar. is referred to impetuosity. Symmachus translates, after the Samar. (which Hitzig approves of): αἱ ὁρμαὶ αὐτοῦ ὁρμαὶ πύρινοι; the Venet., after Kimchi, ἄνθρακες, for he exchanges רֶשֶׁף with the probably non.-cogn. רִצְפָּה; others render it all with words which denote the bright glancings of fire. רִשְׁפֵי (so here, according to the Masora; on the contrary, at Ps. lxxvi. 4, וְרִשְׁפֵי) are effulgurations; the pred. says that these are not only of a bright shining, but of a fiery nature, which, as they proceed from fire, so also produce fire, for they set on fire and kindle.[1] Love, in its flashings up, is like fiery flashes of lightning; in short, it is שַׁלְהֶבֶתְיָה,[2] which is thus to be written as one word with ה raphatum, according to the Masora; but in this form of the word יה is also the name of God, and more than a meaningless superlative strengthening of the idea. As לֶהָבָה is formed from the Kal לָהַב, to flame (R. לב, to lick, like לָהַט, R. לט, to twist), so is שַׁלְהֶבֶת, from the Shafel שִׁלְהֵב, to cause to flame; this active stem is frequently found, especially in the Aram., and has in the Assyr. almost wholly supplanted the Afel (vid. Schrader in Deut. Morg. Zeit. xxvi. 275). שלהבת is thus related primarily to להבה, as inflammatio to (Ger.) Flamme; יה thus presents itself the more naturally to be interpreted as gen. subjecti. Love of a right kind is a flame not kindled and inflamed by man (Job xx. 26), but by God—the divinely-influenced free inclination of two souls to each other, and at the same time, as is now further said, 7a, 7b, a situation supporting all adversities and assaults, and a pure personal relation conditioned by nothing material. It is a fire-flame which mighty waters (רַבִּים, great and many, as at Hab. iii. 15; cf. עַזִּים, wild, Isa. xliii. 16) cannot extinguish, and streams cannot overflow it (cf. Ps. lxix. 3, cxxiv. 4) or sweep it away (cf. Job xiv. 19; Isa. xxviii. 17). Hitzig adopts the latter signification, but the figure of the fire makes the former more natural; no heaping up of adverse circumstances can extinguish true love, as many waters extinguish elemental

---

[1] The Phoen. Inscriptions, Citens. xxxvii., xxxviii., show a name for God, רשפי חץ, or merely רשף, which appears to correspond to Ζεὺς Κεραύνιος on the Inscriptions of Larnax (vid. Vogué's Mélanges Archéologiques, p. 19). רשפי are thus not the arrows themselves (Grätz), but these are, as it were, lightnings from His bow (Ps. lxxvi. 4).

[2] Thus in the Biblia Rabbinica and P. H. with the note מלהחדא ולא מפיק. Thus by Ben-Asher, who follows the Masora. Cf. Liber Psalmorum Hebr. atque Lat. p. 155, under Ps. cxviii. 5; and Kimchi, Wörterb., under אפל and שלהב. Ben-Naphtali, on the other hand, reads as two words, שַׁלְהֶבֶת יָהּ. [Except in this word, the recensions of Ben-Asher and Ben-Naphtali differ only "de punctis vocalibus et accentibus." Strack's Prolegomena, p. 28.]

fire ; no earthly power can suppress it by the strength of its assault,
as streams drench all they sweep over in their flow—the flame of
Jah is inextinguishable.

Nor can this love be bought; any attempt to buy it would be
scorned and counted madness.   The expression is like Prov. vi. 30 f. ;
cf. Num. xxii. 18 ; 1 Cor. xiii. 3.   Regarding הון (from הון, (Arab.) *han*,
levem esse), convenience, and that by which life is made comfortable,
vid. at Prov. i. 13.   According to the shepherd-hypothesis, here occurs
the expression of the peculiar point of the story of the intercourse
between Solomon and Shulamith ; she scorns the offers of Solomon ;
her love is not to be bought, and it already belongs to another.
But of offers we read nothing beyond i. 11, where, as in the following ver. 12, it is manifest that Shulamith is in reality excited in
love.   Hitzig also remarks under i. 12 : " When the speaker says
the fragrance of her nard is connected with the presence of the king,
she means that only then does she smell the fragrance of nard, *i.e.*
only his presence awakens in her heart pleasant sensations or sweet
feelings."   Shulamith manifestly thus speaks, also emphasizing vi.
12, the spontaneousness of her relation to Solomon ; but Hitzig adds :
" These words, i. 12, are certainly spoken by a court lady."   But the
Song knows only a chorus of the " Daughters of Jerusalem "—that
court lady is only a phantom, by means of which Hitzig's ingenuity
seeks to prop up the shepherd-hypothesis, the weakness of which
his penetration has discerned.   As we understand the Song, ver. 7
refers to the love with which Shulamith loves, as decidedly as 6*b* to
the love with which she is loved.   Nothing in all the world is able
to separate her from loving the king; it is love to his person, not
love called forth by a desire for riches which he disposes of, not
even by the splendour of the position which awaited her, but free,
responsive love with which she answered free love making its
approach to her.   The poet here represents Shulamith herself as
expressing the idea of love embodied in her.   That apple tree, where
he awaked first love in her, is a witness of the renewal of their
mutual covenant of love ; and it is significant that only here, just
directly here, where the idea of the whole is expressed more fully,
and in a richer manner than at vii. 7, is God denoted by His
name, and that by His name as revealed in the history of redemption.   Hitzig, Ewald, Olshausen, Böttcher, expand this concluding
word, for the sake of rhythmic symmetry, to שַׁלְהֶבֶת יָהּ שַׁלְהֲבֹתֶיהָ [its
flames are flames of Jah] ; but a similar conclusion is found at Ps.
xxiv. 6, xlviii. 7, and elsewhere.

" I would almost close the book," says Herder in his *Lied der*

Lieder (Song of Songs), 1778, " with this divine seal. It is even as good as closed, for what follows appears only as an appended echo." Daniel Sanders (1845) closes it with ver. 7, places ver. 12 after i. 6, and cuts off vers. 8–11, 13, 14 as not original. Anthologists, like Döpke and Magnus, who treat the Song as the Fragmentists do the Pentateuch, find here their confused medley sanctioned. Umbreit also, 1820, although as for the rest recognising the Song as a compact whole, explains viii. 8–12, 13, 14 as a fragment, not belonging to the work itself. Hoelemann, however, in his *Krone des Hohenliedes* [Crown of the Song], 1856 (thus he names the " concluding Act," viii. 5–14), believes that there is here represented, not only in vers. 6, 7, but further also in vers. 8–12, the essence of true love—what it is, and how it is won ; and then in viii. 13 f. he hears the Song come to an end in pure idyllic tones. We see in ver. 8 ff. the continuation of the love story practically idealized and set forth in dramatic figures. There is no inner necessity for this continuance. It shapes itself after that which has happened ; and although in all history divine reason and moral ideas realize themselves, yet the material by means of which this is done consists of accidental circumstances and free actions passing thereby into reciprocal action. But ver. 8 ff. is the actual continuance of the story on to the completed conclusion, not a mere appendix, which might be wanting without anything being thereby missed. For after the poet has set before us the loving pair as they wander arm in arm through the green pasture-land between Jezreel and Sunem till they reach the environs of the parental home, which reminds them of the commencement of their love relations, he cannot represent them as there turning back, but must present to us still a glimpse of what transpired on the occasion of their visit there. After that first Act of the concluding scene, there is yet wanting a second, to which the first points.

SECOND SCENE OF THE FIFTH ACT, VIII. 8–14.

The locality of this scene is Shulamith's parental home. It is she herself who speaks in these words :

> Ver. 8 We have a sister, a little one,
> And she has no breasts :
> What shall we do with our sister
> In the day when she will be sued for?

Between vers. 8 and 7 is a blank. The figure of the wanderers

is followed by the figure of the visitors.   But who speaks here?
The interchange of the scene permits that Shulamith conclude the
one scene and begin the other, as in the first Act; or also that
at the same time with the change of scene there is an interchange
of persons, as *e.g.* in the third Act.   But if Shulamith speaks, all
her words are not by any means included in what is said from ver. 8
to ver. 10.   Since, without doubt, she also speaks in ver. 11 f., this
whole second figure consists of Shulamith's words, as does also the
second of the second Act, iii. 1–5.   But there Shulamith's address
presents itself as the narrative of an experience, and the narrative
dramatically framed in itself is thoroughly penetrated by the *I* of the
speaker; but here, as *e.g.* Ewald, Heiligst., and Böttch. explain, she
would begin with a dialogue with her brothers referable to herself,
one that had formerly taken place—that little sister, Ewald remarks
under ver. 10, stands here now grown up; she took notice of that
severe word formerly spoken by her brothers, and can now joyfully
before all exclaim, taking up the same flowery language, that she is
a wall, etc.   But that a monologue should begin with a dialogue
without any introduction, is an impossibility; in this case the poet
ought not to have left the expression, " of old my mother's sons
said," to be supplemented by the reader or hearer.   It is true, at
iii. 2, v. 3, we have a former address introduced without any
formal indication of the fact; but it is the address of the narrator
herself.   With ver. 8 there will thus begin a colloquy arising out
of present circumstances.   That in this conversation ver. 8 appertains to the brothers, is evident.   This harsh *entweder oder* (*aut . . . aut*)
is not appropriate as coming from Shulamith's mouth; it is her
brothers alone, as Hoelemann rightly remarks, who utter these words,
as might have been expected from them in view of i. 6.   But does
ver. 8 belong also to them?   There may be two of them, says
Hitzig, and the one may in ver. 9 reply to the question of the
other in ver. 8; Shulamith, who has heard their conversation, suddenly interposes with ver. 10.   But the transition from the first to
the second scene is more easily explained if Shulamith proposes the
question of ver. 8 for consideration.   This is not set aside by Hitzig's
questions: " Has she to determine in regard to her sister? and has
she now for the first time come to do nothing in haste? "   For (1)
the dramatic figures of the Song follow each other chronologically,
but not without blanks; and the poet does not at all require us to
regard ver. 8 as Shulamith's first words after her entrance into her
parental home; (2) but it is altogether seeming for Shulamith, who has
now become independent, and who has been raised so high, to throw

out this question of loving care for her sister. Besides, from the
fact that with ver. 8 there commences the representation of a present
occurrence, it is proved that the sister here spoken of is not
Shulamith herself. If it were Shulamith herself, the words of
vers. 8, 9 would look back to what had previously taken place,
which, as we have shown, is impossible. Or does vi. 9 require that
we should think of Shulamith as having no sister ? Certainly not, for
so understood, these words would be purposeless. The " only one,"
then, does not mean the only one numerically, but, as at Prov. iv. 3,
it is emphatic (Hitzig); she is called by Solomon the " only one "
of her mother in this sense, that she had not one her equal.

Thus it is Shulamith who here speaks, and she is not the " sister "
referred to. The words, " we have a sister . . .," spoken in the family
circle, whether regarded as uttered by Shulamith or not, have something strange in them, for one member of a family does not need
thus to speak to another. We expect: With regard to our sister,
who is as yet little and not of full age, the question arises, What
will be done when she has grown to maturity to guard her innocence ?
Thus the expression would have stood, but the poet separates it into
little symmetrical sentences ; for poetry presents facts in a different
style from prose. Hoelem. has on this remarked that the words are
not to be translated: we have a little sister, which the order of the
words אָחוֹת קְ' וּגוֹ' would presuppose, Gen. xl. 20 ; cf. 2 Sam. iv. 4,
xii. 2 f.; Isa. xxvi. 1, xxxiii. 21. " Little " is not immediately connected with " sister," but follows it as an apposition ; and this
appositional description lays the ground for the question : We may
be now without concern ; but when she is grown up and will be
courted, what then ? " Little " refers to age, as at 2 Kings v. 2;
cf. Gen. xliv. 20. The description of the child in the words, " she
has no breasts," has neither in itself nor particularly for Oriental
feeling anything indecent in it (cf. *mammae sororiarunt*, Ezek.
xvi. 7). The ל following מַה־נַּעֲשֶׂה is here not thus purely the *dat.
commodi*, as *e.g.* Isa. lxiv. 3 (to act for some one), but indiff. dat.
(what shall we do for her ?); but מה is, according to the connection,
as at Gen. xxvii. 37, 1 Sam. x. 2, Isa. v. 4, equivalent to : What
conducing to her advantage ? Instead of בַּיּוֹם, the form בְּיוֹם lay
syntactically nearer (cf. Ex. vi. 28); the art. in בַּיּוֹם is, as at Eccles.
xii. 3, understood demonst.: that day when she will be spoken for,
i.e. will attract the attention of a suitor. בְּ after דֻּבַּר may have
manifold significations (*vid.* under Ps. lxxxvii. 3) ; thus the general
signification of " concerning," 1 Sam. xix. 3, is modified in the sense
of courting a wife, 1 Sam. xxv. 39. The brothers now take speech

in hand, and answer Shulamith's question as to what will have to be done for the future safety of their little sister when the time comes that she shall be sought for:

> Ver. 9 If she be a wall,
> We will build upon her a pinnacle of silver;
> And if she be a door,
> We will block her up with a board of cedar-wood.

The brothers are the nearest guardians and counsellors of the sister, and, particularly in the matter of marriage, have the precedence even of the father and mother, Gen. xxiv. 50, 55, xxxiv. 6–8. They suppose two cases which stand in contrast to each other, and announce their purpose with reference to each case. Hoelem. here affects a synonymous instead of the antithetic parallelism; for he maintains that אִם (וְאִם) . . . אִם nowhere denotes a contrast, but, like *sive . . . sive*, essential indifference. But examples such as Deut. xviii. 3 (*sive bovem, sive ovem*) are not applicable here; for this correl. אִם . . . אִם, denoting essential equality, never begins the antecedents of two principal sentences, but always stands in the component parts of one principal sentence. Wherever אִם . . . וְאִם commences two parallel conditional clauses, the parallelism is always, according to the contents of these clauses, either synonymous, Gen. xxxi. 50, Amos ix. 2–4, Eccles. xi. 3 (where the first וְאִם signifies *ac si*, and the second *sive*), or antithetic, Num. xvi. 29 f.; Job xxxvi. 11 f.; Isa. i. 19 f. The contrast between חוֹמָה (from חָמָה, Arab. *ḥaman*, Modern Syr. *chamo*, to preserve, protect) and דֶּלֶת (from דָּלַל, to hang loose, of doors, Prov. xxvi. 14, which move hither and thither on their hinges) is obvious. A wall stands firm and withstands every assault if it serves its purpose (which is here presupposed, where it is used as a figure of firmness of character). A door, on the contrary, is moveable; and though it be for the present closed (דלת is intentionally used, and not פֶּתַח, *vid.* Gen. xix. 6), yet it is so formed that it can be opened again. A maiden inaccessible to seduction is like a wall, and one accessible to it is like a door. In the apodosis, 9*a*, the LXX. correctly renders טירת by ἐπάλξεις; Jerome, by *propugnacula*. But it is not necessary to read טִירֹת. The verb טוּר, cogn. דּוּר, signifies to surround, whence *tirah* (= Arab. *duâr*), a round encampment, Gen. xxv. 16, and, generally, a habitation, Ps. lxix. 25; and then also, to range together, whence טוּר, a rank, row (cf. Arab. *thur* and *daur*, which, in the manifoldness of their meanings, are parallel with the French *tour*), or also *tirah*, which, Ezek. xlvi. 23 (*vid.* Keil), denotes the row or layer of masonry,—in the passage before us, a row of battlements (Ew.), or a crown of the wall (Hitz.), *i.e.* battlements as a wreath on the summit of a wall. Is she a wall,—*i.e.* does she firmly and successfully withstand all immoral approaches ?— then they will adorn this wall with silver pinnacles (cf. Isa. liv. 12), *i.e.* will bestow upon her the high honour which is due to her maidenly purity and firmness ; silver is the symbol of holiness, as gold is the symbol of nobility. In the apodosis 9*b*, צוּר עָל is not otherwise meant than when used in a military sense of enclosing by means of besieging, but, like Isa. xxix. 3, with the obj.-accus., of that which is pressed against that which is to be excluded ; צוּר here means, forcibly to press against, as סגר, Gen. ii. 21, to unite by closing up.

לוּחַ אֶרֶז is a board or plank (cf. Ezek. xxvii. 5, of the double planks of a ship's side) of cedar wood (cf. Zeph. ii. 14, אַרְזָה, cedar wainscot). Cedar wood comes here into view not on account of the beautiful polish which it takes on, but merely because of its hardness and durability. Is she a door, *i.e.* accessible to seduction ? they will enclose this door around with a cedar plank, *i.e.* watch her in such a manner that no seducer or lover will be able to approach her. By this morally stern but faithful answer, Shulamith is carried back to the period of her own maidenhood, when her brothers, with good intention, dealt severely with her. Looking back to this time, she could joyfully confess :

> Ver. 10 I was a wall,
> And my breasts like towers ;
> Then I became in his eyes
> Like one who findeth peace.

In the language of prose, the statement would be : Your conduct is good and wise, as my own example shows ; of me also ye thus faithfully took care ; and that I met this your solicitude with strenuous self-preservation, has become, to my joy and yours, the happiness of my life. That in this connection not חוֹמה אני, but אני חוֹמה has to be used, is clear : she compares herself with her sister, and the praise she takes to herself she takes to the honour of her brothers. The comparison of her breasts to towers is suggested by the comparison of her person to a wall ; Kleuker rightly remarks that here the comparison is not of thing with thing, but of relation with relation : the breasts were those of her person, as the towers were of the wall, which, by virtue of the power of defence which they conceal within themselves, never permit the enemy, whose attention they attract, to approach them. The two substantival clauses, *murus et ubera mea instar turrium,* have not naturally a retrospective signification, as they would in a historical connection (*vid.* under Gen. ii. 10) ; but they become retrospective by the following " then I became," like Deut. xxvi. 5, by the historical tense following, where, however, it is to be remarked that the expression, having in itself no relation to time, which is incapable of being expressed in German, mentions the past not in a way that excludes the present, but as including it. She was a wall, and her breasts like the towers, *i.e.* all seductions rebounded from her, and ventured not near her awe-inspiring attractions; then (אָז, temporal, but at the same time consequent; thereupon, and for this reason, as at Ps. xl. 8, Jer. xxii. 15, etc.) she became in his (Solomon's) eyes as one who findeth peace. According to the shepherd-hypothesis, she says here: he deemed it good to forbear any further attempts, and to let me remain in peace (Ewald, Hitz., and others). But how is that possible? מצא שָׁלוֹם בעיני is a variation of the frequently occurring מצא חֵן בעיני, which is used especially of a woman gaining the affections of a man, Esth. ii. 17, Deut. xxiv. 1, Jer. xxxi. 2 f.; and the expression here used, "thus I was in his eyes as one who findeth peace," is only the more circumstantial expression for, "then I found (אז מָצָאתִי) in his eyes peace," which doubtless means more than: I brought it to this, that he left me further unmolested; שלום in this case, as syn. of חן, means inward agreement, confidence, friendship, as at Ps. xli. 10; there it means, as in the salutation of peace and in a hundred other cases, a positive good. And why should she use שלום instead of חן, but that she might form a play upon the name which she immediately, 11*a*, thereafter utters, שלמה, which signifies, 1 Chron. xxii. 9, "The man of peace." That *Shulamith* had found *shalom* (peace) with *Sh'lomoh* (Solomon), cannot be intended to mean that uninjured she escaped from him, but that she had entered into a relation to him which seemed to her a state of blessed peace. The delicate description, "in his eyes," is designed to indicate that she appeared to him in the time of her youthful discipline as one finding peace. The כ is כ *veritatis*, *i.e.* the comparison of the fact with its idea, Isa. xxix. 2, or of the individual with the general and common, Isa. xiii. 6; Ezek. xxvi. 10; Zech. xiv. 3. Here the meaning is, that Shulamith appeared to him corresponding to the idea of one finding peace, and thus as worthy to find peace with him. One "finding peace" is one who gains the heart of a man, so that he enters into a relation of esteem and affection for her. This generalization of the idea also opposes the notion of a history of seduction. מוֹצֵאת is from the ground-form *matsiat*, the parallel form to מוֹצֵאת, 2 Sam. xviii. 22. Solomon has won her, not by persuasion or violence; but because she could be no other man's, he entered with her into the marriage covenant of peace (cf. Prov. ii. 17 with Isa. liv. 10).

It now lies near, at least rather so than remote, that Shulamith, thinking of her brothers, presents her request before her royal husband :

> Ver. 11 Solomon had a vineyard in Baal-hamon ;
> He committed the vineyard to the keepers,
> That each should bring for its fruit
> A thousand in silver.
> 12 I myself disposed of my own vineyard :
> The thousand is thine, Solomon,
> And two hundred for the keepers of its fruit !

The words כֶּרֶם הָיָה לִשׁ' are to be translated after כרם וגו', 1 Kings xxi. 1, and לְיִדִידִי . . ., Isa. v. 1, " Solomon had a vineyard " (cf. 1 Sam. ix. 2 ; 2 Sam. vi. 23, xii. 2 ; 2 Kings i. 17 ; 1 Chron. xxiii. 17, xxvi. 10), not " Solomon has a vineyard," which would have required the words כרם לְשׁ', with the omission of היה. I formerly explained, as also Böttcher : a vineyard became his, thus at present is his possession ; and thus explaining, one could suppose that it fell to him, on his taking possession of his government, as a component part of his domain ; but although in itself היה לו can mean, " this or that has become one's own " (e.g. Lev. xxi. 3), as well as " it became his own," yet here the historical sense is necessarily connected by היה with the נתן foll. : Solomon has had . . ., he has given ; and since Solomon, after possessing the vineyard, would probably also preserve it, Hitzig draws from this the conclusion, that the poet thereby betrays the fact that he lived after the time of Solomon. But these are certainly words which he puts into Shulamith's mouth, and he cannot at least have forgotten that the heroine of his drama is a contemporary of Solomon ; and supposing that he had forgotten this for a moment, he must have at least once read over what he had written, and could not have been so blind as to have allowed this היה which had escaped him to stand. We must thus assume that he did not in reality retain the vineyard, which, as Hitzig supposes, if he possessed it, he also " probably " retained, whether he gave it away, or exchanged it, or sold it, we know not ; but the poet might suppose that Shulamith knew it, since it refers to a piece of land lying not far from her home. For בַּעַל הָמוֹן, LXX. Βεελαμών, is certainly the same as that mentioned in Judith viii. 3, according to which Judith's husband died from sunstroke in Bethulia, and was buried beside his fathers " between *Dothaim* and *Balamōn* "[1]

---

[1] This is certainly not the *Baal-Meon* (now *Maïn*) lying half an hour to the south of Heshbon ; there is also, however, a *Meon* (now *Maïn*) on this [the west] side of Jordan, Nabal's Maon, near to Carmel. *Vid.* art. " Maon," by Kleuker in Schenkel's *Bibl. Lex.*

(probably, as the sound of the word denotes, *Belmen*, or, more accurately, *Belmaïn*, as it is also called in Judith iv. 4, with which Kleuker in Schenkel's *Bibl. Lex.*, de Bruyn in his *Karte*, and others, interchange it; and חַמּוֹן, Josh. xix. 28, lying in the tribe of Asher). This *Balamōn* lay not far from Dothan, and thus not far from *Esdräelon;* for Dothan lay (cf. Judith iii. 10) south of the plain of Jezreel, where it has been discovered, under the name of *Tell Dotan*, in the midst of a smaller plain which lies embosomed in the hills of the south.[1]   The ancients, since Aquila, Symm., Targ., Syr., and Jerome, make the name of the place Baal-hamon subservient to their allegorizing interpretation, but only by the aid of soap-bubble-like fancies; *e.g.* Hengst. makes *Baal-hamon* designate the world; *nothrim* [keepers], the nations; the 1000 pieces in silver, the duties comprehended in the ten commandments.   *Hamon* is there under-stood of a large, noisy crowd.   The place may, indeed, have its name from the multitude of its inhabitants, or from an annual market held there, or otherwise from revelry and riot; for, according to Hitzig,[2] there is no ground for co-ordinating it with names such as *Baal-Gad* and *Baal-Zephon*, in which *Baal* is the general, and what follows the special name of God.   *Amon*, the Sun-God, specially worshipped in Egyptian Thebes, has the bibl. name אָמוֹן, with which, after the sound of the word, accords the name of a place lying, according to *Jer. Demaï* ii. 1, in the region of Tyrus, but not המן. The reference to the Egypt. *Amon Ra*, which would direct rather to Baalbec, the Coele-Syrian Heliupolis, is improbable; because the poet would certainly not have introduced into his poem the name of the place where the vineyard lay, if this name did not call forth an idea corresponding to the connection.   The Shulamitess, now become Solomon's, in order to support the request she makes to the king, relates an incident of no historical value in itself of the near-lying Sunem (Sulem), situated not far from Baal-hamon to the north, on the farther side of the plain of Jezreel.   She belongs to a family whose inheritance consisted in vineyards, and she herself had acted in the capacity of the keeper of a vineyard, i. 6,—so much the less therefore is it to be wondered at that she takes an interest in the vineyard of Baal-hamon, which Solomon had let out to keepers on the condition that they should pay to him for its fruit-harvest the sum of 1000 shekels of silver (*shekel* is, according to Ges. § 120. 4, Anm. 2, to be supplied).   יָבִא, since we have interpreted היה retro-

---

[1] *Vid.* Robinson's *Physical Geogr. of the Holy Land*, p. 113; Morrison's *Recovery of Jerusalem* (1871), p. 463, etc.

[2] Cf. also Schwarz' *Das heilige Land*, p. 37.

spectively, might also indeed be rendered imperfect. as equivalent to *afferebat*, or, according to Ewald, § 136*c*, *afferre solebat;* but since נָתַן = ἐξέδοτο, Matt. xxi. 33, denotes a gift laying the recipients under an obligation, יָבִא is used in the sense of יָבִא (אֲשֶׁר) לְמַעַן; however, לְמַעַן is not to be supplied (Symm. ἐνέγκῃ), but יָבִא in itself signifies *afferre debebat* (he ought to bring), like 'עַי, Dan. i. 5, they should stand (wait upon), Ewald, § 136*g*. Certainly נטרים does not mean tenants, but watchers,—the post-bibl. language has חָכַר, to lease, קִבֵּל, to take on lease, חִכּוּר, rent, *e.g. Mezîa* ix. 2,—but the subject here is a *locatio conductio ;* for the vine-plants of that region are entrusted to the "keepers" for a rent, which they have to pay, not in fruits but in money, as the equivalent of a share of the produce (the ב in בְּפֶר' is the ב *pretii*). Isa. vii. 23 is usually compared; but there the money value of a particularly valuable portion of a vineyard, consisting of 1000 vines, is given at "1000 silverlings" (1 shekel); while, on the other hand, the 1000 shekels here are the rent for a portion of a vineyard, the extent of which is not mentioned. But that passage in Isaiah contains something explanatory of the one before us, inasmuch as we see from it that a vineyard was divided into portions of a definite number of vines in each. Such a division into *mᵉkomoth* is also here supposed. For if each "keeper" to whom the vineyard was entrusted had to count 1000 shekels for its produce, then the vineyard was at the same time committed to several keepers, and thus was divided into small sections (Hitzig). It is self-evident that the gain of the produce that remained over after paying the rent fell to the "keepers;" but since the produce varied, and also the price of wine, this gain was not the same every year, and only in general are we to suppose from 12*b*, that it yielded on an average about 20 per cent. For the vineyard which Shulamith means in 12*b* is altogether different from that of Baal-hamon. It is of herself she says, i. 6, that as the keeper of a vineyard, exposed to the heat of the day, she was not in a position to take care of her own vineyard. This her own vineyard is not her beloved (Hoelem.), which not only does not harmonize with i. 6 (for she there looks back to the time prior to her elevation), but her own person, as comprehending everything pleasant and lovely which constitutes her personality (iv. 12–v. 1), as *kerem* is the sum-total of the vines which together form a vineyard.

Of this figurative vineyard she says : כַּרְמִי שֶׁלִּי לְפָנָי. This must mean, according to Hitzig, Hoelem., and others, that it was under her protection ; but although the idea of affectionate care may, in certain circumstances, be connected with לְפָנַי, Gen. xvii. 18, Prov.

iv. 3, yet the phrase: this or that is לְפָנַי, wherever it has not merely a local or temporal, but an ethical signification, can mean nothing else than : it stands under my direction, Gen. xiii. 9, xx. 15, xlvii. 6 ; 2 Chron. xiv. 6 ; Gen. xxiv. 51 ; 1 Sam. xvi. 16. Rightly Heiligst., after Ewald: *in potestate mea est.* Shulamith also has a vineyard, which she is as free to dispose of as Solomon of his at Baal-hamon. It is the totality of her personal and mental endowments. This vineyard has been given over with free and joyful cordiality into Solomon's possession. This vineyard also has keepers (one here sees with what intention the poet has chosen in 11*a* just that word נטרים) — to whom Shulamith herself and to whom Solomon also owes it that as a chaste and virtuous maiden she became his possession. These are her brothers, the true keepers and protectors of her innocence. Must these be unrewarded ? The full thousands, she says, turning to the king, which like the annual produce of the vineyard of Baal-hamon will thus also be the fruit of my own personal worth, shall belong to none else, O Solomon, than to thee, and two hundred to the keepers of its fruit ! If the keepers in Baal-hamon do not unrewarded watch the vineyard, so the king owes thanks to those who so faithfully guarded his Shulamith. The poetry would be reduced to prose if there were found in Shulamith's words a hint that the king should reward her brothers with a gratification of 200 shekels. She makes the case of the vineyard in Baal-hamon a parable of her relation to Solomon on the one hand, and of her relation to her brothers on the other. From מָאתַיִם, one may conclude that there were two brothers, thus that the rendering of thanks is thought of as מַעֲשֵׂר (a tenth part); but so that the 200 are meant not as a tax on the thousand, but as a reward for the faithful rendering up of the thousand.

The king, who seems to this point to have silently looked on in inmost sympathy, now, on being addressed by Shulamith, takes speech in hand ; he does not expressly refer to her request, but one perceives from his words that he heard it with pleasure. He expresses to her the wish that she would gratify the companions of her youth who were assembled around her, as well as himself, with a song, such as in former times she was wont to sing in these mountains and valleys.

> Ver. 13 O thou (who art) at home in the gardens,
>   Companions are listening for thy voice ;
>   Let me hear !

We observe that in the rural paradise with which she is surrounded, she finds herself in her element. It is a primary feature of her character which herein comes to view : her longing after quietness and peace, her love for collectedness of mind and for contemplation ; her delight in thoughts of the Creator suggested by the vegetable world, and particularly by the manifold soft beauty of flowers ; she is again once more in the gardens of her home, but the address, " O thou at home in the gardens ! " denotes that wherever she is, these gardens are her home as a fundamental feature of her nature. The חֲבֵרִים are not Solomon's companions, for she has come hither with Solomon alone, leaning on his arm. Also it is indicated in the expression : " are listening for thy voice," that they are such as have not for a long time heard the dear voice which was wont to cheer their hearts. The חבר׳ are the companions of the former shepherdess and keeper of a vineyard, i. 6 f., the playmates of her youth, the friends of her home. With a fine tact the poet does not represent Solomon as saying חֲבֵרָיִךְ nor חֲבֵרֵינוּ : the former would be contrary to the closeness of his relation to Shulamith, the latter contrary to the dignity of the king. By חברים there is neither expressed a, one-sided reference, nor is a double-sided excluded. That " for thy voice " refers not to her voice as speaking, but as the old good friends wish, as singing, is evident from הַשְׁמִיעִנִי in connection with ii. 14, where also קוֹלֵךְ is to be supplied, and the voice of song is meant. She complies with the request, and thus begins :

> Ver. 14 Flee, my beloved,
> And be thou like a gazelle,
> Or a young one of the harts,
> Upon spicy mountains.

Hitzig supposes that with these words of refusal she bids him away from her, without, however, as " my beloved " shows, meaning them in a bad sense. They would thus, as Renan says, be bantering coquetry. If it is Solomon who makes the request, and thus also he who is addressed here, not the imaginary shepherd violently introduced into this closing scene in spite of the words " (the thousand) is thine, Solomon " (ver. 12), then Shulamith's ignoring of his request is scornful, for it would be as unseemly if she sang of her own accord to please her friends, as it would be wilful if she kept silent when requested by her royal husband. So far the Spanish author, Soto Major, is right (1599): *jussa et rogata id non debuit nec potuit recusare.* Thus with " flee " she begins a song which she sings, as at ii. 15 she commences one, in reponse to a similar request, with " catch us." Hoelem. finds in her present happiness, which fills her more than ever, the thought here expressed that her beloved, if he again went from her for a moment, would yet

very speedily return to his longing, waiting bride.[1] But apart from
the circumstance that Shulamith is no longer a bride, but is married,
and that the wedding festival is long past, there is not a syllable of
that thought in the text; the words must at least have been בְּרַח אֵלַי,
if ברח signified generally to hasten hither, and not to hasten forth.
Thus, at least as little as סב, ii. 17, without אֵלִי, signifies "turn thyself hither," can this בְּרַח mean "flee hither." The words of the
song thus invite Solomon to disport himself, i.e. give way to
frolicsome and aimless mirth on these spicy mountains. As sov
l⁰cha is enlarged to sov d⁰meh-l⁰cha, ii. 17, for the sake of the added
figures (vid. under ii. 9), so here b⁰rahh-l⁰cha (Gen. xxvii. 43) is
enlarged to b⁰rahh ud⁰meh (udămeh) l⁰cha. That "mountains of
spices" occurs here instead of "cleft mountains," ii. 17b, has its
reason, as has already been there remarked, and as Hitzig, Hoelem.,
and others have discovered, in the aim of the poet to conclude the
pleasant song of love that has reached perfection and refinement with
an absolutely pleasant word.

But with what intention does he call on Shulamith to sing to
her beloved this בְּרַח, which obviously has here not the meaning of
escaping away (according to the fundamental meaning, transversum
currere), but only, as where it is used of fleeting time, Job ix. 25,
xiv. 2, the sense of hastening? One might suppose that she whom
he has addressed as at home in gardens replies to his request with the
invitation to hasten forth among the mountains,—an exercise which
gives pleasure to a man. But (1) Solomon, according to ii. 16,
vi. 2 f., is also fond of gardens and flowers; and (2) if he took
pleasure in ascending mountains, it doubled his joy, according to
iv. 8, to share this joy with Shulamith; and (3) we ask, would this
closing scene, and along with it the entire series of dramatic pictures,
find a satisfactory conclusion, if either Solomon remained and gave
no response to Shulamith's call, or if he, as directed, disappeared
alone, and left Shulamith by herself among the men who surrounded
her? Neither of these two things can have been intended by the
poet, who shows himself elsewhere a master in the art of composition. In ii. 17 the matter lies otherwise. There the love-relation
is as yet in progress, and the abandonment of love to uninterrupted
fellowship places a limit to itself. Now, however, Shulamith is
married, and the summons is unlimited. It reconciles itself neither

[1] Similarly Godet: The earth during the present time belongs to the earthly
power; only at the end shall the bridegroom fetch the bride, and appear as the
heavenly Solomon to thrust out the false and fleshly, and to celebrate the heavenly
marriage festival.

with the strength of her love nor with the tenderness of the relation, that she should with so cheerful a spirit give occasion to her husband to leave her alone for an indefinite time. We will thus have to suppose that, when Shulamith sings the song, "Flee, my beloved," she goes forth leaning on Solomon's arm out into the country, or that she presumes that he will not make this flight into the mountains of her native home without her. With this song breaking forth in the joy of love and of life, the poet represents the loving couple as disappearing over the flowery hills, and at the same time the sweet charm of the Song of Songs, leaping gazelle-like from one fragrant scene to another, vanishes away.

APPENDIX

REMARKS ON THE SONG BY DR. J. G. WETZSTEIN.

HE following aphoristic elucidations of the Song are partly collected from epistolary communications, but for the most part are taken from my friend's " Treatise on the Syrian thrashing-table " (in Bastian's *Zeitsch. für Ethnographie*, 1873), but not without these extracts having been submitted to him, and here and there enlarged by him.

The thrashing-table (*lô°ḥ ed-derâs*) is an agricultural implement in common use from ancient times in the countries round the Mediterranean Sea. It consists of two boards of nut-tree wood or of oak, bound together by two cross timbers. These boards are bent upwards in front, after the manner of a sledge, so as to be able to glide without interruption over the heaps of straw; underneath they are set with stones (of porous basalt) in oblique rows, thus forming a rubbing and cutting apparatus, which serves to thrash out the grain and to chop the straw; for the thrashing-table drawn by one or two animals yoked to it, and driven by their keeper, moves round on the straw-heaps spread on the barn floor. The thrashing-table may have sometimes been used in ancient times for the purpose of destroying prisoners of war by a horrible death (2 Sam. xii. 31); at the present day it serves as the seat of honour for the bride and bridegroom, and also as a bier whereon the master of the house is laid when dead. The former of these its two functions is that which has given an opportunity to Wetzstein to sketch in that Treatise, under the title of " The Table in the King's-week," a picture of the marriage festival among the Syrian peasantry. This sketch contains not a few things that serve to throw light on the Song, which we here place in order, intermixed with other remarks by Wetzstein with reference to the Song and to our commentary on it.

i. 6. In August 1861, when on a visit to the hot springs *El-hamma*, between *Domeir* and *Roheiba* to the north of Damascus, I was the guest of the Sheik *'Id*, who was encamped with his tribe, a branch of the *Solêb*, at the sulphurous stream there (*nahar el-mukebret*).

Since the language of this people (who inhabited the Syrian desert previous to the Moslem period, were longest confessors of Christianity among the nomads, and therefore kept themselves free from intermingling with the tribes that at a later period had migrated from the peninsula) possesses its own remarkable peculiarities, I embraced the opportunity of having dictated and explained to me, for three whole days, Solebian poems. The introduction to one of these is as follows : " The poet is *Solêbî Tuwês*, nephew of (the already mentioned) *Râshid*. The latter had had a dispute with a certain *Bishr;* that Tuwês came to know, and now sent the following *kasidah* (poem) to Bishr, which begins with praise in regard to his uncle, and finally advises Bishr to let that man rest, lest he (Tuwês) should become his adversary and that of his party." The last verse is in these words :

" That say I to you, I shall become the adversary of the disturber of the peace,
Bend my right knee before him, and, as a second Zir, show myself on the field of battle (the *menâch*)."

Zir is a hero celebrated in the Dîwân of Benî Hilâl; and to bend the right knee is to enter into a conflict for life or death : the figure is derived from the sword-dance.[1]

So much regarding the poem of Ṣolêbî. From this can nothing be gained for the explanation of נֶחֱרוּ־בִי of the Song ? This is for the most part interpreted as the *Niph.* of חָרָה or חָרַר (to be inflamed, to be angry with one) ; but why not as the *Pih.* of נָחַר ? It is certainly most natural to interpret this נחר in the sense of *nakhar*, to breathe, snort; but the LXX., Symm., Theod., in rendering by μαχέσαντο (διεμαχέσαντο), appear to have connected with *nihharu* the meaning

---

[1] If this dance, *e.g.*, is danced to celebrate a victory, it not seldom happens that the spectators call out to a young man particularly struck by the dancer : Kneel to her. He who is thus challenged steps into the circle, sinks down on his right knee, in which inconvenient attitude he endeavours to approach the dancer, who on her part falls down on both her knees ; sliding and fencing according to the beat of the music, she retreats, and at the same time seeks with all her might to keep her assailant back with a sword. He parries the strokes with his left arm, while he attempts to gain his object. viz. with his right hand to touch the head of the dancer. If he succeeds in this, he cries out, " Dancer, I touch ! " With that the play ends, and the victor leaves the arena amid the approving shouts of the throng, often bleeding from many wounds. Many a one has forfeited his life in his attempt to touch a celebrated beauty. Since such death was self-chosen, the maiden goes unpunished. If the assailant, as often happens, is the brother or father's brother's son of the dancer, in which case the venture is less perilous, he has the right to kiss the vanquished damsel, which is always for the spectator a great amusement.

of that (Arab.) *tanaḥar*, which comes from *taḥrn*, the front of the neck. The outstretched neck of the camel, the breast, the head, the face, the brow, the nose, are, it is well known in the Arab., mere symbols for that which stands forward according to place, time, and rank. Of this *naḥrn*, not only the Old Arab. (*vid. Ḳâmûs* under the word) but also the Modern Arab. has denom. verbal forms. In Damascus they say, *alsyl naḥara min alystan*, " the torrent tore away a part of the garden opposing it ;" and according to the *Deutsch. morg. Zeitschr.* xxii. 142, *naḥḥar flana* is " to strive forward after one." Hence *tanaḥarua*, to step opposite to (in a hostile manner), like *takabalua*, then to contend in words, to dispute; and *naḥir* is, according to a vulgar mode of expression, one who places himself *coram* another, sits down to talk, discourses with him. These *denominativa* do not in themselves and without further addition express in the modern idioms the idea of " to take an opponent by the neck," or " to fight hand to hand with him."

i. 7. For עֹטְיָה the Arab. עֲצִיָּה presents itself for comparison; with inhabitants of the town, as well as of the desert (*Haḍar* and *Bedu*), *alghadwat*, " the (maiden) languishing with love," a very favourite designation for a maiden fatally in love ; the mas. *alghady* (plur. *alghudat*) is used in the same sense of a young man. According to its proper signification, it denotes a maiden with a languishing eye, the deeply sunk glimmerings of whose eyelids veil the eye. In Damascus such eyes are called *'iwan dubbal*, " pressed down eyes ;" and in the Haurân, *'iwan mugharribat*, " broken eyes ;" and they are not often wanting in love songs there. Accordingly, she who speaks seeks to avoid the neighbourhood of the shepherds, from fear of the *hatkalsitr*, *i.e.* for fear lest those who mocked would thus see the secret of her love, in accordance with the verse :

" By its symptoms love discovers itself to the world,
As musk which one carries discovers itself by its aroma."

i. 17. The cypress never bears the name *ṣnawbar*, which always denotes only the pine, one of the pine tribe. The cypress is only called *serwa*, collect. *seru*. Since it is now very probable that ברות (ברוֹשׁ) is the old Heb. name of the cypress, and since there can at no time have been cypresses on the downs of Beirût, the connection of بيروت with ברות is to be given up. Instead of the difficult Heb. word *rahhithēnu*, there is perhaps to be read *v'hhēthēnu* (from *hhäith* = *hhäits*), " and our walls." The word-form حَائِط may have come from the idiom of the Higâz, or from some other impure source, into the written language ; the living language knows only *hayṭ*

(חַיִט), plur. *ḥîṭân* (Syr. Egypt.) and *ḥijûṭ* (Berbery). The written language itself has only the plur. *ḥîṭân*, and uses חַיִט as an actual sing. For the transition of the letter *tsade* into *teth* in the Song, cf. נטר.

ii. 11. " For lo, the winter is past, the rain is over—is gone."

These are the words of the enticing love of the bridegroom to his beloved, whom he seeks to raise to the rank of queen. " The fairest period in the life of a Syrian peasant," thus Wetzstein's description begins, " are the first seven days after his marriage, in which, along with his young wife, he plays the part of king (*melik*) and she of queen (*melika*), and both are treated and served as such in their own district and by the neighbouring communities." The greater part of village weddings take place for the most part in the month of March, the most beautiful month of the Syrian year, called from its loveliness (*sahh^ar*) *âdâr* = "*prachtmonat*" (magnificent month), to which the proverb refers: " If any one would see Paradise in its flowery splendour (*fî ezhârihâ*), let him contemplate the earth in its month of splendour (*fî âdârihâ*). Since the winter rains are past, and the sun now refreshes and revives, and does not, as in the following months, oppress by its heat, weddings are celebrated in the open air on the village thrashing-floor, which at this time, with few exceptions, is a flowery meadow. March is also suitable as the season for festivals, because at such a time there is little field labour, and, moreover, everything then abounds that is needed for a festival. During the winter the flocks have brought forth their young,—there are now lambs and kids, butter, milk, and cheese, and cattle for the slaughter, which have become fat on the spring pasture; the neighbouring desert yields for it brown, yellow, and white earth-nuts in such abundance, that a few children in one day may gather several camel-loads." The description passes over the marriage day itself, with its pomp, the sword-dance of the bride, and the great marriage feast, and begins where the newly married, on the morning after the marriage night,—which the young husband, even to this day, like the young Tobiah, spends sometimes in prayer,—appear as king and queen, and in their wedding attire receive the representative of the bride's-men, now their minister (*mezêr*), who presents them with a morning meal. Then the bride's-men come, fetch the thrashing-table (" corn-drag ") from the straw storehouse (*metben*), and erect a scaffolding on the thrashing-floor, with the table above it, which is spread with a variegated carpet, and with two ostrich-feather cushions studded with gold, which is the seat of honour (*merteba*) for the king and queen during the seven days. This beautiful custom has a good reason for it, and also fulfils a noble end. For the more oppressive, troublesome, and unhappy the condition of the Syro-Palestinian peasant, so much the more reasonable does it appear that he should be honoured for a few days at least, and be celebrated and made happy. And considering the facility and wantonness of divorces in the Orient, the recollection of the marriage week, begun so joyfully, serves as a counterpoise to hinder a separation.

iii. 11. עֲטָרָה. The custom of crowning the bridegroom no longer exists in Syria. The bride's crown, called in Damascus *tâg-el-'arûs*, is called in the Haurân *'orga* (עֶרְגָה). This consists of a silver circlet, which is covered with a net of strings of corals of about three fingers' breadth. Gold coins are fastened in rows to this net, the largest being on the lowest row, those in the other rows upward becoming always smaller. At the wedding feast the hair of the bride is untied, and falls freely down over her neck and breast; and that it might not lose its wavy form, it is only oiled with some fragrant substances. The crowning thus begins: the headband is first bound on her head,—which on this day is not the *Sembar* (*vid. Deut. morg. Zeit.* xxii. 94), but the *Kesmâja*, a long, narrow, silken band, interwoven with dark-red and gold, and adorned at both ends with fringes, between which the *Sumûch*, silver, half-spherical little bells, hang down. The ends of the Kesmâja fall on both sides of the head, the one on the breast and the other on the back, so that the sound of the *Sumûch* is distinctly perceptible only during the sword-dance of the bride. Over the Kesmâja the crown is now placed in such a way that it rests more on the front of the head, and the front gold pieces of the under row come to lie on the naked brow. In the *Sahka*, partly referred to under vii. 2, the poet addresses the goldsmith:

"And beat (for the bride) little bells, which constantly swing and ring like
    the tymbals (*nakkârât*) ; [1]
And (beat) the crown, one of four rows, and let Gihâdîs [2] be on the brow."

---

[1] By *nakkârât* are meant those little tymbals (kettledrums) which are used to keep time with the dancing-song, when that is not done by the tambourine. The ladies of Damascus take them with them to every country party, where frequently, without any singing, they are the only accompaniment of the dance. They are thus used: a damsel seats herself on the bare ground, places the two (scarcely is there ever only one) saucers—large copper hemispheres—before her breast, and beats against them with two wooden mallets. Their strings are made of the skins of goats or gazelles, while, for the tambourine, preference is given to the throat-bag of the pelican. These tymbals, like our own, have an unequal sound; when out of tune, they are rectified by being heated over a brazier.

[2] The *Gihâdî* is a rare Turkish gold piece of money, of old and beautiful

Etymologically considered, I believe that the word 'orga must be regarded as parallel with 'argún (עַרְגֻן), which in the Haurán is the foot-buckle; so that, from the root 'arag, "to be bent," it is the designation of a bow or circlet, which the word taj also certainly means. However, on one occasion in Korêa (to the east of Boṣrâ), while we were looking at a bride's crown, one said to me: "They call it 'orga, because the coral strings do not hang directly down, but, running oblique (mu'arwajat), form a net of an elongated square."

iv. 14. אֲהָלוֹת. Who recognises in the Moorish nif, "the nose," the Heb. אַף? And yet the two words are the same. The word אַנְף, enf, "the nose," is used by the wandering Arabs, who are fond of the dimin. אֲנֵיף, "néf, which is changed into נֵיף; for א in the beginning of a word, particularly before a grave and accented syllable, readily falls away. From néf (neif), finally, comes nif, because the idiom of the Moorish Arabians rejects the diphthong ei.

Thus, also, it fared with the word אֲהָלוֹת, "the little tent," "the little house," as the three-cornered capsules of the cardamum are called,—an aromatic plant which is to the present day so ardently loved by the Hadar and the Bedu, on account of its heat, and especially its sweet aroma, that one would have been led to wonder if it were wanting in this passage of the Song. From אֹהֶל there is formed the dimin. אֲהֵיל, and this is shortened into hél, which is at the present day the name of the cardamum, while the unabbreviated °hel is retained as the caritative of the original meaning,—we say, já °héli, "my dear tent- (i.e. tribal) companions." This linguistic process is observable in all the Semitic languages; it has given rise to a mass of new roots. That it began at an early period, is shown by the Phoenician language; for the bibl. names Hiram and Huram are abbreviated from Ahi-ram and Ahu-ram; and the Punic stones supply many analogues, e.g. the proper names Himilcath (= Ahhi-Milcath, restrictus reginae coeli) with Hethmilcath (= Ahith-Milcath) and the like. On one of the stones which I myself brought from Carthage is found the word דֹן instead of אֲדֹן, "sir, master." In a similar way, the watering-place which receives so many diverse names by travellers, the Wéba (Weiba), in the Araba valley, will be an abbreviation of אֲוֵיבָה, and this the dimin. of אֹבוֹת, the name of an encampment of the Israelites in the wilderness (Num. xxi. 10). It had the name 'ēn ovoth, "the fountain of the water-bottles," perhaps

coinage, thin but very large, and of the finest gold. It was carried as a charm against the evil eye. On a bride's crown it forms the lowermost row of coins.

from the multitude of water-bottles filled here by water-drawers, waiting one after another. This encampment has been sought elsewhere—certainly incorrectly. Of the harbour-town *Elath* (on the Red Sea), it has been said, in the geography of *Ibn el-Bennâ* (MSS. of the Royal Lib. in Berlin, Sect. Spr. Nr. 5), published in Jerusalem about the year 1000: " *Weila*, at the north end of the (eastern) arm of the Red Sea; prosperous and distinguished; rich in palms and fishes; the harbour of Palestine, and the granary of Higâz; is called *Aila* by the common people; but *Aila* is laid waste,—it lies quite in the neighbourhood." Thus it will be correct to say, that the name *Weila* is abbreviated from אֲוֵילָה, " Little-Aila," and designated a settlement which gradually grew up in the neighbourhood of the old Aila, and to which, when the former was at last destroyed, the name was transferred, so that " Little-Aila " became Aila; therefore it is that the later Arab. geographers know nothing of *Weila*. I have already elsewhere mentioned, that at the root of the name of the well-known Port *Suês* lies the Arab. *'sâs* (= אָשִׁישׁ), which, among all the Syrian tribes, has lost the initial letter *Elif*, and takes the form of *Sâs*. Hence the name *Suês* (*Suwês*), the diminutive. The place has its name from this, that it was built on the foundations of an older harbour.

Silv. de Sacy already (*vid.* Gesen. *Thes.* p. 33*b*) conjectured that אֲהָלוֹת means cardamums. But, as it appears, he based his proof less on the identity of the two words *hêl* and *ahalôt*, than on the circumstance that he found the word *kâkula*—the Jemanic, and perhaps originally Indian name of cardamums — in the *hâhula* of the Egyptians of the present day. But the Egyptian does not pronounce the *k* like *h*; he does not utter it at all, or at most like a *Hamza*, so that *kâkula* is sounded by him not *hâhula*, but *'â'ula*. And who could presuppose the antiquity of this word, or that of its present pronunciation, in a land which has so radically changed both its language and its inhabitants as Egypt? And why should the Palestinians have received their Indian spices, together with their names, from Egypt? Why not much rather from *Aila*, to which they were brought from Jemen, either by ships or by the well-organized caravans (*vid.* Strabo, xvi. 4) which traded in the maritime country *Tihâma*? Or from *Têma*, the chief place in the desert (Job vi. 19; Isa. xxi. 14), whither they were brought from *'Akir*, the harbour of *Gerrha*, which, according to Strabo (as above), was the great Arab. spice market? But if Palestine obtained its spices from thence, it would also, with them, receive the foreign name for them unchanged,—*kakula*,—since all the Arab tribes express the *ḳ* sound very distinctly. In short, the word אהלות has nothing to do with *kâḳula;* it is shown to be a pure Semitic word by the plur. formations *ahaloth* and *ahalim* (Prov. vii. 17). The punctuation does not contradict this. The inhabitants of Palestine received the word, with the thing itself, through the medium of the Arabs, among whom the Heb. אֹהֶל is at the present time, as in ancient times, pronounced אֲהַל; thus the Arab vocalization is simply retained to distinguish it from אֹהֶל in its proper signification, without the name of the spice becoming thereby a meaningless foreign word. That the living language had a sing. for "a cardamum capsule" is self-evident. Interesting is the manner and way in which the modern Arabs help themselves with reference to this sing. Since *hêl* does not discover the mutilated אהל, and the Arab. اهل, besides, has modified its meaning (it signifies tent- and house-companions), the *nom. unit. hêla,* "a cardamum capsule," is no longer formed from *hêl;* the word *geras,* "the little bell," is therefore adopted, thereby forming a comparison of the firmly closed seed capsules, in which the loose seeds, on being shaken, give forth an audible rustling, with the little bells which are hung round the bell-wether and the leading camel. Thus they say: take three or four little bells (*egrâs*), and not: *telât, arbaʿ hêlât* (which at most, as a mercantile expression, would denote, "parcels or kinds" of cardamum); they speak also of *geras-el-hêl* ("*hêl* little bells") and *geras-et-tib* ("*spice* little bells"). This "little bell" illustrates the ancient אהל. Supposing that *kâḳula* might have been the true name of the cardamum, then these would have been called אהלות קקלה, "*kaḳula*-capsules," by the Heb. traders in spicery, who, as a matter of course, knew the foreign name; while, on the contrary, the people, ignoring the foreign name, would use the words אֲהָלוֹת (אֲהָלֵי) בִּשֶׂם, "spice-capsules," or only *ahaloth.* Imported spices the people named from their appearance, without troubling themselves about their native names. An Arabian called the nutmeg *gôz-et-tib,* "spice-nut," which would correspond to a Heb. אֱגוֹז בִּשֶׂם. So he called the clove-blossom *mismâr-et-tib,* "spice-cloves," as we do, or merely *mismâr,* "clove." The spice-merchant knows only the foreign word *gurumful,* "clove." It is very probable that *hêl,* divested of its appellative signification by the word *geras,* in process of time disappeared from the living language.

That pounded cardamum is one of the usual ingredients in Arab. coffee, we see from a poem, only a single very defective copy of which could be obtained by Wallin (*vid. Deutsch. morg. Zeit.*

vi. 373). The verse alluded to, with a few grammatical and metrical changes which were required, is as follows :

> "With a pot (of coffee) in which must be cardamum and nutmeg,
> And twenty cloves, the right proportion for connoisseurs."

The nut is not, as Wallin supposes, the cocoa-nut (*gôz-el-Hind*), but the nutmeg ; and '*ûd* = " the small piece of wood," is the clove, as Wallin also, rightly ; elsewhere '*ûd* and '*ûda* is the little stalk of the raisin.

v. 1. " Eat, friends, drink and be drunken, beloved." With רֵעִים here is compared מֵרֵעִים, Judg. xiv. 11, where thirty companions are brought to Samson when he celebrated for seven days his marriage in Timnath, the so-called bride's-men, who are called in post-bibl. Heb. שׁוֹשְׁבֵנִים, and at the present day in Syria, *shebâb el-'arîs, i.e.* the bridegroom's young men; their chief is called the *Shebîn.* " The designation ' bride's-men ' (Nymphagogen) is not wholly suitable. Certainly they have also to do service to the bride ; and if she is a stranger, they form the essential part of the armed escort on horse-back which heads the marriage procession (*el-fârida*), and with mock fighting, which is enacted before the bride and the bride's-maids (*el-ferrâdât*), leads it into the bridegroom's village ; but the chief duties of the *shebâb* on the marriage day and during the ' king's week' belong properly to the bridegroom. This escort must be an ancient institution of the country. Perhaps it had its origin in a time of general insecurity in the land, when the ' young men ' formed a watch-guard, during the festival, against attacks." The names רֵעַ and מֵרֵעַ Wetzstein derives from a רִיע, " to be closely connected," which is nearly related to רעה ; for he takes רֵיעַ, Job vi. 27, as the etymologically closer description of the former, and מֵרֵעַ (= מִרֵעַ) he places parallel to the Arab. word *mirjâ'*, which signifies " the inseparable companion," and among all the Syrian nomad tribes is the designation of the bell-wether, because it follows closely the steps of the shepherd, carries his bread-pouch, and receives a portion at every meal-time.

> vii. 1. What would ye see in Shulamith?—
> " As the dance of Mahanaim."

" The sports during the days of the marriage festival are from time to time diversified with dances. The various kinds of dances are comprehended under the general names of *sahka* and *debka*. The *sahka*, pronounced by the Beduin *sahée* (= *sahtsche*), is a graceful solitary dance, danced by a single person, or in itself not involving several persons. The *debka*, " hanging dance," because the dancers link themselves together by their little fingers; if they were linked together by their hands, this would give the opportunity of pressing hands, which required to be avoided, because Arab ladies would not permit this from men who were strangers to them. For the most part, the *debḳa* appears as a circular dance. If it is danced by both sexes, it is called *debḳa muwaddaʻa* = ʻthe variegated *debḳa*.ʼ The *saḥḳa* must be of Beduin origin, and is accordingly always danced with a *ḳasidah* (poem or song) in the nomad idiom; the *debḳa* is the peculiar national dance of the Syrian peasantry (*Ḥadarî*), and the songs with which it is danced are exclusively in the language of the *Ḥadarî*. They have the prevailing metre of the so-called Andalusian ode ($- \cup - - \mid - \cup - - \mid - \cup -$), and it is peculiar to the *debḳa*, that its strophes hang together like the links of a chain, or like the fingers of the dancers, while each following strophe begins with the words with which the preceding one closes [similar to the step-like rhythm of the psalms of degrees; *vid. Psalmen*, ii. 257]. For the *saḥḳa* and the *debḳa* they have a solo singer. Whenever he has sung a verse, the chorus of dancers and spectators takes up the *kehrvers* (*meredd*), which in the *debḳa* always consists of the two last lines of the first strophe of the poem. Instrumental music is not preferred in dancing; only a little timbrel (*deff*), used by the solo singer, who is not himself (or herself) dancing, gently accompanies the song to give the proper beat" (cf. Ex. xv. 20 f., and Ps. lxviii. 26).

To the *saḥḳa*, which is danced after a *ḳasidah* (for the most part with the metre $- - \cup - \mid - - \cup - \mid - - \cup - \mid - - \cup -$) without the *kehrvers* in $\frac{2}{4}$ time, belongs the sword-dance, which the bride dances on her marriage day. Wetzstein thus describes it in *Deutsch. morg. Zeit.* xxii. 106, having twice witnessed it: "The figure of the dancer (*el-ḥâshî*, ʻshe who fills the ring,ʼ or *abû ḥ°wêsh*, ʻ she who is in the ringʼ), the waving dark hair of her locks cast loose, her serious noble bearing, her downcast eyes, her graceful movements, the quick and secure step of her small naked feet, the lightning-like flashing of the blade, the skilful movements of her left hand, in which the dancer holds a handkerchief, the exact keeping of time, although the song of the *munshid* (the leader) becomes gradually quicker and the dance more animated—this is a scene which has imprinted itself indelibly on my memory. It is completed by the ring (*ḥ°wêsh*), the one half of which is composed of men and the other of women. They stand upright, gently move their shoulders, and accompany the beat of the time with a swaying to and fro of the upper part of their bodies, and a gentle beating of their hands stretched upwards before their breasts. The whole scene is brightened by a fire that has been kindled. The constant repetition of the words *jâ halâlî jâ mâli*, O my own, O my possession! [*vid. Psalmen*, ii. 384, Anm.], and the sword with which the husband protects his family and his property in the hand of the maiden, give to the *sahka*, celebrated in the days of domestic happiness, the stamp of an expression of thanks and joy over the possession of that which makes life pleasant—the family and property; for with the *Hadarî* and the *Bedawî* the word *halâl* includes wife and child."

"When the *sahka* is danced by a man, it is always a sword-dance. Only the form of this dance (it is called *sahkat el-Gawâfina*), as it is performed in Gôf, is after the manner of the *contre*-dance, danced by two rows of men standing opposite each other. The dancers do not move their hands, but only their shoulders; the women form the ring, and sing the refrain of the song led by the *munshid*, who may here be also one of the dancers."

vii. 2. "How beautiful are thy steps in the shoes, O prince's daughter!"

After the maidenhood of the newly married damsel has been established (cf. Deut. xxii. 13–21) before the tribunal (*divân*) of the wedding festival, there begins a great dance; the song sung to it refers only to the young couple, and the inevitable *wasf*, *i.e.* a description of the personal perfections and beauty of the two, forms its principal contents. Such a *wasf* was sung also yesterday during the sword-dance of the bride; that of to-day (the first of the seven wedding-festival days) is wholly in praise of the queen; and because she is now a wife, commends more those attractions which are visible than those which are veiled. In the Song, only vii. 2–6 [1] is compared to this *wasf*. As for the rest, it is the lovers themselves who reciprocally sing. Yet this may also have been done under the

---

[1] According to Wetzstein's opinion, v. 2 ff. is also a *wasf*, to which the narrative, vv. 5–7, aims at giving only an agreeable commencement; the songs of the Song which he does not regard as Solomonic, nor as a dramatic united whole, particularly the *Wasf*-portions, appear to him to have been received into the Canon in order to preserve for the people some beautiful hallowed marriage songs, and to give good examples for imitation to the occasional poets whose productions may in ancient times, among the Hebrews, as in our own day among ourselves, have overstepped the limits of propriety and good taste. The allegorical or mystical interpretation appeared later, and was in this case something lying far nearer than *e.g.* with those love-songs which were sung by the singers of the mosque of the Omajads at the festival *thalilat*, at the grave of John the Baptist. "Place, time, and circumstance," says the Damascene, "give to a song its meaning."

influence of the custom of the *wasf.* The repetition, iv. 1–5 and vi. 4–7, are wholly after the manner of the *wasf;* in the Syrian wedding songs also, these encomiums are after one pattern.

We quote here by way of example such an encomium. It forms the conclusion of a *sahka,* which had its origin under the following circumstances : When, some forty years ago, the sheik of *Nawâ* gave away his daughter in marriage, she declared on her wedding day that she would dance the usual sword-dance only along with a *kasidah,* composed specially for her by a noted Hauran poet. Otherwise nothing was to be done, for the Hauranian chief admired the pride of his daughter, because it was believed it would guard her from errors, and afford security for her family honour. The most distinguished poet of the district at that time was *Kasîm el-Chinn,* who had just shortly before returned from a journey to Mesopotamia to the phylarch of the *Gerbâ* tribe, who had bestowed on him royal gifts. He lived in the district of *Gâsim,*[1] famed from of old for its poets, a mile (German) to the north of *Nawâ.* A messenger on horseback was sent for him. The poet had no time to lose ; he stuck some writing materials and paper into his girdle, mounted his ass, and composed his poem whilst on the way, the messenger going before him to announce his arrival. When Ḳâsim came, the fire was already kindled on the ground, the wedding guests were waiting, and the dancer in bridal attire, and with the sword in her hand, stood ready. Ḳâsim kissed her hand and took the place of leader of the song, since from want of time no one could repeat the poem ; moreover, Ḳâsim had a fine voice. When the dance was over, the bride took her *kesmâja* from off her head, folded twenty *Gâzi* (about thirty thalers) in it, and threw it to the poet,—a large present considering the circumstances, for the *kesmâja* of a rich bride is costly. On the other hand, she required the poem to be delivered up to her. The plan of the poem shows great skill. *Nawâ,* lying in the midst of the extremely fruitful Batanian plain, is interested in agriculture to an extent unequalled in any other part of Syria and Palestine ; its sheik is proud of the fact that formerly Job's 500 yoke ploughed there, and *Nawâ* claims to be Job's town.[2] Since the peasant, according to the well-known proverb, *de bobus arator,* has thought and concern for nothing more than for agriculture ; so the poet might

---

[1] Abû-Temmâm, the collector of the Hamâsa, was also a native of *Gâsim.* [*Vid.* Delitzsch's *Jud.-Arab. Poesien* of the pre-Muhammed period, p. 1.]

[2] It is not improbable that *Nawâ* is an abbreviation of נָוֶה־אִיּוֹב, as *Medina* is of *Medinat-en-Nebî.* Regarding the supposed grave of Job in the neighbourhood of *Nawâ. vid. Comment.* on Job by Fr. Delitzsch.

with certainty reckon on an understanding and an approbation of his poem if he makes it move within the sphere of country life. He does this. He begins with this, that a *shekâra, i.e.* a benefice, is sown for the dancer, which is wont to be sown only to the honour of one of great merit about the place. That the benefice might be worthy of the recipient, four *sauwâmen* (a *sauwâma* consists of six yoke) are required, and the poet has opportunity to present to his audience pleasing pictures of the great *shekâra,* of harvests, thrashings, measuring, loading, selling. Of the produce of the wheat the portion of the dancer is now bought, first the clothes, then the ornaments; both are described. The *wasf* forms the conclusion, which is here given below. In the autumn of 1860, I received the poem from a young man of Nawâ at the same time along with other poems of Kâsim's, all of which he knew by heart. The rest are much more artistic and complete in form than the *sahka.* Who can say how many of the (particularly metrically) weak points of the latter are to be attributed to the poet, and to the rapidity with which it was composed; and how many are to be laid to the account of those by whom it was preserved?

> " Here hast thou thy ornament, O beautiful one! put it on, let nothing be
>   forgotten!
> Put it on, and live when the coward and the liar are long dead.
> She said: Now shalt thou celebrate me in song, describe me in verse
>   from head to foot!
> I say: O fair one, thine attractions I am never able to relate,
> And only the few will I describe which my eyes permit me to see:
> Her head is like the crystal goblet, her hair like the black night,
> Her black hair like the seven nights, the like are not in the whole year;[1]
> In waves it moves hither and thither, like the rope of her who draws
>   water,
> And her side locks breathe all manner of fragrance, which kills me.
> The new moon beams on her brow, and dimly illuminated are the balances,[2]

---

[1] These seven nights are the last four of February and the first three of March (of the old calendar). They are very cloudy, rainy, and dark, and are called *el-mustakridât,* "the borrowing nights," either because they have a share of the clouds, rain, and darkness of all the other nights of the year, as if borrowed from them, or because the seven reciprocally dispose of their shares, so that, *e.g.,* the darkness of each of these nights is sevenfold. The frequent hail which falls during these cold disagreeable days is called " old wives' teeth " (*asnân-el-'agâiz*), because many old people die during these days.

[2] While sometimes the light of the new moon is weak and that of the balances is very strong; the contrary is the case here. The balances are two constellations: the one is called the right balance (*mînzân-el-ḥakk*), and consists of three very bright stars; the other is called the false balance (*m. el-butl*), and consists of two bright and one dimmer star.

And her eyebrows like the arch of the *Nûn* drawn by an artist's hand.[1]

The witchery of her eyes makes me groan as if they were the eyes of a Kufic lady ;[2]

Her nose is like the date of Irâk,[3] the edge of the Indian sword;

Her face like the full moon, and heart-breaking are her cheeks.

Her mouth is a little crystal ring, and her teeth rows of pearls,

And her tongue scatters pearls; and, ah me, how beautiful her lips!

Her spittle pure virgin honey, and healing for the bite of a viper.

Comparable to elegant writing, the *Seijal*[4] waves downwards on her chin,

Thus black seeds of the fragrant *Kezha*[5] show themselves on white bread.

The *Mâni* draws the neck down to itself with the spell written in Syrian letters ;

Her neck is like the neck of the roe which drinks out of the fountain of *Kanawât*.[6]

Her breast like polished marble tablets, as ships bring them to *Sêdâ* (Sidon),

Thereon like apples of the pomegranate two glittering piles of jewels.

Her arms are drawn swords, peeled cucumbers—oh that I had such !

And incomparably beautiful her hands in the rose-red of the *Hinnâ*-leaf ;

Her smooth, fine fingers are like the writing reed not yet cut ;

The glance of her nails like the Dura-seeds which have lain overnight in milk ;[7]

Her body is a mass of cotton wool which a master's hand has shaken into down,[8]

And her legs marble pillars in the sacred house of the Omajads.

---

[1] The eyebrows are compared to the arch of the Arab. letter ن inverted ; this comparison, in which the rural poets imitate the insipid city poets, is only admissible when one has before him a *Nûn* written by a caligraphic hand.

[2] The eyes of the Kufic or Babylonian lady (*bâbilîja*) are perfectly black, which for the Arabians are particularly dangerous. Also with the Babylonian sorceress *Zuhara*, who led astray the two angels *Hârût* and *Mârût* (*vid. Korân* ii. 26), her charms lay in her black eyes.

[3] The date of '*Irâk* is white and small, not too long and very sweet.

[4] The *Seijal* is a *dakka*, *i.e.* a tattooed arabesque in the form of final *Mim's* (م) standing over one another. The *Mâni* (ver. 20), another *dakka*, is applied to the top of the windpipe. It consists for the most part of a ring, in which is engraved as a talisman a Syrian, *i.e.* a feigned angel's name ending in ىـٮ.

[5] The *Kezah, n. unit. Kezha*, is the *nigella sativa* with which fine pastry is sprinkled.

[6] Here it is not the well of the *Wâdy Kanawât* on the Haurân range that is meant, but the *Kanawât* stream, an arm of the *Baradâ*, which fills the tanks of the Damascus houses, so that the thought would be that the neck of the bride is white like that of a lady of the city, not brown like that of a peasant.

[7] The *Dura* of the Haurân is the millet, which, when laid in milk, receives a white glance, and enlarges, so that it may be compared to a finger-nail.

[8] The upholsterer (*neddâf*, usually called *hallâg*) has a bow above one fathom long, the string of which, consisting of a very thick gut-string, he places in contact with the wool or cotton-wool which is to be shaken loose, and then

There hast thou, fair one, thy attractions, receive this, nothing would be
    forgotten,
And live and flourish when the coward and the liar are long ago dead!"

vii. 3. " Thy body a heap of wheat, set round with lilies."

In the fifth Excursus regarding the winnowing shovel and the
winnowing fork in my *Comment. on Isaiah,* Wetzstein's illustration
of this figure was before me. The dissertation regarding the thrashing-table contains many instructive supplements thereto. When the
grain is thrashed, from that which is thrashed (*derîs*), which consists
of corn, chopped straw, and chaff, there is formed a new heap of
winnowings, which is called *'arama.* " According to its derivation
(from *'aram,* to be uncovered), *'arama* means heaps of rubbish
destitute of vegetation ; *'arama, 'oreima, 'irâm,* are, in the Haurân
and Golân, proper names of several *Puys* (conical hills formed
by an eruption) covered with yellow or red volcanic rubbish.
In the terminology of the thrashing-floor, the word always and
without exception denotes the *derîs*-heaps not yet winnowed ; in the
Heb., on the contrary, corn-heaps already winnowed. Such a heap
serves (Ruth iii. 7) Boaz as a pillow for his head when he lay down
and watched his property. Luther there incorrectly renders by
' behind a *Mandel,'* *i.e.* a heap of (fifteen) sheaves ; on the contrary,
correctly at the passage before us (Song vii. 3), ' like a heap of
wheat,' viz. a heap of winnowed wheat. The wheat colour (*el-lôn
el-ḥinṭi*) is in Syria regarded as the most beautiful colour of the
human body."

strikes it with a short wooden mallet. By the violent and rapid vibration of the
string, the wool, however closely it may have been pressed together and entangled,
is changed with surprising quickness into the finest down.

THE BOOK OF ECCLESIASTES

THE BOOK OF ECCLESIASTES

INTRODUCTION.

IF we look at the world without God, it appears what it is,—a magnificent, graduated combination of diverse classes of beings, connected causes and effects, well-calculated means and ends. But thus contemplated, the world as a whole remains a mystery. If, with the atheist, we lay aside the idea of God, then, notwithstanding the law of causation, which is grounded in our mental nature, we abandon the question of the origin of the world. If, with the pantheist, we transfer the idea of God to the world itself, then the effect is made to be as one with the cause,—not, however, without the conception of God, which is inalienable in man, reacting against it; for one cannot but distinguish between substance and its phenomena. The mysteries of the world which meet man as a moral being remain, under this view of the world, altogether without solution. For the moral order of the world presupposes an absolutely good Being, from whom it has proceeded, and who sustains it; it demands a Lawgiver and a Judge. Apart from the reference to this Being, the distinction between good and evil loses its depth and sharpness. Either there is no God, or all that is and happens is a moment in the being and life of God Himself, who is identical with the world : thus must the world - destructive power of sin remain unrecognised. The opinion as to the state of the world will, from a pantheistic point of view, rise to optimism ; just as, on the other hand, from an atheistic point of view, it will sink to pessimism. The commanding power of goodness even the atheist may recognise by virtue of the inner law peculiar to man as a moral being, but the divine consecration is wanting to this goodness ; and if human life is a journey from nothing to nothing, then this will be the best of all goodness : that man set himself free from the evil reality, and put his confidence in nothing. " Him who views the world," says Buddhism, " as a water-bubble, a phantom, the king of death does not terrify. What pleasure, what joy is in this world ? Behold the changing form—it is undone by old age ; the diseased body— it dissolves and corrupts ! ' I have sons and treasures ; here will I dwell in the season of the cold, and there in the time of the heat :' thus thinks the fool ; and cares not for, and sees not, the hindrances thereto. Him who is concerned about sons and treasures,— the man who has his heart so entangled,—death tears away, as the torrent from the forest sweeps away the slumbering village."

The view taken of the world, and the judgment formed regarding it, in the Book of Ecclesiastes, are wholly different. While in the Book of Esther faith in God remains so much in the background that there is nowhere in it express mention made of God, the name of God occurs in Ecclesiastes no fewer than thirty-seven times,[1] and that in such a way that the naming of Him is at the same time the confession of Him as the True God, the Exalted above the world, the Governor and the Ruler over all. And not only that : the book characterizes itself as a genuine product of the Israelitish Chokma by this, that, true to its motto, it places the command, " Fear thou God," v. 6 [7], xii. 13, in the foremost rank as a fundamental moral duty ; that it makes, viii. 12, the happiness of man to be dependent thereon ; that it makes, vii. 18, xi. 9, xii. 14, his final destiny to be conditioned by his fearing God ; and that it contemplates the world as one that was created by God very good, iii. 11, vii. 29, and as arranged, iii. 14, and directed so that men should fear Him. These primary principles, to which the book again and again returns, are of special importance for a correct estimate of it.

Of like decisive importance for the right estimate of the theistic, and at the same time also the pessimistic, view of the world presented by Koheleth is this, that he knows of no future life compensating for the troubles of the present life, and resolving its mystery. It is true that he says, xii. 7, that the life-spirit of the man who dies returns to God who gave it, as the body returns to the dust of which it is formed ; but the question asked in iii. 21 shows that this preferring of the life-spirit of man to that of a beast was not, in his regard, raised above all doubt. And what does this return to

---

[1] הָאֱלֹהִים, ii. 24, 26, iii. 11, 14 (twice), 15, 17, 18, iv. 17, v. 1, 5, 6, 17, 18a, 19, vi. 2 (twice), vii. 13, 14, 26, 29, viii. 15, 17, ix. 1, 7, xi. 5, 9, xii. 7, 13, 14. אֱלֹהִים, iii. 10, 13, v. 3, 18b, vii. 18, viii. 2, 13.

God mean? By no means such a return unto God as amounts to the annihilation of the separate existence of the spirit of man; for, in the first place, there is the supposition of this separate existence running through the Bible; in the second place, נתנה, xii. 7*b*, does not point to an emanation; and in the third place, the idea of Hades prevailing in the consciousness of the ages before Christ, and which is also that of Koheleth, proves the contrary. Man exists also beyond the grave, but without the light and the force of thought and activity characterizing his present life, ix. 5, 10. The future life is not better, but is worse than the present, a dense darkness enduring "for ever," ix. 6, xi. 8, xii. 5*b*. It is true, indeed, that from the justice of God, and the experiences of the present life as standing in contradiction thereto, viii. 14, the conclusion is drawn, xii. 14, xi. 9, that there is a last decisive judgment, bringing all to light; but this great thought, in which the interest of the book in the progress of religious knowledge comes to a climax, is as yet only an abstract postulate of faith, and not powerful enough to brighten the future; and therefore, also, not powerful enough to lift us above the miseries of the present.

That the author gives utterance to such thoughts of the future as xii. 7 and xi. 9, xii. 14,—to which Wisd. iii. 1 ("The souls of the righteous are in God's hand, and no trouble moves them") and Dan. xii. 2 ("Many that sleep in the dust of the earth shall awake, some to everlasting life, and some to shame and everlasting contempt") are related, as being their expansion,—warrants the supposition that he disputes as little as Job does in chap. xiv. the reality of a better future; but only that the knowledge of such a future was not yet given to him. In general, for the first time in the N. T. era, the hope of a better future becomes a common portion of the church's creed, resting on the basis of faith in the history of redemption warranting it; and is advanced beyond the isolated prophetic gleams of light, the mere postulates of faith that were ventured upon, and the unconfirmed opinions, of the times preceding Christ. The N. T. Scripture shows how altogether different this world of sin and of change appears to be since a world of recompense and of glory has been revealed as its background; since the Lord has pronounced as blessed those who weep, and not those who laugh; and since, with the apostle (Rom. viii. 18), we may be convinced that the sufferings of this present time are not worthy to be compared with the glory that shall be revealed to us. The goal of human life, with its labour and its sufferings, is now carried beyond the grave. That which is done under the sun appears only as a segment of the universal and everlasting operation, governed by the wisdom of God, the separate portions of which can only be understood in their connection with the whole. The estimate taken of this present world, apart from its connection with the future, must be one-sided. There are two worlds : the future is the solution of the mystery of the present.

A N. T. believer would not be able to write such a book as that of Job, or even as that of Ecclesiastes, without sinning against revealed truth ; without renouncing the better knowledge meanwhile made possible ; without falling back to an O. T. standpoint. The author of the Book of Ecclesiastes is related to revealed religion in its O. T. manifestation,—he is a believer before the coming of Christ ; but not such an one as all, or as most were, but of peculiar character and position. There are some natures that have a tendency to joyfulness, and others to sadness. The author of this book does not belong to the latter class ; for if he did, the call to rejoice, xi. 9, viii. 15, etc., would not as it does pervade his book, as the χαίρετε, though in a deeper sense, pervades the Epistle to the Philippians. Neither does he belong to those superficial natures which see almost everything in a rosy light, which quickly and easily divest themselves of their own and of others' sorrows, and on which the stern earnestness of life can make no deep and lasting impressions. Nor is he a man of feeling, whom his own weakness makes a prophet of evil ; not a predominatingly passive man, who, before he could fully know the world, withdrew from it, and now citicises it from his own retired corner in a careless, inattentive mood ; but a man of action, with a penetrating understanding and a faculty of keen observation ; a man of the world, who, from his own experience, knows the world on all its sides ; a restless spirit, who has consumed himself in striving after that which truly satisfies. That this man, who was forced to confess that all that science and art, all that table dainties, and the love of women, and riches, and honour yielded him, was at last but vanity and vexation of spirit, and who gained so deep an insight into the transitoriness and vanity of all earthly things, into the sorrows of this world of sin and death, and their perplexing mysteries, does not yet conclude by resigning himself to atheism, putting " Nothing " (Nirvâna), or blind Fate, in the place of God, but firmly holds that the fear of God is the highest duty and the condition of all true prosperity, as it is the highest truth and the surest knowledge—that such is the case with him may well excite our astonishment ; as well as this also, that he penetrates the known illusory character of earthly things in no overstrained manner, despising the world in itself, and also the gifts of God in it, but that he places his ultimatum as to the pure enjoyment of life within the limits of the fear of God, and extends it as widely as God permits. One might therefore call the Book of Koheleth, "The Song of the Fear of God," rather than, as H. Heine does, "The Song of Scepticism;" for however great the sorrow of the world which is therein expressed, the religious conviction of the author remains in undiminished strength; and in the midst of all the disappointments in the present world, his faith in God, and in the rectitude of God, and in the victory of the good, stands firm as a rock, against which all the waves dash themselves into foam. "This book," says another recent author,[1] "which contains almost as many contradictions as verses, may be regarded as the Breviary of the most modern materialism, and of extreme licentiousness." He who can thus speak has not read the book with intelligence. The appearance of materialism arises from this, that the author sees in the death of man an end similar to that of beasts; and that is certainly so far true, but it is not the whole truth. In the knowledge of the reverse side of the matter he does not come beyond the threshold, because His hand was not yet there—viz. the hand of the Arisen One—which could help him over it. And as for the supposed licentiousness, ix. 7-9 shows, by way of example, how greatly the fear of God had guarded him from concluding his search into all earthly things with the disgust of a worn-out libertine.

But there are certainly self-contradictions in the Book of Ecclesiastes. They have a twofold ground. They are, on the one hand, the reflection of the self-contradicting facts which the author affirms. Thus, e.g., iii. 11, he says that God has set eternity in the heart of man, but that man cannot find out from the beginning to the end the work which God maketh; iii. 12, 13, that the best thing in this world is for a man to enjoy life ; but to be able to do this, is a gift of God; viii. 12, 14, that it goes well with them that fear God, but ill with the godless. But there is also the contrary—which is just the ground-tone of the book, that everything has its *But ;* only the fear of God, after all that appertains to the world is found to be as *vanitas vanitatum,* remains as the kernel without the shell, but the commandment of the fear of God as a categorical imperative, the knowledge that the fear of God is in itself the highest happiness, and fellowship with God the highest good, remain unexpressed ; the fear of God is not combined with the love of God, as *e.g.* in Ps. lxxiii. it serves only for warning and not for comfort. On the

[1] Hartmann's *Das Lied vom Ewigen*, St. Galle 1859, p. 12.

other hand, the book also contains contradictions, which consist in
contrasts which the author is not in a condition to explain and
adjust. Thus, *e.g.*, the question whether the spirit of a dying man,
in contrast to that of a beast, takes its way upwards, iii. 21, is proposed as one capable of a double answer; but xii. 7 answers it
directly in the affirmative; the author has good grounds for the
affirmative, but yet no absolute proofs. And while he denies the
light of consciousness and the energy of activity to those who have
gone down to Hades, ix. 10, he maintains that there is a final
decisive judgment of a holy and righteous God of all human conduct,
xi. 9, xii. 14, which, since there is frequently not a righteous
requital given on earth, viii. 14, and since generally the issue here
does not bring to light, ix. 2, the distinction between the righteous
and the wicked, will take place in eternity; but it is difficult to
comprehend how he has reconciled the possibility of such a final
judgment with the shadowy nature of existence after death.

The Book of Koheleth is, on the one side, a proof of the power
of revealed religion which has grounded faith in God, the One God,
the All-wise Creator and Governor of the world, so deeply and firmly
in the religious consciousness, that even the most dissonant and
confused impressions of the present world are unable to shake it;
and, on the other side, it is a proof of the inadequacy of revealed
religion in its O. T. form, since the discontent and the grief which
the monotony, the confusion, and the misery of this earth occasion,
remain thus long without a counterbalance, till the facts of the history
of redemption shall have disclosed and unveiled the heavens above
the earth. In none of the O. T. books does the Old Covenant appear
as it does in the Book of Koheleth, as "that which decayeth and
waxeth old, and is ready to vanish away" (Heb. viii. 13). If the
darkness of earth must be enlightened, then a New Covenant must
be established; for heavenly love, which is at the same time heavenly
wisdom, enters into human nature and overcomes sin, death, and
Hades, and removes the turning-point of the existence of man from
this to the future life. The finger of prophecy points to this new era.
And Koheleth, from amid his heaps of ruins, shows how necessary
it is that the heavens should now soon open above the earth.

It is a view of the world, dark, and only broken by scattered
gleams of light, not disowning its sullenness even where it recommends the happy enjoyment of life, which runs through the book in
a long series of dissonances, and gives to it a peculiar character. It
is thus intentionally a homogeneous whole; but is it also divided
into separate parts according to a plan? That we may be able to

answer this question, we subject the contents of the book to a searching analysis, step by step, yet steadily keeping the whole in view. This will at the same time also serve as a preparation for the exposition of the book.

Here below, all things under the sun are vanity. The labour of man effects nothing that is enduring, and all that is done is only a beginning and a vanishing away again, repeating itself in a never-ending circle : these are the thoughts of the book which stand as its motto, i. 2–11.

Koheleth-Solomon, who had been king, then begins to set forth the vanity of all earthly things from his own experience. The striving after secular knowledge, i. 12 ff., has proved to him unsatisfactory, as has also the striving after happiness in pleasure and in procuring the means of all imaginable gratifications, ii. 1–11 ; wisdom is vanity, for the wise man falls under the stroke of death as well as the fool, and is forgotten, ii. 12–17 ; and riches are vanity, for they become the inheritance, one knows not whether of a worthy or of an unworthy heir, ii. 18–21 ; and, besides, pure enjoyment, like wisdom and know-ledge, depends not merely on the will of man, but both are the gift of God, ii. 22 ff. Everything has its time appointed by God, but man is unable to survey either backwards or forwards the work of God, which fills eternity, notwithstanding the impulse to search into it which is implanted within him; his dependence in all things, even in pure enjoyment, must become to him a school in which to learn the fear of God, who maintains all things unchangeably, who forms the course of that which is done, iii. 1–15. If he sees injustice pre-vailing in the place of justice, God's time for righteous interference has not yet come, iii. 16, 17. If God wishes to try men, they shall see that they are dependent like the beasts, and liable to death without any certain distinction from the beasts—there is nothing better than that this fleeting life should be enjoyed as well as may be, iii. 18 ff.

Koheleth now further records the evils that are under the sun : oppression, in view of which death is better than life, and not to have been at all is better than both, iv. 1–3 ; envy, iv. 4 ; the restlessness of labour, from which only the fool sets himself free, iv. 5, 6 ; the aimless trouble and parsimony of him who stands alone, iv. 7–12 ; the disappointment of the hopes placed on an upstart who has reached the throne, iv. 13–16.

Up to this point there is connection. There now follow rules, externally unconnected, for the relation of man to Him who is the Disposer of all things ; regarding his frequenting the house of God, iv. 17 [v. 1]; prayer, v. 2 ; and praise, v. 3–6.

Then a catalogue of vanities is set forth : the insatiable covetous plundering of the lowly by those who are above them in despotic states, whereat the author praises, v. 7, 8, the patriarchal state based on agriculture ; and the nothingness and uncertainty of riches, which do not make the rich happier than the labourer, v. 9–11 ; which sometimes are lost without any to inherit them, v. 12–14 ; and which their possessor, at all events, must leave behind him when he dies, v. 15, 16. Riches have only a value when by means of them a purer enjoyment is realized as the gift of God, v. 17 ff. For it happens that God gives to a man riches, but to a stranger the enjoyment thereof, vi. 1, 2. An untimely birth is better than a man who has an hundred children, a long life, and yet who has no enjoyment of life even to his death, vi. 3–6. Desire stretching on into the future is torment ; only so much as a man truly enjoys has he of all his labour, vi. 7–9 ; what man shall be is predestinated, all contendings against it are useless : the knowledge of that which is good for him, and of the future, is in the power of no man, vi. 10 ff.

There now follow, without a premeditated plan, rules for the practical conduct of life, loosely connecting themselves with the " what is good," vi. 12, by the catchword " good:" first six (probably originally seven) proverbs of two things each, whereof the one is better than the other, vii. 1–9 ; then three with the same catchword, but without comparison, vii. 10, 11–12, 13–14. This series of proverbs is connected as a whole, for their ultimatum is a counsel to joy regulated by the fear of God within the narrow limits of this life, constituted by God of good and bad days, and terminating in the darkness of death. But this joy is also itself limited, for the deep seriousness of the *memento mori* is mingled with it, and sorrow is declared to be morally better than laughter.

With vii. 15, the *I*, speaking from personal experience, again comes into the foreground ; but counsels and observations also here follow each other aphoristically, without any close connection with each other. Koheleth warns against an extreme tendency to the side of good as well as to that of evil : he who fears God knows how to avoid extremes, vii. 15–18. Nothing affords a stronger protection than wisdom, for (?) with all his righteousness a man makes false steps, vii. 19, 20. Thou shalt not always listen, lest thou hear something about thyself,—also thou thyself hast often spoken harshly regarding others, vii. 21, 22. He has tried everything, but in his strivings after wisdom, and in his observation of the distinction between wisdom and folly, he has found nothing more dangerous than the snares of women; among a thousand men he found one man; but one woman such as she ought to be, he found not; he found in general that God made men upright, but that they have devised many kinds of by-ways, vii. 23 ff.

As the wise man considers women and men in general, wisdom teaches him obedience to the king to whom he has sworn fealty, and, under despotic oppression, patient waiting for the time of God's righteous interference, viii. 1–9. In the time of despotic domination, it occurs that the godless are buried with honour, while the righteous are driven away and forgotten, viii. 10. God's sentence is to be waited for, the more deliberately men give themselves to evil; God is just, but, in contradiction to His justice, it is with the righteous as with the wicked, and with the wicked as with the righteous, here on earth, viii. 11–14. In view of these vanities, then, it is the most desirable thing for a man to eat and drink, and enjoy himself, for that abides with him of his labour during the day of his life God has given him, viii. 15. Restless labour here leads to nothing; all the efforts of man to comprehend the government of God are in vain, viii. 16 ff. For on closer consideration, it appears that the righteous also, with all their actions, are ruled by God, and generally that in nothing, not even in his affections, is man his own master; and, which is the worst thing of all, because it impels men to a wicked, mad abuse of life, to the righteous and the unrighteous, death at last comes alike; it is also the will of God towards man that he should spend this transient life in cheerful enjoyment and in vigorous activity before it sinks down into the night of Hades, ix. 1–10. The fruits of one's labour are not to be gained by force, even the best ability warrants it not, an incomprehensible fate finally frustrates all, ix. 11, 12.

There now follows, but in loose connection as to thought with the preceding, a section relating to wisdom and folly, and the discordances as to the estimate of both here below, along with diverse kinds of experiences and proverbs, ix. 13–x. 15. Only one proverb is out of harmony with the general theme, viz. x. 4, which commends resignation under the ebullition of the wrath of the ruler. The following proverb, x. 5, 6, returns to the theme, but connecting itself with the preceding; the relation of rulers and the ruled to each other is kept principally in view by Koheleth.

With a proverb relating to kings and princes, good and bad, a new departure is made. Riotous living leads to slothfulness; and in contrast to this (but not without the intervention of a warning not to curse the king) follow exhortations to provident, and, at the same time, bold and all-attempting activity; for the future is God's, and not to be reckoned on, x. 16–xi. 6. The light is sweet; and life, however long it may last, in view of the uncertain dark future, is worthy of being enjoyed, xi. 7, 8. Thus Koheleth, at the end of this last series of proverbs, has again reached his *Ceterum censeo;* he formulates it, in an exhortation to a young man to enjoy his life—but without forgetting God, to whom he owes it, and to whom he has to render an account—before grey-haired old age and death overtake him, into a full-toned *finale*, xi. 9–xii. 7. The last word of the book, xii. 8, is parallel with the first (i. 1): "O! vanity of vanities; All is vain!"

An epilogue, from the same hand as the book, seals its truth: it is written as from the very soul of Solomon; it issues from the same fountain of wisdom. The reader must not lose himself in reading many books, for the sum of all knowledge that is of value to man is comprehended in one sentence: "Fear God, for He shall bring every work into judgment," xii. 9 ff.

If we look back on this compendious reproduction of the contents and of the course of thought of the book, there appears everywhere the same view of the world, along with the same *ultimatum;* and as a pictorial *overture* opens the book, a pictorial *finale* closes it. But a gradual development, a progressive demonstration, is wanting, and so far the grouping together of the parts is not fully carried out; the connection of the thoughts is more frequently determined by that which is external and accidental, and not unfrequently an incongruous element is introduced into the connected course of kindred matters. The Solomonic stamp impressed on chap. i. and ii. begins afterwards to be effaced. The connection of the confessions that are made becomes aphoristic in chap. iii.; and the proverbs that are introduced do not appropriately fall into their place. The grounds, occasions, and views which determine the author to place confessions and moral proverbs in such an order after one another, for the most part withdraw themselves from observation. All attempts to show, in the whole, not only oneness of spirit, but also a genetic progress, an all-embracing plan, and an organic connection, have hitherto failed, and must fail.[1]

---

[1] "*Ajunt Hebraei, quum inter cetera scripta Salomonis, quae antiquata sunt nec in memoria duraverunt, et hic liber obliterandus videretur, et quod vanas assereret Dei creaturas et totum putaret esse pro nihilo, et potum et cibum et delicias transeuntes praeferret omnibus, ex hoc uno capitulo* (xii. 13) *meruisse auctoritatem, ut in divinorum voluminum numero poneretur.*"—JEROME.

In presenting this view of the spirit and plan of the Book of Koheleth, we have proceeded on the supposition that it is a post-exilian book, that it is one of the most recent of the books of the O. T. It is true, indeed, that tradition regards it as Solomonic. According to *Bathra* 15*a*, the Hezekiah - *Collegium* [*vid.* Del. on *Proverbs*, vol. I. p. 5] must have " written "—that is, collected into a written form—the Book of Isaiah, as also of the Proverbs, the Song, and Koheleth. The Midrash regards it as Solomon's, and as written in the evening of his days; while the Song was written in his youth, and the Proverbs when he was in middle age (*Jalkut*, under i. 1). If in *Rosch haschana* 21*b* it is said that Koheleth sought to be a second Moses, and to open the one of the fifty gates of knowledge which was unopened by Moses, but that this was denied to him, it is thereby assumed that he was the incomparable king, as Moses was the incomparable prophet. And Bloch, in his work on the origin and era of the Book of Koheleth (1872), is right in saying that all objections against the canonicity of the book leave the Solomonic authorship untouched. In the first Christian century, the Book of Koheleth was an *antilegomenon*. In the Introduction to the Song (p. 14) we have traced to their sources the two collections of legal authorities according to which the question of the canonicity of the Book of Koheleth is decided. The Synod of Jabne (Jamnia), about 90, decided the canonicity of the book against the school of Shammai. The reasons advanced by the latter against the canonicity are seen from *Shabbath* 30*b*, and *Megilla* 7*a*. From the former we learn that they regarded the words of the book, particularly ii. 2 (where they must have read מְהֻלָּל, " worthy to be praised "), cf. vii. 3, and viii. 15, cf. 22, as contradictory (cf. *Proverbs*, vol. I. p. 44); and from the latter, that they hence did not recognise its inspiration. According to the *Midrash Koheleth*, under xi. 9, they were stumbled also by the call to the enjoyment of pleasure, and to walk in the way of the desire of the heart, which appeared to stand in contra-diction to the *Tôra* (cf. xi. 9 with Num. xv. 39), and to savour of heresy. But belief in the Solomonic authorship remained, notwith-standing, uninjured; and the admonitions to the fear of God, with reference to the future judgment, carried them over the tendency of these observations. Already, at the time of Herod the Great (*Bathra* 4*a*), and afterwards, in the time of R. Gamaliel (*Shabbath* 30*b*), the book was cited as Holy Scripture; and when, instead of the book, the author was named, the formula of citation mentioned the name of Solomon; or the book was treated as equally Solomonic with Proverbs and the Song (*Erubin* 21*b*).

Even the doubtfulness of its contents could give rise to no manner of doubt as to the author. Down till the new era beginning with Christianity, and, in the main, even till the Reformation-century, no attention was paid to the inner and historico-literary marks which determine the time of the origin of a book. The Reformation first called into existence, along with the criticism of dogmatic traditions, at the same time also biblical criticism, which it raised to the place of an essential part of the science of Scripture. Luther, in his *Tischreden* (*Table-Talk*), is the first who explained the Preacher as one of the most recent books of the O. T.: he supposed that the book had not reached us in its completed form; that it was written by Sirach rather than by Solomon; and that it might be, "as a Talmud, collected from many books, perhaps from the library of King Ptolemy Euergetes, in Egypt." [1] These are only passing utterances, which have no scientific value; among his contemporaries, and till the middle of the century following, they found no acceptance. Hugo Grotius (1644) is the first who, like Luther, rejects its Solomonic authorship, erroneously supposing, with him, that it is a collection of diverse sayings of the wise, περὶ τῆς εὐδαιμονίας; but on one point he excellently hits the nail on the head: *Argumentum ejus rei habeo multa vocabula, quae non alibi quam in Daniele, Esdra et Chaldaeis interpretibus reperias.* This observation is warranted. If the Book of Koheleth were of old Solomonic origin, then there is no history of the Hebrew language. But Bernstein (*Quaestiones nonnullae Kohelethanae*, 1854) is right in saying that the history of the Hebrew language and literature is certainly divided into two epochs by the Babylonish exile, and that the Book of Koheleth bears the stamp of the post-exilian form of the language.

List of the Hapaxlegomena, and of the Words and Forms in the Book of Koheleth belonging to a more recent Period of the Language.

Aviyonah, xii. 5; cf. *Ma'seroth* iv. 6, *Berachoth* 36a.

Adam, opp. *ishah*, only at vii. 28.

Izzen, Pi., only xii. 9; not Talm.

אִי, x. 16; אִילּוֹ, iv. 10, instead of the older אוֹי; cf. הִי, Ezek. ii. 10; like אִי לְ, *Shemoth rabba*, c. 46; אִי מ', "Alas, how bad!"

---

[1] *Tischreden*, ed. Förstemann-Bindseil, p. 400 f. The expression here almost appears as if Luther had confounded *Ecclesiastes* (Koheleth) with *Ecclesiasticus* (Sirach). At a later period he maintained that the book contained a collection of Solomonic sayings, not executed, however, by Solomon himself.

Targ. Jer. ii., Lev. xxvi. 29 ; 'ע יא, " Alas for the meek!"
Berachoth 6b ; cf. Sanhedrin 11a.

Illu, " if," vi. 6 ; Esth. vii. 4, of אִם (אִין) and לֹי (לֹא, read לָא, Ezek.
iii. 6) ; Targ. Deut. xxxii. 29 = Heb. לֹי, common in the
Mishna, e.g. Maccoth i. 10.

Asurim, only vii. 26 ; cf. Judg. xv. 14 ; Seder olam rabba, c. 25 ; cf.
at iv. 14.

Baale asupoth, only xii. 11 ; cf. Sanhedrin 12a, Jer. Sanhedrin x. 1.

Bihel, only v. 1, vii. 9 ; as Hiph. Esth. vi. 14 ; cf. the transitive use of
the Pih. Esth. ii. 9, like Targ. bahel (= ithbᵉhel) and bᵉhilu, haste.

Bur, only ix. 1 ; cf. the Talm. al buriv, altogether free from error
and sin.

Bᵉhuroth, only xi. 9, xii. 1 ; cf. Mibᵉhurav, Num. xi. 28.

Batel, xii. 3 ; elsewhere only in the Chald. of Ezra ; common in the
Mishna, e.g. Aboth i. 5.

Beth olam (cf. Ezek. xxvi. 20), xii. 5 ; cf. Tosifta Berachoth iii.,
Targ. Isa. xiv. 18, xlii. 11.

Bᵉchen, viii. 10 ; Esth. iv. 16 ; elsewhere only Targ., e.g. Isa. xvi. 5.

Baal hallashon, x. 11 ; cf. baal bashar, corpulent, Berachoth 13b;
baal hahhotam, the large-nosed, carrying the nose high,
Taanith 29a.

Gibber, only at x. 10, to exert oneself ; elsewhere : to prevail.

Gummats, only x. 8, Syr., and in the Targ. of the Hag. (cf. Targ.
Ps. vii. 16).

Divrath, vid. under ש.

Hoveh, ii. 22 ; cf. Shabbath vi. 6, Erubin i. 10, Jebamoth xv. 2.

Holeloth, i. 17, ii. 12, vii. 25, ix. 3 ; and holeluth, madness, only in
the Book of Koheleth, x. 13.

Zichron, as primary form, i. 11, ii. 16 ; vid. at Lev. xxiii. 24, the
connecting form.

Zᵉman, iii. 1 ; Neh. ii. 6 ; Esth. ix. 27, 31 ; elsewhere only in the
bib. Chald. with שָׁעָה, ὥρα, the usual Mishnic word for καιρός
and χρόνος.

Holah (malum), aegrum, v. 12, 15 ; for this nahhlah is used in Isa.
xvii. 11 ; Nah. iii. 19 ; Jer. x. 19, xiv. 17.

Ben-hhorim (liber, in contrast to ĕvĕd, servus), x. 17 ; cf. חרות (freedom)
on the coins of the Revolution of the Roman period ; the
usual Talm. word, even of possessions, such as praedium
liberum, aedes liberae of the Roman law.

Hhuts min, only at ii. 25 (Chald. bar min) ; frequent in the Mishna,
e.g. Middoth ii. 3.

Hhush, ii. 25 ; in the Talm. and Syr. of sorrowful experiences ; here (cf. Job xx. 2), of the experiences derived from the senses, and experiences in general, as in the Rabb. the five senses are called חושים.

Hhayalim, x. 10; everywhere else, also in Aram., meaning war-hosts, except at Isa. xxx. 6, where it denotes *opes*, treasures.

Hhesron, i. 15, a common word in the post-bibl. language.[1]

Hēphĕts, iii. 1, 17, v. 7, viii. 6; cf. Isa. lviii. 3, 13. The primary unweakened meaning is found at v. 3, xii. 1, 10. The weakening of the original meaning may have already early begun; in the Book of Koheleth it has advanced as far as in the language of the Mishna, *e.g. Mezia* iv. 6.

Hheshbon, vii. 25, 27, ix. 10. Plur. at vii. 29, *machinationes;* only in 2 Chron. xxvi. 15 in the sense of *machinae bellicae;* but as in Koheleth, so also in *Shabbath* 150a.

Hhathhhatim, only at xii. 5.

Tahhanah, xii. 4; cf. *t'hhon*, Lam. v. 3, which is foreign to the Mishna, but is used as corresponding to the older *rehhaim*, in the same way as the vulgar Arab. *mathanat* and *ṭahwan*, instead of the older *raha.*[2]

יאשׁ, *Pih.*, only ii. 20. Talm. *Nithpa.* נתיאשׁ, to abandon hope, *e.g. Kelim* xxvi. 8.

Y'giyah, only xii. 12; an abstract such as may be formed from all verbs, and particularly is more frequently formed in the more modern than in the more ancient language.

Yother, as a participial adj.: "that which remains" (cf. 1 Sam. xv. 15) = "gain," vi. 11, vii. 11; or "superiority," vi. 8. As an adv.: "more" (cf. Esth. vi. 6), "particularly," ii. 15, vii. 16; xii. 9, xii. 12. In the Talm. Heb., used in the sense of "remaining over" (*Kiddushin* 24b); and as an adv., in the sense of *plus* or *magis* (*e.g. Chullin* 57b).

Yaphĕh, iii. 11, v. 17, as *e.g. Jer. Pesachim* ix. 9 (*b. Pesachim* 99a): "Silence is well-becoming (יפה) the wise; how much more fools!"

Yithron, ii. 13 (twice), vii. 12 (synon. *mothar*, iii. 1); more frequently "real gain," i. 3, ii. 11, iii. 9, v. 15, x. 10; "superiority and gain," v. 8. Peculiar (= Aram. *yuthran*) to the Book of Koheleth, and in Rabb., whence it is derived.

K'ĕhhad, xi. 6, Isa. lxv. 25, Chron., Ezra, Nehem., the Chald. *kahhada;* Syr. *okchado;* frequent in the Mish., *e.g. Bechoroth* vii. 4; *Kilajim* i. 9.

---

[1] *Vid.* my *Geschichte der jüd. Poesie*, p. 187 f.

[2] *Vid.* Eli Smith in my *Jud.-Arab. Poesien aus vormuh. Zeit.* (1874), p. 40.

K‘var, adv., i. 10, ii. 12, 16, iii. 15, iv. 2, vi. 10, ix. 6, 7; common in the Mishna, *e.g. Erubin* iv. 2, *Nedarim* v. 5; in Aram., more frequently in the sense of " perhaps " than of " formerly."

Kasher, xi. 6, Esth. viii. 5; in the Mishna, the word commonly used of that which is legally admissible; *Hiph.* verbal noun, *hachshēr*, only at x. 10; in the Mishna, of arranging according to order; in the superscription of the tract, *macshirin*, of making susceptible of uncleanness. Cf. *e.g. Menachoth* 48*b*. The word is generally pointed הֻכְשַׁר, but more correctly הֻכְשֵׁר.[1]

Kishron, only at ii. 21, iv. 4, v. 10; not found in the Mishna.

L‘vad, *tantummodo*, vii. 29; similar, but not quite the same, at Isa. xxvi. 13.

Lăhăg, exclusively xii. 12; not Talm.; from the verb *lāhăg* (R. לה), to long eagerly for; Syr. *lahgoz*, vapour (of breathing, *exhalare*); cogn. *higgāyon* (*hĕgĕh*), according to which it is explained in *Jer. Sanhedrin* x. 1 and elsewhere.

Lavah, viii. 15, as in the Mishna: to conduct a guest, to accompany a traveller; whence the proverb: לווי לוויה, he who gives a convoy to the dead, to him it will be given, *Kethuboth* 72*a*; cf. שֵׁם לִוּי, a standing surname, *Negaïm* xiv. 6.

M‘dinah, v. 7, and in no book besides before the Exile.

Madda', x. 20; elsewhere only in the Chron. and Dan.; Targ. מַנְדַּע.

M‘leah, *gravida*, only xi. 5, as in the Mishna, *e.g. Jebamoth* xvi. 1.

Mălāk, v. 5; cf. Mal. ii. 7, in the sense of the later *sh‘luahh shamaïm*, delegated of God.[2]

Miskēn, only iv. 13, ix. 15, 16; but cf. *miskenuth*, Deut. viii. 9, and *m‘sukan*, Isa. xl. 20.

Masm‘roth, xii. 11 = מַסְ', Jer. x. 4; cf. Isa. xli. 7; 1 Chron. xxii. 3; 2 Chron. iii. 9.

M‘attim, v. 1; a plur. only at Ps. cix. 8.

Mikrĕh, more frequently in the Book of Koheleth than in any other book; and at iii. 19, used as explained in the Comm.

Mĕrots, exclusively ix. 11 (elsewhere *m‘rutsah*).

Māshăk, ii. 3; cf. *Chagiga* 14*a*, *Sifri* 135*b*, ed. Friedmann.

Mishlahhath, viii. 8 (cf. Ps. lxxviii. 49).

Nāgă', *Hiph.* with *ĕl*, viii. 14, as at Esth. ix. 26; Aram. מְטָא לְ, *e.g.* Targ. Jer. to Ex. xxxiii. 13.

---

[1] *Vid.* my *Heb. Römerbrief*, p. 79. Cf. Stein's *Talm. Termin.* (1869), under כָּשֵׁר and הֻכְשֵׁר.

[2] *Vid.* my " Discussion der Amtsfrage in Mishna u. Gemara," *Luth. Zeitsch.* (1854), pp. 446–449.

Nāhăg, ii. 3, as in the Mishna, *e.g. Aboda Zara* iii. 4, 54*b ;* cf. Targ. Koh. x. 4.

Nahhath, vi. 5, as in the common phrase *nahhath ruahh;* cf. נוח לו ונו׳, " It were better for him," etc., *Jer. Berachoth* i. 2.   This נוח לו, for Koheleth's נחת לו, is frequent.

Nātă', xii. 11 (for which, Isa. xxii. 23, *tākă';* Mishna, קבע ; *Jer. Sanhedrin* x. 1), as Dan. xi. 45.

סבל, *Hithpa.,* only at xii. 5.

Sof, iii. 11, vii. 2, xii. 13 ; Joel ii. 20 ; 2 Chron. xx. 16, the more modern word which later displaced the word *ahharith,* vii. 8, x. 13 (cf. *Berachoth* i. 1), but which is not exactly equivalent to it ; for *sof dāvār,* xii. 13,[1] which has the meaning of *summa summarum, ahharith davar,* would be inapplicable.

Sāchāl, ii. 19, vii. 17, x. 3 (twice), 14 ; Jer. iv. 22, v. 21 ; in the Book of Koheleth, the synon. of the yet more frequently used פְּסִיל, the Targ. word.

Sĕchĕl, exclusively x. 6.

Sichluth, i. 17 (here with ש), ii. 3, 12, 13, vii. 25, x. 1, 13 (synon. *kᵉsiluth,* Prov. ix. 13).

סכן, *Niph.* x. 9 ; cf. *Berachoth* i. 3.   The Targ.-Talm. *Ithpa.* אִסְתַּכַּן, " to be in danger," corresponds with the *Niph.*

'*Avād,* exclusively ix. 1, like the Syr. '*bad,* Jewish-Aram. עוֹבֵד.

'*Adĕn* (formed of עַד־הֵן), *adhuc,* with לא, *nondum,* iv. 3.

'*Adĕnāh* (of *ăd-hĕnnāh*), *adhuc,* iv. 2 ; Mishnic עֲדַיִן, *e.g. Nedarim* xi. 10.

עות, *Hithpa.* only at xii. 3.

'*Amăd,* ii. 9, viii. 3, as Jer. xlviii. 11 ; Ps. cii. 27.

Ummăth, vid. under ש.

'*Anāh,* v. 19, x. 19.

Inyān, exclusively in the Book of Koheleth, i. 13, ii. 23, 26, iii. 10, iv. 8, v. 2, 13, viii. 16, one of the most extensive words of the post-bibl. Heb. ; first, of the object of employment, *e.g. Kiddushin* 6*a,* " occupied with this object ;" also Aram. *Bathra* 114*b.*

'*Atsăltăyim,* double impurity, *i.e.* where the one hand is as impure as the other, only at x. 18.

'*Asāh,* with *lĕhhĕm,* x. 19, as at Dan. v. 1 : *ăvăd lĕhhĕm ;* in the N. T. Mark vi. 21, ποιεῖν δεῖπνον.   Otherwise Ezek. iv. 15, where *asah lehhem* is used of preparing food.   With the obj. of the time of life, vi. 12 ; cf. Acts xv. 33.   With *tov,* not

---

[1] Vid. *Heb. Römerbrief,* pp. 81, 84.

only "to do good," vii. 20, but also "to act well," "to spend a pleasant life," iii. 12.

Pardēs (Song iv. 13 ; Neh. ii. 8), plur. ii. 5, flower-gardens, parks, as *Mezi͑a* 103a, פרדיסי.

Pēshĕr, explicatio, viii. 1, elsewhere only in the Chald. parts of Dan. Aram. for the older פִּתְרוֹן and שֵׁבֶר, of which the Targ. word is פְּשַׁר and פּוּשָׁן, Talm. פְּשָׁרָה, "adjustment of a controverted matter."

Pithgam in the Chald. parts of Ezra and Daniel, but only as a Hebraised Persian word in viii. 11, Esth. i. 20 ; common in the Targ. and in the Syr., but not in the Talm.

Kilkăl (*Kālāl,* Ezek. i. 7 ; Dan. x. 6), exclusively at x. 10 (on the contrary, at Ezek. xxi. 26, it means "to agitate").

R͑uth, only v. 10 ; *Keri,* for which *Chethib* ראית, which may be read רְאָיַת, רְאִית (cf. Ezek. xxviii. 17), or רְאִיַת ; the latter two of these forms are common in the Mishna, and have there their special meanings proceeding from the fundamental idea of seeing.

רדף, *Niph. part.,* only iii. 15.

R͑uth, besides the Chald. parts of Ezra, occurs only seven times in the Book of Koheleth, i. 14, ii. 11, 17, 26, iv. 4, 6, vi. 9.

Ra͑yon, i. 17, ii. 22, iv. 16 ; elsewhere only in the Chald. parts of Daniel and in the Targ.

שׁ, this in and of itself is in no respect modern, but, as the Babyl.-Assyr. *sa,* the Phoen. אשׁ, shows, is the relative (originally demonstrative) belonging to the oldest period of the language; which in the Mishna has altogether supplanted the אֲשֶׁר of the older Heb. book-language. It is used in the Book of Koheleth quite in the same way as in the Mishna, but thus, that it stands first on the same line (rank) with אשׁר, and makes it doubtful whether this or that which occurs more frequently in the book (שׁ, according to Herzfeld, 68 times, and אשׁר 89 times) has the predominance (cf. *e.g.* i. 13 f., viii. 14, x. 14, where both are used *promiscue*). The use of *asher* as a relative pronoun and relative conjunction is not different from the use of this in the older literature : *'ad asher lo,* in the sense of "before," xii. 1, 2, 6, Mishnic עד שׁלא, is only a natural turn to the fundamental meaning "till that not" (2 Sam. xvii. 13 ; 1 Kings xvii. 17); and *mib͑li asher lo = nisi quod non,* iii. 11 (cf. *bilti,* Dan. xi. 18), for which the Mishnic ובלבד שׁלא (*e.g. Erubin* i. 10),

is only accidentally not further demonstrable. But how far
the use of שׁ has extended, will be seen by the following
survey, from which we exclude שׁ, standing alone as a relative pronoun or relative conjunction :—

Beshekvar, ii. 16. B'shel asher, eo quod, viii. 17 (cf. Jonah
i. 7, 8, 12), corresponding to the Talm. דְּבְדִיל. Kol
שׁ, ii. 7, 9, and xi. 8. Kol-ummath שׁ, v. 15, corresponding to the Chald. kol-kavel דְּ, Dan. ii. 40, etc. כְּשׁ,
v. 14, xii. 7, and in the sense of quum, ix. 12, x. 3.
mah-שׁ, i. 9, iii. 15, vi. 10, vii. 24, viii. 7, x. 14 ; meh
שׁ, iii. 22. מְשׁ, v. 4. 'Al-divrath shĕllo, vii. 14 (cf.
iii. 18, viii. 2). Shĕgam, ii. 15, viii. 14.

Shiddah and plur. Shiddoth, exclusively ii. 8.
Shaharuth, exclusively xi. 10, to be understood after Nedarim iii. 8,
"the black-headed," opposed to בעלי השׁיבות, "the grey-
haired."
שׂכח, Hithpa., only viii. 10, the usual word in the Talm., e.g. San-
hedrin 13b.
Shalat, ii. 19, viii. 9, besides only in Nehemiah and Esther (cf.
Bechoroth, vii. 6, etc.) ; Hiph. v. 18, vi. 2, elsewhere only
Ps. cxix. 133.
Shilton, viii. 4, 8, nowhere else in O. T. Heb., but in the Mishna,
e.g. Kiddushin iii. 6.
Shallith, with בּ, only viii. 8 (cf. Ezek. xvi. 30); on the contrary,
vii. 19, x. 5, as Gen. xlii. 6, in the political signification of
a ruler.
שׁמם, Hithpo., vii. 16.
Shiphluth, x. 18, elsewhere only Targ. Jer. xlix. 24.
Shithi, only x. 17.
Tahath hashshĕmĕsh, i. 3, agreeing with the Greek ὑφ' ἡλίῳ, or ὑπὸ
τὸν ἥλιον.
Takkiph, in O. T. Heb. only vi. 10 ; elsewhere in the Chald., Targ.,
Talm.
Takan, i. 15 ; Pih. vii. 13, xii. 9, a Mishna-word used in the Pih.
and Hiph., whence tikkun (" putting right," e.g. in the text-
hist. terminus technicus, tikkun sopherim, and " arrangement,"
e.g. Gittin iv. 2, " the ordering of the world ") and tikkānāh
(e.g. Gittin iv. 6, " welfare," frequently in the sense of
" direction," " arrangement ").

This survey of the forms peculiar to the Book of Koheleth, and
only found in the most recent books of the O. T., partly only in

the Chaldee portions of these, and in general use in the Aramaic, places it beyond all doubt that in this book we have a product of the post-exilian period, and, at the earliest, of the time of Ezra-Nehemiah. All that Wagenmann (*Comm.* 1856), von Essen (*Der Predeger Salomo's*, 1856), Böhl (*De Aramaismis libri Coheleth*, 1860), Hahn (*Comm.* 1860), Reusch (*Tübinger Quartalschr.* 1860), Warminski (*Verfasser u. Abfassungszeit des B. Koheleth*, 1867), Prof. Taylor Lewis (in the American ed. of Lange's *Bibelwerk*, 1869), Schäfer (*Neue Untersuchungen ü d. B. Koheleth*, 1870), Vegni (*L'Ecclesiaste secondo il testo Ebraico*, Florenz 1871) have advanced to the contrary, rests on grounds that are altogether untenable. If we possessed the original work of Sirach, we should then see more distinctly than from fragments [1] that the form of the language found in Koheleth, although older, is yet one that does not lie much further back; it is connected, yet loosely, with the old language, but at the same time it is in full accord with that new Heb. which we meet with in the Mishna and the Barajtha-Literature, which groups itself around it. To the modern aspects of the Heb. language the following forms belong:—

1. Verbs *Lamed-Aleph*, which from the first interchange their forms with those of verbs *Lamed-He*, are regularly treated in certain forms of inflexion in the Mishna as verbs *Lamed-He; e.g.* יָצְאָה is not used, but יָצְתָה.[2] This interchange of forms found in the later language reveals itself here in יָצָא, x. 5, used instead of יָצְאת; and if, according to the Masora, חוֹטָא (הֹטֵא) is to be always written like מוֹצֵא at vii. 26 (except vii. 26b), the traditional text herein discloses a full and accurate knowledge of the linguistic character of the book. The Aram. יִשְׁנָא for יְשַׁנֶּה, at viii. 1, is not thus to be accounted for.

2. The richness of the old language in mood-forms is here disappearing. The optative of the first person (the cohortative) is only represented by אֲחַכְּמָה, vii. 23. The form of the subjunctive (jussive) is found in the prohibitive clauses, such as vii. 16, 17, 18, x. 4; but elsewhere the only certain examples found are שִׁלֵּךְ, *quod auferat secum*, v. 14, and וִיגִּיד, x. 10. In xii. 7, וְיָשֹׁב may also be read, although וְיָשֻׁב, under the influence of "ere ever" (xii. 6), is also admissible. On the contrary, יָהוּא, xi. 3, is indic. after the Mishn. יְהֵא, and so also is וְיָנֵאץ (derived from נֵץ, not נוּץ), xii. 5. Yet more characteristic, however, is the circumstance that the historic tense,

---

[1] *Vid.* the collection of the Heb. fragments of the Book of Ben-Sira in my *Gesch. der jüd. Poesie*, p. 204 f.

[2] *Vid.* Geiger's *Lehrbuch der Mishna-Sprache*, p. 46.

the so-called *fut. consecutivum,* which has wholly disappeared from the
Mishna-language, also here, notwithstanding the occasions for its
frequent use, occurs only three times, twice in the unabbreviated
form, iv. 1, 7, and once in the form lengthened by the intentional *ah,*
i. 17, which before its disappearance was in frequent use. It probably belonged more to the written than to the spoken language of
the people (cf. the Song vi. 9*b*).

3. The complexion of the language peculiar to the Book of
Koheleth is distinguished also by this, that the designation of the
person already contained in the verbal form is yet particularly expressed, and without there being a contrast occasioning this emphasis,
by the personal pronoun being added to and placed after it, *e.g.* i. 16,
ii. 1, 11, 12, 13, 15, 18, 20, iii. 17, 18, iv. 1, 4, 7, v. 17, vii. 25,
viii. 15, ix. 15. Among the more ancient authors, Hosea has the
same peculiarity (cf. the Song v. 5); but there the personal pronoun
stands always before the verb, *e.g.* viii. 13, xii. 11. The same thing
is found in Ps. xxxix. 11, lxxxii. 6, etc. The inverse order of the
words is found only at ii. 14, after the scheme of Job i. 15, as also
ii. 15 follows the scheme of Gen. xxiv. 27. Mishna-forms of expressions such as מֹוֹדְרְנִי, *Nedarim* i. 1, מְקֻבְּלְנִי, *Jebamoth* xvi. 7, are not
homogeneous with that manner of subordinating the personal pro-
noun (cf. vii. 26, iv. 2). Thus we have here before us a separation
of the subject and the predicate, instead of which, in the language of
the Mishna, the form הָיִיתִי אֹמֵר (אני) and the like (*e.g. Berachoth* i. 5)
is used, which found for itself a place in the language of Koheleth,
in so far as this book delights in the use of the participle to an extent
scarcely met with in any other book of Scripture (*vid. e.g.* i. 6,
viii. 12, x. 19).

4. The use of the demonstrative pronoun זֶה bears also a
Mishnic stamp. We lay no particular stress on the fact that the
author uses it, as regularly as the Mishna, always without the
article; but it is characteristic that he always, where he does not
make use of the masculine from in a neuter sense (as vii. 10, 18,
29, viii. 9, ix. 1, xi. 6, keeping out of view cases determined by
attraction), employs no other feminine form than זֹה, Mishnic זוֹ,
in this sense, ii. 2, v. 15, 18, vii. 23, ix. 13. In other respects
also the use of the pronouns approaches the Mishna language. In
the use of the pronoun also in i. 10 and v. 18 there is an approach
to the Mishnic זֶהוּ, *hic est,* and זֶהִי, *haec est.* And the use of הוּא and
הֵמָּה for the personal verb reaches in iii. 18, ix. 4 (*vid.* Comm.), the
extreme.

The enumeration of linguistic peculiarities betokening a late origin is not yet exhausted; we shall meet with many such in the course of the Exposition. Not only the language, however, but also the style and the artistic form of the book, show that it is the most recent product of the Bibl. *Chokma* literature, and belongs to a degenerated period of art. From the fact that the so-called metrical accent system of the three books—Psalms, Job, and Proverbs—is not used in Ecclesiastes, it does not follow that it is not a poetical book in the fullest sense of the word; for the Song and Lamentations, these masterpieces of the שִׁיר and קִינָה, the Minnesong and the Elegy, are also excluded from that more elevated, more richly expressive, and more melodious form of discourse, perhaps to preserve the spiritual character of the one, and not to weaken the elegiac character of the other, to which a certain melancholy monotone *andante* is suitable. So also, to apply that system of accentuation to the Book of Koheleth was not at all possible, for the symmetrical stichs to which it is appropriate is for the most part wanting in Koheleth, which is almost wholly written in eloquent prose: unfolding its instruction in the form of sentences without symmetrical stichs.—It is, so to speak, a philosophical treatise in which "I saw," and the like, as the expression of the result of experience; "I said," as the expression of reflection on what was observed; "I perceived," as the expression of knowledge obtained as a conclusion from a process of reasoning; and "this also," as the expression of the result,—repeat themselves nearly terminologically. The reasoning tone prevails, and where the writer passes into gnomic poetry he enters into it suddenly, *e.g.* v. 9*b*, or holds himself ready to leave it quickly again, *e.g.* v. 12, vii. 13 f. Always, indeed, where the Mashal note is struck, the discourse begins to form itself into members arranged in order; and then the author sometimes rises in language, and in the order of his words, into the true classic form of the proverb set forth in parallel members, *e.g.* vii. 7, 9, ix. 8. The symmetry of the members is faultless, v. 5, viii. 8, ix. 11; but in other places, as v. 1, vii. 26, xi. 9, it fails, and in the long run the book, altogether peculiar in its stylistic and artistic character, cannot conceal its late origin: in the elevated classical style there quickly again intermingles that which is peculiar to the author, as representing the age in which he lived, *e.g.* vii. 19, x. 2 f., 6, 8–10, 16 f., xi. 3, 6. That in the age of the Mishna they knew how to imitate classic masterpieces, is seen from the beautiful enigma, in the form of a heptastich, by Bar-Kappara, *jer. Moëd katan* iii. 1, and the elegy, in the form of a hexastich on the death of R. Abina, by Bar-Kippuk, *b. Moëd katan*

25*b*.[1] One would thus be in error if he regarded such occasional classical pieces in the Book of Koheleth as borrowed. The book, however fragmentary it may seem to be on a superficial examination, is yet the product of one author.[2] In its oratorical ground-form, and in the proverbs introduced into it, it is a side-piece to Prov. i.–ix. We have shown, in the introduction to the Book of Proverbs, that in these proverbial discourses which form the introduction to the older Solomonic Book of Proverbs, which was probably published in the time of Jehoshaphat, the Mashal appears already rhetorically decomposed. This decomposition is much further advanced in the Book of Ecclesiastes. To it is applicable in a higher degree what is there (*Proverbs*, vol. I. 12 f.) said of Prov. i.–ix. The distich is represented in the integral, vii. 13, synonymous, xi. 4, and synthetic, vii. 1, and also, though rarely, in the antithetic form, vii. 4; but of the emblematic form there is only one example, x. 1. The author never attempted the beautiful numerical and priamel forms; the proverbial form also, beyond the limits of the distich, loses the firmness of its outline. The tetrastich, x. 20, is, however, a beautiful exception to this. But splendour of form would not be appropriate to such a sombre work as this is. Its external form is truly in keeping with its spirit. In the checkered and yet uniform manner of the book is reflected the image of the author, who tried everything and yet was satisfied with nothing; who hastened from one thing to another because nothing was able to captivate him. His style is like the view he takes of the world, which in its course turned to him only its dark side. He holds fast to the fear of God, and hopes in a final judgment; but his sceptical world-sorrow remains unmitigated, and his forced eudaemonism remains without the right consecration: these two stars do not turn the night into day; the significance of the book, with reference to the history of redemption, consists in the actual proof that humanity, in order to its being set free from its unhappiness, needs to be illuminated by the sun of a new revelation. But although the manner of the author's representation is the reflection of his own inner relation to the things represented, yet here and there he makes his representation, not without con-

---

[1] Given and translated in *Wissenchaft, Kunst, Judenthum* (1838), p. 231 f.

[2] Renan, in his *Histoire des Langues Sémitiques*, supposes that a work of so bold a scepticism as Ecclesiastes could not have originated in the post-exilian period of the severely legal rabbinical Judaism; it may be an old Solomonic work, but as it now lies before us, revised by a more recent hand,—an untenable expedient for establishing an arbitrary supposition.

sciousness and art, the picture of his own manner of thought. Thus, *e.g.*, the drawling tautologies in viii. 14, ix. 9, certainly do not escape from him against his will. And as was rightly remarked under Gen. ii. 1–3, that the discourse there is extended, and forms itself into a picture of rest after the work of the creation, so Koheleth, in i. 4–11 and xii. 2–7, shows himself a master of eloquence; for in the former passage he imitates in his style the everlasting unity of the course of the world, and in the latter he paints the exhausted and finally shattered life of man.

Not only, however, by the character of its thought and language and manner of representation, but also by other characteristic features, the book openly acknowledges that it was not written by Solomon himself, but by a Jewish thinker of a much later age, who sought to conceive of himself as in Solomon's position, and clothed his own life-experiences in the confessions of Solomon. The very title of the book does not leave us in doubt as to this. It is in these words : *The words of Koheleth, the son of David, king in Jerusalem.* The apposition, "king in Jerusalem," appertains, like *e.g.* 2 Chron. xxxv. 3, to the name of the speaker who is introduced ; for nothing is here said as to the place in life held by David, but to that held by him who is thus figuratively named. The indeterminate "king" of itself would be untenable, as at Prov. xxxi. 1. As there the words "king of Massa" are to be taken together, so here "king" is determined by "in Jerusalem" added to it, so far that it is said what kind of king Koheleth was. That by this name Solomon is meant, follows, apart from i. 12 ff., from this, that David had only one son who was king, viz. Solomon. The opinion of Krochmal, that a later David, perhaps a governor of Jerusalem during the Persian domination, is meant,[1] is one of the many superfluities of this learned author. Koheleth is Solomon, but he who calls him "king in Jerusalem" is not Solomon himself. Solomon is called "king of Israel," *e.g.* 2 Kings xxiii. 13 ; and as in i. 12 he names himself "king over Israel," so, Neh. xiii. 26, he is called "king of Israel," and along with this designation, "king over all Israel;" but the title, "king in Jerusalem," nowhere else occurs. We read that Solomon "reigned in Jerusalem over all Israel," 1 Kings xi. 42, cf. xiv. 21 ; the title, "king in Jerusalem," is quite peculiar to the title of the book before us. Eichhorn supposes that it corresponds to the time subsequent to the division of the kingdom, when there were two different royal residences ;

---

[1] Vid. *Kerem chemed* v. 89, and his *More neboche ha-seman* (*Director errantium nostrae aetatis*), edited by Zunz, 1851, 4.

but against this view Bloch rightly remarks, that the contrasted "in Samaria" occurs only very rarely (as 2 Kings xiv. 23). We think that in this expression, "king in Jerusalem," there is revealed a time in which Israel had ceased to be an independent kingdom, in which Jerusalem was no more a royal city.

That the book was not composed immediately by Solomon, is indicated by the circumstance that he is not called Solomon, nor Jedidiah (2 Sam. xii. 25), but is designated by a hitherto unheard of name, which, by its form, shows that it belongs, at earliest, to the Ezra-Nehemiah age, in which it was coined. We consider the name, first, without taking into account its feminine termination. In the Arab., *ḳahal* (cogn. *ḳaḥal*) signifies to be dry, hard, from the dryness and leather-like toughness of the skin of an old man; and, accordingly, Dindorf (*Quomodo nomen Coheleth Salomoni tribuatur*, 1791) and others understand *Koheleth* of an old man whose life is worn out; Coccejus and Schultens, with those of their school, understand it of the penitent who is dead to the world. But both views are opposed by this, that the form קָהֵל (קֵהֶל, cf. בֵּהֵל) would be more appropriate; but above all by this, that קהל, in this meaning, *aridum, marcidum esse*, is a verbal stem altogether foreign to the northern Semitic. The verb קהל signifies, in the Heb., Aram., and Assyr., to call (cf. the Syr. *kahlonitho*, a quarrelsome woman), and particularly to call together; whence קָהָל, of the same Sanscrit-Semit. root as the words ἐκ-κλη-σία and *con-cil-ium*,[1]—an extension of the root קל, which, on another side, is extended in the Arab. *kalah*, Aethiop. *kalʿha*, to cry. This derivation of the name Koheleth shows that it cannot mean συναθροιστής (Grotius, not Aquila), in the sense of *collector sententiarum;* the Arab. translation *alajam'at* (also van Dyk) is faultless, because *jam'* can signify, to collect men as well as things together; but קהל is not used in that sense of *in unum redigere*. In close correspondence with the Heb. word, the LXX. translates, ὁ ἐκκλησιαστής; and the Graec. Venet., ἡ ἐκκλησιάστρια (xii. 9: ἡ ἐκκλησιάζουσα). But in the nearest signification, "the collector," this would not be a significant name for the king represented as speaking in this book. In Solomon's reign there occurred an epoch-making assembly in Jerusalem, 1 Kings viii. 1, 2 Chron. v. 2—viz. for the purpose of consecrating the temple. The O. T. does not afford any other historical reference for the name; for although, in Prov. v. 14, xxvi. 26, בְּקָהָל signifies *coram populo, publice*, yet it does not occur directly of the public appearance of Wisdom; the expressions for this are different, i. 20 f.,

---

[1] *Vid.* Friedr. Delitzsch's *Indogermanisch-Semitische Studien*, p. 90.

viii. 1–4, ix. 3, though cognate. But on that great day of the consecration of the temple, Solomon not only called the people together,
but he also preached to them,—he preached indirectly, for he consecrated the temple by prayer; and directly, for he blessed the
people, and exhorted them to faithfulness, 1 Kings viii. 55–61.
Thus Solomon appears not only as the assembler, but also as the
preacher to those who were assembled; and in this sense of a
teacher of the people (cf. xii. 9), *Koheleth* is an appropriate name of
the king who was famed for his wisdom and for his cultivation of
the popular *Mashal*. It is known that in proper names the *Kal* is
frequently used in the sense of the *Hiph.* Thus *Koheleth* is not
immediately what it may be etymologically = קֹרֵא, caller, proclaimer;
but is = מַקְהֵלֶת, from הקהיל, to assemble, and to speak to the assembly,
contionari; according to which Jerome, under i. 1, rightly explains:
ἐκκλησιαστής, *Graeco sermone appellatur qui coetum, id est ecclesiam
congregat, quem nos nuncupare possumus contionatorem, eo quod
loquatur ad populum et ejus sermo non specialiter ad unum, sed ad
universos generaliter dirigatur.* The interpretation: assembly =
academy or *collectivum*, which Döderlein (*Salomon's Prediger u. Hohes-
lied,* 1784) and Kaiser (*Koheleth, Das Collectivum der Davidischen
Könige in Jerusalem,* 1823) published, lightly disregards the form
of the *n. agentis;* and Spohn's (*Der Prediger Salomo,* 1785) "O
vanity of vanities, said the philosopher," itself belongs to the
vanities.

Knobel in his Comm. (1836) has spoken excellently regarding
the feminine form of the name; but when, at the close, he says:
"Thus *Koheleth* properly signifies preaching, the office and business of the public speaker, but is then = קֹהֵל׳, מַקְהִיל, public speaker
before an assembly," he also, in an arbitrary manner, interchanges
the *n. agentis* with the *n. actionis.* His remark, that "the rule that
concreta, if they have a fem. termination, become *abstracta*, must
also hold for *participia*," is a statement that cannot be confirmed.
As הֹתֶמֶת signifies that which impresses (a seal), and כֹּתֶרֶת that
which twines about (chapiter), so also חֹבֶרֶת, Ex. xxvi. 10, that which
joins together (the coupling); one can translate such fem. particip.,
when used as substantives, as *abstracta, e.g.* כָּלָה (from כָּלָה), destruction, utter ruin; but they are *abstracta* in themselves as little as
the *neutra* in τὸ ταὐτόν, which may be translated by "identity,"
or in *immensum altitudinis*, by immensity (in height). Also Arab.
names of men with fem. forms are *concreta.* To the participial
form *Koheleth* correspond, for the most part, such names as (Arab.)
rawiyaton, narrator of tradition (fem. of *rawyn*); but essentially cogn.

also are such words as '*allamat*, greatly learned man ; also *khalyfaton*, which is by no means an inf. noun, like the Heb. חֲלִיפָה, but is the fem. of the verbal adj. *khalyf*, successor, representative. The Arabic grammarians say that the fem. termination gives to the idea, if possible, a collective signification, *e.g. jarrar*, the puller, *i.e.* the drawer of a ship (*helciarius*), and *jarrarat*, the multitude drawing, the company (*taife*) drawing the boat up the stream ; or it also serves " as an exhaustive designation of the properties of the genus ;" so that, *e.g.*, '*allamat* means one who unites in himself that which is peculiar to the very learned, and represents in his own person a plurality of very learned men. They also say that the fem. termination serves in such cases to strengthen the idea. But how can this strengthening result from a change in the gender ? Without doubt the fem. in such cases discharges the function of a neut. ; and since *doctissimus* is heightened to *doctissimum*, it is thereby implied that such an one is a pattern of a learned man,—the reality of the idea, or the realized ideal of such an one.

From these Arab. analogues respecting the import of the name *Koheleth*, it follows that the fem. is not to be referred to *Chokma* in such a way as that Solomon might be thereby designated as the representative, and, as it were, the incarnation of wisdom (Ewald, Hitzig, etc.),—an idea which the book by no means supports ; for if the author had designed, in conformity with that signification of the name, to let Wisdom herself speak through Solomon's mouth, he would have let him speak as the author of Prov. i.-ix. speaks when he addresses the reader by the title, " my son," he would not have put expressions in his mouth such as i. 16–18, vii. 23 f. One should not appeal to vii. 27 ; for there, where the subject is the dangers of the love of women, *Koheleth*, in the sense of Wisdom preaching, is as little appropriate as elsewhere ; just here was the masculine gender of the speaker to be accented, and *Amrah Koheleth* is thus an incorrect reading for *Amar Hakkoheleth* (xii. 8). The name Koheleth, without *Chokma* being supplied, is a man's name, of such recent formation as *Sophereth*, Neh. vii. 5, for which Ezra ii. 55, *Hassophereth;* cf. also Ezra ii. 57, הַצְּ כֹּ֫פ. The Mishna goes yet further in the coining of such names for men *generis fem.* As it generally prefers to use the *part. passivi* in an active sense, *e.g.* סָבוּר, thinking ; רָכוּב, riding ; שָׁתוּי, having drunk ; so also it forms fem. plurals with a masculine signification,—as *Hadruchoth*, press-treaders, *Terumoth* iii. 4 ; *Hammᵉshuhhoth*, surveyors, *Erubin* iv. 11 ; *Hallᵉuᵗoth*, speakers in a foreign tongue, *Megilla* ii. 1,—and construes these with mas. predicates.[1] In these there can be nowhere anything said of a heightening of the idea effected by the transition to fem. forms. But the persons acting, although they are men, are thought of as neut.; and they appear, separated from the determination of their gender, as the representatives of the activity spoken of. According to this, *Koheleth* is, without regard to the gender, a preaching person. The Book of Koheleth thus bears, in its second word, as on its very forehead, the stamp of the Ezra-Nehemiah era to which it belongs.

As the woman of Endor, when she raised Samuel out of Hades at the request of Saul, sees "gods ascending out of the earth" (1 Sam. xxviii. 13), so it is not the veritable Solomon who speaks in this book, but his spirit, for which this neut. name *Koheleth* is appropriate. When he says, i. 12, "I, Koheleth, have been king over Israel in Jerusalem," he recognises himself not as the reigning monarch, but as having been king. The Talmudic *Aggada* has joined to this הייתי, the fable that Solomon was compelled to descend from the throne on account of his transgression of the law, which was then occupied by an angel in his stead, but externally bearing his likeness; and that he now went about begging, saying: "I, Koheleth, have been king over Israel in Jerusalem;" but that they struck him with a stick, and set before him a plate of groats; for they said to him: "How canst thou speak thus? There the king sits in his palace on his throne."[2] In this fiction there is at least grammatical intelligence. For it is a vain delusion for one to persuade himself that Solomon in his advanced age could say, with reference to the period of his life as ruler, "I have been king," *fui rex*—he was certainly always so during the forty years of his reign, and on to the last moment of his life. Or can the words הייתי מלך mean *sum rex?* The case is as follows: הייתי is never the expression of the abstract present, or of existence without regard to time; "I am a king" is expressed in this sense by the substantival clause *ani mělĕk*. In every case where one can translate הייתי by "I am," *e.g.* Ps. lxxxviii. 5, the present being is thought of as the result of an historical past (*sum = factus sum*). But at the most, הייתי, when it looks from the present back upon the past, out of which it arose, signifies "I have become," Gen. xxxii. 11; Ps. xxx. 8; Jer. xx. 7; or when it looks back into the past as

---

[1] *Vid.* Geiger, *Lehrbuch*, § xvi. 6, and cf. Weiss' *Studien*, p. 90, who arbitrarily explains away this linguistic usage. Duke, in his *Sprache der Mishna*, p. 75, avoids the difficulty by the supposition of inadmissible ellipses.

[2] *Jer. Sanhedrin* ii. 6 goes further into the story; *b. Gittin* 68*b*, where the angel is designated by the Persian name *Ashmodee*, cf. Jellinek's *Sammlung kleiner Midrashim* 2. xxvi.

such, "I have been," Josh. i. 5; Judg. xii. 2; Ps. xxxvii. 25.
Whether this word, in the former sense, corresponds to the Greek
perfect, and in the latter to the Greek aorist, is determined only by
the situation and connection. Thus in Ex. ii. 22 it signifies, "I
have become a stranger" (γέγονα = εἰμί); while, on the other hand,
in Deut. xxiii. 8, "thou hast been a stranger" (ἐγένου, *fuisti*). That
where the future is spoken of, הייתי can, by virtue of the *consecutio
temporum*, also acquire the meaning of "I shall become, I shall
be," *e.g.* 1 Kings i. 21, cf. 1 Chron. xix. 12, is of no importance to
us here. In the more modern language the more delicate syntax,
as well as that idea of "becoming," primarily inherent in the verb
היה, is disappearing, and הייתי signifies either the past purely, "I have
been," Neh. xiii. 6, or, though not so frequently, the past along with
the present, "I was," *e.g.* Neh. i. 11. Accordingly, Solomon while
still living would be able to say הייתי מלך only in the sense of "I
have become (and still am) king;" but that does not accord with
the following retrospective perfects.[1] This also does not harmonize
with the more modern linguistic usage which is followed by Koheleth, *e.g.* i. 9, מה־ש', *id quod fuit*; i. 10, כבר היה, *pridem fuit*. In
conformity with this, the LXX. translates הייתי by ἐγενόμην, and
the Graec. Venet. by ὑπῆρξα. But "I have been king," Solomon,
yet living, cannot say, only *Salomo redivivus* here introduced, as the
preacher can use such an expression.

The epilogue, xii. 9 ff., also furnishes an argument in favour of
the late composition of this book, on the supposition that it is an
appendix, not by another hand, but by the author himself. But
that it is from the author's own hand, and does not, as Grätz
supposes, belong to the period in which the school of Hillel had
established the canonicity of the book, follows from this, that it is
composed in a style of Hebrew approaching that used in the
Mishna, yet of an earlier date than the Mishna; for in the Talmuds
it is, clause by clause, a subject of uncertain interpretation,—
the language used is plainly, for the Talmudic authorities, one that
is antiquated, the expressions of which, because not immediately
and unambiguously clear, need, in order to their explanation, to be
translated into the language then in use. The author of the book
makes it thus manifest that here in the epilogue, as in the book
itself, Solomon is intentionally called *Koheleth*; and that the manner
of expression, as well as of the formation of the sentences in this

---

[1] If וְאֶתֵּן followed, then הייתי (as Reusch and Hengstenberg interpret) might
be a circumstantial perfect; *vid.* under Gen. i. 2.

epilogue, can in all particulars be supported from the book itself. In "fear God," xii. 13a, the saying in v. 6, which is similarly formed, is repeated; and "this is the whole of man," xii. 13b, a thought written as it were more in cipher than *in extenso*, is in the same style as vi. 10a. The word יותר ("moreover"), frequently used by the author, and בעל, used in the formation of attributive names, x. 11, 20, v. 10, 12, viii. 8, we meet with also here. And as at xii. 9, 10, 11 a third idea connected ἀσυνδέτως follows two ideas connected by *vav*, so also at i. 7, vi. 5. But if this epilogue is the product of the author's own hand, then, in meaning and aim, it presents itself as its sequel. The author says that the *Koheleth* who appears in this book as "wise" is the same who composed the beautiful people's-book *Mishle;* that he sought out not only words of a pleasing form, but also all words of truth; that the words of the wise are like goads and nails which stand in collected rows and numbers—they are given from one Shepherd. The author of the book thereby denotes that the sentences therein collected, even though they are not wholly, as they lie before us, the words of Solomon, yet that, with the Proverbs of Solomon, and of the wise men generally, they go back to one giver and original author. The epilogue thus, by its historic reference to Solomon, recognises the fiction, and gives the reader to understand that the book loses nothing in its value from its not having been immediately composed by Solomon.

Of untruthfulness, of a so-called *pia fraus*, we cannot therefore speak. From early times, within the sphere of the most ancient Israelitish authorship, it was regarded as a justifiable undertaking for an author to reproduce in a rhetorical or poetical form the thoughts and feelings of memorable personages on special occasions. The Psalter contains not a few psalms bearing the superscription *le-David*, which were composed not by David himself, but by unknown poets, placing themselves, as it were, in David's position, and representing him, such *e.g.* as cxliv., which in the LXX. excellently bears the superscription πρὸς τὸν Γολιάδ. The chronicler, when he seeks to give the reader an idea of the music at the festival of the consecration of the tabernacle and then of the completed temple, allows himself so great freedom, that he puts into the mouth of David the Beracha of the fourth book of the Psalms (cvi. 48), along with the preceding verse of Ps. cvi. (1 Chron. xvi. 35 f.), and into Solomon's mouth verses of Ps. cxxxii. (2 Chron. vi. 41 f.). And the prophetical discourses communicated in the O. T. historical books are certainly partly of this sort, that they either may be regarded as original, as *e.g.* 1 Sam. ii. 27 ff., or must be so regarded, as 2 Kings xviii.–xx.;

but not merely where the utterances of the prophets are in general
terms reproduced, as at Judg. vi. 8–10, 2 Kings xvii. 13, xxi.
10–15, but also elsewhere in most of the prophetic discourses
which we read in the Books of Kings and Chronicles, the style of
the historian makes itself perceptible. Consequently (as also Caspari
in his work on the Syro-Ephraimite War, 1849, finds) the discourses
in the Chronicles, apart from those which are common to them, bear an
altogether different homogeneous character from those of the Book
of Kings. It is the same as with the speeches, for instance, which
are recorded in Thucydides, Dionysius of Halicarnassus, Livy, and
other Greek and Roman historians. Classen may be right in the
opinion, that the speeches in Thucydides are not mere inventions,
but that, nevertheless, as they lie before us, they are the work of
the historian ; even the letters that passed between Pausanias and
Xerxes bear his stamp, although he composed them on the ground
of the verbal reports of the Spartans. It is thus also with the
speeches found in Tacitus. They are more Ciceronian than his own
style is, and the discourses of Germans have less elaborated periods
than those of the Romans ; but so greatly was the writing of history
by the ancients influenced by this custom of free reproduction,
that even a speech of the Emperor Claudius, which is found engraven
on brass, is given by Tacitus not in this its original, but in another
and freer form, assimilated to his own manner of representation.
So also sacred history, which in this respect follows the general
ancient custom, depends not on the identity of the words, but of
the spirit : it does not feign what it represents the historical
person as saying, it follows traditions ; but yet it is the power
of its own subjectivity which thus recalls the past in all that was
essential to it in actual life. The aim is not artistically to represent the imitation which is made as if it were genuine. The arts
by which it is sought to impart to that which is introduced
into a more recent period the appearance of genuineness, were unknown to antiquity. No pseudonymous work of antiquity shows
any such imitation of an ancient style as, *e.g.*, does Meinhold's
Bernsteinhexe, or such a forgery as Wagenfeld's *Sanchuniathon*.
The historians reproduce always in their own individual way,
without impressing on the speeches of different persons any distinct individual character. They abstain from every art aimed at
the concealment of the actual facts of the case. It is thus also
with the author of the Book of Koheleth. As the author of the
" *Wisdom of Solomon* " openly gives himself out to be an Alexandrian, who makes Solomon his organ, so the author of the

Book of Koheleth is so little concerned purposely to veil the fiction of the Solomon - discourse, in which he clothes his own peculiar life-experiences, that he rather in diverse ways discovers himself as one and the same person with the *Salomo redivivus* here presenting himself.

We do not reckon along with these such proverbs as have for their object the mutual relationship between the king and his subjects, viii. 3–5, x. 4, 16 f., 20, cf. v. 8 ; these do not betray in the speaker one who is an observer of rulers and not a ruler himself ; for the two collections of " Proverbs of Solomon" in the Book of Proverbs contain a multitude of proverbs of the king, xvi. 10, 12–15, xix. 12, xx. 2, 8, 26, 28, xxv. 2, 3, 4 f., 6 f., which, although objectively speaking of the king, may quite well be looked on as old Solomonic,—for is there not a whole princely literature regarding princely government, as *e.g.* Friedrich II.'s *Anti-Machiavel ?* But in the complaints against unrighteous judgment, iii. 16, iv. 1, v. 7, one is to be seen who suffers under it, or who is compelled to witness it without the power to change it ; they are not appropriate in the mouth of the ruler, who should prevent injustice. It is the author himself who here puts his complaints into the mouth of Solomon ; it is he who has to record life-experiences such as x. 5–7. The time in which he lived was one of public misgovernment and of dynastic oppression, in contrast with which the past shone out in a light so much the rosier, vii. 10, and it threw long dark shadows across his mind when he looked out into the world, and mediately also upon the confessions of his Koheleth. This Koheleth is not the historical Solomon, but an abstraction of the historical ; he is not the theocratic king, but the king among the wise men ; the actual Solomon could not speak, ii. 18, of the heir to his throne as of " the man that shall be after him,"—and he who was led astray by his wives into idolatry, and thus became an apostate (1 Kings xi. 4), must have sounded an altogether different note of penitential contrition from that which we read at vii. 26–28. This Solomon who tasted all, and in the midst of his enjoyment maintained the position of a wise man (ii. 9), is described by the author of this book from history and from sayings, just as he needs him, so as to make him an organ of himself ; and so little does he think of making the fiction an illusion difficult to be seen through, that he represents Koheleth, i. 16, ii. 7, 9, as speaking as if he had behind him a long line of kings over the whole of Israel and Judah, while yet not he, but the author of the book, who conceals himself behind *Salomo redivivus,* could look back on such a series of kings in Jerusalem.

When did this anonymous author, who speaks instead of his Solomon, live and write ?   Let us first of all see what conclusion may be gathered regarding the book from the literary references it contains.   In its thoughts, and in the form of its thoughts, it is an extremely original work.   It even borrows nothing from the Solomonic Book of Proverbs, which in itself contains so many repetitions ; proverbs such as vii. 16–18 and Prov. iii. 7 are somewhat like, but only accidentally.   On the contrary, between v. 14 and Job i. 21, as well as between vii. 14 and Job ii. 10, there undoubtedly exists some kind of connection ; here there lie before us thoughts which the author of the Book of Koheleth may have read in the Book of Job, and have quoted them from thence—also the mention of an untimely birth, vi. 3, cf. Job iii. 16, and the expression " one among a thousand," vii. 28, cf. Job ix. 3, xxxiii. 23, may perhaps be reminiscences from the Book of Job occurring unconsciously to the author.   This is not of any consequence as to the determination of the time of the composition of the Book of Koheleth, for the Book of Job is in any case much older.   Dependence on the Book of Jeremiah would be of greater importance, but references such as vii. 2, cf. Jer. xvi. 8, ix. 11, cf. Jer. ix. 22, are doubtful, and guide to no definite conclusion.   And who might venture, with Hitzig, to derive the golden lamp, xii. 10, from the vision of Zechariah, iv. 2, especially since the figure in the one place has an altogether different signification from what it has in the other ?   But we gain a more certain *terminus a quo* by comparing v. 5 with Mal. ii. 7. Malachi there designates the priests as messengers (delegated) of Jahve of hosts, along with which also there is the designation of the prophets as God's messengers, iii. 1, Hag. i. 13.   With the author of the Book of Koheleth " the messenger " is already, without any name of God being added, a priestly title not to be misunderstood ; מלאך [1] (messenger) denotes the priest as *vicarius Dei*, the delegate of God, שלוח דרחמנא, according to the later title (*Kiddushin* 23b).   And a *terminus ad quem*, beyond which the reckoning of the time of its composition cannot extend, is furnished by the " Wisdom of Solomon," which is not a translation, but a work written originally in Alexandrine Greek ; for that this book is older than the Book of Koheleth, as Hitzig maintains, is not only in itself improbable, since the latter shows not a trace of Greek influence, but in the light of the history of doctrine is altogether impossible, since it represents, in the history of the development of the doctrine of wisdom and the

---

[1] *Vid.* my dissertation: Die Discussion der Amtsfrage im Mishna u. Gemara, in the *Luth. Zeitschrift* 1854, pp. 446–449.

last things, the stage immediately preceding the last B.C., as Philo does the last; it is not earlier than the beginning of the persecution of the Jews by the Egyptians under Ptolemy VII., Physkon (Joseph. *c. Ap.* ii. 5), and at all events was written before Philo, since the combination of the *Sophia* and the *Logos* is here as yet incomplete. This Book of Wisdom must stand in some kind of historical relation to the Book of Koheleth. The fact that both authors make King Solomon the organ of their own peculiar view of the world, shows a connection that is not accidental. Accident is altogether excluded by the circumstance that the Alexandrian author stands in the same relation to the Palestinian that James stands in to the Pauline letters. As James directs himself not so much against Paul as against a Paulinism misleading to fatal consequences, so the Book of Wisdom is certainly not directly a work in opposition to the Book of Koheleth, as is assumed by J. E. Ch. Schmidt (*Salomo's Prediger,* 1794), Kelle (*Die salom. Schriften,* 1815), and others; but, as Knobel and Grimm assert, against a one-sided extreme interpretation of views and principles as set forth by Koheleth, not without an acquaintance with this book. The lovers of pleasure, who speak in Wisd. ii. 1–9, could support that saying by expressions from the Book of Koheleth, and the concluding words there sound like an appropriation of the words of Koheleth iii. 22, v. 17 (cf. LXX.); it is true they break off the point of the Book of Koheleth, for the exhortation to the fear of God, the Judge of the world, is not echoed; but to break off this point did not lie remote, since the old Chokma watchword, " fear God," hovered over the contents of the book rather than penetrated them. It is as if the author of the Book of Wisdom, i.-v., wished to show to what danger of abuse in the sense of a pure materialistic eudaemonism the wisdom presented in the Book of Koheleth is exposed. But he also opposes the pessimistic thoughts of Koheleth in the decided assertions of the contrary : (1) Koheleth says : " There is one event to the righteous and to the wicked," ix. 2; but he says : there is a difference between them wide as the heavens, Wisd. iii. 2 f., iv. 7, v. 15 f.; (2) Koheleth says : "He that increaseth knowledge increaseth sorrow," i. 18 ; but he says: wisdom bringeth not sorrow, but pure joy with it, Wisd. viii. 16; (3) Koheleth says that wisdom bringeth neither respect nor favour, ix. 11 ; but he says : it brings fame and honour, Wisd. viii. 10 ; (4) Koheleth says : " There is no remembrance of the wise more than of the fool for ever," ii. 16 ; but he says of wisdom in contrast to folly : " I shall obtain by it a deathless name, and shall leave to my descendants an everlasting remembrance," Wisd. viii. 13.

The main distinction between the two books lies in this, that the comfortless view of Hades running through the Book of Koheleth is thoroughly surmounted by a wonderful rising above the O. T. stand-point by the author of the Book of Wisdom, and that hence there is in it an incomparably more satisfying *Theodicee* (cf. Wisd. xii. 2–18 with Eccles. vii. 15, viii. 14), and a more spiritual relation to this present time (cf. Wisd. viii. 21, ix. 17, with Eccles. ii. 24, iii. 13, etc.). The " Wisdom of Solomon " has indeed the appearance of an anti-Ecclesiastes, a side-piece to the Book of Koheleth, which aims partly at confuting it, partly at going beyond it; for it represents, in opposition to Koheleth not rising above earthly enjoyment with the *But* of the fear of God, a more ideal, more spiritual Solomon. If Koheleth says that God "hath made everything beautiful in his time," iii. 11, and hath made man upright, vii. 29 ; so, on the other hand, Solomon says that He hath made all things εἰς τὸ εἶναι, Wisd. i. 14, and hath made man ἐπ' ἀφθαρσίᾳ, ii. 23.   There are many such parallels, *e.g.* v. 9, cf. Koh. viii. 13 ; viii. 5, cf. Koh. vii. 12 ; ix. 13–16, cf. Koh. iii. 10 f., but particularly Solomon's confession, vii. 1–21, with that of Koheleth, i. 12–18.   Here, wisdom appears as a human acquisition ; there (which agrees with 1 Kings iii. 11–13), as a gracious gift obtained in answer to prayer, which brings with it all that can make happy.   If one keeps in his eye this mutual relation between the two books, there can be no doubt as to which is the older and which the younger.   In the Book of Koheleth the Old Covenant digs for itself its own grave.   It is also a "school-master to Christ," in so far as it awakens a longing after a better Covenant than the first.[1]   But the Book of Wisdom is a precursor of this better covenant.   The composition of the Book of Koheleth falls between the time of Malachi, who lived in the time of Nehe-miah's second arrival at Jerusalem, probably under Darius Nothus (423–405 B.C.), and the Book of Wisdom, which at the earliest was written under Ptolemy Physkon (145–117), when the O. T. was already for the most part translated into the Greek language.[2]

Hitzig does not venture to place the Book of Koheleth so far back into the period of the Ptolemies ; he reaches with his chain of evidence only the year 204, that in which Ptolemy Epiphanes (204–181) gained, under the guardianship of the Romans, the throne of his father,—he must be the minor whom the author has in his eye, x. 16.   But the first link of his chain of proof is a *falsum*.   For it is not true that Ptolemy Lagus was the first ruler who exacted from the Jews the " oath of God," viii. 2, *i.e.* the oath of fidelity ; for

[1] *Vid.* Oehler's *Theol. des A. T.*, II. p. 324.
[2] Cf. ii. 12a with Isa. iii. 10, LXX., and xv. 10a with Isa. xliv. 20, LXX.

Josephus (*Antt.* xii. 1. 1) says directly, that Ptolemy Lagus did this with reference to the fidelity with which the Jews had kept to Alexander the Macedonian the oath of allegiance they had sworn to Darius, which he particularly describes, *Antt.* xi. 8. 3 ; besides, the covenant, *e.g.* 2 Sam. v. 3, concluded in the presence of Jahve with their own native kings included in it the oath of allegiance, and the oath of vassalage which, *e.g.*, Zedekiah swore to Nebuchadnezzar, 2 Chron. xxxvi. 13, cf. Ezek. xvii. 13–19, had at the same time binding force on the citizens of the state that was in subjection. Also that " the oath of God " must mean the oath of allegiance sworn to a foreign ruler, and not that sworn to a native ruler, which would rather be called " the oath of Jahve," does not stand the test : the author of the Book of Koheleth drives the cosmopolitism of the Chokma so far, that he does not at all make use of the national name of God connected with the history of redemption, and Nehemiah also, xiii. 25, uses an oath " of God " where one would have expected an oath " of Jahve." The first link of Hitzig's chain of proof, then, shows itself on all sides to be worthless. The author says, viii. 2, substantially the same as Paul, Rom. xiii. 5, that one ought to be subject to the king, not only from fear of punishment, but for conscience' sake.

Thus, then, viii. 10 will also stand without reference to the carrying away of the Jews captive by Ptolemy Lagus, especially since the subject there is by no means that of a mass-deportation; and, besides, those who were carried into Egypt by Lagus were partly from the regions round about Jerusalem, and partly from the holy city itself (Joseph. *Antt.* 12. 1. 1). And the old better times, vii. 10, were not those of the first three Ptolemies, especially since there are always men, and even in the best and most prosperous times, who praise the old times at the expense of the new. And also women who were a misfortune to their husbands or lovers there have always been, so that in vii. 26 one does not need to think of that Agathoclea who ruled over Ptolemy Philopator, and even had in her hands the power of life and death. Passages such as vii. 10 and vii. 26 afford no help in reference to the chronology. On the other hand, the author in ix. 13–16 relates, to all appearance, what he himself experienced. But the little city is certainly not the fortified town of Dora, on the sea-coast to the west of Carmel, which was besieged by Antiochus the Great (Polybius, v. 66) in the year 218, as at a later period, in the year 138, it was by Antiochus VII., Sidetes (Joseph. *Bell.* i. 2. 2) ; for this Dora was not then saved by a poor wise man within it,—of whom Polybius knows nothing,—but "by the strength of the place, and the help of those with Nicholaus." A definite historical event is also certainly found in iv. 13–16. Hitzig sees in the old foolish king the spiritually contracted, but so much the more covetous, high priest Onias, under Ptolemy Euergetes ; and in the poor but wise youth, Joseph (the son of Tobias), who robbed Onias of his place in the state, and raised himself to the office of general farmer of taxes. But here nothing agrees but that Onias was old and foolish, and that Joseph was then a young wise man (Joseph. *Antt.* xii. 4. 2) ; of the poverty of the latter nothing is heard—he was the nephew of Onias. And besides, he did not come out of the house "of prisoners" (הָסוּרִים) ; this word is pointed by Hitzig so as to mean, out of the house "of fugitives" (הַפּוּרִים), perhaps, as he supposes, an allusion to the district Φιχόλα, which the author thus interprets as if it were derived from φεύγειν. Historical investigation has here degenerated into the boldest subjectivism. The Heb. tongue has never called "fugitives" הסורים ; and to whom could the Heb. word פיקולה (cf. *Berachoth* 28b) suggest—as Φύγελα did to Pliny and Mela—the Greek φεύγειν !

We have thus, in determining the time of the authorship of this book, to confine ourselves to the period subsequent to the Diadochs. It may be regarded as beyond a doubt that it was written under the Persian domination. Kleinert (*Der Prediger Salomo,* 1864) is in general right in saying that the political condition of the people which the book presupposes, is that in which they are placed under Satraps : the unrighteous judgment, iii. 16 ; and the despotic oppression, iv. 1, viii. 9, v. 7 ; the riotous court-life, x. 16–19 ; the raising of mean men to the highest places of honour, x. 5–7 ; the inexorable severity of the law of war-service, viii. 8 ;[1] the prudence required by the organized system of espionage [2] existing at such a time,—all these things were characteristic of this period. But if the Book of Koheleth is not at all older than Malachi, then it was written somewhere within the last century of the Persian kingdom, between Artaxerxes I., Longimanus (464–424), and Darius Codomannus (335–332): the better days for the Jewish people, of the Persian supremacy under the first five Achaemenides, were past (vii. 10). Indeed, in vi. 3 there appear to be reminiscences of Artaxerxes II., Mnemon (died about 360), who was 94 years old, and, according to Justin (x. 1), had 115 sons, and of Artaxerxes III., Ochus his successor, who was poisoned by the chief eunuch Bagoas, who, according to Aelian, *Var. Hist.* vi. 8, threw his (Ochus') body to the cats, and

---

[1] *Vid.* Herod. iv. 84, vii. 38 f.
[2] *Vid.* Duncker's *Gesch. des Alterthums,* Bd. 2 (1867), p. 894.

caused sword-handles to be made from his bones. The book altogether contains many examples to which concrete instances in the Persian history correspond, from which they might be abstracted, in which strict harmony on all sides with historical fact is not to be required, since it did not concern the author. The event recorded iv. 13-16 refers to Cyrus rising to the supremacy of world-ruler (after dispossessing the old Median King Astyages), who left [1] nothing but misery to posterity. Such a rich man as is described in vi. 2, who had to leave all his treasures to a stranger, was Croesus, to whom Solon, as vii. 8a (cf. Herod. i. 32. 86), said that no one ought to be praised before his end. A case analogous at least to ix. 14–16, was the deliverance of Athens by the counsel of Themistocles (Justin, ii. 12), who finally, driven from Athens, was compelled to seek the protection of the Persian king, and ended his life in despair.[2] If we were not confined, for the history of the Persian kingdom and its provinces, from Artaxerxes I. to the appearance of Alexander of Macedon, to only a few and scanty sources of information (we know no Jewish events of this period, except the desecration of the temple by Bagoses, described by Josephus, *Antt.* xi. 7), we might probably be better able to understand many of the historical references of the Book of Koheleth. We should then be able to say to whom the author refers by the expression, " Woe to thy land when thy king is a child," x. 16 ; for Artaxerxes I., who, although only as yet a boy at the time of the murder of his father Xerxes (Justin, iii. 1), soon thereafter appeared manly enough, cannot be thought of. We should then, perhaps, be also in possession of the historical key to viii. 10 ; for with the reference to the deportation of many thousands of Jewish prisoners (Josephus, *c. Ap.* i. 22)—which, according to Syncellus and Orosius, must have occurred under Artaxerxes III., Ochus—the interpretation of that passage does not accord.[3] We should then also, perhaps, know to what political arrangement the

---

[1] According to Nicolaus of Damascus (Müller's *Fragm. hist. Graec.* III. 398), Cyrus was the child of poor parents ; by " prison-house" (iv. 14), reference is made to his confinement in Persia, where access to him was prevented by guards (Herod. i. 123). Justin, i. 5: "A letter could not be openly brought to him, since the guards appointed by the king kept possession of all approaches to him."

[2] *Vid.* Spiegel's *Erânische Alterthumskunde*, II. pp. 409, 413. Bernstein suggests the deliverance of Potidea (Herod. viii. 128) or Tripolis (Diodor. xvi. 41); but neither of these cities owed its deliverance to the counsel of a wise man. Burger (*Comm. in Ecclesiasten*, 1864) thinks, with greater probability, of Themistocles, who was celebrated among the Persians (Thucyd. i. 138), which Ewald also finds most suitable, provided the author had a definite fact before his eye.

[3] *Vid.* Bernstein's *Quaestiones Kohelethanae*, p. 66.

author points when he says, vii. 19, that wisdom is a stronger protection to a city than "ten mighty men;" Grätz refers this to the *decuriones* of the Roman municipal cities and colonies; but probably it refers to the dynasties[1] (cf. Assyr. *salaṭ*, governor) placed by the Persian kings over the cities of conquered countries. And generally, the oppressed spirit pervading the book would be so much clearer if we knew more of the sacrifices which the Jewish people in the later time of the Persians had to make, than merely that the Phoenicians, at the same time with "the Syrians in Palestine," had to contribute (Herod. vii. 87) to Xerxes for his Grecian expedition three hundred triremes; and also that the people who "dwelt in the Solymean mountains" had to render him assistance in his expedition against Greece (Joseph. *c. Ap.* i. 22).

The author was without doubt a Palestinian. In iv. 17 he speaks of himself as dwelling where the temple was, and also in the holy city, viii. 10; he lived, if not actually in it, at least in its near neighbourhood, x. 15; although, as Kleinert remarks, he appears, xi. 1, to make use of a similitude taken from the corn trade of a seaport town. From iv. 8 the supposition is natural that he was alone in the land, without children or brothers or sisters; but from the contents and spirit of the whole book, it appears more certain that, like his Koheleth, he was advanced in years, and had behind him a long checkered life. The symptoms of approaching death presenting themselves in old age, which he describes to the young, xii. 2 ff., he probably borrowed from his own experience. The whole book bears the marks of age, — a production of the Old Covenant which was stricken in age, and fading away.

The literature, down to 1860, of commentaries and monographs on the Book of Koheleth is very fully set forth in the English Commentary of Ginsburg, and from that time to 1867, in Zöckler's Commentary, which forms a part of Lange's *Bibelwerk*. Keil's *Einleitung*, 3d ed. 1873, contains a supplement to these, among which, however, the *Bonner Theolog. Literaturblatt*, 1874, Nr. 7, misses Pusey's and Reusch's (cf. the *Tübingen Theol. Quartalschrift*, 1860, pp. 430–469). It is not possible for any man to compass this literature. Zedner's *Catalogue of the Hebrew books in the Library of the British Museum*, 1867, contains a number of Jewish commentaries omitted by Ginsburg and Zöckler, but far from all. For example, the Commentary of Ahron B. Josef (for the first time printed at Eupatoria, 1834) now lies before me, with those of Moses Frankel (Dessau, 1809), and of Samuel David Luz-

---

[1] *Vid.* Duncker's *Gesch. des Alterthums*, II. p. 910.

zatto, in the journal, *Ozar Nechmad* 1864. Regarding the literature of English interpretation, see the American translation, by Tayler Lewis (1870), of Zöckler's Commentary. The catalogue there also is incomplete, for in 1873 a Commentary by Thomas Pelham Dale appeared; and a Monograph on chap. xii., under the title of *The Dirge of Coheleth*, by the Orientalist C. Taylor, appeared in 1874. The fourth volume of the *Speaker's Commentary* contains a Commentary on the Song by Kingsbury, and on Ecclesiastes by W. T. Bullock, who strenuously maintains its Solomonic authorship. The opinion that the book represents the conflict of two voices, the voice of true wisdom and that of pretended wisdom, has lately found advocates not only in a Hebrew Commentary by Ephraim Hirsch (Warsaw, 1871), but also in the article "Koheleth" by Schenkel in his *Bibellexikon* (vol. III., 1871). For the history and refutation of this attempt to represent the book in the form of a dialogue, we might refer to Zöckler's Introd. to his Commentary.

The old translations have been referred to at length by Ginsburg. Frederick Field, in his *Hexapla* (Poet. vol. 1867), has collected together the fragments of the Greek translations. Ge. Janichs, in his *Animadversiones criticae* (Breslau, 1871), has examined the Peshito of Koheleth and Ruth; *vid.* with reference thereto, Nöldeke's *Anzeige* in the *Liter. Centralblatt* 1871, Nr. 49, and cf. Middeldorpf's *Symbolae exegetico-criticae ad librum Ecclesiastis*, 1811. The text of the *Graecus Venetus* lies before us now in a more accurate form than that by Villoison (1784), in Gebhardt's careful edition of certain Venetian manuscripts (Leipzig, Brockhaus 1874), containing this translation of the O. T. books.

EXPOSITION OF THE BOOK OF ECCLESIASTES

" Ostendit omnia esse vanitati subjecta: in his quae propter homines facta sunt vanitas est mutabilitatis; in his quae ab hominibus facta sunt vanitas est curiositatis; in his quae in hominibus facta sunt vanitas mortalitatis."

HUGO OF ST. VICTOR († 1140).

HE title, i. 1, *The words of Koheleth, son of David, king in Jerusalem*, has been already explained in the Introduction. The verse, which does not admit of being properly halved, is rightly divided by " son of David " by the accent *Zakef;* for the apposition, " king in Jerusalem," does not belong to " David," but to " Koheleth." In several similar cases, such as Ezek. i. 3, the accentuation leaves the designation of the oppositional genitive undefined; in Gen. x. 21*b* it proceeds on an erroneous supposition; it is rightly defined in Amos i. 1*b*, for example, as in the passage before us. That " king " is without the article, is explained from this, that it is determined by " in Jerusalem," as elsewhere by " of Israel " (" Judah "). The expression (cf. 2 Kings xiv. 23) is singular.

PROLOGUE : THE EVERLASTING SAMENESS.—I. 2–11.

The book begins artistically with an opening section of the nature of a preamble. The ground-tone of the whole book at once sounds in ver. 2, which commences this section, " O vanity of vanities, saith Koheleth, O vanity of vanities ! All is vain." As at Isa. xl. 1 (*vid. l.c.*) it is a question whether by " saith " is meant a future or a present utterance of God, so here and at xii. 8 whether " saith " designates the expression of Koheleth as belonging to history or as presently given forth. The language

218

admits both interpretations, as *e.g.* " saith," with God as the subject, 2 Sam. xxiii. 3, is meant historically, and in Isa. xlix. 5
of the present time. We understand " saith " here, as *e.g.* Isa.
xxxvi. 4, " Thus saith . . . the king of Assyria," of something said
now, not of something said previously, since it is those presently
living to whom the Solomon *redivivus*, and through him the
author of this book, preaches the vanity of all earthly things. The
old translators take " vanity of vanities " in the nominative, as if it
were the predicate; but the repetition of the expression shows that
it is an exclamation = *O vanitatem vanitatum*. The abbreviated
connecting form of הֶבֶל is here not punctuated הַבַל, after the form
(חֲדַר) חֲדָר and the like, but הֲבֵל, after the manner of the Aram.
ground-form עֲבַד; cf. Ewald, § 32*b*. Jerome read differently: *In*
Hebraeo pro vanitate vanitatum ABAL ABALIM scriptum est, quod
exceptis LXX. interpretibus omnes similiter transtulerunt ἀτμὸς ἀτ-
μίδων sive ἀτμῶν. *Hĕvĕl* primarily signifies a breath, and still bears
this meaning in post-bibl. Heb., *e.g. Schabbath* 119*b*: " The world
exists merely for the sake of the breath of school-children " (who
are the hope of the future). Breath, as the contrast of that which
is firm and enduring, is the figure of that which has no support, no
continuance. Regarding the superlative expression, " Vanity of
vanities," *vid.* the Song i. 1. " Vanity of vanities " is the *non plus*
ultra of vanity,—vanity in the highest degree. The double exclamation is followed by a statement which shows it to be the result
of experience. " All is vain "—the whole (of the things, namely,
which present themselves to us here below for our consideration and
use) is vanity.

Ver. 3. With this verse commences the proof for this exclamation and statement: " What profit hath a man of all his labour which
he laboureth in under the sun?!" An interrogative exclamation,
which leads to the conclusion that never anything right, *i.e.* real,
enduring, satisfying, comes of it. יִתְרוֹן, profit, synon. with *mothar*,
iii. 19, is peculiar to this book (= Aram. יִתְרָן). A primary form, יְתָרוֹן,
is unknown. The punctator Simson (Cod. 102*a* of the Leipzig
University Lib. f. 5*a*) rightly blames those who use וְיִתָרוֹ, in a
liturgical hymn, of the Day of Atonement. The word signifies that
which remains over, either, as here, clear gain, profit, or that which
has the pre-eminence, *i.e.* superiority, precedence, or is the foremost.
" Under the sun " is the designation of the earth peculiar to
this book,—the world of men, which we are wont to call the sub-
lunary world. שׁ has not the force of an accusative of manner, but
of the obj. The author uses the expression, " Labour wherein I

have laboured," ii. 19, 20, v. 17, as Euripides, similarly, μοχθεῖν μόχθον. He now proceeds to justify the negative contained in the question, " What profit ? "

Ver. 4. " One generation passeth away,. and another generation cometh : and the earth remaineth for ever." The meaning is not that the earth remains standing, and thus (Hitz.) approaches no limit (for what limit for it could be had in view ?) ; it is by this very immoveable condition that it fulfils, according to the ancient notion, its destiny, Ps. cxix. 90. The author rather intends to say that in this sphere nothing remains permanent as the fixed point around which all circles ; generations pass away, others appear, and the earth is only the firm territory, the standing scene, of this ceaseless change. In reality, both things may be said of the earth : that it stands for ever without losing its place in the universe, and that it does not stand for ever, for it will be changed and become something else. But the latter thought, which appertains to the history of redemption, Ps. cii. 26 f., is remote from the Preacher ; the stability of the earth appears to him only as the foil of the growth and decay everlastingly repeating themselves. Elster, in this fact, that the generations of men pass away, and that, on the contrary, the insensate earth under their feet remains, rightly sees something tragic, as Jerome had already done : *Quid hac vanius vanitate, quam terram manere, quae hominum causa facta est, et hominem ipsum, terrae dominum, tam repente in pulverem dissolvi ?* The sun supplies the author with another figure. This, which he thinks of in contrast with the earth, is to him a second example of ceaseless change with perpetual sameness. As the generations of men come and go, so also does the sun.

Ver. 5. " And the sun ariseth, the sun goeth down, and it hasteth (back) to its place, there to rise again." It rises and sets again, but its setting is not a coming to rest ; for from its place of resting in the west it must rise again in the morning in the east, hastening to fulfil its course. Thus Hitzig rightly, for he takes " there to rise again " as a relative clause ; the words may be thus translated, but strictly taken, both participles stand on the same level ; שׁוֹאֵף (panting, hastening) is like בָּא in ver. 4, the expression of the present, and 'וז that of the *fut. instans: ibi (rursus) oriturus;* the accentuation also treats the two partic. as co-ordinate, for *Tiphcha* separates more than *Tebir ;* but it is inappropriate that it gives to וְאֶל־קְ׳ the greater disjunctive *Zakef Quaton* (with *Kadma* going before). Ewald adopts this sequence of the accents, for he explains : the sun goes down, and that to its own place, viz. hastening back to it just by its going down, where, panting, it again ascends. But that the sun goes down to the place of its ascending, is a distorted thought. If "to its place" belongs to "goeth," then it can refer only to the place of the going down, as e.g. Benjamin el-Nahawendi (Neubauer, *Aus der Petersb. Bibl.* p. 108) explains : "and that to its place," viz. the place of the going down appointed for it by the Creator, with reference to Ps. civ. 19, "the sun knoweth his going down." But the שָׁם, which refers back to "its place," opposes this interpretation ; and the phrase שֹׁאֵף cannot mean "panting, rising," since שָׁאַף in itself does not signify to pant, but to snatch at, to long eagerly after anything, thus to strive, panting after it (cf. Job vii. 2 ; Ps. cxix. 131), which accords with the words "to its place," but not with the act of rising. And how unnatural to think of the rising sun, which gives the impression of renewed youth, as panting! No, the panting is said of the sun that has set, which, during the night, and thus without rest by day and night, must turn itself back again to the east (Ps. xix. 7), there anew to commence its daily course. Thus also Rashi, the LXX., Syr., Targ., Jerome, Venet., and Luther. Instead of שֹׁאֵף, Grätz would read שָׁב אַף, *redit (atque) etiam;* but שֹׁאֵף is as characteristic of the Preacher's manner of viewing the world as סוֹבֵב וְגוֹ, 6b, and יֵשׁ, 8a. Thus much regarding the sun. Many old interpreters, recently Grätz, and among translators certainly the LXX., refer also 6a to the sun. The Targ. paraphrases the whole verse of the state of the sun by day and night, and at the spring and autumn equinox, according to which Rashi translates הָרוּחַ, *la volonté (du soleil).* But along with the sun, the wind is also referred to as a third example of restless motion always renewing itself. The division of the verses is correct ; 6a used of the sun would overload the figure, and the whole of ver. 6 therefore refers to the wind.

Ver. 6. "It goeth to the south, and turneth to the north; the wind goeth ever circling, and the wind returneth again on its circuits." Thus designedly the verse is long-drawn and monotonous. It gives the impression of weariness. שָׁב may be 3d pret. with the force of an abstract present, but the relation is here different from that in 5a, where the rising, setting, and returning stand together, and the two former lie backwards indeed against the latter; here, on the contrary, the circling motion and the return to a new beginning stand together on the same line ; שָׁב is thus a part., as the Syr. translates it. The participles represent continuance in motion. In ver. 4 the subjects stand foremost, because the ever anew beginning motion belongs to the subject ; in vv. 5 and 6, on the contrary, the pred. stands foremost, and the subject in ver. 6 is therefore placed thus far back, because the first two pred. were not sufficient, but required a third for their completion. That the wind goes from the south (דָּרוֹם, R. דר, the region of the most intense light) to the north (צָפוֹן, R. צָפַן, the region of darkness), is not so exclusively true of it as it is of the sun that it goes from the east to the west; this expression requires the generalization " circling, circling goes the wind," *i.e.* turning in all directions here and there; for the repetition denotes that the circling movement exhausts all possibilities. The near defining part. which is subordinated to " goeth," elsewhere is annexed by " and," *e.g.* Jonah i. 11; cf. 2 Sam. xv. 30; here סֹבֵב ו סוֹבֵב, in the sense of סָבִיב ו סָבִיב, Ezek. xxxvii. 2 (both times with *Pasek* between the words), precedes. סְבִיבָה is here the *n. actionis* of סבב. And " on its circuits " is not to be taken adverbially : it turns back on its circuits, *i.e.* it turns back on the same paths (Knobel and others), but עַל and שׁב are connected, as Prov. xxvi. 11; cf. Mal. iii. 24; Ps. xix. 7 : the wind returns back to its circling movements to begin them anew (Hitzig). " The wind " is repeated (cf. ii. 10, iv. 1) according to the figure Epanaphora or Palindrome (*vid.* the Introd. to Isaiah, c. xl.–lxvi.). To all regions of the heavens, to all directions of the compass, its movement is ceaseless, ever repeating itself anew; there is nothing permanent but the fluctuation, and nothing new but that the old always repeats itself. The examples are thoughtfully chosen and arranged. From the currents of air, the author now passes to streams of water.

Ver. 7. "All rivers run into the sea, and the sea becomes not full; to the place whence the rivers came, thither they always return again." Instead of *n*e*hhárim*, *n*e*hhalim* was preferred, because it is the more general name for flowing waters, brooks, and rivers ; נַחַל (from נחל, *cavare*), אָפִיק (from אפק, *continere*), and (Arab.) *wadin* (from the root-idea of stretching, extending), all three denote the channel or bed, and then the water flowing in it. The sentence, " all rivers run into the sea," is consistent with fact. Manifestly the author does not mean that they all immediately flow thither ; and by " the sea " he does not mean this or that sea ; nor does he think, as the Targ. explains, of the earth as a ring (וּלְשִׁפְּנָקָא, Pers. *angusht-báne*, properly " finger-guard ") surrounding the ocean: but the sea in general is meant, perhaps including also the ocean that is hidden. If we include this internal ocean, then the rivers which lose themselves in hollows, deserts, or inland lakes, which have no visible outlet, form no exception. But the expression refers first of all to the visible sea-basins, which gain no apparent increase by these masses of water being emptied into them: "the sea, it becomes not full ;" אֵינֶנּוּ

(Mishn. אֵינוֹ) has the reflex. pron., as at Ex. iii. 2, Lev. xiii. 34, and elsewhere. If the sea became full, then there would be a real change; but this sea, which, as Aristophanes says (*Clouds*, 1294 f.), οὐδὲν γίγνεται ἐπιρρεόντων τῶν ποταμῶν πλείων, represents also the eternal sameness. In ver. 7b, Symm., Jer., Luther, and also Zöckler, translate שׁ in the sense of "from whence;" others, as Ginsburg, venture to take שָׁם in the sense of מִשָּׁם; both interpretations are linguistically inadmissible. Generally the author does not mean to say that the rivers return to their sources, since the sea replenishes the fountains, but that where they once flow, they always for ever flow without changing their course, viz. into the all-devouring sea (Elst.); for the water rising out of the sea in vapour, and collecting itself in rain-clouds, fills the course anew, and the rivers flow on anew, for the old repeats itself in the same direction to the same end. מְקוֹם is followed by what is a virtual genitive (Ps. civ. 8); the accentuation rightly extends this only to הֹלְכִים; for אֲשֶׁר, according to its relation, signifies in itself *ubi*, Gen. xxxix. 20, and *quo*, Num. xiii. 27; 1 Kings xii. 2 (never *unde*). שָׁם, however, has after verbs of motion, as *e.g.* Jer. xxii. 27 after שׁוּב, and 1 Sam. ix. 6 after הלך, frequently the sense of שָׁמָּה. And שׁוּב with לְ and the infin. signifies to do something again, Hos. xi. 9, Job vii. 7, thus: to the place whither the rivers flow, thither they flow again, *eo rursus eunt*. The author here purposely uses only participles, because although there is constant change, yet that which renews itself is ever the same. He now proceeds, after this brief but comprehensive induction of particulars, to that which is general.

Ver. 8. " All things are in activity; no man can utter it; the eye is not satisfied with seeing, and the ear is not full with hearing." All translators and interpreters who understand *d'varim* here of words (LXX., Syr., and Targ.) go astray; for if the author meant to say that no words can describe this everlasting sameness with perpetual change, then he would have expressed himself otherwise than by "all words weary" (Ew., Elst., Hengst., and others); he ought at least to have said לָרִיק יג'. But also " all things are wearisome " (Knob., Hitz.), or " full of labour " (Zöck.), *i.e.* it is wearisome to relate them all, cannot be the meaning of the sentence; for יָגֵעַ does not denote that which causes weariness, but that which suffers weariness (Deut. xxv. 18; 2 Sam. vii. 2); and to refer the affection, instead of to the narrator, to that which is to be narrated, would be even for a poet too affected a *quid pro quo*. Rosenmüller essentially correctly: *omnes res fatigantur h. e. in perpetua versantur vicissitudine, qua fatigantur quasi.* But יְגֵעִים is not appropriately rendered by *fatigantur;* the word means, becoming wearied, or perfectly feeble, or also : wearying oneself (cf. x. 15, xii. 12), working with a strain on one's strength, fatiguing oneself (cf. יְגִיעַ, that which is gained by labour, work). This is just what these four examples are meant to show, viz. that a restless activity reaching no visible conclusion and end, always beginning again anew, pervades the whole world—all things, he says, summarizing, are in labour, *i.e.* are restless, hastening on, giving the impression of fatigue. Thus also in strict sequence of thought that which follows : this unrest in the outer world reflects itself in man, when he contemplates that which is done around him ; human language cannot exhaust this coming and going, this growth and decay in constant circle, and the *quodlibet* is so great, that the eye cannot be satisfied with seeing, nor the ear with hearing ; to the unrest of things without corresponds the unrest of the mind, which through this course, in these ever repeated variations, always bringing back the old again to view, is kept in ceaseless activity. The object to *dăbbēr* is the totality of things. No words can comprehend this, no sensible perception exhaust it. That which is properly aimed at here is not the unsatisfiedness of the eyes (Prov. xxvii. 20), and generally of the mind, thus not the ever-new attractive power which appertains to the eye and the ear of him who observes, but the force with which the restless activity which surrounds us lays hold of and communicates itself to us, so that we also find no rest and contentment. With שָׂבַע, to be satisfied, of the eye, there is appropriately interchanged נִמְלָא, used of the funnel-shaped ear, to be filled, *i.e.* to be satisfied (as at vi. 7). The *min* connected with this latter word is explained by Zöck. after Hitz., "away from hearing," *i.e.* so that it may hear no more. This is not necessary. As *sāvă'* with its *min* may signify to be satisfied with anything, *e.g.* vi. 3, Job xix. 22, Ps. civ. 13 ; so also *nimlā*, with its *min*, to be full of anything, Ezek. xxxii. 6 ; cf. *Kal,* Isa. ii. 6, *Pih.* Jer. li. 34, Ps. cxxvii. 5. Thus *mishsh'moa'* is understood by all the old translators (*e.g.* Targ. מִלְּמִשְׁמַע), and thus also, perhaps, the author meant it : the eye is not satisfied with seeing, and the ear is not filled (satisfied) with hearing ; or yet more in accordance with the Heb. expression : there is not an eye, *i.e.* no eye is satisfied, etc., restlessly hastening, giving him who looks no rest, the world goes on in its circling course without revealing anything that is in reality new.

Ver. 9. "That which hath been is that which shall be, and that which is done is that which shall be done ; and there is nothing new under the sun."—The older form of the language uses only אֲשֶׁר instead of מַה־שֶּׁ, in the sense of *id quod,* and in the sense of *quid-*

quid, כל אשׁר (vi. 10, vii. 24); but *măh* is also used by it with the
extinct force of an interrogative, in the sense of *quodcunque,* Job
xiii. 13, *aliquid (quidquam),* Gen. xxxix. 8, Prov. ix. 13 ; and *mi*
or *mi asher,* in the sense of *quisquis,* Ex. xxiv. 14, xxxii. 33. In
הוּא שׁ (cf. Gen. xlii. 14) are combined the meanings *id (est) quod* and
idem (est) quod ; hu is often the expression of the equality of two
things, Job iii. 19, or of self-sameness, Ps. cii. 28. The double clause,
quod fuit . . . quod factum est, comprehends that which is done in
the world of nature and of men,—the natural and the historical.
The bold clause, *neque est quidquam novi sub sole,* challenges contradiction ; the author feels this, as the next verse shows.

Ver. 10. "Is there anything whereof it may be said : See, this
is new ?—it was long ago through the ages (aeons) which have been
before us." The Semit. substantive verb יֵשׁ (Assyr. *isu*) has here the
force of a hypothetical antecedent : supposing that there is a thing of
which one might say, etc. The זֶה, with *Makkeph,* belongs as subject, as
at vii. 27, 29 as object, to that which follows. כְּבָר (*vid.* List, p. 193)
properly denotes length or greatness of time (as כִּבְרָה, length of
way). The לְ of לְעֹ is that of measure : this "long ago" measured
(Hitz.) after infinitely long periods of time. מִלְּ, *ante nos,* follows
the usage of מִלְּפָ, Isa. xli. 26, and לְפָ, Judg. i. 10, etc. ; the past
time is spoken of as that which was before, for it is thought of as
the beginning of the succession of time (*vid.* Orelli, *Synon. der Zeit u.*
Ewigkeit, p. 14 f.). The singular הָיָה may also be viewed as pred. of
a *plur. inhumanus* in order ; but in connection, ii. 7, 9 (Gesen. § 147,
An. 2), it is more probable that it is taken as a neut. verb. That
which newly appears has already been, but had been forgotten ; for
generations come and generations go, and the one forgets the other.

Ver. 11. "There is no remembrance of ancestors ; and also of
the later ones who shall come into existence, there will be no remembrance for them with those who shall come into existence after
them." With זִכְרוֹן (with *Kametz*) there is also זִכְרֹן, the more common
form by our author, in accordance with the usage of his age ; Gesen.,
Elst., and others regard it here and at ii. 16 as constr., and thus
לְרִא as virtually object-gen. (Jerome, *non est priorum memoria*) ; but
such refinements of the old *syntaxis ornata* are not to be expected in
our author : he changes (according to the traditional punctuation)
here the initial sound, as at i. 17 the final sound, to *oth* and *uth.*
אֵין לְ is the contrast of הָיָה לְ : to attribute to one, to become partaker
of. The use of the expression, "for them," gives emphasis to the
statement. "With those who shall come after," points from the
generation that is future to a remoter future, cf. Gen. xxxiii. 2. The

Kametz of the prep. is that of the recompens. art.; cf. Num. ii. 31, where it denotes "the last" among the four hosts; for there 'הָא is meant of the last in order, as here it is meant of the remotely future time.

KOHELETH'S EXPERIENCES AND THEIR RESULTS.—I. 12–IV. 16.

The Unsatisfactoriness of striving after Wisdom, i. 12–18.

After this prelude regarding the everlasting sameness of all that is done under the sun, Koheleth-Solomon unfolds the treasure of his life-experience as king.

Ver. 12. " I, Koheleth, have been king over Israel in Jerusalem." That of the two possible interpretations of הָיִיתִי, " I have become " and " I have been," not the former (Grätz), but the latter, is to be here adopted, has been already shown (p. 205). We translate better by " I have been "—for the verb here used is a pure perfect —than by " I was " (Ew., Elst., Hengst., Zöck.), with which Bullock (*Speaker's Comm.*, vol. IV., 1873) compares the expression *Quand j'étois roi!* which was often used by Louis XIV. towards the end of his life. But here the expression is not a cry of complaint, like the "*fuimus Troes*," but a simple historical statement, by which the Preacher of the vanity of all earthly things here introduces himself,—it is Solomon, resuscitated by the author of the book, who here looks back on his life as king. " Israel " is the whole of Israel, and points to a period before the division of the kingdom; a king over Judah alone would not so describe himself. Instead of " king עַל (over) Israel," the old form of the language uses frequently simply " king of Israel," although also the former expression is sometimes found; cf. 1 Sam. xv. 26; 2 Sam. xix. 23; 1 Kings xi. 37. He has been king,— king over a great, peaceful, united people; king in Jerusalem, the celebrated, populous, highly-cultivated city,—and thus placed on an elevation having the widest survey, and having at his disposal whatever can make a man happy; endowed, in particular, with all the means of gaining knowledge, which accorded with the disposition of his heart searching after wisdom (cf. 1 Kings iii. 9–11, v. 9).

But in his search after worldly knowledge he found no satisfaction.

Ver. 13. " And I gave my heart to seek and to hold survey with wisdom over all that is done under the sun : a sore trouble it is which God has given to the children of men to be exercised therewith." The synonyms דָּרַשׁ (to seek) and תּוּר (to hold survey over) do not represent a lower and a higher degree of search (Zöck.), but two kinds of searching: one penetrating in depth, the other going out in extent; for the former of these verbs (from the root-idea of grinding, testing) signifies to investigate an object which one already has in hand, to penetrate into it, to search into it thoroughly; and the latter verb (from the root-idea of moving round about)[1] signifies to hold a survey,— look round in order to bring that which is unknown, or not comprehensively known, within the sphere of knowledge, and thus has the meaning of *bǎkkēsh*, one going the rounds. It is the usual word for the exploring of a country, *i.e.* the acquiring personal knowledge of its as yet unknown condition; the passing over to an intellectual search is peculiar to the Book of Koheleth, as it has the phrase נָתַן לֵב ?, *animum advertere*, or *applicare ad aliquid*, in common only with Dan. x. 12. The *beth* of *bahhochᵉmah* is that of the instrument; wisdom must be the means (*organon*) of knowledge in this searching and inquiry. With עַל is introduced the sphere into which it extends. Grotius paraphrases: *Historiam animalium et satorum diligentissime inquisivi.* But נַעֲשָׂה does not refer to the world of nature, but to the world of men; only within this can anything be said of actions, only this has a proper history. But that which offers itself for research and observation there, brings neither joy nor contentment. Hitzig refers הוּא to human activity; but it relates to the research which has this activity as its object, and is here, on that account, called "a sore trouble," because the attainment and result gained by the laborious effort are of so unsatisfactory a nature. Regarding עִנְיָן, which here goes back to עָנָה בְּ, to fatigue oneself, to trouble oneself with anything, and then to be engaged with it, *vid.* p. 194. The words עִנְיַן רָע would mean trouble of an evil nature (*vid.* at Ps. lxxviii. 49; Prov. vi. 24); but better attested is the reading עִנְיָן רָע, "a sore trouble." הוּא is the subj., as at ii. 1 and elsewhere; the author uses it also in expressions where it is pred. And as frequently as he uses *asher* and שׁ, so also, when form and matter commend it, he uses the scheme of the attributive clause (elliptical relative clause), as here (cf. iii. 16), where certainly, in conformity with the old style, נִתַּן was to be used.

Ver. 14. He adduces proof of the wearisomeness of this work of research: "I saw all the works that are done under the sun; and, behold, all is vanity and striving after the wind." The point of the sentence lies in וָאֶרְאֶה וְהִ׳ = וְהִנֵּה, so that thus *raïthi* is the expression of the parallel fact (circumst. perfect). The result of his seeing,

---

[1] *Vid.* the investigation of these roots (Assyr. *utir*, he brought back) in Ethé's *Schlafgemach der Phantasie*, pp. 86–89.

and that, as he has said ver. 13, of a by no means superficial and limited seeing, was a discovery of the fleeting, unsubstantial, fruitless nature of all human actions and endeavours. They had, as *hevel* expresses, no reality in them; and also, as denoted by *rᵉuth ruahh* (the LXX. render well by προαίρεσις πνεύματος), they had no actual consequences, no real issue. Hos. xii. 2 [1] also says: "Ephraim feedeth on wind," *i.e.* follows after, as the result of effort obtains, the wind, *roëh ruahh;* but only in the Book of Koheleth is this sentence transformed into an abstract *terminus technicus* (*vid.* under *Rᵉuth*, p. 195).

Ver. 15. The judgment contained in the words, "vanity and a striving after the wind," is confirmed: "That which is crooked cannot become straight; and a deficit cannot be numerable," *i.e.* cannot be taken into account (thus Theod., after the Syro-Hex.), as if as much were present as is actually wanting; for, according to the proverb, "Where there is nothing, nothing further is to be counted." Hitzig thinks, by that which is crooked and wanting, according to vii. 13, of the divine order of the world: that which is unjust in it, man cannot alter; its wants he cannot complete. But the preceding statement refers only to labour under the sun, and to philosophical research and observation directed thereto. This places before the eyes of the observer irregularities and wants, brings such irregularities and wants to his consciousness,—which are certainly partly brought about and destined by God, but for the most part are due to the transgressions of man himself,—and what avails the observer the discovery and investigation?—he has only lamentation over it, for with all his wisdom he can bring no help. Instead of לִתְקֹן (*vid.* under תקן, p. 196), לְתַקֵן was to be expected. However, the old language also formed intransitive infinitives with transitive modification of the final vowels, *e.g.* יבֹשׁ, etc. (cf. שִׁישׁוֹן, v. 11).

Having now gained such a result in his investigation and research by means of wisdom, he reaches the conclusion that wisdom itself is nothing.

Vv. 16–18. "I have communed with mine own heart, saying: Lo, I have gained great and always greater wisdom above all who were before me over Jerusalem; and my heart hath seen wisdom and knowledge in fulness. And I gave my heart to know what was in wisdom and knowledge, madness and folly—I have perceived that this also is a grasping after the wind." The evidence in which he bears witness to himself that striving after wisdom and knowledge brings with it no true satisfaction, reaches down to the close of ver. 17; יָדַעְתִּי is the conclusion which is aimed at. The manner of expression is certainly so far involved, as he speaks of his heart to his heart what it had experienced, and to what he had purposely directed it. The אֲנִי leads us to think that a king speaks, for whom it is appropriate to write a capital *I*, or to multiply it into *we;* *vid.* regarding this "I," more pleonastic than emphatic, subordinated to its verb, § 3, p. 198. It is a question whether עִם־לִבִּי, after the phrase (אֶת) עִם דִּבֶּר, is meant of speaking with any one, *colloqui*, or of the place of speaking, as in "thou shalt consider in thine heart," Deut. viii. 5, it is used of the place of consciousness ; cf. Job xv. 9, (עִמָּדִי) עִמִּי הָיָה = σύνοιδα ἐμαυτῷ, and what is said in my *Psychol.* p. 134, regarding συνείδησις, consciousness, and συμμαρτυρεῖν. בְּלִבִּי, interchanging with עִם־לִבִּי, ii. 1, 15, cf. xv. 1, commends the latter meaning : in my heart (LXX., Targ., Jerome, Luther) ; but the cogn. expressions, *mᵉdabbĕrĕth ăl-libbah*, 1 Sam. i. 13, and *lᵉdabbēr ĕl-libbi*, Gen. xxiv. 45, suggest as more natural the former rendering, viz. as of a dialogue, which is expressed by the Gr. Venet. (more distinctly than by Aquila, Symm., and Syr.) : διείλεγμαι ἐγὼ ξὺν τῇ καρδίᾳ μου. Also לֵאמֹר, occurring only here in the Book of Koheleth, brings it near that the following *oratio directa* is directed to the heart, as it also directly assumes the form of an address, ii. 1, after בלבי. The expression, הִגְ׳ הכ׳, " to make one's wisdom great," *i.e.* " to gain great wisdom," is without a parallel ; for the words, הג׳ תו׳, Isa. xxviii. 29, quoted by Hitzig, signify to show and attest truly useful (beneficial) knowledge in a noble way. The annexed וְהו׳ refers to the continued increase made to the great treasure already possessed (cf. ii. 9 and 1 Kings x. 7). The *al* connected therewith signifies, " above" (Gen. xlix. 26) all those who were over Jerusalem before me. This is like the *sarrâni âlik mahrija*, " the kings who were my predecessors," which was frequently used by the Assyrian kings. The Targumist seeks to accommodate the words to the actual Solomon by thus distorting them : " above all the wise men who have been in Jerusalem before me," as if the word in the text were בירושלם,[1] as it is indeed found in several Codd., and according to which also the LXX., Syr., Jerome, and the Venet. translate. Rather than think of the wise (חַכִּימַיָּא), we are led to think of all those who from of old stood at the head of the Israelitish community. But there must have been well-known great men with whom Solomon measures

---

[1] In F the following note is added : " Several Codd. have, erroneously, *birushalam* instead of *al-yᵉrushalam*." Kennicott counts about 60 such Codd. It stands thus also in J ; and at first it thus stood in H, but was afterwards corrected to *al-yᵉrushalam*. Cf. Elias Levita's *Masoreth hamasoreth*, II. 8, at the end.

himself, and these could not be such dissimilarly great men as the Canaanitish kings to the time of Melchizedek; and since the Jebusites, even under Saul, were in possession of Zion, and Jerusalem was for the first time completely subdued by David (2 Sam. v. 7, cf. Josh. xv. 63), it is evident that only one predecessor of Solomon in the office of ruler over Jerusalem can be spoken of, and that here an anachronism lies before us, occasioned by the circumstance that the *Salomo redivivus,* who has behind him the long list of kings whom in truth he had before him, here speaks. Regarding אֲשֶׁר הָיָה, *qu'il y eut,* for אֲשֶׁר הָיוּ, *qui furent, vid.* at i. 10*b*. The seeing here ascribed to the heart (here = νοῦς, *Psychol.* p. 249) is meant of intellectual observation and apprehension; for "all perception, whether it be mediated by the organs of sense or not (as prophetic observing and contemplating), comprehends all, from mental discernment down to suffering, which veils itself in unconsciousness, and the Scripture designates it as a seeing" (*Psychol.* 234); the Book of Koheleth also uses the word רָאָה of every kind of human experience, bodily or mental, ii. 24, v. 17, vi. 6, ix. 9. It is commonly translated: "My heart saw much wisdom and knowledge" (thus *e.g.* Ewald); but that is contrary to the gram. structure of the sentence (Ew. § 287*c*). The adject. *harbēh*[1] is always, and by Koheleth also, ii. 7, v. 6, 16, vi. 11, ix. 18, xi. 8, xii. 9, 12, placed after its subst.; thus it is here adv., as at v. 19, vii. 16 f. Rightly the Venet.: ἡ καρδία μου τεθέαται κατὰ πολὺ σοφίαν καὶ γνῶσιν. *Chokma* signifies, properly, solidity, compactness; and then, like πυκνότης, mental ability, secular wisdom; and, generally, solid knowledge of the true and the right. *Dăăth* is connected with *chokma* here and at Isa. xxxiii. 6, as at Rom. xi. 33 γνῶσις is with σοφία. Baumgarten-Crusius there remarks that σοφία refers to the general ordering of things, γνῶσις to the determination of individual things; and Harless, that σοφία is knowledge which proposes the right aim, and γνῶσις that which finds the right means thereto. In general, we may say that *chokma* is the fact of a powerful knowledge of the true and the right, and the property which arises out of this intellectual possession; but *dăăth* is knowledge penetrating into the depth of the essence of things, by which wisdom is acquired and in which wisdom establishes itself.

Ver. 17. By the consecutive *modus* וָאֶתְּנָה (aor. with *ah,* like Gen. xxxii. 6, xli. 11, and particularly in more modern writings; *vid.* p. 198, regarding the rare occurrence of the aorist form in the Book of Koheleth) he bears evidence to himself as to the end

---

[1] Regarding the form הַרְבֵּה, which occurs once (Jer. xlii. 2), *vid.* Ew. § 240*e*.

which, thus equipped with wisdom and knowledge, he gave his heart to attain unto (cf. 13*a*), *i.e.* toward which he directed the concentration of his intellectual strength. He wished to be clear regarding the real worth of wisdom and knowledge in their contrasts; he wished to become conscious of this, and to have joy in knowing what he had in wisdom and knowledge as distinguished from madness and folly. After the statement of the object *lādăăth*, stands *v'daath*, briefly for וּלְדַעַת. Ginsburg wishes to get rid of the words *holēloth v'sikluth*, or at least would read in their stead תְּבוּנִית וְשִׂכְלוּת (rendering them "intelligence and prudence"); Grätz, after the LXX. παραβολὰς καὶ ἐπιστήμην, reads מְשָׁלוֹת וְשִׂכְלוֹת. But the text can remain as it is: the object of Koheleth is, on the one hand, to become acquainted with wisdom and knowledge; and, on the other, with their contraries, and to hold these opposite to each other in their operations and consequences. The LXX., Targ., Venet., and Luther err when they render *sikluth* here by ἐπιστήμη, etc. As *sikluth*, insight, intelligence, is in the Aram. written with the letter *samek* (instead of *sin*), so here, according to the Masora סכלות, madness is for once written with שׂ, being everywhere else in the book written with ס; the word is an ἐναντιόφωνον,[1] and has, whether written in the one way or in the other, a verb, *sakal* (שׂכל, סכל), which signifies "to twist together," as its root, and is referred partly to a complication and partly to a confusion of ideas. הֹלֵלוֹת, from הָלַל, in the sense of "to cry out," "to rage," always in this book terminates in *ôth*, and only at x. 13 in *ûth* (*vid.* p. 191); the termination *ûth* is that of the abstr. sing.; but *ôth*, as we think we have shown at Prov. i. 20, is that of a fem. plur., meant intensively, like *bogdoth*, Zeph. ii. 4; *binoth, chokmoth,* cf. *bogdim*, Prov. xxiii. 28; *hhovlim*, Zech. xi. 7, 14; *toqim*, Prov. xi. 15 (Böttch. § 700*g* E). Twice *v'sikluth* presents what, speaking to his own heart, he bears testimony to before himself. By *yādă'ti*, which is connected with *dibbarti* (ver. 16) in the same rank, he shows the *facit.* זֶה refers to the striving to become conscious of the superiority of secular wisdom and science to the love of pleasure and to ignorance. He perceived that this striving also was a grasping after the wind; with רְעוּת, 14*b*, is here interchanged רַעְיוֹן (*vid.* p. 195). He proves to himself that nothing showed itself to be real, *i.e.* firm and enduring, unimpeachable and imperishable. And why not?

Ver. 18. "For in much wisdom is much grief; and he that increaseth knowledge increaseth sorrow." The German proverb: "Much wisdom causeth headache," is compared, xii. 12*b*, but not

---

[1] *Vid.* Th. M. Redslob's *Die Arab. Wörter, u.s.w.* (1873).

here, where בַּעַס and מַכְאוֹב express not merely bodily suffering, but also mental grief. Spinoza hits one side of the matter in his *Ethics*, IV. 17, where he remarks: "*Veram boni et mali cognitionem saepe non satis valere ad cupiditates coercendas, quo facto homo imbecillitatem suam animadvertens cogitur exclamare: Video meliora proboque, deteriora sequor.*" In every reference, not merely in that which is moral, there is connected with knowledge the shadow of a sorrowful consciousness, in spite of every effort to drive it away. The wise man gains an insight into the thousand-fold woes of the natural world, and of the world of human beings, and this reflects itself in him without his being able to change it; hence the more numerous the observed forms of evil, suffering, and discord, so much greater the sadness (בַּעַס, R. כס, cogn. הם, *perstringere*) and the heart-sorrow (מַכְאוֹב, *crève-cour*) which the inutility of knowledge occasions. The form of 18a is like v. 6, and that of 18b like *e.g.* Prov. xviii. 22a. We change the clause *v'yosiph daath* into an antecedent, but in reality the two clauses stand together as the two members of a comparison: if one increaseth knowledge, he increaseth (at the same time) sorrow. "יוֹסִיף, Isa. xxix. 14, xxxviii. 5, Eccles. ii. 18," says Ewald, § 169a, "stands alone as a *part. act.*, from the stem reverting from *Hiph.* to *Kal* with ־ִ instead of ־ֵ." But this is not unparalleled; in הנ' יוֹסִף the verb יוֹסִף is fin., in the same manner as יִסַּד, Isa. xxviii. 16; תוֹמִיךְ, Ps. xvi. 5, is *Hiph.*, in the sense of *amplificas*, from יָמַךְ; יָפִיחַ, Prov. vi. 19 (*vid. l.c.*), is an attribut. clause, *qui efflat*, used as an adj.; and, at least, we need to suppose in the passage before us the confusion that the *ē* of *kātēl* (from *kātil*, originally *kātal*), which is only long, has somehow passed over into *î*. Böttcher's remark to the contrary, "An impersonal *fiens* thus repeated is elsewhere altogether without a parallel," is set aside by the proverb formed exactly thus: "He that breathes the love of truth says what is right," Prov. xii. 17.

The Unsatisfying Nature of Worldly Joy, ii. 1–11.

After having proved that secular wisdom has no superiority to folly in bringing true happiness to man, he seeks his happiness in a different way, and gives himself up to cheerful enjoyment.

ii. 1. "I have said in mine heart: Up then, I will prove thee with mirth, and enjoy thou the good! And, lo, this also is vain." Speaking in the heart is not here merely, as at i. 16, 17a, speaking to the heart, but the words are formed into a direct address of the heart. The Targ. and Midrash obliterate this by interpreting as

if the word were אֲנַסֶּכָה, "I will try it" (vii. 23).   Jerome also, in
rendering by *vadam et affluam deliciis et fruar bonis*, proceeds contrary to the usual reading of 'אֶנ (*Niph.* of נסך, *vid.* at Ps. ii. 6), as
if this could mean, "I will pour over myself."   It is an address of
the heart, and בְּ is, as at 1 Kings x. 1, that of the means: I will
try thee with mirth, to see whether thy hunger after satisfaction
can be appeased with mirth.   וּרְאֵה also is an address; Grätz sees
here, contrary to the Gramm., an infin. continuing the בְּשִׂ': *urēh*,
Job x. 15, is the connect. form of the particip. adj. *rāĕh;* and if
r̆ēh could be the inf. after the forms *naqqēh, hinnāqqēh*, it would be
the *inf. absol.*, instead of which וּרְאוֹת was to be expected.   It is the
imper.: See good, sinking thyself therein, *i.e.* enjoy a cheerful life.
Elsewhere the author connects ראה less significantly with the accus.-
obj., v. 17, vi. 6, ii. 24.

This was his intention; but this experiment also to find out the
summum bonum proves itself a failure: he found a life of pleasure
to be a hollow life; that also, viz. devotedness to mirth, was to him
manifestly vanity.

Ver. 2. "To laughter I said: It is mad; and to mirth: What
doth it issue in?"   Laughter and mirth are personified; *m̆holāl* is
thus not neut. (Hitz., a foolish matter), but mas.   The judgment
which is pronounced regarding both has not the form of an address;
we do not need to supply אַתָּה and אַתְּ, it is objectively like an
oratio obliqua: that it is mad; cf. Ps. xlix. 12.   In the midst of
the laughter and revelling in sensual delight, the feeling came over
him that this was not the way to true happiness, and he was compelled to say to laughter, It has become mad (*part. Poal*, as at Ps.
cii. 9), it is like one who is raving mad, who finds his pleasure in
self-destruction; and to joy (mirth), which disregards the earnestness of life and all due bounds, he is constrained to say, What does
it result in? = that it produces nothing, *i.e.* that it brings forth no
real fruit; that it produces only the opposite of true satisfaction;
that instead of filling, it only enlarges the inner void.   Others, *e.g.*
Luther, "What doest thou?" *i.e.* How foolish is thy undertaking!
Even if we thus explain, the point in any case lies in the inability
of mirth to make man truly and lastingly happy,—in the inappro-
priateness of the means for the end aimed at.   Therefore עֹשָׂה is
thus meant just as in עָשָׂה פְּרִי (Hitz.), and מעשׂה, effect, Isa. xxxii. 17.
Thus Mendelssohn: What profit dost thou bring to me?   Regarding זוֹ,
vid. p. 198 ; מַה־זֹּה is = *mah-zoth*, Gen. iii. 13, where it is shown that
the demonstrative pronoun serves here to sharpen the interrogative:
What then, what in all the world!

After this revelling in sensual enjoyment has been proved to be a fruitless experiment, he searches whether wisdom and folly cannot be bound together in a way leading to the object aimed at.

Ver. 3. "I searched in my heart, (henceforth) to nourish my body with wine, while my heart had the direction by means of wisdom; and to lay hold on folly, till I might see what it was good for the children of men that they should do, all the number of the days of their life." After he became conscious that unbridled sensual intoxication does not lead to the wished-for end, he looked around him farther, and examined into the following receipt for happiness. Inappropriately, Zöckl., with Hengst.: "I essayed in my heart to nourish . . ." תּוּר does not mean *probare*, but *explorare*, to spy out, Num. x. 33, and frequently in the Book of Koheleth (here and at i. 13, vii. 25) of mental searching and discovery (Targ. אַלֵּל). With לִמְשׁוֹךְ there then follows the new thing that is contrived. If we read מֹשֵׁךְ and נֹהֵג in connection, then the idea of drawing a carriage, Isa. v. 18, cf. Deut. xxi. 3, and of driving a carriage, 2 Sam. vi. 3, lies near; according to which Hitzig explains: "Wine is compared to a draught beast such as a horse, and he places wisdom as the driver on the box, that his horse may not throw him into a ditch or a morass." But *moshēk* is not the wine, but the person himself who makes the trial; and *nohēg* is not the wisdom, but the heart,—the former thus only the means of guidance; no man expresses himself thus: I draw the carriage by means of a horse, and I guide it by means of a driver. Rightly the Syr.: "To delight (למבסמן, from בְּסַם, *oblectare*) my flesh with wine." Thus also the Targ. and the Venet., by "drawing the flesh." The metaphor does not accord with the Germ. *ziehen* = to nourish by caring for (for which רִבָּה is used); it is more natural, with Gesen., to compare the passing of *trahere* into *tractare*, e.g. in the expression *se benignius tractare* (Horace, *Ep.* i. 17); but apart from the fact that *trahere* is a word of doubtful etymology,[1] *tractare* perhaps attains the meaning of attending to, using, managing, through the intermediate idea of moving hither and thither, which is foreign to the Heb. משׁך, which means only to draw,—to draw to oneself, and hold fast (*attractum sive prehensum tenere*). As the Talm. משׁך occurs in the sense of "to refresh," e.g. *Chagiga* 14a: "The Haggadists (in contradistinction to the Halachists) refresh the heart of a man as with water" (*vid.* p. 193); so here, "to draw the flesh" = to bring it into willing obedience by means of pleasant attractions.[2]

[1] *Vid.* Corssen's *Nachtr. zur lat. Formenlehre*, pp. 107–109.
[2] Grätz translates: to embrocate my body with wine, and remarks that in

The phrase which follows: *v'libbi noh̄eg bahhochmāh*, is conditioning: While my heart had the direction by means of wisdom; or,
perhaps in accordance with the more modern *usus loq. (vid.* p.
194): While my heart guided, demeaned, behaved itself with wisdom. Then the inf. *limshok*, depending on *tarti* as its obj., is
carried forward with *v'lĕĕhhoz b'sichluth*. Plainly the subject treated
of is an intermediate thing (Bardach: מְמֻצָּעַת). He wished to have
enjoyment, but in measure, without losing himself in enjoyment,
and thereby destroying himself. He wished to give himself over
to sweet *desipere*, but yet with wise self-possession (because it is
sadly true that *ubi mel ibi fel*) to lick the honey and avoid the
gall. There are drinkers who know how to guide themselves so
that they do not end in drunken madness; and there are habitual
pleasure-seekers who yet know how so far to control themselves,
that they do not at length become *roués*. Koheleth thus gave himself to a foolish life, yet tempered by wisdom, till there dawned
upon him a better light upon the way to true happiness.

The expression of the *donec viderem* is old Heb. Instead of אֵי־זֶה
טוֹב, *quidnam sit bonum* in indirect interrog. (as xi. 6, cf. Jer. vi. 16),
the old form מַה־טּוֹב (vi. 12) would lie at least nearer. *Asher yăăsu*
may be rendered: *quod faciant* or *ut faciant;* after ii. 24, iii. 22,
v. 4, vii. 18, the latter is to be assumed. The accus. designation
of time, "through the number of the days of their life," is like
v. 17, vi. 12. We have not, indeed, to translate with Knobel:
"the few days of their life," but yet there certainly lies in מִסְפַּר
the idea that the days of man's life are numbered, and that thus
even if they are not few but many (vi. 3), they yet do not endure
for ever.

The king now, in the verse following, relates his undertakings
for the purpose of gaining the joys of life in fellowship with
wisdom, and first, how he made architecture and gardening serviceable to this new style of life.

Vv. 4–6. "I undertook great works, built me houses, planted me
vineyards. I made me gardens and parks, and planted therein all
kinds of fruit-trees. I made me water-pools to water therewith a
forest bringing forth trees." The expression, "I made great my works,"
is like i. 16; the verb contains the adj. as its obj. The love of
wisdom, a sense of the beautiful in nature and art, a striving after
splendour and dignity, are fundamental traits in Solomon's character.

this lies a *raffinement*. But why does he not rather say, "to bathe in wine"?
If משׁח can mean "to embrocate," it may also mean "to bathe," and for יין may
be read יוני : in Grecian, *i.e.* Falernian, Chian, wine.

His reign was a period of undisturbed and assured peace. The nations far and near stood in manifold friendly relations with him. Solomon was "the man of rest," 1 Chron. xxii. 9; his whole appearance was as it were the embodied glory itself that had blossomed from out of the evils and wars of the reign of David. The Israelitish commonwealth hovered on a pinnacle of worldly glory till then unattained, but with the danger of falling and being lost in the world. The whole tendency of the time followed, as it were, a secular course, and it was Solomon first of all whom the danger of the love of the world, and of worldly conformity to which he was exposed, brought to ruin, and who, like so many of the O. T. worthies, began in the spirit and ended in the flesh. Regarding his buildings,—the house of the forest of Lebanon, the pillared hall (porch), the hall of judgment, the palace intended for himself and the daughter of Pharaoh,—vid. the description in 1 Kings vii. 1–12, gathered from the annals of the kingdom; 1 Kings ix. 15–22 = 2 Chron. viii. 3–6, gives an account of Solomon's separate buildings (to which also the city of Millo belongs), and of the cities which he built; the temple, store-cities, treasure-cities, etc., are naturally not in view in the passage before us, where it is not so much useful buildings, as rather buildings for pleasure (1 Kings ix. 19), that are referred to. Vineyards, according to 1 Chron. xxvii. 27, belonged to David's royal domain; a vineyard in Baal-hamon which Solomon possessed, but appears at a later period to have given up, is mentioned at the close of the Song. That he was fond of gardening, appears from manifold expressions in the Song; delight in the life and movements of the natural world, and particularly in plants, is a prominent feature in Solomon's character, in which he agrees with Shulamith. The Song, vi. 2, represents him in the garden at the palace. We have spoken under the Song, vi. 11 f., of the gardens and parks at Etam, on the south-west of Bethlehem. Regarding the originally Persian word *pardēs* (plur. *pardesim*, Mishnic *pardesoth*), *vid.* under Song iv. 13; regarding the primary meaning of *bᵉrēchah* (plur. const. *bᵉrēchoth*, in contradistinction to *birchoth*, blessings), the necessary information is found under Song vii. 5. These Solomonic pools are at the present day to be seen near old Etam, and the clause here denoting a purpose, " to water from them a forest which sprouted trees, *i.e.* brought forth sprouting trees," is suitable to these; for verbs of flowing and swarming, also verbs of growing, thought of transitively, may be connected with obj.-accus., Ewald, § 281b; cf. under Isa. v. 6. Thus, as he gave himself to the building of houses, the care of gardens, and the erection of pools, so also to the cultivation of forests, with the raising of new trees.

Another means, wisely considered as productive of happiness, was a large household and great flocks of cattle, which he procured for himself.

Ver. 7. "I procured servants and maidens, and also I obtained servants born in the house; also the possession of flocks; I obtained many horned and small cattle before all who were in Jerusalem before me." The obtaining of these possessions is, according to Gen. xvii. 12 ff., to be understood of purchase. There is a distinction between the slaves, male and female (*mancipia*), obtained by purchase, and those who were home-born (*vernae*), the בְּנֵי (יְלִידֵי) בַיִת, who were regarded as the chief support of the house (Gen. xiv. 14), on account of their attachment to it, and to this day are called (Arab.) *fada wayyt*, as those who offer themselves a sacrifice for it, if need be. Regarding היה לי, in the sense of increasing possession, *vid.* Song, p. 155; and regarding הָיָה for הָיוּ, *vid.* at i. 10, 16; at all events, the sing. of the pred. may be explained from this, that the persons and things named are thought of in the mass, as at Zech. xi. 5, Joel i. 20 (although the idea there may be also individualizing); but in the use of the pass., as at Gen. xxxv. 26, Dan. ix. 24, the Semite custom is different, inasmuch as for it the passive has the force of an active without a definite subject, and thus with the most general subject; and as to the case lying before us in ver. 7, we see from Ex. xii. 49, cf. Gen. xv. 17, that היה (יהיה) in such instances is thought of as neut. According to Gen. xxvi. 14 and the passage before us, מִקְנֶה lay nearer than מִקְנֵה, but the primary form instead of the connecting form is here the traditional reading; we have thus apposition (*Nebenordnung*) instead of subordination (*Annexion*), as in *z'vahim sh'lamim*, Ex. xxiv. 5, and in *habbaqar hann'hhosheth*, 2 Kings xvi. 17, although *vaqar vatson* may also be interpreted as the accus. of the more accurate definition: the possession of flocks consisting in cattle and sheep. But this manner of construction is, for a book of so late an origin, too artificial. What it represents Solomon as saying is consistent with historical fact; at the consecration of the temple he sacrificed hecatombs, 1 Kings viii. 63; and the daily supply for the royal kitchen, which will at the same time serve to show the extent of the royal household, was, according to 1 Kings v. 2 f., enormous.

There now follows the enumeration of riches and jewels which were a delight to the eye; and finally, the large provision made for revelling in the pleasures of music and of sensual love.

Ver. 8. "I heaped up for myself also silver and gold, and the peculiar property of kings and of countries; I gat me men singers and women singers, and the delights of the children of men: mistress and mistresses." The verb כָּנַס בְּנַס, συνάγειν, is common to all Semitic dialects (also to the Assyr.), and especially peculiar to the more recent Heb., which forms from it the name of the religious community συναγωγή, כְּנֶסֶת; it is used here of that which is brought together merely for the purpose of possession. S⁽ᵉ⁾gŭllah (from sagal, Targ., to make oneself possess), properly possession, and that something which specially and peculiarly belongs to one as his property; the word is here meant collect., as at 1 Chron. xxix. 3: that which only kings and individual countries possess. The interchange of m⁽ᵉ⁾lachim, which is without the article, with the determ. hamm⁽ᵉ⁾dinoth, is arbitrary: something special, such as that which a king possesses, the specialities which countries possess,—one country this, and another that. The hamm⁽ᵉ⁾dinoth are certainly not exclusively the regions embraced within the dominion of Solomon (Zöckl.), as, according to Esth. i. 1, the Persian kingdom was divided into 127 m⁽ᵉ⁾dinoth. Solomon had a fleet which went to Ophir, was in a friendly relation with the royal house of Tyre, the metropolis of many colonies, and ruled over a widely-extended kingdom, bound by commerce with Central Asia and Africa.—His desires had thus ample opportunity to stretch beyond the limits of his own kingdom, and facilities enough for procuring the peculiar natural and artistic productions which other lands could boast of. M⁽ᵉ⁾dinah is, first of all, a country, not as a territory, but as under one government (cf. v. 7); in the later philosophical language it is the Heb. word for the Greek πολιτεία; in the passage before us, m⁽ᵉ⁾dinoth is, however, not different from אֲרָצוֹת.

From the singing men and singing women who come into view here, not as appertaining to the temple service (vid. the Targ.), with which no singing women were connected, but as connected with the festivities of the court (2 Sam. xix. 36; cf. Isa. v. 12), advance is made to shiddah v⁽ᵉ⁾shiddoth; and since these are designated by the preceding וְתַעֲנֻגוֹת (not ותענגות) b⁽ᵉ⁾ne hā͏ādam, especially as objects and means of earthly pleasure, and since, according to vii. 7, sexual love is the fairest and the most pleasant, in a word, the most attractive of all earthly delights (Solomon's luxus, also here contradicting the law of the king, Deut. xvii. 17, came to a height, according to 1 Kings xi. 3, after the example of Oriental rulers, in a harem of not fewer than one thousand women, princesses and concubines), of necessity, the expression shiddah v⁽ᵉ⁾shiddoth must denote a multitude of women whom the king possessed for his own pleasure. Cup-bearers, male and female (Syr., LXX.), cannot at all be understood, for although it may be said that the enumeration thus connects itself with the before-named בָּנַי, yet this class of female attendants are not numbered among the highest human pleasures; besides, with such an explanation one must read שָׁרָה וְשֹׁרוֹת, and, in addition, שְׁרָא (to throw, to pour to, or pour out), to which this Heb. שרה may correspond, is nowhere used of the pouring out of wine. Rather might שדה, like שרא, *hydria*, be the name of a vessel from which one pours out anything, according to which Aq. translates by κυλίκιον καὶ κυλίκια, Symmachus, after Jerome, by *mensurarum* (read *mensarum* [1]) *species et appositiones*, and Jerome, *scyphos et urceos in ministerio ad vina fundenda*; but this word for *kᵉlē mashkēh*, 1 Kings x. 21 (= 2 Chron. ix. 20), is not found. Also the Targ., which translates by *dimasaya uvē vᵉnavan*, public baths (δημόσια), and *balneae*, vindicates this translation by referring the word to the verb שְׁרָא, "with pipes which pour out (דִּשִׁדְיָן) tepid water, and pipes which pour out hot water." But this explanation is imaginary; שִׁדָּה occurs in the Mishna, *Mikwaoth* (of plunge-baths) vi. 5, but there it denotes a chest which, when it swims in the water, makes the plunge-bath unsuitable. Such an untenable conceit also is the translation suggested by Kimchi, בְּלִי זמר, according to which the Venet. σύστημα καὶ συστήματα (in a musical sense: *concentus*), and Luther: "all kinds of musical instruments;" the word has not this meaning; Orelli, *Sanchuniathon*, p. 33, combines therewith Σιδών, according to the Phoenician myth, the inventress of the artistic song. The explanation by Kimchi is headed, "Splendour of every kind;" Ewald, Elster, and Zöckler find therein a general expression, following *taanugoth*: great heap and heaps = in great abundance [*die Hülle und Fülle*]. But the synon. of כבוד, "splendour," is not שֵׁד, but עֹי; and that שָׂרֵד, like עצם, is referred to a great number, is without proof. Thus *shiddah vᵉshiddoth* will denote something definite; besides, "a large number" finds its expression in the climactic union of words. In the Jerus. Talm. *Taanith* iv. 5, *shiddah* must, according to the gloss, be the name of a chariot, although the subject there is not that of motion forward, or moving quickly; it is there announced that *Sichin*, not far from Sepphoris, a place famed also for its pottery, formerly possessed 80 such *shiddoth* wholly of metal. The very same word is explained by Rashi, *Baba kamma* ix. 3, *Shabbath* 120a, *Erubin* 30b, *Gittin* 8b, 68a, *Chagiga* 25a, and elsewhere, of a carriage of wood, and especially of a chariot for

---

[1] Thus, according to Vallarsi, a *Cod. Vat.* and *Cod. Palat.* of the first hand.

women and distinguished persons. The combination of the synonyms, *shiddah uthivah umigdal*, does not in itself mean more than a chest; and Rashi himself explains, *Kethuboth* 65a, *quolphi dashidah* of the lock of a chest (*argaz*); and the author of *Aruch* knows no other meaning than that of a repository such as a chest. But in passages such as *Gittin* 8b, the *shiddah* is mentioned as a means of transport; it is to all appearance a chest going on wheels, moved forward by means of wheels, but on that very account not a state-chariot. Rashi's tradition cannot be verified. Böttcher, in the *Neue Aehrenlese*, adduces for comparison the Syr. *Shydlo*, which, according to Castelli, signifies *navis magna, corbita, arca;* but from a merchant ship and a portable chest, it is a great way to a lady's palanquin. He translates : palanquin and palinquins = one consignment to the harem after another. Gesen., according to Rödiger, *Thes.* 1365b, thinks that women are to be understood; for he compares the Arab. *z'ynat*, which signifies a women's carriage, and then the woman herself (cf. our *Frauenzimmer*, women's apartment, women, like *Odaliske*, from the Turk. *oda*, apartment). But this all stands or falls with that gloss of Rashi's : *'agalah l^emerkavoth nashim usarim.* Meanwhile, of all the explanations as yet advanced, this last [of splendid coaches, palanquins] is the best; for it may certainly be supposed that the words *shiddah v^eshiddoth* are meant of women. Aben Ezra explains on this supposition, *shiddoth = sh^evuyoth*, females captured in war; but unwarrantably, because as yet Solomon had not been engaged in war ; others (*vid.* Pinsker's *Zur Gesch. des Karaismus*, p. 296), recently Bullock, connect it with *shadäim*, in the sense of (Arab.) *nahidah* (a maiden with swelling breast); Knobel explains after *shadad*, to barricade, to shut up, *occlusa*, the female held in custody (cf. *b^ethulah*, the separated one, virgin, from *bathal*, cogn. *badal*); Hitzig, " cushions," " bolsters," from *shanad*, which, like (Arab.) *firash*, λέχος, is then transferred to the *juncta toro.* Nothing of all that is satisfactory. The Babyl. Gemara, *Gittin* 68a, glosses וגו' וְתַעֲנֻ by " reservoirs and baths," and then further says that in the west (Palestine) they say שִׁדְּתָא, chests (according to Rashi: chariots); but that here in this country (*i.e.* in Babylon) they translate *shiddah v^eshiddoth* by *shēdah v^eshēdathin*, which is then explained, " demons and demonesses," which Solomon had made subservient to him.[1] This haggadic-mytholog. interpreta-

---

[1] A demon, and generally a superhuman being, is called, as in Heb. שֵׁד, so in the Babyl.-Assyr. *sîdu*, vid. Norris' *Assyrian Dictionary*, II. p. 668; cf. Schrader, in the *Jena. Lit. Zeit.* 1874, p. 218 f., according to which *sîdu*, with *alap*, is the usual name of Adar formed like an ox.

tion is, linguistically at least, on the right track. A demon is not so named from fluttering or moving to and fro (Levy, Schönhak), for there is no evidence in the Semitic language of the existence of a verb שׁוּד, to flee; also not from a verb *sadad*, which must correspond to the Heb. הִשְׁתַּחֲוָה, in the sense of to adore (Oppert's *Inscription du palais de Khorsabad*, 1863, p. 96); for this meaning is more than doubtful, and, besides, שֵׂד is an active, and not a passive idea,— much rather שֵׂד, Assyr. *sîd*, Arab. *sayyid*, signifies the mighty, from שׁוּד, to force, Ps. xci. 6.[1] In the Arab. (cf. the Spanish *Cid*) it is uniformly the name of a lord, as subduing, ruling, mastering (*sabid*), and the fem. *sayyidat*, of a lady, whence the vulgar Arab. *sitti* = my lady, and *sîdi* = my lord. Since שָׂרַד means the same as שׁוּד, and in Heb. is more commonly used than it, so also the fem. form שֵׁדָה is possible, so much the more as it may have originated from שִׁידָה, v. שִׁיד = שֵׂד, by a sharpening contraction, like סַנִּים, from סִינִים (Olsh. § 83c), perhaps intentionally to make שֵׁדָה, a demoness, and the name of a lady (*donna = domina*) unlike. Accordingly we translate, with Gesen. and Meyer in their *Handwört.*: "lady and ladies;" for we take *shiddoth* as a name of the ladies of the harem, like *shēglath* (Assyr. *saklâti*) and *l^ehhenath* in the book of Daniel, on which Ahron b. Joseph the Karaite remarks: *shedah hinqaroth shagal.*

The connection expressing an innumerable quantity, and at the same time the greatest diversity, is different from the genitival *dor dorim*, generation of generations, *i.e.* lasting through all generations, Ps. lxxii. 5, from the permutative heightening the idea: *rahham rahhamathaim*, one damsel, two damsels, Judg. v. 30, and from that formed by placing together the two gram. genders, comprehending every species of the generic conception: *mash'ēn umash'enah*, Isa. iii. 3 (*vid.* comm. *l.c.*, and Ewald, § 172b). Also the words cited by Ewald (Syr.), *rogo urógo*, "all possible pleasures" (Cureton's *Spicil.* p. 10), do not altogether accord with this passage, for they heighten, like *m^eod m^eod*, by the repetition of the same expression. But similar is the Arab. scheme, *mal wamwal*, "possession and possessions," *i.e.* exceeding great riches, where the collective idea, in itself affording by its indetermination free scope to the imagination, is multiplied by the plur. being further added.

After Koheleth has enumerated all that he had provided for the purpose of gratifying his lusts, but without losing himself therein, he draws the conclusion, which on this occasion also shows a perceptible deficit.

[1] *Vid.* Friedrich Delitzsch's *Assyr. Thiernamen*, p. 37.

Vv. 9–11. " And I became great, and was always greater than all that were before me in Jerusalem : also my wisdom remained with me.   And all that mine eyes desired I kept not from them, I refused not any kind of joy to my heart ; for my heart had joy of all my labour : and this was my portion of all my labour.   And I turned myself to all the works which my hands had done, and to the-labour which I had laboured to accomplish : and, behold, all was vain, and windy effort, and there was no true profit under the sun." In *v⁰hosaphti* there is here no obj. as at i. 16 ; the obj. is the *g⁰dullah*, the greatness, to be concluded and thought of from *v⁰gadalti*, " and I became great."   To the impers. הָיָה for הָיוּ, 7*b*, cf. 7*a*, i. 16, 10. He became great, and always greater, viz. in the possession of all the good things, the possession of which seemed to make a man happy on this earth.   And what he resolved upon, in the midst of this *dulcis insania*, viz. to deport himself as a wise man, he suc-ceeded in doing : his wisdom forsook him not, viz. the means adapted to the end, and ruling over this colossal apparatus of sensual lust ; אַף, as *e.g.* at Ps. xvi. 6, belongs to the whole clause ; and עָמַד, with לְ, does not mean here to stand by, sustain (Herzfeld, Ewald, Elster), which it might mean as well as עָמַד עַל, Dan. xii. 1, but to continue (*vid.* p. 194), as Jerome, and after him, Luther, translates : *sapientia quoque perseveravit mecum ;* the Targ. connects the ideas of continu-ance (LXX., Syr., Venet.) and of help ; but the idea intended is that of continuance, for נהג, *e.g.*, does not refer to helping, but self-maintaining.

Ver. 10. Thus become great and also continuing wise, he was not only in a condition to procure for himself every enjoyment, but he also indulged himself in everything ; all that his eyes desired, *i.e.* all that they saw, and after which they made him lust (Deut. xiv. 26) (cf. 1 John ii. 16), that he did not refuse to them (אָצַל, *subtra-here*), and he kept not back his heart from any kind of joy (מִנֵּעַ, with *min* of the thing refused, as at Num. xxiv. 11, etc., oftener with *min*, of him to whom it is refused, *e.g.* Gen. xxx. 2), for (here, after the foregoing negations, coinciding with *immo*) his heart had joy of all his work ; and this, viz. this enjoyment in full measure, was his part of all his work.   The palindromic form is like i. 6, iv. 1 ; cf. *Isa.* p. 411.   We say in Heb. as well as in German : to have joy in (*an*, בְּ) anything, joy over (*über*, עַל) anything, or joy of (*von*, מִן) anything ; Koheleth here purposely uses *min*, for he wishes to express not that the work itself was to him an object and reason of joy, but that it became to him a well of joy (cf. Prov. v. 18 ; 2 Chron. xx. 27).   Falsely, Hahn and others : after my work (*min*, as *e.g.*

Ps. lxxiii. 20), for thereby the causative connection is obliterated: *min* is the expression of the mediate cause, as the concluding sentence says : Joy was that which he had of all his work—this itself brought care and toil to him ; joy, made possible to him thereby, was the share which came to him from it.

Ver. 11. But was this חֵלֶק a יִתְרוֹן.—was this gain that fell to him a true, satisfying, pure gain ? With the words *uphanithi ani* (*vid*. p. 198) he proposes this question, and answers it. פָּנָה (to turn to) is elsewhere followed by expressions of motion to an end ; here, as at Job vi. 28, by בְּ, by virtue of a *constructio praegnans* : I turned myself, fixing my attention on all my works which my hands accomplished. *La'asoth* is, as at Gen. ii. 3 (*vid. l.c.*), equivalent to *perficiendo*, carrying out, viz. such works of art and of all his labour. The exclamation " behold " introduces the *summa summarum*. Regarding יִתְרוֹן, *vid.* i. 3. Also this way of finding out that which was truly good showed itself to be false. Of all this enjoyment, there remained nothing but the feeling of emptiness. What he strove after appeared to him as the wind ; the satisfaction he sought to obtain at such an expense was nothing else than a momentary delusion. And since in this search after the true happiness of life he was in a position more favourable for such a purpose than almost any other man, he is constrained to draw the conclusion that there is no יתרון, *i.e.* no real enduring and true happiness, from all labour under the sun.

The End of the Wise Man the same as that of the Fool, ii. 12–17.

After Koheleth has shown, i. 12 ff., that the striving after wisdom does not satisfy, inasmuch as, far from making men happy, its possession only increases their inward conflicts, he proposes to himself the question, whether or not there is a difference between wisdom and folly, whether the former does not far excel the latter. He proceeds to consider this question, for it is more appropriate to him, the old much-experienced king, than to others.

Ver. 12. " And I turned myself to examine wisdom, and madness, and folly : for what is the man who could come after the king, him whom they have made so long ago !" Mendelssohn's translation, 12a : " I abandoned my design of seeking to connect wisdom with folly and madness," is impossible, because for such a rendering we should have had at least מִלְּרְאוֹת instead of לִרְאוֹת. Hitzig, otherwise followed by Stuart : " I turned myself to examine me wisdom, and, lo, it was madness as well as folly." This rendering is impossible also, for in such a case וְהִנֵּה ought to have stood as the result, after

חכמה. The passage, Zech. xiv. 6, cited by Hitz., does not prove the possibility of such a brachyology, for there we read not *v^eqaroth v^eqeppayon*, but *'qaroth iq^eppaūn* (the splendid ones, *i.e.* the stars, will draw themselves together, *i.e.* will become dark bodies). The two *vavs* are not correlative, which is without example in the usage of this book, but copulative : he wishes to contemplate (Zöckler and others) wisdom on the one side, and madness and folly on the other, in their relation to each other, viz. in their relative worth. Hitzig's ingenuity goes yet further astray in 12*b* : "For what will the man do who comes after the king? (He shall do) what was long ago his (own) doing, *i.e.* inheriting from the king the throne, he will not also inherit his wisdom." Instead of *āsūhū*, he reads *ăsōhū*, after Ex. xviii. 18 ; but the more modern author, whose work we have here before us, would, instead of this anomalous form, use the regular form עשׂוֹתוֹ ; but, besides, the expression *ēth asher-k^evar 'asotho*, " (he will do) what long ago was his doing," is not Heb. ; the words ought to have been *k^easotho k^evar khen i^esah*, or at least *'asāhū*. If we compare 12*b* with 18*b*, the man who comes after the king appears certainly to be his successor.[1] But by this supposition it is impossible to give just effect to the relation (assigning a reason or motive) of 12*b* to 12*a* expressed by כִּי. When I considered, Knobel regards Koheleth as saying, that a fool would be heir to me a wise man, it appeared strange to me, and I was led to compare wisdom and folly to see whether or not the wise man has a superiority to the fool, or whether his labour and his fate are vanity, like those of the fool. This is in point of style absurd, but it is much more absurd logically. And who then gave the interpreter the right to stamp as a fool the man who comes after the king? In the answer : "That which has long ago been done," must lie its justification ; for this that was done long ago naturally consists, as Zöckler remarks, in foolish and perverse undertakings, certainly in the destruction of that which was done by the wise predecessor, in the lavish squandering of the treasures and goods collected by him. More briefly, but in the same sense, Burger: *Nihil quod a solita hominum agendi ratione recedit.* But in ver. 19, Koheleth places it as a question whether his successor will be a wise man or a fool, while here he would presuppose that " naturally," or as a matter of course, he will be a fool. In the matter of style, we have nothing to object to the translation on which Zöckler, with Ramb., Rosenm., Knobel, Hengst.,

[1] The LXX. and Symm. by *hammĕlĕk* think of *m^elak*, counsel, βουλή, instead of *mĕlĕk*, king ; and as Jerome, so also Bardach understands by the king the *rex factor*, *i.e.* God the Creator.

and others, proceeds ; the supplying of the verb יַעֲשֶׂה to *meh hāādām*
[= what can the man do ?] is possible (cf. Mal. ii. 15), and the neut.
interpret. of the suffix of עָשׂוּהוּ is, after vii. 13, Amos i. 3, Job
xxxi. 11, admissible; but the reference to a successor is not connected with the course of the thoughts, even although one attaches
to the plain words a meaning which is foreign to them. The words
עָשׂוּהוּ . . . אֵת are accordingly not the answer to the question proposed,
but a component part of the question itself. Thus Ewald, and with him
Elster, Heiligst., construes : " How will the man be who will follow
the king, compared with him whom they made (a king) long ago, *i.e.*
with his predecessor ? " But אֵת, in this pregnant sense, " compared
with," is without example, at least in the Book of Koheleth, which
generally does not use it as a prep.; and, besides, this rendering, by
introducing the successor on the throne, offends against the logic of
the relation of 12*b* to 12*a*. The motive of Koheleth's purpose, to
weigh wisdom and folly against each other as to their worth, consists
in this, that a king, especially such an one as Solomon was, has in
the means at his disposal and in the extent of his observation so
much more than every other, that no one who comes after him will
reach a different experience. This motive would be satisfactorily
expressed on the supposition that the answer begins with אֵת, if one
should read עָשָׂהוּ for עָשׂוּהוּ : he will be able to do (accomplish)
nothing but what he (the king) has long ago done, *i.e.* he will only
repeat, only be able to confirm, the king's report. But if we take
the text as it here stands, the meaning is the same ; and, besides, we
get rid of the harsh ellipsis *meh hāādām* for *meh yáǎseh hāādām*.
We translate : for what is the man who might come after the king,
him whom they have made so long ago! The king whom they
made so long ago is Solomon, who has a richer experience, a more
comprehensive knowledge, the longer the time (viz. from the present
time backwards) since he occupied the throne. Regarding the expression *eth asher = quem*, instead of the *asher* simply, *vid.* Köhler
under Zech. xii. 10. עָשׂוּהוּ, with the most general subj., is not
different from נֶעֱשָׂה, which, particularly in the Book of Daniel (*e.g.*
iv. 28 f.), has frequently an active construction, with the subject
unnamed, instead of the passive (Gesen. § 137, margin). The author
of the Book of Koheleth, alienated from the theocratic side of the
kingdom of Israel, makes use of it perhaps not unintentionally ;
besides, Solomon's elevation to the throne was, according to 1 Kings i.,
brought about very much by human agency ; and one may, if he will,
think of the people in the word *'asuhu* also, according to 1 Kings
i. 39, who at last decided the matter. *Meh* before the letters *hheth*

and *ayin* commonly occurs : according to the Masora, twenty-four times ; before other initial letters than these, eight times, and three of these in the Book of Koheleth before the letter *he*, ii. 12, 22, vii. 10. The words are more an exclamation than a question ; the exclamation means : What kind of a man is that who could come after the king ! cf. " What wickedness is this !" etc., Judg. xx. 12, Josh. xxii. 16, Ex. xviii. 14, 1 Kings ix. 13, *i.e.* as standing behind with reference to me—the same figure of *extenuatio*, as *mah adam*, Ps. cxliv. 3 ; cf. viii. 5.

There now follows an account of what, on the one side, happened to him thus placed on a lofty watch-tower, such as no other occupied. Vv. 13, 14*a*. " And I saw that wisdom has the advantage over folly, as light has the advantage over darkness. The wise man has eyes in his head ; but the fool walketh in darkness." In the sacred Scriptures, "light" is generally the symbol of grace, Ps. xliii. 3, but also the contrast of an intellectually and morally darkened state, Isa. li. 4. To know a thing is equivalent to having light on it, and seeing it in its true light (Ps. xxxvi. 10) ; wisdom is thus compared to light ; folly is once, Job xxxviii. 19, directly called "darkness." Thus wisdom stands so much higher than folly, as light stands above darkness. יִתְרוֹן, which hitherto denoted actual result, enduring gain, signifies here preference (*vid.* p. 192) ; along with כִּיתְרוֹן [1] there is also found the form כִּיתְרוֹן [2] (*vid.* Prov. xxx. 17). The fool walks in darkness : he is blind although he has eyes (Isa. xliii. 8), and thus has as good as none,—he wants the spiritual eye of understanding (x. 3) ; the wise man, on the other hand, his eyes are in his head, or, as we also say : he has eyes in his head,—eyes truly seeing, looking at and examining persons and things. That is the one side of the relation of wisdom to folly as put to the test.

The other side of the relation is the sameness of the result in which the elevation of wisdom above folly terminates. Vv. 14*b*, 15. " And I myself perceived that one experience happeneth to them all. And I said in my heart, As it will happen to the fool, it will happen also to me ; and why have I then been specially wise ? Thus I spake then in my heart, that this also is vain." Zöckler gives to גַּם an adversative sense ; but this *gam* (= ὅμως, *similiter*) stands always at the beginning of the clause, Ewald, § 354*a*. *Gam-ani* corresponds to the Lat. *ego idem*, which gives two predicates to one subject ; while *et ipse* predicates the same of the one of two subjects as it does of the other (Zumpt, § 697). The second *gam*-

---

[1] Thus written, according to J and other authorities.

[2] Thus Ven. 1515, 1521 ; *vid.* Comm. under Gen. xxvii. 28, 29 ; Ps. xlv. 10.

ani serves for the giving of prominence to the object, and here precedes, after the manner of a substantival clause (cf. Isa. xlv. 12 ; Ezek. xxxiii. 17 ; 2 Chron. xxviii. 10), as at Gen. xxiv. 27 ; cf. Gesen. § 121. 3. *Miqrĕh* (from קָרָה, to happen, to befall) is *quiquid alicui accidit* (in the later philosoph. terminol. *accidens;* Venet. συμβεβηκός) ; but here, as the connection shows, that which finally puts an end to life, the final event of death. By the word יָד' the author expresses what he had observed on reflection ; by בִּל' . . . 'אָמַ, what he said inwardly to himself regarding it ; and by דִּבַּ' בִל', what sentence he passed thereon with himself. *Lammah* asks for the design, as *maddu'a* for the reason. אָן is either understood temporally : then when it is finally not better with me than with the fool (Hitz. from the standpoint of the dying hour), or logically : if yet one and the same event happeneth to the wise man and to the fool (Elst.) ; in the consciousness of the author both are taken together. The זֶה of the conclusion refers, not, as at i. 17, to the endeavouring after and the possession of wisdom, but to this final result making no difference between wise men and fools. This fate, happening to all alike, is הֶבֶל, a vanity rendering all vain, a nullity levelling down all to nothing, something full of contradictions, irrational. Paul also (Rom. viii. 20) speaks of this destruction, which at last comes upon all, as a ματαιότης.

The author now assigns the reason for this discouraging result.

Ver. 16. " For no remembrance of the wise, as of the fool, remains for ever ; since in the days that are to come they are all forgotten. And how dieth the wise man ? as the fool !" As in i. 11, so here זִכְרוֹן is the principal form, not different from זִכָּרוֹן. Having no remembrance for ever, is equivalent to having no eternal endurance, having simply no onward existence (ix. 6). עִם is both times the comparat. combin., as at vii. 11 ; Job ix. 26, xxxvii. 18 ; cf. יַחַד, Ps. xlix. 11. There are, indeed, individual historically great men, the memory of whom is perpetuated from generation to generation in words and in monuments ; but these are exceptions, which do not always show that posterity is able to distinguish between wise men and fools. As a rule, men have a long appreciating recollection of the wise as little as they have of the fools, for long ago (*vid.* *b'shekvar*, p. 196) in the coming days (הַיָּ' הַבָּ', accus. of the time, like the ellipt. הב', Isa. xxvii. 6) all are forgotten ; הַכֹּל is, as at Ps. xiv. 3, meant personally : the one as the other ; and נִשְׁכָּח is rendered by the Masora, like ix. 6, כְּבָ' אָבָ', as the pausal form of the finite ; but is perhaps thought of as part., denoting that which only in the coming days will become too soon a completed fact, since those who

survive go from the burial of the one, as well as from that of the
other, to the ordinary duties of the day.   Death thus sinks the wise
man, as it does the fool, in eternal oblivion ; it comes to both, and
brings the same to both, which extorted from the author the cry :
How dieth the wise man ? as the fool ! Why is the fate which awaits
both thus the same !   This is the pointed, sarcastic אֵיךְ (how !) of the
satirical Mashal, e.g. Isa. xiv. 4, Ezek. xxvi. 17 ; and יָמוּת is =
moriendum· est, as at 2 Sam. iii. 3, moriendum erat.   Rambach well :
אֵיךְ est h. l. particula admirationis super rei indignitate.

What happened to the author from this sorrowful discovery he
now states.

Ver. 17.   " Then life became hateful to me ; for the work which
man accomplishes under the sun was grievous to me : because all is
vain and windy effort."   He hated life ; and the labour which is
done under the sun, i.e. the efforts of men, including the fate that
befalls men, appeared to him to be evil (repugnant).   The LXX.
translate : πονηρὸν ἐπ' ἐμέ ; the Venet. : κακὸν ἐπ' ἐμοί ; and thus
Hitzig : as a woful burden lying on me.   But רַע עָלַי is to be
understood after tov al, Esth. iii. 9, etc., cf. Ps. xvi. 6, and as synon.
with בְּעֵינַי or לְפָנַי (cf. Dan. iii. 32), according to which Symmachus :
κακὸν γάρ μοι ἐφάνη.   This al belongs to the more modern usus
loq., cf. Ewald, § 217i.   The end of the song was also again the
grievous ceterum censeo : Vanity, and a labour which has wind as its
goal, wind as its fruit.

The Vanity of Wealth gathered with Care and Privation, ii. 18–23.

In view of death, which snatches away the wise man equally
with the fool, and of the night of death, which comes to the
one as to the other, deep dejection came upon him from another
side.

Ver. 18.   " And I hated all my labour with which I laboured
under the sun, that I should leave it to the man who shall be after
me ; " i.e. not : who shall come into existence after me, but : who shall
occupy my place after me.   The fiction discovers itself here in the
expression : " The king," who would not thus express himself indefinitely and unsympathetically regarding his son and successor on
the throne, is stripped of his historical individuality.   The first
and third שֶׁ are relat. pron. (quem, after the schema etymologicum
עָמָל עָמַל, ver. 11, ix. 9, and qui), the second is relat. conj. (eo) quod.
The suffix of שֶׁאֲנִי refers to the labour in the sense of that which
is obtained by wearisome labour, accomplished or collected with

labour; cf. בֻּל, product, fruit, Gen. iv. 12; עֲבוֹרָה, effect, Isa. xxxii. 17.

How this man will be circumstanced who will have at his disposal that for which he has not laboured, is uncertain.

Ver. 19. "And who knoweth whether he shall be wise or foolish? and he will have power over all my labour with which I had wearied myself, and had acted wisely, under the sun: this also is vain." אוֹ ... הֲ, instead of אִם ... הֲ, in the double question, as at Job xvi. 3. What kind of a man he will be no one can previously know, and yet this person will have free control (cf. שָׁלַט, p. 196) over all the labour that the testator has wisely gained by labour—a hendiadys, for חָכַם with the obj. accus. is only in such a connection possible: " my labour which I, acting wisely, gained by labour."

In view of this doubtful future of that which was with pains and wisely gained by him, his spirit sank within him.

Ver. 20. "Then I turned to give up my heart on account of [= to despair of] all the labour with which I wearied myself under the sun." As at 1 Sam. xxii. 17 f., Song ii. 17, Jer. xli. 14, סבב has here the intrans. meaning, to turn about (LXX. ἐπέστρεψα = ἐπεστρεψάμην). Hitzig remarks that פנה and שוב signify, "to turn round in order to see," and סבב, on the contrary, "to turn round in order to do." But פנה can also mean, "to turn round in order to do," e.g. Lev. xxvi. 9; and סבב, "to turn in order to examine more narrowly," vii. 25. The distinction lies in this, that פנה signifies a clear turning round; סבב, a turning away from one thing to another, a turning in the direction of something new that presents itself (iv. 1, 7, ix. 11). The phrase, יִאֵשׁ אֶת־לִבּוֹ[1] closely corresponds to the Lat. despondet animum, he gives up his spirits, lets them sink, i.e. he despairs. The old language knows only נוֹאָשׁ, to give oneself up, i.e. to give up hope in regard to anything; and נוֹאָשׁ, given up, having no prospect, in despair. The Talm., however, uses along with nithyāēsh (vid. p. 192) not only noāsh, but also יִאֵשׁ, in the sense of despair, or the giving up of all hope (subst. יֵאוּשׁ), Mezîa 21b, from which it is at once evident that יִאֵשׁ is not to be thought of as causative (like the Arab. ajjasa and aiasa), but as simply transitive, with which, after the passage before us, לבו is to be thought of as connected. He turned round to give up all heart. He had no more any heart to labour.

---

[1] With Pathach under the yod in the text in Biblia Rabb. and the note ל. Thus also in the MS. Parva Masora, and e.g. Cod. P.

Ver. 21. "For there is a man who labours with wisdom, and knowledge, and ability; and to a man who has not laboured for it, must he leave it as his portion: also that is vain, and a great evil." Ewald renders: whose labour aims after wisdom. But בְּחָ 'וגו' do not denote obj. (for the obj. of עמל is certainly the portion which is to be inherited), but are particular designations of the way and manner of the labour. Instead of שֶׁעָמֵל, there is used the more emphatic form of the noun: שֶׁעֲמָלוֹ, who had his labour, and performed it; 1 Sam. vii. 17, cf. Jer. ix. 5 [6], "Thine habitation is in the midst of deceit," and Hitz. under Job ix. 27. *Kishron* is not ἀνδρεία (LXX.), manliness, moral energy (Elster), but aptness, ability, and (as a consequence connecting itself therewith) success, good fortune, thus skilfulness conducting to the end (*vid.* p. 193). בּוֹ refers to the object, and יִתְּנֶנּוּ to the result of the work; חֶלְקוֹ is the second obj.-accus., or, as we rather say, pred.-accus.: as his portion, viz. inheritance.

That what one has gained by skill and good fortune thus falls to the lot of another who perhaps recklessly squanders it, is an evil all the greater in proportion to the labour and care bestowed on its acquisition.

Vv. 22, 23. "For what has man of all his labour, and the endeavours of his heart with which he wearies himself under the sun? All his days are certainly in sorrows, and his activity in grief; his heart resteth not even in the night: also this is vain." The question literally is: What is (comes forth, results) to a man from all his labour; for "to become, to be, to fall to, happen to," is the fundamental idea of הוה (whence here הֹוֶה, γινόμενον, as at Neh. vi. 6, γενησόμενος) or היה, the root signification of which is *deorsum ferri, cadere*, and then *accidere, fieri,* whence הַוָּה, eagerness precipitating itself upon anything (*vid.* under Prov. x. 3), or object.: fall, catastrophe, destruction. Instead of שֶׁהוּא, there is here to be written שֶׁהוּא,[1] as at iii. 18 שֶׁהֵם. The question looks forward to a negative answer. What comes out of his labour for man? Nothing comes of it, nothing but disagreeableness. This negative contained in the question is established by כִּי, 23a. The form of the clause, "all his days are sorrows," viz. as to their condition, follows the scheme, "the porch was 20 cubits," 2 Chron. iii. 4, viz. in measurement; or, "their feast is music and wine," Isa. v. 12, viz. in its combination (*vid.* Philippi's *Stat. Const.* p. 90 ff.). The parallel clause is וְכַעַס עִנְיָנוֹ, not וְכַ'; for the final syllable, or that having the accent on the penult., immediately preceding the *Athnach*-word, takes *Kametz*, as

---

[1] Thus according to tradition, in H, J, P, *vid. Michlol* 47b, 215b, 216a; *vid.* also Norzi.

e.g. Lev. xviii. 5 ; Prov. xxv. 3 ; Isa. lxv. 17 (cf. Olsh. § 224, p. 440).[1]
Many interpreters falsely explain : *at aegritudo est velut quotidiana
occupatio ejus.* For the sake of the parallelism, עינו (from ענה, to
weary oneself with labour, or also to strive, aim ; *vid. Psalmen,*
ii. 390) is subj. not pred. : his endeavour is grief, *i.e.* brings only grief
or vexation with it. Even in the night he has no rest ; for even
then, though he is not labouring, yet he is inwardly engaged about
his labour and his plans. And this possession, acquired with such
labour and restlessness, he must leave to others ; for equally with
the fool he falls under the stroke of death : he himself has no enjoyment, others have it ; dying, he must leave all behind him,—a
threefold הבל, vv. 17, 21, 23, and thus הבל הבלים.

The Condition of Pure Enjoyment, ii. 24–26.

Is it not then foolish thus restlessly and with so much self-
torment to labour for nothing ? In view of the night of darkness
which awaits man, and the uncertain destiny of our possessions, it is
better to make use of the present in a way as pleasant to ourselves
as possible.

Ver. 24. " There is nothing better among men, than that one eat
and drink, and that he should pamper his soul by his labour : this
also have I seen, that it is in the hand of God." The LXX., as
well as the other Greek transl., and Jerome, had before them the
words באדם שיאכל. The former translates : " Man has not the good
which he shall eat and drink," *i.e.* also this that he eats . . . is for
him no true good ; but the direct contrary of this is what Koheleth
says. Jerome seeks to bring the thought which the text presents
into the right track, by using the form of a question : *nonne melius
est comedere . . .* ; against this iii. 12, 22, viii. 15, are not to be cited
where אין טוב stands in the dependent sentence ; the thought is not
thus to be improved ; its form is not this, for טוב, beginning a sentence, is never interrog., but affirm. ; thus אין טוב is not = הלא טוב,
but is a negative statement. It is above all doubt, that instead
of באדם שֶׁיֹּ we must read באדם מִשֶׁיֹ, after iii. 12, 22, viii. 15 ; for, as
at Job xxxiii. 17, the initial letter *mem* after the terminal *mem*
has dropped out. Codd. of the LXX. have accordingly corrected
ὃ into πλὴν ὃ or εἰ μὴ ὃ (thus the Compl. Ald.), and the Syr. and
Targ. render שׁ here by דְּ אלא and דְּ אלהן [unless that he eat] ;

<hr>

[1] But cf. also וְלֹא with *Zakeph Katan*, 2 Kings v. 17 ; וְגוּ' וְאָר' with *Tiphcha,*
Isa. xxvi. 19 ; and וְרִיב under Ps. lv. 10.

Jerome also has *non est bonum homini nisi quod* in his *Comm.; only the Venet.* seeks to accommodate itself to the traditional text. Besides, only מ is to be inserted, not כי אם; for the phrase כי אם לֶאֱכֹל is used, but not כי אם שֶׁ. Instead of *bāādām,* the form *lāādām* would be more agreeable, as at vi. 12, viii. 15. Hitzig remarks, without proof, that *bāādām* is in accordance with later grammatical forms, which admit ב = "for" before the object. ב, x. 17, is neither prep. of the object, nor is ἐν, Sir. iii. 7, the exponent of the dative (*vid.* Grimm). *Bāādām* signifies, as at 2 Sam. xxiii. 3, and as ἐν ἀνθ., Sir. xi. 14, *inter homines;* also iii. 12 designates by טוֹב בָּם what among them (men) has to be regarded as good. It is interesting to see how here the ancient and the modern forms of the language run together, without the former wholly passing over into the latter; מֹשִׂי, *quam ut edat,* is followed by norm. perfects, in accordance with that comprehensive peculiarity of the old syntax which Ewald, by an excellent figure, calls the dissolution of that which is coloured into grey. טוֹב . . . הִרְ' is equivalent to הֵי' לוֹ, Ps. xlix. 19, the causative rendering of the phrase רָאָה טוֹב, iii. 13, or ר' טוֹבָה, v. 17, vi. 6. It is well to attend to בַּעֲמָלוֹ [by his labour], which forms an essential component part of that which is approved of as good. Not a useless sluggard-life, but a life which connects together enjoyment and labour, is that which Koheleth thinks the best in the world. But this enjoyment, lightening, embellishing, seasoning labour, has also its *But : etiam hoc vidi e manu Dei esse* (*pendere*). The order of the words harmonizes with this Lat.; it follows the scheme referred to at Gen. i. 4; cf. on the contrary, iii. 6. Instead of נַם־זֶה, neut. by attraction, there is here the immediately neut. נַּם־זֹה; the book uniformly makes use of this fem. form instead of זֹאת (*vid.* p. 198). This or that is "in the hand of God," *i.e.* it is His gift, iii. 13, v. 18, and it is thus conditioned by Him, since man cannot give it to himself; cf. *minni,* Isa. xxx. 1; *mimmĕnni,* Hos. viii. 4; *mimmĕnnu,* 1 Kings xx. 33.

This dependence of the enjoyment of life on God is established.

Ver. 25. "For who can eat, and who can have enjoyment, without [= except from] Him?" Also here the traditional text is untenable: we have to read חוּץ ממנו, after the LXX. (which Jerome follows in his *Comm.*) and the Syr. If we adopt the text as it lies before us, then the meaning would be, as given by Gumpel,[1] and thus translated by Jerome: *Quis ita devorabit et deliciis effluet ut ego?* But (1) the question thus understood would require יוֹתֵר מִמֶּנּי, which Gumpel and others silently substitute in place of חוּץ מ';

---

[1] *Vid.* regarding his noteworthy *Comm.* on Koheleth, my *Jesurun,* pp. 183 and 195. The author bears the name among Christians of Professor Levisohn.

(2) this question, in which the king adjudicates to himself an unparalleled right to eat and to enjoy himself, would stand out of
connection with that which precedes and follows. Even though
with Ginsburg, after Rashi, Aben Ezra, and Rashbam, we find in
ver. 25 the thought that the labourer has the first and nearest title
to the enjoyment of the fruit of his labour (מ' חוץ thus exemplif. as
iv. 8, 'ע . . . למי), the continuation with כִּי, ver. 26, is unsuitable;
for the natural sequence of the thoughts would then be this: But
the enjoyment, far from being connected with the labour as its self-
consequence and fruit, is a gift of God, which He gives to one and
withholds from another. If we read מִמֶּנּוּ, then the sequence of the
thoughts wants nothing in syllogistic exactness. חוּשׁ here has
nothing in common with חוּשׁ = حاس, to proceed with a violent,
impetuous motion, but, as at Job xx. 2, is = حس, *stringere* (whence
ḥiss, a sensible impression); the experience (*vid.* p. 191) here meant
is one mediated by means of a pleasant external enjoyment. The
LXX., Theod., and Syr. translate: (and who can) drink, which Ewald
approves of, for he compares (Arab.) *ḥasa* (inf. *ḥasy*), to drink, to sip.
But this Arab. verb is unheard of in Heb.; with right, Heiligst.
adheres to the Arab., and at the same time the modern Heb. *ḥass*, חוּשׁ,
sentire, according to which Schultens, *quis sensibus indulserit*. חוץ
ממנו is not = מ' ולא, "except from him" (Hitz., Zöckl.), but מן חוץ together mean "except;" cf. *e.g.* the Mishnic למ' חוץ, חוץ לומנה וחוץ, beyond the
time and place suitable for the thank-offering, חוץ מאחד מהם, excepting one of the same, *Menachoth* vii. 3, for which the old Heb. would
in the first case use בלא, and in the second זולת or לְבַד מִן (= Aram.
בַּר מִן) (*vid.* p. 191). Accordingly חוץ ממנו means *praeter eum* (*Deum*),
i.e. unless he will it and make it possible, Old Heb. מִבַּ', Gen. xli. 44.

In enjoyment man is not free, it depends not on his own will:
labour and the enjoyment of it do not stand in a necessary connection; but enjoyment is a gift which God imparts, according as He
regards man as good, or as a sinner.

Ver. 26. " For to a man who appears to Him as good, He gave
wisdom, and knowledge, and joy; but to the sinner He gave the work
of gathering and heaping up, in order to give it to him who appears
to Him as good: this also is vain, and grasping after the wind;"
viz. this striving after enjoyment in and of the labour—it is
" vain," for the purpose and the issue lie far apart; and " striving
after the wind," because that which is striven for, when one thinks
that he has it, only too often cannot be grasped, but vanishes into
nothing. If we refer this sentence to a collecting and heaping up

(Hengst., Grätz, and others), then the author would here come back to what has already been said, and that too in the foregoing section ; the reference also to the arbitrary distribution of the good things of life on the part of God (Knobel) is inadmissible, because " this, although it might be called הבל, could not also be called רעות רוח " (Hitz.) ; and perfectly inadmissible the reference to the gifts of wisdom, knowledge, and joy (Bullock), for referred to these the sentence gains a meaning only by introducing all kinds of things into the text which here lie out of the connection.   Besides, what is here said has indeed a deterministic character, and לפניו, especially if it is thought of in connection with ולח',[1] sounds as if to the good and the bad their objective worth and distinction should be adjudicated ; but this is not the meaning of the author ; the unreasonable thought that good or bad is what God's arbitrary ordinance and judgment stamp it to be, is wholly foreign to him.   The "good before Him " is he who appears as good before God, and thus pleases Him, because he is truly good ; and the חוטא, placed in contrast, as at vii. 26, is the sinner, not merely such before God, but really such ; here לפניו has a different signification than when joined with טוב : one who sins in the sight of God, i.e. without regarding Him (Luke xv. 18, ἐνώπιον), serves sin.   Regarding עָנְיָן, vid. under 23a : it denotes a business, negotium ; but here such as one fatigues himself with, quod negotium facessit.   Among the three charismata, joy stands last, because it is the turning-point of the series of thoughts : joy connected with wise, intelligent activity, is, like wisdom and intelligence themselves, a gift of God.   The obj. of לָתֵת (that He may give it) is the store gathered together by the sinner ; the thought is the same as that at Prov. xiii. 22, xxviii. 8, Job xxvii. 16 f.   The perfect we have so translated, for that which is constantly repeating itself is here designated by the general expression of a thing thus once for all ordained, and thus always continued.

The Short-sightedness and Impotence of Man over against God the All-conditioning, iii. 1–15.

As pure enjoyment stands not in the power of man, much rather is a gift of God which He bestows or denies to man according to His own will, so in general all happens when and how God wills, according to a world-plan, comprehending all things which man can

---

[1] Written with *segol* under ט in P, *Biblia Rabb.*, and elsewhere. Thus correctly after the Masora, according to which this form of the word has throughout the book *segol* under ט, with the single exception of vii. 26. Cf. *Michlol* 124*b*, 140*b*.

neither wholly understand, nor in any respect change,—feeling himself in all things dependent on God, he ought to learn to fear Him.

All that is done here below is ordered by God at a time appointed, and is done without any dependence on man's approbation, according to God's ordinance, arrangement, and providence.

iii. 1. " Everything has its time, and every purpose under the heavens its hour." The Germ. language is poor in synonyms of time. Zöckler translates : Everything has its *Frist* . . ., but by *Frist* we think only of a fixed term of duration, not of a period of beginning, which, though not exclusively, is yet here primarily meant ; we have therefore adopted Luther's excellent translation. Certainly זְמָן (from זָמַן, cogn. סָמַן, *signare*), belonging to the more modern Heb. (*vid.* p. 191), means a *Frist* (*e.g.* Dan. ii. 16) as well as a *Zeitpunkt*, point of time ; in the Semit. (also Assyr. *simmu, simanu,* with ס) it is the most common designation of the idea of time. עֵת is abbreviated either from עֶדֶת (וְעַד, to determine) or from עֶנֶת (from עָנָה, cogn. אנה, to go towards, to meet). In the first case it stands connected with מוֹעֵד on the one side, and with עִדָּן (from עָדַד, to count) on the other ; in the latter case, with עוֹנָה, Ex. xxi. 10 (perhaps also עַ and עֶנֶת in כְּעָן, כְּעֶנֶת). It is difficult to decide this point ; proportionally more, however, can be said for the original עֶנֶת (Palest.-Aram. עֶנְתָּא), as also the prep. of participation אֵת is derived from אֲנֶת [1] (meeting, coming together). The author means to say, if we have regard to the root signification of the second conception of time—(1) that everything has its fore-determined time, in which there lies both a determined point of time when it happens, and a determined period of time during which it shall continue ; and (2) that every matter has a time appointed for it, or one appropriate, suitable for it. The Greeks were guided by the right feeling when they rendered זמן by χρόνος, and עת by καιρός. Olympiodorus distinguishes too sharply when he understands the former of duration of time, and the latter of a point of time ; while the state of the matter is this, that by χρόνος the idea comprehends the *termini a quo* and *ad quem,* while by καιρός it is limited to the *terminus a quo.* Regarding חֵפֶץ, which proceeds from the ground-idea of being inclined to, and intention, and thus, like πρᾶγμα and χρῆμα, to the general signification of design, undertaking, *res gesta, res, vid.* p. 192.

The illustration commences with the beginning and the ending

[1] *Vid.* Orelli's work on the *Heb. Synon. der Zeit u. Ewigkeit,* 1871. He decides for the derivation from וְעַד ; Fleischer (Levy's *Chald. W.B.* II. 572) for the derivation from עָנָה, the higher power of אֲנֶת, whence (Arab.) *inan,* right time. We have, under Job xxiv. 1, maintained the former derivation.

of the life of man and (in near-lying connection of thought) of plants.

Ver. 2.[1] "To be born has its time, and to die has its time ; to plant has its time, and to root up that which is planted has its time." The inf. לָלֶדֶת signifies nothing else than to bring forth ; but when that which is brought forth comes more into view than she who brings forth, it is used in the sense of being born (cf. Jer. xxv. 34, 'לְהִטָּבֵחַ = לְטִ); ledah, Hos. ix. 11, is the birth; and in the Assyr., li-id-tu, li-i-tu, li-da-a-tu, designates posterity, progenies. Since now lālĕdĕth has here lāmuth as contrast, and thus does not denote the birth-throes of the mother, but the child's beginning of life, the translation, "to be born has its time," is more appropriate to what is designed than "to bring forth has its time." What Zöckler, after Hitzig, objects that by lĕdĕth a הפץ [an undertaking], and thus a conscious, intended act must be named, is not applicable ; for לַבֹּל standing at the beginning comprehends doing and suffering, and death also (apart from suicide) is certainly not an intended act, frequently even an unconscious suffering. Instead of לָמַעַת (for which the form לְפַּעַת [2] is found, cf. לָמוֹט, Ps. lxvi. 9), the older language uses לִנְטֹעַ, Jer. i. 10. In still more modern Heb. the expression used would be ליטע, i.e. לִטַּע (Shebîith ii. 1). עָקַר has here its nearest signification : to root up (denom. of עָקָר, root), like עָקַר, 2 Kings iii. 25, where it is the Targ. word for הֹפִיל (to fell trees).

From out-rooting, which puts an end to the life of plants, the transition is now made to putting to death.

Ver. 3. "To put to death has its time, and to heal has its time; to pull down has its time, and to build has its time." That harog (to kill) is placed over against "to heal," Hitzig explains by the remark that harog does not here include the full consequences of the act, and is fitly rendered by "to wound." But "to put to death" is nowhere = "nearly to put to death,"—one who is harug

---

[1] These seven verses, 2–8, are in Codd and Edd., like Josh. xii. 9 ff., and Esth. ix. 7 ff., arranged in the form of a song, so that one עֵת (time) always stands under another, after the scheme described in Megilla 16b, Massecheth Sofrim xiii. 3, but without any express reference to this passage in Koheleth. J has a different manner of arranging the words, the first four lines of which we here adduce [read from right to left] :—

'ēth	lāmoth v'eth	lalĕdĕth 'ēth
'ēth	nathu'ă lă'ăqor v'eth	lathă'ăth
'ēth	lirpō veeth	lāhărog
'ēth	livnoth v'eth	liphrots

[2] This Abulwalid found in a correct Damascus MS., Michlol 81b.

is not otherwise to be healed than by resurrection from the dead, Ezek. xxxvii. 6. The contrast has no need for such ingenuity to justify it. The striking down of a sound life stands in contrast to the salvation of an endangered life by healing, and this in many situations of life, particularly in war, in the administration of justice, and in the defence of innocence against murder or injury, may be fitting. Since the author does not present these details from a moral point of view, the time here is not that which is morally right, but that which, be it morally right or not, has been determined by God, the Governor of the world and Former of history, who makes even that which is evil subservient to His plan. With the two pairs of γένεσις καὶ φθορά there are two others associated in ver. 3; with that, having reference, 2b, to the vegetable world, there here corresponds one referring to buildings; to פָּרוֹץ (synon. הֲרוֹס, Jer. i. 10) stands opposed בָּנוֹת (which is more than גָּדוֹר), as at 2 Chron. xxxii. 5.

These contrasts between existence and non-existence are followed by contrasts within the limits of existence itself:—

Ver. 4. "To weep has its time, and to laugh has its time; to mourn has its time, and to dance has its time." It is possible that the author was led by the consonance from *livnoth* to *livkoth*, which immediately follows it; but the sequence of the thoughts is at the same time inwardly mediated, for sorrow kills and joy enlivens, Sir. xxxii. 21–24. סָפוֹד is particularly lamentation for the dead, Zech. xii. 10; and רְקוֹד, dancing (in the more modern language the usual word for *hholēl, kirkēr, hhāgǎg*) at a marriage festival and on other festal occasions.

It is more difficult to say what leads the author to the two following pairs of contrasts:—

Ver. 5. "To throw stones has its time, and to gather together stones has its time; to embrace has its time, and to refrain from embracing has its time." Did the old Jewish custom exist at the time of the author, of throwing three shovelfuls of earth into the grave, and did this lead him to use the phrase חָשׁ אֲבָ'? But we do not need so incidental a connection of the thought, for the first pair accords with the specific idea of life and death; by the throwing of stones a field is destroyed, 2 Kings iii. 35, or as expressed at ver. 19. is marred; and by gathering the stones together and removing them (which is called סִקֵּל), it is brought under cultivation. Does לְחַ', to embrace, now follow because it is done with the arms and hands? Scarcely; but the loving action of embracing stands beside the hostile, purposely injurious throwing of stones into a field, not exclusively (2 Kings iv. 16), but yet chiefly (as *e.g.* at Prov. v. 20) as referring to love for women; the intensive in the second member is introduced perhaps only for the purpose of avoiding the paronomasia *lirhhoq mahhavoq.*

The following pair of contrasts is connected with the avoiding or refraining from the embrace of love :—

Ver. 6. " To seek has its time, and to lose has its time; to lay up has its time, and to throw away has its time." Vaihinger and others translate לְאַבֵּד, to give up as lost, which the *Pih.* signifies first as the expression of a conscious act. The older language knows it only in the stronger sense of bringing to ruin, making to perish, wasting (Prov. xxix. 3). But in the more modern language, אִבֵּד, like the Lat. *perdere,* in the sense of "to lose," is the trans. to the intrans. אָבַד, *e.g. Tahoroth* viii. 3, " if one loses (הַמְאַבֵּד) any-thing," etc.; *Sifri,* at Deut. xxiv. 19, " he who has lost (מְאַבֵּד) a shekel," etc. In this sense the Palest.-Aram. uses the *Aphel* אוֹבֵד, *e.g. Jer. Mezîa* ii. 5, "the queen had lost (אובדת) her ornament." The intentional giving up, throwing away from oneself, finds its expres-sion in לְהַשׁ'.

The following pair of contrasts refers the abandoning and pre-serving to articles of clothing :—

Ver. 7*a.* " To rend has its time, and to sew has its time." When evil tidings come, when the tidings of death come, then is the time for rending the garments (2 Sam. xiii. 31), whether as a spontaneous outbreak of sorrow, or merely as a traditionary custom. —The tempest of the affections, however, passes by, and that which was torn is again sewed together.

Perhaps it is the recollection of great calamities which leads to the following contrasts :—

Ver. 7*b.* " To keep silence has its time, and to speak has its time." Severe strokes of adversity turn the mind in quietness back upon itself; and the demeanour most befitting such adversity is silent resignation (cf. 2 Kings ii. 3, 5). This mediation of the thought is so much the more probable, as in all these contrasts it is not so much the spontaneity of man that comes into view, as the pre-determination and providence of God.

The following contrasts proceed on the view that God has placed us in relations in which it is permitted to us to love, or in which our hatred is stirred up :—

Ver. 8. " To love has its time, and to hate has its time; war has its time, and peace has its time." In the two pairs of contrasts here, the contents of the first are, not exclusively indeed (Ps. cxx. 7),

but yet chiefly referred to the mutual relations of peoples. It is
the result of thoughtful intention that the *quodlibet* of 2 × 7 pairs
terminates this *for* and *against* in " peace ;" and, besides, the author
has made the termination emphatic by this, that here " instead of
infinitives, he introduces proper nouns " (Hitz.).

Ver. 9. Since, then, everything has its time depending not on
human influence, but on the determination and providence of God,
the question arises : " What gain hath he that worketh in that wherewith he wearieth himself ? " It is the complaint of i. 3 which is
here repeated. From all the labour there comes forth nothing
which carries in it the security of its continuance ; but in all he does
man is conditioned by the change of times and circumstances and
relations over which he has no control. And the converse of this
his weakness is short-sightedness.

Vers. 10, 11. " I saw the travail, which God gave to the children
of men to fatigue themselves with it— : He hath well arranged everything beautiful in its appointed time ; He hath also put eternity in
their heart, so that man cannot indeed wholly search through from
beginning to end the work which God accomplisheth." As at i. 14,
רָאִיתִי is here seeing in the way of research, as elsewhere, *e.g.* at ii. 24,
it is as the result of research. In ver. 10 the author says that he
closely considered the labour of men, and in ver. 11 he states the
result. It is impossible to render the word עִנְיָן everywhere by the
same German (or English) word : i. 13, wearisome trouble ; ii. 26,
business ; here : *Geschäftigkeit,*—the idea is in all the three places the
same, viz. an occupation which causes trouble, costs effort. What
presented itself to the beholder was—(1) that He (viz. God, cf. ver. 10
and ver. 11) has made everything beautiful in its time. The author
uses יָפֶה as synon. of טוב (v. 17) ; also in other languages the idea of
the beautiful is gradually more and more generalized. The suffix in
בְּעִתּוֹ does not refer to God, but to that which is in the time ; this
word is = ἐν καιρῷ ἰδίῳ (Symm.), at its proper time (*vid.* Ps. i. 3,
civ. 27 ; Jer. v. 24, etc.), since, as with יַחְדָּו (together with) and
כֻּלּוֹ (every one), the suffix is no longer thought of as such. Like יפה,
בעתו as pred. conception belongs to the verb : He has made everything beautiful ; He has made everything (falling out) at its appointed
time.—The beauty consists in this, that what is done is not done
sooner or later than it ought to be, so as to connect itself as a constituent part to the whole of God's work. The pret. עָשָׂה is to be
also interpreted as such : He " has made," viz. in His world-plan,
all things beautiful, falling out at the appointed time ; for that which
acquires an actual form in the course of history has a previous ideal

existence in the knowledge and will of God (*vid.* under Isa. xxii. 11, xxxvii. 26).

That which presented itself to the beholder was—(2) the fact that He (God) had put אֶת־הָעֹלָם in their hearts (*i.e.* the hearts of men). Gaab and Spohn interpret *'olam* in the sense of the Arab. *'ilam*, knowledge, understanding; and Hitz., pointing the word accordingly עֵלֶם, translates : " He has also placed understanding in their heart, without which man," etc. The translation of מִבְּלִי אֲשֶׁר is not to be objected to ; 'מִבְּ is, however, only seldom a conjunction, and is then to be translated by *eo quod*, Ex. xiv. 11, 2 Kings i. 3, 6, 16, which is not appropriate here ; it will thus be here also a prep., and with *asher* following may mean " without which," as well as " without this, that " = " besides that " (Venet. ἄνευ τοῦ ὅτι, " except that "), as frequently אֶפֶס כִּי, *e.g.* at Amos ix. 8. But that Arab. *'ilam* is quite foreign to the Heb., which has no word עֹלָם in the sense of "to rise up, to be visible, knowable," which is now also referred [1] to for the Assyr. as the stem-word of עֵילָם = highland. It is true Hitzig believes that he has found the Heb. עֹלָם = wisdom, in Sir. vi. 21, where there is a play on the word with נעלם, " concealed :" σοφία γὰρ κατὰ τὸ ὄνομα αὐτῆς ἐστι, καὶ οὐ πολλοῖς ἐστι φανερά. Drusius and Eichhorn have here already taken notice of the Arab. *'ilam ;* but Fritzsche with right asks, " Shall this word as Heb. be regarded as traceable only here and falsely pointed only at Eccles. iii. 11, and shall no trace of it whatever be found in the Chald., Syr., and Rabbin. ? " We have also no need of it. That Ben-Sira has etymologically investigated the word חכמה as going back to חכם, R. חכ, " to be firm, shut up, dark " (*vid.* at Ps. x. 8), is certainly very improbable, but so much the more probable (as already suggested by Drusius) that he has introduced [2] into חכמה, after the Aram. אֲכַם, *nigrescere*, the idea of making dark. Does *eth-ha'olam* in this passage before us then mean " the world " (Jerome, Luther, Ewald), or " desire after the knowledge of the world " (Rashi), or " worldly-mindedness " (Gesen., Knobel) ? The answer to this has been already given in my *Psychol.* p. 406 (2d ed.): " In post-bibl. Heb. *'olam* denotes not only ' eternity ' backwards and forwards as

---

[1] *Vid.* Fried. Delitzsch's *Assyr. Stud.* (1874), p. 39. Otherwise Fleischer, who connects *'alima*, " to know," with *'alam*, " to conceal," so that to know = to be concealed, sunk deep, initiated in something (with *ba* of the obj., as *sh'ar*, whence *shâ'ir*, the poet as " one who marks ").

[2] Grätz translates *eth-ha'olam* by " ignorance " (*vid.* Orelli, p. 83). R. Achwa in the Midrash has added here the *scriptio defectiva* with the remark, 'שהועלם ונו, " for the mysterious name of God is concealed from them."

infinite duration, but also 'the world' as that which endures for
ever (*αἰών, seculum*); the world in this latter sense is, however, not
yet known[1] to the bibl. language, and we will thus not be able to
interpret the words of Koheleth of the impulse of man to reflect on
the whole world." In itself, the thought that God has placed the
whole world in man's heart is not untrue: man is, indeed, a *micro-
cosmos*, in which the *macrocosmos* mirrors itself (Elster), but the connection does not favour it; for the discussion does not proceed from
this, that man is only a member in the great universe, and that God
has given to each being its appointed place, but that in all his
experience he is conditioned by time, and that in the course of
history all that comes to him, according to God's world-plan, happens
at its appointed time. But the idea by which that of time, אֵת
(עֵת), is surpassed is not the world, but eternity, to which time
is related as part is to the whole (Cicero, *Inv.* i. 26. 39, *tempus est
pars quaedam aeternitatis*). The Mishna language contains, along
with the meaning of world, also this older meaning of *'olam*, and
has formed from it an adv. עוֹלָמִית, *aeterne*. The author means
to say that God has not only assigned to each individually his
appointed place in history, thereby bringing to the consciousness
of man the fact of his being conditioned, but that He has also
established in man an impulse leading him beyond that which is
temporal toward the eternal: it lies in his nature not to be contented with the temporal, but to break through the limits which it
draws around him, to escape from the bondage and the disquietude
within which he is held, and amid the ceaseless changes of time to
console himself by directing his thoughts to eternity.

This saying regarding the *desiderium aeternitatis* being planted
in the heart of man, is one of the profoundest utterances of Koheleth.
In fact, the impulse of man shows that his innermost wants cannot
be satisfied by that which is temporal. He is a being limited by
time, but as to his innermost nature he is related to eternity. That
which is transient yields him no support, it carries him on like a
rushing stream, and constrains him to save himself by laying hold
on eternity. But it is not so much the practical as the intellectual
side of this endowment and this peculiar dignity of human nature
which Koheleth brings here to view.

It is not enough for man to know that everything that happens
has its divinely-ordained time. There is an instinct peculiar to his

---

[1] In the Phoen. also, *'olam*, down to a late period, denotes not the world, but
eternity: *melek 'olam*, βασιλεὺς αἰῶνος (αἰώνιος), *seculo frugifero* on a coin = the
fruit-bringing *'olam* (Αἰών).

nature impelling him to pass beyond this fragmentary knowledge and to comprehend eternity; but his effort is in vain, for (3) " man is unable to reach unto the work which God accomplisheth from the beginning to the end." The work of God is that which is completing itself in the history of the world, of which the life of individual men is a fragment. Of this work he says, that God has wrought it עָשָׂה ; because, before it is wrought out in its separate "time," it is already completed in God's plan. Eternity and this work are related to each other as the accomplished and the being accomplished, they are interchangeably the πλήρωμα to each other. יִמְצָא is potential, and the same in conception as at viii. 17, Job xi. 7, xxxvii. 23 ; a knowledge is meant which reaches to the object, and lays hold of it. A laying hold of this work is an impossibility, because eternity, as its name 'olam denotes, is the concealed, i.e. is both forwards and backwards immeasurable. The desiderium aeternitatis inherent in man thus remains under the sun unappeased. He would raise himself above the limits within which he is confined, and instead of being under the necessity of limiting his attention to isolated matters, gain a view of the whole of God's work which becomes manifest in time; but this all-embracing view is for him unattainable.

If Koheleth had known of a future life—which proves that as no instinct in the natural world is an illusion, so also the impulse toward the eternal, which is natural to man, is no illusion—he would have reached a better ultimatum than the following:—

Ver. 12. "Thus I then perceived that among them (men) there is nothing better than to enjoy themselves, and indulge themselves in their life." The resignation would acquire a reality if לַעֲשׂ֫וֹת טוֹב meant "to do good," i.e. right (LXX. Targ. Syr. Jer. Venet.); and this appears of necessity to be its meaning according to vii. 20. But, with right, Ginsburg remarks that nowhere else—neither at ii. 24, nor iii. 22, v. 17, viii. 15, ix. 7—is this moral rendering given to the ultimatum; also וְרָ' טוֹב, 13a, presupposes for לַעֲשׂ֫וֹת טוֹב a eudemonistic sense. On the other hand, Zöckler is right in saying that for the meaning of עֲשׂוֹת טוֹב, in the sense of "to be of good cheer" (Luth.), there is no example. Zirkel compares εὖ πράττειν, and regards it as a Graecism. But it either stands ellipt. for לַעֲשׂוֹת לוֹ טוֹב (= לְהֵיטִיב לוֹ), or, with Grätz, we have to read לִרְאוֹת טוֹב; in any case, an ethical signification is here excluded by the nearest connection, as well as by the parallels; it is not contrary to the view of Koheleth, but this is not the place to express it. Bam is to be understood after baadam, ii. 24. The plur., comprehending men, here, as at ver. 11, wholly passes over into the individualizing sing.

But this enjoyment of life also, Koheleth continues, this advisedly the best portion in the limited and restrained condition of man, is placed beyond his control :—

Ver. 13. "But also that he should eat and drink, and see good in all his labour, is for every man a gift of God." The inverted and yet anacoluthistic formation of the sentence is quite like that at v. 18. כָּל־הָאָ֥ signifies, properly, the totality of men = all men, e.g. Ps. cxvi. 11 ; but here and at v. 18, xii. 13, the author uses the two words so that the determ. second member of the *st. constr.* does not determine the first (which elsewhere sometimes occurs, as *b'thulath Israel*, a virgin of Israel, Deut. xxii. 19) : every one of men (cf. πᾶς τις βροτῶν). The subst. clause *col-haadam* is subject : every one of men, in this that he eats . ... is dependent on God. Instead of מִיַּד the word מַיַּד (abbrev. from מַתְּנַת) is here used, as at v. 18. The connection by *v'gam* is related to the preceding adversat.: and (= but) also (= notwithstanding that), as at vi. 7, Neh. v. 8, cf. Jer. iii. 10, where *gam* is strengthened by *b'col-zoth*. As for the rest, it follows from ver. 13, in connection with ii. 24–26, that for Koheleth εὐποΐα and εὐθυμία reciprocally condition each other, without, however, a conclusion following therefrom justifying the translation "to do good," 12*b*. Men's being conditioned in the enjoyment of life, and, generally, their being conditioned by God the Absolute, has certainly an ethical end in view, as is expressed in the conclusion which Koheleth now reaches :—

Ver. 14. "Thus I discerned it then, that all that God will do exists for ever ; nothing is to be added to it, and nothing taken from it : God has thus directed it, that men should fear before Him." This is a conclusion derived from the facts of experience, a truth that is valid for the present and for the time to come. We may with equal correctness render by *quidquid facit* and *quidquid faciet*. But the pred. shows that the fut. expression is also thought of as fut.; for הוּ֥א יִֽהְ֥יֶ֥ה לְעֹ֥ does not mean: that is for ever (Hitz.), which would be expressed by the subst. clause הוּא לְעוֹלָם ; but: that shall be for ever (Zöck.), *i.e.* will always assert its validity. That which is affirmed here is true of God's directing and guiding events in the natural world, as well as of the announcements of His will and His controlling and directing providence in the history of human affairs. All this is removed beyond the power of the creature to alter it. The meaning is not that one ought not to add to or to take from it (Deut. xiii. 1 ; Prov. xxx. 6), but that such a thing cannot be done

(*vid.* Sir. xviii. 5). And this unchangeableness characterizing the
arrangements of God has this as its aim, that men should fear Him
who is the All-conditioning and is Himself unconditioned: He has
done it that they (men) should fear before Him, שׁ עשׂה, *fecit ut ;* cf.
Ezek. xxxvi. 27. ποιεῖν ἵνα, Rev. xiii. 15 ; and " fear before Him," as
at viii. 12 f.; cf. 1 Chron. xvi. 30 with Ps. xcvi. 9. The unchangeableness of God's action shows itself in this, that in the course of
history similar phenomena repeat themselves ; for the fundamental
principles, the causal connections, the norms of God's government,
remain always the same.

Ver. 15. "That which is now hath been long ago; and that
which will be hath already been: God seeketh after that which was
crowded out." The words : " hath been long ago " (כְּבָר הוּא), are used
of that which the present represents as something that hath been, as
the fruit of a development; the words : "hath already been" (כְּבָר הָיָה),
are used of the future (אֲשֶׁר לְ', τὸ μέλλον, *vid.* Gesen. § 132. 1), as
denying to it the right of being regarded as something new. The
government of God is not to be changed, and does not change ; His
creative as well as His moral ordering of the world produces with
the same laws the same phenomena (the ו corresponds to this line
of thought here, as at 14*b*)—God seeks אֶת־נִ (cf. vii. 7 ; Ewald,
§ 277*d*). Hengstenberg renders : God seeks the persecuted (LXX.
Symm. Targ. Syr.), *i.e.* visits them with consolation and comfort
Nirdaph here denotes that which is followed, hunted, pressed, by
which we may think of that which is already driven into the past ;
that God seeks, seeks it purposely, and brings it back again into the
present; for His government remains always, and brings thus always
up again that which hath been. Thus Jerome : *Deus instaurat quod
abiit ;* the Venet. : ὁ θεὸς ζητήσει τὸ ἀπεληλαμένον ; and thus Geier,
among the post-Reform. interpreters : *praestat ut quae propulsa sunt
ac praeterierunt iterum innoventur ac redeant ;* and this is now the
prevailing exposition, after Knobel, Ewald, and Hitzig. The thought
is the same as if we were to translate : God seeks after the analogue.
In the Arab., one word in relation to another is called *muradif,*
if it is cogn. to it ; and *mutaradifat* is the technical expression
for a synonym. In Heb. the expression used is שֵׁמוֹת נִרְדָּפִים, they
who are followed the one by another,—one of which, as it were,
treads on the heels of another. But this designation is mediated
through the Arab. In evidence of the contrary, ancient examples
are wanting.

The godless Conduct of Men left to themselves, and their End like that of the Beasts, iii. 16–22.

Ver. 16. "And, moreover, I saw under the sun the place of judgment, that wickedness was there; and the place of righteousness, that wickedness was there." The structure of the verse is palindromic, like i. 6, ii. 10, iv. 1. We might also render מְקוֹם as the so-called *casus absol.*, so that 'שָׁמָ . . . 'מק is an emphatic בִּמְקוֹם (Hitz.), and the construction like Jer. xlvi. 5; but the accentuation does not require this (cf. Gen. i. 1); and why should it not be at once the object to רָאִיתִי, which in any case it virtually is? These two words שָׁמָּה הָרֶשַׁע might be attribut. clauses: where wickedness (prevails), for the old scheme of the attributive clause (the *sifat*) is not foreign to the style of this book (*vid.* i. 13, *nathan* = *nᵉthano*; and v. 12, *raithi* = *rᵉithiha*); but why not rather virtual pred. accus.: *vidi locum juris* (*quod*) *ibi impietas?* Cf. Neh. xiii. 23 with Ps. xxxvii. 25. The place of "judgment" is the place where justice should be ascertained and executed; and the place of "righteousness," that where righteousness should ascertain and administer justice; for *mishpat* is the rule (of right), and the objective matter of fact; *tsedek*, a subjective property and manner of acting. רֶשַׁע is in both cases the same: wickedness (see under Ps. i. 1), which bends justice, and is the contrary of *tsĕdĕk, i.e.* upright and moral sternness. רֶשַׁע elsewhere, like *mĕlĕk, tsĕdĕk*, preserves *in p.* its *e*, but here it takes rank along with חֶסֶד, which in like manner fluctuates (cf. Ps. cxxx. 7 with Prov. xxi. 21). שָׁמָּה is here = שָׁם, as at Ps. cxxii. 5, etc.; the locative *ah* suits the question Where? as well as in the question Whither?—He now expresses how, in such a state of things, he arrived at satisfaction of mind.

Ver. 17. "I said in mine heart: God shall judge the righteous as well as the wicked: for there is there a time for every purpose and for every work." Since "the righteous" stands first, the word יִשְׁפֹּט has here the double sense of judging [*richtens* = setting upright] = acting uprightly, justly by one, as in the *shofteni* of Ps. vii. 9, xxvi. 1, etc., and of judging = inflicting punishment. To the righteous, as well as to the wicked,[1] God will administer that which of right belongs to them. But this does not immediately happen, and has to be waited for a long time, for there is a definite time for every undertaking

---

[1] The LXX. (in Aquila's manner): σὺν τὸν δίκαιον καὶ σὺν τὸν ἀσεβῆ—according to the Talm. hermeneut. rule, that where the obj. is designated by אֵת, with that which is expressly named, something else is associated, and is to be thought of along with it.

(iii. 1), and for (עַל, in the more modern form of the language, interchanges *promiscue* with אֶל and לְ, *e.g.* Jer. xix. 15 ; Ezek. xxii. 3 ; Ewald, § 217*i*) every work there is a " time." This שָׁם, defended by all the old interpreters, cannot have a temporal sense : *tunc = in die judicii* (Jerome, Targ.), cf. Ps. xiv. 5, xxxvi. 13, for " a time of judgment there is for all one day " is not intended, since certainly the שָׁם (day of judgment) is this time itself, and not the time of this time. Ewald renders שָׁם as pointing to the past, for he thus construes : the righteous and the unrighteous God will judge (for there is a time for everything), and judge (*vav* thus explicat., " and that too," " and indeed ") every act there, *i.e.* everything done before. But this שָׁם is not only heavy, but also ambiguous and purposeless ; and besides, by this parenthesizing of the words כִּי עֵת וגו׳ [for there is a time for everything], the principal thought, that with God everything, even His act of judgment, has its time, is robbed of its independence and of the place in the principal clause appropriate to it. But if שָׁם is understood adverbially, it certainly has a local meaning connected with it : there, viz. with God, *apud Deum ;* true, for this use of the word Gen. xlix. 24 affords the only example, and it stands there in the midst of a very solemn and earnest address. Therefore it lies near to read, with Houbig., Döderl., Palm., and Hitz., שָׂם, " a definite time . . . has He (God) ordained ;" שׂוּם (שִׂים) is the usual word for the ordinances of God in the natural world and in human history (Prov. viii. 29 ; Ex. xxi. 13 ; Num. xxiv. 23 ; Hab. i. 12, etc.), and, as in the Assyr. *simtuv,* so the Heb. שִׂימָה (שׂוּמָה), 2 Sam. xiii. 32, signifies lot or fate, decree.[1] With this reading, Elster takes exception to the position of the words ; but at Judg. vi. 19 also the object goes before שָׁם, and " unto every purpose and for every work " is certainly the complement of the object-conception, so that the position of the words is in reality no other than at x. 20*a ;* Dan. ii. 17*b.* Quite untenable is Herzfeld's supposition (Fürst, Vaih.), that שָׁם has here the Talm. signification: *aestimat, taxat,* for (1) this שׁוּם = Arab. *sham,* has not עַל, but the accus. after it ; (2) the thought referring to the time on which ver. 18 rests is thereby interrupted. Whether we read שָׁם, or take שָׁם in the sense of עִמּוֹ (Job xxv. 2, xxiii. 14, etc.), the thought is the same, and equally congruous : God will judge the innocent and the guilty ; it shall be done some time, although not so soon as one might wish it, and think necessary, for God has for every undertaking and for every work its fixed time, also its judicial decision (*vid.* at Ps. lxxv. 3) ; He

---

[1] *Vid.* Schrader's *Keilsch. u. A. T.* p. 105, *simtu ubilsu, i.e.* fate snatched him away) Heb. *simah hovilathhu*), cf. Fried. Delitzsch's *Assyr. Stud.* p. 66 f.

permits wickedness, lets it develope itself, waits long before He interposes (*vid.* under Isa. xviii. 4 f.).

Reflecting on God's delay to a time hidden from men, and known only to Himself, Koheleth explains the matter to himself in the following verse :—

Ver. 18. " Thus I said then in mine heart : (it happeneth) for the sake of the children of men that God might sift them, and that they might see that they are like the cattle, they in themselves." Regarding עַל־דִּבְרַת [for the sake of = on account of] as at viii. 2, *vid.* under Ps. cx. 4, where it signifies after (κατά) the state of the matter, and above at p. 195. The infin. לְבָ is not derived from בּוּר. —לָבוּר, ix. 1, is only the metaplastic form of לָבֹר or לִבְרֹר,—but only from בָּרַר, whose infin. may take the form בַּר, after the form רֵד, to tread down, Isa. xlv. 1, שַׁךְ, to bow, Jer. v. 26 ; but nowhere else is this infin. form found connected with a suff.; קְחָם, Hos. xi. 3, would be in some measure to be compared, if it could be supposed that this = בְּקָחְתָּם, *sumendo eos.* The root בר proceeds, from the primary idea of cutting, on the one side to the idea of separating, winnowing, choosing out ; and, on the other, to that of smoothing, polishing, purifying (*vid.* under Isa. xlix. 2). Here, by the connection, the meaning of winnowing, *i.e.* of separating the good from the bad, is intended, with which, however, as in לְבָרֵר, Dan. xi. 35, the meaning of making clear, making light, bringing forward into the light, easily connects itself (cf. *Shabbath* 138*a*, 74*a*), of which the meaning to winnow (cf. לְהָבֵר, Jer. iv. 11) is only a particular form ;[1] cf. Sanhedrin 7*b:* " when a matter is clear, בְּרוּר, to thee (free from ambiguity) as the morning, speak it out; and if not, do not speak it." In the expression לְבָ הָאֱלֹ', the word הָאֱל' is, without doubt, the subject, according to Gesen. § 133. 2. 3 ; Hitz. regards הָאֱל' as genit., which, judged according to the Arab., is correct ; it is true that for *li-imti-hánihim allahi* (with genit. of the subj.), also *allahu* (with nominat. of the subj.) may be used ; but the former expression is the more regular and more common (*vid.* Ewald's *Gramm. Arab.* § 649), but not always equally decisive with reference to the Heb. *usus loq.* That God delays His righteous interference till the time appointed beforehand, is for the sake of the children of men, with the intention, viz., that God may sift them, *i.e.* that, without breaking in upon the free development of their characters before the time, He may permit the distinction between the good and the bad to become manifest. Men,

---

[1] Not " to sift," for not בָּרַר, but רִקֵּד, means " to sift" (properly, " to make to leap up," " to agitate ") ; cf. *Shebiith* v. 9.

who are the obj. to 'לב, are the subject to וְלִרְאוֹת to be supplied : *et
ut videant ;* it is unnecessary, with the LXX., Syr., and Jerome,
to read וְלִרְאוֹת (= וּלְהַרְ'): *ut ostenderet.* It is a question whether
הַפֶּה [1] is the expression of the copula : *sunt (sint)*, or whether *hēmmah
lahĕm* is a closer definition, co-ordinate with *sh^ehem b^ehēmah.* The
remark of Hitzig, that *lahĕm* throws back the action on the sub-
ject, is not clear.   Does he suppose that *lahem* belongs to *liroth ?*
That is here impossible.   If we look away from *lahem,* the need-
lessly circumstantial expression שׁה' . . . 'הם can still be easily
understood : *hemmah* takes up, as an echo, *b^ehemah,* and completes
the comparison (compare the battology in Hos. xiii. 2).   This play
upon words musically accompanying the thought remains also,
when, according to the accentuation שֶׁה' בהמ' ה' לה', we take *hemmah* along with *lahem,* and the former as well as the latter of
these two words is then better understood.   The ל in להם is not
that of the pure dat. (Aben Ezra : They (are like beasts) to themselves, *i.e.* in their own estimation), but that of reference, as at
Gen. xvii. 20, " as for Ishmael ;" cf. Ps. iii. 3 ; 2 Kings v. 7 ; cf. אֶל,
1 Sam. i. 27, etc.   Men shall see that they are cattle (beasts), they
in reference to themselves, *i.e.* either they in reference to themselves
mutually (Luther : among themselves), or : they in reference to
themselves.   To interpret the reference as that of mutual relation,
would, in looking back to ver. 16, commend itself, for the condemnation and oppression of the innocent under the appearance of justice
is an act of human brutishness.   But the reason assigned in ver. 19
does not accord with this reciprocal rendering of *lahem.*   Thus
lahem will be meant reflexively, but it is not on that account
pleonastic (Knobel), nor does it ironically form a climax : *ipsissimi*
= *höchstselbst* (Ewald, § 315*a*); but " they in reference to themselves " is = they in and of themselves, *i.e.* viewed as men (viewed
naturally).   If one disregards the idea of God's interfering at a
future time with the discordant human history, and, in general, if
one loses sight of God, the distinction between the life of man and
of beast disappears.

Ver. 19. " For the children of men are a chance, and the beast
a chance, and they both have once chance : as the death of the one,
so the death of the other, and they have all one breath ; and there
is no advantage to a man over a beast, for all is vain."   If in both
instances the word is pointed מִקְרֶה (LXX.), the three-membered
sentence would then have the form of an emblematical proverb (as

_____

[1] שֶׁהֶם בְּהֵמָה הֵפֶּה thus accented rightly in F. Cf. *Michlol* 216*a.*

e.g. Prov. xxv. 25) : " For as the chance of men, so (*vav* of comparison) the chance of the beast ; they have both one chance." מִקְרֶה
with *segol* cannot possibly be the connecting form (Luzz.), for in
cases such as מַעֲשֵׂ מ׳, Isa. iii. 24, the relation of the words is appositional, not genitival. This form מִקְרֶ׳, thus found three times, is
vindicated by the Targ. (also the Venet.) and by Mss. ; Joseph
Kimchi remarks that " all three have *segol*, and are thus forms of the
absolutus." The author means that men, like beasts, are in their
existence and in their death influenced accidentally, *i.e.* not of
necessity, and are wholly conditioned, not by their own individual
energy, but by a power from without—are dependent beings, as Solon
(Herod. i. 32) says to Croesus : " Man is altogether συμφορή," *i.e.*
the sport of accident. The first two sentences mean exclusively
neither that men (apart from God) are, like beasts, the birth
of a blind accident (Hitz.), nor that they are placed under the same
law of transitoriness (Elst.); but of men, in the totality of their
being, and doing, and suffering, it is first said that they are
accidental beings; then, that which separates them from this, that
they all, men like beasts, are finally exposed to one, *i.e.* to the same
fate. As is the death of the one, so is the death of the other ; and
they all have one breath, *i.e.* men and beasts alike die, for this
breath of life (רוּחַ חַיִּים, which constitutes a beast—as well as a man
a נֶפֶשׁ חַיָּה) departs from the body (Ps. civ. 29). In זֶה ... זֶה (as at
vi. 5, Ex. xiv. 20, and frequently), לָהֶם (mas. as *genus potius*) is
separately referred to men and beasts. With the Mishnic כְּמוֹת =
bibl. כְּמוֹ (cf. *Maaser Sheni,* v. 2), the כְּמוֹת here used has manifestly
nothing to do. The noun מוֹתָר, which in the Book of Proverbs
(xiv. 23, xxi. 5, not elsewhere) occurs in the sense of profit, gain, is
here in the Book of Koheleth found as a synon. of יִתְרוֹן., " preference,"
advantage which is exclusively peculiar to it. From this, that men
and beasts fall under the same law of death, the author concludes
that there is no preference of a man to a beast ; he doubtless means
that in respect of the end man has no superiority ; but he expresses
himself thus generally because, as the matter presented itself to
him, all-absorbing death annulled every distinction. He looks only
to the present time, without encumbering himself with the historical
account of the matter found in the beginning of the *Tôra;* and he
adheres to the external phenomenon, without thinking, with the
Psalmist in Ps. xlix., that although death is common to man with
the beast, yet all men do not therefore die as the beast dies. That
the beast dies because it must, but that in the midst of this necessity of nature man can maintain his freedom, is for him out of view.

הַכֹּל הֶבֶל, the ματαιότης, which at last falls to man as well as to
the beast, throws its long dark shadows across his mind, and wholly
shrouds it.

Ver. 20. "All goes hence to one place; all has sprung out of
the dust, and all returns to the dust again." The "one place" is
(as at vi. 6) the earth, the great graveyard which finally receives all
the living when dead. The art. of the first הֶעָפָר is that denoting
species; the art. of the second is retrospective: to the dust whence
he sprang (cf. Ps. civ. 29, cxlvi. 4); otherwise, Gen. iii. 19 (cf. Job
xxxiv. 15), "to dust shalt thou return," shalt become dust again.
From dust to dust (Sir. xl. 11, xli. 10) is true of every living
corporeal thing. It is true there exists the possibility that with
the spirit of the dying man it may be different from what it is with
the spirit of the dying beast, but yet that is open to question.

Ver. 21. "Who knoweth with regard to the spirit of the children
of men, whether it mounteth upward; and with regard to the spirit
of a beast, whether it goeth downward to the earth?" The interrogative meaning of העלה and הירדת is recognised by all the old translators: LXX., Targ., Syr., Jerome, Venet., Luther. Among the
moderns, Heyder (vid. Psychol. p. 410), Hengst., Hahn, Dale, and
Bullock take the ה in both cases as the article: "Who knoweth the
spirit of the children of men, that which goeth upward ...?" But
(1) thus rendered the question does not accord with the connection,
which requires a sceptical question; (2) following "who knoweth,"
after ii. 19, vi. 12, cf. Josh. ii. 14, an interrogative continuance of
the sentence was to be expected; and (3) in both cases הִיא stands
as designation of the subject only for the purpose of marking the
interrogative clause (cf. Jer. ii. 14), and of making it observable that
ha'olah and hayorĕdĕth are not appos. belonging as objects to רוח and
ורוח. It is questionable, indeed, whether the punctuation of these
words, הָעֹלָה and הַיֹּרֶדֶת, as they lie before us, proceeds from an interrogative rendering. Saadia in Emunoth c. vi., and Juda Halevi in the
Kuzri ii. 80, deny this; and so also do Aben Ezra and Kimchi.
And they may be right. For instead of הָעֹלָה, the pointing ought to
have been הַעֹלָה (cf. הֶעָלָה, Job xiii. 25) when used as interrog. an
ascendens; even before א the compens. lengthening of the interrog.
ha is nowhere certainly found [1] instead of the virtual reduplication;
and thus also the parallel הַיֹּר' is not to be judged after הֲיִי', Lev.

---

[1] For ה is to be read with a Pattach in Judg. vi. 31, xii. 5; Neh. vi. 11; cf.
under Gen. xix. 9, xxvii. 21. In Num. xvi. 22 the ה of הָאִישׁ is the art., the question is not formally designated. Cf. also הַעַ' with ה interrog., Jer. xii. 9; and
הָעַ' with ה as the art., Gen. xv. 11.

x. 19, 'הִדְ, Ezek. xviii. 29,—we must allow that the punctation seeks, by the removal of the two interrog. הֲ (ה), to place that which is here said in accord with xii. 7. But there is no need for this. For מִי יוֹדֵעַ does not quite fall in with that which Lucretius says (*Lib.* I.):

> "*Ignoratur enim quae sit natura animai,*
> *Nata sit an contra nascentibus insinuetur?*
> *An simul intereat nobiscum morte diremta?*"

It may certainly be said of *mi yode'a*, as of *ignoratur*, that it does not exclude every kind of knowledge, but only a sure and certain knowledge resting on sufficient grounds; *interire* and ירד לְמַ' are also scarcely different, for neither of the two necessarily signifies annihilation, but both the discontinuance of independent individual existence. But the putting of the question by Koheleth is different, for it discloses more definitely than this by Lucretius, the possibility of a different end for the spirit of a man from that which awaits the spirit of a beast, and thus of a specific distinction between these two principles of life. In the formation even of the dilemma : Whether upwards or downwards, there lies an inquiring knowledge; and it cannot surprise us if Koheleth finally decides that the way of the spirit of a man is upwards, although it is not said that he rested this on the ground of demonstrative certainty. It is enough that, with the moral necessity of a final judgment beyond the sphere of this present life, at the same time also the continued existence of the spirit of man presented itself to him as a postulate of faith. One may conclude from the *desiderium aeternitatis* (iii. 11) implanted in man by the Creator, that, like the instincts implanted in the beasts, it will be calculated not for deception, but for satisfaction; and from the לְמַעְלָה, Prov. xv. 24,—*i.e.* the striving of a wise man rising above earthly, temporary, common things,—that death will not put an end to this striving, but will help it to reach its goal. But this is an indirect proof, which, however, is always inferior to the direct in force of argument. He presupposes that the Omnipotence and Wisdom which formed the world is also at the same time Love. Thus, though at last, it is faith which solves the dilemma, and we see from xii. 7 that this faith held sway over Koheleth. In the Book of Sirach, also, the old conception of Hades shows itself as yet dominant; but after the οὐκ ἀθάνατος υἱὸς ἀνθρώπου, xvii. 25, we read towards the end, where he speaks of Elias: καὶ γὰρ ἡμεῖς ζωῇ ζησόμεθα, xlviii. 11. In the passage before us, Koheleth remains in doubt, without getting over it by the hand of faith. In a certain reference the question he here proposes is to the present day unanswered; for the soul, or, more correctly, accord-

ing to the biblical mode of conception, the spirit from which the
soul-life of all corporeal beings proceeds, is a monas, and as such is
indestructible. Do the future of the beast's soul and of man's soul not
then stand in a solidaric mutual relation to each other ? In fact, the
future life presents to us mysteries the solution of which is beyond
the power of human thought, and we need not wonder that Koheleth,
this sober-minded, intelligent man, who was inaccessible to fantastic
self-deception, arrives, by the line of thought commenced at ver. 16,
also again at the *ultimatum*.

Ver. 22. "Thus I then saw that there is nothing better than that
a man should rejoice in his works, for that is his portion ; for who
can bring him to this, that he gains an insight into that which shall
be after him ? " Hengstenberg, who has decided against the interrog.
signification of the twice-repeated ה in ver. 21, now also explains
בְּמֶה . . . אַחֲרָיו, not : What shall become of him after it (his death) ?
but : What further shall be done after the state in which he now
finds himself ? Zöckler, although rightly understanding both ה as
well as אחריו (after him = when he will be separated, or separates
from this life, vii. 14, ix. 3 ; cf. Gen. xxiv. 67), yet proceeds on
that explanation of Hengstenberg's, and gives it the rendering : how
things shall be on the earth after his departure. But (1) for this
thought, as vi. 12 shows, the author had a more suitable form
of expression ; (2) this thought, after the author has, ver. 21, explained it as uncertain whether the spirit of a man in the act of
death takes a different path from that of a beast, is altogether aside
from the subject, and it is only an apologetic tendency not yet fully
vanquished which here constrains him. The chain of thought is
however this : How it will be with the spirit of a man when he
dies, who knows ? What will be after death is thus withdrawn
from human knowledge. Thus it is best to enjoy the present, since
we connect together (ii. 24) labour and enjoyment mediated thereby.
This joy of a man in his work—*i.e.* as v. 18 : which flows from his
work as a fountain, and accompanies him in it (viii. 15)—is his
portion, *i.e.* the best which he has of life in this world. Instead
of בְּמַה־שֶּׁ, the punctuation is בַּמֶּה, because שֶׁיִּהְיֶה אַחֲרָיו is a kindred
idea ; *vid.* regarding מֶה under ii. 22. And לִרְאוֹת בְּ is used, because
it is not so much to be said of the living, that he cannot foresee
how it shall be with him when he dies, as that he can gain no
glimpse into that world because it is an object that has for him no
fixity.

The Wrongs suffered by Man from Man embittering the Life of the Observer, iv. 1–3.

From unjust decisions a transition is now made to the subject of the haughty, unmerciful cruelty of the wide-extended oppressions inflicted by men.

iv. 1. "And again I saw all the oppressions that are done under the sun: and behold there the tears of the oppressed, and they have no comforter; and from the hand of their oppressors goeth forth violence; and they have no comforter." Incorrectly Hahn: And anew I saw,—the observation is different from that of iii. 16, though cognate. Thus: And again I saw,—the expression follows the syntactic scheme of Gen. xxvi. 18; regarding the *fut. consec.* brought into view here and at ver. 7, *vid.* above, p. 197, 2. The second הֶעָשׂ׳ is *part. pass.;* the first, as at Job xxxv. 9, and also at Amos iii. 9, is abstract (*i.e.* bringing the many separate instances under one general idea) *pluraletantum* (cf. פְּדֻיֵי, *redemti,* Isa. xxxv. 10; and *redemtio, pretium redemtionis,* Num. iii. 46); the plur. אֲשֶׁר נע׳ need not appear strange, since even חַיִּים is connected with the plur. of the pred., *e.g.* Ps. xxxi. 11, lxxxviii. 4. דִּמְעַת has, as at Isa. xxv. 8 (cf. Rev. xxiv. 4, πᾶν δάκρυον), a collective sense. The expression וּמִיַּד . . . כֹּחַ is singular. According to the most natural impression, it seems to signify: "and from the hand of their oppressors no power of deliverance" (carrying forward אֵין); but the parallelism of the palindromically constructed verse (as at i. 6, ii. 10, iii. 16) excludes this meaning. Thus כֹּחַ is here once—nowhere else—used, like the Greek βία, in the sense of violence; Luzzatto prefers the reading וּבְיָד, by which the expression would be in conformity with the linguistic usage; but also מִיד is explained: the force which they have in their hands is, in going forth from their hands, thought of as abused, and, as taking the form of שֹׁד or חֲזָקָה. In view of this sorrow which men bring upon their fellow-men, life for Koheleth lost all its worth and attraction.

Vers. 2, 3. "And I praised the dead who were long ago dead, more than the living who are yet in life; and as happier than both, him who has not yet come into existence, who hath not seen the evil work which is done under the sun." וְשַׁבֵּחַ is hardly thought of as part., like מִיקְשִׁים = יֻקְשִׁים, ix. 12; the מ of the *part. Pih.* is not usually thrown away, only מַהֵר, Zeph. i. 14, is perhaps = מְמַהֵר, but for the same reason as בֵּית־אֵל, 2 Kings ii. 3, is = בְּבֵית־אֵל. Thus וְשַׁבֵּחַ, like וְנָתוֹן, viii. 9, is *inf. absol.,* which is used to continue, in an adverbially subord. manner, the preceding finite with the same sub-

ject,[1] Gen. xli. 43 ; Lev. xxv. 14 ; Judg. vii. 19, etc.; cf. especially
Ex. viii. 11: "Pharaoh saw ... and hardened (וְהַכְבֵּד) his heart;"
just in the same manner as וְשַׁבֵּחַ here connects itself with וֹש׳ אני
וְאָ. Only the annexed designation of the subject is peculiar; the
syntactic possibility of this connection is established by Num. xix. 35,
Ps. xv. 5, Job xl. 2, and, in the second rank, by Gen. xvii. 10,
Ezek. v. 14. Yet אני might well enough have been omitted had
וֹש׳ אני וא׳ not stood too remote. Regarding עֲדֶנָה [2] and עֶדֶן, *adhuc, vid.*
p. 194. The circumstantial form of the expression : *prae vivis qui
vivi sunt adhuc,* is intentional : they who are as yet living must be
witnesses of the manifold and comfortless human miseries.

It is a question whether ver. 3 begins a new clause (LXX.,
Syr., and Venet.) or not. That אֶת, like the Arab. *aiya,* sometimes
serves to give prominence to the subject, cannot be denied (*vid.*
Böttcher, § 516, and Mühlau's remarks thereto). The Mishnic expressions אוֹתוֹ הַיּוֹם, that day, אוֹתָהּ הָאָרֶץ, that land, and the like
(Geiger, § 14. 2), presuppose a certain preparation in the older
language ; and we might, with Weiss (*Stud. ueber d. Spr. der Mishna,*
p. 112), interpret אֶת אֲשֶׁר in the sense of אוֹתִי אשר, *is qui.* But the
accus. rendering is more natural. Certainly the expression שַׁבֵּחַ טוֹב,
"to praise," "to pronounce happy," is not used; but to טוב it is
natural to suppose וְקִרָאתִי added. Jerome accordingly translates : *et
feliciorem utroque judicavi qui necdum natus est.* הָרָע has the double
Kametz, as is generally the case, except at Ps. liv. 7 and Mic. vii. 3.[3]
Better than he who is born is the unborn, who does not become
conscious of the wicked actions that are done under the sun. A
similar thought, with many variations in its expression, is found in
Greek writers ; see regarding these shrill discordances, which run
through all the joy of the beauty and splendour of Hellenic life, my
Apologetik, p. 116. Buddhism accordingly gives to *nirvâna* the
place of the highest good. That we find Koheleth on the same
path (cf. vi. 3, vii. 1), has its reason in this, that so long as the central point of man's existence lies in the present life, and this is not
viewed as the fore-court of eternity, there is no enduring consolation
to lift us above the miseries of this present world.

---

[1] Also 1 Chron. v. 20, the subject remains virtually the same : *et ita quidem
ut exaudirentur.*

[2] Thus punctuated with *Segol* under *Daleth,* and נ, *raphatum,* in F. H. J. P.
Thus also Kimchi in *W.B.* under עד.

[3] *Vid.* Heidenheim, *Meor Enajim,* under Deut. xvii. 7.

Miserable Rivalry and Restless Pursuit, iv. 4–6.

There follow two other observations, mutually related and issuing in " windy effort :"—

Ver. 4. " And I saw all the labour and all the skill of business, that it is an envious surpassing of the one by the other : also this is vain and windy effort." The הִיא refers to this exertion of vigorous effort and skill. The Graec. Venet., by rendering here and at ii. 24 כִּשְׁרוֹן by καθαρότης, betrays himself as a Jew. With כִּי, *quod*, that which forms the pred. follows the object. The *min* in *mere'ehu* is as in *amatz min*, Ps. xviii. 18, and the like—the same as the compar.: *aemulatio qua unus prae altero eminere studet.* All this expenditure of strength and art has covetousness and envy, with which one seeks to surpass another, as its poisoned sting.

Ver. 5. There ought certainly to be activity according to our calling; indolence is self-destruction : "The fool foldeth his hands, and eateth his own flesh." He layeth his hands together (Prov. vi. 10 = xxiv. 33),—placeth them in his bosom, instead of using them in working,—and thereby he eateth himself up, *i.e.* bringeth ruin upon himself (Ps. xxvii. 2 ; Mic. iii. 3 ; Isa. xlix. 26) ; for instead of nourishing himself by the labour of his hands, he feeds on his own flesh, and thus wasteth away. The emphasis does not lie on the subject (the fool, and only the fool), but on the pred.

Ver. 6. The fifth verse stands in a relation of contrast to this which follows : "Better is one hand full of quietness, than both fists full of labour and windy effort." Mendelssohn and others interpret ver. 5 as the objection of the industrious, and ver. 6 as the reply of the slothful. Zöckler agrees with Hitz., and lapses into the hypothesis of a dialogue otherwise rejected by him (*vid.* above, p. 217). As everywhere, so also here it preserves the unity of the combination of thoughts. נַחַת signifies here, as little as it does anywhere else, the rest of sloth; but rest, in contrast to such activity in labour as robs a man of himself, to the hunting after gain and honour which never has enough, to the rivalry which places its goal always higher and higher, and seeks to be before others—it is rest connected with well-being (vi. 5), gentle quietness (ix. 17), resting from self-activity (Isa. xxx. 15); cf. the post-bibl. נַחַת רוּחַ, satisfaction, contentment, comfort. In a word, *nahath* has not here the sense of being idle or lazy. The sequence of the thoughts is this : The fool in idleness consumes his own life-strength ; but, on the other hand, a little of true rest is better than the labour of windy effort, urged on by rivalry yielding no rest. כַּף is the open hollow hand, and חֹפֶן

(Assyr. *ḥupunnu*) the hand closed like a ball, the fist. "Rest" and "labour and windy effort" are the accusatives of that to which the designation of measure refers (Gesen. § 118. 3); the accus. connection lay here so much the nearer, as מָלֵא is connected with the accus. of that with which anything is full. In "and windy effort" lies the reason for the judgment pronounced. The striving of a man who laboriously seeks only himself and loses himself in restlessness, is truly a striving which has wind for its object, and has the property of wind.

The Aimless Labour and Penuriousness of him who stands alone, iv. 7–12.

Another sorrowful spectacle is the endless labour and the insatiable covetousness of the isolated man, which does good neither to himself nor to any other:

Vers. 7, 8. "There is one without a second, also son and brother he has not; and there is no end of his labour; his eyes nevertheless are not satisfied with riches: For whom do I labour, then, and deny all good to my soul? Also this is vain, and it is a sore trouble." That וָאַיִן, as in Ps. civ. 25, cv. 34, has the meaning of בְּאַיִן, *absque*, Nolde has already observed in his *Partik.-Concordanz*: a *solitarius*, without one standing by his side, a second standing near him, *i.e.* without wife and without friend; also, as the words following show, without son and brother. Regarding וְאַיִן, for which, with the connect. accus., וְאֵין might be expected (cf. also ii. 7, וָאֵין with *Mahpach*; and, on the other hand, ii. 23, וָכַעַס with *Pashta*), *vid.* under Ps. lv. 10. *Gam* may be interpreted in the sense of "also" as well as of "nevertheless" (Ewald, 354*a*); the latter is to be preferred, since the endless labour includes in itself a restless striving after an increase of possession. The *Kerî*, in an awkward way, changes עיניו into עֵינוֹ; the taking together the two eyes as one would here be unnatural, since the avaricious man devours gold, silver, and precious things really with both his eyes, and yet, however great be his wealth, still more does he wish to see in his possession; the sing. of the pred. is as at 1 Sam. iv. 15; Mic. iv. 11. With *ulmi ani*, Koheleth puts himself in the place of such a friendless, childless man; yet this change of the description into a self-confession may be occasioned by this, that the author in his old age was really thus isolated, and stood alone. Regarding חָסֵר with the accus. of the person, to whom, and *min* of the matter, in respect of which there is want, *vid.* under Ps. viii. 6. That the author stands in sympathy with the sorrowful condition here exposed, may also be remarked from the fact that he now proceeds to show the value of companionship and the miseries of isolation :

Ver. 9. " Better are two together than one, seeing they have a good reward in their labour." By *hashsh^{e}näim*, the author refers to such a pair ; *häehhad* is one such as is just described. The good reward consists in this, that each one of the two has the pleasant consciousness of doing good to the other by his labour, and especially of being helpful to him. In this latter general sense is grounded the idea of the reward of faithful fellowship :

Ver. 10. " For if they fall, the one can raise up his fellow : but woe to the one who falleth, and there is not a second there to lift him up." Only the Targ., which Grätz follows, confounds אֵילוֹ [1] with אֵלוֹ (*vid.* above, pp. 191 and 192) ; it is equivalent to אוֹי לוֹ, Isa. iii. 9, or הוֹי לוֹ, Ezek. xiii. 18. *Häehhad* is appos. connecting itself to the pronominal suff., as, *e.g.*, in a far more inappropriate manner, Ps. lxxxvi. 2 ; the prep. is not in appos. usually repeated, Gen. ii. 19, ix. 4 (exceptions : Ps. xviii. 51, lxxiv. 14). Whether we translate שֶׁיִּפֹּל by *qui ceciderit* (xi. 3), or by *quum ceciderit* (Jerome), is all one. יָקִים is potential : it is possible and probable that it will be done, provided he is a חָבֵר טוֹב, *i.e.* a true friend (*Pirke aboth*, ii. 13).

Ver. 11. " Moreover, if two lie together, then there is heat to them : but how can it be warm with one who is alone ? " The marriage relation is not excluded, but it remains in the background ; the author has two friends in his eye, who, lying in a cold night under one covering (Ex. xxii. 26 ; Isa. xxviii. 20), cherish one another, and impart mutual warmth. Also in *Aboth de-Rabbi Nathan*, c. 8, the sleeping of two together is spoken of as an evidence of friendship. The *vav* in *v^{e}hham* is that of the consequent ; it is wanting, 10a, according to rule, in *häehhad*, because it commonly comes into use with the verb, seldom (*e.g.* Gen. xxii. 1) with the preceding subj.

Ver. 12. " And if one shall violently assail him who is alone, two shall withstand him ; and (finally) a threefold cord is not quickly broken asunder." The form *yithq^{e}pho* for *yithq^{e}phehu*, Job xv. 24, is like *yird^{e}pho*, Hos. viii. 3 = *yird^{e}phehu*, Judg. ix. 40. If we take תקף in the sense of to overpower, then the meaning is : If one can overpower him who is alone, then, on the contrary, two can maintain their ground against him (Herzf.); but the two אִם, vers. 10, 11, which are equivalent to ἐάν, exclude such a pure logical εἰ. And why should תקף, if it can mean overpowering, not also

---

[1] With *Munach* and *Rebia* in one word, which, according to the Masora, occurs in only four other places. *Vid. Mas. magna* under this passage, and *Mishpete hateamin* 26a.

mean doing violence to by means of a sudden attack? In the
Mishnic and Arab. it signifies to seize, to lay hold of; in the Aram.
אֲתְקָף = הֶחֱזִיק, and also at Job xiv. 20, xv. 24 (vid. Comm.), it may
be understood of a violent assault, as well as of a completed subjugation; as נשׂא means to lift up and carry; עמד, to tread and to stand.
But whether it be understood inchoat. or not, in any case הָאֶחָד is
not the assailant, who is much rather the unnamed subj. in יתקפי, but
the one (the solitarius) who, if he is alone, must succumb; the
construction of yithqᵉpho häehhad follows the scheme of Ex. ii. 6,
" she saw it, the child." To the assault expressed by תקף, there
stands opposed the expression עמד נגד, which means to withstand
any one with success; as עמד לפני, 2 Kings x. 4, Ps. cxlvii. 17,
Dan. viii. 7, means to maintain one's ground. Of three who hold
together, 12a says nothing; the advance from two to three is thus
made in the manner of a numerical proverb (vid. Proverbs, vol. I.
p. 13). If two hold together, that is seen to be good; but if there
be three, this threefold bond is likened to a cord formed of three
threads, which cannot easily be broken. Instead of the definite
specific art. הַח' הַמ', we make use of the indefinite. Funiculus triplex
difficile rumpitur is one of the winged expressions used by Koheleth.

The People's Enthusiasm for the new King, and its Extinction, iv. 13–16.

A political observation follows in an aphoristic manner the observations relating to social life, viz. how popularity vanishes away
and passes even into its opposite. The author, who here plainly
quotes from actual events, begins with a general statement:
Ver. 13. " Better is a youth poor and wise, than a king old and
foolish, who no longer understands how to be warned,"—*i.e.* who
increases his folly by this, that he is " wise in his own eyes,"
Prov. xxvi. 12; earlier, as עוֹד denotes, he was, in some measure,
accessible to the instruction of others in respect of what was wanting to him; but now in his advanced age he is hardened in his
folly, bids defiance to all warning counsel, and undermines his throne.
The connection of the verb ידע with ל and the inf. (for which elsewhere only the inf. is used) is a favourite form with the author;
it means to know anything well, v. 1, vi. 8, x. 15; here is meant
an understanding resting on the knowledge of oneself and on the
knowledge of men. נזְהָר is here and at xii. 12, Ps. xix. 12, a
Niph. tolerativum, such as the synon. נוֹסָר, Ps. ii. 10: to let oneself be cleared up, made wiser, enlightened, warned. After this
contrast, the idea connected with חכם also defines itself. A young

man (יֶלֶד, as at Dan. i. 4, but also Gen. iv. 23) is meant who (vid. above, p. 193, under misken) yet excels the old imbecile and childish king, in that he perceives the necessity of a fundamental change in the present state of public matters, and knows how to master the situation to such a degree that he raises himself to the place of ruler over the neglected community.

Ver. 14. " For out of the prison-house he goeth forth to reign as king, although he was born as a poor man in his kingdom." With כִּי the properties of poverty and wisdom attributed to the young man are verified,—wisdom in this, that he knew how to find the way from a prison to a throne. As harammim, 2 Chron. xxii. 5 = haarammim, 2 Kings viii. 28, so hasurim = haasurim (cf. masoreth = maasoreth, Ezek. xx. 37) ; beth haasirim (Kerî: haasurim), Judg. xvi. 21, 25, and beth haesur, Jer. xxxvii. 15, designate the prison; cf. Moëd katan, iii. 1. The modern form of the language prefers this elision of the א, e.g. אֶפְלוֹ = אֵלוּ אַף אַף, אַל־אַחַר = אֵל־אַחַר, בָּתַר post = בָּאתַר contra, etc. The perf. יָצָא is also thought of as such ; for the comparison, ver. 13, would have no meaning if the poor and wise youth were not thought of as having reached the throne, and having pre-eminence assigned to him as such. He has come forth from the prison to become king, כִּי . . . רָשׁ. Zöckler translates : " Whereas also he that was born in his kingdom was poor," and adds the remark : " כי נם, after the כי of the preceding clause, does not so much introduce a verification of it, as much rather an intensification ; by which is expressed, that the prisoner has not merely transitorily fallen into such misery, but that he was born in poor and lowly circumstances, and that in his own kingdom בְּמַ', i.e. in the same land which he should afterwards rule as king." But כי נם is nowhere used by Koheleth in the sense of "ja auch " (= whereas also); and also where it is thus to be translated, as at Jer. xiv. 18, xxiii. 11, it is used in the sense of " denn auch " (= for also), assigning proof. The fact is, that this group of particles, according as כי is thought of as demonst. or relat., means either "denn auch," iv. 16, vii. 22, viii. 16, or " wenn auch " = ἐὰν καί, as here and at viii. 12. In the latter case, it is related to כִּי נַם (sometimes also merely נַם, Ps. xcv. 9 ; Mal. iii. 15), as ἐὰν (εἰ) καί, although, notwithstanding, is to καὶ ἐάν (εἰ), even although.[1] Thus 14b, connecting itself with לִמְלֹךְ, is to be translated : " although he was born (נוֹלַד, not נוֹלָד) in his kingdom as a poor man." [2] We cannot also concur with Zöckler in the view

---

[1] That the accentuation separates the two words כי נם־ is to be judged from this, that it almost everywhere prefers כי אם־ (vid. under Comm. to Ps. i. 2).

[2] נולד רש cannot mean "to become poor." Grätz appeals to the Mishnic

that the suff. of במ׳ refers to the young upstart: in the kingdom
which should afterwards become his ; for this reason, that the suff.
of הח׳, ver. 16*b*, refers to the old king, and thus also that this
designation may be mediated, במ׳ must refer to him. מלכות signifies
kingdom, reign, realm; here, the realm, as at Neh. ix. 35, Dan. v. 11,
vi. 29. Grätz thinks vers. 13–16 ought to drive expositors to
despair. But hitherto we have found no room for despair in obtaining a meaning from them. What follows also does not perplex us.
The author describes how all the world hails the entrance of the
new youthful king on his government, and gathers together under his
sceptre.

Vers. 15, 16*a*. " I saw all the living which walk under the sun
on the side of the youth, the second who shall enter upon the place
of the former : no end of all the people, all those at whose head he
stands." The author, by the expression " I saw," places himself
back in the time of the change of government. If we suppose that
he represents this to himself in a lively manner, then the words are
to be translated : of the second who shall be his successor ; but
if we suppose that he seeks to express from the standpoint of the
past that which, lying farther back in the past, was now for the first
time future, then the future represents the time to come in the past,
as at 2 Kings iii. 27 ; Ps. lxxviii. 6 ; Job xv. 28 (Hitz.) : of the
second who should enter on his place (עָמַד, to step to, to step forth,
of the new king, Dan. viii. 23, xi. 2 f.; cf קוּם, 1 Kings viii. 20).
The designation of the crowd which, as the pregnant עַם expresses,
gathered by the side of the young successor to the old king, by
" all the living, those walking under the sun (הַמֶה׳, perhaps intentionally the pathetic word for הֹלְכִים, Isa. xlii. 5)," would remain a hyperbole, even although the throne of the Asiatic world-ruler had been
intended ; still the expression, so absolute in its universality, would
in that case be more natural (*vid.* the conjectural reference to Cyrus
and Astyages, above, at p. 215). הַשֵּׁנִי, Ewald refers to the successor to
the king, the second after the king, and translates : "to the second man
who should reign in his stead ; " but the second man in this sense
has certainly never been the child of fortune ; one must then think
of Joseph, who, however, remains the second man. Hitzig rightly :
" The youth is the second שֵׁנִי, not אַחֵר, in contrast to the king, who,
as his predecessor, is the first." " Yet," he continues, " הילד should
be the appos. and השׁני the principal word," *i.e.* instead of : with the
second youth, was to be expected : with the second, the youth. It
language ; but no intelligent linguist will use נולד רש of a man in any other sense
than that he is originally poor.

is true, we may either translate : with the second youth, or : with the second, the youth,—the form of expression has in it something incorrect, for it has the appearance as if it treated of two youths. But similar are the expressions, Matt. viii. 21, ἕτερος κ.τ.λ., " another, and that, too, one of His disciples ;" and Luke xxiii. 32, ἤγοντο κ.τ.λ. All the world ranks itself by the side (thus we may also express it) of the second youthful king, so that he comes to stand at the head of an endless multitude. The LXX., Jerome, and the Venet. render incorrectly the all (the multitude) as the subject of the relative clause, which Luther, after the Syr., corrects by reading לפניו for לפניהם : of the people that went for him there was no end. Rightly the Targ.: at whose head (= בְּרֵישֵׁיהוֹן) he had the direction, לְפְנֵי, as with יצא ובא, 1 Sam. xviii. 16 ; 2 Chron. i. 10 ; Ps. lxviii. 8, etc. All the world congregates about him, follows his leadership ; but his history thus splendidly begun, viewed backwards, is a history of hopes falsified.

Ver. 16b. " And yet they who come after do not rejoice in him : for that also is vain, and a grasping after the wind." For all that, and in spite of that (gam has here this meaning, as at vi. 7 ; Jer. vi. 15 ; Ps. cxxix. 2 ; Ewald, § 354a), posterity (הָאַ, as at i. 11 ; cf. Isa. xli. 4) has no joy in this king,—the hopes which his contemporaries placed in the young king, who had seized the throne and conquered their hearts, afterwards proved to be delusions ; and also this history, at first so beautiful, and afterwards so hateful, contributed finally to the confirmation of the truth, that all under the sun is vain. As to the historical reminiscence from the time of the Ptolemies, in conformity with which Hitzig (in his Comm.) thinks this figure is constructed, vid. above, p. 213 ; Grätz here, as always, rocks himself in Herodian dreams. In his Comm., Hitz. guesses first of Jeroboam, along with Rehoboam the יֶלֶד שֵׁנִי, who rebelled against King Solomon, who in his old age had become foolish. In an essay, " Zur Exeg. u. Kritik des B. Koheleth," in Hilgenfeld's Zeitschr. XIV. 566 ff., Saul, on the contrary, appears to him to be the old and foolish king, and David the poor wise youth who rose to the throne, and took possession of the whole kingdom, but in his latter days experienced desertion and adversities ; for those who came after (the younger men) had no delight in him, but rebelled against him. But in relation to Saul, who came from the plough to be king, David, who was called from being a shepherd, is not נולד רש ; and to Jewish history this Saul, whose nobler self is darkened by melancholy, but again brightens forth, and who to his death maintained the dignity of a king of Israel, never at any time appears as מלך ... וכסיל. Moreover, by both combinations of that which is related with the בֵּית הַסּוּרִים (for which 'הַפ is written) of the history of the old Israelitish kings, a meaning contrary to the usage of the language must be extracted. It is true that סוּר, as the so-called *particip. perfecti*, may mean "gone aside (to a distance)," Isa. xlix. 21, Jer. xvii. 13; and we may, at any rate, by סוּרים, think on that poor rabble which at first gathered around David, 1 Sam. xxii. 2, regarded as outcasts from honourable society.   But בֵּית will not accord therewith.   That David came forth from the house (home) of the estranged or separated, is and remains historically an awkward expression, linguistically obscure, and not in accordance with the style of Koheleth.   In order to avoid this incongruity, Böttcher regards Antiochus the Great as the original of the ילד. He was the second son of his father, who died 225.   When a hopeful youth of fifteen years of age, he was recalled to the throne from a voluntary banishment into Farther Asia, very soon gained against his old cousin and rival Achaeus, who was supported by Egypt, a large party, and remained for several years esteemed as a prince and captain ; he disappointed, however, at a later time, the confidence which was reposed in him.   But granting that the voluntary exile of Antiochus might be designated as בֵּית הָאֵס', he was yet not a poor man, born poor, but was the son of King Seleucus Callinicus ; and his older relative and rival Achaeus wished indeed to become king, but never attained unto it.   Hence הַשֵׁני is not the youth as second son of his father, but as second on the throne, in relation to the dethroned king reckoned as the first.   Thus, far from making it probable that the Book of Koheleth originated in the time of the Diadochs, this combination of Böttcher's also stands on a feeble foundation, and falls in ruins when assailed.

The section i. 12–iv. 16, to which we have prefixed the superscription, "Koheleth's Experiences and their Results," has now reached its termination, and here for the first time we meet with a characteristic peculiarity in the composition of the book: the narrative sections, in which Koheleth, on the ground of his own experiences and observations, registers the vanities of earthly life, terminate in series of proverbs in which the *I* of the preacher retires behind the objectivity of the exhortations, rules, and principles obtained from experience, here recorded.   The first of these series of proverbs which here follows is the briefest, but also the most complete in internal connection.

FIRST CONCLUDING SECTION.

PROVERBS REGARDING THE WORSHIP OF GOD.—IV. 17 [V. 1]–V. 6 [7]

As an appendix and interlude, these proverbs directly follow the personal section preceding. The first rule here laid down refers to the going to the house of God.

iv. 17 [v. 1]. "Keep thy foot when thou goest to the house of God, and to go to hear is better than that fools give a sacrifice ; for the want of knowledge leads them to do evil." The "house of God" is like the "house of Jahve," 2 Sam. xii. 20, Isa. xxxvii. 1, the temple ; אֶל, altogether like אֶל־מְ־אֶל, Ps. lxxiii. 17. The *Chethîb* רַגְלֶיךָ is admissible, for elsewhere also this plur. ("thy feet") occurs in a moral connection and with a spiritual reference, *e.g.* Ps. cxix. 59 ; but more frequently, however, the comprehensive sing. occurs, Ps. cxix. 105, Prov. i. 15, iv. 26 f., and the *Kerî* thus follows the right note. The correct understanding of what follows depends on פִּי־ . . . רָע. Interpreters have here adopted all manner of impossible views. Hitzig's translation: "for they know not how to be sorrowful," has even found in Stuart at least one imitator ; but עֲשׂוֹת רָע would, as the contrast of '*asoth tov*, iii. 12, mean nothing else than, "to do that which is unpleasant, disagreeable, bad," like '*asah ra'ah*, 2 Sam. xii. 18. Gesen., Ewald (§ 336*b*), Elster, Heiligst., Burger, Zöckl., Dale, and Bullock translate: "they know not that they do evil ;" but for such a rendering the words ought to have been עֲשׂוֹתָם רָע (cf. Jer. xv. 15) ; the only example for the translation of לַעֲשׂוֹת after the manner of the *acc. c. inf.* = *se facere malum*—viz. at 1 Kings xix. 4— is incongruous, for לָמוּת does not here mean *se mori*, but *ut moreretur*. Yet more incorrect is the translation of Jerome, which is followed by Luther: *nesciunt quid faciant mali*. It lies near, as at ii. 24 so also here, to suppose an injury done to the text. Aben Ezra intro- duced רַק before לַעְשׂ', but Koheleth never uses this limiting particle ; we would have to write כִּי אִם־לְעֲשׂוֹת, after iii. 12, viii. 15. Anything thus attained, however, is not worth the violent means thus used ; for the ratifying clause is not ratifying, and also in itself, affirmed of the כְּסִילִים, who, however, are not the same as the *r^esha'im* and the *hattäim*, is inappropriate. Rather it might be said : they know not to do good (thus the Syr.) ; or : they know not whether it be good or bad to do, *i.e.* they have no moral feeling, and act not from moral motives (so the Targ.). Not less violent than this remodelling of the text is the expedient of Herzberg, Philippson, and Ginsburg, who from לִשְׁמֹעַ derive the subject - conception of the obedient (הַשֹּׁמְעִים) : " For those understand not at all to do evil ; " the subj. ought to have been expressed if it must be something different from the immediately preceding כסילים. We may thus render *enam yod'im*, after Ps. lxxxii. 5, Isa. lvi. 10, as complete in itself : they (the fools) are devoid of knowledge to do evil = so that they do evil ; *i.e.*, want of knowledge brings them to this, that they do evil. Similarly also Knobel : they concern themselves not,—are unconcerned (viz. about the right mode of worshipping God),—so that they do evil, with the correct remark that the consequence of their perverse conduct is here represented as their intention. But לא ידע, absol., does not mean to be unconcerned (wanton), but to be without knowledge. Rashbam, in substance correctly : they are predisposed by their ignorance to do evil ; and thus also Hahn ; Mendelssohn translates directly : "they sin because they are ignorant." If this interpretation is correct, then for לִשְׁמֹעַ it follows that it does not mean "to obey" (thus *e.g.* Zöckler), which in general it never means without some words being added to it (cf. on the contrary, 1 Sam. xv. 22), but " to hear,"—viz. the word of God, which is to be heard in the house of God,—whereby, it is true, a hearing is meant which leads to obedience. In the word הוֹרוֹת, priests are not perhaps thought of, although the comparison of ver. 5 (המלאך) with Mal. ii. 7 makes it certainly natural ; priestly instruction limited itself to information regarding the performance of the law already given in Scripture, Lev. x. 11, Deut. xxxiii. 9 f., and to deciding on questions arising in the region of legal praxis, Deut. xxiv. 8 ; Hag. ii. 11. The priesthood did not belong to the teaching class in the sense of preaching. Preaching was never a part of the temple cultus, but, for the first time, after the exile became a part of the synagogue worship. The preachers under the O. T. were the prophets,—preachers by a supernatural divine call, and by the immediate impulse of the Spirit ; we know from the Book of Jeremiah that they sometimes went into the temple, or there caused their books of prophecy to be read ; yet the author, by the word לִשְׁמֹעַ of the foregoing proverb, scarcely thinks of them. But apart from the teaching of the priests, which referred to the realization of the letter of the law, and the teaching of the prophets to the realization of the spirit of the law, the word formed an essential part of the sacred worship of the temple : the *Tefilla*, the *Beracha*, the singing of psalms, and certainly, at the time of Koheleth, the reading of certain sections of the Bible. When thou goest to the house of God, says Koheleth, take heed to thy step, well reflecting whither thou goest and how thou hast there to appear ;

and (with this ׀ he connects with this first *nota bene* a second) drawing near to hear exceeds the sacrifice-offering of fools, for they are
ignorant (just because they hear not), which leads to this result, that
they do evil. מִן, *prae*, expresses also, without an adj., precedence in
number, Isa. x. 10, or activity, ix. 17, or worth, Ezek. xv. 2. קְרוֹב
is *inf. absol.* Böttcher seeks to subordinate it as such to שְׁמֹר : take
heed to thy foot ... and to the coming near to hear more than to ...
But these obj. to שמר would be incongruous, and מתת וגו' clumsy and
even distorted in expression; it ought rather to be מִתִּתְּךָ כִּכְסִילִים זֶבַח.
As the *inf. absol.* can take the place of the obj., Isa. vii. 15, xlii. 24,
Lam. iii. 45, so also the place of the subj. (Ewald, § 240*a*), although
Prov. xxv. 27 is a doubtful example of this.   That the use of the
inf. absol. has a wide application with the author of this book, we
have already seen under iv. 2.   Regarding the sequence of ideas in
מִתֵּת ... זֶבַח (first the subj., then the obj.), *vid.* Gesen. § 133. 3, and
cf. above at iii. 18.   זֶבַח (וּזְבָחִים), along with its general signification
comprehending all animal sacrifices, according to which the altar
bears the name מִזְבֵּחַ, early acquired also a more special signification :
it denotes, in contradistinction to עֹלָה, such sacrifices as are only
partly laid on the altar, and for the most part are devoted to a
sacrificial festival, Ex. xviii. 12 (cf. Ex. xii. 27), the so-called
sh^elamim, or also *zivhhe sh^elamim*, Prov. vii. 14.   The expression נתן
זבח makes it probable that here, particularly, is intended the festival
(1 Kings i. 41) connected with this kind of sacrifice, and easily de-
generating to worldly merriment (*vid.* under Prov. vii. 14) ; for the
more common word for תֵּת would have been הַקְרִיב or שָׁחוֹט ; in תֵּת it
seems to be indicated that it means not only to present something
to God, but also to give at the same time something to man.   The
most recent canonical Chokma-book agrees with Prov. xxi. 3 in this
depreciation of sacrifice.   But the Chokma does not in this stand
alone.   The great word of Samuel, 1 Sam. xv. 22 f., that self-
denying obedience to God is better than all sacrifices, echoes through
the whole of the Psalms.   And the prophets go to the utmost in
depreciating the sacrificial cultus.

The second rule relates to prayer.

v. 1, 2 [2, 3]. "Be not hasty with thy mouth, and let not thy
heart hasten to speak a word before God : for God is in heaven, and
thou art upon earth ; therefore let thy words be few.   For by much
business cometh dreaming, and by much talk the noise of fools."
As we say in German : *auf Flügeln fliegen* [to flee on wings], *auf
Einem Auge nicht sehen* [not to see with one eye], *auf der Flöte
blasen* [to blow on the flute], so in Heb. we say that one slandereth

with (*auf*) his tongue (Ps. xv. 3), or, as here, that he hasteth with
his mouth, *i.e.* is forward with his mouth, inasmuch as the word goes
before the thought. It is the same usage as when the post-bibl.
Heb., in contradistinction to הַתּוֹרָה שֶׁבִּכְתָב, the law given in the
Scripture, calls the oral law הת׳ שֶׁבְּעַל־פֶּה, *i.e.* the law mediated עַל־פֶּה,
oraliter = oralis traditio (*Shabbath* 31*a*; cf. *Gittin* 60*b*). The instrument and means is here regarded as the *substratum* of the action
—as that which this lays as a foundation. The phrase: "to take on
the lips," Ps. xvi. 4, which needs no explanation, is different. Regarding בָּהֵל, *festinare*, which is, like מִהֵר, the intens. of *Kal*, vid.
above, p. 191; once it occurs quite like our "*sich beeilen*" [to
hasten], with reflex. accus. suff., 2 Chron. xxxv. 21. Man, when
he prays, should not give the reins to his tongue, and multiply words
as one begins and repeats over a form which he has learnt, knowing
certainly that it is God of whom and to whom he speaks, but
without being conscious that God is an infinitely exalted Being,
to whom one may not carelessly approach without collecting his
thoughts, and irreverently, without lifting up his soul. As the
heavens, God's throne, are exalted above the earth, the dwelling-place
of man, so exalted is the heavenly God above earthly man, standing
far beneath him; therefore ought the words of a man before God to
be few,—few, well-chosen reverential words, in which one expresses
his whole soul. The older language forms no plur. from the subst.
מְעַט (fewness) used as an adv.; but the more recent treats it as an
adj., and forms from it the plur. מְעַטִּים (here and in Ps. cix. 8, which
bears the superscription *le-david*, but has the marks of Jeremiah's
style); the post-bibl. places in the room of the apparent adj. the
particip. adj. מוֹעֵט with the plur. מוֹעֲטִים (מוֹעֲטִין), *e.g. Berachoth* 61*a:*
"always let the words of a man before the Holy One (blessed be His
name!) be few" (מוע׳). Few ought the words to be; for where they
are many, it is not without folly. This is what is to be understood,
ver. 2, by the comparison; the two parts of the verse stand here in
closer mutual relation than vii. 1,—the proverb is not merely syn-
thetical, but, like Job v. 7, parabolical. The בְ is both times that
of the cause. The dream happens, or, as we say, dreams happen
בְּרֹב עִנְיָן; not: by much labour; for labour in itself, as the expenditure of strength making one weary, has as its consequence, v. 11,
sweet sleep undisturbed by dreams; but: by much self-vexation in
a man's striving after high and remote ends beyond what is possible
(Targ., in manifold project-making); the care of such a man trans-
plants itself from the waking to the sleeping life, if it does not
wholly deprive him of sleep, v. 11*b*, viii. 16,—all kinds of images of

the labours of the day, and fleeting phantoms and terrifying pictures hover before his mind. And as dreams of such a nature appear when a man wearies himself inwardly as well as outwardly by the labours of the day, so, with the same inward necessity, where many words are spoken folly makes its appearance. Hitzig renders כסיל, in the connection קוֹל כְּ', as adj.; but, like אֱוִיל (which forms an adj. ĕvīlī), כסיל is always a subst., or, more correctly, it is a name occurring always only of a living being, never of a thing. There is sound without any solid content, mere blustering bawling without sense and intelligence. The talking of a fool is in itself of this kind (x. 14); but if one who is not just a fool falls into much talk, it is scarcely possible but that in this flow of words empty bombast should appear.

Another rule regarding the worship of God refers to vowing.

Vers. 3 [4]-6 [7]. "When thou hast made a vow to God, delay not to fulfil it; for there is no pleasure in fools: that which thou hast vowed fulfil. Better that thou vowest not, than that thou vowest and fulfillest not. Let not thy mouth bring thy body into punishment; and say not before the messenger of God that it was precipitation: why shall God be angry at thy talk, and destroy the work of thy hands? For in many dreams and words there are also many vanities: much rather fear God!" If they abstained, after *Shabbath* 30*b*, from treating the Book of Koheleth as apocryphal, because it begins with דברי תורה (cf. at i. 3) and closes in the same way, and hence warrants the conclusion that that which lies between will also be דברי תורה, this is in a special manner true of the passage before us regarding the vow which, in thought and expression, is the echo of Deut. xxiii. 22-24. Instead of *kaashĕr tiddor*, we find there the words *ki tiddor*; instead of *lelohim* (= *lĕĕlohim*, always only of the one true God), there we have *lahovah ĕlohĕcha*; and instead of *al-tᵉahher*, there *lo tᵉahher*. There the reason is: "for the Lord thy God will surely require it of thee; and it would be sin in thee;" here: for there is no pleasure in fools, *i.e.* it is not possible that any one, not to speak of God, could have a particular inclination toward fools, who speak in vain, and make promises in which their heart is not, and which they do not keep. Whatever thou vowest, continues Koheleth, fulfil it; it is better (Ewald, § 336*a*) that thou vowest not, than to vow and not to pay; for which the *Tôra* says: "If thou shalt forbear to vow, it shall be no sin in thee" (Deut. xxiii. 22). נֶדֶר, which, according to the stem-word, denotes first the vow of conse-cration or setting apart (cogn. Arab. *nadar*, to separate, נזר, whence נָזִיר), the so-called אֱסָר [*vid.* Num. xxx. 3], is here a vow in its

widest sense; the author, however, may have had, as there, the law
(cf. ver. 24), especially *shalme nĕdĕr*, in view, *i.e.* such peace-offerings
as the law does not enjoin, but which the offerer promises (cogn.
with the *shalme n'davah*, *i.e.* such as rest on free-will, but not on any
obligation arising from a previous promise) from his own inclination,
for the event that God may do this or that for him. The verb שִׁלֵּם
is not, however, related to this name for sacrifices, as חִטֵּא is to חַטָּאת,
but denotes the fulfilling or discharge as a performance fully accordant
with duty. To the expression חֵטְא . . . הָיָה (twice occurring in the
passage of Deut. referred to above) there is added the warning : let
not thy mouth bring thy body into sin. The verb *nathan*, with
Lamed and the inf. following, signifies to allow, to permit, Gen.
xx. 6 ; Judg. i. 34 ; Job xxxi. 30. The inf. is with equal right
translated : not to bring into punishment; for חָטָא—the syncop.
Hiph. of which, according to an old, and, in the Pentateuch, favourite
form, is לְהַחְטִיא—signifies to sin, and also (*e.g.* Gen. xxxix. 9 ; cf. the
play on the word, Hos. viii. 11) to expiate sin ; sin-burdened and
guilty, or liable to punishment, mean the same thing. Incorrectly,
Ginsburg, Zöck., and others : "Do not suffer thy mouth to cause thy
flesh to sin ;" for (1) the formula : "the flesh sins," is not in
accordance with the formation of O. T. ideas ; the N. T., it is true,
uses the expression σὰρξ ἁμαρτίας, Rom. viii. 3, but not ἁμαρτά-
νουσα, that which sins is not the flesh, but the will determined by
the flesh, or by fleshly lust; (2) the mouth here is not merely
that which leads to sin, but the person who sins through thought-
less haste,—who, by his haste, brings sin upon his flesh, for this
suffers, for the breach of vow, by penalties inflicted by God; the
mouth is, like the eye and the hand, a member of the ὅλον τὸ
σῶμα (Matt. v. 24 f.), which is here called בָּשָׂר ; the whole man
in its sensitive nature (*opp.* לֵב, ii. 3, xi. 10 ; Prov. xiv. 30)
has to suffer chastisement on account of that which the mouth
hath spoken. Gesen. compares this passage, correctly, with Deut.
xxiv. 4, for the meaning *peccati reum facere;* Isa. xxix. 21 is also
similar.

The further warning refers to the lessening of the sin of a rash
vow unfulfilled as an unintentional, easily expiable offence : "and say
not before the messenger of God that it was a שְׁגָגָה, a sin of weakness." Without doubt *hammălāch* is an official byname of a priest
(*vid.* above, p. 193), and that such as was in common use at the
time of the author (*vid.* p. 210). But as for the rest, it is not easy to
make the matter of the warning clear. That it is not easy, may be
concluded from this, that with Jewish interpreters it lies remote to

think of a priest in the word *hammălāch*. By this word the Targ. understands the angel to whom the execution of the sentence of punishment shall be committed on the day of judgment; Aben Ezra: the angel who writes down all the words of a man; similarly Jerome, after his Jewish teacher. Under this passage Ginsburg has an entire excursus regarding the angels. The LXX. and Syr. translate "before God," as if the words of the text were נֶגֶד אֵל, Ps. cxxxviii. 1, or as if *hammalach* could of itself mean God, as presenting Himself in history. Supposing that *hammalach* is the official name of a man, and that of a priest, we appear to be under the necessity of imagining that he who is charged with the obligation of a vow turns to the priest with the desire that he would release him from it, and thus dissolve (bibl. הֵפִיר, Mishnic הִתִּיר) the vow. But there is no evidence that the priests had the power of releasing from vows. Individual cases in which a husband can dissolve the vow of his wife, and a father the vow of his daughter, are enumerated in Num. xxx.; besides, in the traditional law, we find the sentence: "A vow, which one who makes it repents of, can be dissolved by a learned man (חכם), or, where none is present, by three laymen," *Bechoroth* 36*b*; the matter cannot be settled by any middle person (שליח), but he who has taken the vow (הנודר) must appear personally, *Jore deah* c. 228, § 16. Of the priest as such nothing is said here. Therefore the passage cannot at all be traditionally understood of an official dissolution of an oath. Where the Talm. applies it juristically, *Shabbath* 32*b*, etc., Rashi explains *hammalach* by *gizbar shĕl-haqdesh*, *i.e.* treasurer of the revenues of the sanctuary; and in the *Comm.* to Koheleth he supposes that some one has publicly resolved on an act of charity (צדקה), *i.e.* has determined it with himself, and that now the representative of the congregation (שליח) comes to demand it. But that is altogether fanciful. If we proceed on the idea that *liphne hammalach* is of the same meaning as *liphne hakkohen*, Lev. xxvii. 8, 11, Num. ix. 6, xxvii. 2, etc., we have then to derive the figure from such passages relating to the law of sacrifice as Num. xv. 22–26, from which the words *ki sh°gagah hi* (Num. xv. 25*b*) originate. We have to suppose that he who has made a vow, and has not kept it, comes to terms with God with an easier and less costly offering, since in the confession (וִדּוּי) which he makes before the priest he explains that the vow was a *sh°gagah*, a declaration that inconsiderately escaped him. The author, in giving it to be understood that under these circumstances the offering of the sacrifice is just the direct contrary of a good work, calls to the conscience of the inconsiderate נודר: why should God be angry on account of thy voice with which thou dost excuse thy sins of omission, and destroy (vid. regarding חִבֵּל under Isa. x. 27) the work of thy hands (vid. under Ps. xc. 17), for He destroys what thou hast done, and causes to fail what thou purposest? The question with lammah resembles those in Ezra iv. 22, vii. 23, and is of the same kind as at vii. 16 f.; it leads us to consider what a mad self-destruction that would be (Jer. xliv. 7, cf. under Isa. i. 5).

The reason [for the foregoing admonition] now following places the inconsiderate vow under the general rubric of inconsiderate words. We cannot succeed in interpreting ver. 6 [7] (in so far as we do not supply, after the LXX. and Syr. with the Targ.: ne credas; or better, with Ginsburg, היא = it is) without taking one of the vavs in the sense of " also." That the Heb. vav, like the Greek καί, the Lat. et, may have this comparative or intensifying sense rising above that which is purely copulative, is seen from e.g. Num. ix. 14, cf. also Josh. xiv. 11. In many cases, it is true, we are not under the necessity of translating vav by " also ; " but since the " and " here does not merely externally connect, but expresses correlation of things homogeneous, an " also " or a similar particle involuntarily substitutes itself for the " and," e.g. Gen. xvii. 20 (Jerome): super Ismael quoque; Ex. xxix. 8: filios quoque; Deut. i. 32: et nec sic quidem credidistis; ix. 8: nam et in Horeb; cf. Josh. xv. 19; 1 Sam. xxv. 43; 2 Sam. xix. 25; 1 Kings ii. 22, xi. 26; Isa. xlix. 6, " I have also given to thee." But there are also passages in which it cannot be otherwise translated than by " also." We do not reckon among these Ps. xxxi. 12, where we do not translate " also my neighbours," and Amos iv. 10, where the words are to be translated, " and that in your nostrils." On the contrary, Isa. xxxii. 7 is scarcely otherwise to be translated than " also when the poor maketh good his right," like 2 Sam. i. 23, " also in their death they are not divided." In 2 Chron. xxvii. 5, in like manner, the two vavs are scarcely correlative, but we have, with Keil, to translate, " also in the second and third year." And in Hos. viii. 6, וְהוּא, at least according to the punctuation, signifies " also it," as Jerome translates: ex Israele et ipse est. According to the interpunction of the passage before us, וְּ הַרְ׳ is the pred., and thus, with the Venet., is to be translated: " For in many dreams and vanities there are also many words." We could at all events render the vav, as also at x. 11, Ex. xvi. 6, as vav apod.; but בְּרֹב וגו׳ has not the character of a virtual antecedent,—the meaning of the expression remains as for the rest the same; but Hitzig's objection is of force against it (as also against Ewald's disposition of the words, like that of Symmachus, Jerome, and Luther: "for where there are many dreams, there are also vanities, and many words"), that it does not accord with the connection, which certainly in the first place requires a reason referable to inconsiderate talk, and that the second half is, in fact, erroneous, for between dreams and many words there exists no necessary inward mutual relation. Hitzig, as Knobel before him, seeks to help this, for he explains: "for in many dreams are also vanities, *i.e.* things from which nothing comes, and (the like) in many words." But not only is this assumed carrying forward of the ב doubtful, but the principal thing would be made a secondary matter, and would drag heavily. The relation in ver. 2 is different where *vav* is that of comparison, and that which is compared follows the comparison. Apparently the text (although the LXX. had it before them, as it is before us) has undergone dislocation, and is thus to be arranged : כי ברב חלמות ודברים הרבה והבלים : for in many dreams and many words there are also vanities, *i.e.* illusions by which one deceives himself and others. Thus also Bullock renders, but without assigning a reason for it. That dreams are named first, arises from a reference back to ver. 2, according to which they are the images of what a man is externally and mentally busied and engaged with. But the principal stress lies on ודברים הרבה, to which also the too rash, inconsiderate vows belong. The pred. והבלים, however, connects itself with " vanity of vanities," which is Koheleth's final judgment regarding all that is earthly. The כי following connects itself with the thought lying in 6*a*, that much talk, like being much given to dreams, ought to be avoided: it ought not to be ; much rather (*imo*, Symm. ἀλλά) fear God, Him before whom one should say nothing, but that which contains in it the whole heart.

CONTINUATION OF THE CATALOGUE OF VANITIES.

THE GRADATIONS OF OPPRESSION IN DESPOTIC STATES.—V. 7, 8 [8, 9].

"Fear God," says the proverb (Prov. xxiv. 21), "and the king." The whole Book of Koheleth shows how full its author is of this fundamental thought. Thus the transition to the theme now following was at least inwardly mediated. The state-government, however, although one should be subject to it for conscience' sake, corresponds very little to his idea : the ascending scale of the powers is an ascending scale of violence and oppression.

Ver. 7 [8]. "If thou seest the oppression of the poor and the robbery of right and of justice in the state, marvel not at the matter: for one higher watches over him who is high; and others are high above both." Like *rash, mishpat vatsĕdĕq* are also the gen. of the obj.; "robbery of the right and of justice" is an expression not found elsewhere, but not on that account, as Grätz supposes, impossible: *mishpat* is right, rectitude, and conformity to law; and *tsĕdĕq*, judicial administration, or also social deportment according to these norms; גֵּזֶל, a wicked, shameless depriving of a just claim, and withholding of the showing of right which is due. If one gets a sight of such things as these in a *mᵉdinah, i.e.* in a territorial district under a common government, he ought not to wonder at the matter. תָּמַהּ means to be startled, astonished, and, in the sense of "to wonder," is the word commonly used in modern Heb. But חֵפֶץ has here the colourless general signification of *res*, according to which the Syr. translates it (*vid.* under iii. 1); every attempt in passages such as this to retain the unweakened primary meaning of the word runs out into groundless and fruitless subtlety. Cf. *Berachoth* 5*a*, אדם ... חפץ לח, "a man who buys a thing from another." On the other hand, there is doubt about the meaning of the clause assigning the reason. It seems to be intended, that over him who is high, who oppresses those under him, there stands one who is higher, who in turn oppresses him, and thereby becomes the executor of punishment upon him; and that these, the high and the higher, have over them a Most High, viz. God, who will bring them to an account (Knobel, Ew., Elst., Vaih., Hengst., Zöckl.). None of the old translators and expositors rises, it is true, to the knowledge that גְּבֹהִים may be *pl. majestatis*,[1] but the first גָּבֹהַּ the Targ. renders by אֵל אַדִּיר. This was natural to the Jewish *usus loq.*, for נבוה in the post-bibl. Heb. is a favourite name for God, *e.g. Beza* 20*b, Jebamoth* 87*a, Kamma* 13*a*: "from the table of God" (משלחן נבוה), *i.e.* the altar (cf. Heb. xiii. 10; 1 Cor. x. 21).[2] The interpretation of נב', however, as the *pl. majest.*, has in the Book of Koheleth itself a support in בּוֹרְאֶיךָ, xii. 1; and the thought in which 7*b* climactically terminates accords essentially with iii. 17. This explanation, however, of 7*b* does not stand the test. For if an unrighteous

---

[1] That is surprising, since the Talm. interpretation, *Menachoth* 110*a*, even brings it about that 'לב, v. 10, is to be understood of God.

[2] חלק נבוה is also a common Rabbin. name for the tithes and offerings (cf. *e.g.* Nachmani under Gen. xiv. 20). Along with חלק הגבוה, the sacrifices are also called (in Hurwitz' work on the Heb. rites, known by the abbreviated title לה"שׁ) המורם לגבוה; *vid.* 85*b* of the ed. 1764, and 23*b* of the Amsterdam ed. 1707 of the abridgment.

administration of justice, if violence is in vogue instead of right, that is an actual proof that over him who is high no human higher one watches who may put a check upon him, and to whom he feels that he is responsible. And that above them both one who is Most High stands, who will punish injustice and avenge it, is a consolatory argument against vexation, but is no explanatory reason of the phenomenon, such as we expect after the *noli mirari*; for אל־תתמה does not signify "be not offended" (John xvi. 1), or, "think it not strange" (1 Pet. iv. 12), which would be otherwise expressed (cf. under Ps. xxxvii. 1), but μὴ θαυμάσῃς (LXX.). Also the contrast, ver. 8, warrants the conclusion that in ver. 7 the author seeks to explain the want of legal order from the constitution of a despotic state as distinguished from patriarchal government. For this reason שֹׁמֵר will not be meant of over-watching, which has its aim in the execution of legal justice and official duty, but of egoistic watching,—not, however, as Hitzig understands it: "they mutually protect each other's advantage; one crow does not peck out the eyes of another,"—but, on the contrary, in the sense of hostile watching, as at 1 Sam. xix. 11, 2 Sam. xi. 16, as B. Bardach understands it: "he watches for the time when he may gain the advantage over him who is high, who is yet lower than himself, and may strengthen and enrich himself with his flesh or his goods." Over the one who is high, who oppresses the poor and is a robber in respect of right and justice, there stands a higher, who on his part watches how he can plunder him to his own aggrandisement; and over both there are again other high ones, who in their own interest oppress these, as these do such as are under them. This was the state of matters in the Persian Empire in the time of the author. The satrap stood at the head of state officers. In many cases he fleeced the province to fatten himself. But over the satrap stood inspectors, who often enough built up their own fortunes by fatal denunciations; and over all stood the king, or rather the court, with its rivalry of intrigues among courtiers and royal women. The cruel death-punishments to which disagreeable officials were subjected were fearful. There was a gradation of bad government and arbitrary domination from high to low and from low to high, and no word is more fitting for this state of things in Persia than שמר; for watching, artfully lurking as spies for an opportunity to accomplish the downfall of each other, was prevalent in the Persian Empire, especially when falling into decay.

Ver. 8 [9]. The author, on the other hand, now praises the patriarchal form of government based on agriculture, whose king takes pride, not in bloody conquests and tyrannical caprice, but in the peaceful promotion of the welfare of his people : " But the advantage of a country consists always in a king given to the arable land." What impossibilities have been found here, even by the most recent expositors ! Ewald, Heiligst., Elster, Zöckl. translate : *rex agro factus = terrae praefectus ;* but, in the language of this book, not עבד but עשׂה מלך is the expression used for " to make a king." Gesen., Win., de Wette, Knobel, Vaih. translate : *rex qui colitur a terra (civibus).* But could a country, in the sense of its population in subjection to the king, be more inappropriately designated than by שָׂדֶה ? Besides, עבד certainly gains the meaning of *colere* where God is the object ; but with a human ruler as the object it means *servire* and nothing more, and נֶעֱבָּד [1] can mean nothing else than "*dienstbar gemacht*" [made subject to], not " honoured." Along with this signification, related denom. to עָבַד, נעבד, referred from its primary signification to שָׂדֶה, the open fields (from שָׂדָה, to go out in length and breadth), may also, after the phrase עבד האדמה, signify cultivated, wrought, tilled ; and while the phrase " made subject to " must be certainly held as possible (Rashi, Aben Ezra, and others assume it without hesitation), but is without example, the *Niph.* occurs, *e.g.* at Ezek. xxxvi. 9, in the latter signification, of the mountains of Israel : " ye shall be tilled." Under 8*a*, Hitzig, and with him Stuart and Zöckler, makes the misleading remark that the *Chethîb* is בְּכָל־הִיא, and that it is = בְּכָל־זאת, according to which the explanation is then given : the protection and security which an earthly ruler secures is, notwithstanding this, not to be disparaged. But היא is *Chethîb*, for which the *Kerî* substitutes הוא ; בְּבָל is *Chethîb* without *Kerî ;* and that בְּכֹל is thus a modification of the text, and that, too, an objectionable one, since בכל־היא, in the sense of " in all this," is unheard of. The *Kerî* seeks, without any necessity, to make the pred. and subj. like one another in gender ; without necessity, for היא may also be neut. : the advantage of a land is this, viz. what follows. And how בְּבֹל is to be understood is seen from Ezra x. 17, where it is to be explained : And they prepared [2] the sum of the men, *i.e.* the list of the men, of such as had married strange wives ; cf. 1 Chron. vii. 5. Accordingly בכל here means, as the author generally uses הכל mostly in the impersonal sense of *omnia : in omnibus,* in all things = by all means ; or : *in universum,*

---

[1] Thus pointed rightly in J., with *Sheva* quiesc. and *Dagesh* in *Beth ; vid.* Kimchi in *Michlol* 63*a*, and under עבד.

[2] That בְּ כלה may mean "to be ready with anything," Keil erroneously points to Gen. xliv. 12 ; and Philippi, *St. Const.* p. 49, thinks that *văkol ănāshim* can be taken together in the sense of *vakol haanashim.*

in general. Were the words accentuated מֶלֶךְ לְשָׂדֶה נֶעֱבָד, the adject. connection of לְשׂ' נע' would thereby be shown ; according to which the LXX. and Theod. translate τοῦ ἀγροῦ εἰργασμένου ; Symm., with the Syr., τῇ χώρᾳ εἰργασμένῃ : "a king for the cultivated land," *i.e.* one who regards this as a chief object. Luzz. thus indeed accentuates ; but the best established accentuation is מֶלֶךְ לְשָׂדֶה נֶעֱבָד. This separation of נעבד from לְשׂ' can only be intended to denote that נעבד is to be referred not to it, but to מֶלֶךְ, according to which the Targ. paraphrases. The meaning remains the same : a king subject (who has become a *servus*) to the cultivated land, *rex agro addictus*, as Dathe, Rosenm., and others translate, is a still more distinct expression of that which "a king for the well-cultivated field" would denote : an agriculture-king,—one who is addicted, not to wars, lawsuits, and sovereign stubbornness in his opinions, but who delights in the peaceful advancement of the prosperity of his country, and especially takes a lively interest in husbandry and the cultivation of the land. The order of the words in 8*b* is like that at ix. 2 ; cf. Isa. viii. 22, xxii. 2. The author thus praises, in contrast to a despotic state, a patriarchal kingdom based on agriculture.

THE UNCERTAINTY OF RICHES, AND THE CHEERFUL ENJOYMENT OF LIFE WHICH ALONE IS PRAISEWORTHY.—V. 9 [10]–VI. 6.

If we fix our attention on the word תְּבוּאָה, 9*a*, which properly denotes that which comes into the barn from without (*e.g.* Prov. xiv. 4), ver. 9 seems to continue the praise of husbandry, as Rashi, Aben Ezra, Luzzatto, Bardach, and others have already concluded. But the thought that one cannot eat money is certainly not that which is intended in 9*a ;* and in 9*b* the thought would be awkwardly and insufficiently expressed, that it is vain to love riches, and not, on the contrary, the fruit of agriculture. Therefore we are decidedly of opinion that here (cf. above, p. 182), with ver. 9, the foregoing series of proverbs does not come to a close, but makes a new departure.

Ver. 9 [10]. "He who loveth silver is not satisfied with silver ; and he whose love cleaveth to abundance, hath nothing of it : also this is vain." The transition in this series of proverbs is not unmediated ; for the injustice which, according to ver. 7, prevails in the state as it now is becomes subservient to covetousness, in the very nature of which there lies insatiableness : *semper avarus eget, hunc nulla pecunia replet.* That the author speaks of the "*sacra fames argenti*" (not *auri*) arises from this, that not זהב, but כסף, is the specific word for coin.[1] Mendelssohn-Friedländer also explains : "He who loveth silver is not satisfied with silver," *i.e.* it does not make him full ; that might perhaps be linguistically possible (cf. *e.g.* Prov. xii. 11), although the author would in that case probably have written the words מִן־הַכֶּסֶף, after vi. 3 ; but "to be not full of money" is, after i. 8, and especially iv. 8, Hab. ii. 5, cf. Prov. xxvii. 20 = never to have enough of money, but always to desire more.

That which follows, 9 *aβ*, is, according to Hitz., a question : And who hath joy in abundance, which bringeth nothing in ? But such questions, with the answer to be supplied, are not in Koheleth's style ; and what would then be understood by capital without interest ? Others, as Zöckler, supply יִשְׂבַּע : and he that loveth abundance of possessions (is) not (full) of income ; but that which is gained by these hard ellipses is only a tautology. With right, the Targ., Syr., Jerome, the Venet., and Luther take *lo t*'*vuah* as the answer or conclusion : and who clings to abundance of possessions with his love ?—he has no fruit thereof ; or, with a weakening of the interrog. pronoun into the relative (as at i. 9 ; cf. under Ps. xxxiv. 13) : he who . . . clings has nothing of it. *Hamon* signifies a tumult, a noisy multitude, particularly of earthly goods, as at Ps. xxxvii. 16 ; 1 Chron. xxix. 16 ; Isa. lx. 5. The connection of אהב with בּ, occurring only here, follows the analogy of חָפֵץ בּ and the like. The conclusion is synon. with *l*'*vilti ho'il ; e.g.* Isa. xliv. 10 ; Jer. vii. 8. All the Codd. read לֹא ; לוֹ in this sense would be meaningless.[2] The designation of advantage by *t*'*vuah* may be occasioned by the foregoing agricultural proverb. In the *t*'*vuah*, the farmer enjoys the fruit of his labour ; but he who hangs his heart on the continual tumult, noise, pomp of more numerous and greater possessions if possible, to him all real profit — *i.e.* all pleasant, peaceful enjoyment—is lost. With the increase of the possessions there is an increase also of unrest, and the possessor has in reality nothing but the sight of them.

Ver. 10 [11]. "When property and goods increase, they become many who consume them ; and what advantage hath the owner thereof but the sight of [them with] his eyes ? " The verb רָבָה signifies to increase, and רָבַב, to be many ; but also (which Böttch. denies) inchoatively : to become many, Gen. vi. 1 ; rightly, the LXX., ἐπληθύν-

---

[1] A Jewish fancy supposes that כסף is chosen because it consists of letters rising in value (20, 60, 80) ; while, on the contrary, זהב consists of letters decreasing in value (7, 5, 2).

[2] In *Maccoth* 10*a*, לוֹ is read three times in succession ; the Midrash *Wajikra*, c. 22, reads לֹא, and thus it is always found without *Keri* and without variation.

θησαν. The author has not a miser in view, who shuts up his money in chests, and only feeds himself in looking at it with closed doors; but a covetous man, of the sort spoken of in Ps. xlix. 12, Isa. v. 8. If the *hattovah*, the possession of such an one, increases, in like manner the number of people whom he must maintain increases also, and thus the number of those who eat of it along with him, and at the same time also his disquiet and care, increase; and what advantage, what useful result (*vid.* regarding *Kishron*, above, p. 193, and under ii. 21) has the owner of these good things from them but the beholding of them (*rᵉith; Kerî, rᵉuth;* cf. the reverse case, Ps. cxxvi. 4)?—the possession does not in itself bring happiness, for it is never great enough to satisfy him, but is yet great enough to fill him with great care as to whether he may be able to support the demands of so great a household: the fortune which it brings to him consists finally only in this, that he can look on all he has accumulated with proud self-complacency.

Ver. 11 [12]. He can also eat that which is good, and can eat much; but he does not on that account sleep more quietly than the labourer who lives from hand to mouth: "Sweet is the sleep of the labourer, whether he eats little or much; but, on the contrary, the abundance of the rich does not permit him to sleep." The LXX., instead of "labourer," uses the word "slave" (δούλου), as if the original were הָעֶבֶד. But, as a rule, sound sleep is the reward of earnest labour; and since there are idle servants as well as active masters, there is no privilege to servants. The Venet. renders rightly by "of the husbandman" (ἐργάτου), the עֹבֵד הָאֲדָמָה; the "labourer" in general is called עָמֵל, iv. 8 and Judg. v. 26, post-bibl. פֹּעֵל. The labourer enjoys sweet, *i.e.* refreshing, sound sleep, whether his fare be abundant or scanty—the labour rewards him by sweet sleep, notwithstanding his poverty; while, on the contrary, the sleep of the rich is hindered and disturbed by his abundance, not: by his satiety, viz. repletion, as Jerome remarks: *incocto cibo in stomachi angustiis aestuante;* for the labourer also, if he eats much, eats his fill; and why should sufficiency have a different result in the one from what it has in the other? As שָׂבָע means satiety, not over-satiety; so, on the other hand, it means, objectively, sufficient and plentifully existing fulness to meet the wants of man, Prov. iii. 10, and the word is meant thus objectively here: the fulness of possession which the rich has at his disposal does not permit him to sleep, for all kinds of projects, cares, anxieties regarding it rise within him, which follow him into the night, and do not suffer his mind to be at rest, which is a condition of sleep. The expression הַשָּׂ' לֶע' is the *circum-*

locutio of the genit. relation, like 'לב . . . 'חל, Ruth ii. 3 ; 'נע . . . 'אם
(LXX. *Ἀμνὼν τῆς Ἀχινόαμ*), 2 Sam. iii. 2. Heiligstedt remarks
that it stands for שְׁבַע העשׁיר; but the nouns שֶׁבַע, רֶעַב, צָמָא form no
const., for which reason the *circumloc.* was necessary; שְׂבַע is the
constr. of שָׂבֵעַ. Falsely, Ginsburg: "*aber der Ueberfluss den Reichen
—er lässt ihn nicht schlafen*" [but superabundance the rich—it
doth not suffer him to sleep]; but this construction is neither in
accordance with the genius of the German nor of the Heb. language.
Only the subject is resumed in אֵינֶנּוּ (as in i. 7); the construction of
הִנִּיחַ is as at 1 Chron. xvi. 21 ; cf. Ps. cv. 14. Of the two *Hiphil*
forms, the properly Heb. הֵנִיחַ and the Aramaizing הִנִּיחַ, the latter is
used in the weakened meaning of *ἐᾶν*, *sinere*.

After showing that riches bring to their possessor no real gaïn,
but, instead of that, dispeace, care, and unrest, the author records as a
great evil the loss, sometimes suddenly, of wealth carefully amassed.

Vers. 12, 13 [13, 14]. "There is a sore evil which I have seen
under the sun, riches kept by their possessor to his hurt: the same
riches perish by an evil event; and he hath begotten a son, thus this
one hath nothing in his hand." There is a gradation of evils. רָעָה
חוֹלָה (cf. חֳלִי רָע, vi. 2) is not an ordinary, but a morbid evil, *i.e.* a
deep hurtful evil ; as a wound, not a common one, but one particularly severe and scarcely curable, is called נַחְלָה, *e.g.* Nah. iii. 19.
רָא 'השׁ ... is, as at x. 5, an ellipt. relat. clause ; cf. on the other hand,
vi. 1; the author elsewhere uses the scheme of the relat. clause without
relat. pron. (*vid.* under i. 13, iii. 16); the old language would use רְאִיתִיהָ,
instead of רָאִיתִי, with the reflex. pron. The great evil consists in
this, that riches are not seldom kept by their owner to his own
hurt. Certainly שָׁמוּר לְ can also mean that which is kept for another,
1 Sam. ix. 24; but how involved and constrained is Ginsburg's
explanation: "hoarded up (by the rich man) for their (future)
owner," viz. the heir to whom he intends to leave them ! That
לְ can be used with the passive as a designation of the subj., *vid.*
Ewald, § 295*c ;* certainly it corresponds as little as מִן with the
Greek *ὑπό*, but in Greek we say also *πλοῦτος φυλαχθεὶς τῷ κεκ-
τημένῳ*, *vid.* Rost's *Syntax*, § 112. 4. The suff. of *lᵉraʼatho* refers to
bᵉʻalav, the plur. form of which can so far remain out of view, that we
even say *adonim qosheh*, Isa. xix. 4, etc. "To his hurt," *i.e.* at the
last suddenly to lose that which has been carefully guarded. The
narrative explanation of this, "to his hurt," begins with *vav explic.*
Regarding *ʼinyan raʼ*, *vid.* above, p. 194. It is a *casus adversus* that
is meant, such a stroke upon stroke as destroyed Job's possessions.
The perf. וְהוֹ supposes the case that the man thus suddenly made

poor is the father of a son ; the clause is logically related to that
which follows as hypothet. antecedent, after the scheme, Gen.
xxxiii. 13*b*. The loss of riches would of itself make one who is
alone unhappy, for the misfortune to be poor is less than the misfortunes to be rich and then to become poor ; but still more unfortunate is the father who thought that by well-guarded wealth he
had secured the future of his son, and who now leaves him with
an empty hand.

What now follows is true of this rich man, but is generalized
into a reference to every rich man, and then is recorded as a second
great evil. As a man comes naked into the world, so also he
departs from it again without being able to take with him any of
the earthly wealth he has acquired.

Ver. 14 [15]. " As he came forth from his mother's womb, naked
shall he again depart as he came, and not the least will he carry
away for his labour, which he could take with him in his hand." In
13*a* the author has the case of Job in his mind ; this verse before
us is a reminiscence from Job i. 21, with the setting aside of the
difficult word שָׁמָּה found there, which Sirach xl. 1 exhibits. With
" naked " begins emphatically the main subject ; כַּאֲשֶׁר בָּא = כְּשֶׁבָּא is
the intensifying resumption of the comparison ; the contrast of לָכֶת,
going away, *excedere vitâ*, is בּוֹא of the entrance on life, coming into
the world. מְאוּמָה (according to the root meaning and use, corresponding to the French *point*, Olsh. § 205*a*) emphatically precedes
the negation, as at Judg. xiv. 6 (cf. the emphasis reached in a different way, Ps. xlix. 18). נָשָׂא signifies here, as at ver. 18, Ps.
xxiv. 5, to take hence, to take forth, to carry away. The בּ of בַּעֲ' is
not partitive (Aben Ezra compares Lev. viii. 32), according to which
Jerome and Luther translate *de labore suo*, but is the *Beth pretii*, as
e.g. at 1 Kings xvi. 34, as the Chald. understands it ; Nolde cites
for this *Beth pretii* passages such as ii. 24, but incorrectly. Regarding the subjunctive שֶׁיֹּלֵךְ, *quod auferat*, vid. above, No. 2, p. 197.
We might also with the LXX. and Symm. punctuate שֶׁיֵּלֵךְ : which
might accompany him in his hand, but which could by no means
denote, as Hitzig thinks : (for his trouble), which goes through his
hand. Such an expression is not used ; and Hitzig's supposition,
that here the rich man who has lost his wealth is the subject, does
not approve itself.

Ver. 15 [16]. A transition is now made to rich men as such, and
the registering formula which should go before ver. 14 here follows :
" And this also is a sore evil : altogether exactly as he came, thus
shall he depart : and what gain hath he that laboureth in the wind ?"

Regarding הִי, *vid.* above, No. 4, p. 198 ; and regarding שׁ 'בְּלַ־עֲ,[1] *vid.*
p. 196.   The writing of these first two as one word [*vid.* note below]
accords with Ibn-Giat's view, accidentally quoted by Kimchi, that the
word is compounded of כ of comparison, and the frequently occurring
לְעֻמַּת always retaining its לְ, and ought properly to be pointed 'בְּלַ
(cf. 'מִלְ, 1 Kings vii. 20).   עֻמָּה signifies combination, society, one
thing along with or parallel to another ; and thus לעמת bears no כ,
since it is itself a word of comparison, כָּל־עֻמַּת " altogether parallel,"
" altogether the same."   The question : what kind of advantage (*vid.*
i. 3) is to him (has he) of this that . . ., carries its answer in itself.
Labouring for the wind or in the wind, his labour is (רַעְיוֹן) רְעוּת
רוּחַ, and thus fruitless.   And, moreover, how miserable an existence
is this life of labour leading to nothing !

Ver. 16 [17].   " Also all his life long he eateth in darkness and
grieveth himself much, and oh for his sorrow and hatred ! "   We
might place ver. 16 under the regimen of the שׁ of 'שִׁיע of ver. 15*b;*
but the Heb. style prefers the self-dependent form of sentences to
that which is governed.   The expression 16*a* has something strange.
This strangeness disappears if, with Ewald and Heiligst., after the
LXX. and Jerome, for יֹאכֵל we read וְאֵבֶל : καὶ ἐν πένθει ; Böttch.
prefers וָאֹפֶל, " and in darkness."   Or also, if we read יֵלֵךְ for יאכל ; thus
the Midrash here, and several codd. by Kennicott ; but the Targ., Syr.,
and Masora read יאכל.   Hitzig gets rid of that which is strange in
this passage by taking כָּל־יָמָיו as accus. of the obj., not of the time :
all his days, his whole life he consumes in darkness ; but in Heb. as
in Lat. we say : *consumere dies vitae,* Job xxi. 13, xxxvi. 11, but not
comedere ; and why should the expression, " to eat in darkness," not
be a figurative expression for a faithless, gloomy life, as elsewhere
" to sit in darkness " (Mic. vii. 8), and " to walk in darkness " ?   It
is meant that all his life long he ate לֶחֶם אוֹנִים, the bread of sorrow,
or לֶחֶם לַחַץ, prison fare ; he did not allow himself pleasant table
comforts in a room comfortably or splendidly lighted, for it is unnecessary to understand חֹשֶׁךְ subjectively and figuratively (Hitz.,
Zöck.).

In 16*b* the traditional punctuation is וְכָעַס.[2]   The *perf.* ruled by the
preceding *fut.* is syntactically correct, and the verb כָּעַס is common with

---

[1] In H. written as one word : בַּלְעֲמַת.   Parchon (*Lex.* under עמת) had this form
before him.   In his *Lex.* Kimchi bears evidence in favour of the correct writing as
two words.

[2] Thus in correct texts, in H. with the note : מלרע 'ב, viz. here and at Ps.
cxii. 10, only there ע has, according to tradition, the *Kametz.*   Cf. *Mas. fin.* 52*b*,
and Baer's Ed. of Psalter, under Ps. cxii. 10.

the author, vii. 9. Hitzig regards the text as corrupt, and reads בְּחָלִיו
and פַּעַם, and explains: and (he consumes or swallows) much grief in
his, etc.; the phrase, " to eat sorrow," may be allowed (cf. Prov.
xxvi. 6, cf. Job xv. 16); but יאכל, as the representative of two so
bold and essentially different metaphors, would be in point of style
in bad taste. If the text is corrupt, it may be more easily rectified
by reading וְכַעַס הרבה וְחָלִי לוֹ וק': and grief in abundance, and sorrow
has he, and wrath. We merely suggest this. Ewald, Burger, and
Böttch. read only וּכַעַס הרבה וְחָלִי ; but לוֹ is not to be dispensed with,
and can easily be reduced to a mere vav. Elster retains וּכַעַס, and
reads, like Hitzig, בחליו: he grieves himself much in his sorrow and
wrath; but in that case the word וקצפו was to be expected; also in this
way the ideas do not psychologically accord with each other. However the text is taken, we must interpret וחליו וקצף as an exclamation,
like הֵף', Isa. xxix. 16; תֵּף', Jer. xlix. 16; Ewald, § 328a, as we
have done above. That וְח' of itself is a subst. clause = וחלי לו is
untenable; the rendering of the noun as forming a clause, spoken of
under ii. 21, is of a different character.[1] He who by his labour
and care aims at becoming rich, will not only lay upon himself unnecessary privations, but also have many sorrows; for many of his
plans fail, and the greater success of others awakens his envy, and
neither he himself nor others satisfy him; he is morbidly disposed,
and as he is diseased in mind, so also in body, and his constantly
increasing dissatisfaction becomes at last קצף, he grumbles at himself, at God, and all the world. From observing such persons, Paul
says of them (1 Tim. vi. 6 f.): "They have pierced themselves
through (transfoderunt) with many sorrows."

In view of these great evils, with which the possession of riches
also is connected: of their deceitful instability, and their merely
belonging to this present life, Koheleth returns to his ceterum censeo.
Ver. 17 [18]. "Behold then what I have seen as good, what as
beautiful (is this): that one eat and drink and see good in all his
labour with which he wearieth himself, under the sun, throughout
the number of the days of his life which God hath given him; for
that is his portion." Toward this seeing, i.e. knowing from his own
experience, his effort went forth, according to ii. 3; and what he here,
vers. 17, 18, expresses as his resultat, he has already acknowledged
at ii. 24 and iii. 12 f. With "behold" he here returns to it; for
he says, that from the observations just spoken of, as from others, no

---

[1] Rashi regards וחליו as a form like חָיְתוֹ. This o everywhere appears only
in a gen. connection.

other *resultat* befell him. Instead of ר' טוֹבָה (here and at vi. 6), he as often uses the words רָאה טוֹב, iii. 13, ii. 24, or בְּטוֹב, ii. 1. In רָא', the seeing is meant of that of mental apperception ; in 'לרָא, of immediate perception, experience. Our translation above does not correspond with the accentuation of the verse, which belongs to the class of dis-proportionably long verses without *Athnach ;* cf. Gen. xxi. 9 ; Num. ix. 1 ; Isa. xxxvi. 1 ; Jer. xiii. 13, li. 37 ; Ezek. xlii. 10 ; Amos v. 1 ; 1 Chron. xxvi. 26, xxviii. 1; 2 Chron. xxiii. 1. The sentence

אָנִי ... הנה (with pausal *āni* with *Rebîa*) constitutes the beginning of the verse, in the form, as it were, of a superscription ; and then its second part, the main proposition, is divided by the disjunctives following each other : *Telisha Gedhola, Geresh, Legarmeh, Rebîa, Tebir, Tifcha, Silluk* (cf. Jer. viii. 1, where *Pazer* instead of *Telisha Gedhola ;* but as for the rest, the sequence of the accents is the same). Among the moderns, Hengst. holds to the accents, for he translates in strict accord-ance therewith, as Tremellius does : " Behold what I have seen : that it is fine and good (Trem. *bonum pulchrum*) to eat . . ." The *asher* in the phrase, *tov asher-yapheh,* then connects it together : good which is at the same time beautiful ; Grätz sees here the Greek καλὸν κἀγαθόν. But the only passage to which, since Kimchi, reference is made for this use of *asher,* viz. Hos. xii. 8, does not prove it ; for we are not, with Drusius, to translate there by : *iniquitas quae sit peccatum,* but by *quae poenam mereat.* The accentuation here is not correct. The second *asher* is without doubt the resumption of the first ; and the translation—as already Dachselt in his *Biblia Accentuata* indicated : *ecce itaque quod vidi bonum, quod pulchrum (hoc est ut quis edat)*— presents the true relation of the component parts of the sentence. The suffix of עֲמָלוֹ refers to the general subj. contained in the inf. ; cf. viii. 15. The period of time denoted by מִסְפַּר is as at ii. 3, vi. 12. Also we read 'חֶל . . . כִּי־, iii. 22, in the same connection.

Ver. 18 [19]. This verse, expressing the same, is constructed anakolouthistically, altogether like iii. 13 : " Also for every man to whom God hath given riches and treasures, and hath given him power to eat thereof, and to take his portion, and to rejoice in his labour ; just this is a gift of God." The anakolouthon can be rendered [into English] here as little as it can at iii. 13 ; for if we allow the phrase, " also every man," the " also " remains fixed to the nearest conception, while in the Heb. it governs the whole long sentence, and, at the nearest, belongs to זֶה. Cheerful enjoyment is in this life that which is most advisable ; but also it is not made possible in itself by the possession of earthly treasures,—it is yet a special gift of God added thereto. *N°chasim,* besides here, occurs also in Josh. xxii. 8 ; 2 Chron. i. 11 f. ; and in the Chald. of the Book of Ezra, vi. 8, vii. 26. Also *hishlit,* to empower, to make possible, is Aram., Dan. ii. 38, 48, as well as Heb., Ps. cxix. 133 ; the prevalence of the verbal stem שׁלט is characteristic of the Book of Koheleth. *Helqo,* "his portion," is just the cheerful enjoyment as that which man has here below of life, if he has any of it at all.

Ver. 19 [20]. Over this enjoyment he forgets the frailty and the darkened side of this life. It proves itself to be a gift of God, a gift from above : " For he doth not (then) think much of the days of his life ; because God answereth the joy of his heart." Such an one, permitted by God to enjoy this happiness of life, is thereby prevented from tormenting himself by reflections regarding its transitoriness. Incorrectly, Hengst. : Remembrance and enjoyment of this life do not indeed last long, according to Ewald, who now, however, rightly explains : He will not, by constant reflection on the brevity of his life, too much embitter this enjoyment ; because God, indeed, grants to him true heart-joy as the fairest gift. The meaning of 19b is also, in general, hit upon. The LXX. translates : " because God occupies him with the joy of his heart ; " but for that we ought to have had the word מַעֲנֵהוּ ; Jerome helps it, for he reads בשמהה instead of בשמחת : *eo quod Deus occupet deliciis cor ejus.* But also, in this form, this explanation of מענה is untenable ; for עָנָה בְ, the causat. of which would be מענה, signifies, in the style of Koheleth, not in general to busy oneself with something, but to weary oneself with something ; hence עה בש׳ cannot mean : to be occupied with joy, and thereby to be drawn away from some other thing. And since the explanation : " he makes him sing," needs no argument to dispose of it, מענה thus remains only as the *Hiph.* of ענה, to meet, to respond to, grant a request. Accordingly, Hitz., like Aben Ezra and Kimchi, comparing Hos. ii. 23 f. : God makes to answer, *i.e.* so works that all things which have in or of themselves that which can make him glad, must respond to his wish. But the omission of the obj.—of which Hitz. remarks, that because indefinite it is left indefinite—is insufferably hard, and the explanation thus ambiguous. Most interpreters translate : for God answers (Gesen. *Heb. Wört. B.,* incorrectly: answered) him with joy of his heart, *i.e.* grants this to him in the way of answer. Ewald compares Ps. lxv. 6 ; but that affords no voucher for the expression : to answer one with something = to grant it to him ; for ענה is there connected with a double accus., and בְּצֶדֶק is the adv. statement of the way and manner. But above all, against this interpretation is the fact of the want of the personal obj.

The author behoved to have written מענהו or מענה אֹתוֹ. We take the
Hiph. as in the sense of the *Kal*, but give it its nearest signification :
to answer, and explain, as in a similar manner Seb. Schmid, Rambam,
and others have already done : God answers to the joy of his heart,
i.e. He assents to it, or (using an expression which is an exact equivalent), He corresponds to it. This makes the joy a heart-joy, *i.e.* a
joy which a man feels not merely externally, but in the deepest
recess of his heart, for the joy penetrates his heart and satisfies it
(Song iii. 11 ; Isa. xxx. 29 ; Jer. xv. 16). A similar expression,
elsewhere not found, we had at ver. 9 in אֹהֵב בְּ. Why should not
עָנָה בְּ (הֵעֵנָה) be possible with עָנָהוּ, just as ἀμείβεσθαι πρός τι is with
ἀμείβεσθαί τινα ? For the rest, בְּשׂ׳ לֵב is not needed as obj.; we can
take it also as an expression of the state or condition : God gives
answer in the heart-joy of such an one. In עָנָה, to answer, to hear
the answer, is thought of as granting a request ; here, as giving assent
to. Job xxxv. 9 affords a twofold suitable example, that the *Hiph.*
can have an enlarged *Kal* signification.

After the author has taken the opportunity of once more expressing his *ultimatum*, he continues to register the sad evils that
cling to wealth.

vi. 1, 2. "There is an evil which I have seen under the sun,
and in great weight it lies upon man : a man to whom God giveth
riches, and treasures, and honour, and he wanteth nothing for his
soul of all that he may wish, but God giveth him not power to
have enjoyment of it, for a strange man hath the enjoyment : that
is vanity and an evil disease." The author presents the result of personal observation ; but inasmuch as he relates it in the second tense,
he generalizes the matter, and places it scenically before the eyes of
the reader. A similar introduction with יֵשׁ, but without the unnecessary *asher*, is found at v. 12, x. 5. Regarding רַבָּה, *vid.* under
viii. 6 ; עַל does not denote the subj., as at ii. 17 : it appears great
to a man, but it has its nearest lying local meaning ; it is a great
(ii. 21) evil, pressing in its greatness heavily upon man. The evil
is not the man himself, but the condition in which he is placed,
as when, *e.g.*, the kingdom of heaven is compared to a merchant
(Matt. xiii. 45 f.),—not the merchant in himself, but his conduct and
life is a figure of the kingdom of heaven.

Ver. 2. To עֹשֶׁר וּנְכָ׳, as at 2 Chron. i. 11, וְכָ׳ [and honour] is
added as a third thing. What follows we do not translate : " and
there is nothing wanting . . . ;" for that אֵינֶנּוּ with the pleonastic suff.
may mean : " there is not," is not to be proved from Gen. xxxix. 9,
thus : and he spares not for his soul (LXX. καὶ οὐκ κ.τ.λ.) what he

always desires. חָסֵר is adj. in the sense of wanting, lacking, as
at 1 Sam. xxi. 16 ; 1 Kings xi. 22 ; Prov. xii. 9. לְנַפְשׁוֹ, " for his
soul," *i.e.* his person, is = the synon. לְעַצְמוֹ found in the later usage
of the language ; מִן (different from the *min*, iv. 8) is, as at Gen. vi. 2,
partitive. The נָכְרִי, to whom this considerable estate, satisfying
every wish, finally comes, is certainly not the legal heir (for that he
enters into possession, in spite of the uncertainty of his moral character, ii. 19, would be in itself nothing less than a misfortune, yet
perfectly in order, v. 13 [14]), but some stranger without any just
claim, not directly a foreigner (Heiligst.), but, as Burger explains :
talis qui proprie nullum habet jus in bona ejus cui נכרי *dicitur* (cf.
נָכְרִיָּה of the unmarried wife in the Book of Proverbs).

That wealth without enjoyment is nothing but vanity and an
evil disease, the author now shows by introducing another historical
figure, and thereby showing that life without enjoyment is worse than
never to have come into existence at all :

Ver. 3. " If a man begat an hundred, and lived many years, and
the amount of the days of his years was great, and his soul satisfied
not itself in good, and also he had no grave, then I say : Better than
he is the untimely birth." The accentuation of 3*a* is like that of 2*a*.
The disjunctives follow the *Athnach*, as at 2 Kings xxiii. 13, only
that there *Telisha Gedhola* stands for *Pazer*. Hitzig finds difficulty
with the clause וגם־ . . . לו, and regards it as a marginal gloss to 5*a*,
taken up into the text at a wrong place. But just the unexpected
form and the accidental nature, more than the inward necessity of
this feature in the figure, leads us to conclude that the author here
connects together historical facts, as conjecturally noted above at
pp. 214, 215, into one fanciful picture. מֵאָה is obviously to be supplemented by בנים (ובנות) ; the Targ. and Midrash make this man to
be Cain, Ahab, Haman, and show at least in this that they extend
down into the time of the Persian kingdom a spark of historical
intelligence. שְׁנֵי רַב׳ interchanges with שְׁנֵי הַר׳, xi. 8, as at Neh.
xi. 30. In order to designate the long life emphatically, the author
expresses the years particularly in days : " and if it is much which
(Heiligst.: *multum est quod*) the days of his years amount to ;" cf.
וַיִּהְיוּ יְמֵי in Gen. v. With *v'naphsho* there follows the reverse side of
this long life with many children : (1) his soul satisfies not itself,
i.e. has no self-satisfying enjoyment of the good (*min*, as at Ps.
civ. 13, etc.), *i.e.* of all the good things which he possesses,—in a
word, he is not happy in his life ; and (2) an honourable burial is
not granted to him, but קְב׳ חַם׳, Jer. xxii. 19, which is the contrary
of a burial such as becomes a man (the body of Artaxerxes Ochus

was thrown to the cats); whereupon Elster rightly remarks that in an honourable burial and an honourable remembrance, good fortune, albeit shaded with sadness, might be seen. But when now, to one so rich in children and so long-lived, neither enjoyment of his good fortune nor even this shaded glory of an honourable burial is allowed, the author cannot otherwise judge than that the untimely birth is better than he. In this section regarding the uncertainty of riches, we have already, v. 14, fallen on a reminiscence from the Book of Job; it is so much the more probable that here also Job iii. 16 has an influence on the formation of the thought. נֵפֶל is the foetus which comes lifeless from the mother's womb.

Vers. 4, 5. The comparison of an untimely birth with such a man is in favour of the former: "For it cometh in nothingness and departeth in darkness; and with darkness its name is covered. Moreover, it hath not seen the sun, and hath not known: it is better with it than with that other." It has entered into existence, בַּהֶבֶל, because it was a lifeless existence into which it entered when its independent life should have begun; and בַּחֹשֶׁךְ, it departeth, for it is carried away in all quietness, without noise or ceremony, and "with darkness" its name is covered, for it receives no name and remains a nameless existence, and is forgotten as if it had never been. Not having entered into a living existence, it is also (gam) thus happy to have neither seen the sun nor known and named it, and thus it is spared the sight and the knowledge of all the vanities and evils, the deceptions and sorrows, that are under the sun. When we compare its fate with the long joyless life of that man, the conclusion is apparent: נַחַת . . . מִ, plus quietis est huic quam illi, which, with the generalization of the idea of rest (Job iii. 13) in a wider sense (vid. above, p. 194), is = melius est huic quam illi (זֶה . . . זֶה, as at iii. 19). The generalization of the idea proceeds yet further in the Mishn. נוח לו, e.g.: "It is better (נוח לו לאדם) for a man that he throw himself into a lime-kiln than that (ואל), etc." From this usage Symm. renders מִ . . . נַחַת as obj. to לֹא יָדַע, and translates: οὐδὲ ἐπειράθη διαφορᾶς ἑτέρου πράγματος πρὸς ἕτερον; and Jerome: neque cognovit distantiam boni et mali,—a rendering which is to be rejected, because thus the point of the comparison in which it terminates is broken, for 5b draws the facit. It is true that this contains a thought to which it is not easy to reconcile oneself. For supposing that life were not in itself, as over against non-existence, a good, there is yet scarcely any life that is absolutely joyless; and a man who has become the father of an hundred children, has, as it appears, sought the enjoyment of life principally in sexual love, and then also has found it richly. But also, if we consider his life less as relating to sense : his children, though not all, yet partly, will have been a joy to him; and has a family life, so lengthened and rich in blessings, only thorns, and no roses at all ? And, moreover, how can anything be said of the rest of an untimely birth, which has been without motion and without life, as of a rest excelling the termination of the life of him who has lived long, since rest without a subjective reflection, a rest not felt, certainly does not fall under the point of view of more or less, good or evil ? The saying of the author on no side bears the probe of exact thinking. In the main he designs to say : Better, certainly, is no life than a joyless life, and, moreover, one ending dishonourably. And this is only a speciality of the general clause, iv. 2 f., that death is better than life, and not being born is better than both. The author misunderstands the fact that the earthly life has its chief end beyond itself; and his false eudaemonism, failing to penetrate to the inward fountain of true happiness, which is independent of the outward lot, makes exaggerated and ungrateful demands on the earthly life.

Ver. 6. A life extending to more than even a thousand years without enjoyment appears to him worthless : "And if he has lived twice a thousand years long, and not seen good—Do not all go hence to one place ?" This long period of life, as well as the shortest, sinks into the night of Sheol, and has advantage over the shortest if it wants the 'ט רָאוֹת, i.e. the enjoyment of that which can make man happy. That would be correct if "good" were understood inwardly, ethically, spiritually; but although, according to Koheleth's view, the fear of God presides over the enjoyment of life, regulating and hallowing it, yet it remains unknown to him that life deepened into fellowship with God is in itself a most real and blessed, and thus the highest good. Regarding אִלּוּ (here, as at Esth. vii. 4, with perf. foll.: etsi vixisset, tamen interrogarem: nonne, etc.), vid. above, p. 191 ; it occurs also in the oldest liturgical Tefilla, as well as in the prayer Nishmath (vid. Baer's Siddur, Abodath Jisrael, p. 207). 'פ . . . אֶלֶף, a thousand years twice, and thus an Adam's life once and yet again. Otherwise Aben Ezra : 1000 years multiplied by itself, thus a million, like עֶשְׂרִים פְּעָמִים, 20 × 20 = 400 ; cf. Targ. Isa. xxx. 26, which translates שִׁבְעָתַיִם by 343 = 7 × 7 × 7. Perhaps that is right; for why was not the expression אֲלָפִים שָׁנָה directly used ? The "one place" is, as at iii. 20, the grave and Hades, into which all the living fall. A life extending even to a million of years is worthless, for it terminates at last in nothing. Life has only as much value as it yields of enjoyment.

OBTAINING BETTER THAN DESIRING.—VI. 7-9.

All labour aims at enjoyment, and present actual enjoyment is always better than that which is sought for in the future.

Ver. 7. "All the labour of man is for his mouth, and yet his soul has never enough;" or, properly, it is not filled, so that it desires nothing further and nothing more; נִמְלָא used as appropriately of the soul as of the ear, i. 8; for that the mouth and the soul are here placed opposite to one another as "organs of the purely sensual and therefore transitory enjoyment, and of the deeper and more spiritual and therefore more lasting kind of joys" (Zöck.), is an assertion which brings out of the text what it wishes to be in it,—נֶפֶשׁ and פֶה stand here so little in contrast, that, as at Prov. xvi. 26, Isa. v. 14, xxix. 8, instead of the soul the stomach could also be named; for it is the soul longing, and that after the means from without of self-preservation, that is here meant; נפש יפה, "beautiful soul," *Chullin* iv. 7, is an appetite which is not fastidious, but is contented. וְגַם, καὶ ὅμως, ὅμως δέ, as at iii. 13; Ps. cxxix. 2. All labour, the author means to say, is in the service of the impulse after self-preservation; and yet, although it concentrates all its efforts after this end, it does not bring full satisfaction to the longing soul. This is grounded in the fact that, however in other respects most unlike, men are the same in their unsatisfied longing.

Ver. 8. "For what hath the wise more than the fool; what the poor who knoweth to walk before the living?" The old translators present nothing for the interpretation, but defend the traditional text; for Jerome, like the Syr., which translates freely, follows the Midrash (fixed in the Targ.), which understands החיים, contrary to the spirit of the book, of the blessed future. The question would be easier if we could, with Bernst. and Ginsburg, introduce a comparat. *min* before יוֹדֵעַ; we would then require to understand by him who knows to walk before the living, some one who acts a part in public life; but how strange a designation of distinguished persons would that be! Thus, as the text stands, יודע is attrib. to לֶעָנִי, what preference hath the poor, such an one, viz., as understands (*vid.* regarding יודע instead of היודע, under Ps. cxliii. 10); not: who is intelligent (Aben Ezra); יודע is not, as at ix. 11, an idea contained in itself, but by the foll. 'הַח ... לַהֲ (cf. iv. 13, 17; and the inf. form, Ex. iii. 19; Num. xxii. 13; Job xxxiv. 23) obtains the supplement and colouring required: the sequence of the accents (*Zakeph, Tifcha, Silluk,* as *e.g.* at Gen. vii. 4) is not against this. How the LXX. understood its πορευθῆναι κατέναντι τῆς ζωῆς, and the Venet. its ἀπιέναι ἀντικρὺ τῆς ζωῆς, is not clear; scarcely as Grätz, with Mendelss.: who, to go against (נגד, as at iv. 12) life, to fight against it, has to exercise himself in self-denial and patience; for "to fight with life" is an expression of modern coinage. הַחַי signifies here, without doubt, not life, but the living. But we explain now, not as Ewald, who separates יודע from the foll. inf. לחלך: What profit has then the wise man, the intelligent, patient man, above the fool, that he walks before the living?—by which is meant (but how does this interrog. form agree thereto?), that the wise, patient man has thereby an advantage which makes life endurable by him, in this, that he does not suffer destroying eagerness of desire so to rule over him, but is satisfied to live in quietness. Also this meaning of a quiet life does not lie in the words הלך ... הח׳. "To know to walk before the living" is, as is now generally acknowledged = to understand the right rule of life (Elst.), to possess the *savoir vivre* (Heiligst.), to be experienced in the right art of living. The question accordingly is: What advantage has the wise above the fool; and what the poor, who, although poor, yet knows how to maintain his social position? The matter treated of is the insatiable nature of sensual desire. The wise seeks to control his desire; and he who is more closely designated poor, knows how to conceal it; for he lays upon himself restraints, that he may be able to appear and make something of himself. But desire is present in both; and they have in this nothing above the fool, who follows the bent of his desire and lives for the day. He is a fool because he acts as one not free, and without consideration; but, in itself, it is and remains true, that enjoyment and satisfaction stand higher than striving and longing for a thing.

Ver. 9. "Better is the sight of the eyes than the wandering of the soul: also this is vain and windy effort." We see from the inf. הֲלָךְ־נֶ֫ interchanging with מֵ֫ that the latter is not meant of the object (xi. 9), but of the action, viz. the "rejoicing in that which one has" (Targ.); but this does not signify *grassatio*,—i.e. *impetus animae appetentis*, ὁρμὴ τῆς ψυχῆς (cf. *Marcus Aurelius*, iii. 16), which Knobel, Heiligst., and Ginsburg compare (for הלך means *grassari* only with certain subjects, as fire, contagion, and the like; and in certain forms, as יַהֲלֹךְ for יֵלֵךְ, to which הֲלָךְ = לֶכֶת does not belong),—but *erratio*, a going out in extent, roving to a distance (cf. הֵלֶךְ, wanderer), ῥεμβασμὸς ἐπιθυμίας, Wisd. iv. 12.—Going is the contrast of rest; the soul which does not become full or satisfied goes out, and seeks and reaches not its aim. This insatiableness, characteristic of the soul, this endless unrest, belongs also to the miseries of this present life; for to have and to enjoy is better than this constant

Hungern und Lungern [hungering and longing]. More must not be put into 9*a* than already lies in it, as Elster does: "the only enduring enjoyment of life consists in the quiet contemplation of that which, as pleasant and beautiful, it affords, without this mental joy mingling with the desire for the possession of sensual enjoyment." The conception of "the sight of the eyes" is certainly very beautifully idealized, but in opposition to the text. If 9*a* must be a moral proverb, then Luther's rendering is the best: "It is better to enjoy the present good, than to think about other good."

THE WEAKNESS AND SHORT-SIGHTEDNESS OF MAN OVER AGAINST HIS DESTINY.——VI. 10–12.

The future, toward which the soul stretches itself out to find what may satisfy it, is not man's: a power against which man is helpless fashions it.

Ver. 10. "That which hath been, its name hath long ago been named; and it is determined what a man shall be: and he cannot dispute with Him who is stronger than he." According to the usage of the tense, it would be more correct to translate: That which (at any time) has made its appearance, the name of which was long ago named, *i.e.* of which the *What?* and the *How?* were long ago determined, and, so to speak, formulated. This 'שֶׁ ... כְּבָר does not stand parallel to כבר הָיָה, i. 10; for the expression here does not refer to the sphere of that which is done, but of the predetermination. Accordingly, וְנוֹ' ... אָדָם is also to be understood. Against the accents, inconsistently periodizing and losing sight of the comprehensiveness of אשר ... אדם, Hitzig renders: "and it is known that, if one is a man, he cannot contend," etc., which is impossible for this reason, that הוא אדם cannot be a conditional clause enclosed within the sentence אשר ... יוכל. Obviously וְנוֹדַע, which in the sense of *constat* would be a useless waste of words, stands parallel to נקרא שְׁמוֹ, and signifies known, viz. previously known, as passive of ידע, in the sense of Zech. xiv. 7; cf. Ps. cxxxix. 1 f. Bullock rightly compares Acts xv. 18. After ידע, *asher*, like *ki*, which is more common, may signify "that," viii. 12, Ezek. xx. 26; but neither "that he is a man" (Knobel, Vaih., Luzz., Hengst., Ginsb.), nor "that he is the man" (Ewald, Elst., Zöckler), affords a consistent meaning. As *mah* after *yada'* means *quid*, so *asher* after it may mean *quod* = that which (cf. Dan. viii. 19, although it does not at all stand in need of proof); and *id quod homo est* (we cannot render הוא without the expression of a definite conception of time) is intended to mean that the whole being of a man, whether of this one or that one, at all times and on all sides, is previously known; cf. to this pregnant substantival sentence, xii. 13. Against this formation of his nature and of his fate by a higher hand, man cannot utter a word. The thought in 10*b* is the same as that at Isa. xlv. 9; Rom. ix. 20 f. The *Chethîb* שֶׁהַתִּקִיף [1] is not inadmissible, for the stronger than man is מִנֶּה ... מְרִי. Also הִתְקִיף might in any case be read: with one who overcomes him, has and manifests the ascendency over him. There is indeed no *Hiph.* הִתְ found in the language of the Bible (Herzf. and Fürst compare הִגְ, Ps. xii. 5); but in the Targ., אַתְקֵף is common; and in the school-language of the Talm., הִתְ is used of the raising of weighty objections, *e.g. Kamma* 71*a*. The verb, however, especially in the perf., is in the passage before us less appropriate. In לֹא־יוּכַל lie together the ideas of physical (cf. Gen. xliii. 32; Deut. xii. 17, xvi. 5, etc.) and moral inability.

Ver. 11. "For there are many words which increase vanity: What cometh forth therefrom for man?" The dispute (objection), רִין, takes place in words; דְּבָרִים here will thus not mean "things" (Hengst., Ginsb., Zöckl., Bullock, etc.), but "words." As that wrestling or contending against God's decision and providence is vain and worthless, nothing else remains for man but to be submissive, and to acknowledge his limitation by the fear of God; thus there are also many words which only increase yet more the multitude of vanities already existing in this world, for, because they are resultless, they bring no advantage for man. Rightly, Elster finds herein a hint pointing to the influence of the learning of the Jewish schools already existing in Koheleth's time. We know from Josephus that the problem of human freedom and of God's absoluteness was a point of controversy between opposing parties: the Sadducees so emphasized human freedom, that they not only excluded (*Antt.* xiii. 5. 9; *Bell.* ii. 8. 14) all divine predetermination, but also co-operation; the Pharisees, on the contrary, supposed an interconnection between divine predetermination (εἱμαρμένη) and human freedom (*Antt.* xiii. 5. 9, xviii. 1. 3; *Bell.* ii. 8. 14). The Talm. affords us a glance at this controversy; but the statement in the Talm. (in *Berachoth* 33*a*, and elsewhere), which conditions all by the power of God manifesting itself in history, but defends the freedom of the religious-moral self-determination of man, may be regarded as a Pharisaic maxim. In Rom. ix., Paul places himself on

---

[1] With *He* unpointed, because it is omitted in the *Keri*, as in like manner in כְּשֶׁה, x. 3, שֶׁה, Lam. v. 18. In the bibl. Rabb., the ה is noted as superfluous.

this side; and the author of the Book of Koheleth would subscribe this passage as his testimony, for the "fear God" is the "*kern und stern*" [kernel and star] of his pessimistic book.

Ver. 12. Man ought to fear God, and also, without dispute and murmuring, submit to His sway: "For who knoweth what is good for man in life during the number of the days of his vain life, and which he spendeth like a shadow? No one can certainly show a man what shall be after him under the sun." We translate אֲשֶׁר only by "*ja*" ("certainly"), because in Germ. no interrogative can follow "*dieweil*" ("because"). The clause with *asher* (as at iv. 9, viii. 11, x. 15; cf. Song, under v. 2), according to its meaning not different from *ki*, is related in the way of proof to that beginning with *ki*. Man is placed in our presence. To be able to say to him what is good for him,—*i.e.* what position he must take in life, what direction he must give to his activity, what decision he must adopt in difficult and important cases,—we ought not only to be able to penetrate his future, but, generally, the future; but, as *Tropfen* [drops] in the stream of history, we are poor *Tröpfe* [simpletons], who are hedged up within the present. Regarding the accus. of duration, מִסְפַּר וגו׳, pointing to the brevity of human life, *vid.* at ii. 3. With הֶבְלוֹ, the attribute of breath-like transitiveness is assigned to life (as at vii. 15, ix. 9) (as already in the name given to Abel, the second son of Adam), which is continued by וְיַעֲשֵׂ בְּ׳ with the force of a relative clause, which is frequently the case after preceding part. attrib., *e.g.* Isa. v. 23. We translate: which he spendeth like the (a) shadow [in the nom.] (after viii. 13; Job xiv. 2); not: like a shadow [in the accus.]; for although the days of life are also likened to a shadow, Ps. cxliv. 4, etc., yet this use of עשׂה does not accord therewith, which, without being a Graecism (Zirkel, Grätz), harmonises with the Greek phrase, ποιεῖν χρόνον, Acts xv. 33; cf. Prov. xiii. 23, LXX. (also with the Lat. *facere dies* of Cicero, etc.). Thus also in the Syr. and Palest.-Aram. *lacad* is used of time, in the sense of *transigere*. *Aharav* does not mean: after his present condition (Zöckl.); but, as at iii. 22, vii. 14: after he has passed away from this scene. Luzz. explains it correctly: Whether his children will remain in life? Whether the wealth he has wearied himself in acquiring will remain and be useful to them? But these are only illustrations. The author means to say, that a man can say, neither to himself nor to another, what in definite cases is the real advantage; because, in order to say this, he must be able to look far into the future beyond the limits of the individual life of man, which is only a small member of a great whole.

SECOND CONCLUDING SECTION.

PROVERBS OF BETTER THINGS, THINGS SUPPOSED TO BE BETTER, GOOD
THINGS, GOOD AND BAD DAYS.—VII. 1–14.

We find ourselves here in the middle of the book. Of its 220 verses, vi. 10 is that which stands in the middle, and with vii. 1 begins the third of the four *Sedarim* [1] into which the Masora divides the book. The series of proverbs here first following, vii. 1–10, has, as we remarked above, p. 189, the word *tov* as their common catchword, and *mah-tov*, vi. 12, as the hook on which they hang. But at least the first three proverbs do not stand merely in this external connection with the preceding; they continue the lowly and dark estimate of the earthly life contained in vi. 3 ff.

The first proverb is a synthetic distich. The thought aimed at is that of the second half of the distich.

vii. 1. " Better is a name than precious ointment; and better is the day of death than the day when one is born." Like רָאָה and יָרֵא, so שֵׁם and שֶׁמֶן stand to each other in the relation of a paronomasia (*vid.* Song under i. 3). Luther translates : " *Ein gut Gerücht ist besser denn gute Salbe* " [" a good odour (= reputation) is better than good ointment]. If we substitute the expression *denn Wolgeruch* [than sweet scent], that would be the best possible rendering of the paronomasia. In the arrangement שֵׁם טוֹב . . . טוֹב, *tov* would be adj. to *shem* (a good reputation goes beyond sweet scent) ; but *tov* standing first in the sentence is pred., and *shem* thus in itself alone, as in the cogn. prov., Prov. xxii. 1, signifies a good, well-sounding, honourable, if not venerable name ; cf. *anshē hashshem,* Gen. vi. 4 ; *v'li-shem,* nameless, Job xxx. 8. The author gives the dark reverse to this bright side of the distich : the day of death better than the day in which one (a man), or he (the man), is born ; cf. for this reference of the pronoun, iv. 12, v. 17. It is the same lamentation as at iv. 2 f., which sounds less strange from the mouth of a Greek than from that of an Israelite ; a Thracian tribe, the Trausi, actually celebrated their birthdays as days of sadness, and the day of death as a day of rejoicing (*vid.* Bähr's Germ. translat. of *Herodotus,* v. 4).—Among the people of the Old Covenant this was not possible ; also a saying such as 1*b* is not in the spirit of the O. T. revelation of religion ;

---

[1] Of three books the Masora gives only the number of verses : Ruth, 85 verses; Shir (the Song), 117 verses; and Kinoth (Lamentations), 154 ; but no sections (*Sedarim*).

yet it is significant that it was possible [1] within it, without apostasy from it; within the N. T. revelation of religion, except in such references as Matt. xxvi. 24, it is absolutely impossible without apostasy from it, or without rejection of its fundamental meaning. Ver. 2. Still more in the spirit of the N. T. (cf. *e.g.* Luke vi. 25) are these words of this singular book which stands on the border of both Testaments: "It is better to go into a house of mourning than to go into a house of carousal (drinking): for that is the end of every man; and the living layeth it to heart." A house is meant in which there is sorrow on account of a death; the lamentation continued for seven days (Sirach xxii. 10), and extended sometimes, as in the case of the death of Aaron and Moses, to thirty days; the later practice distinguished the lamentations (אֲנִינוּת) for the dead till the time of burial, and the mournings for the dead (אֲבֵלוּת), which were divided into seven and twenty-three days of greater and lesser mourning; on the return from carrying away the corpse, there was a *Trostmahl* (a comforting repast), to which, according as it appears to an ancient custom, those who were to be partakers of it contributed (Jer. xvi. 7; Hos. ix. 4; Job iv. 17, *funde vinum tuum et panem tuum super sepulchra justorum*).[2] This feast of sorrow the above proverb leaves out of view, although also in reference to it the contrast between the "house of carousal" and "house of mourning" remains, that in the latter the drinking must be in moderation, and not to drunkenness.[3] The going into the house of mourning is certainly thought of as a visit for the purpose of showing sympathy and of imparting consolation during the first seven days of mourning (John xi. 31).[4] Thus to go into the house of sorrow, and to show one's sympathy with the mourners there, is better than to go into a house of drinking, where all is festivity and merriment; viz. because the former (that he is mourned over as dead) is the end of every man, and the survivor takes it to heart, viz. this, that he too must die. הוּא follows attractionally the gender of סוֹף (cf. Job xxxi. 11, *Kerî*). What is said at iii. 13 regarding כָּל־הָ' is appropriate to the passage before us. יִחַי is rightly vocalised; regarding the

---

[1] "The reflections of the Preacher," says Hitzig (*Süd. deut. ev. protest. Woch. Blatt*, 1864, No. 2), "present the picture of a time in which men, participating in the recollection of a mighty religious past, and become sceptical by reason of the sadness of the present time, grasping here and there in uncertainty, were in danger of abandoning that stedfastness of faith which was the first mark of the religion of the prophets."

[2] Cf. Hamb. *Real Encyc. für Bibel u. Talmud* (1870), article "Trauer."

[3] Maimuni's *Hilchoth Ebel*, iv. 7, xiii. 8.

[4] *Ibid.* xiii. 2.

form הָתַי, vid. Baer in the critical remarks of our ed. of Isaiah under iii. 22. The phrase נָתַן אֶל־לֵב here and at ix. 1 is synon. with שִׂים עַל־לֵב, שִׂים אֶל־לֵב (e.g. Isa. lvii. 1) and שִׂים בְּלֵב. How this saying agrees with Koheleth's ultimatum : There is nothing better than to eat and drink, etc. (ii. 24, etc.), the Talmudists have been utterly perplexed to discover ; Manasse ben-Israel in his Conciliador (1632) loses himself in much useless discussion.[1] The solution of the difficulty is easy. The ultimatum does not relate to an unconditional enjoyment of life, but to an enjoyment conditioned by the fear of God. When man looks death in the face, the two things occur to him, that he should make use of his brief life, but make use of it in view of the end, thus in a manner for which he is responsible before God.

Vers. 3, 4. The joy of life must thus be not riot and tumult, but a joy tempered with seriousness : " Better is sorrow than laughter : for with a sad countenance it is well with the heart. The heart of the wise is in the house of mourning, and the heart of fools in the house of mirth." Grief and sorrow, כַּעַס, whether for ourselves or occasioned by others, is better, viz. morally better, than extravagant merriment ; the heart is with רֹעַ פָּ' (inf. as רַע, Jer. vii. 6 ; cf. פְּנֵ' רְ', Gen. xl. 7 ; Neh. ii. 2), a sorrowful countenance, better than with laughter, which only masks the feeling of disquiet peculiar to man, Prov. xiv. 13. Elsewhere יִיטַב לֵב = " the heart is (may be) of good cheer," e.g. Ruth iii. 7, Judg. xix. 6 ; here also joyful experience is meant, but well becoming man as a religious moral being. With a sad countenance it may be far better as regards the heart than with a merry countenance in boisterous company. Luther, in the main correct, after Jerome, who on his part follows Symmachus : " The heart is made better by sorrow." The well-being is here meant as the reflex of a moral : bene se habere.

Sorrow penetrates the heart, draws the thought upwards, purifies, transforms. Therefore is the heart of the wise in the house of sorrow ; and, on the other hand, the heart of fools is in the house of joy, i.e. the impulse of their heart goes thither, there they feel themselves at home ; a house of joy is one where there are continual feasts, or where there is at the time a revelling in joy. That ver. 4 is divided not by Athnach, but by Zakef, has its reason in this, that of the words following אֵבֶל, none consists of three syllables ; cf. on the contrary, vii. 7, חֶכְם. From this point forward the internal relation of the contents is broken up, according to which this series of

---

[1] Vid. the English translation by Lindo (London 1842), vol. ii. pp. 306–309.

sayings as a concluding section hangs together with that containing
the observations going before in ch. vi.

Vers. 5, 6. A fourth proverb of that which is better (מן טוב)
presents, like the third, the fools and the wise over against each
other: " Better to hear the reproof of a wise man, than that one
should hear the song of fools. For like the crackling of *Nesseln*
(nettles) under the *Kessel* (kettle), so the laughter of the fool : also this
is vain." As at Prov. xiii. 1, xvii. 10, גְּעָרָה is the earnest and severe
words of the wise, which impressively reprove, emphatically warn,
and salutarily alarm. שִׁיר in itself means only song, to the exclusion,
however, of the plaintive song ; the song of fools is, if not immoral,
yet morally and spiritually hollow, senseless, and unbridled madness.
Instead of מִשְׁמֹעַ, the words שׁ' מֵאִ' are used, for the twofold act of
hearing is divided between different subjects. A fire of thorn-twigs
flickers up quickly and crackles merrily, but also exhausts itself
quickly (Ps. cxviii. 12), without sufficiently boiling the flesh in the
pot ; whilst a log of wood, without making any noise, accomplishes
this quietly and surely. We agree with Knobel and Vaihinger in
copying the paronomasia [*Nessel—Kessel*]. When, on the other hand,
Zöckler remarks that a fire of nettles could scarcely crackle, we advise
our friend to try it for once in the end of summer with a bundle of
stalks of tall dry nettles. They yield a clear blaze, a quickly expiring
fire, to which here, as he well remarks, the empty laughter of foolish
men is compared, who are devoid of all earnestness, and of all deep
moral principles of life. This laughter is vain, like that crackling.
There is a hiatus between vers. 6 and 7. For how ver. 7 can be
related to ver. 6 as furnishing evidence, no interpreter has as yet
been able to say. Hitzig regards 6*a* as assigning a reason for ver. 5,
but 6*b* as a reply (as ver. 7 containing its motive shows) to the
assertion of ver. 5,—a piece of ingenious thinking which no one
imitates. Elster translates : " Yet injustice befools a wise man,"
being prudently silent about this " yet." Zöckler finds, as Knobel
and Ewald do, the mediating thought in this, that the vanity of
fools infects and also easily befools the wise. But the subject
spoken of is not the folly of fools in general, but of their singing and
laughter, to which ver. 7 has not the most remote reference.
Otherwise Hengst. : " In ver. 7, the reason is given why the happiness of fools is so brief ; first, the *mens sana* is lost, and then
destruction follows." But in that case the words ought to have
been יהולל כסיל ; the remark, that חכם here denotes one who ought to
be and might be such, is a pure *volte*. Ginsburg thinks that the
two verses are co-ordinated by כי ; that ver. 6 gives the reason for

5b, and ver. 7 that for 5a, since here, by way of example, one accessible to bribery is introduced, who would act prudently in letting
himself therefore be directed by a wise man. But if he had wished
to be thus understood, the author would have used another word
instead of חכם, 7a, and not designated both him who reproves and
him who merits reproof by the one word—the former directly, the
latter at least indirectly. We do not further continue the account
of the many vain attempts that have been made to bring ver. 7 into
connection with vers. 6 and 5. Our opinion is, that ver. 7 is the
second half of a tetrastich, the first half of which is lost, which
began, as is to be supposed, with tov. The first half was almost the
same as Ps. xxxvii. 16, or better still, as Prov. xvi. 8, and the whole
proverb stood thus:

טוֹב מְעַט בִּצְדָקָה

מֵרֹב תְּבוּאוֹת בְּלֹא מִשְׁפָּט:

[and then follows ver. 7 as it lies before us in the text, formed into
a distich, the first line of which terminates with חָכָם]. We go still
further, and suppose that after the first half of the tetrastich was
lost, that expression, " also this is vain," added to ver. 6 by the
punctuation, was inserted for the purpose of forming a connection
for כי עשק: Also this is vain, that, etc. (כי, like asher, viii. 14).

Ver. 7. Without further trying to explain the mystery of the כי,
we translate this verse : " . . . For oppression maketh wise men
mad, and corruption destroyeth the understanding." From the lost
first half of the verse, it appears that the subject here treated of is
the duties of a judge, including those of a ruler into whose hands his
subjects, with their property and life, are given. The second half
is like an echo of Ex. xxiii. 8, Deut. xvi. 19. That which שֹׁחַד
there means is here, as at Prov. xv. 27, denoted by מַתָּנָה; and
עֹשֶׁק is accordingly oppression as it is exercised by one who constrains
others who need legal aid and help generally to purchase it by means
of presents. Such oppression for the sake of gain, even if it does
not proceed to the perversion of justice, but only aims at courting
and paying for favour, makes a wise man mad (הוֹלֵל, as at Job
xii. 17 ; Isa. xliv. 25), i.e. it hurries him forth, since the greed
of gold increases more and more, to the most blinding immorality
and regardlessness ; and such presents for the purpose of swaying
the judgment, and of bribery, destroys the heart, i.e. the understanding (cf. Hos. iv. 11, Bereschith rabba, ch. lvi.), for they obscure
the judgment, blunt the conscience, and make a man the slave of
his passion. The conjecture הָעֹשֶׁר (riches) instead of the word

הָעֹשֶׁק (Burger, as earlier Ewald) is accordingly unnecessary; it has the parallelism against it, and thus generally used gives an untrue thought. The word הולל does not mean "gives lustre" (Desvoeux), or "makes shine forth = makes manifest" (Tyler); thus also nothing is gained for a better connection of ver. 7 with ver. 6. The Venet. excellently: ἐκστήσει. Aben Ezra supposes that מתנה is here = דְּבַר מת׳; Mendelssohn repeats it, although otherwise the consciousness of the syntactical rule, Gesen. § 147a, does not fail him.

Vers. 8, 9. There now follows a fourth, or, taking into account the mutilated one, a fifth proverb of that which is better: "Better the end of a thing than its beginning; better one who forbears than one who is haughty. Hasten thyself not in thy spirit to become angry: for anger lieth down in the bosom of fools." The clause 8a is first thus to be objectively understood as it stands. It is not without limitation true; for of a matter in itself evil, the very contrary is true, Prov. v. 4, xxiii. 32. But if a thing is not in itself evil, the end of its progress, the reaching to its goal, the completion of its destination, is always better than its beginning, which leaves it uncertain whether it will lead to a prosperous issue. An example of this is Solon's saying to Croesus, that only he is to be pronounced happy whose good fortune it is to end his life well in the possession of his wealth (*Herod.* i. 32).

The proverb 8b will stand in some kind of connection with 8a, since what it says is further continued in ver. 9. In itself, the frequently long and tedious development between the beginning and the end of a thing requires expectant patience. But if it is in the interest of a man to see the matter brought to an issue, an אֶרֶךְ אַפּ׳ will, notwithstanding, wait with self-control in all quietness for the end; while it lies in the nature of the גְּבַהּ רוּחַ, the haughty, to fret at the delay, and to seek to reach the end by violent means; for the haughty man thinks that everything must at once be subservient to his wish, and he measures what others should do by his own measureless self-complacency. We may with Hitzig translate: "Better is patience (אֹרֶךְ = אֶרֶךְ) than haughtiness" (גְּבַהּ, inf., as שְׁפַל, xii. 4; Prov. xvi. 19). But there exists no reason for this; גְּבַהּ is not to be held, as at Prov. xvi. 5, and elsewhere generally, as the connecting form of גָּבֹהַּ, and so אֶרֶךְ for that of אָרֹךְ; it amounts to the same thing whether the two properties (characters) or the persons possessing them are compared.

Ver. 9. In this verse the author warns against this pride which, when everything does not go according to its mind, falls into passionate excitement, and thoughtlessly judges, or with a violent rude hand anticipates the end. אַל־תְּב׳ : do not overturn, hasten not, rush not, as at v. 1. Why the word בְּרוּחֵךְ, and not בנפשך or בלבך, is used, *vid. Psychol.* pp. 197–199 : passionate excitements overcome a man according to the biblical representation of his spirit, Prov. xxv. 28, and in the proving of the spirit that which is in the heart comes forth in the mood and disposition, Prov. xv. 13. כְּעוֹס is an infin., like יָשׁוֹן, v. 11. The warning has its reason in this, that anger or (כעס, taken more potentially than actually) fretfulness rests in the bosom of fools, *i.e.* is cherished and nourished, and thus is at home, and, as it were (thought of personally, as if it were a wicked demon), feels itself at home (יָנוּחַ, as at Prov. xiv. 33). The haughty impetuous person, and one speaking out rashly, thus acts like a fool. In fact, it is folly to let oneself be impelled by contradictions to anger, which disturbs the brightness of the soul, takes away the considerateness of judgment, and undermines the health, instead of maintaining oneself with equanimity, *i.e.* without stormy excitement, and losing the equilibrium of the soul under every opposition to our wish.

From this point the proverb loses the form " better than," but *tov* still remains the catchword of the following proverbs. The proverb here first following is so far cogn., as it is directed against a particular kind of *ka'as* (anger), viz. discontentment with the present.

Ver. 10. " Say not : How comes it that the former times were better than these now ? for thou dost not, from wisdom, ask after this." Cf. these lines from Horace (*Poet.* 173, 4) :

> " *Difficilis, querulus, laudator temporis acti*
> *Se puero, censor castigatorque minorum.*"

Such an one finds the earlier days—not only the old days described in history (Deut. iv. 32), but also those he lived in before the present time (cf. *e.g.* 2 Chron. ix. 29)—thus by contrast so much better than the present ones, that in astonishment he asks : " What is it = how comes it that ? " etc. The author designates this question as one not proceeding from wisdom : מֶה, like the Mishnic מִתּוֹךְ חכמה, and שָׁאַל עַל, as at Neh. i. 2 ; *'al-zeh* refers to that question, after the ground of the contrast, which is at the same time an exclamation of wonder. The כי, assigning a reason for the dissuasion, does not mean that the cause of the difference between the present and the good old times is easily seen ; but it denotes that the supposition of this difference is foolish, because in truth every age has its bright and its dark sides ; and this division of light and shadow between the past and the present betrays a want of understanding of the signs of the times and of the ways of God. This proverb does not furnish any point of support for the determination of the date of the authorship of the Book of Koheleth (*vid.* above, p. 213). But if it was composed in the last century of the Persian domination, this dissatisfaction with the present times is explained, over against which Koheleth leads us to consider that it is self-deception and one-sidedness to regard the present as all dark and the past as all bright and rosy.

Vers. 11, 12. Externally connecting itself with "from wisdom," there now follows another proverb, which declares that wisdom along with an inheritance is good, but that wisdom is nevertheless of itself better than money and possessions: "Wisdom is good with family possessions, and an advantage for those who see the sun. For wisdom affordeth a shadow, money affordeth a shadow; yet the advantage of knowledge is this, that wisdom preserveth life to its possessor." Most of the English interpreters, from Desvoeux to Tyler, translate: "Wisdom is as good as an inheritance;" and Bullock, who translates: "with an inheritance," says of this and the other translations: "The difference is not material." But the thought is different, and thus the distinction is not merely a formal one. Zöckl. explains it as undoubted that עִם here, as at ii. 16 (*vid. l.c.*), means *aeque ac;* but (1) that *aeque ac* has occurred to no ancient translator, till the Venet. and Luther, nor to the Syr., which translates: "better is wisdom than weapons (מאנא זינא)," in a singular way making 11a a *duplette* of ix. 18a; (2) instead of "wisdom is as good as wealth," would much rather be said: "wisdom is better than wealth," as *e.g.* Prov. viii. 11; (3) the proverb is formed like *Aboth* ii. 2, "good is study connected with a citizen-like occupation," and similar proverbs; (4) one may indeed say: "the wise man dieth with (together with) the fool" = just as well as the fool; but "good is wisdom with wealth" can neither be equivalent to "as well as wealth," nor: "in comparison with wealth" (Ewald, Elster), but only: "in connection with wealth (possessions);" *aeque ac* may be translated for *una cum* where the subject is common action and suffering, but not in a substantival clause consisting of a subst. as subject and an adj. as pred., having the form of a categorical judgment. נַחֲלָה denotes a possession inherited and hereditary (cf. Prov. xx. 21); and this is evidence in favour of the view that עִם is meant not of comparison, but of connection; the expression would otherwise be עִם־עֹשֶׁר. וְיֹתֵר is now also explained. It is not to be rendered: "and better still" (than wealth), as Herzf., Hitz., and Hengst. render it; but in spite of Hengst., who decides in his own way, "יותר never means advantage, gain," it denotes a prevailing good, *avantage* (*vid.* above, p. 192); and it is explained also why men are here named "those who see the sun"—certainly not merely thus describing them poetically, as in Homer ζώειν is described and coloured by ὁρᾶν φάος ἠελίοιο. To see the sun, is = to have entered upon this earthly life, in which, along with wisdom, also no inheritance is to be despised. For wisdom affords protection as well as money, but the former still more than the latter. So far, the general meaning of ver. 12 is undisputed. But how is 12*a* to be construed? Knobel, Hitz., and others regard בּ as the so-called *beth essentiae*: a shadow (protection) is wisdom, a shadow is money,—very expressive, yet out of harmony, if not with the language of that period, yet with the style of Koheleth; and how useless and misleading would this doubled בּ be here! Hengstenberg translates: in the shadow of wisdom, in the shadow of silver; and Zöckler introduces between the two clauses "it is as." But (1) here the shadow of wisdom, at least according to our understanding of ver. 11, is not likened to the shadow of silver; but in conformity with that עֵם, it must be said that wisdom, and also that money, affords a shadow; (2) but that interpretation goes quite beyond the limits of gnomic brachyology. We explain: for in the shadow (בְּצֵל, like בְּצֵל, Jonah iv. 5) is wisdom, in the shadow, money; by which, without any particularly bold poetic licence, is meant that he who possesses wisdom, he who possesses money, finds himself in a shadow, *i.e.* of pleasant security; to be in the shadow, spoken of wisdom and money, is = to sit in the shadow of the persons who possess both.

Ver. 12*b*. The exposition of this clause is agreed upon. It is to be construed according to the accentuation: and the advantage of knowledge is this, that "wisdom preserveth life to its possessors." The Targ. regards דַּעַת הַחָכְמָה as connected genit.; that might be possible (cf. i. 17, viii. 16), but yet is improbable. Wherever the author uses דַּעַת as subst., it is an independent conception placed beside חכ׳, i. 16, ii. 26, etc. We now translate, not: wisdom gives life (LXX., Jerome, Venet., Luther) to its possessors; for חִיָּה always means only either to revive (thus Hengst., after Ps. cxix. 25; cf. lxxi. 20) or to keep in life; and this latter meaning is more appropriate to this book than the former,—thus (cf. Prov. iii. 18): wisdom preserves in life,—since, after Hitzig, it accomplishes this, not by rash utterances of denunciation,—a thought lying far behind ver. 10, and altogether too mean,—but since it secures it against self-destruction by vice and passions and emotions, *e.g.* anger (ver. 9), which consume life. The shadow in which wisdom (the wise man) sits keeps it fresh and sound,—a result which the shadow in which money (the

capitalist) sits does not afford: it has frequently the directly contrary effect.

Vers. 13, 14. There now follows a proverb of devout submission
to the providence of God, connecting itself with the contents of
ver. 10: "Consider the work of God: for who can make that
straight which He hath made crooked! In the good day be of good
cheer, and in the day of misfortune observe: God hath also made
this equal to that, to the end that man need not experience anything (further) after his death." While רְאֵה, i. 10, vii. 27, 29, is not
different from הַנֵּה, and in ix. 9 has the meaning of "enjoy," here the
meaning of contemplative observation, mental seeing, connects itself
both times with it. כִּי before מִי can as little mean *quod*, as *asher*,
vi. 12, before *mi* can mean *quoniam*. "Consider God's work"
means: recognise in all that is done the government of God, which
has its motive in this, that, as the question leads us to suppose, no
creature is able (cf. vi. 10 and i. 15) to put right God's work in cases
where it seems to contradict that which is right (Job viii. 3, xxxiv.
12), or to make straight that which He has made crooked (Ps. cxlvi. 9).

Ver. 14a a. The call here expressed is parallel to Sir. xiv. 14
(Fritz.): "Withdraw not thyself from a good day, and let not thyself
lose participation in a right enjoyment." The ב of בְּטוֹב is, as little
as that of בְּצֵל, the *beth essentiae*—it is not a designation of quality, but
of condition: in good, *i.e.* cheerful mood. He who is, Jer. xliv. 17,
personally *tov*, cheerful (= *tov lev*), is *b^etov* (cf. Ps. xxv. 13, also Job
xxi. 13). The reverse side of the call, 14aβ, is of course not to be
translated: and suffer or bear the bad day (Ewald, Heiligst.), for in
this sense we use the expression רָאָה רָעָה, Jer. xliv. 17, but not
רָאָה בְרָעָה, which much rather, Obad. 13, means a malicious contemplation of the misfortune of a stranger, although once, Gen. xxi. 16,
ראה בְ also occurs in the sense of a compassionate, sympathizing look,
and, moreover, the parall. shows that ביום רעה is not the obj., but the
adv. designation of time. Also not: look to = be attentive to
(Salomon), or bear it patiently (Burger), for רְאֵה cannot of itself have
that meaning.[1] But: in the day of misfortune observe, *i.e.* perceive
and reflect: God has also made (cf. Job ii. 10) the latter לְעֻמַּת corresponding, parallel, like to (cf. under v. 15) the former.

So much the more difficult is the statement of the object of this
mingling by God of good and evil in the life of man. It is translated: that man may find nothing behind him; this is literal, but
it is meaningless. The meaning, according to most interpreters, is

[1] Similarly also Sohar (Par. מצורע): הוי וגו', *i.e. cave et circumspice*, viz. that
thou mayest not incur the judgment which is pronounced.

this : that man may investigate nothing that lies behind his present time,—thus, that belongs to the future; in other words : that man may never know what is before him. But *aharav* is never (not at vi. 12) = in the future, lying out from the present of a man ; but always = after his present life. Accordingly, Ewald explains, and Heiligst. with him : that he may find nothing which, dying, he could take with him. But this rendering (cf. v. 14) is here unsuitable. Better, Hitzig : because God wills it that man shall be rid of all things after his death, He puts evil into the period of his life, and lets it alternate with good, instead of visiting him therewith after his death. This explanation proceeds from a right interpretation of the words : *idcirco ut* (cf. iii. 18) *non inveniat homo post se quidquam, scil. quod non expertus sit,* but gives a meaning to the expression which the author would reject as unworthy of his conception of God. What is meant is much more this, that God causes man to experience good and evil that he may pass through the whole school of life, and when he departs hence that nothing may be outstanding (in arrears) which he has not experienced.

CONTINUATION OF EXPERIENCES AND THEIR RESULTS.—VII. 15–IX. 12.

The Injuriousness of Excesses, vii. 15–18.

The concluding section, vii. 1–14, is now followed by *I*-sections, *i.e.* advices in the form of actually experienced facts, in which again the *I* of the author comes into the foreground.

Vers. 15–18. The first of these counsels warns against extremes, on the side of good as well as on that of evil : "All have I seen in the days of my vanity : there are righteous men who perish by their righteousness, and there are wicked men who continue long by their wickedness. Be not righteous over-much, and show not thyself wise beyond measure : why wilt thou ruin thyself ? Be not wicked over-much, and be no fool : why wilt thou die before thy time is ? It is good that thou holdest thyself to the one, and also from the other withdrawest not thine hand : for he that feareth God accomplisheth it all." One of the most original English interpreters of the Book of Koheleth, T. Tyler (1874), finds in the thoughts of the book—composed, according to his view, about 200 B.C.—and in their expression, references to the post-Aristotelian philosophy, particularly to the Stoic, variously interwoven with orientalism. But here, in vers. 15–18, we perceive, not so much the principle of the Stoical ethics—τῇ φύσει ὁμολογουμένως ζῆν—as that of the Aristotelian,

according to which virtue consists in the art μέσως ἔχειν, the art of
holding the middle between extremes.[1] Also, we do not find here
a reference to the contrasts between Pharisaism and Sadduceeism
(Zöckl.), viz. those already in growth in the time of the author; for
if it should be also true, as Tyler conjectures, that the Sadducees had
such a predilection for Epicurism,—as, according to Josephus (*Vit.*
c. 2), "the doctrine of the Pharisees is of kin to that of the Stoics,"
—yet צדקה and רִשְׁעָה are not apportioned between these two parties,
especially since the overstraining of conformity to the law by the
Pharisees related not to the moral, but to the ceremonial law. We
derive nothing for the right understanding of the passsge from referring the wisdom of life here recommended to the tendencies of
the time. The author proceeds from observation, over against which
the O. T. saints knew not how to place any satisfying theodicee.
יְמֵי הֶבְלִי (*vid.* vi. 12) he so designates the long, but for the most part
uselessly spent life lying behind him. אֶת־הַכֹּל is not "everything
possible" (Zöckl.), but "all, of all kinds" (Luth.), which is defined
by 15*b* as of two kinds; for 15*a* is the introduction of the following
experience relative to the righteous and the unrighteous, and thus
to the two classes into which all men are divided. We do not
translate: there are the righteous, who by their righteousness, etc.
(Umbr., Hitzig, and others); for if the author should thus commence,
it would appear as if he wished to give unrighteousness the preference to righteousness, which, however, was far from him. To
perish in or by his righteousness, to live long in or by his wickedness (מַאֲרִיךְ, *scil.* יָמִים, viii. 13, as at Prov. xxviii. 2), is = to die in
spite of righteousness, to live in spite of wickedness, as *e.g.* Deut. i. 32:
" in this thing " = in spite of, etc. Righteousness has the promise
of long life as its reward; but if this is the rule, it has yet its exceptions, and the author thence deduces the doctrine that one should
not exaggerate righteousness; for if it occurs that a righteous man,
in spite of his righteousness, perishes, this happens, at earliest, in the
case in which, in the practice of righteousness, he goes beyond the
right measure and limit. The relative conceptions הַרְבֵּה and יוֹתֵר have
here, since they are referred to the idea of the right measure, the
meaning of *nimis.* תִּתְחַכַּם could mean, "to play the wise man;"
but that, whether more or less done, is objectionable. It means, as
at Ex. i. 10, to act wisely (cf. Ps. cv. 25, הִתְ, to act cunningly).
And הִשׁ', which is elsewhere used of being inwardly torpid, *i.e.* being
astonished, *obstupescere*, has here the meaning of placing oneself in a

[1] Cf. Luthardt's *Lectures on the Moral Truths of Christianity*, 2d ed. Edin.,
T. and T. Clark.

benumbed, disordered state, or also, passively, of becoming disconcerted; not of becoming desolate or being deserted (Hitz., Ginsburg, and others), which it could only mean in highly poetic discourse (Isa. liv. 1). The form תִּשּׁוֹמֵם is syncop., like תֵּכ׳, Num. xxi. 27; and the question, with לָמָּה, here and at 17b, is of the same kind as v. 5; Luther, weakening it: "that thou mayest not destroy thyself."

Ver. 17. Up to this point all is clear: righteousness and wisdom are good and wholesome, and worth striving for; but even in these a transgressing of the right measure is possible (Luther remembers the *summum jus summa injuria*), which has as a consequence, that they become destructive to man, because he thereby becomes a caricature, and either perishes rushing from one extreme into another, or is removed out of the way by others whose hatred he provokes. But it is strange that the author now warns against an excess in wickedness, so that he seems to find wickedness, up to a certain degree, praiseworthy and advisable. So much the stranger, since "be no fool" stands as contrast to "show not thyself wise," etc.; so that "but also be no wicked person" was much rather to be expected as contrast to "be not righteous over-much." Zöckler seeks to get over this difficulty with the remark: "Koheleth does not recommend a certain moderation in wickedness as if he considered it allowable, but only because he recognises the fact as established, that every man is by nature somewhat wicked." The meaning would then be: man's life is not free from wickedness, but be only not too wicked! The offensiveness of the advice is not thus removed; and besides, 18a demands, in a certain sense, an intentional wickedness,—indeed, as 18b shows, a wickedness in union with the fear of God. The correct meaning of "be not wicked over-much" may be found if for תִרְשַׁע we substitute תֶּחֱטָא; in this form the good counsel at once appears as impossible, for it would be immoral, since "sinning," in all circumstances, is an act which carries in itself its own sentence of condemnation. Thus רֶשַׁע must here be a setting oneself free from the severity of the law, which, although sin in the eyes of the over-righteous, is yet no sin in itself; and the author here thinks, in accordance with the spirit of his book, principally of that fresh, free, joyous life to which he called the young, that joy of life in its fulness which appeared to him as the best and fairest reality in this present time; but along with that, perhaps also of transgressions of the letter of the law, of shaking off the scruples of conscience which conformity to God-ordained circumstances brings along with it. He means to say: be not a narrow rigorist,—enjoy life, accommodate thyself to life; but let not the reins be too loose; and be no fool who wantonly places himself above law and discipline: Why wilt thou destroy thy life before the time by suffering vice to kill thee (Ps. xxxiv. 22), and by want of understanding ruin thyself (Prov. x. 21)?[1]

Ver. 18. "It is good that thou holdest fast to the one,"—viz. righteousness and wisdom,—and withdrawest not thy hand from the other,—viz. a wickedness which renounces over-righteousness and over-wisdom, or an unrestrained life;—for he who fears God accomplishes all, *i.e.* both, the one as well as the other. Luther, against the Vulg.: "for he who fears God escapes all." But what "all"? Tyler, Bullock, and others reply: "All the perplexities of life;" but no such thing is found in the text here, however many perplexities may be in the book. Better, Zöckler: the evil results of the extreme of false righteousness as of bold wickedness. But that he does not destroy himself and does not die before his time, is yet only essentially one thing which he escapes; also, from ver. 15, only one thing, אֲבָד, is taken. Thus either: the extremes (Umbr.), or: the extremes together with their consequences. The thought presents a connected, worthy conclusion. But if *ĕth-kullam*, with its retrospective suffix, can be referred to that which immediately precedes, this ought to have the preference. Ginsburg, with Hitzig: "Whoso feareth God will make his way with both;" but what an improbable phrase! Jerome, with his vague *nihil negligit*, is right as to the meaning. In the Bible, the phrase 'הָ . . . יָצָא, *egressus est urbem*, Gen. xliv. 4, cf. Jer. x. 20, is used; and in the Mishna, יָצָא אֶת־יְדֵי חוֹבָתוֹ, *i.e.* he has discharged his duty, he is quit of it by fulfilling it. For the most part, יצא merely is used: he has satisfied his duty; and לֹא יָצָא, he has not satisfied it, *e.g. Berachoth* ii. 1. Accordingly יָצָא—since *ĕth-kullam* relates to, "these ought ye to have done, and not to leave the other undone," Matt. xxiii. 23—here means: he who fears God will set himself free from all, will acquit himself of the one as well as of the other, will perform both, and thus preserve the golden *via media*.

What protects him who with all his Righteousness is not free from Sin, and what becomes him, vii. 19–22.

The thought with which the following sentence is introduced is not incongruous to that going before. But each one of these moral proverbs and aphorisms is in itself a little whole, and the deeper connections, in the discovery of which interpreters vie with each other,

---

[1] An old proverb, *Sota* 3a, says: "A man commits no trangression unless there rules in him previously the spirit of folly."

are destitute of exegetical value. One must not seek to be over-wise; but the possession of wisdom deserves to be highly valued.

Ver. 19. "Wisdom affords strong protection to the wise man more than ten mighty men who are in the city." We have to distinguish, as is shown under Ps. xxxi. 3, the verbs עָזַז, to be strong, and עוז, to flee for refuge; יָעֹז is the fut. of the former, whence מָעֹז, stronghold, safe retreat, protection, and with לְ, since עוז means not only to be strong, but also to show oneself strong, as at ix. 20, to feel and act as one strong; it has also the trans. meaning, to strengthen, as shown in Ps. lxviii. 29, but here the intrans. suffices: wisdom proves itself strong for the wise man. The ten *shallithim* are not, with Gins-burg, to be multiplied indefinitely into "many mighty men." And it is not necessary, with Desvoeux, Hitz., Zöckl., and others, to think of ten chiefs (commanders of forces), including the portions of the city garrison which they commanded. The author probably in this refers to some definite political arrangement (*vid.* above, p. 216), perhaps to the ten archons, like those Assyrian *salat*, vice-regents, after whom as eponyms the year was named by the Greeks. שַׁלִּיט, in the Asiatic kingdom, was not properly a military title. And did a town then need protection only in the time of war, and not also at other times, against injury threatening its trade, against encroachments on its order, against the spread of infectious diseases, against the force of the elements? As the Deutero-Isaiah (lx. 17) says of Jerusalem: " I will make thy officers peace, and thine exactors righteousness," so Koheleth says here that wisdom affords a wise man as strong a protection as a powerful decemvirate a city; cf. Prov. xxiv. 5a: " A wise man is *ba'oz,*" *i.e.* mighty.

Ver. 20. " For among men there is not a righteous man on the earth, who doeth good, and sinneth not." The original passage, found in Solomon's prayer at the consecration of the temple, is briefer, 1 Kings viii. 46: " There is no man who sinneth not." Here the words might be אֵין אָדָם צַדִּיק וגו', there is no righteous man ... *Adam* stands here as representing the species, as when we say in Germ.: *Menschen gibt es keine gerechten auf Erden* [men, there are none righteous on earth]; cf. Ex. v. 16: " Straw, none was given." The verification of ver. 19 by reference to the fact of the common sinfulness from which even the most righteous cannot free himself, does not contradict all expectation to the same degree as the *ki* in vii. 7; but yet it surprises us, so that Mercer and Grätz, with Aben Ezra, take ver. 20 as the verification of ver. 16, here first adduced, and Knobel and Heiligst. and others connect it with vers. 21, 22, translating: " Because there is not a just man . . ., therefore it is also the part of wisdom to take no heed unto all words," etc. But these are all forced interpretations ; instead of the latter, we would rather suppose that ver. 20 originally stood after ver. 22, and is separated from its correct place. But yet the sequence of thought lying before us may be conceived, and that not merely as of necessity, but as that which was intended by the author. On the whole, Hitzig is correct : " For every one, even the wise man, sins ; in which case virtue, which has forsaken him, does not protect him, but wisdom proves itself as his means of defence." Zöckler adds : " against the judicial justice of God ; " but one escapes from this by a penitent appeal to grace, for which there is no need for the personal property of wisdom ; there is thus reason rather for thinking on the dangerous consequences which often a single false step has for a man in other respects moral ; in the threatening complications in which he is thereby involved, it is wisdom which then protects him and delivers him. Otherwise Tyler, who by the עֹז, which the wise has in wisdom, understands power over evil, which is always moving itself even in the righteous. But the sinning spoken of in ver. 20 is that which is unavoidable, which even wisdom cannot prevent or make inefficacious. On the contrary, it knows how to prevent the destruction which threatens man from his transgressions, and to remove the difficulties and derangements which thence arise. The good counsel following is connected by *gam* with the foregoing. The exhortation to strive after wisdom, contained in ver. 19, which affords protection against the evil effects of the failures which run through the life of the righteous, is followed by the exhortation, that one conscious that he himself is not free from transgression, should take heed to avoid that tale-bearing which finds pleasure in exposing to view the shortcomings of others.

Vers. 21, 22. " Also give not thy heart to all the words which one speaketh, lest thou shouldest hear thy servant curse thee. For thy heart knoweth in many cases that thou also hast cursed others." The talk of the people, who are the indef. subj. of יְדַבְּרוּ (LXX., Targ., Syr. supply ἀσεβεῖς), is not about "thee who givest heed to the counsels just given" (Hitz., Zöckl.), for the restrictive עָלֶיךָ is wanting ; and why should a servant be zealous to utter imprecations on the conduct of his master, which rests on the best maxims ? It is the babbling of the people in general that is meant. To this one ought not to turn his heart (לְ . . . נָתַן, as at i. 13, 17, viii. 9, 16), *i.e.* give wilful attention, *ne* (פֶּן = אֲשֶׁר לֹא, which does not occur in the Book of Koheleth) *audias servum tuum tibi maledicere ;* the particip. expression of the pred. obj. follows the analogy of Gen. xxi. 9, Ewald, § 284*b*, and is not a Graecism ; for since in this place hearing is meant, not immediately, but mediated through others, the expression would not in good Greek be with the LXX. ... τοῦ δούλου σου καταρωμένου σε, but τὸν δοῦλόν σου καταρᾶσθαι σε. The warning has its motive in this, that by such round-about hearing one generally hears most unpleasant things; and on hearsay no reliance can be placed. Such gossiping one should ignore, should not listen to it at all; and if, nevertheless, something so bad is reported as that our own servant has spoken words of imprecation against us, yet we ought to pass that by unheeded, well knowing that we ourselves have often spoken harsh words against others. The expression יָדַע וגו', "thou art conscious to thyself that," is like פֶּעַ רַ', 1 Kings ii. 44, not the obj. accus. dependent on יָדַע (Hitz.), "many cases where also thou ...," but the adv. accus. of time to קִלֵּלְתָּ; the words are inverted (Ewald, § 336b), the style of Koheleth being fond of thus giving prominence to the chief con-ception (ver. 20, v. 18, iii. 13). The first gam, although it belongs to "thine, thy," as at 22b it is also connected with "thou,"[1] stands at the beginning of the sentence, after such syntactical examples as Hos. vi. 11; Zech. ix. 11; and even with a two-membered sentence, Job ii. 10.

The not-found, and the found the bitterest—a Woman, vii. 23-29.

The author makes here a pause, looks back at the teaching regarding prudence, already given particularly from ver. 15, and ac-knowledges wisdom as the goal of his effort, especially, however, that for him this goal does not lie behind him, but before him in the remote distance.

Ver. 23. "All this have I proved by wisdom: I thought, Wise I will become; but it remained far from me." The בְ in בְּחָכְמָה is, as at i. 13, that designating the *organon*, the means of knowledge. Thus he possessed wisdom up to a certain degree, and in part; but his purpose, comprehended in the one word אֶחְכָּמָה (*vid.* above, p. 197, § 2), was to possess it fully and completely; *i.e.* not merely to be able to record observations and communicate advices, but to adjust the contradictions of life, to expound the mysteries of time and eternity, and generally to solve the most weighty and important questions which perplex men. But this wisdom was for him still in the remote distance. It is the wisdom after which Job, chap. xxviii., made

[1] נַּם־אָתְּ, on account of the half pause, accented on the penult, according to the Masora.

inquiry in all regions of the world and at all creatures, at last to discover that God has appointed to man only a limited share of wisdom. Koheleth briefly condenses Job xxviii. 12–22 in the words following:

Ver. 24. "For that which is, is far off, and deep,—yes, deep; who can reach it?" Knobel, Hitz., Vaih., and Bullock translate: for what is remote and deep, deep, who can find it? *i.e.* investigate it; but *mah-shehayah* is everywhere an idea by itself, and means either *id quod fuit*, or *id quod exstitit*, i. 9, iii. 15, vi. 10; in the former sense it is the contrast of *mah-shĕihyĕh*, viii. 7, x. 14, cf. iii. 22; in the latter, it is the contrast of that which does not exist, because it has not come into existence. In this way it is also not to be translated: For it is far off what it (wisdom) is (Zöckl.) [= what wisdom is lies far off from human knowledge], or: what it is (the essence of wisdom), is far off (Elst.)—which would be expressed by the words מַה־שֶׁהִיא. And if מה־שהיה is an idea complete in itself, it is evidently not that which is past that is meant (thus *e.g.* Rosenm., *quod ante aderat*), for that is a limitation of the obj. of knowledge, which is unsuitable here, but that which has come into existence. Rightly, Hengst.: that which has being, for wisdom is τῶν ὄντων γνῶσις ἀψευδής, Wisd. vii. 17. He compares Judg. iii. 11, "the work which God does," and viii. 17, "the work which is done under the sun." What Koheleth there says of the totality of the historical, he here says of the world of things: this (in its essence and its grounds) remains far off from man; it is for him, and also in itself and for all creatures, far too deep (עָמֹק עָמֹק, the ancient expression for the superlative): Who can intelligibly reach (יִמְצָ, from מָצָא, *assequi*, in an intellectual sense, as at iii. 11, viii. 17; cf. Job xi. 7) it (this all of being)? The author appears in the book as a teacher of wisdom, and emphatically here makes confession of the limitation of his wisdom; for the consciousness of this limitation comes over him in the midst of his teaching.

Ver. 25. But, on the other side, he can bear testimony to himself that he has honestly exercised himself in seeking to go to the foundation of things: "I turned myself, and my heart was there to discern, and to explore, and to seek wisdom, and the account, and to perceive wickedness as folly, and folly as madness." Regarding *sabbothi*, *vid.* under ii. 20: a turning is meant to the theme as given in what follows, which, as we have to suppose, was connected with a turning away from superficiality and frivolity. Almost all interpreters—as also the accentuation does—connect the two words אֲנִי וְלִבִּי; but "I and my heart" is so unpsychological an expression, without example, that many Codd. (28 of Kennicott, 44 of de Rossi) read בְּלִבִּי [with my heart]. The erasure of the *vav* (as *e.g.* Luther: "I applied my heart") would at the same time require the change of סבותי into הֲסַבּוֹתִי. The Targ., Jerome, and the Venet. render the word בלבי; the LXX. and Syr., on the contrary, ולבי; and this also is allowable, if we place the disjunctive on אני and take ולבי as consequent: my heart, *i.e.* my striving and effort, was to discern (Aben Ezra, Herzf., Stuart),—a substantival clause instead of the verbal וְנָתַתִּי אֶת־לִבִּי, i. 13, i. 17. Regarding *tur* in an intellectual sense, *vid.* i. 13. *Hhĕshbon* (*vid.* above, p. 192), with *hhochmah*, we have translated by "*Rechenschaft*" [account, *ratio*]; for we understand by it a knowledge well grounded and exact, and able to be established,—the *facit* of a calculation of all the facts and circumstances relating thereto; נתן חשבון is Mishnic, and = the N. T. λόγον ἀποδιδόναι. Of the two accus. 25*b* following לָדַעַת, the first, as may be supposed, and as the determination in the second member shows, is that of the obj., the second that of the pred. (Ewald, § 284*b*): that רֶשַׁע, *i.e.* conduct separating from God and from the law of that which is good, is *kĕsĕl*, *Thorheit*, folly (since, as Socrates also taught, all sinning rests on a false calculation, to the sinner's own injury); and that *hassichluth*, *Narrheit*, foolishness, *stultitia* (*vid. sachal*, p. 194, and i. 17), is to be thus translated (in contradistinction to כֶּסֶל), *i.e.* an intellectual and moral obtuseness, living for the day, rising up into foolery, not different from *holeloth*, fury, madness, and thus like a physical malady, under which men are out of themselves, rage, and are mad. Koheleth's striving after wisdom thus, at least in the second instance (ולדעת), with a renunciation of the transcendental, went towards a practical end. And now he expresses by ומוצא one of the experiences he had reached in this way of research. How much value he attaches to this experience is evident from the long preface, by means of which it is as it were distilled. We see him there on the way to wisdom, to metaphysical wisdom, if we may so speak—it remains as far off from him as he seeks to come near to it. We then see him, yet not renouncing the effort after wisdom, on the way toward practical wisdom, which exercises itself in searching into the good and the bad; and that which has presented itself to him as the bitterest of the bitter is— a woman.

Ver. 26. "And I found woman more bitter than death; she is like hunting-nets, and like snares is her heart, her hands are bands: he who pleaseth God will escape from her; but the sinner is caught by them." As 'אֶ 'שֵׁ, iv. 2, so here 'מ 'אֶ (*vid.* above, p. 197, 1, and

198, 3) gains by the preceding וְסַבּוֹתִי אֲנִי a past sense;[1] the particip. clause stands frequently thus, not only as a circumstantial clause, Gen. xiv. 12 f., but also as principal clause, Gen. ii. 10, in an historical connection. The preceding pred. מַר, in the mas. ground-form, follows the rule, Gesen. § 147. Regarding the construction of the relative clause, Hitzig judges quite correctly : " הִיא is copula between subj. and pred., and precedes for the sake of the contrast, giving emphasis to the pred. It cannot be a nomin., which would be taken up by the suff. in לְבָּה, since if this latter were subject also to מְצ', הִיא would not certainly be found. Also *asher* here is not a conj." This הוּא (הִיא), which in relative substantival clauses represents the copula, for the most part stands separated from *asher*, e.g. Gen. vii. 2, xvii. 12, Num. xvii. 5, Deut. xvii. 15 ; less frequently immediately with it, Num. xxxv. 31 ; 1 Sam. x. 19 ; 2 Kings xxv. 19 ; Lev. xi. 26 ; Deut. xx. 20. But this *asher hu* (*hi*) never represents the subj., placed foremost and again resumed by the reflex. pronoun, so as to be construed as the accentuation requires : *quae quidem retia et laquei cor ejus = cujus quidem cor sunt retia et laquei* (Heiligst.). מָצוֹד is the means of searching, *i.e.* either of hunting : hunting-net (*mitsodah*, ix. 12), or of blockading : siege-work, bulwarks, ix. 14 ; here it is the plur. of the word in the former meaning. חֲרֵם, Hab. i. 14, plur. Ezek. xxvi. 5, etc. (perhaps from חרם, to pierce, bore through), is one of the many synon. for fishing-net. אֲסוּרִים, fetters, the hands (arms) of voluptuous embrace (cf. above, p. 191). The primary form, after Jer. xxxvii. 15, is אֱסוּר, אָסוּר ; cf. אָבוּס, אֵבוּס ; אַב, Job xxxix. 9. Of the three clauses following *asher*, vav is found in the second and is wanting to the third, as at Deut. xxix. 22, Job xlii. 9, Ps. xlv. 9, Isa. i. 13 ; cf. on the other hand, Isa. xxxiii. 6. Similar in their import are these Leonine verses :

"*Femina praeclara facie quasi pestis amara,*
        Et quasi fermentum corrumpit cor sapientum."

That the author is in full earnest in this harsh judgment regarding woman, is shown by 26*b* : he who appears to God as good (cf. ii. 26) escapes from her (the fut. of the consequence of this his relation to God) ; but the sinner (וְחוֹטֵא, cf. above, p. 254, note) is caught by her, or, properly, in her, viz. the net-like woman, or the net to which she is compared (Ps. ix. 16 ; Isa. xxiv. 18). The harsh judgment is, however, not applicable to woman as such, but

---

[1] With reference to this passage and Prov. xviii. 22, it was common in Palestine when one was married to ask מָצָא אוֹ מוֹצֵא = happy or unhappy ? *Jebamoth* 63*b*.

to woman as she is, with only rare exceptions; among a thousand women he has not found one corresponding to the idea of a woman. Vers. 27, 28. "Behold what I have found, saith Koheleth, adding one thing to another, to find out the account: What my soul hath still sought, and I have not found, (is this): one man among a thousand have I found; and a woman among all these have I not found." It is the ascertained result, "one man, etc.," which is solemnly introduced by the words preceding. Instead of אָמְ' קֹהֶ', the words אָמַר הַקֹּהֶ' are to be read, after xii. 8, as is now generally acknowledged; errors of transcription of a similar kind are found at 2 Sam. v. 2; Job xxxviii. 12. Ginsburg in vain disputes this, maintaining that the name *Koheleth*, as denoting wisdom personified, may be regarded as fem. as well as mas.; here, where the female sex is so much depreciated, was the fem. self-designation of the stern judge specially unsuitable (cf. above, p. 204). Hengst. supposes that *Koheleth* is purposely fem. in this one passage, since true wisdom, represented by Solomon, stands opposite to false philosophy. But this reason for the fem. rests on the false opinion that woman here is heresy personified; he further remarks that it is significant for this fem. personification, that there is "no writing of female authorship in the whole canon of the O. and N. T." But what of Deborah's triumphal song, the song of Hannah, the *magnificat* of Mary? We hand this absurdity over to the Clementines! The woman here was flesh and blood, but *pulchra quamvis pellis est mens tamen plena procellis;* and *Koheleth* is not incarnate wisdom, but the official name of a preacher, as in Assyr., for חַנֵּים, curators, overseers, *hazanâti*[1] is used. זֶה, 27a, points, as at i. 10, to what follows. אַחַת לְ, one thing to another (cf. Isa. xxvii. 12), must have been, like *summa summarum* and the like, a common arithmetical and dialectical formula, which is here subordinate to מְצֹא, since an adv. inf. such as לְקֹחַ is to be supplemented: taking one thing to another to find out the חֶשְׁבּוֹן, *i.e.* the balance of the account, and thus to reach a *facit*, a *resultat*.[2]

That which presented itself to him in this way now follows. It was, in relation to woman, a negative experience: "What my soul sought on and on, and I found not, (is this)." The words are like the superscription of the following result, in which finally the זֶה of 27a terminates. Ginsburg, incorrectly: "what my soul is still seeking," which would have required מְבַקֶּשֶׁת. The pret. בִּקְשָׁה (with

---

[1] *Vid.* Fried. Delitzsch's *Assyr. Stud.* (1874), p. 132.

[2] Cf. *Aboth* iv. 29, לִיתֵּן וגו', "to give account;" הכל וגו', "all according to the result."

ק without *Dagesh*,[1] as at ver. 29) is retrospective ; and עוֹד, from
עוּד, means *redire*, again and again, continually, as at Gen. xlvi. 29.
He always anew sought, and that, as *biqshah naphshi* for בִּקְשָׁתִי
denotes, with urgent striving, violent longing, and never found, viz.
a woman such as she ought to be : a man, one of a thousand, I
have found, etc.   With right, the accentuation gives *Garshayim* to
adam ; it stands forth, as at ver. 20, as a general denominator—the
sequence of accents, *Geresh, Pashta, Zakef*, is as at Gen. i. 9.   "One
among a thousand" reminds us of Job xxxiii. 23, cf. ix. 3 ; the old
interpreters (*vid.* Dachselt's *Bibl. Accentuata*), with reference to these
parallels, connect with the one man among a thousand all kinds of
incongruous christological thoughts.   Only, here *adam*, like the
Romanic *l'homme* and the like, means man in sexual contrast to
woman.   It is thus ideally meant, like *ish*, 1 Sam. iv. 9, xlvi. 15,
and accordingly also the parall. אִשָּׁה.   For it is not to be supposed
that the author denies thereby perfect human nature to woman.
But also Burger's explanation : "a human being, whether man or
woman," is a useless evasion.   Man has the name *adam* κατ᾽ ἐξ.
by primitive hist. right : "for the man is not of the woman, but the
woman of the man," 1 Cor. xi. 8.   The meaning, besides, is not
that among a thousand human beings he found one upright man, but
not a good woman (Hitz.),—for then the thousand ought to have had
its proper denominator, בְּנֵי אָדָם,—but that among a thousand persons of the male sex he found only one man such as he ought to be,
and among a thousand of the female sex not one woman such as she
ought to be ; "among all these" is thus = among an equal number.
Since he thus actually found the ideal of man only seldom, and that
of woman still seldomer (for more than this is not denoted by the
round numbers), the more surely does he resign himself to the
following *resultat*, which he introduces by the word לְבַד (only, alone),
as the clear gain of his searching :

Ver. 29. "Lo, this only have I found, that God created man upright ; but they seek many arts."   Also here the order of the words
is inverted, since זֶה, belonging as obj. to מָצָ֫א (have I found), which is
restricted by לְבַד (*vid.* above, p. 193), is amalgamated with רְאֵה (Lo !
see !).   The author means to say : Only this (*solummodo hocce*) have I
found, that . . . ; the רְאֵה is an interjected *nota bene*.   The expression :
God has made man יָשָׁר, is dogmatically significant.   Man, as he came
from the Creator's hand, was not placed in the state of moral decision,

---

[1] As generally the *Piel* forms of the root בקשׁ, Masor. all have *Raphe* on the
ק, except the imper. בַּקְּשׁוּ ; *vid.* Luzzatto's *Gramm.* § 417.

nor yet in the state of absolute indifference between good and evil; he was not neither good nor bad, but he was טוב, or, which is the same thing, יָשָׁר; *i.e.* in every respect normal, so that he could normally develope himself from this positively good foundation. But by the expression עָשָׂה יָשָׁר, Koheleth has certainly not exclusively his origin in view, but at the same time his relative continuation in the propagation of himself, not without the concurrence of the Creator; also of man after the fall the words are true, עָשָׂה יָשָׁר, in so far as man still possesses the moral ability not to indulge sinful affections within him, nor suffer them to become sinful actions. But the sinful affections in the inborn nature of weak sinful man have derived so strong a support from his freedom, that the power of the will over against this power of nature is for the most part as weakness; the dominance of sin, where it is not counteracted by the grace of God, has always shown itself so powerful, that Koheleth has to complain of men of all times and in all circles of life: they seek many arts (as Luther well renders it), or properly, calculations, inventions, devices (*hhishsh^evonoth*,[1] as at 2 Chron. xxvi. 15, from *hhishsh^evon*, which is as little distinguished from the formation *hhĕshbon*, as *hhizzayon* from *hhĕzyon*), viz. of means and ways, by which they go astray from the normal natural development into abnormities. In other words: inventive refined degeneracy has come into the place of moral simplicity, ἁπλότης (2 Chron. xi. 3). As to the opinion that caricatures of true human nature, contrasts between the actual and that which ought to be (the ideal), are common, particularly among the female sex, the author has testimonies in support of it from all nations. It is confirmed by the primitive history itself, in which the woman appears as the first that was led astray, and as the seducer (cf. *Psychol.* pp. 103–106). With reference to this an old proverb says: "Women carry in themselves a frivolous mind," *Kiddushin* 80*b*.[2] And because a woman, when she has fallen into evil, surpasses a man in fiendish superiority therein, the Midrash reckons under this passage before us fifteen things of which the one is worse than the other; the thirteenth is death, and the fourteenth a bad woman.[3] Hitzig supposes that the author has before him as his model Agathoclea, the mistress of the fourth Ptolemy Philopator. But also the history of the Persian Court affords dreadful examples of the truth of the proverb: "Woe to the age whose leader is a woman;"[4] and generally the harem is a den of female wickedness.

---

[1] If we derive this word from *hhĕshbon*, the *Dagesh* in the שׁ is the so-called *Dag. dirimens.*   [2] Cf. Tendlau's *Sprichw.* (1860), No. 733.

[3] Duke's *Rabb. Blumenl.* (1844), No. 32.   [4] *Ibid.* No. 118.

Wise Conduct towards the King and under Despotic Oppression,
viii. 1–9.

If now the sentence first following sings the praise of wisdom, it does not stand out of connection with the striving after wisdom, which the author, vii. 23 f., has confessed, and with the experiences announced in vii. 25 ff., which have presented themselves to him in the way of the search after wisdom, so far as wisdom was attainable. It is the incomparable superiority of the wise man which the first verse here announces and verifies.

viii. 1. " Who is like the wise ? and who understandeth the interpretation of things ? The wisdom of a man maketh his face bright, and the rudeness of his face is changed." Unlike this saying: " Who is like the wise ? " are the formulas מִי חָכָם, Hos. xiv. 10, Jer. xi. 11, Ps. cvii. 43, which are compared by Hitzig and others. " Who is like the wise ? " means : Who is equal to him? and this question, after the scheme מִי־כָמֹכָה, Ex. xv. 11, presents him as one who has not his like among men. Instead of בְּהֶ 'the word כְּהֶחָכָם might be used, after לֶחָכָם, ii. 16, etc. The syncope is, as at Ezek. xl. 25, omitted, which frequently occurs, particularly in the more modern books, Ezek. xlvii. 22 ; 2 Chron. x. 7, xxv. 10, xxix. 27 ; Neh. ix. 19, xii. 38. The regular giving of *Dagesh* to כ after מִי, with *Jethib*, not *Mahpach*, is as at ver. 7 after כִּי ; *Jethib* is a disjunctive. The second question is not וּמִי כְּיוֹדֵעַ, but וּמִי יֹדֵעַ, and thus does not mean : who is like the man of understanding, but : who understands, viz. as the wise man does; thus it characterizes the incomparably excellent as such. Many interpreters (Oetinger, Ewald, Hitz., Heiligst., Burg., Elst., Zöck.) persuade themselves that פֵּשֶׁר דָּבָר is meant of the understanding of the proverb, 8*b*. The absence of the art., says Hitzig, does not mislead us: of a proverb, viz. the following ; but in this manner determinate ideas may be made from all indeterminate ones. Rightly, Gesenius : *explicationem ullius rei; better*, as at vii. 8 : *cujusvis rei*. Ginsburg compares נְבוֹן דָּבָר, 1 Sam. xvi. 18, which, however, does not mean him who has the knowledge of things, but who is well acquainted with words. It is true that here also the chief idea פֵּשֶׁר first leads to the meaning *verbum* (according to which the LXX., Jer., the Targ., and Syr. translate ; the Venet.: ἑρμηνείαν λόγου) ; but since the unfolding or explaining (*pĕshĕr*) refers to the actual contents of the thing spoken, *verbi* and *rei* coincide. The wise man knows how to explain difficult things, to unfold mysterious things ; in short, he understands how to go to the foundation of things.

What now follows, 1*b*, might be introduced by the confirming

כִּי, but after the manner of synonymous parallelism it places itself in the same rank with 1a, since, that the wise man stands so high, and no one like him looks through the centre of things, is repeated in another form : "Wisdom maketh his face bright" is thus to be understood after Ps. cxix. 130 and xix. 9, wisdom draws the veil from his countenance, and makes it clear; for wisdom is related to folly as light is to darkness, ii. 13. The contrast, 'שֵׁ . . . וְעֹז (" and the rudeness of his face is changed "), shows, however, that not merely the brightening of the countenance, but in general that intellectual and ethical transfiguration of the countenance is meant, in which at once, even though it should not in itself be beautiful, we discover the educated man rising above the common rank. To translate, with Ewald : and the brightness of his countenance is doubled, is untenable ; even supposing that יְשֻׁנֶּא can mean, like the Arab. *yuthattay, duplicatur*, still עֹז, in the meaning of brightness, is in itself, and especially with פָּנָיו, impossible, along with which it is, without doubt, to be understood after *az panim*, Deut. xxviii. 50, Dan. viii. 23, and *hē'ēz panim*, Prov. vii. 13, or *b'phanim*, Prov. xxi. 29, so that thus עֹז פָנִים has the same meaning as the post-bibl. עַזּוּת פָּנִים, stiffness, hardness, rudeness of countenance = boldness, want of bashfulness, regardlessness, *e.g. Shabbath* 30b, where we find a prayer in these words: O keep me this day from עַזֵי פנים and from עזות פ' (that I may not incur the former or the latter). The Talm. *Taanith* 7b, thus explaining, says: " Every man to whom עזות פ' belongs, him one may hate, as the scripture says, יְשֻׁנֶּא . . . וְעֹז (do not read יִשָּׂנֵא)." The LXX. translates μισηθήσεται [will be hated], and thus also the Syr.; both have thus read as the Talm. has done, which, however, bears witness in favour of יְשֻׁנֶּא as the traditional reading. It is not at all necessary, with Hitzig, after Zirkel, to read יְשַׁנֶּא : but boldness disfigureth his countenance ; עֹז in itself alone, in the meaning of boldness, would, it is true, along with פניו as the obj. of the verb, be tenable ; but the change is unnecessary, the passive affords a perfectly intelligible meaning: the boldness, or rudeness, of his visage is changed, viz. by wisdom (Böttch., Ginsb., Zöckl.). The verb שָׁנָה (שְׁנָא, Lam. iv. 1) means, Mal. iii. 6, merely " to change, to become different ;" the *Pih.* שִׁנָּה, Jer. lii. 33, שִׁנָּא, 2 Kings xxv. 29, denotes in these two passages a change *in melius*, and the proverb of the Greek, Sir. xiii. 24,—

Καρδία ἀνθρώπου ἀλλοιοῖ τὸ πρόσωπον αὐτοῦ,
ἐάν τε εἰς ἀγαθὰ ἐάν τε εἰς κακά,

is preserved to us in its original form thus :

לֵב אָדָם יָשֵׂנָּא פָּנָיו

בֵּין לְטוֹב וּבֵין לְרָע׃

so that thus שֵׂנָּא, in the sense of being changed as to the sternness
of the expression of the countenance, is as good as established.
What Ovid says of science: *emollit mores nec sinit esse feros*, thus
tolerably falls in with what is here said of wisdom: Wisdom gives
bright eyes to a man, a gentle countenance, a noble expression; it
refines and dignifies his external appearance and his demeanour; the
hitherto rude external, and the regardless, selfish, and bold deportment, are changed into their contraries. If, now, ver. 1 is not to be
regarded as an independent proverb, it will bear somewhat the
relation of a prologue to what follows. Luther and others regard 1*a*
as of the nature of an epilogue to what goes before; parallels, such
as Hos. xiv. 10, make that appear probable; but it cannot be
yielded, because the words are not מי חכם, but מי כהח׳. But that
which follows easily subordinates itself to ver. 1, in as far as fidelity
to duty and thoughtfulness amid critical social relations are proofs
of that wisdom which sets a man free from impetuous rudeness, and
fits him intelligently and with a clear mind to accommodate himself
to the time.

Ver. 2. The faithfulness of subjects, Koheleth says, is a religious
duty: " I say: Observe well the king's command, and that because
of the oath of God." The author cannot have written 2*a* as it here
stands; אֲנִי hovers in the air. Hitzig reads, with Jerome, שְׂמֹר, and
hears in vers. 2–4 a servile person speaking who veils himself in the
cloak of religion; in vers. 5–8 follows the *censura* of this corrupt
theory. But we have already (*vid.* above, p. 213) remarked that
ver. 2 accords with Rom. xiii. 5, and is thus not a corrupt theory;
besides, this distribution of the expressions of the Book of Koheleth
between different speakers is throughout an expedient resting on a
delusion. Luther translates: I keep the word of the king, and thus
reads אֶשְׂמֹר; as also does the *Jer. Sanhedrin* 21*b*, and *Koheleth rabba*,
under this passage: I observe the command of the king, of the
queen. In any case, it is not God who is meant here by "the king;"
the words: " and that because of the oath of God," render this impossible, although Hengst. regards it as possible; for (1) " the oath of
God" he understands, against all usage, of the oath which is taken to
God; and (2) he maintains that in the O. T. scarcely any passage is
to be found where obedience to a heathen master is set forth as a
religious duty. But the prophets show themselves as morally great
men, without a stain, just in this, that they decidedly condemn and

unhesitatingly chastise any breach of faith committed against the
Assyrian or Chaldean oppressor, *e.g.* Isa. xxviii. 15, xxx. 1 ; Ezek.
xvii. 15 ; cf. Jer. xxvii. 12. However, although we understand
mĕlĕk not of the heavenly, but of an earthly king, yet אֶשְׁמֹר does
not recommend itself, for Koheleth records his experience, and derives
therefrom warnings and admonitions ; but he never in this manner
presents himself as an example of virtue. The paraenetic imper.
שְׁמֹר is thus not to be touched. Can we then use *ani* elliptically, as
equivalent to " I say as follows " ? Passages such as Jer. xx. 10
(Elst.), where לֵאמֹר is omitted, are not at all the same. Also Ezek.
xxxiv. 11, where הנני is strengthened by *ani*, and the expression is
not elliptical, is not in point here. And Isa. v. 9 also does not apply
to the case of the supposed ellipsis here. In an ingenious bold
manner the Midrash helps itself in Lev. xviii. and Num. xiv., for
with reference to the self-introduction of royal words like אני פרעה it
explains : " Observe the *I* from the mouth of the king." This explanation is worthy of mention, but it has little need of refutation ;
it is also contrary to the accentuation, which gives *Pashta* to *ani*, as

to רָאֹה, vii. 27, and לְבַד, vii. 29, and thus places it by itself. Now,

since this elliptical *I*, after which we would place a colon, is insufferably harsh, and since also it does not recommend itself to omit it, as
is done by the LXX., the Targ., and Syr.,—for the words must then
have a different order, שְׁמֹר פִי המלך,—it is most advisable to supply
אָמַרְתִּי, and to write 'אני אָמַ or 'אָמַ אני, after ii. 1, iii. 17, 18. We find
ourselves here, besides, within an *I* section, consisting of sentences
interwoven in a Mashal form. The admonition is solemnly introduced,
since Koheleth, himself a king, and a wise man in addition, gives it
the support of the authority of his person, in which it is to be
observed that the religious motive introduced by ו *explic.* (*vid.* Ewald,
§ 340*b*) is not merely an appendix, but the very point of the admonition.
Kleinert, incorrectly : " Direct thyself according to the mouth of the
king, and that, too, as according to an oath of God." Were this the
meaning, then we might certainly wish that it were a servile Alexandrian court-Jew who said it. But why should that be the meaning ? The meaning "*wegen*" [because of], which is usually attributed to the word-connection על־דברת here and at iii. 18, vii. 14,
Kleinert maintains to be an arbitrary invention. But it alone fits these
three passages, and why an arbitrary invention ? If עַל־דְּבַר, Ps. xlv. 5,
lxxix. 9, etc., means "*von wegen*" [on account of], then also על־דברת
will signify "*propter rationem, naturam,*" as well as (Ps. cx. 4) *ad
rationem.* 'שֵׁב אֶל is, as elsewhere 'שב 'יה, *e.g.* Ex. xxii. 10, a pro-

mise given under an appeal to God, a declaration or promise strengthened by an oath. Here it is the oath of obedience which is meant, which the covenant between a king and his people includes, though it is not expressly entered into by individuals. The king is designated neither as belonging to the nation, nor as a foreigner; that which is said is valid also in the case of the latter. Daniel, Nehemiah, Mordecai, etc., acted in conformity with the words of Koheleth, and the oath of vassalage which the kings of Israel and Judah swore to the kings of Assyria and of Babylon is regarded by the prophets of both kingdoms as binding on king and people (vid. above, p. 213).

Ver. 3. The warning, corresponding to the exhortation, now follows: One must not thoughtlessly avoid the duty of service and homage due to the king: "Hasten not to go away from him: join not in an evil matter; for he executeth all that he desireth." Regarding the connection, of two verbs with one idea, lying before us in תֵּלֵךְ . . . אַל־, as e.g. at Zech. viii. 15, Hos. i. 6, vid. Gesen. § 142. 3b. Instead of this sentence, we might use אַל־תִּבָהֵל לָלֶכֶת מִפָּנָיו, as e.g. Aboth v. 8 : "The wise man does not interrupt another, and hastens not to answer," i.e. is not too hasty in answering. As with עִם, to be with the king, iv. 15 = to hold with him, so here הָלַךְ מִפָּנָיו means to take oneself away from him, or, as it is expressed in x. 4, to leave one's station; cf. Hos. xi. 2: "They (the prophets of Jahve) called to them, forthwith they betook themselves away from them." It is possible that in the choice of the expression, the phrase נִבְהַל מִפְּנֵי, "to be put into a state of alarm before any one," Job xxiii. 15, was not without influence. The indef. דְּבָר רָע, Deut. xvii. 1, xxiii. 10, cf. xiii. 12, xix. 20, 2 Kings iv. 41, etc., is to be referred (with Rosenm., Knobel, Bullock, and others) to undertakings which aim at resisting the will of the king, and reach their climax in conspiracy against the king's throne and life (Prov. xxiv. 21b). אַל־תַּעֲמֹד בְּ might mean: persist not in it; but the warning does not presuppose that the entrance thereon had already taken place, but seeks to prevent it, thus: enter not, go not, engage not, like 'amad b'derek, Ps. i. 1; 'amad babrith, 2 Kings xxiii. 3; cf. Ps. cvi. 23; Jer. xxiii. 18. Also the Arab. 'amada li = intendit, proposuit sibi rem, is compared; it is used in the general sense of "to make toward something, to stretch to something." Otherwise Ewald, Elst., Ginsb., and Zöckl.: stand not at an evil word (of the king), provoking him to anger thereby still more,—against ver. 5, where דבר רע, as generally (cf. Ps. cxli. 4), means an evil thing, and against the close connection of עמד בְּ, which is to be presupposed. Hitzig even: stand not at an evil command, *i.e.* hesitate not to do even that which is evil, which the king commands, with the remark that here a *servilismus* is introduced as speaking, who, in saying of the king, " All that pleaseth him he doeth," uses words which are used only of God the Almighty, John i. 14, Ps. xxxiii. 9, etc. Hengst., Hahn, Dale, and others therefore dream of the heavenly King in the text. But proverbs of the earthly king, such as Prov. xx. 2, say the very same thing; and if the Mishna *Sanhedrin* ii. 2, to which Tyler refers, says of the king, " The king cannot himself be a judge, nor can any one judge him; he does not give evidence, and no evidence can be given against him," a sovereignty is thus attributed to the king, which is formulated in 3*b* and established in the verse following.

Ver. 4. " Inasmuch as the word of a king is powerful; and who can say to him: What doest thou ? " The same thing is said of God, Job ix. 12, Isa. xlv. 9, Dan. iv. 32, Wisd. xii. 12, but also of the king, especially of the unlimited monarch of a despotic state. *Baasher* verifies as בְּשׁ at ii. 16; cf. Gen. xxxix. 9, 23; Greek, ἐν ᾧ and ἐφ᾽ ᾧ. Burger arbitrarily: *quae dixit* (דִּבֶּר for דָּבָר), *rex, in ea potestatem habet.* The adjectival impers. use of the noun *shilton* = *potestatem habens*, is peculiar; in the Talm. and Midrash, *shilton*, like the Assyr. *siltannu*,[1] means the ruler (*vid.* under v. 8). That which now follows is not, as Hitzig supposes, an opposing voice which makes itself heard, but as ver. 2 is compared with Rom. xiii. 5, so is ver. 5 with Rom. xiii. 3.

Ver. 5. " Whoso remaineth true to the commandment will experience nothing evil; and the heart of the wise man will know a time and judicial decision." That by מִצְוָה is here to be understood not the commandment of God, at least not immediately, as at Prov. xix. 16 (Ewald), but that of the king, and generally an injunction and appointment of the superior authority, is seen from the context, which treats not of God, but of the ruler over a state. Knobel and others explain: He who observeth the commandment engageth not with an evil thing, and the wise mind knoweth time and right. But יָדַע is never thus used (the author uses for this, עָמַד בְּ), and the same meaning is to be supposed for the repeated יֵדַע: it means to arrive at the knowledge of; in the first instance: to suffer, Ezek. xxv. 14; cf. Isa. ix. 8; Hos. ix. 7; in the second, to experience, Josh. xxiv. 31; Ps. xvi. 11. It may also, indeed, be translated after ix. 12: a wise heart knoweth time and judgment, viz. that they will not fail; but why should we not render יֵדַע both times fut., since nothing stands in the way? We do not translate: a wise heart,

---

[1] *Vid.* Fried. Delitzsch's *Assyr. Stud.* p. 129 f.

a wise mind (Knobel), although this is possible, 1 Kings iii. 12 (cf.
Ps. xc. 12), but: the heart of a wise man, which is made more natural
by x. 2, Prov. xvi. 23. The heart of a wise man, which is not hurried
forward by dynastic oppression to a selfish forgetfulness of duty, but
in quietness and hope (Lam. iii. 26) awaits the interposition of
God, will come to the knowledge that there is an *eth*, a time, when
oppression has an end, and a *mishpat*, when it suffers punishment.
Well adapted to the sense in which *eth* is here used is the remark
of Elia Levita in his *Tishbi*, that זְמָן corresponds to the German *Zeit*
and the Romanic *tempo*, but עֵת to the German *Ziel* and the Romanic
termino. The LXX. translates καιρὸν κρίσεως ; and, in fact, עֵת וּמ׳ is
a hendiadays, which, however, consists in the division of one conception into two. The heart of the wise man remaining true to duty
will come to learn that there is a terminus and judicial decision, for
everything has an end when it falls under the fate for which it is
ripe, especially the sinner.

    Ver. 6. "For there is a time and decision for everything, for the
wickedness of man becomes too great." From 6*a* there follow four
clauses with כִּי ; by such monotonous repetition of one and the same
word, the author also elsewhere renders the exposition difficult, affording too free a space for understanding the כי as confirming, or as
hypothetical, and for co-ordinating or subordinating to each other the
clauses with כי. Presupposing the correctness of our exposition of
5*a*, the clause 6*a* with כי may be rendered parenthetically, and that
with כי in 6*b* hypothetically: " an end and decision the heart of the
wise man will come to experience (because for everything there is
an end and decision), supposing that the wickedness of man has
become great upon him, *i.e.* his burden of guilt has reached its full
measure." We suppose thereby (1) that רַבָּה, which appears from the
accent on the ult. to be an adj., can also be the 3d pret., since before
עַ the tone has gone back to *áh* (cf. Gen. xxvi. 10 ; Isa. xi. 1), to
protect it from being put aside ; but generally the accenting of such
forms of עַ״עַ hovers between the penult. and the ult., *e.g.* Ps. lxix. 5,
lv. 22 ; Prov. xiv. 19. Then (2) that עָלָיו goes back to הָאָדָם, without
distinction of persons, which has a support in vi. 1, and that thus a
great רָעָה is meant lying upon man, which finally finds its punishment.
But this view of the relation of the clauses fails, in that it affords no
connection for ver. 7. It appears to be best to co-ordinate all the
four כי as members of one chain of proof, which reaches its point in
8*b*, viz. in the following manner : the heart of a wise man will see
the time and the judgment of the ruler, laying to his heart the temptation to rebellion; for (1) as the author has already said, iii. 17 : " God

will judge the righteous as well as the wicked, for there is with Him a time for every purpose and for every act;" (2) the wickedness of man (by which, as ver. 9 shows, despots are aimed at) which he has committed, becomes great upon him, so that suddenly at once the judgment of God will break in upon him; (3) he knows not what will be done; (4) no one can tell him how (*quomodo*) it, the future, will be, so that he might in any way anticipate it—the judgment will overwhelm him unexpectedly and irretrievably : wickedness does not save its possessor.

Vers. 7 and 8 thus continue the *For* and *For:* "For he knoweth not that which shall be ; for who can tell him how it will be ? There is no man who has power over the wind, to restrain the wind ; and no one has authority over the day of death; and there is no discharge in the war ; and wickedness does not save its possessor." The actor has the sin upon himself, and bears it ; if it reaches the terminus of full measure, it suddenly overwhelms him in punishment, and the too great burden oppresses its bearer (Hitzig, under Isa. xxiv. 20). This עת ומש׳ comes unforeseen, for he (the man who heaps up sins) knoweth not *id quod fiet ;* it arrives unforeseen, for *quomodo fiet,* who can show it to him ? Thus, *e.g.,* the tyrant knows not that he will die by assassination, and no one can say to him how that will happen, so that he might make arrangements for his protection. Rightly the LXX. καθὼς ἔσται; on the contrary, the Targ., Hitzig, and Ginsburg : when it will be ;[1] but כַּאֲשֶׁר signifies *quum,* iv. 17, v. 3, viii. 16, but not *quando,* which must be expressed by מָתִי (Mishnic אֵימָתַי, אֵימָת).

Now follows the concluding thought of the four כי, whereby 5b is established. There are four impossibilities enumerated ; the fourth is the point of the enumeration constructed in the form of a numerical proverb. (1) No man has power over the wind, to check the wind. Ewald, Hengst., Zöckl., and others understand רוּחַ, with the Targ., Jerome, and Luther, of the Spirit (רוח חיים) ; but man can limit this physically when he puts a violent termination to life, and must restrain it morally by ruling it, Prov. xvi. 32, xxv. 28. On the contrary, the wind הרוח is, after xi. 5, incalculable, and to rule over it is the exclusive prerogative of Divine Omnipotence, Prov. xxx. 4.

The transition to the second impossibility is mediated by this, that in רוח, according to the *usus loq.,* the ideas of the breath of animal life, and of wind as the breath as it were of the life of the whole of nature, are interwoven. (2) No one has power over the

---

[1] The Venet. ἐν ᾧ, as if the text had בַּאֲשֶׁר.

day of death : death, viz. natural death, comes to a man without his being able to see it before, to determine it, or to change it. With שַׁלִּיט there here interchanges שִׁלְטוֹן, which is rendered by the LXX. and Venet. as abstr., also by the Syr. But as at Dan. iii. 2, so also above at ver. 4, it is concr., and will be so also in the passage before us, as generally in the Talm. and Midrash, in contradistinction to the abstr., which is שָׁלְטָן, after the forms אָבְדָן, דָּרְבָן, etc., e.g. Bereshith rabba, c. 85 extr. : "Every king and ruler שׁלטון who had not a שׁולטן, a command (government, sway) in the land, said that that did not satisfy him, the king of Babylon had to place an under-Caesar in Jericho," etc.[1] Thus : no man possesses rule or is a ruler . . .

A transition is made from the inevitable law of death to the inexorable severity of the law of war ; (3) there is no discharge, no dispensation, whether for a time merely (missio), or a full discharge (dimissio), in war, which in its fearful rigour (vid. on the contrary, Deut. xx. 5-8) was the Persian law (cf. above, p. 214). Even so, every possibility of escape is cut off by the law of the divine requital ; (4) wickedness will not save (מַלֵּט, causative, as always) its lord (cf. the proverb : " Unfaithfulness strikes its own master ") or possessor ; i.e. the wicked person, when the עֵת וּמ' comes, is hopelessly lost. Grätz would adopt the reading עֹשֶׁר instead of רֶשַׁע ; but the fate of the בַּעַל רֶשַׁע, or of the רָשָׁע, is certainly that to which the concatenation of thought from ver. 6 leads, as also the disjunctive accent at the end of the three first clauses of ver. 8 denotes. But that in the words ba'al resha' (not בַּעֲלֵי) a despotic king is thought of (בְּעָלָיו, as at v. 10, 12, vii. 12 ; Prov. iii. 27 ; cf. under Prov. i. 19), is placed beyond a doubt by the epilogistic verse :

Ver. 9. "All that I have seen, and that, too, directing my heart to all the labour that is done under the sun : to the time when a man rules over a man to his hurt." The relation of the clauses is mistaken by Jerome, Luther, Hengst., Vaih., Ginsburg, and others, who begin a new clause with עֵת : " there is a time," etc. ; and Zöckl., who ventures to interpret עֵת וגו' as epexegetical of כָּל־מֵעֲ וגו' (" every work that is done under the sun "). The clause וְנָתוֹן is an adverbial subordinate clause (vid. under iv. 2) : et advertendo quidem animum. עֵת is accus. of time, as at Jer. li. 33 ; cf. Ps. iv. 8, the relation of 'eth asher, like מִק' שֶׁ, i. 7, xi. 3. All that, viz. the wisdom of patient fidelity to duty, the perniciousness of revolutionary selfishness, and the suddenness with which the judgment comes, he has

---

[1] Regarding the distinction between שִׁלְטוֹן and שָׁלְטָן, vid. Baer's Abodath Jisrael, p. 385.

seen (for he observed the actions done under the sun), with his own eyes, at the time when man ruled over man לֹו לְרַע, not : to his own [the ruler's] injury (Symm., Jerome), but : to the injury (LXX., Theod., τοῦ κακῶσαι αὐτόν, and thus also the Targ. and Syr.) of this second man ; for after 'eth asher, a description and not a judgment was to be expected. The man who rules over man to the hurt of the latter rules as a tyrant ; and this whole section, beginning with viii. 1, treats of the right wisdom of life at a time of tyrannical government.

It is with the Righteous as with the Wicked, and with the Wicked as with the Righteous,—it is best to enjoy Life as long as God grants it, viii. 10-15.

The theme of the following section shows itself by " and then " to be cognate. It is the opposition of the fate of the wicked and of the righteous to the inalienable consciousness of a moral government of the world ; this opposition comes forth, under the unhappy tyrannical government of which the foregoing section treats, as a prominent phenomenon.

Ver. 10. " And then I have seen the wicked buried, and they came to rest ; but away from the holy place they had to depart, and were forgotten in the city, such as acted justly : also this is vain." The double particle בְּכֵן signifies, in such a manner, or under such circumstances ; with " I have seen " following, it may introduce an observation coming under that which precedes (בכן = Mishnic בְּכֵן), or, with the force of the Lat. *inde*, introduce a further observation of that ruler ; this temporal signification " then " (= אָז), according to which we have translated, it has in the Targ. (*vid.* Levy's *W. B.*).[1] Apparently the observation has two different classes of men in view, and refers to their fate, contradicting, according to appearance, the rectitude of God. Opposite to the רָשָׁע (" the wicked ") stand they who are described as אֲשֶׁר וגו' : they who have practised what is rightly directed, what stands in a right relation (*vid.* regarding כֵּן, as noun, under Prov. xi. 19), have brought the morally right into practice, *i.e.* have acted with fidelity and honour (עָשָׂה כֵן, as at 2 Kings vii. 9). Koheleth has seen the wicked buried ; ראה is followed by the particip. as predic. obj., as is שמע, vii. 21 ; but קְבוּרִים is not followed by וּבָאִים (which, besides not being distinct enough as *part. perfecti*, would be, as at Neh. xiii. 22, *part. praes.*), but, according to the

---

[1] Cf. וְכֵן, 2 Chron. xxxii. 31 ; Ewald, § 354*a* ; Baer's *Abodath Jisrael*, pp. 384, 386.

favourite transition of the particip. into the finite, Gesen. § 134. 2,

by וְבָאוּ, not וּבָאוּ; for the disjunctive *Rebîa* has the fuller form with

וֹ; cf. Isa. xlv. 20 with Job xvii. 10, and above, at ii. 23. "To
enter in" is here, after Isa. xlvii. 2, = to enter into peace, come
to rest.[1] That what follows וּמִמְּ does not relate to the wicked, has
been mistaken by the LXX., Aquila, Symm., Theod., and Jerome,
who translate by ἐπῃνήθησαν, *laudabantur*, and thus read יִשְׁתַּבְּחוּ (the
Hithpa., Ps. cvi. 47, in the pass. sense), a word which is used in the
Talm. and Midrash along with יִשְׁתַּכְּחוּ.[2] The latter, testified to by
the Targ. and Syr., is without doubt the correct reading: the structure of the antithetical parallel members is chiastic; the naming of
the persons in 1 *a a* precedes that which is declared, and in 1 *a β* it
follows it; cf. Ps. lxx. 5 *b*, lxxv. 9 *b*. The fut. forms here gain, by
the retrospective perfects going before, a past signification. מְק' קָד',
"the place of the holy," is equivalent to מְקוֹם קָדוֹשׁ, as also at Lev.
vii. 6. Ewald understands by it the place of burial: "the upright
were driven away (cast out) from the holy place of graves." Thus
e.g. also Zöckl., who renders: but wandered far from the place of the
holy . . . those who did righteously, *i.e.* they had to be buried in
graves neither holy nor honourable. But this form of expression is
not found among the many designations of a burial-place used by
the Jews (*vid.* below, xii. 5, and Hamburger's *Real-Encykl. für Bibel
u. Talm.*, article "Grab"). God's-acre is called the "good place,"[3]
but not the "holy place." The "holy place," if not Jerusalem itself,
which is called by Isaiah II. (xlviii. 2), Neh., and Dan., *'ir haqqodesh*
(as now *el-kuds*), is the holy ground of the temple of God, the τόπος
ἅγιος (Matt. xxiv. 15), as Aquila and Symm. translate. If, now, we
find *min* connected with the verb *halak*, it is to be presupposed that
the *min* designates the point of departure, as also הִשְׁלַךְ מִן, Isa. xiv. 19.
Thus not: to wander far from the holy place; nor as Hitz., who
points יְהַלֵּכוּ: they pass away (perish) far from the holy place. The
subject is the being driven away from the holy place, but not as if יְהַל'
were causative, in the sense of יוֹלִיכוּ, and meant *ejiciunt*, with an indef.
subj. (Ewald, Heiligst., Elst.),—it is also, iv. 15, xi. 9, only the intens.
of *Kal*,—but יְהַלֵּךְ denotes, after Ps. xxxviii. 7, Job xxx. 28, cf.
xxiv. 10, the meditative, dull, slow walk of those who are compelled

---

[1] Cf. Zunz, *Zur Gesch. u. Literatur*, pp. 356–359.

[2] The Midrash *Tanchuma*, Par. יתרו, *init.*, uses both expressions; the Talm.
Gittin 56*b*, applies the passage to Titus, who took away the furniture of the temple
to magnify himself therewith in his city.

[3] *Vid.* Tendlau's *Sprichw.*, No. 431.

against their will to depart from the place which they love (Ps. xxvi. 8, lxxxiv. 2 ff.). They must go forth (whither, is not said, but probably into a foreign country; cf. Amos vii. 17), and only too soon are they forgotten in the city, viz. the holy city; a younger generation knows nothing more of them, and not even a gravestone brings them back to the memory of their people. Also this is a vanity, like the many others already registered—this, viz., that the wicked while living, and also in their death, possess the sacred native soil; while, on the contrary, the upright are constrained to depart from it, and are soon forgotten. Divine rectitude is herein missed. Certainly it exists, and is also recognised, but it does not show itself always when we should expect it, nor so soon as appears to us to be salutary.

Ver. 11. "Because judgment against the work of the wicked man is not speedily executed, for this reason the heart of the children of men is full within them, to this, that they do evil." The clause with *asher* is connected first with the foregoing *gam-zeh havel*: thus vain, after the nature of a perverted world (*inversus ordo*), events go on, because . . . (*asher*, as at iv. 3, vi. 12*b*; cf. Deut. iii. 24); but the following clause with '*al-ken* makes this clause with *asher* reflex. an antecedent of itself (*asher* = '*al-asher*)—originally it is not meant as an antecedent. פִּתְגָם [1] (here to be written after נַעֲשֹׁה, with פ *raph.*, and, besides, also with ג *raph.*), in the post-exilian books, is the Persian *paigam*, Armen. *patgam*, which is derived from the ancient Pers. *paiti-gama* : "Something that has happened, tidings, news." The Heb. has adopted the word in the general sense of "sentence;" in the passage before us it signifies the saying or sentence of the judge, as the Pers. word, like the Arab. *naban*, is used principally of the sayings of a prophet (who is called *peighâm-bar*). Zirkel regards it as the Greek φθέγμα; but thus, also, the words אָמֵל, אַפִּרְיוֹן strangely agree in sound with σμίλη, φορεῖον, without being borrowed from the Greek. The long *a* of the word is, as Elst. shows, i. 20, invariable; also here פִּתְגָם is the constr. To point פִּתְגָם, with Heiligst. and Burg., is thus unwarrantable. It is more remarkable that the word is construed fem. instead of mas. For since אַיִן is construed [2] neither in the bibl. nor in the Mishnic

<hr/>

[1] With ג *raph.* in H. P. and the older edd., as also Esth. i. 20; Dan. iii. 16. Thus also the punctuator Jekuthiél in his *En hakore* to Esth. i. 20.

[2] Ginsburg points in favour of נַעֲשֹׂה as fin. to Ex. iii. 2, but there אָכַל is particip.; to Jer. xxxviii. 5, but there יוּכַל (if it is not to be read יָבוֹא) represents an attributive clause; and to Job xxxv. 15, but there the word is rightly pointed אַיִן, not אֵין; and this, like the vulg. Arab. *laysa*, is used as an emphatic לֹא.

style with the finite of the verb, נַעֲשָׂה is not the 3d *pret.*, but the particip. It is not, however, necessary, with Hitz., to read נַעֲשָׂה. The foreign word, like the (Arab.) *firdans*, παράδεισος, admits of use in the double gend. (Ewald, § 174*g*) ; but it is also possible that the fem. נַעֲשָׂה is *per. attract.* occasioned by הָרָעָה, as Kimchi, *Michlol* 10*a*, supposes (cf. besides, under x. 15). מַעֲשֵׂה is const. governed by *phithgam*, and *hara'ah* is thus obj. gen. The LXX., Syr., and Jerome read מֵעֹשֵׂי, which would be possible only if *phithgam min*—after the analogy of the Heb.-Aram. phrase, *niphra'* ('*ithp°ra*') *min*, to take one's due of any one, *i.e.* to take vengeance on him, to punish him —could mean the full execution of punishment on any one ; but it means here, as Jerome rightly translates, *sententia ;* impossible, however, with *me'ose hara'ah, sententia contra malos.* Hengst. supposes that not only the traditional text, but also the accentuation, is correct, for he construes : because a sentence (of the heavenly Judge) is not executed, the work of wickedness is haste, *i.e.* speedy. Thus also Dachselt in the *Biblia accentuata.* Mercerus, on the contrary, remarks that the accents are not in the first instance marks of interpunction, but of cantillation. In fact, genit. word-connections do not exclude the keeping them asunder by distinctives such as *Pashta* and *Tiphcha*, Isa. x. 2, and also *Zakeph*, as *e.g.* Esth. i. 4. The LXX. well renders : "Therefore the heart of the sons of men is fully persuaded in them to do evil ; " for which Jerome, freely, after Symm. : *absque timore ullo filii hominum perpetrant mala.* The heart of one becomes full to do anything, is = it acquires full courage thereto (Luzzatto, § 590 : *gli blastò l'animo*) ; cf. Esth. vii. 5 : " Where is he who has his heart filled to do ? " (thus rightly, Keil), *i.e.* whom it has encouraged to so bold an undertaking. בָּהֶם in itself unnecessarily heightens the expression of the inwardness of the destructive work (*vid. Psychol.* p. 151 f.). The sentence of punishment does not take effect *m°hera*, hastily (adv. accus. for *bimherah*, iv. 12), therefore men are secure, and they give themselves with full, *i.e.* with fearless and shameless, boldness to the practice of evil. The author confirms this further, but not without expressing his own conviction that there is a righteous requital which contradicts this appearance.

Vers. 12, 13. "Because a sinner doeth evil an hundred times, and he becometh old therein, although I know that it will go well with them that fear God, that fear before Him : but it will not go well with the wicked, and he shall not live long, like a shadow ; because he feareth not before God." Ewald (whom Heiligst., Elst., and Zöckl. follow), as among the ancients, *e.g.* Mendelssohn, translates ver. 12: "Though a sinner do evil an hundred times, and live long, yet I know," etc. That an antecedent may begin with *asher* is admissible, Lev. iv. 22, Deut. xviii. 22; but in the case lying before us, still less acceptable than at ver. 11. For, in the first place, this *asher* of the antecedent cannot mean "although," but only "considering that;" and in places such as vi. 3, where this "considering that" may be exchanged with "although," there follows not the part., but the fut. natural to the concessive clause; then, in the second place, by this antecedent rendering of *asher* a closer connection of 12a and 12b is indeed gained, but the mediation of ver. 12 and ver. 11 is lost; in the third place, כי גם, in the meaning "however" (*gam, ὅμως*, with affirmative *ki*), is not found; not *asher*, but just this *ki gam*,[1] signifies, in the passage before us, as at iv. 14, εἰ καί, although,—only a somewhat otherwise applied *gam ki*, Ewald, § 362b, as כי על־כן is a somewhat otherwise applied על־כן כי. Rightly, Hitzig: "In 12a, 11a is again resumed, and it is explained how tardy justice has such a consequence." The sinner is thereby encouraged in sinning, because he does evil, and always again evil, and yet enjoys himself in all the pleasures of long life. Regarding חמא for חמא, *vid.* above, p. 197, 1. מאת is = מאה פעמים, an hundred times, as אחת, Job xl. 5, is = פעם אחת; Hengst. and others, inexactly: an hundredfold, which would have required the word מאתים; and falsely, Ginsburg, with the Targ.: an hundred years, which would have required מאה, *scil.* שנה, Gen. xvii. 17. This *centies* (Jerome) is, like מאה, *scil.* בנים, vi. 3, a round number for a great many, as at Prov. xvii. 10, and frequently in the Talm. and Midrash, *e.g. Wajikra rabba*, c. 27: "an hundred deeply-breathed sighs (מאה פעיות) the mother gave forth."[2] The meaning of ומאריך לו is in general clear: he becomes therein old. Jerome, improbable: *et per patientiam sustentatur*, as Mendelssohn: he experiences forbearance, for they supply אפו (Isa. xlviii. 9), and make God the subject. לו is in any case the so-called *dat. ethic.;* and the only question is, whether the doing of evil has to be taken from עשה רע,[3] as obj. to 'ומא: he practises it to him long, or whether, which is more probable, ימים is

---

[1] That גַּם is not pointed גַם, has its reason in the disjunctive *Jethib* with כִּי, which is not interchanged with the conjunctive *Mahpach*. Thus, viii. 1, מִי כְּ', and viii. 7, כִּי כַ'.

[2] *Vid.* Jac. Reifmann in the *Zeitsch.*, המגיד, 1874, p. 342.

[3] We expect these two words (cf. Gen. xxxi. 12) with the retrogression of the tone; but as this ceases, as a rule, with *Mercha* before *Tifcha* and *Pashta*, Gen. xlvii. 3, Ex. xviii. 5, Deut. iv. 42, xix. 4, Isa. x. 14 (cf. the penult. accent of יאבל, Lev. xxii. 10, 19, and בִּנֵה, Gen. iv. 17, with the ult. accent Lev. xxii. 14; Hab.

to be supplied after 13*a*, so that הַאֲרִיךְ signifies to live long, as at Prov. xxviii. 2, to last long; the *dat. ethic.* gives the idea of the feeling of contentment connected with long life: he thereupon sins wantonly, and becomes old in it in good health.

That is the actual state of the case, which the author cannot conceal from himself; although, on the other hand, as by way of limitation he adds *ki . . . ani*, he well knows that there is a moral government of the world, and that this must finally prevail. We may not translate: that it should go well, but rather: that it must go well; but there is no reason not to interpret the fut. as a pure indic.: that it shall go well, viz. finally,—it is a postulate of his consciousness which the author here expresses; that which exists in appearance contradicts this consciousness, which, however, in spite of this, asserts itself. That to לִיר׳ הָאֱל' the clause אֲשֶׁר מִלּ', explaining *idem per idem*, is added, has certainly its reason in this, that at the time of the author the name " fearers of God " [*Gottesfürchtige*] had come into use. " The fearers of God, who fear before (מִלְּפְנֵי, as at iii. 14) Him," are such as are in reality what they are called.

In ver. 13, Hitzig, followed by Elster, Burg., and Zöckl., places the division at יָמִים: like the shadow is he who fears not before God. Nothing can in point of syntax be said against this (cf. 1 Chron. xxix. 15), although כַּצֵּל אֲשֶׁר, " like the shadow is he who," is in point of style awkward. But that the author did not use so rude a style is manifest from vi. 12, according to which כצל is rightly referred to וְלֹא־ . . . יָמִים. Is then the shadow, asks Hitzig, because it does not " prolong its days," therefore קְצַר יָמִים? How subtle and literal is this use of יָמִים! Certainly the shadow survives not a day; but for that very reason it is short-lived, it may even indeed be called קְצַר יָמִים, because it has not existence for a single day. In general, *q^etsel*, ὡς σκιά, is applicable to the life of all men, Ps. cxliv. 4 , Wisd. ii. 5, etc. It is true of the wicked, if we keep in view the righteous divine requital, especially that he is short-lived like the shadow, " because he has no fear before God," and that in consequence of this want of fear his life is shortened by his sin inflicting its own punishment, and by the act of God. *Asher*, 13*b*, as at 11*a*, 12*a*, is the relative conj. Also in ver. 14, אֲשֶׁר (שׁ) as a pronoun, and אֲשֶׁר (שׁ) as a conj., are mixed together. After the author has declared the reality of a moral government of the world as an inalienable fact of human consciousness, and particularly of his own consciousness, he places over against this fact ii. 12), so with *Mercha* sometimes also before other disjunctives, as here before *Tebir*.

of consciousness the actual state of things partly at least contradicting it.

Ver. 14. " There is a vanity which is done on the earth ; that
there be just men, to whom it happeneth according to the conduct
of the wicked ; and that there be wicked men, to whom it happeneth
according to the conduct of the righteous—I said, that also this is
vain." The limiting clause with *ki gam*, 12*b*, 13, is subordinated to
the observation specified in vers. 10–12*a*, and the confirmation of it
is continued here in ver. 14. Regarding הִגִּיעַ, to happen, *vid.* above,
p. 193, under נָגַע. Jerome translates כְּמַ הַרְ׳ by *quasi opera egerint
impiorum*, and כמ׳ הַצַּ׳ by *quasi justorum facta habeant; instar operis
. . .* would be better, such as is conformable to the mode of acting of
the one and of the other; for כ is in the Semitic style of speech
a *nomen*, which annexes to itself the word that follows it in the
genitive, and runs through all the relations of case. This contradictory distribution of destiny deceives, misleads, and causes to err ;
it belongs to the illusory shadowy side of this present life, it is a
hevel. The concluding clause of this verse : " I said, that also this
is vain," begins to draw the *facit* from the observation, and is continued in the verse following.

Ver. 15. " And I commended joy, that there is nothing better
for a man under the sun than to eat and drink and enjoy himself ;
and that this accompanies him in his labour throughout all the days
of his life, which God hath given him under the sun." We already
read the *ultimatum*, 15*a*, in a similar form at ii. 24, iii. 12, 22 ; cf.
v. 17. With הוּא יִלְ׳ either begins a new clause, and the fut. is then
jussive : " let this accompany him," or it is subordinate to the foregoing infinitives, and the fut. is then subjunctive : *et ut id eum
comitetur.* The LXX. and other Greeks translate less appropriately
indicat.: καὶ αὐτὸ συμπροσέσται αὐτῷ. Thus also Ewald, Hengst.,
Zöckl., and others : and this clings to him, which, however, would
rather be expressed by והוא יִתְרוֹן לו or וה׳ חֶלְקוֹ. The verb לוה (R.
לו, to twist, to bend) does not mean to cling to = to remain, but to
adhere to, to follow, to accompany ; cf. under Gen. xviii. 16. The
possibility of the meaning, " to accompany," for the *Kal*, is supported
by the derivatives לִוְיָה and לוּי (particularly לְוָיַת הַמֵּתִים, convoy of the
dead) ; the verb, however, in this signification extra-bibl. is found
only in *Pih.* and *Hiph.*[1]

[1] *Vid.* Baer in *Abodath Jisrael*, p. 39.

The Fruitlessness of all Philosophizing, viii. 16, 17.

Like the distributions of destiny, so also labour and toil here below appear to the author to be on all sides an inextricable series of mysteries. Far from drawing atheistical conclusions therefrom, he sees in all that is done, viewed in its last causality, the work of God, *i.e.* the carrying out into execution of a divine law, the accomplishment of a divine plan. But this work of God, in spite of all his earnest endeavours, remains for man a subject of research for the future. Treating of this inexplicable difficulty, the words here used by the author himself are also hard to be understood.

Vers. 16, 17. " When I gave my heart to know wisdom, and to view the business which is done on the earth (for neither day nor night doth he see sleep with his eyes): then have I seen all the work of God, that a man is unable to find out the work which is done under the sun : therefore that a man wearieth himself to seek out, and yet findeth not ; and although a wise man taketh in hand to know,—he is unable to find." A long period without a premeditated plan has here formed itself under the hand of the author. As it lies before us, it is halved by the *vav* in *v'raithi* (" then I have seen ") ; the principal clause, introduced by " when I gave," can nowhere otherwise begin than here ; but it is not indicated by the syntactical structure. Yet in Chron. and Neh. apodoses of כאשר begin with the second consec. modus, *e.g.* 1 Chron. xvii. 1, Neh. iv. 1, and frequently ; but the author here uses this modus only rarely, and not (*vid.* iv. 1, 7) as a sign of an apodosis.

We consider, first, the protasis, with the parenthesis in which it terminates. The phrase נתן את־הלב לֹ, to direct the heart, to give attention and effort toward something, we have now frequently met with from i. 13 down. The aim is here twofold: (1) " to know wisdom " (cf. i. 17), *i.e.* to gain the knowledge of that which is wisdom, and which is to be regarded as wisdom, viz. solid knowledge regarding the essence, causes, and objects of things ; (2) by such knowledge about that which wisdom is in itself " to see earthly labour," and—this arises from the combination of the two resolutions —to comprehend this labour in accordance with the claims of true wisdom from the point of view of its last ground and aim. Regarding *'inyan, vid.* under iii. 10. " On the earth " and " under the sun " are parallel designations of this world.

With כִּי נַם begins a parenthetical clause. *Ki* may also, it is true, be rendered as at 17*a* : the labour on the earth, that he, etc. (Zöckl.) ; but this restlessness, almost renouncing sleep, is thereby pressed too much into the foreground as the special obj. of the *r*ᵉ*uth* (therefore Ginsburg introduces " how that ") ; thus better to render this clause with *ki gam*, as establishing the fact that there is *'inyan*, self-tormenting, restless labour on the earth. Thus also אֵינֶנּוּ is easier explained, which scarcely goes back to *läadam*, 15*a* (Hitz.), but shows that the author, by *'inyan*, has specially men in view. גַּם . . . וּבְכָל? is = נַם בִּי' נַם בְּל' : as well by day as by night, with the negat. following (cf. Num. xxiii. 25 ; Isa. xlviii. 8) : neither by day nor by night ; not only by day, but also in the night, not. " To see sleep " is a phrase occurring only here ; cf. Terence, *Heautontim.* iii. 1. 82, *Somnum hercle ego hac nocte oculis non vidi meis*, for which we use the expression : " In this whole night my eyes have seen no sleep." The not wishing to sleep, and not being able to sleep, is such an hyperbole, carrying its limitation in itself, as is found in Cicero (*ad Famil.* vii. 30) : *Fuit mirifica vigilantia, qui toto suo consulatu somnum non vidit.*

With וּר', " Then I have seen," begins the apodosis : *vidi totum Dei opus non posse hominem assequi.* As at ii. 24*b*, the author places the obj. in the foreground, and lets the pred. with *ki* follow (for other examples of this so-called antiposis, *vid.* under Gen. i. 4). He sees in the labour here below one side of God's work carrying itself forward amid this restless confusion, and sets forth this work of God, as at iii. 11 (but where the connection of the thoughts is different), as an object of knowledge remaining beyond the reach of man. He cannot come to it, or, as מצא properly means, he reaches not to it, therefore " that a man wearies himself to seek, and yet finds not," *i.e.* that the search on the part of a man with all his endeavours comes not to its aim. בכל אשר [Ewald's emendation, instead of the words of the text before us] : for all this, that *quantumcunque* (Ewald, § 362*c*), which seems to have been approved of by the LXX., Syr., and Jerome, is rightly rejected by Hitzig ; *b*ᵉ*shel asher* is Heb., exactly equivalent to Aram. דְּבִדיל, *e.g.* Gen. vi. 3 ; and is rightly glossed by Rashi, Kimchi, *Michlol* 47*b*, by שֶׁ בִּשְׁבִיל and בַּעֲבוּר שֶׁ. The accent dividing the verse stands on *yimᵉtsa*, for to this word extends the first half of the apodosis, with *v*ᵉ*gam* begins the second. *Gam im* is = εἰ καί, as *gam ki* is = ἐὰν καί. יאמר is to be understood after אמ' אח', vii. 23 : also if (although) the wise man resolves to know, he cannot reach that which is to be known. The characteristic mark of the wise man is thus not so much the possession as the striving after it. He strives after knowledge, but the highest problems remain unsolved by him, and his ideal of knowledge unrealized.

The Power of Fate, and the best possible Thing for Man in his Want of Freedom, ix. 1–12.

He cannot attain unto it, for to the thoughts as well as to the acts of man God has put a limit.

ix. 1. " For all this I brought to my consciousness, and all this I sought to make clear to me, that the righteous, and the wise, and their deeds, are in God's hands : neither love nor hatred stands in the knowledge of man, all lies before them." With *ki* follows the verification of what is said in viii. 17*b*, " is unable to find out," from the fact of men, even the best and the wisest of men, being on all sides conditioned. This conditioning is a fact which he layeth to his heart (vii. 2), or (since he here presents himself less as a feeling than as a thinking man, and the heart as reflecting) which he has brought to his consciousness, and which he has sought to bring out into clearness. וְלָבוּר has here not the force of an *inf. absol.*, so that it subordinates itself in an adverbial manner (*et ventilando quidem*)— for it nowhere stands in the same rank with the *inf. absol.* ; but the inf. with ל (לְ) has the force of an intentional (with a tendency) fut., since the governing הָיִיתִי, as at iii. 15*a*, הָיָה, and at Hab. i. 17*b*, יִהְיֶה, is to be supplied (*vid.* comm. on these passages, and under Isa. xliv. 14) : *operam dedi ut ventilarem* (*excuterem*), or shorter : *ventilaturus fui*. Regarding the form לָבוּר, which is metapl. for לָבֹר, and the double idea of sifting (particularly winnowing, *ventilare*) of the R. בר, *vid.* under iii. 18. In the post-bibl. Heb. the words להעמיד על בוריו would denote the very same as is here expressed by the brief significant word לָבוּר ; a matter in the clearness of its actual condition is called דבר על בוריו (from בְּרִי, after the form חֲלִי, purity, *vid.* Buxtorf's *Lex. Talm.* col. 366). The LXX. and Syr. have read ולבי ראה instead of ולבור, apparently because they could not see their way with it : " And my heart has seen all this." The expression " all this " refers both times to what follows ; *asher* is, as at viii. 12, relat. conj., in the sense of ὅτι, *quod*, and introduces, as at vii. 29, cf. viii. 14, the unfolding of the זֶה,—an unfolding, viz., of the conditioning of man, which viii. 17 declared on one side of it, and whose further verification is here placed in view with *ki*, 1*a*. The righteous, and the wise, and their doings, are in God's hand, *i.e.* power (Ps. xxxi. 16 ; Prov. xxi. 1 ; Job xii. 10, etc.) ; as well their persons as their actions, in respect of their last cause, are conditioned by God, the Governor of the world and the Former of history ; also the righteous and the wise learn to feel this dependence, not only in their being and in what befalls them, but also in their conduct ; also this is not fully attained, לֹא

ידם, they are also therein not sufficient of themselves. Regarding 'avadēhĕm, corresponding to the Aram. 'ovadēhon, vid. 'avad, p. 194.

The expression now following cannot mean that man does not know whether he will experience the love or hatred of God, i.e. providences of a happy nature proceeding from the love of God, or of an unhappy nature proceeding from the hatred of God (J. D. Michaelis, Knobel, Vaih., Hengst., Zöckl.), for אַהֲבָה and שִׂנְ' are too general for this,—man is thus, as the expression denotes, not the obj., but the subj. to both. Rightly, Hitz., as also Ewald: "Since man has not his actions in his own power, he knows not whether he will love or hate." Certainly this sounds deterministic; but is it not true that personal sympathies and antipathies, from which love and hatred unfold themselves, come within the sphere of man, not only as to their objects, in consequence of the divine arrangement, but also in themselves anticipate the knowledge and the will of man? and is it less true that the love which he now cherishes toward another man changes itself, without his previous knowledge, by means of unexpected causes, into hatred, and, on the other hand, the hatred into love? Neither love nor hatred is the product of a man's self-determination; but self-determination, and with it the function of freedom, begins for the first time over against those already present, in their beginnings. In הַכֹּל לִפְ', "by all that is before him," that is brought to a general expression, in which לִפְנֵי has not the ethical meaning proceeding from the local: before them, prae = penes eos (vid. Song, under viii. 12a), but the purely local meaning, and referred to time: love, hatred, and generally all things, stand before man; God causes them to meet him (cf. the use of הִקְרָה); they belong to the future, which is beyond his power. Thus the Targ., Symm., and most modern interpreters; on the contrary, Luther: "neither the love nor the hatred of any one which he has for himself," which is, linguistically, purely impossible; Kleinert: "Neither the love nor the hatred of things does man see through, nor anything else which is before his eyes," for which we ought at least to have had the words גם הכל אשר לפניו; and Tyler: "Men discern neither love nor hatred in all that is before them," as if the text were בכל אשר. The future can, it is true, be designated by אַחֲרִית, and the past by לְפָנִים, but according to the most natural way of representation (vid. Orelli's Synon. der Zeit, p. 14) the future is that which lies before a man, and the past that which is behind him. The question is of importance, which of the two words הכל לפ' has the accent. If the accent be on לפ', then the meaning is, that all lies before men deprived of their freedom; if the accent be on הכל, then the meaning is, that all

things, events of all kinds, lie before them, and that God determines
which shall happen to them. The latter is more accordant with the
order of words lying before us, and shows itself to be that which is
intended by the further progress of the thoughts. Every possible
thing may befall a man—what actually meets him is the determination and providence of God. The determination is not according to
the moral condition of a man, so that the one can guide to no certain conclusion as to the other.

Ver. 2. "All is the same which comes to all: one event happens
to the righteous and the wicked, to the good and the pure and the
impure; to him that sacrificeth, and to him that sacrificeth not: as
with the good, so is it with the sinner; with him that sweareth, as
with him that feareth an oath." Hitzig translates: "All are alike,
one fate comes on all," adding the remark, that to make מקרה אחד
at the same time pred. to הכל and subj. to כאשר לכל was, for the
punctator, too much. This translation is indeed in matter, as well
as in point of syntax, difficult to be comprehended. Rather, with
Ewald, translate: All is as if all had one fate (death); but why
then this useless *hevel haasher*, only darkening the thought? But
certainly, since in הַכֹּל [1] the past is again resumed, it is to be supposed that it does not mean personally, *omnes*, but neut., *omnia;*
and לַכֹּל, on the contrary, manifestly refers (as at x. 3) to persons.
Herein agreeing with Ewald, and, besides, with Knobel, Zöckl., and
others, we accept the interpunction as it lies before us. The apparently meaningless clause, *omnia sicut omnibus*, gives, if we separate
sicut into *sic* and *ut*, the brief but pregnant thought: All is (thus)
as it happens to all, *i.e.* there is no distinction of their experiences
nor of their persons; all of every sort happens in the same way to
all men of every sort. The thought, written in cyphers in this
manner, is then illustrated; the *lameds* following leave no doubt as
to the meaning of לכל. Men are classified according to their different
kinds. The good and the pure stand opposite the impure; טָמֵא is
thus the defiled, Hos. v. 3, cf. Ezek. xxxvi. 25, in body and soul.
That the author has here in his mind the precepts of the law regarding
the pure and the impure, is to be concluded from the following contrast: he who offers sacrifice, and he who does not offer sacrifice, *i.e.*
he who not only does not bring free-will offerings, but not even the
sacrifices that are obligatory. Finally, he who swears, and he who
is afraid of an oath, are distinguished. Thus, Zech. v. 3, he who

[1] The LXX., Syr., and Aq. have read together the end of ver. 1 and the
beginning of ver. 2. Here Jerome also is dependent on this mode of reading:
sed omnia in futurum servantur incerta (הבל).

swears stands along with him who steals. In itself, certainly,
swearing an oath is not a sin; in certain circumstances (*vid.* viii. 2)
it is a necessary, solemn act (Isa. lxv. 16). But here, in the
passage from Zechariah, swearing of an unrighteous kind is meant,
i.e. wanton swearing, a calling upon God when it is not necessary,
and, it may be, even to confirm an untruth, Ex. xx. 7. Compare
Matt. v. 34. The order of the words שְׁבֻ יָרֵ׳ (cf. as to the expression,
the Mishnic יְרֵא חֵטְא) is as at Nah. iii. 1; Isa. xxii. 2; cf. above,
v. 8*b*. One event befalls all these men of different characters, by
which here not death exclusively is meant (as at iii. 19, ii. 14), but
this only chiefly as the same end of these experiences which are not
determined according to the moral condition of men. In the expression of the equality, there is an example of stylistic refinement
in a threefold change; בַּטּוֹב כַּח׳ denotes that the experience of the
good is the experience of the sinner, and may be translated, "*wie der
Gute so der Sünder*" [as the good, so the sinner], as well as "*so der
Gute wie der Sünder*" [so the good as the sinner] (cf. Köhler, under
Hag. ii. 3). This sameness of fate, in which we perceive the want
of the inter-connection of the physical and moral order of the world,
is in itself and in its influence an evil matter.

Ver. 3. "This is an evil in all that is done under the sun, that
one event happeneth to all: and also the heart of the children of
men is full of evil; and madness possesseth their heart during their
life, and after it they go to the dead." As זה, 1*a*, points to the
asher following, in which it unfolds itself, so here to the *ki* following. We do not translate: This is the worst thing (Jerome: *hoc
est pessimum*), which, after Josh. xiv. 15, Judg. vi. 15, Song i. 8,
would have required the words הָרַע בכל—the author does not designate the equality of fate as the greatest evil, but as an evil mixed
with all earthly events. It is an evil in itself, as being a contradiction to the moral order of the world; and it is such also on account
of its demoralizing influences. The author here repeats what he had
already, viii. 11, said in a more special reference, that because evil
is not in this world visibly punished, men become confident and
bold in sinning. *V'gam* (referable to the whole clause, at the
beginning of which it is placed) stands beside *zeh ra'*, connecting
with that which is evil in itself its evil influences. מָלֵא might be
an adj., for this (only once, Jer. vi. 11), like the verb, is connected
with the accus., *e.g.* Deut. xxxiii. 23. But, since not a statement
but a *factum* had to be uttered, it is finite, as at viii. 11. Thus
Jerome, after Symm.: *sed et cor filiorum hominum repletur malitia et
procacitate juxta cor eorum in vita sua.* Keeping out of view the

false *sed*, this translation corresponds to the accenting which gives the conjunctive *Kadma* to רָע. But without doubt an independent substantival clause begins with וְהוֹ׳: and madness is in their heart (*vid.* i. 17) their life long; for, without taking heed to God's will and to what is pleasing to God, or seeking after instruction, they think only of the satisfaction of their inclinations and lusts.

" And after that they go to the dead "—they who had so given themselves up to evil, and revelled in fleshly lusts with security, go the way of all flesh, as do the righteous, and the wise, and just, because they know that they go beyond all restraining bounds. Most modern interpreters (Hitz., Ew., etc.) render *aharav*, after Jer. li. 46, adverbially, with the suffix understood neut. : afterwards (Jerome, *post haec*). But at iii. 22, vi. 12, vii. 14, the suffix refers to man : after him, him who liveth here = after he has laid down his life. Why should it not be thus understood also here ? It is true בְּחַיָּ׳ precedes it ; but in the reverse way, sing. and plur. also interchange in ver. 1; cf. iii. 12. Rightly the Targ., as with Kleinert and others, we also explain : after their (his) lifetime. A man's life finally falls into the past, it lies behind him, and he goes forth to the dead ; and along with self-consciousness, all the pleasures and joy of life at the same time come to an end.

Ver. 4. "For (to him) who shall be always joined to all the living, there is hope : for even a living dog is better than a dead lion." The interrog. מִי אֲשֶׁר, *quis est qui*, acquires the force of a relative, *quisquis* (*quicunque*), and may be interpreted, Ex. xxxii. 33, 2 Sam. xx. 12, just as here (cf. the simple *mi*, v. 9), in both ways ; particularly the latter passage (2 Sam. xx. 11) is also analogous to the one before us in the formation of the apodosis. The *Chethîb* יבחר does not admit of any tenable meaning. In conformity with the *usus loq.*, Elster reads מִי אֲשֶׁר יִבְחָר, " who has a choice?" But this rendering has no connection with what follows ; the sequence of thoughts fails. Most interpreters, in opposition to the *usus loq.*, by pointing יְבְחַר or יֻבַּחַר, render: Who is (more correctly: will be) excepted? or also: Who is it that is to be preferred (the living or the dead) ? The verb בָּחַר signifies to choose, to select ; and the choice may be connected with an exception, a preference ; but in itself the verb means neither *excipere* nor *praeferre*.[1] All the old translators, with right, follow the *Kerî*, and the Syr. renders it correctly, word for word : to every one who is joined (שׁוּתַף, Aram. = Heb. חֻבַּר) to all the living there is

---

[1] Luther translates, "for to all the living there is that which is desired, namely, hope," as if the text were מָה אֲשֶׁר יִבְחָר.

hope ; and this translation is more probable than that on which
Symm. ("who shall always continue to live ?") and Jerome (*nemo
est qui semper vivat et qui hujus rei habeat fiduciam*) proceed : Who
is he that is joined to the whole ? *i.e.* to the absolute life ; or as
Hitzig : Who is he who would join himself to all the living (like
the saying, "The everlasting Jew ")? The expression בָּטֵּ יֵשׁ does
not connect itself so easily and directly with these two latter renderings as with that we have adopted, in which, as also in the other
two, a different accentuation of the half-verse is to be adopted as
follows :

$$\text{כִּי מִי אֲשֶׁר יְחֻבַּר אֶל־כָּל־הַחַיִּים יֵשׁ בִּטָּחוֹן}$$

The accentuation lying before us in the text, which gives a great
disjunctive to יבחֹר as well as to הח׳, appears to warrant the *Chethîb*
(cf. Hitzig under Ezek. xxii. 24), by which it is possible to interpret
מִי ... יב׳ as in itself an interrog. clause. The *Kerî* יח׳ does not
admit of this, for Dachselt's *quis associabit se* (sc. *mortuis?* = *nemo
socius mortuorum fieri vult*) is a linguistic impossibility ; the reflex
may be used for the pass., but not the pass. for the reflex., which is also
an argument against Ewald's translation : Who is joined to the living
has hope. Also the Targ. and Rashi, although explaining according
to the Midrash, cannot forbear connecting אל כל־הח׳ with יח׳, and
thus dividing the verse at הח׳ instead of at יח׳. It is not, however, to
be supposed that the accentuation refers to the *Chethîb;* it proceeds on
some interpretation, contrary to the connection, such as this : he who
is received into God's fellowship has to hope for the full life (in
eternity). The true meaning, according to the connection, is this :
that whoever (*quicunque*) is only always joined (whether by birth or
the preservation of life) to all the living, *i.e.* to living beings, be
they who they may, has full confidence, hope, and joy ; for in
respect to a living dog, this is even better than a dead lion. Symmachus translates : κυνὶ ζῶντι βέλτιόν ἐστιν ἢ λέοντι τεθνηκότι,
which Rosenm., Herzf., and Grätz approve of. But apart from the
obliquity of the comparison, that with a living dog it is better than
with a dead lion, since with the latter is neither good nor evil (*vid.*
however, vi. 5b), for such a meaning the words ought to have been :
chêlĕv häi tov lo min ha'aryēh hammeth.

As the verifying clause stands before us, it is connected not
with יֵשׁ בָּטֵּ, but with אֶל כָּל־הַח׳, of that which is to be verified ; the לְ
gives emphatic prominence (Ewald, § 310b) to the subject, to which
the expression refers as at Ps. lxxxix. 19, 2 Chron. vii. 21 (cf. Jer.
xviii. 16), Isa. xxxii. 1 : A living dog is better than a dead lion, *i.e.* it

is better to be a dog which lives, than that lion which is dead. The
dog, which occurs in the Holy Scriptures only in relation to a shepherd's dog (Job xxx. 1), and as for the rest, appears as a voracious
filthy beast, roaming about without a master, is the proverbial
emblem of that which is common, or low, or contemptible, 1 Sam.
xvii. 43; cf. "dog's head," 2 Sam. iii. 8; "dead dog," 1 Sam.
xxiv. 15; 2 Sam. ix. 8, xvi. 9. The lion, on the other hand, is the
king, or, as Agur (Prov. xxx. 30) calls it, the hero among beasts.
But if it be dead, then all is over with its dignity and its strength;
the existence of a living dog is to be preferred to that of the dead
lion. The art. in הָאֲרִי הַמֵּת is not that denoting species (Dale), which
is excluded by *hammēth*, but it points to the carcase of a lion which
is present. The author, who elsewhere prefers death and nonentity
to life, iv. 2 f., vii. 1, appears to have fallen into contradiction with
himself; but there he views life pessimistically in its, for the most
part, unhappy experiences, while here he regards it in itself as a good
affording the possibility of enjoyment. It lies, however, in the
nature of his standpoint that he should not be able to find the right
medium between the sorrow of the world and the pleasure of life.
Although postulating a retribution in eternity, yet in his thoughts
about the future he does not rise above the comfortless idea of Hades.

Vers. 5, 6. He sarcastically verifies his comparison in favour of
a living dog. "For the living know that they shall die; but the
dead know not anything, and have no more a reward; for their
memory is forgotten. Their love, as well as their hatred and their
envy, has long ago perished, and they have part no more for ever in
all that is done under the sun." The description of the condition of
death begins sarcastically and then becomes elegiac. "They have no
reward further," viz. in this upper world, since there it is only too
soon forgotten that they once existed, and that they did anything
worthy of being remembered; Koheleth might here indeed, with his
view shrouded in dark clouds, even suppose that God also forgot
them, Job xiv. 13. The suff. of אַהֲבָתָם, etc., present themselves as
subjective, and there is no reason, with Knobel and Ginsburg, to
render them objectively: not merely the objects of their love, and
hatred, and envy, are lost to them, but these their affections and
strivings themselves have ceased (Rosenm., Hitzig, Zöckl., and
others), they lie (*Kᵉvar 'avadah*) far behind them as absolutely gone;
for the dead have no part more in the history which is unfolding
itself amid the light of the upper world, and they can have no more
any part therein, for the dead as not living are not only without
knowledge, but also without feeling and desire. The representation

of the state after death is here more comfortless than anywhere else. For elsewhere we read that those who have been living here spend in *Sheol*, *i.e.* in the deep (R. שׁל, to be loose, to hang down, to go downwards) realm of the dead, as *rᵉphāim* (Isa. xiv. 9, etc.), lying beneath the upper world, far from the love and the praise of God (Ps. vi. 3, xxx. 10), a prospectless (Job vii. 7 f., xiv. 6–12 ; Ps. lxxxviii. 11–13), dark, shadowy existence ; the soul in Hades, though neither annihilated nor sleeping, finds itself in a state of death no less than does the body in the grave. But here the state of death is not even set forth over against the idea of the dissolution of life, the complete annihilation of individuality, much less that a retribution in eternity, *i.e.* a retribution executed, if not here, yet at some time, postulated elsewhere by the author, throws a ray of light into the night of death. The apocryphal book of the Wisdom of Solomon, which distinguishes between a state of blessedness and a state of misery measured out to men in the future following death, has in this surpassed the canonical Book of Koheleth. In vain do the Targ., Midrash, and the older Christian interpreters refer that which is said to the wicked dead ; others regard Koheleth as introducing here the discourse of atheists (*e.g.* Oetinger), and interpret, under the influence of monstrous self-deception, ver. 7 as the voice of the spirit (Hengst.) opposing the voice of the flesh. But that which Koheleth expresses here only in a particularly rugged way is the view of Hades predominating in the O. T. It is the consequence of viewing death from the side of its anger. Revelation intentionally permits this manner of viewing it to remain ; but from premises which the revelation sets forth, the religious consciousness in the course of time draws always more decidedly the conclusion, that the man who is united to God will fully reach through death that which since the entrance of sin into the world cannot be reached without the loss of this present life, *i.e.* without death, viz. a more perfect life in fellowship with God. Yet the confusion of the O. T. representation of Hades remains ; in the Book of Sirach it also still throws its deep shadows (xvii. 22 f.) into the contemplation of the future ; for the first time the N. T. solution actually removes the confusion, and turns the scale in favour of the view of death on its side of light. In this history of the ideas of eternity moving forward amid many fluctuations to the N. T. goal, a significant place belongs to the Book of Koheleth ; certainly the Christian interpreter ought not to have an interest in explaining away and concealing the imperfections of knowledge which made it impossible for the author spiritually to rise above his pessimism. He does not rise, in contrast to his pessimism, above an eudaemonism which is earthly, which, without knowing of a future life (not like the modern pessimism, without *wishing to know* of a future life), recommends a pleasant enjoyment of the present life, so far as that is morally allowable:

Vers. 7–10. " Go, eat thy bread with joy, and drink thy wine with a merry heart; for long ago hath God accepted thy work. Let thy garments be always white; and let not oil be wanting to thy head. Enjoy life with a wife whom thou lovest through all the days of thy vain life, which He hath given thee under the sun—through all thy vain days: for that is thy portion in life, and in thy labour wherewith thou weariest thyself under the sun. All that thy hand may find to do with thy might, that do; for there is not work, and calculation, and knowledge, and wisdom, in the under world, whither thou shalt go." Hengstenberg perceives here the counterpart of the spirit; on the contrary, Oetinger, Mendelssohn, and others, discover also here, and here for the first time rightly, the utterance of an epicurean thought. But, in fact, this לֵךְ down to שֶׁ֫ הוֹלֵךְ is the most distinct personal utterance of the author, his *ceterum censeo* which pervades the whole book, and here forms a particularly copious conclusion of a long series of thoughts. We recapitulate this series of thoughts: One fate, at last the same final event, happens to all men, without making any distinction according to their moral condition,—an evil matter, so much the more evil, as it encourages to wickedness and light-mindedness; the way of man, without exception, leads to the dead, and all further prospect is cut off; for only he who belongs to the class of living beings has a joyful spirit, has a spirit of enterprise: even the lowest being, if it live, stands higher in worth, and is better, than the highest if it be dead; for death is the end of all knowledge and feeling, the being cut off from the living under the sun. From this, that there is only one life, one life on this side of eternity, he deduces the exhortation to enjoy the one as much as possible; God Himself, to whom we owe it, will have it so that we enjoy it, within the moral limits prescribed by Himself indeed, for this limitation is certainly given with His approbation. Incorrectly, the Targ., Rashi, Hengst., Ginsb., and Zöckl. explain: For thy moral conduct and effort have pleased Him long ago—the person addressed is some one, not a definite person, who could be thus set forth as such a witness to be commended. Rather with Grotius and others: *Quia Deus favet laboribus tuis h. e. eos ita prosperavit, ut cuncta quae vitam delectant abunde tibi suppetant.* The thought is wholly in the spirit of the Book of Koheleth; for the fruit of labour and the enjoyment of this fruit of labour, as at ii. 24, iii. 13, etc., is a gift from above ; and besides, this may be said to the person addressed, since 7a presupposes that he has at his disposal heart-strengthening bread and heart-refreshing wine. But in these two explanations the meaning of כְּבָר is not comprehended. It was left untranslated by the old translators, from their not understanding it. Rightly, Aben Ezra : For God wills that thou shouldst thus do [indulge in these enjoyments]; more correctly, Hitzig: Long ago God has beforehand permitted this thy conduct, so that thou hast no room for scruples about it. How significant כבר is for the thought, is indicated by the accentuation which gives to it *Zakef* : from afore-time God has impressed the seal of His approbation on this thy eating with joy, this thy drinking with a merry heart.—The assigning of the reason gives courage to the enjoyment, but at the same time gives to it a consecration; for it is the will of God that we should enjoy life, thus it is self-evident that we have to enjoy it as He wills it to be enjoyed.

Ver. 8. The white garments, לְבָנִים, are in contrast to the black robes of mourning, and thus are an expression of festal joy, of a happy mood ; black and white are, according to the ancients, colour-symbols, the colours respectively of sorrow and joy, to which light and darkness correspond.[1] Fragrant oil is also, according to Prov. xxvii. 9, one of the heart-refreshing things. Sorrow and anointing exclude one another, 2 Sam. xiv. 2 ; joy and oil stand in closest mutual relation, Ps. xlv. 8, Isa. lxi. 3 ; oil which smooths the hair and makes the face shine (*vid.* under Ps. civ. 15). This oil ought not to be wanting to the head, and thus the perpetuity of a happy life should suffer no interruption.

In 9a most translators render : Enjoy life with the wife whom thou lovest; but the author purposely does not use the word הָאִשָּׁה, but אִשָּׁה ; and also that he uses חַיִּים, and not הַחַיִּים, is not without significance. He means : Bring into experience what life, what happiness, is (cf. the indetermin. ideas, Ps. xxxiv. 13) with a wife whom thou hast loved (Jerome : *quaecunque tibi placuerit feminarum*), in which there lies indirectly the call to choose such an one ; whereby the

[1] Cf. *Shabbath* 114a : " Bury me neither in white nor in black garments : not in white, because perhaps I may not be one of the blessed, and am like a bridegroom among mourners ; not in black, because perhaps I may be one of the blessed, and am like a mourner among bridegrooms." *Semachoth* ii. 10 : Him who is outside the congregation, they do not bury with solemnity ; the brothers and relatives of such must clothe and veil themselves in white ; cf. *Joma* 39b. Elsewhere white is the colour of innocence, *Shabbath* 153a, *Midrash* under Prov. xvi. 11 ; and black the colour of guilt, *Kiddushin* 40a, etc.

pessimistic criticism of the female sex, vii. 26–28, so far as the author is concerned, falls into the background, since eudaemonism, the other side of his view of the world, predominates. The accus. designation of time, " through all the days of the life of thy vanity (*i.e.* of thy transient vain life)," is like vi. 12, cf. vii. 15. It is repeated in " all the days of thy vanity ; " the repetition is heavy and unnecessary (therefore omitted by the LXX., Targ., and Syr.); probably like והדרך, Ps. xlv. 5, a *ditto ;* Hitzig, however, finds also here great emphasis. The relative clause standing after the first designation of time refers to "the days which He (האלהים, 7*b*) has granted under the sun." *Hu* in 9*b* refers attractionally to חֶלְקָד (Jerome : *haec est enim pars*), as at iii. 22, v. 17, cf. vii. 2 ; היא of the Babyl. is therefore to be rejected ; this enjoyment, particularly of marriage joys, is thy part in life, and in thy work which thou accomplishest under the sun, *i.e.* the real portion of gain allotted to thee which thou mayest and oughtest to enjoy here below.

Ver. 10. The author, however, recommends no continual *dolce far niente,* no idle, useless sluggard-life devoted to pleasure, but he gives to his exhortation to joy the converse side : " All that thy hand may reach (*i.e.* what thou canst accomplish and is possible to thee, 1 Sam. x. 7 ; Lev. xii. 8) to accomplish it with thy might, that do." The accentuation is ingenious. If the author meant : That do with all might (Jerome : *instanter operare*), then he would have said *b^echol-kohhacha* (Gen. xxxi. 6). As the words lie before us, they call on him who is addressed to come not short in his work of any possibility according to the measure of his strength, thus to a work straining his capacity to the uttermost. The reason for the call, 10*b*, turns back to the clause from which it was inferred : in Hades, whither thou must go (*iturus es*), there is no work, and reckoning (*vid.* vii. 25), and knowledge (וְדַעַת[1]), and no wisdom. Practice and theory have then an end. Thus : Enjoy, but not without working, ere the night cometh when no man can work. Thus spake Jesus (John ix. 4), but in a different sense indeed from Koheleth. The night which He meant is the termination of this present life, which for Him, as for every man, has its particular work, which is either accomplished within the limits of this life, or is not accomplished at all.

---

[1] Not וְדַעַת, because the word has the conjunctive, not the disjunctive accent, *vid.* under Ps. lv. 10. The punctuation, as we have already several times remarked, is not consistent in this ; cf. וְדַעַת, ii. 26, and וְעֹרֵב, Ps. lxv. 9, both of which are contrary to the rule (*vid.* Baer in Abulwalîd's *Rikma*, p. 119, note 2).

The Incalculableness of the Issues and of the Duration of Life,
ix. 11, 12.

Another reflection, so far not without connection in the foregoing,
as the fact of experience, that ability is yet no security for the issue
aimed at and merited, is chiefly referred to wisdom :

Ver. 11. " Further, I came to see under the sun, that the race
belongs not to the swift, and the war not to the heroes, and also not
bread to the wise man, and not riches to the prudent, and not favour
to men of knowledge ; for time and chance happeneth to them all."
The nearest preceding 'רָא, to which this 'שַׁב 'וְרָא suitably connects
itself, is at viii. 17. Instead of *redii et videndo quidem = rursus vidi*
(cf. viii. 9 and under ix. 1), we had at iv. 1 the simpler expression, *redii
et vidi*. The five times repeated ל is that of property, of that, viz., by
virtue of which one is master of that which is named, has power over
it, disposes of it freely. The race belongs not to the swift (מֵרוֹץ, masc.
to מְרוּצָה, only here), *i.e.* their fleetness is yet no guarantee that on
account of it they will reach the goal. Luther freely : " To be
fleet does not help in running," *i.e.* running to an object or goal.
" The war belongs not to the heroes," means that much rather it
belongs to the Lord, 1 Sam. xvii. 47.—God alone gives the victory
(Ps. xxxiii. 16). Even so the gaining of bread, riches, favour (*i.e.*
influence, reputation), does not lie in wisdom, prudence, knowledge
of themselves, as an indispensable means thereto; but the obtaining
of them, or the not obtaining of them, depends on times and circumstances which lie beyond the control of man, and is thus, in the
final result, conditioned by God (cf. Rom. ix. 16 [1]) ; time and fate
happen to all whose ability appears to warrant the issue, they both
[time and fate] encounter them and bar to them the way ; they
are in an inexplicable manner dependent on both, and helplessly
subject to them. As the idea of spiritual superiority is here
expressed in a threefold manner by 'הֶחָ (whence 'לַחֲ of the plur., also
with the art. ix. 1 ; Ex. xxxvi. 4; Esth. i. 13), 'הַנ, and 'הַי, so at Isa.
xi. 2, the gifts of " wisdom," " counsel," and " knowledge " follow each
other. '*Eth* is here "time" with its special circumstances (conjunc-
tures), and *pega'*, " accident," particularly as an adversity, disappointment, for the word is used also without any addition (1 Kings v. 18)
of misfortune (cf. שיר פגעים, Ps. iii., xci.). The masc. 'יְקָ is regulated
after 'וּפ ; '*eth* can, however, be used in the masc., Song ii. 12 ; Böttch.
§ 648, viz. " with the misapprehension of its origin " (v. Orelli).

[1] But not Jer. ix. 22 ; this passage, referred to by Bernstein, is of a different
nature.

This limitation of man in his efforts, in spite of all his capacity, has its reason in this, that he is on the whole not master of his own life :

Ver. 12. " For man also knoweth not his time : like the fishes which are caught in an evil net, and like the birds which are caught in the snare—like them are the sons of men snared in an evil time, when it suddenly breaks in upon them." The particles כִּי גַּם are here not so clearly connected as at viii. 12, iv. 14, where, more correctly, the pointing should be כִּי גַם (*ki* with the conjunct. accent) ; *ki* rules the sentence ; and *gam*, as to its meaning, belongs to *eth-'itto*. The particular has its reason from the general : man is not master of his own time, his own person, and his own life, and thus not of the fruits of his capabilities and his actions, in spite of the previously favourable conditions which appear to place the result beyond a doubt ; for ere the result is reached of which he appears to be able to entertain a certainty, suddenly his time may expire, and his term of life be exhausted.   Jerome translates *'itto* (cf. vii. 17) rightly by *finem suum;* עֵת, with the gen. following, frequently (*vid.* under Job xxiv. 1) means the point of time when the fate of any one is decided,—the *terminus* where a reckoning is made ; here, directly, the *terminus ad quem.*   The suddenness with which men are frequently overtaken with the catastrophe which puts an end to their life, is seen by comparison with the fishes which are suddenly caught in the net, and the birds which are suddenly caught in the snare. With שֶׁ (that are caught) there is interchanged, in two variations of expression, הָאֲחֻזוֹת, which is incorrectly written, by v. d. Hooght, Norzi, and others, הָאֲחֻזּ.[1]   מְצוֹ, a net,—of which the plur. form vii. 26 is used,—goes back, as does the similar designation of a bulwark (14*b*), to the root-conception of searching (hunting), and receives here the epithet " evil."   Birds, צִפֳּרִים (from a ground-form with a short terminal vowel ; cf. Assyr. *iṣṣur*, from *iṣpur*), are, on account of their weakness, as at Isa. xxxi. 5, as a figure of tender love, represented in the fem.

The second half of the verse, in conformity with its structure, begins with כָּהֶם (which more frequently occurs as כְּמוֹהֶם).   יוּקָ' is *part. Pu.* for מְיֻקָּשִׁים (Ewald, § 170*d*) ; the particip. מ is rejected, and ק is treated altogether as a guttural, the impracticable doubling of which is compensated for by the lengthening of the vowel.   The use of the part. is here stranger than *e.g.* at Prov. xi. 13, xv. 32 ; the fact repeating itself is here treated as a property.   Like the fish and the birds are they, such as are caught, etc.   Otherwise Hitz. :

[1] *Vid.* Ed. König, *Gedanke, Laut u. Accent* (1874), p. 72.

Like these are they caught, during the continuance of their life in the evil time . . . ; but the being snared does not, however, according to the double figure, precede the catastrophe, but is its consequence. Rightly, Ginsb.: " Like these are the sons of men ensnared in the time of misfortune." רָעָה might be adj., as at Amos v. 13, Mic. ii. 3 ; but since it lies nearer to refer 'כְּשֶׁתִּ to ra'ah than to 'eth, thus ra'ah, like the frequently occurring yom ra'ah (vii. 14 ; cf. Jer. xvii. 17 with xv. 11), may be thought of as genit. An example of that which is here said is found in the fatal wounding of Ahab by means of an arrow which was not aimed at him, so that he died " at the time of the going down of the sun," 2 Chron. xviii. 33, 34.

THE FURTHER SETTING FORTH OF EXPERIENCES, WITH PROVERBS INTERMIXED.—IX. 13–X. 15.

Experiences and Proverbs touching Wisdom and the Contrasts to it,
ix. 13–x. 3.

With the words, " further, I saw," 11a, the author introduced the fact he had observed, that there is not always a sure and honoured position in life connected with wisdom as its consequence ; here he narrates an experience which, by way of example, shows how little wisdom profits, notwithstanding the extraordinary result it produces.

Ver. 13. " Also this have I come to see as wisdom under the sun, and it appeared great to me." The Venet. construes falsely : " This also have I seen : wisdom under the sun ;" as also Hitzig, who reads זֶה (neut. as at vii. 27). There is no reason thus to break up the sentence which introduces the following experience. *Zoh* is connected with *hhochmah*, but not as Luther renders it : " I have also seen this wisdom," which would have required the words זאת 'הח, but, as Jerome does : *Hanc quoque sub sole vidi sapientiam;* this, however, since *gam-zoh*, as at v. 15, cf. 18, is attractionally related to *hhochmah* as its pred., is = " also in this I saw wisdom," as the LXX. translates, or as Zöckl. : " also this have I seen—come to find out as wisdom,"—also this, viz., the following incident narrated, in which wisdom of exceeding greatness presented itself to me. As Mordecai is called " great among the Jews," Esth. x. 3, so here Koheleth says that the wisdom which came to light therein appeared to him great (אֵלַי, as elsewhere בְּעֵינֵי or לִפְנֵי).

Now follows an experience, which, however, has not merely a

light side, but also a dark side ; for wisdom, which accomplished so great a matter, reaped only ingratitude :

Vers. 14, 15. " A little city, and men therein only a few,—to which a great king came near, and he besieged it, and erected against it high bulwarks.   And he met therein a poor wise man, and who saved the city by his wisdom; and no man thought of that poor man."   What may be said as to the hist. reference of these words has already been noticed ; *vid.* above, p. 215.   The "great king" is probably an Asiatic monarch, and that the Persian ; Jerome trans- lates verbally : *Civitas parva et pauci in ea viri, venit contra eam—* the former is the subj., and the latter its pred. ; the object stands first, plastically rigid, and there then follows what happened to it ; the structure of the sentence is fundamentally the same as Ps. civ. 25.   The expression בֹּא אֶל, which may be used of any kind of coming to anything, is here, as at Gen. xxxii. 9, meant of a hostile approach.   The object of a siege and a hostile attack is usually denoted by עַל, 2 Kings xvi. 5 ; Isa. vii. 1.   Two Codd. of de Rossi's have the word מְצוֹרִים, but that is an error of transcription ; the plur. of מָצוֹר is fem., Isa. xxix. 4.   מְצוֹדִים is, as at vii. 26, plur. of מָצוֹד (from צוּד, to lie in wait) ; here, as elsewhere, בַּחַן and דָּיֵק is the siege-tower erected on the ground or on the rampart, from which to spy out the weak points of the beleaguered place so as to assail it.

The words following וּמָצָא בָהּ are rendered by the Targ., Syr., Jerome, Arab., and Luther : " and there was found in it;" most interpreters explain accordingly, as they point to i. 10, יֹאמַר, *dicat aliquis.*   But that מצא in this sequence of thought is = וְנִמְצָא (Job xlii. 15), is only to be supposed if it were impossible to regard the king as the subject, which Ewald with the LXX. and the Venet. does in spite of § 294*b*.   It is true it would not be possible if, as Vaih. remarks, the finding presupposed a searching ; but cf. on the contrary, *e.g.* Deut. xxiv. 1, Ps. cxvi. 3.   We also say of one whom, contrary to expectation, a superior meets with, that he has found his match, that he has found his man.   Thus it is here said of the great king, he found in the city a poor wise man—met therein with such an one, against whom his plan was shattered.   חָכָם is the adjective of the person of the poor man designated by *ish miskēn* (cf. 2 Chron. ii. 13); the accents correctly indicate this relation.   Instead of וּמִלַּט־הוּא, the older language would use וַיְמַלֵּט ; it does not, like the author here, use pure perfects, but makes the chief factum prominent by the *fut. consec.*   The *ē* of *millēt* is, as at xiii. 9, that of *limmēd* before *Makkeph*, referred back to the original *a*.   The making prominent of the subject contained in *millat* by means of *hu* is favourable to the supposition that *umatsa'* has the king as its subject; while even where no opposition (as *e.g.* at Jer. xvii. 18) lies before us this pleonasm belongs to the stylistic peculiarities of the book (*vid.* above, p. 198, No. 3). Instead of *adam lo,* the older form is *ish lo;* perhaps the author here wishes to avoid the repetition of *ish,* but at vii. 20 he also uses *adam* instead of *ish,* where no such reason existed.

Threatened by a powerful assailant, with whom it could not enter into battle, the little city, deserted by its men to a small remainder capable of bearing arms (this idea one appears to be under the necessity of connecting with מעט ... 'ואי), found itself in the greatest straits; but when all had been given up as lost, it was saved by the wisdom of the poor man (perhaps in the same way as Abel-beth-maacha, 2 Sam. xx., by the wisdom of a woman). But after this was done, the wise poor man quickly again fell into the background; no man thought of him, as he deserved to have been thought of, as the saviour of the city; he was still poor, and remained so, and *pauper homo raro vivit cum nomine claro.* The poor man with his wisdom, Hengst. remarks, is Israel. And Wangemann (1856), generalizing the parable : " The beleaguered city is the life of the individual ; the great king who lays siege to it is death and the judgment of the Lord." But sounder and more appropriate is the remark of Luther : *Est exemplum generale, cujus in multis historiis simile reperitur ;* and : *Sic Themistocles multa bona fecit suis civibus, sed expertus summam ingratitudinem.* The author narrates an actual history, in which, on the one hand, he had seen what great things wisdom can do ; and from which, on the other hand, he has drawn the following lesson :

Ver. 16. " And I said : Better is wisdom than strength ; but the wisdom of the poor is despised, and his words are not heard." With the words, " I saw," the author introduces his observations, and with " I said " his reflections (*vid.* above, No. 3, p. 198). Wisdom is better than strength, since it does more for the wise man, and through him for others, than physical force,—more, as expressed in vii. 19, than ten mighty men. But the *respect* which wisdom otherwise secures for a man, if it is the wisdom of a poor man, sinks into *despect,* to which his poverty exposes him,—if necessity arises, his service, as the above history shows, is valued ; but as a rule his words are unheeded, for the crowd estimate the worth of him whom they willingly hear according to the outward respect in which he is held.

To the lessons gathered from experience, are now added instructive proverbs of kindred contents.

Ver. 17. " The words of the wise, heard in quiet, have the superiority above the cry of a ruler among fools." Instead of *tovim min*, there stands here the simple *min*, *prae*, as at iv. 17, to express the superiority of the one to the other.   Hitzig finds in this proverb the meaning that, as that history has shown, the words of the wise, heard with tranquillity, gain the victory over the cry of a ruler over fools.   But (1) the contrast of נָחַת and זַעֲקַת require us to attribute the tranquillity to the wise man himself, and not to his hearers ; (2) מוֹ' בַּכְּ' is not a ruler over fools, by which it would remain questionable whether he himself was not a fool (cf. Job xli. 26), but a ruler among fools (cf. 2 Sam. xxiii. 3, מוֹ' בָּ', " a ruler among men ;" and Prov. xxxvi. 30, גִּבּ' בַּ', " the hero among beasts "), *i.e.* one who among fools takes the place of chief.   The words of the poor wise man pass by unheeded, they are not listened to, because he does not possess an imposing splendid outward appearance, in accordance with which the crowd estimate the value of a man's words ; the wise man does not seek to gain esteem by means of a pompous violent deportment; his words נִשְׁ' בְּ' are heard, let themselves be heard, are to be heard (cf. *e.g.* Song ii. 12) in quiet (Isa. xxx. 15) ; for, trusting to their own inward power of conviction, and committing the result to God, he despises vociferous pomp, and the external force of earthly expedients (cf. Isa. xlii. 2; Matt. xii. 19); but the words of the wise, which are to be heard in unassuming, passionless quietness, are of more value than the vociferation with which a king among fools, an arch-fool, a *non plus ultra* among fools, trumpets forth his pretended wisdom and constrains his hearers.

Ver. 18.   The following proverb also leans on the history above narrated : " Better is wisdom than weapons of war ; and one sinner destroyeth much good."   The above history has shown by way of example that wisdom accomplishes more than implements of war, כְּלֵי קְ' = בְּלִי מְל' (Assyr. *unut taḥazi*[1]), *i.e.* than all the apparatus belonging to preparation for war.   But the much good which a wise man is accomplishing or has accomplished, one sinner (חוֹטֵא,[2] cf. above, p. 254, note) by treachery or calumny may render vain, or may even destroy, through mere malicious pleasure in evil.   This is a synthetic distich whose two parts may be interpreted independently.   As wisdom accomplishes something great, so a single villain may have a far-reaching influence, viz. such as destroys much good.

x. 1.   The second half of the foregoing double proverb introduces what now follows : " Poisonous flies make to stink, make to ferment the oil of the preparer of ointment ; heavier than wisdom,

---

[1] *Vid.* Fried. Delitzsch's *Assyr. Stud.* p. 129.

[2] The Syr. (not the Targ.) had חְטָא before it, and thus realized it, which appears to correspond better with the parall. חכמה.

than honour, weighs a little folly." We do not need to change
זְבוּבֵי מָוֶת, on account of the foll. sing. of the pred., either into זבובי מ׳
(as possible by Hitz.) or זב׳ יָמוּת (Luzz.); both are inadmissible, for
the style of Koheleth is not adorned with archaisms such as *Chirek
compaginis*; and also such an attrib. clause as זבוב ימות, "a fly which
dies," is for him too refined; but both are also unnecessary, for a
plur. of the subj., in which the plurality of the individuals comes
less into view than the oneness of their character, is frequently
enough followed by the sing. of the pred., *e.g.* Gen. xlix. 22; Joel
i. 20; Isa. lix. 12, etc. It is a question, however, whether by זבובי
מות, death-bringing, *i.e.* poisonous flies (LXX., Targ.,[1] Luther) or dead
flies (Symm., Syr., Jerome) is meant. We decide in favour of the
former; for (1) זבובי מות for זְבוּבִים מֵתִים (ix. 4; Isa. xxxvii. 36),
"death-flies" for "dead flies," would be an affected poetic expression
without analogy; while, on the contrary, "death-flies" for "deadly
flies" is a genit. connection, such as כְּלֵי מות [instruments of death, *i.e.*
deadly instruments] and the like; Böttcher understands dung-flies;
but the expression can scarcely extend to the designation of flies
which are found on dead bodies. Meanwhile, it is very possible that
by the expression זב׳ מ׳, such flies are thought of as carry death from
dead bodies to those that are living; the Assyr. *syllabare* show how
closely the Semites distinguished manifold kinds of זבובים (Assyr.
zumbi = zubbi). (2) In favour of "dead flies," it has been remarked
that that influence on the contents of a pot of ointment is effected
not merely by poison-flies, but, generally, by flies that have fallen
into it.

But since the oil mixed with perfumes may also be of the kind
which, instead of being changed by a dead body, much rather em-
balms it; so it does not surprise us that the exciter of fermentation
is thus drastically described by μυῖαι θανατοῦσαι (LXX.); it happens,
besides, also on this account, because "a little folly" corresponds as
a contrasted figure to the little destructive carcase,—wisdom תְּחַיֶּה בְעָ
("giveth life," vii. 12), a little folly is thus like little deadly flies.
The sequence of ideas יַבְּ׳ יַבִּ׳ (maketh the ointment stink) is natural.
The corrupting body communicates its foul savour to the ointment,
makes it boil up, *i.e.* puts it into a state of fermentation, in consequence of which it foams and raises up small blisters, אבעבועות
(Rashi). To the asyndeton יַבִּ׳ יַבְּ׳, there corresponds, in 1*b*, the
asyndeton מֵחָ׳ מְפ׳; the Targ., Syr., and Jerome,[2] who translate by

---

[1] The Targ. interprets, as the Talm. and Mid. do, deadly flies as a figure of the
prava concupiscentia. Similarly Wangemann: a mind buried in the world.

[2] The LXX. entirely remodels 1*b*: τίμιον κ.τ.λ. ("a little wisdom is more

" and," are therefore not witnesses for the phrase 'וּמָכ, but the Venet. (καὶ τῆς δόξης) had this certainly before it; it is, in relation to the other, inferior in point of evidence.[1]   In general, it is evident that the point of comparison is the hurtfulness, widely extending itself, of a matter which in appearance is insignificant.   Therefore the meaning of 1*b* cannot be that a little folly is more weighty than wisdom, than honour, viz. in the eyes of the blinded crowd (Zöckl., Dächsel).   This limitation the author ought to have expressed, for without it the sentence is an untruth.   Jerome, following the Targ. and Midrash, explains : *Pretiosa est super sapientiam et gloriam stultitia parva,* understanding by wisdom and honour the self-elation therewith connected ; besides, this thought, which Luther limits by the introduction of *zuweilen* [" folly is *sometimes* better than wisdom, etc."], is in harmony neither with that which goes before nor with that which follows.   Luzz., as already Aben Ezra, Grotius, Geiger, Hengst., and the more recent English expositors, transfer the verbs of 1*a* zeugmatically to 1*b* : *similiter pretiosum nomine sapientiae et gloriae virum foetidum facit stoliditas parva.*   But יביע forbids this transference, and, besides, מִן יָקָר, " honoured on account of," is an improbable expression ; also 'יקר מכ presents a tautology, which Luzz. seeks to remove by glossing 'מכ, as the Targ. does, by מרוב עושר ונכסים.   Already Rashi has rightly explained by taking יָקָר (Syr. *jakîr,* Arab. *wakur, wakûr*), in its primary meaning, as synon. of כָּבֵד : more weighty, *i.e.* heavier and weighing more than wisdom, than honour, is a little folly ; and he reminds us that a single foolish act can at once change into their contrary the wisdom and the honour of a man, destroying both, making it as if they had never been, cf. 1 Cor. v. 6.   The sentence is true both in an intellectual and in a moral reference.   Wisdom and honour are

honour than the great glory of folly "), *i.e.* יקר מעט חכמה מכבוד סבלות רב (כבוד in the sense of " great multitude ").   Van der Palm (1784) regards this as the original form of the text.

[1] מִכָּבוֹד ; thus in the *Biblia rabb.* 1525, 1615, Genoa 1618, Plantin 1582, Jablonski 1699, and also v. d. Hooght and Norzi.   In the Ven. 1515, 1521, 1615, וּמִכָּבוֹד is found with the copulat. *vav,* a form which is adopted by Michaelis. Thus also the Concord. cites, and thus, originally, it stood in J., but has been corrected to מִכָּבוֹד.   F., however, has מִכָּבוֹד, with the marginal remark : מכבוד בן קבלתי מני שמשון (Simson ha-Nakdam, to whom the writer of the Frankf. Cod. 1294 here refers for the reading 'מכ, without the copul. *vav,* is often called by him his voucher).   This is also the correct Masoretic reading ; for if 'וּמָכ were to be read, then the word would be in the catalogue of words of which three begin with their initial letter, and a fourth has introduced a *vav* before it (*Mas. fin.* f. 26, *Ochla veochla,* Nr. 15).

swept away by a little *quantum* of folly; it places both in the shade, it outweighs them in the scale; it stamps the man, notwithstanding the wisdom and dignity which otherwise belong to him, as a fool. The expressive שֶׁמֶן רֹקֵחַ is purposely used here; the dealer in ointments (*pigmentarius*) can now do nothing with the corrupted perfume,—thus the wisdom which a man possesses, the honour which he has hitherto enjoyed, avail him no longer; the proportionally small portion of folly which has become an ingredient in his personality gives him the character of a fool, and operates to his dishonour. Knobel construes rightly; but his explanation (also of Heiligst., Elst., Ginsb.): "a little folly frequently shows itself more efficacious and fruitful than the wisdom of an honoured wise man," helps itself with a "frequently" inserted, and weakens מכ' to a subordinated idea, and is opposed to the figure, which requires a personality.

Vers. 2, 3. A double proverb regarding wisdom and folly in their difference: "The heart of a wise man is directed to his right hand, and the heart of the fool to his left. And also on the way where a fool goeth, there his heart faileth him, and he saith to all that he is a fool." Most interpreters translate: The heart of the wise man is at his right hand, *i.e.* it is in the right place. But this designation, meant figuratively and yet sounding anatomically, would be in bad taste[1] in this distinguishing double form (*vid.* on the contrary, ii. 14). The ל is that of direction;[2] and that which is situated to the right of a man is figuratively a designation of the right; and that to the left, a designation of the wrong. The designation proceeds from a different idea from that at Deut. v. 32, etc.; that which lies to the right, as that lying at a man's right hand, is that to which his calling and duty point him; הִשׂ denotes, in the later Hebrew, "to turn oneself to the wrong side."

Ver. 3. This proverb forms, along with the preceding, a tetrastich, for it is divided into two parts by *vav*. The *Kerî* has removed the art. in בש' and שה', vi. 10, as incompatible with the שׁ. The order of the words *v*ᵉ*gam-baderek kᵉshehsachal holek* is inverted for *v*ᵉ*gam kᵉshehsachal baderek holek*, cf. iii. 13, and also *rav shĕyihyn*, vi. 3; so

---

[1] Christ. Fried. Bauer (1732) explains as we do, and remarks, "If we translate: the heart of the wise is at his right hand, but the heart of the fool at his left, it appears as if the heart of the prudent and of the foolish must have a different position in the human body, thus affording to the profane ground for mockery."

[2] Accordingly, ver. 2 has become a Jewish saying with reference to the study of a book (this thought of as Heb.): The wise always turn over the leaves backwards, repeating that which has been read; the fool forwards, superficially anticipating that which has not yet been read, and scarcely able to wait for the end.

far as this signifies, "supposing that they are many." Plainly the
author intends to give prominence to "on the way;" and why, but
because the fool, the inclination of whose heart, according to 2b,
always goes to the left, is now placed in view as he presents himself in his public manner of life.   Instead of חֲסַר לֵב־הוּא we have
here the verbal clause לִבּוֹ חָסֵר, which is not, after vi. 2, to be translated : *corde suo caret* (Herzf., Ginsb.), contrary to the suff. and also
the order of the words, but, after ix. 8 : *cor ejus deficit, i.e.* his
understanding is at fault ; for לב, here and at ver. 2, is thus used in
a double sense, as the Greek νοῦς and the Lat. *mens* can also be
used : there it means pure, formal, intellectual soul-life ; here,
pregnantly (*Psychol.* p. 249), as at vii. 7, cf. Hos. iv. 11, the understanding or the knowledge and will of what is right.   The fool takes
no step without showing that his understanding is not there,—that,
so to speak, he does not take it along with him, but has left it at
home.   He even carries his folly about publicly, and prides himself
in it as if it were wisdom : he says to all that he is a fool, *se esse
stultum* (thus, correctly, most Jewish and Christian interpreters, *e.g.*
Rashi and Rambach).   The expression follows the scheme of Ps.
ix. 21 : May the heathen know *mortales se esse* (*vid. l.c.*).   Otherwise
Luther, with Symm. and Jerome: " he takes every man as a fool ; "
but this thought has no support in the connection, and would undoubtedly be expressed by סְכָלִים הֵמָּה.   Still differently Knobel and
Ewald : he says to all, " it is foolish ; " Hitzig, on the contrary, justly
remarks that סָכָל is not used of actions and things ; this also is true
of כְּסִיל, against himself, v. 2, where he translates *qol kᵉsil* by " foolish
discourses."

The Caprice of Rulers and the Perverted World, x. 4–7.

Wisdom is a strong protection.   To this thought, from which
the foregoing group proceeded, there is here subordinated the following admonition.

Ver. 4. This verse shows what is the wise conduct of a subject,
and particularly of a servant, when the anger of the ruler breaks
forth : " If the ill-humour of the ruler rise up against thee, do not
leave thy post ; for patience leaves out great sins."   Luther connects
ver. 4 and ver. 3 by " therefore ; " for by the potentate he understands such an one as, himself a fool, holds all who contradict him
to be fools : then it is best to let his folly rage on.   But the מֹשֵׁל
is a different person from the סָכָל ; and מִק׳ אַל־תַּנַּח does not mean,
" let not yourself get into a passion," or, as he more accurately ex-

plains in the *Annotationes:* "remain self-possessed" (similarly Hitzig: lose not thy mental state or composure), but, in conformity with תלך . . . אל, viii. 3, "forsake not the post (synon. מַצָּב and מַעֲמָד, Isa. xxii. 19, cf. 23) which thou hast received." The person addressed is thus represented not merely as a subject, but officially as a subordinate officer: if the ruler's displeasure (רוּחַ, as at Judg. viii. 3; Prov. xxix. 11) rises up against him (עָלָה, as elsewhere; cf. אף, Ps. lxxiii. 21; or חֵמָה, 2 Sam. xi. 20), he ought not, in the consciousness that he does not merit his displeasure, hastily give up his situation which has been entrusted to him and renounce submission; for patience, gentleness (regarding מַרְפֵּא, *vid.* Prov. xii. 18) גֵּד' . . . יַ'.

This concluding clause of the verse is usually translated: " It appeaseth (pacifieth) great sins" (LXX. καταπαύσει, Symm. παύσει) The phrase (חמה) הֵנִיחַ אַף is not to be compared, for it signifies. quieting by an exhausting outbreak; on the contrary, יניח in the passage before us must signify quieting, as the preventing of an outbreak (cf. Prov. xv. 1). It appears more correct to render הֵנִיחַ in both cases in the sense of *èàv, missum facere:* to leave great sins is = not to commit them, to give up the lust thereto; for *hinniahh* signifies to let go, to leave off, *e.g.* Jer. xiv. 9; and to indulge, Esth. iii. 8, here as at vii. 18, xi. 6, " to keep the hands from something." The great sins cannot certainly be thought of as those of the ruler; for on his part only one comes into view, if indeed, according to the old legal conception, it could be called such, viz. cruel proceeding with reference to him who wilfully withdraws from him, and thus proves his opposition; much rather we are to think of the great sins into which he who is the object of the ruler's displeasure might fall, viz. treason (viii. 2), insubordination, self-destruction, and at the same time, since he does not stand alone, or make common cause with others who are discontented, the drawing of others into inevitable ruin (viii. 3*b*). All these sins, into which he falls who answers wrath with wrath, patience avoids, and puts a check to them. The king's anger is perhaps justified; the admonition, however, would be otherwise expressed than by מק' אל־תנח, if it were not presupposed that it was not justified; and thus without μετάβασις εἰς ἄλλο γένος an *I*-section follows the reflection regarding wise deportment as over against the king's displeasure, a section which describes from experience and from personal observation the world turned upside down in the state.

Ver. 5. "There is an evil which I have seen under the sun, like an error which proceedeth from the ruler." The introduction by the virtual relative *räithi* is as at v. 12, cf. vi. 1. Knobel, Hengst., and others give to the כ of כְּשֶׁ' the meaning of "according to," or "in consequence of which," which harmonizes neither with *ra'ah* nor with *räithi*. Also Kleinert's translation: "There is a misery—I have seen it under the sun—in respect of an error which proceedeth from the ruler," is untenable ; for by this translation *ra'ah* is made the pred. while it is the subj. to שֶׁי, and *kishgagah* the unfolding of this subject. Hitzig also remarks : "as [*wie ein*] an error, instead of which we have : in respect to [*um einen*] an error;" for he confounds things incongruous. Hitz., however, rightly recognises, as also Kleinert, the כ as *Caph veritatis*, which measures the concrete with the ideal, Isa. xiii. 6, compares the individual with the general which therein comes to view, Ezek. xxvi. 10 ; Neh. vii. 2 ; cf. 2 Sam. ix. 8. Koheleth saw an evil under the sun ; something which was like an error, appeared to him altogether like an error which proceedeth from the ruler. If we could translate שֶׁי' by *quod exiit*, then כ would be the usual *Caph similitudinis;* but since it must be translated by *quod exit*, כשׁ' וגו' places the observed fact under a comprehensive generality : it had the nature of an error proceeding from the ruler. If this is correct, it is so much the less to be assumed that by הַשַׁלִּיט God is to be understood (Dan. v. 21), as Jerome was taught by his *Hebraeus : quod putent homines in hac inaequalitate rerum illum non juste et ut aequum est judicare.* It is a governor in a state that is meant, by whom an error might easily be committed, and only too frequently is committed, in the promotion or degradation of persons. But since the world, with its wonderful division of high and low, appears like as it were an error proceeding from the Most High, there certainly falls a shadow on the providence of God Himself, the Governor of the world ; but yet not so immediately that the subject of discourse is an " error " of God, which would be a saying more than irreverent. יָצָא = יָצָה is the metaplastic form for יָצָאה or יָצָאת (for which at Deut. xxviii. 57 incorrectly יֹצֵת), not an error of transcription, as Olsh. supposes ; *vid.* to the contrary, above, No. 1, p. 197. מִלִּפְנֵי (Symm. ἐξ ἔμπροσθεν) with יצא is the old *usus loq.* There now follows a sketch of the perverted world.

Vers. 6, 7. "Folly is set on great heights, and the rich must sit in lowliness. I have seen servants upon horses, and princes like servants walking on foot." The word הַסֶּכֶל (with double *seghol*, Aram. סַכְלוּ) is used here instead of those in whom it is personified. Elsewhere a multiplicity of things great, such as עַמִּים, מַיִם, and the like, is heightened by רַבִּים (cf. *e.g.* Ps. xviii. 17) ; here " great heights " are such as are of a high, or the highest degree ; *rabbim*, instead of *harabbim*, is more appos. than adject. (cf. Gen. xliii.

14; Ps. lxviii. 28, cxliii. 10 ; Jer. ii. 21), in the sense of " many "
(*e.g.* Ginsburg: " in many high positions ") it mixes with the poetry of
the description dull prose.[1] *'Ashirim* also is peculiarly used : *divites*
= *nobiles* (cf. שׁוֹעַ, Isa. xxxii. 5), those to whom their family inheritance
gives a claim to a high station, who possess the means of training
themselves for high offices, which they regard as places of honour,
not as sources of gain. *Regibus multis*, Grotius here remarks, quot-
ing from Sallust and Tacitus, *suspecti qui excellunt sive sapientia sive
nobilitate aut opibus.* Hence it appears that the relation of slaves
and princes to each other is suggested ; *hoc discrimen*, says Justin,
xli. 3, of the Parthians, *inter servos liberosque est quod servi pedibus,
liberi nonnisi equis incedunt;* this distinction is set aside, princes
must walk *'al-haarĕts*, i.e. *bᵉregel* (*bᵉraglēhĕm*), and in their stead
(Jer. xvii. 25) slaves sit high on horseback, and rule over them (the
princes),—an offensive spectacle, Prov. xix. 10. The eunuch Bagoas
(*vid.* above, p. 214), long all-powerful at the Persian Court, is an
example of the evil consequences of this reversal of the natural
relations of men.

*That which is Difficult exposes to Danger; that which is Improper brings
Trouble; that which comes Too Late is not of use, x.* 8-11.

How much time, thought, and paper have been expended in
seeking to find out a close connection between this group of verses
and that going before ! Some read in them warnings against rising
in rebellion against despots (Ginsb.); others (*e.g.* Zöckl.) place these
proverbs in relation to the by no means enviable lot of those upstarts
(Zöckl.); more simply and more appropriately, Luther here finds
exemplified the thought that to govern (*regere homines et gerere res
humanas*) is a difficult matter; on the other hand, Luzz. finds in 8–11
the thought that all depends on fate, and not on the wisdom of man.
In reality, this section forms a member in the carrying forward of
the theme which the author has been discussing from ix. 13 :
wisdom and folly in their mutual relations, particularly in difficult situations of life. The catchword of the foregoing section is
מַרְפֵּא, patience, resignation, which guards against rendering evil for
evil ; and the catchword of the following section is הַכְשִׁיר, considerate
and provisory straining of the means toward the accomplishment of
that which one purposes to do. The author presents a prelude in

---

[1] Luzz. reads נָתַן : " Folly brings many into high places." The order of the
words, however, does not favour this.

four sentences, which denote by way of example, that whoever undertakes any severe labour, at the same time faces the dangers connected
therewith.

Vers. 8, 9. "He that diggeth a pit may fall into it; whoso
breaketh down walls, a serpent may sting him. Whoso pulleth out
stones may do himself hurt therewith ; he who cleaveth wood may
endanger himself thereby." The futures are not the expression of
that which will necessarily take place, for, thus rendered, these four
statements would be contrary to experience; they are the expression
of a possibility. The fut. יִפּוֹל is not here meant as predicting an
event, as where the clause 8a is a figure of self-punishment arising
from the destruction prepared for others, Prov. xxvi. 27 ; Sir.
xxvii. 26. גּוּמָּץ is, Prov. xxvi. 27, the Targum word for שַׁחַת, ditch,
from שׁוּחַ = גָּמַץ, depressum esse. גָּדֵר (R. גד, to cut), something cutting
off, something dividing, is a wall as a boundary and means of protection drawn round a garden, vineyard, or farm-court; פָּרַץ גָּדֵר is
the reverse of גֹּדֵר פֶּרֶץ, Isa. lviii. 12. Serpents are accustomed to
nestle in the crevices and holes of walls, as well as in the earth (for
a city-wall is called חומה and חֵל) ; thus he who breaks into such a
wall may expect that the serpent which is there will bite him (cf.
Amos v. 19). To tear down stones, hissi'a, is synon. of hhatsav, to
break stones, Isa. li. 1 ; yet hhotsēv does not usually mean the stone-
breaker, but the stone-cutter (stone-mason) ; hissi'a, from nasa',
to tear out, does not also signify, 1 Kings v. 31, " to transport," and
here, along with wood-splitting, is certainly to be thought of as
a breaking loose or separating in the quarry or shaft. Ne'etsav
signifies elsewhere to be afflicted ; here, where the reference is not
to the internal but the external feeling: to suffer pain, or reflex. :
to injure oneself painfully ; the derivat. 'etsev signifies also severe
labour; but to find this signification in the Niph. ("he who has painful
labour ") is contrary to the usus loq., and contrary to the meaning
intended here, where generally actual injuries are in view. Accordingly יִסָּכֶן בָּם, for which the Mishn. יְסַכֵּן בְּעַצְמוֹ,[1] " he brings himself
into danger," would denote, to be placed in danger of life and limb,
cf. Gittin 65b, Chullin 37a ; and it is therefore not necessary, with
Hitzig and others, to translate after the vulnerabitur of Jerome :
" He may wound himself thereby;" there is not a denom. סָכַן, to
cut, to wound, derived from שַׂכִּין (סַכִּין), an instrument for cutting,
a knife.[2]

[1] Vid. above, p. 194.
[2] The Midrash understands the whole ethically, and illustrates it by the example of Rabsake [we know now that the half-Assyr., half-Accad. word rabsak

The sum of these four clauses is certainly not merely that he who undertakes a dangerous matter exposes himself to danger; the author means to say, in this series of proverbs which treat of the distinction between wisdom and folly, that the wise man is every-where conscious of his danger, and guards against it. These two verses (8, 9) come under this definite point of view by the following proverb; wisdom has just this value in providing against the mani-fold dangers and difficulties which every undertaking brings along with it.[1] This is illustrated by a fifth example, and then it is declared with reference to all together.

Ver. 10. " If the iron has become blunt, and he has not whetted the face, then he must give more strength to the effort; but wisdom has the superiority in setting right." This proverb of iron, *i.e.* iron instruments (בַּרְזֶל, from בָּרַז, to pierce, like the Arab. name for iron, *hadîd*, means essentially something pointed), is one of the most difficult in the Book of Koheleth,—linguistically the most difficult, because scarcely anywhere else are so many peculiar and unexampled forms of words to be found. The old translators afford no help for the understanding of it. The advocates of the hypothesis of a Dialogue have here a support in אִם, which may be rendered interrogatively; but where would we find, syntactically as well as actually, the answer? Also, the explanations which understand חֲיָלִים in the sense of war-troops, armies, which is certainly its nearest-lying meaning, bring out no appropriate thought; for the thought that even blunt iron, as far as it is not externally altogether spoiled (*lo-phanim qilqal*), or: although it has not a sharpened edge (Rashi, Rashbam), might be an equipment for an army, or gain the victory, would, although it were true, not fit the context; Ginsburg explains: If the axe be blunt, and he (who goes out against the tyrant) do not sharpen it before-hand (*phanim*, after Jerome, for *lᵉphanim*, which is impossible, and besides leads to nothing, since *lᵉphanim* means *ehedem* [formerly], but not *zuvor* [*prius*], Ewald, § 220*a*), he (the tyrant) only increases his army; on the contrary, wisdom hath the advantage by repairing the mischief (without the war being unequal);—but the " ruler" of the foregoing group has here long ago disappeared, and it is only a bold imagination which discovers in the *hu* of 10*a* the person addressed in ver. 4, and represents him as a rebel, and augments

means a military chief], whom report makes a brother of Manasseh, and a renegade in the Assyrian service.

[1] Thus rightly Carl Lang in his *Salom. Kunst im Psalter* (Marburg 1874). He sees in vers. 8–10 *a* beautiful heptastich. Butas to its contents, ver. 11 also belongs to this group.

him into a warlike force, but recklessly going forth with unwhetted swords. The correct meaning for the whole, in general at least, is found if, after the example of Abulwalîd and Kimchi, we interpret גָּבֵּר חֲיָלִים of the increasing of strength, the augmenting of the effort of strength, not, as Aben-Ezra, of conquering, outstripping, surpassing ; גָּבֵּר means to make strong, to strengthen, Zech. x. 6, 12 ; and חֲיָלִים, as plur. of חַיִל, strength, is supported by גִּבּוֹרֵי חֲיָלִים, 1 Chron. vii. 5, 7, 11, 40, the plur. of נבור חיל ; the LXX. renders by δυνάμεις δυναμώσει [and he shall strengthen the forces], and the Peshito has חַיְלֵי for δυνάμεις, Acts viii. 13, xix. 11 (cf. Chald. Syr. אִתְחַיַּל, to strengthen oneself, to become strengthened). Thus understanding the words יְחַ יְגַ of *intentio virium*, and that not with reference to sharpening (Luth., Grotius), but to the splitting of wood, etc. (Geier, Desvoeux, Mendelss.), all modern interpreters, with the exception of a few who lose themselves on their own path, gain the thought, that in all undertakings wisdom hath the advantage in the devising of means subservient to an end. The diversities in the interpretation of details leave the essence of this thought untouched. Hitz., Böttch., Zöckl., Lange, and others make the wood-splitter, or, in general, the labourer, the subject to קֵהָה, referring והוא to the iron, and, contrary to the accents, beginning the apodosis with *qilqal:* "If he (one) has made the iron blunt, and it is without an edge, he swings it, and applies his strength." לֹא־פָנִים, "without an edge" (*lo* for *b'lo*), would be linguistically as correct as לֹא בָנִים, "without children," 1 Chron. ii. 30, 32; Ewald, § 286*g;* and *qilqal* would have a meaning in some measure supported by Ezek. xxi. 26. But granting that *qilqal*, which there signifies "to shake," may be used of the swinging of an axe (for which we may refer to the Aethiop. *kualkuala, kalkala*, of the swinging of a sword), yet קִלְקְלוֹ (קִלְקַל אֹתוֹ) could have been used, and, besides, פנים means, not like פִי, the edge, but, as a somewhat wider idea, the front, face (Ezek. xxi. 21; cf. Assyr. *pan ilippi*, the forepart of a ship) ; "it has no edge" would have been expressed by (פִּיפִיּוֹת) וְהוּא לֹא פֶה, or by והוא איננו מְלֻטָּשׁ (מוֹרָט, מוּחָד). We therefore translate : if the iron has become blunt, *hebes factum sit* (for the *Pih.* of intransitives has frequently the meaning of an inchoative or desiderative stem, like מְעַט, to become little, *decrescere*, xii. 3 ; כָּהָה, *hebescere, caligare*, Ezek. xxi. 12 ; Ewald, § 120*d*), and he (who uses it) has not polished (whetted) the face of it, he will (must) increase the force. וְהוּא does not refer to the iron, but, since there was no reason to emphasize the sameness of the subject (as *e.g.* 2 Chron. xxxii. 30), to the labourer, and thus makes, as with the other explanation, the change of subject noticeable (as *e.g.* 2 Chron. xxvi. 1). The order of the words קל ... וה, *et ille non faciem (ferri) exacuit,* is as at Isa. liii. 9 ; cf. also the position of *lo* in 2 Sam. iii. 34 ; Num. xvi. 29.

קלקל, or pointed with *Pattach* instead of *Tsere* (cf. *qarqar,* Num. xxiv. 17) in bibl. usage, from the root-meaning *levem esse,* signifies to move with ease, *i.e.* quickness (as also in the Arab. and Aethiop.), to shake (according to which the LXX. and Syr. render it by ταράσσειν, דלח, to shake, and thereby to trouble, make muddy) ; in the Mishn. usage, to make light, little, to bring down, to destroy ; here it means to make light = even and smooth (the contrast of rugged and notched), a meaning the possibility of which is warranted by נח׳ קלל, Ezek. i. 7, Dan. x. 6 (which is compared by Jewish lexicographers and interpreters), which is translated by all the old translators " glittering brass," and which, more probably than Ewald's " to steel " (temper), is derived from the root *qal,* to burn, glow.[1] With *vahhaylim* the apodosis begins ; the style of Koheleth recognises this *vav apod.* in conditional clauses, iv. 11, cf. Gen. xliii. 9, Ruth iii. 13, Job vii. 4, Mic. v. 7, and is fond of the inverted order of the words for the sake of emphasis, xi. 8, cf. Jer. xxxvii. 10, and above, under vii. 22.

In 10*b* there follows the common clause containing the application. Hitzig, Elster, and Zöckl. incorrectly translate : " and it is a profit wisely to handle wisdom ;" for instead of the inf. absol. הכ׳, they unnecessarily read the inf. constr. הכשיר, and connect הכשיר חכמה, which is a phrase altogether unparalleled. *Hichsir* means to set in the right position (*vid.* above, p. 193, *kaser*), and the sentence will thus mean : the advantage which the placing rightly of the means serviceable to an end affords, is wisdom—*i.e.* wisdom bears this advantage in itself, brings it with it, concretely : a wise man is he who reflects upon this advantage. It is certainly also possible that הכש׳, after the manner of the *Hiph.* הצליח and השביל, directly means " to succeed," or causatively : " to make to succeed." We might explain, as *e.g.* Knobel : the advantage of success, or of the causing of prosperity, is wisdom, *i.e.* it is that which secures this gain. But the meaning prevalent in post-bibl. Heb. of making fit, equipping,—a predisposition corresponding to a definite aim or result, —is much more conformable to the example from which the *porisma* is deduced. Buxtorf translates the *Hiph.* as a Mishnic word by *aptare, rectificare.* Tyler suggests along with " right guidance " the meaning " pre-arrangement," which we prefer.[2]

---

[1] Regarding the two roots, *vid.* Fried. Delitzsch's *Indogerm.-Sem. Stud.* p. 91 f.

[2] Also the twofold Haggadic explanation, *Taanith* 8*a,* gives to *hachshir* the

Ver. 11. The last proverb of this series presents for consideration the uselessness of him who comes too late. " If a serpent bite
without enchantment, the charmer is of no use." The Talm. interprets this אם, like that of ver. 10, also as interrog. : Does the serpent
bite without its being whispered to, *i.e.* without a providential determination impelling it thereto ? *Jer. Peah*, i. 1. But לַחַשׁ, except
at Isa. xxvi. 16, where whispering prayers are meant, signifies the
whispering of formulas of charming ; " serpents are not to be charmed
(tamed)," לחשׁ, Jer. viii. 17. Rather for בַּעַל הָלָּ' the meaning of
slander is possible, which is given to it in the Haggada, *Taanith* 8*a* :
All the beasts will one day all at once say to the serpent : the lion
walks on the earth and eats, the wolf tears asunder and eats ; but
what enjoyment hast thou by thy bite ? and it answers them : " Also
the slanderer (לבעל הלשׁון) has certainly no profit." Accordingly the
Targ., Jerome, and Luther translate ; but if אִם is conditional, and the
vav of *v*ᵉ*ēn* connects the protasis and the apodosis, then *ba'al hallashon*
must denote a man of tongue, viz. of an enchanting tongue, and thus
a charmer (LXX., Syr.). This name for the charmer, one of many,
is not unintentional ; the tongue is an instrument, as iron is, ver. 10 :
the latter must be sharp, if it would not make greater effort necessary ;
the former, if it is to gain its object, must be used at the right time.
The serpent bites בְּלֹא לָח', when it bites before it has been charmed
(cf. *b*ᵉ*lo yomo*, Job xv. 32) ; there are also serpents which bite without letting themselves be charmed ; but here this is the point, that it
anticipates the enchantment, and thus that the charmer comes too
late, and can make no use of his tongue for the intended purpose,
and therefore has no advantage from his act. There appropriately
follow here proverbs of the use of the tongue on the part of a wise
man, and its misuse on the part of a fool.

The Worthless Prating and the Aimless Labour of the Fool, x. 12–15.

It is wisdom, as the preceding series of proverbs has shown, to
be on one's guard to provide oneself with the right means, and
to observe the right time. These characteristics of the wise man
ver. 11 has brought to view, by an example from the sphere of
action in which the tongue serves as the instrument. There now
follows, not unexpectedly, a proverb with reference to that which the
words of a wise man and the words of a fool respectively bring about.

meaning of " to set, *à priori*, in the right place." Luther translated *qilqal* twice
correctly, but further follows the impossible rendering of Jerome : *multo labore
exacuetur, et post industriam sequetur sapientia.*

Ver. 12. " The words of a wise man's mouth are grace ; but the lips of a fool swallow him up." The words from a wise man's mouth are חֵן, graciousness, *i.e.* gracious in their contents, their form and manner of utterance, and thus also they gain favour, affection, approbation, for culture (education) produces favour, Prov. xiii. 15, and its lips grace (pleasantness), which has so wide an influence that he can call a king his friend, Prov. xxii. 11, although, according to ix. 11, that does not always so happen as is to be expected. The lips of a fool, on the contrary, swallow him, *i.e.* lead him to destruction. The *Pih.* בִּלַּע, which at Prov. xix. 28 means to swallow down, and at Prov. xxi. 20 to swallow = to consume in luxury, to spend dissolutely, has here the metaphorical meaning of to destroy, to take out of the way (for that which is swallowed up disappears). שִׂפְתוֹת is parallel form to שִׂפְתֵי, like the Aram. סִפְוָת. The construction is, as at Prov. xiv. 3, " the lips of the wise תִּשְׁמֹר preserve them ; " the idea of unity, in the conception of the lips as an instrument of speech, prevails over the idea of plurality. The words of the wise are heart-winning, and those of the fool self-destructive. This is verified in the following verse.

Ver. 13. " The beginning of the words of his mouth is foolishness ; and the end of his mouth is mischievous madness." From folly (absurdity) the words which are heard from a fool's mouth rise to madness, which is compounded of presumption, wantonness, and frenzy, and which, in itself a symptom of mental and moral depravity, brings as its consequence destruction on himself (Prov. xviii. 17). The adjective רָעָה is as in חֳלִי רָע, which interchanges with רָעָה חֹלִי vi. 2, v. 12, etc. The end of his mouth, viz. of his speaking, is = the end of the words of his mouth, viz. the end which they at last reach. Instead of *holeloth*, there is here, with the adj. following, *holeluth*, with the usual ending of *abstracta*. The following proverb says how the words of the fool move between these two poles of folly and wicked madness : he speaks much, and as if he knew all things.

Ver. 14. " And the fool maketh many words : while a man yet doth not know that which shall be ; and what shall be when he is no more, who can show him that ? " The *vav* at the beginning of this verse corresponds to the Lat. *accedit quod.* That he who in 12*b* was named *kᵉsil* is now named *hassachal*, arises from this, that meanwhile *sichluth* has been predicated of him. The relation of 14*b* to 14*a*, Geier has rightly defined : *Probatur absurditas multiloquii a communi ignorantia ac imbecillitate humana, quae tamen praecipue dominatur apud ignaros stultos.* We miss before *lo-yeda'* an " although " (*gam*,

Neh. vi. 1, or *ki gam*, viii. 12); the clause is, after the manner of a clause denoting state or condition, subordinated to the principal clause, as at Ps. v. 10 : " an open grave is their throat 'יֵחָ 'שְׁלִ, although they smooth their tongue, *i.e.* speak flatteringly." The LXX., Syr., Symm., and Jerome seek to rectify the tautology *id quod futurum est et quod futurum est* (cf. on the other hand, viii. 7), for they read 'יה . . . מה שהיה. But the second *quod futurum* certainly preserves by 'מֵאַחֲ its distinguishing nearer definition. Hitzig explains : " What is done, and what after this (that is done) is done." Scarcely correctly: *aharav* of the parallel passage, vi. 12, cf. vii. 14, ix. 3, requires for the suffix a personal reference, so that thus *meaharav*, as at Deut. xxix. 21, means " from his death and onwards." Thus, first, the knowledge of the future is denied to man ; then the knowledge of what will be done after his death ; and generally, of what will then be done. The fool, without any consciousness of human ignorance, acts as if he knew all, and utters about all and everything a multitude of words ; for he uselessly fatigues himself with his ignorance, which remains far behind the knowledge that is possible for man.

Ver. 15. " The labour of the foolish wearieth him who knoweth not how to go to the city." If we do not seek to explain : labour such as fools have wearies him (the fool), then we have here such a *synallage numeri* as at Isa. ii. 8, Hos. iv. 8, for from the plur. a transition is made to the distributive or individualizing sing. A greater anomaly is the treatment of the noun עָמָל as fem. (greater even than the same of the noun *pithgam*, viii. 11, which admitted of attractional explanation, and, besides, in a foreign word was not strange). Kimchi, *Michlol* 10*a*, supposes that עמל is thought of in the sense of יְגִיעַת עמל ; impossible, for one does not use such an expression. Hitzig, and with him Hengst., sees the occasion for the synallage in the discordance of the masc. יִיגְעֶנּוּ ; but without hesitation we use the expressions יָיחֵל, Mic. v. 6, יָיֶפ, Josh. vi. 26, and the like. *'Amal* also cannot be here *fem. unitatis* (Böttch. § 657. 4), for it denotes the wearisome striving of fools as a whole and individually. We have thus to suppose that the author has taken the liberty of using *'amal* once as fem. (*vid.* on the contrary, ii. 18, 20), as the poet, Prov. iv. 13, in the introduction of the Book of Proverbs uses *musar* once as fem., and as the similarly formed צָבָא is used in two genders. The fool kindles himself up and perplexes himself, as if he could enlighten the world and make it happy,—he who does not even know how to go to the city. Ewald remarks : " Apparently proverbial, viz. to bribe the great lords in the city." For us who, notwithstanding ver. 16, do not trouble ourselves any more with the tyrants of ver. 4, such thoughts, which do violence to the connection, are unnecessary. Hitzig also, and with him Elst. and Zöckl., thinks of the city as the residence of the rulers from whom oppression proceeds, but from whom also help against oppression is to be sought. All this is to be rejected. Not to know how to go to the city, is = not to be able to find the open public street, and, like the Syrians, 2 Kings vi. 18 f., to be smitten with blindness. The way to the city is *via notissima et tritissima.* Rightly Grotius, like Aben Ezra: *Multi quaestionibus arduis se fatigant, cum ne obvia quidem norint, quale est iter ad urbem.* אֶל־עִיר is vulgar for אֶל־הָעִיר. In the Greek language also the word πόλις has a definite signification, and Athens is called ἄστυ, mostly without the art. But Stamboul, the name of which may seem as an illustration of the proverbial phrase, " not to know how to go to the city," is = εἰς τὴν πόλιν. Grätz finds here an allusion to the Essenes, who avoided the city—*habeat sibi !*

THIRD CONCLUDING SECTION, WITH THE FINALE AND EPILOGUE

(*A.*) WARNINGS AGAINST IDLE REVELRY AND IMPROVIDENCE, AND A CALL
TO A FRESH EFFORT AFTER A HAPPY IMPROVEMENT OF LIFE.—
X. 16–XI. 7.

The Prosperity of a Country, its Misfortune, and Thoughtful Foresight,
x. 16–20.

Interpreters have sought in every way to discover a close connection between the following proverbs of the bad and good princes, and those that precede. Hitzig, rightly dissatisfied with this forced attempt, cuts the knot by putting vers. 16–19 into the mouth of the fool, ver. 15 : Koheleth, ver. 20, refers to him this rash freedom of speech, and warns him against such language ; for, supposing that vers. 16–19 were the words of Koheleth, in ver. 20 he would contradict himself. This unworthy perversion of the contents of the section rectifies itself. The supposed words of the fool belong to the most peculiar, most impressive, and most beautiful utterances of the חכם which the Book of Koheleth contains, and the warning, ver. 20, against cursing the king, stands in no contradiction to the " woe," ver. 16 ; Isaiah under Ahaz, Jeremiah under Zedekiah, actually show how the two are in harmony; and the apostles even in the times of Nero acted on their " honour the king." Rather it may be said that the author in ver. 16, from fools in general (ver. 15) comes to speak of folly in the position occupied by a king and princes. But " folly " is not the characteristic name for that which is unseemly and indecorous which is blamed in these high lords. From x. 16, the Book of Koheleth turns toward the conclusion ; since it represents itself as a discourse of Solomon's on the subject of the wisdom of life, and all through has a sharp eye on rulers and their surroundings, it is not strange that it treated of it in x. 4–7, and again now returns to the theme it had scarcely left.

Vers. 16, 17. "Woe to thee, O land, whose king is a child, and whose princes sit at table in the early morning ! Happy art thou, O land, whose king is a noble, and whose princes sit at table at the right time, in manly strength, and not in drunkenness !" Regarding אִי, *vid.* above, p. 191. Instead of שֶׁמַּ בַּ ', the older language would rather use the phrase אֲשֶׁר נַעַר מַלְכּוֹ; and instead of *na'ar*, we might correctly use, after Prov. xxx. 22, *'ĕvĕd;* but not as Grätz thinks, who from this verse deduces the reference of the book to Herod (the " slave of the Hasmonean house," as the Talm. names him), in the same meaning. For *na'ar*, it is true, sometimes means—*e.g.* as *Ziba's* by-name (2 Sam. xix. 18 [17])—a servant, but never a slave as such, so that here, in the latter sense, it might be the contrast of בְּרחוֹרִים; it is to be understood after Isa. iii. 12 ; and Solomon, Bishop of Constance, understood this woe rightly, for he found it fulfilled at the time of the last German Karolingian Ludwig III.[1] *Na'ar* is a very extensively applicable word in regard to the age of a person. King Solomon and the prophets Jeremiah and Zechariah show that *na'ar* may be used with reference to one in a high office ; but here it is one of few years of age who is meant, who is incapable of ruling, and shows himself as childish in this, that he lets himself be led by bad guides in accordance with their pleasure. In 16*b*, the author perhaps thinks of the heads of the aristocracy who have the phantom-king in their power : intending to fatten themselves, they begin their feasting with the break of day. If we translate *yochĕlu* by " they eat," 16*b* sounds as if to breakfast were a sin,—with us such an abbreviation of the thought so open to misconception would be a fault in style, but not so with a Hebrew.[2] אֲכֹל (for אֲכֹל לֶחֶם, Ps. xiv. 4) is here eating for eating's sake, eating as its own object, eating which, in the morning, comes in the place of fresh activity in one's calling, consecrated by prayer. Instead of אֵשׁ ', 17*a*, there ought properly to have been אֲשָׁרֵיךְ ; but (1) אַשְׁרֵי has this peculiarity, to be explained from its interjectional usage, that with the suff.

<hr>

[1] Cf. Büchmann's *Geflügelte Worte*, p. 178, 5th ed. (1868).

[2] *Vid. Gesch. d. jüd. Poesie*, p. 188 f.

added it remains in the form of the *st. constr.*, for we say *e.g.* אִשְׁרֵיךָ
for אֲשָׁרֶיךָ; (2) the sing. form אֶשֶׁר, inflected אַשְׁרִי, so substitutes itself
that אַשְׁרֶיךָ, or, more correctly, אַשְׁרֵךָ, and אַשְׁרֵהוּ, Prov. xxix. 19, the
latter for אֲשָׁרָיו, are used (*vid.* under Song ii. 14). Regarding *bĕn-
hhorim, vid.* above, p. 191 ; the root-word signifies to be white (*vid.*
under Gen. xl. 16). A noble is called *hhor*, Isa. xxxiv. 12 ; and
one noble by birth, more closely, or also merely descriptively (Gesen.
Lehrgeb. p. 649), *bĕn-hhorim*, from his purer complexion, by which
persons of rank were distinguished from the common people (Lam.
iv. 7). In the passage before us, *bĕn-hhorim* is an ethical conception, as *e.g.* also *generosus* becomes such, for it connects with the idea
of noble by birth that of noble in disposition, and the latter predominates (cf. Song vii. 2, *nadiv*) : it is well with a land whose king
is of noble mind, is a man of noble character, or, if we give to *bĕn-
hhorim* the Mishnic meaning, is truly a free man (cf. John viii. 36).
Of princes after the pattern of such a king, the contrary of what is
said 16*b* is true: they do not eat early in the morning, but *ba'et*,
"at the right time;" everywhere else this is expressed by *b^eitto*
(iii. 11); here the expression—corresponding to the Greek ἐν καιρῷ,
the Lat. *in tempore*—is perhaps occasioned by the contrast *baboqĕr*,
"in the morning." Eating at the right time is more closely characterized by *bighvurah v^elo vashsh^ethi*. Jerome, whom Luther follows,
translates: *ad reficiendum et non ad luxuriam*. Hitz., Ginsb., and
Zöckl., "for strengthening" (obtaining strength), not: "for feasting;"
but that *beth* might introduce the object aimed at (after Hitz., proceeding from the *beth* of exchange), we have already considered under ii. 4.
The author, wishing to say this, ought to have written לִגְבוּרָה וְלֹא לִשְׁתִי.
Better, Hahn: "in strength, but not in drunkenness,"—as heroes,
but not as drunkards (Isa. v. 22). Ewald's "in virtue, and not in
debauchery," is also thus meant. But what is that : to eat in virtue,
i.e. the dignity of a man? The author much rather represents
them as eating in manly strength, *i.e.* as this requires it (cf. the plur.
Ps. lxxi. 16 and Ps. xc. 10), only not *bashti* ("in drunkenness—
excess"), so that eating and drinking become objects in themselves.
Kleinert, well: as men, and not as gluttons. The Masora makes,
under *bashti*, the note לִית, *i.e.* שְׁתִי has here a meaning which it has
not elsewhere, it signifies drunkenness; elsewhere it means the weft
of a web. The Targ. gives the word the meaning of weakness (חֲלָשׁוּת),
after the Midrash, which explains it by בְּתְשִׁישׁוּ (in weakness);
Menahem b. Saruk takes along with it in this sense נָשְׁתָה, Jer. li. 30.
The Talm. *Shabbath* 10*a*, however, explains it rightly by בִּשְׁתִיָּה שֶׁל־יַיִן.
    Ver. 18. Since, now, ver. 19 has only to do with princes, the

following proverb of the consequences of sloth receives a particular reference in the frame of this mirror for princes: "Through being idle the roof falleth; and through laziness of the hands the house leaketh." Ewald, Redslob, Olsh., Hitz., and Fürst, as already Aben Ezra, understand the dual עֲצַלְ of the two idle hands, but a similar attribut. adject.-dual is not found in Heb.; on the contrary, *ephraim*, *m'rathaim* Jer. l. 21, *rish'athaim*, and, in a certain measure, also *riqmathaim*, speak in favour of the intensification of the dual; *'atsaltaim* is related to *'atslah*, as *Faulenzen* [being idle, living in idleness] to *Faulheit* [laziness], it means doubled, *i.e.* great, constant laziness (Gesen. *H. Wört.*, and Böttch. in the *N. Aehrenl.*, under this passage). If *'atsaltaim* were an attribut. designation of the hands, then *shiphluth yadaim* would be lowness, *i.e.* the hanging down of the hands languidly by the side; the former would agree better with the second than with the first passage. Regarding the difference between *hamm'qareh* (the beams and joists of a house) and *hamqareh* (*contignans*), *vid.* note below.[1] Since exceeding laziness leaves alone everything that could support the house, the beams fall (יִמַּךְ, Niph. מָכַךְ), and the house drops, *i.e.* lets the rain through (יִדְלֹף, with *o*, in spite of the intrans. signification); cf. the Arab. proverb of the three things which make a house insufferable, under Prov. xix. 13. Also the community, whom the king and the nobles represent, is a בַּיִת, as *e.g.* Israel is called the house of Jacob. If the rulers neglect their duty, abusing their high position in obeying their own lusts, then the kingdom (state) becomes as a dilapidated house, affording no longer any protection, and at last a *machshelah*, a ruined building, Isa. iii. 6. It becomes so by slothfulness, and the prodigal love of pleasure associated therewith.

Ver. 19. "Meals they make into a pleasure, and wine cheereth the life, and money maketh everything serviceable." By עֹשִׂים, wicked princes are without doubt thought of,—but not immediately, since 16*b* is too remote to give the subject to ver. 19. The subject which *'osim* bears in itself (= *'osim hēm*) might be syntactically definite, as *e.g.* Ps. xxxiii. 5, אֹהֵב, He, Jahve, loves, thus: those princes, or, from ver. 18: such slothful men; but *'osim* is better rendered, like *e.g. omrim*, Ex. v. 16 (Ewald, § 200*a*), and as in the Mishna we read קוֹרִין and the like with gramm. indef. subj.: they make, but so that by it the slothful just designated, and those of a princely rank are meant (cf. a similar use of the *inf. abs.*, as here of the part. in the

---

[1] הַמְּקָרֶה, with *mem* Dageshed (Masora: לִית דנש); in Ps. civ. 3, on the contrary, the *mem* has *Raphe*, for there it is particip. (*Michlol* 46*a*; Parchon's *Lex.* f. 3, col. 1).

historical style, Isa. xxii. 13). Ginsburg's rendering is altogether at fault: "They turn bread and wine which cheereth life into revelry." If עשׂה and לֶחֶם as its object stand together, the meaning is, "to prepare a feast," Ezek. iv. 15 ; cf. 'avad l'hĕm, Dan. v. 1. Here, as there, 'osim lĕhĕm signifies coenam faciunt (parant). The לְ of לִשְׂ' is not the sign of the factitive obj. (as l'ĕl, Isa. xliv. 17), and thus not, as Hitz. supposes, the conditioning לְ with which adv. conceptions are formed,—e.g. Lam. iv. 5, הָאֹכְ' לְמַעֲ', where Jerome rightly translates, voluptuose (vid. E. Gerlach, l.c.),—but, which is most natural and is very appropriate, it is the לְ of the aim or purpose : non ad debitam corporis refectionem, sed ad mera ludicra et stulta gaudia (Geier). שְׂחוֹק is laughter, as that to which he utters the sentence (ii. 2): Thou art mad. It is incorrect, moreover, to take lĕhĕm v'yaim together, and to render y'sammahh hayaim as an attribut. clause to yain : this epitheton ornans of wine would here be a most unsuitable weakening of the figure intended. It is only an apparent reason for this, that what Ps. civ. 15 says in praise of wine the author cannot here turn into a denunciatory reproach. Wine is certainly fitted to make glad the heart of a man ; but here the subject of discourse is duty-forgetting idlers, to whom chiefly wine must be brought (Isa. v. 12) to cheer their life (this sluggard-life spent in feasting and revelry). The fut. יְשַׂמַּח is meant in the same modal sense as יְנַבֵּר, 10a: wine must accomplish that for them. And they can feast and drink, for they have money, and money יַעֲ' ... הַכֹּל־. Luther hits the meaning: "Money must procure everything for them ;" but the clause is too general ; and better thus, after Jerome, the Zürich Bible: "unto money are all things obedient." The old Jewish interpreters compare Hos. ii. 23 f., where ענה, with accus. petentis, signifies, "to answer a request, to gratify a desire." But in the passage before us הַכֹּל is not the obj. accus. of petentis, but petiti ; for 'anah is connected with the accus. of that to which one answers as well as of that which one answers, e.g. Job xl. 2, cf. ix. 3. It is unnecessary, with Hitzig, to interpret יַעֲנֶה as Hiph.: Money makes all to hear (him who has the money),—makes it that nothing is refused to his wish. It is the Kal: Money answers to every demand, hears every wish, grants whatever one longs for, helps to all ; as Menander says : "Silver and gold,—these are, according to my opinion, the most useful gods ; if these have a place in the house, wish what thou wilt (εὖξαι τί βούλει), all will be thine ;" and Horace, Epod. i. 6. 36 s. :

"Scilicet uxorem cum dote fidemque et amicos
Et genus et formam regina pecunia donat."

The author has now described the king who is a misfortune and him who is a blessing to the land, and princes as they ought to be and as they ought not to be, but particularly luxurious idle courtiers; there is now a warning given which has for its motive not only prudence, but also, according to viii. 2, religiousness.

Ver. 20. " Curse not the king even in thy thought; and in thy bed-chamber curse not the rich ; for the birds of the air carry away the sound, and the winged creature telleth the matter." In the Books of Daniel and Chronicles, מַדָּע, in the sense of γνῶσις, is a synon. of הַשְׂכֵּל and חָכְמָה ; here it is rightly translated by the LXX. by συνείδησις ; it does not correspond with the moral-religious idea of conscience, but yet it touches it, for it designates the quiet, inner consciousness (*Psychol.* p. 134) which judges according to moral criteria : even (*gam*, as *e.g.* Deut. xxiii. 3) in the inner region of his thoughts[1] one must not curse the king (cf. vii. 4 f.) nor the rich (which here, as at 6b, without distinction of the aristocracy of wealth and of birth, signifies those who are placed in a high princely position, and have wealth, the *nervus rerum*, at their disposal) in his bed-chamber, the innermost room of the house, where one thinks himself free from treachery, and thus may utter whatever he thinks without concealment (2 Kings vi. 12) : for the birds of the air may carry forth or bring out (Lat. *deferrent*, whence *delator*) that which is rumoured, and the possessor of a pair of wings (cf. Prov. i. 17), after the *Chethîb* (whose ה of the art. is unnecessarily erased by the *Kerî*,[2] as at iii. 6, 10) : the possessor of wings (double-winged), shall further tell the matter. As to its meaning, it is the same as the proverb quoted by the Midrash : " walls have ears."[3] Geier thinks of the swallows which helped to the discovery of Bessus, the murderer of his father, and the cranes which betrayed the murderer of Ibycus, as comparisons approaching that which is here said. There would certainly be no hyperbole if the author thought of carrier-pigeons (Paxton, Kitto) in the service of espionage. But the reason for the warning is hyperbolical, like an hundred others in all languages :

> "*Aures fert paries, oculos nemus : ergo cavere*
> *Debet qui loquitur, ne possint verba nocere.*"

---

[1] Hengst., not finding the transition from *scientia* to *conscientia* natural, gives, after Hartmann, the meaning of "study-chamber" to the word מַדָּע ; but neither the Heb. nor the Aram. has this meaning, although Ps. lxviii. 13 Targ. touches it.

[2] הַכְּנ׳ with unpointed He, because it is not read in the *Kerî;* similarly הַחֲנִית (1 Sam. xxvi. 22). Cf. *Mas. fin.* f. 22, and *Ochla veochla*, No. 166.

[3] *Vid.* Tendlau's *Sprichwörter*, No. 861.

Act Prudently, but not too Prudently—the Future is God's;
Enjoy Life—the World to come is Dark, xi. 1–8.

There are interpreters (as *e.g.* Zöckl.) who regard the concluding part of the book as commencing with xi. 1, and do not acknowledge any connection with that which immediately precedes; but from x. 16 the book draws to its conclusion. לחם, x. 19, affords an external connection for the proverb here following; but, since the proverb x. 20 lies between, the sequence after the same catchword is uncertain. Whether there is here a more inward connection, and what it is, is determined by the interpretation of xi. 1, which proceeds in two fundamentally different directions, the one finding therein recommended unscrupulous beneficence, the other an unscrupulous spirit of enterprise. We decide in favour of the latter : it is a call, derived from commercial pursuits, to engage in fresh enterprise.

xi. 1. " Let thy bread go forth over the watery mirror : for in the course of many days shalt thou find it." Most interpreters, chiefly the Talm., Midrash, and Targ.,[1] regard this as an exhortation to charity, which although practised without expectation of reward, does not yet remain unrewarded at last. An Aram. proverb of Ben Sira's (*vid.* Buxtorf's *Florilegium,* p. 171) proceeds on this interpretation : " Scatter thy bread on the water and on the dry land ; in the end of the days thou findest it again." Knobel quotes a similar Arab. proverb from Diez' *Denkwürdigkeiten von Asien* (Souvenirs of Asia), II. 106 : " Do good ; cast thy bread into the water : thou shalt be repaid some day." See also the proverb in Goethe's *Westöst. Divan,* compared by Herzfeld. Voltaire, in his *Précis de l'Ecclésiaste en vers,* also adopts this rendering :

> *Repandez vos bienfaits avec magnificence,*
> *Même aux moins vertueux ne les refusez pas.*
> *Ne vous informez pas de leur reconnaissance—*
> *Il est grand, il est beau de faire des ingrats.*

That instead of " into the water (the sea) " of these or similar proverbs, Koheleth uses here the expression, " on the face of (עַל־פְּנֵי) the waters," makes no difference ; Eastern bread has for the most part

---

[1] The Midrash tells the following story : Rabbi Akiba sees a ship wrecked which carried in it one learned in the law. He finds him again actively engaged in Cappadocia. What whale, he asked him, has vomited thee out upon dry land? How hast thou merited this ? The scribe learned in the law thereupon related that when he went on board the ship, he gave a loaf of bread to a poor man, who thanked him for it, saying : As thou hast saved my life, may thy life be saved. Thereupon Akiba thought of the proverb in Eccles. xi. 1. Similarly the Targ. : Extend to the poor the bread for thy support ; they sail in ships over the water.

the form of cakes, and is thin (especially such as is prepared hastily for guests, *'ughoth* or *matstsoth*, Gen. xviii. 6, xix. 3) ; so that when thrown into the water, it remains on the surface (like a chip of wood, Hos. x. 7), and is carried away by the stream. But שְׁלַח, with this reference of the proverb to beneficence, is strange ; instead of it, the word הַשְׁלֵךְ was rather to be expected ; the LXX. renders by ἀπόστειλον ; the Syr., *shadar ;* Jerome, *mitte ;* Venet. πέμπε ; thus by none is the pure idea of casting forth connected with שְׁלַח. And the reason given does not harmonize with this reference : " for in the course of many days (*b^erov yamin,* cf. *mērov yamim,* Isa. xxiv. 22) wilt thou find it " (not " find it again," which would be expressed by תָּשׁוּב תִּמְ'). This indefinite designation of time, which yet definitely points to the remote future, does not thus indicate that the subject is the recompense of noble self-renunciation which is sooner or later rewarded, and often immediately, but exactly accords with the idea of commerce carried on with foreign countries, which expects to attain its object only after a long period of waiting. In the proper sense, they send their bread over the surface of the water who, as Ps. cvii. 33 expresses, " do business in great waters." It is a figure taken from the corn trade of a seaport (*vid.* p. 216), an illustration of the thought: seek thy support in the way of bold, confident adventure.[1] Bread in לֶחֶם' is the designation of the means of making a living or gain, and bread in תִמְצָאֶנּוּ the designation of the gain (cf. ix. 11). Hitzig's explanation : Throw thy bread into the water = venture thy hope, is forced ; and of the same character are all the attempts to understand the word of agricultural pursuits ; *e.g.* by van der Palm : *sementem fac juxta aquas* (or : *in loca irrigua*); Grätz even translates : " Throw thy corn on the surface of the water," and understands this, with the fancy of a Martial, of begetting children. Mendelssohn is right in remarking that the exhortation shows itself to be that of Koheleth-Solomon, whose ships traded to Tarshish and Ophir. Only the reference to self-sacrificing beneficence stands on a level with it as worthy of consideration. With Ginsburg, we may in this way say that a proverb as to our dealings with those who are above us, is followed by a proverb regarding those who are below us ; with those others a proverb regarding judicious courageous venturing, ranks itself with a proverb regarding a rashness which is to be discountenanced ; and the following proverb does not say : Give a portion, distribute of that which is thine, to seven and also to eight : for it is well done that thou gainest for thee friends with the unrighteous

---

[1] The Greek phrase σπείρειν πόντον, " to sow the sea " = to undertake a fruitless work, is of an altogether different character ; cf. Amos vi. 12.

mammon for a time when thou thyself mayest unexpectedly be in want; but it is a prudent rule which is here placed by the side of counsel to bold adventure:

Ver. 2. " Divide the portion into seven, yea, eight (parts); for thou knowest not what evil shall happen on the earth." With that other interpretation, עָלֶיךָ was to be expected instead of 'al-haarets; for an evil spreading abroad over the earth, a calamity to the land, does not yet fall on every one without exception; and why was not the רָעָה designated directly as personal? The impression of the words לְשִׁבְ ... תֵּן, established in this general manner, is certainly this, that on the supposition of the possibility of a universal catastrophe breaking in, they advise a division of our property, so that if we are involved in it, our all may not at once be lost, but only this or that part of it, as Jacob, Gen. xxxii. 9, says. With reference to 1a, it is most natural to suppose that one is counselled not to venture his all in one expedition, so that if this is lost in a storm, all might not at once be lost (Mendelss., Preston, Hitz., Stuart); with the same right, since 1a is only an example, the counsel may be regarded as denoting that one must not commit all to one caravan; or, since in ver. 2 לחמך is to be represented not merely as a means of obtaining gain, that one ought not to lay up all he has gathered in one place, Judg. vi. 11, Jer. xli. 8 (Nachtigal); in short, that one ought not to put all into one business, or, as we say literally, venture all on one card. חֵלֶק is either the portion which one possesses, i.e. the measure of the possession that has fallen to him (Ps. xvi. 5), or נָתַן חֵלֶק means to make portions, to undertake a division. In the first case, the expression נתן ... לְ follows the scheme of Gen. xvii. 20 : make the part into seven, yea, into eight (parts); in the second case, the scheme of Josh. xviii. 5 : make division into seven, etc. We prefer the former, because otherwise that which is to be divided remains unknown; חֵלֶק is the part now in possession : make the much or the little that thou hast into seven or yet more parts. The rising from seven to eight is as at Job v. 19, and like the expression ter quaterque, etc. The same inverted order of words as in 2b is found in Esth. vi. 3 ; 2 Kings viii. 12.

Ver. 3. With this verse there is not now a transition, εἰς ἄλλο γένος (as when one understands ver. 1 f. of beneficence); the thoughts down to ver. 6 move in the same track. " When the clouds are full of rain, they empty themselves on the earth : and if a tree fall in the south, or in the north—the place where the tree falleth, there it lieth." Man knows not—this is the reference of the verse backwards—what misfortune, as e.g. hurricane, flood, scarcity, will come

upon the earth ; for all that is done follows fixed laws, and the binding together of cause and effect is removed beyond the influence of
the will of man, and also in individual cases beyond his knowledge.
The interpunction of 3*a a* : אִם־יִמָּלְאוּ הֶעָבִים גֶּשֶׁם (not as by v. d.
Hooght, Mendelss., and elsewhere הֶעָבִים, but as the Venet. 1515, 21,
Michael. הֶעָבִים, for immediately before the tone syllable *Mahpach* is
changed into *Mercha*) appears on the first glance to be erroneous,
and much rather it appears that the accentuation ought to be

$$\text{אִם־יִמָלְאוּ הֶעָבִים גֶשֶׁם עַל־הָאָרֶץ יָרִיקוּ}$$

but on closer inspection גֶשֶׁם is rightly referred to the conditional
antecedent, for " the clouds could be filled also with hail, and thus
not pour down rain " (Hitz.).   As in iv. 10, the fut. stands in the
protasis as well as in the apodosis.   If A is done, then as a consequence B will be done ; the old language would prefer the words
וְהֵרִיקוּ . . . נִמְלְאוּ (כִּי) אִם, Ewald, § 355*b* : as often as A happens, so
always happens B.   יָרִיקוּ carries (without needing an external object
to be supplied), as internally transitive, its object in itself : if the
clouds above fill themselves with rain, they make an emptying, *i.e.*
they empty themselves downwards.   Man cannot, if the previous
condition is fixed, change the necessary consequences of it.

    The second conditioning clause : *si ceciderit lignum ad austrum
aut ad aquilonem, in quocunque loco ceciderit ibi erit.*   Thus rightly
Jerome (*vid.* above, p. 152).   It might also be said : וְאִם־יִפּוֹל עֵץ אִם
בְּדָרוֹם וְאִם בַּצָּפוֹן, and if a tree falls, whether it be in the south or in
the north ; this *sive . . . sive* would thus be a parenthetic parallel
definition.   Thus regarded, the protasis as it lies before us consists in
itself, as the two *v*'*im* in Amos ix 3, of two correlated halves : " And
if a tree falls on the south side, and (or) if it fall on the north side,"
i.e. whether it fall on the one or on the other.   The *Athnach*, which
more correctly belongs to יָרִיקוּ, sets off in an expressive way the protasis over against the apodosis ; that a new clause begins with *v*'*im
yippol* is unmistakeable ; for the contrary, there was need for a chief
disjunctive to בְּצ'.   *M*'*qom* is *accus. loci* for *bimqom*, as at Esth. iv. 3,
viii. 17.   *Sham* is rightly not connected with the relat. clause (cf.
Ezek. vi. 13) ; the relation is the same as at i. 7.   The fut. יְהוּא is
formed from הָוָה, whence ii. 22, as at Neh. vi. 6, and in the Mishna
(*Aboth*, vi. 1 ;[1] *Aboda zara*, iii. 8) the part. הוֶֹה.   As the jussive form
יְהִי is formed from יִהְיֶה, so יְהוָה (יְהְוֶה) passes into יְהוּ, which is here
written יְהוּא.   Hitzig supposes that, according to the passage before
us and Job xxxvii. 6, the word appears to have been written with א,

[1] *Vid.* Baer, *Abodath Jisrael*, p. 290.

in the sense of " to fall." Certainly הוה has the root-signification of *delabi, cadere,* and derives from thence the meaning of *accidere, exsistere, esse* (*vid.* under Job xxxvii. 6); in the Book of Job, however, הוה may have this meaning as an Arabism ; in the *usus loq.* of the author of the Book of Koheleth it certainly was no longer so used. Rather it may be said that יְהוּ had to be written with an א added to distinguish it from the abbreviated tetragramm, if the א, as in אָבוֹא, Isa. xxviii. 12, and הֵלְֹ, Josh. x. 24, does not merely represent the long terminal vowel (cf. the German-Jewish דוּא = thou, דיא = the, etc.).[1] Moreover, יְהוּא, as written, approaches the Mishnic inflection of the fut. of the verb הוה ; the sing. there is אֱהֵא, תְּהֵא, יְהֵא, and the plur. יְהוּ, according to which Rashi, Aben Ezra, and Kimchi interpret יְהוּא here also as plur ; Luzzatto, § 670, hesitates, but in his Commentary he takes it as sing., as the context requires : there will it (the tree) be, or in accordance with the more lively meaning of the verb הוה : there will it find itself, there it continues to lie. As it is an invariable law of nature according to which the clouds dis-charge the masses of water that have become too heavy for them, so it is an unchangeable law of nature that the tree that has fallen before the axe or the tempest follows the direction in which it is impelled. Thus the future forms itself according to laws beyond the control of the human will, and man also has no certain knowledge of the future ; wherefore he does well to be composed as to the worst, and to adopt prudent preventive measures regarding it. This is the reference of ver. 3 looking backwards. But, on the other hand, from this incalculableness of the future—this is the reference of ver. 3 looking forwards—he ought not to give up fresh venturesome activity, much rather he ought to abstain from useless and impeding calcula-tions and scruples.

Ver. 4. " He who observeth the wind shall not sow ; and he that regardeth the clouds shall not reap." The proverb is not to be understood literally, but in the spirit of the whole *paraenesis :* it is not directed against the provident observation, guided by experience, of the monitions and warnings lying in the present condition of the weather, but against that useless, because impossible, calculation of the coming state of the weather, which waits on from day to day, from week to week, till the right time for sowing and reaping has passed away. The seed-time requires rain so as to open up and moisten the ground ; he who has too much hesitation observes (שׁמר, as at Job xxxix. 1) the wind whether it will bring rain (Prov.

---

[1] Otherwise Ewald, § 192*b :* יְהוּא, Aram. of הוּא (as בּוֹא) = הְוָא.

xxv. 23), and on that account puts off the sowing of the seed till it is too late. The time of harvest requires warmth without rain (Prov. xxvi. 1) ; but the scrupulous and timid man, who can never be sure enough, looks at the clouds (cf. Isa. xlvii. 13), scents rainy weather, and finds now and never any security for the right weather for the gathering in of the fruits of the field. He who would accomplish and gain anything, must have confidence and courage to venture something ; the conditions of success cannot be wholly reckoned upon, the future is in the hand of God, the All-Conditioning.

Ver. 5. "As thou hast no knowledge what is the way of the wind, like as the bones in the womb of her who is with child ; so thou knowest not the work of God who accomplisheth all." Luther, after Jerome, renders rightly : "As thou knowest not the way of the wind, and how the bones in the mother's womb do grow ; so," etc. The clause, *instar ossium in ventre praegnantis,* is the so-called *comparatio decurtata* for *instar ignorantiae tuae ossium,* etc., like thy ignorance regarding the bones, *i.e.* the growth of the bones. כַּעֲצָ,[1] because more closely defined by בְּבֶ' הַמְּ', has not the art. used elsewhere after כ of comparison ; an example for the regular syntax (*vid.* Riehm, under Ps. xvii. 12) is found at Deut. xxxii. 2. That man has no power over the wind, we read at viii. 8 ; the way of the wind he knows not (John iii. 8), because he has not the wind under his control : man knows fundamentally only that which he rules. Regarding the origin and development of the embryo as a secret which remained a mystery to the Israel. Chokma, *vid. Psychol.* p. 209 ff. For עֶצֶם, cf. Ps. cxxxix. 15 and Job x. 11. Regarding *m'leah,* pregnant (like the Lat. *plena*), *vid.* above, p. 193. With fine discrimination, the fut. לֹא תֵדַע in the apodosis interchanges with the particip. אֵינְךָ יוֹדֵעַ in the protasis, as when we say : If thou knowest not that, as a consequence thou shalt also not know this. As a man must confess his ignorance in respect to the way of the wind, and the formation of the child in the mother's womb ; so in general the work of God the All-Working lies beyond his knowledge : he can neither penetrate it in the entireness of its connection, nor in the details of its accomplishment. The idea *'oseh kol,* Isa. xliv. 24, is intentionally unfolded in a fut. relat. clause, because here the fut. in the natural world, as well as in human history, comes principally into view. For that very reason the words אֶת־הַכֹּל are also used, not : (as in passages where there is a reference to the world of creation in its present condition) *eth-kol-elleh,* Isa. lxvi. 2. Also the growth of the

---

[1] The Targ. reads בְּעֲצ, and construes : What the way of the spirit in the bones, *i.e.* how the embryo becomes animated.

child in the mother's womb is compared to the growth of the future
in the womb of the present, out of which it is born (Prov. xxvii. 1 ;
cf. Zeph. ii. 2).　What is established by this proof that man is not
lord of the future,—viz. that in the activity of his calling he should
shake off anxious concern about the future,—is once again inferred
with the combination of what is said in vers. 4 and 2 (according
to our interpretation, here confirmed).

Ver. 6. " In the morning sow thy seed, and towards evening
withdraw not thine hand ; for thou knowest not which shall prosper,
whether this or that, or whether both together shall well succeed."
The cultivation of the land is the prototype of all labour (Gen.
ii. 15*b*), and sowing is therefore an emblem of all activity in one's
pursuit ; this general meaning for אַל־ . . . יָדְךָ (like vii. 18 ; synon.
with אַל־ . . . יָדְךָ, Josh. x. 6, of the older language) is to be accepted.
The parallel word to *babokĕr* is not *ba'ĕrĕv;* for the cessation from work
(Judg. xix. 16 ; Ps. civ. 23) must not be excluded, but incessant labour
(cf. Luke ix. 62) must be continued until the evening.　And as ver.
2 counsels that one should not make his success depend exclusively
on one enterprise, but should divide that which he has to dispose of,
and at the same time make manifold trials ; so here also we have
the reason for restless activity of manifold labour from morning till
evening : success or failure (v. 5*b*) is in the hand of God,—man
knows not which (*quid,* here, according to the sense, *utrum*) will
prosper (*vid.* regarding *kasher,* above, p. 193), whether (הֲ) this or
(אִם) that, and whether (וְאִם), etc. ; *vid.* regarding the three-membered
disjunctive question, Ewald, § 361 ; and regarding *kĕähhad,* above,
p. 192 ; it is in common use in the more modern language, as *e.g.*
also in the last benediction of the *Shemone-Esra:* בָּרְכֵנוּ . . . כְּאֶחָד,
" bless us, our Father, us all together." שְׁנֵיהֶם goes back to the two
זֶה, understood neut. (as at vii. 18 ; cf. on the contrary, vi. 5).　The
LXX. rightly : καὶ ἐὰν (better : εἴτε) τὰ δύο ἐπὶ τὸ αὐτὸ ἀγαθά.
Luther, who translates : "and if both together it shall be better," has
been misled by Jerome.

The proverb now following shows its connection with the
preceding by the copula *vav.*　" The tendency of the advice in
vers. 1, 2, 6, to secure guarantees for life, is justified in ver. 7 : life
is beautiful, and worthy of being cared for."　Thus Hitzig ; but the
connection is simpler.　It is in the spirit of the whole book that,
along with the call to earnest activity, there should be the call to
the pleasant enjoyment of life : he who faithfully labours has a
right to enjoy his life ; and this joy of life, based on fidelity to one's
calling, and consecrated by the fear of God, is the most real and the

highest enjoyment here below. In this sense the *fruere vita* here connects itself with the *labora*:

Vers. 7, 8. "And sweet is the light, and pleasant it is for the eyes to see the sun: for if a man live through many years, he ought to rejoice in them all, and remember the days of darkness; that there will be many of them. All that cometh is vain." Dale translates the copula *vav* introducing ver. 7 by "yes," and Bullock by "truly," both thus giving to it a false colouring. "Light," Zöckler remarks, stands here for "life." But it means only what the word denotes, viz. the light of life in this world (Ps. lvi. 14; Job xxxiii. 30), to which the sun, as the source of it, is related, as מָאוֹר is to אוֹר. Cf. Eurip. *Hippol.*, ὦ λαμπρὸς αἰθὴρ κ.τ.λ., and *Iphigen. in Aulis*, 1218–19, μὴ μ᾽ ἀπολέσῃς κ.τ.λ. : "Destroy not my youth; to see the light is sweet," etc. The לֹ in עֵינֵי has the short vowel *Pattach*, here and at 1 Sam. xvi. 7, after the Masora.[1]

The *ki* beginning ver. 8 is translated by Knobel, Hitz., Ewald, and others by "*ja*" (yes); by Heiligstedt, as if a negative preceded by *immo;* but as the *vav* of 7*a* is copulative "and," so here the *ki* is causal "for." If it had been said: man must enjoy himself as long as he lives, for the light is sweet, etc., then the joy would have its reason in the opportunity given for it. Instead of this, the occasion given for joy has its reason in this, that a man ought to rejoice, viz. according to God's arrangement and ordinance: the light is sweet, and it is pleasant for the eyes to see the sun; for it ought thus to be, that a man, however long he may live, should continue to enjoy his fair life, especially in view of the night which awaits him. *Ki im* are not here, as at iii. 12, viii. 15, where a negative precedes, to be taken together; but *ki* assigns the reason, and *im* begins a hypothetical protasis, as at Ex. viii. 17, and frequently. *Im*, with the conclusion following, presents something impossible, as *e.g.* Ps. l. 12, *si esurirem*, or also the extreme of that which is possible as actual, *e.g.* Isa. vii. 18, *si peccata vestra sint instar coccini*. In the latter case, the clause with the concessive particle may be changed into a sentence with a concessive conjunctive, as at Isa. x. 22 : "for though thy people, O Israel, be as numerous as the sand of the sea;" and here: "though a man may live ever so many years." The second *ki* after וְ is the explicat. *quod*, as at ii. 24, iv. 4, viii. 17, etc. : he must remember the days of darkness, that there shall be many of them, and, at all events, not fewer than the many years available for the happy enjoyment of life. In this connection *kol-shebba'*

---

[1] Cf. on the contrary, at Gen. iii. 6 and Prov. x. 26, where it has the *Kametz*; cf. also *Michlol* 53*b*.

denotes all that will come after this life. If Hitz. remarks that the
sentence: "All that is future is vanity," is a false thought, this may
now also be said of his own sentence extracted from the words : "All
that is, is transitory." For all that is done, in time may pass away ;
but it is not actually transitory (הֶבֶל). But the sentence also respects
not all that is future, but all that comes after this life, which must
appear as vain (hĕvel) to him for whom, as for Koheleth, the future
is not less veiled in the dark night of Hades, as it was for Horace,
i. 4. 16 s.:

> " Jam te premet nox fabulaeque Manes
> Et domus exilis Plutonia."

Also, for Koheleth as for Horace, iv. 7. 16, man at last becomes
pulvis et umbra, and that which thus awaits him is *hĕvel*. Tyler is
right, that "the shadowy and unsubstantial condition of the dead and
the darkness of Sheol" is thus referred to. הַבָּא signifies not that
which is *nascens*, but *futurum*, *e.g. Sanhedrin* 27a, "from the present
ולהבא and for the future" (for which, elsewhere, the expression
לעתיד לָבֹא is used). The Venet. construes falsely: All (the days) in
which vanity will overtake (him); and Luther, referring בא as the
3d pers. to the past, follows the misleading of Jerome. Rightly the
LXX. and Theod.: πᾶν τὸ ἐρχόμενον.

(*B.*) FINALE, WITH AN EPIPHONEMA.—XI. 9–XII. 7, 8.

In xi. 7, 8, having again reached the fundamental saying of
his earthly eudaemonism, the author now discontinues this his
ceterum censeo, and artistically rounds off his book ; for having begun
it with an *ouverture*, i. 2–11, he concludes it with a *finale*, xi. 9–
xii. 7. Man, in view of the long night of death into which he goes
forth, ought to enjoy the life granted to him. This fundamental
thought of the book, to which the author has given a poetic colouring,
xi. 7, 8, now amplifies itself into an animated highly poetical call to
a young man to enjoy life, but not without the consciousness that
he must render unto God an account for it. That the call is
addressed not to a man as such, but to the young man,—including,
however, after the rule *a potiori fit denominatio*, young women,—
is explained from this, that the *terminus a quo* of an intelligent,
responsible enjoyment of life stands over against the *terminus ad
quem*, the night of death, with its pre-intimation in hoary old age.
Without any connecting word, and thus as a new point of departure,
the *finale* begins :

Ver. 9. "Rejoice, young man, in thy youth ; and let thy heart cheer thee in the days of thy youth, and walk in the ways of thine heart, and in the sight of thine eyes : but know, that for all this God will bring thee to judgment." The parallel בִּימֵי shows that the *beth* in בִּילַד (with ד aspirated) does not introduce the reason of the joy, but the time suitable for it. Instead of *v*ᵉ*yithav libb*ᵉ*cha*, "let thy heart be of good cheer," as the expression might also be, the words are *vithiv*ᵉ*cha libb*ᵉ*cha*, "make thy heart of good cheer to thee,"—so, viz., that from this centre brightness may irradiate thy countenance (Prov. xv. 13) and thy whole personality, *vid. Psychologie*, p. 249. *V*ᵉ*hhuroth*, the period of youth, is here and at xii. 1 = Num. xi. 28, *v*ᵉ*hhurim*, as the only once occurring *n*ᵉ*uroth*, Jer. xxxii. 30, is = the elsewhere generally used *n*ᵉ*urim ;* the form in *ôth* is the more modern (cf. *k*ᵉ*luloth*, Jer. ii. 2). "Ways of the heart" are thus ways into which the impulse of the heart leads, and which satisfy the heart. מַר' עֵינ', at vi. 9, designates the pleasure felt in the presence of the object before one ; here, a sight which draws and fastens the eyes upon it. The *Chethîb* has the plur. מַרְאֵי, which is known to the language (Dan. i. 15 ; Song ii. 14), and which would here designate the multitude of the objects which delight the eyes, which is not unsuitable ; the *Pih.* הִלֵּך denotes also elsewhere, frequently, *e.g.* Ps. cxxxi. 1, walking, in an ethical sense ; Hitz., Zöckl., and others interpret the first ב as specifying the sphere, and the second as specifying the norm ("according to the sight of thine eyes") ; but they both introduce that wherein he ought to act freely and joyfully : in the ways of thy heart, into which it draws thee ; and in the sight of thine eyes, towards which they direct themselves with interest. The LXX. B. renders, "and not after the sight of thine eyes." This "not" (μή), which is wanting in A. C., is an interpolation, in view of the warning, Num. xv. 39, against following the impulse of the heart and of the eyes ; the Targ. also therefore has : "be prudent with reference to the sight of thine eyes." But this moralizing of the text is superfluous, since the call to the youthful enjoyment of life is accompanied with the *nota bene:* but know that God will bring thee to an account for all this ; and thus it excludes sinful sensual desire. In the midst of an address, where a yet closer definition follows, בְּמִשׁ' is thus punctuated, xii. 14, Job xiv. 3, Ps. cxliii. 3 ; here, in the conclusion of the sentence, it is בַּמִּשׁ'. Hitzig supposes that there is denoted by it, that the sins of youth are punished by chronic disease and abandonment in old age ; Knobel and others understand by the judgment, the self-punishment of sins by all manner of evil consequences, which the O. T. looks upon as divinely inflicted penalties. But in view of the facts of experience, that God's righteous requital is in this life too frequently escaped, viii. 14, the author, here and at iii. 17, xii. 14, postulates a final judgment, which removes the contradiction of this present time, and which must thus be in the future; he has no clear idea of the time and manner of this final judgment, but his faith in God places the certainty of it beyond all doubt. The call to rejoice is now completed by the call to avoid all that occasions inward and outward sorrow.

Ver. 10. "And remove sorrow from thy heart, and banish evil from thy flesh: for youth and age, not yet grown to grey hairs, are vain." Jerome translates: *aufer iram a corde tuo,* and remarks in his *Comm.: in ira omnes perturbationes animi comprehendit;* but בַּעַס (R. כם, *contundere, confringere*) does not signify anger, but includes both anger and sorrow, and thus corresponds to the specific ideas, "sadness, moroseness, fretfulness." The clause following, Jerome translates: *et amove malitiam a carne tua,* with the remark: *in carnis malitia universas significat corporis voluptates;* but רָעָה is not taken in an ethical, but in a physical sense: כעם is that which brings sorrow to the heart; and רעה, that which brings evil to the flesh (בשׂר, *opp.* לב, ii. 3, Prov. xiv. 30). More correctly than the Vulgate, Luther renders: "banish sorrow from thy heart, and put evil from thy body." He ought to free himself from that which is injurious to the inner and the outer man, and hurtfully affects it; for youth, destined for and disposed to joy, is *hĕvĕl, i.e.* transitory, and only too soon passes away. Almost all modern interpreters (excepting the Jewish), in view of Ps. cx. 3, give to שַׁחֲרוּת the meaning of "the dawn of the morning;" but the connection with יַלְדוּת would then be tautological; the Mishn.-Midrash *usus loq.,* in conformity with which the Targ. translates, "days of black hair," proves that the word does not go back to שַׁחַר, morning dawn, morning-red, but immediately to שָׁחוֹר, black (*vid.* above, p. 196), and as the contrast of שֵׂיבָה (non-bibl. שֵׂיבוּת, סָב׳, כֵּיב׳, סָב׳), *canities,* denotes the time of black hair, and thus, in the compass of its conception, goes beyond ילדות, since it comprehends both the period of youth and of manhood, and thus the whole period during which the strength of life remains unbroken.[1]

With xii. 1 (where, inappropriately, a new chapter begins,

---

[1] The Mishna, *Nedarim* iii. 8, jurist. determines that שְׁחוֹרי הראשׁ denotes men, with the exclusion of women (whose hair is covered) and children. It is disputed (*vid.* Baer's *Abodath Jisrael,* p. 279) whether תִּשְׁחֹרֶת, *Aboth* iii. 16, *Derech erez* c. II., *Midrash* under Lam. ii. 11, is = שַׁחֲרוּת, but without right; *ben-tishhorĕth* is used for a grown-up son in full manly strength.

instead of beginning with xi. 9) the call takes a new course, resting its argument on the transitoriness of youth: " And remember thy Creator in the days of thy youth, ere the days of evil come, and the years draw nigh, of which thou shalt say : I have no pleasure in them." The *plur. majest.* בּוֹרְאֶיךָ is = עֹשִׂים as a designation of the Creator, Job xxxv. 10, Isa. liv. 5, Ps. cxlix. 2 ; in so recent a book it cannot surprise us (cf. above, p. 292), since it is also not altogether foreign to the post-bibl. language. The expression is warranted, and the Midrash ingeniously interprets the combination of its letters.[1] Regarding the words 'ad asher lo, commonly used in the Mishna (*e.g. Horajoth* iii. 3 ; *Nedarim* x. 4), or 'ad shello (Targ. 'ad d'lo), ante-quam, vid. above, p. 195. The days of evil (viz. at least, first, of bodily evil, cf. κακία, Matt. vi. 34) are those of feeble, helpless old age, perceptibly marking the failure of bodily and mental strength; parallel to these are the years of which (asher, as at i. 10) one has to say : I have no pleasure in them (bahěm for bahěn, as at ii. 6, mehěm for mehěn). These evil days, adverse years, are now described symptomatically, and that in an allegorical manner, for the " ere " of 1b is brought to a grand unfolding.

Ver. 2. " Ere the sun becomes dark, and the light, and the moon, and the stars, and the clouds return after the rain." Umbreit, Elster, and Ginsburg find here the thought : ere death overtakes thee ; the figure under which the approach of death is described being that of a gathering storm. But apart from other objections (*vid.* Gurlitt, " zur Erkl. d. B. Koheleth," in *Stud. u. Krit.* 1865), this idea is opposed by the consideration that the author seeks to describe how man, having become old, goes forth (הֹלֵךְ, 5b) to death, and that not till ver. 7 does he reach it. Also Taylor's view, that what precedes 5b is as a dirge expressing the feelings experienced on the day of a person's death, is untenable ; it is discredited already by this, that it confuses together the days of evil, 1b, and the many days of darkness, *i.e.* the long night of Hades, xi. 8 ; and besides, it leaves unanswered the question, what is the meaning of the clouds returning after the rain. Hahn replies : The rain is death, and the return is the entrance again into the nothingness which went before the entrance into this life. Knobel, as already Luther and also Winzer (who had made the exposition of the Book of Koheleth one of the labours of his life), sees in the darkening of the sun, etc., a figure of the decay of hitherto joyful prosperity ; and in the clouds after the

---

[1] It finds these things expressed in it, partly directly and partly indirectly : remember בְּאֵרְךָ, thy fountain (origin) ; בּוֹרְךָ, thy grave ; and בּוֹרַאֲיִךְ, thy Creator. Thus *Jer. Sota* ii. 3, and Midrash under Eccles. xii. 1.

rain a figure of the cloudy days of sorrow which always anew visit
those who are worn out by old age.   Hitz., Ewald, Vaih., Zöckl., and
Tyler, proceeding from thence, find the unity of the separate features
of the figure in the comparison of advanced old age, as the winter
of life to the rainy winter of the (Palestinian) year.   That is right.
But since in the sequel obviously the *marasmus senilis* of the separate parts of the body is set forth in allegorical enigmatic figures, it
is asked whether this allegorical figurative discourse does not probably commence in ver. 2.   Certainly the sun, moon, and stars occur
also in such pictures of the night of judgment, obscuring all the lights
of the heavens, as at Isa. xiii. 10 ; but that here, where the author
thus ranks together in immediate sequence 'וְהַכ . . . 'הַשֶּׁ, and as he
joins the stars with the moon, so the light with the sun, he has not
connected the idea of certain corresponding things in the nature and
life of man with these four emblems of light, is yet very improbable.
Even though it might be impossible to find out that which is represented, yet this would be no decisive argument against the significance of the figures ; the *canzones* in Dante's *Convito*, which he
there himself interprets, are an example that the allegorical meaning
which a poet attaches to his poetry may be present even where it
cannot be easily understood or can only be conjectured.

The attempts at interpreting these figures have certainly been
wholly or for the most part unfortunate.   We satisfy ourselves
by registering only the oldest: their glosses are in matter tasteless,
but they are at least of linguistic interest.   A Barajtha, *Shabbath*
151–152a, seeking to interpret this closing picture of the Book of
Koheleth, says of the sun and the light: "this is the brow and the
nose ;" of the moon: "this is the soul;" of the stars: "this the
cheeks."   Similarly, but varying a little, the Midrash to Lev. c. 18
and to Koheleth : the sun = the brightness of the countenance ;
light = the brow ; the moon = the nose ; the stars = the upper part
of the cheeks (which in an old man fall in).   Otherwise, but following
the Midrash more than the Talmud, the Targum: the sun = the
stately brightness of thy countenance ; light = the light of thine
eyes; the moon = the ornament of thy cheeks; the stars = the
apple of thine eye.   All the three understand the rain of wine
(Talm. בכי), and the clouds of the veil of the eyes (Targ.: " thy
eye-lashes "), but without doing justice to שוב אחר; only one
repulsive interpretation in the Midrash takes these words into
account.   In all these interpretations there is only one grain of
truth, this, viz., that the moon in the Talm. is interpreted of the
נשמה, *anima*, for which the more correct word would have been נפש;

but it has been shown, *Psychol.* p. 154, that the Jewish, like the Arab. psychology, reverses terminologically the relation between רוח (נשמה), spirit, and נפש, soul. The older Christian interpretations are also on the right track. Glassius (as also v. Meyer and Smith in " The portraiture of old age ") sees in the sun, light, etc., emblems of the *interna microcosmi lumina mentis ;* and yet better, Chr. Friedr. Bauer (1732) sees in 2*a* a representation of the thought : " ere understanding and sense fail thee." We have elsewhere shown that רוח חיים (נִשְׁמַת) and נפש חַיָּה (for which nowhere נפש חיים) are related to each other as the *principium principians* and *principium principatum* of life (*Psychol.* p. 79), and as the root distinctions of the male and female, of the predominantly active and the receptive (*Psychol.* p. 103). Thus the figurative language of ver. 3 is interpreted in the following manner. The sun is the male spirit רוח (which, like שֶׁמֶשׁ, is used in both genders) or נשמה, after Prov. xx. 27, a light of Jahve which penetrates with its light of self-examination and self-knowledge the innermost being of man, called by the Lord, Matt. vi. 23 (cf. 1 Cor. ii. 11), "the light that is in thee." The light, viz. the clear light of day proceeding from the sun, is the activity of the spirit in its unweakened intensity : sharp apprehension, clear thought, faithful and serviceable memory. The moon is the soul ; for, according to the Heb. idea, the moon, whether it is called יֶרֵחַ or לְבָנָה, is also in relation to the sun a figure of the female (cf. Gen. xxxvii. 9 f., where the sun in Joseph's dream = Jacob-Israel, the moon = Rachel) ; and that the soul, viz. the animal soul, by means of which the spirit becomes the principle of the life of the body (Gen. ii. 7), is related to the spirit as female σκεῦος ἀσθενέστερον, is evident from passages such as Ps. xlii. 6, where the spirit supports the soul (*animus animam*) with its consolation. And the stars? We are permitted to suppose in the author of the Book of Koheleth a knowledge, as Schrader[1] has shown, of the old Babyl.-Assyr. seven astral gods, which consisted of the sun, moon, and the five planets ; and thus it will not be too much to understand the stars, as representing the five planets, of the five senses (Mishn. הָרְגָּשׁוֹת,[2] later הַיֹּשִׁים, cf. the verb, ii. 25) which mediate the receptive relation of the soul to the outer world (*Psychol.* p. 233). But we cannot see our way further to explain 2*b* patholo.- anatom., as Geier is disposed to do : *Nonnulli haec accommodant ad crassos illos ac pituosos senum vapores ex debili ventriculo in cerebrum adscendentes continuo, ubi itidem imbres* (נשם) *h. e. destillationes creber-*

---

[1] *Vid.* " Sterne " in Schenkel's *Bib. Lex.* and *Stud. u. Krit.* 1874.

[2] Thus the five senses are called, *e.g. Bamidbar rabba,* c. 14.

*rimae per oculos lippientes, per nares guttatim fluentes, per os subinde
excreans cet., quae sane defluxiones, tussis ac catharri in juvenibus non
ita sunt frequentia, quippe ubi calor multo adhuc fortior, consumens
dissipansque humores.* It is enough to understand עֲבִים of cases of
sickness and attacks of weakness which disturb the power of
thought, obscure the consciousness, darken the mind, and which
ahhar haggĕshĕm, after they have once overtaken him and then
have ceased, quickly again return without permitting him long to
experience health. A cloudy day is = a day of misfortune, Joel
ii. 2, Zeph. i. 15; an overflowing rain is a scourge of God, Ezek.
xiii. 13, xxxviii. 22; and one visited by misfortune after misfortune complains, Ps. xlii. 8 [7]: " Deep calleth unto deep at the
noise of thy waterspouts : all thy waves and thy billows are gone
over me."

Ver. 3. To the thought : Ere the mind and the senses begin to
be darkened, and the winter of life with its clouds and storms
approaches, the further details here following stand in a subordinate relation : "That day when the watchers of the house
tremble, and the strong men bow themselves, and the grinders
rest, because they have become few, and the women looking out
of the windows are darkened." Regarding בַּיּוֹם with art. : *eo* (*illo*)
tempore, vid. under Song viii. 8. What follows is regarded by
Winzer, with Mich., Spohr, and partly Nachtigal, as a further description of the night to which old age, ver. 2, is compared :
Watchers then guard the house; labourers are wearied with the
labours and cares of the day; the maids who have to grind at the
mill have gone to rest; and almost all have already fallen asleep;
the women who look out from the windows are unrecognisable,
because it has become dark. But what kind of cowardly watchers
are those who " tremble," and what kind of (*per antiphrasin*) strong
men who " bow themselves " at evening like children when they
have belly-ache ! Ginsburg regards vers. 2–5 as a continuation of
the description of the consequences of the storm under which human
life comes to an end : the last consequence is this, that they who
experience it lose the taste for almonds and the appetite for locusts.
But what is the meaning of this quaint figure ? it would certainly
be a meaningless and aimless digression. Taylor hears in this verse
the mourning for the dead from ver. 2, where death is described :
the watchers of the house tremble; the strong men bow themselves,
viz. from sorrow, because of the blank death has made in the house,
etc. ; but even supposing that this picture had a connection in ver. 2,
how strange would it be !—the lookers out at the windows must

be the "ladies," who are fond of amusing themselves at windows, and who now—are darkened. Is there anything more comical than such little ladies having become darkened (whether externally or internally remains undetermined)? However one may judge of the figurative language of ver. 2, ver. 3 begins the allegorical description of hoary old age after its individual bodily symptoms; interpreters also, such as Knobel, Hitz., and Ewald, do not shrink from seeking out the significance of the individual figures after the old Haggadic manner. The Talm. says of *shomrē habbayith* : these are the loins and ribs ; of the *anshē hehhayil* : these are the bones ; of *harooth baarŭbboth* : these, the eyes. The Midrash understands the watchers of the house, of the knees of the aged man ; the men of strength, of his ribs or arms ; the women at the mill, of the digestive organs (הַמְסֵס,[1] the stomach, from *omasum*) ; those who have become few, of the teeth ; the women looking out at the window, of the eyes ; another interpretation, which by *harooth* thinks of the lungs, is not worth notice.

Here also the Targ. principally follows the Midrash : it translates the watchers of the house by "thy knees;" strong men by "thine arms;" the women at the mill by "the teeth of thy mouth;" the women who look out at the window by "thine eyes." These interpretations for the most part are correct, only those referable to the internal organs are in bad taste ; references to these must be excluded from the interpretation, for weakness of the stomach, emphysema of the lungs, etc., are not appropriate as poetical figures. The most common biblical figures of the relation of the spirit or the soul to the body is, as we have shown, *Psychol.* p. 227, that of the body as of the house of the inner man. This house, as that of an old man, is on all sides in a ruinous condition. The *shomrē habbayith* are the arms terminating in the hands, which bring to the house whatever is suitable for it, and keep away from it whatever threatens to do it injury ; these protectors of the house have lost their vigour and elasticity (Gen. xlix. 24), they tremble, are palsied (יָזֻעוּ, from זוּעַ, *Pilp.* זִעֲזַע, bibl. and Mishn. : to move violently hither and thither, to tremble, to shake[2]), so that they are able neither to grasp securely, to hold fast and use, nor actively to keep back and forcibly avert evil. *Anshē hĕhhayil* designates the legs, for the *shoqē hāish* are the seat of his strength, Ps. cxlvii. 10 ; the legs of a man in the fulness of youthful strength are like marble pillars, Song x. 15 ; but those of the old man *hith'authu* (*Hithpa.* only here) have bowed themselves, they

---

[1] This *hamses* is properly the second stomach of the ruminants, the cellular caul.

[2] *Vid.* Friedr. Delitzsch's *Indogerm.-Sem. Stud.* p. 65 f.

have lost their tight form, they are shrunken (בִּרְעוֹת, Job iv. 4, etc.)
and loose ; 4 Macc. iv. 5 calls this τὴν ἐκ τοῦ γήρως νωθρότητα
ποδῶν ἐπικύφων. To maidens who grind (cf. 'בַּ חֵ ט, Num. xi. 8
and Isa. xlvii. 2) the corn by means of a hand-mill are compared
the teeth, the name of which in the old language is masc., but in the
modern (cf. Prov. xxix. 19), as also in the Syr. and Arab., is fem. ; the
reference of the figure to these instruments for grinding is not to be
missed ; the Arab. *taḥinat* and the Syr. *taḥonto* signify *dens molaris*,
and we now call 6 of the 32 teeth *Mahlzähne* (molar teeth, or
grinders); the Greeks used for them the word μύλαι (Ps. lvii. 7,
LXX.). Regarding בְּטְלוּ, LXX. ἤργησαν (= ἀεργοὶ ἐγενήθησαν), *vid.*
above, p. 191.[1] The clause כִּי מִעֵטוּ (LXX. ὅτι ὠλιγώθησαν) assigns
the reason that the grinders rest, *i.e.* are not at work, that they have
become few : they stand no longer in a row ; they are isolated, and
(as is to be supposed) are also in themselves defective. Taylor
interprets *mi'etu* transitively : the women grinding rest when they
have wrought a little, *i.e.* they interrupt their labour, because on
account of the occurrence of death, guests are now no longer entertained ; but the beautiful appropriate allegory maintains its place
against this supposed lamentation for the dead ; also מִעֵט does not
signify to accomplish a little (Targ.), but to take away, to become
few (LXX., Syr., Jerome, Venet., Luther), as such a *Pih.* as x. 10,
קֵהָה, to become blunt. And by הָרֹאוֹת בָּאֲ 'we are not to think, with
Taylor, of women such as Sisera's mother or Michal, who look out of
the window, but of the eyes, more exactly the apples of the eyes, to
which the *orbita* (LXX. ἐν ταῖς ὀπαῖς ; Symm. διὰ τῶν ὀπῶν) and
the eyelids with the eye-lashes are related as a window is to those
who look out ; אֲרֻבָּה (from אָרַב, R. רב, to entwine firmly and closely)
is the window, consisting of a lattice of wood ; the eyes are, as Cicero
(*Tusc.* i. 20) calls them, *quasi fenestrae animi;* the soul-eyes, so to
speak, without which it could not experience what sight is, look by
means of the external eyes ; and these soul-bodily eyes have become
darkened in the old man, the power of seeing is weakened, and the
experiences of sight are indistinct, the light of the eyes is extinguished
(although not without exception, Deut. xxxiv. 7).

---

[1] We find a similar allegory in *Shabbath* 152a. The emperor asked the Rabbi
Joshua b. Chananja why he did not visit בי אבידן (a place where learned conversation, particularly on religious subjects, was carried on). He answered : " The
mount is snow (= the hair of the head is white), ice surrounds me (= whiskers and
beard on the chin white), its (of my body) dogs bark not (the voice fails), and its
grinders (the teeth) grind not." The proper meaning of בי אבידן, Levy has not
been able clearly to bring to light in his *Neuhebr. u. Chald. W. B.*

Ver. 4. From the eyes the allegory proceeds to the mouth, and the repugnance of the old man to every noise disturbing his rest : " And the doors to the street are closed, when the mill sounds low ; and he rises up at the voice of a bird ; and all the daughters of song must lower themselves." By the door toward the street the Talm. and Midrash understand the pores or the emptying members of the body,—a meaning so far from being ignoble, that even in the Jewish morning prayer a *Beracha* is found in these words : " Blessed art Thou, O Lord our God, King of the world, who hast wisely formed man, and made for him manifold apertures and cavities. It is manifest and well known before the throne of Thy Majesty, that if one of these cavities is opened, or one of these apertures closed, it is impossible for him to exist and to stand before Thee ; blessed art Thou, O Lord, the Physician of the body, and who doest wondrous works ! " The words which follow הַמַּ׳ . . . בִּשְׁ׳ are accordingly to be regarded as assigning a reason for this closing : the non-appearance of excretion has its reason in defective digestion in this, that the stomach does not grind (Talm. : בשביל ¹ קורקבן וגו׳). But the dual דְּלָתַיִם suggests a pair of similar and related members, and בַּשּׁוּק a pair of members open before the eyes, and not such as modesty requires to be veiled. The Targum therefore understands the shutting of the doors properly ; but the mills, after the indication lying in הַטּ׳ [grinding maids], it understands of the organs of eating and tasting, for it translates : " thy feet will be fettered, so that thou canst not go out into the street ; and appetite will fail thee." But that is an awkward amalgamation of the literal with the allegorical, which condemns itself by this, that it separates the close connection of the two expressions required by בִּשְׁפַל, which also may be said of the reference of דלת׳ to the ears, into which no sound, even from the noisy market, penetrates (Gurlitt, Grätz). We have for דלתים a key, already found by Aben Ezra, in Job xli. 6 [2], where the jaws of the leviathan are called דַּלְתֵי פָנָיו ; and as Herzf. and Hitz. explain, so Samuel Aripol in his *Commentary*, which appeared in Constantinople, 1855, rightly : " He calls the jaws דלתים, to denote that not two דלתות in two places, but in one place, are meant, after the manner of a door opening out to the street, which is large, and consists of two folds or wings, דלתות, which, like the lips (הַשְּׂפָתַיִם, better : the jaws), form a whole in two parts ; and the meaning is, that at the time of old age the lips are closed and drawn in, because the teeth have disappeared, or, as the

---

¹ Cf. *Berachoth* 61*b :* The stomach (קוּרְקְבָן) grinds. As *hamses* is properly the caul of the ruminant, so this word קוּרְקְבָן is the crop (bibl. מֻרְאָה) of the bird.

text says, because the noise of the mill is low, just because he has no teeth to grind with." The connection of סֻנְּרוּ and בְּשֵׁפַל is, however, closer still : the jaws of an old man are closed externally, for the sound of the mill is low ; *i.e.* since, when one masticates his food with the jaws of a toothless mouth, there is heard only a dull sound of this chewing (*Mumpfelns, vid.* Weigand's *Deut. W. B.*), *i.e.* laborious masticating. He cannot any more crack or crunch and break his food, one hears only a dull munching and sucking.—The voice of the mouth (Bauer, Hitz., Gurlitt, Zöckl.) cannot be the meaning of קול הט׳ ; the set of teeth (Gurlitt indeed substitutes, 3*b*, the cavity of the mouth) is not the organ of voice, although it contributes to the formation of certain sounds of words, and is of importance for the full sound of the voice.

בַּשּׁוּק, "to the street," is here = on the street side ; שֵׁפֶל is, as at Prov. xvi. 19, infin. (Symmachus : ἀχρειωθείσης τῆς φωνῆς ; the Venet. : ἐν τῷ ταπεινῶσθαι τὴν φωνήν), and is to be understood after Isa. xxix. 4 ; טַחֲנָה stands for רֵחַיִם, as the vulgar Arab. *ṭaḥûn* and *maṭhana* instead of the antiquated *raḥâ.* Winzer now supposes that the picture of the night is continued in 4*b* : *et subsistit* (*vox molae*) *ad cantum galli, et submissius canunt cantatrices* (viz. *molitrices*). Elster, with Umbreit, supposes the description of a storm continued : the sparrow rises up to cry, and all the singing birds sink down (flutter restlessly on the ground). And Taylor supposes the lament for the dead continued, paraphrasing : But the bird of evil omen [owl, or raven] raises his dirge, and the merry voice of the singing girls is silent.

These three pictures, however, are mere fancies, and are also evidently here forced upon the text ; for יקום קול cannot mean *subsistit vox*, but, on the contrary (cf. Hos. x. 14), *surgit* (*tollitur*) *vox* ; and יקום לקול cannot mean : it (the bird) raises itself to cry, which would have required יקום לתת קולו, or at least לְקוֹל, after קום לַמִּלחמה, etc. ; besides, it is to be presumed that צפור is genit., like קול עוגב and the like, not nom. of the subj. It is natural, with Hitz., Ewald, Heiligst., Zöck., to refer *qol tsippor* to the peeping, whispering voice ("childish treble" of Shakespeare) of the old man (cf. *tsiphtseph*, Isa. xxix. 4, xxxviii. 14, x. 14, viii. 19). But the translation : "And it (the voice) approaches a sparrow's voice," is inadmissible, since for קום לְ the meaning, "to pass from one state to another," cannot be proved from 1 Sam. xxii. 13, Mic. ii. 8 ; קום signifies there always "to rise up," and besides, *qol tahhanah* is not the voice of the mouth supplied with teeth, but the sound of the chewing of a toothless mouth. If *l'qol* is connected with a verb of external movement, or of that of the soul, it always denotes the occasion of this movement, Num. xvi. 34 ; Ezek. xxvii. 28 ; Job xxi. 12 ; Hab. iii. 16. In-fluenced by this inalienable sense of the language, the Talm. explains 'וִיקוּם . . . צִפ by "even a bird awakes him." Thus also literally the Midrash, and accordingly the Targ. paraphrasing : "thou shalt awaken out of thy sleep for a bird, as for thieves breaking in at night." That is correct, only it is unnecessary to limit וְיָקוּם (or rather וְיָקֹם,[1] which accords with the still continued subordination of ver. 4 to the *eo die quo* of ver. 3*a*) to rising up from sleep, as if it were synonymous with וְיֵעוֹר : the old man is weak (nervously weak) and easily frightened, and on account of the deadening of his senses (after the figure of ver. 2, the darkening of the five stars) is so liable to mistake, that if even a bird chirps, he is frightened by it out of his rest (cf. *hēkim,* Isa. xiv. 9).

Also in the interpretation of the clause וְיִשַּׁחוּ . . . הַשִּׁיר, the ancients are in the right track. The Talm. explains : even all music and song appear to him like common chattering (שׂוּחָה or, according to other readings, שִׂיחָה) ; the proper meaning of ישׁחוּ is thus Haggad. twisted. Less correctly the Midrash : בנות השיר are his lips, or they are the reins which think, and the heart decides (on this curious psychol. conception, cf. *Chullin* 11*a,* and particularly *Bera-choth* 61*a,* together with my *Psychol.* p. 269). The reference to the internal organs is *à priori* improbable throughout ; the Targ. with the right tact decides in favour of the lips : "And thy lips are untuned, so that they can no more say (sing) songs." In this translation of the Talm. there are compounded, as frequently, two different interpretations, viz. that interpretation of בנ' הֹשׁ', which is proved by the כל going before to be incorrect, because impossible ; and the interpretation of these "daughters of song" of "songs," as if these were synonymous designations, as when in Arab. mis-fortunes are called *banatu binasan,* and the like (*vid.* Lane's *Lex.* I. p. 263) ; בַּת קוֹל, which in Mish. denotes a separate voice (the voice of heaven), but in Syr. the separate word, may be compared. But יִשַּׁחוּ (fut. *Niph.* of שָׁחַח) will not accord with this interpretation. For that בנ' הֹשׁ' denotes songs (Hitz., Heiligst.), or the sound of singing (Böttch.), or the words (Ewald) of the old man himself, which are now softened down so as to be scarcely audible, is yet

---

[1] Vav with *Cholem* in H. F. Thus rightly, according to the Masora, which places it in the catalogue of those words which occur once with a higher (יקֹם) and once with a lower vowel (יקוּם), *Mas. fin.* 2*a b, Ochlaweochla,* No. 5 ; cf. also Aben Ezra's *Comm.* under Ps. lxxx. 19 ; *Zachoth* 23*a, Safa berura* 21*b* (where Lipmann is uncertain as to the meaning).

too improbable ; it is an insipid idea that the old man gives forth these
feeble " daughters of song " from his mouth. We explain יָשֹׁחוּ of a
being bowed down, which is external to the old man, and accordingly
understand *b'noth hashshir* not of pieces of music (Aq. πάντα τὰ τῆς
ᾠδῆς) which must be lowered to *pianissimo*, but according to the
parallel already rightly acknowledged by Desvoeux, 2 Sam. xix. 36,
where the aged Barzillai says that he has now no longer an ear for
the voice of singing men and singing women, of singing birds (cf.
בַּר זְמִירָא of a singing bird in the Syrian fables of Sophos, and *banoth*
of the branches of a fruit tree, Gen. xlix. 22), and, indeed, so that
these are a figure of all creatures skilled in singing, and taking pleasure in it : all beings that are fond of singing, and to which it has
become as a second nature, must lower themselves, viz. the voice of
their song (Isa. xxix. 4) (cf. the *Kal*, Ps. xxxv. 14, and to the modal
sense of the fut. x. 10, יֻגַּבַּר, and x. 19, יִשְׂמַח), *i.e.* must timidly retire,
they dare not make themselves heard, because the old man, who is
terrified by the twittering of a little bird, cannot bear it.

Ver. 5a. From this his repugnance to singing, and music,
and all loud noises, progress in the description is made to the
difficulty such aged men have in motion: "Also they are afraid of
that which is high; and there are all kinds of fearful things in the
way . . ." The description moves forward in a series of independent
sentences ; that שׁ בַּיוֹם to which it was subordinate in ver. 3, and
still also in ver. 4, is now lost sight of. In the main it is rightly
explained by the Talm., and with it the Midrash : " Even a little
hillock appears to him like a high mountain; and if he has to go on
a journey, he meets something that terrifies him ; " the Targ. has
adopted the second part of this explanation. גָּבֹהַ (falsely referred
by the Targ. to the time lying far back in the past) is understood
neut. ; cf. 1 Sam. xvi. 7. Such decrepid old men are afraid of
(יִּרְאוּ, not *videbunt*, as the LXX., Symm., Ar., and the Venet. translate, who seem to have had before them the defective יראו) a height,
—it alarms them as something insurmountable, because their breath
and their limbs fail them when they attempt it; and *hathhhattim*
(plur. of the intensifying form of חַת, *consternatio*, Job xli. 25), *i.e.*
all kinds of *formidines* (not *formido*, Ewald, § 179a, Böttch. § 762,
for the plur. is as in *salsilloth*, '*aph'appim*, etc., thought of as such),
meet them in the way. As the sluggard says : there is a lion in
the way, and under this pretence remains slothfully at home, Prov.
xxiv. 13, xxii. 13, so old men do not venture out; for to them a
damp road appears like a very morass; a gravelly path, as full of
neck-breaking hillocks; an undulating path, as fearfully steep and

precipitous; that which is not shaded, as oppressively hot and exhausting—they want strength and courage to overcome difficulties, and
their anxiety pictures out dangers before them where there are none.

5b. The allegory is now continued in individual independent
figures : "And the almond tree is in blossom." The Talm. explains
וינ הש׳ of the haunch-bone projecting (from leanness); the Midrash,
of the bones of the vertebral column, conceived of as incorruptible
and as that round which will take place the future restoration of the
human body,—probably the cross bone, os sacrum,[1] inserted between
the two thigh bones of the pelvis as a pointed wedge ; cf. Jerome in
his *Comm.: quidam sacram spinam interpretantur quod decrescentibus
natium cornibus spina accrescat et floreat;* לח is an Old Heb., Aram.,
and Arab. name of the almond tree and the almond nut (*vid.* under
Gen. xxx. 37), and this, perhaps, is the reason of this identification of
the emblematic שָׁקֵד with לח (the *os sacrum*, or *vertebra magna*) of the
spine. The Targ. follows the Midrash in translating: the רֵישׁ שֵׁזֵ
(the top of the spine) will protrude from leanness like an almond
tree (viz. from which the leaves have been stripped). In these
purely arbitrary interpretations nothing is correct but (1) that שָׁקֵד
is understood not of the almond fruit, but of the almond tree, as also
at Jer. i. 11 (the rod of an almond tree) ; (2) that ינאץ (notwithstanding that these interpreters had it before them unpointed) is
interpreted, as also by the LXX., Syr., Jerome, and the Venet., in
the sense of blossoming, or the bursting out of blossoms by means of
the opening up of the buds. Many interpreters understand שָׁקֵד of
almond fruit (Winzer, Ewald, Ginsb., Rödiger, etc.), for they derive
יִנָּאץ from נאץ, as Aben Ezra had already done, and explain by:
fastidit amygdalam (nucem), or *fastidium creat amygdala.* But
(1) יִנָּאץ for יִנְאץ (*Hiph.* of נָאץ, to disdain, to treat scornfully) is a
change of vowels unexampled ; we must, with such an explanation,
read either יִנָּאץ, *fastiditur* (Gaab), or יִנְאץ ; (2) almond nuts, indeed,
belong to the more noble productions of the land and the delicacies,
Gen. xliii. 11, but dainties, κατ᾽ ἐξ., at the same time they are not,
so that it would be appropriate to exemplify the blunted sensation
of taste in the old man, by saying that he no more cracks and eats
almonds. The explanation of Hitzig, who reads יִנָאץ, and interprets
the almond tree as at Song vii. 9 the palm, to denote a woman, for he
translates : the almond tree refuses (viz. the old man), we set aside as
too ingenious ; and we leave to those interpreters who derive ינאץ from

[1] The Jewish opinion of the incorruptible continuance of this bone may be
connected with the designation *os sacrum;* the meaning of this is controverted, *vid.*
Hyrtl's *Anatomie,* § 124.

נאץ, and understand השקד[1] of the *glans penis* (Böttch., Fürst, and several older interpreters), to follow their own foul and repulsive criticism. יְנַאץ is an incorrect reading for יֵנֵי, as at Hos. x. 14, קָאם for קָם, and, in Prov., רָאשׁ' for רִשׁ' (Gesen. § 73. 4); and besides, as at Song vi. 11, הַנֵצוּ, regular *Hiph.* of נָצַץ (נרץ, Lam. iv. 15), to move tremblingly (vibrate), to glisten, blossom (cf. נום, to flee, and ניסן, Assyr. *nisannu*, the flower - month). Thus deriving this verbal form, Ewald, and with him Heiligst., interprets the blossoming almond tree as a figure of the winter of life : " it is as if the almond tree blossomed, which in the midst of winter has already blossoms on its dry, leafless stem." But the blossoms of the almond tree are rather, after Num. xvii. 23, a figure of special life-strength, and we must thus, thrown back to יִנאץ from נאץ (to flourish), rather explain, with Furrer (in Schenkel's *B. L.*), as similarly Herzf.: the almond tree refuses, *i.e.* ceases, to blossom ; the winter of old age is followed by no spring ; or also, as Dale and Taylor: the almond tree repels, *i.e.* the old man has no longer a joyful welcome for this messenger of spring. But his general thought has already found expression in ver. 2 ; the blossoming almond tree must be here an emblem of a more special relation. Hengst. supposes that " the juniper tree (for this is the proper meaning of שקד) is in bloom " is = sleeplessness in full blossom stands by the old man; but that would be a meaningless expression. Nothing is more natural than that the blossoming almond tree is intended to denote the same as is indicated by the phrase of the Latin poet : *Intempestivi funduntur vertice cani* (Luther, Geiger, Grot., Vaih., Luzz., Gurlitt, Tyler, Bullock, etc.). It has been objected that the almond blossoms are not pure white, but according to the variety, they are pale-red, or also white ; so that Thomson, in his beautiful *Land and the Book*, can with right say: " The almond tree is the type of old age whose hair is white ; " and why ? " The white blossoms completely cover the whole tree." Besides, Bauer (1732) has already remarked that the almond blossoms, at first tinged with red, when they are ready to fall off become white as snow ; with which may be compared a clause cited by Ewald from Bodenstedt's *A Thousand and One Days in the Orient:* " The white blossoms fall from the almond trees like snow-flakes." Accordingly, Dächsel is right when he explains, after the example of Zöckler: "the almond tree with its reddish flower in late winter, which strews the ground with its blossoms, which have gradually become white like snow-flakes, is an emblem of the winter of old age with its falling silvery hair."

---

[1] Abulwalid understands שקד and חגב sexually, and glosses the latter by *jundub* (the locust), which in Arab. is a figure of suffering and patience.

Ver. 5c. From the change in the colour of the hair, the allegory
now proceeds to the impairing of the elasticity of the thighs and of
their power of bearing a load, the *malum coxae senile* (in a wider than
the usual pathological sense): "And the grasshopper (*i.e.* locust, חָגָב,
Samar. חרנבה = חָרְגֹּל, Lev. xi. 22) becomes a burden." Many interpreters (Merc., Döderl., Gaab, Winz., Gesen., Winer, Dale) find in
these words וְיִסְ' הֶחָ' the meaning that locust-food, or that the chirping of grasshoppers, is burdensome to him (the old man); but even
supposing that it may at once be assumed that he was a keen aerido-
phagus (locusts, steeped in butter, are like crabs (shrimps) spread on
slices of butter and bread), or that he had formerly a particular delight
in the chirping of the τέττιξ, which the ancients number among singing birds (cf. Taylor, *l.c.*), and that he has now no longer any joy in
the song of the *tettix*, although it is regarded as soothing and tending
to lull to rest, and an Anacreon could in his old days even sing his
μακαρίζομέν σε, τέττιξ,—yet these two interpretations are impossible, because יִסְ' may mean to burden and to move with difficulty,
but not "to become burdensome." For the same reason, nothing is
more absurd than the explanation of Kimchi and Gurlitt: Even a
grasshopper, this small insect, burdens him; for which Zöckl., more
naturally: the hopping and chirping of the grasshopper is burdensome to him; as we say, The fly on the wall annoys him. Also
Ewald and Heiligstedt's interpretation: "it is as if the locust
raised itself to fly, breaking and stripping off its old husk," is inadmissible; for הסתבל can mean *se portare laboriose*, but not *ad evolan-
dum eniti*; the comparison (Arab.) *tahmmal* gains the meaning to
hurry onwards, to proceed on an even way, like the Hebr. השבים, to
take upon the shoulder; it properly means, to burden oneself, *i.e.* to
take on one's back in order to get away; but the grasshopper coming
out of its case carries away with it nothing but itself. For us, such
interpretations—to which, particularly, the advocates of the several
hypotheses of a storm, night, and mourning, are constrained—
are already set aside by this, that according to the allegory וְינ' הֹשׁ',
וים הֹח' must also signify something characteristic of the body of an
old man. The LXX., Jerome, and Ar. translate: the locust becomes
fat; the Syr.: it grows. It is true, indeed, that great corpulence,
or also a morbid dropsical swelling of the belly (*ascites*), is one
of the symptoms of advanced old age; but supposing that the
(voracious) locust might be an emblem of a corpulent man, yet הסתבל
means neither to become fat nor to grow. But because the locust
in reality suggests the idea of a corpulent man, the figure cannot
at the same time be intended to mean that the old man is like a

skeleton, consisting as it were of nothing but skin and bone (Lyra, Luther, Bauer, Dathe); the resemblance of a locust to the back-bone and its joints (Glassius, Köhler, Vaih.) is not in view; only the position of the locust's feet for leaping admits the comparison of the prominent *scapulae* (shoulder-blades); but shoulder-blades (*scapulae alatae*), angular and standing out from the chest, are characteristics of a consumptive, not of a senile habit. Also we must cease, with Hitz., Böttch., Luzz., and Gratz, to understand the figure as denoting the φαλλός to be now impotent; for relaxation and shrinking do not agree with הסתבל, which suggests something burdensome by being weighty. The Midrash interprets החגב by "ankles," and the Targ. translates accordingly: the ankles (אִסְתַּוָרֵי, from the Pers. *ustuwâr*, firm) of thy feet will swell—unsuitably, for "ankles" affords no point of comparison with locusts, and they have no resemblance to their springing feet. The Talm., glossing החגב by "these are the buttocks" (*nates*) (cf. Arab. 'ajab, the *os coccygis*, Syn. 'ajuz, as the Talm. עגבות interchanges with עכו), is on the right track. There is nothing, indeed, more probable than that חגב is a figure of the *coxa*, the hinder region of the pelvis, where the lower part of the body balances itself in the hip-joint, and the motion of standing up and going receives its impulse and direction by the muscular strength there concentrated. This part of the body may be called the locust, because it includes in itself the mechanism which the two-membered foot for springing, placed at an acute angle, presents in the locust. Referred to this *coxa*, the loins, יסתבל has its most appropriate meaning: the marrow disappears from the bones, elasticity from the muscles, the cartilage and oily substance from the joints, and, as a consequence, the middle of the body drags itself along with difficulty; or: it is with difficulty moved along (*Hithpa.* as pass., like viii. 10); it is stiff, particularly in the morning, and the old man is accustomed to swing his arms backwards, and to push himself on as it were from behind. In favour of this interpretation (but not deciding it) is the accord of חגב with ענב = κόκκυξ (by which the *os coccygis* is designated as the cuckoo's bone). Also the verbal stem (Arab.) *jahab* supplies an analogous name: not *jahab*, which denotes the air passage (but not, as Knobel supposes, the breath itself; for the verb signifies to separate, to form a partition, Mishn. מחיצה), but (Arab.) *jahabat*, already compared by Bochart, which denotes the point (dual), the two points or projections of the two hip-bones (*vid.* Lane's *Lex.*), which, together with the *os sacrum* lying between, form the ring of the pelvis.

Ver. 5*d.* From the weakening of the power of motion, the allegory passes on to the decay of sensual desires, and of the organs appertaining thereto : " And the caper-berry fails " . . . The meaning " caper " for אָבִיּ is evidenced by the LXX. (ἡ κάππαρις, Arab. *alkabar*), the Syr., and Jerome (*capparis*), and this rendering is confirmed by the Mishnic אביונות, which in contradistinction to חמרות, *i.e.* the tender branches, and קפריסין, *i.e.* the rind of fruit, signifies the berry-like flower-buds of the caper bush,[1] according to Buxtorf (*vid.* above, p. 190). This Talm. word, it is true, is pointed אֲבִיּוֹנוֹת ; but that makes no difference, for אֲבִיּוֹנָה is related to אֲבִיּוֹנָה merely as making the word emphatic, probably to distinguish the name of the caper from the fem. of the adj. אֶבְיוֹן, which signifies *avida*, *egena*. But in the main they are both one ; for that אֲבִיּוֹנָה may designate " desire " (Abulwalîd :[2] *aliradat ;* Parchon : התאוה; Venet. : ἡ ὄρεξις ; Luther : *alle Lust*), or " neediness," " poverty " (the Syr. in its second translation of this clause), is impossible, because the form would be unexampled and incomprehensible ; only the desiring soul, or the desiring, craving member (*vid.* Kimchi), could be so named. But now the caper is so named, which even to this day is used to give to food a more piquant taste (cf. Plutarch's *Sympos.* vi. *qu.* 2). It is also said that the caper is a means of exciting sexual desire (*aphrodisiacum*) ; and there are examples of its use for this purpose from the Middle Ages, indeed, but none from the records of antiquity ; Pliny, *Hist. Nat.* xx. 14 (59), knew nothing of it, although he speaks at length of the uses and effects of the *capparis.* The Talm. explains האבי' by חמדה, the Midrash by תאוה, the Targ. by משכבא, interpreting the word directly without reference to the caper in this sense. If *haaviyonah* thus denotes the caper, we have not thence to conclude that it incites to sexual love, and still less are we, with the Jewish interpreters, whom Böttch. follows, to understand the word of the *membrum virile* itself ; the Arab. name for the caper, *'itar*, which is compared by Grätz, which has an obscene meaning, designates also other aromatic plants. We shall proceed so much the more securely if we turn away from the idea of sexual impulse and hold by the idea of the impulse of self-preservation, namely, appetite for food, since אֶבְיוֹן (from אָבָה, the root-meaning of which, " to desire,"

---

[1] The caper-bush is called in the Mish. צָלָף, and is celebrated, *Beza* 25a, cf. *Shabbath* 30b (where, according to J. S. Bloch's supposition, the disciple who meets Gamaliel is the Apostle Paul), on account of its unconquerable life-power, its quick development of fruit, and manifold products. The caper-tree is planted, says *Berachoth* 36a, " with a view to its branches ;" the eatable branches or twigs here meant are called שׁוּתִי (שׁיתי). Another name for the caper-tree is נצפה, *Demai* i. 1, *Berachoth* 36a, 40b ; and another name for the bud of the caper-blossom is פרחא דבוטיתא, *Berachoth* 36b (cf. Aruch, under the words *aviyonoth* and *tseḷaph*).

[2] In his *Dictionary of Roots* (*kitâb el·uṣûl*), edited by Neubauer, Oxford 1873–4.

is undoubted[1]) denotes a poor man, as one who desires that which is indispensable to the support of life ; the caper is accordingly called *aviyonah*, as being *appetitiva, i.e.* exciting to appetite for food, and the meaning will not be that the old man is like a caper-berry which, when fully ripe, bursts its husks and scatters its seed (Rosenm., Winer in his *R. W.*, Ewald, Taylor, etc.), as also the LXX., Symm. (καὶ διαλυθῇ ἡ ἐπίπονος, *i.e.* as Jerome translates it, *et dissolvetur spiritus fortitudo*, perhaps ἐπίτονος, the strength or elasticity of the spirit), and Jerome understand the figure; but since it is to be presupposed that the name of the caper, in itself significant, will also be significant for the figure : *capparis est irrita sive vim suam non exerit* (וְהֵפֵר as inwardly trans. *Hiph.* of פרר, to break in pieces, frustrate), *i.e.* even such means of excitement as capers, these appetite-berries, are unable to stimulate the dormant and phlegmatic stomach of the old man (thus *e.g.* Bullock). Hitzig, indeed, maintains that the cessation of the enjoyment of love in old age is not to be overlooked ; but (1) the use of artificial means for stimulating this natural impulse in an old man, who is here described simply as such, without reference to his previous life and its moral state, would make him a sensualist ; and (2) moral statistics show that with the decay of the body lust does not always (although this would be in accordance with nature, Gen. xvii. 17; Rom. iv. 19) expire ; moreover, the author of the Book of Koheleth is no Juvenal or Martial, to take pleasure, like many of his interpreters, in exhibiting the *res venereae*.

Ver. 5*e*. And in view of the clause following, the ceasing from nourishment as the last symptom of the certain approach of death is more appropriate than the cessation from sexual desire : " For," thus the author continues after this description of the enfeebled condition of the hoary old man, " man goeth to his everlasting habitation, and the mourners go about the streets." One has to observe that the *antequam* of the *memento Creatoris tui in diebus juventutis tuae* is continued in vers. 6 and 7. The words *'ad asher lo* are thrice repeated. The chief group in the description is subordinated to the second *'ad asher lo ;* this relation is syntactically indicated also in ver. 4 by the subjective form וְיָקוּם, and continues logically in ver. 5, although without any grammatical sign, for וְיָנֵאץ and וְתָפֵר are indicative. Accordingly the clause with כִּי, 5*b*, will not be definitive ; considerately the accentuation does not begin a new verse with כִּי : the symptoms of *marasmus* already spoken of are here explained by this, that man is on his way to the grave, and, as we say, has already one foot in it.

---

[1] *Vid.* Fried. Delitzsch's *Indogerman.-Sem. Stud.* I. p. 62 f. Also the Arab. *âby* in the language of the Negd means nothing else.

The part. הֹלֵךְ is also here not so much the expression of the *fut.
instans* (*iturus est*), like ix. 10, as of the present (Venet.: ἄπεισι);
cf. Gen. xv. 2, where also these two possible renderings stand in
question. "Everlasting house" is the name for the grave of the
dead, according to Diodorus Sic. i. 51, also among the Egyptians, and
on old Lat. monuments also the expression *domus aeterna* is found
(*vid.* Knobel); the comfortless designation, which corresponds[1] to the
as yet darkened idea of Hades, remained with the Jews in spite of the
hope of the resurrection they had meanwhile received; cf. Tob. iii. 6;
Sanhedrin 19*a*, "the churchyard of *Husal*;" "to a churchyard"
(*beth 'olam*); "at the door of the churchyard" (*beth 'olam*), *Vajikra
rabba*, c. 12. Cf. also above, p. 191, and Assyr. *bit 'idii* = בית עד of
the under-world (Bab.-Assyr. Epic, "*Höllenfahrt der Istar*," i. 4).

The clause following means that mourners already go about the
streets (cf. סָבַב, Song iii. 3, and *Pil.* Song iii. 2; Ps. lix. 7) expecting
the death of the dying. We would say: the undertaker tarries in
the neighbourhood of the house to be at hand, and to offer his services.
For *hassophdim* are here, as Knobel, Winz., and others rightly explain,
the mourners, *saphdanin* (*sophdanin*), hired for the purpose of playing
the mourning music (with the horn שיפורא, *Moëd katan* 27*b*, or flute,
חלילים, at the least with two, *Kethuboth* 46*b*; cf. Lat. *siticines*) and
of singing the lament for the dead, *qui conducti plorant in funere*
(Horace, *Poet.* 433), along with whom were mourning women, מקוננות
(Lat. *praeficae*) (cf. Buxtorf's *Lex. Talm.* col. 1524 s.),—a custom
which existed from remote antiquity, according to 2 Sam. iii. 31;
Jer. xxxiv. 5. The Talm. contains several such lamentations for the
dead, as *e.g.* that of a "mourner" (ההוא ספדנא) for R. Abina: "The
palms wave their heads for the palm-like just man," etc.; and of the
famed "mourner" Bar-Kippuk on the same occasion: "If the fire
falls upon the cedar, what shall the hyssop of the walls do?" etc.
(*Moëd katan* 25*b*[2])—many of the ספדנים were accordingly elegiac poets.
This section of ver. 5 does not refer to the funeral itself, for the
procession of the mourners about the bier ought in that case to have
been more distinctly expressed; and that they walked about in the
streets before the funeral (Isa. xv. 3) was not a custom, so far as we
know. They formed a component part of the procession following
the bier to the grave in Judea, as *Shabbath* 153*a* remarks with

---

[1] The Syr. renders *beth 'olam* by *domus laboris sui*, which is perhaps to be understood after Job iii. 17*b*.

[2] Given in full in *Wiss. Kunst Judenth.* p. 230 ff. Regarding the lament for the
dead among the Haurans, *vid.* Wetzstein's treatise on the Syrian Threshing-Table
in Bastian's *Zeitsch. für Ethnologie*, 1873.

reference to this passage, and in Galilee going before it ; to mourn over the death, to reverse it, if possible, was not the business of these mourners, but of the relatives (Hitz.), who were thus not merely called הסופדים. The Targ. translates : " and the angels will go about, who demand an account of thee, like the mourning singers who go about the streets, to record what account of thee is to be given." It is unnecessary to change 'בְּסוֹפְד into 'בְּסְפָּר (instar scribarum). According to the idea of the Targumist, the sophdim go about to collect materials for the lament for the dead. The dirge was not always very scrupulously formed ; wherefore it is said in Berachoth 62a, " as is the estimate of the dead that is given, so is the estimate of the mourners (singers and orators at the funeral), and of those who respond to their words." It is most natural to see the object of the mourners going about in their desire to be on the spot when death takes place.[1]

Vers. 6, 7. A third 'ad asher lo now follows (cf. v. 1, 2) ; the first placed the old man in view, with his désagrément in general ; the second described in detail his bodily weaknesses, presenting themselves as forerunners of death ; the third brings to view the dissolution of the life of the body, by which the separation of the soul and the body, and the return of both to their original condition is completed. " Ere the silver cord is loosed, and the golden bowl is shattered, and the pitcher is broken at the fountain, and the wheel is shattered in the well, and the dust returns to the earth as that which it was, and the spirit returns to God who gave it." Before entering into the contents of these verses, we shall consider the form in which some of the words are presented. The Chethîb ירחק we readily let drop, for in any case it must be said that the silver cord is put out of action ; and this word, whether we read it יְרָחֵק or יֵרָחֵק (Venet. μακρυνθῇ), is too indefinite, and, supposing that by the silver cord a component part of the body is meant, even inappropriate, since the organs which cease to perform their functions are not removed away from the dead body, but remain in it when dead. But the Keri יֵרָתֵק (" is

---

[1] The Arab. funeral dirge furnishes at once an illustration of " and the mourners go about the streets." What Wetzstein wrote to me ought not, I believe, to be kept from the reader : " In Damascus the men certainly take part in the dirge ; they go about the reservoir in the court of the house along with the mourning women, and behave themselves like women ; but this does not take place in the villages. But whether the ' going about the streets ' might seem as an evidence that in old times in the towns, as now in the villages, the menaṣṣa (bed of state) was placed with the mourning tent in the open street without, is a question. If this were the case, the sôphdim might appear publicly ; only I would then understand by the word not hired mourners, but the relatives of the dead." But then מְפֹה, as at Ps. xxvi. 6 מזבח, ought to have been joined to סבב as the object of the going about.

unbound") has also its difficulty. The verb רָתַק signifies to bind together, to chain ; the bibl. Heb. uses it of the binding of prisoners, Nah. iii. 18, cf. Isa. xl. 19 ; the post-bibl. Heb. of binding = shutting up (contrast of פתח, *Pesikta*, ed. Buber, 176*a*, whence *Mezia* 107*b*, שורא וריתקא, a wall and enclosure); the Arab. of shutting up and closing a hole, rent, split (*e.g. murtatik*, a plant with its flower-buds as yet shut up ; *rutûk*, inaccessibleness). The Targumist [1] accordingly understands יֵרָתֵק of binding = lameness (palsy) ; Rashi and Aben Ezra, of shrivelling ; this may be possible, however, for נִרְתַּק, used of a "cord," the meaning that first presents itself, is " to be firmly bound ;" but this affords no appropriate sense, and we have therefore to give to the *Niph.* the contrasted meaning of setting free, *discatenare* (Parchon, Kimchi) ; this, however, is not justified by examples, for a privat. *Niph.* is unexampled, Ewald, § 121*e;* נִלְבַּב, Job xi. 12, does not mean to be deprived of heart (understanding), but to gain heart (understanding). Since, however, we still need here the idea of setting loose or tearing asunder (LXX. ἀνατραπῇ ; Symm. κοπῆναι ; Syr. נתפסק, from פְּסַק, *abscindere;* Jerome, *rumpatur*), we have only the choice of interpreting *yērathēq* either, in spite of the appearance to the contrary, in the meaning of *constringitur*, of a violent drawing together of the cord stretched out lengthwise ; or, with Pfannkuche, Gesen., Ewald, to read יִנָּתֵק (" is torn asunder "), which one expects, after Isa. xxxiii. 20 ; cf. Judg. xvi. 9, Jer. x. 20. Hitzig reaches the same, for he explains יֵרָתֵק=יֵחָרֵק, from (Arab.) *kharak*, to tear asunder (of the sound of the tearing [2]) ; and Böttcher, by adopting the reading יֵחָרֵק ; but without any support in Heb. and Chald. *usus loq.* גֻּלָּה, which is applied to the second figure, is certainly [3] a vessel of a round form (from גָּלַל, to roll, revolve round), like the גֻּלָּה which received the oil and conducted it to the seven lamps of the candlestick in Zech. iv. ; but to understand וְתָרֻץ of the running out of the oil not expressly named (Luther : " and the golden fountain runs out ") would be contrary to the *usus loq.;* it is the metapl. form for וְתֵרַץ, *et confringitur*, as יָרוּץ, Isa. xlii. 4, for יֵרֹץ, from רָצַץ, cogn. רעע, Ps. ii. 9, whence נָרֹץ, 6*b*, the regularly formed *Niph.* (the fut. of which, תֵּרֹץ, Ezek. xxix. 7). We said that oil is

---

[1] Similarly the LXX. understands וְנִרֹץ, καὶ συντροχάσῃ (*i.e.* as Jerome in his *Comm.* explains : *si fuerit in suo funiculo convoluta*), which is impossible.

[2] *Vid.* my treatise, *Physiol. u. Musik, u.s.w.*, p. 31.

[3] The LXX., unsuitably, τὸ ἀνθέμιον, which, *per synecdochen partis pro toto*, signifies the capital (of a pillar). Thus, perhaps, also are meant Symm. τὸ περι-φερές, Jerome *vitta*, Venet. τὸ στέφος, and the Syr. " apple." Among the Arabs, this ornament on the capital is called *tabaryz* (" prominence ").

not expressly named. But perhaps it is meant by הַזָּהָב. The *gullah* above the candlestick which Zechariah saw was, according to ver. 12, provided with two golden pipes, in which were two olive trees standing on either side, which sunk therein the tuft-like end of their branches, of which it is said that they emptied out of themselves *hazzahav* into the oil vessels. Here it is manifest that *hazzahav* means, in the one instance, the precious metal of which the pipes are formed; and in the other, the fluid gold of the oil contained in the olive branches. Accordingly, Hitzig understands *gullath hazzahav* here also; for he takes *gullah* as a figure of the body, the golden oil as a figure of the soul, and the silver cord as a figure of vital energy.

Thus, with Hitz., understanding *gullath hazzahav* after the passage in Zechariah, I have correctly represented the meaning of the figures in my *Psychol.* p. 228, as follows:—" The silver cord = the soul directing and bearing the body as living; the lamp hanging by this silver cord = the body animated by the soul, and dependent on it; the golden oil = the spirit, of which it is said, Prov. xx. 27, that it is a lamp of God." I think that this interpretation of the golden oil commends itself in preference to Zöckler's interpretation, which is adopted by Dächsel, of the precious *fluidum* of the blood; for if *hazzahav* is a metaphorical designation of oil, we have to think of it as the material for burning and light; but the principle of bright life in man is the spirit (*ruahh hhayim* or *nishmath hhayim*); and in the passage in Zechariah also, oil, which makes the candlestick give light, is a figure of the spirit (ver. 6, *ki im-beruhhi*). But, as one may also suppose, it is not probable that here, with the same genit. connection, הכסף is to be understood of the material and the quality; and *hazzahav*, on the contrary, of the contents. A golden vessel is, according to its most natural meaning, a vessel which is made of gold, thus a vessel of a precious kind. A golden vessel cannot certainly be broken in pieces, but we need not therefore understand an earthenware vessel only gilded, as by a silver cord is to be understood only that which has a silver line running through it (Gesen. in the *Thes.*); רָצִץ may also denote that which is violently crushed or broken, Isa. xlii. 3; cf. Judg. ix. 53. If *gullath hazzahav*, however, designates a golden vessel, the reference of the figure to the body, and at the same time of the silver cord to the vital energy or the soul, is then excluded,—for that which animates stands yet above that which is animated,—the two metallic figures in this their distribution cannot be comprehended in this reference. We have thus to ask, since *gullath hazzahav* is not the body itself: What in the human body is compared to a silver cord and to a golden vessel? What, moreover, to a pitcher at the fountain, and to a wheel or a windlass? Winzer settles this question by finding in the two double figures only in general the thoughts represented: *antequam vita ex tenui quasi filo suspensa pereat,* and (which is essentially the same) *antequam machina corporis destruatur.* Gurlitt also protests against the allegorical explanation of the details, but he cannot refrain from interpreting more specially than Winzer. Two *momenta,* he says, there are which, when a man dies, in the most impressive way present themselves to view: the extinction of consciousness, and the perfect cessation, complete ruin, of the bodily organism. The extinction of consciousness is figuratively represented by the golden lamp, which is hung up by a silver cord in the midst of a house or tent, and now, since the cord which holds it is broken, it falls down and is shattered to pieces, so that there is at once deep darkness; the destruction of the bodily organism, by a fountain, at which the essential parts of its machinery, the pitcher and windlass, are broken and rendered for ever useless. This interpretation of Gurlitt's affords sufficient support to the expectation of the allegorical meaning with which we approached ver. 6; and we would be satisfied therewith, if one of the figures did not oppose us, without seeking long for a more special allegorical meaning: the pitcher at the fountain or well (כַּד, not הַכַּד, because determined by *'al-hammabu'a*) is without doubt the heart which beats to the last breath of the dying man, which is likened to a pitcher which, without intermission, receives and again sends forth the blood. That the blood flows through the body like living water is a fact cognizable and perceptible without the knowledge of its course; fountain (מָקוֹר) and blood appear also elsewhere as associated ideas, Lev. xii. 7; and *nishbar,* as here *v'tishshabĕr,* used of a pitcher, is a usual scriptural word for the heart brought into a state of death, or near to death, Jer. xxiii. 9; Ps. lxix. 21. From this *gullath hazzahav* must also have a special allegorical sense; and if, as Gurlitt supposes, the golden vessel that is about to be destroyed is a figure of the perishing self-consciousness (whereby it is always doubtful that, with this interpretation, the characteristic feature of light in the figure is wanting), then it is natural to go further, and to understand the golden vessel directly of the head of a man, and to compare the breaking of the skull, Judg. ix. 53, expressed by *vataritz eth-gulgolto,* with the words here before us, *vatharutz gullath hazzahav;* perhaps by *gullath* the author thought of the cogn.—both as to root and meaning—נֻלְגֹּלֶת; but, besides, the comparison of the head, the bones of which form an oval bowl, with *gullath* is of itself also natural. It is true that, according to the ancient view, not the head, but the heart, is the seat of the life of the spirit; "in the heart, Ephrem said (*Opp. Syr.* ii. 316), the thinking spirit (*chuschobo*) acts as in its palace;" and the understanding, the Arabians[1] also say, sits in the heart, and thus between the ribs. Everything by which בשׂר and נפשׁ is affected—thus, briefly formulated, the older bibl. idea—comes in the לב into the light of consciousness. But the Book of Koheleth belongs to a time in which spiritual-psychical actions began to be placed in mediate causal relation with the head; the Book of Daniel represents this newer mode of conception, ii. 28, iv. 2, vii. 10, vii. 15. The image of the monarchies seen in Nebuchadnezzar's dream, ii. 32, 38, had a golden head; the head is described as golden, as it is the *membrum praecipuum* of the human body; it is compared to gold as to that which is most precious, as, on the other hand, ראשׁ is used as a metaphorical designation of that which is most precious. The breaking to pieces of the head, the death-blow which it receives, shows itself in this, that he who is sick unto death is unable to hold his head erect, that it sinks down against his will according to the law of gravity; as also in this, that the countenance assumes the aspect which we designate the *facies hippocratica*, and that feeling is gradually destroyed; but, above all, that is thought of which Ovid says of one who was dying: *et resupinus humum moribundo vertice pulsat.*

If we now further inquire regarding the meaning of the silver cord, nothing can obviously be meant by it which is locally above the golden bowl which would be hanging under it; also גלת הכסף itself certainly admits no such literal antitype,—the concavity of the גלגלת is below, and that of a גלה, on the other hand, is above. The silver cord will be found if a component part of the structure of the body is pointed to, which stands in a mutually related connection with the head and the brain, the rending asunder of which brings death with it. Now, as is well known, dying finally always depends on the brain and the upper spinal marrow; and the ancients already interpreted the silver cord of the spinal marrow, which is called by a figure terminologically related to the silver cord, חוּט הַשִּׁדְרָה (the spinal cord), and as a cord-like lengthening of the brain into the spinal channel could not be more appropriately named; the centre is grey, but the external coating is white. We do not, however, maintain that *hakkĕsĕph* points to the white colour; but the spinal marrow is related, in the matter of its value for the life of man, to

[1] *Vid.* Noldeke's *Poesien d. alten Araber,* p. 190.

the brain as silver is to gold. Since not a violent but a natural death is the subject, the fatal stroke that falls on the spinal marrow is not some kind of mechanical injury, but, according as יֵרָתֵק [is unbound] is explained or is changed into יְנָּתֵק [is torn asunder], is to be thought of either as constriction = shrinking together, consuming away, exhaustion; or as unchaining = paralysis or disabling; or as tearing asunder = destruction of the connection of the individual parts. The emendation ינתק most commends itself; it remains, however, possible that ירתק is meant in the sense of morbid contraction (vid. Rashi); at any rate, the fate of the גלה is the consequence of the fate of the חבל, which carries and holds the *gullah*, and does not break without at the same time bringing destruction on it; as also the brain and the spinal marrow stand in a relation of solidarity to each other, and the head receives [1] from the spinal marrow (as distinguished from the so-called prolonged marrow) the death-stroke. As the silver cord and the bowl, so the pitcher and the well and the wheel stand in interchangeable relation to each other. We do not say: the wheel at the fountain, as is translated by Hitz., Ewald, and others; for (1) the fountain is called בְּאֵר, not בּוֹר (באר), which, according to the usage (vid. Hitz. under Jer. vii. 9), signifies a pit, and particularly a hole, for holding water, a cistern, reservoir; but for this there was no need for a wheel, and it is also excluded by that which had to be represented; (2) the expression *galgal ĕl-habor* is purposely not used, but *hagalgal ĕl-habor*, that we may not take *ĕl-habor* as virtual adj. to *galgal* (the wheel being at the בור), but as the designation of the place into which the wheel falls when it is shattered. Rightly, the LXX. renders 'al-hammabu'a by ἐπὶ τῇ πηγῇ, and *el-habor* by ἐπὶ τὸν λάκκον. The figure of a well (*mabbu'a*) formed by means of digging, and thus deep, is artistically conceived; out of this the water is drawn by means of a pitcher (כַּד, Gen. xxiv. 14, a word as curiously according with the Greek κάδος as those mentioned in pp. 12 and 74, whence (Arab.) *kadd*, to exhaust, to pitcher-out, as it were; syn. דְלִי, a vessel for drawing out water; Assyr. *di-lu*, the zodiacal sign of the water-carrier), and to facilitate this there is a wheel or windlass placed above (Syr. *gilgla dᵉvira*), by which a rope is wound up and down (vid. Smith's *Bibl. Dict.* under "well").[2] The Midrash refers to the deep draw-

---

[1] Many interpreters (lately Ewald, Hengst, Zöckl., Taylor, and others) understand the silver cord of the thread of life; the spinal marrow is, without any figure, this thread of life itself.

[2] Wetzstein remarks, that it is translated by "cylinder" better than by "wheel," since the *galgal* is here not at a river, but over a draw-well.

well of the hill town of Sepporis, which was supplied with such rollers serving as a pulley (polyspast). Wheel and pitcher stand in as close mutual relation as air and blood, which come into contact in the lungs. The wheel is the figure of the breathing organ, which expands and contracts (winds and unwinds) itself like a draw-rope by its inhaling and exhaling breath. The throat, as the organ of respiration and speech, is called גָּרוֹן (Ps. cxv. 7) and נַּרְגְּרוֹת (vid. under Prov. i. 9), from נָּרָה or גָּרַר, to draw, σπᾶν (τὸν ἀέρα, Wisd. vii. 3). When this wheel makes its last laborious revolution, there is heard the death-rattle. There is a peculiar rattling sound, which they who once hear it never forget, when the wheel swings to an end—the so-called choking rheum, which consists in this, that the secretion which the dying cannot cough up moves up and down in the air-passage, and finally chokes him. When thus the breathings become always weaker, and sometimes are interrupted for a minute, and at last cease altogether, there takes place what is here designated as the breaking to pieces of the wheel in the pit within—-the life is extinguished, he who has breathed his last will be laid as a corpse in the grave (בּוֹר, Ps. xxviii. 1, and frequently), the σῶμα has become a πτῶμα (Mark vi. 29 ; cf. Num. xiv. 32). The dust, i.e. the dust of which the body was formed, goes back to the earth again like as it was (originally dust), and the spirit returns to God who gave it. וְיָשֹׁב subordinates itself to the 'ad asher lo, also in the form as subjunct. ; the interchange of the full and the abbreviated forms occurs, however, elsewhere in the indic. sense, e.g. Job xiii. 27 ; Ewald, § 343b. Shuv 'al occurs also at 2 Chron. xxx. 9 ; and אֶל and עַל interchange without distinction in the more modern language ; but here, as also at 6b, not without intention, the way downwards is to be distinguished from the way upwards (cf. iii. 21). כְּשֶׁהָיָה is = כַּאֲשֶׁר הָיָה, instar ejus quod fuit. The body returns to the dust from which it was taken, Gen. iii. 19, to the dust of its original material, Ps. civ. 29 ; and the spirit goes back to the God of its origin, to whom it belongs.

We have purposely not interrupted our interpretation of the enigmatical figures of ver. 6 by the citation and criticism of diverging views, and content ourselves here with a specification of the oldest expositions. The interpretation of Shabbath 152a does not extend to ver. 6. The Midrash says of the silver cord: זו חוט השדרה (as later, Rashi, Aben Ezra, and many others), of the golden vessel: זו נלנלת (as we), and it now adds only more in jest: "the throat which swallows up the gold and lets the silver run through." The pitcher becoming leaky must be כרם, the belly, which three days after death is wont to burst. And as for *hagalgal*, reference is made to the draw-wells of Sepporis; so for *el havor*, after Job xxi. 33, to the clods of Tiberias: he lies deep below, " like those clods of the deep-lying Tiberias." The Targ. takes its own way, without following the Midrash, and translates: " before thy tongue [this of חבל] is bound and thou art unable to speak any more, and the brain of thy head [this the גלה] is shattered, and thy gall [= כד] is broken with thy liver [= המבוע], and thy body [= הגלגל] hastens away [נרץ of רוץ] into the grave." These interpretations have at least historical and linguistic value; they also contain separate correct renderings. A *quodlibet* of other interpretations [1] is found in my *Psychol.* p. 229, and in Zöckler, *ad loc.* A principal error in these consists in this, that they read Koheleth as if he had been a disciple of Boerhaave, and Harvey, and other masters. Wunderbar in his *Bibl.-Talm. medicin* (1850) takes all in earnest, that the author knew already of the nervous system and the circulation of the blood; for, as he himself says, there is nothing new under the sun. As far as concerns my opinion, says Oetinger in his exposition (*Sämmt. Schrift. herausg. von Ehmann,* IV. p. 254), I dare not affirm that Solomon had a knowledge *systematis nervolymphatici,* as also *circuli sanguinis,* such as learned physicians now possess; yet I believe that the Holy Spirit spake thus through Solomon, that what in subsequent times was discovered as to these matters might be found under these words. This judgment also goes too far; the figure of death which Koheleth presents contains no anticipation of modern discoveries; yet it is not without its value for the historical development of anthropology, for science and poetry combine in it; it is as true to fact as it is poetically beautiful.

The author has now reached the close. His Koheleth-Solomon has made all earthly things small, and at last remains seated on this dust-heap of *vanitas vanitatum.* The motto-like saying, i. 2, is here repeated as a *quod erat demonstrandum,* like a summary conclusion. The book, artistically constructed in whole and in its parts, comes to a close, rounding itself off as in a circle in the epiphonema:

Ver. 8. " O vanity of vanities, saith Koheleth, all is vain." If we here look back to ver. 7, that which is there said of the spirit can be no consolation. With right, Hofmann in his *Schriftbeweis,* I. 490, says: "That it is the personal spirit of a man which returns to God; and that it returns to God without losing its consciousness, is an idea foreign to this proverb." Also, *Psychol.* p. 410, it is willingly conceded that the author wished here to

---

[1] Geiger in the *Deut. Morg. Zeitsch.* xxvii. 800, translates xii. 6 arbitrarily: and the stone-lid (גלגל in the sense of the Mish.-Targ. גולל) presses on the grave.

express, first, only the fact, in itself comfortless, that the component parts of the human body return whence they came. But the comfortless averse of the proverb is yet not without a consoling reverse. For what the author, iii. 21, represents as an unsettled possibility, that the spirit of a dying man goes not downwards like that of a beast, but upwards, he here affirms as an actual truth.[1] From this, that he thus finally decides the question as an advantage to a man above a beast, it follows of necessity that the return of the spirit to God cannot be thought of as a resumption of the spirit into the essence of God (resorption or remanation), as the cessation of his independent existence, although, as also at Job xxxiv. 14, Ps. civ. 29, the nearest object of the expression is directed to the ruin of the soul-corporeal life of man which directly follows the return of the spirit to God. The same conclusion arises from this, that the idea of the return of the spirit to God, in which the author at last finds rest, cannot yet stand in a subordinate place with reference to the idea of Hades, above which it raises itself; with the latter the spirit remains indestructible, although it has sunk into a silent, inactive life. And in the third place, that conclusion flows from the fact that the author is forced by the present contradiction between human experience and the righteousness of God to the postulate of a judgment finally settling these contradictions, iii. 17, xi. 9, cf. xii. 14, whence it immediately follows that the continued existence of the spirit is thought of as a well-known truth (*Psychol.* p. 127). The Targ. translates, not against the spirit of the book: " the spirit will return to stand in judgment before God, who gave it to thee." In this connection of thoughts Koheleth says more than what Lucretius says (ii. 998 ss.):

> *Cedit item retro, de terra quod fuit ante,*
> *In terras, et quod missum est ex aetheris oris*
> *Id rursum caeli rellatum templa receptant.*

A comforting thought lies in the words אֲשֶׁר נְתָנָהּ. The gifts of God are on His side ἀμεταμέλητα (Rom. xi. 29). When He receives back that which was given, He receives it back to restore it again in another manner. Such thoughts connect themselves with the reference to God the Giver. Meanwhile the author next aims at showing the vanity of man, viz. of man as living here. Body and spirit are separated, and depart each in its own direction. Not only the world and the labours by which man is encompassed are " vain," and not only is that which man has and does and experiences " vain," but also

---

[1] In the Rig-Veda that which is immortal in man is called *manas*; the later language calls it *âtman*; vid. Muir in the *Asiatic Journal*, 1865, p. 305.

man himself as such is vain, and thus—this is the *facit*—all is הבל,
" vain."

(*C.*) THE EPILOGUE.—XII. 9–14.

In an unexpected manner there now follows a postscript. Since
the book closes with the epiphonema xii. 8 as having reached the
intended goal, the supposition that what follows xii. 8 is from
another hand is more natural than the contrary. Of the question of
genuineness there cannot be here properly anything said, for only
that which is not what it professes to be and ought to be, is spurious ;
the postscript is certainly according to tradition an integral part
of the Book of Koheleth (Bullock), but not as an original organic
formal part of it, and still less does it expressly bear self-evidence
of this. At the least, those who regard Solomon as the author of the
book ought to contend against the recognition in xii. 9 ff. of an appendix
by a later hand. Hahn, however, regards the same Solomon who
speaks in ver. 8 as continuing to speak in ver. 9, for he interprets
אמר, which, however, only means *inquit,* as perf., looking back to the
completed book, and regards this retrospect as continued in ver. 9 ff.,
without being hindered by the interchange of the *I* and of the following historical *he,* which is contained in " saith Koheleth." Dale even
ventures the assertion, that the Book of Koheleth could have closed
with the unsatisfying pure negative, ver. 8, as little as the Gospel
of Mark with " and they were afraid " (xvi. 8). As if ver. 13 f.
expressed postulates not already contained in the book itself ! The
epilogue has certainly manifestly the object of recommending the
author of the book, Koheleth-Solomon, and of sealing the contents of
the book. If Solomon himself were the author, the epilogue would
stand in the same relation to the book as John xxi. 24 f. to the
fourth Gospel, of the Johannean origin of which a voice from the
apostolic church there bears witness.[1]

It is a serious anachronism when modern interpreters of Scripture occupy the standpoint of the old, who take the name of the
man after whom the book is entitled, without more ado, as the
name of its author from first to last.[2] To what childish puerilities
a bigotry so uncritical descends is seen in the case of Christ.

---

[1] Hoelemann, in *Abth.* II. of his *Bibel-Studien* (1860), draws a parallel between
these two epilogues ; he regards them as original formal parts of the Solomonic
Koheleth and of the Johannean Gospel, and seeks to prove that they stand in more
than external and accidental relation to the two works respectively.

[2] Thus John Miller, in his *Commentary on the Proverbs* (New York, 1872),
regards Solomon as the author of the entire Book of Proverbs and also of Ecclesi-

Fried. Bauer (1732). In this section, vers. 9–12, he says Solomon turns especially to his son Rehoboam, and delivers to him this *Solennel*-discourse or sermon as an instruction for his future life. He recommends it [the sermon] at once on account of the author, ver. 9, and of its contents, ver. 10, which accord, ver. 11, with his other writings, and from which altogether Rehoboam could find sufficient information, so that to write to him several books would be unnecessary. After this apostrophe to his son the preacher turns round to the entire *auditorio*, and addresses them in הַכֹּל נִשְׁמָע. But we are all permitted to hear what is the final aim and intention of this sermon : Fear thou God, and keep His commandments ; for such ought every man to be, etc.

A rationalism not less fruitful in wonderful conceits appeared over against this dreamy irrationalism. Döderlein (1784) says of Koheleth : " As it appears, so the author feigned, that this was a lecture or treatise which Solomon delivered before his literary academy ; for this academy I am inclined to understand under the name ' Koheleth.' " The epilogue appears to him as an appendage by another hand. Such is the opinion also of J. E. Ch. Schmidt (1794), Bertholdt (in his *Einleit.* 1812 ff.), Umbreit (1818, 20), and Knobel (1836), who maintain that this appendage is aimless, in form as in doctrine, out of harmony with the book, revealing by the " endless book-making " a more recent time, and thus is an addition by a later author. This negative critical result Grätz (1871) has sought, following Krochmal (in his *More nebuche hazeman*, 1851, 54), to raise to a positive result. Vers. 9–11 are to him as an apology of the Book of Koheleth, and vers. 12–14 as a clause defining the collection of the Hagiographa, which is completed by the reception into it of the Book of Koheleth ; and this bipartite epilogue as an addition belonging to the period of the Synod of Jabneh, about A.D. 90 (*vid.* above, p. 189).

If, nevertheless, we regard this epilogue as a postscript by the author of the book himself, we have not only Herzfeld on our side, who has given his verdict against all Knobel's arguments, but also Hitzig, who (Hilgenfeld's *Zeitsch.* 1872, p. 566) has rejected Grätz' Herod-hypothesis, as well as also his introduction of the epilogue into the history of the canon, or, as Geiger (*Jüd. Zeitsch.* 1872, p. 123) has expressed himself, has dealt with it according to its

astes. His interpretation of Scripture proceeds on the fundamental principle, in itself commendable, that the Scripture never expresses trivialities (" each text must be a brilliant ") ; but it is not to be forgotten that the O. T., in relation to the high school of the New, is in reality a *trivium*, and that the depth of the words of Scripture is not everywhere the same, but varies according to the author and the times.

merit. Also in Bloch's monograph on the Book of Koheleth (1872) there are many striking arguments against placing the authorship of the book in the Herod-Mishn. period, although the view of this critic, that the book contains notes of Solomon's with interpolations, and an epilogue by the collector, who sought to soften the impression of the gloomy pessimism of these notes, is neither cold nor hot.

We have already (p. 206) shown that the epilogue is written quite in the same style as the book itself; its language is like that of the chronicler; it approaches the idiom of the Mishna, but, with reference to it, is yet somewhat older. That the first part of the epilogue, vers. 9–11, serves an important end, is also proved (p. 206), —it establishes the book as a production of the Chokma, which had Solomon as its pattern; and the second part, vers. 12–14, bears on it the stamp of this Chokma, for it places all the teaching of the book under the double watchword: "Fear God," and "There is a judgment" (Job xxviii. 28, xix. 29; cf. Eccles. v. 6, xi. 9). In the book, Koheleth-Solomon speaks, whose mask the author puts on; here, he speaks, letting the mask fall off, of Koheleth. That in his time (the Persian) too much was done in the way of making books, we may well believe. In addition to authors by profession, there have always been amateurs; the habit of much writing is old, although in the course of time it has always assumed greater dimensions. A complaint in reference to this sounds strange, at least from the mouth of an author who has contented himself with leaving to posterity a work so small, though important. We nowhere encounter any necessity for regarding the author of the book and of the epilogue as different persons. The spirit and tone of the book and of the epilogue are one. The epilogue seals only the distinction between the pessimism of the book and the modern pessimism, which is without God and without a future.

Ver. 9. In connection with ver. 8, where Koheleth has spoken his last word, the author, who has introduced him as speaking hitherto, continues: "And, moreover, because Koheleth was wise, he taught the people knowledge; he applied and searched out and formed many proverbs." The postscript begins with "and" because it is connected with the concluding words of the book—only externally, however; nothing is more unwarrantable than to make ver. 8 the beginning of the postscript on account of the *vav*. The LXX. translate καὶ περισσὸν (Venet. περιττὸν) ὅτι; as Hitz.: "it remains (to be said) that Koheleth was a wise man," etc.; and Dale may be right, that ויתר is in this sense as subj., pointed with *Zakeph gadhol* (cf. Gen. xvi. 16, xx. 4, and the obj. thus pointed, Ex. xxiii. 3). But that Koheleth was "a wise man" is nothing remaining to be said, for as such he certainly speaks in the whole book from beginning to end; the עוֹד, unconnected, following, shows that this his property is presupposed as needing no further testimony. But untenable also is the translation: So much the greater Koheleth was as a wise man, so much the more, etc. (Heinem., Südfeld); עוֹד does not signify *eo magis;* the Heb. language has a different way of expressing such an intensification: כָּל הַגָּדוֹל מֵחֲבֵרוֹ יִצְרוֹ נָדוֹל מִמֶּנּוּ, *i.e.* the higher the position is which one assumes, so much the greater are the temptations to which he is exposed. Rightly, Luther: "This same preacher was not only wise, but," etc. וְיֹתֵר signifies, vii. 11, "and an advance (benefit, gain);" here שֶׁ וְיֹתֵר, "and something going beyond this, that," etc.—thought of as accus.-adv.: "going beyond this, that = moreover, because" (Gesen., Knobel, Vaih., Ginsb., Grätz); *vid.* above, p. 192. Thus *'od* is in order, which introduces that which goes beyond the property and position of a "wise man" as such. That which goes beyond does not consist in this, that he taught the people knowledge, for that is just the meaning of the name *Koheleth;* the statement which *'od* introduces is contained in the concluding member of the compound sentence; the after-word begins with this, that it designates the Koheleth who appears in the more esoteric book before us as חָכָם, as the very same person who also composed the comprehensive people's book, the *Mishle.* He has taught the people knowledge; for he has placed, *i.e.* formed ("*stellen,*" to place, as "*Schriftsteller*" = author; modern Heb. מְחַבֵּר; Arab. *musannif*),[1] many proverbs, as the fruit of mature reflection and diligent research. The obj. *mᵉshalim harbēh* belongs only to *tiqqēn,* which ἀσυνδέτως (according to the style of the epilogue and of the book, as is shown above, p. 207) follows the two preparative mental efforts, whose *resultat* it was. Rightly, as to the syntax, Zöckler, and, as to the matter, Hitzig: "Apparently the author has here not 1 Kings v. 12, but the canonical Book of Proverbs in his eye." The language is peculiar. Not only is תִּקֵּן exclusively peculiar (*vid.* above, p. 196) to the Book of Koheleth, but also אָזַן, *perpendere* (cf. Assyr. *uzunu,* reflection), to consider, and the Pih. חִקֵּר. Regarding the position of *harbeh, vid.* above, p. 230.[2]

---

[1] Cogn. in the meaning "*verfassen*" = to compose, is יסד; *vid.* Zunz' *Aufs.:* "To compose and to translate," expressed in Heb. in *Deut. Morg. Zeitsch.* xxv. p. 435 ff.

[2] *Harbeh bĕchēh,* Ezra x. 1, which signifies "making much weeping," makes no exception in favour of the scribe. Cf. *hatsne'a lecheth,* Mic. vi. 8; *haphlē vaphĕlĕ,* Isa. xxix. 14.

Ver. 10. It is further said of Koheleth, that he put forth efforts
not only to find words of a pleasant form, but, above all, of exact
truth : " Koheleth strove to find words of pleasantness, and, written
in sincerity, words of truth." The unconnected beginning *biqqesh
Koheleth* is like *dibbarti ani*, i. 16, etc., in the book itself. Three
objects follow *limtso*. But Hitz. reads the *inf. absol.* וְכָתוֹב instead of
וְכָתַב, and translates : to find pleasing words, and correctly to write
words of truth. Such a continuance of the *inf. const.* by the *inf.
absol.* is possible ; 1 Sam. xxv. 26, cf. 31. But why should וְכָתוֹב
not be the continuance of the finite (Aq., Syr.), as *e.g.* at viii. 9, and
that in the nearest adverbial sense : *et scribendo quidem sincere verba
veritatis, i.e.* he strove, according to his best knowledge and conscience, to write true words, at the same time also to find out
pleasing words ; thus sought to connect truth as to the matter with
beauty as to the manner ? *V*chathuv* needs no modification in its
form. But it is not to be translated : and that which was right
was written by him ; for the ellipsis is inadmissible, and כָתוּב מִן
is not correct Heb. Rightly the LXX., *καὶ γεγραμμένον εὐθύτητος.*
כָּתוּב signifies " written," and may also, as the name of the Hagiographa
כְּתוּבִים shows, signify " a writing ; " *kakathuvah*, 2 Chron. xxx. 5, is =
" in accordance with the writing ; " and *b*lo kăkathuv*, 2 Chron.
xxx. 18, " contrary to the writing ; " in the post-bibl. the phrase
הַכָּתוּב אֹמֵר = *ἡ γραφὴ λέγει*, is used. The objection made by Ginsburg, that *kathuv* never means, as *k*thav* does, " a writing," is thus
nugatory. However, we do not at all here need this subst. meaning,
וכתוב is neut. particip., and יֹשֶׁר certainly not the genit., as the
LXX. renders (reading וּכְתוֹב), but also not the nom. of the subj.
(Hoelem.), but, since יֹשֶׁר is the designation of a mode of thought and
of a relation, the accus. of manner, like *v*yashar*, Ps. cxix. 18 ; *emeth*,
Ps. cxxxii. 11 ; *emunah*, Ps. cxix. 75. Regarding the common use
of such an accus. of the nearer definition in the passive part., *vid.*
Ewald, § 284c. The asyndeton *v*chathuv yosher divre emeth* is like
that at x. 1, *mehhochmah michvod*. That which follows *limtso* we
interpret as its threefold object. Thus it is said that Koheleth
directed his effort towards an attractive form (cf. *avne-hephets*, Isa.
liv. 12) ; but, before all, towards the truth, both subjectively (יֹשֶׁר)
and objectively (אֱמֶת), of that which was formulated and expressed
in writing.

Ver. 11. From the words of Koheleth the author comes to the
words of the wise man in general ; so that what he says of the
latter finds its application to himself and his book : " Words of the
wise are as like goads, and like fastened nails which are put together

in collections—they are given by one shepherd." The LXX., Aq., and
Theod. translate *darvonoth* by βούκεντρα, the Venet. by βουπλῆγες;
and that is also correct. The word is one of three found in the
Jerus. Gemara, *Sanhedrin* x. 1, to designate a rod for driving (oxen)
—דרבן (from דרב, to sharpen, to point), מַלְמֵד (from למד, to adjust,
teach, exercise), and מַרְדֵּעַ (from רדע, to hold back, *repellere*); we read
ka-dārᵉvonoth; Gesen., Ewald, Hitz., and others are in error in
reading *dorvonoth;* for the so-called light *Metheg*, which under certain circumstances can be changed into an accent, and the *Kametz
chatuph* exclude one another.[1] If דרבן is the goad, the point of
comparison is that which is to be excited intellectually and morally.
Incorrectly, Gesen., Hitz., and others: like goads, because easily and
deeply impressing themselves on the heart as well as on the memory.
For goads, *aculei*, the Hebrews use the word קוֹצִים; *darᵉvonoth* also
are goads, but designed for driving on, thus *stimuli* (Jerome); and is
there a more natural commendation for the proverbs of the wise men
than that they incite to self-reflection, and urge to all kinds of noble
effort? *Divre* and *darᵉvonoth* have the same three commencing
consonants, and, both for the ear and the eye, form a paronomasia.
In the following comparison, it is a question whether *ba'ale asuppoth*
(plur. of *ba'al asuppoth*, or of the double plur. *ba'al asuppah*, like *e.g.*
sare missim, Ex. i. 11, of *sar mas*) is meant of persons, like *ba'al
hallashon*, x. 11, cf. *ba'al kᵉnaphayim*, x. 20, or of things, as *ba'al
piphiyoth*, Isa. xli. 15; and thus, whether it is a designation parallel to
חכמים or to דברי. The Talm. *Jer. Sanhedrin* x. 1, wavers, for there it
is referred first to the members of assemblies (viz. of the *Sanedrium*),
and then is explained by "words which are spoken in the assembly."
If we understand it of persons, as it was actually used in the Talm.
(*vid.* above, p. 191), then by *asuppoth* we must understand the societies
of wise men, and by *ba'ale asuppoth*, of the academicians (Venet.:
δεσπόται ξυναγμάτων; Luther: "masters of assemblies") belonging
to such academies. But an appropriate meaning of this second comparison is not to be reached in this way. For if we translate: and as
nails driven in are the members of the society, it is not easy to see
what this wonderful comparison means; and what is then further said:
they are given from one shepherd, reminds us indeed of Eph. iv. 11,
but, as said of this perfectly unknown great one, is for us incomprehensible. Or if we translate, after Isa. xxviii. 1: and (the words of

---

[1] The *Kametz* is the *Kametz gadhol* (opp. *Kametz chatuph*), and may for this
reason have the accent *Munach* instead of *Metheg*. *Vid. Michlol* 153b, 182b. The
case is the same as at Gen. xxxix. 34, where *mimmachŏrāth* is to be read. Cf.
Baer's *Metheg-Setz.* § 27 and § 18.

the wise are) like the fastened nails of the members of the society, it is as tautological as if I should say : words of wise men are like fastened nails of wise men bound together in a society (as a confederacy, union). Quite impossible are the translations : like nails driven in by the masters of assemblies (thus *e.g.* Lightfoot, and recently Bullock), for the accus. with the pass. particip. may express some nearer definition, but not (as of the genit.) the effective cause ; and : like a nail driven in are the (words) of the masters of assemblies (Tyler : "those of editors of collections "), for ellipt. genit., dependent on a governing word carrying forward its influence, are indeed possible, *e.g.* Isa. lxi. 7, but that a governing word itself, as *ba'ale*, may be the governed genit. of one omitted, as here *divre*, is without example.[1] It is also inconsistent to understand *ba'ale asuppoth* after the analogy of *ba'ale masoreth* (the Masoretes) and the like. It will not be meant of the persons of the wise, but of the proverbs of the wise. So far we agree with Lang and Hoelem. Lang (1874) thinks to come to a right understanding of the "much abused" expression by translating, "lords of troops,"—a designation of proverbs which, being by many acknowledged and kept in remembrance, possess a kind of lordship over men's minds ; but that is already inadmissible, because *asuppoth* designates not any multitude of men, but associations with a definite end and aim. Hoelem. is content with this idea ; for he connects together "planted as leaders of assemblies," and finds therein the thought, that the words of the wise serve as seeds and as guiding lights for the expositions in the congregation ; but *ba'ale* denotes masters, not in the sense of leaders, but of possessors ; and as *ba'ale b'rith*, Gen. xiv. 13, signifies "the confederated," *ba'ale sh'vu'ah*, Neh. vi. 18, "the sworn," and the frequently occurring *ba'ale ha'ir*, "the citizens;" so *ba'ale asuppoth* means, the possessors of assemblies and of the assembled themselves, or the possessors of collections and of the things collected. Thus *ba'ale asuppoth* will be a designation of the "words of the wise" (as in *shalishim*, choice men = choice proverbs, Prov. xxii. 20, in a certain measure personified), as of those which form or constitute collections, and which stand together in order and rank (Hitz., Ewald, Elst., Zöckl., and others). Of such it may properly be said, that they are like nails driven in, for they are secured against separation,—they are, so to speak, made nail-fast, they stand on one common ground ; and their being fixed in such connection not only is a help to the memory,

---

[1] Regarding this omission of the *mudâf* [the governing noun], where this is naturally supplied before a genitive from the preceding, cf. Samachschari's *Mufaṣṣal*, p. 43, l. 8–13.

but also to the understanding of them. The Book of Koheleth itself is such an *asuppah;* for it contains a multitude of separate proverbs, which are thoughtfully ranged together, and are introduced into the severe, critical sermon on the nothingness of all earthly things as oases affording rest and refreshment; as similarly, in the later Talmudic literature, Haggadic parts follow long stretches of hair-splitting dialectics, and afford to the reader an agreeable repose.

And when he says of the " proverbs of the wise," individually and as formed into collections : נִתְּנוּ מֵרֹעֶה אֶחָד, *i.e.* they are the gift of one shepherd, he gives it to be understood that his " words of Koheleth," if not immediately written by Solomon himself, have yet one fountain with the Solomonic Book of Proverbs,—God, the one God, who guides and cares as a shepherd for all who fear Him, and suffers them to want nothing which is necessary to their spiritual support and advancement (Ps. xxiii. 1, xxviii. 9). " *Mēro'eh ehad,*" says Grätz, " is yet obscure, since it seldom, and that only poetically, designates the Shepherd of Israel. It cannot certainly refer to Moses." Not to Moses, it is true (Targ.), nor to Solomon, as the father, the pattern, and, as it were, the patron of " the wise," but to God, who is here named the ἀρχιποίμην as spiritual preserver (provider), not without reference to the figure of a shepherd from the goad, and the figure of household economy from the nails ; for רעה, in the language of the Chokma (Prov. v. 21), is in meaning cogn. to the N. T. conception of edification.[1] Regarding *masmᵉroth* (iron nails), *vid.* above, p. 193 ; the word is not used of tent spikes (Spohn, Ginsb.), —it is masc., the sing. is מַשְׂמֵר (מִסְמֵר), Arab. *mismâr.* נְטוּעִים is = תְּקוּעִים (cf. Dan. xi. 45 with Gen. xxxi. 25), post-bibl. (*vid. Jer. Sanhedrin*) קְבוּעִים (Jerome, *in altum defixi*). *Min* with the pass., as at Job xxi. 1, xxviii. 4, Ps. xxxvii. 23 (Ewald, § 295*b*), is not synonymous with the Greek ὑπό (*vid.* above, p. 67). The LXX. well : " given by those of the counsel from one shepherd." Hitzig reads מִרְעֶה, and accordingly translates : " which are given united as a pasture," but in *mēro'eh ehad* there lies a significant apologetic hint in favour of the collection of proverbs by the younger Solomon (Koheleth) in relation to that of the old. This is the point of the verse, and it is broken off by Hitzig's conjecture.[2]

---

[1] *Vid.* my Heb. *Römerbrief,* p. 97.

[2] J. F. Reimmann, in the preface to his Introduction to the *Historia Litterarum antediluviana*, translates, ver. 11 : " The words of the wise are like hewn-out marble, and the beautiful *collectanea* like set diamonds, which are presented by a good friend." A *Disputatio philologica* by Abr. Wolf, Königsberg 1723, contends against this παρερμηνεία.

Ver. 12. With *v'yother mehemmah* the postscript takes a new departure, warning against too much reading, and finally pointing once more to the one thing needful: "And besides, my son, be warned: for there is no end of much book-making; and much study is a weariness of the body." With "my son," the teacher of wisdom here, as in the Book of Proverbs, addresses the disciple who places himself under his instruction. Hitzig translates, construing *mehemmah* with *hizzaher*: "And for the rest: by these (the 'words of Koheleth,' ver. 10) be informed." But (1) נִזְהַר, according to usage, does not signify in general to be taught, but to be made wiser, warned; particularly the imper. הִזָּהֵר is cogn. with הִשָּׁמֵר (cf. *Targ. Jer. Ex.* x. 28, הִשָּׁמֶר לְךָ = אִזְדְּהַר לָךְ), and in fact an object of the warning follows; (2) *min* after *yothēr* is naturally to be regarded as connected with it, and not with *hizzaher* (cf. Esth. vi. 6, *Sota* vii. 7; cf. Ps. xix. 12). The punctuation of *v'yother* and *mehemmah* is thus not to be interfered with. Either *hēmmah* points back to *divre* (ver. 11): And as to what goes beyond these (in relation thereto) be warned (Schelling: *quidquid ultra haec est, ab iis cave tibi,* and thus *e.g.* Oehler in Herzog's *R. E.* vii. 248); or, which is more probable, since the *divre* are without a fixed beginning, and the difference between true and false "wise men" is not here expressed, *hemmah* refers back to all that has hitherto been said, and *v'yother mehemmah* signifies not the result thereof (Ewald, § 285e), but that which remains thereafter: and what is more than that (which has hitherto been said), *i.e.* what remains to be said after that hitherto said; Lat. *et quod superest, quod reliquum est.*

In 12b, Hitzig also proposes a different interpunction from that which lies before us; but at the same time, in the place of the significant double sentence, he proposes a simple sentence: "to make many books, without end, and much exertion of mind (in making these), is a weariness of the body." The author thus gives the reason for his writing no more. But with xii. 8 he has certainly brought his theme to a close, and he writes no further; because he does not write for hire and without an aim, but for a high end, according to a fixed plan; and whether he will leave off with this his book or not is a matter of perfect indifference to the readers of this one book; and that the writing of many books without end will exhaust a man's mind and bring down his body, is not that a flat truism? We rather prefer Herzfeld's translation, which harmonizes with Rashbam's: "But more than these (the wise men) can teach thee, my son, teach thyself: to make many books there would be no end; and much preaching is fatiguing to the body." But נזהר cannot mean to

" teach oneself," and *ēn qētz* does not mean *non esset finis*, but *non est finis;* and for *lahach* the meaning " to preach" (which Luther also gives to it) is not at all shown from the Arab. *lahjat,* which signifies the tongue as that which is eager (to learn, etc.), and then also occurs as a choice name for tongues in general. Thus the idea of a double sentence, which is the most natural, is maintained, as the LXX. has already rendered it. The *n. actionis* עֲשׂוֹת with its object is the subject of the sentence, of which it is said *ēn qēts,* it is without end ; Hitzig's opinion, that *ēn lach qēts* must mean *non est ei finis,* is not justified ; for *ēn qēts* is a virtual adj., as *ēn 'avel,* Deut. xxxiii. 4, and the like, and as such the pred. of the substantival sentence. Regarding לָהַג, *avidum discendi legendique studium, vid.* above, p. 193. C. A. Bode (1777) renders well : *polygraphiae nullus est finis et polymathia corpus delessat.* Against this endless making of books and much study the postscript warns, for it says that this exhausts the bodily strength without (for this is the reverse side of the judgment) truly furthering the mind, which rather becomes decentralized by this πολυπραγμοσύνη. The meaning of the warning accords with the phrase coined by Pliny (*Ep.* vii. 9), *multum non multa.* One ought to hold by the " words of the wise," to which also the " words of Koheleth," comprehended in the *asuppah* of the book before us, belong ; for all that one can learn by hearing or by reading amounts at last, if we deduct all that is unessential and unenduring, to a *unum necessarium :*

Ver. 13. " The final result, after all is learned, (is this) : Fear God and keep His commandments ; for this is the end of every man." Many expositors, as Jerome, the Venet., and Luther, render נִשְׁמָע as fut. : The conclusion of the discourse we would all hear (Salomon) ; or : The conclusion of the whole discourse or matter let us hear (Panzer, 1773, de Wette-Augusti) ; Hitzig also takes together *soph davar hakol = soph davar kol-haddavar :* The end of the whole discourse let us hear. But הַכֹּל for כֻּלָּנוּ is contrary to the style of the book ; and as a general rule, the author uses הכל for the most part of things, seldom of persons. And also *soph davar hakol,* which it would be better to explain (" the final word of the whole "), with Ewald, § 291*a,* after *yᵉmē-olam mosheh,* Isa. lxiii. 11 (cf. *Proverbs,* vol. II. p. 267, note), than it is explained by Hitzig, although, in spite of Philippi's (*Stat. const.* p. 17) doubt, possible in point of style, and also exemplified in the later period of the language (1 Chron. ix. 13), is yet a stylistic crudeness which the author could have avoided either by writing *soph dᵉvar hakol,* or better, *soph kol-haddavar.* נִשְׁמָע, Ewald, § 168*b,* renders as a particip. by *audiendum ;* but that also does not commend itself, for נִשְׁמָע signifies nothing else than *auditum*, and acquires the meaning of *audiendum* when from the empirical matter of fact that which is inwardly necessary is concluded ; the translation : The final word of the whole is to be heard, *audiendum est*, would only be admissible if also the translation *auditum est* were possible, which is not the case.   Is נִשְׁמָע thus possibly the pausal form of the finite נִשְׁמַע ?   We might explain : The end of the matter (*summa summarum*), all is heard, when, viz., that which follows is heard, which comprehends all that is to be known.   Or as Hoelem. : Enough, all is heard, since, viz., that which is given in the book to be learned contains the essence of all true knowledge, viz., the following two fundamental doctrines.   This retrospective reference of *hakol nishm'a* is more natural than the prospective reference ; but, on the other hand, it is also more probable that *soph davar* denotes the final *resultat* than that it denotes the conclusion of the discourse. The right explanation will be that which combines the retrospective reference of *hakol nishm'a* and the resultative reference of *soph davar*.   Accordingly, Mendelss. appears to us to be correct when he explains : After thou hast heard all the words of the wise . . . this is the final result, etc.   *Finis* (*summa*) *rei, omnia audita* is = *omnibus auditis*, for the sentence denoting the conditions remains externally undesignated, in the same way as at x. 14 ; Deut. xxi. 1 ; Ezra x. 6 (Ewald, § 341b).   After the clause, *soph . . . nishm'a, Athnach* stands where we put a colon : the mediating *hocce est* is omitted just as at vii. 12b (where translate : yet the preference of knowledge is this, that, etc.).

The sentence, *eth-haelohim y'ra* (" fear God "), repeating itself from v. 6, is the kernel and the star of the whole book, the highest moral demand which mitigates its pessimism and hallows its eudaemonism. The admonition proceeding therefrom, "and keep His commandments," is included in *lishmo'a*, iv. 17 [v. 1], which places the hearing of the divine word, viz. a hearing for the purpose of observing, as the very soul of the worship of God above all the *opus operatum* of ceremonial services.

The connection of the clause, *ki-zeh kol-haadam*, Hitzig mediates in an unnecessary, roundabout way : " but not thou alone, but this ought every man."   But why this negative here introduced to stamp כִּי as an *immo* establishing it ?   It is also certainly suitable as the immediate confirmation of the rectitude of the double admonition finally expressing all.   The clause has the form of a simple judgment, it is a substantival clause, the briefest expression for the thought which is intended.   What is that thought ?   The LXX.

renders: ὅτι τοῦτο πᾶς ὁ ἄνθρωπος; also Symm. and the Venet. render *kol haadam* by πᾶς ὁ ἄνθρ., and an unnamed translator has ὅλος ὁ ἄνθρ., according to which also the translation of Jerome is to be understood, *hoc est enim omnis homo.* Thus among the moderns, Herzf., Ewald, Elst., and Heiligst. : for that is the whole man, viz. as to his destiny, the end of his existence (cf. as to the subject-matter, Job xxviii. 28) ; and v. Hofmann (*Schriftbew.* II. 2, p. 456) : this is the whole of man, viz. as Grotius explains : *totum hominis bonum ;* or as Dale and Bullock: " the whole duty of man ;" or as Tyler : " the universal law (כֹּל, like the Mishnic כְּלָל) of man ;" or as Hoelem. : that which gives to man for the first time his true and full worth. Knobel also suggests for consideration this rendering : this is the all of man, *i.e.* on this all with man rests. But against this there is the one fact, that *kol-haadam* never signifies the whole man, and as little anywhere the whole (the all) of a man. It signifies either " all men " (πάντες οἱ ἄνθρωποι, οἱ πά. ἄνθρ. οἱ ἄνθρ. πά.), as at vii. 2, *hu soph kol-haadam*, or, of the same meaning as *kol-haadam*, " every man " (πᾶς ἄνθρωπος), as at iii. 13, v. 18 (LXX., also vii. 2 : τοῦτο τέλος παντὸς ἀνθρώπου) ; and it is yet more than improbable that the common expression, instead of which *haadam kullo* was available, should here have been used in a sense elsewhere un-exampled. Continuing in the track of the *usus loq.*, and particu-larly of the style of the author, we shall thus have to translate : " for this is every man." If we use for it : " for this is every man's," the clause becomes at once distinct ; Zirkel renders *kol-haadam* as genit., and reckons the expression among the Graecisms of the book : παντὸς ἀνθρώπου, viz. πρᾶγμα. Or if, with Knobel, Hitz., Böttch., and Ginsburg, we might borrow a verb to supple-ment the preceding imperat. : " for this ought every man to do," we should also in this way gain the meaning to be expected ; but the clause lying before us is certainly a substantival clause, like *meh haadam,* ii. 12, not an elliptical verbal clause, like Isa. xxiii. 5, xxvi. 9, where the verb to be supplied easily unfolds itself from the לְ of the end of the movement.

We have here a case which is frequent in the Semitic languages, in which subj. and pred. are connected in the form of a simple judg-ment, and it is left for the hearer to find out the relation sustained by the pred. to the subj.—*e.g.* Ps. cx. 3, cix. 4, " I am prayer ;" and in the Book of Koheleth, iii. 19, " the children of men are a chance."[1] In the same way we have here to explain : for that is every man,

[1] *Vid.* Fleischer's *Abh. ü. einige Arten der Nominalapposition,* 1862, and Philippi's *St. const.* p. 90 ff.

viz. according to his destiny and duty; excellently, Luther: for that
belongs to all men.   With right, Hahn, like Bauer (1732), regards
the pronoun as pred. (not subj. as at vii. 2): " this, *i.e.* thus constituted, that they must do this, are all men," or rather : this = under
obligation thereto, is every man.[1]   It is a great thought that is thereby expressed, viz. the reduction of the Israelitish law to its common
human essence.   This has not escaped the old Jewish teachers.
What can this mean: *zeh kol-haadam ?* it is asked, *Berachoth* 6*b;*
and R. Elazar answers: " The whole world is comprehended therein;" and R. Abba bar-Cahana: "This fundamental law is of the same
importance to the universe;" and R. Simeon b. Azzai: " The universe
has been created only for the purpose of being commanded this."[2]

Ver. 14. As we render *zeh kol-haadam* as expressive of the
same obligation lying on all men without exception, this verse appropriately follows: " For God shall bring every work into the judgment
upon all that is concealed, whether it be good or bad."   To bring
into judgment is, as at xi. 9 = to bring to an account.   There the
punctuation is בַּמִּשׁ׳, here בְּמִשׁ׳, as, according to rule, the art. is
omitted where the idea is determined by a relative clause or an
added description; for *b*emishpat 'al kol-ne'llam* are taken together :
in the judgment upon all that is concealed (cf. Rom. ii. 16 ; 1 Cor.
iv. 5, τὰ κρυπτά).   Hitzig, however, punctuates here בְּמִשׁ׳, and explains עַל as of the same meaning as the distributive לְ, *e.g.* Gen.
ix. 5, 10; but in this sense עַל never interchanges with לְ.   And
wherefore this subtlety ?   The judgment upon all that is concealed is
a judgment from the cognition of which nothing, not even the most
secret, can escape; and that מִשׁפט עַל is not a Germanism, is shown
from xi. 9 ; to execute judgment on (Germ. *an*) any one is expressed
by בְ, Ps. cxix. 84, Wisd. vi. 6 ; judgment upon (*über*) any one may
be expressed by the genit. of him whom it concerns, Jer. li. 9 ; but
judgment upon anything (Symm. περὶ παντὸς παροραθέντος) cannot
otherwise be expressed than by עַל.   Rather עַל may be rendered as
a connecting particle: " together with all that is concealed " (Vai'
Hahn); but כל־מעשׂה certainly comprehends all, and with כל־נעלם

---

[1] Hitz. thus renders הִיא, Jer. xlv. 4*b*, predicat. : " And it is such, all the world."

[2] Cf. *Jer. Nedarim* ix. 3 : " Thou oughtest to love thy neighbour as thyself,"
says R. Akiba, is a principal sentence in the Law.   Ben-Azzai says : " The words
zĕh . . . adam (Gen. v. 1) are it in a yet higher degree," because therein the
oneness of the origin and the destiny of all men is contained.   Aben Ezra
alludes to the same thing, when at the close of his *Comm.* he remarks : " The
secret of the non-use of the divine name יהוה in Gen. i.–ii. 3 is the secret of the
Book of Koheleth."

this comprehensive idea is only deepened. The accent dividing the verse stands rightly under מֵעָלָם ;[1] for *sive bonum sive malum* (as at v. 11) is not related to *ne'llam* as disjoining, but to *kol-ma'aseh.*

This certainty of a final judgment of personal character is the Ariadne-thread by which Koheleth at last brings himself safely out of the labyrinth of his scepticism. The prospect of a general judgment upon the nations prevailing in the O. T., cannot sufficiently set at rest the faith (*vid. e.g.* Ps. lxxiii., Jer. xii. 1–3) which is tried by the unequal distributions of present destiny. Certainly the natural, and particularly the national connection in which men stand to one another, is not without an influence on their moral condition; but this influence does not remove accountability,—the *individuum* is at the same time a person; the object of the final judgment will not be societies as such, but only persons, although not without regard to their circle of life. This personal view of the final judgment does not yet in the O. T. receive a preponderance over the national view; such figures of an universal and individualizing personal judgment as Matt. vii. 21–23, Rev. xx. 12, are nowhere found in it; the object of the final judgment are nations, kingdoms, cities, and conditions of men. But here, with Koheleth, a beginning is made in the direction of regarding the final judgment as the final judgment of men, and as lying in the future, beyond the present time. What Job xix. 25–27 postulates in the absence of a present judgment of his cause, and the Apocalyptic Dan. xii. 2 saw as a dualistic issue of the history of his people, comes out here for the first time in the form of doctrine into that universally-human expression which is continued in the announcements of Jesus and the apostles. Kleinert sees here the morning-dawn of a new revelation breaking forth; and Himpel says, in view of this conclusion, that Koheleth is a precious link in the chain of the preparation for the gospel; and rightly. In the Book of Koheleth the O. T. religion sings its funeral song, but not without finally breaking the ban of nationality and of bondage to this present life, which made it unable to solve the mysteries of life, and thus not without prophesying its resurrection in an expanded glorified form as the religion of humanity.

---

[1] Thus rightly pointed in F. with *Dagesh* in *lamed*, to make distinct the ע as quiescent (cf. 1 Kings x. 3; and, on the other hand, Neh. iii. 11, Ps. xxvi. 4). Cf. תֶּחְשַׁ׳ with *Dagesh* in *shin*, on account of the preceding quiescent guttural, like יִחְ׳, ix. 8; הַתָּ׳, Lev. xi. 16; נָחָ׳, Num. i. 7, etc.; cf. *Luth. Zeitsch.* 1863, p. 413.

The synagogal lesson repeats the 13th verse after the 14th, to gain thereby a conclusion of a pleasing sound. The Masoretic *Siman* (*vox memorialis*) of those four books, in which, after the last verse, on account of its severe contents, the verse going before is repeated in reading, is יׄתׄ״קׄקׄ. The יׄ refers to ישעיה (Isaiah), תׄ to תריסר (the Book of the Twelve Prophets), the first קׄ to קהלת, the second קׄ to קינות (Lamentations). The Lamentations and Koheleth always stand together. But there are two different arrangements of the five *Mcgilloth*, viz. that of the calendar of festivals which has passed into our printed editions: the Song, Ruth, Lamentations, Koheleth, and Esther (*vid.* above, p. 3); and the Masoretic arrangement, according to the history of their origin: Ruth, the Song, Koheleth, Lamentations, and Esther.